Social Psychology

Social Psychology

FIRST CANADIAN EDITION

SHARON S. BREHM

Indiana University—Bloomington

SAUL KASSIN

Williams College

STEVEN FEIN

Williams College

TARA M. BURKE

Ryerson University

HOUGHTON MIFFLIN COMPANY Boston New York

Executive Publisher: George Hoffman
Project Manager: Timothy Cullen
Sponsoring Editor: Jane Potter
Development Editor: Glen Herbert
Senior Project Editor: Margaret Park Bridges
New Title Project Manager: James Lonergan
Senior Marketing Manager: David Tonen

Cover image: People Looking at Fish in Aquarium Tank. Courtesy of Eri Morita, Getty Images

Photo credits are found following the References at the end of the book.

Printed in the U.S.A.

Library of Congress Control Number: 2006937981

ISBN-10: 0-618-76724-X
ISBN-13: 978-0-618-76724-3

Instructor's Edition and Student Study supplements are available online. Please contact us for details at Canada@hmco.com

1 2 3 4 5 6 7 8 9-DOW-11 10 09 08 07

We dedicate this book to our families, friends, students, and colleagues.

Brief Contents

Contents

PART TWO Social Influence

Preface

We authors used to think of social psychology as a discipline that is stable and slow to change. As in other sciences, we thought, knowledge accumulates in small increments, one step at a time. There are, after all, no "critical" experiments, and no single study can literally "prove" a theory or hypothesis. While all this remains true, and while future social psychologists will stand firmly on the shoulders of their predecessors, for us the process of revising this textbook has put a spotlight on just how dynamic and responsive our field can be. As the world around us rapidly changes—socially, politically, and technologically—so too does social psychology.

We had two main goals for this book. First, we wanted to accurately and impartially represent the most important recent advances in the field. We have no theoretical or political axes to grind. As such, we sought a balanced presentation of perspectives within the field as a whole—biological and sociocultural, affective and cognitive, basic and applied. Second, we wanted this textbook to serve as a good teacher outside the classroom. To us, this means speaking the student's language while introducing a new one; making connections to current events in politics, sports, business, entertainment, and other life domains; and encouraging students to rethink their commonsense assumptions. Good teachers are dynamic, interactive, and challenging—and so, we think, is this textbook.

What's New to the Canadian Edition

For the Canadian edition, we reorganized this text to reflect the needs and interests of a Canadian readership. We have tried to put our finger on the pulse of social psychology in Canada *today*—so that the reader can feel that pulse in the pages of this textbook.

The Content

Comprehensive, Up-to-Date Scholarship The bedrock of teaching is knowledge. The Canadian edition offers a broad, balanced, mainstream look at social psychology. Thus, there are detailed descriptions of classic studies from the historical warehouse as well as the latest research findings, some hot off the presses, from hundreds of new references.

Connections with Current Events To cover the world of social psychology is one thing. To use the principles to explain events in the real world is quite another.

The Canadian edition includes a commitment to making social psychology *relevant.* Indeed, we invite you to flip the book open to any page and start reading. Soon, you'll come across a passage, a figure, a table, a photo, or a cartoon that refers to people, places, events, and issues that are prominent in contemporary culture. You'll read about Vancouver Canucks' Todd Bertuzzi's late hit on Colorado

Avalanche player Steve Moore; how celebrities such as Don Cherry or Steve Nash can influence our behaviour; the Liberal party's sponsorship scandal; flash mobs; the shooting of Dudley George at Ipperwash Provincial Park; Robert Latimer's conviction for what he argued was the mercy killing of his severely disabled daughter; and the wrongful conviction of Thomas Sophonow.

You will also find—within the margins—various quotations, song lyrics, public opinion poll results, "factoids," and relevant Web site addresses. These high-interest items are designed to further illustrate the connectedness of social psychology to a world beyond the academic institution.

Sociocultural Perspectives Social psychologists have long been fascinated by both similarities and differences—among cultural groups, racial and ethnic groups within cultures, men and women, gays and straights. Our coverage of cross-cultural research, and of studies involving race and ethnicity, gender, and sexual orientation, are fully incorporated in the main body of the text. On virtually all topics—from the social self and perception of others, to attitudes, conformity and obedience, interpersonal behaviour, attraction, group dynamics, leadership, and conceptions of justice—sociocultural perspectives are embedded throughout. More than ever before, social psychology itself has become a truly international discipline, which is why you'll find many new citations to research conducted throughout Europe, Asia, Australia, and other parts of the world. We believe that the study of human diversity—from the perspectives of researchers who themselves are a diverse lot—can help students become more informed about interpersonal relations as well as about ethics and values.

The Organization

Of all the challenges faced by teachers and textbooks, perhaps the greatest is to put information together in a way that is accurate and understandable. A strong organizational framework helps in meeting this challenge. There is nothing worse for a student than having to wade through a "laundry list" of endless studies whose connection with each other remains a profound mystery. A strong structure thus facilitates the development of conceptual understanding.

But the tail should not wag the dog. Since organizational structure is a means to an end, not an end in itself, we believe that it should be kept simple and unobtrusive. We present social psychology within four major parts, a heuristic structure that teachers and students have found sensible and easy to follow. As before, we start with an internal focus on *Social Perception* (Part One), shift outward to *Social Influence* (Part Two) and *Social Relations* (Part Three), and conclude with *Applying Social Psychology* (Part Four). We realize that some instructors prefer to reshuffle the deck to develop a chapter order that better fits their own approach. There is no problem in doing this. Each chapter stands on its own and does not require that others be read first.

The Presentation

Even when the content of a textbook is accurate and up-to-date, and even when its organization is sound, there is still the matter of presentation. As the teacher outside the classroom, a good textbook should facilitate learning. Thus, each and every chapter comes complete with the following pedagogical features:

- A narrative preview, chapter outline, and common sense quiz (beginning with Chapter 3).
- Key terms highlighted in the text, defined in the margin, listed at the end of the chapter, and reprinted in an alphabetized glossary at the end of the

book. Both the list and the glossary provide page numbers for easy location of the term.

- Numerous bar graphs, line graphs, tables, sketches, photographs, flow charts, and cartoons that not only illustrate material in the text but extend, enhance, and enliven that material. Some of these depict classic images and studies from social psychology's past; others are contemporary, often "newsy."
- A comprehensive bulleted review summarizing the major sections and points at the end of each chapter.

Supplemental Materials

For the Instructor

Instructor's Manual • contains learning objectives, lecture outlines, discussion topics, classroom exercises, handouts, and audiovisual resources. Classroom exercises have a "What if This Bombs?" section that gives instructors tips on making the most of every activity—even if it doesn't work.

Printed Test Bank • features an extensive set of multiple-choice and essay questions for every chapter. Three types of objective questions are provided—factual, conceptual, and applied—and each test item is keyed to learning objective, text-page reference, and question type. Sample answers accompany the essay questions.

Text-specific Instructor's Web site* • *www.hmco.ca/brehm • For instructors, in addition to online access to popular instructor manual resources, we offer a new feature designed to help integrate digital media into the classroom, engage students in more active learning, and generally learn about how sound instructional technology can affect learning outcomes.

HMClassPrep with HMTesting CD-ROM • This combined CD includes both the Computerized Test Bank and the HMClass Prep CD. Our HMTesting program offers delivery of test questions in an easy-to-use interface; compatible with both MAC and WIN platforms. The HMClass Prep instructor CD-ROM provides one location for all text-specific preparation materials that instructors might want to have available electronically. It contains PowerPoint lecture outlines and select art from the textbook as well as select material from the Instructor's Manual.

Overhead Transparencies • include some images from the book's illustration program.

Houghton Mifflin Social Psych in Film DVD/VHS • contains clips from popular films illustrating key concepts in social psychology. Clips from films including *Schindler's List*, *Snow Falling on Cedars*, and many others are combined with commentary and discussion questions to help bring psychology alive for students and demonstrate its relevance to contemporary life and culture. Teaching tips and suggested discussion questions are also included.

Social Psychology Lecture Starter Video clips • created especially for this textbook and offers approximately 60 minutes of brief video clips perfectly suited for classroom use.

Content for Course Management Software Blackboard and Web CT • course cartridges are available with this text, allowing instructors to use text-specific material to create an online course on their own campus course management system. The cartridges feature interactive Net Lab exercises, PowerPoint slides and other course preparation, presentation, and student study materials for easy upload.

For the Student

Student CD-ROM • included with the text, this completely revamped CD-ROM is designed to reinforce concepts presented in the textbook as well as in classroom lecture. Instructors can assign review of video stills that demonstrate key concepts from popular films such as *Patch Adams*, *Snow Falling on Cedars*, and *Apollo 13*, as well as classic experiments from the Films for Humanities series. Multiple choice practice tests and essay questions accompany each still to reinforce students' grasp of concepts initially presented in their textbook. Progress reports can be printed and/or emailed to instructors directly from the CD-ROM.

Student Study Guide • facilitates student learning through the use of a chapter outline, learning objectives, a review of key terms and concepts, multiple-choice questions with explanations for why the correct answer is the best choice, and a new set of practice essay questions with sample answers.

Text-specific Student Web site • ***www.hmco.ca/brehm*** • a full service, interactive Web site dedicated to facilitating the learning and teaching of psychology. It offers students access to current events and contemporary issues in psychology, NetLabs interactive activities, practice tests, and more for the introductory course.

Readings in Social Psychology: The Art and Science of Research Reader • contains 16 original articles—each with a brief introduction and questions to stimulate critical thinking about "doing" social psychology. These articles represent some of the most creative and accessible research in the field, both classic and contemporary, of topical interest to students. Related links are included on the student CD-ROM.

Acknowledgments

Textbooks are the product of a team effort. Thanks to everyone within the Houghton Mifflin international division who worked to make this new edition a reality. I'd like to thank Patricia Tutunjian of Houghton Mifflin International for her foresight and dedication to the creation of a Canadian edition, as well as her colleagues in Boston and in Canada who provided guidance on Canadian market needs and trends. Glen Herbert attended to the development of the edition and I am grateful for his guidance and support throughout the project. Thanks to Merrill Peterson and his staff who handled the production phase of the project.

To my colleagues at Ryerson University—Michelle Dionne, Stephen Want, Maria Gurevich, and John Turtle—thank you for your helpful feedback and suggestions. And finally, to Madison and Scott Pincombe, this is for you.

Then there are my colleagues who guided us through their feedback on this and all prior editions. Each of these teachers and scholars has helped to make this a better book. For their invaluable insights, comments, and suggestions, I thank:

Glenn Adams, *University of Toronto*
Theresa Bianco, *Concordia University*
Del Brodie, *St. Thomas University*
Rich Ennis, *University of Waterloo*
Christian Jordan, *Wilfrid Laurier University*
Sara Pawson, *Kwantlen University College*
Jeff Pfeifer, *University of Regina*
Saba Safdar, *University of Guelph*
Brent Snook, *Memorial University*
Joseph Snyder, *Concordia University*

Tara Burke
Ryerson University

About the Authors

Sharon S. Brehm is Professor of Psychology at Indiana University in Bloomington. Born and raised in Roanoke, Virginia, she received a B.A. and a Ph.D. in psychology from Duke University, an A.M. from Harvard University, and completed a clinical psychology internship at the University of Washington Medical Center. After 15 years on the psychology faculty at the University of Kansas, she served as dean of the Harper College of Arts and Sciences at SUNY Binghamton, provost at Ohio University, and chancellor of the Indiana University Bloomington campus. She was an Intra-University Professor at the University of Kansas, a Fulbright Senior Research Scholar at the Ecole des Hautes Etudes en Sciences Sociales, and a visiting professor in Germany and Italy. Her books include *The Application of Social Psychology to Clinical Practice*, a recognized classic in the field, and *Intimate Relationships*, a highly regarded textbook. Her current research interests involve psychology of women and organizational behaviour.

Saul Kassin is Professor of Psychology at Williams College in Williamstown, Massachusetts. Born and raised in New York City, he graduated from Brooklyn College. After receiving his Ph.D. in personality and social psychology from the University of Connecticut, he spent one year at the University of Kansas and two years at Purdue University. In 1984, he was awarded a prestigious U.S. Supreme Court Judicial Fellowship, and in 1985 he worked as a postdoctoral fellow in the Psychology and Law Program at Stanford University. Kassin is author of the textbook *Psychology* (fourth edition) and has coauthored or edited a number of scholarly books, including *Developmental Social Psychology*, *The Psychology of Evidence and Trial Procedure*, and *The American Jury on Trial*. His research interests are in social perception and influence, and their applications to police interrogations and confessions, eyewitness testimony, jury decision making, and other aspects of law.

Steven Fein is Professor of Psychology at Williams College, Williamstown, Massachusetts. Born and raised in Bayonne, New Jersey, he received his A.B. from Princeton University and his Ph.D. in social psychology from the University of Michigan. He has been teaching at Williams College since 1991, with time spent teaching at Stanford University in 1999. His edited books include *Emotion: Interdisciplinary Perspectives*, *Readings in Social Psychology: The Art and Science of Research*, *Motivated Social Perception: The Ontario Symposium*, and *Gender and Aggression: Interdisciplinary Approaches*. He recently completed a term on the executive committee of the Society of Personality and Social Psychology. His research interests concern stereotyping and prejudice, suspicion, and sociocultural and motivational influences on person perception.

Tara Burke is an Assistant Professor of Psychology at Ryerson University in Toronto, Ontario. Born and raised in Toronto, she received her B.A. from the University of Western Ontario and her M.A. and Ph.D. in Social Psychology from the University of Toronto. She has been at Ryerson University since 1999, where she was the recipient of a Teaching Excellence Award, honouring her for her work teaching courses such as Social Psychology, Psychology and Law, and Introductory Psychology. She has published several articles and book chapters in areas related to research ethics, and psychology and law. Her current research interests include social influence (applied to areas such as jury decision-making, pretrial publicity and the psychology of alibis), interpersonal trust, and research ethics.

Social Psychology

1 Introduction

OUTLINE

PREVIEW

THIS CHAPTER introduces you to the study of social psychology. We begin by defining social psychology and identifying how it is distinct from but related to some other areas of study, both outside and within psychology. Next, we review the history of the field. We conclude by looking forward, with a discussion of the important themes and perspectives that are propelling social psychology into a new century.

"Man is a social animal."
—Benedict Spinoza, *Ethics*

A few years from now, you may receive a letter in the mail, inviting you to a high school or university reunion. You'll probably feel a bit nostalgic, and you'll begin to think about those old school days. What thoughts will come to mind first? Will you remember the terrific English teacher you had in Grade 11? Will you think about the excitement you felt when you completed your first chemistry lab? Will a tear form in your eye as you remember how inspiring your social psychology class was?

Perhaps. But what will probably dominate your thoughts are the people you knew in school and the interactions you had with them—the long and intense discussions about everything imaginable; the loves you had, lost, or wanted so desperately to experience; the time you made a fool of yourself at a party; the effort of trying to be accepted by a fraternity, sorority, or clique of popular people; the day you sat in the pouring rain with your friends while watching a football game.

We focus on these social situations because we are social beings. We forge our individual identities not alone but in the context of other people. We work, play, and live together. We hurt and help each other. We define happiness and success for each other. And we don't fall passively into social interactions; we actively seek them. We visit family, make friends, give parties, build networks, play the dating game, pledge an enduring commitment, and decide to have children. We watch others, speculate about them, and predict who will wind up with whom, whether in real life or on "reality" TV shows like *The Lofters* and *Survivor*.

You've probably seen the movie *It's a Wonderful Life*. When the hero, George Bailey, was about to kill himself, the would-be angel Clarence didn't save him by showing him how much personal happiness he'd miss if he ended his life. Instead, he showed George how much his life had touched the lives of others and how many people would be hurt if he were not a part of their world. It was these social relationships that saved George's life, just as they define our own.

Strangers quickly become celebrities as millions of people tune in to watch them relate to each other on "reality" shows, such as this cast from a recent season of U8TV: The Lofters, *where viewers could follow the lives—24 hours a day—of eight young people living in a loft in downtown Toronto. The enormous popularity of shows like these illustrates part of the appeal of social psychology—people are fascinated with how we relate to one another.*

One of the exciting aspects of learning about social psychology is discovering how basic and profoundly important these social relationships are to the human animal. And research continues to find new evidence for and point to new implications of our social nature. Consider, for example, this set of headlines that appeared in media outlets around the world during the course of one month:

- "British Study Finds Going to the Pub Good for the Brain" (*The Times*, London, November 7, 2003)
- "Shock and Distress of Social Rejection Affects Brain in Same Way as Physical Injury, Study Says" (Associated Press, October 9, 2003)
- "Brain Hard-Wired for Empathy: Study" (Reuters Health, November 6, 2003)

Each of these headlines is based on carefully conducted research that illustrates, respectively, that engaging in social interactions, such as socializing in a pub, is associated with improved verbal and numerical ability; that seeing an expression of disgust on someone else's face activates the same part of our brain—the insula—as when we feel disgust ourselves; and that experiencing a social rejection produces activity in the same part of the brain—the anterior cingulate cortex—as when we feel physical pain (Eisenberger et al., 2003; Singh-Manoux et al., 2003; Wicker et al., 2003). Taken together, these studies use cutting-edge methodology and technology to demonstrate how basic and important is our connection to other people, and how much we benefit from social interaction and are hurt—not just metaphorically but even physically—from social isolation or rejection.

Precisely because we need and care so much about social interactions and relationships, the social contexts in which we find ourselves can influence us profoundly. You can find many examples of this kind of influence in your own life. Have you ever laughed at a joke you didn't get just because those around you were laughing? Do you present yourself in one way with one group of people and in quite a different way with another group? The power of the situation can also be much more subtle, and yet more powerful, than in these examples, as when another's unspoken expectations about you literally seem to cause you to become a different person.

Are some people, such as these members of the Canadian Red Cross, naturally altruistic, or can anyone display courage and heroism under the right conditions?

The relevance of social psychology is evident in everyday life, of course, such as when two people become attracted to each other, or when a group tries to coordinate its efforts on a project. Dramatic events can heighten its significance all the more; we seek answers to the kinds of questions that social psychologists study—questions about hatred and violence, about intergroup conflict and suspicion, as well as about heroism, cooperation, and the capacity for understanding across cultural, ethnic, racial, religious, and geographic divides. We are reminded of the need for a better understanding of social psychological issues as we read the latest tragic news coming out of the Middle East, see footage of death and destruction in the Persian Gulf or the Congo, or are confronted with the reality of an all-too-violent world as nearby as our own neighbourhoods and campuses. We also appreciate the majesty and power of social connections as we recognize the courage of a firefighter, read about the charity of a donor, or see the glow in the eyes of a new parent. These are all—the bad and the good, the mundane and the extraordinary—part of the fascinating landscape of social psychology.

You will see evidence of these points throughout this book. What's more, you will learn *how* social psychologists have discovered this evidence. It is an exciting process, and one that we are enthusiastic about sharing with you. The purpose of this first chapter is to provide you with a broad overview of the field of social psychology. By the time you finish it, you should be ready and (we hope) eager for what lies ahead.

What Is Social Psychology?

We begin by previewing the new territory you're about to enter. Then we define social psychology and map out its relationship to sociology and some other disciplines within the field of psychology.

Social psychology is the scientific study of how individuals think, feel, and behave in regard to other people and how individuals' thoughts, feelings, and behaviours are affected by other people. Let's look at each part of this definition.

Defining Social Psychology

Scientific Study There are many approaches to understanding how people think, feel, and behave. We can learn about human behaviour from novels, films, history, and philosophy—to name just a few possibilities. What makes social psychology different from these artistic and humanistic endeavours is that social psychology is a science. It applies the *scientific method* of systematic observation, description, and measurement to the study of the human condition. How, and why, social psychologists do this is explained in Chapter 2.

How Individuals Think, Feel, and Behave Social psychology concerns an amazingly diverse set of topics. People's private, even nonconscious beliefs and attitudes, their most passionate emotions, their heroic, cowardly, or merely mundane public behaviours—these all fall within the broad scope of social psychology. In this way, social psychology differs from other social sciences such as economics and political science. Research on attitudes (see Chapter 6) offers a good illustration. Whereas economists and political scientists may be interested in people's economic and political attitudes, respectively, social psychologists investigate a wide variety of attitudes and contexts. In doing so, they strive to establish general principles of attitude formation and change that apply in a variety of situations, rather than exclusively to particular domains.

Our social relationships and interactions are extremely important to us. Most people seek out and are profoundly affected by other people. This social nature of the human animal is what social psychology is all about.

social psychology The scientific study of how individuals think, feel, and behave in regard to other people and how individuals' thoughts, feelings, and behaviours are affected by other people.

A celebrity like Don Cherry can influence the attitudes and behaviours of millions of people. When he recommended a hat honouring the Canadian Forces Personnel Support Agency during a "Coaches' Corner" segment on Hockey Night in Canada, *sales of the hats skyrocketed.*

Note the word *individuals* in our definition of *social psychology.* This word points to another important way in which social psychology differs from some other social sciences. Sociology, for instance, typically classifies people in terms of their nationality, race, socioeconomic class, and other *group factors.* In contrast, social psychology typically focuses on the psychology of the *individual.* Even when social psychologists study groups of people, they usually emphasize the behaviour of the individual in the group context.

Other People—The Social Element The last part of the definition—"in regard to other people and how individuals' thoughts, feelings, and behaviours are affected by other people"—is where the "social" in social psychology comes into play and how social psychology is distinguished from other branches of psychology. As a whole, the discipline of psychology is an immense, sprawling enterprise, the 800-pound gorilla of the social sciences, concerned with everything from the actions of neurotransmitters in the brain to the actions of music fans in a mosh pit. What makes social psychology unique is its emphasis on the social nature of individuals.

However, the "socialness" of social psychology varies. Attempting to establish general principles of human behaviour, social psychologists sometimes examine nonsocial factors that affect people's thoughts, emotions, motives, and actions. For example, they may study whether heat causes people to behave more aggressively (Anderson et al., 2000; Anderson & Huesmann, 2003). What is social about this is the behaviour: people hurting each other. In addition, social psychologists sometimes study people's thoughts or feelings about nonsocial things, such as people's attitudes toward Nike versus New Balance basketball shoes. How can attitudes toward basketball shoes be of interest to social psychologists? One way is if these attitudes are influenced by something social, such as whether having Steve Nash's endorsement of Nike makes people like Nike and perhaps even ultimately buy Nike shoes. Both examples, determining whether heat causes an increase in aggression or whether Steve Nash causes an increase in sales of Nike shoes, are social psychological pursuits because the thoughts, feelings, or behaviours either (a) concern other people or (b) are influenced by other people.

The "other people" referred to in the definition of *social psychology* do not have to be real or present. Even the implied or imagined presence of others can have important effects on individuals (Allport, 1985). For example, if people imagine receiving positive or negative reactions from others, their self-esteem can be affected significantly (Leary et al., 1998). In fact, Baldwin (1994) found even subliminal presentation of the name of a person known to be either critical or accepting can influence our mood either positively or negatively. And if young people are asked to imagine living a day in the life of a particular older man, their ratings of the elderly on a number of traits can become more positive (Galinsky & Ku, 2004).

Social Psychological Questions and Applications

For those of us fascinated by social behaviour, social psychology is a dream come true. Just look at Table 1.1 and consider a small sample of the questions you'll explore in this textbook. As you can see, the social nature of the human animal is what social psychology is all about. Learning about social psychology is learning about ourselves and our social worlds. And because social psychology is scientific rather than anecdotal, systematic rather than haphazard, it provides insights that would be impossible to gain through intuition or experience alone.

The number and importance of these applications continue to grow. Judges are drawing on social psychological research to render landmark decisions, and lawyers are depending on it to support or refute evidence. Health professionals are increasingly aware of the role of social psychological factors in the prevention and treatment of disease. Indeed, we can think of no other field of study that offers expertise that is more clearly relevant to so many different career paths.

The value of social psychology's perspective on human behaviour is widely recognized. Courses in social psychology are often required for undergraduate majors in business, education, and journalism as well as in psychology and sociology. Although most advanced graduates with a Ph.D. in social psychology hold faculty

TABLE 1.1

Examples of Social Psychological Questions

Social Perception: What Affects the Way We Perceive Ourselves and Others?

- Why do people sometimes sabotage their own performance, making it more likely that they will fail? (Ch. 3)
- How do people in East Asia often differ from North Americans in the way they explain people's behaviour? (Ch. 4)
- Where do stereotypes come from, and why are they so resistant to change? (Ch. 5)

Social Influence: How Do We Influence Each Other?

- Why do we often like what we suffer for? (Ch. 6)
- How do salespeople sometimes trick us into buying things we never really wanted? (Ch. 7)
- Why do people often perform worse in groups than they would have alone? (Ch. 8)

Social Interaction: What Causes Us to Like, Love, Help, and Hurt Others?

- How similar or different are the sexes in what they look for in an intimate relationship? (Ch. 9)
- When is a bystander more or less likely to help you in an emergency? (Ch. 10)
- Does exposure to TV violence, or to pornography, trigger aggressive behaviour? (Ch. 11)

Applying Social Psychology: How Does Social Psychology Help Us Understand Questions About Law?

- Why do people sometimes confess to crimes they did not commit? (Ch. 12)
- Does exposure to pre-trial publicity impact the judgments of jurors? (Ch. 12)

appointments in universities, they also work in medical centres, law firms, government agencies, and a variety of business settings involving investment banking, marketing, advertising, human resources, negotiating, and e-commerce. Social psychologists constantly seek new knowledge and new opportunities to apply what they have learned.

The Power of the Social Context: An Example of a Social Psychology Experiment

The social nature of people runs so deep that even that which seems so personal and unique to ourselves—our own senses of identity, of who we are and what we strive to be—can be influenced subtly but significantly by merely thinking about other people. This point is illustrated in research by Emily Pronin and her colleagues (2004) concerning what they call *identity bifurcation*. Female undergraduate students who cared about and had done well in math participated in this research. These women often confronted a challenge: Math was important to their own identities, but they also were aware of negative stereotypes concerning the relation between math ability and their identity as women. That is, whether or not they believed it to be true, they were aware of the negative stereotypes about the math ability of women relative to men. As we will see in Chapter 5, awareness of negative stereotypes about one's group (such as women) in a particular domain (such as math) can have serious consequences for an individual's performance in and commitment to that domain.

Pronin and her colleagues wondered if one consequence of the conflict between women's math and feminine identities might be that women might try to disavow aspects of their feminine identity that would seem most at odds with success in math, at least as suggested by popular stereotypes. The researchers found that particular traits such as *emotional* were considered by many undergraduates as both feminine and associated with lack of success in math. A trait such as *empathic*, on the other hand, was seen as consistent with femininity but was not seen as particularly relevant to math one way or the other.

These researchers hypothesized that merely being made to think about how other females and males do in math would cause their female participants to exhibit this identity bifurcation. That is, thinking about females generally underperforming in math relative to males would make individual women deny their own identification with aspects of femininity that were associated with negative stereotypes about women and math.

To test this hypothesis, Pronin and her colleagues had the students in the experiment read two scientific articles. For half of these students, one of these articles had nothing to do with gender or math, but the other article reported the results of a study of seventh- and eighth-graders who had taken a standardized math test. The article included a table of average scores for the boys and the girls, and the results indicated that, in general, the boys performed better than the girls on this test. The other half of the students in the study, in contrast, read two scientific articles that were irrelevant to gender and math.

Would reading about the underperformance of a group of seventh- and eighth-grade girls affect how these women felt about their own personalities? The results of this research suggest that it can. After the students read the scientific articles, they rated how strongly they personally identified with each of a series of feminine characteristics. The two bars on the left side of Figure 1.1 show the extent to which students indicated their identification with feminine characteristics that were associated with the negative stereotype of women in math. As you should see, the students who had read the article about gender differences among the seventh- and eighth-graders rated themselves as identifying less with these feminine characteristics (the yellow bar) than did the students who had not read this article (the blue bar). The two bars on the right side of Figure 1.1 show the ratings of the feminine characteristics that were not relevant to the stereotype. For these characteristics, which article the students had read did not make a reliable difference on the students' ratings.

A troubling fact about these results is that the women in this experiment were enrolled in an outstanding American university (Stanford University) and had demonstrated a great deal of ability and interest in math, and therefore they should have been among the best examples of individuals defying the negative stereotype about women and math. And yet, as we shall see in subsequent chapters of this book, the social context can have subtle and profound effects even on individuals who might otherwise seem well protected against it. Knowing the stereotype in their culture, even while defying it, and thinking about others who may have reinforced it were enough to cause the women in this study to become more likely to distance themselves from aspects of their feminine identity. A bit of good news, on the other hand, as we will see as well throughout this book, is that making changes to the social context in a more positive way, such as promoting positive rather than negative expectancies about an individual or group, can have powerfully positive effects.

FIGURE 1.1

Math or Femininity: Do Women Have to Choose?

This graph shows the results of an experiment by Emily Pronin and others (2004) in which female undergraduates rated how much they personally identified with a number of feminine characteristics. The results depicted here show that if the women had read a scientific article about girls underperforming relative to boys on a math test, these women subsequently reported identifying less with feminine characteristics that were relevant to negative stereotypes about women's ability in math than with feminine characteristics that were irrelevant to this stereotype. If the women had read an article having nothing to do with gender and math, however, they did not tend to devalue the feminine characteristics associated with the stereotype. This pattern of results suggests that women who aspire to achieve in math may sometimes feel pressure to disavow aspects of their femininity that some may see as incompatible with success in math. *(Based on Pronin et al., 2004.)*

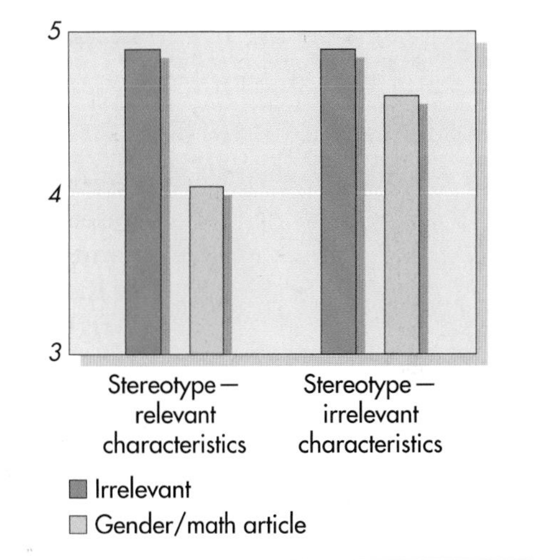

Social Psychology and Related Fields: Distinctions and Intersections

Social psychology is sometimes confused with certain other fields of study. Before we go on, it is important to clarify how social psychology is distinct from these other fields. At the same time, it is important to illustrate some of the ways in which interesting and significant questions can be addressed through interactions between social psychology and these other fields (see Table 1.2).

Social Psychology and Sociology Sociologists and social psychologists share an interest in many issues, such as violence, prejudice, cultural differences, and marriage. As noted, however, sociology tends to focus on the group level, whereas social psychology tends to focus on the individual level. For example, sociologists might track the political attitudes of the middle class in Canada, whereas social psychologists might examine some of the specific factors that make individuals like one political candidate better than another.

In addition, sociologists most often study the relation between people's behaviours and *societal* variables, such as social class. In contrast, social psychologists are more likely to study the relation between people's behaviours and more specific, immediate variables, such as manipulations of mood and exposure to particular models of behaviour. Finally, although there are many exceptions, social psychologists are more likely than sociologists to conduct experiments in which they manipulate some variable and determine the effects of this manipulation using precise, quantifiable measures.

Despite these differences, sociology and social psychology are clearly related. Indeed, many sociologists and social psychologists share the same training and publish in the same journals. When these two fields intersect, the result can be a more complete understanding of important issues. For example, interdisciplinary

TABLE 1.2

Distinctions Between Social Psychology and Related Fields: The Case of Research on Prejudice

To see the differences between social psychology and related fields, consider an example of how researchers in each field might conduct a study of prejudice.

Field of Study	Example of How a Researcher in the Field Might Study Prejudice
Sociology	Examine whether or not racial profiling is used by police officers to assist them in their investigations
Clinical psychology	Test various therapies for people with antisocial personalities who exhibit great degrees of prejudice
Personality psychology	Develop a questionnaire to identify men who are very high or low in degree of prejudice toward women
Cognitive psychology	Manipulate exposure to a member of some category of people and measure the thoughts and concepts that are automatically activated *(A study of prejudice in this field would, by definition, be at the intersection of cognitive and social psychology.)*
Social psychology	Manipulate various kinds of contact between individuals of different groups and examine the effect of these manipulations on the degree of prejudice exhibited

research on stereotyping and prejudice has examined the dynamic roles of both societal and immediate factors, such as how particular social systems or institutional norms and beliefs affect individuals' attitudes and behaviours (Eagly, 2004; Hogg & Ridgeway, 2003; Jost et al., 2004; Pratto, 2002; Schmitt et al., 2003; Tropp & Wright, 2003).

Social Psychology and Clinical Psychology Tell people not very familiar with psychology that you are taking a social psychology class, and they are likely to say things like "Oh, great, now you're going to start psychoanalyzing me" or "Finally, maybe you can tell me why everyone in my family is so messed up." The assumption underlying these reactions, of course, is that you are studying clinical, or abnormal, psychology. Clinical psychologists seek to understand and treat people with psychological difficulties or disorders. Social psychologists do not focus on disorders; rather, they focus on the more typical ways in which individuals think, feel, behave, and influence each other.

There are, however, many fascinating ways in which clinical and social psychology intersect. Both, for example, may address how people cope with anxiety or pressure in social situations; how depressed and nondepressed individuals differ in the way they process and understand social information or seek out interactions; how support, feedback, or rejection from others affects individuals' health and feelings of self-worth; and how stereotypes or social stigmas associated with various psychological disorders can affect individuals labelled with these disorders (e.g., Giesler & Swann, 1999; Hawkley et al., 2003; Lambert et al., 2003; Leary & Tangney, 2003; Major et al., 2004; Plant & Devine, 2003; Scott et al., 2003; Vaughn & Weary, 2002).

Social Psychology and Personality Psychology Both personality psychology and social psychology are concerned with individuals and their thoughts, feelings,

Are young children more likely to become aggressive after watching a television show depicting violence? Do violent video games make teenagers more aggressive? These are some of the questions that social psychology addresses.

and behaviours. However, personality psychology seeks to understand differences between individuals that remain relatively stable across a variety of situations, whereas social psychology seeks to understand how social factors affect most individuals, *regardless of* their different personalities.

In other words, personality psychologists are interested in cross-situational consistency. They may ask, "Is this person outgoing and friendly almost all the time, in just about any setting?" Social psychologists are interested in how different situations cause different behaviours. They may ask, "Are people in general more likely to seek out companionship when they are made anxious by a situation than when they are made to feel relaxed?"

These examples show the contrast between the fields; but in fact, personality psychology and social psychology are very closely linked. The Canadian Psychological Association has more than 25 different divisions, and yet personality psychologists and social psychologists share the same division. The reason for the high degree of connection between social psychology and personality psychology is that the two areas complement each other so well. For example, some social psychologists examine how receiving negative feedback (a situational factor) can have different effects on people as a function of whether their self-esteem is high or low (an individual-difference factor), or whether exposure to violent images on TV (a situational factor) is especially likely to trigger aggressiveness in particular types of children (an individual-difference factor) (Anderson et al., 2004; Vohs & Heatherton, 2001).

Social Psychology and Cognitive Psychology Cognitive psychologists study mental processes such as thinking, learning, remembering, and reasoning. Social psychologists are often interested in these same processes. More specifically, though, social psychologists are interested in how people think, learn, remember, and reason with respect to social information and in how these processes are relevant to social behaviour.

The last two decades have seen an explosion of interest in the intersection of cognitive and social psychology. The study of *social cognition* is discussed in more detail later in this chapter, and it is a focus throughout this text, especially in Part I on Social Perception.

Social Psychology and Common Sense

After reading about a theory or finding of social psychology, you may sometimes think, "Of course. I knew that all along. Anyone could have told me that." This "knew-it-all-along" phenomenon often causes people to question how social psychology is different from common sense, or traditional folk wisdom. After all, why would any of the following social psychological findings be surprising?

- Beauty and brains don't mix: Physically attractive people tend to be seen as less smart than physically unattractive people.
- People will like an activity more if you offer them a large reward for doing it, causing them to associate the activity with the positive reinforcement.
- People think that they're more distinctive than they really are: They tend to underestimate the extent to which others share the same opinions or interests.
- Playing contact sports or violent video games releases aggression and makes people less likely to vent their anger in violent ways.

We will have more to say about each of these statements later.

Common sense may seem to explain many social psychological findings after the fact. The problem is distinguishing common-sense fact from common-sense myth. After all, for most common-sense notions, there is an equally sensible-sounding notion that says the opposite. Is it "Birds of a feather flock together" or "Opposites attract"? Is it "Two heads are better than one" or "Too many cooks spoil the broth"? Which are correct? We have no reliable way to answer such questions through common sense or intuition alone.

Social psychology, unlike common sense, uses the scientific method to put its theories to the test. How it does so will be discussed in greater detail in the next chapter. But before we leave this section, one word of caution: Those four "findings" listed earlier? *They are all false.* Although there may be sensible reasons to believe each of the statements to be true, research indicates otherwise. Therein lies another problem with relying on common sense: Despite offering very compelling predictions and explanations, it is sometimes wildly inaccurate. And even when it is not completely wrong, common sense can be misleading in its simplicity. Often there is no simple answer to a question such as "Does absence make the heart grow fonder?" In reality, the answer is more complex than common sense would suggest, and social psychological research reveals how such an answer depends on a variety of factors.

To emphasize these points, and to encourage you to think critically about social psychological issues *before* as well as after learning about them, this textbook contains a feature called "Putting Common Sense to the Test." Beginning with Chapter 3, each chapter opens with a few statements about social psychological issues that will be covered in that chapter. Some of the statements are true, and some are false. As you read each statement, make a prediction about whether it is true or false, and think about *why* this is your prediction. Marginal notes throughout the chapter will tell you whether the statements are true or false. In reading the chapter, check not only whether your prediction was correct but also whether your reasons for the prediction were appropriate. If your intuition wasn't quite on the mark, think about what the right answer is and how the evidence supports that answer. There are few better ways of learning and remembering than through this kind of critical thinking.

From Past to Present: A Brief History of Social Psychology

"Psychology has a long past, but only a short history."

—Herman Ebbinghaus, *Summary of Psychology*

People have probably been asking social psychological questions for as long as humans could think about each other. Certainly, early philosophers such as Plato offered keen insights into many social psychological issues. But no systematic and scientific study of social psychological issues developed until the end of the nineteenth century. The field of social psychology is therefore a very young one. As a testament to this youth, the social psychologist Dorwin Cartwright said in 1979 that 90 percent of social psychologists who had ever lived were still alive at that time. Recent years have marked a tremendous interest in social psychology and an injection of many new scholars into the field. As social psychology begins its second century, it is instructive to look back to see how the field today has been shaped by the people and events of its first century.

The Birth and Infancy of Social Psychology: 1880s–1920s

Like most such honours, the title "founder of social psychology" has many potential recipients, and not everyone agrees on who should prevail. Most point to the American psychologist Norman Triplett, who is credited with having published the first research article in social psychology at the end of the nineteenth century (1897–1898). Triplett's work was noteworthy because, after observing that bicyclists tended to race faster when racing in the presence of others than when simply racing against a clock, he designed an experiment to study this phenomenon in a carefully controlled, precise way. This scientific approach to studying the effects of the social context on individuals' behaviour can be seen as marking the birth of social psychology.

A case can also be made for the French agricultural engineer Max Ringelmann. Ringelmann's research was conducted in the 1880s but wasn't published until 1913. In an interesting twist of fate, Ringelmann also studied the effects of the presence of others on the performance of individuals. In contrast to Triplett, however, Ringelmann noted that individuals often performed worse on simple tasks such as pulling rope when they performed the tasks with other people. The issues addressed by these two early researchers continue to be of vital interest, as will be seen later in Chapter 8 on Group Processes.

Lance Armstrong (front, yellow jersey) races on the way to winning his seventh Tour de France in July 2005. Would Armstrong and his fellow cyclists have raced faster or slower if they were running individually against the clock rather than running simultaneously with their competitors? More generally, what effect does the presence of others have on an individual's performance? The two founders of social psychology, American psychologist Norman Triplett and French agricultural engineer Max Ringelmann, sought answers to questions such as these. Chapter 8 on Group Processes brings you up-to-date on the latest research in this area.

Despite their place in the history of social psychology, neither Triplett nor Ringelmann actually established social psychology as a distinct field of study. Credit for this creation goes to the writers of the first three textbooks in social psychology: the English psychologist William McDougall (1908) and two Americans, Edward Ross (1908) and Floyd Allport (1924). Allport's book in particular, with its focus on the interaction of individuals and their social context and its emphasis on the use of experimentation and the scientific method, helped establish social psychology as the discipline it is today. These authors announced the arrival of a new approach to the social aspects of human behaviour. Social

What determines whether people are likely to act to conserve their environment, as these students did by volunteering their time to clean up a beach? Built on the legacy of Kurt Lewin, one of the leading figures in the development of the field, applied social psychology contributes to the solution of numerous social problems, such as environmental conservation.

psychology was born. As early as 1913, McGill University offered a course in social psychology (Ferguson, 1992).

A Call to Action: 1930s–1950s

What one person would you guess has had the strongest influence on the field of social psychology? Various social psychologists, as well as psychologists of other areas, might be mentioned in response to this question. But someone who was not a psychologist at all may have had the most dramatic impact on the field: Adolf Hitler.

Hitler's rise to power and the ensuing turmoil caused people around the world to become desperate for answers to social psychological questions about what causes violence, prejudice and genocide, conformity and obedience, and a host of other social problems and behaviours. In addition, many social psychologists living in Europe in the 1930s fled to Canada and the United States and helped establish a critical mass of social psychologists who would give shape to the rapidly maturing field. The years just before, during, and soon after World War II marked an explosion of interest in social psychology.

In 1936, Gordon Allport (younger brother of Floyd, author of the 1924 textbook) and a number of other social psychologists formed the Society for the Psychological Study of Social Issues. The name of the society illustrates these psychologists' concern for making important, practical contributions to society. Also in 1936, a social psychologist named Muzafer Sherif published groundbreaking experimental research on social influence. As a youth in Turkey, Sherif had witnessed groups of Greek soldiers brutally killing his friends. After immigrating to the United States, Sherif drew on this experience and began to conduct research on the powerful influences groups can exert on their individual members. Sherif's research was crucial for the development of social psychology because it demonstrated that it is possible to study complex social processes such as conformity and social influence in a rigorous, scientific manner. This innovation laid the foundation for what was to become one of the major topics in social psychology. Research and theory on social influence are discussed throughout this text, particularly in Part II on Social Influence.

Another great contributor to social psychology, Kurt Lewin, fled the Nazi onslaught in Germany and immigrated to the United States in the early 1930s. Lewin was a bold and creative theorist whose concepts have had lasting effects on the field. Among the fundamental principles of social psychology that Lewin (1935, 1947) helped establish were the following:

What we do depends to a large extent on how we perceive and interpret the world around us. Different people can see the same situation differently, and their behaviour will vary accordingly. This theme continues to be important in social psychology. You will encounter it throughout this textbook, especially in Part I on Social Perception.

Behaviour is a function of the interaction between the person and the environment. Lewin's conviction that both internal and external factors affect behaviour helped create a unified view that was distinct from the other major psychological paradigms during his lifetime: psychoanalysis, with its emphasis on internal motives and fantasies; and behaviourism, with its focus on external rewards and punishments. Lewin's position was an early version of what today is known as the **interactionist perspective** (Blass, 1991). This approach combines personality psychology (stressing internal, psychological differences among individuals) with social psychology (stressing differences among external situations). Throughout this book, we examine the impact of both individual and situational differences, alone and together.

Social psychological theories should be applied to important, practical issues. Lewin researched a number of practical issues, such as how to persuade Americans at home during the war to conserve materials to help the war effort; how to promote more economical and nutritious eating habits; and what kinds of leaders elicit the best work from group members. Through these studies, Lewin showed how social psychology could enlarge our understanding of social problems and contribute to their solutions. Built on Lewin's legacy, applied social psychology flourishes today in areas such as advertising, business, education, environmental protection, health, law, politics, public policy, religion, and sports. Throughout this text, we draw on the findings of applied social psychology to illustrate the implications of social psychological principles for our daily lives. In Chapter 12, the application of social psychology to the legal system is discussed in detail. One of Lewin's statements can be seen as a call to action for the entire field: "No research without action, no action without research."

During World War II, many social psychologists answered Lewin's call as they worked for the Canadian and US governments to investigate how to protect soldiers from the propaganda of the enemy, how to persuade citizens to support the war effort, how to select officers for various positions, and other practical issues. During and after the war, social psychologists sought to understand the prejudice, aggression, and conformity the war had brought to light. The 1950s saw many major contributions to the field of social psychology; Table 1.3 lists just some of them. With this remarkable burst of activity and impact, social psychology was clearly, and irrevocably, on the map.

Confidence and Crisis: 1960s–Mid-1970s

In spectacular fashion, Stanley Milgram's research in the early and middle 1960s linked the post-World War II era with the coming era of social revolution. Milgram's research was inspired by the destructive obedience demonstrated by Nazi officers and ordinary citizens in World War II, but it also looked ahead to the civil disobedience that was beginning to challenge institutions in many parts of the world. Milgram's experiments, which demonstrated individuals' vulnerability to the destructive commands of authority, became the most famous research in the history of social psychology. This research is discussed in detail in Chapter 7.

With its foundation firmly in place, social psychology entered a period of expansion and enthusiasm. In the 1970s the Canadian government expanded its funding programs, attracting many social psychologists from the US (Adair, 2005). The sheer range of its investigations was staggering. Social psychologists considered how people thought and felt about themselves and others. They studied interactions in groups and social problems such as why people fail to help others in distress. They also examined aggression, physical attractiveness, and stress. For the field as a whole, it was a time of great productivity.

interactionist perspective An emphasis on how both an individual's personality and environmental characteristics influence behaviour.

TABLE 1.3

Some Major Contributions to Social Psychology During the 1950s

Contributor	Contribution	Discussed in This Text
Theodor Adorno and colleagues	Published *The Authoritarian Personality,* an influential book on prejudice	Perceiving Groups (Chapter 5)
Gordon Allport	Published *The Nature of Prejudice,* which continues to inspire research on stereotyping and prejudice	Perceiving Groups (Chapter 5)
Solomon Asch	Demonstrated individuals' tendency to conform to an obviously wrong majority; studied how individuals form impressions of others	Conformity (Chapter 7); Perceiving Persons (Chapter 4)
Leon Festinger	Introduced theory of social comparison, concerning how people look to others to learn about themselves; introduced theory of cognitive dissonance, concerning people's desire to maintain consistency in their thoughts and behaviours	The Social Self (Chapter 3), Stereotypes, Prejudice, and Discrimination (Chapter 5); Attitudes (Chapter 6)
Fritz Heider	Introduced attribution theory, concerning how people judge others and the causes of their behaviour; introduced balance theory, concerning people's desire for consistency in their thoughts, feelings, and relationships	Perceiving Persons (Chapter 4); Attraction and Close Relationships (Chapter 9)
Carl Hovland and colleagues	Conducted experiments on attitudes and persuasion, which was influential not only to social psychology but to the rapidly growing advertising industry	Attitudes (Chapter 6)
John Thibaut and Harold Kelley	Studied how people consider costs and rewards in their relationships	Attraction and Close Relationships (Chapter 9)

Ironically, it was also a time of crisis and heated debate. Many of the strong disagreements during this period can be understood as a reaction to the dominant research method of the day: the laboratory experiment. The social psychologists who questioned this type of research maintained that certain practices were unethical (Kelman, 1967), that experimenters' expectations influenced their participants' behaviour (Orne, 1962; Rosenthal, 1976), and that the theories being tested in the laboratory were historically and culturally limited (Gergen, 1973). Those who favoured laboratory experimentation, on the other hand, contended that their procedures were ethical, their results valid, and their theoretical principles widely applicable (McGuire, 1967). For a while, social psychology seemed split in two.

An Era of Pluralism: Mid-1970s–1990s

Fortunately, both sides won. As we will see in the next chapter, more rigorous ethical standards for research were instituted, more stringent procedures to guard against bias were adopted, and more attention was paid to possible cross-cultural differences in behaviour. But the baby was not thrown out with the bath water. Laboratory experiments continued. They did, however, get some company, as a single-minded attachment to one research method evolved into a broader acceptance of many methods. The logic behind a pluralistic approach is compelling (Carr & MacLachlan, 1998; Houts et al., 1986):

- Because different topics require different kinds of investigations, a range of research techniques is needed.
- Because no research method is perfect, a *multimethod* investigation of a topic increases our confidence that the results obtained do not simply reflect the peculiar characteristics of any one approach.

The various research methods used by today's social psychologists are described in the next chapter.

Pluralism in social psychology extends far beyond its methods. There are also important variations in what aspects of human behaviour are emphasized. Some social psychology research takes what we might call a "hot" perspective, focusing on *emotion* and *motivation* as determinants of our thoughts and actions. Other research in this field takes a "cold" perspective that emphasizes the role of *cognition*, examining the ways in which people's thoughts affect how they feel, what they want, and what they do. Of course, some social psychologists examine behaviour from both perspectives separately as well as interactively. Integrating such different perspectives is characteristic of the pluralism that the field has come to embrace in recent years.

Another source of pluralism in social psychology is its development of international and multicultural perspectives. Although, as we have seen, individuals from many countries helped establish the field, social psychology achieved its greatest professional recognition in Canada and the United States. At one point, it was estimated that 75 to 90 percent of social psychologists lived in North America (Smith

Social psychologists are becoming increasingly interested in cross-cultural research, which helps us break out of our culture-bound perspective. Many of our behaviours differ across cultures. In some cultures, for example, people are expected to negotiate about the price of the products they buy, as in this market in Tunisia. In other cultures, such bargaining would be highly unusual and cause confusion and distress.

& Bond, 1993; Triandis, 1994). Indeed, some called social psychology "culture-bound" (Berry et al., 1992) and "largely monocultural" (Moghaddam et al., 1993). However, this aspect of social psychology began to change rapidly in the 1990s, reflecting not only the different geographic and cultural backgrounds of its researchers and participants but also the recognition that many social psychological phenomena once assumed to be universal may actually vary dramatically as a function of culture (Kitayama et al., 2003; Miller-Loessi & Parker, 2003; Nisbett, 2004). While there is a great deal of similarity between the types of research conducted on both sides of the border, Canadian research has a strong focus on our cultural identity as well as uniquely Canadian issues, such as bilingualism and multiculturalism (Adair, 2005).

Social Psychology in a New Century

As we began the twenty-first century, social psychology began its second hundred years. The field today continues to grow in number and diversity of researchers and research topics, areas of the world in which research is conducted, and industries that hire social psychologists and apply their work.

Throughout this text, we emphasize the most current, cutting-edge research in the field, along with the classic findings of the past. In the remainder of the chapter we focus on a few of the exciting themes and perspectives emerging from current research—research that is helping to shape the social psychology of the new century.

Integration of Emotion, Motivation, and Cognition

If any one perspective dominated the final quarter of social psychology's first century, it may have been **social cognition,** the study of how we perceive, remember, and interpret information about ourselves and others. Social psychologists demon-

We are constantly making judgements about our own behaviour, as well as the behaviour of others. Such judgements may help us feel good about ourselves, although at times they may come at the expense of accuracy.

social cognition The study of how people perceive, remember, and interpret information about themselves and others.

strated that these social-cognitive processes are critically important to virtually every area in the field. Social-cognitive explanations were so powerful that the roles of "hotter" influences, such as emotions and motivations, often took a back seat. Social cognition continues to flourish, but one of the more exciting developments in the field is the re-emergence of interest in how individuals' emotions and motivations influence their thoughts and actions. Especially exciting is the fact that the social-cognitive approach is not necessarily seen as being at odds with approaches that emphasize motivations and emotions. Instead, there is a new push to integrate these perspectives, as in research investigating how people's motivations influence nonconscious cognitive processes, and vice versa (Forgas et al., 2004; Kruglanski et al., 2002; Moskowitz et al., 2004; Spencer et al., 2003).

One issue illustrating the integration of "hot" and "cold" variables concerns the conflict between wanting to be right and wanting to feel good about oneself. Most of us hold two very different motivations simultaneously: On the one hand, we want to be accurate in our judgments about ourselves and others. On the other hand, we *don't* want to be accurate if it means we will learn something bad about ourselves or those closest to us. These goals can pull our cognitive processes in very different directions. How we perform the required mental gymnastics is an ongoing concern for social psychologists.

Another theme running through many chapters of this book is the growing interest in distinguishing between automatic and controllable processes and in understanding the dynamic relationship between them (Chaiken & Trope, 1999; Dovidio et al., 2002; Wegner, 2003). For example, there is a great deal of new evidence concerning whether and when stereotypes can be activated in one's mind automatically—that is, quickly and spontaneously, with no awareness, intention, or effort, and possibly even against one's will. On the other hand, there also is growing evidence that even such automatic reactions can be controlled under particular conditions. Individuals' conscious and nonconscious motivations can play important but complex roles in both the activation and suppression of negative stereotypes. The automatic and controlled nature of a variety of processes and behaviours relevant to social psychology will no doubt continue to be an exciting area of research in the coming years.

Biological and Evolutionary Perspectives

As the technology available to researchers evolves, biological perspectives are increasingly being integrated into all branches of psychology, and this integration should continue to grow in social psychology. We are, of course, biological organisms, and it is clear that our brains and bodies influence, and are influenced by, our social experiences.

Social psychologists have been concerned with physiological influences and responses for many years. Examples of this interest can be found throughout the textbook, especially in discussions of self-perception, attribution, attitude change, attraction, and aggression. A particularly exciting recent development is the emergence of the subfield of **social neuroscience**—the study of the relationship between neural and social processes. Social neuroscience is part of a flourishing set of research that explores how the social world affects the brain and biology, and vice versa. Recent research has investigated such issues as the relationship between loneliness and the discharge of particular hormones, and gender differences in neuroendocrine reactivity in response to stress (Bernston & Cacioppo, 2004; Eberhardt & Goff, 2004; Ochsner & Lieberman, 2001). Cunningham and others (2004) have studied the relationship between activity in the amygdala (a structure in the brain) and how one responds to observing black versus white faces. Participants who briefly (30 ms) viewed a black face showed greater activation in the amygdala than

social neuroscience The study of the relationship between neural and social processes.

did those who viewed the same black face for a longer period of time (525 ms); in that case, areas of the brain responsible for inhibition and control were activated. It seems that the initial reaction is an automatic response, but given time, it is possible to overcome—or at least control—one's emotions.

Recent advances in **behavioural genetics**—a subfield of psychology that examines the effects of genes on behaviour—has triggered new research to investigate such matters as the extent to which aggression is an inherited trait and the roles that genes play in individuals' sexual orientation or identity (Miller, 2000; Rowe et al., 1999).

Evolutionary psychology, which uses the principles of evolution to understand human behaviour, is another growing area that is sparking new research in social psychology. According to this perspective, to understand a social psychological issue such as jealousy, we should ask how the psychological mechanisms underlying jealousy today may have evolved from the natural-selection pressures our ancestors faced. Evolutionary psychological theories can then be used to explain and predict gender differences in jealousy, the situational factors most likely to trigger jealousy, and so on (Buss, 2004). This perspective is discussed in many places in the textbook, especially in Part III on Social Relations.

Sociocultural Perspectives

Because of such developments as satellite communications, the Internet, and the globalization of the world's economies, it is faster, easier, and more necessary than ever before for people from vastly different cultures to interact with one another. Thus, our need and desire to understand how we are similar to and different from one another are greater than ever as well. Social psychology is currently experiencing tremendous growth in research designed to give us a better understanding and appreciation of the role of culture in all aspects of social psychology.

Increasing numbers of social psychologists are evaluating the universal generality or cultural specificity of their theories and findings by conducting **cross-cultural research,** in which they examine similarities and differences across a variety of cultures. More and more social psychologists are also conducting **multicultural research,** in which they examine racial and ethnic groups within cultures.

These developments are already profoundly influencing our view of human behaviour. For example, the greater emphasis by European social psychologists on the meaning and impact of group membership has vastly increased the "socialness" of social psychology, and cross-cultural research has revealed important distinctions between the collectivist cultures typically found in Africa, Asia, and Latin America and the individualistic ones more commonly found in North America and Europe (e.g., Heine, 2005; Kim & Markus, 2002; Oyserman & Lauffer, 2002; Waid & Frazier, 2003).

Sociocultural factors clearly contribute to differences between men and women on a number of dimensions; and for years, social psychologists have studied gender differences in a variety of domains, such as conformity, leadership style, and aggression. Recent research is not only extending this tradition, it is sometimes turning it on its ear by illustrating that many previous research programs were flawed as a result of taking a male-dominated approach. New research on aggression, for example, illustrates that most of the older research focused almost exclusively on the forms of aggression typical of boys, thereby failing to recognize important issues relevant to aggression among girls.

These are but a few examples of the sociocultural research taking place today. In this text, we describe studies conducted in dozens of countries, representing every continent on earth. As our knowledge expands, we should be able to see much more clearly both the behavioural differences among cultures and the similarities we all share.

behavioural genetics A subfield of psychology that examines the role of genetic factors in behaviour.

evolutionary psychology A subfield of psychology that uses the principles of evolution to understand human social behaviour.

cross-cultural research Research designed to compare and contrast people of different cultures.

multicultural research Research designed to examine racial and ethnic groups within cultures.

Some social psychology textbooks devote a separate chapter to culture or to culture and gender. We chose not to do so. Because we believe that sociocultural influences are inherent in all aspects of social psychology, we chose instead to integrate discussions of the role of culture and gender throughout the textbook.

New Technologies

Advances in technologies that allow researchers to see images of the brain at work, through noninvasive procedures, have had a profound effect on several areas of psychology, including social psychology. A growing number of social psychologists are using techniques such as *positron emission tomography (PET)* and *functional magnetic resonance imaging (fMRI)* to study the interplay of the brain and discrete thoughts, feelings, and behaviours. Social psychology research today benefits from other technological advances as well, such as new and better techniques to measure hormone levels, to code people's everyday dialogue into quantifiable units, and to present visual stimuli to research participants at fractions of a second and then record the number of milliseconds it takes the participants to respond to these stimuli. Researchers are just beginning to use virtual reality technology to examine a number of social psychological questions. James Blascovich and others have created The Research Center for Virtual Environments and Behavior at the University of California at Santa Barbara and have been conducting fascinating research on issues such as conformity, group dynamics, aggression and altruism, and eyewitness testimony (e.g., Bailenson et al., 2003). Because participants in these experiments are immersed in a virtual reality that the experimenters create for them, the researchers can test questions that would be impractical, impossible, or unethical without this technology.

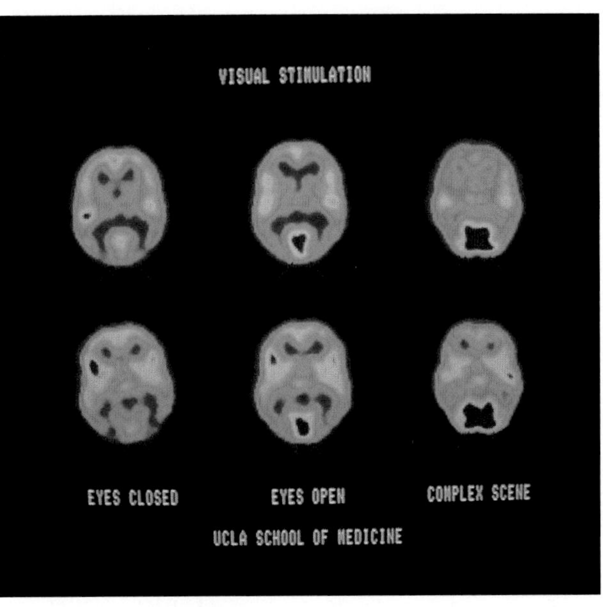

Advances in technology enable social psychologists to extend their research in exciting new directions, such as by using positron emission tomography (PET) *and* functional magnetic resonance imaging (fMRI) *to study activation in the brain in response to various thoughts or stimuli. In this PET scan the areas in red reveal the most intense brain activity as a function of visual stimulation.*

As the Internet expands at a dizzying rate, its role in social psychology research grows along with it. Through the Internet, researchers around the world can now not only communicate and collaborate much more easily but also gain access to research participants from populations that would otherwise never have been available. These developments have sparked the field's internationalization, perhaps its most exciting course in this new century. World War II triggered an explosion of social psychological research in North America; the Internet is extending this research to the rest of the world.

The Internet itself is also becoming a provocative topic of study. As more people interact with each other through email and chat rooms, there is growing interest in studying how attraction, prejudice, group dynamics, and a host of other social psychological phenomena unfold online versus offline (Bargh et al., 2003).

"Awesome" is an overused word, but it surely is appropriate to describe the revolution that is taking place in how we access information and communicate with each other. In writing this new edition of *Social Psychology*, we have been amazed to discover how much more information is available through our computers today than just a few years ago. We would be presumptuous, and probably naive, to try to predict how new communication and computer technologies will influence the ways in which people interact in the coming years; but it probably is safe to predict that their influence will be great. As more and more people fall in love online, or fall into social isolation, or react with anxiety or violence to the loss of individual privacy, social psychology will explore these issues. We expect that some of the students reading this textbook today will be among those explorers in the coming years.

Review

What Is Social Psychology?

Defining Social Psychology

- Social psychology is the scientific study of how individuals think, feel, and behave in regard to other people and how individuals' thoughts, feelings, and behaviours are affected by other people.
- Like other sciences, social psychology relies on the systematic approach of the scientific method.
- Distinctive characteristics of social psychology include a focus on the individual as well as a broad perspective on a variety of social contexts and behaviours.
- The "socialness" of social psychology varies, as social psychologists sometimes examine how nonsocial factors affect social thoughts, feelings, and behaviours and sometimes study how social factors influence nonsocial thoughts, feelings, and behaviours.

Social Psychological Questions and Applications

- Social psychologists study a large variety of fascinating questions about people and their social worlds. The scope and relevance of these questions to so many important aspects of our lives make social psychology applicable to many careers and interests.

The Power of the Social Context: An Example of a Social Psychology Experiment

- In one experiment that illustrates the power of thinking about others, female undergraduate students who cared about math disavowed aspects of their feminine identity that were relevant to negative stereotypes about women and math if they had just read about the underperformance on a math test of a number of seventh- and eighth-grade girls relative to boys.

Social Psychology and Related Fields: Distinctions and Intersections

- Social psychology is related to a number of different areas of study, including sociology, clinical psychology, personality psychology, and cognitive psychology. Important work is being done at the intersection of social psychology and each of these fields.
- Social psychology tends to focus on individuals, whereas sociology tends to focus on groups. In addition, social psychology is less likely than sociology to study the relation between broad societal variables and people's behaviours and is more likely to use experimentation.
- In contrast to clinical psychology, social psychology focuses not on disorders but, rather, on the more typical ways in which individuals think, feel, behave, and interact.
- Personality psychology focuses on differences between individuals that remain relatively stable across a variety of situations; social psychology focuses on how social factors affect most individuals, regardless of their different personalities.
- Cognitive and social psychologists share an interest in mental processes such as thinking, learning, remembering, and reasoning; but social psychologists focus on the relevance of these processes to social behaviour.

Social Psychology and Common Sense

- Many social psychological theories and findings appear to be like common sense. One problem with common sense, however, is that it may offer conflicting explanations and provide no way to test which is correct. Another problem is that common sense is often oversimplified and therefore misleading.

From Past to Present: A Brief History of Social Psychology

The Birth and Infancy of Social Psychology: 1880s–1920s

- Early research by Triplett and Ringelmann established an enduring topic in social psychology: how the presence of others affects an individual's performance.
- The first social psychology textbooks in 1908 and 1924 began to give the emerging field of social psychology its shape.

A Call to Action: 1930s–1950s

- Trying to explain, and offer solutions to, a world at war, social psychology began to flourish.
- Sherif's work laid the foundation for later studies of social influence, and the legacy of Kurt Lewin is still evident throughout much of social psychology.
- The 1940s and 1950s saw a burst of activity in social psychology that firmly established it as a major social science.

Confidence and Crisis: 1960s–Mid-1970s

- Stanley Milgram's experiments demonstrated individuals' vulnerability to the destructive commands of authority.
- While social psychology was expanding in many new directions, there was also intense debate about the ethics of research procedures, the validity of research results, and the generalizability of conclusions drawn from the research.

An Era of Pluralism: Mid-1970s–1990s

- During the 1970s, social psychology began to take a pluralistic approach that continues today in its research methods, views on human behaviour, and development of international and multicultural perspectives.

Social Psychology in a New Century

- Several exciting themes and perspectives are helping to shape the beginning of social psychology's second century.

Integration of Emotion, Motivation, and Cognition

- Researchers are becoming more interested in how emotion, motivation, and cognition can operate together in influencing individuals' thoughts, feelings, and behaviours.
- A great deal of recent social psychological research has explored the automatic versus controllable nature of a number of processes, such as stereotyping.

Biological and Evolutionary Perspectives

- Biological perspectives, including perspectives based on neuroscience, genetics, and evolutionary principles, are being applied to the study of social psychological issues such as gender differences, relationships, and aggression.

Sociocultural Perspectives

- Increasing numbers of social psychologists are evaluating the universal generality or cultural specificity of their theories and findings by examining similarities and differences across cultures as well as between racial and ethnic groups within cultures.

New Technologies

- Advances in technology, such as improved brain imaging techniques, have given rise to groundbreaking research in social psychology.
- The Internet has fostered communication and collaboration among researchers around the world, enabled researchers to study participants from diverse populations, and inspired researchers to investigate whether various social psychological phenomena are similar or different online versus offline.
- As rapidly advancing technologies change how individuals communicate and access information, the ways in which they interact are also likely to change. The social psychology of the next era will explore these issues.
- Virtual reality technology enables researchers to test questions that otherwise would be impractical, impossible, or unethical.

Key Terms

behavioural genetics *(20)*
cross-cultural research *(20)*
evolutionary psychology *(20)*
interactionist perspective *(15)*
multicultural research *(20)*
social cognition *(18)*
social neuroscience *(19)*
social psychology *(5)*

2 Doing Social Psychology Research

OUTLINE

PREVIEW

THIS CHAPTER examines how social psychologists do their research. We begin by asking, "Why should you learn about research methods?" We answer this question by discussing how learning about research methods can benefit you both in this course and beyond. Then we consider how researchers come up with and develop ideas and begin the research process. Next, we provide an overview of the research designs that social psychologists use to test their ideas. Finally, we turn to important questions about ethics and values in social psychology.

"The most exciting phrase to hear in science, the one that heralds new discoveries, is not 'Eureka!' (I found it!) but 'That's funny. . . .'"

—Isaac Asimov

It's a familiar situation. You're starting a new semester at school, and you're just beginning to settle into a new schedule and routine. You're looking forward to your new courses. In general, it's an exciting time. But there's one major catch: As you spend more and more time with your new classmates and new responsibilities, you're leaving someone behind. It could be a boyfriend or girlfriend, a spouse, or a close friend—someone who is not involved in what you are doing now. You may now live far apart from each other, or your new commitments in school may be keeping you apart from each other much more than you'd like. The romantic in you says, "Together forever." Or at least, "No problem." But the realist in you worries a bit. Will your love or friendship be the same? Can it survive the long distance, or the new demands on your time, or the new people in your respective environments? Your friends or family may have advice to offer in this situation. Some might smile and reassure you, "Don't worry. Remember what they say, 'Absence makes the heart grow fonder.' This will only strengthen your relationship." Others might call you aside and whisper, "Don't listen to them. Everybody knows, 'Out of sight, out of mind.' You'd better be careful."

Taking your mind off this problem, you begin to work on a class project. You have the option of working alone or as part of a group. Which should you do? You consult the wisdom of common sense. Maybe you should work in a group. After all, everyone knows that "two heads are better than one." As some members of your group begin to miss meetings and shirk responsibilities, though, you remember that "too many cooks spoil the broth." Will you regret having been so quick to decide to join this group? After all, haven't you been taught to "look before you leap?" Then again, if you had waited and missed the chance to join the group, you might have regretted your inaction, recalling that "he who hesitates is lost."

Questions about the course of relationships, the efficiency of working in groups, and the regret of action versus inaction are social psychological questions. And because we all are interested in predicting and explaining people's behaviours and their thoughts and feelings about each other, we all have our own opinions and intuitions about social psychological matters. If the discipline of social psychology were built on the personal experiences, observations, and intuitions of everyone who is interested in social psychological questions, it would be chock full of interesting theories and ideas; but it would also be a morass of contradictions, ambiguities, and relativism. Instead, social psychology is built on the scientific method.

Scientific? It's easy to see how chemistry is scientific. When you mix two specific compounds in the lab, you can predict exactly what will happen. The compounds will act the same way every time you mix them if the general conditions in the lab are the same. But what happens when you mix together two chemists, or any two people, in a social context? Sometimes you get great chemistry between them; other times you get apathy or even repulsion. How, then, can social behaviour, which seems so variable, be studied scientifically?

To many of us in the field, that's the great excitement and challenge of social psychology—the fact that it is so dynamic and diverse. Furthermore, in spite of these characteristics, social psychology can, and should, be studied according to scientific principles. Social psychologists develop specific, quantifiable hypotheses that can be tested empirically. If these hypotheses are wrong, they can be proven wrong. In addition, social scientists report the details of how they conduct their tests so that others can try to replicate their findings. They integrate evidence from across time and place. And slowly but steadily, they build a consistent and ever more precise understanding of human nature. How social psychologists investigate social psychological questions scientifically is the focus of this chapter. Before we explain the methodology they use, we first explain a bit about why it's important and interesting for you to learn about these matters.

Why Should You Learn About Research Methods?

One very practical reason for learning about research methods is that it will help you better understand and learn the material in this book, which will in turn help you on tests and in subsequent courses. Let's look more closely at why this is so. Because social psychology is so relevant to our everyday lives, and because there are so many common-sense notions about social psychological questions, separating myths from truths can be difficult. Most of us don't have an intuition about particular questions concerning quantum mechanics, but we do have intuitions about, say, whether people work better alone or in groups. If you simply read a list of social psychological findings about issues such as this, without knowing and understanding the evidence that social psychologists have produced to support the findings, you may discover later that the task of remembering which were the actual findings and which were merely your own intuitions is difficult. This task is sometimes especially challenging in multiple-choice exams. The right answer might seem very plausible; but then again, so might some of the wrong answers, just as there are good reasons to believe both that "two heads are better than one" and that "too many cooks spoil the broth."

We are bombarded with information in our everyday lives, such as in the countless advertisements designed to persuade us to buy particular products or adopt particular opinions or attitudes. Learning the methods used in social psychology research can help students become more sophisticated consumers of this information.

But the benefits of learning about research methods go far beyond the academic. Training in research methods in psychology can improve your reasoning about real-life events (Lehman et al., 1988; VanderStoep & Shaughnessy, 1997). It can make you a better, more sophisticated consumer of information in general. We are constantly bombarded with "facts" from the media, from sales pitches, and from other people. Much of this information turns out to be wrong or, at best, oversimplified and misleading. We are told about the health benefits of eating certain kinds of food, or the social status benefits of driving a certain kind of car or wearing a certain kind of shoe. To each of these pronouncements, we should say, "Prove it." What is the evidence? What alternative explanations might there be? For example, a commercial tells us that most doctors prefer a particular (and relatively expensive)

brand of aspirin. So should we buy this brand? Think about what it was compared with. Perhaps the doctors didn't prefer that brand of aspirin over other (and cheaper) brands of aspirin but, rather, were asked to compare that brand of aspirin with several non-aspirin products for a particular problem. In that event, the doctors may have preferred *any* brand of aspirin over non-aspirin products for that need. Thinking like a scientist while reading this text will foster a healthy sense of doubt about claims like these. You will be in a better position to critically evaluate the information to which you're exposed and separate fact from fiction.

"Education is not the filling of a pail, but the lighting of a fire."

—William Butler Yeats

Developing Ideas: Beginning the Research Process

The research process involves coming up with ideas, refining them, testing them, and interpreting the meaning of the results obtained. This section describes the first stage of research, coming up with ideas. It also discusses the role of hypotheses and theories and of basic and applied research.

Asking Questions

Every social psychology study begins with a question. And the questions come from everywhere. As discussed in Chapter 1, the first social psychology experiment published was triggered by the question "Why do bicyclists race faster in the presence of other bicyclists?" (Triplett, 1897–1898). Inspiration can come from a variety of sources, from the distressing, such as a gruesome murder and the inaction of witnesses to that murder (Latané & Darley, 1970), to the amusing, such as the lyrics of a country song suggesting that to the men in a bar, the female patrons seem prettier as closing time approaches (Pennebaker et al., 1979).

Questions also come from reading about research that has already been done. Solomon Asch (1946), for example, read about Muzafer Sherif's (1936) demonstration of how individuals in a group conform to others in the group when making judgments about a very ambiguous stimulus (mentioned in Chapter 1 and described in Chapter 7 on Conformity). Asch questioned whether people would conform to the opinions of others in a group even when it was quite clear that the group was wrong. He tested this question, and the results surprised him and the rest of the field: People often did conform even though it was clear that the group was wrong. Thus, one of the most famous experiments in the field inspired an even more famous experiment.

On April 28, 1999 a 14-year-old boy opened fire at W.R. Myers High School in Taber, Alberta. One student was killed and another injured; the shooter was a former student who had dropped out of high school a year earlier. He had reportedly been the victim of extensive teasing and bullying by his former classmates. The shooting came just eight days after the Littleton, Colorado massacre during which 12 students and one teacher were killed by two students. Over the years, tragic incidents like these have inspired social psychologists to conduct research on violence and a wide range of other important social problems.

Searching the Literature

Once the researcher has an idea, whether it came from personal observation, folk wisdom, a news story, or previous findings, it is important to see what research has already been done on this topic and related topics. Textbooks such as this one offer a starting point. One of the best ways to search for published materials on topics of interest is by using an electronic database. Electronic databases can store tremendous amounts of information on computers, and the information can be accessed very quickly and easily. Some of

"Give people facts and you feed their minds for an hour. Awaken curiosity and they feed their own minds for a lifetime."
—Ian Russell

these databases, such as PsycArticles and PsycINFO, are specific to the psychology literature; others are more general. When you use an electronic database, you can search hundreds of thousands of published articles and books in seconds. You can type in names of authors, key words or phrases, years, or the like and instantly receive summaries of articles that fit your search criteria. In addition to searching databases specific to the psychology literature, you can learn about other research by searching more generally—on the World Wide Web, say, or in databases containing references to newspaper and magazine articles. Once you have found some relevant articles, there is a good chance that they will refer to other articles that are also relevant. Going from article to article, sometimes called *treeing*, can prove very valuable in tracking down information about the research question.

More often than not, the researcher's original question is changed in one way or another during the course of searching the literature. The question should become more precise, more specific to particular sets of conditions that are likely to have different effects, and more readily testable.

Hypotheses and Theories

"The currency of science is not truth, but doubt."
—Dennis Overbye

An initial idea for research may be so vague that it amounts to little more than a hunch or an educated guess. Some ideas vanish with the break of day. But others can be shaped into a **hypothesis**—an explicit, testable prediction about the conditions under which an event will occur. Based on observation, existing theory, or previous research findings, one might test a hypothesis such as "Teenage boys are more likely to be aggressive toward others if they have just played a violent video game for an hour than if they played a nonviolent video game for an hour." This is a specific prediction, and it can be tested empirically. Formulating a hypothesis is a critical step toward planning and conducting research. It allows us to move from the realm of common sense to the rigours of the scientific method.

As hypotheses proliferate and data are collected to test the hypotheses, a more advanced step in the research process may take place: the proposal of a **theory**—an organized set of principles used to explain observed phenomena. Theories are usually evaluated in terms of three criteria: simplicity, comprehensiveness, and their ability to generate new hypotheses. All else being equal, the best theories are elegant and precise; encompass all of the relevant information; and lead to new hypotheses, further research, and better understanding.

In social psychology, there are many theories. Social psychologists do not attempt the all-encompassing grand theory, such as those of Freud or Piaget, which you may have studied in introductory psychology. Instead, they rely on more precise "mini-theories" that address limited and specific aspects of the way people behave, make explicit predictions about behaviour, and allow meaningful empirical investigation. Consider, for example, Daryl Bem's (1967, 1972) self-perception theory, which is discussed in Chapter 3 on the Social Self. Bem proposed that when people's internal states, such as a feeling or attitude, are difficult for them to interpret, they infer this feeling or attitude by observing their own behaviour and the situation in which it takes place. This theory did not apply to all situations; rather, it was specific to situations in which people made inferences about their own actions when their own internal states were somewhat ambiguous. Though more limited in scope than a grand theory of personality or development, self-perception theory did generate numerous specific, empirically testable hypotheses.

Good social psychological theories inspire subsequent research. Specifically, they stimulate systematic studies designed to test various aspects of the theories and the specific hypotheses that are derived from them. A theory may be quite accurate and yet have little worth if it cannot be tested. Conversely, a theory may make an important contribution to the field even if it turns out to be wrong. The research it inspires

hypothesis A testable prediction about the conditions under which an event will occur.

theory An organized set of principles used to explain observed phenomena.

may prove more valuable than the theory itself, as the results shed light on new truths that might not have been discovered without the directions suggested by the theory.

Indeed, when Bem introduced self-perception theory to the field, it generated a great deal of attention and controversy. Part of its value as a good theory was that it helped organize and make sense of evidence that had been found in previous studies. Furthermore, it generated testable new hypotheses. Many scholars doubted the validity of the theory, however, and conducted research designed to prove it wrong. In short, both supporters and doubters of the theory launched a wave of studies, which ultimately led to a greater understanding of the processes described in Bem's theory.

Students new to social psychology are often surprised by the lack of consensus in the field. In part, such disagreement reflects the fact that social psychology is a relatively young science (Kruglanski, 2001). At this stage in its development, premature closure is a worse sin than contradiction or even confusion. But debate is an essential feature of even the most mature science. It is the fate of all scientific theories to be criticized and, eventually, surpassed.

"[Close cooperation between theoretical and applied psychology] can be accomplished . . . if the theorist does not look toward applied problems with highbrow aversion or with a fear of social problems, and if the applied psychologist realizes that there is nothing so practical as a good theory."

—Kurt Lewin

Basic and Applied Research

Is testing a theory the purpose of research in social psychology? For some researchers, yes. **Basic research** seeks to increase our understanding of human behaviour and is often designed to test a specific hypothesis from a specific theory. **Applied research** has a different purpose: to make use of social psychology's theories or methods to enlarge our understanding of naturally occurring events and to contribute to the solution of social problems.

Despite their differences, basic and applied research are closely connected in social psychology. Some researchers switch back and forth between the two—today basic, tomorrow applied. Some studies test a theory and examine a real-world phenomenon simultaneously. As a pioneer in both approaches, Kurt Lewin (1951) set the tone when he encouraged basic researchers to be concerned with complex social problems and urged applied researchers to recognize how important and practical good theories are.

Refining Ideas: Defining and Measuring Social Psychological Variables

No matter what method researchers plan to use to test their hypotheses, they always must decide how they will define and measure the variables in which they are interested. This is sometimes a straightforward process. For example, if you are interested in comparing how quickly people run a 100-metre dash when alone and when racing against another person, you can rely on well-established ways to define and measure the variables in question. Many other times, however, the process is less straightforward. If you are interested in studying the effects of self-esteem on altruistic behaviour, you must first define self-esteem and altruistic behaviour. There may be countless ways to do this. Which ones should you pick?

basic research Research where the goal is to increase the understanding of human behaviour, often by testing hypotheses based on a theory.

applied research Research where the goals are to enlarge the understanding of naturally occurring events and to find solutions to practical problems.

Conceptual Variables and Operational Definitions: From the Abstract to the Specific

When a researcher first develops a hypothesis, the variables typically are in an abstract, general form. These are *conceptual variables*. Examples of conceptual variables

From this picture, we can guess that the boy sitting by himself on the playground is lonely, but how do researchers precisely define and measure conceptual variables like loneliness? Researchers may use any of a number of approaches, such as asking people how they feel or observing their behaviour.

include prejudice, conformity, attraction, love, violence, group pressure, and social anxiety. In order to test specific hypotheses, we must then transform these conceptual variables into variables that can be manipulated or measured in a study. The specific way in which a conceptual variable is manipulated or measured is called the **operational definition** of the variable. For example, a researcher might operationally define "conformity" in a particular study as the number of times a participant indicated agreement with the obviously wrong judgments made by a group of confederates. Part of the challenge and fun of designing research in social psychology is taking an abstract conceptual variable such as love or group pressure and deciding how to operationally define it so as to manipulate or measure it.

Often, there is no single best way to transform a variable from the abstract (conceptual) to the specific (operational). A great deal of trial and error may be involved. However, sometimes there are systematic, statistical ways of checking how valid various manipulations and measures are, and researchers spend a great deal of time fine-tuning their operational definitions to best capture the conceptual variables they wish to study.

Researchers evaluate the manipulation and measurement of variables in terms of their **construct validity.** Construct validity refers to the extent to which (1) the manipulations in an experiment really manipulate the conceptual variables they were designed to manipulate and (2) the measures used in a study (experimental or otherwise) really measure the conceptual variables they were designed to measure. Imagine, for example, wanting to conduct an experiment on the effects of alcohol on aggression. One of the conceptual variables might be whether or not participants are intoxicated. There are several ways of measuring this variable, most of which are relatively straightforward: assessing participants' blood alcohol concentration, measuring their ability to perform simple motor tasks, or asking them how drunk they feel, for example. Thus, one researcher might operationally define intoxication as when a participant has a blood alcohol level of .10, whereas another might define it as when a participant says that he or she feels drunk. A second conceptual variable in this study would be aggression. Measuring aggression in experiments is particularly difficult because of ethical and practical issues—researchers can't let participants in their studies attack each other. Researchers interested in measuring aggression are thus often forced to measure relatively unusual behaviours, such as administering shocks to another person as part of a specific task. Does this really measure aggression? It's hard to tell. Some researchers say that such measures often are valid; others say they often aren't (Anderson et al., 1999; Ritter & Eslea, 2005; Tedeschi & Quigley, 2000).

operational definition The specific procedures for manipulating or measuring a conceptual variable.

construct validity The extent to which the measures used in a study measure the variables they were designed to measure and the manipulations in an experiment manipulate the variables they were designed to manipulate.

Measuring Variables: Self-Reports and Observations

Social psychologists measure variables in many ways, but most can be placed into one of two categories: self-reports and observations.

Self-reports are also affected by the way in which questions are asked (Schwarz, 1999). The importance of well-designed questions and response options may never have been more evident than in the aftermath of the US presidential election in November 2000, when thousands of Palm Beach County, Florida residents who intended to vote for Democratic Party candidate Al Gore mistakenly voted for Reform Party candidate Pat Buchanan. The reason for the apparent error was the confusing "butterfly" ballot design. This confusion very well may have caused Gore to lose the presidency to George W. Bush. The day after the US presidential election, Sinclair, Mark, Moore, Lovis, & Soldat (2000) exposed Canadian college students, as well as shoppers in a suburban mall, to a mock-vote for the Prime Minister of Canada using either a single-column or dual-column ("butterfly") ballot design. Results indicated that both groups found the butterfly ballots extremely confusing, although systematic voting errors were only found for the non-student sample; the authors attributed this to the fact that college students are generally quite adept at filling out optical scanning sheets often used for multiple-choice exams.

Self-Reports: Going Straight to the Source Collecting *self-reports*—in which participants disclose their thoughts, feelings, desires, and actions—is a widely used measurement technique in social psychology. Self-reports can consist of individual questions or sets of questions that together measure a single conceptual variable. One popular self-report measure, the Rosenberg Self-Esteem Scale, consists of a set of questions that measures individuals' overall self-esteem. For example, respondents are asked the extent to which they agree with statements such as "I feel that I have a number of good qualities," and "All in all, I am inclined to feel that I'm a failure." This scale is used in a wide variety of settings, and many researchers consider it to have good construct validity (Heatherton & Wyland, 2003; Griffiths et al., 1999; Robins et al., 2001).

Self-reports give the researcher access to an individual's beliefs and perceptions. But self-reports are not always accurate and can be misleading. For example, the desire to look good to ourselves and others can influence how we respond. As Shakespeare put it in the play *Measure for Measure*, "It oft falls out, to have what we would have, we speak not what we mean." Research using a procedure called the "bogus pipeline" indicates that participants who are led to believe that their responses will be verified by an infallible lie-detector report facts about themselves more accurately and endorse socially unacceptable opinions more frequently than those not told about such a device. The bogus pipeline is, in fact, bogus; no such infallible device exists. But belief in its powers discourages people from lying (Alexander & Fisher, 2003; Gannon, 2006; Plant et al., 2003; Roese & Jamieson, 1993; Tourangeau et al., 1997).

Consider some of the effects of wording and context in the following instances:

- Recent research has uncovered important cultural differences in the assumptions individuals make and the information they tend to give as they respond to questions on a survey (Johnson et al., 2005; Schwarz, 2003). Susanne Haberstroh and others (2002), for example, found that individuals from a culture that promotes interdependent, collectivistic values and self-concepts (such as China) are more likely to take into account question context when completing a questionnaire than are respondents from cultures associated with a more independent, individualistic orientation (such as Germany).

"Clemson here. How may I disappoint you?"

This person would probably score low on Rosenberg's Self-Esteem Scale.

- In one study, 88 percent of participants indicated that they thought condoms were effective in stopping AIDS when condoms were said to have a "95 percent success rate." However, when condoms were said to have a "5 percent failure rate," only 42 percent indicated that they thought condoms were effective (Linville et al., 1992).
- When German adults were asked how many hours a day they watched TV, their answers differed dramatically as a function of the response scale they were given (Schwarz et al., 1985). These results are displayed in Table 2.1.

Another reason self-reports can be inaccurate is that they often ask participants to report on thoughts or behaviours from the past, and participants' memory for these thoughts or behaviours may be suspect. To minimize this problem, psychologists have developed ways to reduce the time that elapses between an actual experience and the person's report of it. For example, some use *interval-contingent* self-reports, in which respondents report their experiences at regular intervals, usually once a day. They may report events since the last report, or how they feel at the moment, or both. Researchers may also collect *signal-contingent* self-reports. Here, respondents report their experiences as soon as possible after being signalled to do so, usually by means of a beeper. Finally, some researchers collect *event-contingent* self-reports, in which respondents report on a designated set of events as soon as possible after such events have occurred. For example, the Rochester Interaction Record (RIR) is an event-contingent self-report questionnaire used by respondents to record every social interaction lasting ten minutes or more that occurs during the course of the study, usually a week or two (Nezlek, 2003; Nezlek & Leary, 2002).

TABLE 2.1

How Many Hours of TV Do You Watch?

German adults in this survey were asked how much TV they watch each day. Depending on the scale given to them, either a small percentage or a much larger percentage of the respondents said that they watched more than 2.5 hours of TV each day. Changing the response alternatives given to respondents can change their self-reports. *(Schwarz et al., 1985.)*

	Percent Who Said "More Than 2.5 Hours"
If they were given a scale ranging from a minimum of "Up to 0.5 hour" to a maximum of "More than 2.5 hours"	16.2
If they were given a scale ranging from a minimum of "Up to 2.5 hours" to a maximum of "More than 4.5 hours"	37.5

Whatever their differences, most self-report methods require participants to provide specific answers to specific questions. In contrast, *narrative studies* collect lengthy responses on a general topic. Narrative materials can be generated by participants at the researcher's request or taken from other sources (such as diaries, speeches, books, or chat room discussions). These accounts are then analyzed in terms of a coding scheme developed by the researcher. For example, the researcher might code descriptions of an event for the use of particular stereotypes, diaries for evidence of the writers' personality styles, and sports articles in newspapers for athletes' explanations for winning or losing (Fink & Kensicki, 2002; Mehl & Pennebaker, 2003; Roesch & Amirkhan, 1997; Salzer, 2000).

Observations: Looking On Self-reports are not the only available window on human behaviour. Researchers can also observe people's actions. Sometimes these observations are very simple, as when a researcher notes which of two items a person selects. At other times, however, the observations are more elaborate and (like the coding of narrative accounts) require that interrater reliability be established. **Interrater reliability** refers to the level of agreement among multiple observers of the same behaviour. Only when different observers agree can the data be trusted.

interrater reliability The degree to which different observers agree on their observations.

Machines, too, can do the watching. Various kinds of equipment are used to measure physiological responses such as changes in heart rate, levels of particular hormones, and sexual arousal. Social psychologists use computers to record the speed with which participants respond to stimuli, such as how quickly they can identify the gender of people in a series of photographs after exposure to stereotypic words about men or women or the race of people in photographs if the faces are hostile or friendly (Hugenberg & Bodenhausen, 2004; Kawakami & Dovidio, 2001). Indeed, throughout social psychology, much of what used to be done by human voice or hand—instructions given, materials presented, measures taken—is now computerized.

Observational methods provide a useful alternative to self-reports. For example, studies of young children, whose verbal skills are limited, often rely on observations.

The advantage of observational methods is that they avoid our sometimes faulty recollections and distorted interpretations of our own behaviour. Actions can speak louder than words. But if individuals know they are being observed, some observational methods are as vulnerable as self-reports to people's desire to present themselves in a favourable light.

Testing Ideas: Research Designs

Social psychologists use several different methods to test their research hypotheses and theories. Although methods vary, the field generally emphasizes objective, systematic, and quantifiable approaches. Social psychologists do not simply seek out evidence that supports their ideas; rather, they test their ideas in ways that could very clearly prove them wrong.

The most popular and preferred research method in social psychology is experimentation, in which researchers can test cause-and-effect relationships, such as whether exposure to a violent television program causes viewers to behave more aggressively. We emphasize the experimental approach in this book. In addition, we report the results of many studies that use another popular approach: correlational research, which looks for associations between two variables without establishing cause and effect. We also report the results of studies that use a relatively new technique called meta-analysis, which integrates the research findings of many different studies. Before describing these approaches, though, we turn to an approach with which we all are very familiar: descriptive research. This is the approach used in opinion polls, ratings of the popularity of TV shows, box scores in the sports section, and the like.

Descriptive Research: Discovering Trends and Tendencies

One obvious way of testing ideas about people is simply to record how frequently or how typically people think, feel, or behave in particular ways. The goal of *descriptive*

Computerized video technology, such as this Perception Analyzer™, allows researchers to track participants' moment-by-moment reactions to events on the screen as was done recently at the University of Waterloo by Correll, Spencer and Zanna (2004). Students watched a videotaped debate about a proposed tuition increase and could indicate their agreement with either speaker by turning a dial on the device; a higher number on the dial reflected a perceived increase in the speaker's persuasiveness. This technology can help researchers study the dynamics of social influence.

research in social psychology is, as the term implies, to describe people and their thoughts, feelings, and behaviours. This method can test questions such as: Do most people support capital punishment? What percentage of people who encounter a person lying on the sidewalk would offer to help that person? What do men and women say are the things most likely to make them jealous of their partner? Particular methods of doing descriptive research include observing people, studying records of past events and behaviours, and surveying people. We discuss each of these methods in this section.

Observational Studies We can learn about other people by simply observing them, of course, and some social psychological questions can be addressed through observational studies. For example, researchers (Hawkins et al., 2001; Pepler & Craig, 1995) wanted to know how common bullying is among schoolchildren in Canada, and how often peers step in to help those who are being bullied. Is bullying an infrequent occurrence, revolving around a handful of bullies, or is it a widespread problem? Are there gender differences in bullying or in peer interventions? To investigate these questions, the researchers used hidden cameras and microphones to record the incidents of bullying and peer interventions in a number of schools in Canada (with the permission of the schools and parents). This peek into the schoolyard enabled the researchers to discover that the problem of bullying is much more pervasive than many people believe, and they were able to report the frequency with which particular forms of aggression, and helping, occurred. This research could be used to suggest strategies for reducing the prevalence and harmful impact of bullying among schoolchildren.

TV news magazine shows including *W5* and *the fifth estate* often use hidden cameras to record people's behaviours. The ethics of this can be troublesome; we return to the issue of ethics in research later in the chapter. In addition to ethical matters, though, questions of accuracy may arise in connection with these news programs. TV reporters and journalists often are more interested in telling a good story than in being scientifically sound, so we should be careful when drawing general conclusions from their presentations. A news program may show footage that is consistent with the point of view of their overall story—for example, footage demonstrating that certain kinds of people are treated worse by car salespeople or auto mechanics than others—but may not show footage that is inconsistent with this point of view. Social psychologists are trained to be systematic and unbiased in their observations and to report all of the data that are relevant to the research question, not just the data that support a particular hypothesis.

Archival Studies Archival research involves examining existing records of past events and behaviours, such as newspaper articles, medical records, diaries, sports statistics, personal ads, crime statistics, or hits on a Web page. A major advantage of archival measures is that, because the researchers are observing behaviour secondhand, they can be sure that they did not influence the behaviour by their presence. A limitation of this approach is that available records are not always complete or sufficiently detailed, and they may have been collected in a nonsystematic manner.

Archival measures are particularly valuable for examining cultural and historical trends. In Chapter 11 on Aggression, for example, we report a number of trends concerning the rate of violent crime in Canada and how it has changed in recent years, and we report differences in homicide rates in countries around the world.

These data come from archival records, such as the records of police stations, or the Royal Canadian Mounted Police (RCMP). Other examples of archival research include a study by Connolly, Price and Read (2006) that investigated the role of social science experts in cases that involve child sexual assault alleged to have been committed long before the case comes to trial, and a study that compared the academic performance of Quebec college students with or without disabilities (Jorgensen et al., 2005).

"Just as we suspected—they're beginning to form a boy band."

Observational research can reveal some fascinating—and sometimes disturbing!—insights into social behaviour.

Surveys It seems that nobody in politics these days sneezes without first conducting an opinion poll. Surveys have become increasingly popular in recent years, and they are conducted on everything from politics, to attitudes about social issues, to the percentages of women and men who squeeze the toothpaste tube from the bottom (O.K., we'll tell you: 37 percent of women and 18 percent of men; Weiss, 1991). Conducting surveys involves asking people questions about their attitudes, beliefs, and behaviours. Surveys can be conducted in person, over the phone, by mail, or via the Internet. Many social psychological questions can be addressed only with surveys because they involve variables that are impossible or unethical to observe directly or manipulate, such as people's sexual behaviours or their optimism about the future.

Although anyone can conduct a survey (and sometimes it seems that everyone does), there is a science to designing, conducting, and interpreting the results of surveys. Like other self-report measures, surveys can be affected strongly by subtle aspects of the wording and context of questions, and survey researchers are trained to consider these issues and to test various kinds of wording and question ordering before conducting their surveys.

One of the most important issues that survey researchers face is how to select the people who will take part in the survey. The researchers first must identify the *population* in which they are interested. Is this survey supposed to tell us about the attitudes of Canadians in general, shoppers at Loblaws, or students in Introduction to Social Psychology at University X, for example? From this general population, the researchers select a subset, or *sample*, of individuals. For a survey to be accurate, the sample must be similar to, or representative of, the population on important characteristics such as age, sex, race, income, education, and cultural background. The best way to achieve this representativeness is to use **random sampling**, a method of selection in which everyone in a population has an equal chance of being selected for the sample. Survey researchers use randomizing procedures, such as tables of randomly distributed numbers generated by computers, to decide how to select individuals for their samples.

To see the importance of random sampling, consider a pair of US presidential elections (Rosnow & Rosenthal, 1993). Just before the 1936 election, a magazine called the *Literary Digest* predicted that Alfred Landon, the Republican governor of Kansas, would win by 14 percentage points over Franklin Roosevelt. The *Digest* based its prediction on a survey of more than 2 million Americans. In fact, though, Landon *lost* the election by 24 percentage points. The magazine, which had been in financial trouble before the election, declared bankruptcy soon after.

random sampling A method of selecting participants for a study so that everyone in a population has an equal chance of being in the study.

Many social psychological questions are addressed using surveys, which can be conducted over the phone, by mail, via the Internet, or face-to-face in field settings such as this street fair.

Twenty years later, the Gallup survey's prediction of Dwight Eisenhower's victory was almost perfect—it was off by less than 2 percent. The size of its sample? Only about 8000. How could the 1936 survey, with its much larger sample, be so wrong and the 1956 survey be so right? The answer is that the 1936 sample was not randomly selected. The *Digest* contacted people through sources such as phone books and club membership lists. In 1936, many people could not afford to have telephones or belong to clubs. The people in the sample, therefore, tended to be wealthier than much of the population, and wealthier people preferred Landon. In 1956, by contrast, Gallup pollsters randomly selected election districts throughout the country and then randomly selected households within those districts. Today, because of improved sampling procedures, surveys conducted on little more than 1000 Canadians can be used to make accurate predictions about the entire Canadian population.

Correlational Research: Looking for Associations

Although there is much to learn from descriptive research, social psychologists typically want to know more. Most research hypotheses in social psychology concern the relationship between variables. For example, is there a relationship between people's gender and their willingness to ask for help from others, or between how physically attractive people are and how much money they make?

One way to test such hypotheses is with correlational research. Like descriptive research, **correlational research** can be conducted using observational, archival, or survey methods. Unlike descriptive research, however, correlational approaches measure the relationship between different variables. The extent to which variables relate to each other, or correlate, can suggest how similar or distinct two different measures are (for example, how related people's self-esteem and popularity are) and how well one variable can be used to predict another (for example, how well we can predict university success from high school grades). It is important to note that researchers doing correlational research typically do not manipulate the variables they study; they simply measure them.

correlational research Research designed to measure the association between variables that are not manipulated by the researcher.

correlation coefficient A statistical measure of the strength and direction of the association between two variables.

Correlation Coefficient When researchers examine the relationship between variables that vary in quantity (such as temperature or degree of self-esteem), they can measure the strength and direction of the relationship between the variables and calculate a statistic called a **correlation coefficient.** Correlation coefficients can range from – 1.0 to + 1.0. The absolute value of the number (the number itself, without the positive or negative sign) indicates how strongly the two variables are associated. The larger the absolute value of the number, the stronger the association between the two variables, and thus the better either of the variables is as a pre-

In the 1948 US presidential election, pollsters nationwide predicted that Thomas Dewey would defeat Harry Truman by a wide margin. As Truman basked in his victory, pollsters realized that their predictions were based on nonrandom samples of voters. Random sampling would have led to much more accurate predictions.

dictor of the other. Whether the coefficient is positive or negative indicates the direction of the relationship. A positive correlation coefficient indicates that as one variable increases, so does the other. For example, smoking and lung cancer are positively correlated; higher levels of smoking are associated with an increased likelihood of developing lung cancer and lower levels of smoking are associated with a decreased chance of developing lung cancer. This correlation is not perfect; some people who are heavy smokers will not develop lung cancer, and some people who never smoke, or smoke very little, will. Therefore, the correlation is less than +1.0; but it is greater than 0, because there is some association between the two. A negative coefficient indicates that the two variables go in opposite directions: As one goes up, the other tends to go down. For example, number of classes missed and GPA are likely to be negatively correlated. And a correlation close to 0 indicates that there is no consistent relationship at all. These three types of patterns are illustrated in Figure 2.1. Because few variables are perfectly related to each other, most correlation coefficients do not approach +1.0 or –1.0 but have more moderate values, such as – .39 or +.57.

Correlations obtained at a single point in time across a number of individuals are called *concurrent*. For example, you might be interested in testing the hypothesis that physically attractive people tend to make more money than less attractive people. You could measure the physical attractiveness of many different people somehow (such as by taking their pictures and asking a dozen other people to rate their physical appearance) and then ask them how much money they make. Correlations also can be obtained at different times from the same individuals. These correlations are called *prospective*. Prospective studies are especially useful in determining whether certain behaviours at a particular age are associated with other behaviours at a later age. For example, you might want to see whether people's degree of optimism at the age of 20 is correlated with how happy they feel at the age of 40. You would record the level of optimism of a number of 20-year-olds by using a questionnaire designed to measure optimism; and 20 years later, you'd ask these same individuals to complete a questionnaire designed to measure how happy they are.

Based on the results of a study of undergraduate students, Scott W. VanderStoep and John J. Shaughnessy (1997) concluded that studying research methods in psychology can give students "some general skills that they can use while watching the evening news, shopping for automobiles, voting, or deciding whether to adopt a new weight-loss technique they saw advertised."

Advantages and Disadvantages of Correlational Research Correlational research has many advantages. It can study the associations of naturally occurring

Being in a relationship is correlated with having similar levels of physical attractiveness. But a correlation cannot identify the cause of this association. Chapter 9 on Attraction and Close Relationships discusses both correlational and experimental research on the role of similarity in the attraction process.

variables that cannot be manipulated or induced—such as gender, race, ethnicity, and age. It can examine phenomena that would be difficult or unethical to create for research purposes, such as love, hate, and abuse. And it offers researchers a great deal of freedom in where variables are measured. Participants can be brought into a laboratory especially constructed for research purposes, or they can be approached in a real-world setting (often called "the field") such as a shopping mall or airport.

Despite these advantages, however, correlational research has one very serious disadvantage. And here it is in bold letters: **Correlation is not causation.**

In other words, a correlation cannot demonstrate a cause-and-effect relationship. Instead of revealing a specific causal pathway from one variable, A, to another variable, B, a correlation between variables A and B contains within it three possible causal effects: A could cause B; B could cause A; or a third variable, C, could cause both A and B. For example, imagine learning that the number of hours per night one sleeps is negatively correlated with the number of colds one gets. This means that as the amount of sleep increases, colds decrease in frequency; conversely, as sleep decreases, colds become more frequent. One reasonable explanation for this relationship is that lack of sleep (variable A) causes people to become more vulnerable to colds (variable B). Another reasonable

FIGURE 2.1

Correlations: Positive, Negative, and None

Correlations reveal a systematic association between two variables. Positive correlations indicate that variables are in sync: Increases in one variable are associated with increases in the other, decreases with decreases. Negative correlations indicate that variables go in opposite directions: Increases in one variable are associated with decreases in the other. When two variables are not systematically associated, there is no correlation.

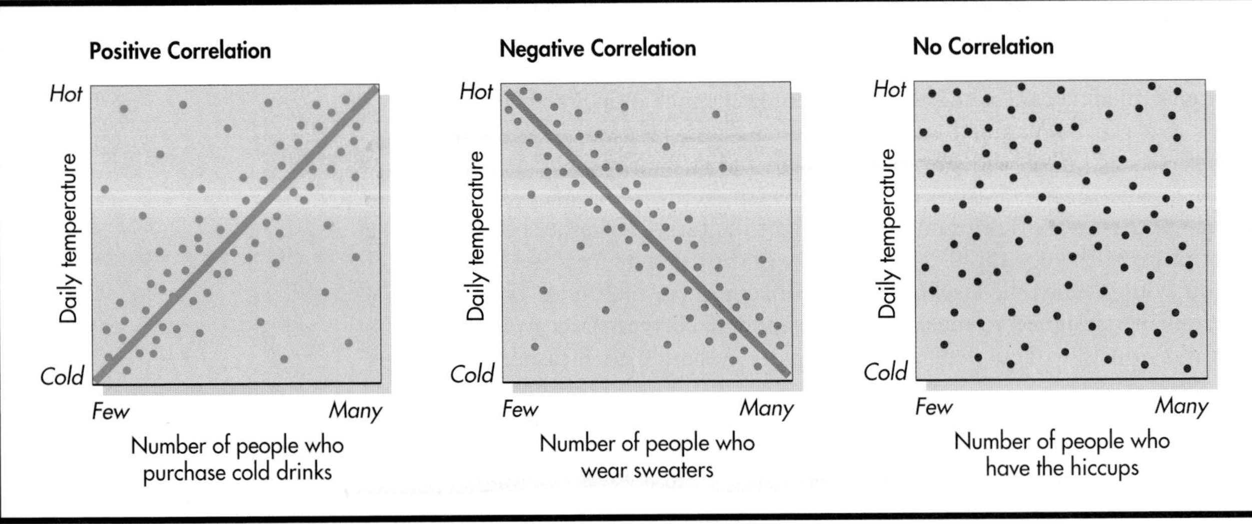

FIGURE 2.2

Explaining Correlations: Three Possibilities

The correlation between one variable (A) and another variable (B) could be explained in three ways. Variable A could cause changes in variable B, or variable B could cause changes in variable A, or a third variable (C) could cause similar changes in both A and B, even if A and B did not influence each other. For example, a correlation between how much TV children watch and how aggressively they behave could be explained in the following ways:

(1) TV watching causes aggressive behaviour;

(2) children who behave aggressively like to watch a lot of TV; or

(3) children who have family troubles, such as parents who are not very involved in the children's development, tend both to watch a lot of TV and to behave aggressively.

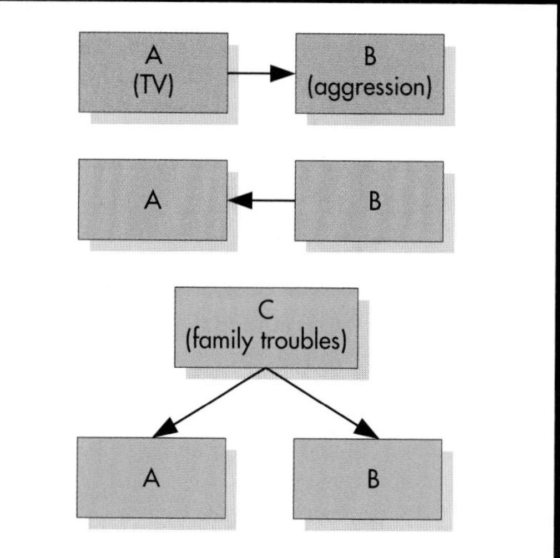

explanation, however, is that people who have colds can't sleep well, and so colds (variable B) cause lack of sleep (variable A). A third reasonable explanation is that some other variable (C) causes both lack of sleep and greater frequency of colds. This third variable could be stress. Indeed, stress has many effects on people, as will be discussed in Chapter 14 on Health. Figure 2.2 describes another correlation that can be explained in many ways—the correlation between TV watching and aggression.

As sure as death and taxes, there will be many, many times in your life when you'll encounter reports in the media that suggest cause-and-effect relationships based on correlational research. One of the great benefits of learning and gaining experience with the material in this chapter is that you can see the flaws in media reports like these and not be taken in by them. Correlation is not causation.

Do we learn nothing, then, from correlations? To say that would be to take caution too far. Correlations tell researchers about the strength and direction of relationships between variables, thus helping them understand these variables better and allowing them to use one variable to predict the other. Correlations can be extremely useful in developing new hypotheses to guide future research. And by gathering large sets of correlations and using complicated statistical techniques to crunch the data, we can develop highly accurate predictions of future events. But still, correlation is not causation.

Experiments: Looking for Cause and Effect

Social psychologists often do want to examine cause-and-effect relationships. Although it is informative to know, for example, that watching a lot of TV is correlated with violent behaviour in real life, the inevitable next question is whether watching a lot of TV *causes* an increase in violent behaviour. If we want to examine cause-and-effect relationships, we need to conduct an **experiment.** Experiments in social psychology range from the very simple to the incredibly elaborate. All of them, however, share two essential characteristics.

1. The researcher has *control* over the experimental procedures, manipulating the variables of interest while ensuring uniformity elsewhere. In other words, all participants in the research are treated in exactly the same manner—except for the specific differences the experimenter wants to create. By exercising control, the researcher attempts to ensure that differences obtained after the experimental manipulation are produced only by that manipulation and are not affected by other events in the experiment.

experiment A form of research that can demonstrate causal relationships because (1) the experimenter has control over the events that occur and (2) participants are randomly assigned to conditions.

2. Participants in the study are *randomly* assigned to the different manipulations (called "conditions") included in the experiment. If there are two conditions, who goes where may be determined by simply flipping a coin. If there are many conditions, a computer program may be used. But however it's done, **random assignment** means that participants are not assigned to a condition on the basis of their personal or behavioural characteristics. Through random assignment, the experimenter attempts to ensure a level playing field: *On average, the participants randomly assigned to one condition are no different from those assigned to another condition.* Differences that appear between conditions after an experimental manipulation can therefore be attributed to the impact of that manipulation and not to any pre-existing differences between participants.

TABLE 2.2
Correlations Versus Experiments

	Correlational Research	Experimental Research
What does it involve?	Measuring variables and the degree of association between them	Random assignment to conditions and control over the events that occur; determining the effects of manipulations of the independent variable(s) on changes in the dependent variable(s)
What is the biggest advantage of using this method?	Enables researchers to study naturally occurring variables, including variables that would be too difficult or unethical to manipulate	Enables researchers to determine cause-and-effect relationships—that is, whether the independent variable can cause a change in the dependent variable

Because of experimenter control and random assignment of participants, an experiment is a powerful technique for examining cause and effect. Both characteristics serve the same goal: to eliminate the influence on participants' behaviour of any factors other than the experimental manipulation. By ruling out alternative explanations for research results, we become more confident that we understand just what has, in fact, caused a certain behaviour to occur. Table 2.2 summarizes the distinctions between correlational and experimental research.

Random Sampling Versus Random Assignment You may recall that we mentioned random sampling earlier, in connection with surveys. It's important to remember the differences between random *sampling* and random *assignment.* Table 2.3 summarizes these differences. Random sampling concerns how individuals are selected to be in a study; it is important for generalizing the results obtained from a sample to a broader population, and it is therefore very important for survey research. Random assignment concerns not who is selected to be in the study but, rather, how participants in the study are assigned to different conditions, as explained previously. Random assignment is essential to experiments because it is necessary for determining cause-and-effect relationships; without it, there is always the possibility that any differences found between the conditions in a study were caused by pre-existing differences among participants. Random sampling, in contrast, is not necessary for establishing causality. For that reason, and because random sampling is difficult and expensive, very few experiments use random sampling. We consider the implications of this fact later in the chapter.

Laboratory and Field Experiments Most experiments in social psychology are conducted in a *laboratory* setting, usually located in a university, so that the environment can be controlled and the participants carefully studied. Social psychology labs do not necessarily look like stereotypical laboratories with liquid bubbling in beakers or expensive equipment everywhere (although many social psychology labs are indeed very "high-tech"). They can resemble ordinary living rooms or even game rooms. The key point here is that the laboratory setting enables researchers to have control over the setting, measure participants' behaviours precisely, and keep conditions identical for participants.

random assignment A method of assigning participants to the various conditions of an experiment so that each participant in the experiment has an equal chance of being in any of the conditions.

Field research is conducted in real-world settings outside of the laboratory. Researchers interested in studying helping behaviour, for example, might conduct an experiment in a public park. The advantage of field experiments is that people are more likely to act naturally in a natural setting than in a laboratory in which they know they are being studied. The disadvantage of field settings is that the experimenter often has less control and cannot ensure that the participants in the various conditions of the experiment will be exposed to the same things.

TABLE 2.3

Random Sampling Versus Random Assignment

	Random Sampling	Random Assignment
What does it involve?	Selecting participants to be in the study so that everyone from a population has an equal chance of being a participant in the study	Assigning participants (who are already in the study) to the various conditions of the experiment so that each participant has an equal chance of being in any of the conditions
What is the biggest advantage of using this procedure?	Enables researchers to collect data from samples that are representative of the broader population; important for being able to generalize the results to the broader population	Equalizes the conditions of the experiment so that it is very unlikely that the conditions differ in terms of pre-existing differences among the participants; essential to determine that the independent variable(s) caused an effect on the dependent variable(s)

Independent and Dependent Variables In an experiment, researchers manipulate one or more **independent variables** and examine the effect of these manipulations on one or more **dependent variables.** For example, in Chapter 1, we described an experiment by Emily Pronin and others (2004). In this study, some students read an article reporting that boys tended to perform better on a standardized math test than did girls, whereas other students read an article unrelated to gender and math. Which article the students were randomly assigned to read was the independent variable in this study; that is, the researchers manipulated this variable to determine its effects on another variable, the dependent variable. In this study, one of the dependent variables was the students' ratings of how strongly they personally identified with each of a series of feminine characteristics. The ratings were the dependent variable because the researchers were interested in seeing if they would *depend* on (that is, be influenced by) the manipulation of the independent variable. As discussed in Chapter 1, the manipulation did have a significant effect on the dependent variable: The students who read the article indicating that boys outperformed girls in math rated themselves as identifying less with the feminine characteristics than did the students who had not read this article.

Subject Variables Some experiments include variables that are neither dependent nor truly independent. In many experiments, some of the participants are male and some are female. The sex of the participants cannot be manipulated and randomly assigned, so it is not a true independent variable; and it is not influenced by the independent variables, so it is not a dependent variable. Variables such as these are called **subject variables**, because they characterize pre-existing differences among the subjects, or participants, in the experiment. If a study includes subject variables but no true, randomly assigned independent variable, it is not a true experiment. But experiments often include subject variables along with independent variables so that researchers can test whether the independent variables have the same or different effects on different kinds of participants.

Main Effects and Interactions Some experiments include multiple predictor variables (i.e., independent or subject variables). Researchers can then examine the separate effects of each predictor variable on the dependent variable and can also study how the different predictor variables combine to create interactive effects. In such cases, researchers can examine (1) the **main effect** of each predictor variable—the overall effect of the independent or subject variable on the dependent variable, ignoring all

independent variables In an experiment, the factors experimenters manipulate to see if they affect the dependent variables.

dependent variables In an experiment, the factors experimenters measure to see if they are affected by the independent variables.

subject variables Variables that characterize pre-existing differences among the participants in a study.

main effect A statistical term indicating the overall effect that an independent variable has on the dependent variable, ignoring all other independent variables.

other predictor variables, and (2) the **interaction** between predictor variables—the change in the relationship between each independent or subject variable and the dependent variable as a function of other predictor variables.

By way of illustration, let's consider an experiment by Joseph Vandello and Dov Cohen (2003, 2005). Vandello and Cohen were interested in cultural differences concerning gender roles, particularly in how a man is perceived as a function of whether his wife is faithful or not to him. As we will see in Chapter 11 on Aggression, researchers have been examining cultural differences in the degree to which a man's honour and status are emphasized, which has implications for how men are expected to protect or reclaim their honour and status. For example, Grandon and Cohen (2002, as cited in Vandello & Cohen, 2003) found 77% of Chileans, compared to only 32% of Canadians, agreed with the statement "a woman's honour must be defended by the men in the family." Vandello and Cohen conducted an experiment to test one particular hypothesis stemming from this body of research: A wife's infidelity would have stronger effects on the husband's reputation in *cultures of honour* than in less honour-focused cultures.

In field research, people are observed in real-world settings. Field researchers may observe children in a schoolyard, for example, to study any of a variety of social psychological issues, such as friendship patterns, group dynamics, conformity, helping, aggression, and cultural differences.

In one study, the researchers had students from either the northern United States or Brazil read a story either about a man whose wife was faithful to him or about a man whose wife was unfaithful to him by having an affair. The variation in culture—northern United States versus Brazil—was a *subject variable* in this study; that is, the participants' culture was a pre-existing condition that they brought with them to the study, rather than a condition to which they were randomly assigned. The researchers treated this subject variable as an independent variable in the analysis, but if this had been the only variation in the study, it would not have been a true experiment because it would have lacked random assignment. (Another subject variable in this study was the gender of the participants—some were male and some female. We'll ignore that variable in this discussion, in part because it did not make a difference in any of the results that Vandello and Cohen found.)

The *independent variable* in this study was the version of the story the students read—participants were randomly assigned to read either the story in which the wife did not cheat on her husband, or the story in which she was unfaithful to him. Table 2.4 summarizes the design of the experiment.

One of the outcomes studied in this research (a *dependent variable*) was the students' ratings of the man's "manliness." Vandello and Cohen took an average of each student's ratings on several dimensions related to the construct of manliness, such as masculinity, courage, and strength. The higher the average rating (on a 5-point scale), the more they saw him as "manly."

What were the researchers looking for in this study? They wanted to test the hypothesis that the students from the more honour-focused culture (i.e., Brazil) would be more affected by the wife's behaviour in their ratings of the man than would the students from the less honour-based culture.

interaction A statistical term indicating the change in the effect of each independent variable as a function of other independent variables.

Figure 2.3 depicts the results of this study. One question we might ask at this point is whether there was a main effect for the independent variable concerning the wife's behaviour. In other words, did the students who read that she cheated on her husband tend to rate the husband as being less manly than did the students who read that she was faithful? Remember, for a main effect, you look at the effect of one independent variable but ignore the effect of any other independent (or subject) variables, so for now we ignore the difference between US and Brazilian participants. If you look closely at the figure, comparing just the average scores of the students in the

TABLE 2.4

Female Infidelity, Male Honour, and Culture: The Conditions

In Vandello and Cohen's experiment, participants from either Brazil or the northern United States read about a man whose wife was either faithful or unfaithful to him. Combining these two variables—culture and the wife's behaviour—creates the four conditions displayed here. *(Based on Vandello & Cohen, 2003, 2005.)*

	Northern United States	Brazil
Wife is faithful	**Condition 1** U.S./ Faithful	**Condition 2** Brazil/ Faithful
Wife is unfaithful	**Condition 3** U.S./ Unfaithful	**Condition 4** Brazil/ Unfaithful

"faithful" conditions with those in the "unfaithful" conditions (ignoring the variable of culture), you should see that the man did tend to be rated as more manly if his wife was faithful than if she was unfaithful. That is, the teal bars tend to be higher than the gold bars. In short, there is a main effect for the manipulation of the wife's behaviour.

Next, we can examine if there is a main effect for culture. Although it is a subject variable, we can treat it as an independent variable in these analyses, to see if there is a difference in the ratings of the man as a function of the students' culture. The figure suggests there is a main effect for culture, since the students from the United States tended to rate the man as more manly than did the students from Brazil. Again, to assess the main effect, we ignore other independent variables, so here we ignore whether the story was about the faithful or unfaithful wife. It does appear, then, that there is a main effect for culture in this study.

Why would the US students rate the husband as more manly than the students from Brazil? If you look closely at the graph, you can see that the difference between the US sample and the Brazilian sample was pretty small when the wife was described as faithful; the difference was large only if the wife was described as unfaithful. This illustrates why it is important to look for the *interaction* between the two independent variables.

To look for the interaction, ask yourself, "Does the effect of one independent variable change as a function of the other independent variable?" To the extent that it does, there is an interaction between the two variables. So, in this study, did the *effect* of the manipulation of the wife's infidelity change as a function of whether the students were from the United States or Brazil? Yes. That is, although *in general* students rated the husband as less manly if his wife was unfaithful, this difference was especially great among students from Brazil. Similarly, although *in general* students from Brazil rated the husband as less manly than did the students from the United States, this difference was especially great if his wife was unfaithful.

So, the researchers' hypothesis was supported by the data. The wife's fidelity did have more of an impact on the man's reputation in

FIGURE 2.3

Female Infidelity, Male Honour, and Culture: The Results

This graph shows how US and Brazilian students rated a man's manliness when his wife was either faithful or unfaithful. In general, students rated a man as less manly if his wife was unfaithful to him than if his wife was faithful. Also in general, students from the northern United States tended to rate the man as more manly than did students from Brazil. But the *interaction* between these two variables is most relevant for this study: The effect of the wife's unfaithfulness on ratings of the man's reputation was much stronger among Brazilian students than among American students. *(Based on Vandello & Cohen, 2003, 2005.)*

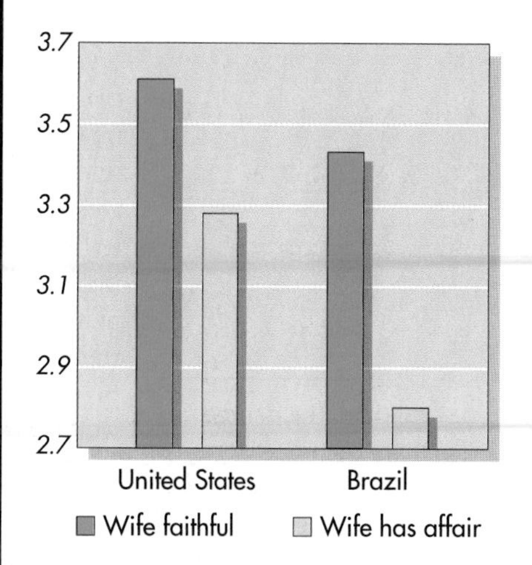

Brazil than in the United States, which is consistent with the theory and research concerning cultures of honour. Vandello and Cohen believe that these results have implications for the issue of domestic violence, and we will return to this issue in Chapter 11 on Aggression.

Statistical Significance Another close look at the results in Figure 2.3 reveals that the average scores in the four conditions in Vandello and Cohen's experiment differed by only fractions of a point on a 5-point scale. Are such differences large enough to be meaningful, or could they simply be due to chance? After all, if you flip a coin ten times, you might get six tails and four heads. Is the difference between six and four a meaningful difference? Surely it isn't—one could expect differences like this from random luck alone. Results obtained in an experiment are examined with statistical analyses that allow the researcher to determine how likely it is that the results could have occurred by chance. The standard convention is that if the results could have occurred by chance five or fewer times in 100 possible outcomes, then the result is *statistically significant* and should be taken seriously.

The fact that results are statistically significant does not mean that they are absolutely certain. In essence, statistical significance is an attractive betting proposition. The odds are quite good (at least 95 out of 100) that the effects obtained in the study were due to the experimental manipulation of the independent variable. But there is still the possibility (as high as five out of 100) that the findings occurred by chance. This is one reason why it is important to try to *replicate* the results of an experiment—to repeat the experiment and see if similar results are found. If similar results are found, the probability that these results could have occurred by chance both times is 5 percent times 5 percent, or one-quarter of 1 percent (which equals one time in 400 possible outcomes).

Internal Validity: Did the Independent Variable Cause the Effect? When an experiment is properly conducted, its results are said to have *internal validity*: There is reasonable certainty that the independent variable did, in fact, cause the effects obtained on the dependent variable (Cook & Campbell, 1979). As noted earlier, both experimenter control and random assignment seek to rule out alternative explanations of the research results, thereby strengthening the internal validity of the research.

Experiments also include *control groups* for this purpose. Typically, a control group consists of participants who experience all of the experimental procedures except the experimental treatment. In Vandello and Cohen's study, for example, the participants in the condition in which the wife was faithful could be considered a control group, which provided a baseline against which to compare the ratings of the husband when the wife was unfaithful. It was in the "unfaithful" condition that the researchers expected to see the cultural difference emerge.

Outside the laboratory, creating control groups in natural settings that examine real-life events raises many practical and ethical problems. For example, research on new medical treatments for deadly diseases, such as AIDS, can create a terrible dilemma. Individuals randomly assigned to the control group receive the standard treatment, but they are excluded for the duration of the study from what could turn out to be a life-saving new intervention. Yet without such a comparison, it is extremely difficult to determine which new treatments are effective and which are useless. Although many AIDS activists used to oppose including control groups in treatment research, they have become more supportive of this approach (Gorman, 1994).

In assessing internal validity, researchers need to consider their own role as well. Unwittingly, they can sometimes sabotage their own research. Here's how:

- Before they conduct a study, experimenters usually make an explicit prediction, or at least have a strong expectation, about the effect of an independent variable.
- If they know what conditions participants have been assigned to, they may, without realizing it, treat participants in different conditions differently.

internal validity The degree to which there can be reasonable certainty that the independent variables in an experiment caused the effects obtained on the dependent variables.

- Because the experimenters' behaviour can affect the participants' behaviour, the results could then be produced by the experimenters' actions rather than by the independent variable.

The best way to protect an experiment from the influence of experimenters' expectations—called **experimenter expectancy effects** (Rosenthal, 1976)—is to keep experimenters uninformed about assignments to conditions. If they do not know the condition to which a participant has been assigned, they cannot treat participants differently as a function of their condition. Of course, there may be times when keeping experimenters uninformed is impossible or impractical. In such cases, the opportunity for experimenter expectancy effects to occur can at least be reduced—specifically, by minimizing the interaction between experimenters and participants. For example, rather than receiving instructions directly from an experimenter, participants can be asked to read the instructions on a computer screen.

External Validity: Do the Results Generalize? In addition to guarding internal validity, researchers are concerned about **external validity**, the extent to which the results obtained under one set of circumstances would also occur in a different set of circumstances (Berkowitz & Donnerstein, 1982). When an experiment has external validity, its findings can be assumed to generalize to other people and to other situations. Both the participants in the experiment and the setting in which it takes place affect external validity.

Because social psychologists often seek to establish universal principles of human behaviour, their ideal sample of participants should be representative of all human beings, all over the world. Such an all-inclusive representative sample has never been seen and probably never will be. Representative samples of more limited populations do exist and can be achieved by random sampling of a population, which was discussed earlier in the chapter. But, as also mentioned earlier, social psychologists rarely study representative samples. Usually, they rely on convenience samples drawn from populations that are readily available to them, which explains why so much social psychological research is conducted on university students. The common practice of using convenience samples in social psychological research poses a crucial question: Is it possible to establish universal principles of human behaviour with research on nonrepresentative samples?

Those who favour the use of convenience samples point to some very real practical issues. Representative samples are fine for surveys requiring short answers to a short list of questions. But what about complex, time-consuming experiments? The expense of bringing participants from diverse geographic areas into the lab would be staggering. And various extraneous variables (travel fatigue, disruptions in regular routines) could distort the results. Advocates of convenience samples also contend that there is no contradiction between universal principles and particular participants. Indeed, the more basic the principle, the less it matters who participates in the research. For example, various people or cultures might differ in the form of aggression they typically exhibit when angry; but the situational factors that cause people to be more likely to exhibit aggressive behaviour, however that aggression is expressed, may be similar for most individuals no matter where they are from or what experiences they have had. Yet in spite of these arguments, the drawbacks to convenience samples are clear—an important consideration given the need for social psychology to become more inclusive. The growing interest in cross-cultural research in the field is certainly one step in the right direction.

External validity is also affected by the setting in which the research is conducted. Because field research occurs in real-life natural settings rather than in the artificial arrangements of a laboratory, aren't its results more generalizable to actual behaviour? The answer depends on where you stand on the issue of mundane versus experimental realism (Aronson & Carlsmith, 1968).

experimenter expectancy effects The effects produced when an experimenter's expectations about the results of an experiment affect his or her behaviour toward a participant and thereby influence the participant's responses.

external validity The degree to which there can be reasonable confidence that the results of a study would be obtained for other people and in other situations.

A teacher in a village in Cameroon, Africa, prepares the day's lesson in the morning calm before hundreds of students arrive to attend classes in dilapidated buildings nearby. Conducting research across a wide range of cultures and contexts has become increasingly important in social psychology today.

Mundane realism refers to the extent to which the research setting resembles the real-world setting of interest. In order to study interpersonal attraction, Theodore Newcomb (1961) set up an entire college dormitory—a striking example of mundane realism. Advocates of mundane realism contend that if research procedures are more realistic, research findings are more likely to reveal what really goes on.

In contrast, **experimental realism** refers to the degree to which the experimental setting and procedures are real and involving to the participant, regardless of whether they resemble real life or not. According to those who favour experimental realism, if the experimental situation is compelling and real to the participants while they are participating in the study, their behaviour in the lab—even if the lab is in the basement of the psychology building—will be as natural and spontaneous as their behaviour in the real world. The majority of social psychologists who conduct experiments emphasize experimental realism.

Researchers who strive to create a highly involving experience for participants often rely on **deception,** providing participants with false information about experimental procedures. Toward this end, social psychologists sometimes employ **confederates,** who act as though they are participants in the experiment but are really working for the experimenter. For example, Regan and Gutierrez (2005) had confederates, pretending to be ordinary shoppers, approach individuals in a supermarket to ask for $0.25 toward various items such as milk (considered a high-need item), cookie dough (a low-need item), or alcohol (low-need with negative connotations). The researchers wanted to see if the sex of the participant and the perceived need associated with the item would influence helping behaviour; in this case, need associated with the item played a greater role in helping than sex of the participant. Deception not only strengthens experimental realism but also confers other benefits: It allows the experimenter to manufacture situations in the laboratory that would be difficult to observe in a natural setting; to study potentially harmful behaviours, such as aggression, in a regulated, safe manner; and to assess people's spontaneous reactions rather than socially acceptable presentations. Studies have shown that participants are rarely bothered by deception and often particularly enjoy studies that use it (Smith & Richardson, 1983). Nevertheless, the use of deception creates some serious ethical concerns, which we examine later in this chapter.

mundane realism The degree to which the experimental situation resembles places and events in the real world.

experimental realism The degree to which experimental procedures are involving to participants and lead them to behave naturally and spontaneously.

deception In the context of research, a method that provides false information to participants.

confederate Accomplice of an experimenter who, in dealing with the real participants in an experiment, acts as if he or she is also a participant.

Meta-Analysis: Combining Results Across Studies

We have seen that social psychologists conduct original descriptive, correlational, and experimental studies to test their hypotheses. Another way to test hypotheses in social psychology is to use a set of statistical procedures to examine, in a new way, relevant research that has already been conducted and reported. This technique is called **meta-analysis.** By "meta-analyzing" the results of a number of studies that have been conducted in different places and by different researchers, a social psychologist can measure precisely how strong and reliable particular effects are. For example, studies published concerning the effects of alcohol on aggression may sometimes contradict each other. Sometimes alcohol increases aggression; sometimes it doesn't. By combining the data from all the studies that are relevant to this hypothesis and conducting a meta-analysis, a researcher can determine what effect alcohol typically has, how strong that effect typically is, and perhaps under what specific conditions that effect is most likely to occur. This technique, which was developed relatively recently, is being used with increasing frequency in social psychology today, and we report the results of many meta-analyses in this textbook.

Ethics and Values in Social Psychology

Regardless of where research is conducted and what method is used, ethical issues must always be considered. Researchers in all fields have a moral and legal responsibility to abide by ethical principles. In social psychology, the use of deception has caused particular concern (Bersoff, 2003; Lawson, 2001; Ortmann & Hertwig, 1997), and several studies have provoked fierce debate about whether they went beyond the bounds of ethical acceptability. For example, Stanley Milgram (1963) designed a series of experiments to address the question "Would people obey orders to harm an innocent person?" To test this question, he put volunteers into a situation in which an experimenter commanded them to administer painful electric shocks to someone they thought was another volunteer participant (in fact, the other person was a confederate who was not actually receiving any shocks). The experiment had extremely high experimental realism—many of the participants experienced a great deal of anxiety and stress as they debated whether they should disobey the experimenter or continue to inflict pain on another person. The details and results of this experiment will be discussed in Chapter 7 on Conformity, but suffice it to say that the results of the study made people realize how prevalent and powerful obedience can be.

Milgram's research was inspired by the obedience displayed by Nazi officers in World War II. No one disputes the importance of his research question. What has been debated, however, is whether the significance of the research topic justified exposing participants to possibly harmful psychological consequences. Under today's provisions for the protection of human participants, Milgram's classic experiments probably could not be conducted in their original form.

Milgram's research was by no means the only social psychological research to trigger debates about ethics. Several studies in the history of social psychology have sparked a great deal of controversy. And it is not only the controversial studies that receive scrutiny. Today, virtually every prospective social psychology study is evaluated for its ethics by other people before the study can be conducted. In the following sections, we describe current policies and procedures as well as continuing concerns about ethics and values in social psychological research.

Research Ethics Boards: The Ethical Watchdogs

In 1994, a Tri-Council Working Group was created by the Canadian Institutes of Health Research (CIHR), the Natural Science and Engineering Research Council (NSERC) and the Social Science and Humanities Research Council (SSHRC) to determine how to deal with ethical issues associated with research in Canada. The

meta-analysis A set of statistical procedures used to review a body of evidence by combining the results of individual studies to measure the overall reliability and strength of particular effects.

result was the Interagency Advisory Panel on Research Ethics (PREA), which is in place to support the Tri-Council Policy Statement: Ethical Conduct for Research Involving Humans (TCPS). The policies of this Council include the requirement that all research involving human subjects be reviewed and approved by an institutional Research Ethics Board (REB).

Although researchers have become accustomed to submitting their proposals to REBs, questions persist about the appropriate role of these boards (Chastain & Landrum, 1999). For example, should REBs act as censors? Few, if any, researchers or board members would endorse such a practice. But an experiment by Stephen Ceci and his colleagues (1985) found that university REBs were more likely to approve politically neutral proposals than socially sensitive ones having implications for societal groups or policies. Socially sensitive topics often raise serious ethical questions that require careful scrutiny by investigators and REBs. Properly conducted, however, socially sensitive research can offer vital information needed to address major societal issues.

Informed Consent: Do You (Really) Want to Participate?

"[Objectivity in science] is the willingness (even the eagerness in truly honorable practitioners) to abandon a favored notion when testable evidence disconfirms key expectations."

—Stephen Jay Gould

Besides submitting their research to government-mandated REBs, researchers must also abide by their profession's code of ethics. The statement of ethics of the Canadian Psychological Association (CPA), called the *Canadian Code of Ethics for Psychologists* (2000), considers a wide range of ethical issues, including those related to research procedures and practices. The CPA *Code* stipulates that researchers are obligated to guard the rights and welfare of all those who participate in their studies.

One such obligation is to obtain **informed consent**. Individuals must be asked whether they wish to participate in the research project and must be given enough information to make an informed decision. Researchers should not proceed if "consent is given under any conditions of coercion, undue pressure, or undue reward."

In principle, informed consent is absolutely essential for the protection of human participants. Only if you know what you will be getting into can you decide whether you want to participate in a study. In practice, however, it can be difficult to ensure that consent is, in fact, informed. Often, the information given to participants is vague because the researchers do not want to tell the participants so much that their responses during the study will be affected. Other times, the information can be so detailed and complex that many participants don't fully understand it. To make the practice of obtaining informed consent as effective as the principle says it should be, we need more research on how best to communicate this information.

Debriefing: Telling All

Have you ever participated in psychological research? If so, what was your reaction to this experience? Have you ever been deceived about the hypothesis or procedures of a study in which you were a participant? If so, how did you feel about it? Most research on participants' reactions indicates that they have positive attitudes about their participation, even when they were deceived about some aspects of a study (Christensen, 1988; Epley & Huff, 1998). Indeed, deceived participants sometimes have expressed more favourable opinions than those who have not been deceived, presumably because studies involving deception are often interesting and creative (Smith & Richardson, 1983).

informed consent An individual's deliberate, voluntary decision to participate in research, based on the researcher's description of what will be required during such participation.

These findings are reassuring, but they do not remove the obligation of researchers to use deception only when nondeceptive alternatives are not feasible. In addition, whenever deception has been used, there is a special urgency to the requirement that, once the data have been collected, researchers fully inform their participants about the nature of the research in which they have participated. This process of disclosure is called **debriefing.** During a debriefing, the researcher goes over all procedures, explaining exactly what happened and why. Deceptions are revealed, the purpose of the research is discussed, and the researcher makes every effort to help the participant feel good about having participated. A skilful debriefing takes time and requires close attention to the individual participant.

Social psychology experiments don't reach this level of deception, nor are participants likely to be so startled by the debriefing! But whenever participants are deceived about research procedures or purposes, it is especially important to provide a full and thorough debriefing.

Values and Science: Points of View

Ethical principles are based on moral values. These values set standards for and impose limits on the conduct of research, just as they influence individuals' personal behaviour. When the potential benefits of research for humankind are high and the potential costs are ethically acceptable, there is a moral imperative to try to carry out the research. But when the human costs are too high in terms of the suffering of participants, the moral imperative is to refrain. Ethical issues are an appropriate focus for moral values in science, but do values affect science in other ways as well? Consider this statement from the *Canadian Code of Ethics for Psychologists*: "Psychologists are not expected to be value-free or totally without self-interest in conducting their activities. However, they are expected to understand how their backgrounds, personal needs, and values interact with their activities, to be open and honest about the influence of such factors, and to be as objective and unbiased as possible under the circumstances" (2000, p. 27).

Infatuated by important topics, wrestling with beliefs about right and wrong, under the thumb of those who control funding for research—all this seems a long way from "objective and unbiased." It's such a long way that perhaps the search for objectivity is only a self-serving illusion. Perhaps the more forthright approach is to adopt a psychology of political advocacy: "championing causes that one believes good for the culture; . . . condemning movements or policies that seem inimical to human welfare" (Gergen, 1994, p. 415).

But there is another view. From this perspective, science can never be completely unbiased and objective because it is a human enterprise. Scientists choose what to study and how to study it; their choices are affected by personal values as well as by professional rewards. To acknowledge these influences, however, is not to embrace them. Quite the contrary. Such influences are precisely why the scientific method is so important.

As Stanley Parkinson (1994) puts it, "Scientists are not necessarily more objective than other people; rather, they use methods that have been developed to minimize self-deception" (p. 137). By scrutinizing their own behaviour and adopting the rigours of the scientific method, scientists attempt to free themselves of their preconceptions and, thereby, to see reality more clearly, even if never perfectly.

You've read what others have said about values and science. But what do you think about all this? How do values influence science? How *should* values affect scientific inquiry?

Your introduction to the field of social psychology is now complete. In these first two chapters, you have gone step-by-step through a definition of social psychology, a review of its history and discussion of its future, an overview of its research methods, and a consideration of ethics and values. As you study the material presented in the coming chapters, the three of us who wrote this book invite you to share our enthusiasm. You can look forward to information that overturns common-sense assumptions, to lively debate and heated controversy, and to a better understanding of yourself and other people. Welcome to the world according to social psychology. We hope you enjoy it!

debriefing A disclosure, made to participants after research procedures are completed, in which the researcher explains the purpose of the research, attempts to resolve any negative feelings, and emphasizes the scientific contribution made by the participants' involvement.

Review

Why Should You Learn About Research Methods?

- Because common sense and intuitive ideas about social psychological issues can be misleading and contradictory, it is important to understand the scientific evidence on which social psychological theories and findings are based.
- Studying research methods in psychology improves people's reasoning about real-life events and information presented by the media and other sources.

Developing Ideas: Beginning the Research Process

Asking Questions

- Ideas for research in social psychology come from everywhere—personal experiences and observations, events in the news, and other research.

Searching the Literature

- Before pursuing a research idea, it is important to see what research has already been done on this and related topics.
- Electronic databases provide access to a wealth of information, both in the psychology literature and in more general sources.

Hypotheses and Theories

- Formulating a hypothesis is a critical step toward planning and conducting research.
- Theories in social psychology are specific rather than comprehensive and generate research that can support or disconfirm them. They should be revised and improved as a result of the research they inspire.

Basic and Applied Research

- The goal of basic research is to increase understanding of human behaviour.
- The goal of applied research is to increase understanding of real-world events and contribute to the solution of social problems.

Refining Ideas: Defining and Measuring Social Psychological Variables

Conceptual Variables and Operational Definitions: From the Abstract to the Specific

- Researchers often must transform abstract, conceptual variables into specific operational definitions that indicate exactly how the variables are to be manipulated or measured.
- Construct validity is the extent to which the operational definitions successfully manipulate or measure the conceptual variables to which they correspond.

Measuring Variables: Self-Reports and Observations

- In self-reports, participants indicate their thoughts, feelings, desires, and actions.
- Self-reports can be distorted by efforts to make a good impression, as well as by the effects of the wording and context of questions.
- To increase the accuracy of self-reports, some approaches emphasize the need to collect self-reports as soon as possible after participants experience the relevant thoughts, feelings, or behaviours.
- Narrative studies analyze the content of lengthy responses on a general topic.
- Observations can be made by human observers or by machines.

Testing Ideas: Research Designs

- Most social psychologists test their ideas by using objective, systematic, and quantifiable methods.

Descriptive Research: Discovering Trends and Tendencies

- In descriptive research, social psychologists record how frequently or typically people think, feel, or behave in particular ways.
- One form of descriptive research is observational research, in which researchers observe individuals systematically, often in natural settings.
- In archival research, researchers examine existing records and documents such as newspaper articles, diaries, and published crime statistics.
- Surveys involve asking people questions about their attitudes, beliefs, and behaviours.
- Survey researchers identify the population to which they want the results of the survey to generalize, and they select a sample of people from that population to take the survey.
- To best ensure a sample that is representative of the broader population, researchers should randomly select people from the population to be in the survey.

Correlational Research: Looking for Associations

- Correlational research examines the association between variables.
- A correlation coefficient is a measure of the strength and direction of the association between two variables.
- Positive correlations indicate that as scores on one variable increase, scores on the other variable increase; and that as scores on one variable decrease, scores on the other decrease.

- Negative correlations indicate that as scores on one variable increase, scores on the other decrease.
- Correlation does not indicate causation; the fact that two variables are correlated does not necessarily mean that one causes the other.
- Correlations can be used for prediction and for generating hypotheses.

Experiments: Looking for Cause and Effect

- Experiments require (1) control by the experimenter over events in the study and (2) random assignment of participants to conditions.
- Random sampling concerns how people are selected to be in a study, whereas random assignment concerns how people who are in the study are assigned to the different conditions of the study.
- Experiments are often conducted in a laboratory so that the researchers can have control over the context and can measure variables precisely.
- Field experiments are conducted in real-world settings outside the laboratory.
- Experiments examine the effects of one or more independent variables on one or more dependent variables.
- Subject variables are variables that characterize pre-existing differences among the participants.
- In a main effect, the levels of a single independent variable produce differences in the dependent variable; this effect is independent of (not related to) the effects of any other independent variables.
- In an interaction, the effect of one independent variable on the dependent variable changes as a function of another independent variable; thus, the independent variables jointly affect the dependent variable.
- Results that are statistically significant could have occurred by chance five or fewer times in 100 possible outcomes.
- Experimental findings have internal validity to the extent that changes in the dependent variable can be attributed to the independent variables.
- Control groups strengthen internal validity; experimenter expectancy effects weaken it.
- Research results have external validity to the extent that they can be generalized to other people and other situations.
- A representative sample strengthens external validity; a convenience sample weakens it.
- Mundane realism is the extent to which the research setting seems similar to real-world situations.
- Experimental realism is the extent to which the participants experience the experimental setting and procedures as real and involving.
- Deception is sometimes used to increase experimental realism.
- Confederates act as though they are participants in an experiment but actually work for the experimenter.

Meta-Analysis: Combining Results Across Studies

- Meta-analysis uses statistical techniques to integrate the quantitative results of different studies.

Ethics and Values in Social Psychology

- Ethical issues are particularly important in social psychology because of the use of deception in some research.

Research Ethics Boards: The Ethical Watchdogs

- Established by the federal government, REBs are responsible for reviewing research proposals to ensure that the welfare of participants is adequately protected.

Informed Consent: Do You (Really) Want to Participate?

- The Canadian Psychological Association's code of ethics requires psychologists to secure informed consent from research participants.

Debriefing: Telling All

- Most participants have positive attitudes about their participation in research, even if they were deceived about some aspects of the study.
- Whenever deception has been used in a study, a full debriefing is essential; the researchers must disclose the facts about the study and make sure that the participant does not experience any distress.

Values and Science: Points of View

- Moral values set standards for and impose limits on the conduct of research.
- There are various views on the relation between values and science. Few believe that there can be a completely value-free science, but some advocate trying to minimize the influence of values on science, whereas others argue that values should be recognized and encouraged as an important factor in science.

Key Terms

applied research *(29)*
basic research *(29)*
confederate *(46)*
construct validity *(30)*
correlation coefficient *(36)*
correlational research *(36)*
debriefing *(49)*
deception *(46)*
dependent variables *(41)*
experiment *(39)*
experimental realism *(46)*
experimenter expectancy effects *(45)*
external validity *(45)*
hypothesis *(28)*
independent variables *(41)*
informed consent *(48)*
interaction *(42)*
internal validity *(44)*
interrater reliability *(32)*
main effect *(41)*
meta-analysis *(47)*
mundane realism *(46)*
operational definition *(30)*
random assignment *(40)*
random sampling *(35)*
subject variables *(41)*
theory *(28)*

3 The Social Self

OUTLINE

PREVIEW

THIS CHAPTER examines three interrelated aspects of the "social self." First, it considers the *self-concept* and the question of how people come to understand their own actions, emotions, and motivations. Second, it considers *self-esteem,* the affective component, and the question of how people evaluate themselves and defend against threats to their self-esteem. Third, it considers *self-presentation,* a behavioural manifestation of the self, and the question of how people present themselves to others. As we will see, the self is complex and multi-faceted.

PUTTING COMMON SENSE TO THE TEST

T / F

____ **Humans are the only animals who recognize themselves in the mirror.**

____ **Smiling can make you feel happier.**

____ **Sometimes the harder you try to control a thought, feeling, or behaviour, the less likely you are to succeed.**

____ **People tend to be overly optimistic about their future.**

____ **People often sabotage their own performance in order to protect their self-esteem.**

____ **It's more adaptive to alter one's behaviour than to stay consistent from one social situation to the next.**

Can you imagine living a meaningful or coherent life without a clear sense of who you are? In *The Man Who Mistook His Wife for a Hat*, neurologist Oliver Sacks (1985) described such a person—a patient named William Thompson. According to Sacks, Thompson suffered from an organic brain disorder that impairs a person's memory of recent events. Unable to recall anything for more than a few seconds, Thompson was always disoriented and lacked a sense of inner continuity. The effect on his behaviour was startling. Trying to grasp a constantly vanishing identity, Thompson would construct one tale after another to account for who he was, where he was, and what he was doing. From one moment to the next, he would improvise new identities—a grocery store clerk, minister, or medical patient, to name just a few. In social settings, Thompson's behaviour was especially intriguing. As Sacks (1985) observed,

> *The presence of others, other people, excite and rattle him, force him into an endless, frenzied, social chatter, a veritable delirium of identity-making and -seeking; the presence of plants, a quiet garden, the nonhuman order, making no social demands upon him, allow this identity-delirium to relax, to subside (p. 110).*

Thompson's plight is unusual, but it highlights two important points—one about the private "inner" self, the other about the "outer" self we show to others. First, the capacity for self-reflection is necessary for people to feel as if they understand their own motives and emotions and the causes of their behaviour. Unable to ponder his own actions, Thompson appeared vacant and without feeling—"desouled," as Sacks put it. Second, the self is heavily influenced by social factors. Thompson himself seemed compelled to put on a face for others and to improvise characters for the company he kept. We all do, to some extent. We may not create a kaleidoscope of multiple identities as Thompson did, but the way we manage ourselves is influenced by the people around us.

This chapter examines several aspects of the self. First, we ask a cognitive question: How do people come to know themselves, develop a self-concept, and maintain a stable sense of identity? Second, we explore an affective, or emotional, question: How do people evaluate themselves, enhance their self-images, and defend against threats to their self-esteem? Third, we confront a behavioural question: How do people regulate their own actions and present themselves to others according to interpersonal demands? As we'll see, the self is a topic that in recent years has attracted unprecedented interest among social psychologists (Baumeister, 1999; Brown, 1998; Leary & Tangney, 2003; Tesser et al., 2002).

The Self-Concept

Have you ever been at a noisy gathering and yet managed to hear someone at the other end of the room mention your name? If so, then you have experienced the "cocktail party effect"—the tendency of people to pick a personally relevant stimulus out of a complex environment (Moray, 1959; Wood & Cowan, 1995). To the cognitive psychologist, this phenomenon shows that people are selective in their attention. To the social psychologist, it also shows that the self is an important object of our own attention.

The term **self-concept** refers to the sum total of beliefs that people have about themselves. But what, specifically, does the self-concept consist of? According to Hazel Markus (1977), the self-concept is made up of cognitive molecules called **self-schemas**: beliefs about oneself that guide the processing of self-relevant information. Self-schemas are to an individual's total self-concept what hypotheses are to a theory, or what books are to a library. You can think of yourself as masculine or feminine, as independent or dependent, as liberal or conservative, as introverted or extroverted. Indeed, any specific attribute may have relevance to the self-concept for some people but not for others. The self-schema for body weight is a good example. People who regard themselves as extremely overweight or underweight, or for whom body image is a conspicuous aspect of the self-concept, are considered *schematic* with respect to weight. For body-weight schematics, a wide range of otherwise mundane events—a trip to the supermarket, new clothing, dinner at a restaurant, a day at the beach, or a friend's eating habits—may trigger thoughts about the self. In contrast, those who do not regard their own weight as extreme or as an important part of their lives are *aschematic* on that attribute (Markus et al., 1987).

Beginnings of the Self-Concept

When you stand in front of a mirror, what do you see? If you were a dog, a cat, or some other animal, you would not realize that the image you see is you, your own reflection. Except for human beings, only great apes—chimpanzees, gorillas, and orangutans—seem capable of self-recognition. How can we possibly know what nonhumans think about mirrors? In a series of studies, Gordon Gallup (1977) placed different species of animals in a room with a large mirror. At first, they greeted their own images by vocalizing, gesturing, and making other social responses. After several days, the great apes—but not the other animals—began to use the mirror to pick food out of their teeth, groom themselves, blow bubbles, and make faces for their own entertainment. From all appearances, they recognized themselves.

In other studies, Gallup anaesthetized the animals, then painted an odourless red dye on their brows, and returned them to the mirror. Upon seeing the red spot, only the apes spontaneously reached for their own brows—proof that they perceived the image as their own. Among apes, this form of self-recognition emerges in young adolescence and is stable across the life span, at least until old age (DeVeer et al., 2003; Povinelli et al., 1997). By using a similar red dye test (but without anaesthetizing the infants), developmental psychologists have found that most human

self-concept The sum total of an individual's beliefs about his or her own personal attributes.

self-schemas Beliefs people hold about themselves that guide the processing of self-relevant information.

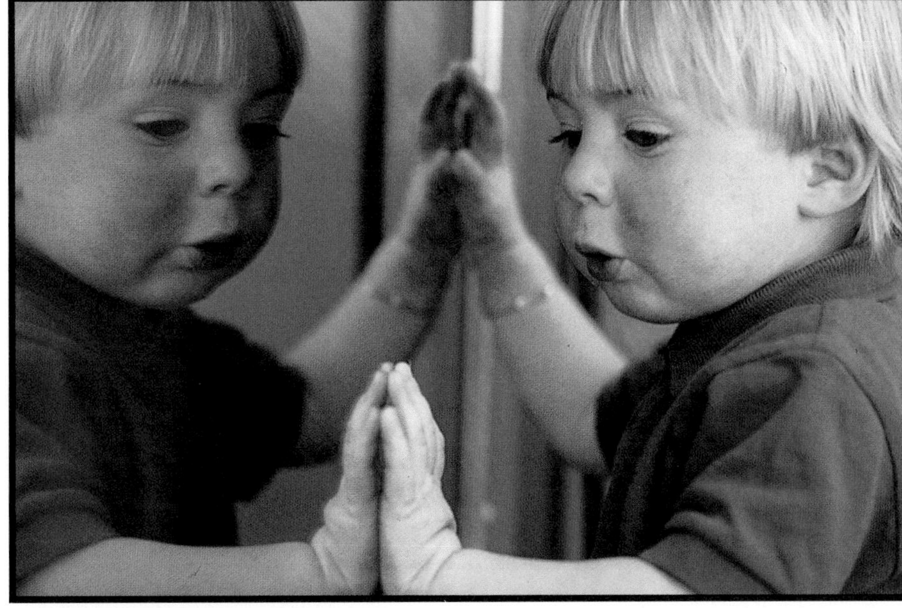

Infants begin to recognize themselves in the mirror at 18 to 24 months of age.

infants begin to recognize themselves in the mirror between the ages of 18 and 24 months (Lewis & Brooks-Gunn, 1979). Today, many researchers believe that self-recognition among great apes and human infants is the first clear expression of the concept "me" (Boysen & Himes, 1999).

The ability to see yourself as a distinct entity is a necessary first step in the evolution and development of a self-concept. The second step involves social factors. Sociologist Charles Horton Cooley (1902) introduced the term *looking-glass self* to suggest that other people serve as a mirror in which we see ourselves. Expanding on this idea, George Herbert Mead (1934) added that we often come to know ourselves by imagining what significant others think of us and then incorporating these perceptions into our self-concepts. More recently, Susan Andersen and Serena Chen (2002) theorized that the self is "relational"—that we draw our sense of who we are from our past and current relationships with the significant others in our lives. It is interesting that when Gallup tested his apes, those that had been raised in isolation—without exposure to peers—did not recognize themselves in the mirror. Only after such exposure did they begin to show signs of self-recognition. Among human beings, our self-concepts match our *perceptions* of what others think of us. But there's a hitch: What we think of ourselves often does not match what specific others *actually* think of us (Felson, 1989; Kenny & DePaulo, 1993; Shrauger & Schoeneman, 1979; Tice & Wallace, 2003).

Humans are the only animals who recognize themselves in the mirror. **False.**

In recent years, social psychologists have broken new ground in the effort to understand the social self. People are not born thinking of themselves as reckless, likeable, shy, or outgoing. So where do their self-concepts come from? In the coming pages, five sources are considered: introspection, perceptions of our own behaviour, the influences of other people, autobiographical memories, and the cultures in which we live.

Introspection

Let's start at the beginning: How do people achieve insight into their own beliefs, attitudes, emotions, and motivations? Common sense makes this question seem ludicrous. After all, don't you know what you think because *you* think it? And don't you know how you feel because *you* feel it? Look through popular books on how to achieve self-insight, and you'll find the answers to these questions to be yes. Whether the prescribed technique is meditation, psychotherapy, religion, dream analysis, or hypnosis, the advice is basically the same: Self-knowledge is derived from introspection, a looking inward at one's own thoughts and feelings.

If these how-to books are correct, it stands to reason that no one can know you as well as you know yourself. Thus, people tend to assume that for others to know you at all, they would need information about your private thoughts, feelings, and other inner states—not just about your behaviour. But is this really the case? Some social psychologists are not sure that this faith in introspection is justified. Several

"Look, babe. At this point, you've reinvented yourself so many times you're back to who you were at the start."

In some ways, our sense of self is malleable and subject to change.

years ago, Richard Nisbett and Timothy Wilson (1977) found that research participants often cannot accurately explain the causes or correlates of their own behaviour. This observation forced researchers to confront a thorny question: Does introspection improve the accuracy of self-knowledge?

In *Strangers to Ourselves*, Wilson (2002) says no, that introspection can sometimes impair self-knowledge. In a series of studies, he found that the attitudes people reported having about different objects corresponded closely to their behaviour toward those objects. The more participants said they enjoyed a task, the more time they spent on it; the more attractive they found a scenic landscape, the more pleasure they revealed in their facial expressions; the happier they said they were with a current dating partner, the longer the relationship ultimately lasted. Ironically, however, after participants were told to analyze the reasons for how they felt, the attitudes they reported no longer corresponded to their behaviour. Human beings keep mentally busy processing information, which is why we often fail to understand our own thoughts, feelings, and behaviours. Apparently, it is possible to think too much and be too analytical, only to get confused.

People also have difficulty projecting forward and predicting how they would feel in response to future emotional events—a process known as **affective forecasting**. How happy would you be six months after winning a million-dollar lottery? Or, how unhappy would you be if injured in an automobile accident? In a series of studies, Timothy Wilson and Daniel Gilbert (2003) asked research participants to predict how they would feel after various positive and negative life events and compared their predictions to how others experiencing those events said they actually felt. Consistently, they found that people overestimate the strength and duration of their emotional reactions, a phenomenon they call the *impact bias*. However, recent research suggests this bias may not be universal. For example, East Asians (who tend to think more holistically), do not exhibit this effect whereas Euro-Canadians (who tend to focus more on individual events) do (Lam et al., 2005).

To become more accurate in our predictions, then, we need to force ourselves to think more broadly, about *all* the events that impact us.

Perceptions of Our Own Behaviour

Regardless of what we can learn from introspection, Daryl Bem (1972) believes that people can learn about themselves the same way outside observers do—by watching their own behaviour. Bem's **self-perception theory** is simple yet profound. To the extent that internal states are weak or difficult to interpret, people infer what they think or how they feel by observing their own behaviour and the situation in which that behaviour takes place. Think about it. Have you ever listened to yourself argue with someone, only to realize with amazement how angry you were? Have you ever devoured a sandwich in record time, only then to conclude that you must have been

affective forecasting
The process of predicting how one would feel in response to future emotional events.

self-perception theory
The theory that when internal cues are difficult to interpret, people gain self-insight by observing their own behaviour.

incredibly hungry? In each case, you made an inference about yourself by watching your own actions.

There are limits to self-perception, of course. According to Bem, people do not infer their own internal states from behaviour that occurred in the presence of compelling situational pressures such as reward or punishment. If you argued vehemently or wolfed down a sandwich because you were paid to do so, you probably would not assume that you were angry or hungry. In other words, people learn about themselves through self-perception only when the situation alone seems insufficient to have caused their behaviour.

A good deal of research supports self-perception theory. When people are gently coaxed into doing something, and when they are not otherwise certain about how they feel, they come to view themselves in ways that are consistent with the behaviour (Chaiken & Baldwin, 1981; Fazio, 1987; Schlenker & Trudeau, 1990). Thus, research participants induced to describe themselves in flattering terms scored higher on a later test of self-esteem than did those who were led to describe themselves more modestly (Jones et al., 1981; Rhodewalt & Agustsdottir, 1986). Similarly, those who were manoeuvered by leading questions into describing themselves as introverted or extroverted—whether or not they really were—came to define themselves as such later on, unless they were certain of this aspect of their personality (Fazio et al., 1981; Swann & Ely, 1984). British author E. M. Forster anticipated the theory well when he asked, "How can I tell what I think 'til I see what I say?"

"I don't sing because I am happy. I am happy because I sing."

As suggested by self-perception theory, we sometimes infer how we feel by observing our own behaviour.

In 1975, Martin Seligman argued that depression results from **learned helplessness**, the acquired expectation that one cannot control important outcomes. In a classic series of experiments, Seligman had found that dogs strapped into a harness and exposed to painful electric shocks soon became passive and gave up trying to escape, even in new situations where escape was possible. In contrast, dogs that had not received uncontrollable shocks quickly learned the escape routine. As applied to humans, this finding suggested that prolonged exposure to uncontrollable events might similarly cause apathy, inactivity, a loss of motivation, and pessimism. Among human research participants, those exposed to inescapable bursts of noise thus failed to protect themselves in a later situation where the noise could be easily avoided. Seligman was quick to note that people who are exposed to uncontrollable events become, in many ways, like depressed individuals: discouraged, pessimistic about the future, and lacking in initiative. Thus, he saw depression as a form of learned helplessness.

The perception of control refers to the expectation that our behaviours can produce satisfying outcomes. But people also differ in the extent to which they believe that they can perform these behaviours in the first place. These concepts seem related; but in fact they refer to different beliefs, both of which are necessary for us to feel that we control the important outcomes in our lives (Skinner, 1996). According to Albert Bandura (1997), these latter expectations are based on feelings of competence, or **self-efficacy**. Some individuals may be generally more confident than others, says Bandura, but self-efficacy is a state of mind that varies from one specific task and situation to another. In other words, you may have high self-efficacy about meeting new people, but not about raising your grades. Or you may have high self-efficacy about solving a math problem but not about writing a paper.

Research on self-efficacy has shown that the more of it you have at a particular task, the more likely you are to take on that task, try hard, persist in the face of

learned helplessness The acquired expectation that one cannot control important outcomes.

self-efficacy A person's belief that he or she is capable of the specific behaviour required to produce a desired outcome in a given situation.

People often have feelings of self-efficacy in some life domains but not others.

failure, and succeed. The implications for mental and physical health are particularly striking. For example, individuals with high self-efficacy on health-related matters are more likely, if they want, to stop smoking, abstain from alcohol, stay physically fit, and tolerate the pain of arthritis, childbirth, and migraine headaches (Bandura, 1999; Maddux, 1995).

Self-Perceptions of Emotion Draw the corners of your mouth back and up and tense your eye muscles. Okay, relax. Now raise your eyebrows, open your eyes wide, and let your mouth drop open slightly. Relax. Now pull your brows down and together and clench your teeth. Relax. If you followed these directions, you would have appeared to others to be feeling first happy, then fearful, and finally angry. The question is: How would you have appeared to yourself?

Social psychologists who study emotion have asked precisely that question. Viewed within the framework of self-perception theory, the **facial feedback hypothesis** states that changes in facial expression can trigger corresponding changes in the subjective experience of emotion. In the first test of this hypothesis, James Laird (1974) told participants that they were taking part in an experiment on activity of the facial muscles. After attaching electrodes to their faces, he showed them a series of cartoons. Before each one, the participants were instructed to contract certain facial muscles in ways that created either a smile or a frown. As Laird predicted, participants rated what they saw as funnier, and reported feeling happier, when they were smiling than when they were frowning. In follow-up research, people were similarly induced through posed expressions to experience fear, anger, sadness, and disgust (Duclos et al., 1989). Facial feedback can evoke and magnify certain emotional states. It's important to note, however, that the face is not *necessary* to the experience of emotion. Neuropsychologists recently tested a 21-year-old woman who suffered from bilateral facial paralysis and found that despite her inability to outwardly *show* emotion, she reported *experiencing* various emotions in response to positive and negative visual images (Keillor et al., 2003).

Other expressive behaviours, such as body posture, can also provide us with sensory feedback and influence the way we feel. When people feel proud, they stand erect with their shoulders raised, chest expanded, and head held high *(expansion)*. When dejected, however, people slump over with their shoulders drooping and head bowed *(contraction)*. Clearly, your emotional state is revealed in the way you carry yourself. But is it also possible that the way you carry yourself affects your emotional state? Can people lift their spirits by expansion or lower their spirits by contraction? Yes. Sabine Stepper and Fritz Strack (1993) arranged for people to sit in either a slumped or an upright position by varying the height of the table they had to write on. Those forced to sit upright reported feeling more pride after succeeding at a task than did those who were placed in a slumped position. In another study, participants who were instructed to lean forward with their fists clenched during the experiment reported feeling anger, while those who sat slumped with their heads down said they felt sadness (Duclos et al., 1989; Flack et al., 1999).

facial feedback hypothesis The hypothesis that changes in facial expression can lead to corresponding changes in emotion.

Self-Perceptions of Motivation Without quite realizing it, Mark Twain was a self-perception theorist. In *The Adventures of Tom Sawyer*, written in the late 1800s, he quipped, "There are wealthy gentlemen in England who drive four-horse passenger coaches twenty or thirty miles on a daily line, in the summer, because the privilege costs them considerable money; but if they were offered wages for the service that would turn it into work then they would resign." Twain's hypothesis—that reward for an enjoyable activity can undermine interest in that activity—seems to contradict our intuition and a good deal of psychological research. After all, aren't we all motivated by reward, as declared by B. F. Skinner and other behaviourists? The answer depends on how *motivation* is defined.

Smiling can make you feel happier. **True.**

As a keen observer of human behaviour, Twain anticipated a key distinction between intrinsic and extrinsic motivation. *Intrinsic motivation* originates in factors within a person. People are said to be intrinsically motivated when they engage in an activity for the sake of their own interest, the challenge, or sheer enjoyment. Eating a fine meal, listening to music, spending time with friends, and engaging in a hobby are among the activities that you might find intrinsically motivating. In contrast, *extrinsic motivation* originates in factors outside the person. People are said to be extrinsically motivated when they engage in an activity as a means to an end, for tangible benefits. It might be for money, grades, or recognition; to fulfill obligations; or to avoid punishment. As the behaviourists have always said, people do strive for reward. The question is: What happens to the intrinsic motivation once that reward is no longer available?

From the standpoint of self-perception theory, Twain's hypothesis makes sense. When someone is rewarded for listening to music, playing a game, or eating a tasty food, his or her behaviour becomes *over*justified, or *over*rewarded, and can be attributed to extrinsic as well as intrinsic motives. This **overjustification effect** can be dangerous: Observing that their own efforts have paid off, people begin to wonder if the activity was ever worth pursuing in its own right.

Research shows that when people start getting "paid" for a task they already enjoy, they sometimes lose interest in it. In an early demonstration of this phenomenon, Mark Lepper and his colleagues (1973) gave preschool children an opportunity to play with colourful felt-tipped markers—an opportunity most could not resist. By observing how much time the children spent on the activity, the researchers were able to measure their intrinsic motivation. Two weeks later, the children were divided into three groups, all about equal in terms of initial levels of intrinsic motivation. In one, the children were simply asked to draw some pictures with the markers. In the second, they were told that if they used the markers they would receive a "Good Player Award," a certificate with a gold star and a red ribbon. In a third group, the children were not offered a reward for drawing pictures, but—like those in the second group—they received a reward when they were done.

About a week later, the teachers placed the markers and paper on a table in the classroom while the experimenters observed through a one-way mirror. Since no rewards were offered on this occasion, the amount of free time the children spent playing with the markers reflected their intrinsic motivation. As predicted, those children who had expected and received a reward for their efforts were no longer as interested in the markers as they had been. Children who had not received a reward were not adversely affected, nor were those who had unexpectedly received the reward. Having played with the markers without the promise of reward, these children remained intrinsically motivated (see Figure 3.1).

The paradox that reward can undermine rather than enhance intrinsic motivation has been observed in many settings and with both children and adults (Deci & Ryan, 1985; Enzle & Anderson, 1993; Pittman & Heller, 1987; Remedios et al., 2005; Tang & Hall, 1995). Accept money for a leisure activity, and before you know it, what used to be "play" comes to feel more like "work." In the long run, this can have negative effects on the quality of performance. In a series of studies, Teresa Amabile (1996) and others had participants write poems, draw or paint pictures, make paper collages, and generate creative solutions to business dilemmas.

overjustification effect The tendency for intrinsic motivation to diminish for activities that have become associated with reward or other extrinsic factors.

FIGURE 3.1

Paradoxical Effects of Reward on Intrinsic Motivation

In this study, an expected reward undermined children's intrinsic motivation to play with felt-tipped markers. Children who received an unexpected reward or no reward did not lose interest. *(Lepper et al., 1973.)*

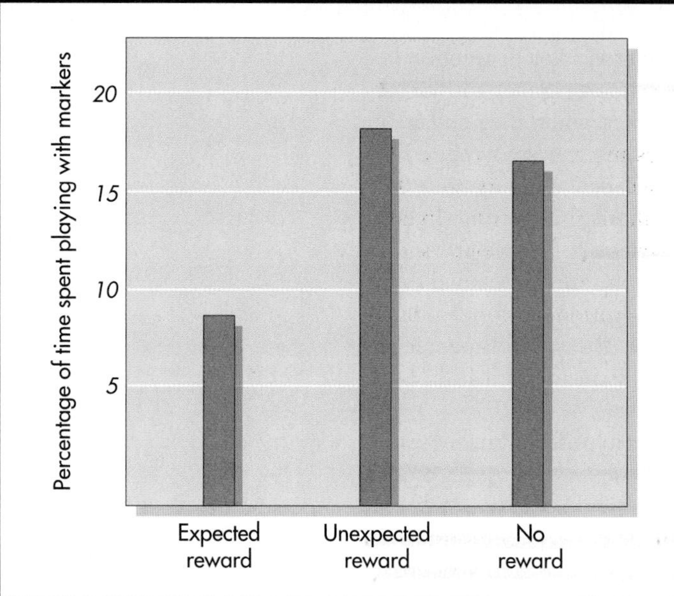

Consistently, they found that people are more creative when they feel interested and challenged by the work itself than when they feel pressured to make money, fulfill obligations, meet deadlines, win competitions, or impress others. In one study, Amabile had art experts rate the works of professional artists and found that the artists' commissioned work (art they were contracted for) was judged as lower in quality than their noncommissioned work. People are likely to be more creative when they are intrinsically motivated in relation to the task, not compelled by outside forces.

But wait. If extrinsic benefits serve to undermine intrinsic motivation, should teachers and parents *not* offer rewards to their children? And are the employee incentive programs so often used in business doomed to fail, as some (Kohn, 1993) have suggested? It all depends on how the reward is perceived—and by whom. If a reward is presented in the form of verbal praise that is perceived to be sincere, or as a special "bonus" for superior performance, then it can actually *enhance* intrinsic motivation by providing positive feedback about competence—as when people win competitions, scholarships, or a pat on the back from people they respect (Cameron & Pierce, 1994; Covington, 2000; Eisenberger & Cameron, 1996; Henderlong & Lepper, 2002).

Individual differences in motivational orientation toward work must also be considered. For intrinsically oriented people who say that "What matters most to me is enjoying what I do" and that "I seldom think about salary and promotions," reward may be unnecessary—and may even be detrimental (Amabile et al., 1994). Yet for people who are highly focused on the achievement of certain goals—whether at school, at work, or in sports—extrinsic inducements such as grades, scores, bonuses, trophies, and the thrill of competition—tend to boost their intrinsic motivation (Harackiewicz & Elliot, 1993; Sansone & Harackiewicz, 2000).

Influences of Other People

As we noted earlier, Cooley's (1902) theory of the looking-glass self emphasized that other people help us define ourselves. In this section, we will see the importance of this proposition to our self-concepts.

Social Comparison Theory Suppose a stranger were to ask, "Who are you?" If you had only a minute or two to answer, would you mention your ethnic or religious background? What about your hometown? Would you describe your talents and your interests or your likes and dislikes? When asked this question, people tend to describe themselves in ways that set them apart from others in their immediate vicinity (McGuire & McGuire, 1988). For example, Kalin and Berry (1995) report on the results of two national surveys conducted in 1974 and 1991 examining multicultural and ethnic attitudes. In the 1991 survey, most Canadians identified themselves as "Canadian" but in Quebec most identified themselves as "Provincial"

(Quebecois), whereas in the 1974 survey, those in Quebec identified themselves as "French Canadian." Interestingly, the researchers found that despite this difference, all respondents maintained a strong attachment to Canada. They explain this by noting that in a country as diverse as Canada, multiple loyalties are possible; "Individuals can feel pride in, and allegiance to, smaller communities (e.g. ethnic groups) nested within the larger community of the nationstate (p. 1)." The implication is intriguing: Change someone's social surroundings, and you can change that person's spontaneous self-description.

This reliance on distinguishing features in self-description indicates that the self is "relative," a social construct, and that we define ourselves in part by using others—sometimes just a best friend—as a benchmark (Mussweiler & Strack, 2000; Mussweiler & Rüter, 2003). Indeed, that is what Leon Festinger (1954) proposed in his **social comparison theory**. Festinger argued that when people are uncertain of their abilities or opinions—that is, when objective information is not readily available—they evaluate themselves through comparisons with similar others. The theory seems reasonable, but is it valid? Over the years, social psychologists have put social comparison theory to the test, focusing on two key questions: (1) *When* do we turn to others for comparative information? (2) Of all the people who inhabit the earth, *with whom* do we choose to compare ourselves? (Suls & Wheeler, 2000).

As Festinger proposed, the answer to the "when" question appears to be that people engage in social comparison in states of uncertainty, when more objective means of self-evaluation are not available. In fact, recent studies suggest that Festinger may have understated the role of social comparison processes—that people may judge themselves in relation to others even when more objective standards are available. For example, William Klein (1997) asked college students to make a series of judgments of artwork. Giving false feedback, he then told the students that 60 percent or 40 percent of their answers were correct—and that this was 20 percent higher or lower than the average among students. When they later rated their own skill at the task, participants were influenced not by their absolute scores, but by where they stood in relation to their peers. For them, it was better to have had a 40 percent score that was above average than a 60 percent score that was below average. However, the tendency to view ambiguous information in a self-enhancing way is more likely when participants receive information about their own and others' performance at the same time (Klein et al., 2006).

The "with whom" question has also been the subject of many studies. The answer seems to be that when we evaluate our own taste in music, value on the job market, or athletic ability, we look to others who are similar—or different—to us in relevant ways (Goethals & Darley, 1977; C. T. Miller, 1984; Wheeler et al., 1982)—a choice that we make automatically, without necessarily being aware of it (Gilbert et al., 1995). For example, Lockwood and Kunda (2000) found that we will make a positive comparison with a role model when we feel it is possible to attain their level of success, but we will be demoralized if we feel it is not. There are exceptions to this rule, of course. Later in the chapter, we will see that people often cope with personal inadequacies by focusing on others who are *less* able or *less* fortunate than themselves.

Two-Factor Theory of Emotion People seek social comparison information to evaluate their abilities and opinions. Do they also turn to others to determine something as personal and subjective as their own emotions? In experiments on affiliation, Stanley Schachter (1959) found that when people were frightened into thinking they would receive painful electric shocks, most sought the company of others who were in the same predicament. Nervous and uncertain about how they should be feeling, participants wanted to affiliate with similar others, presumably for the purpose of comparison. Yet when they were not fearful, and expected only mild shocks,

social comparison theory
The theory that people evaluate their own abilities and opinions by comparing themselves to others.

or when the "others" were not taking part in the same experiment, participants preferred to be alone. As Schachter put it, "Misery doesn't just love any kind of company; it loves only miserable company" (p. 24).

Schachter and Singer's **two-factor theory of emotion** has attracted a good deal of controversy, as some studies have corroborated their findings but others have not. Overall, it now appears that one limited but important conclusion can safely be drawn: When people are unclear about their own emotional states, they sometimes interpret how they feel by watching others (Reisenzein, 1983). The "sometimes" part of the conclusion is important. For others to influence your emotion, your level of physiological arousal cannot be too intense, or else it will be experienced as aversive—regardless of the situation (Maslach, 1979; Zimbardo et al., 1993). Also, research shows that other people must be present as a possible explanation for arousal *before* its onset. Once people are aroused, they turn for an explanation to events that preceded the change in their physiological state (Schachter & Singer, 1979; Sinclair et al., 1994).

In subsequent chapters, we will see that the two-factor theory of emotion has far-reaching implications for passionate love, anger and aggression, and other affective experiences.

Autobiographical Memories

Philosopher James Mill once said, "The phenomenon of the Self and that of Memory are merely two sides of the same fact." If the story of patient William Thompson at the start of this chapter is any indication, Mill was right. Without autobiographical memories—recollections of the sequences of events that have touched your life (Fivush et al., 2003; Rubin, 1996; Thompson et al., 1998)—you would have no coherent self-concept. Think about it. Who would you be if you could not remember your parents or childhood playmates, your successes and failures, the places you lived, the schools you attended, the books you read, and the teams you played for? Clearly, memories shape the self-concept. In this section, we'll see that the self-concept shapes our personal memories as well (Conway & Pleydell-Pearce, 2000).

"The nice thing about having memories is that you can choose."

—William Trevor

When people are prompted to recall their own experiences, they typically report more events from the recent than from the distant past. There are, however, two consistent exceptions to this recency rule. The first is that older adults retrieve a large number of personal memories from their adolescence and early adult years—a "reminiscence peak" that may occur because these years are busy and formative in one's life (Fitzgerald, 1988; Jansari & Parkin, 1996). A second exception is that people tend to remember transitional "firsts." Reflect for a moment on your university career. What events pop to mind—and when did they occur? Did you come up with the day you arrived on campus or the first time you met your closest friend? What about notable classes, parties, or sports events? Obviously, not all experiences leave the same impression. Ask people old enough to remember November 22, 1963, and they probably can tell you exactly where they were, whom they were with, and what was happening the moment they heard the news that US President John F. Kennedy had been shot. Roger Brown and James Kulik (1977) coined the term *flashbulb memories* to describe these enduring, detailed, high-resolution recollections and speculated that humans are biologically equipped for survival purposes to "print" these dramatic events in memory. These flashbulb memories are not necessarily accurate, but they "feel" special and serve as prominent landmarks in the biographies we write about ourselves (Conway, 1995).

two-factor theory of emotion The theory that the experience of emotion is based on two factors: physiological arousal and a cognitive interpretation of that arousal.

By linking the present to the past and providing us with a sense of inner continuity, autobiographical memory is a vital part of—and can be shaped by—our identity. Our current view of ourselves is often affected by our views of our past selves,

Although adults recall more events from the recent than distant past, people are filled with memories from late adolescence and early adulthood. These formative years are nicely captured by high-school yearbook photos—such as those of entertainers Will Smith and Jennifer Lopez. (ClassMates.com, Yearbook Archives.)

as well as our views of our future selves (Wilson & Ross, 2003). In particular, people are often motivated to distort the past in ways that are self-inflated. According to Anthony Greenwald (1980), "The past is remembered as if it were a drama in which the self was the leading player" (p. 604).

For example, Michael Ross (1989) found that after people were persuaded by an expert who said that frequent tooth brushing was desirable, they reported, in the context of a subsequent experiment, having brushed more often in the previous two weeks. Illustrating that memory can be biased rather than objective, these participants "updated" the past in light of their new attitude. More recently, Harry Bahrick and others (1996) had undergraduates recall all of their high school grades and then checked the accuracy of these reports against the actual transcripts. Overall, the majority of grades were recalled correctly. But most of the errors in memory were grade *inflations*—and most of these were made when the actual grades were *low* (see Figure 3.2).

Do these findings support sociologist George Herbert Mead's (1934) contention that our visions of the past are like pure "escape fancies . . . in which we rebuild the world according to our hearts' desires" (pp. 348–349)? Not necessarily. In a series of studies, Ian Newby-Clark and Michael Ross (2003) asked people to recall significant events from their own lives and to anticipate significant events likely to occur in their future. They found that although people are hopeful about the future, anticipating mostly positive events, their recollections from the past are more balanced. Most people feel as if they have been fortunate in their lives, but they are as quick to recall becoming ill or their parents divorcing, as they are to recall meeting a boyfriend or girlfriend, or graduating from high school.

FIGURE 3.2

Distortions in Memory of High School Grades

College students were asked to recall their high school grades, which were then checked against their actual transcripts. These comparisons revealed that most errors in memory were grade inflations. Lower grades were recalled with the least accuracy (and the most inflation). It appears that people sometimes revise their own past to suit their current self-image. *(Bahrick et al., 1996.)*

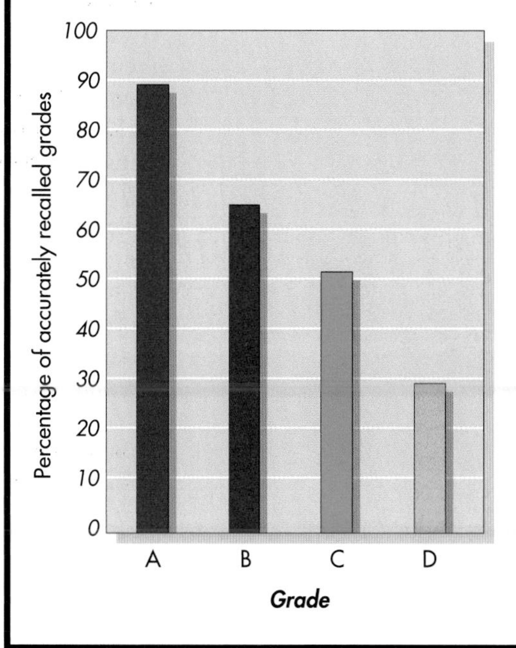

Cultural Perspectives

The self-concept is also influenced by cultural factors. In North America, it is said that "the squeaky wheel gets the grease"; in

Reflecting an interdependent view of the self, children in Japan are taught to fit into the community. Reflecting a more independent view of the self, children in Canada are encouraged to express their individuality.

Japan, it is said that "the nail that stands out gets pounded down." Thus Canadian parents try to raise their children to be independent, self-reliant, and assertive (a "cut above the rest"), whereas Japanese children are raised to fit into their groups and community.

The preceding example illustrates two contrasting cultural orientations. One values *individualism* and the virtues of independence, autonomy, and self-reliance. The other orientation values *collectivism* and the virtues of interdependence, cooperation, and social harmony. Under the banner of individualism, one's personal goals take priority over group allegiances. In collectivist cultures, by contrast, the person is, first and foremost, a loyal member of a family, team, company, church, and state (Triandis, 1994). In what countries are these orientations the most extreme? In a worldwide study of 117 000 employees of IBM, Geert Hofstede (2003) found that the most fiercely individualistic people were from the United States, Australia, the United Kingdom, Canada, and the Netherlands—in that order. The most collectivist people were from Guatemala, Ecuador, Panama, Venezuela, Indonesia, and Pakistan.

It's also important to realize that individualism and collectivism are not simple opposites on a continuum and that the similarities and differences between countries do not fit a simple pattern. Daphna Oyserman and others (2002) conducted a meta-analysis of many thousands of respondents in 83 studies. Within the United States, they found that African Americans were the most individualistic subgroup and that Asian and Latino Americans were the most collectivistic. Comparing nations, they found that Americans as a group are relatively individualistic. Collectivist orientations varied within Asia, however, as the Chinese were more collectivistic than Japanese and Korean respondents. Cheah and Nelson (2004) found that within a Canadian Aboriginal population (a minority culture), not all group members identify with their heritage culture. While Aboriginal students were more likely to endorse collectivist ideals, such as interdependence and the maintenance of group balance and harmony, compared to European Canadian students, this was only found among Aboriginal students who held more traditional values.

Individualism and collectivism are so deeply ingrained in a culture that they mould our very self-conceptions and identities. According to Hazel Markus and Shinobu Kitayama (1991), most North Americans and Europeans have an *independent* view of the self. In this view, the self is an entity that is distinct, autonomous, self-contained, and endowed with unique dispositions. Yet in much of Asia, Africa, and Latin America, people hold an *interdependent* view of the self. Here, the self is part of a larger social network that includes one's family, co-workers, and others with whom one is socially connected. People with an independent view say that "the only person you can count on is yourself" and "I enjoy being unique and different from others." In contrast, those with an interdependent view are more likely to agree that "I'm partly to blame if one of my family members or co-workers fails" and "my happiness depends on the happiness of those around me" (Rhee et al., 1995; Singelis, 1994; Triandis et al., 1998). These contrasting orientations—one focused on the personal self, the other on a collective self—are depicted in Figure 3.3.

Research confirms that there is a close link between cultural orientation and conceptions of the self. David Trafimow and his colleagues (1991) had North American and Chinese college students complete 20 sentences beginning with "I am. . . ." The Americans were more likely to fill in the blank with trait descriptions ("I am shy"), whereas the Chinese were more likely to identify themselves by group affiliations ("I am a college student"). It's no wonder that in China, one's family name comes *before* one's personal name. Similar differences are found between Australians and Malaysians (Bochner, 1994).

These cultural orientations can influence the way we perceive, evaluate, and present ourselves in relation to others. Markus and Kitayama (1991) identified two interesting differences between East and West. The first is that people in individualistic cultures strive for personal achievement, while those living in collectivist cultures derive more satisfaction from the status of a valued group. Thus, whereas North Americans tend to overestimate their own contributions to a team effort, take credit for success, and blame others for failure, people from collectivist cultures underestimate their own role and present themselves in more modest, self-effacing terms in relation to other members of the group (Akimoto & Sanbonmatsu, 1999; Heine et al., 2000).

A second consequence of these differing conceptions of the self is that American college students see themselves as less similar to others than do Asian Indian students. This difference reinforces the idea that individuals with independent conceptions of the self believe they are unique. In fact, our cultural orientations toward conformity or independence may lead us to favour similarity or uniqueness in all things. In a fascinating study, Heejung Kim and Hazel Markus (1999) showed abstract figures to subjects from the United States and Korea. Each figure contained

FIGURE 3.3

Cultural Conceptions of Self

As depicted here, different cultures foster different conceptions of the self. Many westerners have an *independent* view of the self as an entity that is distinct, autonomous, and self-contained. Yet many Asians, Africans, and Latin Americans hold an *interdependent* view of the self that encompasses others in a larger social network. *(Markus & Kitayama, 1991.)*

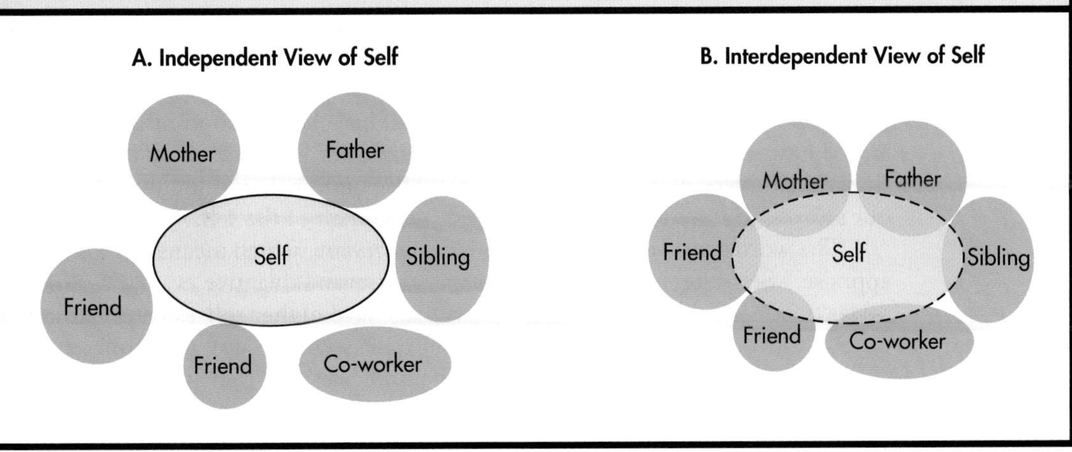

FIGURE 3.4

What's Your Preference: Similarity or Uniqueness?

Which subfigure within each set do you prefer? Kim and Markus (1999) found that Americans tend to like subfigures that "stand out" as unique or in the minority, while Koreans tend to like subfigures that "fit in" with the surrounding group. *(Kim & Markus, 1999.)*

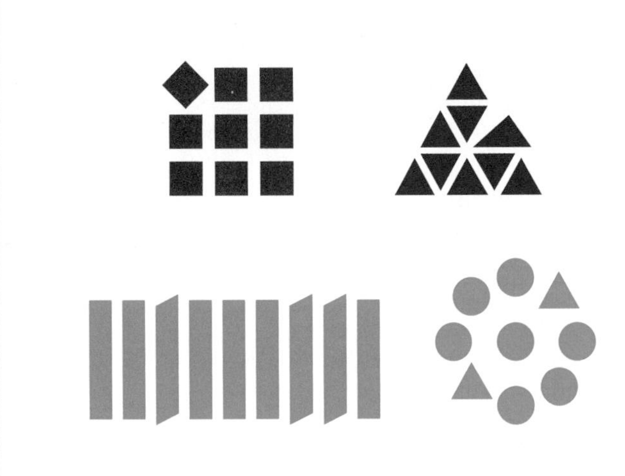

nine parts. Most of the parts were identical in shape, position, and direction. One or more were different. Look at Figure 3.4. Which of the nine subfigures within each group do you like most? The American subjects liked the subfigures that were unique or in the minority, while Korean subjects preferred those that "fit in" as part of the group. In another study, these same researchers approached pedestrians of American and East Asian heritage at San Francisco's International Airport and asked them to fill out a questionnaire. Afterward, as a gift, they offered all the participants a choice of one pen from a handful of pens, three or four of which had the same colour barrel, green or orange. The result: 74 percent of the Americans chose a uniquely coloured pen, and 76 percent of the East Asians selected one of the commonly coloured pens. It seems that our culturally ingrained orientations to conformity and independence leave a mark on us, leading us to form preferences for things that "fit in" or "stand out."

Are people from disparate cultures locked into thinking about the self in either personal or collective terms, or are both aspects of the self present in everyone, to be expressed according to the situation? A study by Ross, Xun and Wilson (2002) demonstrated that it is possible to activate different cultural mindsets that in turn affect bicultural individuals' self-perceptions. Chinese-born students living in Canada were asked to complete self-perception questionnaires in either Chinese or English. Compared to the Canadian-born participants of either Chinese or European descent, the Chinese-born participants responding in Chinese reported higher agreement with Chinese beliefs, were more likely to note their cultural background, and reported significantly lower self-esteem. It appears that each of us have both personal and collective aspects of the self to draw on—and that the part that comes to mind depends on the situation we are in.

Self-Esteem

How do you feel about yourself? Are you generally satisfied with your appearance, personality, abilities, and friendships? Are you optimistic about your future? When it comes to the self, people are hardly cool, objective, dispassionate observers. Rather, we are judgmental, emotional, and highly protective of our **self-esteem**—an affectively charged component of the self.

The word *esteem* comes from the Latin *aestimare*, which means "to estimate or appraise." Self-esteem thus refers to our positive and negative evaluations of ourselves (Coopersmith, 1967). Some individuals have higher self-esteem than others do—an attribute that can have a profound impact on the way they think and feel about themselves. It's important to keep in mind, however, that although some of us have higher self-esteem than others, a feeling of self-worth is not a single trait etched permanently in stone. Rather, it is a state of mind that varies in response to

self-esteem An affective component of the self, consisting of a person's positive and negative self-evaluations.

success, failure, changes in fortune, social interactions, and other life experiences (Heatherton & Polivy, 1991). Also, because the self-concept is made up of many self-schemas, individuals typically view parts of the self differently: Some parts they judge more favourably, or see more clearly or as more important, than other parts (Pelham, 1995; Pelham & Swann, 1989). Indeed, just as individuals differ according to how high or low their self-esteem is, they also differ in the extent to which their self-esteem is stable or unstable. As a general rule, self-esteem is a trait that is stable from childhood through old age (Trzesniewski et al., 2003). Yet for some people in particular, self-esteem seems to fluctuate up and down in response to daily experiences—which makes them highly responsive to praise and overly sensitive to criticism (Baldwin & Sinclair, 1996; Kernis &Waschull, 1995; Schimel et al., 2001).

The Need for Self-Esteem

You and just about everyone else on the planet seem to have a need for self-esteem, as we all want to see ourselves in a positive light. This observation about human motivation is beyond dispute. But let's step back for a moment and ask, why? Why do we have this need for self-esteem?

At present, there are two social psychological answers to this question. One theory, proposed by Mark Leary and Roy Baumeister (2000), is that people are inherently social animals and that the desire for self-esteem is driven by this more primitive need to connect with others and gain their approval. In this way, our sense of self-esteem serves as a "sociometer," a rough indicator of how we're doing in the eyes of others. The threat of social rejection thus lowers self-esteem, which activates the need to regain approval and acceptance.

Alternatively, Jeff Greenberg, Sheldon Solomon, and Thomas Pyszczynski (1997) have proposed Terror Management Theory to help explain our need for self-esteem. According to this theory, we humans are biologically programmed for self-preservation. Yet we are conscious of—and terrified by—the inevitability of our own death. We cope with this deeply rooted fear by constructing and accepting cultural worldviews about how, why, and by whom the earth was created; explanations of the purpose of our existence; and a sense of history filled with heroes, villains, and momentous events. These worldviews provide meaning and purpose and a buffer against anxiety. In a series of experiments, these investigators found that people react to graphic scenes of death, or to the thought of their own death, with intense defensiveness and anxiety. When given positive feedback on a test, however, which boosts their self-esteem, that reaction is muted. As we'll see in later chapters, this theory has been used to explain how Americans are likely to cope with the trauma of 9/11 and the terror that it triggered (Pyszczynski et al., 2002).

In many ways, satisfying the need for self-esteem is critical to our entire outlook on life. People with positive self-images tend to be happy, healthy, productive, and successful. They are also confident, bringing to new challenges a winning and motivating attitude—which leads them to persist longer at difficult tasks, sleep better at night, maintain their independence in the face of peer pressure, and suffer fewer ulcers. In contrast, people with negative self-images tend to be more depressed, pessimistic about the future, and prone to failure. Lacking confidence, they bring to new tasks a losing attitude that traps them in a vicious, self-defeating cycle. Expecting to fail, and fearing the worst, they become anxious, exert less effort, and "tune out" on important challenges. People with low self-esteem don't trust their own positive self-appraisals (Josephs et al., 2003). And when they fail, they tend to blame themselves, which makes them feel even less competent (Brockner, 1983; Brown & Dutton, 1995). Low self-esteem may even be hazardous to your health. Some research suggests that becoming aware of one's own negative attributes adversely affects the activity of certain white blood cells in the immune system, thus compromising the body's capacity to ward off disease (Strauman et al., 1993).

Influences of Gender, Race, and Culture

Just as individuals differ in their self-esteem, so, too, do social and cultural groups. Think about it. If you were to administer a self-esteem test to thousands of people all over the world, would you find that some segments of the population score higher than others? Would you expect to see differences in the averages of men and women, Blacks and Whites, or inhabitants of different cultures? Believing that self-esteem promotes health, happiness, and success, and concerned that some groups are disadvantaged in this regard, researchers have indeed made these types of comparisons.

Are there gender differences in self-esteem? Over the years, a lot has been written in the popular press about the inflated but fragile "male ego," the low self-regard among adolescent girls and women, and the resulting gender-related "confidence gap" (Orenstein, 1994). Despite such claims, a study of 66 schoolchildren, ages 11 and 12 in Southwestern Ontario, found no difference in self-esteem levels between the boys and girls in its sample (Bosacki et al., 1997).

Researchers have also wondered if low self-esteem is a problem for members of stigmatized minority groups—historically, victims of prejudice and discrimination. Does membership in a minority group deflate one's sense of self-worth? Based on the combined results of studies involving more than half a million respondents, Bernadette Gray-Little and Adam Hafdahl (2000) reported that black children, adolescents, and adults consistently score higher—not lower—than their white counterparts on measures of self-esteem (see also Twenge & Crocker, 2002). Such counterintuitive findings have been dubbed the "puzzle of self-esteem" (Simmons, 1978). Some have suggested that perhaps Blacks—more than other minorities—are able to preserve their self-esteem in the face of adversity by attributing negative outcomes to the forces of discrimination and using this adversity to build a sense of group pride. In this regard, Twenge and Crocker found that self-esteem scores of black Americans, relative to those of white, have risen over time—from the pre-civil rights days of the 1950s to the present. It also may be the case that one devalues any attribute upon which one's group does poorly, and instead focuses on those attributes upon which one's group excels; thus a stigmatized group protects its self-esteem (Verkuyten, 2005).

Variations in self-esteem have also been observed among people from different parts of the world. Earlier we saw that inhabitants of individualistic cultures tend to view themselves as distinct and autonomous, whereas those in collectivist cultures view the self as part of an interdependent social network. Do these different orientations have implications for self-esteem? Steven Heine and his colleagues (1999) believe that they do. Comparing the distribution of self-esteem scores in Canada and Japan, they found that whereas most Canadians' scores clustered in the high-end range, the majority of Japanese respondents scored in the centre of that same range.

Is the self-esteem of the Japanese truly less inflated than that of North Americans (a conclusion also suggested by their tendency to talk about themselves in critical, self-effacing terms)? Or do Japanese respondents, high in self-esteem, simply feel compelled to present themselves modestly to others (as a function of the collectivist need to "fit in" rather than "stand out")? To answer this question, researchers have tried to develop indirect, subtle, "implicit" tests that would enable them to measure a person's self-esteem without his or her awareness. In a timed word-association study, for example, Anthony Greenwald and Shelly Farnham (2000) found that despite their non-inflated scores on self-esteem tests, Asian Americans—just like their European American counterparts—were quicker to associate themselves with positive words such as *happy* and *sunshine* than with negative words such as *vomit* and *poison*. Does this mean that people from individualist and collectivist cultures are similarly motivated and that they similarly think highly of themselves? It appears that way. Culture may influence the way we seek to fulfill the need for positive regard—for example, by presenting ourselves as unique and self-confident or as equal members of a group—but the need for people to see themselves in a positive light is universal, or "pancultural" (Sedikides et al., 2003).

Self-Discrepancy Theory

What determines how people feel about themselves? According to E. Tory Higgins (1989), our self-esteem is defined by the match or mismatch between how we see ourselves and how we want to see ourselves. To demonstrate, try the following exercise. On a blank sheet of paper, write down ten traits that describe the kind of person you think you *actually* are (smart? easygoing? sexy? excitable?). Next, list ten traits that describe the kind of person you think you *ought* to be, characteristics that would enable you to meet your sense of duty, obligation, and responsibility. Then make a list of traits that describe the kind of person you would like to be, an *ideal* that embodies your hopes, wishes, and dreams. If you follow these instructions, you should have three lists: your actual self, your ought self, and your ideal self.

Research has shown that these lists can be used to predict your self-esteem and your emotional well-being. The first list is your self-concept. The others represent your personal standards, or *self-guides*. To the extent that you fall short of these standards, you will have lowered self-esteem, negative emotion, and, in extreme cases, a serious affective disorder. The specific consequence depends on which self-guide you fail to achieve. If there's a discrepancy between your actual and ought selves, you will feel guilty, ashamed, and resentful. You might even suffer from excessive fears and anxiety-related disorders. If the mismatch is between your actual and ideal selves, you'll feel disappointed, frustrated, unfulfilled, and sad. In the worst-case scenario you might even become depressed (Boldero & Francis, 2000; Higgins, 1999; Scott & O'Hara, 1993; Strauman, 1992).

It's clear that every one of us must cope with some degree of self-discrepancy. Nobody is perfect. Yet we do not all suffer from the emotional consequences. The reason, according to Higgins, is that self-esteem depends on a number of factors. One is simply the amount of discrepancy. The more of it there is, the worse we feel. Another is the importance of the discrepancy to the self. The more important the domain in which we fall short, again, the worse we feel. A third factor is the extent to which we focus on our self-discrepancies. The more focused we are, the greater the harm. This last observation raises an important question: What causes us to be more or less focused on our personal shortcomings? For an answer, we turn to self-awareness theory.

The Self-Awareness "Trap"

If you carefully review your daily routine—classes, work, chores at home, leisure activities, social interactions, and meals—you will probably be surprised at how little time you actually spend thinking about yourself. In a study that illustrates this point, more than 100 people, ranging in age from 19 to 63, were equipped for a week with electronic beepers that sounded every two hours or so between 7:30 A.M. and 10:30 P.M. Each time the beepers went off, participants interrupted whatever they were doing, wrote down what they were thinking at that moment, and filled out a brief questionnaire. Out of 4700 recorded thoughts, only 8 percent were about the self. For the most part, attention was focused on work and other activities. In fact, when participants were thinking about themselves, they reported feeling relatively unhappy and wished they were doing something else (Csikszentmihalyi & Figurski, 1982).

"I have the true feeling of myself only when I am unbearably unhappy."
—Franz Kafka

Self-Focusing Situations The finding that people may be unhappy while they think about themselves is interesting, but what does it mean? Does self-reflection bring out our personal shortcomings the way staring into a mirror draws our gaze to every blemish on the face? Is self-awareness an unpleasant mental state from which we need to retreat?

Robert Wicklund and others have theorized that the answer is yes (Duval & Wicklund, 1972; Wicklund, 1975; Wicklund & Frey, 1980). According to their **self-awareness theory**, people are not usually self-focused, but certain situations predictably force us to turn inward and become the objects of our own attention. When we talk about ourselves, glance in a mirror, stand before an audience or camera, watch ourselves on videotape, or behave in a conspicuous manner, we enter into a state of heightened self-awareness that leads us naturally to compare our behaviour to some standard. This comparison often results in a negative discrepancy and a temporary reduction in self-esteem as we discover that we fall short. Thus, people often experience a negative mood state when placed in front of a mirror (Fejfar & Hoyle, 2000; Hass & Eisenstadt, 1990). In fact, the more self-focused people are in general, the more likely they are to find themselves in a bad mood (Flory et al., 2000) or depressed (Pyszczynski & Greenberg, 1987). People who are self-absorbed are also more likely to suffer from alcoholism, anxiety, and other clinical disorders (Ingram, 1990; Mor & Winquist, 2002).

Is there a solution? Self-awareness theory suggests two basic ways of coping with such discomfort: (1) "Shape up" by behaving in ways that reduce our self-discrepancies; or (2) "ship out" by withdrawing from self-awareness. According to Charles Carver and Michael Scheier (1981), the solution chosen depends on whether people think they can reduce their self-discrepancy and whether they're pleased with the progress they make once they try (Duval et al., 1992). If so, they tend to match their behaviour to personal or societal standards; if not, they tune out, look for distractions, and turn attention away from the self. This process is depicted in Figure 3.5.

In general, research supports the prediction that when people are self-focused, they tend to behave in ways that are consistent either with their own personal values or with socially accepted ideals (Gibbons, 1990). In an interesting field study, for example, Halloween trick-or-treaters—children wearing masks, costumes, and painted faces—were greeted at a researcher's door and left alone to help themselves from a bowl of candy. Although the children were asked to take only one piece, 34 percent violated the request. When a full-length mirror was placed behind the candy bowl, however, the number of violators dropped to 12 percent. Apparently, the mirror forced the children to become self-focused, leading them to behave in a way that was consistent with public standards of desirable conduct (Beaman et al., 1979). In another study that illustrates this positive effect of self-awareness, C. Neil

self-awareness theory
The theory that self-focused attention leads people to notice self-discrepancies, thereby motivating either an escape from self-awareness or a change in behaviour.

FIGURE 3.5

The Causes and Effects of Self-Awareness

Self-awareness pressures people to reduce self-discrepancies either by matching their behaviour to personal or societal standards or by withdrawing from self-awareness.

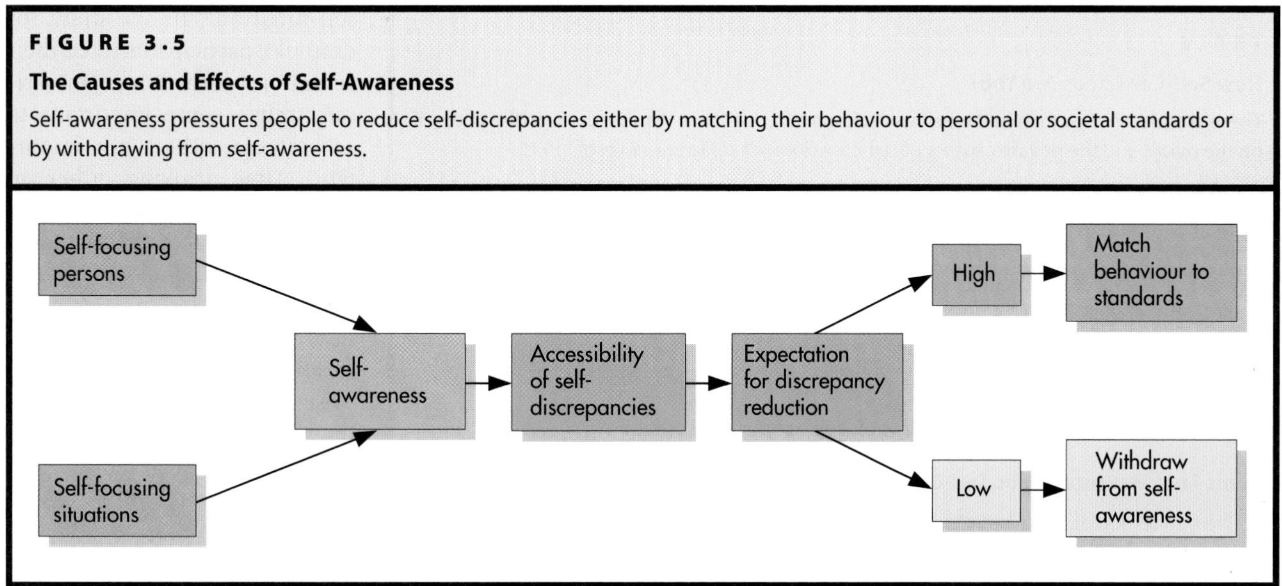

Macrae and his colleagues (1998) found that participants were less likely than normal to use stereotypes in describing others—a social taboo known to us all—when they were seated in front of a mirror, when they could see themselves on a TV monitor, or when their names were flashed briefly on a screen.

Self-awareness theory states that if a successful reduction of self-discrepancy seems unlikely, individuals will take a second route: escape from self-awareness. Roy Baumeister (1991) speculates that drug abuse, sexual masochism, spiritual ecstasy, binge eating, and even suicide all serve this escapist function. Even television may serve as a form of escape. In one study, Sophia Moskalenko and Steven Heine (2003) brought college students into a laboratory and tested their actual-ideal self-discrepancies twice. Half watched a brief TV show on nature before filling out the second measure. In a second study, students were sent home with the questionnaire and instructed to fill it out either before or after watching TV. In both cases, those who watched TV had lower self-discrepancies on the second measure. In yet a third study, students who were told they had done poorly on an IQ test spent more time watching TV while waiting in the lab than those who were told they had succeeded. Perhaps TV and other forms of entertainment enable people to "watch their troubles away."

One particularly disturbing health implication concerns the use of alcohol. According to Jay Hull, people often drown their sorrows in a bottle as a way to escape the negative implications of self-awareness. To test this hypothesis, Hull and Richard Young (1983) administered what was supposed to be an IQ test to male participants and gave false feedback suggesting that they had either succeeded or failed. Supposedly as part of a separate study, those participants were then asked to taste and rate different wines. As they did so, experimenters kept track of how much they drank during a 15-minute tasting period. As predicted, participants who were prone to self-awareness drank more wine after failure than after success, presumably to dodge the blow to their self-esteem. Among participants not prone to self-awareness, there was no difference in alcohol consumption. These results come as no surprise. Indeed, many of us expect alcohol to grant this form of relief (Leigh & Stacy, 1993) and help us manage our emotional highs and lows (Cooper et al., 1995).

Claude Steele and Robert Josephs (1990) believe that alcoholic intoxication provides more than just a means of tuning out on the self. By causing people to lose touch with reality and shed their inhibitions, it also evokes a state of "drunken

TABLE 3.1

How Self-Conscious Are You?

These sample items appear in the Self-Consciousness Scale. How would you describe yourself on the public and the private aspects of self-consciousness? *(Fenigstein et al., 1975.)*

Items That Measure Private Self-Consciousness

- I'm always trying to figure myself out.
- I'm constantly examining my motives.
- I'm often the subject of my fantasies.
- I'm alert to changes in my mood.
- I'm aware of the way my mind works when I work on a problem.

Items That Measure Public Self-Consciousness

- I'm concerned about what other people think of me.
- I'm self-conscious about the way I look.
- I'm concerned about the way I present myself.
- I usually worry about making a good impression.
- One of the last things I do before leaving my house is look in the mirror.

self-inflation." In one study, for example, participants rated their actual and ideal selves on various traits—some important to self-esteem, others not important. After drinking either an 80-proof vodka cocktail or a harmless placebo, they re-rated themselves on the same traits. As measured by the perceived discrepancy between actual and ideal selves, participants who were drinking expressed inflated views of themselves on traits they considered important (Banaji & Steele, 1989).

Self-Focusing Persons Just as *situations* evoke a state of self-awareness, certain *individuals* are characteristically more self-focused than others. Research has revealed an important distinction between **private self-consciousness**—the tendency to introspect about our inner thoughts and feelings—and **public self-consciousness**—the tendency to focus on our outer public image (Buss, 1980; Fenigstein et al., 1975). Table 3.1 presents a sample of items used to measure these traits.

Private and public self-consciousness are distinct traits. People who score high on a test of private self-consciousness tend to fill in incomplete sentences with first-person pronouns, are quick to make self-descriptive statements, and are acutely aware of changes in their internal bodily states (Mueller, 1982; Scheier et al., 1979). In contrast, those who score high on a measure of public self-consciousness are sensitive to the way they are viewed from an outsider's perspective. Thus, when people were asked to draw a capital letter E on their foreheads, 43 percent of those with high levels of public self-consciousness, compared with only 6 percent of those with low levels, oriented the E so that it was backward from their own standpoint but correct for an outside observer (Hass, 1984). People who are high in public self-consciousness are also particularly sensitive to the extent to which others share their opinions (Fenigstein & Abrams, 1993).

The distinction between private and public self-awareness has implications for the ways in which we reduce self-discrepancies. According to Higgins (1989), people are motivated to meet either their own standards or the standards held for them by significant others. If you're privately self-conscious, you listen to an inner voice and try to reduce discrepancies relative to your own standards; if you're publicly self-conscious, however, you try to match your behaviour to socially accepted norms. As illustrated in Figure 3.6, there may be "two sides of the self: one for you and one for me" (Scheier & Carver, 1983, p. 123).

private self-consciousness
A personality characteristic of individuals who are introspective, often attending to their own inner states.

public self-consciousness
A personality characteristic of individuals who focus on themselves as social objects, as seen by others.

Limits of Self-Regulation

To this point, we have seen that self-focused attention can motivate us to control our behaviour and strive toward personal or social ideals. To achieve these goals—which enables us to reduce the self-discrepancies that haunt us—we must engage in self-regulation, the processes by which we seek to control or alter our thoughts, feelings, behaviours, and urges (Carver & Scheier, 1998). From lifting ourselves out of bed in the morning to dieting, running the extra mile, smiling politely at people we really don't like, and working when we have more exciting things to do, the exercise of self-control is something we do all the time.

Mark Muraven and Roy Baumeister (2000) have theorized that self-control is a limited inner resource that can temporarily be depleted by usage. There are two components to their theory. The first is that all self-control efforts draw from a single common reservoir. The second is that exercising self-control is like flexing a muscle: Once used, it becomes fatigued and loses strength, making it more difficult to re-exert self-control—at least for a while, until the resource is replenished. Deny yourself the ice-cream sundae that tickles your sweet tooth and you'll find it more difficult to hold your temper when angered. Try to conceal your stage fright as you stand before an audience and you'll find it harder to resist the urge to watch TV when you should be studying.

Thus far, research supports this provocative hypothesis. In one study, Muraven and Baumeister (1998) had participants watch a brief clip from *Mondo Cane*, an upsetting film that shows scenes of sick and dying animals exposed to radioactive waste. Some of the participants were instructed to stifle their emotional responses to the clip, including their facial expressions; others were told to amplify or exaggerate their emotional responses; a third group received no special instructions. Both before and after the movie, self-control was measured by the length of time that participants were able to squeeze a handgrip exerciser without letting go. As predicted, those who had to inhibit or amplify their emotions during the film—but not those in the third group—lost their willpower in the handgrip task between the first time they tried it and the second (see Figure 3.7).

It appears that we can control ourselves just so much before self-regulation fatigue sets in, causing us to "lose it." What might this mean, then, for people who are constantly regulating their behaviour? To find out, Kathleen Vohs and Todd Heatherton (2000) showed a brief and dull documentary to individual female college students, half of whom were chronic dieters. Placed in the viewing room—either within arm's reach (high temptation) or ten feet away (low temptation)—was a bowl filled with Skittles, M&Ms, Doritos, and salted peanuts that participants were free to sample. After watching the movie, they were taken to another room for an ice-cream taste test and told they could eat as much as they wanted. The question is: How much ice cream did they consume? The researchers predicted that dieters seated within reach of the bowl would have to fight the hardest to avoid snacking—an act of self-control that would cost them later. The prediction was confirmed. As measured by the amount of ice cream consumed in the taste test, dieters in the high-temptation condition ate more ice cream than did all nondieters and dieters in the low-temptation situation. What's more, a second study showed that dieters who had to fight the urge in the high-temptation situation were later less persistent—and quicker to give up—on a set of impossible cognitive problems they were asked to solve.

There's another possible downside to self-control that is often seen in sports when athletes become so self-focused under pressure that they stiffen up and "choke." While many athletes rise to the occasion, the pages of sports history are filled with stories of basketball players who lose their touch in the final minute of a championship game, or of tennis players who lose their serve, all when it matters most. "Choking" seems to be a paradoxical type of failure caused by thinking too much. When you learn a new motor activity, like how to throw a curve ball or land a jump, you must think through the mechanics in a slow and cautious manner. As you get better, however, your movements become automatic, so you do not have to think about timing, breathing, the position of your head and limbs, or the distribution of your weight. You relax and just do it. Unless trained to perform while self-focused,

FIGURE 3.6

Revolving Images of Self

According to self-awareness theory, people try to meet either their own standards or standards held for them by others—depending, perhaps, on whether they are in a state of private or public self-consciousness. As Scheier and Carver (1983, p. 123) put it, there are "two sides of the self: one for you and one for me."
(Snyder et al., 1983)

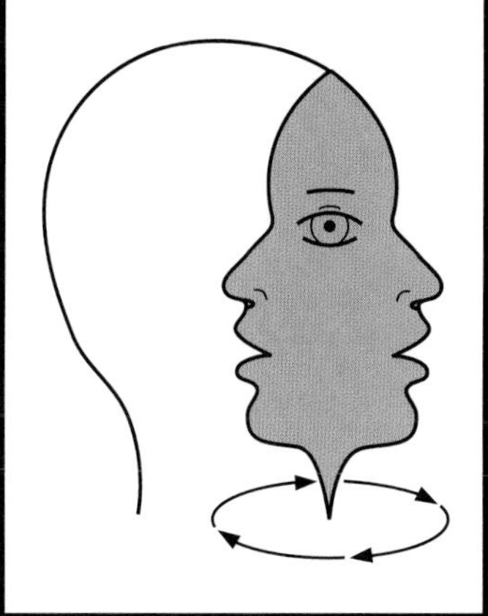

"The highest possible stage in moral culture is when we recognize that we ought to control our thoughts."
—Charles Darwin

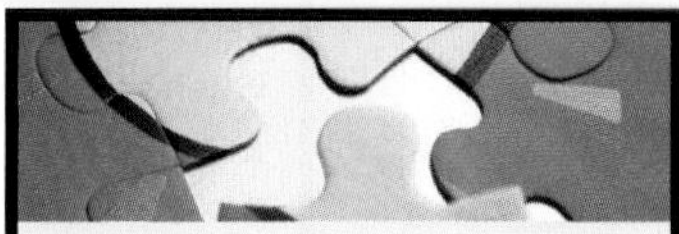

Sometimes the harder you try to control a thought, feeling, or behaviour, the less likely you are to succeed. **True.**

FIGURE 3.7

Self-Control as a Limited Inner Resource

Participants were shown an upsetting film and told to amplify or suppress their emotional responses to it (a third group received no self-control instruction). Before and afterward, self-control was measured by persistence at squeezing a handgrip exerciser. As shown, the two groups that had to control their emotions during the film—but not those in the third group—later lost their willpower on the handgrip. *(Muraven & Baumeister, 1998.)*

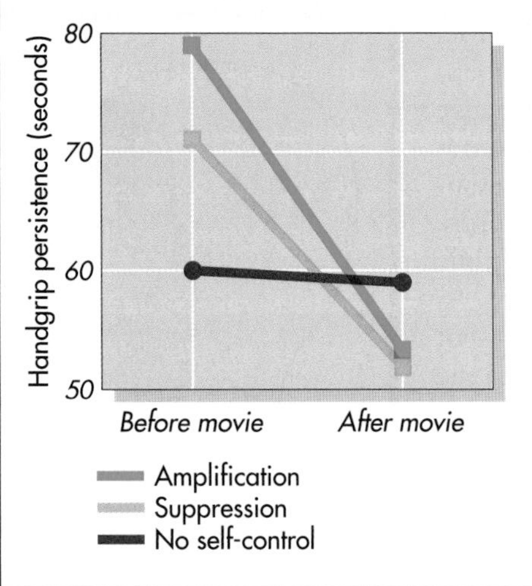

athletes under pressure often try their hardest not to fail, become self-conscious, and think too much—which disrupts the fluid and natural flow of their performance (Baumeister, 1984; Beilock & Carr, 2001; Lewis & Linder, 1997).

The paradoxical effects of attempted self-control are evident in other situations, too. Studying what he calls *ironic processes*, Daniel Wegner (1994) has found that, at times, the harder you try to inhibit a thought, feeling, or behaviour, the less likely you are to succeed. Try not to think about a white bear for the next 30 seconds, he finds, and that very image intrudes upon consciousness with remarkable frequency. Instruct the members of a jury to disregard inadmissible evidence, and the censored material is sure to pop to mind as they deliberate. Try not to worry about how long it's taking to fall asleep, and you'll stay awake. Try not to laugh in class, think about the chocolate cake in the fridge, or scratch the itch on your nose—well, you get the idea.

According to Wegner, every conscious effort at maintaining control is met by a concern about failing to do so. This concern automatically triggers an "ironic operating process" as the person, trying hard *not* to fail, searches his or her mind for the unwanted thought. The ironic process will not necessarily prevail, says Wegner. Sometimes we can put the imaginary white bear out of mind. But if the person is cognitively busy, distracted, tired, hurried, or under stress, then the ironic process, because it "just happens," will prevail over the intentional process, which requires conscious attention and effort. Thus, Wegner (1997) notes that "any attempt at mental control contains the seeds of its own undoing" (p. 148).

Ironic processes have now been observed in a wide range of behaviours. In an intriguing study of this effect on the control of motor behaviour, Wegner and his colleagues (1998) had participants hold a pendulum (a crystalline pendant suspended from a nylon fishing line) over the centre of two intersecting axes on a glass grid, which formed a 1. Some participants were instructed simply to keep the pendulum steady, while others were more specifically told not to allow it to swing back and forth along the horizontal axis. Try this yourself, and you'll see that it's not easy to prevent all movement. In this experiment, however, the pendulum was more likely to swing horizontally when this direction was specifically forbidden. To further examine the role of mental distraction, the researchers instructed some participants to

FIGURE 3.8

Ironic Effects of Mental Control

In this study, participants tried to hold a pendulum motionless over a grid. As illustrated in the tracings shown here, they were better at the task when simply instructed to keep the pendulum steady (*a*) than when specifically told to prevent horizontal movement (*c*). Among participants who were mentally distracted during the task, this ironic effect was even greater (*b* and *d*). *(Wegner et al., 1998.)*

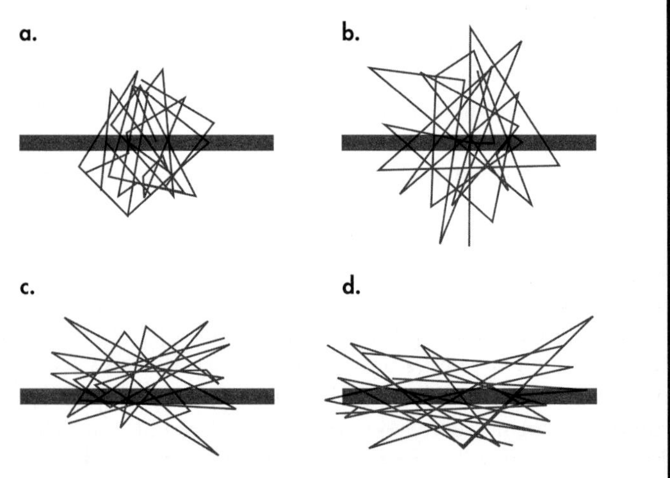

Why do some athletes choke under pressure and others rise to the occasion? After an embarrassing quarter-final loss at the 2002 winter Olympics, Sweden's men's hockey team came back and won gold in Torino in 2006. Team Canada, heavily favoured to win gold going in, and the defending gold-medal champions, left Torino empty-handed.

count backward from a thousand by sevens while controlling the pendulum. In this situation, the ironic effect was even greater. Among those who specifically tried to prevent horizontal movement but could not concentrate fully on the task, the pendulum swayed freely back and forth—in the forbidden direction (see Figure 3.8). Using a similar method, these researchers found that people were most likely to overshoot a golf putt when they specifically tried *not* to overshoot but were distracted while putting. It may seem both comic and tragic, but at times our efforts at self-control backfire, thwarting even the best of intentions.

Mechanisms of Self-Enhancement

We have seen that self-awareness can create discomfort and lower self-esteem by focusing attention on discrepancies. We have seen that people often avoid focusing on themselves and turn away from unpleasant truths, but that such avoidance is not always possible. And we have seen that efforts at self-regulation often fail and sometimes even backfire. How, then, does the average person cope with his or her faults, inadequacies, and uncertain future?

In North American cultures, most people most of the time think highly of themselves. Consistently, research has shown that participants see positive traits as more self-descriptive than negative ones, rate themselves more highly than they rate others, rate themselves more highly than they are rated *by* others, exaggerate their control over life events, and predict that they have a bright future (Taylor, 1989). Research shows that people overrate their effectiveness as speakers to an

"We don't see things as they are, we see them as we are."
—Anaïs Nin

audience (Keysar & Henly, 2002) and overestimate their contributions to a group and the extent to which they would be missed if absent (Savitsky et al., 2003). People also overestimate their intellectual and social abilities across a wide range of domains. What's particularly interesting about this tendency is that those who are least competent are the most likely to overrate their performance. In a series of studies, Justin Kruger and David Dunning (1999) found that American college students with the lowest scores on tests of logic, grammar, and humour were the ones who most grossly overestimated their own abilities (on average, their scores were in the lowest 12 percent among peers, yet they estimated themselves to be in the 62nd percentile). These investigators also found that when the low-scorers were trained to be more competent in these areas, they became more realistic in their self-assessments. Ignorance, as they say, is bliss.

Other research, too, shows that people tend to exhibit **implicit egotism**, a nonconscious and subtle form of self-enhancement. This is well illustrated in the finding that people rate the letters in their name more favourably than other letters of the alphabet (Hoorens & Nuttin, 1993). In an article entitled "Why Susie Sells Seashells by the Seashore," Brett Pelham and his colleagues (2002) argue that we form positive associations to the sight and sound of our own name and thus are drawn to other people, places, and entities that share this most personal aspect of "self." In a thought-provoking series of studies, these researchers examined several important life choices that we make and found that people exhibit small but statistically detectable preferences for things that contain the letters of their own first or last name. For example, men and women are more likely than would be predicted by chance to live in places (Michelle in Manitoba, George in Guelph), attend schools (Wendy from the University of Western Ontario), and choose careers (Dennis and Denise as dentists) whose names resemble their own. In a subtle but remarkable way, we unconsciously seek out reflections of the self in our surroundings.

This recent research on implicit egotism shows that we tend to hold ourselves in high regard. And it's not that we consciously or openly flatter ourselves. The response is more like a reflex. Indeed, when research participants are busy or distracted as they make self-ratings, their judgments are quicker and even more favourable (Hixon & Swann, 1993; Paulhus et al., 1989). We can't all be perfect, nor can we all be better than average. So what supports this common illusion? In this section, we examine four methods that people use to rationalize or otherwise enhance their self-esteem: self-serving cognitions, self-handicapping, basking in the glory of others, and downward social comparisons.

Self-Serving Cognitions When students receive exam grades, those who do well take credit for their success; those who do poorly complain about the instructor and the test questions. When researchers have articles accepted for publication, they credit the quality of their work; when articles are rejected, they blame the editor and reviewers. When gamblers win a bet, they see themselves as skilful; when they lose, they moan and groan about fluke events that transformed near victory into defeat. Whether people are high or low in self-esteem, explain their outcomes publicly or in private, and try to be honest or to make a good impression, there is bias: People tend to take credit for success and to distance themselves from failure (Schlenker et al., 1990).

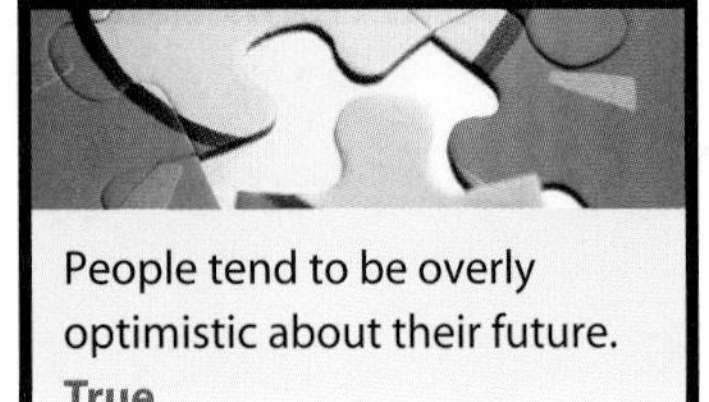

People tend to be overly optimistic about their future. **True.**

Most of us are also unrealistically optimistic. College students who were asked to predict their own future compared with that of the average person believed that they would graduate higher in their class, get a better job, have a happier marriage, and bear a gifted child. They also believed they were less likely to get fired or divorced, have a car accident, become depressed, be victimized by crime, or suffer from a heart attack (Weinstein, 1980). In sports, politics, health, and social issues, people exhibit an optimistic bias about their own future (Helweg-Larsen & Shepperd, 2001).

implicit egotism A nonconscious form of self-enhancement.

Obviously, the future is not always bright, so what supports this unwavering optimism? Ziva Kunda (1987) finds that people bolster their rosy outlook with elaborate theories that link their own personal attributes to desirable outcomes. In one study, for example, people who had been involved in a serious high school relationship said they believed that such an experience promotes a stable marriage. Yet those who had not been romantically involved said they believed that a *lack* of experience promotes a happy-ever-after ending. It is no wonder that those who participated in Kunda's study predicted there was only a 20 percent chance that their own future marriages would end in divorce—despite knowing that the population divorce rate is 50 percent. It's also no wonder that most people harbour illusions of control, overestimating the extent to which they can influence personal outcomes that are not, in fact, within their power to control (Langer, 1975; Thompson, 1999).

In casinos, racetracks, and lotteries, gamblers lose billions of dollars a year. This self-defeating behaviour persists in part because people exaggerate their control over random events. For example, many slot-machine addicts mistakenly think that they can find "hot" machines that have not recently surrendered a jackpot.

Self-Handicapping "My dog ate my homework." "I had a flat tire." "My alarm didn't go off." "My computer crashed." "I had a bad headache." "The referee blew the call." On occasion, people make excuses for their past performance. Sometimes they even come up with excuses in anticipation of future performance. Particularly when people are afraid that they might fail in an important situation, they use illness, shyness, anxiety, pain, trauma, and other complaints as excuses (Kowalski, 1996; Snyder & Higgins, 1988). The reason people do this is simple: By admitting to a limited physical or mental weakness, they can shield themselves from what could be the most shattering implication of failure—a lack of ability.

One form of excuse-making that many of us can relate to is *procrastination*—a purposive delay in starting or completing a task that is due at a particular time (Ferrari et al., 1995). Some people procrastinate chronically, while others do so only in certain situations. There are many reasons why someone might put off what needs to get done—whether it's studying for a test, shopping for Christmas, or preparing for the April 30 tax deadline. According to Joseph Ferrari (1998), one "benefit" of procrastinating is that it helps to provide an excuse for possible failure.

Making verbal excuses is one way to cope with the threatening implications of failure. Under certain conditions, this strategy is taken one step further: Sometimes people actually sabotage their own performance. It seems like the ultimate paradox, but there are times when we purposely set *our*selves up for failure in order to preserve our precious self-esteem. First described by Stephen Berglas and Edward Jones (1978), **self-handicapping** refers to actions people take to handicap their own performance in order to build an excuse for anticipated failure. To demonstrate, Berglas and Jones recruited college students for an experiment supposedly concerning the effects of drugs on intellectual performance. All the participants worked on a 20-item test of analogies and were told that they had done well, after which they expected to work on a second, similar test. For one group, the problems in the first test were relatively easy, leading participants to expect more success in the second test; for a second group, the problems were insoluble, leaving participants confused about their initial success and worried about possible failure. Before

self-handicapping Behaviours designed to sabotage one's own performance in order to provide a subsequent excuse for failure.

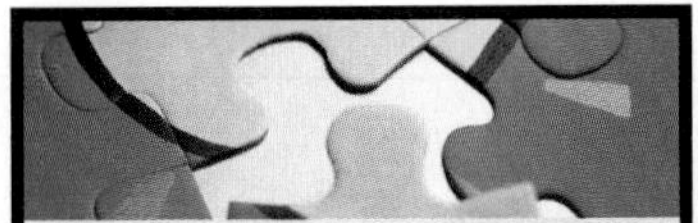

People often sabotage their own performance in order to protect their self-esteem. **True.**

seeing or taking the second test, participants were given a choice of two drugs: Actavil, which was supposed to improve performance, and Pandocrin, which was supposed to impair it.

Although no drugs were actually administered, most participants who were confident about the upcoming test selected the Actavil. In contrast, males—but not females—who feared the outcome of the second test chose the Pandocrin. By handicapping themselves, these men set up a convenient excuse for failure—an excuse, we should add, that may have been intended more for the experimenter's benefit than for the benefit of the participants themselves. Indeed, a follow-up study showed that although self-handicapping occurs when the experimenter witnesses the participants' drug choice, it is reduced when the experimenter is not present while that choice is being made (Kolditz & Arkin, 1982).

Some people use self-handicapping as a defense more than others do (Rhodewalt, 1990), and there are different ways to use it. For example, men often handicap themselves by taking drugs (Higgins & Harris, 1988) or neglecting to practice (Hirt et al., 1991), while women tend to report stress and physical symptoms (Smith et al., 1983). Another tactic is to set one's goals too high, as perfectionists like to do, which sets up failure—but not for a lack of ability (Hewitt et al., 2003; Schultheiss & Brunstein, 2000). Still another paradoxical tactic used to reduce performance pressure is to play down our own ability, lower expectations, and predict for all to hear that we will fail—a self-presentation strategy known as "sandbagging" (Gibson & Sachau, 2000). People also differ in their reasons for self-handicapping. Dianne Tice (1991) found that people who are low in self-esteem use self-handicapping to set up a defensive, face-saving excuse in case they fail, while those who are high in self-esteem use it as an opportunity to claim extra credit if they succeed.

Whatever the tactics and whatever the goal, self-handicapping appears to be an ingenious strategy: With the odds seemingly stacked against us, the self is insulated from failure and enhanced by success. By easing the pressure to succeed, self-handicapping might even enable us to enjoy what we're doing without worrying so much about how well we do it (Deppe & Harackiewicz, 1996). Of course, this strategy is not without a cost. Sabotaging ourselves—by not practicing, or by drinking too much, using drugs, faking illness, or setting goals too high—objectively increases the risk of failure. What's worse, it does not exactly endear us to others. Frederick Rhodewalt and his colleagues (1995) found that participants did not like their partners in an experiment when they thought that these partners had self-handicapped by claiming they did not care, were anxious, or were medically impaired. Women are particularly suspicious and critical of people who self-handicap (Hirt et al., 2003).

Basking in the Glory of Others To some extent, your self-esteem is influenced by individuals and groups with whom you identify. According to Robert Cialdini and his colleagues (1976), people often **bask in reflected glory (BIRG)** by showing off their connections to successful others. Cialdini's team first observed BIRGing on the university campuses of Arizona State, Louisiana State, Notre Dame, Michigan, Pittsburgh, Ohio State, and Southern California. On the Monday mornings after football games, they counted the number of school sweatshirts worn on campus and found that more of them were worn if the team had won its game on the previous Saturday. In fact, the larger the margin of victory, the more school shirts were counted.

bask in reflected glory (BIRG) Increasing self-esteem by associating with others who are successful.

To evaluate the effects of self-esteem on BIRGing, Cialdini gave students a general-knowledge test and rigged the results so half would succeed and half would fail. The students were then asked to describe in their own words the outcome of a recent football game. In these descriptions, students who thought they had just failed a test were more likely than those who thought they had succeeded to share in their team's victory by exclaiming that "*we* won" and to distance themselves from defeat by lamenting how "*they* lost." In another study, participants coming off a recent failure were quick to point out that they had the same birth date as someone known to be successful—thus BIRGing by a merely coincidental association (Cialdini & De Nicholas, 1989).

When the Toronto Blue Jays won the 1992 World Series—the first time the series had ever been played outside the US—baseball fans celebrated across the country. The celebrations continued the following year, when the Jays won yet again. And why not? "We" won!

If self-esteem is influenced by our links to others, how do we cope with friends, family members, teammates, and co-workers of low status? Again, consider sports fans, an interesting breed. As loudly as they cheer in victory, they often turn and jeer their teams in defeat. This behaviour seems fickle, but it is consistent with the notion that people derive part of their self-esteem from associations with others. In one study, participants took part in a problem-solving team that then succeeded, failed, or received no feedback about its performance. Participants were later offered a chance to take home a team badge. In the success and no-feedback groups, 68 and 50 percent, respectively, took badges; in the failure group, only 9 percent did (Snyder et al., 1986). It seems that the tendency to bask in reflected glory is matched by an equally powerful tendency to CORF—that is, to "cut off reflected failure."

Additional research confirms that the failures of others with whom we identify can influence our own sense of well-being. In one study, Edward Hirt and his colleagues (1992) found that avid sports fans temporarily lost faith in their own mental and social abilities after a favourite team suffered defeat. Reflected failure may even have physiological effects on the body. Paul Bernhardt and others (1998) took saliva samples from male college students before and after they watched a basketball or soccer game between their favourite team and an arch rival. By measuring pre- to post-game changes in testosterone levels, these investigators found that men who witnessed their teams in defeat—compared to those who enjoyed victory—exhibited lowered levels of testosterone, the male sex hormone.

Downward Social Comparisons Earlier, we discussed Festinger's (1954) theory that people evaluate themselves by social comparison with similar others. But let's contemplate the *implications*. If the people around us achieve more than we do, what does that do to our self-esteem? Perhaps adults who shy away from class reunions in order to avoid having to compare themselves with former classmates are acting out an answer to that question.

Festinger fully realized that people don't always seek out objective information and that social comparisons are sometimes made in self-defense. When a person's self-esteem is at stake, he or she often benefits from making **downward social comparisons** with others who are less successful, less happy, or less fortunate (Hakmiller, 1966; Wills, 1981; Wood, 1989). Research shows that people who suffer some form of setback or failure adjust their social comparisons in a downward direction (Gibbons et al., 2002)—and these comparisons have an uplifting effect on

downward social comparisons Defensive tendencies to compare ourselves with others who are worse off than we are.

their mood and on their outlook for the future (Aspinwall & Taylor, 1993; Gibbons & McCoy, 1991).

Although Festinger never addressed the issue, Anne Wilson and Michael Ross (2000) at the University of Waterloo note that in addition to making social comparisons between ourselves and similar others, we make *temporal* comparisons between our past and present selves. In one study, these investigators had college students describe themselves; in another, they analyzed the autobiographical accounts of celebrities appearing in popular magazines. In both cases, they counted the number of times the self-descriptions contained references to past selves, to future selves, and to others. The result: People made more comparisons to their own past selves than to others, and most of these temporal comparisons were favourable. Keenly aware of how "I'm better today than when I was younger," people use downward temporal comparisons the way they use downward social comparisons as a means of self-enhancement.

Whether people make upward or downward social comparisons can have striking implications for health-related issues. When victimized by tragic life events (perhaps a crime, an accident, a disease, or the death of a loved one) people like to *affiliate* with others in the same predicament who are adjusting well, role models who offer hope and guidance. But they tend to *compare* themselves with others who are worse off, a form of downward social comparison (Taylor & Lobel, 1989). Clearly, it helps to know that life could be worse, which is why most cancer patients compare themselves with others in the same predicament but who are adjusting less well than they are. In a study of 312 women who had early-stage breast cancer and were in peer support groups, Laura Bogart and Vicki Helgeson (2000) had the patients report every week for seven weeks on instances in which they talked to, heard about, or thought about another patient. They found that 53 percent of all the social comparisons made were downward, to others who were worse off, while only 12 percent were upward, to others who were better off. (The remainder were "lateral" comparisons to similar or dissimilar others.) Bogart and Helgeson also found that the more often patients made these social comparisons, the better they felt.

Interviews of women with breast cancer tell the story. One woman who had only a lump removed wondered "How awful it must be for women who have had a full mastectomy." An older woman who had a mastectomy said: "The people I really feel sorry for are these young gals. To lose a breast when you're so young must be awful." Yet a young mastectomy patient derived comfort from the fact that "if I hadn't been married, this thing would have really gotten to me" (Taylor, 1989, p. 171). As these quotes poignantly illustrate, there's always someone else with whom we can favourably compare—and this downward comparison makes us feel better (VanderZee et al., 1996).

Unfortunately, it's not always possible to defend the self via downward comparison. Think about it. When a sibling, spouse, or close friend has more success than you do, what happens to your self-esteem? Abraham Tesser (1988) predicted two possible reactions. On the one hand, you might feel proud of your association with this successful other, as in the process of basking in reflected glory. If you've ever bragged about the achievements of a loved one as if they were your own, you know how "reflection" can bolster self-esteem. On the other hand, you may feel overshadowed by the success of this other person and experience *social comparison jealousy*—a mixture of emotions that include resentment, envy, and a drop in self-esteem. According to Tesser, the key to whether one feels the pleasure of reflection or the pain of jealousy is whether the other person's success is self-relevant. When close friends surpass us in ways that are vital to our self-concepts, we become jealous and distance ourselves from them in order to keep up our own self-esteem. When intimate others surpass us in ways that are not important, however, we take pride in their triumphs through a process of reflection (Tesser & Collins, 1988; Tesser et al., 1989).

Personal and cultural factors may also influence the way people react to the success of others. For some people—as in those from collectivist cultures, whose concept of self is expanded to include friends, relatives, co-workers, classmates, and others with whom they identify—the success of another may bolster, not threaten, self-esteem. To test this hypothesis, Wendi Gardner and her colleagues (2002) brought pairs of friends into the laboratory together for a problem-solving task. They found that when they led the friends to think in collectivist terms, each derived pleasure, not jealousy and threat, from the other's greater success.

Are Positive Illusions Adaptive?

Psychologists used to maintain that an accurate perception of reality was vital to mental health. In recent years, however, this view has been challenged by research on the mechanisms of self-defense. Consistently, as we have seen, people preserve their self-esteem by deluding themselves and others with biased cognitions, self-handicapping, BIRGing, and downward comparisons. Are these strategies a sign of health and well-being, or are they symptoms of disorder?

When Shelley Taylor and Jonathon Brown (1988) reviewed the relevant research, they found that individuals who are depressed or low in self-esteem actually have more realistic views of themselves than do most others who are better adjusted. Their self-appraisals are more likely to match appraisals of them made by neutral observers; they make fewer self-serving attributions to account for success and failure; they are less likely to exaggerate their control over uncontrollable events; and they make more balanced predictions about their future. Based on these results, Taylor and Brown reached the provocative conclusion that positive illusions promote happiness, the desire to care for others, and the ability to engage in productive work—hallmark attributes of mental health: "These illusions help make each individual's world a warmer and more active and beneficent place in which to live" (p. 205). Research involving people under stress—such as men infected with HIV—shows that perceived control, optimism, and other positive illusions are "health-protective" psychological resources that help people cope with adversity (Taylor et al., 2000). As a result, people with high self-esteem appear better adjusted in personality tests and in interviews that are rated by friends, strangers, and mental health professionals (Taylor et al., 2003).

Not everyone agrees with the notion that it is adaptive in the long run to wear rose-coloured lenses. Roy Baumeister and Steven Scher (1988) warned that positive illusions can give rise to chronic patterns of self-defeating behaviour, as when people escape from self-awareness through alcohol and other drugs, self-handicap themselves into failure and underachievement, deny health-related problems until it's too late for treatment, and rely on the illusion of control to protect them from the tender mercies of the gambling casino. From an interpersonal standpoint, C. Randall Colvin and others (1995) found that people with inflated rather than realistic views of themselves were rated less favourably on certain dimensions by their own friends. In their studies, self-enhancing men were seen as assertive and ambitious—which are okay—but also as boastful, condescending, hostile, and less considerate of others. Self-enhancing women were seen as more hostile, more defensive and sensitive to criticism, more likely to overreact to minor setbacks, and less well-liked. Consistent with these findings, research shows that people filled with very high self-esteem are more likely to lash out angrily and violently in response to criticism, rejection, and other bruises to the ego (Bushman & Baumeister, 1998). Thus, people with inflated self-images may make a good first

FIGURE 3.9

The Dark Side of High Self-Esteem

College students who were high or low in self-esteem were given ego-threatening or nonthreatening feedback about their intelligence before interacting with a fellow student. As shown, the high and low self-esteem students in the no-threat group were liked equally by their partners (left). In the ego-threat group, however, the high self-esteem students were liked less than those with lower self-esteem (right). It seems that high self-esteem people who feel threatened become boastful and abrasive. *(Heatherton & Vohs, 2000.)*

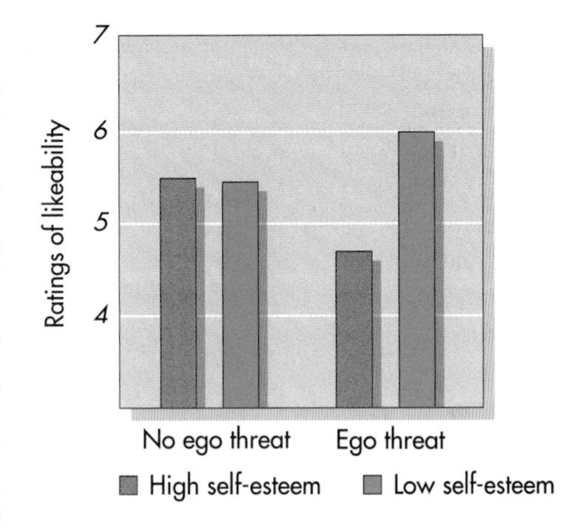

impression on others, but they are liked less and less as time wears on (Paulhus, 1998).

In a study that illustrates this dark side of high self-esteem, Todd Heatherton and Kathleen Vohs (2000) administered a standard self-esteem test to pairs of unacquainted college students and then brought them together for a brief conversation. Just before meeting, one student within each pair took a "Remote Associates Test," which involved finding one word that connects sets of three seemingly unrelated words (for example, *lick*, *sprinkle*, and *mines* were linked by the word *salt*). For half of these target students, the test was pitched as experimental and the problems given to them were easy to solve. Others were told that the test measured achievement potential and were given very difficult problems—leading them to perform, supposedly, worse than average. Did this ego-threatening feedback affect the students' behaviour—and the impressions they made on their interaction partners? Look at Figure 3.9 and you'll see that in the no-ego-threat group, the high and low self-esteem students were equally well liked. In the ego-threat situation, however, students with high self-esteem became less likeable; in fact, they were rated by their partners as rude, unfriendly, and arrogant.

Realism or illusion, which orientation is more adaptive? As social psychologists debate the short-term and long-term effects of positive illusions, it's clear that there is no simple answer. For now, the picture that has emerged is this: People who harbour positive illusions of themselves are likely to enjoy the benefits and achievements of high self-esteem. But these same individuals may pay a price in other ways—as in their relations with others. So what are we to conclude? Do positive illusions motivate personal achievement but alienate us socially from others? Is it adaptive to see oneself in slightly inflated terms, but maladaptive to take a view that is too biased? It will be interesting to see how this thorny debate is resolved in the years to come.

Self-Presentation

The human quest for self-knowledge and self-esteem tells us about the inner self. The portrait is not complete, however, until we paint in the outermost layer, the behavioural expression of the social self. Most people are acutely concerned about the image they present to others. The fashion industry, diet centres, cosmetic surgeries designed to reshape everything from eyelids to breasts, and the endless search for miracle drugs that grow hair, remove hair, whiten teeth, freshen breath, and smooth out wrinkles, all exploit our preoccupation with physical appearance. Similarly, we are concerned about the impressions we convey through our public behaviour. What, as they say, will the neighbours think?

Thomas Gilovich and others (2000) have found that people are so self-conscious in public settings that they are often subject to the *spotlight effect*, a tendency to believe that the social spotlight shines more brightly on them than it really does. In one set of studies, participants were asked to wear a T-shirt with a flattering or embarrassing image into a room full of strangers, after which they estimated how many of those strangers would be able to identify the image. Demonstrating that people self-consciously feel as if all eyes are upon them, the T-shirted participants overestimated by 23–40 percent the number of observers who had noticed and could recall what they were wearing. Follow-up studies have similarly shown that when people commit a public social blunder, they later overestimate the negative impact of their behaviour on those who had observed them (Savitsky et al., 2001).

In *As You Like It*, William Shakespeare wrote, "All the world's a stage, and all the men and women merely players." This insight was first put into social science terms by sociologist Erving Goffman (1959), who argued that life is like a theatre and that each of us acts out certain *lines*, as if from a script. Most important, said Goffman, is that each of us assumes a certain *face*, or social identity, that others politely help us to maintain. Inspired by Goffman's theory, social psychologists study **self-presentation**: the process by which we try to shape what others think of us and what we think of ourselves (Schlenker, 2003). An act of self-presentation may take many different forms. It may be conscious or unconscious, accurate or misleading, intended for an external audience or for ourselves. In this section, we look at the various goals of self-presentation and the ways in which people try to achieve these goals.

The Two Faces of Self-Presentation

There are basically two types of self-presentation, each serving a different motive. *Strategic self-presentation* consists of our efforts to shape others' impressions in specific ways in order to gain influence, power, sympathy, or approval. Prominent examples of strategic self-presentation are everywhere: in personal ads, on Internet message boards, in political campaign promises, in defendants' appeals to the jury. The specific goals include the desire to be seen as likeable, competent, moral, dangerous, or helpless. Whatever the goal may be, people find it less effortful to present themselves in ways that are accurate rather than contrived.

To illustrate this point, Beth Pontari and Barry Schlenker (2000) instructed research participants who were introverted or extroverted to present themselves to a job interviewer in a way that was consistent or inconsistent with their true personality. Without distraction, all participants successfully presented themselves as introverted or extroverted, depending on the task they were given. But could they present themselves as needed if, during the interview, they also had to keep an eight-digit number in mind for a memorization test? In this situation, cognitively busy participants self-presented successfully when asked to convey their true personalities but not when asked to portray themselves in a way that was out of character.

The specific identities that people try to present vary from one person and situation to another. There are, however, two strategic self-presentation goals that are very common. The first is *ingratiation*, a term used to describe acts that are motivated by the desire to "get along" with others and be liked. The other is *self-promotion*, a term used to describe acts that are motivated by a desire to "get ahead" and gain respect for one's competence (Arkin, 1981; Jones & Pittman, 1982).

On the surface, it seems easy to achieve these goals. When people want to be liked, they put their best foot forward, smile a lot, nod their heads, express agreement, and, if necessary, use favours, compliments, and apple-polishing flattery. When people want to be admired for their competence, they try to impress others by talking about themselves and immodestly showing off their status, knowledge, and exploits. In both cases, there are tradeoffs. As the term *brown-nosing* all too graphically suggests, ingratiation tactics need to be subtle or else they will backfire (Jones, 1964). People also do not like those who relentlessly trumpet and brag about their own achievements (Godfrey et al., 1986) or who exhibit a "slimy" pattern of being friendly to their superiors but not to subordinates (Vonk, 1998).

self-presentation Strategies people use to shape what others think of them.

Ingratiation is a strategy often used to curry favour.

Self-presentation may give rise to other problems as well. In a provocative article entitled "Self-Presentation Can Be Hazardous to Your Health," Mark Leary and his colleagues (1994) reviewed evidence suggesting that the need to project a favourable public image can lure us into unsafe patterns of behaviour. For example, self-presentation concerns can increase the risk of AIDS (when men are too embarrassed to buy condoms and talk openly with their sex partners), skin cancer (when people bake under the sun to get an attractive tan), eating disorders (when women overdiet or use amphetamines, laxatives, and forced vomiting to stay thin), drug abuse (when teenagers smoke, drink, and use drugs to impress their peers), and accidental injury (when young men drive recklessly to appear brave and fearless to others).

The second self-presentation motive is *self-verification*: the desire to have others perceive us as we truly perceive ourselves. According to William Swann (1987), people are highly motivated to verify their existing self-concept in the eyes of others. Swann and his colleagues have gathered a great deal of evidence for this hypothesis—and have found, for example, that people selectively elicit, recall, and accept personality feedback that confirms their self-conceptions. In fact, people sometimes bend over backward to correct others whose impressions are positive but mistaken. In one study, participants interacted with a confederate who later said that they seemed dominant or submissive. When the comment was consistent with the participant's self-concept, it was accepted at face value. Yet when it was inconsistent, participants went out of their way to prove the confederate wrong: Those who perceived themselves as dominant but were labelled submissive later behaved more assertively than usual; those who viewed themselves as submissive but were labelled dominant subsequently became even more docile (Swann & Hill, 1982).

Self-verification seems desirable, but wait: Do people who have a negative self-concept want others to share that impression? Nobody is perfect, and everyone has some faults. But do we really want to verify these faults in the eyes of others? Do those of us who feel painfully shy, socially awkward, or insecure about an ability want others to see these weaknesses? Or would we prefer to present ourselves as bold, graceful, or competent? What happens when the desire for self-verification clashes with the need for self-enhancement?

Seeking to answer this question, Swann and his colleagues (1992) asked each participant to fill out a self-concept questionnaire and then choose an interaction partner from two other participants—one who supposedly had evaluated the participant favourably; the other, unfavourably. The result? Although participants with a positive self-concept chose partners who viewed them in a positive light, a majority of those with a negative self-concept preferred partners who confirmed their admitted shortcomings. In a more recent study, 64 percent of participants with low self-esteem, compared with only 25 percent of those with high self-esteem, sought clinical feedback about their weaknesses rather than their strengths when given a choice (Giesler et al., 1996).

If people seek self-verification from laboratory partners, it stands to reason that they would want the same from their close relationships. In a study of married couples, husbands and wives separately answered questions about their self-concepts, spouses, and commitment to the marriage. As predicted, people who had a positive self-concept expressed more commitment to partners who appraised them favourably, while those with a negative self-concept felt more committed to partners who appraised them *un*favourably (Swann et al., 1992).

Regarding important aspects of the self-concept, research shows that people would rather reflect on and learn more about their positive qualities than their negative ones (Sedikides, 1993). Still, it appears that the desire for self-verification is powerful—and can even, at times, overwhelm the need for self-enhancement. We all want to make a good impression, but we also want others in our lives to have an accurate impression, one that is compatible with our own self-concept (Swann, 1999).

Individual Differences in Self-Monitoring

Although self-presentation is a way of life for all of us, it differs considerably among individuals. Some people are generally more conscious of their public image than others. Also, some people are more likely to engage in strategic self-presentation, while others seem to prefer self-verification. According to Mark Snyder (1987), these differences are related to a personality trait he called **self-monitoring**: the tendency to regulate one's own behaviour to meet the demands of social situations.

Individuals who are high in self-monitoring appear to have a repertoire of selves from which to draw. Sensitive to strategic self-presentation concerns, they are poised, ready, and able to modify their behaviour as they move from one situation to another. As measured by the Self-Monitoring Scale (Snyder, 1974; Snyder & Gangestad, 1986), they are likely to agree with such statements as "I would probably make a good actor" and "In different situations and with different people, I often act like very different persons." In contrast, low self-monitors are self-verifiers by nature, appearing less concerned about the propriety of their behaviour. Like character actors always cast in the same role, they express themselves in a consistent manner from one situation to the next, exhibiting what they regard as their true and honest self. On the Self-Monitoring Scale, low self-monitors say that "I can only argue for ideas which I already believe" and "I have never been good at games like charades or improvisational acting" (see Table 3.2).

Social psychologists disagree on whether the Self-Monitoring Scale measures one global trait or a combination of two or more specific traits. They also disagree about whether high and low self-monitors represent two discrete types of people or just points along a continuum. Either way, the test scores do appear to predict important social behaviours (Gangestad & Snyder, 2000). Concerned with public image, high self-monitors go out of their way to learn about others with whom they might interact and about the rules for appropriate conduct. Then, once they have the situation sized up, they modify their behaviour accordingly. If a situation calls for conformity, high self-monitors conform; if the same situation calls for autonomy, they refuse to conform. Low self-monitors, by contrast, maintain a relatively consistent posture across these situations (Snyder & Monson, 1975). Consistent with the finding that high self-monitors are more concerned than lows about what other people think, research conducted in work settings shows that high self-monitors receive higher performance ratings and more promotions, and they are more likely to emerge as leaders (Day et al., 2002).

In the coming chapters, we will see that because so much of our behaviour is influenced by social norms, self-monitoring is relevant to many aspects of social psychology. There are also interesting developmental implications. A survey of 18 to 73-year-olds revealed that self-monitoring scores tend to drop with age—presumably because people become more settled and secure about their personal identities as they get older (Reifman et al., 1989). For now, however, ponder this question: Is it better to be a high or low self-monitor? Is one orientation inherently more adaptive than the other?

self-monitoring The tendency to change behaviour in response to the self-presentation concerns of the situation.

TABLE 3.2

Self-Monitoring Scale

Are you a high or low self-monitor? For each statement, answer True or False. When you are done, give yourself one point if you answered T to items 4, 5, 6, 8, 10, 12, 17, and 18. Then give yourself one point if you answered F to items 1, 2, 3, 7, 9, 11, 13, 14, 15, and 16. Count your total number of points. This total represents your Self-Monitoring Score. Among North American college students, the average score is about 10 or 11. *(Snyder & Gangestad, 1986.)*

1. I find it hard to imitate the behaviour of other people.
2. At parties and social gatherings, I do not attempt to do or say things that others will like.
3. I can only argue for ideas which I already believe.
4. I can make impromptu speeches even on topics about which I have almost no information.
5. I guess I put on a show to impress or entertain others.
6. I would probably make a good actor.
7. In a group of people I am rarely the centre of attention.
8. In different situations and with different people, I often act like very different persons.
9. I am not particularly good at making other people like me.
10. I'm not always the person I appear to be.
11. I would not change my opinions (or the way I do things) in order to please someone or win their favour.
12. I have considered being an entertainer.
13. I have never been good at games like charades or improvisational acting.
14. I have trouble changing my behaviour to suit different people and different situations.
15. At a party I let others keep the jokes and stories going.
16. I feel a bit awkward in company and do not show up quite as well as I should.
17. I can look anyone in the eye and tell a lie with a straight face (if for a right end).
18. I may deceive people by being friendly when I really dislike them.

The existing research does not enable us to make this kind of value judgment. Consider high self-monitors. Quite accurately, they regard themselves as pragmatic, flexible, and adaptive and as able to cope with the diversity of life's roles. But they could also be described as fickle or phoney opportunists, more concerned with appearances than with reality and willing to change colours like a chameleon just to fit in. Now think about low self-monitors. They describe themselves as principled and forthright; they are without pretence, always speaking their minds so others know where they stand. Of course, they could also be viewed as stubborn, insensitive to their surroundings, and unwilling to compromise in order to get along. Concerning the relative value of these two orientations, then, it is safe to conclude that neither high nor low self-monitoring is necessarily undesirable—unless carried to the extreme. Goffman (1955) made the same point many years ago, when he wrote:

It's more adaptive to alter one's behaviour than to stay consistent from one social situation to the next. **False.**

> *Too little perceptiveness, too little savoir faire, too little pride and considerateness, and the person ceases to be someone who can be trusted to take a hint about himself or give a hint that will save others embarrassment. . . Too much savoir faire or too much considerateness and he becomes someone who is too socialized, who leaves others with the feeling that they do not know how they really stand with him, nor what they should do to make an effective long-term adjustment.* (p. 227)

Epilogue: The Multi-faceted Self

Throughout human history, writers, poets, philosophers, and personality theorists have portrayed the self as an enduring aspect of personality, as an invisible "inner core" that is stable over time and slow to change. The struggle to "find yourself" and "be true to yourself" is based on this portrait. Indeed, when people over 85 years old were asked to reflect on their lives, almost all said that despite having changed in certain ways, they had remained essentially the same person (Troll & Skaff, 1997). In recent years, however, social psychologists have focused on change. In doing so, they have discovered that at least part of the self is malleable—moulded by life experiences and varying from one situation to the next. From this perspective, the self has many different faces.

When you look into the mirror, what do you see, one self or many? Do you see a person whose self-concept is enduring or one whose identity seems to change from time to time? Do you see a person whose strengths and weaknesses are evaluated with an objective eye or one who is insulated from unpleasant truths by mechanisms of self-defense? Do you see a person who has an inner, hidden self that is different from the face shown to others?

Based on the material presented in this chapter, the answer to such questions seems always to be the same: The self has all these characteristics. More than 100 years ago, William James (1890) said that the self is not simple but complex and multi-faceted. Based on current theories and research, we can now appreciate just how right James was. Sure, there's an aspect of the self-concept that we come to know only through introspection and that is stable over time. But there's also an aspect that changes with the company we keep and the information we get from others. When it comes to self-esteem, there are times when we are self-focused enough to become acutely aware of our shortcomings. Yet there are also times when we guard ourselves through self-serving cognitions, self-handicapping, BIRGing, and downward social comparisons. Then there is the matter of self-presentation. It's clear that each of us has a private self that consists of our inner thoughts, feelings, and memories. But it is equally clear that we also have an outer self, portrayed by the roles we play and the masks we wear in public. As you read through the pages of this text, you will see that the cognitive, affective, and behavioural components of the self are not separate and distinct but interrelated. They are also of great significance for the rest of social psychology.

Review

The Self-Concept

- The self-concept is the sum total of a person's beliefs about his or her own attributes. It is the cognitive component of the self.

Beginnings of the Self-Concept

- Recognizing oneself as a distinct entity is the first step in the development of a self-concept.
- Human beings and apes are the only animals to recognize their mirror-image reflections as their own.
- Cooley's "looking-glass" self suggests that social factors are a necessary second step.

Introspection

- People believe that introspection is a key to knowing the true self.
- But research shows that introspection sometimes diminishes the accuracy of self-reports.
- People also tend to overestimate their emotional reactions to future positive and negative events.

Perceptions of Our Own Behaviour

- Bem's self-perception theory holds that when internal states are difficult to interpret, we infer our inner states by observing our own behaviour and the surrounding situation.
- Based on self-perception theory, the facial feedback hypothesis states that facial expressions can produce, not

just reflect, an emotion state (smiling can cause us to feel happy).
- But it's unclear if the emotion occurs via self-perception or because facial expressions trigger physiological changes that produce the emotional response.
- Also derived from self-perception theory, studies of the overjustification effect show that people sometimes lose interest in activities for which they are rewarded.
- But if a reward is seen as a "bonus" for superior performance, then it can enhance intrinsic motivation by providing positive feedback.

Influences of Other People

- According to social comparison theory, people often evaluate their own opinions and abilities by comparing themselves to similar others.
- Schachter and Singer proposed that the experience of emotion is based on two factors: physiological arousal and a cognitive label for that arousal.
- Under certain conditions, people interpret their own arousal by watching others in the same situation.

Autobiographical Memories

- Memory of one's life events is critical to the self-concept.
- When people recall life experiences, they typically report more events from the recent past than from the distant past, though some types of memories are generally more vivid and lasting than others.
- Autobiographical memories are shaped by self-serving motives, as people overemphasize their own roles in past events.

Cultural Perspectives

- Cultures foster different conceptions of self.
- Many Europeans and North Americans hold an independent view of the self that emphasizes autonomy.
- People in certain Asian, African, and Latin American cultures hold an interdependent view of the self that encompasses social connections.
- These cultural differences influence the way we perceive, feel about, and present ourselves in relation to others.

Self-Esteem

- Self-esteem refers to a person's positive and negative evaluations of the self.

The Need for Self-Esteem

- People have a need for high self-esteem and want to see themselves in a positive light.
- People with low self-esteem often find themselves caught in a vicious cycle of self-defeating behaviour.

Influences of Gender, Race, and Culture

- Among adolescents and young adults, males have higher self-esteem than females do, though the difference is very small, particularly among older adults.
- African Americans outscore white Americans on self-esteem tests, indicating, perhaps, that stigmatized minorities focus on their positive attributes.
- Cultural differences are also found, suggesting that people from collectivist cultures, compared to those in individualistic cultures, see or present themselves in a modest light relative to others.

Self-Discrepancy Theory

- Self-esteem can be defined by the match between how we see ourselves and how we want to see ourselves. Large self-discrepancies are associated with negative emotional states.
- Discrepancies between the actual and ideal selves are related to feelings of disappointment and depression.
- Discrepancies between the actual and the ought selves are related to shame, guilt, and anxiety.
- These emotional effects depend on the amount of discrepancy and whether we are consciously focused on it.

The Self-Awareness "Trap"

- In general, people spend little time actually thinking about themselves.
- But certain situations (mirrors, cameras, audiences) increase self-awareness, and certain people are generally more self-conscious than others.
- Self-awareness forces us to notice self-discrepancies and can produce a temporary reduction in self-esteem.
- To cope, we either adjust our behaviour to meet our standards or withdraw from the self-focusing situation. Heavy drinking can be viewed as a means of escaping from self-awareness.

Limits of Self-Regulation

- Self-control can temporarily be depleted by usage.
- Due to the operation of ironic processes, our efforts at self-control may also backfire, causing us to think, feel, and act in ways that are opposite to our intentions.

Mechanisms of Self-Enhancement

- Most people think highly of themselves and have unconscious positive associations with things related to the self.
- People protect their self-esteem in four major ways: through self-serving cognitions, such as taking credit for success and denying the blame for failure; self-handicapping, in order to excuse anticipated failure; basking in reflected glory, which boosts their self-esteem through associations with successful others; and downward social comparisons to others who are less well-off.
- When others surpass us in ways that are important to us, we become jealous and distance ourselves from them. When surpassed in ways that are not self-relevant, we feel pride and seek closeness.

Are Positive Illusions Adaptive?

- Recent research suggests that certain positive illusions may foster high self-esteem and mental health.

- An alternative view is that such illusions promote self-defeating behaviour patterns and that people with inflated views of themselves are liked less by others.

Self-Presentation

- We care deeply about what others think of us and often believe that the social spotlight shines more brightly on us than it really does.
- Self-presentation is the process by which we try to shape what others think of us and even what we think of ourselves.

The Two Faces of Self-Presentation

- There are basically two types of self-presentation, each of which serves a different motive: strategic self-presentation (through which we try to shape others' impressions in order to be liked or seen as competent) and self-verification (through which we try to get others to perceive us as we perceive ourselves).

Individual Differences in Self-Monitoring

- Individuals differ in the tendency to regulate their behaviour to meet the demands of social situations.
- High self-monitors modify their behaviour, as appropriate, from one situation to the next.
- Low self-monitors express themselves in a more consistent manner, exhibiting at all times what they see as their true self.

Epilogue: The Multi-faceted Self

- As this chapter has shown, the self is not simple but complex and multifaceted.

Key Terms

affective forecasting *(56)*
bask in reflected glory (BIRG) *(78)*
downward social comparisons *(79)*
facial feedback hypothesis *(58)*
implicit egotism *(76)*
learned helplessness *(57)*
overjustification effect *(59)*
private self-consciousness *(72)*
public self-consciousness *(72)*
self-awareness theory *(70)*
self-concept *(54)*
self-efficacy *(57)*
self-esteem *(66)*
self-handicapping *(77)*
self-monitoring *(85)*
self-perception theory *(56)*
self-presentation *(83)*
self-schemas *(54)*
social comparison theory *(61)*
two-factor theory of emotion *(62)*

PUTTING COMMON SENSE TO THE TEST

Humans are the only animals who recognize themselves in the mirror.

False. *Studies have shown that the great apes (chimpanzees, gorillas, and orangutans) are also capable of self-recognition.*

Smiling can make you feel happier.

True. *Consistent with the facial feedback hypothesis, facial expressions can trigger or amplify the subjective experience of emotion.*

Sometimes the harder you try to control a thought, feeling, or behaviour, the less likely you are to succeed.

True. *Research on ironic processes in mental control has revealed that trying to inhibit a thought, feeling, or behaviour often backfires.*

People tend to be overly optimistic about their future.

True. *In general, people see themselves as more likely than average to have positive outcomes and less likely to have negative ones.*

People often sabotage their own performance in order to protect their self-esteem.

True. *Studies have shown that people often handicap their own performance in order to build an excuse for anticipated failure.*

It's more adaptive to alter one's behaviour than to stay consistent from one social situation to the next.

False. *High and low self-monitors differ in the extent to which they alter their behaviour to suit the situation they are in, but neither style is inherently more adaptive.*

4 Perceiving Persons

OUTLINE

PREVIEW

THIS CHAPTER examines how people come to know, or think that they know, other persons. First, we introduce the elements of social perception—those aspects of persons, situations, and behaviour that guide initial observations. Next, we examine how people make explanations, or attributions, for the behaviour of others and how they form integrated impressions based on initial perceptions and attributions. We then consider confirmation biases, the subtle ways in which initial impressions lead people to distort later information, setting in motion a self-fulfilling prophecy.

PUTTING COMMON SENSE TO THE TEST

T / F

___ **The impressions we form of others are influenced by superficial aspects of their appearance.**

___ **Adaptively, people are skilled at knowing when someone is lying rather than telling the truth.**

___ **Like social psychologists, people are sensitive to situational causes when explaining the behaviour of others.**

___ **People are slow to change their first impressions on the basis of new information.**

___ **The notion that we can create a "self-fulfilling prophecy" by getting others to behave in ways we expect is a myth.**

___ **People are more accurate at judging the personality of friends and acquaintances than of strangers.**

In March 2004, Vancouver Canucks Forward Todd Bertuzzi hit Colorado Avalanche player Steve Moore from behind late in a game, resulting in a broken neck for Moore. The hit came late in the game, and some believed it was retaliation for an incident earlier in the season between Moore and the Canucks' team captain. Others believed that it was simply an unfortunate accident, a natural by-product of an aggressive game, and that the entire episode was blown out of proportion by the media. Bertuzzi apologized to Moore, stating, in part, "I had no intention of hurting you"; was his statement (and apology) sincere, or had he in fact intended to "get back" at Moore during the game?

In October 1993, Saskatchewan farmer Robert Latimer killed his 12-year-old daughter Tracy. Tracy suffered from cerebral palsy, had endured several painful surgeries, and was both physically and mentally disabled. Latimer ran a hose from the exhaust on his truck into the cab where she sat, and then watched while she died. Was he a

In March of 2004, Todd Bertuzzi broke Steve Moore's neck when he hit him from behind in a hockey game. Was the hit intentional, meant as payback for an incident earlier that season? Or was Bertuzzi's tearful apology, when he claimed that he had not intended to hurt Moore, to be believed? As social perceivers, this is the type of question we often ask ourselves in trying to understand other people.

compassionate father, desperate to put his daughter out of her daily misery and relieve her suffering, or was he a callous father, trying to free himself of the exhausting daily rituals required to keep his daughter alive?

Whatever the topic—sports, world politics, or personal events closer to home—we are all active and interested participants in **social perception**, the processes by which people come to understand one another. This chapter is divided into four sections. First we look at the "raw data" of social perception: persons, situations, and behaviour. Second, we examine how people explain and analyze behaviour. Third, we consider how people integrate their observations into a coherent impression of other persons. Fourth, we discuss some of the subtle ways in which our impressions create a distorted picture of reality, often setting in motion a self-fulfilling prophecy. As you read this chapter, you will notice that the various processes are considered from a perceiver's vantage point. Keep in mind, however, that in the events of life, you are both a *perceiver* and a *target* of others' perceptions.

Observation: The Elements of Social Perception

As our opening examples suggest, understanding others may be difficult, but it's a vital part of everyday life. How do we do it? What kinds of evidence do we use? We cannot actually "see" someone's mental or emotional state, motives, or intentions, any more than a detective can see a crime that has already been committed. So, like a detective who tries to reconstruct events by turning up witnesses, fingerprints, blood samples, and other evidence, the social perceiver comes to know others by relying on indirect clues—the elements of social perception. These clues arise from three sources: persons, situations, and behaviour.

Persons: Judging a Book by Its Cover

Have you ever met someone for the first time and immediately formed an impression based only on a quick "snapshot" of information? As children, we were told not to judge a book by its cover, that things are not always what they seem, that appearances are deceptive, and that all that glitters is not gold. As adults, however, we can't seem to help ourselves.

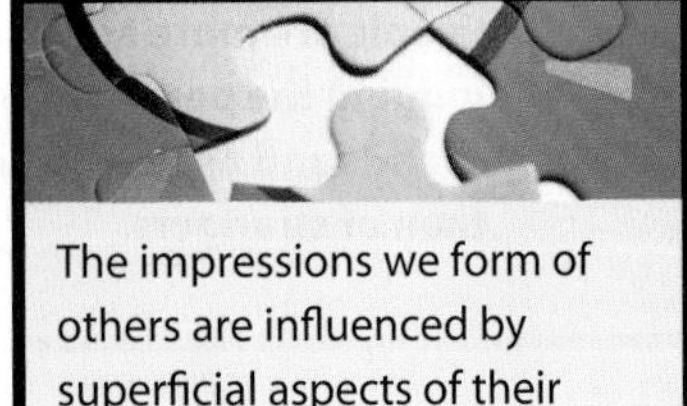

The impressions we form of others are influenced by superficial aspects of their appearance. **True.**

In 500 BCE, the mathematician Pythagoras looked into the eyes of prospective students to determine if they were gifted. At about the same time, Hippocrates, the founder of modern medicine, used facial features to make diagnoses of life and death. In the nineteenth century, Viennese physician Franz Gall introduced a carnival-like science called phrenology and claimed that he could assess people's character by the shape of their skulls. And in 1954, psychologist William Sheldon mistakenly concluded from flawed studies of adult men that there is a strong link between physique and personality.

People may not measure each other by bumps on the head, as phrenologists used to do, but first impressions are influenced in subtle ways by a person's height, weight, skin colour, hair colour, tattoos, eyeglasses, facial beauty, and other aspects of appearance (Alley, 1988; Herman et al., 1986; Rhodes & Zebrowitz, 2002). As social perceivers, we are also influenced by the colour of a person's clothing. For example, Aldert Vrij (1997) found that crime suspects are seen as more aggressive when dressed in black—a colour that is associated with evil and death in many cultures—than when they wear lighter clothing. We may even be influenced by

social perception A general term for the process by which people come to understand one another.

a person's name. For example, Robert Young and others (1993) found that fictional characters with "old generation" names such as Harry, Walter, Dorothy, and Edith are judged less popular and intelligent than those with "young generation" names such as Kevin, Michael, Lisa, and Michelle.

The human face in particular attracts more than its share of attention. Since the time of ancient Greece, human beings have practiced physiognomy—the art of reading character from faces. We may not realize it, but this tendency persists today. For example, Ran Hassin and Yaacov Trope (2000) found that people prejudge others in photographs as kind-hearted rather than mean-spirited based on such features as a full round face, curly hair, long eyelashes, large eyes, a short nose, full lips, and an upturned mouth. Interestingly, these researchers also found that just as people read traits *from* faces, at times they read traits *into* faces based on prior information. In one study, for example, participants who were told that a man was kind—compared to those told he was mean—later judged his face to be fuller, rounder, and more attractive.

What do you see when you look at this man's face? Perhaps you think he looks kind and intelligent. Or maybe weak and dull-witted. Can we really know anything about a person just by looking at a picture?

Similarly, Grant, Button, Hannah and Ross (2002) at Memorial University conducted a series of studies to examine the attitudes that we infer just by looking at someone's face. Students were shown head-and-shoulders shots of individuals ranging from those in their late teens to their late seventies. Participants attributed conservative attitudes to the men in the photos for issues such as homosexuality and child rearing, while they believed the women in the photos were more likely to be conservative when it came to religion. Interestingly, attractive people were deemed to be the most liberal, and older adults the most conservative. In their studies of the human face, Diane Berry and Leslie Zebrowitz-McArthur (1986) found that adults who have baby-faced features—large, round eyes, high eyebrows, round cheeks, a large forehead, smooth skin, and a rounded chin—tend to be seen as warm, kind, naive, weak, honest, and submissive. In contrast, adults who have mature features—small eyes, low brows and a small forehead, wrinkled skin, and an angular chin—are seen as stronger, more dominant, and more competent. Thus, in small-claims court, judges are more likely to favour baby-faced defendants who are accused of intentional wrongdoing, but they tend to rule against baby-faced individuals accused of negligence (Zebrowitz & McDonald, 1991).

What accounts for these findings? And why, in general, are people so quick to judge others by appearances? There are three possible explanations. One is that humans are genetically programmed to respond gently to infantile features so that real babies are treated with tender loving care. Another possibility is that we simply learn to associate infantile features with helplessness and then generalize this expectation to baby-faced adults. Third, maybe there is an actual link between physical appearance and behaviour, a possibility suggested by the fact that research participants exposed only to photos or brief videotapes of strangers formed impressions that correlated with the self-descriptions of these same strangers (Kenny et al., 1992; Zebrowitz et al., 2003).

In the nineteenth century, Franz Gall introduced phrenology, the pseudo-scientific theory that personality traits and abilities could be "seen" in the bumps on the skull.

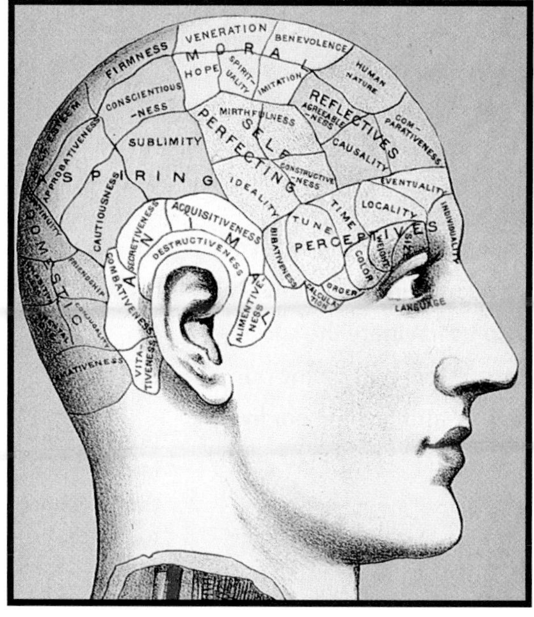

Situations: The Scripts of Life

In addition to the beliefs we hold about persons, each of us has preset notions about certain types of situations—"scripts" that enable us to anticipate the goals, behaviours, and outcomes likely to occur in a particular setting (Abelson, 1981; Read, 1987). Based on

What is your impression of this man? People often make snap judgments of others—judgments that are often wrong. Pictured here, Rocky Mullin is a computer administrator for a financial services company. Despite being all pierced up and tattooed, Mullin is a self-described yuppie: "I'm young, upwardly mobile, and I work in a professional company."

past experience, people can easily imagine the sequences of events likely to unfold in a typical greeting or at the shopping mall or dinner table. The more experience you have in a given situation, the more detail your scripts will contain.

In a study of the North American "first date" script, John Pryor and Thomas Merluzzi (1985) asked students to list the sequence of events that take place in this situation. From these lists, a picture of a typical first date emerged. Sixteen steps were identified, including: (1) male arrives; (2) female greets male at door; (3) female introduces date to parents or roommate; (4) male and female discuss plans and make small talk; (5) they go to a movie; (6) they get something to eat or drink; (7) male takes female home; (8) if interested, he remarks about a future date; (9) they kiss; (10) they say good night. Sound familiar? Pryor and Merluzzi then randomized their list of events and asked participants to arrange them into the appropriate order. They found that those with extensive dating experience were able to organize the statements more quickly than those who had less dating experience. For people who are familiar with a script, the events fall into place like the pieces of a puzzle.

Knowledge of social settings provides an important context for understanding other people's verbal and nonverbal behaviour. For example, this knowledge leads us to expect someone to be polite during a job interview, playful at a picnic, and rowdy at a keg party. Scripts influence social perceptions in two ways. First, we sometimes see what we expect to see in a particular situation. In one study, participants looked at photographs of human faces that had ambiguous expressions. When told that the person in the photo was being threatened by a vicious dog, they saw the expression as fearful; when told that the individual had just won money, participants interpreted the *same* expression as a sign of happiness (Trope, 1986). Second, people use what they know about social situations to explain the causes of human behaviour. As described later in this chapter, an action seems to offer more information about a person when it departs from the norm than when it is common. In other words, you would learn more about someone who is rowdy during a job interview or polite at a keg party than if it were the other way around.

Behavioural Evidence

"Our faces, together with our language, are social tools that help us navigate the social encounters that define our 'selves' and fashion our lives."
—Alan J. Fridlund

An essential first step in social perception is to recognize what someone is doing at a given moment. Identifying actions from movement is surprisingly easy. Even when actors dressed in black move about in a dark room with point lights attached only to the joints of their bodies, people easily recognize such complex acts as walking, running, jumping, exercising, and falling (Johansson et al., 1980).

More interesting, perhaps, is that people derive *meaning* from their observations by dividing the continuous stream of human behaviour into discrete units. By having participants observe someone on videotape and press a button whenever they detect a meaningful action, Darren Newtson and his colleagues (1987) have found that some perceivers break the behaviour stream into a large number of fine units, whereas others break it into a small number of gross units. While watching a baseball game, for example, you might press the button after each pitch, after each batter, after every inning, or only after runs are scored. The manner in which people divide a stream of behaviour can influence perceptions in important ways. Research participants who are told to break an event into fine units rather than gross units attend more closely, detect more meaningful actions, and remember more details about the actor's behaviour than do gross-unit participants (Lassiter et al., 1988). Fine-unit participants become more familiar with the actor they've observed, so they also come to view that actor in more positive terms (Lassiter, 1988). As we will see in Chapter 9, familiarity often heightens attraction.

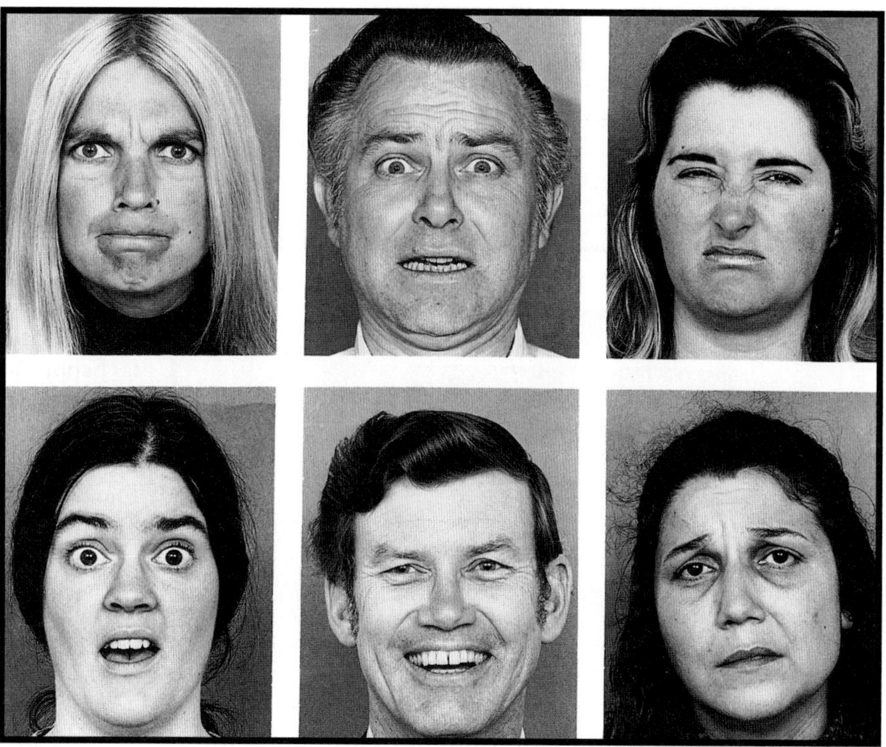

Can you tell how these individuals are feeling? If you are like most people, regardless of your culture, you will have little trouble recognizing the emotions portrayed.

The Silent Language of Nonverbal Behaviour Behavioural cues are used not only to identify someone's actions but also to determine his or her inner states. Knowing how another person is feeling can be tricky because people often try to hide their true emotions. Have you ever had to suppress your rage at someone, mask your disappointment after failure, feign surprise, make excuses, or pretend to like something just to be polite? Sometimes people come right out and tell us how they feel. At other times, however, they do not tell us, they are themselves not sure, or they actively try to conceal their true feelings. For these reasons, we often tune in to the silent language of **nonverbal behaviour**.

What kinds of nonverbal cues do people use in judging how someone else is feeling? In *The Expression of the Emotions in Man and Animals*, Charles Darwin (1872) proposed that the face expresses emotion in ways that are innate and understood by people all over the world. Contemporary research supports this notion. Numerous studies have shown that when presented with photographs similar to those shown earlier, people can reliably identify at least six "primary" emotions: happiness, fear, sadness, anger, surprise, and disgust. In one study, participants from ten different countries—Estonia, Germany, Greece, Hong Kong, Italy, Japan, Scotland, Sumatra, Turkey, and the United States—exhibited high levels of agreement in their recognition of these emotions (Ekman et al., 1987).

From one end of the world to the other, it is clear that a smile is a smile and a frown is a frown, and that just about everyone knows what they mean—even when these expressions are "put on" by actors and not genuinely felt (Gosselin et al., 1995). Still, the results do not fully support the claim that basic emotions are "universally" recognized from the face (Russell, 1994). To determine the extent to which emotions are universally recognized or culturally specific, Hillary Elfenbein and Nalini Ambady (2002) meta-analyzed 97 studies involving a total of 22 148 participants from 42 different countries. As shown in Figure 4.1, they found support for both points of view. On the one hand, people all over the world are able to recognize the primary emotions from photographs of facial expressions. On the other hand, people are 9 percent more accurate at judging faces from their own national,

nonverbal behaviour
Behaviour that reveals a person's feelings without words—through facial expressions, body language, and vocal cues.

FIGURE 4.1

How Good Are People at Identifying Emotions in the Face?

A meta-analysis of emotion recognition studies involving 22 148 participants from 42 countries confirmed that people all over the world can recognize the six basic emotions from posed facial expressions. *(Elfenbein & Ambady, 2002.)*

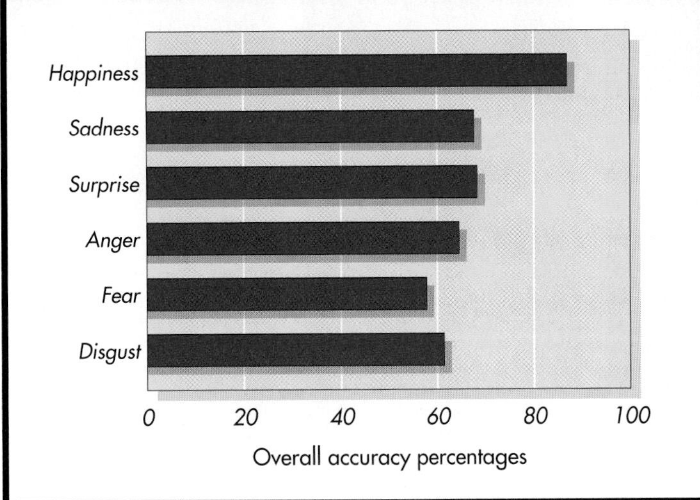

ethnic, or regional groups than from members of less familiar groups—indicating that we enjoy an "ingroup advantage" when it comes to knowing how those who are closest to us are feeling. Darwin believed that the ability to recognize emotion in others has survival value for all members of a species. This hypothesis suggests that it is more important to identify some emotions than others. For example, it may be more adaptive to beware of someone who is angry, and hence prone to lash out in violence, than someone who is happy, a nonthreatening emotion. In fact, studies have shown that angry faces arouse us and cause us to frown even when presented subliminally, without our awareness (Dimberg & Ohman, 1996; Dimberg et al., 2000). Joel Aronoff and others (1992) believe that anger is universally and quickly "seen" in certain fixed geometric patterns in the face—such as triangular eyes that point toward the nose and other hard downward lines in the forehead, cheeks, mouth, and chin.

Disgust is another basic emotion that has adaptive significance. When confronted with an offensive stimulus such as a foul odour, spoiled food, feces, rotting flesh, or the sight of mutilation, people react with an aversion that shows in the way they wrinkle the nose, raise the upper lip, and gape. This visceral reaction is often accompanied by nausea and can facilitate the expulsion of bad food from the mouth (Rozin & Fallon, 1987; Rozin et al., 2000). In nature, food poisoning is a real threat, so it is adaptive for us to recognize disgust in the face of others. In a study published in the journal *Neuron,* Bruno Wicker and others (2003) had 14 men watch video clips of people smelling pleasant, disgusting, or neutral odours. Afterward, these same men were exposed to the odours themselves. If you've ever inhaled the sweet, floury aroma of a bakery or inserted your nose into a carton of soured milk, you'll appreciate the different reactions that would appear on your face. Using functional magnetic resonance imaging, or fMRI, researchers monitored activity in the participants' brains throughout the experiment. They found that a structure in the brain known as the *insula* was activated not only when participants sniffed the disgusting odour but also when they watched *others* sniffing it. This result suggests that people more than recognize the face of disgust; they experience it at a neural level.

Many animals communicate nonverbally. For example, ants send chemical signals to indicate food, and vervet monkeys give off loud alarm calls that differ depending on whether the predator they see is a snake, eagle, or leopard.

It's interesting to note that the social value of the face is evident to those who communicate online. When email first became popular, the written word was often misinterpreted—especially when the writer was trying to be funny—because it lacked the nonverbal cues that normally animate and clarify live interactions. To fill in this gap, emailers created smiley faces and other "emoticons" (emotion icons) from standard keyboard characters. Some routinely used emoticons, which are meant to be viewed with one's head tilted 90 degrees to the left, are shown in Figure 4.2 (Sanderson, 1993).

Other nonverbal cues can also influence social perception, enabling us to make quick and often accurate judgments of others based on "thin slices" of expressive behaviour (Ambady & Rosenthal, 1993). For example, social perceivers are often fluent readers of *body language*—the ways in which people stand, sit, walk, and express themselves with various gestures. In communicating with others, people use conversational hand gestures such as the raised fist, the bye-bye wave, the thumbs up, and the extended middle finger, sometimes referred to as "flipping the bird" (Krauss et al., 1996). People also form impressions of others based on how they walk. Thus, men and women who have a youthful walking style—who sway their hips, bend their knees, lift their feet, and swing their arms—are seen as happier and more powerful than those who walk slowly, take shorter steps, and stiffly drag their feet (Montepare & McArthur, 1988).

FIGURE 4.2

Some Common Email "Emoticons"

In order to clarify the meaning of their written words, emailers often add smiles, winks, and other face-like symbols, or emoticons, to their electronic messages. One set of emoticons is shown here; you may be familiar with others. *(Sanderson, 1993.)*

Wink	Smirk	Said smiling	Said frowning	Sardonic incredulity
'-)	:-,	:-)	:-(	;-)

Disgusted	Kiss, kiss	Clowning around	Said late at night	Said tongue-in-cheek
:-|	:-X	:*)	|-(	:-J

Eye contact, or *gaze*, is another common form of nonverbal communication. People are highly attentive to eyes, often following the gaze of others. Look up, down, left, or right, and someone observing you will likely follow the direction of your eyes (Langton et al., 2000). Controlled studies show that even one-year-old infants tend to follow gaze, looking toward or pointing at the object of an adult researcher's attention (Brooks & Meltzoff, 2002).

Eyes have been called the "windows of the soul." In many cultures, people tend to assume that someone who avoids eye contact is evasive, cold, fearful, shy, or indifferent; that frequent gazing signals intimacy, sincerity, self-confidence, and respect; and that the person who stares is tense, angry, and unfriendly. Typically, however, eye contact is interpreted in light of a pre-existing relationship. If a relationship is friendly, frequent eye contact elicits a positive impression. If a relationship is not friendly, eye contact is seen in negative terms. It has been said that if two people lock eyes for more than a few seconds, they are going to either make love or kill each other (Kleinke, 1986; Patterson, 1983).

Another powerful, primitive form of nonverbal behaviour is *touch*—the congratulatory high-five, the sympathetic pat on the back, the joking elbow in the ribs, and the loving embrace being just a few familiar examples. Physical touching has long been regarded as an expression of friendship, nurturance, and sexual interest. But it may also serve other functions. Several years ago, Nancy Henley (1977) observed that men, older persons, and those of high socioeconomic status were more likely to touch women, younger persons, and individuals of lower status than the other way around. Henley's interpretation: that touching may be an expression not only of intimacy but of dominance and control. Simple forms of touch, as when people greet each other, also provide us with thin slices of behavioural evidence. Think about the handshakes you've received in your life and whether the grips were firm or limp, strong or weak, dry or clammy, brief or lingering. Research suggests that the first impressions we form of others may be influenced by these qualities of a simple handshake (Chaplin et al., 2000).

Anger is universally recognized by hard, downward, and pointed lines in the face—as seen in the protective masks worn by National Hockey League goalies.

As described by Axtell (1993), nonverbal communication norms vary from one culture to the next. So watch out! In Bulgaria, nodding your head means "no" and shaking your head sideways means "yes." In Germany and Brazil, the North American "okay" sign (forming a circle with your thumb and forefinger) is an obscene gesture. Personal-space habits also vary across cultures. Japanese people like to keep a comfortable distance while interacting. But in Puerto Rico and much of Latin America, people stand very close and backing off is considered an insult. Also beware of what you do with your eyes. In Latin

America, locking eyes is a must; yet in Japan, too much eye contact shows a lack of respect. If you're in the habit of stroking your cheek, you should know that in Italy, Greece, and Spain it means that you find the person you're talking to attractive. And whatever you do, don't ever touch someone's head in Buddhist countries, especially Thailand. The head is sacred there.

Different cultures also have vastly different rules for greeting someone. In Finland, you should give a firm handshake; in France, you should loosen the grip; in Zambia, you should use your left hand to support the right; and in Bolivia, you should extend your arm if your hand is dirty. In Japan, people bow; in Thailand, they put both hands together in a praying position on the chest; and in Fiji, they smile and raise their eyebrows. In certain parts of Latin America, it is common for people to hug, embrace, and kiss upon meeting. And in most Arab countries, men greet one another by saying *salaam alaykum*, then shaking hands, saying *kaif halak*, and kissing each other on the cheek.

Distinguishing Truth from Deception Social perception is tricky because people often try to hide or stretch the truth about themselves. Poker players bluff to win money, witnesses lie to protect themselves, public officials make campaign promises they don't intend to keep, and acquaintances pass compliments to each other to be polite and supportive. On occasion, everyone tells something less than "the truth, the whole truth, and nothing but the truth." Can social perceivers tell the difference? Can *you* tell when someone is lying?

Sigmund Freud, the founder of psychoanalysis, once said that "no mortal can keep a secret. If his lips are silent, he chatters with his fingertips; betrayal oozes out of him at every pore" (1905, p. 94). Paul Ekman and Wallace Friesen (1974) revised Freud's observation by pointing out that some pores "ooze" more than others. Specifically, Ekman and Friesen proposed that some channels of communication are difficult for deceivers to control, while others are relatively easy. To test this hypothesis, they showed a series of films—some pleasant, others disgusting—to a group of female nurses. While watching, the nurses were instructed either to report their honest impressions of these films or to conceal their true feelings. Through the use of hidden cameras, these participants were videotaped. Others, acting as observers, then viewed the tapes and judged whether the participants had been truthful or deceptive. The results showed that judgment accuracy rates were influenced by which types of nonverbal cues the observers were exposed to. Observers who watched tapes that focused on the body were better at detecting deception than were those who saw tapes focused on the face. The face can communicate emotion, but it is relatively easy for deceivers to control—unlike nervous movements of the hands and feet. As Bella DePaulo (1994) puts it, "There's nothing like Pinocchio's nose to help judge whether someone is telling the truth."

This study was the first of many. In other studies, too, one group of participants made truthful or deceptive statements while another group read the transcripts, listened to audiotapes or watched videotapes, and then tried to evaluate the statements. This research showed that people frequently make mistakes in their judgments of truth and deception and too often accept what others say at face value. Even more sobering, people don't have a good sense of their own lie-detection skills. Specifically, it seems that people are confident in these judgments regardless of whether they are correct or incorrect (DePaulo et al., 1997). As you might expect, some people are better at the task than others (Frank & Ekman, 1997). Surprisingly, however, professionals who regularly make these kinds of judgments for a living—police detectives, trial judges, psychiatrists, and those who administer lie-detector tests—are, like the rest of us, highly prone to error (Ekman & O'Sullivan, 1991; Memon et al., 2003).

What seems to be the problem? After reviewing over 30 studies, Miron Zuckerman and his colleagues (1981) concluded that there's a *mismatch* between the behavioural cues that actually signal deception and those used by perceivers to detect deception. This conclusion is generally supported by a more recent meta-analysis of results from 120 studies involving thousands of research participants (DePaulo et al., 2003). To be more specific, four channels of communication provide relevant information: words, the face, the body, and the voice. When people have a reason to lie, *words* alone cannot be trusted. The *face* is also controllable. We tend to think that people do not smile when they lie, but it is common for deceivers to mask their real feelings with false smiles that do not stretch up to the eye muscles. Indeed, psychophysiological research confirms that there are two types of smiles, one more genuine than the other (Ekman & Davidson, 1993; Frank et al., 1993). The *body* is somewhat more revealing than the face, as deception is often accompanied by fidgety movements of the hands and feet and by restless shifts in posture. Finally, the *voice* is the leakiest, most revealing cue. When people lie, especially when they are highly motivated to do so, their voices rise in pitch, and the number of speech hesitations increases.

In light of these findings, it appears that social perceivers tune in to the wrong channels of communication. Too easily seduced by the silver tongue and the smiling face, we often fail to notice the restless body and quivering voice. Ironically, research participants become more accurate in their judgments of truth and deception when they are too busy to attend closely to what a speaker says (Gilbert & Krull, 1988). People are also more accurate when they're instructed to pay more attention to the telltale cues of the body or voice than to the face (DePaulo et al., 1982) and when they report having based their judgments more on the voice than on verbal or visual information (Anderson et al., 1999).

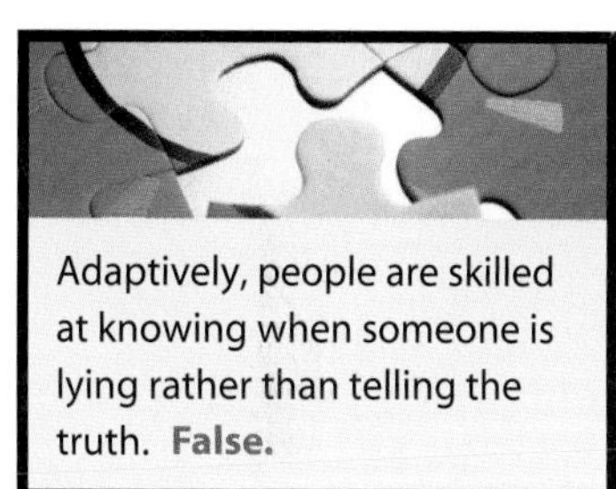

Adaptively, people are skilled at knowing when someone is lying rather than telling the truth. **False.**

Attribution: From Elements to Dispositions

To interact effectively with others, we need to know how they feel and when they can be trusted. But to understand people well enough to predict their future behaviour, we must also identify their inner *dispositions:* stable characteristics such as personality traits, attitudes, and abilities. Since we cannot actually see dispositions, we infer them indirectly from what a person says and does. In this section, we look at the processes that lead us to make these inferences.

People make personal and situational attributions all the time in an effort to make sense of their social world.

Attribution Theories

Do you ever think about the influence that you have on other people? What about the roles of heredity, childhood experiences, and social forces? Do you wonder why some people succeed while others fail? Individuals differ in the extent to which they feel a need to explain the uncertain events of human behaviour (Weary & Edwards, 1994). Among students, for example, psychology majors are more curious about

"It's not you, Frank, it's me—I don't like you."

people than are natural-science majors (Fletcher et al., 1986). Although there are vast differences among us, people in general tend to ask "why?" when they confront important events that are negative or unexpected (Hastie, 1984; Weiner, 1985) and when understanding these events has personal relevance (Malle & Knobe, 1997).

To make sense of our social world, we try to understand the causes of other people's behaviour. But what kinds of explanations do we make, and how do we go about making them? In a classic book entitled *The Psychology of Interpersonal Relations*, Fritz Heider (1958) took the first step toward answering these questions. To Heider, we are all scientists of a sort. Motivated to understand others well enough to manage our social lives, we observe, analyze, and explain their behaviour. The explanations we come up with are called *attributions*, and the theory that describes the process is called **attribution theory**. The questions posed at the beginning of the chapter regarding Todd Bertuzzi and Robert Latimer are questions of attribution.

Ask people to explain why their fellow human beings behave as they do—why they succeed or fail, laugh or cry, work or play, or help or hurt others—and you'll see that they come up with complex explanations often focused on whether the behaviour is intentional or unintentional (Malle et al., 2000). Interested in how people answer these *why* questions, Heider found it particularly useful to group the explanations people give into two categories: *personal* and *situational.* Consider the Bertuzzi case. What led him to hit Moore from behind? Did he intend to hurt him? He said no. But what caused him to lash out? Was it because he had a history of being an aggressive player and had a score to settle (a **personal attribution**), or because of an unfortunate reaction in the heat of the moment (a **situational attribution**). Bertuzzi pleaded guilty and was sentenced to probation and community service. Kafer, Hodkin, Furrow, and Landry (1993) explored the attributions surrounding the horrific massacre of 14 women by Marc Lepine at the École Polytechnique in Montreal in 1989. Lepine, blaming feminists for "ruining his life," walked through the school ordering the men to leave and shooting the women. Was his behaviour the result of a general acceptance in society of violence against women (a situational attribution) or the result of his own rage and pathology? Kafer et al. (1993) found that to some extent women and men differed in their attributions; women were more likely to attribute the massacre to the killer (a **personal attribution**), whereas men were more likely to endorse the societal explanation (a **situational attribution**). The task for the attribution theorist is not to determine the true *causes* of such an event but, rather, to understand people's *perceptions* of causality. For now, two major attribution theories are described.

Jones's Correspondent Inference Theory According to Edward Jones and Keith Davis (1965), each of us tries to understand other people by observing and analyzing their behaviour. Jones and Davis's *correspondent inference theory* predicts that people try to infer from an action whether the act itself corresponds to an enduring personal characteristic of the actor. Is the person who commits an act of aggression a beast? Is the person who donates money to charity an altruist? To answer these kinds of questions, people make inferences on the basis of three factors.

The first factor is a person's degree of *choice*. Behaviour that is freely chosen is more informative about a person than behaviour that is coerced. In one study, participants read a speech, presumably written by a student, that either favoured or opposed Fidel Castro, the communist leader of Cuba. Some participants were told that the student had freely chosen this position, and others were told that the student had been assigned the position by a professor. When asked to determine the student's true attitude, participants were more likely to assume a correspondence between his or her essay (behaviour) and attitude (disposition) when the student had had a choice than when he or she had been assigned to the role (Jones & Harris, 1967; see Figure 4.3). Keep this study in mind. It supports correspondent infer-

attribution theory A group of theories that describe how people explain the causes of behaviour.

personal attribution Attribution to internal characteristics of an actor, such as ability, personality, mood, or effort.

situational attribution Attribution to factors external to an actor, such as the task, other people, or luck.

ence theory; but as we will see later, it also demonstrates one of the most tenacious biases of social perception.

The second factor that leads people to make dispositional inferences is the *expectedness* of behaviour. As previously noted, an action tells us more about a person when it departs from the norm than when it is typical, part of a social role, or otherwise expected under the circumstances (Jones et al., 1961). Thus, people think they know more about a student who wears three-piece suits to class or a citizen who openly refuses to pay taxes than about a student who wears blue jeans to class or a citizen who files tax returns on April 30.

Third, people consider the intended *effects* or consequences of someone's behaviour. Acts that produce many desirable outcomes do not reveal a person's specific motives as clearly as acts that produce only a single desirable outcome (Newtson, 1974). For example, you are likely to be uncertain about exactly why a person stays on a job that is enjoyable, high paying, and in an attractive location—three desirable outcomes, each sufficient to explain the behaviour. In contrast, you may feel more certain about why a person stays on a job that is tedious and low paying but is in an attractive location—only one desirable outcome.

FIGURE 4.3

What Does This Speechwriter Really Believe?

As predicted by correspondent inference theory, participants who read a student's speech (behaviour) were more likely to assume that it reflected the student's true attitude (disposition) when the position taken was freely chosen (left) rather than assigned (right). But also note the evidence for the fundamental attribution error. Even participants who thought the student had been assigned a position inferred the student's attitude from the speech. *(Jones & Harris, 1967.)*

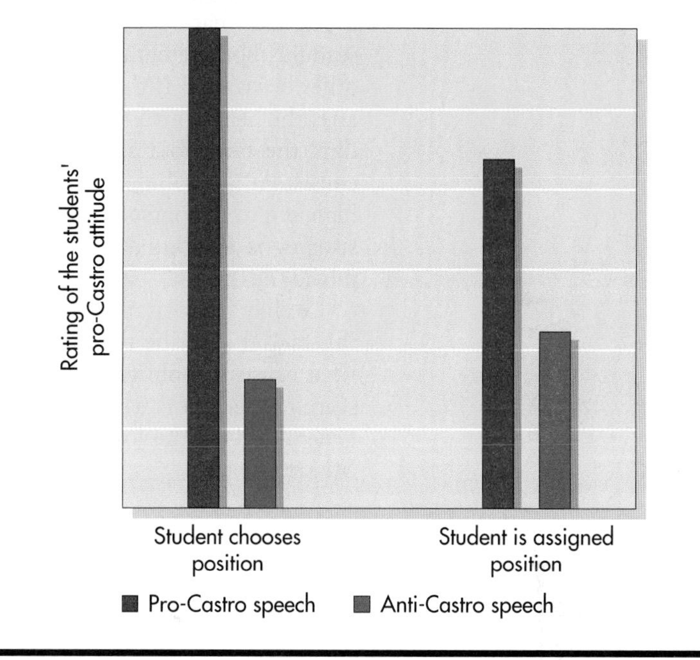

Kelley's Covariation Theory Correspondent inference theory seeks to describe how perceivers try to discern an individual's personal characteristics from a slice of behavioural evidence. However, behaviour can be attributed not only to personal factors but to situational factors as well. How is this distinction made? In the opening chapter, we noted that the causes of human behaviour can be derived only through *experiments*. That is, one has to make more than a single observation and compare behaviour in two or more settings in which everything stays the same except for the independent variables. Like Heider, Harold Kelley (1967) believes that people are much like scientists in this regard. They may not observe others in a laboratory, but they too make comparisons and think in terms of "experiments." According to Kelley, people make attributions by using the **covariation principle**: In order for something to be the cause of a behaviour, it must be present when the behaviour occurs and absent when it does not. Three kinds of covariation information are particularly useful: consensus, distinctiveness, and consistency.

To illustrate these concepts, imagine you are standing on a street corner one hot, steamy evening minding your own business, when all of a sudden a stranger comes out of an air-conditioned movie theatre and blurts out, "Great flick!" Looking up, you don't recognize the movie title, so you wonder what to make of this "recommendation." Was the behaviour (the rave review) caused by something about the person (the stranger), the stimulus (the film), or the circumstances (say, the air-conditioned theatre)? Possibly interested in spending a night at the movies, how would you proceed to explain what happened? What kinds of information would you want to obtain?

covariation principle A principle of attribution theory holding that people attribute behaviour to factors that are present when a behaviour occurs and absent when it does not.

Thinking like a scientist, you might seek out *consensus information* to see how different persons react to the same stimulus. In other words, how do other moviegoers feel about this film? If others also rave about it, the stranger's behaviour is high in consensus and is attributed to the stimulus. If others are critical of the same film, the behaviour is low in consensus and is attributed to the person. Still thinking like a scientist, you might also want to have *distinctiveness information* to see how the same person reacts to different stimuli. In other words, how does this moviegoer react to other films? If the stranger is critical of other films, the target behaviour is high in distinctiveness and is attributed to the stimulus. If the stranger raves about everything, however, then the behaviour is low in distinctiveness and is attributed to the person. Finally, you might seek *consistency information* to see what happens to the behaviour at another time when the person and the stimulus both remain the same. How does this moviegoer feel about this film on other occasions? If the stranger raves about the film on video as well as in the theatre, the behaviour is high in consistency. If the stranger does not always enjoy the film, the behaviour is low in consistency. According to Kelley, behaviour that is consistent is attributed to the stimulus when consensus and distinctiveness are also high and to the person when they are low. In contrast, behaviour that is low in consistency is attributed to transient circumstances, such as the temperature of the movie theatre.

Kelley's theory and the predictions it makes are represented in Figure 4.4. Does this model describe the kinds of information you seek when you try to determine what causes people to behave as they do? Often they do. Research shows that research participants who are instructed to make attributions for various events do, in general, follow the logic of covariation (Cheng & Novick, 1990; Fosterling, 1992; McArthur, 1972).

FIGURE 4.4

Kelley's Covariation Theory

For behaviours that are high in consistency, people make personal attributions when there is low consensus and distinctiveness (top row) and stimulus attributions when there is high consensus and distinctiveness (bottom row). Behaviours that are low in consistency (not shown) are attributed to passing circumstances.

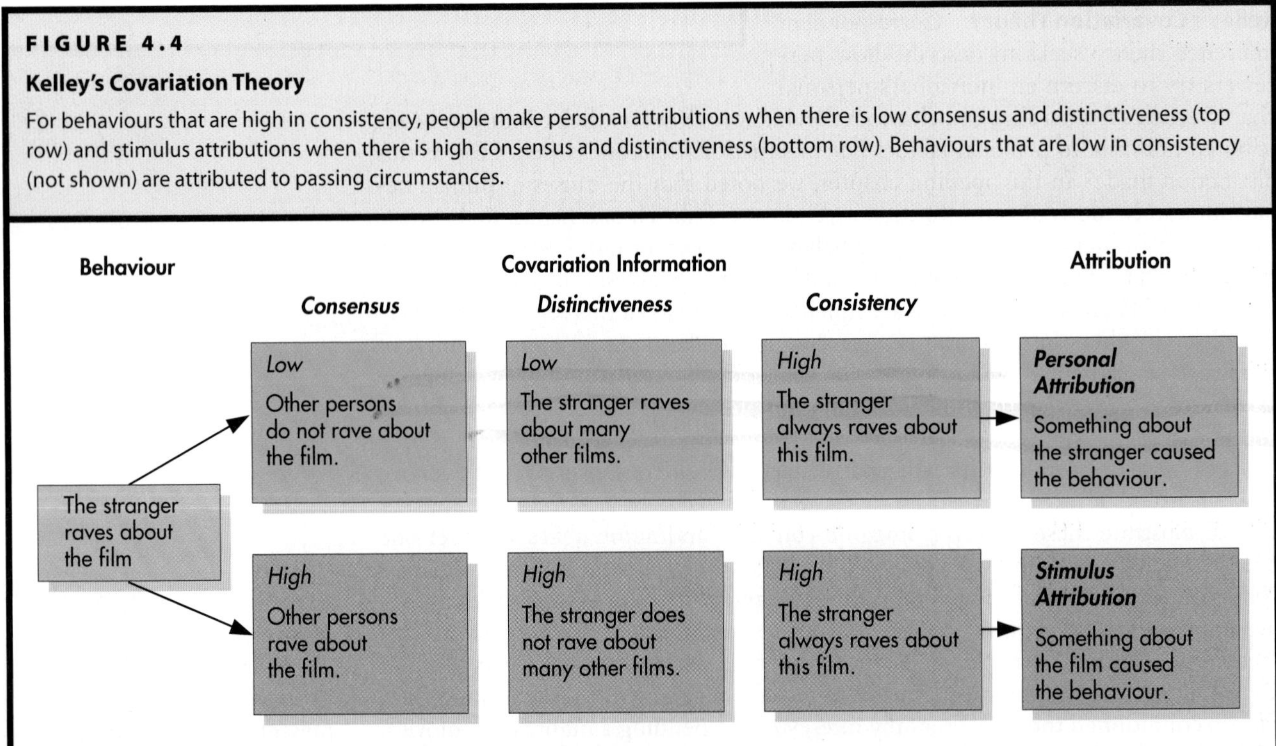

Attribution Biases

When the theories of attribution were first proposed, they were represented by such complicated flow charts, formulas, and diagrams that many social psychologists began to wonder: Do people really analyze behaviour in the way that one might expect of computers? Do people have the time, motivation, or cognitive capacity for such elaborate and mindful processes? The answer is sometimes yes, sometimes no. As social perceivers, we are limited in our ability to process all relevant information, or we may lack the kinds of training needed to employ fully the principles of attribution theory. More important, we often don't make an effort to think carefully about our attributions. With so much to explain and not enough time in a day, people take mental shortcuts, cross their fingers, hope for the best, and get on with life. The problem is that speed brings bias and perhaps even a loss of accuracy. In this section, we examine some of these shortcuts and their consequences.

Cognitive Heuristics According to Daniel Kahneman, Amos Tversky, and others, we often make attributions and other types of social judgments by using cognitive heuristics: information-processing rules of thumb that enable us to think in ways that are quick and easy but that frequently lead to error (Gilovich et al., 2002; Kahneman et al., 1982; Nisbett & Ross, 1980).

One rule of thumb that has particularly troublesome effects on attribution is the **availability heuristic**, a tendency to estimate the odds that an event will occur by how easily instances of it pop to mind. To demonstrate this phenomenon, Tversky and Kahneman (1973) asked research participants: Which is more common, words that start with the letter *r* or words that contain *r* as the third letter? In actuality, the English language has many more words with *r* as the third letter than as the first. Yet most people guessed that more words begin with *r*. The reason? It's easier to bring to mind words in which *r* appears first. Apparently, our estimates of likelihood are heavily influenced by events that are readily available in memory (MacLeod & Campbell, 1992).

The availability heuristic can lead us astray in two ways. First, it gives rise to the **false-consensus effect**, a tendency for people to overestimate the extent to which others share their opinions, attributes, and behaviours. This bias is pervasive. Regardless of whether people are asked to predict how others feel about same sex marriage, the privatization of health care, abortion, certain types of music, or norms for appropriate behaviour, they exaggerate the percentage of others who behave similarly or share their views (Krueger, 1998; Ross, Greene, & House, 1977).

To illustrate the effect, Joachim Krueger and Russell Clement (1994) asked participants in a study to indicate whether they agreed or disagreed with a series of statements taken from a well-known personality test. Later, they were asked to estimate the percentage of people in general who would agree with these same statements. Participants' beliefs about other people were biased by their own responses. In part, the false-consensus bias is a by-product of the availability heuristic. We tend to associate with others who are like us in important ways, so we are more likely to notice and recall instances of similar rather than dissimilar behaviour (Deutsch, 1989). Interestingly, people do *not* exhibit this bias when asked to predict the behaviour of people from groups other than their own (Mullen et al., 1992). People also do not exhibit this bias when predicting aspects of others for which they see themselves as distinct rather than typical (Karniol, 2003).

A second consequence of the availability heuristic is that social perceptions are influenced more by one vivid life story than by hard statistical facts. Have you ever wondered why so many people buy lottery tickets despite the astonishingly low odds or why so many travelers are afraid to fly even though they are more likely to perish in a car accident? These behaviours are symptomatic of the **base-rate fallacy**—the

availability heuristic The tendency to estimate the likelihood that an event will occur by how easily instances of it come to mind.

false-consensus effect The tendency for people to overestimate the extent to which others share their opinions, attributes, and behaviours.

base-rate fallacy The finding that people are relatively insensitive to consensus information presented in the form of numerical base rates.

"A single death is a tragedy; a million is a statistic."
—Joseph Stalin

fact that people are relatively insensitive to numerical base rates, or probabilities, and are influenced instead by graphic, dramatic events such as the sight of a multimillion-dollar lottery winner celebrating on TV or a photograph of bodies being pulled from the wreckage of a plane crash. The base-rate fallacy can thus lead to various misperceptions of risk. Indeed, people overestimate the number of those who die in shootings, fires, floods, and terrorist bombings and underestimate the death toll caused by heart attacks, strokes, diabetes, and other mundane events (Slovic et al., 1982). Made relevant by recently acquired fears of terrorism, research shows that people's perceptions of risk are affected more by fear, anxiety, and other emotions than by cold probabilities (Loewenstein et al., 2001; Slovic, 2000).

People can also be influenced by how easy it is to imagine events that did *not* occur. As thoughtful and curious beings, we often are not content to accept what happens to us or to others without wondering, at least in private, "What if . . . ?" According to Daniel Kahneman and Dale Miller (1986), people's emotional reactions to events are often coloured by **counterfactual thinking**, the tendency to imagine alternative outcomes that might have occurred but did not. There are different types of counterfactual thoughts. If we imagine a result that is better than the actual result, then we're likely to experience disappointment, regret, and frustration. If the imagined result is worse, then we react with emotions that range from relief and satisfaction to elation. Thus, the psychological impact of positive and negative events depends on the way we think about "what might have been" (Roese, 1997; Roese & Olson, 1995). Just as counterfactual thoughts can alter our mood, the mood we are in can influence the kind of counterfactual thinking we do. When people feel good, they imagine how much worse things could be; when down in the dumps, they imagine how much better they could be (Sanna et al., 1999).

People don't immerse themselves in counterfactual thought after every experience, obviously. Research shows that we are more likely to think about what might have been—often with feelings of regret—after negative outcomes that result from actions we take rather than from those we don't take (Byrne & McEleney, 2000; Zeelenberg et al., 1998). Thus, the day trader who takes action by selling 100 shares of a stock before it goes on to climb five points ("I could've made $500 had I not sold") feels worse than the one who fails to act by not selling the 100 shares before the stock drops five points ("I could've saved a $500 loss had I sold").

According to Victoria Medvec and Kenneth Savitsky (1997), certain situations—such as being on the *verge* of a better or worse outcome, just above or below some cut-off point—make it especially easy to conjure up images of what might have been. The implications are intriguing. Imagine, for example, that you are an Olympic athlete and have just won a silver medal—a remarkable feat. Now imagine that you have just won the bronze medal. Which situation would make you feel better? Rationally speaking, you should feel more pride and satisfaction with the silver medal. But what if your achievement had prompted you to engage in counterfactual thinking? What alternative would preoccupy your mind if you had finished in second place? Where would your focus be if you had placed third? Is it possible that the athlete who is better off objectively will feel worse?

During the 1996 Summer Olympics, Nike ran this counterfactual—and controversial—advertisement: "You don't win silver, you lose gold."

To examine this question, Medvec and her colleagues (1995) videotaped 41 athletes in the 1992 Summer Olympic Games at the moment they realized that they had won a silver or a bronze medal and again, later, during the medal ceremony. Then they showed these tapes, without sound, to people who did not know the order of finish. These participants were asked to observe the medalists and rate their emotional states on a scale ranging from "agony" to "ecstasy." The intriguing result, as you might expect, was that the bronze medalists, on average, seemed happier than the silver medalists. Was there any more direct evidence of counterfactual thinking? In a second study, participants who watched interviews with many of these same athletes rated the silver medalists as more negatively focused on finishing second rather than first and the bronze medalists as more positively focused on

counterfactual thinking
A tendency to imagine alternative events or outcomes that might have occurred but did not.

finishing third rather than fourth. For these world-class athletes, feelings of satisfaction were based more on their thoughts of what might have been than on the reality of what was.

The Fundamental Attribution Error By the time you finish reading this textbook, you will know the cardinal lesson of social psychology: People are profoundly influenced by the *situational* context of behaviour. This point is not as obvious as it may seem. For instance, parents are often surprised to hear that their mischievous child, the family monster, is a perfect angel in the classroom. And students are often surprised to observe that their favourite professor, so eloquent in the lecture hall, may stumble over words in less formal gatherings. These reactions are symptomatic of a well-documented aspect of social perception. When people explain the behaviour of others, they tend to overestimate the role of personal factors and overlook the impact of situations. Because this bias is so pervasive, and sometimes so misleading, it has been called the **fundamental attribution error** (Ross, 1977).

Evidence of the fundamental attribution error was first reported in the Jones and Harris (1967) study described earlier, in which participants read an essay presumably written by a student. In that study, participants were more likely to infer the student's true attitude when the position taken had been freely chosen than when they thought that the student had been assigned to it. But look again at Figure 4.3, and you'll notice that even when participants thought that the student had no choice but to assert a position, they still used the speech to infer his or her attitude. This finding has been repeated many times. Whether the essay topic is nuclear power, abortion, drug laws, or the death penalty, the results are essentially the same (Jones, 1990).

People fall prey to the fundamental attribution error even when they are fully aware of the situation's impact on behaviour. In one experiment, the participants themselves were assigned to take a position, whereupon they swapped essays and rated each other. Remarkably, they still jumped to conclusions about each other's attitudes (Miller et al., 1981). In another experiment, participants inferred attitudes from a speech even when they were the ones who had assigned the position to be taken (Gilbert & Jones, 1986).

A fascinating study by Lee Ross and his colleagues (1977) demonstrates the fundamental attribution error in a more familiar setting, the TV quiz show (Ross et al., 1977). By a flip of the coin, participants in this study were randomly assigned to play the role of either the questioner or the contestant in a quiz game while spectators looked on. In front of the contestant and spectators, the experimenter instructed the questioner to write ten challenging questions from his or her own store of general knowledge. If you are a trivia buff, you can imagine how esoteric such questions can be: Who was the founder of eBay? What team won the NHL Stanley Cup in 1968? It is no wonder that contestants correctly answered only about 40 percent of the questions asked. When the game was over, all participants rated the questioner's and contestant's general knowledge on a scale of 0 to 100.

Picture the events that transpired. The questioners appeared more knowledgeable than the contestants. After all, they knew all the answers. But a moment's reflection should remind us that the situation put the questioner at a distinct advantage (there were no differences between the two groups on an objective test of general knowledge). Did participants take the questioners' advantage into account, or did they assume that the questioners actually had greater knowledge? The results were startling. Spectators rated the questioners as above average in their general knowledge and the contestants as below average. The contestants even rated themselves as inferior to their partners. Like the spectators, they too were fooled by the loaded situation (see Figure 4.5).

fundamental attribution error The tendency to focus on the role of personal causes and underestimate the impact of situations on other people's behaviour.

FIGURE 4.5

Fundamental Attribution Error and the TV Quiz Show

Even though the simulated quiz show situation placed questioners in an obvious position of advantage over contestants, observers rated the questioners as more knowledgeable (right). Questioners did not overrate their general knowledge (left); but contestants rated themselves as inferior (middle) and observers rated them as inferior as well. These results illustrate the fundamental attribution error. *(Ross, Amabile, and Steinmetz, 1977.)*

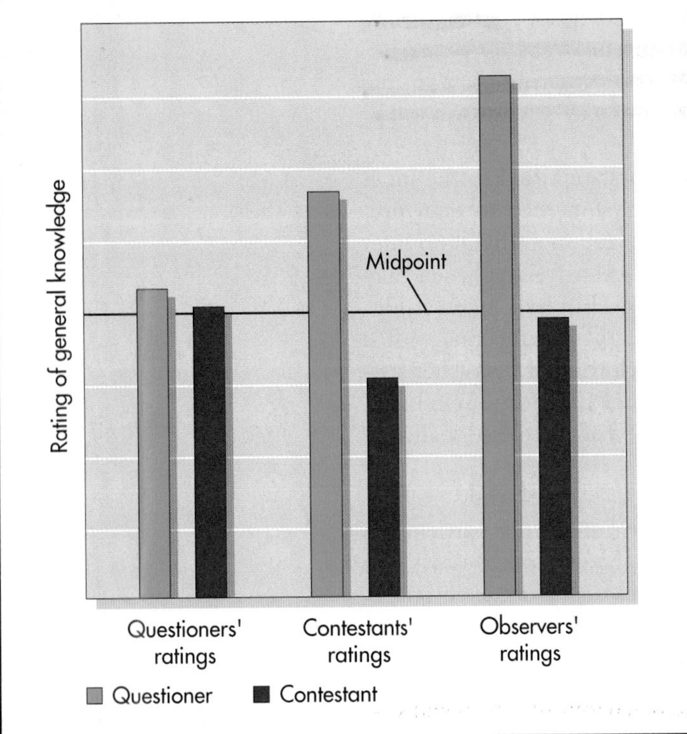

What's going on here? Why do social perceivers consistently make assumptions about persons and fail to appreciate the impact of situations? According to Daniel Gilbert and Patrick Malone (1995), the problem stems in part from *how* we make attributions. Attribution theorists used to assume that people survey all the evidence and then decide on either a personal or a situational attribution. Instead, it now appears that social perception is a two-step process: First we identify the behaviour and make a quick personal attribution; then we correct or adjust that inference to account for situational influences. The first step is simple and automatic, like a reflex; the second requires attention, thought, and effort (see Figure 4.6). At present, social neuroscience researchers are beginning to use neuroimaging to probe the brain for evidence of this model (Lieberman et al., 2004).

Several research findings support this hypothesis. First, without realizing it, people often form quick impressions of others based on a brief glimpse at a face or sample of behaviour (Newman & Uleman, 1989; Todorov & Uleman, 2002). Second, perceivers are *more* likely to commit the fundamental attribution error when they are cognitively busy, or distracted, as they observe the target person than when they pay full attention (Gilbert et al., 1992; Trope & Alfieri, 1997). Since the two-step model predicts that personal attributions are automatic but that the later adjustment for situational factors requires conscious thought, it makes sense to suggest that when attention is divided, when the attribution is

FIGURE 4.6

Two-Step Model of the Attribution Process

Traditional attribution theories assumed that we analyze behaviour by searching for a personal or situational cause. The two-step model suggests that people make personal attributions automatically and then must consciously adjust that inference in order to account for situational factors.

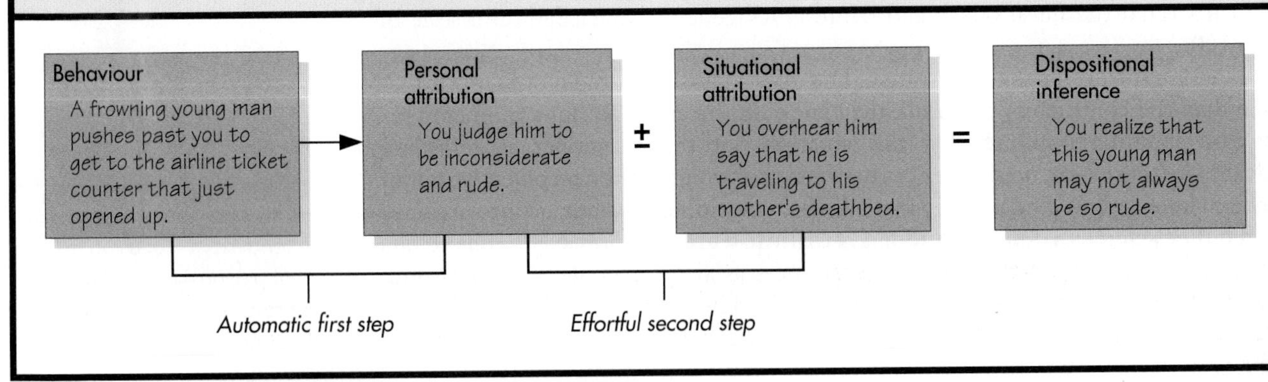

made hastily, or when perceivers lack motivation, the second step suffers more than the first. As Gilbert and his colleagues (1988) put it, "The first step is a snap, but the second one's a doozy" (p. 738).

Why is the first step such a snap, and why does it seem so natural for people to assume a link between acts and personal dispositions? One possible explanation is based on Heider's (1958) insight that people see dispositions in behaviour because of a perceptual bias, something like an optical illusion. When you listen to a speech or watch a quiz show, the actor is the conspicuous *figure* of your attention; the situation fades into the *background* ("out of sight, out of mind," as they say). And according to Heider, people attribute events to factors that are perceptually conspicuous, or *salient.* To test this hypothesis, Shelley Taylor and Susan Fiske (1975) varied the seating arrangements of observers who watched as two actors engaged in a carefully staged conversation. In each session, the participants were seated so that they faced actor A, actor B, or both actors. When later questioned about their observations, they rated the actor they faced as the more dominant member of the pair, the one who set the tone and direction.

How knowledgeable is this man? Alex Trebek has hosted the TV quiz show, Jeopardy! *since 1984. As host, Trebek reads questions to contestants, and then reveals the correct answers. In light of the quiz show study by Ross and others (1977), which illustrates the fundamental attribution error, viewers probably see Trebek as highly knowledgeable—despite knowing that the answers he recites are provided to him as part of his job.*

People may commit the fundamental attribution error when they explain the behaviour of others, but do they exhibit the same bias in explaining their own behaviour? Think about it. Are you shy or outgoing, or does your behaviour depend on the situation? Are you calm or intense, quiet or talkative, lenient or firm? Or, again, does your behaviour in these respects depend primarily on the situation? Now think of a friend, and answer the same questions about his or her behaviour. Do you notice a difference? Chances are, you do. Research shows that people are more likely to say "It depends on the situation" to describe themselves than to describe others. When Lewis Goldberg (1978) administered 2800 English trait words to 14 groups, each containing 100 people, he found that 85 percent checked off more traits for others than for themselves.

The tendency to make personal attributions for the behaviour of others and situational attributions for ourselves is called the **actor-observer effect** and has been widely demonstrated (Jones & Nisbett, 1972; Watson, 1982). In one study, 60 prison inmates and their counsellors were asked to explain why the inmates had committed their offences. The counsellors cited enduring personal characteristics; the prisoners referred to transient situational factors (Saulnier & Perlman, 1981). In a second study, roommates rated themselves or each other in terms of how consistently they exhibited various traits—such as inquisitiveness, happiness, patience, and impulsiveness. Compared with the way students saw themselves, the roommates rated others as more consistent in their behaviour (Krueger, 1998).

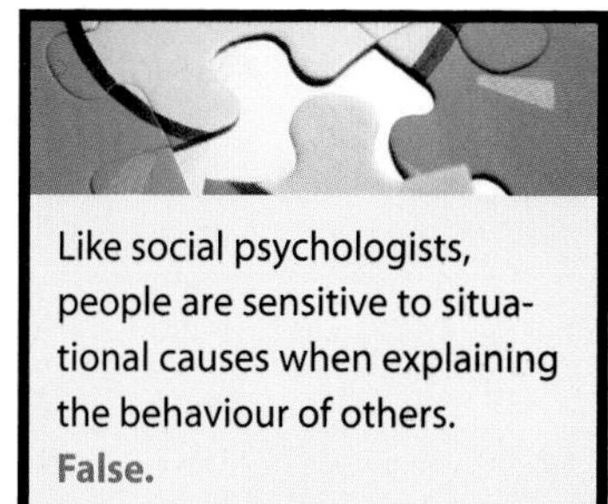

Like social psychologists, people are sensitive to situational causes when explaining the behaviour of others. **False.**

Attributions as Cultural Constructions

Attribution researchers used to assume that people all over the world explained human behaviour in the same ways. It is now clear, however, that the culture in which we live shapes in subtle but profound ways the kinds of attributions we make about people and social situations (Nisbett, 2003). As we saw in Chapter 3, westerners tend to believe that persons are autonomous, motivated by internal forces, and responsible for their own actions. In contrast, people in many nonwestern "collectivist" cultures take a more holistic view that emphasizes the relationship between individuals and their social surroundings.

actor-observer effect The tendency to attribute our own behaviour to situational causes and the behaviour of others to personal factors.

FIGURE 4.7

Fundamental Attribution Error: A Western Bias?

American and Asian Indian participants of varying ages described the causes of negative actions they had observed. Among young children, there were no cultural differences. With increasing age, however, Americans made more personal attributions, and Indian participants made more situational attributions. Explanations for positive behaviours followed a similar pattern. This finding suggests that the fundamental attribution error is a western phenomenon. *(J. G. Miller, 1984.)*

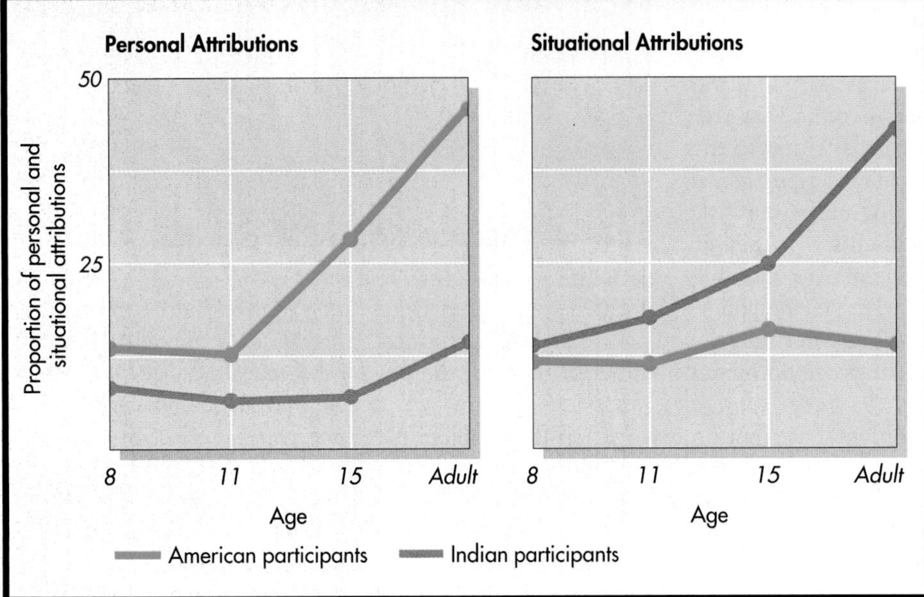

Do these contrasting cultural worldviews influence the attributions we make? Is it possible that the fundamental attribution error is a uniquely western phenomenon? To answer these questions, Joan Miller (1984) asked Americans and Asian Indians of varying ages to describe the causes of positive and negative behaviours they had observed in their lives. Among young children, there were no cultural differences. With increasing age, however, the American participants made more personal attributions, while the Indians made more situational attributions (see Figure 4.7). In another study, Michael Morris and Kaiping Peng (1994) compared students from the United States and China. They found no cultural differences in the perception of *physical* events; but for social behaviours, the American students made attributions that were more personal and less situational. Additional studies show that even within a given culture, people differ in their individualist versus collectivist orientations—differences that are related to

Look at this tropical underwater scene, then turn away and try to recount as much of it as you can. What did you notice? What did you forget? When researchers showed American and Japanese students underwater scenes, they found that while both groups recalled the focal fish (like the large blue one shown here), the Japanese recalled more about the elements of the background.

the attributions they make and the inferences they draw from behaviour (Duff & Newman, 1997; Newman, 1993).

According to Ara Norenzayan and Richard Nisbett (2000), cultural differences in attribution are founded on varying folk theories about human causality. Western cultures, they argue, emphasize the individual person and his or her attributes, whereas East Asian cultures focus on the background or field that surrounds that person. To test this hypothesis, they showed American and Japanese college students underwater scenes featuring a cast of small fish, small animals, plants, rocks, and coral—and one or more large, fast-moving *focal* fish, the stars of the show. Moments later, when asked to recount what they had seen, both groups recalled details about the focal fish to a nearly equal extent, but the Japanese reported far more details about the supporting cast in the background. Other researchers, too, have observed cultural differences in the extent to which people notice, think about, and remember the details of situational contexts (Ishii et al., 2003; Kitayama et al., 2003; Masuda & Nisbett, 2001). Compared to the inhabitants of most western cultures, people from East Asia tend to see humans as more malleable and likelier to be influenced by social groups, situations, and other contextual factors (Choi et al., 1999). As such, they are less prone to commit the fundamental attribution error first identified by Jones and Harris (Miyamoto & Kitayama, 2002).

Clearly, the world is becoming a global village characterized by increasing racial and ethnic diversity within countries. Many people who migrate from one country to another become *bicultural* in their identity, retaining some of their ancestral heritage while adopting some of the lifestyles and values of their new homeland. How do these bicultural individuals make attributions for human behaviour? Is it possible that they view people through one cultural frame or the other, depending on which one is brought to mind? It's interesting that when shown a picture of one fish swimming ahead of a group, and asked why, Americans see the lone fish as *leading* the others (a personal attribution), while Chinese see the same fish as being *chased* by the others (a situational attribution). But what about bicultural social perceivers? In a study of China-born students attending university in California, researchers presented images symbolizing one of the two cultures (such as the U S and Chinese flags), administered the fish test, and found that compared to students exposed to the American images, those who saw the Chinese images made more situational attributions, seeing the lone fish as being chased rather than as leading (see Figure 4.8). Apparently, it is possible for us to hold differing cultural world views at the same time and to perceive others within either frame, depending on which culture is brought to mind (Hong et al., 2000; Peng & Knowles, 2003).

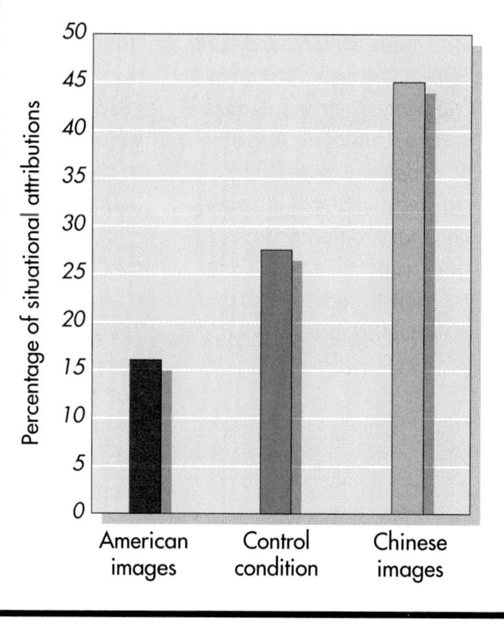

FIGURE 4.8

Attributions Within Cultural Frames

When one fish swims ahead of others in a group, Americans see that fish as *leading* the others (a personal attribution), while Chinese see it as being *chased by* the others (a situational attribution). In a study of bicultural Chinese students attending college in California, Ying-yi Hong and others (2000) displayed visual images that symbolized the United States or China before administering this fish test. As you can see, compared to students who were not first shown any images (centre), the tendency to make situational attributions was more common among those exposed to Chinese images (right) and less common among those exposed to American images (left). For people familiar with both world views, it appears that social perceptions are fluid—and depend on which culture is brought to mind.

Motivational Biases

As objective as we try to be, our social perceptions are sometimes coloured by personal needs, wishes, and preferences. This tendency showed itself in the officiating controversies of the 2002 Winter Olympics. Canadian figure skating pair Jamie Sale and David Pelletier had skated a flawless program and beamed smiles to the cheering crowd. They "knew" they had won the gold medal over Elena Berezhnaya

Jamie Sale and David Pelletier (left) *look at Russian skaters Elena Berezhnaya and Anton Sikharulidze* (right) *during the initial award ceremony at the 2002 Winter Olympics. Because of a judging scandal, the International Olympic Committee later granted gold medals to both pairs. Showing that people tend to see what they want to see, most Canadian fans saw the double gold as just; most Russian fans did not.*

and Anton Sikharulidze of Russia. Yet when the judges' scores came up moments later, the Russian pair was granted first place, unleashing a torrent of disapproval from the Salt Lake Ice Center crowd. Soon, a French judge admitted that she was pressured in her vote, leading the International Olympic Committee to award a second gold to the Canadian skaters. Canadian fans saw the revised decision as fair and just; but many Russians were outraged, insisting that Berezhnaya and Sikharulidze had won outright. This conflict illustrates a powerful bias in social perception: Sometimes we see what we want to see.

People have a strong need for self-esteem, and this motive can lead us to make favourable, self-serving, and one-sided attributions for our own behaviour. In Chapter 3, we saw that research with students, teachers, parents, workers, athletes, and others shows that we take more credit for success than for failure. Similarly, people seek more information about their strengths than about their weaknesses, overestimate their contribution to group efforts, exaggerate their control, and predict a rosy future. The false-consensus effect described earlier also has a self-serving side to it. It seems that we overestimate the extent to which others think, feel, and behave as we do, in part to reassure ourselves that our own ways are correct, normal, and socially appropriate (Alicke & Largo, 1995).

According to David Dunning and his colleagues, the need for self-esteem can bias our social perceptions in other subtle ways, too—even when we don't realize that the self is implicated. For example, do you consider yourself to be a "people-person," or are you more of a "task-oriented" type? And which of the two styles do you think makes for great leadership? It turns out that students who describe themselves as people-oriented see social skills as necessary for good leadership, while those who are more task-focused see a task orientation as better for leadership. Hence, people tend to judge favourably others who are similar to themselves, rather than different, on key characteristics (McElwee et al., 2001).

At times, personal defensive motives lead us to blame others for their misfortunes. Consider the following classic experiment. Participants thought they were taking part in an emotion-perception study. One person, actually a confederate, was selected randomly to take a memory test while the others looked on. Each time the confederate made a mistake, she was jolted by a painful electric shock (actually, there was no shock; what participants saw was a staged videotape). Since participants knew that only the luck of the draw had kept them off the "hot seat," you might think they would react with sympathy and compassion. Not so. In fact, they belittled the hapless confederate (Lerner & Simmons, 1966).

Melvin Lerner (1980) argues that the tendency to be critical of victims stems from our deep-seated **belief in a just world.** According to Lerner, people need to view the world as a just place in which we "get what we deserve" and "deserve what we get"—a world where hard work and clean living always pay off and where laziness and a sinful lifestyle are punished. To believe otherwise is to concede that we, too, are vulnerable to the cruel twists and turns of fate. Research suggests that the belief in a just world can help victims cope and serves as a buffer against stress. But how might this belief system influence our perceptions of *others*? If people cannot help or compensate the victims of misfortune, they turn on them. Thus, it is often assumed that poor people are lazy, that crime victims are careless, that

belief in a just world The belief that individuals get what they deserve in life, an orientation that leads people to disparage victims.

battered wives provoke their violent and abusive husbands, and that gay men with AIDS lack moral integrity. As you might expect, cross-national comparisons reveal that people in poorer countries are less likely than those in more affluent countries to believe in a just world (Furnham, 2003). In addition, a tendency to believe in a just world may be related to one's long-term goals; that is, in order to achieve a long-term goal we need to believe that the world is a fair and just place. That if we work hard to achieve these goals, we will eventually realize them (Hafer et al., 2005).

The tendency to disparage victims may seem like just another symptom of the fundamental attribution error: too much focus on the person and not enough on the situation. But the conditions that trigger this tendency suggest there is more to it. Studies have shown that accident victims are held more responsible for their fate when the consequences of the accident are severe rather than mild (Walster, 1966), when the victim's situation is similar to the perceiver's (Shaver, 1970), and when the perceiver is generally anxious about threats to the self (Thornton, 1992). The more threatened we feel by an apparent injustice, the greater is the need to protect ourselves from the dreadful implication that it could happen to us—an implication we defend by disparaging the victim.

In a laboratory experiment that reveals part of this process at work, participants watched a TV news story about a boy who was robbed and beaten. Some were told that the boy's assailants were captured, tried, and sent to prison. Others were told that the assailants fled the country, never to be brought to trial—a story that strains one's belief in a just world. Afterward, participants were asked to name as quickly as they could the colours in which various words in a list were typed (for example, the word *chair* may have been written in blue, *floor* in yellow, and *wide* in red). When the words themselves were neutral, all participants—regardless of which story they had seen—were equally fast at naming the colours. But when the words pertained to justice (words such as *fair* and *unequal*), those who had seen the justice-threatened version of the story were more distracted by the words and, hence, slower to name the colours. In fact, the more distracted they were, the more they derogated the victim. With their cherished belief in a just world threatened, these participants became highly sensitive to the concept of "justice"—and quick to disparage the innocent victim (Hafer, 2000).

Integration: From Dispositions to Impressions

When behaviour is attributed to situational factors, we do not generally make inferences about the actor. However, personal attributions often lead us to infer that a person has a certain disposition—that the leader of a failing business is incompetent, for example, or that the enemy who extends the olive branch seeks peace. Human beings are not one-dimensional, however, and one trait does not a person make. To have a complete picture of someone, social perceivers must assemble the various bits and pieces into a unified impression.

Information Integration: The Arithmetic

Once personal attributions are made, how are they combined into a single coherent picture of a person? How do we approach the process of **impression formation**?

impression formation The process of integrating information about a person to form a coherent impression.

What sort of impression might people have of convicted killer Karla Homolka? What sort of weighting would you give to any positive information you learned about her?

Do we simply add up all of a person's traits and calculate a mental average, or do we combine the information in more complicated ways? Anyone who has written or received letters of recommendation will surely appreciate the practical implications. Suppose that you're told an applicant is friendly and intelligent, two highly favourable qualities. Would you be more or less impressed if you then learned that this applicant was also prudent and even-tempered, two moderately favourable qualities? If you are more impressed, then you are intuitively following a *summation* model of impression formation: The more positive traits there are, the better. If you are less impressed, then you are using an *averaging* model: The higher the average value of all the various traits, the better.

To quantify the formation of impressions, Norman Anderson (1968) had research participants rate the desirability of 555 traits on a 7-point scale. By calculating the average ratings, he obtained a *scale value* for each trait (*sincere* had the highest scale value; *liar* had the lowest). In an earlier study, Anderson (1965) used similar values and compared the summation and averaging models. Specifically, he asked a group of participants to rate how much they liked a person described by two traits with extremely high scale values *(H, H)*. A second group received a list of four traits, including two that were high and two that were moderately high in their scale values *(H, H, M*1, *M*1*)*. In a third group, participants received two extremely low, negative traits *(L, L)*. In a fourth group, they received four traits, including two that were low and two that were moderately low *(L, L, M*2, *M*2*)*. What effect did the moderate traits have on impressions? As predicted by an averaging model, the moderate traits diluted rather than added to the impact of the highly positive and negative traits. The practical implication for those who write letters of recommendation is clear. Applicants are better off if their letters include only the most glowing comments and omit favourable remarks that are somewhat more guarded in nature.

After extensive amounts of research, it appears that although people tend to combine traits by averaging, the process is somewhat more complicated. Consistent with Anderson's (1981) **information integration theory**, impressions formed of others are based on a combination, or integration, of (1) personal dispositions of the perceiver and (2) a *weighted* average, not a simple average, of the target person's characteristics (Kashima & Kerekes, 1994). Let's look more closely at these two sets of factors.

information integration theory The theory that impressions are based on (1) perceiver dispositions and (2) a weighted average of a target person's traits.

Deviations from the Arithmetic

Like other aspects of our social perceptions, impression formation does not follow the rules of cold logic. Weighted averaging may describe the way most people combine different traits, but the whole process begins with a warm-blooded human perceiver, not a computer. Thus, certain deviations from the "arithmetic" are inevitable.

Perceiver Characteristics To begin with, perceivers differ in the kinds of impressions they form of others. Some people seem to measure everyone with an intellectual yardstick; others look for physical beauty, a warm smile, a good sense of humour, or a firm handshake. Whatever the attribute, each of us is more likely to notice and recall certain traits than others (Bargh et al., 1988; Higgins et al., 1982). Thus, when people are asked to describe a group of target individuals, there's typically more overlap between the various descriptions provided *by* the same *perceiver* than there is between those provided *for* the same *target* (Dornbusch et al., 1965; Park, 1986). Part of the reason for the differences among perceivers is that we tend to use ourselves as a standard, or frame of reference, when evaluating others. Compared with the inert couch potato, for example, the serious jock is more likely to see others as less active and athletic (Dunning & Hayes, 1996). As we saw earlier, people also tend to see their own skills and traits as particularly desirable for others to have (McElwee et al., 2001).

A perceiver's current, temporary *mood* can also influence the impressions formed of others (Forgas, 2000). For example, Joseph Forgas and Gordon Bower (1987) told research participants that they had performed very well or poorly on a test of social adjustment. As expected, this feedback altered their moods; it also affected their outlook on others. When presented with behavioural information about various characters, participants spent more time attending to positive facts and formed more favourable impressions when they were happy than when they were sad. Follow-up research shows that the biasing influence of mood is most pronounced when we are forming impressions of others who are atypical and who require more thought and effort in order to be understood (Forgas, 1992). In short, the combined effects of perceiver differences and fluctuating moods point to an important conclusion: that to some extent, impression formation is in the eye of the beholder.

Priming Effects The characteristics we tend to notice in other people also change from time to time, depending on recent experiences. Have you ever noticed that once a seldom-used word slips into a conversation, it is often repeated over and over again? If so, you have observed **priming**, the tendency for frequently or recently used concepts to come to mind easily and influence the way we interpret new information.

The effect of priming on person impressions was first demonstrated by E. Tory Higgins and others (1977). Research participants were presented with a list of trait words, ostensibly as part of an experiment on memory. In fact, the task was designed as a priming device to plant certain ideas in their minds. Some participants read words that evoked a positive image: *brave, independent, adventurous.* Others read words that evoked a more negative image: *reckless, foolish, careless.* Later, in what they thought to be an unrelated experiment, participants read about a man who climbed mountains, drove in a demolition derby, and tried to cross the Atlantic Ocean in a sailboat. As predicted, their impressions were shaped by the trait words they had earlier memorized. Those exposed to positive words later formed more favourable impressions of the character than those exposed to negative words. All the participants read exactly the same description, yet they formed different impressions depending on what was already on their minds. In fact, priming seems to work best when the prime words are presented so rapidly that people are not even aware of the exposure (Bargh & Pietromonaco, 1982).

Recent research now shows that our motivations, and even our social behaviours, are also subject to the automatic effects of priming without awareness. In one provocative study, John Bargh and Tanya Chartrand (1999) gave participants a "word search" puzzle that contained either neutral words or words associated with achievement motivation (*strive, win, master, compete, succeed*). Afterward, the participants were left alone and given three minutes to write down as many words as

priming The tendency for recently used words or ideas to come to mind easily and influence the interpretation of new information.

FIGURE 4.9

The Priming of Social Behaviour Without Awareness

Would waiting participants interrupt the busy experimenter? Compared with those who had previously been given neutral words to unscramble (centre), participants given politeness words were less likely to cut in (left) and those given rudeness words were more likely to cut in (right). These results show that priming can influence not only our social judgments but our behaviour as well. *(Bargh, Chen, and Burrows, 1996.)*

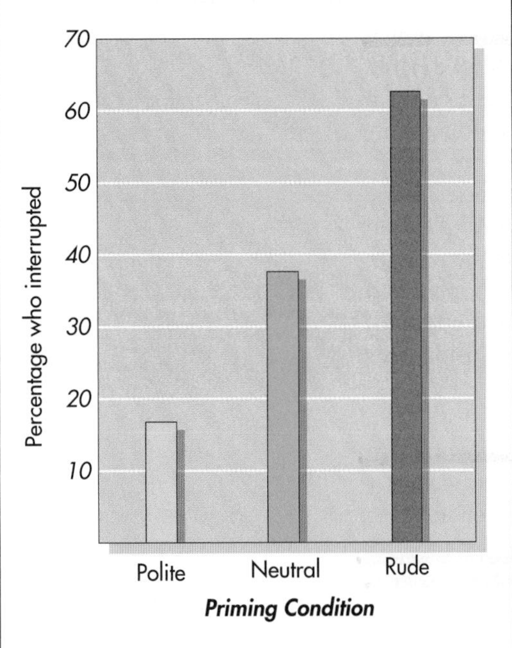

they could from a set of Scrabble™ letter tiles. When the three-minute limit was up, they were signalled over an intercom to stop. Did these participants, driven to obtain a high score, stop on cue or continue to write? Through the use of hidden cameras, the experimenters observed that 57 percent of those primed with achievement-related words continued to write after the stop signal—compared to only 22 percent in the control group.

Looking at priming effects on social behaviour, Bargh, Chen, and Burrows (1996) gave people 30 sets of words presented in scrambled order ("he it hides finds instantly") and told them to use some of the words in each set to form grammatical sentences. After explaining the test, which would take about five minutes, the experimenter told participants to locate him down the hall when they were finished so he could administer a second task. So far, so good. But when participants found the experimenter, he was in the hallway immersed in a conversation—and he stayed in that conversation for ten full minutes without even acknowledging their presence. What's a person to do, wait patiently or interrupt? The participants didn't know it, but some had worked on a scrambled word test that contained many "politeness" words (*yield*, *respect*, *considerate*, *courteous*), while others had been exposed to words related to rudeness (*disturb*, *intrude*, *bold*, *bluntly*). Would these test words secretly prime participants, a few minutes later, to behave in one way or the other? Yes. Compared with those given the neutral words to unscramble, participants primed for rudeness were more likely—and those primed for politeness were less likely—to break in and interrupt the experimenter (see Figure 4.9).

Target Characteristics Just as not all social perceivers are created equal, neither are all traits created equal. In recent years, personality researchers have discovered, across cultures, that individuals can reliably be distinguished from one another along five broad traits, or factors: extroversion, emotional stability, openness to experience, agreeableness, and conscientiousness (De Raad, 2000; McCrae & Costa, 1997; Wiggins, 1996). Some of these factors are easier to judge than others. Based on their review of 32 studies, David Kenny and others (1994) found that social perceivers are most likely to agree in their judgments of a target's extroversion—that is, the extent to which he or she is sociable, friendly, fun-loving, outgoing, and adventurous. It seems that this characteristic is easy to spot—and different perceivers often agree on it even when rating a target person whom they are seeing for the first time.

The valence of a trait—whether it is considered socially desirable or undesirable—also affects its impact on our final impressions. Specifically, research shows that people exhibit a *trait negativity bias*, the tendency for negative information to weigh more heavily than positive information (Rozin & Royzman, 2001; Skowronski & Carlston, 1989). This means that we form more extreme impressions of a person who is said to be untrustworthy than of one who is said to be honest. We tend to view others favourably, so we are quick to take notice and pay careful attention when this expectation is violated (Pratto & John, 1991). One bad trait may be enough to destroy a person's reputation—regardless of other qualities. Research on American political campaigns confirms the point, as public opinion is shaped more by a candidate's "negatives" than by positive information (Klein, 1991; Lau, 1985).

When you think about it, it's probably adaptive for people to stay alert for—and pay particularly close attention to—negative information. Recent research suggests that people are quicker to sense their exposure to subliminally presented negative

Brain research shows that when people are exposed to negative emotional images—such as the car bomb on the right as opposed to the beach scene on the left—activity in certain parts of the brain is more pronounced.

words such as *bomb*, *thief*, *shark*, and *cancer*, than to positive words such as *baby*, *sweet*, *friend*, and *beach* (Dijksterhuis & Aarts, 2003). This sensitivity to negative information can even be "seen" in the brain (Smith et al., 2003). In one study, for example, Tiffany Ito and others (1998) exposed research participants to slides that depicted images that were positive (a red Ferrari, people enjoying a roller coaster), negative (a mutilated face, a handgun pointed at the camera), or neutral (a plate, a hair dryer). Using electrodes attached to participants' scalps, these researchers recorded electrical activity in different areas of the brain during the slide presentation. Sure enough, they observed that certain types of activity were more pronounced when participants saw negative images than when they saw stimuli that were positive or neutral. It appears, as these researchers commented, that "negative information weighs more heavily on the brain" (p. 887).

The impact of trait information on our impressions of others depends not only on characteristics of the perceiver and target but on context as well. Two contextual factors are particularly important in this regard: (1) implicit theories of personality and (2) the order in which we receive information about one trait relative to other traits.

Implicit Personality Theories When Karla Homolka and Paul Bernardo were charged with the rape and murder of two young schoolgirls, people who knew them expressed shock and disbelief that they could be the killers. They had been described as a "perfect couple" although, it later emerged, six months before their "fairy-tale" wedding, they were responsible for the rape and ultimate death of Homolka's younger sister Tammy. It's easy to understand why people initially reacted to the charges with such disbelief. They just didn't seem like *the kind of people* who would commit cold-blooded murders. That reaction was based on an **implicit personality theory**—a network of assumptions that we hold about relationships among various types of people, traits, and behaviours. Knowing that someone has one trait thus leads us to infer that he or she has other traits as well (Bruner & Tagiuri, 1954; Schneider, 1973; Sedikides & Anderson, 1994). For example, you might assume that a person who is unpredictable is also dangerous or that someone who speaks slowly is also slow-witted. You might also assume that certain traits are linked to certain behaviours (Reeder, 1993; Reeder & Brewer, 1979).

Solomon Asch (1946) was the first to discover that the presence of one trait often implies the presence of others. Asch told one group of research participants that an individual was "intelligent, skilful, industrious, warm, determined, practical and

implicit personality theory A network of assumptions people make about the relationships among traits and behaviours.

cautious." Another group read an identical list of traits, except that the word *warm* was replaced by *cold*. Only the one term was changed, but the two groups formed very different impressions. Participants inferred that the warm person was also happier and more generous, good-natured, and humorous than the cold person. When two other words were varied (*polite* and *blunt*), however, the differences were less pronounced. Why? Asch concluded that *warm* and *cold* are **central traits**, meaning that they imply the presence of certain other traits and exert a powerful influence on final impressions. Other researchers have observed similar effects (Stapel & Koomen, 2000). In fact, the impact of central traits is not limited to studies using trait lists. When college students in different classes were led to believe that a guest lecturer was a warm or a cold person, their impressions after the lecture were consistent with these beliefs—even though he gave the same lecture to everyone (Kelley, 1950; Widmeyer & Loy, 1988).

The Primacy Effect The order in which a trait is discovered can also influence its impact. It is often said that first impressions are critical, and social psychologists are quick to agree. Studies show that information often has greater impact when presented early in a sequence rather than late, a common phenomenon known as the **primacy effect**.

In another of Asch's (1946) classic experiments, one group of participants learned that a person was "intelligent, industrious, impulsive, critical, stubborn, and envious." A second group received exactly the same list but in reverse order. Rationally speaking, the two groups should have felt the same way about the person. But instead, participants who heard the first list in which the more positive traits came first formed more favourable impressions than did those who heard the second list. Similar findings were obtained among participants who watched a videotape of a woman taking an aptitude test. In all cases, she correctly answered 15 out of 30 multiple-choice questions. But participants who observed a pattern of initial success followed by failure perceived the woman as more intelligent than did those who observed the opposite pattern of failure followed by success (Jones et al., 1968). There are exceptions, but as a general rule, people tend to be more heavily influenced by the "early returns."

What accounts for this primacy effect? There are two basic explanations. The first is that once perceivers think they have formed an accurate impression of someone, they tend to pay less attention to subsequent information. Thus, when research participants read a series of statements about a person, the amount of time they spent reading the items declined steadily with each succeeding statement (Belmore, 1987). Does this mean we are doomed to a life of primacy? Not at all. If unstimulated, or tired, our attention may wane. But if perceivers are sufficiently motivated to avoid tuning out and are not pressured to form a quick first impression, then primacy effects are diminished (Anderson & Hubert, 1963; Kruglanski & Freund, 1983). Thus, in one study, students "leaped to conclusions" about a target person on the basis of preliminary information when they were mentally fatigued from having just taken a two-hour exam—but not when they were fresh, alert, and motivated to pay attention (Webster et al., 1996). In addition, Arie Kruglanski and Donna Webster (1996) have found that some people are more likely than others to "seize" upon and "freeze" their first impressions. Indeed, they find that individuals differ in their **need for closure**, the desire to reduce ambiguity. People who are low in this regard are open-minded, deliberate, and perhaps even reluctant to draw firm conclusions about others. In contrast, those who are high in the need for closure tend to be impulsive and impatient and to form quick and lasting judgments of others.

More unsettling is the second reason for primacy, known as the *change-of-meaning hypothesis*. Once people have formed an impression, they start to interpret inconsis-

central traits Traits that exert a powerful influence on overall impressions.

primacy effect The tendency for information presented early in a sequence to have more impact on impressions than information presented later.

need for closure A desire to reduce cognitive uncertainty, which heightens the importance of first impressions.

tent information in light of that impression. Asch's research shows just how malleable the meaning of a trait can be. When people are told that a kind person is *calm*, they assume that he or she is gentle, peaceful, and serene. When a cruel person is said to be *calm*, however, the same word is interpreted to mean cool, shrewd, and calculating. There are many examples to illustrate the point. Based on your first impression, the word *proud* can mean self-respecting or conceited, *critical* can mean astute or picky, and *impulsive* can mean spontaneous or reckless.

It is remarkable just how creative we are in our efforts to transform a bundle of contradictions into a coherent, integrated impression. For example, the person who is said to be "good" but also "a thief" can be viewed as a Robin Hood type of character (Burnstein & Schul, 1982). Asch and Henri Zukier (1984) presented people with inconsistent trait pairs and found that they used different strategies to reconcile the conflicts. For example, a brilliant-foolish person may be seen as "very bright on abstract matters, but silly about day-to-day practical tasks," a sociable-lonely person has "many superficial ties but is unable to form deep relations," and a cheerful-gloomy person may simply be someone who is "moody."

Confirmation Biases: From Impressions to Reality

"Please your majesty," said the knave, "I didn't write it and they can't prove I did; there's no name signed at the end." "If you didn't sign it," said the King, "that only makes the matter worse. You must have meant some mischief, or else you'd have signed your name like an honest man."

This exchange, taken from Lewis Carroll's *Alice's Adventures in Wonderland*, illustrates the power of existing impressions. It is striking but often true: Once people make up their minds about something—even if they have incomplete information—they become more and more unlikely to change their minds when confronted with new evidence. Political leaders thus refuse to withdraw their support for government programs that don't work, and scientists stubbornly defend their theories in the face of conflicting research data. These instances are easy to explain. Politicians and scientists have personal investments in their opinions, for pride, funding, and reputation may be at stake. But what about people who more innocently fail to revise their opinions, often to their own detriment? What about the baseball manager who clings to old strategies that are ineffective or the trial lawyer who always selects juries according to false stereotypes? Why are they often so slow to face the facts? As we will see, people are subject to various **confirmation biases**—tendencies to interpret, seek, and create information in ways that verify existing beliefs.

"It is a capital mistake to theorize before you have all the evidence. It biases the judgment."

—Arthur Conan Doyle

Perseverance of Beliefs

Imagine you are looking at a slide that is completely out of focus. Gradually, it becomes focused enough so that the image is less blurry. At this point, the experimenter wants to know if you can recognize the picture. The response you're likely to make is interesting. Participants in experiments of this type have more trouble making an identification if they watch the gradual focusing procedure than if they simply view the final, blurry image. In the mechanics of the perceptual process, people apparently form early impressions that interfere with their subsequent

confirmation bias The tendency to seek, interpret, and create information that verifies existing beliefs.

ability to "see straight" once presented with improved evidence (Bruner & Potter, 1964). As we will see in this section, social perception is subject to the same kind of interference, which is another reason why first impressions often stick like glue even after we are forced to confront information that discredits them.

Consider what happens when you're led to expect something that does not materialize. In one study, John Darley and Paget Gross (1983) asked participants to evaluate the academic potential of a nine-year-old girl named Hannah. One group was led to believe that Hannah came from an affluent community in which both parents were well-educated professionals (high expectations). A second group thought that she was from a run-down urban neighbourhood and that both parents were uneducated blue-collar workers (low expectations). As shown in Figure 4.10, participants in the first group were slightly more optimistic in their ratings of Hannah's potential than were those in the second group. In each of these groups, however, half the participants then watched a videotape of Hannah taking an achievement test. Her performance on the tape seemed average. She correctly answered some difficult questions but missed others that were relatively easy. Look again at Figure 4.10 and you'll see that even though all participants saw the same tape, Hannah now received much lower ratings of ability from those who thought she was poor and higher ratings from those who thought she was affluent. Apparently, presenting an identical body of mixed evidence did not extinguish the biasing effects of beliefs—it *fuelled* these effects.

Events that are ambiguous enough to support contrasting interpretations are like inkblots: We see in them what we want or expect to see. Illustrating this point, researchers had people rate from photographs the extent to which pairs of adults and children resembled each other. Interestingly, the participants did not see more resemblance in parents and offspring than in random pairs of adults and children. Yet when told that certain pairs were related, they did "see" a resemblance, even when the relatedness information was false (Bressan & Dal Martello, 2002).

What about information that plainly disconfirms our beliefs? What then happens to our first impressions? Craig Anderson and his colleagues (1980) addressed this question by supplying participants with false information. After they had time to think about the information, they were told that it was untrue. In one experiment, half the participants read case studies suggesting that people who take risks make better firefighters than do those who are cautious. The others read cases suggesting the opposite conclusion. Next, participants were asked to come up with a theory for the suggested correlation. The possibilities are easy to imagine: "He who hesitates is lost" supports risk-taking, whereas "You have to look before you leap" supports caution. Finally, participants were led to believe that the session was over and were told that the information they had received was false, manufactured for the sake of the experiment. Participants, however, did not abandon their firefighter theories. Instead they exhibited **belief perseverance**, sticking to initial beliefs even after these had been discredited. Apparently, it's easier to get people to build a theory than to convince them to tear it down. Thus, five full months after the terrorist attack on the World Trade Center in New York City, the Gallup Organization interviewed some 10 000 residents of nine Muslim countries and found that 61 percent did *not* believe—as virtually all westerners did—that the attacks were carried out by Arab men (Gallup Organization, 2002).

People are slow to change their first impressions on the basis of new information. **True.**

Why do beliefs often outlive the evidence on which they are supposed to be based? The reason is that when people conjure up explanations that make sense, those explanations take on a life of their own. In fact, once people form an opinion, that opinion becomes strengthened when they merely *think* about the topic, even if they do not articulate the reasons for it (Tesser, 1978). And therein lies a possible solution. By asking people to consider why an *alternative* theory might be true, we can reduce or eliminate the belief perseverance effects to which they are vulnerable (Anderson & Sechler, 1986).

belief perseverance The tendency to maintain beliefs even after they have been discredited.

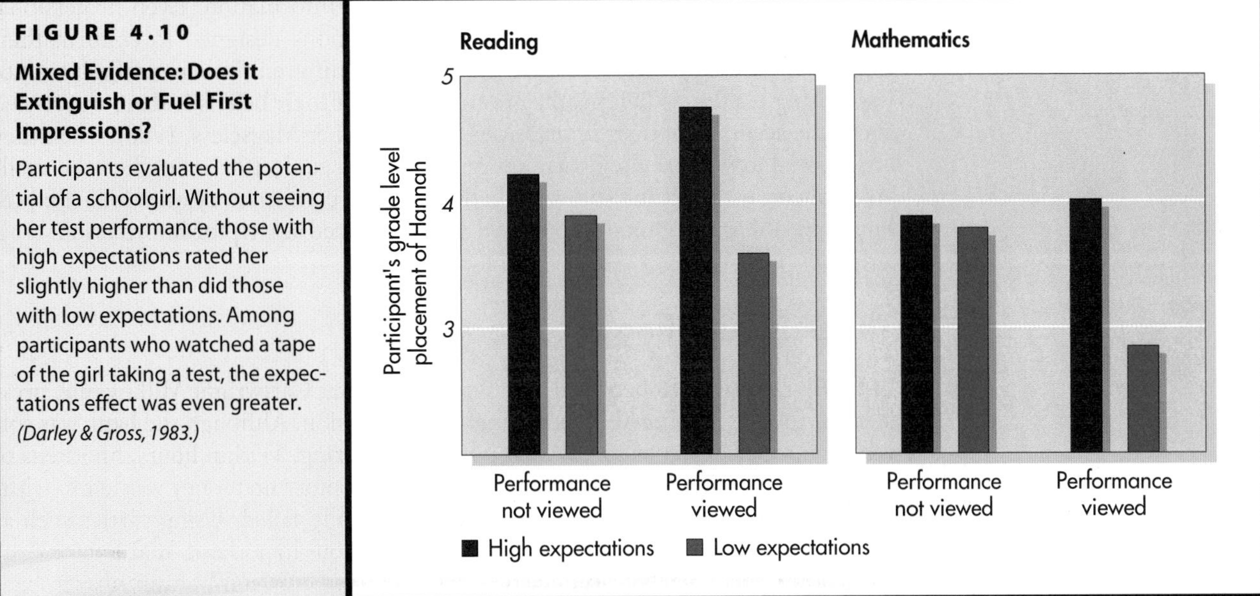

FIGURE 4.10

Mixed Evidence: Does it Extinguish or Fuel First Impressions?

Participants evaluated the potential of a schoolgirl. Without seeing her test performance, those with high expectations rated her slightly higher than did those with low expectations. Among participants who watched a tape of the girl taking a test, the expectations effect was even greater. *(Darley & Gross, 1983.)*

Confirmatory Hypothesis Testing

Social perceivers are not passive recipients of information. Like detectives, we ask questions and actively search for clues. But do we seek information objectively, or are we inclined to confirm the suspicions we already hold?

Mark Snyder and William Swann (1978) addressed this question by having pairs of participants who were strangers to one another take part in a getting-acquainted interview. In each pair, one participant was to interview the other. But first, that participant was falsely led to believe that his or her partner was either introverted or extroverted (actually, the participants were assigned on a random basis to these conditions) and was then told to select questions from a prepared list. Those who thought they were talking to an introvert chose mostly introvert-oriented questions ("Have you ever felt left out of some social group?"), while those who thought they were talking to an extrovert asked extrovert-oriented questions ("How do you liven up a party?"). Expecting a certain kind of person, participants unwittingly sought evidence that confirmed their expectations. By asking loaded questions, in fact, the interviewers actually gathered support for their beliefs. Thus, neutral observers who later listened to the tapes were also left with the mistaken impression that the interviewees really were as introverted or extroverted as the interviewers had assumed.

This last part of the study is powerful but, in hindsight, not all that surprising. Imagine yourself on the receiving end of an interview. Asked about what you do to liven up parties, you would probably talk about organizing group games, playing dance music, and telling jokes. On the other hand, if you were asked about difficult social situations, you might talk about being nervous before oral presentations or about what it feels like to be the new kid on the block. In other words, simply by going along with the questions that are asked, you supply evidence confirming the interviewer's beliefs. Thus, perceivers set in motion a vicious cycle: Thinking someone has a certain trait, they engage in a one-sided search for information; and in doing so, they create a reality that ultimately supports their beliefs (Zuckerman et al., 1995).

Are people so blinded by their existing beliefs that they cannot manage an objective search for evidence? It depends. In the task devised by Snyder and Swann, people conduct a biased, confirmatory search for information. Even professional counsellors trained in psychotherapy select questions designed to confirm their own hypotheses (Haverkamp, 1993). Thankfully, different circumstances produce less biasing results. When people are not certain of their beliefs and are concerned about the accuracy of their impressions (Kruglanski & Mayseless, 1988), when they are allowed to prepare their own interviews (Trope et al., 1984), or when the available nonconfirmatory questions are better than the confirmatory questions (Skov & Sherman, 1986), they tend to pursue a more balanced search for information.

The Self-Fulfilling Prophecy

In 1948, sociologist Robert Merton told a story about Cartwright Millingville, president of the Last National Bank during the Depression. Although the bank was solvent, a rumour began to spread that it was floundering. Within hours, hundreds of depositors were lined up to withdraw their savings before no money was left to withdraw. The rumour was false, but the bank eventually failed. Using stories such as this, Merton proposed what seemed like an outrageous hypothesis: that a perceiver's expectation can actually lead to its own fulfillment, a **self-fulfilling prophecy**.

Merton's hypothesis lay dormant within psychology until Robert Rosenthal and Lenore Jacobson (1968) published the results of a study entitled *Pygmalion in the Classroom*. Noticing that teachers had higher expectations for better students, they wondered if teacher expectations *influenced* student performance rather than the other way around. To address the question, they told teachers in a San Francisco elementary school that certain pupils were on the verge of an intellectual growth spurt. The results of an IQ test were cited but, in fact, the pupils had been randomly selected. Then eight months later, when real tests were administered, the "late bloomers" exhibited an increase in their IQ scores compared with children assigned to a control group. They were also evaluated more favourably by their classroom teachers.

When the Pygmalion study was first published, it was greeted with chagrin. If positive teacher expectations can boost student performance, can negative expectations have the opposite effect? And what about the social implications? Could it be that affluent children are destined for success and disadvantaged children are doomed to failure because educators hold different expectations for them? Many researchers were critical of the study itself and skeptical about the generality of the results. Unfortunately, though, these findings cannot be swept under the proverbial rug. In a review of additional studies, Rosenthal (1985) found that teacher expectations significantly predicted student performance 36 percent of the time. Mercifully, the predictive value of teacher expectancies seems to wear off, not accumulate, as children graduate from one grade to the next (Smith et al., 1999).

How might teacher expectations be transformed into reality? There are two points of view. According to Rosenthal (2002), the process involves covert communication. The teacher forms an initial impression of students early in the school year—based, perhaps, on their background or reputation, physical appearance, initial classroom performance, and standardized-test scores. The teacher then alters his or her behaviour in ways that are consistent with that impression. If initial expectations are high rather than low, the teacher gives the student more praise, attention, challenging homework, and better feedback. In turn, the student adjusts his or her own behaviour. If the signals are positive, the student may become energized, work hard, and succeed. If negative, there may be a loss of interest and self-confidence. The cycle is thus complete and the expectations confirmed.

While recognizing that this effect can occur, Lee Jussim and others (1996) question whether teachers in real life are so prone in the first place to form erro-

self-fulfilling prophecy
The process by which one's expectations about a person eventually lead that person to behave in ways that confirm those expectations.

neous impressions of their students. It's true, in many naturalistic studies, that the expectations teachers have at the start of a school year are later confirmed by their students—a result that is consistent with the notion that the teachers had a hand in producing that outcome. But wait. That same result is also consistent with a more innocent possibility: that perhaps the expectations that teachers form of their students are *accurate*. There are times, Jussim admits, when teachers may stereotype a student and, without realizing it, behave in ways that create a self-fulfilling prophecy. But there are also times when teachers can predict how their students will perform without necessarily influencing that performance (Alvidrez & Weinstein, 1999). Addressing this question in a longitudinal study of mothers and their children, Stephanie Madon and others (2003) found that underage adolescents are more likely to drink when their mothers had expected them to. Statistical analyses revealed that this prophecy was fulfilled in part because the mothers *influenced* their sons and daughters, as Rosenthal's work would suggest, and in part because the mothers were *accurate* in their predictions, as Jussim's model would suggest.

Either way, it's clear that self-fulfilling prophecies are at work in many settings—not only schools but also a wide range of organizations, including the military (Kierein & Gold, 2000; McNatt, 2000). In a study of 1000 men assigned to 29 platoons in the Israeli Defense Forces, Dov Eden (1990) led some platoon leaders but not others to expect that the groups of trainees they were about to receive had great potential (in fact, these groups were of average ability). After ten weeks, the trainees assigned to the high-expectation platoons scored higher than the others on written exams and on the ability to operate a weapon. The process may also be found in the criminal justice system, where police interrogate suspects. In one study, Kassin and others (2003) had some college students but not others commit a mock crime, stealing $100 from a laboratory. All suspects were then questioned by student interrogators who were led to believe that their suspect was probably guilty or innocent. Interrogators who presumed guilt asked more incriminating questions, conducted more coercive interrogations, and tried harder to get the suspect to confess. In turn, this more aggressive style made the suspects sound defensive and led observers who later listened to the tapes to judge them guilty, even when they were innocent. Still other self-fulfilling prophecy studies have shown that judges unwittingly bias juries (Hart, 1995) and that negotiators settle for lesser outcomes if they believe that their counterparts are highly competitive (Diekmann et al., 2003).

The self-fulfilling prophecy is a powerful phenomenon (Darley & Fazio, 1980; Harris & Rosenthal, 1985; Rosenthal, 2002). But how does it work? How do social perceivers transform their own expectations of others into reality? Research indicates that the phenomenon occurs as a three-step process. First, a perceiver forms an impression of a target person—an impression that may be based on interactions with the target or on other information. Second, the perceiver behaves in a manner that is consistent with that first impression. Third, the target person unwittingly adjusts his or her behaviour to the perceiver's actions. The net result: behavioural confirmation of the first impression (see Figure 4.11).

But now let's straighten out this picture. It would be a sad commentary on human nature if each of us were so easily moulded by others' perceptions into appearing brilliant or stupid, introverted or extroverted, competitive or cooperative, warm or cold. The effects are well established, but there are limits. By viewing the self-fulfilling prophecy as a three-step process, social psychologists can identify the links in the chain that can be broken to prevent the vicious cycle.

Consider the first step, the link between one's expectations and one's behaviour toward the target person. In the typical study, perceivers try to get to know the target on only a casual basis and are not necessarily driven to form an accurate impression. But when perceivers are highly motivated to seek the truth (as when they are considering the target as a possible teammate or opponent), they become more

FIGURE 4.11

The Self-Fulfilling Prophecy as a Three-Step Process

How do people transform expectations into reality? (1) A perceiver has expectations of a target person; (2) The perceiver then behaves in a manner consistent with those expectations; (3) The target unwittingly adjusts his or her behaviour according to the perceiver's actions.

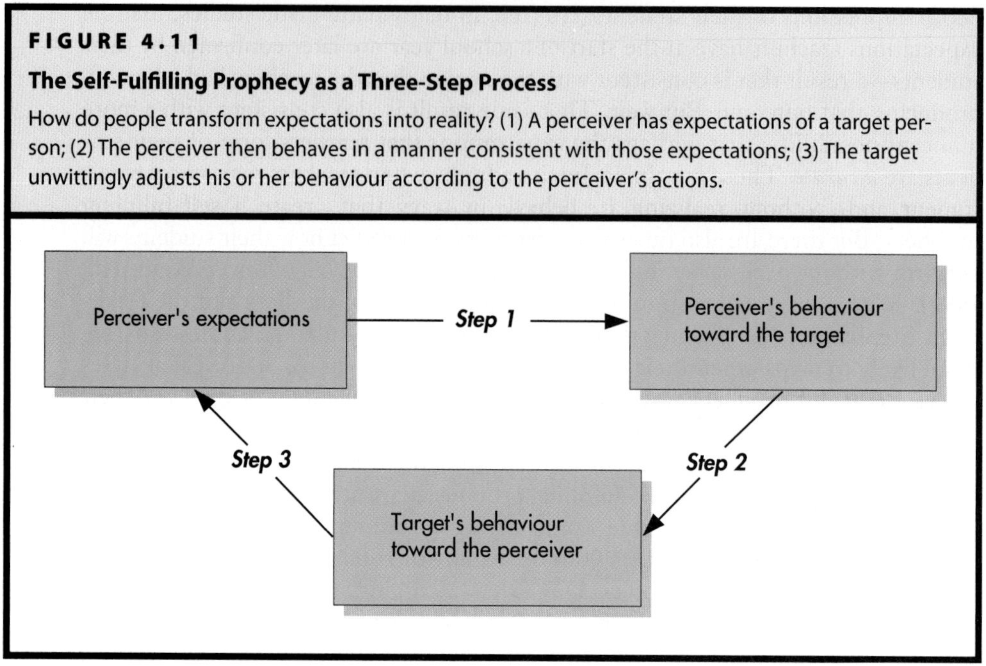

objective—and often do not confirm prior expectations (Harris & Perkins, 1995; Hilton & Darley, 1991).

The link between expectations and behaviour depends in other ways on a perceiver's goals and motivations in the interaction (Snyder & Stukas, 1999). In one study, John Copeland (1994) put either the perceiver or the target into a position of relative power. In all cases, the perceiver interacted with a target who was said to be introverted or extroverted. In half the pairs, the perceiver was given the power to accept or reject the target as a teammate for a money-winning game. In the other half, it was the target who was empowered to choose a teammate. The two participants interacted, the interaction was recorded, and neutral observers listened to the tapes and rated the target person. So, did perceivers cause the targets to behave as introverted or extroverted, depending on initial expectations? Yes and no. Illustrating what Copeland called "prophecies of power," the results showed that high-power perceivers triggered the self-fulfilling prophecy, as in past research, but that low-power perceivers did not. In the low-power situation, the perceivers spent less time getting to know the target person and more time trying to be liked.

Now consider the second step, the link between a perceiver's behaviour and the target's response. In much of the past research, as in much of life, target persons are not aware of the false impressions held by others. Thus, it is unlikely that Rosenthal and Jacobson's (1968) "late bloomers" knew of their teachers' high expectations or that Snyder and Swann's (1978) "introverts" and "extroverts" knew of their interviewers' misconceptions. But what if they had known? How would *you* react if you found yourself being cast in a particular light? When it happened to participants in one experiment, they managed to overcome the effect by behaving in ways that forced the perceivers to abandon their expectations (Hilton & Darley, 1985).

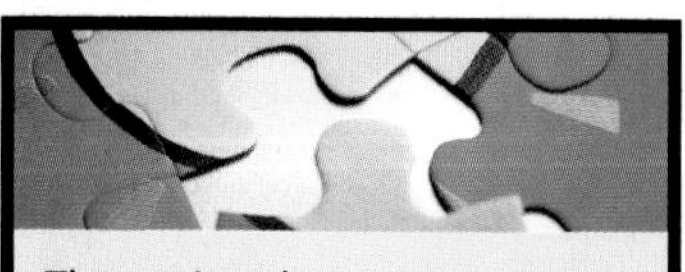

The notion that we can create a "self-fulfilling prophecy" by getting others to behave in ways we expect is a myth. **False.**

As you may recall from the discussion of self-verification in Chapter 3, this result is most likely to occur when perceiver expectations clash with a target person's self-concept. When targets who viewed themselves as extroverted were interviewed by perceivers who believed they were introverted (and vice versa), what changed as a result of the interaction were the perceivers' beliefs, not the targets' behaviour (Swann & Ely, 1984). Social perception is a two-way street—and the persons we judge have their own prophecies to fulfill.

Social Perception: The Bottom Line

Trying to understand people—whether they are professional athletes, business leaders, trial lawyers, or loved ones closer to home—is no easy task. As you reflect on the material in this chapter, you will notice that there are two radically different views of social perception. One suggests that the process is quick and relatively automatic. Without much thought, effort, or awareness, people make rapid-fire snap judgments about others based on physical appearance, preconceptions, or just a hint of behavioural evidence. According to a second view, however, the process is relatively mindful. People observe others carefully and reserve judgment until their analysis of the target person, behaviour, and situation is complete. As suggested by theories of attribution and information integration, the process is eminently logical. In light of recent research, it is now safe to conclude that both accounts of social perception are correct. Sometimes, our judgments are made instantly; at other times, they are based on a more painstaking analysis of behaviour. Either way, we often steer our interactions with others along a path that is narrowed by first impressions, a process that can set in motion a self-fulfilling prophecy. The various aspects of social perception, as described in this chapter, are summarized in Figure 4.12.

At this point, we must confront an important question: How *accurate* are people's impressions of each other? For years, this question has proved provocative but hard to answer (Cronbach, 1955; Kenny, 1994). Granted, people often depart from the ideals of logic and exhibit bias in their social perceptions. In this chapter alone, we have seen that perceivers typically focus on the wrong cues to

FIGURE 4.12

The Processes of Social Perception

Summarizing Chapter 4, this diagram depicts the processes of social perception. As shown, it begins with the observation of persons, situations, and behaviour. Sometimes, we make snap judgments from these cues. At other times, we form impressions only after making attributions and integrating these attributions. Either way, our impressions are subject to confirmation biases and the risk of a self-fulfilling prophecy.

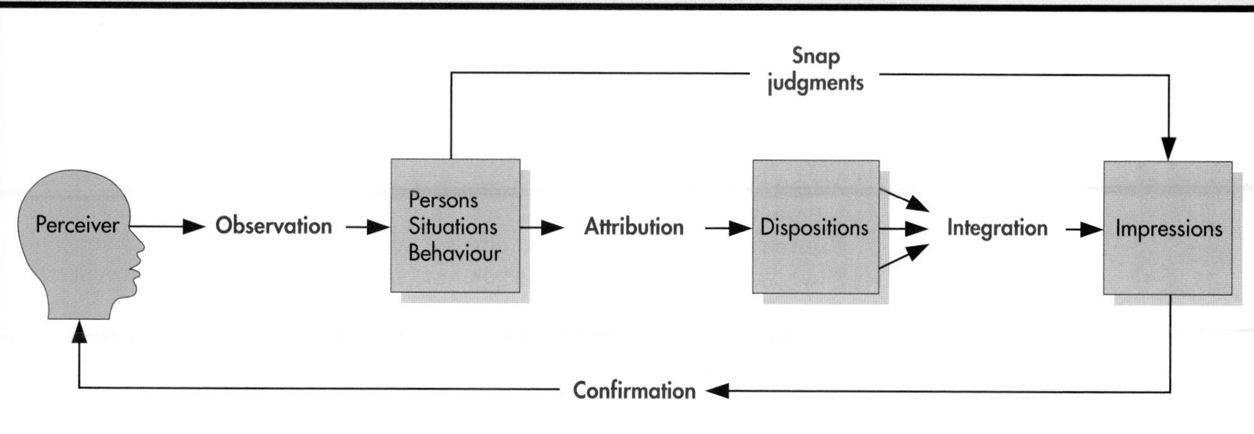

determine if someone is lying; use cognitive heuristics without regard for numerical base rates; overlook the situational influences on behaviour; disparage victims whose misfortunes threaten their sense of justice; form premature first impressions; and interpret, seek, and create evidence in ways that support these impressions.

To make matters worse, we often have little awareness of our limitations, leading us to feel *overconfident* in our judgments. In a series of studies, David Dunning and his colleagues (1990) asked students to predict how a target person would react in various situations. Some made predictions about a fellow student whom they had just met and interviewed, and others made predictions about their roommates. In both cases, participants reported their confidence in each prediction, and accuracy was determined by the responses of the target persons themselves. The results were clear: Regardless of whether they judged a stranger or a roommate, the students consistently overestimated the accuracy of their predictions. In fact, Kruger and Dunning (1999) found that people who scored low rather than high on tests of spelling, logic, grammar, and humour appreciation were later the most likely to overestimate their own performance. Apparently, poor performers are doubly cursed and don't know what they don't know (Dunning et al., 2003).

Standing back from the material presented in this chapter, you may find the list of shortcomings, punctuated by the problem of overconfidence, to be long and depressing. So, how can this list be reconciled with the triumphs of civilization? Or to put it another way, "If we're so dumb, how come we made it to the moon?" (Nisbett & Ross, 1980, p. 249).

A number of years ago, Herbert Simon (1956) coined the term *satisficing* (by combining *satisfying* and *sufficing*) to describe the way people make judgments that, while not logically perfect, are good enough. Today, many psychologists believe that people operate by a principle of "bounded rationality"—that we are rational *within bounds* depending on our abilities, motives, available time, and other factors. In a book entitled *Simple Heuristics That Make Us Smart*, Gerd Gigerenzer and others (1999) noted that people seldom compute intricate probabilities to make decisions; rather, they "reach into an adaptive toolbox filled with fast and frugal heuristics" (p. 5).

It is true that people fall prey to the biases identified by social psychologists and probably even to some that have not yet been noticed. It is also true that we often get fooled by con artists, misjudge our partners in marriage, and hire the wrong job applicants. As Thomas Gilovich (1991) points out, more North Americans believe in ESP than in evolution, and there are 20 times more astrologers in the world than astronomers. The problem is, these biases can have harmful consequences—giving rise, as we'll see in Chapter 5, to stereotypes, prejudice, and discrimination. Yet despite our imperfections, there are four reasons to be guardedly optimistic about our competence as social perceivers:

1. The more experience people have with each other, the more accurate they are. For example, although people have a limited ability to assess the personality of strangers they meet in the laboratory, they are generally better at judging their own friends and acquaintances (Kenny & Acitelli, 2001; Levesque, 1997; Malloy & Albright, 1990).
2. Although we are not good at making global judgments of others (that is, at knowing what people are like across a range of settings), we are able to make more circumscribed predictions of how others will behave in our own presence. You may well misjudge the personality of a roommate or co-worker, but to the extent that you can predict your roommate's actions at home or your coworker's actions on the job, the mistakes may not matter (Swann, 1984).
3. Social perception skills can be enhanced in people who are taught the rules of probability and logic (Kosonen & Winne, 1995; Nisbett et al., 1987). For example, graduate students in psychology—because they take courses in statistics—

tend to improve in their ability to reason about everyday social events (Lehman et al., 1988).

4. People can form more accurate impressions of others when motivated by a concern for accuracy and open-mindedness than when motivated by a need for immediacy, confirmation, and closure (Kruglanski & Webster, 1996). Many studies described in this chapter have shown that people exhibit less bias when there is an incentive for accuracy within the experiment (Kunda, 1990; Neuberg, 1989)—as when the perceiver judges a prospective teammate's ability to facilitate success in a future task (Fiske & Neuberg, 1990) or a future dating partner's *social* competence (Goodwin et al., 2002).

To summarize, research on the accuracy of social perceptions offers a valuable lesson: To the extent that we observe others with whom we have had time to interact, make judgments that are reasonably specific, have some knowledge of the rules of logic, and are sufficiently motivated to form an accurate impression, the problems that plague us can be minimized. Indeed, just being aware of the biases described in this chapter may well be a necessary first step toward a better understanding of others.

People are more accurate at judging the personality of friends and acquaintances than of strangers. **True.**

Review

Observation: The Elements of Social Perception

- To understand others, social perceivers rely on indirect clues—the elements of social perception.

Persons: Judging a Book by Its Cover

- People often make snap judgments of others based on physical appearances (for example, adults with baby-faced features are seen as having childlike qualities).

Situations: The Scripts of Life

- People have preconceptions, or "scripts," about certain types of situations. These scripts guide our interpretations of behaviour.

Behavioural Evidence

- People derive meaning from behaviour by dividing it into discrete, meaningful units.
- Nonverbal behaviours are often used to determine how others are feeling.
- From facial expressions, people all over the world can identify the emotions of happiness, fear, sadness, surprise, anger, and disgust.
- Body language, gaze, and touch are also important forms of nonverbal communication.
- People use nonverbal cues to detect deception but are often not accurate in making these judgments because they pay too much attention to the face and neglect cues that are more revealing.

Attribution: From Elements to Dispositions

- Attribution is the process by which we explain people's behaviour.

Attribution Theories

- People begin to understand others by making personal or situational attributions for their behaviour.
- Correspondent inference theory states that people learn about others from behaviour that is freely chosen, that is unexpected, and that results in a small number of desirable outcomes.
- From multiple behaviours, we base our attributions on three kinds of covariation information: consensus, distinctiveness, and consistency.

Attribution Biases

- People depart from the logic of attribution theory in two major ways.
- First, we use cognitive heuristics—rules of thumb that enable us to make judgments that are quick but often in error.
- Second, we tend to commit the fundamental attribution error, overestimating the role of personal factors and underestimating the impact of situations.

Attributions as Cultural Constructions

- Cultures differ in their implicit theories about the causes of human behaviour.
- Studies show, for example, that East Asians are more likely than Americans to consider the impact of the social and situational contexts of which they are a part.

Motivational Biases

- Our attributions for the behaviour of others are often biased by our own self-esteem motives.
- Needing to believe in a just world, people often criticize victims and blame them for their fate.

Integration: From Dispositions to Impressions

Information Integration: The Arithmetic

- The impressions we form are usually based on an averaging of a person's traits, not on a summation.
- According to information integration theory, impressions are based on perceiver predispositions and a weighted average of individual traits.

Deviations from the Arithmetic

- Perceivers differ in their sensitivity to certain traits and in the impressions they form.
- Differences stem from stable perceiver characteristics, priming from recent experiences, implicit personality theories, and the primacy effect.

Confirmation Biases: From Impressions to Reality

- Once an impression is formed, people become less likely to change their minds when confronted with nonsupportive evidence.
- People tend to interpret, seek, and create information in ways that confirm existing beliefs.

Perseverance of Beliefs

- First impressions may survive in the face of inconsistent information.
- Ambiguous evidence is interpreted in ways that bolster first impressions.
- The effect of evidence that is later discredited perseveres because people formulate theories to support their initial beliefs.

Confirmatory Hypothesis Testing

- Once perceivers have beliefs about someone, they seek further information in ways that confirm those beliefs.

The Self-Fulfilling Prophecy

- As shown by the effects of teacher expectancies on student achievement, first impressions set in motion a self-fulfilling prophecy.
- This is the product of a three-step process: (1) A perceiver forms an expectation of a target person, (2) the perceiver behaves accordingly, and (3) the target adjusts to the perceiver's actions.
- This self-fulfilling prophecy effect is powerful but limited in important ways.

Social Perception: The Bottom Line

- Sometimes, people make snap judgments; at other times, they evaluate others by carefully analyzing their behaviour.
- Research suggests that our judgments are often biased and that we are overconfident.
- Still, there are conditions under which we are more competent as social perceivers.

Key Terms

actor-observer effect *(107)*
attribution theory *(100)*
availability heuristic *(103)*
base-rate fallacy *(103)*
belief in a just world *(110)*
belief perseverance *(118)*
central traits *(116)*
confirmation bias *(117)*
counterfactual thinking *(104)*
covariation principle *(101)*
false-consensus effect *(103)*
fundamental attribution error *(105)*
implicit personality theory *(115)*
impression formation *(111)*
information integration theory *(112)*
need for closure *(116)*
nonverbal behaviour *(95)*
personal attribution *(100)*
primacy effect *(116)*
priming *(113)*
self-fulfilling prophecy *(120)*
situational attribution *(100)*
social perception *(92)*

The impressions we form of others are influenced by superficial aspects of their appearance.

True. *Research shows that first impressions are influenced by height, weight, clothing, facial characteristics, and other aspects of appearance.*

Adaptively, people are skilled at knowing when someone is lying rather than telling the truth.

False. *People frequently make mistakes in their judgments of truth and deception, too often accepting what others say at face value.*

Like social psychologists, people are sensitive to situational causes when explaining the behaviour of others.

False. *In explaining the behaviour of others, people overestimate the importance of personal factors and overlook the impact of situations—a bias known as the "fundamental attribution error."*

People are slow to change their first impressions on the basis of new information.

True. *Studies have shown that once people form an impression of someone, they become resistant to change even when faced with contradictory new evidence.*

The notion that we can create a "self-fulfilling prophecy" by getting others to behave in ways we expect is a myth.

False. *In the laboratory and in the classroom, a perceiver's expectation can actually lead to its own fulfillment.*

People are more accurate at judging the personality of friends and acquaintances than of strangers.

True. *People often form erroneous impressions of strangers but tend to be more accurate in their judgments of friends and acquaintances.*

5 Stereotypes, Prejudice, and Discrimination

PUTTING COMMON SENSE TO THE TEST

T / F

____ Very brief exposure to a member of a stereotyped group does not lead to biased judgments or responses, but longer exposure typically does.

____ Members of low-status, stereotyped groups have lower self-esteem than members of high-status groups.

____ Even brief exposure to sexist television commercials can significantly influence the behaviours of men and women.

____ A black student is likely to perform worse on an athletic task if the task is described as one reflecting sports intelligence than if it is described as reflecting natural athletic ability.

____ Groups with a history of prejudice toward each other tend to become much less prejudiced soon after they are made to interact with each other in a desegregated setting.

PREVIEW

THIS CHAPTER considers how people think, feel, and behave toward members of social groups. We begin by examining stereotypes, beliefs about groups that influence our judgments of individuals. Next, we examine prejudice, negative feelings toward others based on their group membership. To illustrate these problems, we then focus on sexism and racism, forms of discrimination based on a person's gender and racial background. After considering some of the effects of being the targets of these biases, we discuss some ways to reduce stereotypes, prejudice, and discrimination today and in the future.

> "Police receive training to make them more sensitive to weapons, but they don't get training to undo unconscious race stereotypes or biases."
>
> —Anthony Greenwald

On September 6, 1995, at Ipperwash Provincial Park in Ontario, Anthony "Dudley" George was shot and killed by an Ontario Provincial Police (OPP) Officer. George was one of many aboriginal protesters involved in a land dispute; protestors had occupied the land to protect an ancient burial ground located in the park. A day earlier, two OPP officers posing as a television camera crew had carried on a conversation that included racial slurs and comments directed at the protestors; this conversation was recorded on an audiotape, which surfaced after the incident, but was not immediately released to the public. On this tape, one OPP officer suggests setting a trap for the protesters using cases of beer as the bait; someone on the tape then notes that this "works in the South with watermelons" in reference to "baiting" black Americans. The following day, George—who was unarmed—was shot and killed by another OPP officer several metres away. George was carrying a stick, yet the officer who shot him claimed he had seen a muzzle flash and believed that George was carrying a rifle. While the OPP Association did apologize for the comments made by their officers (and the officer was charged with and found guilty of criminal negligence causing death), the case did highlight the fact that racism is still alive and well today. Although the officer was convicted, he was given a two-year suspended sentence and ordered to do community service. Did racism play a role in the death of Dudley George? Or did the officer truly believe that he and other officers were in danger from a gun he believed George was brandishing? Such cases raise the critical question of whether the officer's perception of a gun rather than a stick involved his "eyes" or his "heart." The implied question was whether stereotypes associated with the Aboriginal protesters made the officer more likely to misperceive the stick as a gun. Although we can never know for sure, there is ample research discussed in the present chapter that makes it clear such an effect is possible. Perception of others is profoundly influenced by the act of perceiving them as a member of a group.

Race is but one kind of group membership that can influence perceivers' thoughts, feelings, and actions. Others include gender, sexual orientation, age, physical

The death of Dudley George raises serious issues about racism and prejudice in Canada. Did negative stereotypes about the Aboriginal protesters lead an OPP officer to misperceive a stick that George was carrying as a gun?

appearance, and economic class. Indeed, stereotypes, prejudice, and discrimination are problems worldwide. Watch the news and you might see stories about genocide in Sudan, "ethnic cleansing" in Bosnia, neo-Nazi violence in Germany and France, and hate crimes against gay men in the North America. And for every bit of violence, there are countless other, more subtle ways in which people hurt others as a result of viewing them through the lenses of group identity.

For the purposes of this chapter, a **group** is defined as two or more people perceived as having at least one of the following characteristics: (1) direct interactions with each other over a period of time; (2) joint membership in a social category based on sex, race, or other attributes; (3) a shared, common fate, identity, or set of goals. We see people in fundamentally different ways if we consider them to constitute a group rather than simply an aggregate of individuals. How does this happen, and why? How are people's thoughts, feelings, and behaviours affected? Examining these questions is the focus of this chapter.

The chapter is divided into five parts. First, we consider the causes and effects of **stereotypes**—beliefs that associate a whole group of people with certain traits. Second, we examine **prejudice**, which consists of negative feelings about others because of their connection to a social group. To put these problems in concrete terms, we then focus specifically on sexism and racism, two historically common forms of **discrimination**—negative behaviours directed against persons because of their membership in a particular group. Next, we shift the focus from the perceivers to the perceived: What are some of the ways in which people are affected by being the targets of stereotypes, prejudice, and discrimination? The chapter concludes with a discussion of some ways in which stereotypes, prejudice, and discrimination can be reduced. For the most part, the chapter discusses stereotypes and prejudice separately. Note, however, that our beliefs and feelings influence each other, that both give rise to discrimination, and that discriminatory behaviour, in turn, fuels stereotypes and prejudices (see Figure 5.1).

group Two or more persons perceived as related because of their interactions with each other over time, membership in the same social category, or common fate.

stereotype A belief that associates a group of people with certain traits.

prejudice Negative feelings toward persons based on their membership in certain groups.

discrimination Negative behaviour directed against persons because of their membership in a particular group.

FIGURE 5.1

Perceiving Groups: Three Reactions

There are two paths to discrimination: one based on stereotypes, the other on prejudice. Note also that there are other links among these variables. Discriminatory practices may support stereotypes and prejudice; stereotypes may cause people to become prejudiced; and prejudiced people may use stereotypes to justify their feelings.

Discrimination

Stereotypes

Prejudice

Stereotypes

When you stop to think about it, the list of well-known stereotypes seems endless. Consider some examples: The Japanese are sneaky, athletes are brainless, librarians are quiet, Italians are emotional, accountants are dull, Canadians are polite, white men can't jump, and used-car salespeople can't be trusted as far as you can throw them. Stereotypes are so universal and frequently experienced that they seem almost an essential part of the human condition. For this reason, it may be difficult to consider where they come from and why they are so difficult to extinguish. But to understand stereotypes, it is critical to trace their roots. In this section, we focus on a variety of factors that give rise to, and help maintain, stereotypes.

How Stereotypes Form

The origins of stereotypes can be traced to a number of sources. From a historical perspective, stereotypes spring from past events. Thus, it can be argued that slavery in America gave rise to the portrayal of Blacks as inferior, just as Japanese kamikaze attacks during World War II fostered a belief that the Japanese cannot be trusted. From a political perspective, stereotypes are viewed as a means by which groups in power come to rationalize war, religious intolerance, and economic oppression. And from a sociocultural perspective, it has been argued that real differences between social groups contribute to perceived differences. Each of these perspectives has something unique to offer. Social psychologists, however, also pose an additional question: Regardless of how stereotypes are born within a culture, how do they grow and operate in the minds of individuals?

The formation of stereotypes involves two related processes. The first is *categorization*, in which we sort people into groups. The second is a process by which we perceive groups to which we belong *(ingroups)* as being different from groups to which we do not belong *(outgroups)*. These two processes reflect basic cognitive operations and are influenced by sociocultural and motivational factors, as well as by differences in individuals' theories about groups.

Social Categorization As perceivers, we routinely sort single objects into groups rather than think of each as unique. Biologists classify animals into species; archaeologists divide time into eras; geographers split the earth into regions. Likewise, people sort each other into groups on the basis of gender, race, and other common attributes in a process called **social categorization**. In some ways, social categorization is natural and adaptive. By grouping people the way we group foods, animals, and other objects, we form impressions quickly and use past experience to guide new interactions. With so many things to pay attention to in our social worlds, we can save time and effort by using people's group memberships to make inferences about them (Bodenhausen et al., 2003; Sherman et al., 2004; Wigboldus et al., 2004).

There is, however, a serious drawback to the time and energy saved through social categorization. Like lumping apples and oranges together because both are fruit, categorizing people leads us to overestimate the differences between groups and to underestimate the differences within groups (Ford & Tonander, 1998; Krueger et al., 1989; Spears, 2002; Stangor & Lange, 1994; Wyer et al., 2002). Aware of the social categories to which individuals belong, we can fail even to perceive information about these individuals that does not conform to our stereotypes about their groups (von Hippel et al., 1995). And we may come to believe that the distinctions between social categories are more rigid, even more biologically

social categorization The classification of persons into groups on the basis of common attributes.

rooted, than they are. Many people assume, for example, that there is a clear genetic basis for classifying people by race. The fact is, however, that how societies make distinctions between races can change dramatically as a function of historical contexts. For instance, it was fairly common for Americans in the early part of the twentieth century to consider Irish Americans as distinct from Whites, but today such thinking is quite rare. Moreover, biologists, anthropologists, and psychologists have noted that there is more genetic variation within races than between them (Eberhardt & Goff, 2004; Marks, 1995; Ore, 2000).

Ingroups Versus Outgroups The second process that promotes stereotyping follows directly from the first. Although grouping humans is much like grouping objects, there is a key difference. When it comes to social categorization, perceivers themselves are members or nonmembers of the categories they use. Groups that you identify with—your country, your religion, your political party, even your hometown sports team—are called **ingroups**, whereas groups other than your own are called **outgroups**. This strong tendency to carve the world into "us" and "them" has important consequences.

One consequence is that we exaggerate the differences between our ingroup and other outgroups. Ingroup members often care a great deal about preserving distinctions between their ingroup and outgroups (Castano et al., 2002). For example, many Quebecers (an example of an ingroup, when viewed as separate from the rest of Canada) have repeatedly argued for distinct society status including having French as their sole official language despite the fact that at the federal level, the rest of Canada (a potential outgroup) is officially both French and English. Indeed, Robert Kurzban and Mark Leary (2001) propose that this vigilance has evolutionary origins—that is, it was adaptive for humans to avoid contact with outsiders, who might have posed health or safety risks, and to work in groups that would compete with and possibly exploit other groups.

Another consequence is a phenomenon known as the **outgroup homogeneity effect**, whereby perceivers assume that there is a greater similarity among members of outgroups than among members of one's own group. In other words, there may be fine and subtle differences among "us," but "they" are all alike (Linville & Jones, 1980).

Research shows that outgroup homogeneity effects are common and evident around the world (Bartsch et al., 1997; Linville, 1998; Read & Urada, 2003; Vonk & van Knippenberg, 1995). Indeed, there are many real-life examples. Landed immigrants who arrive from China, Korea, Taiwan, and Vietnam see themselves as different, but to many western eyes they are all Asian. Business majors like to talk about engineering types; engineers talk about business types; liberals lump together all conservatives; and teenagers lump together all older people. To people outside the group, outgroup members can even seem to look alike—people are less accurate in distinguishing and recognizing faces of members of racial groups other than their own, especially to the extent that they are unfamiliar with these other groups (Pezdek et al., 2003; Slone et al., 2000; Wright et al., 2003).

There are two reasons for the tendency to perceive outgroups as homogeneous. First, we often do not notice subtle differences among outgroups because we have little personal contact with them. Think about your family or your favourite sports team, and specific individuals come to mind. Think about an unfamiliar outgroup, however, and you are likely to think in abstract terms about the group as a whole. Indeed, the more familiar people are with an outgroup, the less likely they are to perceive it as homogeneous. A second problem is that people often do not encounter a representative sample of outgroup members. A student from one school who encounters students from a rival school only when they cruise into town for a football game, screaming at the top of their lungs, sees only the most avid rival fans—hardly a diverse lot (Linville et al., 1989; Quattrone, 1986). It has even been

ingroups Groups with which an individual feels a sense of membership, belonging, and identity.

outgroups Groups with which an individual does not feel a sense of membership, belonging, or identity.

outgroup homogeneity effect The tendency to assume that there is greater similarity among members of outgroups than among members of ingroups.

suggested that people perceive their own group to be homogeneous when they first join it, but over time, as they become more familiar with fellow group members, they see their group as more diverse relative to outgroups (Ryan & Bogart, 1997).

Satirist Rick Mercer plays up ingroup and outgroup differences when he asks unsuspecting Americans unusual questions about Canada. For example, he has gotten some Americans to agree that the capital building of Canada is an igloo and others to sign a petition asking the Canadian government to stop putting our elderly citizens on ice floes!

Sociocultural and Motivational Factors Social categorization and ingroup-outgroup distinctions reflect basic cognitive processes; they are, in part, by-products of how humans think and process information about their world. They are also influenced, however, by situational factors, such as the cultural context in which people live and the motivations that people have in particular settings. For example, there are numerous ways in which people can divide others into social categories. Why are some categorizations—such as race, gender, and sexual preference—more likely to dominate our perceptions than others? Why, and when, are people quicker to categorize a black male firefighter as black than as a man or as a firefighter? Cognitive factors can determine this; if perceivers have recently been primed to think about one of the categories, that category becomes more likely to dominate perceptions. But sociocultural and motivational factors can also play important roles (Dijksterhuis & van Knippenberg, 1996; Vescio et al., 1999; Zárate & Sanders, 1999).

Sociocultural factors include how various groups are portrayed by the media and how parents, peers, and schools promote particular ways of dividing people. If, for example, the media tend to portray people very differently as a function of race, or if parents warn their children about playing with children of other races, then race becomes a critically important way to divide up the world (Bar-Tal, 1996; Schaller, 2002). It is often said that people must be taught to hate. People learn stereotypes and prejudice through role models, group norms, and the culture at large (Castelli et al., 2003; Devine, 1989; Guimond, 2000; Pettigrew, 1958). Like hairstyles and musical preferences, individuals' racial prejudices are affected dramatically by those of their peers, family, and other social contacts. Merely overhearing a racial slur by a stranger can increase people's expressions of prejudice (Greenberg & Pyszczynski, 1985). One author of this textbook recalls a time when he was about eight years old and his two best friends suddenly called him a "Jew ball." They had never categorized him as Jewish before, and yet on this day, suddenly Jewishness was relevant—and negative to them. But why *then*, and how did they come up with "Jew ball"? Only much later did it become clear that they had misheard their father say "Jew boy." Trying to model their father's values, they used a version of this expression against their friend, and they would thereafter see him in a different way.

Cultures differ in what categorizations they emphasize and how they make ingroup-outgroup distinctions (Han & Park, 1995; Lee & Ottati, 1995; Meeres & Grant, 1999). For example, Darío Páez and others (1998) have noted that people from collectivistic cultures, which value group harmony, are more likely to perceive ingroup homogeneity than are people from individualistic cultures, which value the distinctiveness of the individual.

Motivational factors also affect how people categorize others. If your house is on fire, you are much more likely to categorize a black male firefighter as a firefighter than as black or male (Bodenhausen & Macrae, 1998). A white man who encounters a black doctor is more likely to categorize him according to his professional rather than racial identity if the white man is motivated to like and respect him (Sinclair & Kunda, 1999). And people in relatively powerful positions in society may be motivated to categorize others in ways that help them maintain the status quo and justify their feelings of superiority (Goodwin et al., 2000; Operario & Fiske, 2001; Ruscher et al., 2000). Motivational factors also influence perceptions of ingroups and outgroups. People who are motivated to protect or affirm their group identity—for example, when they feel that their group's status is under threat—become more likely to see their ingroup as relatively *homogeneous* (Brewer & Brown, 1998; Lorenzi-Cioldi et al., 1998; Pickett & Brewer, 2001).

Relations between groups, as well as their relative status and power in a society, influence the content of the stereotypes that form about them. If an outgroup is seen as threatening to an ingroup's status, its members are likely to be considered competent but hostile. If the outgroup is seen as relatively weak and somewhat dependent on the ingroup, on the other hand, its members may be believed to be warm but incompetent (Eckes, 2002; Fiske et al., 2002; Johannesen-Schmidt & Eagly, 2002).

Implicit Personality Theories About Groups Researchers develop theories about stereotypes, of course, but all of us are likely to develop ideas about how our social worlds work. Chapter 4 discussed *implicit personality theories*—networks of assumptions that people hold about the relationships among traits and behaviours. People also have implicit theories about social groups. For example, individuals may vary in the extent to which they think of social groups as relatively fixed, static entities or as dynamic and malleable (Levy et al., 2001). **Entity theorists** tend to see groups in terms of traits and to expect more similarity and consistency within groups. They may think of a group as having a core essence, and when they perceive and evaluate groups, they process information about them almost as they would about a single person. **Incremental theorists**, in contrast, expect less consistency within a social group, are less likely to see a group in trait terms or as having a core essence, and see the boundaries between groups as fuzzy and changeable.

These differences in implicit theories have numerous implications for stereotyping (Brewer et al., 2004; Hong et al., 2004; Leyens et al., 2004; McConnell, 2001; Yzerbyt & Rocher, 2002). Sheri Levy and her colleagues (1998), for example, found that although entity theorists and incremental theorists were equally aware of common stereotypes in their culture, entity theorists were more likely to believe that these stereotypes applied to the groups and that the stereotypic traits were fixed from birth. In addition, when given information about a new fictitious group, entity theorists more readily and rapidly judged the group in trait, and relatively extreme, terms. In short, they used stereotypes more. In research by Jennifer Eberhardt and others (2002), entity theorists perceived and remembered racially ambiguous faces as more consistent with racial labels than did incremental theorists.

Having a more static or dynamic view of groups is not only a matter of individual differences. Situational factors can make people more likely to adopt one or the other orientation. Matthew Crawford and others (2002), for example, manipulated the use of an entity or incremental approach by varying the information given to participants about different groups. When participants were induced to have a more entitative perspective, they were more likely to take information they learned about one group member and apply it to all group members. In addition, some groups just seem to most people to be more entitative than other groups. Brian Lickel and his colleagues (2000), for example, found that the most important factors in determining how much a group seemed like a fixed entity include whether the group members appear to interact with each other, share common goals and outcomes, and seem similar to each other.

entity theorists People who tend to see social groups as relatively fixed, static entities and the borders between groups as relatively clear and rigid.

incremental theorists People who tend to see social groups as relatively dynamic and changeable, with less consistency within groups and more malleability between groups.

Are Stereotypes Ever Accurate? So many stereotypes are so widespread that one may wonder if they are accurate. Of course, what is meant by "accurate" can be debated. "Accurate" in this context could mean that stereotypes reflect universal, stable, possibly genetic differences; or it could mean that stereotypes reflect differences that exist under particular sets of societal and historic conditions, with no presumption that the differences will persist if these conditions change. Most social psychologists focus on the latter meaning.

Like people, stereotypes are not all alike. Some are more accurate than others. And some researchers have argued that the field has overstated the inaccuracy of stereotypes (Madon et al., 1998). Although many stereotypes are based on completely illusory information or perceptions, some do stem from a kernel of truth, and still others may be fairly accurate. Even when they are based on reality, though, they tend to exaggerate differences and understate similarities between groups (e.g., Diekman et al., 2002; Krueger et al., 2003).

The extent to which individuals see groups as distinct entities can influence their perceptions of group members. For example, entity theorists are more likely than incremental theorists to see this group as similar to each other and distinct from outgroups, and to take information learned about one group member and apply it to all group members.

But the question of accuracy is more complicated than it may appear. As relations between groups change, their stereotypes can change along with them. Stereotyping is a dynamic process, making assessment of accuracy all the more challenging. Moreover, if you believe someone is rude, and you therefore react toward him or her in a cold way, the person might indeed act rudely back to you. Was your expectation of that person accurate? In a sense, it was—the person was rude to you, just as you expected. But clearly your own behaviour may have caused the rudeness. As we will see in the paragraphs to follow, there are a variety of ways in which people perceive others, explain their behaviour, and act toward them in ways that can reinforce stereotypes, often making stereotypes seem more accurate than they really are.

How Stereotypes Survive and Self-Perpetuate

Stereotypes offer us quick and convenient summaries of social groups. It is clear, however, that they often cause us to overlook the diversity within categories and to form mistaken impressions of specific individuals. Given their shortcomings, why do stereotypes endure? We turn now to some of the mechanisms that help perpetuate stereotypes.

"Not everybody's life is what they make it. Some people's life is what other people make it."

—Alice Walker

Illusory Correlations One way in which stereotypes endure is through the **illusory correlation**, a tendency for people to overestimate the link between variables that are only slightly or not at all correlated (Berndsen et al., 2002; Stroessner & Plaks, 2001). Illusory correlations result from two different processes. First, people tend to overestimate the association between variables that are *distinctive*—variables that capture attention simply because they are novel or deviant. To illustrate this, imagine observing 100 behaviours performed by people from group X and 20 behaviours performed by people from group Y (see Table 5.1). Within each group, most individuals behave positively, but a few behave negatively. In this situation, people from group Y are more distinctive than people from group X, because they are in the minority; and negative behaviours are more distinctive than positive behaviours, because they are in the minority. Despite the fact that group Y people are no more likely than group X people to behave negatively, observers tend to overestimate the association between the minority group and minority behaviours. Therefore, they perceive group Y people as more likely to behave poorly than group X people (Hamilton & Gifford, 1976). Even children in second grade may perceive these false associations (Johnston & Jacobs, 2003). The implications for stereotyping are important: Unless otherwise motivated, people overestimate the joint occurrence of distinctive variables such as minority groups and deviant acts.

illusory correlation An overestimate of the association between variables that are only slightly or not at all correlated.

Second, people tend to overestimate the association between variables that they

TABLE 5.1

The Illusory Correlation

Perceivers often overestimate the frequency with which distinctive variables co-occur, such as when minority group members (group Y) behave in a relatively rare, negative way. Although the proportion of group X members who behave negatively is the same as the proportion of group Y members who do, perceivers see group Y members as more likely to behave negatively.

Reality	Perception
100 Group X People	**100 Group X People**
75 positive behaviours (75%)	75 positive behaviours (75%)
25 negative behaviours (25%)	25 negative behaviours (25%)
20 Group Y People	**20 Group Y People**
15 positive behaviours (75%)	10 positive behaviours (50%)
5 negative behaviours (25%)	10 negative behaviours (50%)

already expect to go together. For example, in one study, participants were presented with lists of paired words, such as *lion-tiger*, *lion-eggs*, *bacon-tiger*, and *bacon-egg*. The participants tended to overestimate the frequency of pairings that had meaningful, expected associations (*lion-tiger*, *bacon-eggs*), even if such pairings actually occurred no more frequently than less expected pairings (*lion-eggs*, *bacon-tiger*) (Chapman, 1967). David Hamilton and Terrence Rose (1980) found that stereotypes can lead people to expect social groups and traits to fit together like bacon and eggs and to overestimate the frequency with which they've actually observed these associations. The implications for stereotyping are important here as well: People overestimate the joint occurrence of variables they expect to be associated with each other, such as stereotyped groups and stereotypic behaviours.

Attributions People also maintain their stereotypes through the attributions that they make about other people and their behaviours. Chapter 4 on Perceiving Persons discusses how perceivers attribute other people's behaviours to personal factors, such as their personalities and attitudes, and to situational factors, such as the circumstances in which the behaviours occurred. One important attributional bias discussed in that chapter is the fundamental attribution error, the tendency to focus on the role of personal causes and underestimate the impact of situations on other people's behaviours. This bias can help perpetuate stereotypes. We know, for example, that discrimination can impair the performance of stereotyped individuals; but because of the fundamental attribution error, perceivers may fail to take this effect into account when judging such individuals. In short, the perceivers may see confirmation of the stereotype rather than recognize the consequences of discrimination.

The fundamental attribution error represents a way in which perceivers fail to take into account situational influences. However, when perceivers' expectations about others are violated, they become much *more* likely to think about situational factors—in order to explain the surprising behaviour. Rather than accept a stereotype-disconfirming behaviour at face value, such as a woman defeating a man in an athletic contest, perceivers imagine the situational factors that might explain away this apparent exception to the rule, such as random luck, ulterior motives, or other special circumstances. By explaining the behaviour as caused by situational or circumstantial factors instead of personal traits and abilities, perceivers can more easily maintain their negative stereotypes of these groups (Hilton et al., 1993; Karpinski & von Hippel, 1996; Schnake & Ruscher, 1998; Sekaquaptewa et al., 2003; Wigboldus et al., 2004).

Subtyping and Contrast Effects Have you ever noticed that people often manage to hold negative views about a social group even when they like individual members of that group? One of the unnerving paradoxes of social perception is that stereotypes stubbornly survive one disconfirmation after the next. The question is, why? Gordon Allport (1954) recognized this phenomenon half a century ago. He wrote, "There is a common mental device that permits people to hold prejudgments even in the face of much contradictory evidence. It is the device of admitting exceptions. . . . By excluding a few favoured cases, the negative rubric is kept intact for all other cases" (p. 23). Confronted with a woman who does not seem particularly warm and nurturing, for example, people can either develop a more diversified image of females or toss the mismatch into a special subtype—say, "career women." To the extent that people create this subtype, their existing image of women in general will remain relatively intact (Hewstone & Lord, 1998; Weber & Crocker, 1983; Wilder et al., 1996). Similarly, Kunda & Oleson (1995) had students read about a lawyer described as "introverted," a term that generally does not conform to the more stereotypic view of lawyers as being extroverted. When this was the only information provided, participants were more likely to generalize this information and modify their beliefs about lawyers to include the possibility that they could indeed be introverted. However, some of the participants were given further information: that the lawyer either worked for a large, or a small, firm. While this would appear to be quite innocuous information, participants in these conditions were much more likely to subtype the lawyer; it is easier to make sense of an introverted lawyer either "blending in" to a large firm and avoiding social contact, or seeking out a small firm where social interaction is less likely to occur than it is to change one's stereotypic views.

Women who play rough contact sports—such as these members of the Olympic gold medal-winning Canadian women's hockey team—defy gender stereotypes. But rather than change their gender stereotypes, many perceivers subtype these women and dismiss them as exceptions.

Indeed, exceptions to the rule sometimes can be seen in particularly extreme ways. As a general rule, when something differs only slightly from expectations, the difference is barely noticed, if at all. But when it varies considerably from expectations, the perceived difference may be magnified, a biased perception known as the **contrast effect**. An ambitious, assertive businesswoman may be perceived as more extremely ambitious and assertive than a comparable man. Successful but demanding women are often portrayed in very extreme, super-aggressive ways for actions that they and others have argued would hardly be noticed if not for stereotypes about women.

Confirmation Biases and Self-Fulfilling Prophecies Imagine learning that a mother yelled at a 14-year-old girl, that a lawyer behaved aggressively, and that a Boy Scout grabbed the arm of an elderly woman crossing the street. Now imagine that a construction worker yelled at a 14-year-old girl, that an ex-con behaved aggressively, and that a skinhead grabbed the arm of an elderly woman crossing the street. Do very different images of these actions come to mind? This is a fundamental effect of stereotyping: Stereotypes of groups distort people's perceptions and interpretations of the behaviours of group members. Perceivers are likely to see members of stereotyped groups as more similar to the stereotype than they actually are. This is especially likely when a target of a stereotype behaves in an ambiguous way; perceivers reduce the ambiguity by interpreting the behaviour as consistent with the stereotype (Dunning & Sherman, 1997; Kunda et al., 1997). For example, in one study, black and white sixth-grade boys saw pictures and descriptions of ambiguously aggressive behaviours (such as one child bumping into another). Both the black and the white boys judged the behaviours as more mean and threatening if the behaviours were performed by black boys than white boys (Sagar & Schofield, 1980).

contrast effect A tendency to perceive stimuli that differ from expectations as being even more different than they really are.

Stereotypes' effect on perceptions of individuals is a type of confirmation bias, which, as we saw in Chapter 4, involves people's tendencies to interpret, seek, and

FIGURE 5.2

"White Men Can't Jump"?

Students listened to a basketball game and evaluated one particular player. Half of the students were led to believe that the player was black, the other half, that he was white. Consistent with their stereotypes, the students perceived the player as having more physical ability if they thought he was black and as having more "court smarts" if they thought he was white. *(Stone et al., 1997.)*

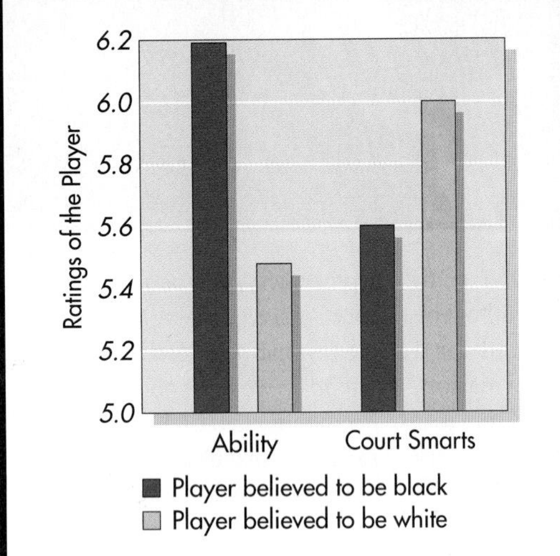

create information that seems to confirm their expectations. In a clever demonstration of this bias (specifically in the context of interpreting information), Jeff Stone and his colleagues (1997) had students listen to a college basketball game. Some were led to believe that a particular player was white; others thought he was black. After listening to the game, all of the students were asked to evaluate how the player had performed in the game. Consistent with racial stereotypes, those students who believed the player was black rated him as having played better and more athletically, whereas those who thought he was white rated him as having played with more intelligence and hustle (see Figure 5.2).

In addition to interpreting information in a biased manner, perceivers often seek information about stereotyped others in a way that prevents them from disconfirming the stereotype. For example, in a study by Yaacov Trope and Erik Thompson (1997), participants were requested to ask questions of another person in order to learn this person's attitudes. As it turns out, they asked fewer questions when led to believe that the other person was a member of a stereotyped group, and the questions they did ask were biased such that virtually all responses to them could be seen as consistent with the stereotype of that group.

Stereotypes are held not just by individuals but typically by many people within a culture, and stereotypes are often perpetuated through repeated communications. In a classic demonstration, Gordon Allport and Leo Postman (1947) showed participants a picture of a subway train filled with passengers. In the picture were a black man dressed in a suit and a white man holding a razor (see Figure 5.3). One participant viewed the scene briefly and then described it to a second participant who had not seen it. The second participant communicated the description to a third participant and so on, through six rounds of communication. The result: In more than half the sessions, the final participant's report indicated that the black man, not the white man, held the razor. Some participants even reported that he had waved it in a threatening manner. As Allport and Postman explained, "The distortion may occur even in participants who have no anti-Negro bias. It is an unthinking cultural stereotype that the Negro is hot tempered and addicted to the use of razors and weapons" (p. 63).

In a more recent experiment, Anthony Lyons and Yoshihisa Kashima (2001) had Australian students read a story about an Australian Rules football player. The students were put in groups of four. One person read the story, and after a delay of a few minutes transmitted the story to the next student, and so on down the four-person chain. The students were supposed to relay the story as accurately as possible. Some of the information in the story was consistent with stereotypes about Australian Rules football players (e.g., "On the way, Gary and his mate drank several beers in the car"), and some of it was inconsistent with the stereotype (e.g., "He switched on some classical music"). Although the first student in the chain was likely to communicate both stereotype-consistent and stereotype-inconsistent information, as the story went from person to person the stereotype-inconsistent information was progressively screened out. By the time the fourth person told the story, the football player seemed much more clearly stereotypical than he had seemed in the original story.

Confirmation biases are bad enough. But even more disturbing are situations in which stereotyped group members themselves are led to behave in stereotype-confirming ways. In other words, stereotypes can create self-fulfilling prophecies. As noted in Chapter 4, a self-fulfilling prophecy occurs when a perceiver's false expectations about a person cause the person to behave in ways that confirm those expectations. Stereotypes can trigger such behavioural confirmation (Rosenthal, 2002). Consider a classic experiment by Carl Word and others (1974) involving a situation of great importance in people's lives: the job interview. White participants, without realizing it, sat farther away, made more speech errors, and held shorter interviews when interviewing black applicants (who were actually experimental confederates) than white applicants. In a second study, white interviewers were asked to treat white job applicants as the black applicants had been treated in the first study (i.e., shorter interviews, farther social distance and so on). Being exposed to this colder interpersonal style then led the white applicants to behave in a nervous and awkward manner; thus the applicants "confirmed" what the interviewers seemed to expect of them and this hurt their overall interview performance. The reality is that stereotypes have the potential to shape both perceptions and behaviour.

FIGURE 5.3

How Racial Stereotypes Distort Social Perceptions

After briefly viewing this picture, one participant described it to a second participant, who described it to a third, and so on. After six rounds of communication, the final report often placed the razor held by the white man into the black man's hand. This study illustrates how racial stereotypes can distort social perception. *(Adapted from Allport & Postman, 1947.)*

Is Stereotyping Inevitable? Automatic Versus Intentional Processes

Stereotypes are defined as beliefs that associate a group of people with certain traits, but part of their power is that they can bias our perceptions and responses even if we don't personally agree with these beliefs. In other words, we don't have to believe a stereotype for it to trigger illusory correlations and self-fulfilling prophecies, or to bias how we think, feel, and behave toward group members. Sometimes just being aware of stereotypes in one's culture is enough to cause these effects. Moreover, stereotypes can be activated without our awareness. Indeed, they can operate at an unconscious, or "implicit" level (Blair, 2001).

These findings raise a provocative, and potentially depressing, question: Is stereotyping inevitable? When we encounter people from other groups, do our stereotypes of these groups always become activated in our minds? Can we do anything to prevent this from happening? Most people believe that they can resist stereotyping others, but recent research paints a far more complex picture.

Stereotypes as (Sometimes) Automatic Patricia Devine (1989) distinguished between automatic and controlled processes in stereotyping. She argued that people have become highly aware of the contents of many stereotypes through sociocultural mechanisms such as lessons learned from parents and images in the media. Because of this high awareness, people automatically activate stereotypes whenever they are exposed to members of groups for which popular stereotypes

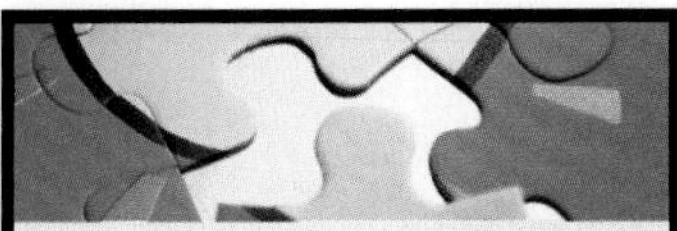

Very brief exposure to a member of a stereotyped group does not lead to biased judgments or responses, but longer exposure typically does. **False.**

exist. Thus, just as many of us are automatically primed to think *eggs* after hearing *bacon*, we are also primed to think of concepts relevant to a stereotype when we think of a stereotyped group. To be sure, we can try to prevent this activated stereotype from influencing our judgments or behaviours. As noted earlier, however, we are often unaware that a particular stereotype has been activated or how it can influence our perceptions and behaviours (Bargh, 1997). Thus, the stereotype can affect us in spite of our good intentions. In her study, Devine exposed white participants to **subliminal presentations** on a computer monitor. For one group, these presentations consisted of words relevant to stereotypes about black people, such as "Africa," "ghetto," "welfare," and "basketball." Subliminally presented information is presented so quickly that perceivers do not even realize that they have been exposed to it. Thus, these students were not consciously aware that they had seen these words. Being subliminally primed with a lot of these words seemed to cause participants to activate the black stereotype more generally, which subsequently biased their interpretations of another person's behaviour, so that they saw it in a more negative, hostile light. These effects occurred *even among participants who did not consciously endorse the stereotypes in question.*

Devine's theory sparked an explosion of interest in these issues. Are we automatically biased by stereotypes, including those we disagree with? And are we inevitably prone to stereotyping after merely being exposed to stereotypes prevalent in our culture? Such questions are very complex, but within the past several years social psychologists have made great strides in addressing them. It is now clear that stereotype activation can be triggered implicitly and automatically, influencing subsequent thoughts, feelings, and behaviours even among perceivers who are relatively low in prejudice. But it also is clear that several factors can make such activation more or less likely to happen.

First, some stereotypes are more likely than others to come to mind quickly and easily for any given person. For example, people in Western Europe may be quicker to activate the "skinhead" stereotype than people in South America. How much exposure individuals have to a stereotype, and therefore how accessible the stereotype is in their mind, varies across time and cultures.

Second, it is important to consider the kind and amount of information that perceivers encounter. If perceivers encounter or are induced to think about information about *some* aspects of the stereotype, they are likely to automatically activate thoughts about the stereotype *in general*, as in the Devine (1989) study. If they are exposed to only very minimal, emotionally neutral information, such as a category label (e.g., "black" or "gay") or a photo of a member of the group, automatic stereotype activation may depend on a perceiver's degree of prejudice. That is, people low in prejudice are less likely to automatically activate the stereotype based on this information than people higher in prejudice (Lepore & Brown, 1997, 2002; Kawakami et al., 1998; Wittenbrink et al., 1997). Another interesting question is *which* stereotype gets activated in response to someone who is a member of multiple stereotyped groups, such as an Asian woman. Here, again, the kind of information available plays an important role, such as whether the Asian woman is seen eating with chopsticks or applying makeup; activation of one stereotype (such as Asian) can inhibit activation of the other (such as woman) (Macrae et al., 1995).

Third, there is a growing recognition of the role that motivational factors can play in stereotype activation (Blair, 2002; Bodenhausen et al., 2003; Gollwitzer & Schaal, 2001; Kunda & Spencer, 2003; Spencer et al., 2003). Whether or not we realize it, we often have particular goals when we encounter others, such as wanting to learn about them, impress them, get to our next task and not be interrupted by them, and so on. Some sets of goals make us more likely to activate stereotypes, and others have the opposite effect. We focus on these goals and their effects in the following section.

subliminal presentation A method of presenting stimuli so faintly or rapidly that people do not have any conscious awareness of having been exposed to them.

Motivation: Fuelling Activation or Putting on the Brakes An important goal that can drive people's perceptions and behaviours is the desire to maintain, protect, and perhaps enhance their self-image and self-esteem. These goals can lead even people low in prejudice to activate negative stereotypes. For example, when their self-esteem is threatened, people may become motivated to stereotype others so that they will feel better about themselves (Fein & Spencer, 1997). Motivated in this way, they may also become more likely to activate stereotypes automatically. To demonstrate these points, Steven Spencer and others (1998) conducted a series of experiments in which they threatened some participants' self-esteem by making them think that they had done poorly on an intelligence test. These participants became more likely to automatically activate negative stereotypes about Blacks or Asians when exposed briefly, even subliminally, to a drawing or videotape of a member of the stereotyped group.

Whether people are likely to immediately categorize this person by her race, gender, or occupation depends on a combination of cognitive, sociocultural, and motivational factors.

Trying to protect one's self-image cannot only promote activation of some stereotypes, but it can also inhibit activation of others. For example, Lisa Sinclair and Ziva Kunda found that when white Canadian students in their study received praise from a black doctor, not only did they activate positive stereotypes about doctors but they also simultaneously *inhibited* activation of negative stereotypes about Blacks—a pattern presumably driven by the desire to see the person who praised them as especially smart and successful. If this is the effect that praise brings about, will criticism have the opposite effect? Sinclair and Kunda's (1999, 2000) research suggests that it can. They found that when a stereotyped group member criticizes or even simply disagrees with participants, the participants become more likely to activate negative stereotypes about the group (see Figure 5.4).

Despite all that we've written so far about the pervasiveness of stereotypes and their effects, there is no question that an important goal for many people today is to *not* use stereotypes or be prejudiced. We will discuss some of the implications of this in the closing section of this chapter, but for now we can ask whether simply wanting to avoid activating stereotypes can be effective against the numerous factors that can make activation automatic under many conditions.

How can something automatic be controllable? Consider the process of driving a car. Especially if the route you're taking is familiar, much of what you do is automatic. Without stopping to think about it, you steer, check the mirrors, and know when and how hard to press your foot against the gas and brake pedals. Indeed, the process is so automatic that you would find it difficult to articulate to someone else exactly what you're doing and how you're doing it. Yet this automatic process can be interrupted—by an unexpected event, say, or a compelling emotion such as concern about making a mistake in front of a parent, blind date, or police officer. By the same token, the often-automatic route from exposure to a stereotyped group member to stereotype activation can be diverted under particular conditions.

The question is: Can you actually prevent yourself from activating a negative stereotype? For instance, what if you try really hard to resist thinking about the stereotype? Research in other contexts suggests that sometimes the harder you try to suppress an unwanted thought, the less likely you are to succeed. Try not to think about a white bear for the next 30 seconds, and that image will come to mind with remarkable frequency. Try not to worry about how long it's taking you to fall asleep, and you'll stay awake. Try not to think about an itch, or the chocolate cheesecake in the fridge, or a particular sexist thought—well, you get the idea (Wegner, 1997).

Research on the effectiveness of trying to suppress stereotyping is mixed. On

FIGURE 5.4

Motivated Stereotype Inhibition and Activation

Participants received either praise or criticism about their performance from either a black man or a white man who they were led to believe was a doctor. A computer task that measured how quickly the participants could respond to various stimuli was used to assess whether they activated stereotypes about Blacks. Compared to the reaction times of participants who received neither praise nor criticism ("no-feedback controls"), quicker reaction times indicate stereotype *activation*, whereas longer reaction times suggest stereotype *suppression*. Participants criticized by the black doctor strongly activated the Black stereotypes, whereas participants praised by the black doctor inhibited black stereotypes. *(Sinclair & Kunda, 1999.)*

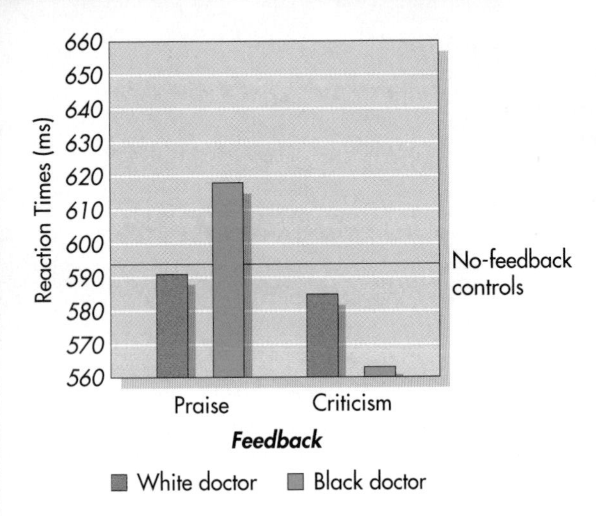

the one hand, trying to suppress a stereotype can sometimes cause a post-suppression rebound: after a person spends energy suppressing a stereotype, the stereotype pops up even more, like a volleyball that's been held under water (e.g., Macrae et al., 1994). Other research suggests that when people are intrinsically motivated to suppress a stereotype that they truly don't believe in, they may be successful at avoiding rebound effects (Monteith et al., 1998; Wyer et al., 2000). And some people are better than others at suppressing thoughts (Brewin & Beaton, 2002). One factor is age. William von Hippel and others (2000) found that older people have a harder time suppressing stereotypes than younger people, which may explain in part why older people often appear more prejudiced than younger people. Individual differences in prejudice are also important. Low-prejudice people in particular may be able to consider personal information about individual members of stereotyped groups and thus have an easier time keeping stereotyped thoughts out of mind. This may indeed be the best strategy for avoiding the influences of stereotypes: Rather than try to suppress thoughts about a stereotyped group, try instead to activate thoughts about the individual who happens to be a member of that group.

New findings suggest additional ways in which stereotype activation can be reduced (see Table 5.2). For example, Kawakami et al. (2000) trained individuals to respond in a non-stereotypic way to members of certain groups. Participants in one condition were asked to press a NO button when faced with a photo of a target person paired with a stereotypic association (i.e., "Skinhead-Hostile" or "Elderly-Weak") and YES when paired with a more positive, non-stereotypic descriptor. This training led to an overall reduction in stereotype activation. Other research has found that taking the perspective of a member of the stereotyped group can also lead to a reduction in stereotype activation (Galinsky & Ku, 2004). In addition, Gordon Moskowitz and others (2004) have identified people who have a particularly strong goal of being fair, or egalitarian, to all people, and when this goal is activated, they are less likely to stereotype others. This research has also found that this goal can be induced temporarily in others if they are made to feel that they have been biased and unfair. When people feel that they have violated their own, their group's, or their culture's standards of fairness and morality, they are less likely to activate negative stereotypes of others (Fein et al., 2003; Son Hing et al., 2002; Monin & Miller, 2001; Monteith & Voils, 2001).

From Activation to Application: When Are Activated Stereotypes Applied? The evidence just discussed indicates that stereotype activation is automatic under some conditions and not others. Once activated, stereotypes can influence our perceptions and reactions in important ways. But activation doesn't necessarily force us to evaluate specific persons only in terms of the stereotype. Research indicates that three factors enable us to overcome stereotypes and judge others on a more individual basis (Brewer, 1988; Fiske & Neuberg, 1990; Fiske et al., 1999).

The first factor is the amount of *personal information* we have about someone. Once such information is available, stereotypes and other preconceptions lose relevance and impact. Thus, when participants in one study read about a man or woman who consistently reacted to difficult situations by behaving assertively or passively, their impressions of that person were influenced more by his or her actions than by gender (Locksley et al., 1980). In fact, people will often set aside their stereotypes even when the personal information they have is not clearly relevant to the judgment they have to make (Hilton & Fein, 1989; Yzerbyt et al., 1998). And the amount of personal information people learn can also dilute stereotyping. In a provocative series of studies, Ziva Kunda and others (2002) exposed white Canadian participants to a videotape of an interview with a black person and found that these participants tended to activate stereotypes associated with this group within 15 seconds of exposure. However, if they continued to be exposed to the individual for 12 minutes and learned more information about him or her, they no longer exhibited any stereotype activation. Interestingly, if they were later provided with information indicating that this black person disagreed with them on a verdict in a court case, the stereotype was once again activated.

TABLE 5.2

Automatic Stereotype Activation: Important Factors

Based on very recent research, we can propose the following sets of factors as important in determining when people are more or less likely to activate stereotypes automatically—that is, without awareness or intention, whether or not they even endorse the stereotypes, upon exposure to minimal cues about a social group or group member. There are other factors that matter, and the effects of each of the factors below may depend on the presence or absence of the other factors, but these general conclusions can be offered at this time.

Factors That Make Automatic Activation More Likely	Factors That Make Automatic Activation Less Likely
Cognitive Factors	
■ Exposure to information consistent with stereotype, or with negative feelings	■ Exposure to minimal, neutral information
■ Stereotype is accessible (e.g., recently activated or primed)	■ Too busy to attend to category cues
	■ Competing stereotypes activated (e.g., target is member of a multiple stereotyped group, such as an Asian woman)
Cultural Factors	
■ Popular stereotype in culture	■ Not common stereotype in culture
Motivational Factors	
■ Motivated to make inferences about the person quickly	■ Motivated to avoid prejudice
■ Motivated to feel superior to other person	■ Motivated to be fair, egalitarian
Personal Factors	
■ Endorse stereotypes, high in prejudice	■ Disagree with stereotypes, low in prejudice

The second factor is our cognitive *ability* to focus on an individual member of a stereotyped group. Stereotypes that already have been activated are most likely to bias a perceiver's judgments of a particular group member when a perceiver's energy or cognitive resources have been impaired by alcohol, strong emotions, arousal, or other demands (Bless et al., 1996; Gilbert & Hixon, 1991; Lambert et al., 2003; von Hippel et al., 1995). In an intriguing test of this ability hypothesis, Galen Bodenhausen (1990) classified participants by their circadian arousal patterns, or biological rhythms, into two types: "morning people" (who describe themselves as most alert early in the morning) and "night people" (who say they peak much later, in the evening). By random assignment, participants took part in an experiment in human judgment that was scheduled at either 9 A.M. or 8 P.M. The result? Morning people were more likely to use stereotypes when tested at night; night owls were more likely to do so early in the morning.

The third factor is *motivation*. When social perceivers are highly motivated to form an accurate impression of someone (say, if they're in an interdependent relationship with the person or if they need to compete against the person), they often manage to set aside their pre-existing beliefs (Fiske, 2000). Sufficiently motivated, people can make individualized judgments of others. But motivation can work in the opposite direction, too. Do you know some people who tend to think a lot about every decision and others who always seem motivated to make quick decisions and never look back? People in the latter category—who have a high need for closure—are particularly unlikely to pay attention to individuating information about group members (Kruglanski & Webster, 1996).

Interestingly, in some cases our judgments are biased by our attempt to *avoid* applying negative stereotypes. For example, Natalie Wyer (2004) found that participants very low in prejudice toward black people showed a bias toward stereotype *dis*confirmation when seeking information and making judgments about black people. So these perceivers were influenced by race, but in the direction that ran counter to the stereotypes.

Prejudice

Categorizing people into groups, and dividing people into ingroups and outgroups, are fundamental to how stereotypes form and endure. But they have implications for not only the way we *think* about groups, but also how we *feel* about the social groups we encounter. If you look back at Figure 5.1, you'll see that stereotypes and prejudice are related but distinct, each influencing the other while also having separate effects on discrimination. In this section, we trace the roots of prejudice—one's negative feelings toward people based on their membership in a group—and examine some of its causes and consequences.

Intergroup Conflict

Clearly, some people are more prejudiced than others. The problem is so widespread, however, that it seems nobody is immune. Social psychologists have thus sought to identify the situational factors that give rise to prejudice. This section describes a classic study of intergroup conflict, a study that sets the stage for theories focusing on the role of social situations.

Robbers Cave: Setting the Stage We begin our analysis in an unlikely place: Robbers Cave State Park, Oklahoma. In the summer of 1954, a small group of 11-year-old boys—all white, healthy, middle-class youngsters, all strangers to one another—arrived at a 200-acre camp located in a densely wooded area of the park. The boys spent the first week or so hiking, swimming, boating, and camping out. After a while, they gave themselves a group name and printed it on their caps and T-shirts. At first, the boys thought they were the only ones at the camp. Soon, however, they discovered that there was a second group and that tournaments had been arranged between the two groups.

What these boys didn't know was that they were participants in an elaborate study conducted by Muzafer Sherif and his colleagues (1961). Parents had given permission for their sons to take part in an experiment for a study of competitiveness and cooperation. The two groups were brought in separately, and only after each had formed its own culture was the other's presence revealed. Now, the "Rattlers" and the "Eagles" were ready to meet. They did so under tense circumstances, competing against each other in football, a treasure hunt, a tug-of-war, and other events. For each event, the winning team was awarded points, and the tournament winner was promised a trophy, medals, and other prizes. Almost overnight, the groups turned into hostile antagonists; and their rivalry escalated into a full-scale war. Group flags were burned, cabins were ransacked, and a food fight that resembled a riot exploded in the mess hall. Keep in mind that the participants in this study were well-adjusted boys, not street-gang members. Yet as Sherif (1966) noted, a naive observer would have thought the boys were "wicked, disturbed, and vicious" (p. 85).

Creating a monster through competition was easy. Restoring the peace, however, was not. First the experimenters tried saying nice things to the Rattlers about the Eagles and vice versa, but the propaganda campaign did not work. Then the two groups were brought together under noncompetitive circumstances, but that didn't help either. What did eventually work was the introduction of **superordinate goals**, mutual goals that could be achieved only through cooperation between the groups. For example, the experimenters arranged for the camp truck to break down, and both groups were needed to pull it up a steep hill. This strategy worked like a charm. By the end of camp, the two groups were so friendly that they insisted on traveling home on the same bus. In just three weeks, the Rattlers and Eagles experienced the kinds of changes that often take generations to unfold: They formed close-knit groups, went to war, and made peace.

The events of Robbers Cave mimicked the kinds of conflict that plague people all over the world. The simplest explanation for this conflict is competition. Assign strangers to groups, throw the groups into contention, stir the pot, and soon there's conflict. Similarly, the intergroup benefits of reducing the focus on competition by activating superordinate goals are also evident around the world. Consider, for example, the remarkable aftermath of the natural disasters that befell Greece and Turkey in 1999. Fraught with conflict and mistrust for generations, Greek-Turkish relations improved dramatically in the wake of earthquakes that rocked both countries. Television images of Turkish rescue workers pulling a Greek child from under a pile of rubble in Athens generated an outpouring of goodwill. Uniting against a shared threat, as the boys in Robbers Cave did when the camp truck broke down, the two nations began to bridge a significant gulf (Kinzer, 1999).

Realistic Conflict Theory The view that direct competition for valuable but limited resources breeds hostility between groups is called **realistic conflict theory** (Levine & Campbell, 1972). As a simple matter of economics, one group may fare better in the struggle for land, jobs, or power than another group. The loser becomes frustrated and resentful, the winner feels threatened and protective—and before long, conflict heats to a rapid boil. Chances are, a good deal of prejudice in the world is driven by the realities of competition (Duckitt & Mphuthing, 1998; Stephan et al., 1999; Taylor & Moghaddam, 1994).

But there is much more to prejudice than real competition. First, the "realistic" competition for resources may in fact be imagined—a perception in the mind of an individual who is not engaged in any real conflict. Second, people may become resentful of other groups not because of their conviction that their own security or resources are threatened by these groups but because of their sense of **relative deprivation**—the belief that they fare poorly compared with others (Hong et al., 2001; Walker & Smith, 2002). What matters to the proverbial Smiths is not the size of their house per se but whether it is larger than the Jones's house next door. Third, even if people don't feel personally threatened or deprived, their perceptions of threats to their group can trigger prejudice (Smith et al., 1999). For example, Ellemers and Bos (1998) found that native shopkeepers in Amsterdam felt threatened by the emergence of immigrant stores but this was not related to personal gains or losses; rather they were afraid that as a group the native shopkeepers were somehow falling behind.

superordinate goals Shared goals that can be achieved only through cooperation among individuals or groups.

realistic conflict theory The theory that hostility between groups is caused by direct competition for limited resources.

relative deprivation Feelings of discontent aroused by the belief that one fares poorly compared with others.

Social Identity Theory

Why are people so sensitive about the status and integrity of their ingroups relative to rival outgroups, even when personal interests are not at stake? Could it be that

On July 1 each year, Canadians enjoy a national holiday and celebrate their Canadian identity.

personal interests really *are* at stake, that our protectiveness of ingroups is nourished by a concern for the self? If so, could that explain why people all over the world believe that their own nation, culture, language, and religion are better and more deserving than others?

These questions were first raised in a study of high school boys in Bristol, England, conducted by Henri Tajfel and his colleagues (1971). The boys were shown a series of dotted slides, and their task was to estimate the number of dots on each. The slides were presented in rapid-fire succession, so the dots could not be counted. Later, the experimenter told the participants that some people are chronic "overestimators" and that others are "underestimators." As part of a second, entirely separate task, participants were supposedly divided for the sake of convenience into groups of overestimators and underestimators (in fact, they were divided randomly). Knowing who was in their group, participants were told to allocate points to each other, points that could be cashed in for money.

This procedure was designed to create *minimal groups*—persons categorized on the basis of trivial, minimally important similarities. Tajfel's overestimators and underestimators were not long-term rivals, did not have a history of antagonism, were not frustrated, did not compete for a limited resource, and were not even acquainted with each other. Still, participants consistently allocated more points to members of their own group than to members of the other group. This pattern of discrimination, called **ingroup favouritism**, has been found in studies performed in many countries and using a variety of measures (Capozza & Brown, 2000). The preference for ingroups is so powerful that its effects can be elicited simply by the language we use. Charles Perdue and others (1990) found that subtly priming "ingroup" pronouns such as *we*, *us*, and *ours* triggered positive emotions in participants, while "outgroup" pronouns such as *they*, *them*, and *theirs* elicited negative emotions.

To explain ingroup favouritism, Tajfel (1982) and John Turner (1987) proposed **social identity theory**. According to this theory, each of us strives to enhance our self-esteem, which has two components: a *personal* identity and various collective or *social* identities that are based on the groups to which we belong. In other words, people can boost their self-esteem through their own personal achievements or through affiliation with successful groups. What's nice about the need for social identity is that it leads us to derive pride from our connections with others, even if we don't receive any direct benefits from these others (Gagnon & Bourhis, 1996). What's sad, however, is that we often feel the need to belittle "them" in order to feel secure about "us." Religious fervour, racial and ethnic conceit, and patriotism may all fulfill this more negative side of our social identity. The theory is summarized in Figure 5.5.

ingroup favouritism The tendency to discriminate in favour of ingroups over outgroups.

social identity theory The theory that people favour ingroups over outgroups in order to enhance their self-esteem.

Basic Predictions Two basic predictions arise from social identity theory: (1) Threats to one's self-esteem heighten the need for ingroup favouritism, and (2) expressions of ingroup favouritism enhance one's self-esteem. Research generally sup-

FIGURE 5.5

Social Identity Theory

Tajfel and Turner claim that people strive to enhance self-esteem, which has two components: a personal identity and various social identities that derive from the groups to which we belong. Thus, people may boost their self-esteem by viewing their ingroups more favourably than outgroups.

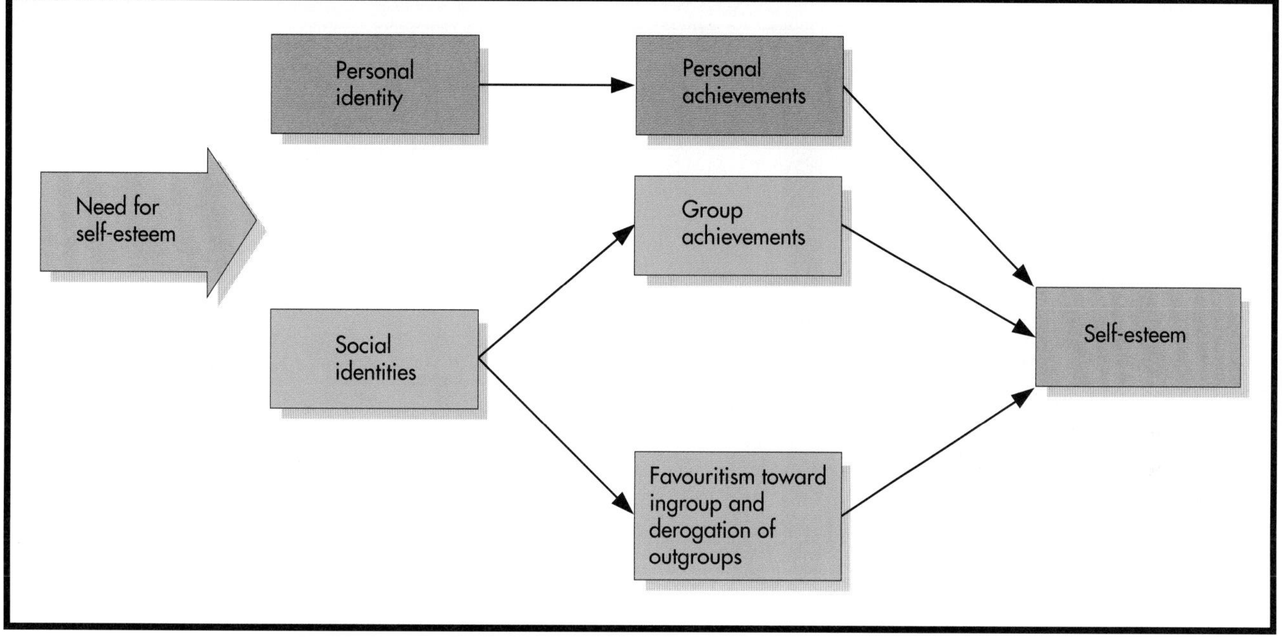

Need for self-esteem
Personal identity
Social identities
Personal achievements
Group achievements
Favouritism toward ingroup and derogation of outgroups
Self-esteem

ports these predictions (Brewer & Brown, 1998; Petersen & Blank, 2003; Rubin & Hewstone, 1998). In one study, Steven Fein and Steven Spencer (1997) gave participants positive or negative feedback about their performance on a test of social and verbal skills—feedback that temporarily raised or lowered their self-esteem. These participants then took part in what was supposed to be a second experiment in which they evaluated a job applicant. All participants received a photograph of a young woman, her résumé, and a videotape of a job interview. In half the cases, the woman was called Maria D'Agostino and depicted as Italian; in the other half, she was called Julie Goldberg and depicted as Jewish (on the campus where the study was held, there was a popular negative stereotype of the "Jewish American Princess," often targeting upper-middle-class Jewish women from New York).

As predicted by social identity theory, there were two important results (see Figure 5.6). First, among participants whose self-esteem had been lowered by negative feedback, Julie Goldberg was rated more negatively than Maria D'Agostino—even though their pictures and their credentials were the same. Second, negative-feedback participants given a chance to belittle the Jewish woman later exhibited a post-experiment increase in self-esteem. A blow to one's self-image evokes prejudice—and the expression of prejudice helps to restore that image. Interestingly, recent research suggests that self-esteem is not always what it appears to be. Jordan, Spencer, and Zanna (2005) describe how some people with high self-esteem are outwardly (or explicitly) quite secure in this view, whereas others who consciously consider themselves to have high self-esteem may be harbouring doubts and require more reinforcement of their positive self-view. Participants in their study, all of whom were initially chosen for their high scores on an explicit measure of self-esteem, were given negative feedback about their performance on a bogus intelligence test.

FIGURE 5.6

Self-Esteem and Prejudice

Participants received positive or negative feedback and then evaluated a female job applicant believed to be Italian or Jewish. There were two key results: (1) participants whose self-esteem had been lowered by negative feedback evaluated the woman more negatively when she was Jewish than when she was Italian (left); and (2) negative-feedback participants given the opportunity to belittle the Jewish woman showed a post-experiment increase in self-esteem (right). *(Fein & Spencer, 1997.)*

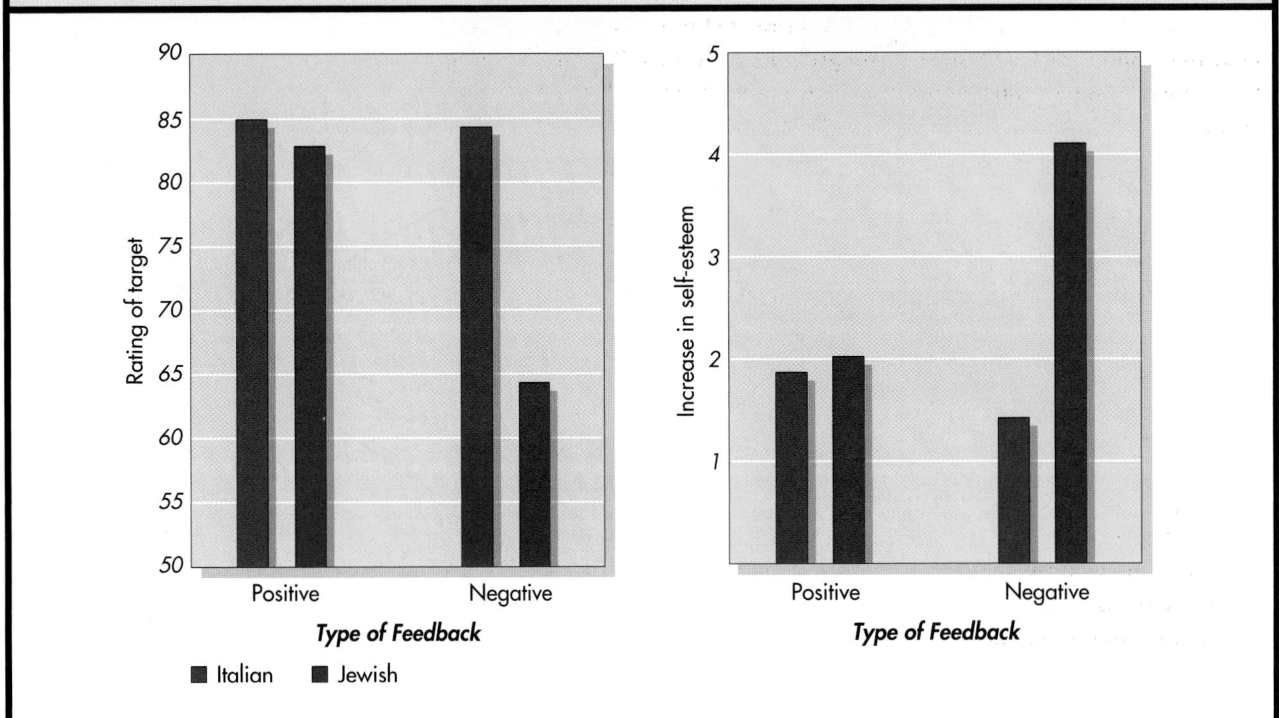

They then read about a case of student misconduct; some read that the student was a member of the First Nations, whereas others read that the student was White. They were then given the opportunity to suggest an appropriate punishment for the offender. What they found was that participants with lower implicit self-esteem (i.e., those who were less confident in their outward belief in their high self-esteem) recommended more severe punishments for the First Nations student than for the white student while participants with high implicit self-esteem recommended similar punishments in both conditions.

According to Jamie Arndt and others (2002; Castano et al., 2002), when people feel threatened by thoughts of their own mortality, they tend to seek greater affiliation with their ingroups and exhibit greater prejudice against outgroups, in part to reaffirm their sense of place in the world. A case in point is the finding that Christian participants rated Christian targets more positively and Jewish targets more negatively when they were made to think about their own mortality (Greenberg et al., 1990). More recently, Pyszczynski and his colleagues (2003) applied this theory in predicting the wave of ingroup pride and outgroup hostilities that many Americans displayed in the days and weeks following the terrorist attacks of September 11, 2001.

Situational, Individual, and Cultural Differences Recent work has extended social identity theory by making more specific distinctions among various types of esteem-relevant threats (such as whether the threat is to the group's status or to the individual's role within the group) and among different ingroup members (such as whether they are strongly or weakly identified with their group) (Aharpour & Brown, 2002; Castano et al., 2002; Doosje & Branscombe, 2003; Lalonde, 2002; Roccas, 2003). Greater ingroup identification, for example, has been found across many studies to be associated with stronger social identity effects. Shana Levin and her colleagues (2003) reported that the Lebanese participants in their study who most strongly felt identified with the group "Arabs" were especially likely to report supporting terrorist organizations and feeling that the September 11, 2001 attacks on the United States were justified. And Manfred Schmitt and Juergen Maes (2002) found that the more East Germans identified with East Germany, the more they showed increased ingroup bias when making comparisons with West Germany during the German unification process—an effect heightened by increased feelings of relative deprivation during unification. Identification with a superordinate group (such as Europeans), on the other hand, can reduce expressions of bias between particular subgroups (such as Greeks and Turks), particularly when the superordinate group is made salient (e.g., Klein et al., 2003; Lipponen et al., 2003).

Being part of a small, close-knit group can be an important, rewarding part of one's personal identity.

Although our membership in various social groups gives us an important part of our personal identity, not all of the groups to which we belong are equally likely to be important to our sense of self. According to Marilynn Brewer and Cynthia Pickett (1999; Brewer, 2003), one important consideration is the relative size and distinctiveness of one's ingroup. Noting that people want to belong to groups that are small enough for them to feel unique, Brewer and Pickett observed that ingroup loyalty and outgroup prejudice are more intense for groups that are in the minority than for members of large and inclusive majorities.

Another important factor is a person's status relative to others in the ingroup. Jeffrey Noel and his colleagues (1995) found that people are most motivated to derogate outsiders when their ingroup status is marginal—such as when they are pledges (under initiation) rather than active (fully initiated) members of fraternities and sororities, and when they are in the presence of fellow ingroup members. Wanting to prove themselves worthy members of the group, they publicly derogate outsiders in part to win the favour of fellow ingroup members.

Cultural differences can also influence social identity processes. Steven Heine and Darrin Lehman (1997) propose that people from collectivist cultures such as those in Asia are less likely than people from individualist cultures such as those in North America to show biases favouring their ingroups in order to boost their self-esteem. In one study, for example, Japanese students exhibited less ingroup-enhancing bias than Japanese-Canadian students, who, in turn, exhibited less bias than European-Canadian students. However, collectivists are not completely immune from showing ingroup-enhancing biases (Capozza et al., 2000; Chen et al., 2002). Collectivists may be less likely to overtly exaggerate the strengths of their ingroups, but some research indicates that they draw sharper distinctions between ingroup and outgroup members than individualists do (Gudykunst & Bond, 1997). Among a sample of sixth-graders in Korea, for example, children who were more collectivistic exhibited greater discrimination between ingroup and outgroup members than did more individualistic children (Han & Park, 1995). In any event, given these sometimes contradictory findings, there is a clear need for more cross-cultural research on social identity processes.

Reactions to Low Status Social identity theory poses another interesting question: If self-esteem is influenced by the status of our ingroups relative to outgroups, how do people cope with ingroups of low status or with weak ingroup members? How do you cope with associations you find embarrassing? The theory predicts two possible reactions: Risk a loss of self-esteem or distance yourself from those in question. So which is it? To examine the question, José Marques and others (1988) have conducted studies in which participants had to evaluate ingroup and outgroup members who behaved in positive or negative ways. In one study, Belgian participants judged attractive Belgian students more favourably than attractive North African students, but they judged unattractive Belgian students more unfavourably than unattractive North African students. To preserve the integrity of the ingroup, people may be excessively harsh in their treatment of less able fellow members—at least when the ingroup is important to their social identities (Branscombe et al., 1993).

Even if people don't or can't distance themselves from weak ingroup members, their self-esteem may not be deflated by being members of low-status ingroups: People who are members of low-status, stereotyped groups do not tend to have lower overall self-esteem than people in high-status groups (Twenge & Crocker, 2002; Wolfe & Crocker, 2003). Self-esteem is a flexible quality (e.g., Major et al., 2004). If an ingroup is relatively low in status in a particular domain (such as academics), ingroup members may de-emphasize the importance of this domain and instead invest their self-esteem in domains for which their ingroups have higher status (such as popularity) (Hinkle et al., 1998; Steele, 1997). In addition, Heather Smith and Tom Tyler (1997) propose that although pride in the status of one's ingroup is important for one's self-esteem, so, too, is the respect that one feels within the ingroup. Thus, even if the ingroup is low in status, individuals who are high in status within the ingroup can derive positive self-esteem from it.

Members of low-status, stereotyped groups have lower self-esteem than members of high-status groups. **False.**

Implicit Theories and Ideologies

Earlier in the chapter we discussed how stereotyping is influenced by individuals' implicit theories about their social worlds, such as whether they see groups more as fixed entities or as dynamic and malleable. These implicit theories also play an important role in prejudice in general, and in social identity in particular. Seeing groups as fixed entities promotes the exaggeration of intragroup similarity and intergroup differences, makes people more anxious about accepting outsiders into one's ingroup, and creates a greater tendency for ingroup favouritism (Corneille et al., 2001; Hong et al., 2004; Levy et al., 2001).

People also vary in their ideologies about intergroup relations in society, such as concerning equality and access to power and social mobility. For example, a growing body of research has examined the **social dominance orientation**—a desire to see one's ingroups as dominant over other groups and a willingness to adopt cultural values that facilitate oppression over other groups (Levin, 2004; Sidanius et al., 2004). Felicia Pratto, Jim Sidanius, and others have found in numerous countries throughout the world that ingroup identification and outgroup derogation can be especially strong among people with a social dominance orientation (Pratto et al., 2000; Sidanius et al., 2000).

social dominance orientation
A desire to see one's ingroups as dominant over other groups and a willingness to adopt cultural values that facilitate oppression over other groups.

Social dominance orientations promote self-interest. But some ideologies support a social structure that may actually oppose one's self-interest, depending on the status of one's groups. John Jost and his colleagues (2004) have focused on what they call *system justification*—processes that endorse and legitimize existing social arrangements. System-justifying beliefs protect the status quo. Groups with power, of course, may promote the status quo to preserve their own advantaged position. But groups that are disadvantaged may be better off challenging the current economic or political system, and yet these group members may hold system-justifying beliefs. To the extent that they do, members of low-status groups may show *out*group favouritism—toward more powerful outgroups.

So far, we have traced the roots and examined some consequences of stereotypes and prejudice. We now concentrate more specifically on two forms of prejudice and discrimination: sexism and racism. There are many other forms of prejudice and discrimination, of course. For example, there is a growing interest in *ageism*—prejudice and discrimination against people because of their age. Researchers today are also studying prejudice and discrimination toward people based on their sexual orientation, physical appearance, and physical and mental challenges. Sexism and racism, however, have received by far the most attention in social psychology research.

Sexism

When a baby is born, the first words uttered ring loud and clear: "It's a boy!" or "It's a girl!" In many hospitals, the newborn boy immediately is given a blue hat and the newborn girl a pink hat. The infant receives a gender-appropriate name and is showered with gender-appropriate gifts. Over the next few years, the typical boy is supplied with toy trucks, baseballs, pretend tools, guns, and chemistry sets; the typical girl is furnished with dolls, stuffed animals, pretend make-up kits, kitchen sets, and tea sets. As they enter school, many expect the boy to earn money by delivering newspapers and to enjoy math and computers, while they expect the girl to babysit and to enjoy crafts, music, and social activities. These distinctions persist in university, as more male students major in economics and the sciences and more female students in the arts, languages, and humanities. In the work force, more men become doctors, construction workers, auto mechanics, airplane pilots, investment bankers, and engineers. In contrast, more women become secretaries, schoolteachers, nurses, flight attendants, bank tellers, and homemakers. Back on the home front, the life cycle begins again when a man and woman have their first baby and discover that "It's a girl!" or "It's a boy!"

The traditional pinks and blues are not as distinct today as they used to be. Many gender barriers of the past have broken down, and the colours have somewhat blended together. Nevertheless, **sexism**—prejudice and discrimination based on a person's gender—still exists. Indeed, it begins with the fact that sex is the most conspicuous social category we use to identify ourselves and others (Stangor et al., 1992).

Gender Stereotypes: Blue for Boys, Pink for Girls

What do people say when asked to describe the typical man and woman? Males are said to be more adventurous, assertive, aggressive, independent, and task-oriented; females are thought to be more sensitive, gentle, dependent, emotional, and people-oriented. These images are so universal that they were reported by 2800

sexism Prejudice and discrimination based on a person's gender.

The Blues and the Pinks. *Even a very quick look at a toy store illustrates dramatic differences in how boys and girls are socialized. For example, boys are encouraged to play active, loud, and violent games (top), while girls are encouraged to engage in quieter, nurturing role-play (bottom).*

students from 30 different countries of North and South America, Europe, Africa, Asia, and Australia (Williams & Best, 1982). The images are also salient to young children—who identify themselves and others as boys or girls by three years of age, form gender-stereotypic beliefs about toys and other objects soon after that, and then use their simplified stereotypes in judging others and favouring their own gender over the other in intergroup situations (Golombok & Hines, 2002). Preschool boys and girls like a new toy less if they are told that it is a toy that opposite-sex children like (Martin et al., 1995). Even infants and toddlers can tell the difference. In one study, nine-month-olds who were shown pictures of only male or only female faces spent less and less time looking—until a face of the opposite sex appeared. This result tells us what the infants themselves could not: that they distinguish between men and women (Leinbach & Fagot, 1993). They also begin quite early to distinguish between stereotypically masculine and feminine behaviours. One recent study, for instance, found that by their second birthday, toddlers exhibited more surprise when adults performed behaviours inconsistent with gender roles (Serbin et al., 2002).

Beliefs about males and females are so deeply ingrained that they influence the behaviour of adults literally the moment a baby is born. In a fascinating study, the first-time parents of 15 girls and 15 boys were interviewed within 24 hours of the babies' births. There were no differences between the male and female newborns in height, weight, or other aspects of physical appearance. Yet the parents of girls rated their babies as softer, smaller, and more finely featured. The fathers of boys saw their sons as stronger, larger, more alert, and better coordinated (Rubin et al., 1974). Could it be there really were differences that only the parents were able to discern? Doubtful. In one recent study, Emily Mondschein and others (2000) found that mothers of 11-month-old girls underestimated their infants' crawling ability, whereas mothers of 11-month-old boys overestimated it.

As they develop, boys and girls receive many divergent messages, in many different settings. Barbara Morrongiello and Tess Dawber (2000) conducted a study that was relevant to this point. They showed mothers videotapes of children engaging in somewhat risky activities on a playground and asked them to stop the tape and indicate whatever they would ordinarily say to their own child in the situation shown. Mothers of daughters intervened more frequently and more quickly than did mothers of sons. As shown in Table 5.3, mothers of daughters were more likely to caution the child about getting hurt, whereas mothers of sons were more likely to encourage the child's risky playing. Another study by Morrongiello and others (2000) revealed that although boys typically experience more injuries from risky playing than girls, all children by the age of six tend to think that girls are at greater risk of injury than boys.

Clearly, then, children have ample opportunity to learn gender stereotypes and roles from their parents and other role models. A recent meta-analysis of more than 40 studies showed a significant correlation between parents' gender stereotypes and their children's gender-related thinking (Tenenbaum & Leaper, 2002).

But this correlation, and gender-related thinking and behaviours in general, may have biological and evolutionary roots as well. Gerianne Alexander (2003), for example, proposes that boys' and girls' preferences for objects such as toys may stem from evolutionary factors, combined with contemporary gender socialization. Indeed, a fascinating recent study reported that vervet monkeys showed sex differences in toy preferences similar to those seen in human children (Alexander & Hines, 2002).

TABLE 5.3

What Mothers Would Say

Mothers of young children watched a videotape of another child playing on a playground and engaging in risky behaviours, such as standing on top of a structure and leaning far over to look underneath. They were asked to stop the videotape whenever they would say something to the child if the child were theirs, and to indicate what they would say. Mothers of daughters stopped the tape much more often than mothers of sons to express caution ("Be careful!"), worry about injury ("You could fall!"), and directives to stop ("Stop that this instant!"). In contrast, mothers of sons were more likely to indicate encouragement ("Good job! Let me see you go higher."). *(Adapted from Morrongiello & Dawber, 2000.)*

Context of Statement	Frequency of Statement by: Mothers of Girls	Mothers of Boys
Caution	3.9	0.7
Worry about injury	9.2	0.2
Directive to stop	9.3	0.6
Encouragement	0.5	3.0

According to a recent Statistics Canada poll, men and women are much more likely to share household responsibilities than they were 20 years ago. Whereas only 54 percent of married men with children reported helping out around the house in 1986, that number has risen to 71 percent today (Statistics Canada, 2006).

Why Do Gender Stereotypes Endure?

Gender stereotypes often are based on a kernel of truth, but they tend to oversimplify and exaggerate that truth (Allen, 1995). Like the cartoonist who draws caricatures, we tend to stretch, expand, and enlarge the ways in which men and women differ. If men and women are more similar than people think, why do exaggerated perceptions of difference endure? Earlier in this chapter, we described several reasons why a stereotype, like the proverbial cat, can have many lives. The same mechanisms—illusory correlations, biased attributions, confirmation biases, and self-fulfilling prophecies—apply to perceptions of gender. But there is an additional reason for why gender stereotypes in particular are so enduring: Gender stereotypes are distinct from virtually all other stereotypes in that they are *prescriptive* rather than merely *descriptive*; that is, they indicate what the majority of people in a given culture believe men and women *should* be. Few Canadians, for example, think that gays should be artistic and sensitive or that old people should be forgetful and conservative; but many more think that women should be nurturing and that men should be unemotional. Even though ambition and drive are valued in our society, women who exhibit such traits may be viewed in especially harsh terms. These values put pressure on women and men to conform to gender stereotypes, and they increase perceivers' resistance against accepting stereotype-inconsistent evidence (Cuddy et al., 2005; Prentice & Carranza, 2002; Rudman & Glick, 2001).

Other sociocultural explanations have been proposed to explain why gender stereotypes are so stubborn. One focuses on media images and popular culture; another concerns the social roles that people occupy.

Media Images and Popular Culture Sociocultural factors, such as societal institutions and popular culture, foster male-female distinctions in many ways. Gone are the days when the media almost exclusively portrayed women in stereotypical,

Although looking at images of attractive people is a pleasant experience for many people, these popular images may also produce negative consequences—perpetuating stereotypes and promoting dangerous behaviours among those who try to achieve what are often impossible, unhealthy standards of masculinity and femininity.

powerless roles. Still, research indicates that some gender stereotyping persists—for example, in TV commercials and programs in countries around the world (Bartsch et al., 2000; Coltraine & Messineo, 2000; Furnham et al., 2001), children's books (Turner-Bowker, 1996), magazine advertisements (Kang, 1997), and music videos (Gan et al., 1997; Signorielli et al., 1994). In an analysis of 1 699 television commercials, for example, the characters who exhibited the greatest degree of prominence and authority were generally either white or male (Coltraine & Messineo, 2000).

More to the point is the fact that media depictions can influence viewers, often without their realizing it. Think about TV commercials for beer or men's cologne. There's a good chance that the commercials that come to mind include images of women as sex objects whose primary purpose in the ads is to serve as "the implied 'reward' for product consumption" (Rudman & Borgida, 1995, p. 495). Can these commercials affect not only men's attitudes toward women but their immediate behaviour as well? Yes, according to research by Laurie Rudman and Eugene Borgida (1995). Male undergraduates in their study watched a videotape containing either sexist TV commercials or TV commercials for similar products that contained no sexual imagery. After watching the commercials, each participant went to a room to meet and interview a woman, who actually was a confederate of the experimenter. Each student's interaction with the woman was secretly videotaped. Later, female judges watched these videotaped interactions and evaluated the male students' behaviour toward the female confederate on several dimensions. The results revealed that the men who had seen sexist commercials were rated as behaving in a more sexualized, objectifying manner than the men who had seen the neutral ads. Having been primed with images of women as sex objects on TV, the men treated the woman in objectifying ways.

TV commercials influence women's behaviour as well. Studies have shown that female students who had just watched a set of commercials in which the female characters were portrayed in stereotypic fashion tended to express lower self-confidence, less independence, and fewer career aspirations than did those who viewed stereotype-irrelevant or counter-stereotypical ads. They even performed more poorly on a difficult math test (Davies et al., 2002; Geis et al., 1984; Jennings et al., 1980). Whether or not consumers purchase the products explicitly advertised on television, they do seem to buy the implicit messages about gender—messages that may set in motion a self-fulfilling prophecy.

Donna and Eaaron Henderson-King and Lisa Hoffman (2001) examined the effects not only of objectifying media images but also of the social context in which these images are seen. In one of their studies, female undergraduates saw slides of either idealized images of women or neutral images, taken from popular magazines. Each woman watched these slides along with a few other women or with a mix of a few women and men. In addition, for the groups containing some men, the researchers manipulated the behaviour of the men so that in half the sessions the men (who were confederates) made brief comments during the presentation of some slides, such as "Nice," "All right," and "Yeah." In the other half of the mixed-sex sessions, the men made no comments.

The results of the study can be seen in Figure 5.7. When no men were present, the manipulation of media images did not have a significant effect on women's feelings about their weight. When men were merely present in the room (but did not make any comments), however, women felt worse about their weight if they had seen the idealized images than if they had seen the neutral images. But, interestingly enough, if men made comments, the effect was eliminated. In fact, the women who had seen the idealized images tended to feel *best* about their weight in the condition in which men made the comments. Why would the men's somewhat crude comments result in the women feeling better? The researchers believe that women may be most vulnerable to sexualized, objectifying images when they are not very mindful of them. While standing in the checkout line, flipping through a magazine, or half-watching a TV commercial, women process these images but may not think much about them in terms of the potentially dangerous messages they convey. These messages can sneak in under the radar and have unnerving effects. However, when made more mindful of the exaggerated or sexist implications of these images, as when men make sexist or sexualized comments, women may respond to these images very differently, such as by seeing them as exaggerations or unreal fantasies, and so they are better armed against their threatening implications.

FIGURE 5.7

Effects of Idealized Images of Women: The Role of Social Context

Female students saw slides of images from advertisements and layouts that contained either neutral imagery or many idealized images of women. They saw these slides either with a few other women or with both women and men. In the condition with the men present, the men (who were confederates) either made no comments or made a few comments about some of the images. After seeing the slides, the women completed questions about how they felt about their bodies, including on dimensions most relevant to weight. With no men present, the women's feelings about their weight did not vary as a function of the images they had seen. But with men present who did not make a comment, the women felt worse about their weight after seeing the idealized images. Interestingly, this effect was eliminated in the condition in which men made comments; in fact, the women who saw idealized images felt best about their weight when men made comments about some of the images. *(Henderson-King et al., 2001.)*

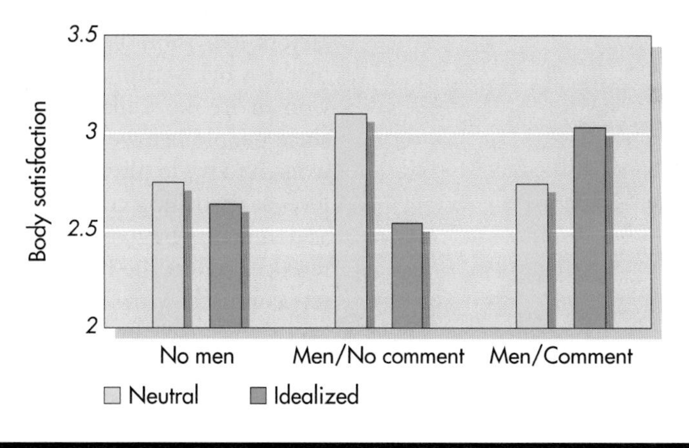

Immersed in popular culture, people implicitly learn stereotypes about how men and women are supposed to look. Media images of impossibly thin models are implicated in the near-epidemic incidence of eating disorders and debilitating anxiety over physical appearance, particularly among young white women (Milkie, 1999; Thompson & Heinberg, 1999). An even more recent phenomenon is the growing number of teenage boys and men who are hurting themselves through their obsession with their bodies—trying to gain muscle mass while remaining extremely lean. Here, too, the media appear to play a critical role; indeed, graphic displays of images of muscular and lean male models have become increasingly prevalent of late (McCabe et al., 2002; Pope et al., 2000). The media's impact may be especially negative among individuals who already have concerns about their appearance or are particularly concerned with other people's opinions (Henderson-King & Henderson-King, 1997; Ricciardelli et al., 2000).

Even brief exposure to sexist television commercials can significantly influence the behaviours of men and women. **True.**

Social Role Theory The media and popular culture are not the only sociocultural factors that contribute to the durability of gender stereotypes. Imagine a secretary typing a letter for a corporate president. Did you visualize a *female* secretary working for a *male* president? Alice Eagly's (1987; Eagly et al., 2004) **social role theory** states that although the perception of sex differences may be based on actual differences,

social role theory The theory that small gender differences are magnified in perception by the contrasting social roles occupied by men and women.

FIGURE 5.8

Eagly's Social Role Theory of Gender Stereotypes

According to social role theory, stereotypes of men as dominant and women as subordinate persist because men occupy higher-status positions in society. This division of labour, a product of many factors, leads men and women to behave in ways that fit their social roles. But rather than attribute the differences to these roles, people attribute the differences to gender.

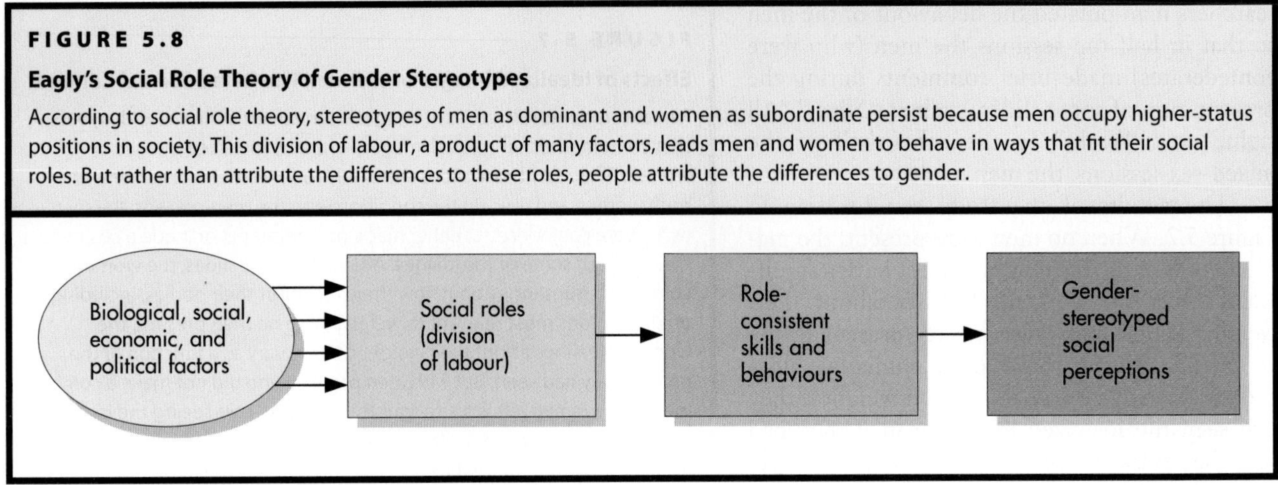

it is magnified by the unequal social roles occupied by men and women. The process involves three steps. First, through a combination of biological and social factors, a division of labour between the sexes has emerged over time—at home and in the work setting. Men are more likely to work in construction or business; women are more likely to care for children and to take lower-status jobs. Second, since people behave in ways that fit the roles they play, men are more likely than women to wield physical, social, and economic power. Third, these behavioural differences provide a continuing basis for social perception, leading us to perceive men as dominant "by nature" and women as domestic "by nature," when in fact the differences reflect the roles they play. In short, sex stereotypes are shaped by—and often confused with—the unequal distribution of men and women into different social roles (see Figure 5.8). According to this theory, perceived differences between men and women are based on real behavioural differences that are mistakenly assumed to arise from gender rather than from social roles.

Sex Discrimination: A Double Standard?

It could be argued that variety is the spice of life and that there's nothing inherently wrong with gender stereotypes as long as men and women are portrayed as different but equal. But are masculine and feminine attributes equally valued? Are men and women judged by the same standard, or is there a "double standard"?

Many years ago, Philip Goldberg (1968) asked female students to evaluate the content and writing style of some articles. When the material was supposedly written by John McKay rather than Joan McKay, it received higher ratings, a result that led Goldberg to wonder if even women were prejudiced against women. Certain other studies showed that people often devalue the performance of women who take on tasks usually reserved for men (Lott, 1985) and attribute their achievements to luck rather than ability (Deaux & Emswiller, 1974; Nieva & Gutek, 1981). It now appears, however, that the devaluation of women is not common. More than 100 studies modeled after Goldberg's indicate that people are not generally biased by gender in the evaluation of performance (Swim et al., 1989, 1996; Top, 1991).

In other ways, however, sex discrimination still exists. How many female airline pilots have you met lately? What about male secretaries? Look at Table 5.5, and you'll notice some striking results regarding women's occupational choices. Sex discrimination during the early school years may pave the way for diverging career paths in adulthood. Then, when equally qualified men and women compete for a job, gender considerations enter in once again, as some research indicates that

TABLE 5.5

Women in Work Settings Around the World

International labour statistics indicate that in most of the countries represented, women are especially likely to work in clerical occupations (e.g., as secretaries or bookkeepers), sales occupations (e.g., as salespeople, real estate agents, or insurance agents), and service occupations (e.g., as caretakers, cooks, hairdressers, or barbers), and especially unlikely to work in production/transport occupations (e.g., as woodworkers, miners, or shipping clerks). *(Data from International Labor Office, 1996.)*

	Percent of Workers Who Are Women														
	Australia	**Brazil**	**Canada**	**Costa Rica**	**Egypt**	**Israel**	**Italy**	**Japan**	**Mexico**	**Netherlands**	**New Zealand**	**Niger**	**Spain**	**USA**	**UK**
Total	42%	39%	45%	30%	20%	42%	35%	40%	32%	41%	44%	8%	34%	46%	45%
Professional/ technical	25	63	56	45	30	54	15	43	45	45	50	8	48	53	44
Administrative/ managerial	43	39	42	33	12	19	54	9	20	17	24	8	12	43	33
Clerical	47	41	80	49	35	71	34	60	55	59	77	30	51	79	76
Sales	10	86	45	37	14	38	50	38	51	47	48	—	45	50	64
Service	78	35	57	58	6	59	46	55	39	65	65	—	58	60	66
Production/ transport	29	25	14	19	4	13	22	28	19	10	16	2	12	18	15

business professionals favour men for so-called masculine jobs (such as a manager for a machinery company) and women for so-called feminine jobs (such as a receptionist) (Eagly, 2004). Even when women and men have comparable jobs, the odds are good that the women will be paid less than their male counterparts. They are also frequently confronted with a hostile, unfair work environment. Canadian estimates of workplace sexual harassment towards women range from 42 percent to 80 percent (National Forum on Health, 2000). Women vying for jobs and career advancement are often confronted with a virtually impossible dilemma: They are seen as more competent if they present themselves with stereotypically masculine rather than feminine traits; yet they are also perceived as less socially skilled and attractive—a perception that may ultimately cost them the job or career advancement they were seeking (Eagly, 2004; Jackson et al., 2001; Rudman & Glick, 2001).

Ambivalent Sexism

The bind that women can find themselves in is that if they act more consistently with gender stereotypes, they may be liked more but respected less. These contradictory messages reflect the complex, ambivalent nature of sexism. Overall, stereotypes of women tend to be more positive than stereotypes about men (Eagly et al., 1994); however, the positive traits associated with women are less valued in important domains such as business than the positive traits associated with men.

These contradictions are reflected in Peter Glick and Susan Fiske's (2001) concept of **ambivalent sexism**. Ambivalent sexism consists of two elements: *hostile sexism*, characterized by negative, resentful feelings about women's abilities, value, and ability to challenge men's power; and *benevolent sexism*, characterized by affectionate, chivalrous feelings founded on the potentially patronizing belief that women need and deserve protection. Although hostile sexism is clearly more negative and many women feel favourably toward what Glick and Fiske call benevolent sexism

ambivalent sexism A form of sexism characterized by attitudes about women that reflect both negative, resentful beliefs and feelings and affectionate, chivalrous, but potentially patronizing beliefs and feelings.

FIGURE 5.9

Hostile Sexism Across Countries

Respondents from 19 countries completed measures of hostile and benevolent sexism. The average hostile sexism scores for male respondents from 11 of these countries are depicted here. The countries are listed from left to right in order of how unequal the sexes are in terms of political and economic power as defined by United Nations' criteria. It is clear both from this figure and from the data more generally that hostile sexism is positively correlated with gender inequality. Though not depicted in this graph, benevolent sexism is also positively correlated with gender inequality. *(Data from Glick, based on author correspondence.)*

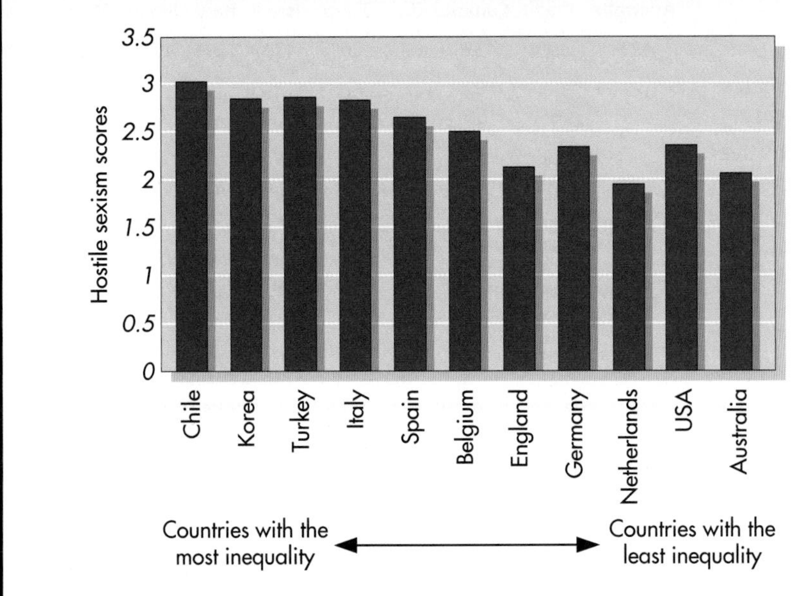

(Kilianski & Rudman, 1998), the two forms of sexism are positively correlated. In a study of 15 000 men and women in 19 nations across six continents, Glick, Fiske, and others (2000) found strong support for the notion of prevalent ambivalent sexism around the world. Among their most intriguing findings is the fact that people from countries with the greatest degree of economic and political inequality between the sexes tend to exhibit the most hostile *and* benevolent sexism. Figure 5.9 depicts the average hostile sexism scores for each of several countries.

Racism

In 1996, *National Geographic* magazine featured a story about Toronto, Ontario. While the article itself was quite complimentary towards the Canadian city, quotes from known Holocaust-denier, Ernst Zundel, were included. He blamed Blacks in Canada for rapes and drive-by shootings, and reportedly stated, "I'm objecting to allowing hordes of racially unabsorbable populations to invade the living space of a specific race." Zundel, who lived in Canada for 40 years, immigrated here when he was 19 to avoid being conscripted into the German army. In the late 1970s Zundel began distributing pamphlets with titles such as "The Hitler We Loved and Why" and "Did Six Million Really Die?" He spent his years in Canada distributing hate literature (to a not-insubstantial mailing list) until his mailing privileges were suspended and also maintained a controversial Web site where he freely posted his racist views about whomever he pleased.

In 2003 he was deemed a threat to Canadian society and human rights and was deported back to Germany in March 2005. The outrage expressed by the Canadian people at Zundel's statements indicates that societal standards and values are changing, so that blatant **racism** is increasingly less acceptable. But racism can also be much more subtle, lurking beneath surfaces and behind corners. We may see its shadow and not be sure whether it is real or an apparition. Subtle, undercover forms of racism can be just as hurtful as more blatant forms, in part because their subtlety allows them to slip through people's defenses. In this section of the chapter, we consider some of the blatant and subtle forms and consequences of racism.

None of us is completely immune from racism, whether as perpetrators or targets. But it is important to realize that racism exists at several different levels. At the *individual* level, any of us can be racist toward anyone else. And at the *institutional* and *cultural* levels, some people are privileged while others are discriminated against.

There is nothing subtle about the racism exhibited by Holocaust-denier Ernst Zundel. Before being deported from Canada, he distributed hate literature and maintained a Web site where he posted his racist views.

Going Under Cover: Modern and Implicit Racism

A close examination of legislation, opinion polls, sociological data, and social psychological research indicates that racial prejudice and discrimination have been lessening in North American over the last several decades (Dovidio & Gaertner, 1998; Dovidio et al., 2002)—although they may once again be on the rise in Western Europe (Pettigrew, 1998b). In a classic study of ethnic stereotypes published in 1933, Daniel Katz and Kenneth Braly found that white college students viewed the average white American as smart, industrious, and ambitious. Yet they saw the average African American as superstitious, ignorant, lazy, and happy-go-lucky. In multiple follow-up surveys with demographically similar samples of white students conducted from 1951 through 1993, these negative images of Blacks largely faded (Dovidio et al., 1996). For example, in 1987 only 48 percent of participants agreed with the statement "It's all right for Blacks and Whites to date each other" compared to 69 percent agreement in 1997 (Peterson, 1997).

Modern Racism As noted earlier, researchers have pointed to the existence of subtle, covert forms of racism. One example is **modern racism**—a subtle form of prejudice that surfaces in direct ways whenever it is safe, socially acceptable, or easy to rationalize. In short, the overt symptoms of racism may have changed, but the underlying disease remains. According to theories of modern racism, many people are racially ambivalent. They want to see themselves as fair, but they still harbour feelings of anxiety and discomfort concerning other racial groups (Hass et al., 1992). There are several specific theories of modern racism, but they all emphasize contradictions and tensions that lead to subtle, often unconscious forms of prejudice and discrimination.

In modern racism, prejudice against minorities surfaces primarily under circumstances when the expression of prejudice is safe, socially acceptable, and easy to rationalize because of its ambiguity. For example, in a study by John Dovidio,

racism Prejudice and discrimination based on a person's racial background.

modern racism A form of prejudice that surfaces in subtle ways when it is safe, socially acceptable, and easy to rationalize.

Jennifer Smith, and others (1997), white participants read about a trial in which the defendant was found guilty of murdering a white police officer. Some were led to believe that the defendant was black; others, that he was white. High-prejudice participants were more likely to recommend the death penalty if the defendant was black than if he was white. Low-prejudice white participants, however, exhibited a more complex pattern of results, reflecting modern racism: They tended to be *less* likely to recommend death if the defendant was black than if he was white—unless they learned that a black juror advocated the death penalty, in which case they were more likely to recommend death if the defendant was black. In short, knowing that a black juror had advocated the death penalty may have rendered their judgments more ambiguous with respect to racism. The implication is that when circumstances allow Whites to excuse a negative response, they become more likely to discriminate against Blacks.

Ambivalence concerning race is evident in situations where people's desire to be fair and unbiased is coupled with their knowledge or fear of failing to achieve this goal. In fact, many Whites who consider themselves nonprejudiced admit that on some occasions they do not react toward Blacks, or other groups such as gay men, as they should—an insight that causes them to feel embarrassed, guilty, and ashamed of themselves (Monteith et al., 2002). Indeed, when they have reason to suspect that racism could bias their judgments, low-prejudice whites may show an *opposite* bias on explicit, consciously controlled tasks, responding more favourably to Blacks than to Whites (Dovidio et al., 1997; Fein et al., 1997; Wyer, 2004).

Just as with any other form of prejudice, individuals differ in the degree to which they exhibit underlying racist tendencies. But because of the covert nature of these tendencies, measuring the differences is difficult. Several questionnaires have been developed to ask individuals relatively subtle, indirect questions about their attitudes toward particular groups, including the Modern Racism Scale (McConahay, 1986) and scales designed to measure subtle forms of racism in Western Europe and modern forms of sexism (Pettigrew & Meertens, 1995; Swim et al., 1995; Tougas et al., 1995). Although these scales have been used successfully in many studies (e.g., Wittenbrink et al., 1997), other research has demonstrated that people who are highly motivated to control their expressions of prejudice may score low on them, even if they do harbour prejudiced attitudes (Dunton & Fazio, 1997; Plant & Devine, 1998). Part of the limitation of these scales is that they *explicitly* ask respondents about their attitudes toward various groups, when research today is showing more and more how *implicit* these attitudes can be (Blair, 2001; Fazio & Olson, 2003).

Implicit Racism Just as stereotypes can be activated and applied without conscious awareness or intent, so, too, racism and other forms of prejudice and discrimination can operate unconsciously and unintentionally. Undetected by individuals who want to be fair and unbiased, implicit racism can skew their judgments, feelings, and behaviours—without inducing the guilt or motivation to make amends that more obvious, explicit forms of racism would trigger.

Again, the question of how to detect and measure implicit racism is a challenging one. Because of its implicit nature, covert measures that do not require individuals to answer questions about their attitudes typically are used. Russell Fazio and others (1995), for example, developed a procedure they call a *bona fide pipeline*, which never asks participants a single question about their attitudes but instead measures how quickly they can make particular judgments. In this procedure, participants are presented a series of adjectives on a computer screen and are asked to judge as quickly as they can whether each adjective is good (e.g., *wonderful*) or bad (e.g., *annoying*). The computer records how many milliseconds these decisions take. In the critical trials, a picture of a person's face is presented immediately before each adjective. The participants think their memory for these faces will be tested later. What they don't realize is that the race of the person they see can influence how quickly they make a positive or negative judgment about the adjective. In one study, for example, white participants were slower to rate a positive adjective as good if the adjective was presented immediately after an image of a black student than if it was presented after an image of a white student. Black participants were faster to rate a negative adjective as bad if the adjective was presented immediately after an image of a white student. Individuals' degree of prejudice is measured by the degree to which their responses are influenced by the race of the people seen in the pictures. Indeed, Fazio and his colleagues found that their measure predicted white participants' nonverbal behaviours toward Blacks in an interaction much better than did these participants' scores on the Modern Racism Scale.

Another useful implicit measure is the Implicit Association Test (IAT), first developed and tested by Anthony Greenwald and others (1998). The IAT measures the extent to which two concepts are associated. Implicit racism toward Blacks, for example, is detected to the extent that participants can associate black cues, such as a black face, faster with negative concepts and slower with positive concepts, relative to how fast they can make the same kinds of associations with white cues. The IAT is discussed in more detail in Chapter 6 on Attitudes. It has sparked an explosion of research in the past few years concerning racism and other forms of prejudice and discrimination, and it has been so popular that between October 1998 and October 2003 approximately 2.5 million IATs were completed by visitors to the IAT Web site (Nosek, 2003).

Additional measures of implicit biases are being added to researchers' toolboxes. For example, Brian Nosek and Mahzarin Banaji (2001) have created a variation of the IAT called the Go/No-Go Association Task (GNAT), which enables researchers to measure bias against a single group at a time rather than only in comparison to another. Denise Sekaquaptewa and her colleagues (2003) have developed a very different implicit measure of racial stereotyping that focuses on how individuals respond to descriptions of behaviours that are either consistent or inconsistent with stereotypes.

Interracial Perceptions and Interactions

Among the ways in which racism differs from sexism, one of the most dramatic is the extent to which members of the ingroups and outgroups interact with each other, in terms of both frequency and intimacy. While women and men often live with each other, are in the same family, and often seek each other for love and support, the divides between racial and ethnic groups tend to be more vast and may promote stronger feelings of hostility, fear, and distrust. In addition, in contemporary society, the stigma of being perceived as racist typically is much worse than being perceived as sexist. These factors—less contact, stronger negative emotions, and anxiety about appearing racist—combine to make interracial perception and interaction particularly challenging and fraught with tension.

For example, Kurt Hugenberg and Galen Bodenhausen (2003) found that individuals' levels of implicit racism predicted how biased they were in perceiving hostility in black faces. White participants watched brief movies of facial expressions of white or black targets. In their first study, the facial expression began as displaying hostility and gradually became more neutral. In a second study, the expression began as neutral and gradually became more hostile. The participants' task was to indicate when the face no longer expressed the initial emotion—in other words, when did the emotion change from hostile to neutral in the first study, or from neutral to hostile in the second study? The researchers found that participants with relatively high levels of implicit bias, as measured by the IAT, saw the black faces as staying hostile longer in the first study, and becoming hostile quicker in the second study, relative to the white faces. Participants who showed relatively low racism on the IAT did not show this bias.

These studies illustrate that for perceivers high in implicit racism, seeing a black person may prime them to perceive hostility. These researchers have also found that seeing hostility may prime such individuals to perceive someone as black. In another study (Hugenberg & Bodenhausen, 2004), participants who showed a strong race bias on the IAT were more likely to categorize a racially ambiguous face as black if the face expressed hostility than if it expressed happiness.

Not only can perceptions be influenced by racial labels and implicit racism, but the emotional reactions triggered by these perceptions can as well. Just perceiving a member of a racial outgroup may trigger different, more emotional reactions than perceiving an ingroup member. This is a conclusion suggested by a study by Allen Hart and others (2000). They monitored the brain activity of white and black participants using a functional magnetic resonance imaging (fMRI) technique while they presented the participants with pictures of individuals from their racial ingroup or outgroup. The fMRI revealed differential responses in the amygdala, a structure in the brain associated with emotion. Pictures of racial outgroup members tended to elicit stronger amygdala activation than did pictures of ingroup members. Elizabeth Phelps and others (2000) also found that white participants showed greater amygdala activation in response to black than white faces. In addition, this greater activation was associated with higher levels of implicit prejudice.

If perceptions of a member of a racial outgroup are associated with various biases and emotional reactions, interracial interactions may be all the more complex and challenging. This is evident in a study by Wendy Mendes and others (2002), in which participants who were not black interacted with either a black or a white confederate on a series of tasks. Participants were more likely to exhibit cardiovascular reactions (such as changes in the amount of blood pumped by the heart per minute) associated with feelings of threat if the confederate was black than if the confederate was white. According to Jacquie Vorauer (2003), individuals engaging in intergroup interactions often activate *metastereotypes*, or thoughts about the outgroup's stereotypes about them, and worry about being seen as consistent with these stereotypes.

When engaging in interracial interactions, Whites may be concerned about a number of things, including not wanting to be, or appear to be, racist. They may therefore try to regulate their behaviours, become particularly vigilant for signs of distrust or dislike from their interaction partners, and so on. What should ideally be a smooth-flowing normal interaction can become awkward, and even exhausting. This, in turn, can affect their partner's perceptions of them, possibly leading to the ironic outcome of their appearing to be racist because they were trying not to be. A number of researchers have been examining such phenomena (e.g., Devine et al., 2004; Dovidio et al., 2002; Richeson et al., 2003; Shelton, 2003). Jennifer Richeson and Nicole Shelton (2003), for example, found that white participants who scored relatively high on a measure of implicit racism showed impaired performance on a basic cognitive task after they had interacted with a black rather than with a white confederate, presumably because their attempt to not appear racist was so taxing. Indeed, such participants are more likely than less prejudiced individuals to show activity of brain regions thought to involve self-regulation and control in response to images of black faces (Richeson et al., 2003).

This illustration highlights (in red) areas of the brain that showed significantly greater activation in response to black faces than white faces, among relatively prejudiced participants in a study by Jennifer Richeson and others (2003). This pattern of increased activation suggests that participants were trying to control their prejudiced reactions to black faces.

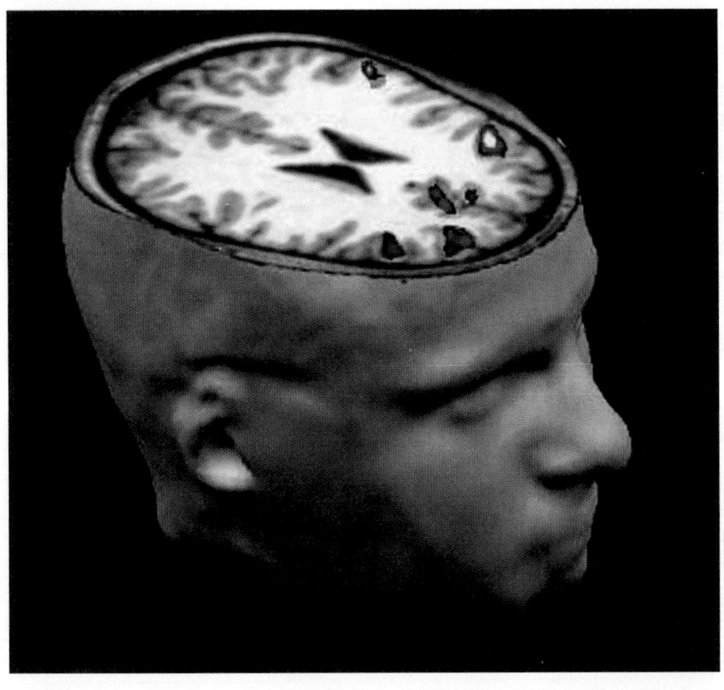

Unfortunately, the vast majority of the work on interracial perceptions and interactions focuses on whites' perceptions of and behaviours toward Blacks. There is an obvious need to expand this research to look at the more diverse and dynamic nature of interracial perception and interaction, and social psychologists are beginning to pursue this (e.g., Shelton, 2003). They are also examining interactions across other social groups. Irene Blair and others (2003), for example, are studying anxiety experienced by straight individuals as they anticipate interacting with gays.

A Threat in the Air: Effects on Stigmatized Targets

We are all the targets of other people's stereotypes and prejudices. We are stereotyped and treated differently based on how we look, how we talk, and where we come from. People infer numerous things about us by whether we are "morning people" or "night owls," what sports teams we root for, and whether we drink Coke or Pepsi. None of us is immune from having our work evaluated in a biased way, our motives questioned, or our attempts at making new friends rejected because of stereotypes and prejudices.

But for the targets of some stereotypes and prejudices, these concerns are relentless and profound. For them, there seem to be few safe havens. Social psychologists often refer to these targets as *stigmatized*—"individuals who, by virtue of their membership in a particular social group, or by possession of particular characteristics, are targets of negative stereotypes, are vulnerable to being labelled as deviant, and are devalued in society" (Major & Crocker, 1993, p. 345). What are some of the effects of being stigmatized by stereotypes and prejudice? In this section we first examine some of the effects that perceiving discrimination can have on individuals; we then focus on the impact that the perceived threat of being stereotyped can have on academic achievement, particularly that of women and minorities.

Perceiving Discrimination

Members of different groups disagree dramatically about the prevalence and magnitude of discrimination that is directed at their groups. Many surveys have shown, for example, that white Americans and black Americans have very different impressions of the degree to which racism still exists (Dovidio et al., 2002; Major et al., 2002). The more covert, subtle forms of racism characterized as modern racism may often be barely visible to observers, but their effects can be humiliating to their targets. In *Color-Blind*, writer Ellis Cose (1997), who is black, tells a story about how he was treated in a job interview 20 years ago. He was an award-winning newspaper reporter at the time and was hoping to land a job with a national magazine. The editor he met with was pleasant and gracious, but he said that the magazine didn't have many black readers. "All the editor saw was a young black guy, and since *Esquire* was not in need of a young black guy, they were not in need of me . . . he had been so busy focusing on my race that he was incapable of seeing *me* or my work" (p. 150). Then a few years later, and in light of affirmative action, Cose was asked if he was interested in a position in a firm as corporate director of equal opportunity. "I was stunned, for the question made no sense. I was an expert neither on personnel nor on equal employment law; I was, however, black, which seemed to be the most important qualification" (p. 156).

The targets of stigmatizing stereotypes wonder frequently whether and to what extent others' impressions of them are distorted through the warped lens of social categorization. Over time, such suspicions can be deeply frustrating. In particular situations, however, they can have both positive and negative consequences. In a study by Jennifer Crocker and her colleagues (1991), black participants described themselves on a questionnaire, supposedly to be evaluated by an unknown white student who sat in an adjacent room. Participants were told that they were either liked or disliked by this student on the basis of the questionnaire; then they took a self-esteem test. If the participants thought that the white student could not see them and did not know their race, their self-esteem scores predictably rose after positive feedback and declined after negative feedback. But when participants thought the evaluating student had seen them through a one-way mirror, negative feedback did *not* lower their self-esteem. In this situation, participants blamed the unfavourable evaluations on prejudice. However, there was a drawback: One-way mirror participants who received positive feedback showed a *decrease* in self-esteem. The reason? Instead of internalizing the credit for success, these participants attributed the praise to patronizing, reverse discrimination.

Attributing negative feedback to discrimination can sometimes protect one's self-esteem, but it can have costs as well. First, such an attribution can sometimes be inaccurate, and the recipient of the feedback might miss an opportunity to learn information relevant for self-improvement. Consider the dilemma faced by a white teacher who wants to give negative feedback to black students regarding the term paper they have handed in. If the students dismiss this criticism as biased, they may fail to learn from their mistakes and the teacher's advice. But if the teacher sugar-coats the feedback in an attempt to avoid the appearance of racism, the students may likewise fail to learn. Studying this dilemma in a pair of experiments, Geoffrey Cohen and others (1999) came up with a twofold prescription for solving it. What they found was that black students responded most positively to negative feedback when the teacher both (a) made it clear that he or she had high standards and (b) assured the students that they had the capacity to achieve those standards.

Second, although attributing negative feedback to discrimination can protect one's overall self-esteem, it can also make people feel as if they have less personal control over their lives. Individuals from low-status groups may be threatened by this vulnerability to discrimination and thus feel worse about themselves when they perceive that they were discriminated against—especially if they have reason to think that the discrimination against them could persist over time (Schmitt et al., 2002). There are ways in which members of stigmatized groups can assert some control over their situation. For example, if they suspect that they are about to interact with a person who is prejudiced against them, they may try to compensate by working particularly hard at getting this person to like them or to see them in a nonstereotypical way (Miller & Myers, 1998).

Whether a person is more or less likely to perceive discrimination based on his or her group membership, or to be affected negatively by such perceptions, depends in part on how and to what extent the target identifies with his or her stigmatized group (Major et al., 2002, 2004; Sellers & Shelton, 2003). For example, people who are highly identified with their group are more likely to perceive discrimination against them than are people who are less identified. In a study by Brenda Major and others (2003), for instance, female participants received negative feedback from a male confederate about their performance on a test of their creativity. The women also learned information about the man that either clearly indicated that he was sexist ("he never picks a girl to be a team leader"), indicated nothing about whether he was sexist, or offered ambiguous cues about his sexism ("he grades guys and girls differently"). Later, the women were asked to indicate the extent to which the feedback they received about their test performance was due to discrimination. As can be seen in Figure 5.10, participants who exhibited strong gender identification (such as agreeing strongly with the statement "Being a woman is an important reflection of who I am") were no more likely than less identified women to attribute the feedback to discrimination if there were no cues about sexism or if the cues were very clear that the man was sexist. But gender identification did make a difference when the cues were ambiguous: Highly identified women were significantly more likely to attribute the negative feedback to sex discrimination than were less identified women.

FIGURE 5.10

Identification with Ingroup and Attributions to Discrimination

Women who considered their gender to be either a very important ("high group identification") or not very important ("low group identification") part of their identity received negative performance feedback from a man. The women learned information about him that suggested either very clearly that he tends to be sexist ("clear cues"), that indicated nothing about his sexism ("no cues"), or that offered ambiguous information about his sexism ("ambiguous cues"). When the cues were clear or absent, women's judgment of whether the man's criticism of them was due to sexism did not differ as a function of their degree of gender identification. When ambiguous cues were present, however, high-identification women attributed his criticism to sexism significantly more than low-identification women did. *(Major et al., 2004.)*

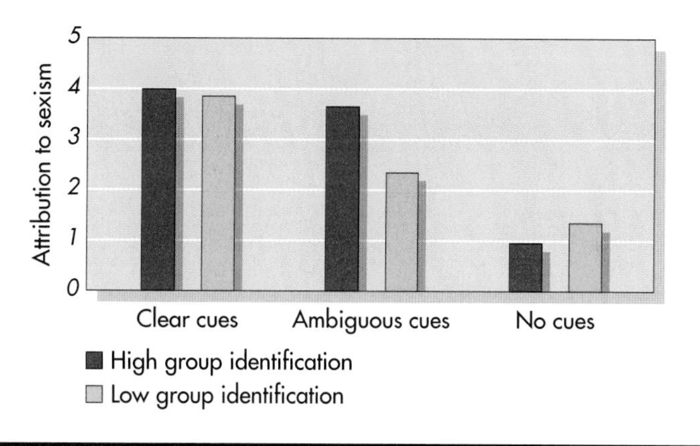

Stereotype Threat and Academic Achievement

Claude Steele proposes that in situations in which a negative stereotype can apply to certain groups, members of these groups can fear being seen "through the lens of diminishing stereotypes and low expectations" (1999, p. 44). Steele (1997) calls this predicament *stereotype threat*, for it hangs like "a threat in the air" while the individual is in the stereotype-relevant situation. The predicament can be particularly threatening for individuals whose identity and self-esteem are invested in domains for which the stereotype is relevant. Steele argues that stereotype threat plays a crucial role in influencing the intellectual performance and identity of stereotyped group members. More recently, Steele and his colleagues (2002) have broadened the scope of their analysis to include *social identity threats* more generally, which are not necessarily tied to specific stereotypes but instead reflect a more general devaluing of a person's social group.

Threats to Blacks and Women Steele cites disturbing statistics pointing to the underperformance of black students in school and of women in domains requiring advanced math skills. According to his theory, stereotype threat can hamper achievement in academic domains in two ways. First, reactions to the "threat in the air" can directly interfere with performance—for example, by increasing anxiety and triggering distracting thoughts. Second, if this stereotype threat is chronic in the academic domain, it can cause individuals to *disidentify* from that domain—to dismiss the domain as no longer relevant to their self-esteem and identity (Arndt et al., 2002; Cokley, 2002; Steele, 1997). To illustrate, imagine a black student and a white student who enter high school equally qualified in academic performance. Imagine that while taking a particularly difficult test at the beginning of the school year, each student struggles on the first few problems. The white student may begin to worry about failing, but the black student may have a whole set of additional worries about appearing to confirm a negative stereotype of Blacks. Even if the black student doesn't believe the stereotype at all, the threat of being reduced to a stereotype in the eyes of those around her can trigger anxiety and distraction, impairing her performance. And if she experiences this threat in school frequently—perhaps because she stands out as one of only a few black students in the school or because she is treated by others in a particular way—the situation may become too threatening to her self-esteem. To buffer herself against the threat, she may disidentify with school; if so, her academic performance will become less relevant to her identity and self-esteem. In its place, some other domain of life, such as social

FIGURE 5.11

Stereotype Threat and Academic Performance

Black and white students took a very difficult standardized verbal test. Before taking the test, some students were told that it was a test of their intellectual ability, but others were told that it was simply a laboratory task unrelated to intellectual ability. All students' scores on this test were adjusted based on their scores from standardized college entrance verbal examinations. Despite this adjustment, black students did significantly worse than white students on the test if it had been introduced as a test of intellectual ability (left). In contrast, among the students who had been told that the test was unrelated to ability, black students and white students performed equally well (right). *(Steele & Aronson, 1995.)*

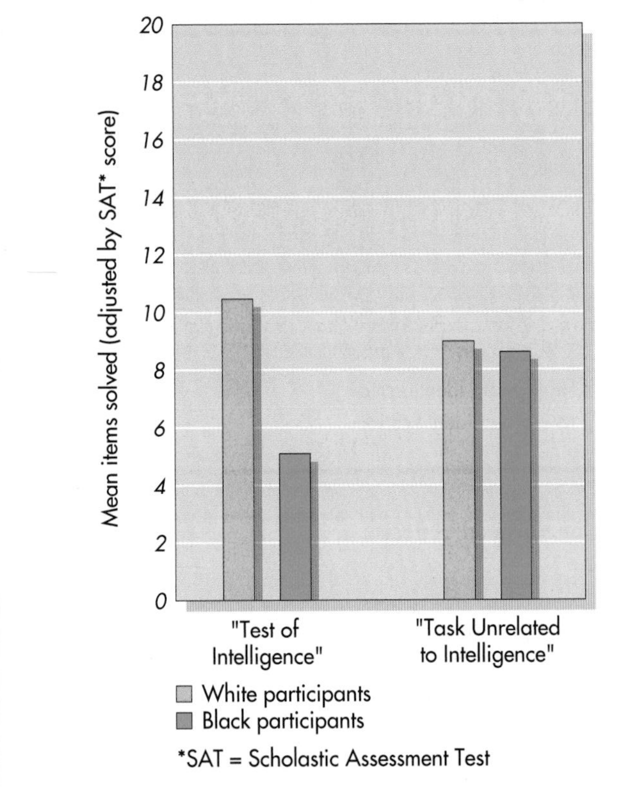

success or a particular non-academic talent will become a more important source of identity and pride.

Steele and others conducted a series of experiments in which they manipulated factors likely to increase or decrease stereotype threat as students took academic tests. For example, Steele and Joshua Aronson (1995) had black and white students from a highly selective university take a very difficult standardized verbal test. To some participants, it was introduced as a test of intellectual ability; to others, it was a laboratory problem-solving task unrelated to ability. Steele and Aronson reasoned that because of the difficulty of the test, *all* the students would struggle with it. If the test was said to be related to intellectual ability, however, the black students would also feel the threat of a negative stereotype. In contrast, if the test was simply a laboratory task and not a real test of intelligence, then negative stereotypes would be less applicable, and the stereotype threat would be reduced. In that case, black students would be less impaired while taking the test. As shown in Figure 5.11, the results supported these predictions.

Thus, a seemingly minor change in the setting—a few words about the meaning of a test—had a powerful effect on the black students' performance. In a second study, the researchers used an even more subtle manipulation of stereotype threat: whether or not the students were asked to report their race just before taking the test (which was described as unrelated to ability). Making them think about race for a few seconds just before taking the test impaired the performance of black students but had no effect on white students.

Steele's theory predicts that because negative stereotypes concerning women's advanced math skills are prevalent, women may often experience stereotype threat in settings relevant to these skills. Reducing stereotype threat in these settings, therefore, should reduce the underperformance that women tend to exhibit in these areas. To test this idea, Steven Spencer and others (1999) recruited male and female students who were good at math and felt that math was important to their identities. The researchers gave these students a very difficult standardized math test, one on which all of them would perform poorly. Before taking the test, some students were told that the test generally showed no gender differences—thereby implying that the negative stereotype of women's ability in math was *not* relevant to this particular test. Other students were told that the test *did* generally show gender differences. As Steele's theory predicted, women performed worse than men when they were told that the test typically produced gender differences, but they performed as well as men when told that the test typically did not produce gender differences. Paul Davies and others (2002) found that women performed worse on a math test after watching a series of TV commercials that depicted women in stereotypic ways than after watching neutral commercials.

Moreover, women who saw the stereotypic ads showed signs of disidentifying with math and related fields. In another study, Debra Oswald and Richard Harvey (2000–2001) demonstrated that a cartoon joking about women's math abilities triggered stereotype threat for women. On the other hand, women who tend to cope with stressful situations with humour, or women induced to think of examples of women who have been successful in math and related fields, have been found to be less vulnerable to these effects (Ford et al., 2004; McIntyre et al., 2003).

An interesting experiment by Barbara Fredrickson and others (1998) also examined how the math performance of women can be affected by the context in which they are tested. Male and female participants in their study were asked to evaluate some consumer products, including an item of clothing that they tried on and wore for some amount of time. For some participants, the clothing was a one-piece swimsuit; for others, it was a crewneck sweater. While wearing the clothing alone in a room in front of a mirror, each participant took a math test. Fredrickson and her colleagues proposed that because women in our society are made to feel more shame and anxiety about their bodies than are men, they should feel more anxious when taking the test while wearing the swimsuit, whereas men should be relatively unaffected by the manipulation of clothing. As can be seen in Figure 5.12, the results supported their predictions. After adjusting the participants' test scores based on their past performance on standardized math tests, these researchers found that women did significantly worse when wearing a swimsuit than a sweater, whereas men's performance was unaffected by the clothing manipulation.

FIGURE 5.12

The Swimsuit Becomes You

While wearing either a sweater or swimsuit in front of a mirror, male and female students took a challenging standardized math test. All students' scores on this test were adjusted based on their scores from standardized college entrance math examinations. The men's scores were unaffected by what clothes they were wearing (left). The women's scores were affected (right): Women did significantly worse on the test if they were wearing a swimsuit than if they were wearing a sweater. *(Fredrickson et al., 1998.)*

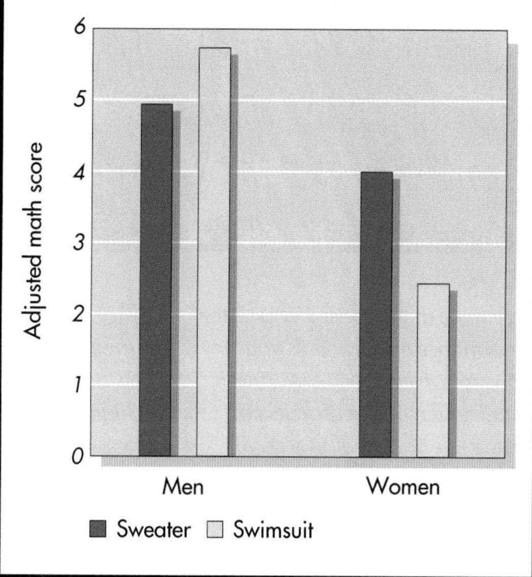

Diversity of Stereotype Threats Stereotype threats can affect any group for which strong, well known, negative stereotypes are relevant in particular settings. For example, many white athletes feel stereotype threat whenever they step onto a court or playing field where they comprise the minority. Will the white athlete feel the added weight of this threat while struggling against other athletes in a game? To address this question, Jeff Stone and others (1999) had black and white students play miniature golf. When the experimenters characterized the game as diagnostic of "natural athletic ability," the white students did worse. But when they characterized it as diagnostic of "sports intelligence," the black students did worse. In a subsequent series of experiments, Stone (2002) found that white students who were made to experience stereotype threat about their athletic ability practiced less than nonthreatened students before an athletic task. Thus they exhibited a form of self-handicapping, which, as discussed in Chapter 3, involves sabotaging one's own performance in order to provide an excuse for failure.

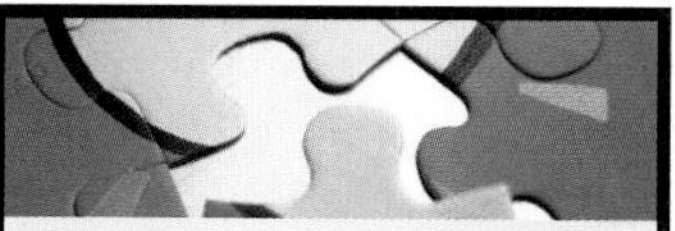

A black student is likely to perform worse on an athletic task if the task is described as one reflecting sports intelligence than if it is described as reflecting natural athletic ability. **True.**

Because individuals are members of multiple groups, they can feel either threatened or emboldened by a stereotype—depending on which of their social identities has been activated. Consider, for example, a study by Margaret Shih and others (1999) in which Asian women were examined. In North America, there is a negative stereotype about women and math but a positive stereotype about Asians and math. The researchers found that these women performed worse on a math test when their gender identity was made salient (by means of questions they had to answer about their gender before taking the test), whereas they performed better on the test when their ethnic identity was made salient. In an interesting follow-up, though, Sapna Cheryan and Galen Bodenhausen (2000) reported that if the high expectations of Asian women's math abilities are made particularly salient to them

Stereotype threat can undermine the performance of individuals from any group for which strong, well known, negative stereotypes are relevant. White male basketball players, for example, may experience stereotype threat in the presence of a black majority.

as they are about to take a math test, the concern about living up to these expectations can itself be distracting, leading to a "choking" effect and worse performance.

In general, members of a group (such as men) that has the relative advantage of being compared to an outgroup targeted by a negative stereotype (such as women in math) may benefit from what Gregory Walton and Geoffrey Cohen (2004) call *stereotype lift*. In a meta-analysis of 43 relevant studies, members of non-stereotyped groups tended to perform better on tasks when the stereotype threat against the outgroup was relevant than when it was reduced. Reducing the threat, such as reassuring the targeted group that a particular test is not relevant to a negative stereotype, therefore not only improves the performance of the targeted group but also seems to remove some of the boost that the non-stereotyped group members get from being in the allegedly "superior" group.

Since Claude Steele introduced the concept of stereotype threat, the amount of research it has inspired is staggering. Stereotype threat effects have been demonstrated with a wide variety of groups: white men on a math test when compared with Asians; women on a math test in a coed rather than same-sex setting; low-socioeconomic-status French students on a verbal test when the test was said to be diagnostic of intellectual ability; Latina women on a test of math and spatial ability; individuals with a history of mental illness on a reasoning test when they revealed their illness; and women or men on a negotiation task, depending on whether success on the task was said to be associated with masculine or feminine traits (Aronson et al., 1999; Ben-Zeev et al., 2005; Croizet & Claire, 1998; Gonzales et al., 2002; Kray et al., 2002; Quinn et al., 2004; Sekaquaptewa & Thompson, 2003). And the list goes on.

How exactly does stereotype threat interfere with performance? And who within a target group is most vulnerable to these effects? These are among the questions currently being investigated. It is clear that one does not need to *believe in* a negative stereotype in order for it to have an effect. Just knowing about the stereotype seems to be enough—particularly if the individual identifies strongly with the group and cares about performing well (McFarland et al., 2003; Schmader, 2002; Steele et al., 2002). Recent work suggests that stereotype threat can trigger physiological arousal in individuals, which may interfere with their ability to perform well on the task at hand (Ben-Zeev et al., 2004; Blascovich et al., 2001; O'Brien & Crandall, 2003). Stereotype threat may also cause threatened individuals to try to suppress thoughts about the stereotype, which can have the ironic effect of draining cognitive resources away from the task they are working on (Steele et al., 2002). People performing under stereotype threat do show impaired working memory (Croizet et al., 2004; Schmader & Johns, 2003).

But although stereotype threat effects are widespread, the growing body of research on this subject also gives us reason to hope. Through changes in the situational factors that give rise to this phenomenon, the tremendous weight of negative stereotypes can be reduced, allowing the targets of stereotypes to perform to their potential. In fact, outside of the laboratory, Steele and his colleagues have applied their theory in a university setting. By creating what Steele calls a "wise" environment that fosters interracial contact and cooperation and reduces factors that contribute to stereotype threat, these researchers found that the black students in their program showed almost no underperformance in their grades and were much less likely than other black students to drop out of school (Steele, 1997).

Reducing Stereotypes, Prejudice, and Discrimination

The description of the Dudley George tragedy that opened this chapter and the exciting research of Claude Steele and others that closed the last section illustrate some of the problems and prospects concerning stereotypes, prejudice, and discrimination. In this final section, we focus more specifically on some of the approaches that have been suggested for combating stereotypes, prejudice, and discrimination, and we point to directions we expect future research to follow on the road toward more progress.

Intergroup Contact

One of the classic books written on prejudice is Gordon Allport's (1954) *The Nature of Prejudice.* The book was unprecedented in its scope and gave important insights into the social psychology of prejudice. One of the many enduring ideas that Allport advanced was the **contact hypothesis**, which states that under certain conditions, direct contact between members of rival groups will reduce stereotyping, prejudice, and discrimination.

Around the time of the publication of this book, in the historic 1954 case of *Brown* v. *Board of Education of Topeka*, the US Supreme Court ruled that racially separate schools were inherently unequal, in violation of the *Constitution.* In part, the decision was informed by empirical evidence supplied by 32 eminent social scientists on the harmful effects of segregation on the self-esteem and academic achievement of black students as well as on race relations (Allport et al., 1953). The Supreme Court's decision propelled the nation into a large-scale social experiment.

(Left) Students at Central High School in Little Rock, Arkansas, in September 1957, shout insults at Elizabeth Eckford, 16, as she walks toward the school entrance. National Guardsmen blocked the entrance and would not let her enter. (Right) Jackie Robinson and Branch Rickey discuss Robinson's contract with the Brooklyn Dodgers. In 1947 Robinson became the first black player to cross "the colour line" and play Major League Baseball, thereby beginning the integration of major league sports.

contact hypothesis The theory that direct contact between hostile groups will reduce prejudice under certain conditions.

TABLE 5.7

The Contact Hypothesis: Critical Conditions

Four conditions are deemed very important for intergroup contact to serve as a treatment for racism. However, many desegregated schools have failed to create a setting that meets these conditions.

1. ***Equal status*** The contact should occur in circumstances that place the two groups in an equal status.
2. ***Personal interaction*** The contact should involve one-on-one interactions among individual members of the two groups.
3. ***Cooperative activities*** Members of the two groups should join together in an effort to achieve superordinate goals.
4. ***Social norms*** The social norms, defined in part by relevant authorities, should favour intergroup contact.

What would be the effect? In Ontario, the law allowing segregation of black and white students wasn't repealed until 1964, when the law was criticized by Leonard Braithwaite, Ontario's first black MPP. The last segregated school in Ontario closed in 1965.

Despite the US Court's ruling, desegregation proceeded slowly. There were stalling tactics, lawsuits, and vocal opposition to busing. Many schools remained untouched until the early 1970s. Then, as the dust began to settle, research brought the grave realization that little had changed—that contact between black and white schoolchildren was not having the intended effect. Walter Stephan (1986) reviewed studies conducted during and after desegregation and found that although 13 percent reported a decrease in prejudice among whites, 34 percent reported no change, and 53 percent reported an *increase*. These findings forced social psychologists to challenge the wisdom of their testimony to the Supreme Court and to re-examine the contact hypothesis that had guided that advice in the first place.

Is the original contact hypothesis wrong? No. Although desegregation did not immediately produce the desired changes, it's important to realize that the conditions necessary for successful intergroup contact did not exist in the public schools. Nobody ever said that deeply rooted prejudices could be erased just by throwing groups together. According to the contact hypothesis, four conditions must exist for contact to succeed (See Table 5.7). In a recent meta-analysis involving research conducted on approximately 90 000 subjects from 25 different nations, Thomas Pettigrew and Linda Tropp (2000) found that when intergroup contact satisfies the chief requirements of the contact hypothesis, it does indeed tend to be successful in reducing prejudice. Furthermore, their analysis suggests that these conditions do not all have to be present for contact to reduce prejudice, although their presence clearly does enhance the positive effects of contact. Although many problems have plagued school and other desegregation efforts, such findings offer cause for optimism.

One of the most successful demonstrations of desegregation took place on the baseball diamond. In 1945, the Montreal Royals, a triple-A minor league affiliate of the Brooklyn Dodgers, signed a young black man, Jackie Robinson, to play on the team. Robinson's opportunity came through Dodgers owner Branch Rickey, who felt that integrating baseball was both moral and good for the game (Pratkanis & Turner, 1994). Rickey knew all about the contact hypothesis and was assured by a social scientist friend that a team could furnish the conditions needed for it to work: equal status among teammates, personal interactions, dedication to a common goal, and a positive climate from the owner, managers, and coaches. Montreal—a city that for the most part embraced Jackie—provided stark contrast to his initial days traveling with the team, when he faced many obstacles on the road, including death threats. When the Royals won the "Little World Series" in 1946, thanks in large part to Jackie, he was promoted to the Dodgers. On April 15, 1947, Jackie Robinson became the first black man to break the colour barrier in American sports. The rest is history. Although Robinson did face a great deal of racism, he endured, and baseball was integrated. At the end of his first year, Jackie Robinson was named rookie of the year; and in 1962, he was elected to the Baseball Hall of Fame. At his induction ceremony, Robinson asked three people to stand beside him: his mother, his wife, and his friend Branch Rickey.

"See that man over there?"
"Yes."
"Well, I hate him."
"But you don't know him."
"That's why I hate him."
—Gordon Allport

The Jigsaw Classroom

As the third condition in Table 5.7 indicates, cooperation and shared goals are necessary for intergroup contact to be successful. Yet the typical classroom is filled with competition, exactly the wrong ingredient. Picture the scene. The teacher stands in front of the class and asks a question. Many children wave their hands, each straining to catch the teacher's eye. Then, as soon as one student is called on, the others groan in frustration. In the competition for the teacher's approval, they are losers—hardly a scenario suited to positive intergroup contact. To combat this problem in the classroom, Elliot Aronson and his colleagues (1978) developed a cooperative learning method called the *jigsaw classroom*. In newly desegregated public schools, they assigned the Grade 5 students to small racially and academically mixed groups. The material to be learned within each group was divided into subtopics, much the way a jigsaw puzzle is broken into pieces. Each student was responsible for learning one piece of the puzzle, after which all members took turns teaching their material to one another. In this system, everyone—regardless of race, ability, or self-confidence—needs everyone else if the group as a whole is to succeed.

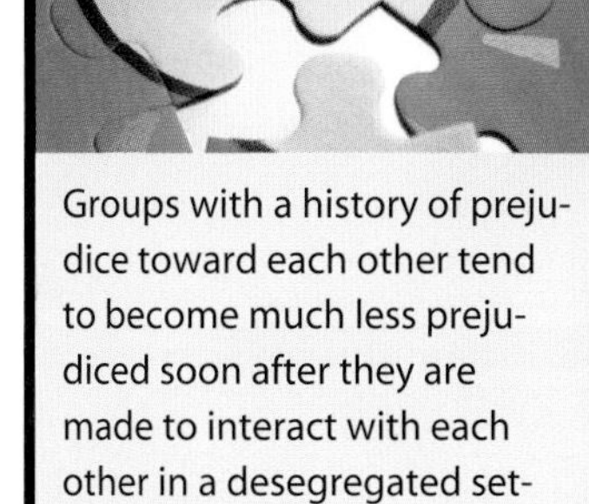

Groups with a history of prejudice toward each other tend to become much less prejudiced soon after they are made to interact with each other in a desegregated setting. **False.**

The method produced impressive results. Compared with children in traditional classes, those in jigsaw classrooms grew to like each other more, liked school more, were less prejudiced, and had higher self-esteem. What's more, academic test scores improved for minority students and remained the same for white students. Much like an interracial sports team, the jigsaw classroom offers a promising way to create a truly integrated educational experience. It also provides a model of how to use interpersonal contact to promote greater tolerance of diversity.

Decategorization and Recategorization

One important consequence of the jigsaw classroom technique is that individuals became more likely to classify outgroup members as part of their own ingroup. Instead of seeing racial or ethnic "others" within the classroom, the students now see fellow classmates, all in the same boat together. A growing body of research has emerged in support of the idea that intergroup contact emphasizing shared goals and fates, and involving the cross-cutting of group memberships (such that an individual in one's outgroup in one context will be in his or her ingroup in another context), can be very successful at reducing prejudice and discrimination—specifically by changing how group members categorize each other (Bettencourt & Dorr, 1998; Brewer, 2000).

According to the Common Ingroup Identity Model developed by John Dovidio, Samuel Gaertner, and others (Gaertner & Dovidio, 2000; Nier et al., 2001), this change comes about through two separate processes: *de*categorization and *re*categorization. *Decategorization* leads people not only to pay less attention to categories and intergroup boundaries but also to perceive outgroup members as individuals. *Recategorization*, in turn, leads people to change their conception of groups, allowing them to develop a more inclusive sense of the diversity characterizing their own ingroup. By recognizing members of an outgroup as ingroup members, just as the Rattlers and Eagles did when they converted from competitors to collaborators in Robbers Cave, "they" becomes "we," and a common ingroup identity can be forged.

Changing Cultures and Motivations

jigsaw classroom A cooperative learning method used to reduce racial prejudice through interaction in group efforts.

Earlier in the chapter we reported some of the research showing the role that popular media can play in perpetuating stereotypes and prejudice. Exposure to images that reflect the diversity within social groups, in contrast, can help weaken stereotypes and combat their automatic activation. It might also change people's implicit theories away from seeing groups as relatively fixed entities and toward seeing them as dynamic and with less rigid borders.

Motivations and values can change as well. Here again popular culture can and does play a critically important role. People—especially younger people—look to images in popular culture for a sense of current fashions and interests, but also, typically without realizing it, for what attitudes and behaviours are cool or out of date. We also look to our peers to get a sense of the local norms around us, including norms about stereotypes and prejudice (e.g., Crandall & Eshleman, 2003; Fein et al., 2003; Stangor et al., 2001). In a particular high school, a student might feel comfortable calling a friend a "fag" and mean little by it and think nothing of it, and yet several months later in university this student might realize how wrong that would be to do in his or her new setting, and feel guilty for ever having done so. If this lesson is learned, it's more likely to have been learned by watching and interacting with one's peers than from having been lectured to about diversity and sensitivity by a campus speaker. Learning these norms can make us motivated to adopt them. Legislating against hate speech, unequal treatment, and hostile environments can also be an important weapon, of course. Although they can create resistance and backlashes, laws and policies requiring behavioural change can—if done right, with no suggestion of compromise, and with important leaders clearly behind them—cause hearts and minds to follow (Aronson, 1992).

Social psychologists today recognize that more and more people are motivated to not be prejudiced. The motivation may begin as a concern with not appearing to others to be prejudiced, but for many it becomes internalized—a much more effective antidote (Devine et al., 2004; Monteith et al., 2002).

Much of the hope, therefore, rests with what is at the very core of social psychology: the social nature of the human animal. Some of our baser instincts, such as intergroup competition breeding intergroup biases, may always be present, but we also can learn from each other the thoughts, values, and goals that make us less vulnerable to perpetuating or being the targets of stereotypes, prejudice, and discrimination.

Review

- Stereotypes are beliefs that associate groups of people with certain characteristics.
- Prejudice refers to negative feelings toward persons based on their membership in certain groups.
- Discrimination concerns negative behaviours directed against persons because of their membership in a particular group. It is influenced by both beliefs and feelings about social groups.

Stereotypes

How Stereotypes Form

- The formation of stereotypes begins with the tendency for people to group themselves and others into social categories.
- Social categories can be energy-saving devices, allowing perceivers to make quick inferences about group members; but these can lead to inaccurate judgments.
- Social categorization spawns the outgroup homogeneity effect, a tendency to assume that there is more similarity among members of outgroups than ingroups.
- Sociocultural and motivational factors can influence social categorization and outgroup homogeneity effects.
- Entity theorists, who tend to see groups more in trait terms and expect more similarity and consistency within groups, are more likely to use stereotypes when judging group members than are incremental theorists, who tend to see groups as more dynamic and malleable.
- Judging the accuracy of stereotypes is challenging, in part because "accuracy" can have different meanings. Some stereotypes are more accurate than others, but, in general, stereotypes exaggerate intergroup differences and understate intergroup similarities.

How Stereotypes Survive and Self-Perpetuate

- People perceive illusory correlations between groups and traits when the traits are distinctive or when the correlations fit prior notions.
- People tend to make attributions about the causes of group members' behaviours in ways that help maintain their stereotypes.
- Group members who do not fit the mould are often subtyped, leaving the overall stereotype intact. They force a revision of beliefs only when they are otherwise typical members of the group.
- Behaviours that differ markedly from stereotypic expectations can be judged even more discrepant than they really are as the result of a contrast effect.
- In general, though, people tend to interpret and remember information in ways that confirm existing stereotypes.
- The stereotypes that people hold about group members can lead them to behave in biased ways toward those members, sometimes causing the latter to behave consistently with the stereotypes and, hence, producing a self-fulfilling prophecy.

Is Stereotyping Inevitable? Automatic Versus Intentional Processes

- Stereotypes are often activated without our awareness and operate at an unconscious, or "implicit" level.
- Stereotype activation occurs automatically under some conditions, but it can also be influenced by a number of factors, including the accessibility of various stereotypes in perceivers' minds, the kind and amount of information perceivers have about a group member, how prejudiced the perceivers are, and what the perceivers' motivations are.
- Some motivations make stereotype activation more likely to occur, and others make it less likely.
- Recent research suggests a variety of strategies—such as training, taking the perspective of others, and having egalitarian goals—that can help suppress automatic activation of stereotypes.
- Perceivers can ignore stereotypes and form more individualized impressions of others when they have personal information and the ability and motivation to use that information.
- Already activated stereotypes are more likely to be applied to specific judgments and behaviours when perceivers are busy, distracted, or otherwise cognitively impaired.
- When perceivers are highly motivated to form an accurate impression of someone, they are less likely to rely on stereotypes.

Prejudice

Intergroup Conflict

- In the Robbers Cave study, boys divided into rival groups quickly showed intergroup prejudice, which was reduced when they were brought together through tasks that required intergroup cooperation.
- Realistic conflict theory maintains that direct competition for resources gives rise to prejudice.
- Prejudice is aroused by perceived threats to an important ingroup.

Social Identity Theory

- Participants categorized into arbitrary minimal groups discriminate in favour of the ingroup.
- Social identity theory proposes that self-esteem is influenced by the fate of social groups with which we identify.
- Research shows that threats to the self cause derogation of outgroups, which in turn increases self-esteem.
- Ingroup favouritism is more intense among people whose identity and self-esteem are closely tied to their group, people in relatively small minority groups, and people who need to secure or elevate their ingroup status because of their tenuous position in the group.
- Cultural differences can influence social identity processes, with individualists more likely to show overt ingroup-enhancing biases but collectivists possibly drawing sharper distinctions between ingroups and outgroups.
- People sometimes distance themselves from ingroups, or from individual members, that fail. Even so, people can derive positive self-esteem from low-status groups.

Implicit Theories and Ideologies

- People with a social dominance orientation exhibit a desire to see one's ingroups as dominant over other groups, and tend to show stronger ingroup identification and outgroup derogation.
- People who tend to endorse and legitimize existing social arrangements can show signs of outgroup favouritism when their group holds a relatively disadvantaged position in society.

Sexism

- Sexism is a form of prejudice and discrimination based on a person's gender.

Gender Stereotypes: Blue for Boys, Pink for Girls

- Across the world, men are described as assertive, independent, and task-oriented; women as sensitive, dependent, and people-oriented.
- Gender stereotypes are so deeply ingrained that they bias perceptions of males and females from the moment they are born.

Why Do Gender Stereotypes Endure?

- Unlike most other stereotypes, gender stereotypes are more than just descriptive: They also indicate what the majority of people in a society believe men and women *should* be.

- Cultural institutions foster gender distinctions in portrayals of males and females.
- Stereotypic media images of women and men have been implicated in the increased incidence of eating disorders and anxiety about physical appearance, and can affect both men's and women's behaviour.
- Perceived differences between men and women are magnified by the contrasting social roles they occupy.

Sex Discrimination: A Double Standard?

- There are some striking sex differences in occupational choices.
- Men and women are judged more favourably when they apply for jobs that are consistent with gender stereotypes.
- Women often face a difficult dilemma: If they behave consistently with gender stereotypes, they may be liked more but respected less.

Ambivalent Sexism

- Ambivalent sexism reflects both hostile sexism, characterized by negative, resentful feelings toward women, and benevolent sexism, characterized by affectionate, chivalrous, but potentially patronizing feelings toward women.
- Individuals from countries with the greatest degree of economic and political inequality between men and women tend to exhibit high levels of both hostile and benevolent sexism.

Racism

- Racism is a form of prejudice and discrimination based on a person's racial background.
- Individual, institutional, and cultural factors fuel racism.

Going Under Cover: Modern and Implicit Racism

- Over the years, surveys have recorded a decline in negative views of black Americans.
- However, more subtle, modern racism surfaces in less direct ways when people can rationalize racist behaviour.
- People's ambivalence concerning race can lead them to exhibit biases in favour of or against particular groups, depending on the context.
- Racism often works implicitly, inasmuch as stereotypes and prejudice can fuel discrimination without conscious intent or awareness on the part of perceivers.
- Researchers use covert measures to detect and measure modern and implicit racism and other subtle forms of prejudice and discrimination.

Interracial Perceptions and Interactions

- White perceivers are more likely to perceive hostility in the facial expressions of a black person than in a white person.
- Seeing a member of a racial outgroup is associated with increased activation in the amygdala, a brain structure associated with emotion.
- Interracial interactions can feel threatening, anxiety-provoking, and cognitively draining, particularly among people relatively high in implicit racism.

A Threat in the Air: Effects on Stigmatized Targets

- Stigmatized groups are negatively stereotyped and devalued in society.

Perceiving Discrimination

- When members of stigmatized groups perceive others' reactions to them as discrimination, they experience both benefits and drawbacks to their self-esteem and feelings of control.
- The frequency, and effects, of such perceptions depend in part on how and to what extent the target identifies with his or her stigmatized group.

Stereotype Threat and Academic Achievement

- Situations that activate stereotype threat cause individuals to worry that others will see them in negative, stereotypic ways.
- Stereotype threat can impair the intellectual performance and identity of stereotyped group members.
- Stereotype threat can cause African American and female students to fail to perform to their potential in academic settings.
- Research has documented a huge and growing list of groups whose members show underperformance and performance-impairing behaviours when a negative stereotype about their abilities is made relevant.
- Some new evidence points to increased arousal, attempts at suppressing negative stereotypes, and impaired working memory as mechanisms through which stereotype threat creates underperformance.
- Reducing stereotype threat through slight changes in a setting can dramatically improve the performance of stereotyped group members.

Reducing Stereotypes, Prejudice, and Discrimination

Intergroup Contact

- In its 1954 ruling in *Brown* v. *Board of Education*, the US Supreme Court ordered public schools to desegregate.
- Although, according to the contact hypothesis, desegregation should reduce prejudice, it did not cure the problem in the absence of key conditions of intergroup contact: equal status, personal interactions, the need to achieve a common goal, and social norms. When these conditions are met, intergroup contact tends to be much more successful in reducing prejudice.

The Jigsaw Classroom

- Schools often fail to meet the conditions for reducing prejudice, often because competition is too great. A program that is designed to foster intergroup cooperation and interdependence suggests that the right kinds of contact can improve attitudes and behaviours in a school setting.

Decategorization and Recategorization

- Recent research has demonstrated that changing how group members categorize each other can reduce prejudice and discrimination.

Changing Cultures and Motivations

- Changes in the kinds of information perpetuated in one's culture can alter how we perceive social groups.
- As the general culture, and local norms, change to promote values consistent with fairness and diversity and inconsistent with prejudice and discrimination, individuals' motives can change accordingly.

Key Terms

ambivalent sexism *(157)*
contact hypothesis *(169)*
contrast effect *(137)*
discrimination *(130)*
entity theorists *(134)*
group *(130)*
illusory correlation *(135)*
incremental theorists *(134)*
ingroup favouritism *(146)*
ingroups *(132)*
jigsaw classroom *(171)*
modern racism *(159)*
outgroup homogeneity effect *(132)*
outgroups *(132)*
prejudice *(130)*
racism *(158)*
realistic conflict theory *(145)*
relative deprivation *(145)*
sexism *(151)*
social categorization *(131)*
social dominance orientation *(150)*
social identity theory *(146)*
social role theory *(155)*
stereotype *(130)*
subliminal presentation *(140)*
superordinate goals *(145)*

Very brief exposure to a member of a stereotyped group does not lead to biased judgments or responses, but longer exposure typically does.

False. *Even very brief exposure to a member of a stereotyped group can activate the stereotype about the group, and this activation can bias subsequent judgments and reactions. Learning more information about the individual, however, sometimes reduces the effects of the stereotype.*

Members of low-status, stereotyped groups have lower self-esteem than members of high-status groups.

False. *Because people are adaptive in terms of what they emphasize and take pride in, membership in a low-status, stereotyped group often does not cause an individual to develop low self-esteem.*

Even brief exposure to sexist television commercials can significantly influence the behaviours of men and women.

True. *Exposure to sexist commercials can make men behave in more sexist ways toward women and can make women engage in more stereotypical behaviours.*

A black student is likely to perform worse on an athletic task if the task is described as one reflecting sports intelligence than if it is described as reflecting natural athletic ability.

True. *Research on stereotype threat suggests that black students are likely to be concerned about being seen through the lens of negative stereotypes concerning their intelligence if the task is described as one that is diagnostic of their sports intelligence—a situation that could undermine their performance. White students tend to show the opposite effect: Their performance is worse if the task is described as reflecting natural athletic ability.*

Groups with a history of prejudice toward each other tend to become much less prejudiced soon after they are made to interact with each other in a desegregated setting.

False. *When the contact between groups involves unequal status between them, lacks personal interaction between individual group members, and does not involve cooperation to achieve shared goals, contact is not likely to reduce prejudice.*

6 Attitudes

OUTLINE

PREVIEW

THIS CHAPTER examines social influences on attitudes. We define *attitudes* and then discuss how they are measured and when they are related to behaviour. Then we consider two methods of changing attitudes. First, we look at source, message, and audience factors that win persuasion through the media of communication. Second, we consider theories and research showing that people often change their attitudes as a consequence of their own actions.

PUTTING COMMON SENSE TO THE TEST

T / F

___ **Researchers can tell if someone has a positive or negative attitude by measuring physiological arousal.**

___ **In reacting to persuasive communications, people are influenced more by superficial images than by logical arguments.**

___ **People are most easily persuaded by commercial messages that are presented without their awareness.**

___ **The more money you pay people to tell a lie, the more they will come to believe it.**

___ **People often come to like what they suffer for.**

Abortion. Same sex marriages. Gun control. Immigration. Aboriginal autonomy. Liberals and Conservatives. Israelis and Palestinians. Anyone who follows recent events knows how passionately people feel about the issues of the day. Attitudes and the mechanisms of attitude change, or persuasion, are a vital part of human social life. This chapter addresses three sets of questions: (1) What is an attitude, how can it be measured, and what is its link to behaviour? (2) What kinds of persuasive communications lead people to change their attitudes? (3) Why do we often change our attitudes as a result of our own actions?

The Study of Attitudes

Should smoking be prohibited in public places? Would you rather listen to rock music or jazz, drink Coke™ or Pepsi™, work on a PC or a Mac? Should Quebec secede from the rest of Canada? As these questions suggest, each of us has positive and negative reactions to various persons, objects, and ideas. These reactions are called **attitudes**. Skim the chapters in this book, and you'll see just how pervasive attitudes are. You'll see, for example, that self-esteem is an attitude we hold about ourselves, that attraction is a positive attitude toward another person, and that prejudice is a negative attitude often directed against certain groups. Indeed, the study of attitudes—what they are, where they come from, how they can be measured, what causes them to change, and how they interact with behaviour—is central to the whole field of social psychology (Ajzen, 2001; Eagly & Chaiken, 1999; Petty & Chaiken, 2004; Wood, 2000).

attitude A positive, negative, or mixed reaction to a person, object, or idea.

FIGURE 6.1

Four Possible Reactions to Attitude Objects

As shown, people evaluate objects along both positive and negative dimensions. As a result, our attitudes can be positive, negative, ambivalent, or indifferent. *(Cacioppo et al., 1997.)*

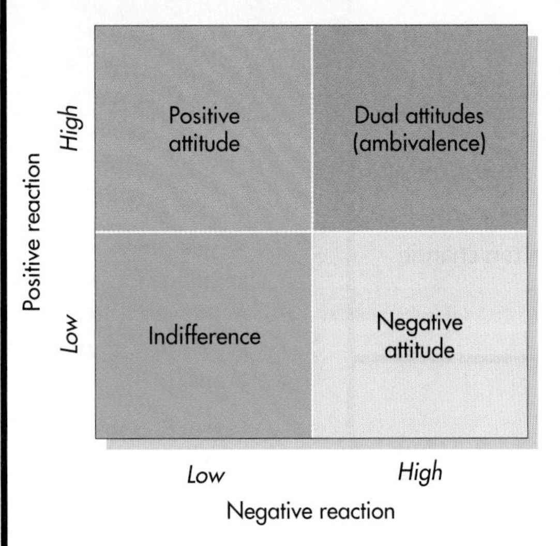

An attitude is a positive, negative, or mixed evaluation of an object, expressed at some level of intensity—nothing more, nothing less. *Like, love, dislike, hate, admire,* and *detest* are the kinds of words that people use to describe their attitudes. It's important to realize that attitudes cannot simply be represented along a single continuum ranging from wholly positive to wholly negative—as you might expect if attitudes were like the balance knob on a stereo that directs sound to the left or right speaker or like the lever on a thermostat that raises or lowers temperature. Rather, as depicted in Figure 6.1, our attitudes can vary in strength along both positive and negative dimensions. In other words, we can react to something with positive affect, with negative affect, with ambivalence (strong but mixed emotions), or with apathy and indifference (Cacioppo et al., 1997). In fact, at times people can have both positive and negative reactions to the same attitude object without feeling conflict. For example, MacDonald and Zanna (1998) found that men with ambivalent attitudes towards feminists indicated admiration for them but not affection. Someone who is openly positive toward racial minorities but unconsciously harbours prejudice is a case in point (Wilson et al., 2000).

Everyone routinely forms positive and/or negative evaluations of the people, places, objects, and ideas they encounter. In fact, this process is often instantaneous and automatic, like a reflex action (Bargh et al., 1996; Cunningham et al., 2003; Duckworth et al., 2002). It now appears, however, that individuals differ in the extent to which they tend to react to stimuli in strong positive and negative terms. What about you—do you form opinions easily? Do you have strong likes and dislikes? Or do you tend to react in more objective, non-evaluative ways? People who describe themselves as high rather than low in the *need for evaluation* are more likely to view their daily experiences in judgmental terms. They are also more opinionated on a whole range of social, moral, and political issues (Jarvis & Petty, 1996).

Before we examine the elusive science of measuring people's attitudes, let's stop for a moment and ponder this question: Why do we bother to have attitudes? Does forming positive and negative judgments of people, objects, and ideas serve a useful purpose? Over the years, researchers have found that attitudes serve important functions, such as enabling us to judge, quickly and without much thought, whether something we encounter is good or bad, helpful or hurtful, and to be sought or avoided (Maio & Olson, 2000). The problem is that having pre-existing attitudes about persons, objects, and ideas can lead us to become closed-minded, bias the way we interpret new information, and make us more resistant to change. Russell Fazio and others (2000) found that people who were focused on their positive or negative attitudes toward computerized faces, compared to those who were not, were later slower to notice when the faces were "morphed" and no longer the same. On the global stage, five full months after the terrorist attack on the World Trade Center in the United States, the Gallup Organization interviewed thousands of adults from nine Islamic countries and found that 61 percent did *not* believe, as most westerners did, that the attacks were carried out by Arab men (Gallup Poll Editors, 2002).

How Attitudes Are Measured

In 1928, Louis Thurstone published an article entitled *Attitudes Can Be Measured.* What Thurstone failed to anticipate, however, is that attitude measurement is a tricky business. One review of research uncovered more than 500 different methods of determining an individual's attitudes (Fishbein & Ajzen, 1972).

As seen in this pro-marijuana rally, people are often very passionate about their attitudes.

Self-Report Measures The easiest way to assess a person's attitude about something is to ask. All over the world, public opinion is assessed on a range of issues—in politics, the economy, health care, foreign affairs, science and technology, sports and entertainment, and lifestyles. Simply by asking, Ipsos-Reid polls conducted in 2006 revealed that the majority of Canadians prefer a public (versus private) health-care system; believe that gun violence is a result of gangs, drugs and lenient judges; that Canadian children prefer grilled cheese to peanut-butter and jelly sandwiches (**http://www.ipsos.ca/pa/polls.cfm**).

Self-report measures are direct and straightforward. But attitudes are sometimes too complex to be measured by a single question. As you may recall from Chapter 2, one problem recognized by public opinion pollsters is that responses to attitude questions can be influenced by their wording, the context in which they are asked, and other extraneous factors (Schwarz, 1999; Tourangeau et al., 2000).

Recognizing the shortcomings of single-question measures, researchers who study people's social and political opinions often use multiple-item questionnaires known as **attitude scales** (Robinson et al., 1991, 1998). Attitude scales come in different forms, perhaps the most popular being the *Likert Scale*, named after its inventor, Rensis Likert (1932). In this technique, respondents are presented with a list of statements about an attitude object and are asked to indicate on a multiple-point scale how strongly they agree or disagree with each statement. Each respondent's total attitude score is derived by summing his or her responses to all the items. However, regardless of whether attitudes are measured by one question or by a full-blown scale, the results should be taken with caution. All self-report measures assume that people express their true opinions. Sometimes this assumption is reasonable and correct, but often it is not. Wanting to make a good impression on others, people are generally reluctant to admit to their failures, vices, weaknesses, unpopular opinions, and prejudices.

One approach to this problem is to increase the accuracy of self-report measures. To get respondents to answer attitude questions more truthfully, researchers sometimes use the **bogus pipeline**, an elaborate mechanical device that supposedly records our true feelings like a lie-detector test. While the machine actually has no ability to detect anything, participants are convinced that it does. Not wanting to get caught in a lie, respondents tend to answer attitude questions with less social desirability bias when they think that deception would be detected by the bogus pipeline (Jones & Sigall, 1971; Roese & Jamieson, 1993). For example, Roger Tourangeau and others (1997) found that people were more likely to admit to drinking too much, using cocaine, having frequent oral sex, and not exercising enough when the bogus pipeline was used than when it was not.

Covert Measures A second general approach to the self-report problem is to collect indirect, covert measures of attitudes that cannot be controlled. One possibility in this regard is to use observable behaviour such as facial expressions, tone of voice,

attitude scale A multiple-item questionnaire designed to measure a person's attitude toward some object.

bogus pipeline A phoney lie-detector device that is sometimes used to get respondents to give truthful answers to sensitive questions.

As this polling station in Vancouver illustrates, attitude measurement is all around us.

and body language. In one study, Gary Wells and Richard Petty (1980) secretly videotaped college students as they listened to a speech and noticed that when the speaker took a position that the students agreed with (that tuition costs should be lowered), most made vertical head movements. But when the speaker took a contrary position (that tuition costs should be raised), head movements were in a horizontal direction. Without realizing it, the students had signalled their attitudes by nodding and shaking their heads.

Although behaviour provides clues, it is far from perfect as a measure of attitudes. Sometimes, we nod our heads because we agree; at other times, we nod to be polite. The problem is that people monitor their overt behaviour just as they monitor self-reports. But what about internal, physiological reactions that are difficult, if not impossible, to control? Does the body betray how we feel? In the past, researchers tried to divine attitudes from involuntary physical reactions such as perspiration, heart rate, and pupil dilation. The result, however, was always the same: Measures of arousal reveal the intensity of one's attitude toward an object but not whether that attitude is positive or negative. On the physiological record, love and hate look very much the same (Petty & Cacioppo, 1983).

Although physiological arousal measures cannot distinguish between positive and negative attitudes, some exciting alternatives have been discovered. One is the **facial electromyograph (EMG)**. As shown in Figure 6.2, certain muscles in the face contract when we are happy, and different facial muscles contract when we are sad. Some of the muscular changes cannot be seen with the naked eye, however, so the facial EMG is used. To determine whether the EMG can be used to measure the affect associated with attitudes, John Cacioppo and Richard Petty (1981) recorded facial muscle activity of college students as they listened to a message with which they agreed or disagreed. The agreeable message increased activity in the cheek muscles—the facial pattern characteristic of happiness. The disagreeable message sparked activity in the forehead and brow area—the facial patterns associated with sadness and distress. Outside observers who later watched the participants were unable to see these subtle changes. Apparently, the muscles in the human face reveal smiles, frowns, and other reactions to attitude objects that otherwise are hidden from view (Cacioppo et al., 1986; Tassinary & Cacioppo, 1992).

From a social neuroscience perspective, electrical activity in the brain may also assist in the measure of attitudes. In 1929, Hans Burger invented a machine that could detect, amplify, and record "waves" of electrical activity in the brain through electrodes pasted to the surface of the scalp. The instrument is called an *electroencephalograph*, or EEG, and the information it provides takes the form of line tracings called *brain waves*. Based on an earlier discovery, that certain patterns of electrical brain activity are triggered by exposure to stimuli that are novel or inconsistent, Cacioppo and his colleagues (1993) had participants list ten items they liked and ten they did not like within various object categories (fruits, sports, movies, universities, etc.). Later, these participants were brought into the laboratory, wired to an EEG, and presented with a list of category words that depicted the objects they liked and disliked. The result: Brain-wave patterns normally triggered by inconsistency increased more when a disliked stimulus appeared after a string of positive items, or

facial electromyograph (EMG) An electronic instrument that records facial muscle activity associated with emotions and attitudes.

when a liked stimulus was shown after a string of negative items, than when either stimulus evoked the same attitude as the items that preceded it. In another study, researchers used fMRI to record brain activity in participants as they read names of famous figures, such as Adolph Hitler and Bill Cosby. When the names were read, they observed greater activity in the amygdala, a structure in the brain associated with emotion—regardless of whether or not participants were asked to evaluate the famous figures (Cunningham et al., 2003). This suggests that people react automatically to positive and negative attitude objects. Although more research is needed, it appears that attitudes may be measurable by electrical activity in the brain.

FIGURE 6.2

The Facial EMG: A Covert Measure of Attitudes?

The facial EMG makes it possible to detect differences between positive and negative attitudes. Notice the major facial muscles and recording sites for electrodes. When people hear a message with which they agree rather than disagree, there is a relative increase in EMG activity in the depressor and zygomatic muscles but a relative decrease in the corrugator and frontalis muscles. These changes cannot be seen with the naked eye. *(Cacioppo & Petty, 1981.)*

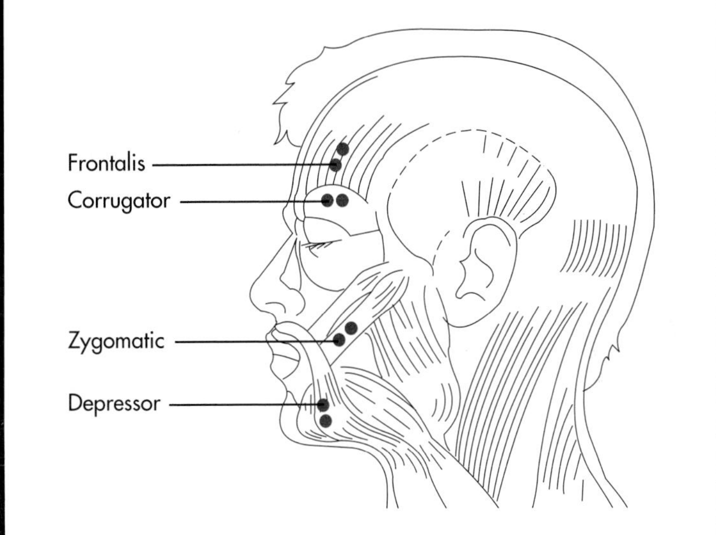

The Implicit Association Test (IAT) When it comes to covert measurement, one particularly interesting development is based on the notion that each of us has **implicit attitudes** that we *cannot* self-report in questionnaires because we are not aware of having them (Fazio & Olson, 2003). To measure these attitudes, Anthony Greenwald, Mahzarin Banaji, Brian Nosek, and others have developed the *Implicit Association Test*, or *IAT*. As we saw in Chapter 5, the IAT measures the speed with which people associate pairs of concepts (Greenwald et al., 1998). To see how it works, try visiting the IAT Web site by typing **"Implicit Association Test"** in a search engine or **www.yale.edu/implicit**.

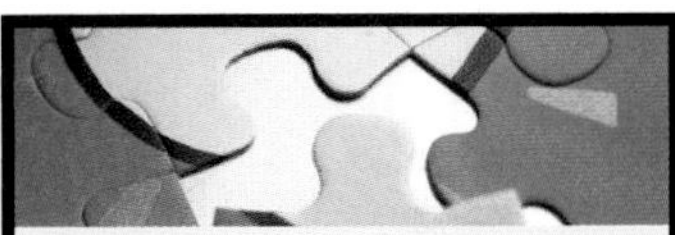

Researchers can tell if someone has a positive or negative attitude by measuring physiological arousal. **False.**

You can complete tests that measure your implicit attitudes about race, age, gender, and many other constructs. Part of the task asks you to quickly respond to two concepts (such as *black* and *wonderful*, or *elderly* and *good*); the more closely linked those associations are, the easier it is for you to respond to them —therefore your reaction time will be faster. Using the IAT, your implicit attitudes about Blacks can thus be detected by the speed it takes you to respond to *black-bad/white-good* pairings relative to *black-good/white-bad* pairings. The test takes only about ten minutes to complete. When you're done, you receive the results of your test and an explanation of what it means (see Figure 6.3).

Starting in 1998, for the next five years visitors to this site completed 2.5 million tests. In questionnaires, interviews, and public opinion polls, people don't tend to reveal their stereotypes, prejudices, or other unpopular attitudes. Yet on the IAT, respondents have exhibited an average implicit preference for self over other, white over black, young over old, and the stereotype that links males with careers and females with family (Greenwald et al., 2003; Nosek et al., 2002).

Implicit Association Test (IAT) A covert measure of unconscious attitudes, it is derived from the speed at which people respond to pairings of concepts—such as *Blacks* or *Whites* with *good* or *bad*.

implicit attitude An attitude—such as prejudice—that one is not aware of having.

The Link Between Attitudes and Behaviour

People take for granted the notion that attitudes influence behaviour. We assume that voters' opinions of opposing candidates predict the decisions they make on election day, that consumers' attitudes toward competing products influence the purchases they make, and that feelings of prejudice trigger negative acts of discrimination. Yet

FIGURE 6.3

The Implicit Association Test (IAT)

Through a sequence of tasks, the IAT measures implicit racial attitudes toward for example, Blacks by measuring how quickly people respond to *black-bad/white-good* word pairings relative to *black-good/white-bad* pairings. Responding faster to the first pairing indicates a negative association to Blacks. *(Greenwald et al., 2003.)*

as sensible as these assumptions seem, the link between attitudes and behaviour is far from perfect.

Sociologist Richard LaPiere (1934) was the first to notice that attitudes and behaviour don't always go hand in hand. In the 1930s, LaPiere took a young Chinese American couple on a three-month, 10 000-mile automobile trip, visiting 250 restaurants, campgrounds, and hotels across the United States. Although prejudice against Asians was widespread at the time, the couple was refused service only once. Yet when LaPiere wrote back to the places they had visited and asked if they would accept Chinese patrons, more than 90 percent of those who returned an answer said they would not. Self-reported attitudes did not correspond with behaviour.

This study was provocative but seriously flawed. LaPiere measured attitudes several months after his trip, and during that time the attitudes may have changed. He also did not know whether those who responded to his letter were the same people who had greeted the couple in person. It was even possible that the Chinese couple were served wherever they went only because they were accompanied by LaPiere himself.

Despite these problems, LaPiere's study was the first of many to reveal a lack of correspondence between attitudes and behaviour. In 1969, Allan Wicker reviewed the applicable research and concluded that attitudes and behaviour are correlated only weakly, if at all. Sobered by this conclusion, researchers were puzzled: Could it be that the votes we cast do *not* follow from our political opinions, that consumer purchases are *not* based on their attitudes toward a product, or that discrimination is *not* related to underlying prejudice? Is the study of attitudes useless to those interested in human social behaviour? No, not at all. During the next few years, researchers went on to identify some of the conditions under which attitudes and behaviour are correlated. When Stephen Kraus (1995) analyzed all of this research, he concluded that "attitudes significantly and substantially predict future behaviour" (p. 58). In fact, Kraus calculated that there would have to be 60 983 new studies reporting a zero correlation before this conclusion would have to be revised.

Attitudes in Context One important factor is the level of *correspondence*, or similarity, between attitude measures and behaviour. Perhaps the reason that LaPiere (1934) did not find a correlation between self-reported prejudice and discrimination was that he had asked proprietors about Asians in general but then observed their actions toward only one couple. To predict a single act of discrimination, he should have measured people's more specific attitudes toward a young, well-dressed, attractive Chinese couple accompanied by an American professor.

Analyzing more than a hundred studies, Icek Ajzen and Martin Fishbein (1977) found that attitudes correlate with behaviour only when attitude measures closely match the behaviour in question. Illustrating the point, Andrew Davidson and James Jaccard (1979) tried to use attitudes to predict whether women would use birth control pills within the next two years. Attitudes were measured in a series of questions ranging from very general ("How do you feel about birth control?") to very specific ("How do you feel about using birth control pills during the next two years?"). The more specific the initial attitude question was, the better it predicted the behaviour. Other researchers as well have replicated this finding (Kraus, 1995).

FIGURE 6.4

Theory of Planned Behaviour

According to the theory of planned behaviour, attitudes toward a specific behaviour combine with subjective norms and perceived control to influence a person's intentions. These intentions, in turn, guide but do not completely determine behaviour. This theory places the link between attitudes and behaviour within a broader context. *(Ajzen, 1991.)*

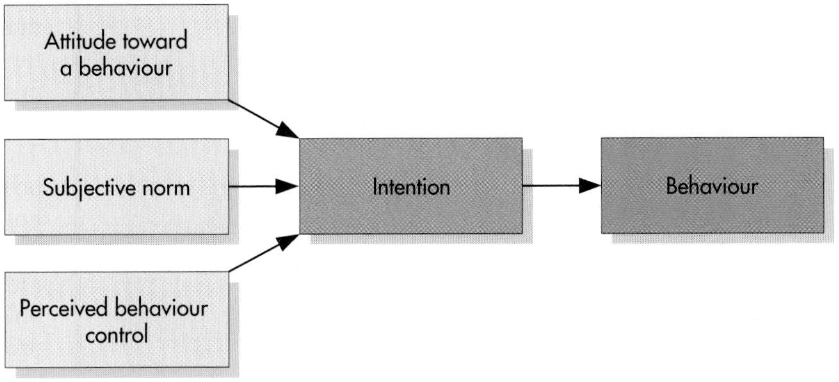

Attitude toward a behaviour
Subjective norm
Perceived behaviour control
Intention
Behaviour

The link between our feelings and our actions should also be placed within a broader context. Attitudes are one determinant of social behaviour, but there are other determinants as well. This limitation formed the basis for Fishbein's (1980) theory of reasoned action, which Ajzen (1991) then expanded into his **theory of planned behaviour**. According to these theories, our attitudes influence our behaviour through a process of deliberate decision making—and their impact is limited in four respects (see Figure 6.4).

First, as just described, behaviour is influenced less by general attitudes than by attitudes toward a specific behaviour. Second, behaviour is influenced not only by attitudes but also by *subjective norms*—our beliefs about what others think we should do. As we'll see in Chapter 7, social pressures to conform often lead us to behave in ways that are at odds with our inner convictions. Third, according to Ajzen, attitudes give rise to behaviour only when we perceive the behaviour to be within our *control*. To the extent that people lack confidence in their ability to engage in some behaviour, they are unlikely to form an intention to do so. Fourth, although attitudes (along with subjective norms and perceived control) contribute to an *intention* to behave in a particular manner, people often do not or cannot follow through on their intentions.

A good deal of research supports the theories of reasoned action and planned behaviour (Madden et al., 1992). Indeed, this general approach, which places the link between attitudes and behaviours in a broader context, has successfully been used to predict a wide range of important and practical behaviours—such as using condoms, obeying speed limits, and eating healthy foods (Albarracin et al., 2001; Conner et al., 2002; Elliott et al., 2003).

Strength of the Attitude According to the theories of reasoned action and planned behaviour, specific attitudes combine with social factors to produce behaviour. Sometimes attitudes have more influence on behaviour than do other factors; sometimes they have less influence. In large part, it depends on the importance, or *strength*, of the attitude. Each of us has some views that are nearer and dearer to the heart than others. Computer jocks often become attached to PCs or Macs, while political activists have fiery passions for one political party over others. In

theory of planned behaviour The theory that attitudes toward a specific behaviour combine with subjective norms and perceived control to influence a person's actions.

FIGURE 6.5

Genetic Influences on Attitudes

In this study, 672 twins individually rated their attitudes on a range of issues and activities. Indicating the role of genetic factors, there were higher correlations among pairs of identical twins than among pairs of fraternal twins. *(Olson et al., 2001.)*

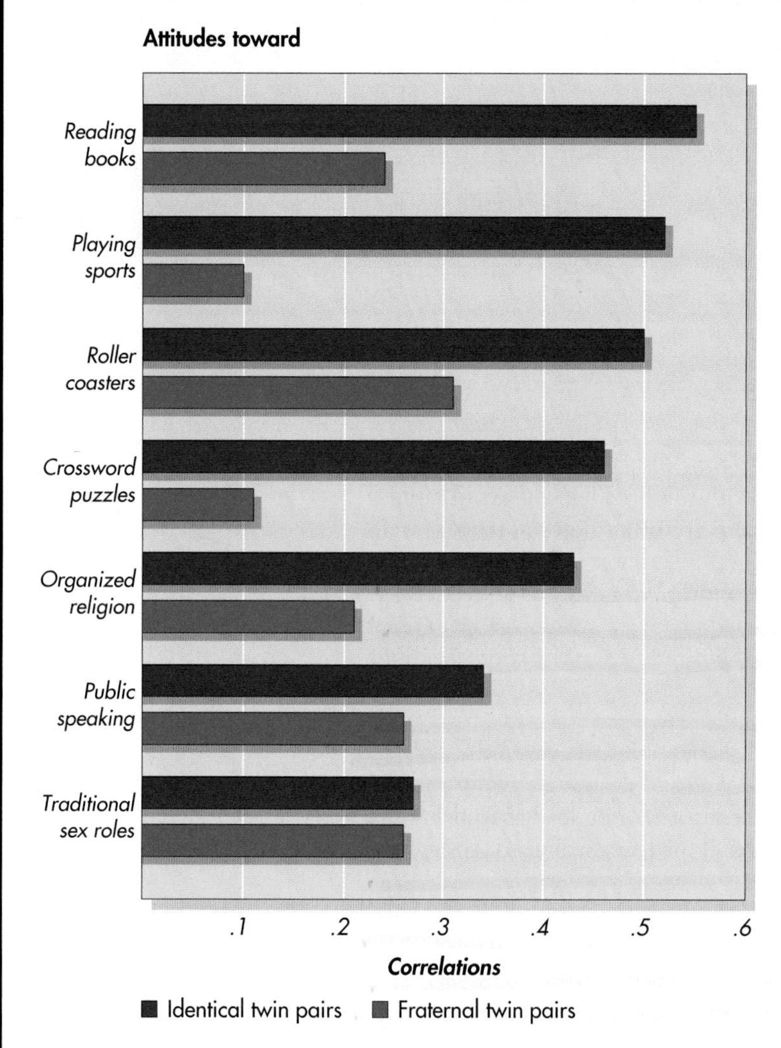

each case, the attitude is held with great confidence and is difficult to change (Petty & Krosnick, 1995).

Why are some attitudes stronger than others? One provocative hypothesis, first advanced by Abraham Tesser (1993), is that strong likes and dislikes are rooted in our genetic make-up. Research shows that on some issues, the attitudes of identical twins are more similar than those of fraternal twins; and twins raised apart are as similar to each other as are those raised in the same home. This pattern of evidence suggests that people may be predisposed by nature to hold certain attitudes. Indeed, Tesser found that when asked about attitudes for which there seems to be a genetic link (such as attitudes toward sexual promiscuity, religion, and the death penalty), research participants were quicker to respond and less likely to alter their views in the direction of social norms. Tesser speculated that as a result of inborn physical, sensory, and cognitive skills, temperament, and personality traits, individuals are biologically predisposed to hold certain strong attitudes. As illustrated in Figure 6.5, other twin studies, too, have supported the notion that people differ in their attitudes toward a range of issues, in part, because of differences in their genetic make-up (Olson et al., 2001).

Whether or not there is a genetic link, David Boninger and others (1995) have identified three psychological factors that consistently seem to distinguish between our strongest and weakest attitudes. They found that the attitudes people held most passionately were those that concerned issues that (1) directly affected their own outcomes and self-interests; (2) related to deeply held philosophical, political, and religious values; and (3) were of concern to their close friends, family, and social ingroups.

Several factors indicate the strength of an attitude and its link to behaviour. One is that people tend to behave in ways that are consistent with their attitudes when they are well informed. For example, in one study, students were questioned about their views on various environmental issues and later were asked to take action—to sign petitions, participate in a recycling project, and so on. The more informed students were, the more consistent their environmental attitudes were with their behaviour (Kallgren & Wood, 1986).

Second, the strength of an attitude is indicated not only by the *amount* of information on which it is based but also by *how* that information was acquired. Research shows that attitudes are more stable and more predictive of behaviour when they are born of direct personal experience than when based on indirect, secondhand information. In a series of experiments, for example, Russell Fazio and Mark Zanna (1981) introduced two groups of participants to a set of puzzles. One group worked on sample puzzles; the other group merely watched someone else work on them. All participants were then asked to rate their interest in the puzzles (attitude) and were given an opportunity to spend time on them (behaviour). As it turned out, attitudes and behaviours were more consistent among participants who had previously sampled the puzzles.

Chances are, these identical twins have more in common than being firefighters. Research suggests that people may be genetically predisposed to hold certain attitudes.

Third, an attitude can be strengthened, ironically, by an attack against it from a persuasive message. According to Zakary Tormala and Richard Petty (2002), people hold attitudes with varying degrees of certainty, and they become more confident after they successfully resist changing that attitude in response to a persuasive communication. In one study, for example, researchers confronted university students with an unpopular proposal to add senior comprehensive exams as a graduation requirement. Each student read a pro-exam argument that was described as strong or weak, after which they were asked to write down counterarguments and indicate their attitude toward the policy. The result: Students who continued to oppose the policy despite reading what they thought to be a strong argument became even more certain of their opinion. In fact, additional studies have shown that people who believe they have resisted a strong message become more certain of their attitude and more likely to form a behavioural intention that is consistent with it.

A fourth key factor is that strong attitudes are highly accessible to awareness, which means they are quickly and easily brought to mind (Fazio, 1990). To return to our earlier examples, computer jocks think often about their computer preferences, and political activists think often about their party allegiances. It turns out that many attitudes—not just those we feel strongly about—are easily brought to mind by the mere sight or even just the mention of an attitude object (Bargh et al., 1992). Of course, situational factors can also bring an attitude into awareness. Attitudes thus correlate with behaviour more when people become self-focused by staring into a mirror (Gibbons, 1978), when they overhear others discussing the issue (Borgida & Campbell, 1982), or when they are questioned repeatedly about it (Powell & Fazio, 1984). Regardless of how or why an attitude we hold pops to mind, it can trigger behaviour in a quick, spontaneous way or by leading us to think carefully about how we feel and how to respond (Fazio & Towles-Schwen, 1999).

To summarize, research on the link between attitudes and behaviour leads to an important conclusion. Our evaluations of an object do not always determine our actions because other factors must be taken into account. However, when attitudes are strong and specific to a behaviour, the effects are beyond dispute. Under these conditions, voting *is* influenced by political opinions, consumer purchasing *is* affected by product attitudes, and racial discrimination *is* rooted in feelings of prejudice. Attitudes are important determinants of behaviour. The question now is, How can attitudes be changed?

Persuasion by Communication

Television provides a major outlet for commercial persuasion. The average Canadian watches just over 21 hours of TV per week—and views roughly 30 000 commercials per year. (Statistics Canada, 2004).

On a day-to-day basis, we are all involved in the process of changing attitudes. Advertisers flood consumers with ad campaigns designed to sell cars, soft drinks, sneakers, computers, and Internet services. Likewise, politicians make speeches, pass out bumper stickers, and kiss babies to win votes. Attitude change is sought whenever parents socialize their children, scientists advance theories, religious groups seek converts, financial analysts recommend stocks, or trial lawyers argue cases to a jury. Some appeals work; others do not. Some are soft and subtle; others are hard and blatant. Some serve the public interest, whereas others serve personal interests. The point is, there is nothing inherently evil or virtuous about changing attitudes, a process known as **persuasion**. We do it all the time.

If you wanted to change someone's attitude on an issue, you'd probably try by making a persuasive *communication*. Appeals made in person and through the mass media rely on the spoken word, the written word, and the image that is worth 1000 words. What determines whether an appeal succeeds or fails? To understand why certain approaches are effective while others are not, social psychologists have, for many years, sought to understand *how* and *why* persuasive communications work. For that, we need a road map of the persuasion process.

Two Routes to Persuasion

It's a familiar scene in politics: Every few years, various candidates launch extensive campaigns for office. In a way, if you've seen one election, you've seen them all. The names and dates may change; but over and over again, opposing candidates accuse each other of ducking the issues and turning the election into a flag-waving popularity contest. True or not, these accusations show that politicians are keenly aware that they can win votes through two different methods. They can stick to the issues, or they can base their appeals on other grounds.

To account for these alternative approaches, Richard Petty and John Cacioppo (1986) proposed a dual-process model of persuasion. This model assumes that we do not always process communications the same way. When people think critically about the contents of a message, they are said to take a **central route to persuasion** and are influenced by the strength and quality of the arguments. When people do not think critically about the contents of a message but focus instead on other cues, they take a **peripheral route to persuasion**. As we'll see, the route taken depends on whether one is willing and able to scrutinize the information contained in the message itself. Over the years, this model has provided an important framework for understanding the factors that elicit persuasion (Petty & Wegener, 1999).

persuasion The process by which attitudes are changed.

central route to persuasion The process by which a person thinks carefully about a communication and is influenced by the strength of its arguments.

peripheral route to persuasion The process by which a person does not think carefully about a communication and is influenced instead by superficial cues.

The Central Route In the first systematic attempt to study persuasion, Carl Hovland and his colleagues (1949, 1953) started the Yale Communication and Attitude Change Program. They proposed that for a persuasive message to have influence, the recipients of that message must learn its contents and be motivated to accept it. According to this view, people can be persuaded only by an argument they attend to, comprehend, and retain in memory for later use. Regardless of whether the message takes the form of a personal appeal, a newspaper editorial, a Sunday sermon, a TV commercial, or an advertising banner on a Web site, these basic requirements remain the same.

A few years later, William McGuire (1969) reiterated the information-processing steps necessary for persuasion and, like the Yale group before him, distinguished between the learning, or *reception*, of a message, a necessary first step, and its later *acceptance.* In fact, McGuire (1968) used this distinction to explain the surprising finding that a recipient's self-esteem and intelligence are unrelated to persuasion. In McGuire's scheme, these characteristics have opposite effects on reception and acceptance. People who are smart or high in self-esteem are better able to learn a message but are less likely to accept its call for a change in attitude. People who are less smart or low in self-esteem are more willing to accept the message but may have trouble learning its contents. Overall, then, neither group is generally more vulnerable to persuasion than the other—a prediction that is supported by a good deal of research (Rhodes & Wood, 1992).

In elections, candidates try to win votes by addressing the issues, as in speeches (the central route), or through the use of celebrities, music, "spontaneous" photo-ops, and other theatrics (the peripheral route).

Anthony Greenwald (1968) and others then argued that persuasion requires a third, intermediate step: **elaboration**. To illustrate, imagine you are offered a job and your prospective employer tries to convince you over lunch to accept. You listen closely, learn the terms of the offer, and understand what it means. But if it's an important interview, your head will spin with questions as you weigh the pros and cons and contemplate the implications: Would I have to move? Is there room for growth? Am I better off staying where I am? When confronted with personally significant messages, we don't just listen for the sake of collecting information—we think about that information. The message is then effective to the extent that it leads us to focus on favourable rather than unfavourable thoughts.

These theories of attitude change all share the assumption that the recipients of persuasive appeals are attentive, active, critical, and thoughtful. This assumption is correct—some of the time. When it is, and when people consider a message carefully, their reaction to it depends on the strength of its contents. In these instances, messages have greater impact when they are easily learned rather than difficult, when they are memorable rather than forgettable, and when they stimulate favourable rather than unfavourable elaboration. Ultimately, strong arguments are persuasive, and weak arguments are not. On the central route to persuasion, the process is eminently thoughtful.

It's important to note, however, that thinking carefully about a persuasive message does not mean that the process is objective or that it necessarily promotes truth-seeking. At times, each of us prefers to hold a particular attitude—which leads us to become biased in our processing of information (Petty & Wegener, 1999). To further complicate matters, there are times when people want to hold the right attitudes, but believing they may be biased or overly influenced by nonrelevant factors, they try to correct for that bias—sometimes with an ironic result: overcorrection. In one study, for example, audience members who were forewarned that people are prone to agree with speakers they like later exhibited more attitude change in response to a speaker who was clearly *not* likeable (Petty et al., 1998).

elaboration The process of thinking about and scrutinizing the arguments contained in a persuasive communication.

The Peripheral Route "The receptive ability of the masses is very limited, their understanding small; on the other hand, they have a great power of forgetting." The author of this statement was Adolf Hitler (1933, p. 77). Believing that people are incompetent processors of information, Hitler relied heavily in his propaganda on the use of slogans, uniforms, marching bands, flags, and other symbols. For Hitler, "Meetings were not just occasions to make speeches, they were carefully planned theatrical productions in which settings, lighting, background music, and the timing of entrances were devised to maximize the emotional fervor of an audience" (Qualter, 1962, p. 112). Do these ploys work? Can the masses be so handily manipulated into persuasion? History shows that they can. Audiences are not always thoughtful. Sometimes people do not follow the central route to persuasion but instead take a shortcut through the peripheral route. Rather than try to learn the message and think through the issues, they respond with little effort on the basis of superficial, peripheral cues.

On the peripheral route to persuasion, people will often evaluate a communication by using simple-minded heuristics, or rules of thumb (Chaiken, 1987; Chen & Chaiken, 1999). If a communicator has a good reputation, speaks fluently, or writes well, we tend to assume that his or her message must be correct. And when a speaker has a reputation for being honest, people think less critically about the contents of his or her communication (Priester & Petty, 1995). Likewise, we assume that a message must be correct if it contains a long litany of arguments, or statistics, or an impressive list of supporting experts; if it's familiar; if it elicits cheers from an audience; or if the speaker seems to be arguing against his or her own interests. In some cases, simply knowing that an argument has majority support will get people to change their attitudes (Giner-Sorolla & Chaiken, 1997).

On the mindless peripheral route, people are also influenced by a host of attitude-irrelevant factors, such as cues from their own body movements. In one study, participants were induced to nod their heads up and down (as if saying "yes") or shake them from side to side (as if saying "no") while listening via headphones to an editorial, presumably to test whether the headphones could endure the physical activity. Those coaxed into nodding later agreed more with the arguments (Wells & Petty, 1980). In other studies, participants viewed and rated graphic symbols or word-like stimuli (*surtel*, *primet*) while using an exercise bar to either stretch their arms out (which mimics what we do to push something away) or flex their arms in (which we do to bring something closer). These stimuli were later judged to be more pleasant when associated with the flexing of the arm than with the stretching-out motion (Cacioppo et al., 1993; Priester et al., 1996).

Route Selection Thanks to Petty and Cacioppo's (1986) two-track distinction between the central and peripheral routes, we can better understand why the persuasion process seems so logical on some occasions yet so illogical on others—why voters may select candidates according to issues or images, why juries may base their verdicts on evidence or a defendant's appearance, and why consumers may base their purchases on marketing reports or product images. The process that is engaged depends on whether the recipients of a persuasive message have the *ability* and the *motivation* to take the central route or whether they rely on peripheral cues instead.

To understand the conditions that lead people to take one route or the other, it's helpful to view persuasive communication as the outcome of three factors: a *source* (who), a *message* (says what and in what context), and an *audience* (to whom). Each of these factors influences a recipient's approach to a persuasive communication. If a source speaks clearly, if the message is important, if there is a bright, captive, and involved audience that cares deeply about the issue and has time to absorb the information, then audience members will be willing and able to take the effortful central route. But if the source speaks at a rate too fast to comprehend, if the message is trivial or too complex to process, or if audience members are distracted, pressed for time, or uninterested, then the less strenuous peripheral route is taken.

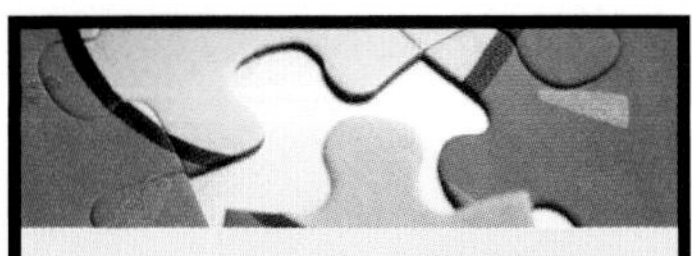

In reacting to persuasive communications, people are influenced more by superficial images than by logical arguments. **False.**

Figure 6.6 presents a road map of persuasive communication. In the next three sections, we will follow this map from the input factors (source, message, and audience), through the central or peripheral route processing strategies, to the final destination: persuasion.

The Source

Basketball player Steve Nash has been paid millions of dollars per year to endorse Nike and other commercial products. Why is Nash considered an effective spokesperson? What makes some communicators, in general, more effective than others? As we'll see, there are two key attributes: credibility and likeability.

Credibility Imagine you are waiting in line in a supermarket, and you catch a glimpse of a swollen headline: "Doctors Discover Cure for AIDS!" As your eye wanders across the front page, you discover that you are reading the sensationalistic *National Enquirer.* What would you think? Next, imagine that you are reading through scientific periodicals in a university library, and you come across a similar article—but this time it appears in the *New England Journal of Medicine.* Now what would you think?

Chances are, you'd react with more excitement to the medical journal than to the supermarket tabloid—even though both sources report the same news item. In a study conducted during the cold war era of the 1950s, participants read a speech advocating the development of nuclear submarines. The speech elicited more agreement when it was attributed to an eminent American physicist than when the source was said to be the Soviet government newspaper *Pravda* (Hovland & Weiss, 1951). Likewise, when participants read a speech favouring more lenient treatment of juvenile offenders, they changed their attitudes more when they thought the speaker was a judge rather than a convicted drug dealer (Kelman & Hovland, 1953).

Why are some sources more believable than others? Why were the medical journal, the physicist, and the judge more credible than the tabloid, *Pravda,* and the drug dealer? For communicators to be seen as credible, they must have two distinct characteristics: (1) competence, or expertise, and (2) trustworthiness. *Competence*

FIGURE 6.6

Two Routes to Persuasion

Based on characteristics of the source, message, and audience, recipients of a communication take either a central or a peripheral route to persuasion. On the central route, people are influenced by strong arguments and evidence. On the peripheral route, persuasion is based more on heuristics and other superficial cues. This two-process model helps explain how persuasion can seem logical on some occasions and illogical on others.

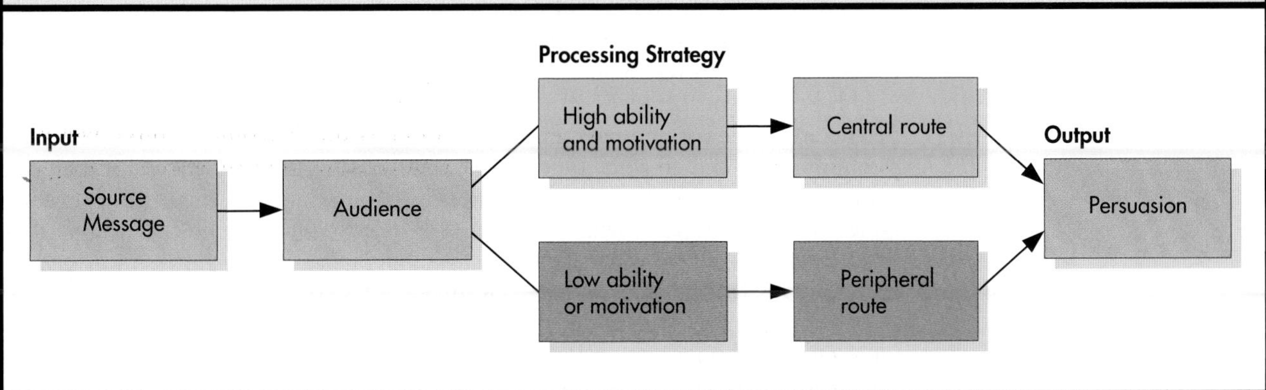

Can attractive sources help to sell products? Targeting the peripheral route to persuasion, the advertising industry seems to think so.

refers to a speaker's ability. People who are knowledgeable, smart, or well spoken or who have impressive credentials are persuasive by virtue of their expertise (Hass, 1981). Experts can have a disarming effect on us. We assume they know what they're talking about. So when they speak, we listen. And when they take a position, even one that is extreme, we often yield. Unless an expert contradicts us on issues that are personally important, we tend to accept what he or she says without too much scrutiny (Maddux & Rogers, 1980)—even when the message itself is ambiguous (Chaiken & Maheswaran, 1994).

Still, we are confronted by plenty of experts in life whose opinions do not sway us. The reason is that expertise alone is not enough. To have credibility, communicators must also be *trustworthy*—that is, they must be seen as willing to report what they know truthfully and without compromise. What determines whether we trust a communicator? To some extent, we make these judgments on the basis of stereotypes. Recently, for example, a poll conducted by Ipsos-Reid for *Reader's Digest* magazine asked about 1000 Canadians to rate the trustworthiness levels associated with various occupational categories. They found that pharmacists, airline pilots, and doctors were rated the highest, while politicians and car salespeople were at the bottom (2003).

In judging the credibility of a source, we are armed by common sense with a simple rule of caution: Beware of those who have something to gain from successful persuasion. If a speaker has been bought off, has an axe to grind, or is simply telling us what we want to hear, we suspect him or her of bias. This rule sheds light on a classic dilemma in advertising concerning the value of celebrity spokespersons: The more products a celebrity endorses, the less trustworthy he or she appears to consumers (Tripp et al., 1994). In the courtroom, the same rule of caution can be used to evaluate witnesses. In one study, research participants served as jurors in a mock trial in which a man claimed that his exposure to an industrial chemical at work had caused him to contract cancer. Testifying in support of this claim was a biochemist who was paid either $4800 or $75 for his expert testimony. You might think that jurors would be more impressed by the scientist when he commanded the higher fee. Yet, when highly paid, the expert was perceived to be a "hired gun"—and was, as a result, less believable and less persuasive (Cooper & Neuhaus, 2000).

The self-interest rule has other interesting implications. One is that people are impressed by others who take unpopular stands or argue against their own interests. When research participants read a political speech accusing a large corporation of polluting a local river, those who thought that the speechmaker was a pro-environment candidate addressing a staunch environmentalist group perceived him to be biased, while those who thought he was a pro-business candidate talking to company supporters assumed he was sincere (Eagly et al., 1978). Trust is also established by speakers who are not purposely trying to change our views. Thus, people are influenced more when they think that they are accidentally overhearing a communication than when they receive a sales pitch clearly intended for their ears (Walster & Festinger, 1962). That's why advertisers sometimes use the "overheard communicator" trick, in which the source tells a buddy about a new product that really works. Feeling as if they are eavesdropping on a personal conversation, viewers assume that what one friend says to another can be trusted.

Likeability As Dale Carnegie (1936) implied in the title of his classic bestseller, *How to Win Friends and Influence People*, being liked and being persuasive go hand in hand. The question is, What makes a communicator likeable? As we'll see in Chapter 9, two factors that spark attraction are *similarity* and *physical attractiveness.*

The effect of source similarity on persuasion has obvious implications for those who wish to exert influence. We're all similar to one another in some respects. We might agree in politics, share a common friend, have similar tastes in food, or enjoy spending summers on the same beach. Aware of the social benefits of similarity, the astute communicator can thus use common bonds to enhance his or her impact on an audience. This approach is particularly effective when the similarities seem relevant to the content of the communication (Berscheid, 1966).

When it comes to physical attractiveness, advertising practices presuppose that beauty is also persuasive. After all, billboards, magazine ads, and TV commercials are filled with young and glamourous "supermodels" who are tall and slender (for women) or muscular (for men) and who have glowing complexions and radiant smiles. Sure, these models can turn heads, you may think, but can they change attitudes and behaviours?

In a study that addressed this question, Shelly Chaiken (1979) had male and female US college students approach others on campus. They introduced themselves as members of an organization that wanted the university to stop serving meat during breakfast and lunch. In each case, these student assistants gave reasons for the position and then asked respondents to sign a petition. The result: Attractive communicators were able to get 41 percent of respondents to sign the petition, whereas those who were less attractive succeeded only 32 percent of the time. Sometimes, a speaker's physical appearance matters more than the quality of his or her arguments (Kahle & Homer, 1985; Pallak, 1983). In advertising, sheer beauty is particularly persuasive when the physical "image" is important to the product being sold (Shavitt et al., 1994).

Advertisers are so convinced that beauty sells products that they pay millions of dollars for supermodels to appear in their ads. Here, top models Esther Canadas, from Spain, and Mark Vanderloo, her Dutch husband, launched the ad campaign for the new DKNY fragrance for women at Macy's in New York City.

When What You Say Is More Important Than Who You Are To this point, it must seem as if the source of a persuasive message is more important than the message itself. Is this true? Advertisers have long debated the value of high-priced celebrity endorsements. David Ogilvy (1985), a leader in advertising, used to say that celebrities are not effective because viewers know they've been bought and paid for. Ogilvy was not alone in his skepticism. Still, many advertisers scramble furiously to sign high-priced models, entertainers, and athletes. The bigger the star, supposedly, the more valuable the endorsement.

Compared with the contents of a message, does the source really make the difference that advertisers pay for? Are we so impressed by the expert, and so drawn to the charming face, that we embrace whatever they have to say? And are we so scornful of non-experts and unattractive people that their presentations fall on deaf ears? In light of what is known about the central and peripheral routes to persuasion, the answer to these questions is "it depends."

First, a recipient's level of involvement plays an important role. When a message has personal relevance to your life, you pay attention to the source and think critically about the message, arguments, and implications. When a message does not have relevance, however, you may take the source at face value and spend little time scrutinizing the information. For example, Richard Petty and others (1981) had students listen to a speaker who proposed that seniors should be required to take comprehensive exams in order to graduate. Three aspects of the communication situation were varied. First, participants were led to believe that the speaker was either an education professor at Princeton University or a high school student. Second, participants heard either well-reasoned arguments and hard evidence or a weak message based only on anecdotes and personal opinion. And third, participants were told either that the proposed exams might be used the following year (Uh oh, that means me!) or that they would not take effect for another ten years (Who cares, I'll be long gone by then!).

As predicted, personal involvement determined the relative impact of source expertise and speech quality. Among participants who would not be affected by the proposed change, attitudes were based largely on the speaker's credibility: The professor was persuasive, the high school student was not. Among participants who thought that the proposed change would affect them directly, attitudes were based on the quality of the speaker's proposal: Strong arguments were persuasive, weak arguments were not. As depicted in Figure 6.7, people followed the source rather than the message under low levels of involvement, illustrating the peripheral route to persuasion. But message factors outweighed the source under high levels of involvement, when participants cared enough to take the central route to persuasion. Likewise, research has shown that the tilt toward likeable and attractive communicators is reduced when recipients take the central route (Chaiken, 1980).

There is a second limit to source effects. It is often said that time heals all wounds. Well, it may also heal the effects of a bad reputation. Hovland and Weiss (1951) varied communicator credibility (for example, the physicist versus *Pravda*) and found that the change had a large and immediate effect on persuasion. But when they remeasured attitudes four weeks later, the effect had vanished. Over time, the attitude change produced by the credible source decreased, and the change caused by the noncredible source increased. This latter finding of a delayed persuasive impact of a low-credibility communicator is called the **sleeper effect**.

To explain this unforeseen result, the Hovland research group proposed the *discounting cue hypothesis*. According to this hypothesis, people immediately discount the arguments made by noncredible communicators; but over time, they dissociate what was said from who said it. In other words, we tend to remember the message but forget the source (Pratkanis et al., 1988). To examine the role of memory in this process, Kelman and Hovland (1953) reminded a group of participants of the source's identity before reassessing their attitudes. If the sleeper effect was due to forgetting, they reasoned, then it could be eliminated through reinstatement of the link between the source and the message. As shown in Figure 6.8, they were right. When participants' attitudes were measured after three weeks, those who were not reminded of the source showed the usual sleeper effect. Those who were reminded of the source did not. For the latter participants, the effects of high and low credibility endured. Recent studies by cognitive psychologists have confirmed that, over time, people "forget" the connection between a message and its source (Underwood & Pezdek, 1998).

The sleeper effect generated a good deal of controversy. There was never a doubt that credible communicators lose some impact over time. But researchers had a harder time finding evidence for delayed persuasion by noncredible sources. Exasperated by their own failures to obtain this result, Paulette Gillig and Anthony Greenwald (1974) thus wondered, "Is it time to lay the sleeper effect to rest?" The answer, as it turned out, was no. More recent research showed that the sleeper effect is reliable—provided that participants do not learn who the source is until *after* they have received the original message (Greenwald et al., 1986; Gruder et al., 1978; Pratkanis et al., 1988).

To appreciate the importance of timing, imagine that you're surfing the Internet and you come across what appears to be a review of a new CD. Before you begin

sleeper effect A delayed increase in the persuasive impact of a noncredible source.

reading, however, you notice in the fine print that this so-called review is really an advertisement. Aware that you can't always trust what you read, you skim the ad and reject it. Now imagine the same situation, except that you read the entire ad before realizing what it is. Again, you reject it. But notice the difference. This time, you have read the message with an open mind. You may then have rejected it; but after a few weeks, the information sinks in and influences your evaluation of the CD. This experience illustrates the sleeper effect.

FIGURE 6.7

Source Versus Message: The Role of Audience Involvement

People who were high or low in their personal involvement heard a strong or weak message from an expert or nonexpert. For high-involvement participants (left), persuasion was based on the strength of arguments, not on source expertise. For low-involvement participants (right), persuasion was based more on the source than on the arguments. Source characteristics have more impact on those who don't care enough to take the central route to persuasion. *(Petty et al., 1981.)*

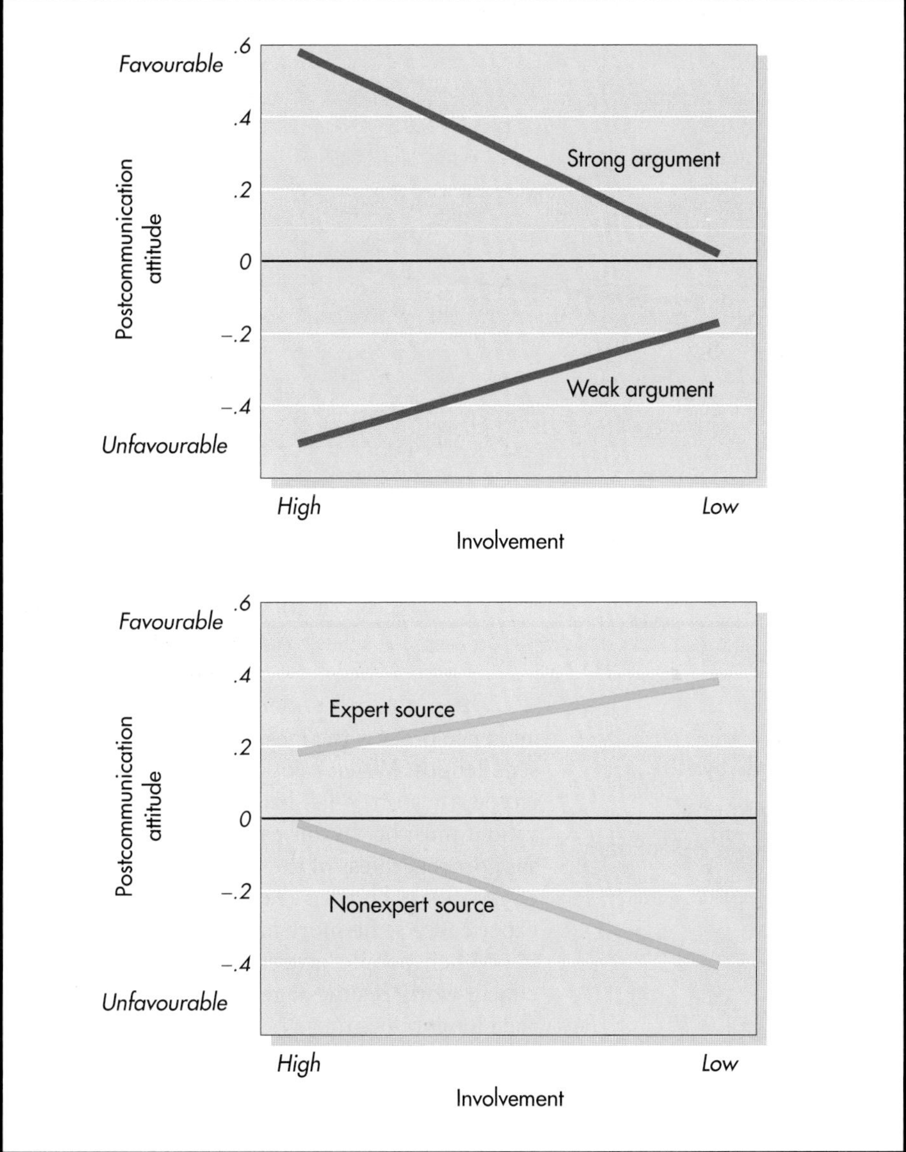

The Message

Obviously, not all sources are created equal; some are more credible or likeable than others. On the peripheral route to persuasion, audiences are influenced heavily, maybe too heavily, by these and other source characteristics. But when people care about an issue, the strength of a message determines its success. On the central route to persuasion, what matters most is whether a scientist's theory is supported by the data, whether a company has a sound product. Keep in mind, however, that the target of a persuasive appeal comes to know a message only through the medium of communication: *what* a person has to say and *how* that person says it.

Informational Strategies Communicators often struggle over how to present an argument to maximize its impact. Should a message be long and crammed with facts or short and to the point? Is it better to present a highly partisan, one-sided message or to take a more balanced, two-sided approach? And how should the various arguments be ordered—from strongest to weakest or the other way around? These are the kinds of questions often studied by persuasion researchers (Petty & Wegener, 1998; Petty et al., 1997).

FIGURE 6.8

The Sleeper Effect

In Experiment 1, participants changed their immediate attitudes more in response to a message from a high-credibility source than in response to a message from a low-credibility source. When attitudes were remeasured after three weeks, the high-credibility source lost impact, and the low-credibility source gained impact—the sleeper effect. In Experiment 2, the sleeper effect disappeared when participants were reminded of the source. *(Kelman & Hovland, 1953.)*

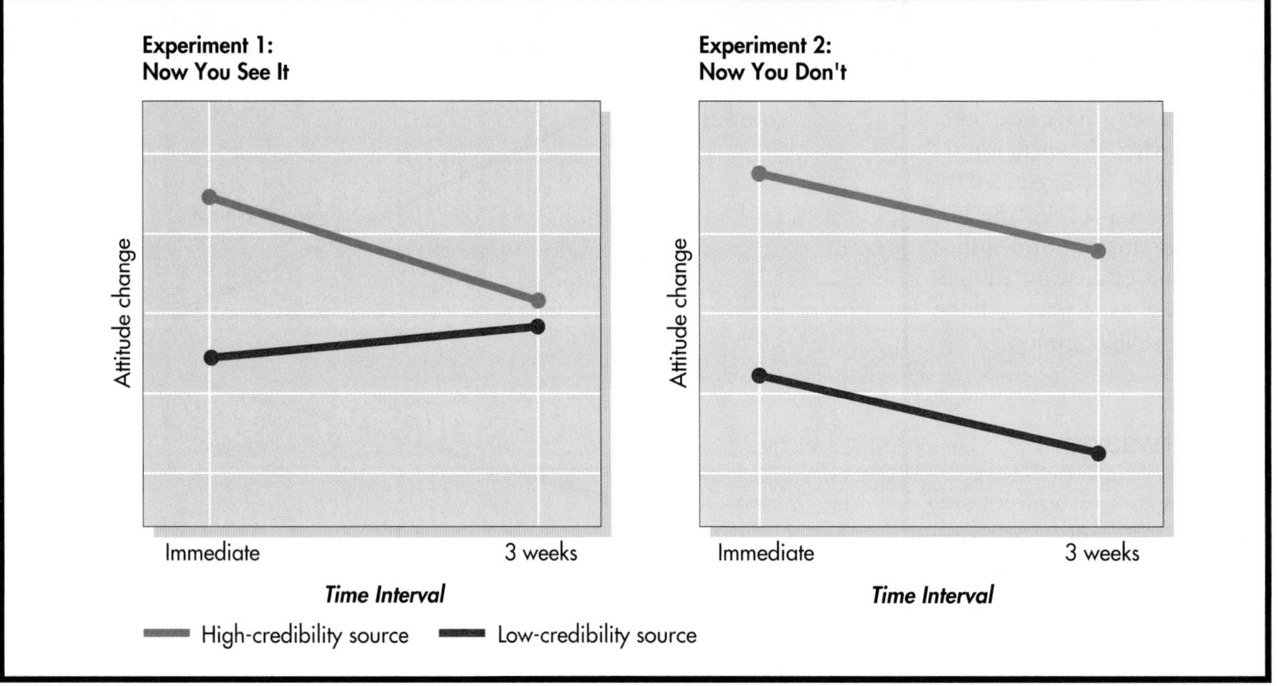

"The truth is always the strongest argument."

—Sophocles

Often, the most effective strategy to use depends on whether members of the audience process the message on the central or the peripheral route. Consider message length. When people process a message lazily, with their eyes and ears half-closed, they often fall back on a simple heuristic: The longer a message, the more valid it must be. In this case, word length gives the superficial appearance of factual support regardless of the quality of the arguments (Petty & Cacioppo, 1984; Wood et al., 1985). Thus, as David Ogilvy (1985) concluded from his years of advertising experience, "The more facts you tell, the more you sell" (p. 88).

When people process a communication carefully, however, length is a two-edged sword. If a message is long because it contains lots of supporting information, then longer does mean better. The more supportive arguments you can offer, or the more sources you can find to speak on your behalf, the more persuasive will be your appeal (Harkins & Petty, 1981). But if the added arguments are weak, or if the new sources are redundant, then an alert audience will not be fooled by length alone. When adding to the length of a message dilutes its quality, an appeal might well *lose* impact (Friedrich et al., 1996; Harkins & Petty, 1987).

When opposing sides try to persuade an audience, presentation order becomes a relevant factor as well. Imagine you are a juror in a high-profile criminal case. The Crown has the chance to present their case first, and then it is the Defence's turn. Do you think this order provides an advantage to one side over the other? If you believe that information presented first has more impact, you'd predict a *primacy effect* (advantage to the Crown). If you believe that the information presented last has the edge, you'd predict a *recency effect* (advantage to the Defence).

There are good reasons for both predictions. On the one hand, first impressions are important. On the other hand, memory fades over time, and people often recall only the last argument they hear before making a decision. In light of these contrasting predictions, Norman Miller and Donald Campbell (1959) searched for the "missing link" that would determine the relative effects of primacy and recency. They discovered that the missing link is *time.* In a jury simulation study, they had people (1) read a summary of the plaintiff's case, (2) read a summary of the defendant's case, and (3) make a decision. The researchers varied how much time separated the two messages and then how much time elapsed between the second message and the decisions. When participants read the second message right after the first and then waited a whole week before reporting their opinion, a primacy effect prevailed, and the side that came first was favoured. Both messages faded equally from memory, so only the greater impact of first impressions was left. Yet when participants made a decision immediately after the second message but a full week after the first, there was a recency effect. The second argument was fresher in memory, thus favouring the side that went last. Using these results as a guideline, let's return to our original question: What is the impact on a jury in terms of the order of presentation? It appears that if the Defence proceeds immediately after the Crown finishes its case (no delay), there is no effect of presentation order (Table 6.1).

Message Discrepancy Persuasion is a process of changing attitudes. But just how much change should be sought? Before addressing an audience, speakers confront what is perhaps the most critical strategic question: How extreme a position should they take? How *discrepant* should a message be from the audience's existing position in order to have the greatest impact? Common sense suggests two opposite answers. One approach is to take an extreme position in the hope that the more change you advocate, the more you get. Another approach is to exercise caution and not push for too much change so that the audience will not reject the message outright. Which approach seems more effective? Imagine trying to convert your politically conservative friends into liberals, or the other way around. Would you stake out a radical position in order to move them toward the centre, or would you preach moderation so as not to be cast aside?

Research shows that communicators should adopt the second, more cautious approach. To be sure, some discrepancy is needed to produce a change in attitude. But the relationship to persuasion can be pictured as an upside-down U with the most change being produced at moderate amounts of discrepancy (Bochner & Insko, 1966). A study by Kari Edwards and Edward Smith (1996) helps to explain why taking a more extreme counter-attitudinal position is counterproductive. These investigators first measured people's attitudes on a number of hot social issues—for example, whether lesbian and gay couples should adopt children, whether employers should give preference in hiring to minorities, and whether the death penalty should be abolished. Several weeks later, they asked these same people to read, think about, and rate arguments that were either consistent or inconsistent with their own prior attitudes. The result: When given arguments to read that preached attitudes that were discrepant from their own, the participants spent more time scrutinizing the material and judged the arguments to be weak. Apparently, people are quick to refute and reject persuasive messages they don't agree with. In fact, the more

TABLE 6.1

Effects of Presentation Order and Timing on Persuasion

A study by Miller and Campbell (1959) demonstrated the effect of presentation order and the timing of opposing arguments on persuasion.

Conditions					Results
1. **Message 1**	**Message 2**	One week	Decision		**Primacy**
2. **Message 1**	One week	**Message 2**	Decision		**Recency**
3. **Message 1**	**Message 2**	Decision			None
4. **Message 1**	One week	**Message 2**	One week	Decision	None

personally important an issue is to us, the more stubborn and resistant to change we become (Zuwerink & Devine, 1996).

Before her death in 2005, Heather Crowe became a well-known face of the anti-smoking movement in Canada. Despite never having smoked a day in her life, she died of lung cancer. She believed this was the result of spending more than 40 years of her life as a waitress in a restaurant where she was surrounded by second-hand smoke.

Fear Appeals Many trial lawyers say that to win cases, they have to appeal to jurors through the heart rather than through the mind. The evidence is important, they admit; but what really matters is whether the jury reacts to their client with anger, disgust, sympathy, or sadness. Of course, very few messages are entirely based on rational argument or on emotion. And it's possible that the best approach to take depends on whether the attitude is rooted more in a person's beliefs or in his or her feelings about the object or issue in question (Edwards, 1990; Millar & Millar, 1990).

The use of fear appeals is particularly common. Certain religious cults use scare tactics to indoctrinate new members. So do public health organizations that graphically portray the victims of cigarette smoking, drugs, overeating, and unsafe sex. Political campaigns are notorious for negative advertising. The most hard-hitting and controversial ever was a TV commercial that aired just once, on September 7, 1964. In an ad to re-elect Democratic President Lyndon Johnson, running against Republican Barry Goldwater, a young girl pictured in a field counted to ten as she picked the petals off a daisy. As she reached nine, an adult voice broke in and counted down from ten to zero, followed by a nuclear explosion and this message: "Vote for President Johnson on November 3. The stakes are too high for you to stay home."

Is fear effective? If so, is it better to arouse a little nervousness or to trigger a full-blown anxiety attack? To answer these questions, social psychologists have compared the effects of communications that vary in their fearfulness. In the first such study, Irving Janis and Seymour Feshbach (1953) found that high levels of fear arousal did not generate increased agreement with a communication. Since then, however, research has shown that high fear often does motivate change—in part, by increasing our incentive to think carefully about the persuasive arguments contained in the message (Baron et al., 1994).

Fear arousal increases the incentive to change for those who do not actively resist it, but its ultimate impact depends on the strength of the arguments and on whether the message also contains reassuring advice on how to avoid the threatened danger (Keller, 1999; Leventhal, 1970; Rogers, 1983; Witte, 1992). This last point is important. Without specific instructions on how to cope, people feel helpless, panic, and tune out. In one study, for example, participants with a chronic fear of cancer were less likely than others to detect the logical errors in a message that called for regular cancer checkups (Jepson & Chaiken, 1990). When clear instructions are included, however, high dosages of fear can be effective. Anti-smoking films that tell smokers how to quit thus elicit more negative attitudes about cigarettes when they show gory lung-cancer operations than charts filled with dry statistics (Leventhal et al., 1967). Driving-safety films are more effective when they show broken bones and bloody accident victims than controlled collisions involving plastic crash dummies (Rogers & Mewborn, 1976). The more vulnerable people feel about a threatened outcome, the more attentive they are and the more influenced they are by the recommendations contained within the fear appeal (Das et al., 2003).

Positive Emotions It's interesting that just as fear helps to induce a change in attitude, so do positive emotions. In one study, people were more likely to agree with a series of controversial arguments when they snacked on peanuts and soda than when they did not eat (Janis et al., 1965). In another study, participants liked a TV commercial more when it was embedded in a program that was upbeat rather than sad (Mathur & Chattopadhyay, 1991). Research shows that people are "soft touches" when they are in a good mood. Depending on the situation, food, drinks, a soft reclining chair, tender memories, a success experience, breathtaking scenery, and pleasant music can lull us into a positive emotional state ripe for persuasion (Schwarz et al., 1991).

According to Alice Isen (1984), people see the world through rose-coloured glasses when they are feeling good. Filled with high spirits, we become more sociable, more generous, and generally more positive in our outlook. We also make decisions more quickly and with relatively little thought. The result: Positive feelings activate the peripheral route to persuasion, facilitating change and allowing superficial cues to take on added importance (Petty et al., 1993; Worth & Mackie, 1987).

What is it about feeling good that leads us to take shortcuts rather than the more effortful central route to persuasion? There are three possible explanations. One is that a positive emotional state is cognitively distracting, causing the mind to wander and impairing our ability to think critically about the persuasive arguments (Mackie & Worth, 1989; Mackie et al., 1992). A second explanation is that when people are in a good mood, they assume that all is well, let down their guard, and become somewhat lazy processors of information (Schwarz, 1990). A third explanation is that when people are happy, they become motivated to savour the moment and maintain their happy mood, not spoil it by thinking critically about new information (Wegener & Petty, 1994).

This last notion raises an interesting question: What if happy people were presented with a positive, uplifting persuasive message? Would they still appear cognitively distracted, or lazy, or would they pay close attention in order to prolong the rosy glow? To find out, Duane Wegener and his colleagues (1995) showed some US college students a funny segment from the TV show *Late Night with David Letterman*. Others, less fortunate, watched a sombre scene from an HBO movie, *You Don't Have to Die*. All students were then asked to read and evaluate either an uplifting, pro-attitudinal article about a new plan to cut tuition or a distressing, counter-attitudinal article about a new plan to raise tuition. In half the cases, the article they read contained strong arguments; in the others, the arguments were weak. Did the students read the material carefully enough to distinguish between the strong and weak arguments? Those in the sombre condition clearly did. Among those in the happy condition, however, the response depended on whether they expected the message to be one they wanted to hear. When the happy students read about a tuition increase, they tuned out and were equally persuaded by the strong and weak arguments. When they read about the proposal to cut tuition, however, they were persuaded more when the arguments were strong than when they were weak. Being in a good mood, and receiving a pro-attitudinal message that would not spoil it, these happy students took the effortful central route to persuasion.

Subliminal Messages In 1957, Vance Packard published *The Hidden Persuaders*, an exposé of Madison Avenue. As the book climbed the bestseller list, it awakened in the public a fear of being manipulated by forces they could not see or hear. What had Packard uncovered? In the 1950s, amid growing fears of communism and the birth of rock 'n' roll, a number of advertisers were said to have used *subliminal advertising*, the presentation of commercial messages outside of conscious awareness. It all started in a drive-in movie theatre in New Jersey, where the words "Drink Coke" and "Eat popcorn" were secretly flashed on the screen during intermissions for a third of a millisecond. Although the audience never noticed the message, Coke™ sales were said to have increased 18 percent and popcorn sales 58 percent over a six-week period (Brean, 1958).

For years, advertisers have defended against the charge that they embed suggestive and sexual images in print ads. This piece by the American Association of Advertising Agencies addresses the claim.

This incident was followed by many others. In 1958, Canadian Broadcasting Corporation announced that they were going to present a subliminal message during a half-hour show, although the specific message ("telephone now") was not made public. While no increase in telephone usage was found, many viewers reported they were suddenly hungry, or thirsty. Apparently they erroneously attributed these feelings to the subliminal message. Later, in books entitled *Subliminal Seduction* (1973) and *The Age of Manipulation* (1989), William Bryan Key charged that advertisers routinely sneak faint sexual images in visual ads to heighten the appeal of their products. Several years ago, concerns were also raised about subliminal messages in rock music. In one case, the families of two boys who committed suicide blamed the British rock group Judas Priest for subliminal lyrics ("Do it") that promoted Satanism and suicide (*National Law Journal*, 1990). Although the families lost their case, it's clear that many people believe in the power of hidden persuaders.

At the time of the New Jersey theatre scandal, research on the topic was so sketchy, and the public so outraged by the sinister implications, that the matter was quickly dropped. But today there is renewed interest in subliminal influences, as well as new research developments. In one recent field study, for example, researchers played traditional German or French music, on alternating days for two weeks, at a supermarket display of wines. Keeping track of sales they found that, of the total number of wines bought, 83 percent were German on German-music days and 65 percent were French on French-music days. Yet when asked the reasons for their choices, customers did not cite the music as a factor, suggesting that they were not aware of the effect it had on them (North et al., 1999).

In what has become a multimillion-dollar industry, companies today sell self-help videos, tapes, and CDs that play new age music or nature sounds and also contain fleeting messages that promise to help you relax, lose weight, stop smoking, make friends, raise self-esteem, and even improve your sex life. Can subliminal messages really trigger behaviour without our awareness? In 1982, Timothy Moore reviewed the existing research and concluded that "what you see is what you get"—nothing, "complete scams." Moore was right. The original Coke-and-popcorn incident was later exposed as a publicity stunt, a hoax (Pratkanis, 1992). And controlled experiments on subliminal self-help tapes—to raise self-esteem, improve memory, or lose weight, show that they offer no therapeutic benefits (Greenwald et al., 1991; Merikle & Skanes, 1992).

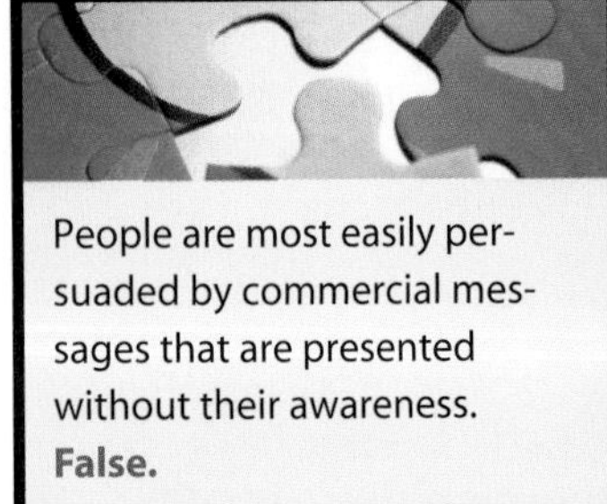

People are most easily persuaded by commercial messages that are presented without their awareness. **False.**

If there is no solid evidence of subliminal influence, why, you may wonder, does research demonstrate perception without awareness in studies of mere exposure and priming, described elsewhere in this book, but not in studies of subliminal persuasion? If you think about it, the two sets of claims are different. In the laboratory, subliminal exposures have a short-term effect on simple judgments and actions. But in claims of subliminal persuasion, the exposure is presumed to have long-term effects on eating and drinking, consumer purchases, voter sentiment, or even the most profound of violent acts, suicide. Psychologists agree that people can process information at an unconscious level, but they're also quick to note that this processing is "analytically limited" (Greenwald, 1992).

Erin Strahan and others (2002) suggest that although people *perceive* subliminal cues, those cues will not *persuade* them to take action unless they are already motivated to do so. To test this hypothesis, they brought thirsty University of Waterloo students into the lab for a marketing study and provided drinking water to some but not to others. Then, as part of a test administered by computer, they subliminally exposed these students to neutral words (*pirate*, *won*) or thirst-related words (*thirst*, *dry*). Did the subliminal "thirsty" message later lead the students, like automatons, to drink more in a taste test of the Kool-Aid™ beverages? Yes and no. Figure 6.9 shows that the subliminal thirst primes had little impact on students whose thirst had just been quenched, but they quite clearly increased consumption among those who were water-deprived and thirsty. For a subliminal message to influence behaviour, it has to strike "while the iron is hot."

FIGURE 6.9

Subliminal Influence

Thirsty and nonthirsty research participants were subliminally exposed to neutral or thirst-related words. Afterward they participated in a beverage taste test in which the amount they drank was measured. You can see that the subliminal thirst cues had little impact on nonthirsty participants but they did increase consumption among those who were thirsty. Apparently, subliminal cues can influence our behaviour when we are otherwise predisposed. *(Strahan et al., 2002.)*

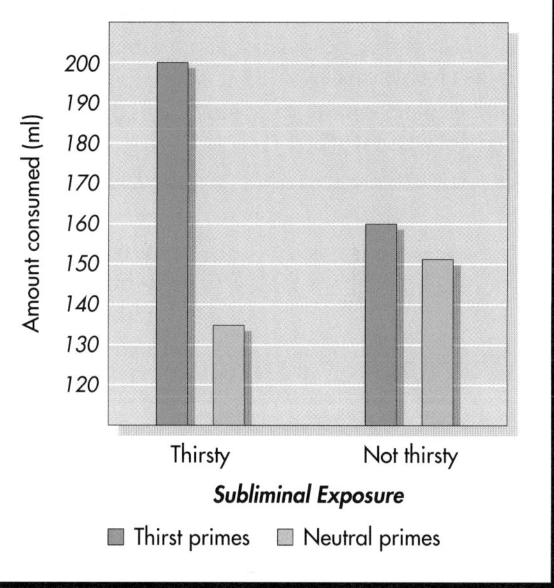

The Audience

Although source and message factors are important, the astute communicator must also take his or her audience into account. Presentation strategies that succeed with some people fail with others. Audiences on the central route to persuasion, for example, bear little resemblance to those found strolling along the peripheral route. In this section, we'll see that the impact of a message is influenced by two additional factors: the recipient's personality and his or her expectations.

Right from the start, social psychologists tried to identify types of people who were more or less vulnerable to persuasion. But it turned out that very few individuals are *consistently* easy or difficult to persuade. Based on this insight, the search for individual and group differences is now guided by an interactionist perspective. Assuming that each of us can be persuaded more in some settings than in others, researchers look for an appropriate "match" between characteristics of the message and the audience. Thus we ask, What kinds of messages turn *you* on?

The Need For Cognition Earlier, we saw that people tend to process information more carefully when they are highly involved. Involvement can be determined by the importance and self-relevance of a message. According to Cacioppo and Petty (1982), however, there are also individual differences in the extent to which people become involved and take the central route to persuasion. Specifically, they have found that individuals differ in the extent to which they enjoy and participate in effortful cognitive activities, or, as they call it, the **need for cognition (NC)**. People who are high rather than low in their need for cognition like to work on hard problems, search for clues, make fine distinctions, and analyze situations. These differences can be identified by the items contained in the Need for Cognition Scale, some of which appear in Table 6.2.

The need for cognition has interesting implications for changing attitudes. If people are prone to approach or avoid effortful cognitive activities, then the prepared communicator could design messages unique to a particular audience. In theory, the high-NC audience should receive information-oriented appeals, and the low-NC audience should be treated to appeals that rely on the use of peripheral cues. The theory is fine, but does it work? Can a message be customized to fit the information-processing style of its recipients? In one test of this hypothesis, participants read an editorial that consisted of either a strong or a weak set of arguments. As predicted, the higher their NC scores were, the more the participants thought about the material, the better they later recalled it, and the more persuaded they

need for cognition (NC) A personality variable that distinguishes people on the basis of how much they enjoy effortful cognitive activities.

TABLE 6.2

Need for Cognition (NC) Scale: Sample Items

Are you high or low in the need for cognition? These statements are taken from the NC Scale. If you agree with items 1, 3, and 5 and disagree with items 2, 4, and 6, you would probably be regarded as high in NC. *(Cacioppo & Petty, 1982.)*

1. I really enjoy a task that involves coming up with new solutions to problems.
2. Thinking is not my idea of fun.
3. The notion of thinking abstractly is appealing to me.
4. I like tasks that require little thought once I've learned them.
5. I usually end up deliberating about issues even when they do not affect me personally.
6. It's enough for me that something gets the job done; I don't care how or why it works.

were by the strength of its arguments (Cacioppo et al., 1983). In contrast, people who are low in the need for cognition are persuaded by cues found along the peripheral route—such as a speaker's reputation and physical appearance, the reactions of others in the audience, and a positive mood state (Cacioppo et al., 1996). At times, they are mindlessly influenced by a reputable source even when his or her arguments are weak (Kaufman et al., 1999).

Self-Monitoring Just as people high in the need for cognition crave information, other personality traits are associated with an attraction to other kinds of messages. Consider the trait of *self-monitoring*. As described in Chapter 3, high self-monitors regulate their behaviour from one situation to another out of concern for public self-presentation. Low self-monitors are less image conscious and behave instead according to their own beliefs and preferences. In the context of persuasion, high self-monitors may be particularly responsive to messages that promise desirable social images. Whether the product is beer, soda, blue jeans, or cars, this technique is common in advertising, where often the image is the message.

To test the self-monitoring hypothesis, Mark Snyder and Kenneth DeBono (1985) showed image- or information-oriented print ads to high and low self-monitors. In an ad for Irish Mocha Mint coffee, for example, a man and woman were depicted as relaxing in a candlelit room over a steamy cup of coffee. The image-oriented version promised to "Make a chilly night become a cozy evening," while the informational version offered "A delicious blend of three great flavours—coffee, chocolate, and mint." As predicted, high self-monitors were willing to pay more for products after reading imagery ads, while low self-monitors were influenced more by the information-oriented appeals (see Figure 6.10). Imagery can even influence the way high self-monitors evaluate a product, independent of its quality. DeBono and others (2003) presented people with one of two perfume samples packaged in more or less attractive bottles. Whereas low self-monitors preferred the more pleasant-scented fragrance, high self-monitors preferred whatever scent came from the more attractive bottles.

The Cultural Context A message is persuasive to the extent that it meets the psychological needs of its audience. In this regard, cultural factors also play a subtle but important role. In Chapter 3, we saw that cultures differ in the extent to which they are oriented toward individualism versus collectivism. In light of these differences, Sang-Pil Han and Sharon Shavitt (1994) compared the contents of magazine advertisements in the United States, an individualistic country, and Korea, a country with a collectivistic orientation. They found that while US advertising slogans were focused more on personal benefits, individuality, competition, and self-improvement ("She's got a style all her own," "Make your way through the crowd"), Korean ads appealed more to the integrity, achievement, and well-being of one's family and other ingroups ("An exhilarating way to provide for your family," "Celebrating a half-century of partnership"). Clearly, there are different ways to appeal to the members of these two cultures. In a second study, Han and Shavitt created two sets of ads for various products. One set portrayed individuals ("Treat yourself to a breath-freshening experience"), and the other set featured groups ("Share this breath-freshening experience"). Both sets were presented to American and Korean participants. The result: Americans were persuaded more by individualistic ads, and Koreans preferred collectivistic ads. Similar differences are found in comparisons of Americans, who are drawn to products that promise "separateness," and Chinese, who like these products more when they offer "togetherness" (Wang et al., 2000). To be persuasive, a message should appeal to the culturally shared values of its audience.

FIGURE 6.10

Informational and Image-Oriented Ads: The Role of Self-Monitoring

High and low self-monitors estimated how much they would pay for products presented in image-oriented or informational magazine ads. As shown, high image-oriented self-monitors preferred products depicted in image-oriented ads (left), while low self-monitors preferred those depicted in informational ads (right). *(Snyder & DeBono, 1985.)*

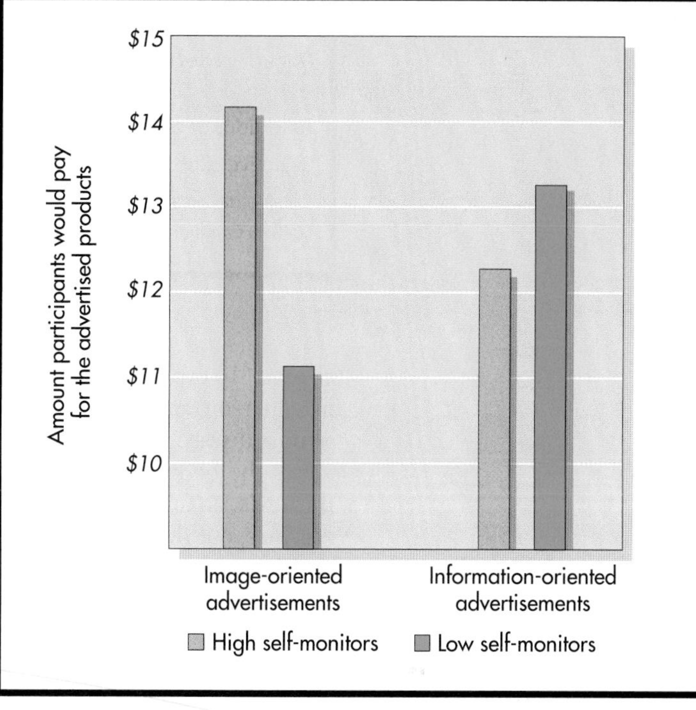

Forewarning and Resistance When our attitudes or values come under attack, we can succumb to the challenge and change the attitude, or we can resist it and maintain the attitude. There are different means of resistance. In a series of studies, Julia Jacks and Kimberly Cameron (2003) asked people to describe and rate the ways in which they manage to resist persuasion in their attitudes on abortion, or the death penalty. They identified seven strategies—the most common being attitude bolstering ("I think about all the reasons I believe the way I do") and the least common being source derogation ("I look for faults in the person who challenges my belief"). These means of resistance are listed in Table 6.3.

What leads people to invoke these mechanisms of resistance? Does it help to be forewarned that your attitude is about to come under attack? Perhaps the toughest audience to persuade is the one that knows you're coming. When people are aware that someone is trying to change their attitude, they become more likely to resist. All they need is some time to collect their thoughts and come up with a good defence. Jonathan Freedman and David Sears (1965) first discovered this when they told high school seniors to expect a speech on why teenagers should not be allowed to drive (an unpopular position, as you can imagine). The students were warned either two or ten minutes before the talk began or not at all. Those who were the victims of a sneak attack were the most likely to succumb to the speaker's position. Those who had a full ten minutes' warning were the least likely to agree. To be forewarned is to be forearmed. But why?

At least two processes are at work here. To understand them, let's take a closer look at what forewarning does. Participants in the Freedman and Sears (1965) study were put on notice in two ways: (1) They were informed of the position the speaker would take, and (2) they were told that the speaker intended to change their attitudes. Psychologically, these two aspects of forewarning have different effects.

The first effect is purely cognitive. Knowing in advance what position a speaker will take enables us to come up with counter-arguments and, as a result, to become more resistant to

In a series of print ads, Apple Computer paid tribute to Albert Einstein, Muhammad Ali, Pablo Picasso, and other creative geniuses who dared to "think different." In a highly individualistic campaign, Apple saluted "The crazy ones. The misfits. The rebels. The troublemakers. The round pegs in the square holes. The ones who see things differently."

TABLE 6.3
Strategies for Resisting Persuasion

Strategy	Example
Attitude bolstering	"I reassure myself of facts that support the validity of my belief."
Counterarguing	"I would talk to myself and play devil's advocate."
Social validation	"I also rely on others with the same opinion to be there for me."
Negative affect	"I tend to get angry when someone tries to change my beliefs."
Assertions of confidence	"I doubt anybody could change my viewpoint."
Selective exposure	"Most of the time I just ignore them."
Source derogation	"I look for faults in the person presenting the challenging belief."

(Jacks & Cameron, 2003.)

change. To explain this effect, William McGuire (1964) drew an analogy: Protecting a person's attitudes from persuasion, he said, is like inoculating the human body against disease. In medicine, injecting a small dose of infection into a patient stimulates the body to build up a resistance to it. According to this **inoculation hypothesis**, an attitude can be immunized the same way. As with flu shots and other vaccines, our defences can be reinforced by exposure to weak doses of the opposing position before we actually encounter the full presentation. Studies of negative political ads show that inoculation can be used to combat the kinds of attack messages that sometimes win elections (Pfau et al., 1990). It has even been suggested that parents can protect children from advertising propaganda by exposing them to small doses of TV commercials and then critically discussing the claims that are made (Pratkanis & Aronson, 1992).

Simply knowing that someone is trying to persuade us also elicits a motivational reaction as we brace ourselves to resist the attempt regardless of what position is taken. As a TV viewer, you have no doubt heard the phrase "And now, we pause for a message from our sponsor." What does this warning tell us? Not knowing yet who the sponsor is, even the grouchiest among us is in no position to object. Yet imagine how you would feel if an experimenter said to you, "In just a few minutes, you will hear a message prepared according to well-established principles of persuasion and designed to induce you to change your attitudes." If you are like the participants who actually heard this forewarning, you might be tempted to reply, "Oh yeah? Try me!" Indeed, subjects rejected that message without counterargument and without much advance notice (Hass & Grady, 1975).

"To do just the opposite is also a form of imitation."
—Lichtenberg

When people think that someone is trying to change their attitude or otherwise manipulate them, a red flag goes up. That red flag is called **psychological reactance**. According to Jack Brehm's theory of psychological reactance, all of us want the freedom to think, feel, and act as we (not others) choose. When we sense that a cherished freedom is being threatened, we become motivated to maintain it. And when we sense that a freedom is slipping away, we try to restore it (Brehm & Brehm, 1981). One possible result is that when a communicator comes on too strong, we may react with *negative attitude change*, by moving in the direction opposite to the one advocated—even, ironically, when the speaker's position agrees with our own (Heller et al., 1973). Sometimes, the motive to protect our freedom to think as we choose trumps our desire to hold a specific opinion.

inoculation hypothesis The idea that exposure to weak versions of a persuasive argument increases later resistance to that argument.

psychological reactance The theory that people react against threats to their freedom by asserting themselves and perceiving the threatened freedom as more attractive.

However, forewarning does not always increase resistance to persuasion, because the effects are not that simple. Based on a meta-analysis of 48 experiments, Wendy Wood and Jeffrey Quinn (2003) found that when people are forewarned about an impending persuasive appeal on a topic that is personally not that important, they start to agree before they even receive the message in order to keep from appearing vulnerable to influence. Yet when people are forewarned about a persuasive appeal on a topic that is of personal importance, they feel threatened and think up counter-arguments to bolster their attitude. This cognitive response strengthens their resistance to change once that appeal is delivered.

Persuasion by Our Own Actions

Anyone who has ever acted on stage knows how easy it is to become so absorbed in a role that the experience seems real. Feigned laughter can make an actor feel happy, and crocodile tears can turn into sadness.

Role-Playing: All the World's a Stage

People frequently engage in attitude-discrepant behaviour as part of a job, for example, or to please others. As commonplace as this seems, it raises a profound question. When we play along, saying and doing things that are privately discrepant from our own attitudes, do we begin to change those attitudes as a result? How we feel can determine the way we act. Is it also possible that the way we act can determine how we feel?

In a job interview, candidates typically try their best to show thay are a good "fit" to the organization, even if this is a little bit of an act. But what happens after they get the job? Do their existing attitudes determine their actions, or does their new role ultimately reshape their attitudes?

According to Irving Janis (1968), attitude change persists more when it is inspired by our own behaviour than when it stems from passive exposure to a persuasive communication. Janis conducted a study in which one group of participants listened to a speech that challenged their positions on a topic and others were handed an outline and asked to give the speech themselves. As predicted, participants changed their attitudes more after giving the speech than after listening to it (Janis & King, 1954). According to Janis, role-playing works because it forces people to learn the message. That is why people remember arguments they come up with on their own better than they remember arguments provided by others (Slamecka & Graff, 1978). In fact, attitude change is more enduring even when people who read a persuasive message merely *expect* that they will later have to communicate it to others (Boninger et al., 1990).

But there's more to role-playing than improved memory. The effects of enacting a role can be staggering, in part because it is so easy to confuse what we do, or what we say, with how we really feel. Think about the times you've dished out compliments you didn't mean, or smiled at someone you didn't like, or nodded your head in response to a statement you disagreed with. We often shade what we say just to please a particular listener. What's fascinating is not that we make adjustments to suit others but that this role-playing has such powerful effects on our own private attitudes. For example, participants in one study read about a man and then described him to someone else, who supposedly liked or disliked him. As you might expect, participants described the man in more positive terms when their listener was favourably disposed. In the process, however, they also convinced themselves. At least to some extent, "saying is believing" (Higgins & Rholes, 1978).

Consider the implications. We know that attitudes influence behaviour—as when people help those whom they like and hurt those whom they dislike. But research on role-playing emphasizes the flip side of the coin—that behaviour can determine attitudes. Perhaps we come to like people because we have helped them and blame people whom we have hurt. To change people's inner feelings, then, maybe we should begin by focusing on their behaviour. Why do people experience changes of attitude in response to changes in their own behaviour? One answer to this question is provided by the theory of cognitive dissonance.

Cognitive Dissonance Theory: The Classic Version

Many social psychologists believe that people are motivated by a desire for cognitive consistency—a state of mind in which one's beliefs, attitudes, and behaviours are all compatible with each other (Abelson et al., 1968). Cognitive consistency theories seem to presuppose that people are generally logical. However, Leon Festinger (1957) turned this assumption on its head. Struck by the irrationalities of human behaviour, Festinger proposed **cognitive dissonance theory**, which states that a powerful motive to maintain cognitive consistency can give rise to irrational and sometimes maladaptive behaviour.

According to Festinger, all of us hold many cognitions about ourselves and the world around us. These cognitions include everything we know about our own beliefs, attitudes, and behaviour. Although generally our cognitions coexist peacefully, at times they clash. Consider some examples. You say you're on a diet, yet you just dived headfirst into a chocolate mousse. Or you waited in line for hours to get into a rock concert, and then the band was disappointing. Or you baked for hours under the hot summer sun, even though you knew of the health risks. Each of these scenarios harbours inconsistency and conflict. You have already committed yourself to one course of action, yet you realize that what you did is inconsistent with your attitude.

"Man is the only animal that learns by being hypocritical. He pretends to be polite and then, eventually, he becomes polite."

—Jean Kerr

Under certain specific conditions, discrepancies such as these can evoke an unpleasant state of tension known as cognitive dissonance. But discrepancy doesn't always produce dissonance. If you broke a diet for a Thanksgiving dinner with the family, your indiscretion would not lead you to experience dissonance. Or if you mistakenly thought the mousse you ate was low in calories, only later to find out the truth, then, again, you would not experience much dissonance. As we'll see, what really hurts is knowing that you committed yourself to an attitude-discrepant behaviour freely and with some knowledge of the consequences. When that happens, dissonance is aroused, and you become motivated to reduce it. There are many possible ways to do so, as shown in Table 6.4. Often, the easiest is to change your attitude to bring it in line with your behaviour.

Right from the start, cognitive dissonance theory captured the imagination. Festinger's basic proposition is simple, yet its implications are far-reaching. In this section, we examine three research areas that demonstrate the breadth of what dissonance theory has to say about attitude change.

cognitive dissonance theory The theory that holding inconsistent cognitions arouses psychological tension that people become motivated to reduce.

Justifying Attitude-Discrepant Behaviour: When Doing Is Believing Imagine for a moment that you are a participant in a classic study by Leon Festinger and

J. Merrill Carlsmith (1959). As soon as you arrive, you are greeted by an experimenter who says that he is interested in various measures of performance. Wondering what that means, you all too quickly find out. The experimenter hands you a wooden board containing 48 square pegs in square holes and asks you to turn each peg a quarter turn to the left, then a quarter turn back to the right, then back to the left, then back again to the right. The routine seems endless. After 30 minutes, the experimenter comes to your rescue. Or does he? Just when you think things are looking up, he hands you another board, another assignment. For the next half-hour, you are to take 12 spools of thread off the board, put them back, take them off, and put them back again. By now, you're just about ready to tear your hair out. As you think back over better times, even the first task begins to look good.

TABLE 6.4

Ways to Reduce Dissonance

"I need to be on a diet, yet I just dived headfirst into a chocolate mousse." If this were you, how would you reduce dissonance aroused by the discrepancy between your attitude and your behaviour?

Techniques	Examples
Change your attitude.	"I don't really need to be on a diet."
Change your perception of the behaviour.	"I hardly ate any chocolate mousse."
Add consonant cognitions.	"Chocolate mousse is very nutritious."
Minimize the importance of the conflict.	"I don't care if I'm overweight—life is short!"
Reduce perceived choice.	"I had no choice; the mousse was prepared for this special occasion."

Finally, you're done. After one of the longest hours of your life, the experimenter lets you in on a secret: There's more to this experiment than meets the eye. You were in the control group. To test the effects of motivation on performance, other participants are being told that the experiment will be fun and exciting. You don't realize it, but you are now being set up for the critical part of the study. Would you be willing to tell the next participant that the experiment is enjoyable? As you hem and haw, the experimenter offers to pay for your services. Some participants are offered $1; others are offered $20. In either case, you agree to help out. Before you know it, you find yourself in the waiting room trying to dupe an unsuspecting fellow student (who is really a confederate).

By means of this elaborate, staged presentation, participants were goaded into an attitude-discrepant behaviour, an action that was inconsistent with their private attitudes. They knew how dull the experiment really was, yet they raved about it. Did this conflict arouse cognitive dissonance? It depends on how much the participants were paid. Suppose you were one of the lucky ones offered $20 for your assistance. By today's standards, that payment would be worth $80—surely a sufficient justification for telling a little white lie, right? Feeling well compensated, these participants experienced little if any dissonance. But wait. Suppose you were paid only $1. Surely your integrity is worth more than that, don't you think? In this instance, you have **insufficient justification** for going along—so you need a way to cope. According to Festinger (1957), unless you can deny your actions (which is not usually possible), you'll feel pressured to change your attitude about the task. If you can convince yourself that the experiment wasn't that bad, then saying it was interesting is all right.

One way to reduce dissonance is to minimize the importance of the conflict.

"It's a crazy idea, but it just might work."

The results were just as Festinger and Carlsmith had predicted. When the experiment was presumably over, participants were asked how they felt about the peg-board tasks. Those in the control group who did not mislead a confederate openly admitted that the tasks were boring. So did those in the $20 condition, who had ample justification for what they did. However, participants who were paid only $1 rated the experiment as somewhat enjoyable. Having engaged in an attitude-

FIGURE 6.11

The Dissonance Classic

Participants in a boring experiment (attitude) were asked to say that it was enjoyable (behaviour) to a fellow student. Those in one group were paid $1 to lie; those in a second group were offered $20. Members of a third group, who did not have to lie, admitted that the task was boring. So did the participants paid $20—ample justification for what they did. Participants paid only $1, however, rated the task as more enjoyable. Behaving in an attitude-discrepant manner without justification, the $1 participants reduced dissonance by changing their attitude. *(Festinger & Carlsmith, 1959.)*

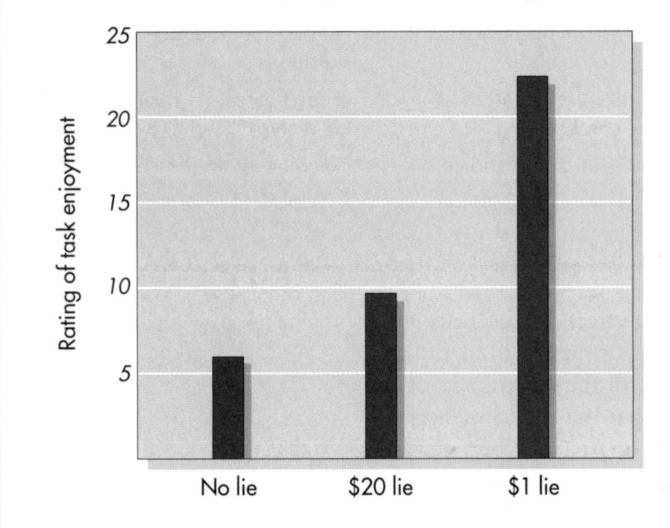

discrepant act without sufficient justification, these participants reduced cognitive dissonance by changing their attitude. The results can be seen in Figure 6.11.

Two aspects of this classic study are noteworthy. First, it showed the phenomenon of self-persuasion: When people behave in ways that contradict their attitudes, they sometimes go on to change those attitudes—without exposure to a persuasive communication. Demonstrating the power of this phenomenon, Michael Leippe and Donna Eisenstadt (1994) found that white college students who were coaxed into writing essays in favour of new scholarship funds only for black students later reported more favourable attitudes in general toward African Americans. The second major contribution of Festinger and Carlsmith's results is that they contradicted the time-honoured belief that big rewards produce greater change. In fact, the more money participants were offered for their inconsistent behaviour, the more justified they felt and the less likely they were to change their attitudes.

Just as a small reward provides insufficient justification for attitude-discrepant behaviour, mild punishment is **insufficient deterrence** for attitude-discrepant *non*behaviour. Think about it. What happens when people refrain from doing something they really want to do? Do they devalue the activity and convince themselves that they never really wanted to do it in the first place? In one study, children were prohibited from playing with an attractive toy by being threatened with a mild or a severe punishment. All participants refrained. As cognitive dissonance theory predicts, however, only those faced with the mild punishment—an insufficient deterrent—later showed disdain for the forbidden toy. Those who confronted the threat of severe punishment did not (Aronson & Carlsmith, 1963). Once again, cognitive dissonance theory turned common sense on its head: The less severe the threatened punishment, the greater the attitude change produced.

Justifying Effort: Coming to Like What We Suffer For Have you ever spent tons of money or tried really hard to achieve something, only to discover later that it wasn't worth all the effort? This kind of inconsistency between effort and outcome can arouse cognitive dissonance and motivate a change of heart toward the unsatisfying outcome. The hypothesis is simple but profound: We alter our attitudes to justify our suffering.

insufficient justification A condition in which people freely perform an attitude-discrepant behaviour without receiving a large reward.

insufficient deterrence A condition in which people refrain from engaging in a desirable activity, even when only mild punishment is threatened.

In a classic test of this hypothesis, Elliot Aronson and Judson Mills (1959) invited female students to take part in a series of group discussions about sex. But there was a hitch. Because sex is a sensitive topic, participants were told that they would have to pass an "embarrassment test" before joining the group. The test consisted of reading sexual material aloud in front of a male experimenter. One group of participants experienced what amounted to a *severe* initiation in which they had to recite obscene words and lurid passages taken from paperback novels. A second group underwent a *mild* initiation in which they read a list of more ordinary words pertaining to sex. A third group was admitted to the discussions without an initiation test.

Moments later, all participants were given headphones and permitted to eavesdrop on the group they would soon be joining. Actually, what they heard was a tape-recorded discussion about "secondary sex behaviour in the lower animals." It was dreadfully boring. When it was over, participants were asked to rate how much they liked the group members and their discussion. Keep in mind what dissonance theory predicts: The more time or money or effort you choose to invest in something, the more anxious you will feel if the outcome proves disappointing. One way to cope with this inconsistency is to alter your attitudes. That's exactly what happened. Participants who had endured a severe initiation rated the discussion group more favourably than did those who had endured little or no initiation.

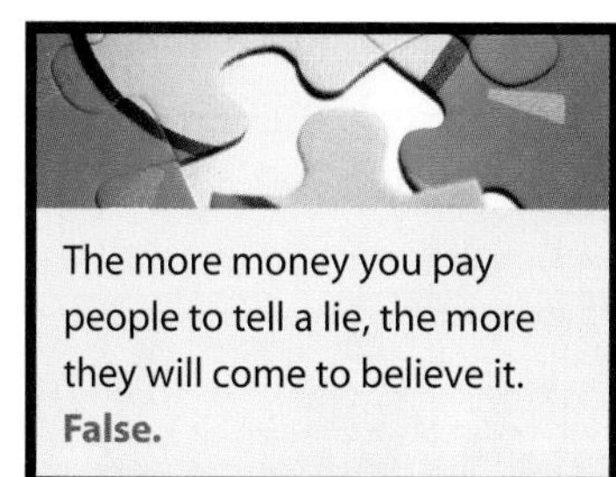

The more money you pay people to tell a lie, the more they will come to believe it. **False.**

It's important to note that embarrassment is not the only kind of "effort" we feel the need to justify to ourselves. As a general rule, the more you pay for something—whether you pay in physical exertion, pain, time, or money—the more you will come to like it. This principle has provocative implications. For example, research suggests that the harder psychotherapy patients have to work at their own treatment, the more likely they are to feel better when that treatment is over (Axsom, 1989; Axsom & Cooper, 1985).

Justifying Difficult Decisions: When Good Choices Get Even Better Whenever we make difficult decisions—whether to marry, what school to attend, or what job to accept—we feel dissonance. By definition, a decision is difficult when the alternative courses of action are about equally desirable. Marriage offers comfort and stability; staying single enables us to seek out exciting new relationships. One job might pay more money; the other might involve more interesting work. Once people make tough decisions like these, they are at risk, as negative aspects of the chosen alternatives and positive aspects of the alternatives not chosen are at odds with their decisions. According to dissonance theory, people rationalize whatever they decide by exaggerating the positive features of the chosen alternative and the negative features of the unchosen alternative.

In an early test of this hypothesis, Jack Brehm (1956) asked female participants to evaluate various consumer products, presumably as part of a marketing research project. After rating a toaster, a coffee pot, a radio, a stopwatch, and other products, participants were told that they could take one home as a gift. In the high-dissonance condition, they were offered a difficult choice between two items they found equally attractive. In the low-dissonance group, they were offered an easier choice between a desirable and an undesirable item. After receiving the gift, participants read a few research reports and then re-evaluated all the products. The results provided strong support for dissonance theory. In the low-dissonance group, the participants' post-decision ratings were about the same as their predecision ratings. But in the high-dissonance condition, ratings increased for the chosen item and decreased for the nonchosen item. Participants torn between two equivalent alternatives coped by reassuring themselves that they had made the right choice.

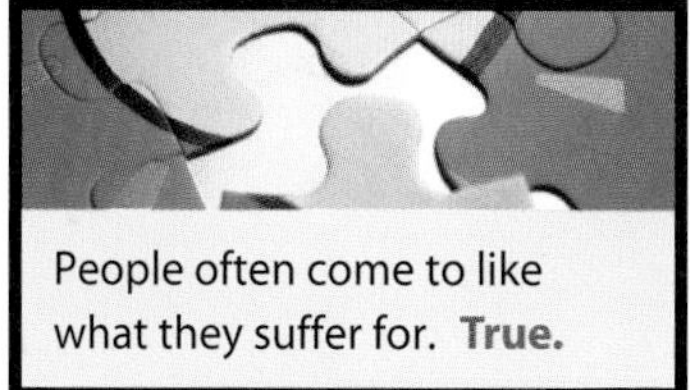

People often come to like what they suffer for. **True.**

This phenomenon appears in a wide range of settings. For example, Robert Knox and James Inskter (1968) took dissonance theory to the racetrack and found that bettors who had already placed $2 bets on a horse were more optimistic about winning than were those still standing in line. Similarly, Dennis Regan and Martin Kilduff (1988) visited several polling stations on election day and found that voters were more likely to think that their candidates would win when interviewed after submitting their ballots than before. Since bets and votes cannot be taken back, people who had committed themselves to a decision were motivated to reduce post-decision dissonance. So they convinced themselves that the decision they made was right.

Suggesting that people need to justify difficult irrevocable decisions to quell the dissonance they arouse, researchers found that gamblers who had already bet on a horse rated themselves as more certain of winning than those who were still waiting to place a bet.

Cognitive Dissonance Theory: A New Look

Following in Festinger's bold footsteps, generations of social psychologists have studied and refined the basic theory (Harmon-Jones & Mills, 1999). Nobody disputes the fact that when people are gently coaxed into performing an attitude-discrepant behaviour, they often go on to change their attitudes. In fact, people will feel discomfort and change their attitudes when they see inconsistent behaviour from someone else with whom they identify—a process of *vicarious* dissonance (Norton et al., 2003). Through systematic research, however, it became evident early on that Festinger's (1957) original theory was not to be the last word. People do change their attitudes to justify attitude-discrepant behaviour, effort, and difficult decisions. But for dissonance to be aroused, certain conditions must be present. As first summarized by Joel Cooper and Russell Fazio's (1984) "new look" at dissonance theory, we now have a pretty good idea of what those conditions are.

According to Cooper and Fazio, four steps are necessary for the arousal and reduction of dissonance. First, the attitude-discrepant behaviour must produce unwanted *negative consequences*. Recall the initial Festinger and Carlsmith (1959) study. Not only did participants say something they knew to be false, they also deceived a fellow student into taking part in a painfully boring experiment. Had these participants lied without causing hardship, they would *not* have changed their attitudes to justify the action (Cooper et al., 1974). To borrow an expression from schoolyard basketball, "no harm, no foul." In fact, it appears that negative consequences arouse dissonance even when people's actions are consistent with their attitudes—as when college students who wrote against fee hikes were led to believe that their essays had backfired, prompting a university committee to favour an increase (Scher & Cooper, 1989).

The second necessary step in the process is a feeling of *personal responsibility* for the unpleasant outcomes of behaviour. Personal responsibility consists of two factors. The first is the freedom of *choice*. When people believe they had no choice but to act as they did, there is no dissonance and no attitude change (Linder et al., 1967). Had Festinger and Carlsmith coerced participants into raving about the boring experiment, the participants would not have felt the need to further justify what they did by changing their attitudes. But the experimental situation led participants to think that their actions were voluntary and that the choice was theirs. Pressured without realizing it, participants believed that they did not have to comply with the experimenter's request.

For people to feel personally responsible, they must also believe that the potential negative consequences of their actions were *foreseeable* at the time (Goethals et al., 1979). When the outcome could not realistically have been anticipated, then there's no dissonance and no attitude change. Had Festinger and Carlsmith's participants lied in private, only later to find out that their statements had been tape-recorded for subsequent use, then, again, they would not have felt the need to further justify their behaviour.

The third necessary step in the process is physiological *arousal*. Right from the start, Festinger viewed cognitive dissonance as a state of discomfort and tension that people seek to reduce—much like hunger, thirst, and other basic drives. Research has shown that this emphasis was well placed. In a study by Robert Croyle and Joel Cooper (1983), participants wrote essays that supported or contradicted their own attitudes. Some were ordered to do so, but others were led to believe that the choice was theirs. During the session, electrodes were attached to each participant's fingertips to record physiological arousal. As predicted by cognitive dissonance theory, those who freely wrote attitude-discrepant essays were the most aroused—an observation made by other researchers as well (Elkin & Leippe, 1986). In fact, participants who write attitude-discrepant essays in a "free-choice" situation report feeling high levels of discomfort—which subside once they change their attitudes (Elliot & Devine, 1994).

The fourth step in the dissonance process is closely related to the third. It isn't enough to feel generally aroused. The person must also make an *attribution* for that arousal to his or her own behaviour. Suppose you just lied to a friend, or studied for an exam that was cancelled, or made a tough decision that you might soon regret. Suppose further that although you are upset, you believe that your discomfort is caused by some external factor, not by your dissonance-producing behaviour. Under these circumstances, will you exhibit attitude change as a symptom of cognitive dissonance? Probably not. When participants were led to attribute their dissonance-related arousal to a drug they had supposedly taken (Zanna & Cooper, 1974), to the anticipation of painful electric shocks (Pittman, 1975), or to a pair of prism goggles that they had to wear (Losch & Cacioppo, 1990), attitude change did not occur. Figure 6.12 summarizes these steps in the production and reduction of dissonance.

In addition, there are cross-cultural findings demonstrating that dissonance reduction is not universal. Heine and Lehman (1997) compared Japanese participants (who come from a culture based on an interdependent view of oneself) to a Canadian sample (where one is likely to view oneself as independent) in a free-choice paradigm. Canadian participants were much more likely to provide rationalizations for their choices in the task, whereas the Japanese participants did not; there was no dissonance reduction in this group. To this day, social psychologists continue to debate the "classic" and "new look" theories of cognitive dissonance. On the one hand, research has shown that attitude-discrepant actions do not always produce dissonance, in part because not everyone cares about being cognitively consistent (Cialdini et al., 1995) and in part because a change in attitude often seems to require the production of negative consequences (Johnson et al., 1995). On the other hand, some researchers have found that inconsistency alone can trigger cognitive dissonance, even without the negative consequences. For example, Eddie Harmon-Jones and others (1996) had people drink a Kool-Aid™ beverage that was mixed with sugar or vinegar. The researchers either told participants (no choice) or asked them (high choice) to state in writing that they liked the beverage and then toss these notes, which were not really needed, into the wastebasket. Afterward, they rated how much they really liked the drink. You may have noticed that this experiment parallels the Festinger and Carlsmith study, with

FIGURE 6.12

Necessary Conditions for the Arousal and Reduction of Dissonance

Research suggests that four steps are necessary for attitude change to result from the production and reduction of dissonance.

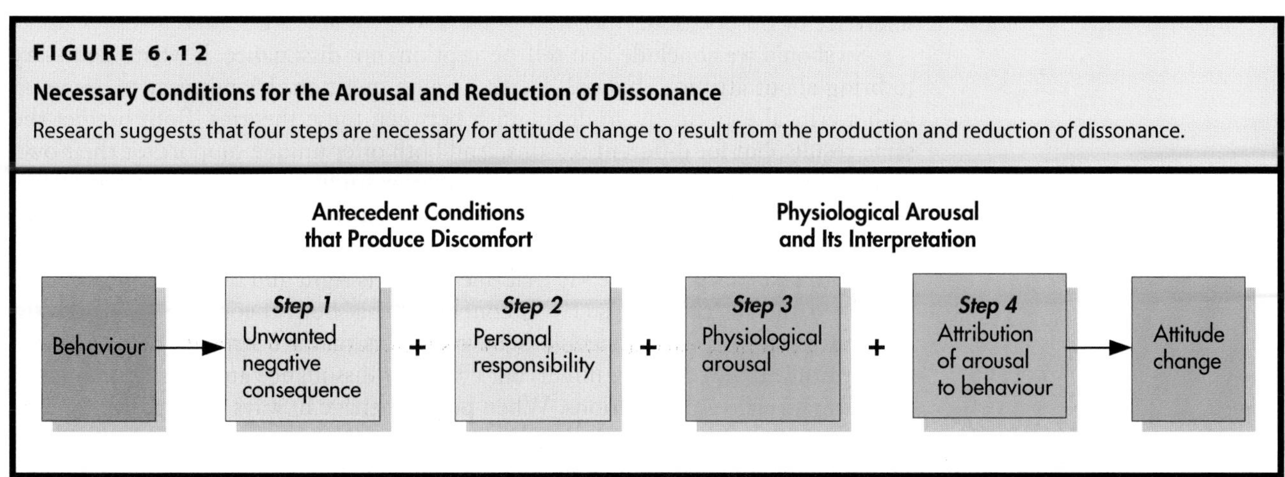

one key exception: For participants in the high-choice situation who consumed vinegar and said they liked it, the lie—although it contradicted their true attitudes—did not cause harm to anyone. Did they experience dissonance that they would have to reduce by overrating the vinegar Kool-Aid™? Yes. Compared with participants who lied about the vinegar in the no-choice situation, those in the high-choice situation rated its taste as more pleasant. The lie was harmless, but the feeling of inconsistency still forced a change in attitude.

Alternative Routes to Self-Persuasion

It is important to distinguish between the empirical facts as uncovered by dissonance researchers and the theory that is used to explain them. The facts themselves are clear: Under certain conditions, people who behave in attitude-discrepant ways go on to change their attitudes. Whether this phenomenon reflects a human need to reduce dissonance, however, is a matter of some controversy. Over the years, three other explanations have been proposed.

Self-Perception Theory Daryl Bem's (1965) *self-perception theory*, as described in Chapter 3, posed the first serious challenge to dissonance theory. Noting that people don't always have first-hand knowledge of their own attitudes, Bem proposed that we infer how we feel by observing ourselves and the circumstances of our own behaviour. This sort of self-persuasion is not fuelled by the need to reduce tension or justify our actions. Instead, it is a cool, calm, and rational process in which people interpret ambiguous feelings by observing their own behaviour. But can Bem's theory replace dissonance theory as an explanation of self-persuasion?

Bem confronted this question head-on. What if neutral observers who are not motivated by the need to reduce dissonance were to read a step-by-step description of a dissonance study and predict the results? This approach to the problem was ingenious. Bem reasoned that observers can have the same behavioural information as the participants themselves but not experience the same personal conflict. If observers generate the same results as real participants, it shows that dissonance arousal is not necessary for the resulting changes in attitudes.

To test his hypothesis, Bem (1967) described the Festinger and Carlsmith study to observers and had them guess participants' attitudes. Some were told about the $1 condition, some were told about the $20 condition, and others read about the control group procedure. The results closely paralleled the original study. As observers saw it, participants who said the task was interesting for $20 didn't mean it—they just went along for the money. But those who made the claim for only $1 must have been sincere. Why else would they have gone along? As far as Bem was concerned, participants themselves reason the same way. No conflict, no arousal—just inference by observation.

So should we conclude that self-perception, not dissonance, is what's necessary to bring about attitude change? That's a tough question. It's not easy to come up with a critical experiment to distinguish between these theories. Both predict the same results, but for different reasons. And both offer unique support for their own points of view. On the one hand, Bem's observer studies show that dissonance-like results *can* be obtained without arousal. On the other hand, the subjects of dissonance manipulations *do* experience arousal, which seems necessary for attitude change to take place. Can we say that one theory is right and the other wrong?

Fazio and his colleagues (1977) concluded that both theories are right but in different situations. When people behave in ways that are strikingly at odds with their attitudes, they feel the unnerving effects of dissonance and change their attitudes to rationalize their actions. When people behave in ways that are not terribly discrepant from how they feel, however, they experience relatively little tension and form their attitudes as a matter of inference. In short, highly discrepant behaviour produces attitude change through dissonance, whereas slightly discrepant behaviour produces change through self-perception.

Impression-Management Theory Another alternative to a dissonance view of self-persuasion is based on *impression-management theory*, which says that what matters is not a motive to *be* consistent but a motive to *appear* consistent. Nobody wants to be called fickle or be seen by others as a hypocrite. So we calibrate our attitudes and behaviours only publicly just to present ourselves to others in a particular light (Baumeister, 1982; Tedeschi et al., 1971). Or perhaps we are motivated not by a desire to appear consistent but by a desire to avoid being held responsible for the unpleasant consequences of our actions (Schlenker, 1982). Either way, this theory places the emphasis on our concern for self-presentation. According to this view, participants in the Festinger and Carlsmith study simply did not want the experimenter to think they had sold out for a paltry sum of money.

If the impression-management approach is correct, then cognitive dissonance does not produce attitude change at all—only reported change. In other words, if research participants were to state their attitudes anonymously, or if they were to think that the experimenter could determine their true feelings through covert measures, then dissonance-like effects should vanish. Sometimes, the effects do vanish; but other times, they do not. In general, studies have shown that although self-persuasion can be motivated by impression management, it can also occur in situations that do not clearly arouse self-presentation concerns (Baumeister & Tice, 1984).

Self-Esteem Theory A third competing explanation relates self-persuasion to the self. According to Elliot Aronson, acts that arouse dissonance do so because they threaten the self-concept, making the person feel guilty, dishonest, or hypocritical, and motivating a change in attitude or future behaviour (Aronson, 1999; Stone et al., 1997). This being the case, perhaps Festinger and Carlsmith's participants needed to change their attitudes toward the boring task in order to repair damage to the self, not to resolve cognitive inconsistency.

If cognitive dissonance is aroused only by behaviour that lowers self-esteem, then people with already low expectations of themselves should not be affected: "If a person conceives of himself as a 'schnook,' he will expect to behave like a schnook" (Aronson, 1968, p. 24). In fact, Jeff Stone (2003) found that when college students were coaxed into writing an essay in favour of a tuition increase (a position that contradicted their attitude) and into thinking about their own standards of behaviour, those who had high self-esteem changed their attitude to meet their behaviour, as dissonance theory would predict, more than those who had low self-esteem. Claude Steele (1988) takes the notion two steps further. First, he suggests that a dissonance-producing situation—engaging in attitude-discrepant behaviour, exerting wasted effort, or making a difficult decision—sets in motion a process of *self-affirmation* that serves to revalidate the integrity of the self-concept. Second, this revalidation can be achieved in many ways, not just by resolving dissonance. Self-affirmation theory makes a unique prediction: If the active ingredient in dissonance situations is a threat to the self, then people who have an opportunity to affirm the self in other ways will not suffer from the effects of dissonance. Give Festinger and Carlsmith's $1 participants a chance to donate money, help a victim in distress, or solve a problem, and their self-concepts should bounce back without further need to justify their actions.

Research provides support for this hypothesis. For example, Steele and his colleagues (1993) gave people positive or negative feedback about a personality test they had taken. Next, they asked them to rate ten popular music albums and then

FIGURE 6.13

When Self-Affirmation Fails

Students gave a dissonant speech advocating a ban on a popular campus tradition. Compared to those in a low-choice situation, students in a high-choice group changed their attitude more to favour the ban. As self-affirmation theory predicts, those given a chance to express their values afterward did not then favour the ban—unless their values were poorly received. Self-affirmation can repair the dissonance-damaged self. When it fails, however, cognitive dissonance returns to pressure the change in attitude. *(Galinsky et al., 2000.)*

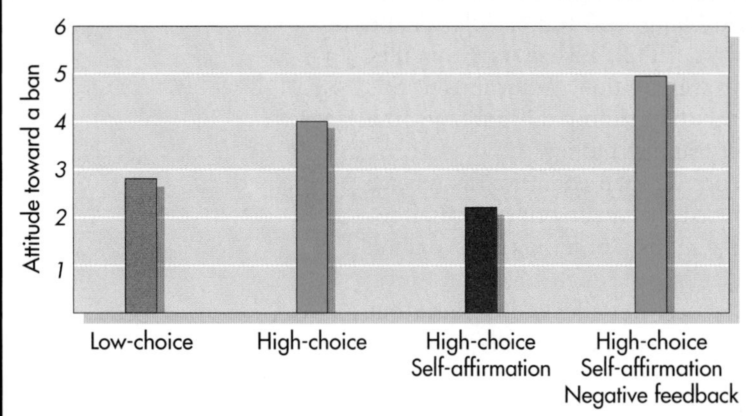

offered them a choice of keeping either their fifth- or sixth-ranked album. Soon after making the decision, participants were asked to re-rate the albums. As predicted by dissonance theory, most inflated their ratings of the chosen album relative to the album that was not chosen. The key word, however, is *most.* Among positive-feedback participants, ratings did not change. Why not? According to Steele, these participants had just enjoyed a self-affirming experience—enough to overcome the need to reduce dissonance.

Steele's research suggests that there are many possible ways to repair the dissonance-damaged self. But if these efforts at indirect self-affirmation fail, would cognitive dissonance return and pressure a change in attitude? Yes. In one study, college students were asked (high-choice) or told (low-choice) to deliver an attitude-discrepant speech advocating that a popular campus tradition (running nude on the evening of the first snowfall) be banned. For those in the high-choice condition, cognitive dissonance was aroused, pressuring a change in attitude favouring the ban. Students in a third group who were subsequently given an opportunity to self-affirm by expressing some cherished values felt less discomfort and exhibited less attitude change. For them, self-affirmation provided the necessary relief. However, among students in a fourth group—who self-affirmed but then received negative feedback about the values they expressed—cognitive dissonance returned, pressuring a change in attitude toward the ban. In essence, cognitive dissonance and its impact on attitudes re-emerged from the failed attempt at self-affirmation (Galinsky et al., 2000; see Figure 6.13).

To summarize, dissonance theory maintains that people change their attitudes to justify their attitude-discrepant behaviours, efforts, and decisions. Self-perception theory argues that the change occurs because people infer how they feel by observing their own behaviour. Impression-management theory claims that the attitude change is spurred by self-presentation concerns. And self-affirmation theory says that the change is motivated by threats to the self (see Figure 6.14).

Attitudes and attitude change are an important part of social life. In this chapter, we have seen that persuasion can be achieved in different ways. The most common approach is through communication from *others.* Faced with newspaper editorials, junk mail, books, TV commercials, Internet ads, and other messages, we take one of two routes to persuasion. On the central route, attitude change is based on the merits of the source and his or her communication. On the peripheral route, it is based on superficial cues. A second, less obvious means of persuasion originates within *ourselves.* When people behave in ways that run afoul of their true convictions, they often go on to change their attitudes. Once again, there is not one route to change, but many. In this regard, dissonance, self-perception, impression management, and self-affirmation are among the possible avenues.

FIGURE 6.14

Theories of Self-Persuasion: Critical Comparisons

Here we compare the major theories of self-persuasion. Each alternative challenges a different aspect of dissonance theory. Self-perception theory assumes that attitude change is a matter of inference, not motivation. Impression-management theory maintains that the change is more apparent than real, reported for the sake of public self-presentation. Self-affirmation theory contends that the motivating force is a concern for the self and that attitude change will not occur when the self-concept is affirmed in other ways.

	Theories			
	Cognitive Dissonance	*Self-Perception*	*Impression Management*	*Self-Affirmation*
Is the attitude change motivated by a desire to reduce discomfort?	Yes	No	Yes	Yes
Does a person's private attitude really change?	Yes	Yes	No	Yes
Must the change be directly related to the attitude-discrepant behaviour?	Yes	Yes	Yes	No

Review

The Study of Attitudes

- An attitude is an affective, evaluative reaction toward a person, place, issue, or object.

How Attitudes Are Measured

- The most common way to measure attitudes is through self-reports, such as attitude scales.
- To get respondents to answer questions honestly, the bogus pipeline may be used.
- Covert measures may also be used. Such measures include nonverbal behaviour, the facial electromyograph (EMG), brain-wave patterns, and the Implicit Association Test (IAT).

The Link Between Attitudes and Behaviour

- Attitudes do not necessarily correlate with behaviour; but under certain conditions, there is a high correlation.
- Attitudes predict behaviour best when they're specific rather than general and strong rather than weak.
- Attitudes compete with other influences on behaviour.

Persuasion by Communication

- The most common approach to changing attitudes is through a persuasive communication.

Two Routes to Persuasion

- When people think critically about a message, they take the central route to persuasion and are influenced by the strength of the arguments.
- When people do not think carefully about a message, they take the peripheral route to persuasion and are influenced by peripheral cues.
- The route taken depends on whether people have the ability and the motivation to fully process the communication.

The Source

- Attitude change is greater for messages delivered by a source that is credible (competent and trustworthy).
- Attitude change is also greater when the source is likeable (similar and attractive).
- When an audience has a high level of personal involvement, source factors are less important than message quality.
- The sleeper effect shows that people often forget the source but not the message, so the effects of source credibility dissipate over time.

The Message

- On the peripheral route, lengthy messages are persuasive. On the central route, length works only if the added information does not dilute the message.

- Whether it is best to present an argument first or second depends on how much time elapses—both between the two arguments and between the second argument and the final decision.
- Messages that are moderately discrepant from an audience's attitudes will inspire change, but highly discrepant messages will be scrutinized and rejected.
- High-fear messages motivate attitude change when they contain strong arguments and instructions on how to avoid the threatened danger.
- Positive emotion also facilitates attitude change because people are easier to persuade when they're in a good mood.
- Research shows that subliminal messages do not produce meaningful or lasting changes in attitudes.

The Audience

- People are not consistently difficult or easy to persuade. Rather, different kinds of messages influence different kinds of people.
- People who are high in the need for cognition are persuaded more by the strength of the arguments.
- People who are high in self-monitoring are influenced more by appeals to social images.
- To be persuasive, a message should also appeal to the cultural values of its audience.
- Forewarning increases resistance to persuasive influence. It inoculates the audience by providing the opportunity to generate counter-arguments, and it arouses psychological reactance.

Persuasion by Our Own Actions

Role-Playing: All the World's a Stage

- The way people act can influence how they feel, as behaviour can determine attitudes.

Cognitive Dissonance Theory: The Classic Version

- Under certain conditions, inconsistency between attitudes and behaviour produces an unpleasant psychological state called cognitive dissonance.
- Motivated to reduce the tension, people often change their attitudes to justify (1) attitude-discrepant behaviour, (2) wasted effort, and (3) difficult decisions.

Cognitive Dissonance Theory: A New Look

- According to the "new look" version of cognitive dissonance theory, four conditions must be met for dissonance to be aroused: (1) an act with unwanted consequences, (2) a feeling of personal responsibility, (3) arousal or discomfort, and (4) attribution of the arousal to the attitude-discrepant act.
- Social psychologists continue to debate whether dissonance can be aroused by cognitive inconsistency when no unwanted consequences are produced.

Alternative Routes to Self-Persuasion

- Alternative explanations of dissonance-related attitude change have been proposed.
- Self-perception theory states that people logically infer their attitudes by observing their own behaviour.
- Impression-management theory says that people are motivated only to appear consistent to others.
- Self-affirmation theory states that dissonance is triggered by threats to the self and can be reduced indirectly, without a change in attitude, through self-affirming experiences.

Key Terms

attitude *(177)*
attitude scale *(179)*
bogus pipeline *(179)*
central route to persuasion *(186)*
cognitive dissonance theory *(204)*
elaboration *(187)*
facial electromyograph (EMG) *(180)*
Implicit Association Test (IAT) *(181)*
implicit attitude *(181)*
inoculation hypothesis *(202)*
insufficient deterrence *(206)*
insufficient justification *(205)*
need for cognition (NC) *(199)*
peripheral route to persuasion *(186)*
persuasion *(186)*
psychological reactance *(202)*
sleeper effect *(192)*
theory of planned behaviour *(183)*

Researchers can tell if someone has a positive or negative attitude by measuring physiological arousal.

False. *Measures of arousal can reveal how intensely someone feels, but not whether the person's attitude is positive or negative.*

In reacting to persuasive communications, people are influenced more by superficial images than by logical arguments.

False. *As indicated by the dual-process model of persuasion, people can be influenced by images or arguments—depending on their ability and motivation to think critically about the information.*

People are most easily persuaded by commercial messages that are presented without their awareness.

False. *There is no research evidence to support the presumed effects of subliminal ads.*

The more money you pay people to tell a lie, the more they will come to believe it.

False. *Cognitive dissonance studies show that people believe the lies they are underpaid to tell as a way to justify their own actions.*

People often come to like what they suffer for.

True. *Studies show that the more people work or suffer for something, the more they come to like it as a way to justify their effort.*

7 Conformity

OUTLINE

PREVIEW

THIS CHAPTER examines ways in which social influences are "automatic." We then look at three processes. First, we consider the reasons why people exhibit *conformity* to group norms. Second, we describe the strategies used to elicit *compliance* with direct requests. Third, we analyze the causes and effects of *obedience* to the commands of authority. The chapter concludes with a discussion of the *continuum of social influence.*

PUTTING COMMON SENSE TO THE TEST

T / F

____ **When all members of a group give an incorrect response to an easy question, most people most of the time conform to that response.**

____ **An effective way to get someone to do you a favour is to make a first request that is so large the person is sure to reject it.**

____ **In experiments on obedience, most participants who were ordered to administer severe shocks to an innocent person refused to do so.**

____ **As the number of people in a group increases, so does their impact on an individual.**

____ **Conformity rates vary across different cultures and from one generation to the next.**

On August 27, 2005, 200 people, strangers to one another, gathered in downtown Vancouver outside of an art gallery. Acting like zombies, they marched as a group around various points of the city until they eventually dispersed. On November 13, 2005 more than 200 people converged in downtown Toronto where they proceeded to engage in a massive pillow fight. In London, a large crowd descended upon a furniture store, admired the sofas, and talked on cell phones without using the letter *o*. In Rome, 300 people entered a music and bookshop and asked the staff for titles that did not exist. In Paris, people congregated under the pyramid of the Louvre and fell lifelessly to the ground. Illustrating the power of the Internet to serve as a vehicle for social influence, each of these crowds was a "flash mob"—a group of people who received instructions over the Internet, gathered voluntarily at a set time and place, performed some silly but harmless action, and dispersed. While it appears that the flash mob has its origins in the United States in 2003, flash mobs have since come together in Amsterdam, Berlin, Oslo, Melbourne, Budapest, and other cities around the world.

Sometimes, the social influences that move us are not entertaining and funny but potentially hazardous to our health. Consider the unusual events that occurred on a Vancouver bus in 2004 when several people, including the bus driver and the paramedics called to treat him, became violently ill and had to be hospitalized. It was initially believed that a "suspicious" passenger had poisoned them, after the driver reported an "unusual odour." All quickly recovered and no medical explanation for their illness was ever found. An epidemiologist at the University of British Columbia labelled it a case of "mass psychogenic illness"—a profound form of social influence previously documented by Jones (2000).

Flash mobs reveal the awesome power of social influence. The effects that people have on each other can also be seen in the most mundane of human events. Thus, sports fans spread the "wave" around a stadium or chant "de-fence" in a spectacular show of unison. TV producers insert canned laughter into sitcoms to increase viewer responsiveness. Political candidates trumpet the inflated results of their own favourable public opinion polls to attract new voters to their side. And bartenders, waiters, and waitresses stuff dollar bills into their tip jars as a way to get customers to follow suit. As they say, "Monkey see, monkey do."

You don't need to be a social psychologist to know that we have an impact on each other's behaviour. The question is, how, and with what effect? The term *social influence*

"We are discreet sheep; we wait to see how the drove is going and then go with the drove."

—Mark Twain

This flash mob, following instructions they received over the Internet, gathered at the Louvre in Paris in August of 2003. Once they had congregated under the pyramid entrance, they fell lifelessly to the ground.

refers to the ways in which people are affected by the real and imagined pressures of others (Cialdini & Goldstein, 2004; Kiesler & Kiesler, 1969). The kinds of influences brought to bear on an individual come in different shapes and sizes. In this chapter, we look at social influences that are *automatic;* then we consider three forms of influence that vary in the degree of pressure exerted on an individual—*conformity, compliance*, and *obedience.* As depicted in Figure 7.1, conformity, compliance, and obedience are not distinct, qualitatively different "types" of influence. In all three cases, the influence may emanate from a person, a group, or an institution. And in all instances, the behaviour in question may be constructive (helping oneself or others), or destructive (hurting oneself or others), or neutral. It is useful to note, once again, that social influence varies, as points along a continuum, according to the degree of pressure exerted on the individual. It is also useful to note that we do not always succumb under pressure. People may conform or maintain their independence from others; they may comply with direct requests or react with assertiveness; they may obey the commands of authority or oppose powerful others in an act of defiance. In this chapter, we examine the factors that lead human beings to yield to or resist social influence.

Social Influence as "Automatic"

Before we consider the explicit forms of social influence depicted in Figure 7.1, whereby individuals choose whether or not to "go along," it's important to note that, as social animals, humans are vulnerable to a host of subtle, almost reflex-like influences. Without realizing it, we often yawn when we see others yawning and laugh when we hear others laughing. In an early study, Stanley Milgram and others (1969) had research confederates stop on a busy street in New York City, look up, and gawk at the sixth-floor window of a nearby building. Films shot

FIGURE 7.1

Continuum of Social Influence

Social influences vary in the degree of pressure they bring to bear on an individual. People may (1) *conform* to group norms or maintain their independence, (2) *comply* with requests or be assertive, and (3) *obey* or defy the commands of authority.

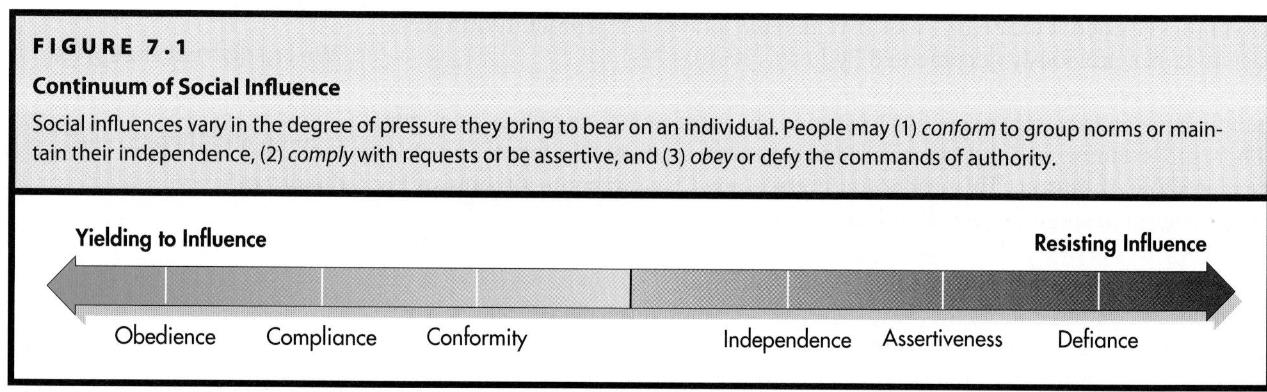

from behind the window indicated that about 80 percent of passers-by stopped and gazed up when they saw the confederates.

Do we really imitate one another automatically, without thought and without conflict? It appears that we do. In recent years, controlled studies of human infants have shown that within 72 hours of birth, babies not only look at faces but—to the delight of parents all over the world—often mimic gestures such as moving the head, pursing the lips, and sticking out the tongue (Bremner, 2002; Gopnik et al., 1999).

Often we are not aware of the influence other people have on our behaviour.

You may not realize it, but human adults unwittingly mimic each other all the time. To demonstrate, Tanya Chartrand and John Bargh (1999) set up participants to work on a task with a partner, a confederate who exhibited the habit of rubbing his face or shaking his foot. Hidden cameras recording the interaction revealed that, without realizing it, participants mimicked these motor behaviours, rubbing their face or shaking a foot to match their partner's behaviour. Chartrand and Bargh dubbed this phenomenon the "chameleon effect," after the lizard that changes colours according to its physical environment (see Figure 7.2). The reason for this nonconscious form of imitation, they speculated, is that people interact more smoothly when they are behaviourally "in sync" with one another. Accordingly, Chartrand and Bargh turned the tables in a second study, instructing their confederate to match in subtle ways the mannerisms of some participants but not others. Sure enough, participants who had been mimicked liked the confederate more than those who had not.

FIGURE 7.2

The Chameleon Effect

This graph shows the number of times per minute participants rubbed their face or shook their foot when with a confederate who was rubbing his face or shaking his foot. *(Chartrand & Bargh, 1999.)*

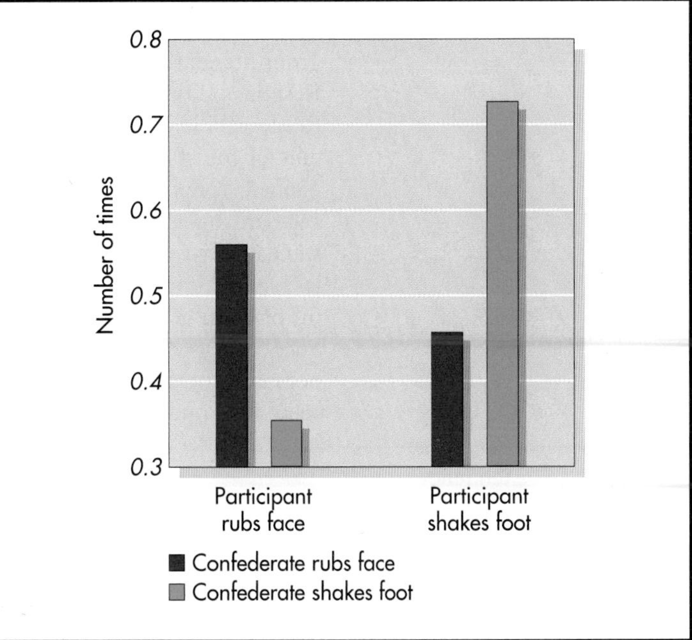

Further demonstrating the social function of mimicry, people mimic others more when they are motivated to affiliate than when they are not (Lakin & Chartrand, 2003). This may explain why women, who are generally more affiliative than men, tend to smile more in social situations (LaFrance et al., 2003).

The human impulse to mimic others may have adaptive social value, but these types of effects can also be found in nonsocial situations—and colour our emotional states. In one study, Ulf Dimberg and others (2000) exposed people to rapid-fire subliminal pictures of happy or angry faces. The participants were not conscious of having seen the images. Yet by recording facial muscle activity through the use of electrodes (as described in Chapter 6, the facial EMG can be used to record subtle changes in facial expression that often cannot be seen with the naked eye), these researchers found that the happy and angry faces evoked muscle reactions associated, respectively, with smiling and frowning. In another study, Roland Neumann and Fritz Strack (2000) had people listen to an abstract philosophical speech that was recited on tape in a happy, sad, or neutral voice. Afterward, participants rated their own mood as more positive when they heard the happy voice and as more negative when they heard the sad voice. Apparently, even though the participants and speakers never interacted, the speaker's emotional state was socially contagious—an automatic effect that can be described as a form of "mood contagion."

Conformity

It is hard to find behaviours that are *not* in some way affected by exposure to the actions of others. When social psychologists talk of **conformity**, they specifically refer to the tendency of people to change their perceptions, opinions, and behaviour in ways that are consistent with group norms. With this definition in mind, would you call yourself a conformist or a nonconformist? For instance, do you ever feel inclined to follow what others are doing? At first, you may deny the tendency to conform and, instead, declare your individuality. But think about it. When was the last time you appeared at a formal wedding dressed in blue jeans or remained seated during the national anthem at a sports event? People find it difficult to breach social norms. In an interesting demonstration of this point, social psychology research assistants were supposed to ask subway passengers to give up their seats—a conspicuous violation of the norm of acceptable conduct. Many of the assistants could not carry out their assignment. In fact, some of those who tried it became so anxious that they pretended to be ill just to make their request appear justified (Milgram & Sabini, 1978).

With conformity being so widespread, it is interesting and ironic that research participants (at least in North America) who are coaxed into conforming to a group norm will often not admit it. In one study, Buehler and Griffin (1994) had students at the University of Waterloo read a story based on newspaper reports describing a real-life incident where a white police officer shot and killed a black teenager who was driving a stolen car. Participants in the Police Responsibility condition were told that previous research participants believed that the officer was 75 percent responsible; those in the Victim Responsibility condition were told others believed the officer was 25 percent responsible. Participants were asked to indicate their agreement with the group standard and then assign what they believed was the appropriate amount of police responsibility. One week later they were asked to relate the details of the shooting incident in their own words. Results indicated that the participants agreed with the group standards equally often; 38 percent agreed with the group norm in the Police Responsibility condition and 41 percent agreed with the group norm in the Victim Responsibility condition. One week later, participants were more likely to recall details of the shooting in a way that supported the group norm. As the authors explained, "people followed up their decision to conform to or dissent from a group standard by reconstructing the facts and rewriting history" (p. 993). People understandably have mixed feelings about conformity. After all, some degree of conformity is essential if individuals are to coexist peacefully, as when people assume their rightful place in a waiting line. Yet at other times, conformity can have harmful consequences, as when people drink too heavily at parties or tell offensive ethnic jokes because others are doing the same. For the social psychologist, the goal is to understand the conditions that promote conformity and the reasons for that behaviour.

conformity The tendency to change our perceptions, opinions, or behaviour in ways that are consistent with group norms.

The Early Classics

In 1936, Muzafer Sherif published a classic laboratory study of how norms develop in small groups. His method was ingenious. Male students, who believed they were participating in a visual perception experiment, sat in a totally darkened room. Approximately 4.5 metres in front of them, a small dot of light appeared for two seconds, after which participants were asked to estimate how far it had moved. This procedure was repeated several times. Although participants didn't realize it, the dot of light always remained motionless. The movement they thought they saw was merely an optical illusion known as the *autokinetic effect:* In darkness, a stationary point of light appears to move, sometimes erratically, in various directions.

FIGURE 7.3

A Classic Case of Suggestibility

This graph, taken from Sherif's study, shows how three participants' estimates of the apparent movement of light gradually converged. Before they came together, their perceptions varied considerably. Once in groups, however, participants conformed to the norm that had developed. *(Sherif, 1936.)*

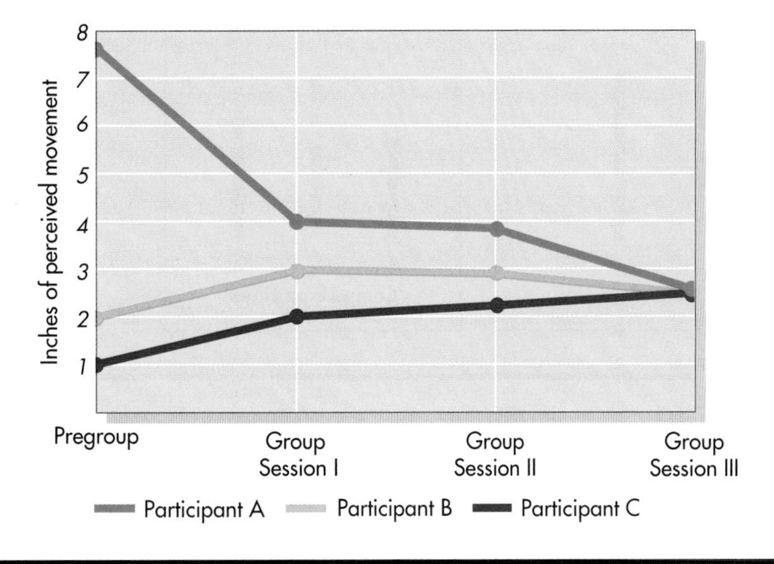

At first, participants sat alone and reported their judgments to the experimenter. After several trials, Sherif found that they settled in on their own stable perceptions of movement, with most estimates ranging from two to 25 centimetres. During the next three days, people returned to participate in three-person groups. As before, lights were flashed, and participants, one by one, announced their estimates. As shown in Figure 7.3, initial estimates varied considerably, but participants later converged on a common perception. Eventually, each group established its own set of norms.

Some 15 years after Sherif's demonstration, Solomon Asch (1951) constructed a very different task for testing how people's beliefs affect the beliefs of others. To appreciate what Asch did, imagine yourself in the following situation. You sign up for a psychology experiment and when you arrive, you find six other students waiting around a table. Soon after you take an empty seat, the experimenter explains that he is interested in the ability to make visual discriminations. As an example, he asks you and the others to indicate which of three comparison lines is identical in length to a standard line.

That seems easy enough. The experimenter then says that after each set of lines is shown, you and the others should take turns announcing your judgments out loud in the order of your seating position. Beginning on his left, the experimenter asks the first person for his judgment. Seeing that you are in the next-to-last position, you patiently await your turn. The opening moments pass uneventfully. The discriminations are clear, and everyone agrees

After two uneventful rounds in Asch's study, the participant (seated second from the right) faces a dilemma. The answer he wants to give in the third test of visual discrimination differs from that of the first five confederates, who are all in agreement. Should he give his own answer, or conform to theirs?

FIGURE 7.4

Line Judgment Task Used in Asch's Conformity Studies

Which comparison line—A, B, or C—is the same in length as the standard line? What would you say if you found yourself in the presence of a unanimous majority that answered A or C? The participants in Asch's experiments conformed to the majority about a third of the time. *(Asch, 1955.)*

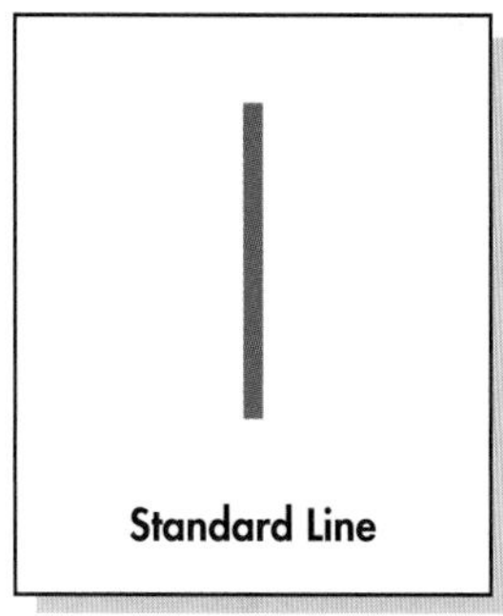

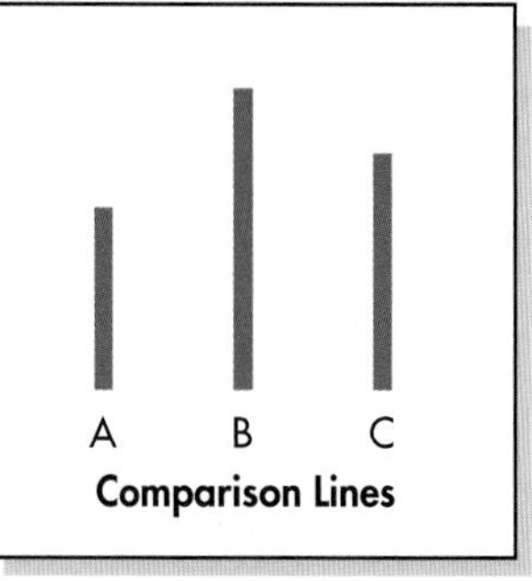

on the answers. On the third set of lines, however, the first participant selects what is quite clearly the wrong line. Huh? What happened? Did he suddenly lose his mind, his eyesight, or both? Before you have the chance to figure this one out, the next four participants choose the same wrong line. Now what? Feeling as if you have entered the Twilight Zone, you wonder if you misunderstood the task. And you wonder what the others will think if you have the nerve to disagree. It's your turn now. You rub your eyes and take another look. What do you see? More to the point, what do you do?

Figure 7.4 gives an idea of the bind in which Asch's participants found themselves—caught between the need to be right and the desire to be liked (Insko et al., 1982; Ross et al., 1976). As you may suspect by now, the other "participants" were actually confederates—and had been trained to make incorrect judgments on 12 out of 18 presentations. There seems little doubt that the real participants knew the correct answers. In a control group, where they made judgments in isolation, they made almost no errors. Yet Asch's participants went along with the incorrect majority about 37 percent of the time—far more often than most of us would ever predict. Not everyone conformed, of course. About 25 percent refused to agree on any of the incorrect judgments. Yet 50 percent went along on at least half of the critical presentations, with the remaining participants conforming on an occasional basis. Similarly high levels of conformity were observed when Asch's study was repeated 30 years later and in recent studies involving other cognitive tasks (Larsen, 1990; Schneider & Watkins, 1996).

Nonconformists often pay a price for dissent. Nelson Mandela spent 27 years in prison for speaking out against apartheid in South Africa.

Looking at Sherif's and Asch's research, let's compare these classic studies of social influence. Obviously, both demonstrate that our visual perceptions can be heavily influenced by others. But how similar are they, really? Did Sherif's and Asch's participants exhibit the same kind of conformity, and for the same reasons, or was the resemblance in their behaviour more apparent than real?

From the start, it was clear that these studies differed in some important ways. In Sherif's research, participants were quite literally "in the dark," so they naturally turned to others for guidance. When physical reality is ambiguous and we are uncertain of our own judgments, as in the autokinetic situation, others can serve as a valuable source of information (Festinger, 1954). Asch's participants found themselves in a much more awkward position. Their task was relatively simple, and they could see with their own eyes what answers were correct. Still, they often followed the incorrect majority. In interviews, many of

Asch's participants reported afterward that they went along with the group even though they were not convinced. Many of those who did not conform said they felt "conspicuous" and "crazy," like a "misfit" (Asch, 1956, p. 31).

In 2002, more than 600 million people worldwide had access to communication over the Internet (Manasian, 2003). This being the case, you may wonder: Do the social forces that influence people in the face-to-face encounters studied by Sherif and Asch also operate in virtual groups, where members are somewhat anonymous? The answer is yes. McKenna and Bargh (1998) observed behaviour in a number of Internet newsgroups in which people with common interests posted and responded to messages on a range of topics, from obesity and sexual orientation to money and the stock market. The social medium in this situation was "remote." Still, these researchers found that in newsgroups that brought together people with "hidden identities" (such as gays and lesbians who had concealed their sexuality from others), members were highly responsive to social feedback. Those who posted messages that were met with approval rather than disapproval later became more active participants of the newsgroup. When it comes to social support and rejection, even virtual groups have the power to shape our behaviour (Bargh & McKenna, 2004; Williams et al., 2000).

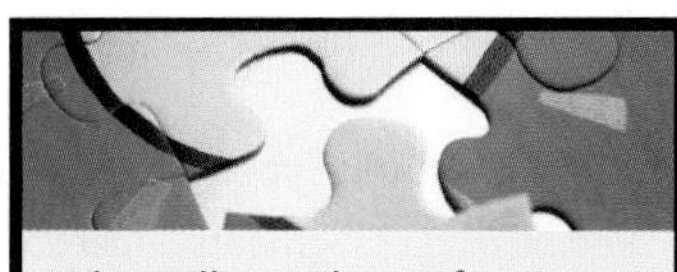

When all members of a group give an incorrect response to an easy question, most people most of the time conform to that response. **False.**

Why Do People Conform?

The Sherif and Asch studies demonstrate that people conform for two very different reasons: one informational, the other normative (Crutchfield, 1955; Deutsch & Gerard, 1955). Through **informational influence**, people conform because they want to be correct in their judgments and they assume that when others agree on something, they must be right. In Sherif's autokinetic task, as in other difficult or ambiguous tasks, it's natural to assume that four eyes are better than two. Hence, research shows that eyewitnesses trying to recall a crime or some other event will alter their recollections—and even create false memories—in response to what they hear other witnesses report (Gabbert et al., 2003; Roediger et al., 2001). **Normative influence**, however, leads people to conform because they fear the consequences of appearing deviant. It's easy to see why. Research shows that individuals who stray from a group norm are often disliked, rejected, ridiculed, and laughed at (Levine, 1989; Schachter, 1951). These negative social reactions are hard to take. In a series of controlled studies, people who were socially *ostracized*—by being neglected, ignored, and excluded in a live or Internet chat room conversation—reacted by feeling hurt, angry, and alone (Williams et al., 2002). In fact, MacDonald and Leary (2005) suggest that both physical pain and social pain are adaptive, as they lead us out of harm's way and guide us toward those who may help, and similar physiological systems seem to play a role in how our bodies react to either type of threat. For example, in a brain-imaging study, young people who were left out by other players in a three-person Internet game called "Cyberball" exhibited elevated activity in a part of the brain normally associated with physical pain (Eisenberger et al., 2003). In *Ostracism: The Power of Silence*, Kipling Williams (2001) notes that some people get so distressed when they are rejected that they become passive, numb, and lethargic—"as though they had been hit with a stun gun" (p. 159).

Usually, informational and normative influences operate jointly (Insko et al., 1983). Even some of Asch's participants admitted that they came to agree with their group's erroneous judgments. Still, the distinction between the two types of influence is important, not just for understanding why people conform but because the two types of influence produce different types of conformity: private and public (Allen, 1965; Kelman, 1961). Like beauty, conformity may be skin deep, or it may penetrate beneath the surface. **Private conformity**, also called true acceptance or conversion, describes instances in which others cause us to change not only our overt behaviour but our minds as well. To conform at this level is to be truly

informational influence Influence that produces conformity when a person believes others are correct in their judgments.

normative influence Influence that produces conformity when a person fears the negative social consequences of appearing deviant.

private conformity The change of beliefs that occurs when a person privately accepts the position taken by others.

FIGURE 7.5

Distinguishing Types of Conformity

People made judgments under conditions in which they had a high or a low level of motivation. Regardless of whether the judgment task was difficult or easy, there were moderate levels of conformity when participants had low motivation (left). But when they were highly motivated (right), participants conformed more when the task was difficult. *(Baron et al., 1996.)*

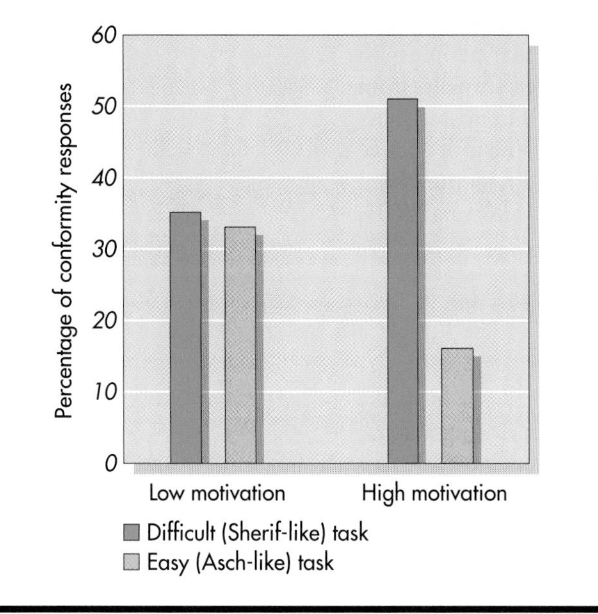

persuaded that others are correct. In contrast, **public conformity** (sometimes called compliance, a term that is used later in this chapter to describe a different form of influence) refers to a superficial change in behaviour. People often respond to normative pressures by pretending to agree even when privately they do not. This often happens when we want to curry favour with others. The politician who tells constituents whatever they want to hear is a case in point.

How, you might be wondering, can social psychologists ever tell the difference between the private and public conformist? After all, both exhibit the same change in their observable behaviour. The difference is that compared with someone who merely acquiesces in public, the individual who is truly persuaded maintains that change long after the others are out of the picture. When this distinction is applied to Sherif's and Asch's research, the results come out as expected. At the end of his study, Sherif (1936) retested participants alone and found that their estimates continued to reflect the norm previously established in their group—even among those who were re-tested a full year after the experiment (Rohrer et al., 1954). In contrast, when Asch (1956) had participants write their answers privately, their level of conformity dropped sharply (Deutsch & Gerard, 1955; Mouton et al., 1956).

In a study that demonstrates both processes, Robert S. Baron and others (1996) had people, in groups of three (one participant and two confederates), act as eyewitnesses: First they would see a picture of a person, then they would try to pick that person out of a line-up. In some groups, the task was difficult, like Sherif's, since participants saw each picture only once, for half a second. For other groups, the task was easier, like Asch's, in that they saw each picture twice for a total of ten seconds. How often did participants conform when the confederates made the wrong identification? It depended on how motivated they were. When the experimenter downplayed the task as only a "pilot study," the conformity rates were 35 percent when the task was difficult and 33 percent when it was easy. But when participants were offered a financial incentive to do well, conformity went up to 51 percent when the task was difficult—and down to 16 percent when it was easy (see Figure 7.5). With pride and money on the line, the Sherif-like participants conformed more, and the Asch-like participants conformed less.

Table 7.1 summarizes the comparison of Sherif's and Asch's studies and the depths of social influence that they demonstrate. Looking at this table, you can see that the difficulty of the task is crucial. When reality cannot easily be validated by physical evidence, as in the autokinetic situation, people turn to others for information and conform because they are truly persuaded by that information. When reality is clear, however, the cost of dissent becomes the major issue. As Asch found, it can be difficult to depart too much from others even when you know that they—not you—are wrong. So you play along. Privately, you don't change your mind. But you nod your head in agreement anyway.

public conformity A superficial change in overt behaviour, without a corresponding change of opinion, produced by real or imagined group pressure.

Majority Influence

Realizing that people often succumb to peer pressure is only the first step in understanding the process of social influence. The next step is to identify the situational

TABLE 7.1

Two Types of Conformity

A comparison of Sherif's and Asch's studies suggests different kinds of conformity for different reasons. Sherif used an ambiguous task, so others provided a source of information and influenced the participants' true opinions. Asch used a task that required simple judgments of a clear stimulus, so most participants exhibited occasional public conformity in response to normative pressure but privately did not accept the group's judgments.

Experimental Task	Primary Effect of Group	Depth of Conformity Produced
Sherif's ambiguous autokinetic effect	Informational influence	Private acceptance
Asch's simple line judgments	Normative influence	Public conformity

and personal factors that make us more or less likely to conform. We know that people tend to conform when the social pressure is intense and they are insecure about how to behave. But what creates these feelings of pressure and insecurity? Here, we look at four factors: the size of the group, a focus on norms, the presence of an ally, and the personal characteristics of the individual.

Group Size: The Power in Numbers Common sense would suggest that as the number of people in a majority increases, so should their impact. Actually, it is not that simple. Asch (1956) varied the size of groups, using 1, 2, 3, 4, 8, or 15 confederates, and he found that conformity increased with group size—but only up to a point. Once there were three or four confederates, the amount of *additional* influence exerted by the rest was negligible. Other researchers have obtained similar results (Gerard et al., 1968).

Beyond the presence of three or four others, additions to a group are subject to the law of "diminishing returns" (Knowles, 1983; Mullen, 1983). As we will see later, Bibb Latané (1981) likens the influence of people on an individual to the way light bulbs illuminate a surface. When a second bulb is added to a room, the effect is dramatic. When the tenth bulb is added, however, its impact is barely felt, if at all. Economists say the same about the perception of money. An additional dollar seems greater to the person who has only $3 than to the person who has $300.

Another possible explanation is that as more and more people express the same opinion, an individual is likely to suspect that they are acting either in "collusion" or as "spineless sheep." According to David Wilder (1977), what matters is not the actual number of others but one's perception of how many distinct others, thinking independently, there are. Indeed, Wilder found that people were more influenced by two groups of two than by one four-person group and by two groups of three than by one six-person group. Conformity increased even further when people were exposed to three two-person groups. When faced with a majority opinion, we do more than just count the number of warm bodies—we try to assess the number of independent minds.

A Focus on Norms The size of a majority may influence the amount of pressure that is felt, but social norms give rise to conformity only when we know and focus on those norms. This may sound like an obvious point, yet we often misperceive what is normative—particularly when others are too afraid or embarrassed to publicly present their true thoughts, feelings, and behaviours.

Whether in sports stadiums or on the streets, social norms influence us when they are brought to awareness by the current or past behaviour of others.

One common example of this "pluralistic ignorance" concerns perceptions of alcohol usage. In a survey of university students, Neighbours, Dillard, Lewis, Bergstrom, and Neil (2006) found that most students overestimated both the frequency and the amount of alcohol consumed by their peers, and this predicted the students' own drinking patterns, up to a year later. In addition, students who believed their peers drank more, and more often, were more likely to be consuming greater quantities of alcohol a year later.

People's willingness to express prejudice is also influenced by what they think the norms are. In a series of studies, Christian Crandall and his colleagues (2002) assessed people's attitudes toward 105 social groups, such as drug users, male nurses, country music fans, cheerleaders, blind people, environmentalists, and auto mechanics. They found that it is more normatively acceptable to harbour prejudice against some groups than against others (people agree, for example, that it is okay to dislike drug users but not blind people)—and the more acceptable a prejudice is, the more willing people are to express it, joke about it, and discriminate against group members in dating, housing, and employment settings.

Knowing how others are behaving in a situation is necessary for conformity, but these norms are likely to influence us only when they are brought to our awareness, or "activated." Robert Cialdini and his colleagues have demonstrated this point in studies on littering (Kallgren et al., 2000). In one study, researchers had confederates pass out handbills to amusement park visitors and varied the amount of litter that appeared in one section of the park (an indication of how others behave in that setting). The result: The more litter there was, the more likely visitors were to toss their handbills to the ground (Cialdini et al., 1990). A second study showed that passers-by were most influenced by the prior behaviour of others when their attention was drawn to the existing norm. In this instance, people were observed in a parking garage that was either clean or cluttered with cigarette butts, candy wrappers, paper cups, and trash. In half of the cases, the norm that was already in place—clean or cluttered—was brought to participants' attention by a confederate who threw paper to the ground as he walked by. In the other half, the confederate passed by without incident. As participants reached their cars, they found a "Please Drive Safely" handbill tucked under the windshield wiper. Did they toss the paper to the ground or take it with them? The results showed that people were most likely to conform (by littering more when the garage was cluttered than when it was clean) when the confederate had littered—an act that drew attention to the norm (Cialdini et al., 1991).

An Ally in Dissent: Getting By with a Little Help In Asch's initial experiment, participants found themselves pitted against unanimous majorities. But what if they had an ally, a partner in dissent? Asch investigated this issue and found that the presence of a single confederate who agreed with the participant reduced conformity by almost 80 percent. This finding, however, does not tell us why the presence of an ally was so effective. Was it because he or she *agreed* with the participant or because he or she *disagreed* with the majority? In other words, were the views of the participants strengthened because a dissenting confederate offered validating information or because dissent per se reduced *normative* pressures?

A series of experiments explored these two possibilities. In one, Vernon Allen and John Levine (1969) led participants to believe they were working together with four confederates. Three of these others consistently agreed on the wrong judgment. The fourth then either followed the majority, agreed with the participant, or made a third judgment, which was also incorrect. This last variation was the most interesting: Even when the confederate did not validate their own judgment, participants conformed less often to the majority. In another study, Allen and Levine (1971) varied the competence of the ally. Some participants received support from an average person. In contrast, others found themselves supported by someone who wore very thick glasses and complained that he could not see the visual displays. Not a very reassuring ally, right? Wrong. Even though participants derived less comfort from this supporter than from one who seemed more competent at the task, his presence still reduced their level of conformity.

Two important conclusions follow from this research. First, it is substantially more difficult for people to stand alone for their convictions than to be part of even a tiny minority. Second, *any* dissent—whether it validates an individual's opinion or not—can break the spell cast by a unanimous majority and reduce the normative pressures to conform.

Gender Differences Are there gender differences in conformity? Based on Asch's initial studies, social psychologists used to think that women, once considered the "weaker" sex, conform more than men. In light of more recent research, however, it appears that two additional factors have to be considered. First, sex differences depend on how comfortable people are with the experimental task. Frank Sistrunk and John McDavid (1971) had male and female participants answer questions on stereotypically masculine, feminine, and gender-neutral topics. Along with each question, participants were told the percentage of others who agreed or disagreed. Although females conformed to the contrived majority more on the masculine items, males conformed more on the feminine items (there were no sex differences on the neutral questions). This finding suggests that one's familiarity with the issue at hand, not gender, is what affects conformity. Ask about football or video war games, and most women acquiesce more than most men. Ask about family planning and fashion design, and the pattern is reversed (Eagly & Carli, 1981).

A second factor is the type of social pressure people face. As a general rule, sex differences are weak and unreliable. But there is an important exception: In face-to-face encounters, where people must openly disagree with each other, small differences do emerge. In fact, when participants think they are being observed, women conform more and men conform less than they do in a more private situation (Eagly & Chravala, 1986; Eagly et al., 1981). Why does being "in public" create such a divergence in behaviour? Alice Eagly (1987) argues that in front of others, people worry about how they come across and feel pressured to behave in ways that are viewed as acceptable within traditional gender-role constraints. At least in public, men make it a point to behave with fierce independence and autonomy, while women play a gentler, more docile role.

Cultural Influences Linked together by space, language, religion, and a common history, each cultural group has its own ideologies, folklore, music, fashions, foods, laws, and customs. As many tourists and exchange students have come to learn, sometimes the hard way, the social norms that influence human conduct can vary in

In Canada, where cows are considered mainly a food source, we would likely be surprised to see one on the sidewalk. In India, however, cows are considered sacred and are welcome to roam freely on the streets.

significant ways from one part of the world to another.

In *Do's and Taboos Around the World,* R. E. Axtell (1993) warns world travelers about some of these differences. Dine in an Indian home, he notes, and you should leave food on the plate to show the host that the portions were generous and that you had enough to eat. Yet as a dinner guest in Bolivia, you would show your appreciation by cleaning your plate. Shop in an outdoor market in Iraq, and you should expect to negotiate the price of everything you buy. Plan an appointment in Brazil, and the person you're scheduled to meet is likely to be late. Nothing personal. Even the way we space ourselves from each other is culturally determined. Americans, Canadians, British, and Northern Europeans keep a polite distance between themselves and others—and feel "crowded" by the touchier, nose-to-nose style of the French, Greeks, Arabs, Mexicans, and people of South America.

Just as cultures differ in their social norms, so, too, they differ in the extent to which people adhere to those norms. As we saw in Chapter 3, there are two different cultural orientations toward persons and their relationships to groups. Some cultures value **individualism** and the virtues of independence, autonomy, and self-reliance, while others value **collectivism** and the virtues of interdependence, cooperation, and social harmony. Under the banner of individualism, personal goals take priority over group allegiances. Yet in collectivistic cultures, the person is, first and foremost, a loyal member of a family, team, company, church, and state. Generally, conformity rates are higher in cultures that are collectivistic rather than individualistic in their orientation (Bond & Smith, 1996).

Minority Influence

It's not easy for individuals to express unpopular views or enlist support from others. Philosopher Bertrand Russell once said, "Conventional people are roused to frenzy by departure from convention, largely because they regard such departure as criticism of themselves." He may have been right. Although people who stand up for their beliefs against the majority are generally seen as competent and honest, they are also disliked and often rejected (Bassili & Provencal, 1988; Levine, 1989). It's no wonder that people think twice before expressing positions that are unpopular. In a series of survey studies that revealed what he called the "minority slowness effect," John Bassili (2003) asked people about their attitudes on social policy issues like affirmative action or about their likes and dislikes for various celebrities, sports, foods, places, and activities. Consistently, and regardless of topic, respondents who held minority opinions were slower to answer the questions than those in the majority.

Resisting the pressure to conform and maintaining one's independence may be socially difficult, but not impossible. History's famous heroes, villains, and creative minds are living proof: Joan of Arc, Muhammad, Charles Darwin, and Gandhi, to name just a few, were dissenters of their time who continue to capture the imagination. Then there's human behaviour in the laboratory. Social psychologists were so intrigued by Asch's initial finding that participants conformed 37 percent of the time that textbooks such as this one routinely refer to "Asch's conformity study." Yet the overlooked flip side of the coin is that Asch's participants refused to acquiesce

individualism A cultural orientation in which independence, autonomy, and self-reliance take priority over group allegiances.

collectivism A cultural orientation in which interdependence, cooperation, and social harmony take priority over personal goals.

63 percent of the time—thus also indicating the power of independence (Friend et al., 1990).

Thanks to Serge Moscovici, Edwin Hollander, and others, we now know quite a bit about **minority influence** and about the strategies that effective nonconformists use to act as agents of social change (De Dreu & De Vries, 2001; Hollander, 1985; Maass & Clark, 1984; Moscovici et al., 1985; Mugny & Perez, 1991).

The Power of Style According to Moscovici, majorities are powerful by virtue of their sheer *numbers* and inherent power, while nonconformists derive power from the *style* of their behaviour. It is not just what they say that matters, but how they say it. To exert influence, says Moscovici, those in the minority must be forceful, persistent, and unwavering in support of their position. Yet at the same time, they must appear flexible and open-minded. Confronted with a consistent but even-handed dissenter, members of the majority will sit up, take notice, and rethink their own positions.

Why should a consistent behavioural style prove effective? One possible reason is that unwavering repetition draws attention from those in the mainstream, which is a necessary first step to social influence. Another possibility is that consistency signals that the dissenter is unlikely to yield, which leads those in the majority to feel pressured to seek compromise. A third possible reason is that when confronted with someone who has the self-confidence and dedication to take an unpopular stand without backing down, people assume that he or she must have a point. Unless a dissenter is perceived in negative terms—as biased, obstinate, or just plain crazy—this situation stimulates others to re-examine their own views (Moskowitz, 1996). Of course, it helps to be seen as part of "us" rather than "them." Research shows that dissenters have more influence when people identify with them and perceive them to be similar in ways that are positive and relevant (Turner, 1991; Wood et al., 1996).

Based on a meta-analysis of 97 experiments investigating minority influence, Wendy Wood and her colleagues (1994) concluded that there is strong support for the consistency hypothesis. In one classic study, for example, Moscovici and others (1969) turned Asch's procedure on its head by confronting people with a *minority* of confederates who made incorrect judgments. In groups of six, participants took part in what was supposed to be a study of colour perception. They viewed a series of slides—all blue, but varying in intensity. For each slide, the participants took turns naming the colour. The task was simple, but two confederates announced that the slides were green. When the confederates were *consistent*—that is, when both made incorrect green judgments for all slides—they had a surprising degree of influence. About a third of all participants incorrectly reported seeing at least one green slide, and eight percent of all responses were incorrect. Subsequent research confirmed that the perception of consistency increases minority influence (Clark, 2001; Crano, 2000).

A Chip Off the Old Block? Regardless of which strategy is used, minority influence is a force to be reckoned with. But does it work just like the process of conformity, or is there something different about the way that minorities and majorities effect change? Some theorists believe that a *single process* accounts for both directions of social influence—that minority influence is just like a "chip off the old block" (Latané & Wolf, 1981; Tanford & Penrod, 1984). Others have taken a *dual-process* approach (Moscovici, 1980; Nemeth, 1986). In this second view, majorities and minorities exert influence in very different ways. Majorities, because they have power and control, elicit public conformity by bringing stressful normative pressures to bear on the individual. But minorities, because they are seen as seriously committed to their views, produce a deeper and more lasting form of private conformity, or *conversion*, by leading others to rethink their original positions.

To evaluate these single- and dual-process theories, researchers have compared the effects of majority and minority viewpoints on participants who are otherwise neutral on an issue in dispute. On the basis of this research, two conclusions can be

minority influence The process by which dissenters produce change within a group.

drawn. First, the relative impact of majorities and minorities depends on whether the judgment that is being made is objective or subjective, a matter of fact or opinion. In a study conducted in Italy, Ann Maass and others (1996) found that majorities have greater influence on factual questions, for which only one answer is correct ("What percentage of its raw oil does Italy import from Venezuela?"), but that minorities exert equal impact on opinion questions, for which there is a range of acceptable responses ("What percentage of its raw oil *should* Italy import from Venezuela?"). People feel freer to stray from the mainstream on matters of opinion—when there is no right or wrong answer.

The second conclusion is that the relative effects of majority and minority viewpoints depend on how conformity is measured. To be sure, majorities have a decisive upper hand on direct or public measures of conformity. After all, people are reluctant to stray conspicuously from the group norm. But on more indirect or private measures of conformity—when participants can respond without a fear of appearing deviant—minorities exert a strong impact (Clark & Maass, 1990; Moscovici & Personnaz, 1991; Wood et al., 1996). As Moscovici so cogently argued, each of us is changed in a meaningful but subtle way by minority opinion. Because of social pressures, we may be too intimidated to admit it; but the change is unmistakable (Wood et al., 1994).

According to Charlan Nemeth (1986), dissenters serve a valuable purpose regardless of whether their views are correct. Simply by their willingness to stay independent, minorities can force other group members to think more carefully, more openly, and more creatively about a problem, thus enhancing the quality of a group's decision making. In one study, participants exposed to a minority viewpoint on how to solve anagram problems later found more novel solutions themselves (Nemeth & Kwan, 1987). In a second study, those exposed to a consistent minority view on how to recall information later recalled more words from a list they were trying to memorize (Nemeth et al., 1990). And in a third study, interacting groups that contained one dissenting confederate produced more original analyses of complex business problems (Van Dyne & Saavedra, 1996).

Compliance

In conformity situations, people follow implicit group norms. But another common form of social influence occurs when others make direct *explicit* requests of us in the hope that we will comply. Situations calling for **compliance** take many forms. These include a friend's request for help, sheepishly prefaced by the question "Can you do me a favour?" They also include the pop-up ad on the Internet designed to lure you into clicking onto a commercial site and the salesperson's pitch for business prefaced by the dangerous words "Have I got a deal for you!" Sometimes, the request itself is up front and direct; what you see is what you get. At other times, it is part of a subtle and more elaborate manipulation.

How do people get others to comply with self-serving requests? How do police interrogators get crime suspects to confess? How do TV evangelists draw millions of dollars in contributions for their ministries? How do *you* exert influence over others? Do you use threats, promises, politeness, deceit, or reason? Do you hint, coax, sulk, negotiate, throw tantrums, or pull rank whenever you can? To a large extent, the compliance strategies we use depend on how well we know a person, our status within a relationship, our personality, culture, and the nature of the request.

compliance Changes in behaviour that are elicited by direct requests.

By observing the masters of influence—advertisers, fund raisers, politicians, and business leaders—social psychologists have learned a great deal about the subtle but effective strategies that are commonly used. What we see is that people often get others to comply with their requests by setting traps. Once caught in one of these traps, the unwary victim often finds it difficult to escape.

Con artists prosper from the tendency for people to respond mindlessly to requests that sound reasonable but offer no real basis for compliance.

The Language of Request

How a request is phrased can affect our levels of compliance. Consider, for example, requests that sound reasonable but offer no real reason for compliance. Ellen Langer and her colleagues (1978) have found that words alone can sometimes trick us into submission. In their research, an experimenter approached people who were using a library photocopier and asked to cut in. Three different versions of the request were used. In one, participants were simply asked, "Excuse me. I have five pages. May I use the Xerox machine?" In a second version, the request was justified by the added phrase "because I'm in a rush." As you would expect, more participants stepped aside when the request was justified (94 percent) than when it was not (60 percent). A third version of the request, however, suggests that the reason offered had little to do with the increase in compliance. In this case, participants heard the following: "Excuse me. I have five pages. May I use the Xerox machine because I have to make some copies?" If you read this request closely, you'll see that it really offered no reason at all. Yet 93 percent in this condition complied! It was as if the appearance of a reason, triggered by the word *because*, was all that was necessary. Indeed, Langer (1989) finds that the mind is often on "automatic pilot," as we respond *mindlessly* to words without fully processing the information they are supposed to convey. At least for requests that are small, "sweet little nothings" may be enough to win compliance.

It is interesting that although the state of mindlessness can make us vulnerable to compliance, it can also have the opposite effect. For example, many city dwellers automatically walk past panhandlers on the street looking for a handout. Perhaps the way to increase compliance in such situations is to disrupt this mindless refusal response by making a request that is so unusual that it piques the target person's interest. In one study, a confederate approached people on the street and made a request that was either typical ("Can you spare a quarter?") or atypical ("Can you spare 17¢?"). The result: Atypical pleas elicited more comments and questions from those who were targeted—and produced a 60 percent increase in the number of people who gave money (Santos et al., 1994). In another study, researchers went door-to-door selling holiday cards and gained more compliance when they disrupted the mindless process and reframed the sales pitch. They sold more cards when they said the price was "300 pennies—that's $3, it's a bargain" than when they simply asked for $3 (Davis & Knowles, 1999).

The Norm of Reciprocity

A simple, unstated, but powerful rule of social behaviour known as the *norm of reciprocity* dictates that we treat others as they have treated us (Gouldner, 1960). On the negative side, this norm can be used to sanction retaliation against those who cause us harm: "An eye for an eye." On the positive side, it leads us to feel obligated to repay others for acts of kindness. Thus, when we receive gifts, invitations, and free samples, we usually go out of our way to return the favour.

The norm of reciprocity contributes to the predictability and fairness of social interaction. However, it can also be used to exploit us. Dennis Regan (1971) examined this possibility in the following study. Individuals were brought together with a confederate—who was trained to act in a likeable or unlikeable manner—for an experiment on "aesthetics." In one condition, the confederate did the participant an unsolicited favour. He left during a break and returned with two bottles of Coca-Cola™, one for himself and the other for the participant. In a second condition, he returned from the break empty-handed. In a third condition, participants were treated to a Coke™—but by the experimenter, not the confederate. The confederate then told participants in all conditions that he was selling raffle tickets at 25¢ apiece and asked if they would be willing to buy any. On the average, participants bought more raffle tickets when the confederate had earlier brought them a soft drink than when he had not. The norm of reciprocity was so strong that they returned the favour even when the confederate was not otherwise a likeable character. In fact, participants in this condition spent an average of 43¢ on raffle tickets. At a time when soft drinks cost less than a quarter, the confederate made a handsome quick profit on his investment!

It's clear that the norm of reciprocity can be used to trap us into compliance. Research conducted in restaurants shows that waiters and waitresses can increase their tip percentages by writing, "Thank you" on the back of the customer's check, by drawing a happy face on it, or by placing candy on the check tray (Rind & Strohmetz, 2001; Strohmetz et al., 2002). But does receiving a favour make us feel indebted forever, or is there a time limit to this social rule of thumb? In an experiment designed to answer this question, Jerry Burger and others (1997) used Regan's soft drink favour and had the confederate try to "cash in" with a request either immediately or one week later. The result: Compliance levels increased in the immediate condition but not after a full week had passed. People may feel compelled to reciprocate, but that feeling—at least for small acts of kindness—is relatively short-lived.

Some people are more likely than others to exploit the reciprocity norm. According to Martin Greenberg and David Westcott (1983), individuals who use reciprocity to elicit compliance are called "creditors" because they always try to keep others in their debt so they can cash in when necessary. On a questionnaire that measures *reciprocation ideology*, people are identified as creditors if they agree with such statements as "If someone does you a favour, it's good to repay that person with a greater favour." On the receiving end, some people more than others try not to accept favours that might later set them up to be exploited. On a scale that measures *reciprocation wariness*, people are said to be wary if they express the suspicion, for example, that "asking for another's help gives them power over your life" (Eisenberger et al., 1987).

Setting Traps: Sequential Request Strategies

People who raise money or sell for a living know that it often takes more than a single plea to win over a potential donor or customer. Social psychologists share this knowledge and have studied several compliance techniques that are based on making two or more related requests. *Click!* The first request sets the trap. *Snap!* The second captures the prey. In a fascinating book entitled *Influence: Science and Practice*, Robert Cialdini (2001) describes a number of sequential request tactics in vivid detail. These methods are presented in the following pages.

The Foot in the Door Folk wisdom has it that one way to get a person to comply with a sizable request is to start small. First devised by traveling salespeople peddling vacuum cleaners, hairbrushes, cosmetics, magazine subscriptions, and encyclopaedias, the trick is to somehow get your "foot in the door." The expression need not be taken literally, of course. The point of the **foot-in-the-door technique** is to break the ice with a small initial request that the customer can't easily refuse. Once that first commitment is elicited, the chances are increased that another, larger request will succeed.

foot-in-the-door technique A two-step compliance technique in which an influencer sets the stage for the real request by first getting a person to comply with a much smaller request.

Jonathan Freedman and Scott Fraser (1966) tested the impact of this technique in a series of field experiments. In one, an experimenter pretending to be employed by a consumer organization telephoned a group of female homemakers in Palo Alto, California, and asked if they would be willing to answer some questions about household products. Those who consented were then asked a few innocuous questions and thanked for their assistance. Three days later, the experimenter called back and made a considerable, almost outrageous, request. He asked the women if they would allow a handful of men into their homes for two hours to rummage through their drawers and cupboards so they could take an inventory of household products.

The foot-in-the-door technique proved to be very effective. When participants were confronted with only the very intrusive request, 22 percent consented. Yet among those surveyed earlier, the rate of agreement more than doubled, to 53 percent. This basic result has now been repeated over and over again. People are more likely to donate time, money, blood, the use of their home, and other resources once they have been induced to go along with a small initial request. Although the effect is seldom as dramatic as that obtained by Freedman and Fraser, it does appear in a wide variety of circumstances—and increases compliance rates, on average, by about 13 percent (Burger, 1999).

The practical implications of the foot-in-the-door technique are obvious. But why does it work? Several explanations have been suggested. One that seems plausible is based on self-perception theory—that people infer their attitudes by observing their own behaviour. This explanation suggests that a two-step process is at work. First, by observing your own behaviour in the initial situation, you come to see yourself as the kind of person who is generally cooperative when approached with a request. Second, when confronted with the more burdensome request, you seek to respond in ways that maintain this new self-image. By this logic, the foot-in-the-door technique should succeed only when you attribute an initial act of compliance to your own personal characteristics.

Based on a review of dozens of studies, Jerry Burger (1999) concludes that the research generally supports the self-perception account. Thus, if the first request is too trivial or if participants are paid for the first act of compliance, they won't later come to view themselves as inherently cooperative. Under these conditions, the technique does *not* work. Likewise, the effect occurs only when people are motivated to be consistent with their self-images. If participants are unhappy with what the initial behaviour implies about them, if they are too young to appreciate the implications, or if they don't care about behaving in ways that are personally consistent, then again the technique does not work. Other processes may be at work, but it appears that the foot opens the door by altering *self*-perceptions. In fact, this process can occur even when a person tries to comply with the initial small request but fails. In a series of studies, Dariusz Dolinski (2000) found that when people were asked if they could find directions to a nonexistent street address or decipher an unreadable message—small favours they could not satisfy—they, too, become more compliant with the next request.

Knowing that a foot in the door increases compliance is both exciting and troubling—exciting for the owner of the foot, troubling for the owner of the door. As Cialdini (2001) put it, "You can use small commitments to manipulate a person's self-image; you can use them to turn citizens into 'public servants,' prospects into 'customers,' prisoners into 'collaborators.' And once you've got a person's self-image where you want it, he or she should comply *naturally* with a whole range of requests that are consistent with this new self-view" (p. 67).

Low-Balling Another two-step trap, perhaps the most unscrupulous of all compliance techniques, is also based on the "start small" idea. Imagine yourself in the following situation. You're at a local automobile dealership. After some negotiation, the salesperson offers a great price on the car of your choice. You cast aside other considerations and shake hands on the deal; and as the salesperson goes off to "write it up," you begin to feel the thrill of owning the car of your dreams. Absorbed in fantasy, you are interrupted by the sudden return of the salesperson. "I'm sorry," he

Low-balling is a common technique used in selling cars. Notice the fact that "up to" is placed to the side, in a smaller font, than the dollar amount.

says. "The manager would not approve the sale. We have to raise the price by another $450. I'm afraid that's the best we can do." As the victim of an all-too-common trick known as **low-balling,** you are now faced with a tough decision. On the one hand, you're wild about the car. You've already enjoyed the pleasure of thinking it's yours; and the more you think about it, the better it looks. On the other hand, you don't want to pay more than you bargained for, and you have an uneasy feeling in the pit of your stomach that you're being duped. What do you do?

Salespeople who use this tactic are betting that you'll go ahead with the purchase despite the added cost. If the way research participants behave is any indication, they are often right. In one study, experimenters phoned introductory psychology students and asked if they would be willing to participate in a study for extra credit. Some were told up front that the session would begin at the uncivilized hour of 7 A.M. Knowing that, only 31 percent volunteered. But other participants were low-balled. Only *after* they agreed to participate did the experimenter inform them of the 7 A.M. starting time. Would that be okay? Whether or not it was, the procedure achieved its objective—the sign-up rate rose to 56 percent (Cialdini et al., 1978).

Low-balling is an interesting technique. Surely, once the low ball has been thrown, many recipients suspect that they were misled. Yet they go along. Why? The reason appears to be based on the psychology of commitment (Kiesler, 1971). Once people make a particular decision, they justify it to themselves by thinking of all its positive aspects. As they get increasingly committed to a course of action, they grow more resistant to changing their mind, even if the initial reasons for the action have been changed or withdrawn entirely. In the automobile dealership scenario, you might very well have decided to purchase the car because of the price. But then you would have thought about its sleek appearance, the leather interior, the sunroof, and the CD player. By the time you learned that the price would be more than you'd bargained for, it was too late—you were already hooked.

Low-balling also produces another form of commitment. When people do not suspect duplicity, they feel a nagging sense of unfulfilled obligation to the person with whom they negotiated. Thus, even though the salesperson was unable to complete the original deal, you might feel obligated to buy anyway, having already agreed to make the purchase. This commitment to the other person may account for why low-balling works better when the second request is made by the same person who made the initial request than when it is made by someone else (Burger & Petty, 1981). It may also explain why people are most vulnerable to the low-ball when they make their commitment in public rather than in private (Burger & Cornelius, 2003).

low-balling A two-step compliance technique in which the influencer secures agreement with a request but then increases the size of that request by revealing hidden costs.

door-in-the-face technique A two-step compliance technique in which an influencer prefaces the real request with one that is so large that it is rejected.

The Door in the Face Although shifting from an initial small request to a larger one can be effective, as in the foot-in-the-door and low-ball techniques, oddly enough the opposite is also true. In *Influence,* Cialdini (2001) describes the time he was approached by a Boy Scout and asked to buy two $5 tickets to an upcoming circus. Having better things to do with his time and money, he declined. Then the boy asked if he would be interested in buying chocolate bars at a dollar apiece. Even though he doesn't like chocolate, Cialdini—an expert on social influence—bought two of them! After a moment's reflection, he realized what had happened. Whether the Boy Scout planned it that way or not, Cialdini had fallen for what is known as the **door-in-the-face technique**.

The technique is as simple as it sounds. An individual makes an initial request that is so large it is sure to be rejected and then comes back with a second, more reasonable request. Will the second request fare better after the first one has been declined? Plagued by the sight of uneaten chocolate bars, Cialdini and others (1975) tested the effectiveness of the door-in-the-face technique. They stopped students on campus and asked if they would volunteer to work without pay at a counselling centre for juvenile delinquents. The time commitment would be forbidding: roughly two hours a week for the next two years! Not surprisingly, everyone who was approached politely slammed the proverbial door in the experimenter's face. But then the experimenter followed up with a more modest proposal, asking the students if they would be willing to take a group of delinquents on a two-hour trip to the zoo. The strategy worked like a charm. Only 17 percent of the students confronted with only the second request agreed. But of those who initially declined the first request, 50 percent said yes to the zoo trip. You should note that the door-in-the-face technique does not elicit only empty promises. Most research participants who comply subsequently do what they've agreed to do (Cialdini & Ascani, 1976).

Why is the door-in-the-face technique such an effective trap? One possibility involves the principle of *perceptual contrast:* To the person exposed to a very large initial request, the second request "seems smaller." In this case, $2 worth of candy bars is not bad compared with $10 for circus tickets. Likewise, taking a group of kids to the zoo seems trivial compared with two years of volunteer work. As intuitively sensible as this explanation seems, Cialdini and others (1975) concluded that perceptual contrast is only partly responsible for the effect. When participants heard the large request without actually having to reject it, their rate of compliance with the second request (25 percent) was only slightly larger than the 17 percent rate of compliance exhibited by those who heard only the small request.

A second, more compelling explanation for the effect involves the notion of *reciprocal concessions.* A close cousin of the reciprocity norm, this refers to the pressure to respond to changes in a bargaining position. When an individual backs down from a large request to a smaller one, we view that move as a concession that we should match by our own compliance. Thus, the door-in-the-face technique does not work if the second request is made by a different person (Cialdini et al., 1975). Nor does it work if the first request is so extreme that it comes across as an insincere "first offer" (Schwarzwald et al., 1979). On an emotional level, refusing to help on one request may trigger feelings of guilt—which we can reduce by complying with the second, smaller request (O'Keefe & Figge, 1997; Millar, 2002).

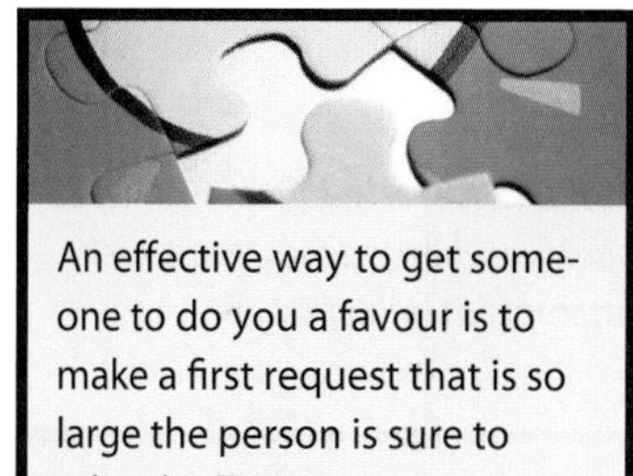

An effective way to get someone to do you a favour is to make a first request that is so large the person is sure to reject it. **True.**

That's Not All, Folks! If the notion of reciprocal concessions is correct, then a person shouldn't actually have to refuse the initial offer in order for the shift to a smaller request to work. Indeed, another familiar sales strategy manages to use concession without first eliciting refusal. In this strategy, a product is offered at a particular price; but then, before the buyer has a chance to respond, the seller adds, "And that's not all!" At that point, either the original price is reduced, or a bonus is offered to sweeten the pot. The seller, of course, intends all along to make the so-called concession.

This ploy, called the **that's-not-all technique**, seems awfully transparent, right? Surely, no one falls for it, right? Jerry Burger (1986) was not so sure. He predicted that people are more likely to make a purchase when a deal seems to have improved than when the same deal is offered right from the start. To test this hypothesis, Burger set up a booth at a campus fair and sold cupcakes. Some customers who approached the table were told that the cupcakes cost 75¢ each. Others were told that they cost a dollar; but then, before they could respond, the price was reduced to 75¢. Rationally speaking, Burger's manipulation did not affect the ultimate price, so it should not have affected sales. But it did. When customers were led to believe that the final price represented a reduction, sales increased from 44 to 73 percent.

that's-not-all technique
A two-step compliance technique in which the influencer begins with an inflated request, then decreases its apparent size by offering a discount or bonus.

TABLE 7.2

Sequential Request Strategies

Various compliance techniques are based on a sequence of two related requests. *Click!* The first request sets the trap. *Snap!* The second captures the prey. Research has shown that the four sequential request strategies summarized in this table are all effective.

Request Shifts	Technique	Description
From small to large	Foot in the door	Begin with a very small request; secure agreement; then make a separate, larger request.
	Low-balling	Secure agreement with a request, and then increase the size of that request by revealing hidden costs.
From large to small	Door in the face	Begin with a very large request that will be rejected; then follow that up with a more modest request.
	That's not all	Begin with a somewhat inflated request; than immediately decrease the apparent size of that request by offering a discount or bonus.

At this point, let's step back and look at the various compliance techniques described in this section. All of them are based on a two-step process that involves a shift from a request of one size to another. What differs is whether the small or large request comes first and how the transition between steps is made (see Table 7.2). Moreover, all these strategies work in subtle ways by manipulating the target person's self-image, commitment to the product, feelings of obligation to the seller, or perceptions of the real request. It is even possible to increase compliance by prefacing the request with "How are you feeling?"—a question that tends to elicit a favourable first response from strangers (Howard, 1990a). When you consider these various traps, you have to wonder whether it's ever possible to escape.

Assertiveness: When People Say No

Compliance techniques are likely to backfire when seen as transparent attempts at influence.

Cialdini (2001) opens his book with a confession: "I can admit it freely now. All my life I've been a patsy." As a past victim of compliance traps, he is not alone. Many people find it difficult to be assertive in interpersonal situations. Faced with an unreasonable request from a friend, spouse, or stranger, they become anxious at the mere thought of putting a foot down and refusing to comply. Indeed, there are times when it is uncomfortable for anyone to say no. However, just as we can maintain our autonomy in the face of conformity pressures, we can also refuse direct requests—even clever ones. The trap may be set, but you don't have to get caught.

"Your Honour, has anyone ever told you what a wry, sensuous mouth you have?"

According to Cialdini, being able to resist the pressure of compliance rests, first and foremost, on being vigilant. If a stranger hands you a gift and then launches into a sales pitch, you should recognize the tactic for what it is and not feel indebted by the norm of reciprocity. And if you strike a deal with a salesperson who later reneges on the terms, you should be aware that you're being thrown a low ball. Indeed, that is exactly what happened to one of the authors of this book. After a full Saturday afternoon of careful negotiation at a local car dealer, he and his wife finally came to terms on a price. Minutes later, however, the salesperson returned with the news that the manager would not approve the deal. The cost of an air conditioner, which was originally to be included, would have to be added on to the price. Familiar with the research, the author turned to his wife and exclaimed, "It's a trick; they're low-balling us!" Realizing what was happening, she became furious, went straight to the manager, and made such a scene in front of other customers that he backed down and honoured the original deal.

What happened in this instance? Why did recognizing the attempted manipulation produce such anger and resistance? As this story illustrates, compliance techniques work smoothly only if they are hidden from view. The problem is not only that they are attempts to influence us but that they are deceptive. Flattery, gifts, and other ploys often elicit compliance—but not if they are perceived as insincere (Jones, 1964) and not if the target has a high level of reciprocity wariness (Eisenberger et al., 1987). Likewise, the sequential request traps are powerful to the extent that they are subtle and cannot be seen for what they are (Schwarzwald et al., 1979). People don't like to be hustled. In fact, feeling manipulated typically leads us to react with anger, psychological reactance, and stubborn noncompliance . . . unless the request is a command and the requester is a figure of authority.

"Knowledge is power, and if you know when a clever technique is being used on you, then it becomes easier to ignore it."

—Burke Leon

Obedience

From the day we are born, we are taught that it's important to respect legitimate forms of leadership. Most people think twice before defying parents, teachers, employers, coaches, and government officials. The problem is, mere symbols of authority—titles, uniforms, badges, or the trappings of success, even without the necessary credentials—can sometimes turn ordinary people into docile servants. Leonard Bickman (1974) demonstrated this phenomenon in a series of studies in which a male research assistant stopped passers-by on the street and ordered them to do something unusual. Sometimes, he pointed to a paper bag on the ground and said, "Pick up this bag for me!" At other times, he pointed to an individual standing beside a parked car and said, "This fellow is over-parked at the meter but doesn't have any change. Give him a dime!" Would anyone really take this guy seriously? When he was dressed in street clothes, only a third of the people stopped and followed his orders. But when he wore a security guard's uniform, nearly nine out of every ten people obeyed! Even when the uniformed assistant turned the corner and walked away after issuing his command, the vast majority of passers-by followed his orders. Clearly, uniforms signify the power of authority (Bushman, 1988).

Blind **obedience** may seem funny; but if people are willing to take orders from a total stranger, how far will they go when it really matters? As the pages of history attest, the implications are sobering. In World War II, Nazi officials participated in the deaths of millions of Jews, as well as Poles, Russians, Gypsies, and homosexuals. Yet when tried for these crimes, their defence was always the same: "I was following orders."

Surely, you may be thinking, the Holocaust was a historical anomaly that says more about the Nazis as prejudiced, frustrated, and sick individuals than about the situations that lead people in general to commit acts of destructive obedience. In *Hitler's Willing Executioners*, historian Daniel Goldhagen (1996) argues on the basis of past records that many Germans were willing anti-Semitic participants in the Holocaust—not ordinary people forced to follow orders. But two lines of evidence suggest that attaching responsibility to the German people is far too simple an explanation of what happened. First, interviews with Nazi war criminals and doctors who worked in concentration camps have suggested the provocative and disturbing conclusion that these people were "utterly ordinary" (Arendt, 1963; Lifton, 1986;

obedience Behaviour change produced by the commands of authority.

Taken to the extreme, blind obedience can have devastating results. In World War II, Nazi officials killed millions, many said, "because I was just following orders."

Von Lang & Sibyll, 1983). Second, the monstrous events of World War II do not stand alone in modern history. Even today, crimes of obedience, including torture, are being committed throughout the world (Kelman & Hamilton, 1989; Haritos-Fatouros, 2002). On extraordinary occasions, obedience is carried to its limit. In 1978, 900 members of the People's Temple cult obeyed an order from the Reverend Jim Jones to kill themselves. In 1997, in a small Quebec town, five disciples of the Order of the Solar Temple took sedatives and then blew up their cottage; according to the doctrines of the cult, this allowed them to ascend to the stars. Fanatic cult members have committed mass suicide before, and they will likely do so again (Galanter, 1999). As we will discuss in Chapter 8, these horrific acts often occur when seemingly rational people find themselves in a group situation; for example, the 1993 beating death of an unarmed Somali teen by a group of elite Canadian peacekeepers (discussed in more detail in the next chapter) was a shameful mark on our nation's history. The soldiers even took pictures showing their grinning faces next to the young man's badly beaten body. While we cannot excuse such an act, social psychologists do strive to understand what factors may have contributed to this disgraceful behaviour.

Milgram's Research: Forces of Destructive Obedience

"Far more, and far more hideous, crimes have been committed in the name of obedience than have ever been committed in the name of rebellion."

—C. P. Snow

During the time that Adolf Eichmann was being tried for his Nazi war crimes, Stanley Milgram (1963) began a dramatic series of experiments that culminated in his 1974 book *Obedience to Authority*. For many years, the ethics of this research has been the focus of much debate. Those who say it was not ethical point to the potential psychological harm to which the participants were exposed. In contrast, those who believe that Milgram's research met appropriate ethical standards emphasize the contribution it makes to our understanding of an important social problem. They conclude that, on balance, the extreme danger that destructive obedience poses for all humankind justified Milgram's unorthodox methods. Consider both sides of the debate, which were summarized in Chapter 2, and make your own judgment. Now, however, take a more personal look. Imagine yourself as one of the approximately 1000 participants who found themselves in the following situation.

The experience begins when you arrive at a Yale University laboratory and meet two men. One is the experimenter, a stern young man dressed in a grey lab coat and carrying a clipboard. The other is a middle-aged gentleman named Mr. Wallace, an accountant who is slightly overweight and average in appearance. You exchange introductions, and then the experimenter explains that you and your co-participant will take part in a study on the effects of punishment on learning. After lots have been drawn, it is determined that you will serve as the teacher and that Mr. Wallace will be the learner. So far, so good.

Soon, however, the situation takes on a more ominous tone. You find out that your job is to test the learner's memory and administer electric shocks of increasing

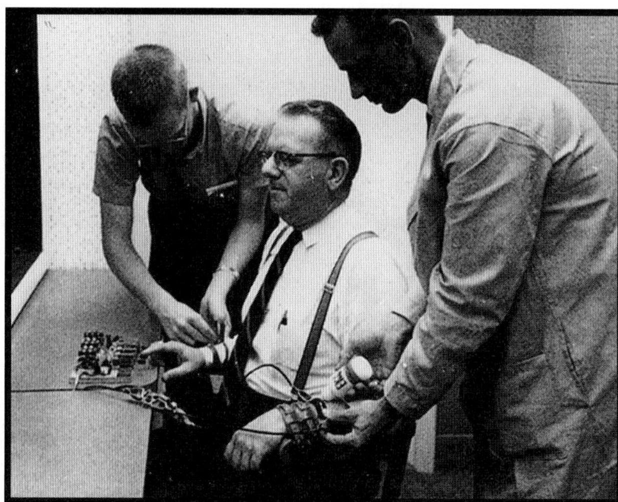

By using Milgram's shock generator (left), participants in Milgram's studies believed they were shocking Mr. Wallace, the man being strapped into his chair (right).

intensity whenever he makes a mistake. You are then escorted into another room, where the experimenter straps Mr. Wallace into a chair, rolls up his sleeves, attaches electrodes to his arms, and applies "electrode paste" to prevent blisters and burns. As if that isn't bad enough, you may overhear Mr. Wallace telling the experimenter that he has a heart problem. The experimenter responds by conceding that the shocks will be painful but reassures Mr. Wallace that they will not cause "permanent tissue damage." In the meantime, you can personally vouch for how painful the shocks are because the experimenter stings you with one that is supposed to be mild. From there, the experimenter takes you back to the main room, where you are seated in front of a "shock generator," a machine with 30 switches that range from 15 volts, labelled "slight shock," to 450 volts, labelled "XXX."

Your role in this experiment is straightforward. First you read a list of word pairs to Mr. Wallace through a microphone. Then you test his memory with a series of multiple-choice questions. The learner answers each question by pressing one of four switches that light up signals on the shock generator. If his answer is correct, you move on to the next question. If it is incorrect, you announce the correct answer and shock him. When you press the appropriate shock switch, a red light flashes above it, relay switches click inside the machine, and you hear a loud buzzing sound go off in the learner's room. After each wrong answer, you're told, the intensity of the shock should be increased by 15 volts.

You aren't aware, of course, that the experiment is rigged and that Mr. Wallace—who is actually a confederate—is never really shocked. As far as you know, he gets zapped each time you press one of the switches. As the session proceeds, the learner makes more and more errors, leading you to work your way up the shock scale. As you reach 75, 90, and 105 volts, you hear the learner grunt in pain. At 120 volts, he begins to shout. If you're still in it at 150 volts, you hear the learner cry out, "Experimenter! That's all. Get me out of here. My heart's starting to bother me now. I refuse to go on!" Screams of agony and protest continue. At 300 volts, he says he absolutely refuses to continue. By the time you surpass 330 volts, the learner falls silent and fails to respond—not to be heard from again. Table 7.3 lists his responses in grim detail.

Somewhere along the line, you turn to the experimenter for guidance. "What should I do? Don't you think I should stop? Shouldn't we at least check on him?" You might even confront the experimenter head-on and refuse to continue. Yet in answer to your inquiries, the experimenter—firm in his tone and seemingly unaffected by the learner's distress—prods you along as follows:

- Please continue (or please go on).
- The experiment requires that you continue.

TABLE 7.3

The Learner's Protests in the Milgram Experiment

As participants administered progressively more intense shocks, they heard the learner moan, groan, protest, and complain. All participants heard the same programmed set of responses. Eventually, the learner fell silent and ceased to respond. *(Milgram, 1974.)*

75 volts	Ugh!
90 volts	Ugh!
105 volts	Ugh! *(louder)*
120 volts	Ugh! Hey this really hurts.
135 volts	Ugh!!
150 volts	Ugh!!! Experimenter! That's all. Get me out of here. I told you I had heart trouble. My heart's starting to bother me now. Get me out of here, please. My heart's starting to bother me. I refuse to go on. Let me out.
165 volts	Ugh! Let me out! *(shouting)*
180 volts	Ugh! I can't stand the pain. Let me out of here! *(shouting)*
195 volts	Ugh! Let me out of here. Let me out of here. My heart's bothering me. Let me out of here! You have no right to keep me here! Let me out! Let me out of here! Let me out! Let me out of here! My heart's bothering me. Let me out! Let me out!
210 volts	Ugh!! Experimenter! Get me out of here. I've had enough. I won't be in the experiment any more.
225 volts	Ugh!
240 volts	Ugh!
255 volts	Ugh! Get me out of here.
270 volts	*(Agonized scream.)* Let me out of here. Let me out of here. Let me out of here. Let me out. Do you hear? Let me out of here.
285 volts	*(Agonized scream.)*
300 volts	*(Agonized scream.)* I absolutely refuse to answer any more. Get me out of here. You can't hold me here. Get me out. Get me out of here.
315 volts	*(Intensely agonized scream.)* I told you I refuse to answer. I'm no longer part of this experiment.
330 volts	*(Intense and prolonged agonized scream.)* Let me out of here. Let me out of here. My heart's bothering me. Let me out, I tell you. *(Hysterically)* Let me out of here. Let me out of here. You have no right to hold me here. Let me out! Let me out! Let me out! Let me out of here! Let me out! Let me out!

- It is absolutely essential that you continue.
- You have no other choice; you must go on.

What do you do? In a situation that begins to feel more and more like a bad dream, do you follow your own conscience or obey the experimenter?

Milgram described this procedure to psychiatrists, students, and middle-class adults, and he asked them to predict how they would behave. On average, these groups estimated that they would call it quits at the 135-volt level. Not a single person thought he or she would go all the way to 450 volts. When asked to predict the percentage of *other* people who would deliver the maximum shock, those interviewed gave similar estimates. The psychiatrists estimated that only one out of 1000 people would exhibit that kind of extreme obedience. They were wrong. In Milgram's initial study, involving 40 men from the surrounding New Haven community, participants exhibited an alarming degree of obedience, administering an average of 27 out of 30 possible shocks. In fact, 26 of the 40 participants—*65 percent*—delivered the ultimate punishment of 450 volts. The complete results are shown in Table 7.4.

The Obedient Participant At first glance, you may see these results as a lesson in the psychology of cruelty and conclude that Milgram's participants were seriously disturbed. But research does not support such a simple explanation. To begin with, those in a control group who were not prodded along by an experimenter refused to continue early in the shock sequence. Moreover, Milgram found that virtually all participants, including those who administered severe shocks, were tormented by the experience. Many of them pleaded with the experimenter to let them stop. When he refused, they went on. But in the process, they trembled, stuttered, groaned, perspired, bit their lips, and dug their fingernails into their flesh. Some burst into fits of nervous laughter. On one occasion, said Milgram, "we observed a [participant's] seizure so violently convulsive that it was necessary to call a halt to the experiment" (1963, p. 375).

Was Milgram's 65 percent baseline level of obedience attributable to his unique sample of male participants? Not at all. Forty women who participated in a later study exhibited precisely the same level of obedience: 65 percent threw the 450-volt switch. Before you jump to the conclusion that something was amiss in New Haven, consider the fact that Milgram's basic finding has been obtained in several different countries and with children as well as students and older adults (Shanab & Yahya, 1977, 1978). Obedience in the Milgram situation is so universal that it led one author to ask, "Are we all Nazis?" (Askenasy, 1978).

The answer, of course, is no. An individual's character can make a difference; and some people, depending on the situation, are far more obedient than others. In the aftermath of World War II, a group of social scientists, searching for the root causes of prejudice, sought to identify individuals with an *authoritarian personality* and developed a questionnaire known as the F-Scale to measure it (Adorno et al., 1950; Stone et al., 1993). What they found is that people who get high scores on the F-Scale (F stands for "Fascist") are rigid, dogmatic, sexually repressed, ethnocentric, intolerant of dissent, and punitive. They are submissive toward figures of authority but aggressive toward subordinates. Indeed, people with high F scores are also more willing than low scorers to administer high-intensity shocks in Milgram's obedience situation (Elms & Milgram, 1966). Examining the scores of more than 4000 Canadian university students and more than 2500 of their parents, Robert Altemeyer (2004) has concluded that those who score the highest on authoritarian scales are also among the most prejudiced in society.

TABLE 7.4

Milgram's Baseline Results

In Milgram's original experiment, participants exhibited a troubling inclination to obey blindly. This table shows the number and percentage of male participants who delivered shocks of varying maximum intensity in response to the experimenter's commands. *(Milgram, 1974.)*

	Participants Who Stopped at This Level	
Shock Level (Volts)	Number	Percent
300	5	12.5
315	4	10.0
330	2	5.0
345	1	2.5
360	1	2.5
375	1	2.5
450	26	65.0

Although personality characteristics may make someone vulnerable or resistant to destructive obedience, what seems to matter most is the situation in which people find themselves. By carefully altering particular aspects of his basic scenario, in more than 20 variations of the basic experiment, Milgram was able to identify factors that increase and decrease the 65 percent baseline rate of obedience (see Figure 7.6). Three factors in particular are important: the authority figure, the proximity of the victim, and the experimental procedure (Blass, 1992; Miller, 1986).

The Authority What is most remarkable about Milgram's findings is that a lab-coated experimenter is *not* a powerful figure of authority. Unlike a military superior, employer, or teacher, the psychology experimenter in Milgram's research could not ultimately enforce his commands. Still, his physical presence and his apparent legitimacy played major roles in drawing obedience. When Milgram diminished the experimenter's status by moving his lab from the distinguished surroundings of Yale University to a rundown urban office building in nearby Bridgeport, Connecticut, the rate of total obedience dropped to 48 percent. When the experimenter was replaced by an ordinary person—supposedly another participant—there was a sharp reduction to 20 percent. Similarly, Milgram found that when the experimenter was in charge but issued his commands by telephone, only 21 percent fully obeyed. (In fact, when the experimenter was not watching, many participants in this condition feigned obedience by pressing the 15-volt switch.) One conclusion, then, is clear. At least in the Milgram setting, destructive obedience requires the physical presence of a prestigious authority figure.

If an experimenter can exert such control over research participants, imagine the control wielded by truly powerful authority figures—present or not. An intriguing field study examined the extent to which hospital nurses would obey unreasonable orders from a doctor they did not know. Using a fictitious name, a male physician called several female nurses on the phone and told them to administer a drug to a specific patient. His order violated hospital regulations: The drug was uncommon, the dosage was too large, and the effects could have been harmful. Yet out

FIGURE 7.6

Factors That Influence Obedience

Milgram varied many factors in his research program. Without commands from an experimenter, fewer than 3 percent of the participants exhibited full obedience. Yet in the standard baseline condition, 65 percent of male and female participants followed the orders. To identify factors that might reduce this level, Milgram varied the location of the experiment, the status of the authority, the participant's proximity to the victim, and the presence of confederates who rebel. The effects of these variations are illustrated here. *(Milgram, 1974.)*

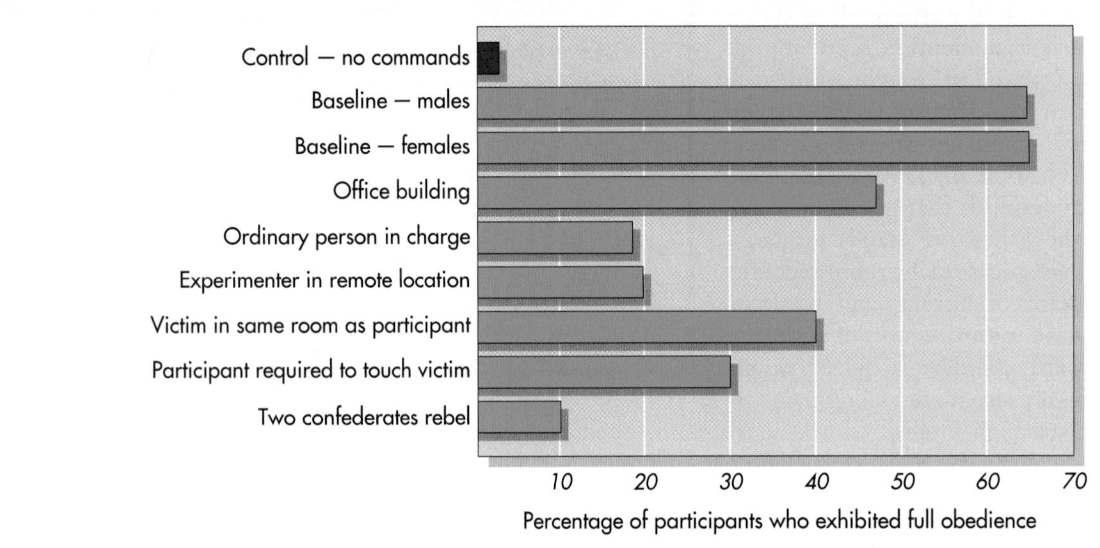

of the 22 nurses who were contacted, 21 had to be stopped as they prepared to obey the doctor's orders (Hofling et al., 1966).

The Victim Situational characteristics of the victim are also important in destructive obedience. Milgram noted that Nazi war criminal Adolf Eichmann felt sick when he toured concentration camps but only had to shuffle papers from behind a desk to play his part in the Holocaust. Similarly, the B-29 pilot who dropped the atom bomb on Hiroshima in World War II said of his mission, "I had no thoughts, except what I'm supposed to do" (Miller, 1986, p. 228). These events suggest that because Milgram's participants were physically separated from the learner, they were able to distance themselves emotionally from the consequences of their actions.

To test the impact of a victim's proximity on destructive obedience, Milgram seated the learner in one of his studies in the same room as the participant. Under these conditions, only 40 percent fully obeyed. When participants were required to physically grasp the victim's hand and force it onto a metal shock plate, full obedience dropped to 30 percent. These findings represent significant reductions from the 65 percent baseline. Still, three out of ten participants were willing to use brute force in the name of obedience.

The Procedure Finally, there is the situation created by Milgram. A close look at the dilemma his participants faced reveals two important aspects of the experimental procedure. First, participants were led to feel relieved of any personal sense of *responsibility* for the victim's welfare. The experimenter said up front that he was accountable. When participants were led to believe that *they* were responsible, their levels of obedience dropped considerably (Tilker, 1970). The ramifications of this finding are immense. In the military and other organizations, individuals often occupy positions in a hierarchical chain of command. Eichmann was a middle-level bureaucrat who received orders from Hitler and transmitted them to others for implementation. Caught between individuals who make policy and those who carry it out, how personally responsible do those in the middle feel? Wesley Kilham and Leon Mann (1974) examined this issue in an obedience study that cast participants in one of two roles: the *transmitter* (who took orders from the experimenter and passed them on) and the *executant* (who actually pressed the shock levers). As they predicted, transmitters were more obedient (54 percent) than executants (28 percent).

The second feature of Milgram's scenario that promoted obedience is gradual escalation. Participants began the session by delivering mild shocks and then, only gradually, escalated to voltage levels of high intensity. After all, what's another 15 volts compared with the current level? By the time participants realized the frightening implications of what they were doing, it had become more difficult for them to escape (Gilbert, 1981). This sequence is much like the foot-in-the-door technique. In Milgram's words, people become "integrated into a situation that carries its own momentum. The subject's problem . . . is how to become disengaged from a situation which is moving in an altogether ugly direction" (1974, p. 73). We should point out that obedience by momentum is not unique to Milgram's research paradigm. As reported by Amnesty International, many countries today torture political prisoners—and those who are recruited for the dirty work are trained, in part, through an escalating series of commitments (Haritos-Fatouros, 2002).

Milgram in the Twenty-First Century

When Stanley Milgram published the results of his first experiment in 1963, at the age of 28, a *New York Times* headline read: "Sixty-Five Percent in Test Blindly Obey Order to Inflict Pain." Milgram had pierced the public consciousness and was poised to become one of the most important and controversial figures in psychology—and beyond. In a fascinating biography, *The Man Who Shocked the World,* Thomas Blass (2004) tells of how Milgram became interested in obedience and the impact his studies have had on social scientists, legal scholars, the military, and popular culture around the world (Milgram's obedience book has been translated into 11 languages).

Today, with the air we breathe filled with threats of global conflict, fanaticism, and terrorism, obedience to authority is an issue of such massive importance that social psychologists all over the world continue to ponder its ramifications (Blass, 2000).

Would the same results as Milgram's be repeated today, in a different but analogous situation? To answer this question, Dutch researchers Wim Meeus and Quinten Raaijmakers (1995) constructed a moral dilemma like Milgram's. Rather than command participants to inflict physical pain, however, they arranged for them to cause psychological harm. When participants arrived at a university laboratory, they met a confederate supposedly there to take a test as part of a job interview. If the confederate passed the test, he'd get the job; if he failed, he would not. As part of a study of performance under stress, the experimenter told participants to distract the test-taking applicant by making an escalating series of harassing remarks. On cue, the applicant pleaded with participants to stop, became angry, faltered, and eventually fell into a state of despair and failed. As in Milgram's research, the question was straightforward: How many participants would obey orders through the entire set of 15 stress remarks, despite the apparent harm caused to a real-life job applicant? In a control group that lacked a prodding experimenter, no one persisted. But when the experimenter ordered them to go on, 92 percent exhibited complete obedience despite seeing the task as unfair and distasteful. It appears that obedience is a powerful aspect of human nature brought about by the docile manner in which people relate to figures of authority—even today.

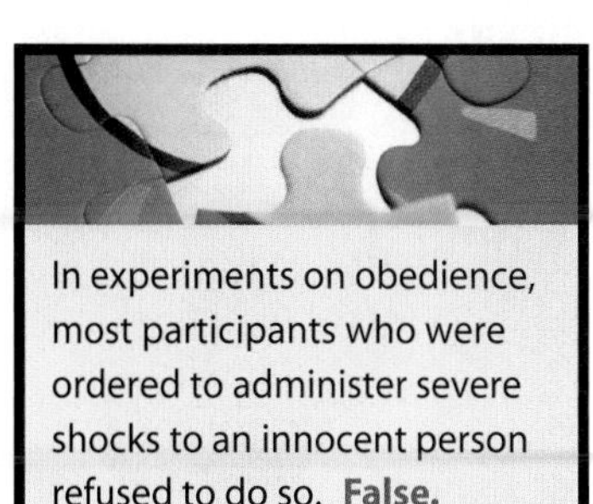

In experiments on obedience, most participants who were ordered to administer severe shocks to an innocent person refused to do so. **False.**

Before leaving the Milgram studies, consider an awkward but important moral question: By providing a situational explanation for the evils of Nazi Germany or of modern-day terrorism, are social psychologists unwittingly excusing the perpetrators? Does blaming what they did on the situation let them off the responsibility hook? In a series of studies, Arthur Miller and others (1999) found that after people were asked to come up with explanations for acts of wrongdoing, they tended to be more forgiving of the individuals who committed those acts—and were seen as more forgiving by others. This appearance of forgiveness was certainly not Milgram's intent, nor is it the intent of other researchers today who seek to understand cruelty, even while continuing to condemn it. Miller and his colleagues are thus quick to caution, "To explain is not to forgive" (p. 265).

Defiance: When People Rebel

"A little rebellion now and then is a good thing."
—Thomas Jefferson

It is easy to despair in light of the impressive array of forces that compel people toward blind obedience. But there's also good news. Just as social influence processes can breed subservience to authority, they can also breed rebellion and defiance. Few people realize it, but this phenomenon, too, was seen during World War II. In *Resistance of the Heart*, historian Nathan Stoltzfus (1996) describes a civil protest in Berlin in which the non-Jewish wives of 2 000 newly captured Jews congregated outside the prison. The women were there, initially, seeking information about their husbands. Soon they were filling the streets chanting and refusing to leave. After eight straight days of protest, the defiant women prevailed. Fearing the negative impact on public opinion, the Nazis backed down and released the men.

Are the actions of a group harder to control than the behaviour of a single individual? Consider the following study. Pretending to be part of a marketing research firm, William Gamson and others (1982) recruited people to participate in a supposed discussion of "community standards." Scheduled in groups of nine, participants were told that their discussions would be videotaped for a large oil company that was suing the manager of a local service station who had spoken out against higher gas prices. After receiving a summary of the case, most participants sided with the station manager. But there was a hitch. The oil company wanted evidence to win its case, said the experimenter—posing as the discussion coordinator. He told each of the group members to get in front of the camera and express the company's viewpoint. Then he told them to sign an affidavit giving the company permission to edit the tapes for use in court.

Political protests allow the public to express their displeasure at the decisions made by their political leaders. Research shows that it is easier for people to behave defiantly in groups than alone.

You can see how the obedience script was supposed to unfold. Actually, only one of 33 groups even came close to following the script. In all others, people became incensed by the coordinator's behaviour and refused to continue. Some groups were so outraged that they planned to take action. One group even threatened to blow the whistle on the firm by calling the local newspapers. Faced with one emotionally charged mutiny after another, the researchers had to discontinue the experiment.

Why did this study produce such active, often passionate revolt when Milgram's revealed such utterly passive obedience? Could it reflect a change in values from the 1960s, when Milgram's studies were run? Many students believe that people would conform less today than in the past, but an analysis of obedience studies has revealed that there is no correlation between the year a study was conducted and the level of obedience that it produced (Blass, 1999). So what accounts for the contrasting results? One key difference is that people in Milgram's studies took part alone and those in Gamson's were in groups. As Michael Walzer noted, "Disobedience, when it is not criminally but morally, religiously, or politically motivated, is always a *collective* act" (cited in R. Brown, 1986, p. 17).

Our earlier discussion of conformity indicated that the mere presence of one ally in an otherwise unanimous majority gives individuals the courage to dissent. Perhaps the same holds true for obedience. Notably, Milgram never had more than one participant present in the same session. But in one experiment, he did use two confederates who posed as co-teachers along with the real participant. In these sessions, one confederate refused to continue at 150 volts, and the second refused at 210 volts. These models of disobedience had a profound influence on participants' willingness to defy the experimenter: In their presence, only 10 percent delivered the maximum level of shock (see Figure 7.6).

We should add that the presence of a group is not a perfect safeguard against destructive obedience. Groups can trigger aggression, as we'll see in Chapter 11. For example, the followers of Jim Jones were together when they collectively followed his command to die. And lynch mobs are just that—groups, not individuals. Clearly, there is power in sheer numbers. That power can be destructive, or it can be used for constructive purposes. Indeed, the presence and support of others often provide the extra ounce of courage that people need to resist orders they find offensive.

The Continuum of Social Influence

As we have seen, social influence on behaviour ranges from the implicit pressure of group norms, to the traps set by direct requests, to the powerful commands of authority. In each case, people choose whether to react with conformity or independence, compliance or assertiveness, obedience or defiance. At this point, let's step back and ask two important questions. First, although different kinds of pressure influence us for different reasons, is it possible to predict all effects with a single, overarching principle? Second, what does the theory and research on social influence say about human nature?

Social Impact Theory

In 1981, Bibb Latané proposed that a common bond among the different processes involved in social influence leads people toward or away from such influence. Specifically, Latané proposed **social impact theory**, which states that social influence of any kind—the total impact of others on a target person—is a function of the others' strength, immediacy, and number. According to Latané, social forces act on individuals in the same way that physical forces act on objects. Consider, for example, how overhead lights illuminate a surface. The total amount of light cast on a surface depends on the strength of the bulbs, their distance from the surface, and their number. As illustrated in the left portion of Figure 7.7, the same factors apply to social impact.

The *strength* of a source is determined by his or her status, ability, or relationship to a target. The stronger the source, the greater the influence. When people view the other members of a group as competent, they are more likely to conform in their judgments. When it comes to compliance, sources enhance their strength by making targets feel obligated to reciprocate a small favour. And to elicit obedience, authority figures gain strength by wearing uniforms or flaunting their prestigious affiliations.

Immediacy refers to a source's proximity in time and space to the target. The closer the source, the greater its impact. Milgram's research offers the best example. Obedience rates were higher when the experimenter issued commands in person rather than from a remote location; and when the victim suffered in close proximity to the participant, he acted as a contrary source of influence and obedience levels dropped. Consistent with this hypothesis, Latané and others (1995) asked individuals to name up to seven people in their lives and to indicate how far away those

social impact theory The theory that social influence depends on the strength, immediacy, and number of source persons relative to target persons.

According to social impact theory, this "intervention" should prove persuasive.

people lived and how many memorable interactions they'd had with them. In three studies, the correlation was the same: The closer others are, geographically, the more impact they have on us.

Finally, the theory predicts that as the *number* of sources increases, so does their influence—at least up to a point. You may recall that when Asch (1956) increased the number of live confederates in his line-judgment studies from one to four, conformity levels rose; yet further increases had only a negligible additional effect.

Social impact theory also predicts that people sometimes resist social pressure. According to Latané, this resistance is most likely to occur when social impact is *divided* among many strong and distant *targets*, as seen in the right part of Figure 7.7. There should be less impact on a target who is strong and far from the source than on one who is weak and close to the source; and there should be less impact on a target who is accompanied by other target persons than on one who stands alone. Thus, we have seen that conformity is reduced by the presence of an ally and that obedience rates drop when people are in the company of rebellious peers.

Over the years, social impact theory has been challenged, defended, and refined on various grounds (Jackson, 1986; Mullen, 1985; Sedikides & Jackson, 1990). On the one hand, critics say that it does not enable us to *explain* the processes that give rise to social influence or answer *why* questions. On the other hand, the theory enables us to *predict* the emergence of social influence and determine *when* it will occur. Whether the topic is conformity, compliance, or obedience, this theory has set the stage for interesting new research in the years to come.

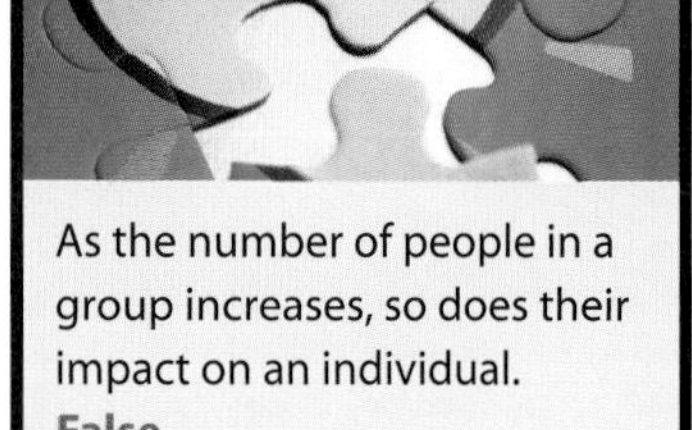

As the number of people in a group increases, so does their impact on an individual. **False.**

A number of social psychologists have recently argued that social impact is a fluid, dynamic, ever-changing process (Vallacher et al., 2002). Latané and L'Herrou (1996) thus refined the theory in that vein. By having large groups of participants interact through email, for example, and by controlling their lines of communication, they found that the individuals within the network formed "clusters." Over time, neighbours (participants who were in direct contact) became more similar to each other than did those who were more distant (not in direct contact) within the network. Referring to the geometry of social space, Latané and L'Herrou note that in

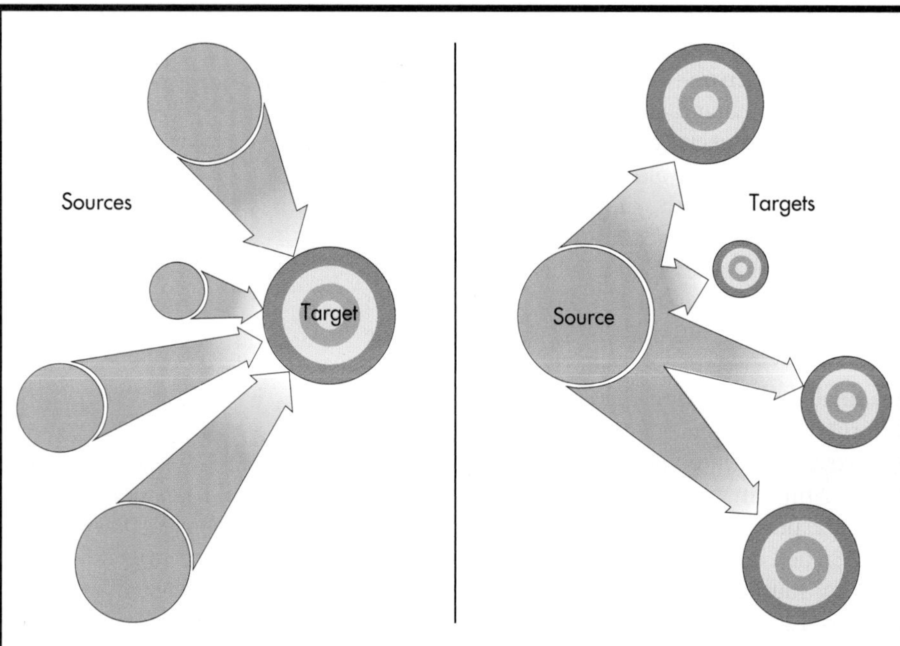

FIGURE 7.7

Social Impact: Source Factors and Target Factors

According to social impact theory, the total influence of other people on a target individual depends on three factors related to the source persons: their strength (size of source circles), immediacy (distance to the target), and number (number of source circles). Similarly, the total influence is diffused, or reduced, by the strength (size of target circles), immediacy (distance from source circle), and number of target persons. *(Latané, 1981.)*

the real world, immediacy cannot be defined strictly in terms of physical distance. "Walls between houses, rivers through towns, open spaces between cities, these and other spatial discontinuities all tend to prevent the equal flow of influence among all members of a population" (p. 1229). Speculating on the role of computer technology, they also note that social impact theory has to account for the fact that, more and more, people interact in cyberspace—perhaps making physical proximity a less relevant factor.

According to social impact theory, an officer will exert influence to the extent that he is strong (in a position of power), immediate (physically close), and numerous (backed by others in the institution) relative to his trainees.

Perspectives on Human Nature

From the material presented in this chapter, what general conclusions might you draw about human nature? Granted, social influence is more likely to occur in some situations than in others. But are people generally malleable or unyielding? Is there a tilt toward accepting influence or toward putting up resistance?

There is no single, universal answer to these questions. As we saw earlier, some cultures value autonomy and independence, while others place more emphasis on conformity to one's group. Even within a given culture, values may change over time. To demonstrate the point, ask yourself: If you were a parent, what traits would you like your child to have? When this question was put to American mothers in 1924, they chose "obedience" and "loyalty," key characteristics of conformity. Yet when mothers were asked the same question in 1978, they cited "independence" and "tolerance of others," key characteristics of autonomy. Similar trends were found in surveys conducted in West Germany, Italy, England, and Japan (Remley, 1988)—and in laboratory experiments, where conformity rates are somewhat lower today than in the past (Bond & Smith, 1996).

Is it possible that today's children—tomorrow's adults—will exhibit greater resistance to the various forms of social influence? If so, what effects will this trend have on society as a whole? Cast in a positive light, conformity, compliance, and obedience are good and necessary human responses. They promote group solidarity and agreement—qualities that keep groups from being torn apart by dissension. Cast in a negative light, a lack of independence, assertiveness, and defiance are undesirable behaviours that lend themselves to narrow-mindedness, cowardice, and destructive obedience—often with terrible costs. For each of us, and for society as a whole, the trick is to strike a balance.

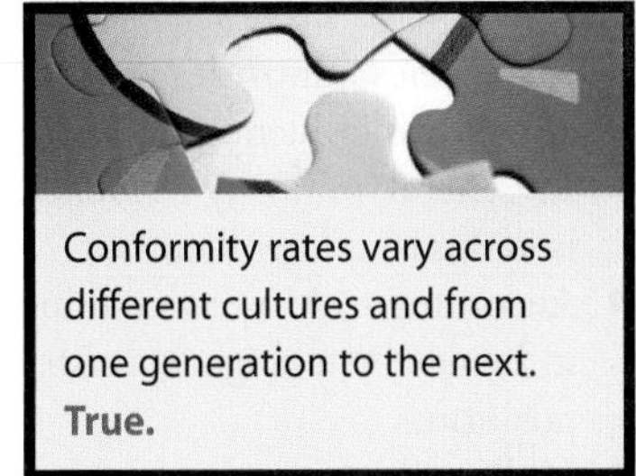

Conformity rates vary across different cultures and from one generation to the next. **True.**

Review

- Conformity, compliance, and obedience are three kinds of social influence, varying in the degree of pressure brought to bear on an individual.

Social Influence as "Automatic"

- Sometimes we are influenced by other people without our awareness.
- Studies show that people mimic each other's behaviours and moods, perhaps as a way of smoothing social interactions.

Conformity

- Conformity is the tendency for people to change their behaviour to be consistent with group norms.

The Early Classics

- Two classic experiments illustrate contrasting types of conformity.
- Sherif presented groups of participants with an ambiguous task and found that their judgments gradually converged.
- Using a simpler line-judgment task, Asch had confederates make incorrect responses and found that participants went along about a third of the time.

Why Do People Conform?

- Sherif found that people exhibit private conformity, using others for information in an ambiguous situation.
- Asch's studies indicated that people conform in their public behaviour to avoid appearing deviant.

Majority Influence

- As the size of an incorrect unanimous majority increases, so does conformity—up to a point.
- People conform to perceived social norms when these norms are brought to mind.
- The presence of one dissenter reduces conformity, even when he or she disagrees with the participant and lacks competence at the task.
- Women conform more than men on "masculine" tasks and in face-to-face settings, but not on "feminine" or gender-neutral tasks or in private settings.
- Conformity rates are higher in cultures that value collectivism than in those that value individualism.

Minority Influence

- Sometimes minorities resist pressures to conform and are able to influence majorities.
- In general, minority influence is greater when the source is an ingroup member.
- According to Moscovici, minorities can exert influence by taking a consistent and unwavering position.
- Hollander claims that to exert influence, a person should first conform, then dissent.
- Majority influence is greater on direct and public measures of conformity, but minorities show their impact in indirect or private measures of conformity.
- By forcing other group members to think more openly about a problem, minorities enhance the quality of a group's decision making.
- People gain courage to resist conformity pressures after watching others do the same.

Compliance

- A common form of social influence occurs when we respond to direct requests.

The Language of Request

- People are more likely to comply when they are taken by surprise and when the request *sounds* reasonable.

The Norm of Reciprocity

- We often comply when we feel indebted to a requester who has done us a favour.
- People differ in the extent to which they use reciprocity for personal gain and are wary of falling prey to this strategy.

Setting Traps: Sequential Request Strategies

- Four compliance techniques are based on a two-step request: The first step sets a trap, and the second elicits compliance.
- Using the foot-in-the-door technique, a person sets the stage for the "real" request by first getting someone to comply with a smaller request.
- In low-balling, one person gets another to agree to a request but then increases the size of it by revealing hidden costs. Despite the increase, people often follow through on their agreement.
- With the door-in-the-face technique, the real request is preceded by a large one that is rejected. People then comply with the second request because they see it as a concession to be reciprocated.
- The that's-not-all technique begins with a large request. Then the apparent size of the request is reduced by the offer of a discount or bonus.

Assertiveness: When People Say No

- Many people find it hard to be assertive. Doing so requires that we be vigilant and recognize the traps.

Obedience

- When the request is a command, and the requester is a figure of authority, the resulting influence is called obedience.

Milgram's Research: Forces of Destructive Obedience

- In a series of experiments, participants were ordered by an experimenter to administer increasingly painful shocks to a confederate.
- Sixty-five percent obeyed completely but felt tormented by the experience.
- Obedience levels are influenced by various situational factors, including a participant's physical proximity to both the authority figure and the victim.
- Two other aspects of Milgram's procedure also contributed to the high levels of obedience: (1) participants did not feel personally responsible, and (2) the orders escalated gradually.
- In more recent studies, people exhibited high rates of obedience when told to inflict psychological harm on another person.

Milgram in the Twenty-First Century

- Milgram's studies have remained relevant and controversial into the twenty-first century.
- Researchers note that a situational explanation for acts of destructive obedience does not forgive them.

Defiance: When People Rebel

- Just as processes of social influence breed obedience, they can also support acts of defiance, since groups are more difficult to control than individuals.
- Provision of a situational explanation for cruel behaviour does not excuse that behaviour.

The Continuum of Social Influence

Social Impact Theory

- Social impact theory predicts that social influence depends on the strength, immediacy, and number of sources who exert pressure relative to target persons who absorb that pressure.

Perspectives on Human Nature

- There is no single answer to the question of whether people are conformists or nonconformists.
- There are cross-cultural differences in social influence, and values change over time even within specific cultures.

Key Terms

collectivism *(228)*
compliance *(230)*
conformity *(220)*
door-in-the-face technique *(234)*
foot-in-the-door technique *(232)*
individualism *(228)*
informational influence *(223)*
low-balling *(234)*
minority influence *(229)*
normative influence *(223)*
obedience *(237)*
private conformity *(223)*
public conformity *(224)*
social impact theory *(245)*
that's-not-all technique *(235)*

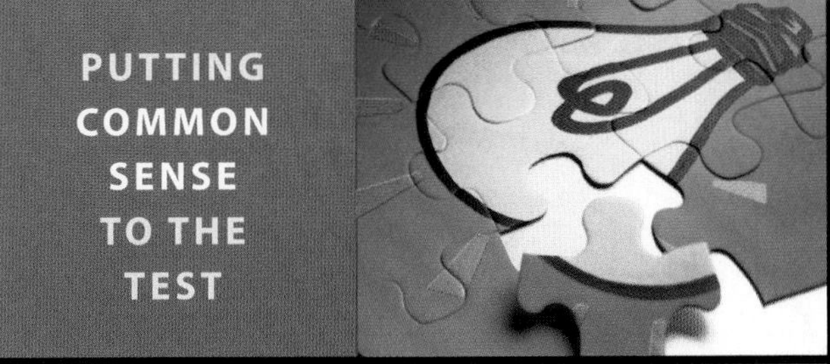

When all members of a group give an incorrect response to an easy question, most people most of the time conform to that response.

False. *In Asch's classic conformity experiments, respondents conformed only about a third of the time.*

An effective way to get someone to do you a favour is to make a first request that is so large the person is sure to reject it.

True. *This approach, known as the door-in-the-face technique, increases compliance by making the person feel bound to make a concession.*

In experiments on obedience, most participants who were ordered to administer severe shocks to an innocent person refused to do so.

False. *In Milgram's classic research, 65 percent of all participants obeyed the experimenter and administered the maximum possible shock.*

As the number of people in a group increases, so does their impact on an individual.

False. *Increasing group size boosts the impact on an individual only up to a point, beyond which further increases have very little added effect.*

Conformity rates vary across different cultures and from one generation to the next.

True. *Research shows that conformity rates are higher in cultures that are collectivistic rather than individualistic in orientation, and values change over time even within cultures.*

8 Group Processes

OUTLINE

PREVIEW

THIS CHAPTER examines social influence in a group context. First, we focus on *collective processes*, the effects of the presence of others on an individual's behaviour. Then we turn to *group processes*, in which individuals directly interact with each other, and discuss why the whole (the group decision or performance) is different from the sum of its parts (the attitudes and abilities of the group members). In the final section, on *cooperation, competition*, and *conflict*, we examine how groups intensify or reconcile their differences.

December 17, 2003, marked the 100th anniversary of one of the landmark achievements in history. A century before, fantasy as old as human history had finally, remarkably, become reality, as Orville and Wilbur Wright's plane flew precariously through the cold, windy air near Kitty Hawk, North Carolina. Given how many people had tried and failed to accomplish such a feat, it wouldn't have been surprising if progress in aviation would continue to be painstakingly slow after 1903. But looking back now, the speed of this progress seems as close to miraculous as anything humans have achieved. After its long history as an earthbound species, within a few decades of Orville's first 12-second flight, people would fly across vast lands and oceans. Within one person's lifetime, humans would go from celebrating a dozen seconds of staying above earth to celebrating men walking on the moon.

But in the world of aviation, 2003 was a year of mourning as well as celebration. Just as the anniversary of the Wright brothers' ascent was a great leap for humanity, so the descent of the space shuttle *Columbia* back toward Earth on February 1, 2003, was a tragic fall. Sixteen days after its launch into space, *Columbia* was only minutes away from its scheduled landing when it disintegrated during re-entry into the atmosphere, killing all seven crew members on board.

The fact that humans could achieve so much in one century, from learning how to fly several feet above the ground to launching probes to the ends of the solar system, is a testament to what can be accomplished when people work together. The Wright brothers could not have achieved their great feat without each other and without the help, expertise, and fresh perspectives that several others offered. And certainly the numerous, stunning achievements since then were possible only through people collaborating in groups. But as we will see in this chapter, the tragedy of the *Columbia* also reveals a cautionary lesson about groups and about how group processes can lead to bad, even catastrophic, decision making.

For example, several days before *Columbia* exploded, a team of engineers at the US National Aeronautics and Space Administration (NASA) reviewed a video of foam breaking off the *Columbia* during launch and hitting the area near the left wing, and they speculated about whether the impact could have damaged the heat-shielding tiles there. One engineer, Rodney Rocha, made more than a half dozen

PUTTING COMMON SENSE TO THE TEST

T / F

___ **People will cheer louder when they cheer as part of a group than when they cheer alone.**

___ **Group members' attitudes about a course of action usually become more moderate after group discussion.**

___ **People brainstorming as a group come up with a greater number of better ideas than the same number of people working individually.**

___ **Groups are less likely than individuals to invest more and more resources in a project that is failing.**

___ **Large groups are more likely than small groups to exploit a scarce resource that the members collectively depend on.**

While most of us don't typically play a role in decisions affecting life and death, as those involved in the Challenger *shuttle mission, we all take part in group processes. Like them, the more we can harness the benefits of the process, while being aware of possible pitfalls, the better.*

requests of NASA managers to go outside the agency and seek images from spy satellite photos or powerful telescopes that could provide a better look at the possible damage to the *Columbia* while it was in space. These requests were ignored or rejected. One manager said that he refused to be a "Chicken Little." The flight director emailed his rejection of the engineer's request: "I consider it to be a dead issue" (Glanz & Schwartz, 2003).

As investigators concluded months later, aspects of the "culture" at NASA were to blame for the failure to adequately consider concerns like these. In the end, the investigators pointed to the group dynamics at NASA as much as to the physical problems in explaining what led the *Columbia* and its crew to disaster.

And one of the most disturbing revelations was this: Although the physical causes in this incident were very different from those implicated in the 1986 NASA tragedy, when the space shuttle *Challenger* exploded during its ascent, the flawed group dynamics were shockingly similar. Several engineers at the Morton Thiokol Corporation, which had made the *Challenger*'s solid rocket boosters, warned that launching in cold temperatures could cause the O-ring seals in the rocket boosters to fail, which would cause a catastrophic explosion. Some wanted to ban a liftoff if the temperature was below 50 degrees. On the morning of January 28, 1986, the temperature at the launch pad was below freezing. But high-level officials at Morton Thiokol and NASA were motivated not to delay the launch. NASA had heavily promoted the mission because it marked the first time that "an ordinary citizen," a New Hampshire high school teacher named Christa McAuliffe, would travel into space along with the astronauts. The decision was made to launch. Seventy-three seconds after liftoff, the *Challenger* exploded, killing all seven people on board. Apparently, the O-ring seals had indeed failed.

In both cases, group members recognized the very problems that would cause the catastrophes and tried to warn people higher up in the chain of command, but aspects of the culture and structure of their organization created obstacles that prevented these warnings from being heeded.

On a much more mundane, earthbound scale, we all work in groups, and we are all affected by them. And the same kinds of group processes that contributed to both the accomplishments and tragedies of the first century of flight affect our own lives in countless ways. Most of us won't learn "rocket science," but we can and should learn about group processes. The more we learn how to harness the good that groups can bring, and avoid their pitfalls, the better our lives will be.

People are often at their best—and their worst—in groups. It is through groups that individuals form communities, pool resources, and share successes. But it is also through groups that stereotypes turn into oppression, frustrations turn into mob violence, and conflicts turn into wars.

Clearly, it is important that we understand how groups work and how individuals influence, and are influenced by, groups. The research reported in this chapter reveals a fascinating fact: *Groups can be quite different from the sum of their parts.* When you think about that statement, it suggests something almost mystical or magical about groups, like quantum physics (or the enduring careers of any of several untalented actors or pop stars!). How can a group be better, or worse, than the individuals that constitute it? The math may not seem to add up, but the theory and research discussed in this chapter will help answer this question. We examine groups on several levels: At the individual level, we explore how individuals are influenced by groups; at the group level, we explore how groups perform; and at the intergroup level, we explore how groups interact with each other in cooperation and competition.

Collective Processes: The Presence of Others

In Chapter 5, we focused on how individuals perceive groups and group members. In that context, we characterized a group as two or more people perceived as having at least one of the following characteristics: (1) direct interactions with each other over a period of time; (2) joint membership in a social category based on sex, race, or other attributes; (3) a shared, common fate, identity, or set of goals. The current chapter focuses on groups themselves rather than others' perceptions of groups and group members. In this context, we emphasize the first and third criteria: direct interactions among group members over a period of time and a shared, common fate, identity, or set of goals.

"You think because you understand 'one,' you must understand 'two,' because one and one make two. But you must also understand 'and.' "
—Ancient Sufi saying

Also in Chapter 5, we discussed how groups may vary in the extent to which they are seen as distinct entities, often with a fundamental essence and with rigid boundaries making them distinct from other groups. In other words, some groups seem more "groupy" than others (Brewer et al., 2004). Richard Moreland and Jamie McMinn (2004) distinguish between these perceptions of how entitative particular groups seem and the actual degree of *social integration* of groups, which is the extent to which group members act, think, and feel like a single individual.

On the very low end of the dimensions of entity or social integration would be people attending a concert or working out near each other in a gym. These are not real groups. Such assemblages are sometimes called **collectives**—people engaging in a common activity but having little direct interaction with each other (Milgram & Toch, 1969). Although several important social psychological processes are unique to real groups, some processes that affect groups also affect collectives. We begin our discussion by examining these *collective processes*, which influence individuals when they are in the presence of others, whether in real groups or collectives. We turn later to processes that are specific to real groups.

Social Facilitation: When Others Arouse Us

Social psychologists have long been fascinated by how the presence of others affects behaviour. In Chapter 1, we reported that one of the founders of social psychology was Norman Triplett, whose article *The Dynamogenic Factors in Pace-making and Competition* (1897–1898) is often cited as the earliest publication in the field. Triplett began his research by studying the official bicycle records from the Racing Board of the League of American Wheelmen for the 1897 season. He noticed that cyclists who competed against others performed better than those who cycled alone against the clock. After dismissing various theories of the day (our favourite is "brain worry"), he proposed his own hypothesis: The presence of another rider releases the competitive instinct, which increases nervous energy and enhances performance. To test this proposition, Triplett got 40 children to wind up fishing reels, alternating between performing alone and working in parallel. On the average, winding time was faster when the children worked side by side than when they worked alone.

Later research following Triplett's studies proved disappointing. Sometimes the presence of others (side by side or with an audience out front) enhanced performance; at other times, performance declined. It seemed that Triplett's promising lead had turned into a blind alley, and social psychologists had largely abandoned this research by World War II. But years later, Robert Zajonc (1965, 1980) saw a way to reconcile the contradictory results by integrating research from experimental psychology with social psychological research. Zajonc offered an elegant solution: The presence of others increases arousal, which can affect performance in different ways, depending on the task at hand. Let's see how this works.

collective People engaged in common activities but having minimal direct interaction.

The Zajonc Solution According to Zajonc, the road from presence to performance requires three steps.

1. The presence of others creates general physiological *arousal*, which energizes behaviour. Based on experimental psychology research and principles of evolution, Zajonc argued that all animals, including humans, tend to become aroused when in the presence of *conspecifics*—that is, members of their own species.
2. Increased arousal enhances an individual's tendency to perform the *dominant response*. The dominant response is the reaction elicited most quickly and easily by a given stimulus. Here again, Zajonc drew from experimental psychology research, particularly research concerning learning.
3. The quality of an individual's performance varies according to the type of *task*. On an easy task (one that is simple or well learned), the dominant response is usually correct or successful. But on a difficult task (one that is complex or unfamiliar), the dominant response is often incorrect or unsuccessful.

Putting these three steps together (see Figure 8.1) yields the following scenarios. Suppose you are playing the violin. If you're an excellent player and are performing a well-learned, familiar arrangement, having other people around should enhance your performance—the presence of others will increase your arousal, which will enhance your dominant response. Because this arrangement is so well learned, your dominant response will be to perform it well. However, if you are just learning to play the violin and you are unfamiliar with this arrangement, the presence of others is the last thing you'll want. The increase in arousal should enhance the dominant response, which in this case would be *unsuccessful* violin playing.

When you think about it, this makes intuitive sense. If you are just learning how to perform some complicated task, such as playing the violin or riding a bike, it helps if you are not aroused. In contrast, if you are already good at the task, you may need the extra "juice" that comes from performing in front of others to help you rise to new heights and perform even better than you would if performing alone. Sports fans may be able to think of many instances in which the best athletes seem to rise to the occasion when the pressure is on, while lesser athletes "choke" under the same kind of pressure. And physical performances are not the

FIGURE 8.1

Social Facilitation: The Zajonc Solution

According to Zajonc, the presence of others increases arousal, which strengthens the dominant response to a stimulus. On an easy task, the dominant response is usually correct, and thus the presence of others enhances performance. On a difficult task, the dominant response is often incorrect, and thus the presence of others impairs performance.

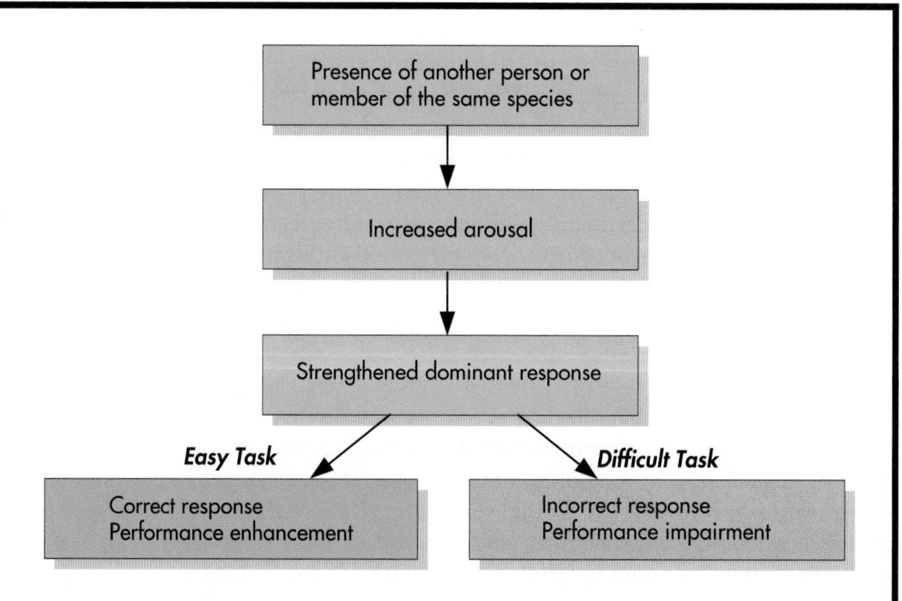

only ones influenced; the effects also hold for social judgment or cognitive tasks, such as forming impressions of others or applying stereotypes (Lambert et al., 2003; Thomas et al., 2002).

Taken as a package, these two effects of the presence of others—helping performance on easy tasks but hurting performance on difficult tasks—are known as **social facilitation**. Unfortunately, this term has been a prime source of confusion for countless students. The trick is to remember that the presence of others facilitates the *dominant* response, not necessarily the task itself. This facilitation of the dominant response does, in effect, facilitate easy tasks, but it makes difficult tasks even more difficult.

Zajonc says that social facilitation is universal—occurring not only in human activities but also among other animals, even insects. Consider, for instance, cockroaches. How fast will they run? In a study by Zajonc and his colleagues (1969), participating insects were placed in a brightly lit start box connected to a darkened goal box. When the track was a simple one, with a straight runway between the start box and the goal box, cockroaches running in pairs ran more quickly toward the goal box than did those running alone. But in a more complex maze, with a right turn required to reach the goal box, solitary cockroaches outraced pairs. In a particularly creative follow-up experiment, Zajonc and his colleagues found that cockroaches completed the easy maze faster, and the difficult maze slower, if they raced in front of a crowd of spectator cockroaches than if they raced with no audience. You may wonder, how did the researchers get cockroaches to participate as spectators? The researchers placed cockroaches in Plexiglas "audience boxes" along either side of the maze, and this "audience" produced social facilitation.

Through social facilitation, seasoned performers like this fire-eater in Barcelona, Spain, benefit from the presence of an audience when performing well-learned routines. On the other hand, when first learning a difficult—and dangerous—act like this, a performer would be advised not to try it in front of an arousing crowd!

Zajonc's formulation revived interest in the issues raised by Triplett's early research, and suddenly the inconsistent findings that had been reported began to make sense. The results of a meta-analysis of 241 studies were consistent with much of Zajonc's account (Bond & Titus, 1983). Moreover, Jim Blascovich and others (1999) have recently found physiological evidence supporting and extending Zajonc's theory: The presence of others triggered arousal in individuals performing a task, and the specific pattern of cardiovascular responses associated with this arousal was consistent with findings of facilitated performance on well-learned tasks and impaired performance on unlearned tasks. And as technology makes more and more of our lives "watched" by others, understanding social facilitation effects may become increasingly important. Most of us, for example, have had the experience of talking with a sales representative on the phone and hearing that our "call may be monitored." Workers' actions on the job are coming under increasing surveillance, as the number of computer key strokes they make per hour or the content of their calls, emails, or Internet browsing can be recorded electronically. According to John Aiello and Elizabeth Douthitt (2001), this electronic monitoring can produce social facilitation effects on performance at work.

And so social facilitation effects have been replicated across many domains, but not all of Zajonc's theory has received universal support. Zajonc proposed that the **mere presence** of others is sufficient to produce social facilitation. Indeed, one recent experiment suggests that even a computer can serve as the "other" and can cause social facilitation if the computer interface is designed to look like another person (Sproull et al., 1996). Some have argued, however, that the presence of others will produce social facilitation only when the others have certain characteristics or have certain effects on the individual who is performing. These issues have produced various alternative explanations of social facilitation, and we turn now to two of the major variations on Zajonc's theme.

social facilitation A process whereby the presence of others enhances performance on easy tasks but impairs performance on difficult tasks.

mere presence theory A theory holding that the mere presence of others is sufficient to produce social facilitation effects.

Evaluation Apprehension The first and most thoroughly researched alternative, **evaluation apprehension theory**, proposes that performance will be enhanced or impaired only in the presence of others who are in a position to evaluate that performance (Geen, 1991; Henchy & Glass, 1968). In other words, it's not simply because others are around that I'm so aroused and therefore inept as I try to learn to snowboard on a crowded mountain. Rather, it's because I worry that the others are watching and probably laughing at me. I imagine them telling stories about me at dinner, or perhaps sending a videotape of my performance to one of those "funniest videos" shows. These concerns increase my dominant response, which is falling.

Usually, presence and potential evaluation go hand in hand. To pry them apart, researchers have come up with some rather unusual procedures. In one study, for example, participants worked on a task alone, in the presence of two other supposed participants (actually confederates), or in the presence of two blindfolded confederates supposedly preparing for a perception study. Compared with participants working alone, those working in the presence of seeing confederates were more likely to come up with dominant responses. In the presence of the blindfolded confederates, however, dominant responses were no more frequent than among participants working alone (Cottrell et al., 1968).

People may experience evaluation apprehension when they are targets of negative stereotypes about their group's ability to perform in a particular domain. As discussed in Chapter 5, women taking a math test, for instance, may fail to perform to their potential because of concerns about negative stereotypes of women's ability in math. Talia Ben-Zeev and her colleagues (2005) wondered recently whether this stereotype threat could cause women to feel aroused while about to take a math test, which in turn would trigger social facilitation effects, even on a completely unrelated task. To test this, Ben-Zeev et al. ran an experiment in which students were told they would be taking a difficult math test. In all conditions, the tests were run in small groups, and so the mere presence of others was held constant. But in one condition, female students' concerns about the negative stereotype were abated by instructions that informed them that the math test they were about to take produced no gender differences—that males and females allegedly scored equally on it. In the other condition, the instructions said nothing about gender differences, thereby allowing the negative stereotype of women and math to remain potentially relevant. In reality, the students never actually took a math test—they only thought that they were about to.

While thinking they were about to take the test, the students were asked first to perform a quick task. For some, this task could not have been much easier: They were asked to write their name (first and last) quickly, but legibly, as many times as they could for 20 seconds. For the other participants, the task was similar, but with a twist that made it annoyingly difficult: They were asked to repeatedly write their name (first name only), but *backward*. To do this, students would have to go against their instinct to spell their name correctly. Ben-Zeev et al. hypothesized that women under stereotype threat about math would be aroused, and therefore they would perform the simple, straightforward task better, but the difficult, backward task worse, relative to women who thought they would be taking a math test for which no relevant stereotype existed. As can be seen in Figure 8.2, this is exactly what Ben-Zeev et al. found. Concern about a stereotype facilitated performance on the easy unrelated task but impeded performance on a difficult unrelated task. For male students, who had no reason to be concerned about negative stereotypes of them, there was no evidence of social facilitation.

evaluation apprehension theory A theory holding that the presence of others will produce social facilitation effects only when those others are seen as potential evaluators.

distraction-conflict theory A theory holding that the presence of others will produce social facilitation effects only when those others distract from the task and create attentional conflict.

Distraction Another approach to social facilitation, **distraction-conflict theory**, points out that being distracted while we're working on a task creates attentional conflict (Baron, 1986; Sanders, 1981). We're torn between focusing on the task and inspecting the distracting stimulus. Conflicted about where to pay attention, our arousal increases. Surprisingly, the distraction caused by the presence of others can actually enhance individuals' performance on some tasks—especially when such distraction is countered by a narrowing of attention. In one study, Pascal Huguet and his colleagues (1999) found that this "tunnel vision" response helped people's performance on a task in which focused attention was beneficial, but it hurt their performance on a task in which peak performance required the use of a broader, more complex array of information.

Distraction-conflict theory maintains that there's nothing uniquely social about "social" facilitation. People, of course, can be distracting; but so can crashing objects, blaring music, and glittering lights. The effect of mere presence has also been called into question. People are not always distracting; a familiar presence that we take for granted will likely leave our performance untouched.

Consider again the three theories of social facilitation we have described. Is one of them right and the others wrong? Probably not. For example, the mere presence account can explain social facilitation among cockroaches better than the evaluation apprehension account can, but evaluation apprehension is better than mere presence at explaining why blindfolded others have less impact than others who are not blindfolded. Comprehensive reviews of the research evidence have drawn different conclusions about which theory has the best track record (Bond & Titus, 1983; Guerin, 2003). It seems likely that all three of the basic elements described by these theories (mere presence, evaluation, and attention) contribute to the impact others have on our own performance. But as we are about to see in the next section, there is even more to the story of how individuals are affected by the presence of others.

FIGURE 8.2

Stereotype Threat and Social Facilitation

Students thought they were about to take a difficult math test, under conditions designed to make female students feel either threatened or not by negative stereotypes about women and math. While waiting for the test to begin, participants performed either an easy, familiar task (writing their first and last name as many times as possible for 20 seconds) or a difficult, novel task (writing their first name backward as many times as possible for 20 seconds). The researchers hypothesized that women under stereotype threat would feel aroused, causing social facilitation effects on the unrelated task. As predicted, women under stereotype threat performed better on the easy task (that is, they were able to write their names more frequently within the allotted time) and worse on the difficult task compared to women not under threat. *(Ben-Zeev et al., 2005.)*

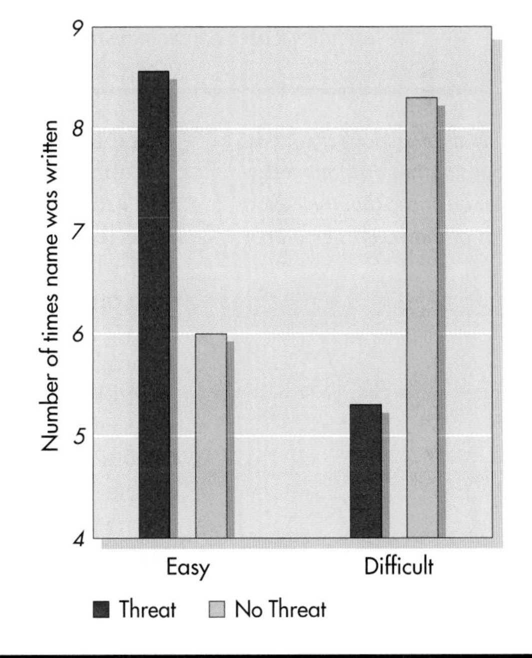

Social Loafing: When Others Relax Us

The tasks employed in research on social facilitation produce individually identifiable results. That is, behaviour can be identified and evaluated. But on some tasks, efforts are pooled so that the specific performance of any one individual cannot be determined. That other founder of social psychology, French agricultural engineer Max Ringelmann, investigated group performance on these kinds of collective endeavours. In research conducted during the 1880s, Ringelmann discovered that, compared with what people produced when they worked on their own, individual output declined when they worked together on simple tasks like pulling a rope or pushing a cart (Kravitz & Martin, 1986; Ringelmann, 1913).

Why did individual output decline? One explanation is that the individuals exerted less effort when they acted collectively, but another explanation is that the individuals simply demonstrated poor coordination when working together—some pulled while others relaxed and vice versa. How can you distinguish lack of effort from poor coordination in a task like this? Nearly 100 years after Ringelmann's research, Alan Ingham and his colleagues (1974) answered this question by using a rope-pulling machine and blindfolding participants. In one condition, participants were led to *think* that they were pulling with a bunch of other participants; and in another condition, the participants were informed that they were pulling alone

"We just haven't been flapping them hard enough."

Individuals often don't try as hard in groups as they do alone. If they can be convinced that their efforts will pay off, however, their output can soar.

(which, in fact, they were). The researchers told the participants to pull as hard as they could. Ingham and colleagues were able to measure exactly how hard each individual participant pulled, and they observed that the participants pulled almost 20 percent harder when they thought they were pulling alone than when they thought they were pulling with others. Naoki Kugihara (1999) recently found a similar decline in rope-pulling among Japanese men (but not women) in a collective setting.

Bibb Latané and his colleagues (1979) found that group-produced reductions in individual output, which they called **social loafing**, are common in other types of tasks as well. For example, imagine being asked as part of a psychology experiment to cheer or clap as loudly as you can. Common sense might lead you to think that you would cheer and clap louder when doing this together with others in a group than when performing alone because you would be less embarrassed and inhibited if others were doing the same thing as you. But Latané and his colleagues found that when performing collectively, individual students loafed—they exerted less effort. The sound pressure generated by each individual decreased as the size of the group increased (see Figure 8.3). This social loafing occurred even among cheerleaders, who are supposed to be experts at cheering and clapping with others! And social loafing is not restricted to simple motor tasks. Sharing responsibility with others reduces the amount of effort that people put into more complex motor tasks, such as swimming in a relay race; cognitive tasks, such as trying to remember information or working on math or verbal tests; and important, enduring real-world behaviours, such as working on collective farms or working collaboratively on classroom projects (Latané et al., 1979; Miles & Greenberg, 1993; North et al., 2000; Plaks & Higgins, 2000; Weldon et al., 2000). When others are there to pick up the slack, people slack off.

Steven Karau and Kipling Williams (1993) conducted a meta-analysis of 78 studies and found social loafing to be a reliable phenomenon, displayed across numerous tasks and in countries around the world. But social loafing is not inevitable; a number of factors can reduce it. Social loafing is less likely to occur when one of the following conditions is present:

- People believe that their own performance can be identified and thus evaluated, by themselves or others.
- The task is important or meaningful to those performing it.
- People believe that their own efforts are necessary for a successful outcome.
- The group expects to be punished for poor performance.
- The group is small.
- The group is cohesive—that is, membership in the group is valuable and important to the members, and the individuals like each other.

In addition, although men and women in a wide variety of populations and cultures exhibit social loafing, it is less prevalent among women than men and less prevalent among people from eastern, collectivist cultures (such as China, Japan, and Taiwan) than among people from western, individualist cultures (such as Canada and the United States). Individual differences matter as well. For example, Brian Smith and others (2001) report that individuals with a relatively high need for

social loafing A group-produced reduction in individual output on easy tasks where contributions are pooled.

cognition did not socially loaf on a cognitively engaging task, whereas those lower in need for cognition did. (As was discussed in Chapter 6, the need for cognition is the extent to which people enjoy effortful cognitive activities.)

Several researchers have constructed theoretical accounts to explain the findings about when social loafing is more or less likely to occur (e.g., Guerin, 2003; Shepperd & Taylor, 1999). One influential analysis is by Karau and Williams (2001), who proposed the **collective effort model**. This model asserts that individuals try hard on a collective task when they think their efforts will help them achieve outcomes that they personally value. If the outcome is important to individual members of the group, and if they believe that they can help achieve the desired outcome, then these individuals are likely to engage in *social compensation*—specifically, by increasing their efforts on collective tasks to try to compensate for the anticipated social loafing or poor performance of other group members. Conversely, if the outcome is not personally important to individual members, if they believe that their contribution won't affect the outcome very much, or if they feel they are unable to compensate for the anticipated social loafing of other members, then they are likely to exert less effort. This is sometimes called the *sucker effect:* Nobody wants to be the "sucker" who does all the work while everyone else goofs off, so everyone withholds effort, and the result is very poor group performance (Houldsworth & Mathews, 2000; Kerr, 1983; Shepperd, 1993a). The next time you work on a group project, such as a paper that you and several other students are supposed to write together, consider the factors that increase and decrease social loafing. You might want to try to change aspects of the situation so that all group members are motivated to do their share of the work.

FIGURE 8.3

Social Loafing: When Many Produce Less

Social loafing is a group-produced reduction in individual output on simple tasks. In this study, college students were told to cheer or clap as loudly as they could. The sound pressure produced by each of them decreased as the size of the group increased. *(Latané et al., 1979.)*

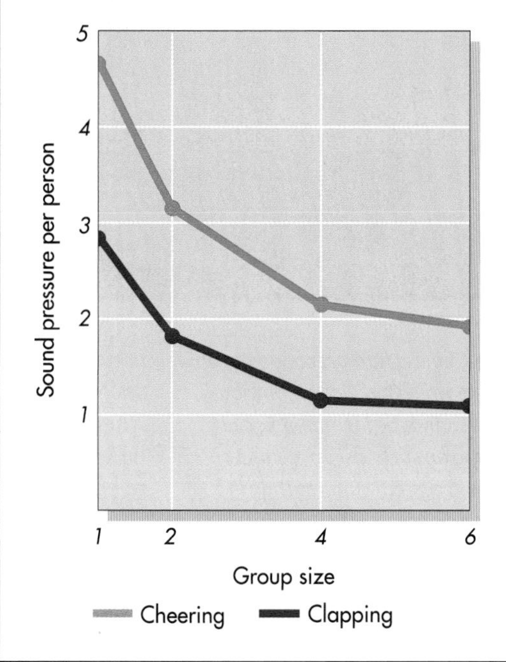

Facilitation and Loafing: Unifying the Paradigms

Social facilitation and social loafing represent two separate research traditions, but the connection between them—the fact that both arise in the presence of others—has prompted some investigators to attempt a unified approach that highlights the arousal associated with possible performance evaluation (Guerin, 2003; Harkins & Szymanski, 1987; Sanna, 1992).

- When individual contributions can be identified (social facilitation), the presence of others *increases* arousal and the possibility of being evaluated: The individual is in the spotlight.
- When individual contributions are pooled (social loafing), the presence of others *decreases* arousal and the possibility of being evaluated: Each person's performance is swallowed up in the group product, and the individual can relax and be lost in the crowd.

Now, how do arousal and possible evaluation affect performance? It depends on the difficulty of the task to be performed. Four predictions can be made.

- When the presence of others increases the possibility of evaluation of an individual's work: (1) Performance on easy tasks is enhanced because the individual is more motivated. That's social facilitation, part one. (2) Performance on difficult tasks is impaired because the pressure gets to the individual. That's social facilitation, part two.

People will cheer louder when they cheer as part of a group than when they cheer alone. **False.**

collective effort model The theory that individuals will exert effort on a collective task to the degree that they think their individual efforts will be important, relevant, and meaningful for achieving outcomes that they value.

Here, Chinese farmers cooperate on a task in which individual contributions cannot be identified. Social loafing on such tasks occurs less often in eastern cultures than in western ones.

- When the presence of others decreases the possibility of evaluation of an individual's work: (3) Performance on easy tasks is impaired because the individual is uninspired. That's social loafing. (4) Performance on difficult tasks is enhanced because being lost in the crowd frees the individual from anxiety. There's no official name for this effect, but we're inclined to call it "social security."

These predictions have been confirmed in several studies using different methods and measures (Jackson & Williams, 1985; Sanna, 1992). The typical pattern of results is diagrammed in Figure 8.4. A unified view of social facilitation and social loafing has important practical implications for maximizing performance when individuals are working together. In team sports, for example, coaches would be well advised to evaluate each player's performance against a weak opponent but to stress team spirit and overall group effort during a tough game. Unification is also historically satisfying: the two founders of social psychology, Triplett and Ringelmann, together at last.

Deindividuation: When People Lose Control

Some pioneers in social psychology regarded the presence of others as considerably more profound and more troubling. Based on their research in France, Gabriel Tarde (1890) and Gustave Le Bon (1895) thought of collective influence as virtually mesmerizing. They maintained that, under the sway of the crowd, people turn into copycat automatons or, worse still, uncontrollable mobs.

In December of 1992, members of the elite Canadian Airborne Regiment were sent to Somalia to help keep the peace; while there, the soldiers did little to hide their racial slurs and epithets aimed at Somali citizens. One colonel reportedly offered a prize of a "case or a bottle of champagne to the first one who gets or kills a Somali" (*Macleans*, 1995). In March of 1993, Shidane Arone, a Somali teenager, entered the aid camp claiming he was looking for food, although the soldiers later claimed he was in actuality a thief looking for something to steal. He was grabbed by drunken Canadian soldiers, tortured, and eventually beaten to death. A photo of one of the soldiers grinning beside the dying teenager was widely broadcast by the Canadian media. Due to the ensuing scandal, the Canadian Airborne Regiment was disbanded. What would cause these Canadian soldiers to display such shocking and horrific behaviour? Was it simply that the soldiers involved were "bad apples," or was there more to it? Did being part of this elite regiment somehow play a role in their behaviour? As we discussed in Chapter 5, being part of an ingroup can be a powerful motivator, and these soldiers were part of a very elite ingroup. Did this allow them to hide behind the group mentality? There is no doubt that the destructive capacity of collectives has left a bloody trail through human history. What turns

FIGURE 8.4

Unifying the Paradigms: Presence and Evaluation

The relationship between the presence of others and the potential for evaluation is the key to a unified paradigm of social facilitation and social loafing. When individual performance can be evaluated, the presence of others enhances performance on easy tasks but impairs performance on difficult endeavours. When contributions are pooled across individuals, the pattern reverses, as performance declines on easy tasks but improves on difficult ones. *(Adapted from Jackson & Williams, 1985; Sanna, 1992.)*

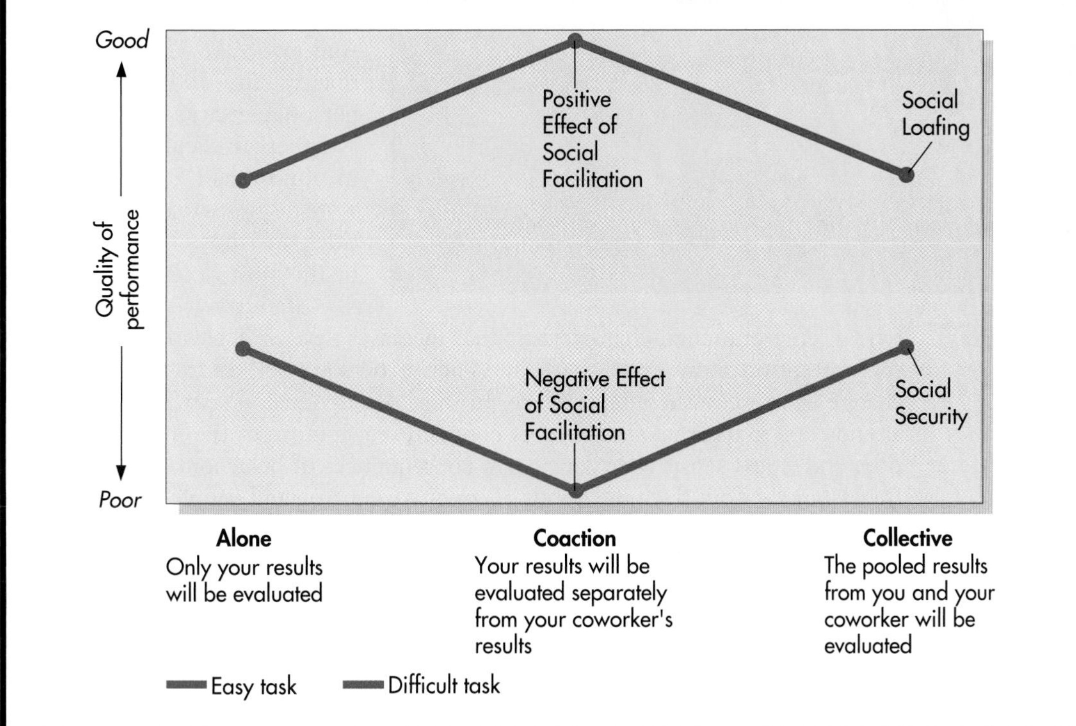

an unruly crowd into a violent mob? It is clear that many of the factors described in Chapter 11 on Aggression contribute to violence by groups as well as by individuals. Possible factors include imitation of aggressive models, intense frustration, high temperatures, alcohol consumption, and the presence of weapons that trigger aggressive thoughts and actions. But there's also **deindividuation,** the loss of a person's sense of individuality and the reduction of normal constraints against deviant behaviour. Most investigators believe that deindividuation is a collective phenomenon that occurs only in the presence of others (Diener et al., 1976; Festinger et al., 1952). Philip Zimbardo (1969) observed that arousal, anonymity, and reduced feelings of individual responsibility together contribute to deindividuation.

Environmental Cues In order to understand deindividuation, we must examine the physical and social environment in which it takes place. According to Steven Prentice-Dunn and Ronald Rogers (1982, 1983), two types of environmental cues—accountability cues and attentional cues—increase deviant behaviour.

Accountability cues affect the individual's cost-reward calculations. When accountability is low, those who commit deviant acts are less likely to be caught and punished, and people may deliberately choose to engage in gratifying but usually inhibited behaviours. Consider, for instance, features of the environment that

deindividuation The loss of a person's sense of individuality and the reduction of normal constraints against deviant behaviour.

create anonymity (such as being in a large crowd or wearing a mask or hood). What would *you* do if you could be totally anonymous—indeed, invisible—for 24 hours? Among college students asked this question, their most frequent responses involved criminal acts; the single most common response was "rob a bank" (Dodd, 1985). Andrew Silke (2003) observed that of the 500 violent interpersonal attacks he studied in Northern Ireland, the offenders in almost half of the incidents wore disguises to mask their identities, and those attacks tended to be the most violent.

It has become fairly commonplace in recent years for celebrations by groups of fans after their team's victory in a championship to escalate from joy to mayhem and destruction.

Attentional cues, the second type of environmental characteristic that increases deviant behaviour, focus a person's attention away from the self. When a person's self-awareness declines, a change in consciousness takes place. In this "deindividuated state," the individual attends less to internal standards of conduct, reacts more to the immediate situation, and is less sensitive to long-term consequences of behaviour (Diener, 1980). Behaviour slips out from the bonds of cognitive control, and people act on impulse.

Have you ever been at a party with flashing strobe lights and music so loud that you could feel the room vibrate? If so, did it seem that you were somehow merging with the pulsating crowd and that your individual identity was slipping away? Intense stimulation from the environment is probably the most common attentional cue reducing self-awareness. In laboratory research, groups of participants placed in a highly stimulating environment (loud music, colourful video games) were more uninhibited, extreme, and aggressive in their actions (Diener, 1979; Spivey & Prentice-Dunn, 1990).

One particularly creative set of field experiments by Edward Diener and Arthur Beaman and their colleagues (Beaman et al., 1979; Diener et al., 1976) demonstrated how accountability cues and attentional cues can affect behaviour on a night when many otherwise well-behaved individuals act in antisocial ways: Halloween. When you think about it, Halloween can be a perfect time to study deindividuation; children often wear costumes with masks, travel in large groups at night, and are highly aroused. In one study, the researchers unobtrusively observed more than 1 300 children who came trick-or-treating to 27 homes spread around Seattle. At each of these homes, a researcher met and greeted the children, who were either alone or in groups. In one condition, the researcher asked the children their names and where they lived; in another condition, the researcher did not ask them any questions about their identities. When asked to identify themselves, the children should have become more self-aware and more accountable for their actions. Children who were not asked to reveal their identities should have felt relatively deindividuated, safe and anonymous in their costumes.

The children were then invited to take *one* item from a bowl full of candy and were left alone with the bowl. Hidden observers watched to see how many pieces of candy each child took. What did the observers see? The children took the most candy when they were the most deindividuated: when they were in a group and had not been asked to identify themselves. In another experiment, the researchers placed a mirror behind the candy bowl in some conditions. As noted in Chapter 3, the presence of a mirror tends to increase people's self-awareness. Children who had been asked their names, especially older children, were much less likely to steal candy if there was a mirror present than if there wasn't. Older children are more likely to have internal standards against stealing, and making these children self-aware made them more likely to act according to those standards.

Being in a large crowd can decrease both accountability and self-awareness. Perhaps because of this double impact, larger groups are associated with greater violence (Mullen, 1986). For example, in 1997, 14-year-old Vancouver teenager Rena Virk became a victim of "swarming"; she was severely beaten and then held underwater until she died. She was attacked by six girls and one boy whose ages ranged from 14 to 17. Sadly, Leon Mann (1981) found that when a crowd gathers to watch someone who is threatening to commit suicide by jumping from a building or other tall structure, those in the crowd are more likely to jeer and taunt the person if the crowd is large rather than small—especially at night, when the people in the crowd can feel more anonymous.

Moving from Personal to Social Identity Despite the association between crowds and violence, the loss of personal identity does not always produce antisocial behaviour. In a study conducted by Robert Johnson and Leslie Downing (1979), female undergraduates donned garments resembling either robes worn by Ku Klux Klan members or nurses' uniforms. Half of the participants were individually identified throughout the study; the others were not. All of the participants were then given the opportunity to increase or decrease the intensity of electric shocks delivered to a supposed other participant (actually, an experimental confederate) who had previously behaved in an obnoxious manner. Participants wearing Ku Klux Klan costumes increased shock levels in both the identified and anonymous conditions. However, among those in nurse's apparel, anonymous participants *decreased* shock intensity four times more frequently than did identified participants!

These findings (displayed in Figure 8.5) make a telling point: Sometimes becoming less accountable, or less self-aware, allows us to be more responsive to the needs of others. According to the *social identity model of deindividuation effects (SIDE)*, whether deindividuation affects people for better or for worse seems to reflect the characteristics and norms of the group immediately surrounding the individual (Douglas & McGarty, 2002; Postmes & Spears, 2002; Reicher, 2001). As personal identity and internal controls are submerged, social identity emerges and conformity to the group increases. If a group defines itself ("us") in terms of prejudice and hatred against another group ("them"), deindividuation can ignite an explosion of violence. But if a group defines itself in terms of concern for the welfare of others, deindividuation can spark an expansion of goodness. The consequences of losing your personal identity depend on what you lose it to.

FIGURE 8.5

Deindividuation and Social Identity

Regardless of whether they were individually identified or anonymous, female participants wearing KKK robes increased the intensity of shocks they administered to an experimental confederate. Among those wearing nurses' uniforms, however, anonymous participants *decreased* shock intensity much more than did individually identified participants. *(Data from Johnson & Downing, 1979.)*

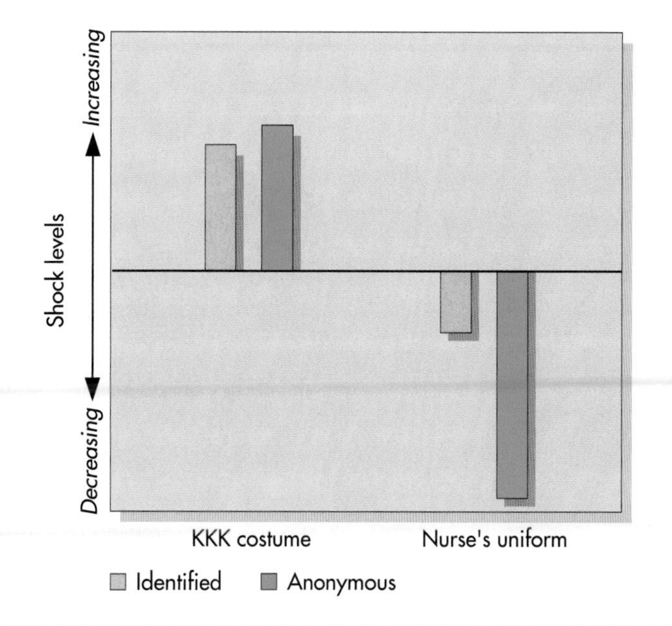

Group Processes: Interacting with Others

Influential as they can be, collectives are only minimally social. People are in the same place at the same time working on a common task or reacting to the same event, but they don't engage in extensive interaction with each other. In this section, we examine social influence and other processes in groups, where interaction among members is more direct and meaningful.

Joining a Group

Groups come in all shapes and sizes: large and small, highly organized and quite informal, short term and long lasting. Sometimes group membership is involuntary. You didn't choose your family. But membership in most groups is voluntary. You decide to join an existing group or get together with others to create a brand-new one. Why do people join groups? How do groups develop over time? We address these questions next.

Why Join a Group? There are several reasons for joining groups. At a fundamental level, people may have an innate need to belong to groups, stemming from evolutionary pressures that increased people's chances of survival and reproduction when in groups rather than in isolation (Baumeister & Tweng, 2003; Kurzban & Leary, 2001). This need may also be driven by the desire to feel protected against threat and uncertainty in everyday life or to gain a greater sense of personal and social identity (Aharpour & Brown, 2002; Schmitt et al., 2003; Taubman-Ben-Ari et al., 2002). Further, people join specific groups in order to accomplish things that they cannot accomplish as individuals. Neither symphonies nor football games can be played by one person alone, and many types of work require team effort. People also join groups because of the social status and identity that they offer. According to social identity theory, which was discussed in Chapter 5 on Perceiving Groups, an important part of people's feelings of self-worth comes from their identification with particular groups. Even a relatively low-status group can be a source of pride for individuals who are held in high esteem within the group; being big fish in small ponds can make people feel good about themselves, particularly people from individualist cultures (Gagnon & Bourhis, 1996; McFarland & Buehler, 1995). People may also join groups simply because they like the members and want to have the opportunity to interact with them. Whatever our reasons for joining a particular group, when we join a group we usually are optimistic that we will benefit by belonging (Brinthaupt et al., 1991). In contrast, being rejected by a group is one of life's most painful experiences (Eisenberger et al., 2003; Leary et al., 2003; Williams, 2001).

Members of the University of Western Ontario Hindu Student's Association celebrate the Hindu Holi festival on campus in London, Ontario. The celebration of good over evil involves bright colours to represent good.

Group Development Once an individual has joined a group, a process of adjustment takes place. The individual assimilates into the group, making whatever changes are necessary to fit in. At the same time, the group accommodates to the newcomer, making whatever changes are necessary to include that individual. Socialization of a new member into a group often relies heavily on the relationship between newcomers and established members (Arrow & Burns, 2004; Levine et al., 2004). Newcomers model their behaviour on what the old-timers do; old-timers may hold explicit training sessions for newcomers. Acting as mentors, old-timers may also develop close personal relationships with newcomers to help them be successful in the group. Having a mentor is useful to anyone joining a new group but may be especially helpful to those, such as women and people of colour, who are joining groups from which they were previously excluded (Irons & Moore, 1985). Many men, on the other hand, resent having a woman mentor (Armstrong et al., 2002). In general, whether or not mentors are used, the quicker and more effectively new members are socialized into the group, the more productive the group is likely to be (Ardts et al., 2001).

The socialization of group members is one way in which groups develop and maintain themselves. Group development may proceed through several stages. Group members first investigate and evaluate each other and the group as a whole. To the extent that the members accept each other and the group at large, their commitment to the group increases. Eventually, however, individuals may begin to diverge from the group, and the group may try to re-socialize them. If the re-socialization is unsuccessful, these individuals may exit the group, or the group may dissolve (Levine et al., 2004; Moreland & Levine, 2002).

Bruce Tuckman (1965; Tuckman & Jensen, 1977) proposed a particularly memorable set of stages through which groups often develop: forming, storming, norming, performing, and adjourning. These stages are described in Table 8.1. According to this model, groups gradually progress from a period of initial orientation through stages of conflict, compromise, and action, followed by a period of withdrawal if the group no longer satisfies members' needs. Although many groups seem to pass through these stages, not all groups do. Contemporary theory on group development offers more complex models of group development, including the recognition that groups often develop in ways that are not linear and that different groups may develop in different ways (e.g., Chidambaram & Bostrom, 1997; Seers & Woodruff, 1997). For example, Connie Gersick (1988, 1994) observes that groups often do not proceed gradually through a uniform series of stages but instead operate in starts and stops, going through periods of relative inactivity until triggered by awareness of time and deadlines. According to Gersick, many groups adopt a problem-solving strategy very quickly—much quicker than Tuckman's theory suggests—but then they procrastinate until they have wasted about half the time they have allotted for the task, after which point they spring into action. Think about the work groups that *you've* been a part of: Do the stages described in Table 8.1 seem to apply, or do the groups described by Gersick seem more familiar to you?

Roles, Norms, and Cohesiveness

Despite their variation in specific characteristics, all groups can be described in terms of three essential components: roles, norms, and cohesiveness (Forsyth, 1999; Levine & Moreland, 1990). We consider each of these in the following sections.

Roles People's *roles* in a group, their set of expected behaviours, can be formal or informal. Formal roles are designated by titles: teacher or student in a class, vice president or account executive in a corporation. Informal roles are less obvious but still powerful. For example, Robert Bales (1958) proposed that regardless of people's

TABLE 8.1

Stages of Group Development

- **Forming:** Members try to orient themselves to the group. They often act in polite, exploratory ways with each other.
- **Storming:** Members try to influence the group so that it best fits their own needs. They become more assertive about the group's direction and what roles they would like to play in the group. A great deal of conflict and hostility may arise, along with feelings of excitement about what might be achieved.
- **Norming:** Members try to reconcile the conflicts that emerged during storming and develop a common sense of purpose and perspective. They establish norms and roles and begin to feel more commitment to the group.
- **Performing:** Members try to perform their tasks and maximize the group's performance. They operate within their roles in the group and try to solve problems to allow them to achieve their shared goals.
- **Adjourning:** Members disengage from the group, distancing themselves from the other members and reducing their activities within the group. This may occur if members believe that the benefits of staying in the group no longer outweigh the costs.

(Based on Tuckman, 1965; Tuckman & Jensen, 1977.)

titles, enduring groups give rise to two fundamental types of roles: an *instrumental* role to help the group achieve its tasks and an *expressive* role to provide emotional support and maintain morale. The same person can fill both roles, but often they are assumed by different individuals, and which of these roles is emphasized in groups may fluctuate over time depending on the needs of the group.

Having a set of clear roles is beneficial to a group. A meta-analysis of studies involving more than 11 000 individuals found a significant negative correlation between role ambiguity and job performance—the more role ambiguity, the worse one's job performance (Tubre & Collins, 2000). Teams often strive to organize themselves and to distribute task roles based on group members' particular skills and preferences. The better a team does in assigning roles that match the individual's characteristics, the better the individual will function in the group. However, when a person's role in the group is ambiguous, conflicts with other roles the person has (as when a group member needs to be demanding but also is the person who typically provides emotional support to others), or changes over time, stress and loss of productivity are likely to result (Bettencourt & Sheldon, 2001; Hechanova et al., 2003; Jackson & Schuler, 1985; Stempfle et al., 2001).

Norms In addition to roles for its members, groups also establish *norms*, rules of conduct for members. Like roles, norms may be either formal or informal. Fraternities and sororities, for example, usually have written rules for the behaviour expected from their members. Informal norms are more subtle. What do I wear? How hard can I push for what I want? Who pays for this or that? Figuring out the unwritten rules of the group can be a time-consuming and, sometimes, anxiety-provoking endeavour.

Researchers have investigated the development and consequences of a huge array of group norms, involving everything from binge drinking, smoking, sexual behaviour, and prejudice to the use of language and symbols in Internet chat groups (Crandall & Eshleman, 2002; Johnston & White, 2003; Sassenberg, 2002; Schofield et al., 2003; Selvan et al., 2001). Brendan McAuliffe and others (2003) found that even a group norm of individualism can be established, resulting in members conforming to the norm of not conforming! You probably know of groups that vary in this way, with some fostering individuality and others emphasizing solidarity. These norms can play a role in group cohesiveness, which we discuss next.

Cohesiveness The third characteristic of groups, *cohesiveness*, refers to the forces exerted on a group that push its members closer together (Cartwright & Zander, 1960; Festinger, 1950). Various factors contribute to cohesiveness, including commitment to the group task, attraction to group members, group pride, and number and intensity of interactions (Carless & De Paola, 2000; Cota et al., 1995; Dion, 2000). Outside forces, too, affect cohesiveness. Groups in dangerous or unusual

Group members are often the same, but different. That is, while they may appear similar, they can still maintain unique attributes.

environments and groups threatened by other groups often become more cohesive—especially if the groups' members think that they can cope with these forces effectively as a group (Depret & Fiske, 1999; Dion, 1979; Harrison & Connors, 1984; Lanzetta, 1955). However, threats from within the group—in the form of envy between group members, say—can tear apart group cohesion (Duffy & Shaw, 2000).

Cohesiveness and group performance are causally related, but the relationship is not a simple one. When a group is cohesive, group performance improves, and when a group performs well, it becomes more cohesive. In their meta-analysis of the research on cohesiveness and group performance, Brian Mullen and Carolyn Copper (1994) found more evidence for an effect of performance on cohesiveness than for an effect of cohesiveness on performance. They also found that the positive relationship between cohesiveness and group performance may depend on the size of the group: The relationship tended to be stronger in small groups than in large ones.

A separate meta-analysis conducted by Stanley Gully and others (1995) indicates that the positive relationship between cohesiveness and performance is much stronger for tasks that require interdependence among group members than for tasks that do not require interdependence. Interdependent tasks are those in which group members must interact, communicate, cooperate, and observe each other (as in a military operation or a game of football). Cohesiveness should help performance on such tasks, but it can hurt performance in situations where creative, innovative ideas and behaviours are needed (as when designing a new advertising campaign for a product that is not selling well). Possibly because women tend to value interdependence more than men, a recent meta-analysis of 46 studies of cohesiveness in sports teams found not only a generally positive correlation between cohesiveness and team performance, but also that the relationship was particularly strong for female sports teams (Carron et al., 2002).

Finally, the effect of cohesiveness on group performance depends on the norms that have been established in the group. If the norms are positive and consistent with an organization's goals, then high cohesiveness should improve group performance. If, however, a group has established negative, counterproductive norms, then high cohesiveness should lead to *poor* group performance. For example, a group of workers might establish a relatively low work standard as a norm. If this group is cohesive, its members may threaten or socially reject any group member who deviates from the others by working harder than the norm; so cohesiveness promotes poor performance. In contrast, other groups set very ambitious goals for each other and establish positive norms; the more cohesive these groups are, the more likely they are to push each other to succeed (Langfred, 1998; Prapavessis & Carron, 1997; Stogdill, 1972).

Sometimes, breaking a norm in a cohesive group can be very difficult and even traumatic for a group member. Coworkers are especially reluctant to report the unethical behaviour of others on their work teams, fearing the social consequences of reporting on a member of the group. Consultants involved in employee relations

In 1994, former Olympian Myriam Bedard was working in marketing for Via Rail. She became suspicious of some invoices from Groupaction Marketing—one of the companies implicated in a sponsorship scandal. She claims that when she voiced her concerns, she was fired from her job.

frequently observe the dilemma that workers in cohesive teams face when they witness unethical conduct. As one consultant noted, "[Team workers] have a fear they'll be seen as divisive. We're social animals, and we so very much want to belong" (Armour, 1998, p. 6B).

In 1995, the Liberal government set up a fund to help promote Canadian sovereignty, particularly in Quebec, by funding social and cultural events. The rules for the disbursement of this fund were not clear, although the company Groupaction Marketing was paid more than $500 000 to prepare a report than no one ever saw. Ultimately, further investigation revealed a massive misappropriation of funds, with millions of dollars paid to various companies—friends of the Liberal government—without any clear accounting of the money, or benefit to Canadians in general. Public Works employee Alan Cutler was the first to blow the whistle on the scandal.

Group Polarization: Gaining Conviction

Once a group has formed—with roles, norms, and some degree of cohesiveness—it begins to make decisions and take actions. The issues faced by groups range from the trivial ("Where do we party?") to the profound ("Should we make war—or peace?"). Whatever the issue, the attitudes of group members affect what they do. How does being in a group influence people's opinions?

The key to answering this question is to realize that most groups consist of individuals who hold roughly similar views. People are attracted to groups that share their attitudes, and those who disagree with the group usually leave by their own choice or are ejected by the others. But similar does not mean identical. Although the range of opinion is relatively restricted, there are still differences.

What do you think should be the result of a group discussion of these differing points of view? For example, imagine that a group is discussing whether someone should behave in a risky or a cautious manner, such as whether an entrepreneur should risk trying to expand his or her business or whether an employee in a stable but boring job should quit and take a more creative job in a new but unproven Internet company. Are groups more likely to advocate risky or cautious decisions about issues like these?

"A committee is a cul-de-sac down which ideas are lured and then quietly strangled."
—Barnett Cock

Common sense suggests two alternative predictions. Perhaps the most reasonable prediction is that after the group members discuss their differing points of view, the group decision will represent an overall compromise as everyone moves toward the group average. But common sense also suggests another prediction. Many people familiar with committees agree that forming a committee is a good way *not* to get something done. The idea is that individuals are willing to take risks and implement new ideas, whereas groups tend to be cautious and slow moving. Wary of leading the group toward a risky decision, people become more cautious in their views as they discuss them with the other group members.

So, which prediction is the correct one—movement toward the average attitude or movement toward caution? James Stoner (1961) tested this question by comparing decisions made by individuals with decisions made by groups, and he found that *neither* prediction was correct: Group decisions tended to be *riskier* than individuals' decisions. Was this a fluke? Several subsequent studies found similar results, and the tendency for groups to become riskier than the average of the individuals became known as the *risky shift* (Cartwright, 1971).

But the story doesn't end there. Later studies seemed to contradict the idea of the risky shift, finding that for some choices, groups tended to become more *cautious* (Knox & Safford, 1976). How can we make sense of these contradictory findings?

Researchers concluded that group discussion tends to enhance or exaggerate the initial leanings of the group. Thus, if most group members initially lean toward a risky position on a particular issue, the group's position becomes even riskier after the discussion; but if group members in general initially lean toward a cautious position, the group discussion leads to greater caution. This effect is called **group polarization**—the exaggeration through group discussion of initial tendencies in the thinking of group members (Moscovici & Zavalloni, 1969; Myers & Lamm, 1976).

Group polarization is not restricted to decisions involving risk versus caution. Any group decision can be influenced by group polarization, such as a sorority's decision about what theme to use at its next party (Chandrashekaran et al., 1996). Group polarization is more likely to occur when important, rather than unimportant, issues are being discussed, however (Kerr, 1992). Consider, for example, racial prejudice. In one study, high school students responded to an initial questionnaire and were classified as high, medium, or low on racial prejudice. Groups of like-minded students then met for a discussion of racial issues, with their individual attitudes on these issues assessed before and after their interaction. Group polarization was dramatic. Students low in prejudice to begin with were even less prejudiced after the group discussion; students moderate or high in prejudice became even more prejudiced (Myers & Bishop, 1970).

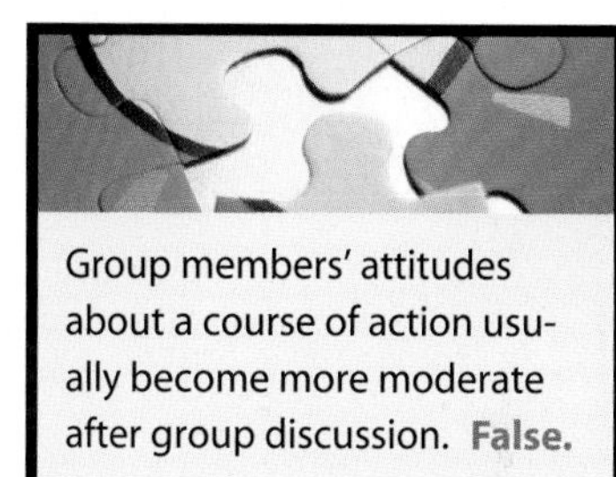

Group members' attitudes about a course of action usually become more moderate after group discussion. **False.**

What creates group polarization? Three processes are usually emphasized:

1. According to *persuasive arguments theory*, the greater the number and persuasiveness of the arguments to which group members are exposed, the more extreme their attitudes become (Vinokur & Burnstein, 1974). Some arguments provide new information to group members hearing them for the first time. If most group members favour a cautious decision, for example, most of the arguments discussed will favour caution, giving the members more and more reason to want to be cautious. In addition, realizing that others favour caution, members may focus on pro-caution arguments when talking to each other and fail to bring up pro-risk arguments that may also be important to consider (Pavitt, 1994). Simply hearing others repeat our arguments (without offering any new ones) can validate our own reasoning, giving us more confidence in what may originally have been only a slight leaning (Baron et al., 1996; Brauer et al., 1995).
2. Group polarization is also created as group members simply discover other people's opinions, even if no arguments are presented (Brown, 1965; Sanders & Baron, 1977). Here, *social comparison* is at work. As described in Chapter 3, individuals develop their view of social reality by comparing themselves with others. The construction of social reality in like-minded groups is a two-step process. First, people discover more support for their own opinion than they had originally anticipated. Second, this discovery sets up a new, more extreme norm and motivates group members to go beyond that norm. If believing X is good, then believing double X is even better. By adopting a more extreme attitudinal position, people can distinguish themselves in the group in a manner approved by the group (Lamm & Myers, 1978).
3. In addition, group polarization is influenced by a concept you may recall from Chapter 5: *social categorization*, the tendency for people to categorize themselves and others in terms of social groups. The social categorization approach compares how individuals react to information from ingroups (to which they belong or want to belong) and outgroups (to which they don't belong and don't want to). Ingroup members may want to distinguish their group from other groups, and so they overestimate the extremity of their group's position and distance themselves from the position of an outgroup (Hogg et al., 1990; McGarty et al., 1992).

group polarization The exaggeration through group discussion of initial tendencies in the thinking of group members.

Groupthink: Losing Perspective

The processes involved in group polarization may set the stage for an even greater, and perhaps more dangerous, bias in group decision making. Recall the discussion at the opening of this chapter about the NASA catastrophes in 1986 and 2003. These were not the only cases in which high-level groups made decisions that in hindsight seem remarkably ill-conceived.

For example, in May, 2000 a criminal investigation began in Walkerton, Ontario, after 7 people died and more than 2000 residents became ill after drinking local water. It turned out that the town's water supply contained the deadly *E. coli* bacteria after a storm caused cow manure to wash into a town well. The investigation revealed that many people who worked for the city were aware that the water was contaminated, but rather than warning the public and cleaning it up, they covered it up. The chlorination system, which may have helped to avert the tragedy, was not working at the time the storm occurred, and in fact had not been working properly for some time. Rather than fixing this, those in charge instead falsified the logs for any required water tests.

Or consider one of the greatest fiascos in US history: the decision to invade Cuba in 1961. When John Kennedy became president of the United States in 1961, he assembled one of the most impressive groups of advisers in the history of American government. These individuals—highly intelligent, educated at the best universities, led by a new president brimming with ambition, charisma, and optimism—were called "the best and the brightest" (Halberstam, 1972). But the Kennedy administration had inherited a plan from the previous administration to invade Cuba at the Bay of Pigs in order to spark a people's revolt that would overthrow Fidel Castro's government. Kennedy and his advisers, after much deliberation, eventually approved an invasion plan that, in hindsight, was hopelessly flawed. For example, once the invaders landed at the Bay of Pigs, they were to be supported by anti-Castro guerrillas camped in the mountains nearby. But had Kennedy and his advisers consulted a map, they might have noticed that the invaders were actually set to land 80 miles away from these mountains and were separated from them by a huge swamp. Ultimately, the invasion failed miserably. The invaders were quickly killed or captured, the world was outraged at the United States, and Cuba allied itself more closely with the Soviet Union—exactly the opposite of what Kennedy had intended. The United States was humiliated. After the fiasco, Kennedy himself wondered, "How could we have been so stupid?" (Janis, 1982).

"'It is always best on these occasions to do what the mob do. 'But suppose there are two mobs?' suggested Mr. Snodgrass. 'Shout with the largest,' replied Mr. Pickwick."

—Charles Dickens

According to Irving Janis (1982), the answer to this question, and similar questions that could be posed of any of the other fiascos we've described, lies in a particular kind of flawed group dynamic, which he called **groupthink**, an excessive tendency to seek concurrence among group members. Groupthink emerges when the need for agreement takes priority over the motivation to obtain accurate information and make appropriate decisions. Figure 8.6 outlines the factors that contribute to groupthink, along with its symptoms and consequences.

Janis believed that three characteristics contribute to the development of groupthink:

1. Since *highly cohesive groups* are more likely to reject members with deviant opinions, Janis thought they would be more susceptible to groupthink.
2. *Group structure* is also important. Groups that are composed of people from similar backgrounds, isolated from other people, directed by a strong leader, and lacking in systematic procedures for making and reviewing decisions should be particularly likely to fall prey to groupthink.
3. Finally, Janis emphasized that *stressful situations* can provoke groupthink. Under stress, urgency can overrule accuracy, and the reassuring support of other group members becomes highly desirable.

groupthink A group decision-making style characterized by an excessive tendency among group members to seek concurrence.

In Janis's formulation, groupthink is a kind of social disease, and infected groups display the behavioural symptoms indicated in the middle of Figure 8.6. For example, Kennedy and his advisers exhibited *overestimation of the group*, assuming that as "the best and the brightest," they could pull off a little invasion, even if some of the details were worrisome. And the refusal of those in charge of the Walkerton water supply to ask for outside help once they realized there was a problem clearly illustrated the symptom of *closed-mindedness*. Another symptom, *pressures toward uniformity*, was evident in both these examples. In groupthink, group members may censor their own thoughts or act as "mindguards" to discourage deviant thoughts by other group members. During the planning of the Bay of Pigs invasion, the president's brother, Robert Kennedy, served as a mindguard and warned dissenting members to keep quiet. And, as we indicated earlier, when a vice president for engineering argued to delay launching the *Challenger*, he was told by a manager to take off his "engineering hat" and put on his "management hat." He switched hats, and his vote. In the end, this helped foster an illusion of unanimity because top-level managers at NASA never knew of all the dissent voiced by the engineers that morning.

When alternatives are not considered, the behavioural symptoms of groupthink can result in the defective decision making outlined in Figure 8.6. In turn, a defective decision-making process increases the likelihood that a group will make bad decisions.

FIGURE 8.6

Charting the Course of Groupthink

Irving Janis depicted groupthink as a kind of social disease, complete with antecedents, symptoms, and long-term consequences. *(Based on Janis, 1982.)*

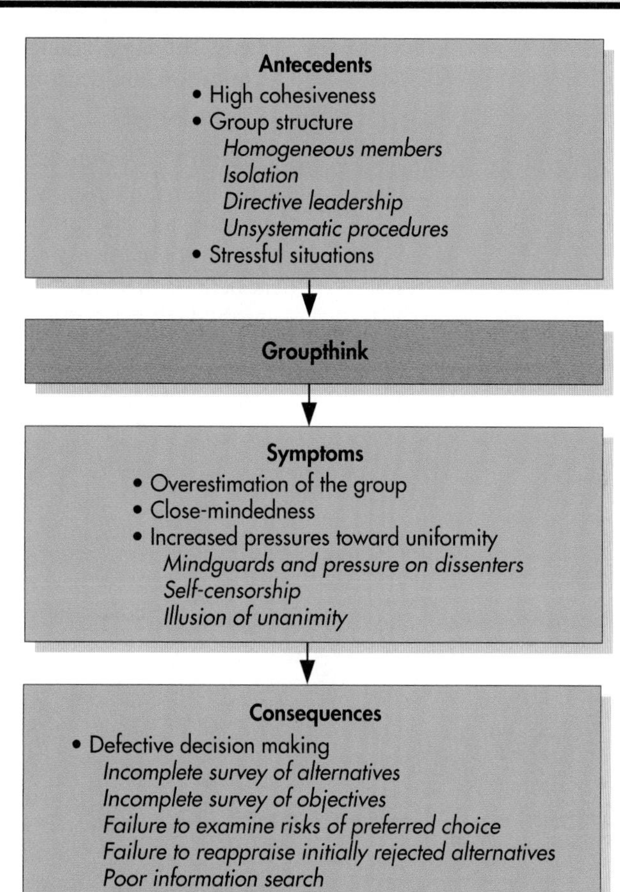

Research on Groupthink Groupthink is a rather distinctive theory in social psychology. On the one hand, its impact has been unusually broad: It is discussed in a variety of disciplines outside psychology, including business, political science, and communication, and it has spawned numerous workshops as well as a best-selling management training video. Yet, on the other hand, there is not a great deal of empirical support for the model, certainly not in proportion to its fame. This may be partly due to the difficulty of experimentally testing such a broad set of variables in high-pressure group settings. However, research has been conducted on various aspects of Janis's model, typically through case studies and historical analyses of groups and organizational settings around the world, and some experimental research has been done as well (Eaton, 2001; Esser, 1998).

Some researchers disagree with Janis about the specific conditions that make groups vulnerable to groupthink (Choi & Kim, 1999; Kramer, 1998; 't Hart et al., 1995; Tetlock, 1998; Whyte, 1998). But when multiple antecedents of groupthink are evident simultaneously, such as high cohesiveness, a strong and controlling leader, and a great deal of stress, groups are particularly vulnerable to the kinds of faulty decision making that Janis described (Esser, 1998; Mullen et al., 1994).

Preventing Groupthink To guard against groupthink, Janis urged groups to make an active effort to process information more carefully and accurately. He recommended that decision-making groups use the following strategies:

- To avoid isolation, groups should consult widely with outsiders.
- To reduce conformity pressures, leaders should explicitly encourage criticism and not take a strong stand early in the group discussion.
- To establish a strong norm of critical review, subgroups should separately discuss the same issue, a member should be assigned to play devil's advocate and question all decisions and ideas, and a "second chance" meeting should be held to reconsider the group decision before taking action.

Recent research has shown empirical support for the effectiveness of some strategies in curtailing groupthink tendencies. These include inserting someone in the group to play the role of a "reminder" who is responsible for informing the group about the dangers of biased decision making; making individual group members believe that they will be held personally responsible for the outcome of their group's decisions; increasing the diversity of group members; and creating a group norm encouraging critical thinking and discouraging the search for concurrence (Kroon et al., 1991; Postmes et al., 2001; Schultz et al., 1995; 't Hart, 1998). And computer-based technology can be used during meetings to help avoid groupthink (Miranda, 1994). Table 8.2 lists some of the ways in which computerized *group support systems*, in which groups use specialized, interactive computer programs to guide their meetings, can enhance group decision making.

"On second thought, don't correct me if I'm wrong."

A controlling leader who discourages disagreement can promote groupthink, leading to bad decisions.

In recent research, Laura Kray and Adam Galinsky (2003; Liljenquist et al., 2004) point to the effectiveness of encouraging groups to engage in counterfactual thinking, which, as discussed in Chapter 4, involves imagining alternative events or outcomes that might have occurred but did not. In a set of clever experiments, Kray and Galinsky had groups of students discuss and make decisions about a problem that was modeled after the space shuttle *Challenger* disaster. To prevent participants from realizing what the case was really about, details were changed so that the problem was whether or not a race car team should go ahead with a race despite cold weather, which could affect car engines. Prior to making decisions about this scenario, however, groups were exposed to a different, unrelated scenario, which for some groups was designed so that the groups would easily imagine a desired, counterfactual alternative outcome. Kray and Galinsky found that the groups primed to think of counterfactuals were much more likely than the other groups to seek disconfirmatory information when discussing whether to go ahead with the race, and as a result their decisions were much more accurate. Two-thirds of the groups primed with counterfactual thinking made the correct decision to pull out of the race, whereas fewer than a quarter of the groups not primed did so.

Group Performance: Are More Heads Better than One?

Group polarization and groupthink are examples of how groups can go wrong, ending up with attitudes that are too extreme and decisions that are seriously flawed. But aren't two, or more, heads generally better than one? How does the performance of a group compare with the performance of the same number of people working individually? Researchers investigating this question have uncovered a number of important factors that affect group performance, as we will see in the sections that follow.

TABLE 8.2

How Computerized Group Support Systems Help Groups Avoid Groupthink

1. Allow group members to raise their concerns anonymously through the computer interface, enabling them to risk challenging group consensus without fear of direct attacks
2. Reduce the directive role of the leader
3. Enable group members to provide input simultaneously, so they don't have to wait for a chance to raise their ideas
4. Allow the least assertive group members to state their ideas as easily as the most dominating
5. Provide a systematic agenda of information gathering and decision making
6. Keep the focus in the group meetings on the ideas themselves rather than on the people and relationships within the group

(Based on Miranda, 1994.)

Types of Tasks and Process Loss According to Ivan Steiner (1972), how a group's performance compares to the potential of its individuals depends on the type of task. For instance, on an *additive* task, the group product is the *sum* of all the members' contributions. Donating to a charity is an additive task, and so is making noise at a pep rally. As we have seen, people often indulge in social loafing during additive tasks. Even so, groups usually outperform a single individual. Each member's contribution may be less than it would be if that person worked alone, but the group total is still greater than what could be provided by one person.

On a *conjunctive* task, the group product is determined by the individual with the *poorest* performance. Mountain-climbing teams are engaged in such a task; the "weakest link" will determine their success or failure. Because of this vulnerability to the poor performance of a single group member, group performance on conjunctive tasks tends to be worse than the performance of a single, average individual.

Just as the strength of a chain depends on its weakest link, the group product of a conjunctive task is determined by the individual with the poorest performance. In mountain climbing, for example, if one person slips or falls, the whole team is endangered.

On a *disjunctive* task, the group product is (or can be) determined by the performance of the individual with the *best* performance. Trying to solve a problem or develop a strategy is a disjunctive task: What the group needs is a single successful idea, regardless of the number of failures. In principle, groups have an edge on individuals in the performance of disjunctive tasks: The more people involved, the more likely it is that someone will make a breakthrough. In practice, however, group processes can interfere with coming up with ideas and getting them accepted—a phenomenon that Steiner called **process loss**.

Process loss is not restricted to disjunctive tasks. It can result from lack of motivation, as in social loafing on additive tasks. Lack of coordination can also cause process loss, as when the group is slowed down by weaker members on conjunctive tasks. On disjunctive tasks, groups may not realize which group members have the best ideas or are most expert. Unless the best solution for a particular problem is easily identifiable once it has been suggested, the group may fail to implement it; as a result, the group performs worse than its best members (Gigone & Hastie, 1997; Laughlin & Ellis, 1986; Stasser et al., 1995; Stasson & Bradshaw, 1995). Have you

process loss The reduction in group performance due to obstacles created by group processes, such as problems of coordination and motivation.

ever had the experience of *knowing* you had the right idea but being unable to convince others in your group until it was too late? If so, then you have experienced first-hand the problem of process loss on a disjunctive task. Fortunately, as groups gain experience with each other, they can become better at recognizing and utilizing the expertise of their members (Bonner et al., 2002; Henry et al., 1996).

On some kinds of tasks, groups can even show *process gain*, in which they outperform even the best members. Of course, the expectation of process gain is one of the key reasons to work in groups in the first place, but as we have seen, there are many obstacles in the way. Patrick Laughlin and his colleagues (2002) propose that groups can perform better than the best individuals on tasks in which the correct answer is clearly evident to everyone in the group once it is presented and in which the work can be divided up so that various subgroups work on different aspects of the task.

Setting Goals Groups, like individuals, tend to perform better on a task when they have specific, challenging, and reachable goals—particularly if the group members are committed to the goals and believe they have the ability to achieve them. Such goals are generally more effective than "do your best" goals or no goals at all (Locke & Latham, 2002; Wegge, 2000). You've probably worked in many groups in which the goal was simply to "do your best." Despite the popularity of such goals, the research clearly shows that they are not as effective as specific goals. As Edwin Locke and Gary Latham (2002) concluded from their review of 35 years' worth of studies, "When people are asked to do their best, they do not do so" (p. 706). People are indeed capable of better than their vaguely defined "best." Even specific goals can lead to underperformance, however, if the goals are set too low. Verlin Hinsz (1995) found that the goals selected by groups tend to be less ambitious than those selected by individuals. Social loafing may provide a partial explanation for this outcome. Even though groups tend to set less ambitious goals than individuals, when groups do set goals, they typically perform much better than groups that do not (O'Leary-Kelly et al., 1994). Moreover, as group members gain more experience with their tasks and with each other, they begin to set more challenging goals (Forsyth, 1999; Harkins & Lowe, 2000).

Brainstorming: Coming Up with Ideas During the 1950s, advertising executive Alex Osborn developed a technique called **brainstorming**, designed to enhance the creativity and productivity of problem-solving groups. The ground rules for brainstorming call for a freewheeling, creative approach:

- Express *all* ideas that come to mind, even if they sound crazy.
- The more ideas, the better.
- Don't worry whether the ideas are good or bad, and don't criticize anyone's ideas; they can be evaluated later.
- All ideas belong to the group, so members should feel free to build on each other's work.

Osborn (1953) claimed that by using these procedures, groups could generate more and better ideas than could individuals working alone. The gimmick caught on. Brainstorming was soon a popular exercise in business, government, and education; and it remains so today. But when the research caught up with the hype, it turned out that Osborn's faith in the group process was unfounded. In fact, "nominal groups" (several individuals working alone) produce a greater number of better ideas than do real groups in which members interact with each other. Brainstorming can indeed be effective, but people brainstorming individually produce more and higher-quality ideas than the same number of people brainstorming together. One meta-analysis concluded that brainstorming groups are only about half as productive as an equal number of individuals working alone (Mullen et al., 1991). Rather than being inspired by each other and building on each other's ideas, people

brainstorming A technique that attempts to increase the production of creative ideas by encouraging group members to speak freely without criticizing their own or others' contributions.

brainstorming in a group underperform (Nijstad et al., 2003; Paulus & Brown, 2003).

The top half of Table 8.3 presents several possible explanations that have been proposed for why brainstorming is ineffective. It's particularly ironic, then, that people who engage in group brainstorming typically think that it works wonderfully. Despite the research evidence, brainstorming is still a popular device in many organizations. People who participate in interactive brainstorming groups evaluate their own performance more favourably than do individuals in nominal groups. They also enjoy themselves more. And those who have not participated in an interactive brainstorming group believe that such groups are highly productive. Both the experienced and the inexperienced cling to the illusion that group brainstorming is much better than individual brainstorming (Nijstad et al., 2003; Paulus & Brown, 2003).

TABLE 8.3

Brainstorming in Groups: Problems and Solutions

Factors That Reduce the Effectiveness of Group Brainstorming

- **Production blocking:** When people have to wait for their turn to speak, they may forget their ideas, may be too busy trying to remember their ideas to listen to others or to generate new ones, or may simply lose interest.
- **Free riding:** As others contribute ideas, individuals may feel less motivated to work hard themselves. They see their own contributions as less necessary or less likely to have much impact.
- **Evaluation apprehension:** In the presence of others, people may be hesitant to suggest wild, off-the-wall ideas for fear of looking foolish and being criticized. Even if they are willing to suggest such ideas, they may spend time preparing to justify them—time that they otherwise could have spent coming up with more ideas.
- **Performance matching:** Group members work only as hard as they see others work. Once the other three factors have reduced the performance of a brainstorming group, performance matching can help maintain this relatively inferior performance.

Why Electronic Brainstorming Is Effective

- Production blocking is reduced because members can type in ideas whenever they come to mind.
- Free riding can be reduced by having the computer keep track of each member's input.
- Evaluation apprehension is reduced because group members contribute their ideas anonymously.
- Performance matching is reduced because group members spend less time focusing on the performance of others as they type in their own ideas. In addition, performance matching is less of a problem because the initial performance of groups brainstorming electronically is likely to be high.
- Group members can benefit by seeing the ideas of others, which can inspire new ideas that they might not otherwise have considered.

Group brainstorming may indeed benefit the group in indirect ways—for example, it can be a fun experience that promotes good will and cohesion—but, as we have seen, its effect on idea generation is much poorer than most group members realize. One strategy to improve productivity while also promoting the enjoyment that group brainstorming can produce is to alternate brainstorming sessions, having members brainstorm together and then individually (Paulus & Brown, 2003). Another strategy is to use a facilitator trained to understand the factors that impair group brainstorming. The facilitator can cut people off who stray from the task, discourage evaluation, call on individuals to prevent them from free riding, and keep motivating them to do more ("Come on, a few more ideas and we break 50!"). Again, see the top half of Table 8.3 (Kramer et al., 2001).

People brainstorming as a group come up with a greater number of better ideas than the same number of people working individually. **False.**

Computers offer a new and promising way to improve group brainstorming. Electronic brainstorming combines the freedom of working alone at a computer with the stimulation of receiving the ideas of others on a screen. The bottom of Table 8.3 presents some of the factors that make this type of brainstorming effective. The research on electronic brainstorming is encouraging, suggesting that interactive groups often perform about as well as nominal groups, and—in some situations, such as when the group is relatively large—may even perform better than nominal groups (Dennis & Williams, 2003). Brainstorming may have found its true home in a technology that Osborn could have only dreamed about a half century before.

"A committee should consist of three men, two of whom are absent."

—Hebert Beerbohm Tree

Biased Sampling and Communication: Getting Ideas on the Table Brainstorming stresses the need for creativity. On some tasks, however, simply sharing information is crucial for good performance. Unfortunately, as Garold Stasser (1992; Stasser et al., 2002) points out, not all the information available to individual members will necessarily be brought before the group. Rather, information that is known to many group members is more likely to enter the group discussion than information known to only one or a few group members. Imagine, for example, that your group is discussing which of several candidates should be supported in an election. You have read some potentially damaging personal information about one of the candidates, and you assume that the others are also aware of it. If you observe during group discussion that nobody else mentions this information, you may further assume that the others don't think the information is relevant or credible; so you may not mention it yourself. Stasser calls this process *biased sampling*. Because of biased sampling, a group may fail to consider important information that is not common knowledge in the group. Inadequately informed, the group may make a bad decision.

Recent research has discovered several conditions in which biased sampling is less likely to occur. When group members are aware that not everyone has access to the same information, they are more likely to share their information with the group (Schittekatte & van Hiel, 1996; Stasser & Birchmeier, 2003). Leaders who encourage a lot of group participation are more likely to elicit unshared (as well as shared) information during group discussions than are more directive leaders (Larson et al., 1998). In addition, when two group members know the uncommon information, it is more likely to be discussed and used by the rest of the group than if only one person knows this information, possibly because the other person can validate the information if it is brought up (Schittekatte & van Hiel, 1996). It is important, however, that group members who introduce new information are trusted and taken seriously. In one study, for example, Kathleen Propp (1995) found that when the unique information was presented by a woman, it was less likely to be used by the group to make decisions than if it was presented by a man.

As with so many aspects of group dynamics, the norms that develop in a group can play a crucial role in determining its effectiveness. Norms often exist about how and what the group communicates, such as whether the group members tend to reinforce or challenge the dominant ideas that have been expressed. Tom Postmes and others (2001) conducted an experiment in which they manipulated the establishment of group norms that promoted either consensus or critical thinking. They did this by having some groups work on creating a collage—a collective, creative task in which collaboration (consensus) was essential. Other groups worked on assessing a controversial campus policy to which the group members would be strongly opposed—a task that encouraged critical thinking. Although the group members would quickly agree on their opposition to this policy, the task fostered independent, critical analysis because each group member could contribute numerous arguments attacking this policy. The researchers presumed that working on these different types of tasks would create two different types of group norms, which would then carry over and influence a group's performance on a subsequent task.

For both types of groups, the subsequent task was evaluating a set of three candidates for a teaching position at the university. Within each group, each member received information about the candidates that all the other group members had, but each member also had information that the other members did not have. Previous studies using this task had shown that groups tend to discuss the shared but not the unshared information. But only if individuals brought the unshared information to the table could the group have enough information to realize that one candidate was clearly the best one for the job. If they relied only on shared information, they typically would reach an incorrect judgment.

As can be seen in Figure 8.7, when group members first received their information but had not discussed it with each other, they were very unlikely to make a correct decision. Only through a discussion of the unshared information could groups recognize the best candidate. But if groups focused only on shared information during their discussion, their chances of making the correct decision would not improve. This is what happened for the groups that had engaged first in the consensus-norm task. These groups did not discuss the unshared information much, so their post-discussion decisions were not significantly better than their pre-discussion decisions. But the groups that had engaged first in the task that promoted critical thinking were much more likely to make the correct decision after the discussion, because they discussed unshared information.

Other kinds of mindsets can also promote more thorough information sharing in groups. For instance, Adam Galinsky and Laura Kray (2004) found that priming some groups to think counterfactually—that is, to imagine alternative outcomes that easily could have happened but did not—prompted these groups to discuss unshared information, and to make the correct decision, significantly more often than the groups that were not primed.

FIGURE 8.7

Sharing Information in a Group: The Role of Group Norms

Groups that had been induced to establish a group norm of either consensus or critical thinking worked on a task in which they were to decide which of three candidates was best suited for a job. Each group member had some information about the candidates that everyone else also knew, but each also had unique information. Only by discussing the unshared as well as shared information would the group be likely to make a correct decision. Before getting the chance to have any discussion of the information, groups rarely chose the best-qualified candidate. But would their performance improve after they had a discussion? Relative to the consensus-norm groups, the critical-norm groups were much more likely to make the right decision after discussion because they were much more likely to bring the unshared information into their discussions. *(Postmes et al., 2001.)*

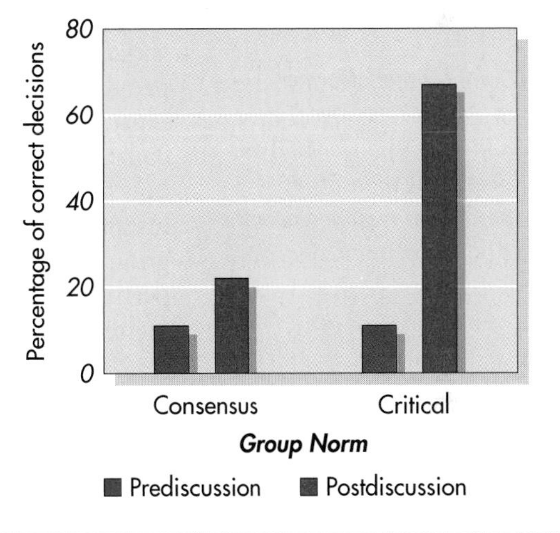

Escalation Effects A trap that can be very costly to organizations and businesses is known as the **escalation effect** (and is sometimes referred to as *entrapment*). Escalation effects occur when commitment to a failing course of action is increased to justify investments already made (Arkes & Ayton, 1999; Karlsson et al., 2002; Staw, 1997; Tan & Yates, 2002). Laboratory experiments show that groups are more likely to escalate commitment to a failing project, and are likely to do so in more extreme ways, than are individuals (Dietz-Uhler, 1996; Whyte, 1993). In numerous instances, groups, businesses, and governments have incurred huge costs because they kept throwing more money, time, and other resources into a project that should have been terminated long before. One example is British Columbia's escalation of its commitment to host a world's fair in 1986 despite rapidly growing budget deficits (from a projection of $6 million in 1978 to a projection of over $300 million in 1985) (Ross & Staw, 1986). Similarly, in 1999, the city of Toronto made a "deal" to lease computers for three years from MFP Financial Services Limited. While the original quote was for $43 million, taxpayers were outraged to discover that the final bill was for more than $80 million. And, to make matters worse, the inquiry into the resulting computer scandal cost *more than $19 million!*

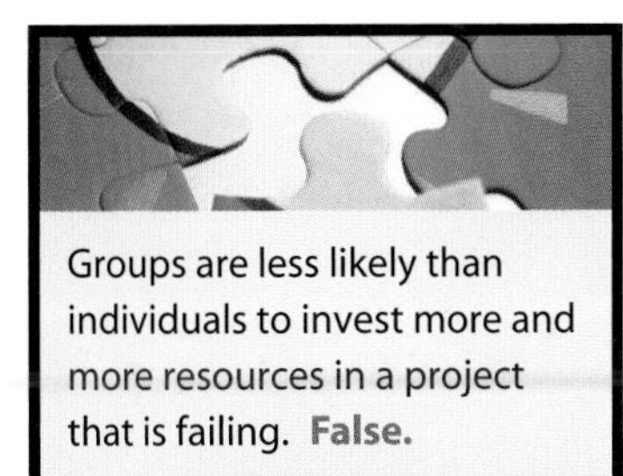

Groups are less likely than individuals to invest more and more resources in a project that is failing. **False.**

Information Processing Once a group has all the available information, group members must process that information and use it to make judgments or perform tasks. How well do groups process information, compared with individuals? In general, groups are susceptible to the same information-processing biases as individuals—only more so. For example, Chapter 4 reported people's tendency to fall prey to the base-rate fallacy—the tendency to underutilize numerical base rates, or probabilities, when making judgments and to rely instead on more vivid but less predictive information. Some research suggests that groups may exaggerate this individual bias (Argote et al., 1990). In reviewing the research on group information processing, Verlin Hinsz and others (1997) concluded, "If some bias, error, or tendency predisposes individuals to process information in a particular way, then groups exaggerate this tendency. However, if this bias, error, or tendency is unlikely

escalation effect The condition in which commitments to a failing course of action are increased to justify investments already made.

Dash Domi, brother of former Toronto Maple Leafs player Tie Domi and a salesman for MFP, was implicated in the sponsorship scandal. He was investigated for the alleged bribery of a city councillor.

among individuals processing the information (e.g., less than half the sample), then groups are even less likely to process information in this fashion" (pp. 49–50).

Groups can divide a large body of information into smaller portions and delegate different members to remember these more manageable portions, ideally by matching information to individuals based on their expertise and interest. This shared process is known as **transactive memory** and helps groups remember more information more efficiently than individuals (Austin, 2003; Lewis, 2003; Wegner et al., 1991). But process loss can occur in this domain as well. Some studies have found that the combined memory of individuals working alone surpasses the memory of groups working together. In other words, although five people remember more information than any one individual, if the five people work separately, their combined memory can exceed the memory of five people working collaboratively in a group (Basden et al., 1997; Weldon & Bellinger, 1997). And how groups delegate the information to each other may be inefficient or biased. For instance, Andrea Hollingshead and Samuel Fraidin (2003) found that, in mixed-sex groups, men and women tended to use gender stereotypes to infer differences in expertise for male and female group members and to assign information to group members accordingly.

"Nor is the people's judgment always true: The most may err as grossly as the few."
—John Dryden

In some domains, however, groups do tend to process information well. As we discussed earlier concerning biased sampling of information, groups can perform particularly well when working on problems whose solutions can be clearly demonstrated to group members and when dealing with complex tasks that require the use of multiple sources of information or evidence (Laughlin & Bonner, 1999; Laughlin et al., 2002). And just as individuals can learn and improve their skills over time, so can groups. As groups gain experience in production, for example, their productivity often improves significantly—particularly when group membership is stable (Argote et al., 1995).

Computer Technology and Group Support Systems Some of the obstacles that get in the way of good group discussion and decision making can be reduced through the use of interactive computer-mediated programs. Recently there has been an explosion of research on the use of such programs. Often referred to as *group support systems (GSSs)* or *group decision support systems (GDSSs)*, these programs help remove communication barriers and provide structure and incentives for group discussions and decisions. You may recall our earlier reference to the benefits of computer-mediated brainstorming (see Table 8.3). Many of the same benefits apply to information processing and discussion in groups. Multiple people can "speak" at the same time; they can read and be inspired by each other's ideas; and they can remain anonymous and yet still be held accountable for their individual input. Compared to groups employing more conventional face-to-face modes of discussion, groups that use these systems often do a better job of sampling infor-

transactive memory A shared system for remembering information that enables multiple people to remember information together more efficiently than they could alone.

mation, communicating, and arriving at good decisions (Froehle et al., 1999; Lam & Schaubroek, 2000; Postmes & Lea, 2000).

Students from schools in rural areas around Bangalore, India, get connected to the rest of the world as part of a program in November 2003, that gave 27 000 schoolchildren a chance to learn about the Internet. As new technology allows more and more diverse groups to communicate and work together, it is more important than ever that groups learn how to utilize the great benefits and minimize the costs of diversity in group processes.

Diversity As we begin the twenty-first century, groups around the world, whether in schools, organizations, businesses, sports, arts, or governments, are becoming increasingly diverse, most obviously in terms of sex, race, ethnicity, and cultural background. How does diversity affect group performance? How can a group best use diversity to its advantage? The answers to such questions—and even the meaning of *diversity*—are likely to change as society changes in terms of its demographics and attitudes. Thus, the issues surrounding diversity are particularly challenging. In the meantime, though, a great deal of new research is addressing these issues, and some tentative conclusions can be offered.

The evidence from empirical research concerning the effects of diversity on group performance is decidedly mixed. Diversity often is associated with negative group dynamics (Levine & Moreland, 1998; Maznevski, 1994). Miscommunications and misunderstandings are more likely to arise among heterogeneous group members, causing frustration and resentment and damaging group performance by weakening coordination, morale, and commitment to the group. Cliques often form in diverse groups, causing some group members to feel alienated (Jackson et al., 1995; Maznevski, 1994). And even if diversity doesn't appear to hurt a group in any objective way, group members may *think* that it does. For example, S. Gayle Baugh and George Graen (1997) compared how diverse and homogeneous project teams rated their own effectiveness. Project teams that were diverse in terms of gender and race rated themselves as less effective—even though external evaluators judged the diverse teams to be no less effective than the homogeneous teams.

Research has also demonstrated positive effects of diversity. Diversity can give a group flexibility, creativity, and the ability to succeed on tasks that require innovative approaches (Levine & Moreland, 1998; Nemeth & Nemeth-Brown, 2003; Paulus, 2000). As more and more organizations try to attract customers and investors from diverse cultures, diversity in personnel should offer more and more advantages. In one study, for example, ethnically diverse groups and all-white groups brainstormed to come up with ideas to get more tourists to visit the United States, a topic that the researchers chose for its relevance to diversity. The ideas produced by the ethnically diverse groups were judged to be more effective and feasible than the ideas produced by the all-white groups (McLeod et al., 1996).

In reviewing the literature on diversity and group performance, Martha Maznevski (1994) concluded that diversity can enhance a group's performance if the group is integrated. Heterogeneity is not as likely to help a group if there are many cliques, if there is little communication or equal-status interaction among the diverse group members, and if there is a lack of shared identity. Maznevski proposes that strategies to improve communication can promote true integration of diverse group members, which should help groups reap the benefits that diversity can offer.

William Swann and his colleagues (2003) note that people often think that for diversity in groups to work, group members must de-emphasize their individuality and instead emphasize their commonality as group members. Although there is some value to this idea, it also clashes with one of the fundamental reasons to encourage diversity in the first place! According to Swann and his colleagues, diversity in small groups is more likely to succeed when individuals feel that their personal identity is verified and accepted by the other group members.

Cooperation, Competition, and Conflict: Responding to Differences

The importance of group performance is crystal clear for some of the crucial issues confronting our world today. What determines whether people will act responsibly to protect the environment? What factors contribute to the escalation of conflict? Are there ways to reduce conflict once it has started? For answers to these questions, both individual characteristics and group processes must be considered. Here, we describe individual and group influences on cooperation, competition, and conflict. When there are differences between us, how do we respond?

Mixed Motives and Social Dilemmas

Imagine that you have to choose between cooperating with others in your group and pursuing your own self-interests, which can hurt the others. Examples of these mixed-motive situations are everywhere. An actor in a play may be motivated to try to "steal" a scene, a basketball player may be inclined to hog the ball, an executive may want to keep more of the company's profits, a family member may want to eat more than her fair share of the leftover birthday cake, and a citizen of the Earth may want to use more than his fair share of finite, valuable resources. In each case, the individual can gain something by pursuing his or her self-interests; but if everyone in the group pursues self-interests, all of the group members will ultimately be worse off than if they had cooperated with each other. Each option, therefore, has possible benefits along with potential costs. When you are in a situation like this, you may feel torn between wanting to cooperate and wanting to compete, and these mixed motives create a difficult dilemma. What do you do?

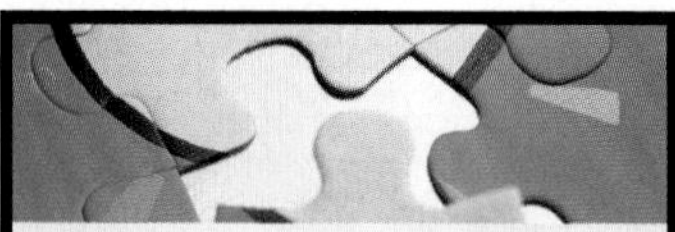

Large groups are more likely than small groups to exploit a scarce resource that the members collectively depend on. **True.**

The notion that the pursuit of self-interest can sometimes be self-destructive forms the basis for what is called a **social dilemma**. In a social dilemma, what is good for one is bad for all. If everyone makes the most self-rewarding choice, everyone suffers the greatest loss. This section examines how people resolve the tension between their cooperative and competitive inclinations in social dilemmas.

The Prisoner's Dilemma We begin with a detective story. Two partners in crime are picked up by the police for questioning. Although the police believe they have committed a major offence, there is only enough evidence to convict them on a minor charge. In order to sustain a conviction for the more serious crime, the police will have to convince one of them to testify against the other. Separated during questioning, the criminals weigh their alternatives (see Figure 8.8). If neither confesses, they will both get light sentences on the minor charge. If both confess and plead guilty, they will both receive moderate sentences. But if one confesses and the other stays silent, the confessing criminal will secure immunity from prosecution while the silent criminal will pay the maximum penalty.

social dilemma A situation in which a self-interested choice by everyone creates the worst outcome for everyone.

prisoner's dilemma A type of dilemma in which one party must make either cooperative or competitive moves in relation to another party; typically designed in such a way that competitive moves are more beneficial to either side, but if both sides make competitive moves, they are both worse off than if they both cooperated.

This story forms the basis for the research paradigm known as the **prisoner's dilemma**. In the two-person prisoner's dilemma, participants are given a series of choices in which they have the option of cooperating or competing with each other, but either option has potential costs. Consider an example: Imagine that you're Prisoner A in Figure 8.8. It appears that no matter what Prisoner B does, you're better off if you compete with B and confess. If B doesn't confess to the police (in other words, if he cooperates with you), you get a lighter sentence if you do confess (you'd get no jail time) than if you don't confess (you'd get 1 year in jail). If B does confess, you still get a lighter sentence if you confess than if you don't—5 versus 10 years. So, clearly, you should confess, right? But here's the dilemma: If you *both* confess, each of you gets 5 years. If *neither* of you confesses, each of you gets only 1 year. It's really a perplexing situation. What do you think you would do?

FIGURE 8.8

The Prisoner's Dilemma

In the original prisoner's dilemma, from which the game took its name, each of two criminals is offered immunity from prosecution in exchange for a confession. If both stay silent, both get off with a light sentence on a minor charge (upper left). If both confess, both receive a moderate sentence (lower right). But if one confesses while the other stays mum, the confessing criminal goes free and the silent one spends a long time in jail.

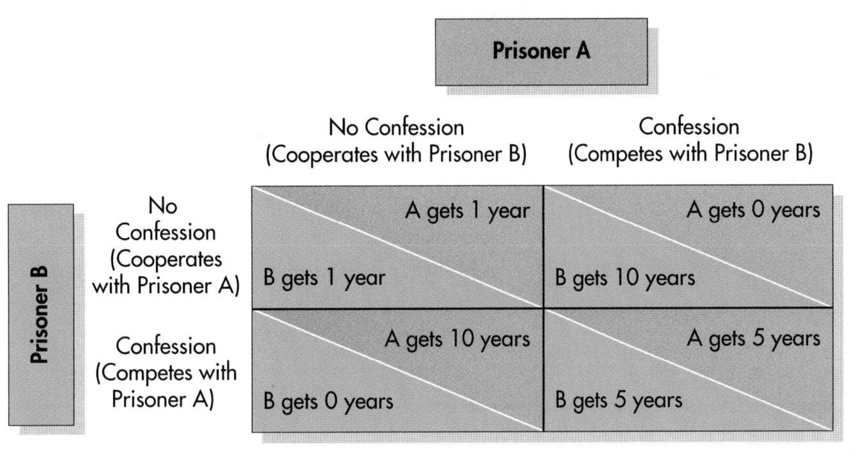

This kind of social dilemma is not limited to situations involving only two individuals at a time. Imagine, for example, being in a burning building or a sinking ship. Everyone might want to race for the exit or the lifeboats as quickly as possible and push others out of the way; but if everyone does that, more people will die in the panic. More lives will be saved if people leave in an orderly fashion. Soldiers engaged in combat may be better off individually if they take no chances and duck for cover, but if their comrades did the same thing, they all would be slaughtered by the enemy. Nations face such dilemmas as well. Two countries locked in an arms race would be better off if they stopped spending money and resources on weapons of mass destruction, but neither country wants to risk falling behind the other (Dawes, 1980).

By now, thousands of participants in research on the prisoner's dilemma have confronted various versions of this mixed-motive problem. One strategy that many people eventually adopt over the course of multiple trials is known as *tit-for-tat*—a reciprocal strategy in which cooperation by one elicits cooperation by the other, while competition by one provokes competition by the other. This strategy tends to result in relatively positive joint outcomes for the people involved in the dilemma, eliciting higher levels of cooperation than most other strategies (Au & Komorita, 2002; Axelrod, 1984; Pruitt, 1998). But cooperation and competitiveness are not equally powerful. Competitiveness is a very strong determinant of reciprocity. Once one party makes a competitive move, the other party is highly likely to follow suit (Kelley & Stahelski, 1970). In contrast, a cooperative move may not elicit cooperation: People who are consistently and unconditionally cooperative can be exploited and taken advantage of (Komorita et al., 1993). A case in point is when British Prime Minister Neville Chamberlain tried to prevent war in the 1930s by cooperating with Hitler; this behaviour only gave Hitler the opportunity to become more aggressive.

Would you like to try participating in a prisoner's dilemma game online? Some Web sites offer a chance for you to do this. To find them, search for "Prisoner's dilemma" in a search engine.

An alternative to simple reciprocity that is often successful is *win-stay, lose-shift*—a strategy consistent with basic learning principles and conditioning. Using this strategy, individuals continue to compete or cooperate as long as the payoff they receive is high, but they shift to the opposite action whenever the payoff is low (Kraines & Kraines, 1995; Nowak & Sigmund, 1993).

Resource Dilemmas The prisoner's dilemma sets up a trap for those who play it: Attempts to gain an advantage will backfire if the other party also makes the competitive choice. This conflict of motives also forms the basis for another category of social dilemmas: **resource dilemmas**, which concern how two or more people

resource dilemmas Social dilemmas concerning how two or more people share a limited resource.

share a limited resource. Resource dilemmas come in two basic types: (1) commons dilemmas and (2) public goods dilemmas.

The *commons dilemma* is a situation in which, if people take as much as they want of a limited resource that does not replenish itself, nothing will be left for anyone. Robyn Dawes (1980) called this situation the *take-some dilemma,* one popular version of which is known as the "tragedy of the commons" (Hardin, 1968). In earlier times, people would let their animals graze on the town's lush, grassy commons. But if all the animals grazed to their hearts' content, and to their owners' benefit, the commons would be stripped, the animals' food supply diminished, and the owners' welfare threatened. Today, the tragedy of the commons is a clear and present danger on a global scale. Deforestation, air pollution, ocean dumping, massive irrigation, over-fishing, commercial development of wilderness areas, a rapidly increasing population in some developing countries, and an over-consuming population in the richest nations—all pit individual self-interest against the common good. Selfish responses to commons dilemmas are social sins of commission; people take too much.

In *public goods dilemmas,* all of the individuals are supposed to contribute resources to a common pool. Examples of these public goods include the blood supply, public broadcasting, schools, libraries, roads, and parks. If no one gives, the service can't continue (Olson, 1965). If club members don't pay their dues or contribute their time, the club will fail. Again, private gain conflicts with the public good.

TABLE 8.4

Solving Social Dilemmas

Behaviour in a social dilemma is influenced by both psychological factors and structural arrangements. The characteristics listed here contribute to the successful solution of social dilemmas.

Psychological Factors

- Individual and cultural differences
  - Having a prosocial, cooperative orientation
  - Trusting others
  - Being a member of a collectivistic culture
- Situational factors
  - Being in a good mood
  - Having had successful experience managing resources and working cooperatively
  - Seeing unselfish models
  - Having reason to expect others to cooperate
- Group dynamics
  - Acting as an individual rather than in a group
  - Being in a small group rather than in a large group
  - Sharing a social identity or superordinate goals

Structural Arrangements

- Creating a payoff structure that rewards cooperative behaviour and/or punishes selfish behaviour
- Removing resources from the public domain and handing them over to private ownership
- Establishing an authority to control the resources

Solving Social Dilemmas

When does individual desire prevail in social dilemmas? When, in contrast, do people see beyond their own immediate potential for gain and consider the long-term benefits of cooperation? Social dilemmas pose a serious threat to the quality of life and even to life itself. How do people try to solve them? What factors make them more or less cooperative when faced with these dilemmas? There is a huge body of research on these questions. Table 8.4 summarizes some of the factors that extensive research has identified as facilitating the best solutions to social dilemmas.

For example, many investigators have found that although people around the world are susceptible to exploiting each other in social dilemmas, there are individual and cultural differences that predict whether one is more or less likely to resolve social dilemmas in cooperative ways. One individual difference concerns people's social value orientations. People with a *prosocial, cooperative* orientation seek to maximize joint gains, those with an *individualist* orientation seek to maximize their own gain, and those with a *competitive* orientation seek to maximize their own gain relative to that of others. People with a cooperative orientation are less likely to behave in a competitive, resource-consuming fashion than are people with individualistic or competitive orientations (De Cremer & van Lange, 2001; Joireman et al., 2003; Parks et al., 2003; Rusbult & van Lange, 2003).

Groups tend to be more competitive in mixed-motive situations than individuals. The competitiveness of groups has its roots in fear and greed—the fear that the other group will exploit one's own group and the greedy desire to maximize the outcomes achieved by one's own group at the other group's expense. Individuals, too, can be driven by fear and greed, but competition between groups intensifies such motives. Another reason why groups are more competitive than individuals is that group members feel less identifiable by members of the other group. The greater anonymity that a group offers frees individual group members to act in a self-interested, aggressive manner (Wildschut et al., 2003). This is one reason why large groups are more likely to exploit scarce resources than are small ones (Pruitt, 1998; Seijts & Latham, 2000).

The fact remains that social dilemmas also involve very large groups—a city, a province, a nation, the whole world. In these circumstances, the structural factors we have listed in Table 8.4 may be most appropriate. The importance of resolving social dilemmas well is crucial for maintaining the quality of our lives, both immediately but even more so for the future. Understanding the psychological and structural factors that affect groups' behaviours when confronted with these dilemmas is therefore one of the most vital contributions that social psychological research can make.

Conflict Escalation

Social dilemmas can create important conflicts between groups, and how groups resolve these dilemmas can make the difference between war and peace. There are, of course, many other sources of conflict between groups. The very fact that groups differ from each other on any of a number of dimensions—religious, ethnic, racial, cultural, political—can spark conflict. Again and again, throughout human history, differences between groups explode in hatred and bloodshed. What fans the flames of an escalating conflict? And what can extinguish these flames? We address these questions in the remaining sections of the chapter.

Conflicts between groups are caused by many factors, including competition for scarce resources, stereotypes and prejudice, and competing ideologies. But once a conflict is in place, it can feed on itself. Indeed, *conflict spirals* are frequent, as one party annoys the other party, who retaliates, prompting a more extreme reaction from the first party, and so on (Brett et al., 1998; Rubin et al., 1994). Table 8.5 lists several factors that contribute to conflict escalation. The first three concern group processes discussed earlier in the chapter. The fourth one, concerning the capacity to use threat, may seem more surprising.

Threat Capacity It seems obvious that the ability to punish someone who engages in a prohibited behaviour can act as a deterrent to conflict escalation. You're less likely to mess with someone who can mess right back with you. If both parties hold their fire, a balance of terror can work. But having the capacity to attack can present an irresistible temptation to do so.

A classic study conducted by Morton Deutsch and Robert Krauss (1960) makes the point. These investigators had pairs of female participants engage in a simulated work environment in which each was in charge of a trucking company carrying merchandise over a road to a specific destination. Because they had to share parts of the road, they had to coordinate their efforts. However, in one condition of the

Group conflict is tragically hard to stop. After Israeli and Palestinian leaders reached an agreement at a crisis summit held in Egypt in October 2000 to end the spiral of violence, many ignored the calls to stop the daily clashes. In the midst of the fighting depicted here, a boy is shot in the stomach.

study, one of the women in each pair had the capacity to take control of the road and block the other's progress, which would increase her own profit and reduce the other participant's profit. In another condition, both participants in each pair had this capacity. What was the result?

In general, when a participant had the ability to block the other, she did—and both participants suffered. Overall, participants earned more money if neither could block the other than if one of them could, and when *both* members of the pair could block the other, the participants earned least of all. These results suggest that once coercive means are available, people tend to use them, even when doing so damages their own outcomes.

Perceptions of the Other The fifth factor listed in Table 8.5 calls to mind our earlier discussion of stereotypes and prejudice, including the favouring of ingroups over outgroups (see Chapter 5). During conflict, the opposing group and its members are often perceived as "the other"—strange, foreign, alien. They are characterized in simplistic, exaggerated ways. Held at a psychological distance, the other becomes a screen on which it is possible to project one's worst fears. Indeed, groups often see each other as *mirror images:* They see in their enemies what their enemies see in them. As Urie Bronfenbrenner (1961) discovered when he visited the former Soviet Union during the cold war, the Soviets saw Americans as aggressive, exploitative, and untrustworthy—just as the Americans saw them. The same is true of Israelis and Palestinians today.

Taken to extremes, negative views of the other can result in *dehumanization*, the perception that people lack human qualities or are "subhuman." Jeroen Vaes, Jacques-Philippe Leyens, and others call this *infrahumanization* and propose that it plays an important role in intergroup prejudice and conflict (Leyens et al., 2004; Vaes et al., 2003). Based on malicious stereotypes about outgroups, dehumanization is both a consequence of hostility between groups and an incitement to intergroup conflict (Bandura, 2002; Opotow, 2001). Aggression against the outgroup is justified by dehumanization, which is used to excuse more aggression, which requires more dehumanization to justify, and so on. As the Nazis began the Holocaust, they released propaganda that characterized Jews as less than human—as rats that spread disease and needed to be exterminated. Dehumanization is the ultimate version of "us"

TABLE 8.5

Factors That Promote and Sustain the Escalation of Between-Group Conflict

- The group polarization process, which increases the extremity of group members' attitudes and opinions
- Pressures for conformity, such as group cohesiveness and groupthink, which make it difficult for individuals to oppose the group's increasingly aggressive position
- Escalation of commitment, which seeks to justify past investments through the commitment of additional resources
- Premature use of threat capacity, which triggers aggressive retaliation
- Negative perceptions of "the other," which promote acceptance of aggressive behaviour and enhance cohesiveness of the ingroup "us" against the outgroup "them"

versus "them," removing all religious and ethical constraints against the taking of human life. As George Orwell (1942) discovered during the Spanish Civil War, the cure for dehumanization is to restore the human connection. Sighting an enemy soldier holding up his trousers with both hands while running beside a nearby trench, Orwell was unable to take the easy shot: "I had come here to shoot at 'Fascists'; but a man who is holding up his trousers isn't a 'Fascist,' he is visibly a fellow creature, similar to yourself, and you don't feel like shooting at him" (p. 254).

Negotiations are both important and complex, involving nations with different resources, needs, relationships, and cultures. This highlights the usefulness of social psychological research, which has specified a number of factors that can make negotiations more or less likely to succeed.

Reducing Conflict

With all the forces pressing it forward (see Table 8.5 for a summary), conflict escalation is hardly surprising. In this section, we examine the kind of sustained effort that peacemaking requires.

GRIT Every once in a while, individual leaders try to break the gridlock of intergroup conflict by taking a unilateral step toward peace. Egyptian President Anwar Sadat flew to Jerusalem uncertain of the reception he would receive; Soviet General Secretary Mikhail Gorbachev withdrew Soviet forces from Afghanistan before meeting with US President Ronald Reagan in Moscow. The notion that unilateral concessions can reverse an escalating conflict is central to a peacemaking strategy developed by Charles Osgood (1962): **graduated and reciprocated initiatives in tension-reduction (GRIT)**.

To see how GRIT works, imagine that two groups, A and B, are in conflict. (1) The members of group A state their intention to reduce conflict, announce a few tension-reducing initiatives, and invite the other side to reciprocate. (2) Group A carries out these initiatives, putting public pressure on group B to respond cooperatively. (3) If group B makes a cooperative move, group A quickly reciprocates with a move that risks at least as much as—and, if possible, more than—group B's cooperative behaviour. (4) Group A maintains a retaliatory capability in order to deter exploitation by group B. If group B attacks, group A retaliates at precisely the same level. Once it has retaliated, it resumes its unilateral tension-reducing efforts.

Reciprocal, tit-for-tat strategies like GRIT are maximally responsive: Cooperation is met with cooperation, attack with attack. Because the other party is given a greater sense of control over the interaction, the perceived risk of being cooperative is reduced. GRIT also prevents exploitation by allowing for retaliation if it is necessary and avoids conflict escalation by keeping retaliatory actions within the level established by the other party. But GRIT is not simply reactive. It patiently, persistently, and proactively seeks peace. Research on GRIT is encouraging; even people with a competitive orientation tend to respond cooperatively to this strategy, and the positive effects of GRIT can be enduring (Lindskold & Han, 1988; Stone et al., 1996). These findings also suggest that it is not necessary to like an opponent to cooperate on various ventures. Instead, the essential elements are establishing at least a minimal level of trust and recognizing that one's own interests will benefit.

graduated and reciprocated initiatives in tension-reduction (GRIT) A strategy for unilateral, persistent efforts to establish trust and cooperation between opposing parties.

Negotiating Unilateral concessions are useful for beginning the peace process, but extended negotiations are usually required to reach a final agreement. Negotiations on complex issues such as nuclear arms control and international environmental protection, as well as efforts to make peace in volatile regions such as the Middle East, often go on for years or even decades.

But negotiations are not restricted to the international scene. Unions and management engage in collective bargaining to establish employee contracts. Divorcing couples negotiate the terms of their divorce, by themselves or through their lawyers. Dating couples negotiate about which movie to attend. Families negotiate about who does which annoying household chores. Indeed, negotiations occur whenever there is a conflict that the parties wish to resolve without getting into an open fight or relying on an imposed legal settlement. There is an immense amount of research on negotiation and bargaining (Bazerman et al., 2000; De Dreu & Carnevale, 2003; Lewicki et al., 1999). Here, we focus on those findings most relevant to conflict reduction.

Conflicts can be reduced through successful negotiation. But what constitutes success in this context? Perhaps the most common successful outcome is a 50-50 compromise. Here, the negotiators start at extreme positions and gradually work toward a mutually acceptable midpoint. Some negotiators, however, achieve an even higher level of success. Most negotiations are not simply fixed-sum situations in which each side must give up something until a middle point is reached. Instead, there often exist ways in which both sides can benefit (Bazerman & Neale, 1992). When an **integrative agreement** is reached, both parties obtain outcomes that are superior to a 50-50 split.

Take, for instance, the tale of the orange and the two sisters (Follett, 1942). One sister wanted the juice to drink; the other wanted the peel for a cake. So they sliced the orange in half and each one took her portion. These sisters suffered from an advanced case of the *"fixed-pie" syndrome.* They assumed that whatever one of them won, the other lost. In fact, however, each of them could have had the whole thing: all of the juice for one, all of the peel for the other. An integrative agreement was well within their grasp, but they failed to see it. Unfortunately, research indicates that this happens all too often. Leigh Thompson and Dennis Hrebec (1996) conducted a meta-analysis of 32 experiments and found that in over 20 percent of negotiations that could have resulted in integrative agreements, the participants agreed to settlements that were worse for both sides. The ability to achieve integrative agreements is an acquired skill: Experienced negotiators obtain them more often than do inexperienced ones (Thompson, 1990).

What are the characteristics of experienced negotiators? Negotiators who can appear both flexible and strong are particularly successful. (McGillicuddy et al., 1984; Nemeth & Brilmayer, 1987). Two other key elements are communicating and trying to understand the point of view of the other person. It is always difficult for participants in a dispute to listen carefully to each other and to reach some reasonable understanding of each other's perspective. Communication difficulties are especially likely during negotiations between individuals and groups from different cultures (Carnevale & Leung, 2001; Gelfand & Brett, 2003). Table 8.6 lists some common assumptions made by negotiators from western countries that are not always shared by representatives from other cultures (Kimmel, 1994, 2000). If negotiators are not aware of these kinds of cross-cultural differences, the inevitable misunderstandings may prevent them from achieving a successful outcome. Interestingly, negotiators from collectivist cultures tend to achieve better joint outcomes than do negotiators from individualist cultures (Arunachalam et al., 1998; Gelfand & Christakopoulou, 1999). In addition to culture, gender and gender stereotypes can also play a role in how negotiations proceed. In a series of experiments, Laura Kray and her colleagues (2004) found that when negotiators were given information linking masculine traits with negotiator effectiveness, negotiated outcomes became more one-

integrative agreement A negotiated resolution to a conflict in which all parties obtain outcomes that are superior to what they would have obtained from an equal division of the contested resources.

sided in favour of the negotiator who had more power. On the other hand, when feminine traits were said to be associated with negotiator effectiveness, more integrative outcomes resulted.

Communication in which both sides disclose their goals and needs is critically important in allowing each side to see opportunities for joint benefits. This may seem obvious, and yet people in negotiations very often fail to communicate their goals and needs. For one thing, negotiators tend to think that their goals and objectives are clearer to the other party than they actually are (Vorauer & Claude, 1998). Furthermore, in conflict negotiations each party is likely to distrust and fear the other. Neither wants to reveal too much for fear of losing power at the bargaining table. Again, this is part of the fixed-pie syndrome. But if one party does disclose information, the disclosure can have dramatic effects. If one side discloses, the other party becomes much more likely to do so, enhancing the likelihood of integrative agreement (Thompson, 1991).

TABLE 8.6

Cultural Assumptions About Negotiating

People from different cultures make different assumptions about the negotiation process. This table summarizes some assumptions commonly made by western negotiators. It also presents some alternative assumptions that may be held by negotiators from other cultures. As you can see, such different assumptions could make it very difficult to reach a successful agreement. *(Based on Kimmel, 1994, 2000.)*

Assumptions Made by Negotiators from the U.S. and Other Western Countries	Alternatives
Negotiation is a business, not a social activity.	The first step in negotiating is to develop a trusting relationship between the individual negotiators.
Substantive issues are more important than social and emotional issues.	If you don't feel strongly about an issue, then it isn't important to you.
Communication is direct and verbal.	Some of the most important communications are nonverbal.
Written contracts are binding; oral commitments are not.	Written contracts are less meaningful than oral communications because the nonverbal context clarifies people's intentions.
Current information and ideas are more valid than historical or traditional opinions and information.	History and tradition are more valid than current information and ideas.
Time is very important; punctuality is expected; deadlines should be set and adhered to.	Building a relationship takes time and is more important than punctuality; setting deadlines is an effort to humiliate the other party.

In addition to disclosure of information, several other factors can improve negotiations and increase the chances that both sides will benefit. These factors include training negotiators in conflict-resolution techniques and using computerized negotiation support systems (Davis & Hall, 2003; Shakun, 1999; Thompson et al., 2000). Being aware of the group processes we have covered in this chapter puts you in a good position to help reduce conflicts.

During particularly difficult or significant negotiations, outside assistance may be sought. Some negotiations rely on an *arbitrator*, who has the power to impose a settlement. But it is more common for conflicting parties to request the participation of a *mediator*, who works with them to try to reach a voluntary agreement. Traditionally, mediators have been employed in labour-management negotiations and international conflicts. But increasingly, mediators help resolve a wide range of other disputes, such as those involving tenants and landlords, divorcing couples, and feuding neighbours. Trained in negotiation and conflict management, mediators can often increase the likelihood of reaching a cooperative solution (Bercovitch & Houston, 2000; Bowling & Hoffman, 2000; Carnevale, 2002; Wilkenfeld et al., 2003).

Finding Common Ground Every conflict is unique, as is every attempt at conflict resolution. Still, all efforts to find a constructive solution to conflict require some common ground to build upon. Recognition of a *superordinate identity* is one way to establish common ground between groups in conflict. When group members

Germans demonstrate against neo-Nazi groups and anti-Semitism. The sign, "I am a foreigner worldwide," proclaims that since we are all foreigners somewhere, there is no "them," only a superordinate human identity as "us."

perceive that they have a shared identity—a sense of belonging to something larger than and encompassing their own groups—the attractiveness of outgroup members increases, and interactions between the groups often become more peaceful.

Superordinate goals have another valuable characteristic: They can produce a superordinate identity. The experience of intergroup cooperation increases the sense of belonging to a single superordinate group (Gaertner & Dovidio, 2000). Even the mere expectation of a cooperative interaction increases empathy (Lanzetta & Englis, 1989), which, in turn, enhances helpfulness and reduces aggression. Indeed, empathic connections between various members of each group can lay the foundation for an inclusive, rather than exclusive, social identity.

On the road to peace, both kinds of common ground are needed. Cooperation to meet shared goals makes similarities more visible, and a sense of a shared identity makes cooperation more likely. Those who would make peace, not war, realize that it is in their own self-interest to do so and understand that the cloak of humanity is large enough to cover a multitude of lesser differences.

Review

Collective Processes: The Presence of Others

- In collectives, people engage in common activities but have minimal direct interaction.

Social Facilitation: When Others Arouse Us

- In an early experiment, Triplett found that children performed faster when they worked side-by-side rather than alone.
- Social facilitation refers to two effects that occur when individual contributions are identifiable: The presence of others enhances performance on easy tasks but impairs performance on difficult tasks.
- The theories of mere presence, evaluation apprehension, and distraction-conflict give different answers to questions concerning (1) whether social facilitation is necessarily social and (2) whether the mere presence of others is sufficient to affect performance.

Social Loafing: When Others Relax Us

- In early research on easy tasks involving pooled contributions, Ringelmann found that individual output declined when people worked with others.
- But social loafing is reduced or eliminated when people think their individual efforts will be important, relevant, and meaningful. In such cases, individuals may engage in social compensation in an effort to offset the anticipated social loafing of others.

Facilitation and Loafing: Unifying the Paradigms

- A unified paradigm integrates social facilitation, social loafing, and what we've called "social security": when the presence of others enhances performance on difficult tasks involving pooled contributions.

Deindividuation: When People Lose Control

- Deindividuation diminishes a person's sense of individuality and reduces constraints against deviant behaviour.
- Two types of environmental cues can increase deviant behaviour: (1) Accountability cues, such as anonymity, signal that individuals will not be held responsible for their actions; and (2) attentional cues, such as intense environmental stimulation, produce a deindividuated state in which the individual acts impulsively.
- Large crowds can both increase anonymity and decrease self-awareness, which together can increase violent or other deviant behaviour.
- The effects of deindividuation depend on the characteristics of the immediate group. In the context of an antagonistic social identity, antisocial behaviour increases; in the context of a benevolent social identity, prosocial behaviour increases.

Group Processes: Interacting with Others

Joining a Group

- People join a group for a variety of reasons, including to perform tasks that can't be accomplished alone, to enhance self-esteem and social identity, to gain a sense of identity, and to interact with group members.
- The socialization of newcomers into a group relies on the relationships they form with old-timers, who act as models, trainers, and mentors.
- Groups often proceed through several stages of development, from initial orientation through periods of conflict, compromise, and action.
- Some groups pass through periods of inactivity followed by sudden action in response to time pressures.

Roles, Norms, and Cohesiveness

- Interacting groups have three major features: an expected set of behaviours for members (roles), rules of conduct for members (norms), and forces that push members together (cohesiveness).
- Establishing clear roles can help a group; but when members' roles are ambiguous, conflict with other roles, or change, stress and poor performance can result.
- The relationship between cohesiveness and group performance is complex, depending on factors such as the size of the group, the kind of task that the group is performing, and the kinds of norms that have been established.

Group Polarization: Gaining Conviction

- When individuals who have similar, though not identical, opinions participate in a group discussion, their opinions become more extreme.
- Explanations for group polarization emphasize the number and persuasiveness of arguments heard, social comparison with a perceived group norm, and the influence of one's own ingroup.

Groupthink: Losing Perspective

- Groupthink refers to an excessive tendency to seek concurrence among group members.
- The symptoms of groupthink produce defective decision making, which can lead to a bad decision.
- A highly cohesive group is more likely to experience groupthink if other contributors to groupthink are present, such as a controlling leader and a stressful situation.
- Self-managed work teams, though increasingly popular, may be particularly susceptible to groupthink.
- Strategies that have been successful in helping groups avoid groupthink include consulting with outsiders, having the leader play a less controlling role, encouraging criticism and thorough information search, and having a group member play the devil's advocate and challenge the consensus.
- Computer-based technology can help groups avoid groupthink by guiding them to follow systematic agendas and focus on ideas.
- Encouraging counterfactual thinking can also be effective.

Group Performance: Are More Heads Better than One?

- Group performance is influenced by the type of task at hand (additive, conjunctive, or disjunctive).
- Because of process loss, a group may perform worse than it would if every individual performed up to his or her potential.
- Among the factors that create process loss are social loafing, poor coordination, and failure to recognize the expertise of particular group members.
- Groups can do better than even the best members of the group on tasks that can be divided among subgroups and in which the correct answer is clearly demonstrable to the rest of the group members.
- Groups often set goals that are not sufficiently challenging. Setting specific, ambitious goals can improve group performance.
- Contrary to illusions about the effectiveness of interactive brainstorming, groups in which members interact face-to-face produce fewer creative ideas than the same number of people working alone.
- Computer-based technology can improve group brainstorming.
- Biased sampling refers to the tendency for groups to pay more attention to shared information than to unshared information.
- Information may not be communicated adequately in a group because of problems in the group's communication network, such as suppression of relevant information at some point in the decision-making chain.

- Group norms fostering critical thinking can prevent biased sampling.
- Groups are susceptible to an escalation effect, which occurs when commitment to a failing course of action is increased to justify investments already made. Instead of cutting their losses, they essentially throw good money and time after bad.
- Groups are also susceptible to the same information-processing biases as individuals—only more so.
- Groups can remember more information than individuals through transactive memory, a shared process in which the information can be divided among the group members.
- Many groups and businesses today use interactive computer-mediated systems that are designed to improve how groups process and communicate information, leading to better decisions.
- The effects of diversity on group performance depend on the nature of the task, how well integrated the group is, and whether group members feel their individual identities are verified by the others.

Cooperation, Competition, and Conflict: Responding to Differences

Mixed Motives and Social Dilemmas

- In mixed-motive situations, such as the prisoner's dilemma, there are incentives for both competition and cooperation.
- In a social dilemma, personal benefit conflicts with the overall good.
- Resource dilemmas involve sharing limited resources. In the commons dilemma, a group of people can take resources from a common pool; whereas in the public goods dilemma, the maintenance of a common resource requires the contributions of a group of people.
- Behaviour in a social dilemma is influenced by psychological factors—including individual and cultural differences, situational factors, and group dynamics—as well as structural arrangements.

Conflict Escalation

- Conflicts can escalate for many reasons, including conflict spirals and escalation of commitment.
- The premature use of the capacity to punish can elicit retaliation and escalate conflict.
- Perceptions of the other that contribute to conflict escalation include unfavourable mirror images and dehumanization.

Reducing Conflict

- GRIT—an explicit strategy for the unilateral, persistent pursuit of trust and cooperation between opposing parties—is a useful strategy for beginning the peace process.
- Many negotiations have the potential to result in integrative agreements, in which outcomes exceed a 50-50 split; but negotiators often fail to achieve such outcomes.
- Flexibility, communication, and an understanding of the other party's perspective are key ingredients of successful negotiation.
- Communication difficulties are especially likely during negotiations between individuals and groups from different cultures.
- Gender stereotypes can affect performance in negotiations.
- Mediators can often be helpful in achieving success in negotiations.
- Superordinate goals and a superordinate identity increase the likelihood of a peaceful resolution of differences.

Key Terms

brainstorming *(274)*
collective *(253)*
collective effort model *(259)*
deindividuation *(261)*
distraction-conflict theory *(256)*
escalation effect *(277)*
evaluation apprehension theory *(256)*
graduated and reciprocated initiatives in tension-reduction (GRIT) *(285)*
group polarization *(269)*
groupthink *(270)*
integrative agreement *(286)*
mere presence theory *(255)*
prisoner's dilemma *(280)*
process loss *(273)*
resource dilemmas *(281)*
social dilemma *(280)*
social facilitation *(255)*
social loafing *(258)*
transactive memory *(278)*

People will cheer louder when they cheer as part of a group than when they cheer alone.

False. *People tend to put less effort into collective tasks, such as group cheering, than into tasks when their individual performance can be identified and evaluated.*

Group members' attitudes about a course of action usually become more moderate after group discussion.

False. *Group discussion often causes attitudes to become more extreme as the initial tendencies of the group are exaggerated.*

People brainstorming as a group come up with a greater number of better ideas than the same number of people working individually.

False. *Groups in which members interact face-to-face produce fewer creative ideas when brainstorming than the same number of people brainstorming alone.*

Groups are less likely than individuals to invest more and more resources in a project that is failing.

False. *Although individuals often feel entrapped by previous commitments and make things worse by throwing good money (and other resources) after bad, groups are even more prone to having this problem.*

Large groups are more likely than small groups to exploit a scarce resource that the members collectively depend on.

True. *Large groups are more likely to behave selfishly when faced with resource dilemmas, in part because people in large groups feel less identifiable and more anonymous.*

9 Attraction and Close Relationships

OUTLINE

PREVIEW

THIS CHAPTER examines how people form relationships with each other. First, we describe the fundamental human need for *being with others,* why people affiliate, and the problem of loneliness. Then we consider various personal and situational factors that influence our *initial attraction* to specific others. Third, we examine different types of *close relationships*—what makes them rewarding, how they differ, the types of love they arouse, and the factors that keep them together or break them apart.

PUTTING COMMON SENSE TO THE TEST

T / F

___ **People seek out the company of others, even strangers, in times of stress.**

___ **Infants do not discriminate between faces considered attractive and unattractive in their culture.**

___ **People who are physically attractive are happier and have higher self-esteem than those who are unattractive.**

___ **When it comes to romantic relationships, opposites attract.**

___ **Men are more likely than women to interpret friendly gestures by the opposite sex in sexual terms.**

___ **After the honeymoon period, there is an overall decline in levels of marital satisfaction.**

No topic fascinates the people of this planet more than interpersonal attraction. Needing to belong, we humans are obsessed about friendships, romantic relationships, dating, love, sex, reproduction, sexual orientation, marriage, and divorce. Playwrights, poets, and musicians write with eloquence and emotion about loves desired, won, and lost. North American television is filled with relationship-centred reality TV shows like *The Bachelor*, *Hooked up*, or *Fairy Tale*, the first Canadian reality show for gays, lesbians bisexual and transgendered individuals. More and more, people are meeting romantic partners online, in Internet chat rooms and dating services such as Lavalife or It's Just Lunch. Both in our hearts and in our minds, the relationships we seek and enjoy with other people are more important than anything else.

At one time or another, all of us have been startled by our reaction to someone we've met. Why, in general, are human beings drawn to each other? Why are we attracted to some people and yet indifferent to, or even repelled by, others? What determines how our intimate relationships evolve? What does it mean to love someone, and what problems are likely to arise along the way? As these questions reveal, attraction among people—from the first spark through the flames of an intimate connection—often seems like a kind of wild card in the deck of human behaviour. This chapter unravels some of the mysteries.

Being with Others: A Fundamental Human Motive

Although born helpless, human infants are equipped with reflexes that orient them toward people. They are uniquely responsive to human faces, they turn their head toward voices, and they are able to mimic certain facial gestures on cue. Then, a few weeks later, there is the baby's first smile, surely the warmest sign of all. Much to the delight of parents all over the world, the newborn seems an inherently social animal. But wait. If you reflect on the amount of time you spend talking to, being with, flirting with, pining for, confiding in, or worrying about other people, you'll realize that we are all social animals. It seems that people need people.

According to Roy Baumeister and Mark Leary (1996), the need to belong is a basic human motive, "a pervasive drive to form and maintain at least a minimum quantity of lasting, positive, and significant interpersonal relationships" (p. 497). This general proposition is supported by everyday observation and a great deal of research. All over the world, people feel joy when they form new social attachments and react with anxiety and grief when these bonds are broken—as when separated from a loved one by distance, divorce, or death. The need to belong runs deep, which is why people are distressed when they are neglected by others, rejected, excluded, stigmatized, or ostracized, all forms of "social death" (Leary, 2001; Williams et al., 2002).

We care deeply about what others think of us, which is why we spend so much time and money to make ourselves presentable and attractive. In fact, some people are so worried about how they come across to others that they suffer from *social anxiety*, intense feelings of discomfort in situations that invite public scrutiny (Leary & Kowalski, 1995). One very familiar example is public speaking anxiety, or "stage fright"—a performer's worst nightmare. If you've ever had to make a presentation, only to feel weak in the knees and hear your voice quiver, you will have endured a hint of this disorder. When sufferers are asked what there is to fear, the most common responses are: shaking and showing other signs of anxiety, going blank, saying something foolish, and being unable to continue (Stein et al., 1996). For people with high levels of social anxiety, the problem is also evoked by other social situations, such as eating at a public lunch counter, signing a cheque in front of a store clerk, and, for males, urinating in a crowded men's room. In extreme cases, the reaction can become so debilitating that the person just stays at home (Beidel & Turner, 1998; Crozier & Alden, 2001).

Our need to belong is a fundamental human motive. People who have a network of close social ties—in the form of lovers, friends, family members, and coworkers—tend to be happier and more satisfied with life than those who are more isolated (Diener et al., 1999). In fact, people who are socially connected are also physically healthier and less likely to die a premature death (Cohen et al., 2000; House et al., 1988; Uchino et al., 1996).

The Thrill of Affiliation

As social beings, humans are drawn to each other. We work together, play together, live together, and often make lifetime commitments to grow old together. This social motivation begins with the **need for affiliation**, defined as a desire to establish social contact with others (McAdams, 1989). Individuals differ in the strength of their need for affiliation, but it seems that people are motivated to establish and maintain an *optimum* balance of social contact—sometimes craving the company of others, sometimes wanting to be alone—the way the body maintains a certain level of caloric intake. In an interesting study, Bibb Latané and Carol Werner (1978) found that laboratory rats were more likely to approach others of their species after a period of isolation and were less likely to approach others after prolonged contact. These researchers suggested that rats, like many other animals, have a built-in "sociostat" (social thermostat) to regulate their affiliative tendencies.

Is there evidence of a similar mechanism in humans? Shawn O'Connor and Lorne Rosenblood (1996) recruited students to carry portable beepers for four days. Whenever the beepers went off (on average, every hour), the students wrote down whether, at the time, they were *actually* alone or in the company of other people and whether, at the time, they *wanted* to be alone or with others. The results

need for affiliation The desire to establish and maintain many rewarding interpersonal relationships.

showed that the students were in the state they desired two-thirds of the time—and that the situation they wished to be in on one occasion predicted their actual situation the next time they were signalled. Whether it was solitude or social contact that the students sought, they successfully managed to regulate their own personal needs for affiliation.

People may well differ in the strength of their affiliative needs, but there are times when we all want to be with other people. It is common to find the streets of major cities across North America filled with fans whenever the home team wins the final championship game. From one city to the next, jubilant fans stay long after the game ends, milling about and exchanging high-fives, slaps on the back, hugs, and kisses. In each of these cities, it's clear that people want to celebrate together rather than alone. Affiliating can satisfy us for other reasons as well. From others, we get energy, attention, stimulation, information, and emotional support (Hill, 1987).

People are motivated to establish and maintain an optimum level of social contact.

One condition that strongly arouses our need for affiliation is stress. Have you ever noticed the way neighbours who never stop to say hello come together in snowstorms, hurricanes, power failures, and other major crises? Many years ago, Stanley Schachter (1959) theorized that external threat triggers fear and motivates us to affiliate—particularly with others who face a similar threat. In a laboratory experiment that demonstrated the point, Schachter found that people who were expecting to receive painful electric shocks chose to wait with other nervous participants rather than alone. So far, so good. But when Irving Sarnoff and Philip Zimbardo (1961) led participants to expect that they would be engaging in an embarrassing behaviour—sucking on large nipples and pacifiers—their desire to be with others fell off. It seemed puzzling. Why do people in fearful misery love company, while those in embarrassed misery seek solitude?

Yacov Rofé (1984) proposed a simple answer: utility. Rofé argued that stress increases the desire to affiliate only when being with others is seen as useful in reducing the negative impact of the stressful situation. Schachter's participants had good reason to believe that affiliation would be useful. They would have the opportunity to compare their emotional reactions with those of others to determine whether they really needed to be fearful. For those in the Sarnoff and Zimbardo study, however, affiliation had little to offer. Facing embarrassment, being with others is more likely to increase the stress than reduce it.

Returning to Schachter's initial study, what specific benefit do people get from being in the presence of others in times of stress? Research suggests that people facing an imminent threat seek each other out in order to gain *cognitive clarity* about the danger they are in. In one study, James Kulik and Heike Mahler (1989) found that hospital patients waiting for open-heart surgery preferred to have as roommates other patients who were post-operative rather than pre-operative, presumably because they were in a position to provide information about the experience. Patients in a second study who had been assigned post-operative rather than pre-operative roommates became less anxious about the experience and were later quicker to recover from the surgery (Kulik et al., 1996).

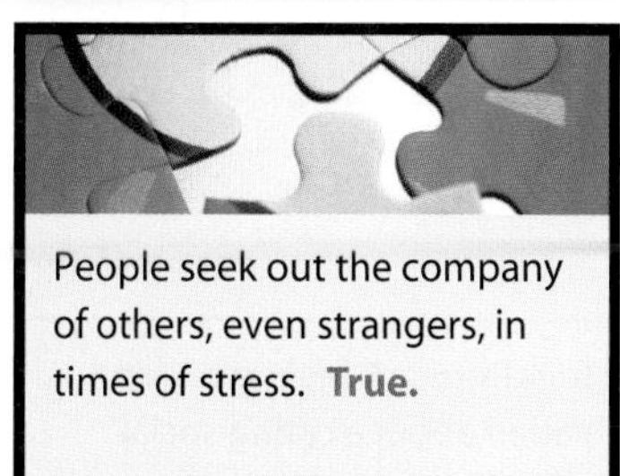

People seek out the company of others, even strangers, in times of stress. **True.**

Even in a laboratory setting, Kulik and others (1994) found that people anticipating the painful task of soaking a hand in ice-cold water (compared with those told that the task would not be painful) preferred to wait with someone who had already completed the task than with someone who had not. They also asked more questions of these experienced peers. Under stress, we adaptively become motivated to affiliate with others who can help us cope with an impending threat. Summarizing his own work, Schachter (1959) had noted that misery loves miserable company. Based on their more recent studies, Gump and Kulik (1997) further amended this assertion: "Misery loves the company of those in the same miserable situation" (p. 317).

"Loneliness and the feeling of being unwanted is the most terrible poverty."
—Mother Teresa

The Agony of Loneliness

People need other people—to celebrate, share news with, commiserate with, talk to, and learn from. But some people are painfully shy, socially awkward, inhibited, and reluctant to approach others (Bruch et al., 1989). Shyness is a pervasive problem. Roughly 49 percent of all Americans describe themselves as shy, as do 31 percent in Israel, 40 percent in Germany, 55 percent in Taiwan, and 57 percent in Japan (Henderson & Zimbardo, 1998). In fact, it is estimated that 3 percent of the Canadian population suffers from social anxiety disorder—an extreme form of shyness, and less than half of those individuals seek help (*Canadian Community Health Survey (CCHS): Mental Health and Well-being*, 2002). People who are shy find it difficult to approach strangers, make small talk, telephone someone for a date, participate in small groups, or mingle at parties. What's worse, they often reject others—perhaps because they fear being rejected themselves. The sad result is a pattern of risk avoidance that sets them up for unpleasant and unrewarding interactions (Crozier, 2001).

Shyness can arise from different sources. In some cases, it may be an inborn personality trait. Jerome Kagan (1994) and others have found that some infants are highly sensitive to stimulation, inhibited, and cautious shortly after birth. In other cases, shyness develops as a learned reaction to failed interactions with others. Thus, interpersonal problems of the past can ignite social anxieties about the future (Leary & Kowalski, 1995). Not all infants grow up to become inhibited adults. But longitudinal research indicates that there is some continuity—that this aspect of our personalities may be predictable from our temperament and behaviour as young children. Thus, toddlers observed to be inhibited, shy, and fearful at age 3 were more likely than toddlers who were more outgoing to be socially isolated and depressed at age 21 (Caspi, 2000).

Whatever the source, shyness is a real problem—and it has painful consequences. Studies show that shy people evaluate themselves negatively, expect to fail in their social encounters and blame themselves when they do. As a result, many shy people go into self-imposed isolation, which makes them feel lonely (Cheek & Melchior, 1990; Jackson et al., 2002). In part, the problem stems from a paralyzing fear of rejection, which inhibits people from making friendly or romantic overtures to those they are interested in. If you ever wanted to approach someone you liked, only to stop yourself, you know that this situation often triggers an approach-avoidance conflict, pulling you between the desire for contact and a fear of being rejected. What's worse, research shows that people who fear rejection think that their friendly or romantic interest is transparent to others, which leads them to back off (Vorauer et al., 2003).

Loneliness is a sad and heart-wrenching emotion. To be lonely is to feel deprived about the nature of one's existing social relations. Some researchers have maintained that loneliness is triggered by a discrepancy between the level of social contact that a person has and the level he or she wants (Peplau & Perlman, 1982). Others find, more simply, that the less social contact people have, the lonelier they feel (Archibald et al., 1995). Who is lonely, and when? Loneliness is most likely to occur during times of transition or disruption—as in the first year at university, after a romantic break-up, or when a loved one moves far away. Surveys show that people who are unattached are lonelier than those who have romantic partners—but that those who are widowed, divorced, and separated are lonelier than people who have never been married. Contrary to the stereotypic image of the lonely old

loneliness A feeling of deprivation about existing social relations.

man passing time on a park bench, the loneliest groups in North American society are adolescents and young adults 18- to 30-years-old. In fact, loneliness seems to decline over the course of adulthood—at least until health problems in old age limit social activities (Peplau & Perlman, 1982).

How do people cope with this distressing state? When students were asked about the behavioural strategies they use to combat loneliness, 96 percent said they sometimes or often tried harder to be friendly to other people; 94 percent took their mind off the problem by reading or watching TV; and 93 percent tried extra hard to succeed at another aspect of life. Others said that they distracted themselves by running, shopping, washing the car, or staying busy at other activities. Still others sought new ways to meet people, tried to improve their physical appearance, or talked to a friend, relative, or therapist about the problem. Though fewer in number, some are so desperate that they use alcohol or drugs to wash away feelings of loneliness (Rook & Peplau, 1982).

The Initial Attraction

Affiliation is a necessary first step in the formation of a social relationship. But each of us is drawn to some people more than to others. If you've ever had a crush on someone, felt the tingly excitement of a first encounter, or enjoyed the first few moments of a new friendship, then you know the meaning of the term *attraction*. When you meet someone for the first time, what do *you* look for? Does familiarity breed fondness or contempt? Do birds of a feather flock together, or do opposites attract? Is beauty the object of your desire, or do you believe that outward appearances are deceiving? And what is it about a situation, or the circumstances of an initial meeting, that draws you in for more?

According to one perspective, people are attracted to others with whom a relationship is rewarding (Byrne & Clore, 1970; Lott & Lott, 1974). The rewards may be direct—as when people provide us with attention, support, money, status, information, and other valuable commodities. Or the rewards may be indirect—as when it feels good to be with someone who is beautiful, smart, or funny, or who happens to be in our presence when times are good. A new perspective on attraction has also emerged in recent years—that of evolutionary psychology, the subdiscipline that uses principles of evolution to understand human social behaviour. According to this view, human beings all over the world exhibit patterns of attraction and mate selection that favour the conception, birth, and survival of their offspring. This approach has a great deal to say about differences in this regard between men and women (Buss, 2004; Simpson & Kenrick, 1997).

Recognizing the role of rewards and the call of our evolutionary past provides broad perspectives for understanding human attraction. But there's more to the story. Much more. Over the years, social

Dating services, such as Internet dating or speed dating, enable strangers to meet. Interested in first encounters of this nature, attraction researchers try to determine what factors draw people to each other. Here, aboard the Ocean Princess, *100 singles meet for the first time in Match.com's "World's largest floating blind date."*

psychologists have identified many determinants of attraction and the development of intimate relationships (Berscheid & Reis, 1998; Brehm et al., 2001). It's important to note that most of the research has focused on heterosexuals, so we often do not know how well specific findings apply to the homosexual population. We do know that in Ontario, where same sex marriages have been legal since 2003, more than 4000 same-sex couples married within the first year. Therefore, we'll see that many of the basic processes described in this chapter affect the development of close relationships—regardless of whether the individuals involved are gay, lesbian, or straight (Kurdek, 2000).

Familiarity: Being There

It seems so obvious that people tend to overlook it: We are most likely to become attracted to someone whom we have seen and become familiar with. So let's begin with two basic and necessary factors in the attraction process: proximity and exposure.

The Proximity Effect The single best predictor of whether two people will get together is physical proximity, or nearness. Sure, we interact at remote distances with the help of telephones, email, online chat rooms, and message boards. These days it's common for people to find friends, lovers, and sexual partners on the Internet. Still, our most impactful social interactions occur among people who are in the same place at the same time (Latané et al., 1995). Even in the virtual neighbourhoods of cyberspace, people intersect more often with some message-posters than others—particularly through the use of "buddy lists" that tell us when the people we seek happen to be online (Wallace, 1999).

To begin with, where we live influences the friends we make. Many years ago, Leon Festinger and his colleagues (1950) studied friendship patterns in married-student housing and found that people were more likely to become friends with residents of nearby apartments than with those who lived farther away. More recent research has also shown that students—who live in off-campus apartments, dormitories, or fraternity and sorority houses—tend to date those who live either nearby (Hays, 1985) or in the same type of housing as they do (Whitbeck & Hoyt, 1994).

The Mere Exposure Effect Proximity does not necessarily spark attraction, but to the extent that it increases frequency of contact, it's a good first step. Folk wisdom often suggests a dim view of familiarity, which is said to "breed contempt." Not so. In a series of experiments, Robert Zajonc (1968) found that the more often people saw a novel stimulus—whether it was a foreign word, a geometric form, or a human face—the more they came to like it. This phenomenon, which Zajonc called the **mere exposure effect**, has since been observed in more than 200 experiments (Bornstein, 1989).

People do not even have to be aware of their prior exposures for this effect to occur. In a typical study, participants are shown pictures of several stimuli, each for one to five milliseconds, which is too quick to register in awareness and too quick for anyone to realize that some stimuli are presented more often than others. After the presentation, participants are shown each of the stimuli and asked two questions: Do you like it, and have you ever seen it before? Perhaps you can predict the result. The more frequently the stimulus is presented, the more people like it. Yet when asked if they've ever seen the liked stimulus before, they say no. These results demonstrate that the mere exposure effect can influence us without our awareness (Kuntz-Wilson & Zajonc, 1980). In fact, the effect is stronger under these conditions (Bornstein & D'Agostino, 1992; Zajonc, 2001).

To appreciate the implications in a naturalistic situation, imagine yourself in a psychology class that is held in a large lecture hall. Three times a week, you trudge

mere exposure effect The phenomenon whereby the more often people are exposed to a stimulus, the more positively they evaluate that stimulus.

over to class, shake the cobwebs out of your head, and try your best to be alert. The room holds several hundred students. You come in and look down the tiered seats to the front where your instructor stands. During the semester, you're vaguely aware of another student who sits up front, but you never talk to her, and you probably would not recognize her if you saw her somewhere else. Then, at the end of the semester, you attend a special session where you are shown photographs of four women and asked some questions about them. Only then do you learn that you have participated in a study of the mere exposure effect.

Now view the same events from the perspective of Richard Moreland and Scott Beach (1992). These researchers selected four women who looked like typical students to be confederates in this study. One had a very easy job: She had her picture taken. But the other three also attended the class—either 5, 10, or 15 times. Did the frequency of exposure spark attraction among the real students in this situation? Yes. In questionnaires they completed after viewing pictures of all four women, students rated each woman on various traits (such as popularity, honesty, intelligence, and physical attractiveness) and recorded their beliefs about how much they would like her, enjoy spending time with her, and want to work with her on a mutual project. The results lined up like ducks in a row: The more classes a woman attended, the more attracted the students were to her.

Familiarity can even influence our self-evaluations. Imagine that you had a portrait photograph of yourself developed into two pictures—one that depicted your actual appearance and the other a mirror-image copy. Which image would you prefer? Which would a friend prefer? Theodore Mita and his colleagues (1977) tried this interesting experiment with female students and found that most preferred their own mirror images, while their friends liked the actual photos. In both cases, the preference was for the view of the face that was most familiar.

Physical Attractiveness: Getting Drawn In

"Beauty is a greater recommendation than any letter of introduction."
—Aristotle

What do you look for in a friend or romantic partner? Intelligence? Kindness? A sense of humour? How important, really, is a person's looks? As children, we were told that "beauty is only skin deep" and that we should not "judge a book by its cover." Yet as adults, we react more favourably to others who are physically attractive than to those who are not. Inspiring Nancy Etcoff's (1999) book, *Survival of the Prettiest*, studies have shown that in the affairs of our social world, beauty is a force to be reckoned with (Hatfield & Sprecher, 1986; Langlois et al., 2000).

The bias for beauty is pervasive. In one study, fifth-grade teachers were given background information about a boy or girl, accompanied by a photograph. All teachers received identical information, yet those who saw an attractive child saw that child as being smarter and more likely to do well in school (Clifford & Walster, 1973). In a second study, male and female experimenters approached students on a university campus and tried to get them to sign a petition. The more attractive the experimenters were, the more signatures they were able to get (Chaiken, 1979). In a third study, Texas judges set lower bail and imposed smaller fines on suspects who were rated as attractive rather than unattractive on the basis of photographs (Downs & Lyons, 1991). In a fourth study conducted in Canada and the United States, economists discovered that across occupational groups, physically attractive men and women earn more money than others who are comparable except for being less attractive (Hamermesh & Biddle, 1994). Across a range of job situations, people fare better if they are attractive than if they are not (Hosoda et al., 2003).

It all seems so shallow, so superficial. But before we go on to accept the notion that people prefer others who are physically attractive, let's stop for a moment and consider a fundamental question: What constitutes physical beauty? Is it an objective and measurable human characteristic like height, weight, or hair colour? Or is

Perceptions of facial beauty are largely consistent across cultures. Those regarded as good-looking in one culture also tend to be judged as attractive by people from other cultures. The individuals pictured here are from Venezuela, Kenya, Japan, and the United States.

beauty a subjective quality, existing in the eye of the beholder? There are advocates on both sides.

What Is Beauty? Some researchers believe that certain faces are inherently more attractive than others. There are three sources of evidence for this proposition.

First, when people are asked to rate faces on a ten-point scale, there is typically a high level of agreement—among children and adults, men and women, and people from the same or different cultures (Langlois et al., 2000). For example, Michael Cunningham and others (1995) asked Asian and Latino students, along with black and white American students, to rate the appearance of women from all these groups. Overall, the ratings were highly consistent, leading these investigators to argue that people everywhere share an image of what is beautiful. People also tend to agree about what constitutes an attractive body. For example, men tend to be drawn to the "hourglass" figure seen in women of average weight whose waists are a third narrower than their hips—a shape thought to be associated with reproductive fertility. In contrast, women like men with a waist-to-hip ratio that forms a tapering V-shaped physique (Singh, 1993, 1995). If marriage statistics are any indication, women also seem to have a preference for height. Comparisons made in Europe indicate that married men are a full inch taller, on average, than unmarried men (Pawlowski et al., 2000).

"There is no known culture in which people do not paint, pierce, tattoo, reshape or simply adorn their bodies."
—Enid Schildkrout, anthropologist

Second, some researchers have identified physical features of the human face that are reliably associated with judgments of attractiveness (Rhodes et al., 2001). Particularly intriguing are studies showing that people like faces in which the eyes, nose, lips, and other features are not too different from the average. Judith Langlois and Lori Roggman (1990) showed students both actual yearbook photos and computerized facial composites that "averaged" features from 4, 8, 16, or 32 of the photos. Time and again, they found that the students preferred the averaged composites to the individual faces—and that the more faces used to form the composite, the more highly it was rated. Other studies have since confirmed this result (Langlois et al., 1994; Rhodes et al., 1999).

It seems odd that "averaged" faces are judged attractive when, after all, the faces we find the most beautiful are anything but average. What accounts for these findings? Langlois and others (1994) believe that people like averaged faces because they are more prototypically face-like and, as such, seem more familiar to us. Consistent with this notion, research shows that just as people are more attracted to averaged faces than to individual faces, they also prefer averaged dogs, birds, fish, automobiles, and wristwatches (Halberstadt & Rhodes, 2000, 2003). Other studies indicate that computerized averaging produces faces that are also symmetrical—and that symmetry is what we find attractive (Grammer & Thornhill, 1994; Mealey et al., 1999). Why do people prefer symmetrical faces in which the paired features on the right and left sides mirror each other? Although the research support is mixed, some evolutionary psychologists have speculated that symmetry is naturally associated with health, fitness, and fertility—qualities that are highly desirable in a mate (Rhodes et al., 2001; Shackelford & Larsen, 1999; Thornhill & Gangestad, 1993).

A third source of evidence for the view that beauty is an objective quality is that babies who are far too young to have learned the culture's standards of beauty exhibit a nonverbal preference for faces considered attractive by adults. Picture the scene in an infant laboratory: A baby, lying on her back in a crib, is shown a series of faces previously rated by students. The first face appears and a clock starts ticking as the baby stares at it. As soon as the baby looks away, the clock stops and the next face is presented. The result: young infants spend more time tracking and looking at attractive faces than at unattractive ones—regardless of whether the faces are young or old, male or female, or black or white (Game et al., 2003; Langlois et al., 1991). In contrast to this objective perspective, other researchers argue that physical attractiveness is subjective, and they point for evidence to the influences of culture, time, and the circumstances of our perception. One source of support for this view is that people from different cultures enhance their beauty in very different ways through face painting, makeup, plastic surgery, scarring, tattoos, hairstyling, the moulding of bones, the filing of teeth, braces, and the piercing of ears and other body parts—all contributing to the "enigma of beauty" (Newman, 2000). What people find attractive in one part of the world is often seen as repulsive in another part of the world (Landau, 1989).

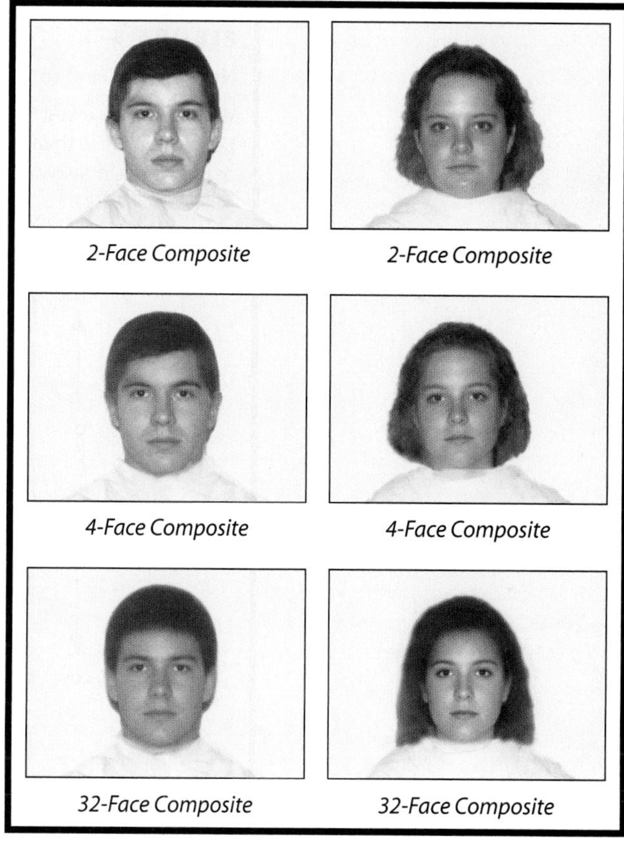

Computer-generated images that "average" the features of different faces are seen as more attractive than the individual faces on which they were based. Shown here are sets of male and female composites that combine 2, 4, and 32 faces. Which do you prefer? (Langlois & Roggman, 1990.)

Ideals also vary when it comes to bodies. Looking at preferences for female body size in 54 cultures, Judith Anderson and others (1992) found that heavy women are judged more attractive than slender women in places where food is frequently in short supply. In one study, for example, Douglas Yu and Glenn Shepard (1998) found that Matsigenka men living in the Andes mountains of southeastern Peru see female forms with "tubular" shapes—as opposed to hourglass shapes—as healthier, more attractive, and more desirable in a mate.

Standards of beauty also change over time, from one generation to the next. Brett Silverstein and others (1986) examined the measurements of female models appearing in women's magazines from 1901 to 1981, and they found that "curvaceousness" (as measured by the bust-to-waist ratio) varied over time, with a boyish, slender look becoming particularly desirable in recent years. Recently, researchers took body measurements from a men's magazine beginning with the first issue, in 1953, through the last issue of 2001 and found that over time, models became thinner and had lower bust-to-waist ratios—away from the ample "hourglass" to a more slender, athletic, sticklike shape (Voracek & Fisher, 2002).

Still other evidence for the subjective nature of beauty comes from many research laboratories. Time and again, social psychologists have found that our judgments of someone's beauty can be inflated or deflated by various circumstances. Research shows, for example, that people often see others as more physically attractive after they have grown to like them (Gross & Crofton, 1977). In fact, the more in love people are with their partners, the less attracted they are to others of the opposite sex (Johnson & Rusbult, 1989; Simpson et al., 1990). On the other hand, men who viewed ravishing nude models in *Playboy* and *Penthouse* magazines

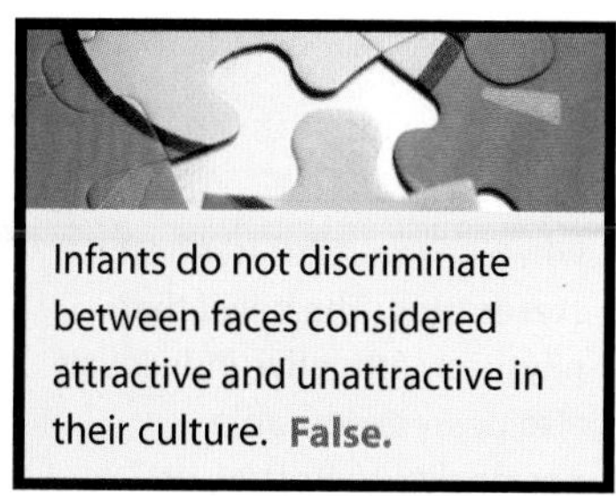

Infants do not discriminate between faces considered attractive and unattractive in their culture. **False.**

FIGURE 9.1

How Does It Feel to See a Perfect 10?

When people viewed facial photos of same-sex individuals, those who saw highly attractive people felt worse than those who saw average people. However, when viewing photos of opposite-sex individuals, those who saw highly attractive people felt better. *(Data from Kenrick et al., 1993.)*

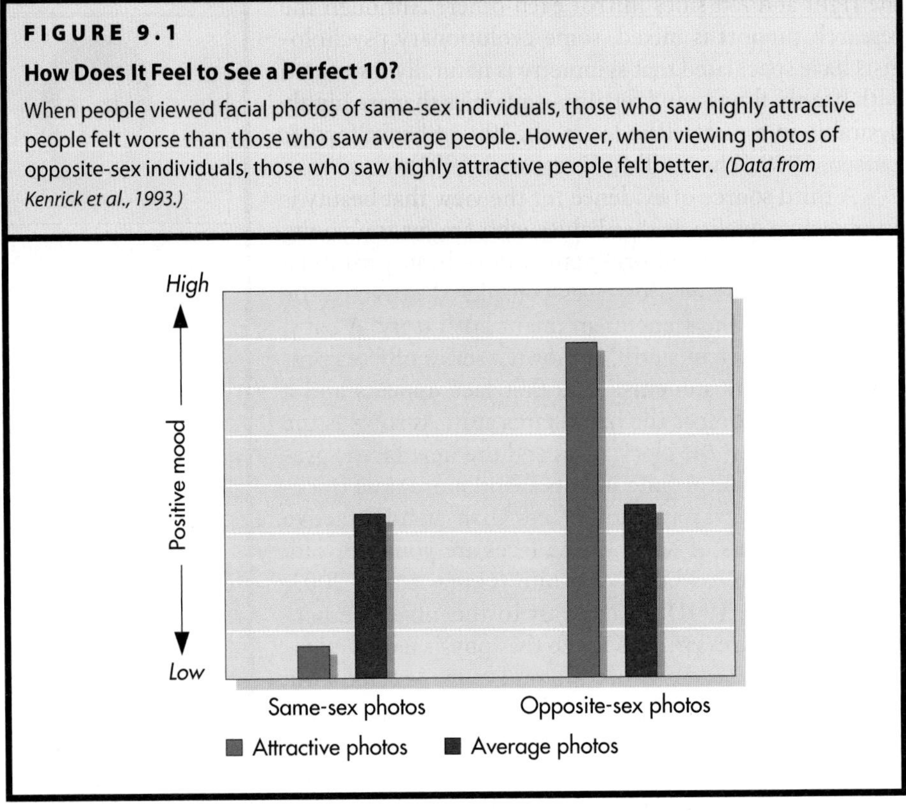

"Cyberdating works because the courting process is reversed; people get to know each other from the inside out."
—Trish McDermott, **match.com**

later gave lower attractiveness ratings to average-looking women, including their own wives—the unfortunate result of a contrast effect (Kenrick et al., 1989). Even our self-evaluations are malleable in this regard. Research shows that people feel less attractive after viewing supermodel-like members of the same sex than after viewing homelier persons (Thornton & Moore, 1993). Douglas Kenrick and others (1993) found that while exposure to highly attractive members of the opposite sex put people into a good mood, exposure to attractive members of the same sex had the opposite effect (see Figure 9.1).

Why Are We Blinded by Beauty? Regardless of how beauty is defined, it's clear that people seen as physically attractive are at a social advantage. Perhaps that's why billions of dollars a year are spent on makeup, hair products, and cosmetic surgery to plump up sunken skin, peel and scrape wrinkles from the face, vacuum out fat deposits, lift faces, reshape noses, tuck in tummies, and enlarge breasts.

What creates the bias for beauty, and why are we drawn like magnets to people who are physically attractive? One possibility is that it is inherently rewarding to be in the company of people who are aesthetically appealing—that we derive pleasure from beautiful men and women the same way that we enjoy a breathtaking landscape or a magnificent work of art. Or perhaps the rewards are more extrinsic. Perhaps, for example, we expect the glitter of another's beauty to rub off on us. When average-looking men and women are seen alongside someone else of the same sex, they are rated as more attractive when the other person is good-looking and as less attractive when he or she is plain-looking (Geiselman et al., 1984).

what-is-beautiful-is-good stereotype The belief that physically attractive individuals also possess desirable personality characteristics.

A second possible reason for the bias for beauty is that people tend to associate physical attractiveness with other desirable qualities—an assumption known as the **what-is-beautiful-is-good stereotype** (Dion et al., 1972). Think about children's fairy tales, where Snow White and Cinderella are portrayed as beautiful *and* kind, while the witch and stepsisters are said to be both ugly *and* cruel. This link between beauty and goodness can even be seen in Hollywood movies. Stephen Smith and others (1999) asked people to watch and rate the main characters who appeared in the 100 top-grossing movies between 1940 and 1990. They found that the more attractive the characters were, the more frequently they were portrayed as virtuous, romantically active, and successful. In a second study, these investigators showed students a film that depicted either a strong or a weak link between the beauty and goodness of the characters. Then, in a supposedly unrelated experiment, these students were asked to evaluate two graduate school applicants whose credentials were equivalent but whose photographs differed in terms of physical attractiveness. The result was both interesting and disturbing: Students who had watched a film depicting the beautiful-is-good stereotype were more likely than those who had watched a nonstereotypic film to favour the physically attractive applicant in their evaluations (see Figure 9.2). It appears that the entertainment industry unwittingly helps to foster and perpetuate our tendency to judge people by their physical appearance.

FIGURE 9.2

Media Influences on the Bias for Beauty

In this study, participants evaluated graduate school applicants who differed in their physical attractiveness. Indicating the power of the media to influence us, those who had first watched a stereotypic film in which beauty was associated with goodness were more likely to favour the attractive applicant than those who had first seen a nonstereotypic film. *(Smith et al., 1999.)*

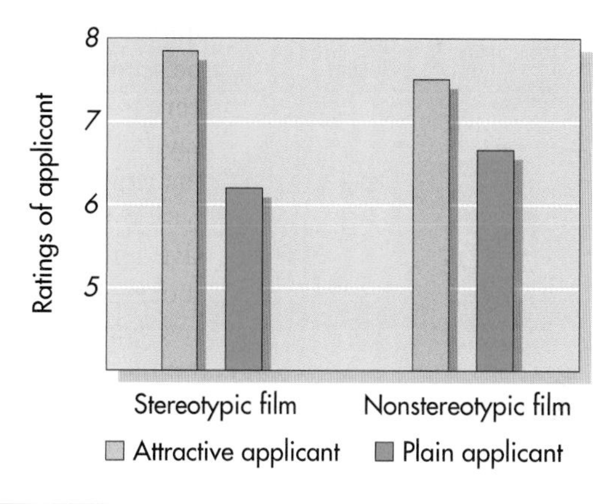

Studies have shown that good-looking people are judged to be smart, successful, happy, well-adjusted, socially skilled, confident, and assertive—though also vain (Eagly et al., 1991). So, is this physical attractiveness stereotype accurate? Only to a limited extent. Research shows that good-looking people do have more friends, better social skills, and a more active sex life. But beauty is *not* related to objective measures of intelligence, personality, adjustment, or self-esteem. In these domains, popular perceptions appear to exaggerate the reality (Feingold, 1992b). It also seems that the specific nature of the stereotype depends on cultural conceptions of what is "good." When Ladd Wheeler and Youngmee Kim (1997) asked people in Korea to rate photos of various men and women, they found that people seen as physically attractive were also assumed to have "integrity" and "a concern for others"—traits that are highly valued in this collectivist culture. In contrast to what is considered desirable in more individualistic cultures, attractive people in Korea were not assumed to be dominant or assertive. What is beautiful is good; but what is good is, in part, culturally defined.

If the physical attractiveness stereotype is true only in part, why does it endure? One possibility is that each of us creates support for the bias via the *self-fulfilling prophecy* model described in Chapter 4. In a classic study of interpersonal attraction, Mark Snyder and others (1977) brought together unacquainted pairs of male and female students. All the students were given biographical sketches of their partners. Each man also received a photograph of a physically attractive or unattractive woman, supposedly his partner. At that point, the students rated each other on several dimensions and had a phone-like conversation over headphones. The results were provocative. Men who thought they were interacting with a woman who was attractive (1) formed more positive impressions of her personality and (2) were friendlier in their conversational behaviour. And now for the clincher: (3) The female students whose partners had seen the attractive picture were later rated by listeners to the conversation as warmer, more confident, and more animated. Fulfilling the prophecies of their own expectations, men who expected an attractive partner actually created one. These findings call to mind the Greek myth of Pygmalion, who fell in love with a statue he had carved—and brought it to life.

This painting depicts a Greek myth in which Pygmalion, the King of Cyprus, sculpted his ideal woman in an ivory statue he called Galatea. Illustrating the power of a self-fulfilling prophecy, Pygmalion fell in love with his creation, caressed it, adorned it with jewellery, and eventually brought it to life.

The Benefits and Costs of Beauty No doubt about it, good-looking people have a significant edge. As a result, they are more popular, more sexually experienced, and more socially skilled. In light of these advantages, it's interesting that physical attractiveness is not a sure ticket to health, happiness, or high self-esteem (Diener et al., 1995; Feingold, 1992b; Langlois et al., 2000).

One problem is that highly attractive people can't always tell if the attention and praise they receive from others are due to their talent or just their good looks. A study by Brenda Major and others (1984) illustrates the point. Male and female participants who saw themselves as attractive or unattractive wrote essays that were later positively evaluated by an unknown member of the opposite sex. Half the participants were told that their evaluator would be watching them through a one-way mirror as they wrote the essay; the other half were led to believe that they could not be seen. In actuality, there was no evaluator, and all participants received identical, very positive evaluations of their work. Participants were then asked why their essay had been so favourably reviewed. The result: Those who saw themselves as unattractive felt better about the quality of their work after getting a glowing evaluation from someone who had seen them. Yet those who saw themselves as attractive and thought they had been seen attributed the glowing feedback to their looks—not to the quality of their work. For people who are highly attractive, positive feedback is sometimes hard to interpret (see Figure 9.3). This distrust may be well founded. In one study, many men and women openly admitted that they would lie in order to present themselves well to prospective dates—when those dates are highly attractive (Rowatt et al., 1999).

Another cost of having physical attractiveness as a social asset is the pressure to maintain one's appearance. In contemporary American society, such pressure is particularly strong when it comes to the body. This focus on the human form can produce a healthy emphasis on nutrition and exercise. But it can also have distinctly unhealthy consequences—as when men pop steroids to build muscles or when women over-diet in order to lose weight. Particularly among young women, an obsession with thinness can give rise to serious eating disorders such as *bulimia* (food binges followed by purging) and *anorexia nervosa* (self-imposed starvation, which can be fatal). Although estimates vary, recent studies indicate that fewer than 1 percent of women suffer from anorexia, that 2 to 3 percent have bulimia, and that these rates are higher among female students than among nonstudents (Fairburn & Brownell, 2002; Striegel-Moore & Smolak, 2001).

FIGURE 9.3

When Being Seen Leads to Disbelief

People who believed they were physically unattractive were more likely to cite the quality of their work as the reason for receiving a positive evaluation when they thought they were seen by the evaluator. However, people who believed they were attractive were less likely to credit the quality of their work when they thought they were seen. *(Major et al., 1984.)*

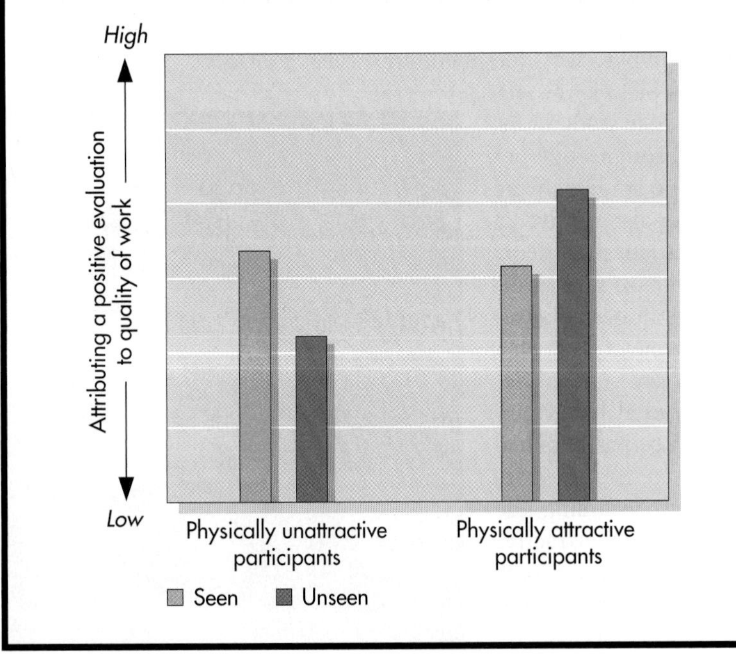

Women are more likely than men to suffer from what Janet Polivy and others (1986) call the "modern mania for slenderness." This slender ideal is projected in the mass media. Studies have shown that young women who see magazine ads or TV commercials that feature ultra-thin models become more dissatisfied with their own bodies than those who view neutral materials (Posavac et al., 1998). Trying to measure up to the multi-million-dollar supermodels can only prove frustrating to most. What's worse, the cultural ideal for thinness may be set early in childhood. Kevin Norton and others (1996) recently projected the life-size dimensions of the world-popular Ken and Barbie dolls and found that both were unnaturally thin compared with the average young adult. In fact, the estimated odds that any young woman will have Barbie's shape are approximately 1 in 100 000.

In sum, being beautiful may be a mixed blessing. There are some real benefits that cannot be denied, but there may be some costs as well. This trade-off makes you wonder about the long-term effects. Some years ago, Ellen Berscheid and others (1972) compared the physical attractiveness levels of students (based on yearbook pictures) to their adjustment when they reached middle age. There was little relationship between their appearance in youth and their later happiness. Those who were especially good-looking in university were more likely to be married, but they were not more satisfied with marriage or more content with life. Beauty may confer advantage, but it is not destiny.

People who are physically attractive are happier and have higher self-esteem than those who are unattractive. **False.**

First Encounters: Getting Acquainted

Proximity increases the odds that we will meet someone, familiarity puts us at ease, and beauty draws us in like magnets to a first encounter. But what determines whether sparks will fly in the early getting-acquainted stages of a relationship? In this section, we consider three characteristics of others that can influence our attraction: similarity, liking, and being hard to get.

Liking Others Who Are Similar The problem with proverbial wisdom is that it very often contradicts itself. Common sense tells us that "birds of a feather flock together." Yet we also hear that "opposites attract." So which is it? Before answering this question, imagine sitting at a computer, meeting someone in an online chat room, and striking up a conversation about politics, sports, restaurants, where you live, or your favourite band—only to realize that the two of you have a lot in common. Now imagine the opposite experience, of chatting with someone who is very different from you in his or her background, interests, values, and outlook on life. Which of the two strangers would you want to meet, the one who is similar or the one who is different?

Over the years, research has consistently shown that people tend to associate with others who are similar to themselves. On a whole range of demographic variables—including age, education, race, religion, height, level of intelligence, and socioeconomic status—people who go together as friends, dates, or partners in marriage resemble each other more than randomly paired couples (Warren, 1966).

These correlations cannot be used to prove that similarity causes attraction. A more compelling case could be made, however, by first measuring people's demographic characteristics and then determining whether these people, when they met others, liked those who were similar to them more than those who were dissimilar. This is what Theodore Newcomb (1961) did. In an elaborate study, Newcomb set up an experimental dormitory and found that students who were similar in their backgrounds grew to like each other more than did those who were dissimilar. Is demographic similarity still a factor even today, with all the choices we have in our diverse and multicultural society? Yes. Commenting on the persistently magnetic appeal of similarity, sociologist John Macionis (2003) notes that "Cupid's arrow is aimed by society more than we like to think." One unfortunate result, as we saw in Chapter 5, is that by associating only with similar others, people form social niches that are homogeneous—and divided along the lines of race, ethnic background, age, religion, level of education, and occupation (McPherson et al., 2001).

People can also be similar to us in other ways we find attractive—as when we share certain opinions, interests, and values. The drawing power of similarity is particularly evident on the Internet, where chat rooms and message boards bring together sports fans, political junkies, stock market investors, collectors, singles, and people from various geographical areas. What is the effect? Again Newcomb's (1961) experimental dormitory provided a unique setting for tracking attraction over time. During the course of the school year, he found that students who liked each other right from the start also perceived each other to be similar in attitudes. Since this link was established before the students knew each other, attraction was the active ingredient.

What about the role of *attitude* similarity in attraction? Here, the time course is slower, because people have to get to know each other first. In Newcomb's study, the link between actual similarity and liking increased gradually during the school year. Laboratory experiments have confirmed the point. For example, Donn Byrne (1971) had people give their opinions on a whole range of issues and then presented them with an attitude survey supposedly filled out by another person (the responses were actually rigged). In study after study, he found that participants liked this other person better when they perceived his or her attitudes as being more similar to theirs (Byrne, 1997).

The link between attitudes and attraction can also be seen in dating and married couples, as research shows that the more similar two people are in the roles they like to play and the ways they like to spend leisure time, the more compatible they are (Houts et al., 1996). Apparently, birds of a feather that flock together also stay together. But wait. Does this necessarily mean that similarity breeds attraction, or might attraction also breed similarity? In all likelihood, both mechanisms are at work. Studies of dating couples show that when partners who are close discover that they disagree on important moral issues, they bring their views on these issues into alignment and become more similar from that point on (Davis & Rusbult, 2001).

According to Milton Rosenbaum (1986), attraction researchers have overplayed the role of attitudinal similarity. Similarity does not spark attraction, he says; rather, *dis*similarity triggers repulsion—the desire to avoid someone. Rosenbaum maintains that people expect most others to be similar, which is why others who are different grab our attention. Taking this hypothesis one step further, David Lykken and Auke Tellegen (1993) argue that in mate selection, *all* forms of interpersonal similarity are irrelevant. After a person discards the 50 percent of the population who are least similar, they claim, a random selection process takes over.

So which is it: Are we turned on by others who are similar in their attitudes, or are we turned off by those who are different? As depicted in Figure 9.4, Donn Byrne and his colleagues proposed a two-step model that takes both reactions into account. First, they claim, we avoid associating with others who are dissimilar; then, among those who remain, we are drawn to those who are most similar (Byrne et al., 1986; Smeaton et al., 1989). Our reactions may also be influenced by expectations. People expect similarity from ingroup members—like fellow Liberals or Conservatives, or fellow straights or gays. In a series of studies, Fang Chen and Douglas Kenrick (2002) thus found that research participants were particularly attracted to outgroup members who expressed similar attitudes, and they were most repulsed by ingroup members who expressed dissimilar attitudes.

In addition to demographics and attitudes, there is a third source of similarity and difference also at work, at least in romantic relationships. Have you ever noticed the way people react to couples in which one partner is gorgeous and the other plain? Typically, we are startled by "mismatches" of this sort, as if expecting people to pair off with others who are similarly attractive—not more, not less. This reaction has a basis in reality. Early on, laboratory studies showed that both men and women yearn for partners who are highly attractive. Thus, when incoming first-year students at the University of Minnesota were randomly coupled for a dance, their desire for a second date was influenced more by their partner's physical attractiveness than by any other variable (Walster et al., 1966). In real-life situations,

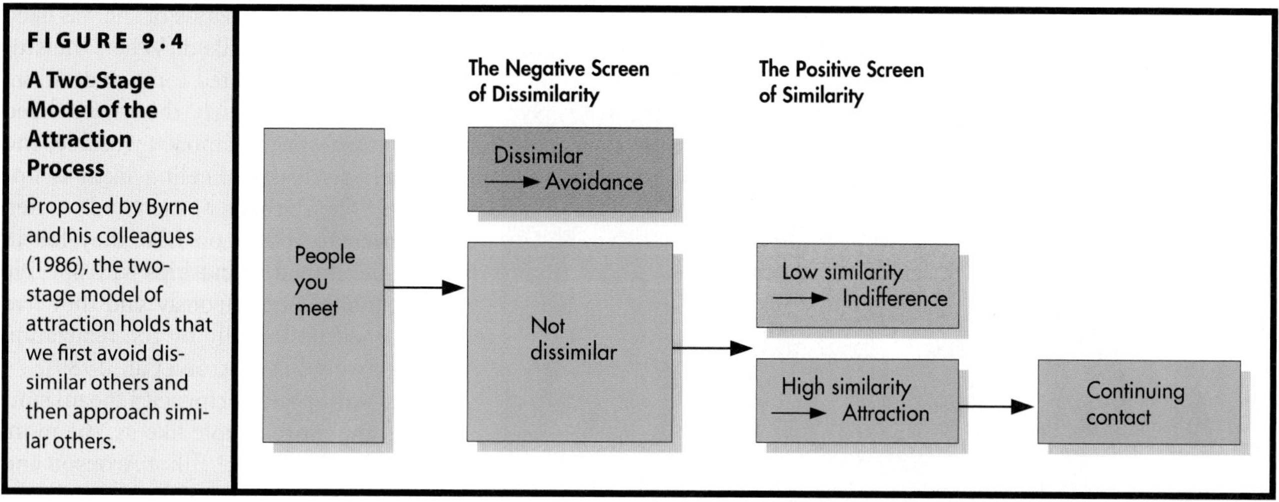

FIGURE 9.4

A Two-Stage Model of the Attraction Process

Proposed by Byrne and his colleagues (1986), the two-stage model of attraction holds that we first avoid dissimilar others and then approach similar others.

however, where one can be accepted or rejected by a prospective partner, people shy away from romantic encounters with others who are "out of their league" (Berscheid et al., 1971). Correlational studies of couples who are dating, engaged, living together, or married thus support a **matching hypothesis**—the idea that people tend to become involved romantically with others who are equivalent in their physical attractiveness (Feingold, 1988).

Matching is also predictive of progress in a relationship. When paired with others who were similar rather than dissimilar in their attractiveness, clients of a professional dating service were more likely to begin and then continue dating (Folkes, 1982)—and couples were more likely to grow closer and more in love (Murstein, 1972). In the romantic marketplace, physical matching seems to occur automatically, as people seek the best but settle for what they can get (Kalick & Hamilton, 1986).

Before concluding that similarity is the key to attraction, though, what about the common-sense notion that opposites attract? Many years ago, sociologists proposed the *complementarity* hypothesis, which holds that people seek others whose needs "oppose" their own—that people who need to dominate, for example, are drawn to those who are submissive (Winch et al., 1954). Is there any support for this view? Surprisingly, the answer is no. Sure, most human beings are romantically attracted to others of the opposite sex. But when it comes to fitting mutual needs and personality traits the way keys fit locks, research shows that complementarity does not influence attraction (O'Leary & Smith, 1991).

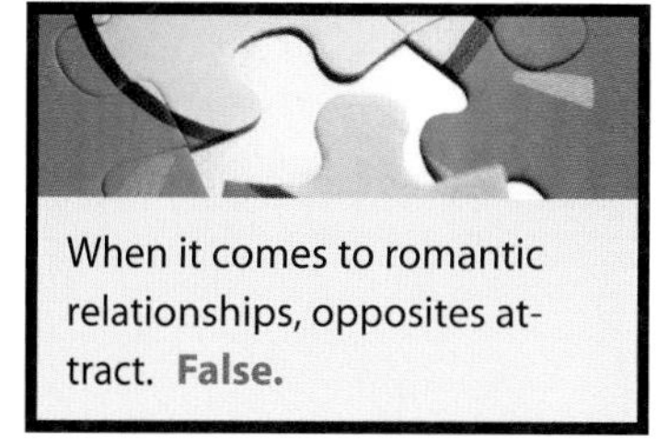

When it comes to romantic relationships, opposites attract. **False.**

Liking Others Who Like Us Many years ago, Fritz Heider (1958) theorized that people prefer relationships that are psychologically "balanced" and that a state of imbalance causes distress. In groups of three or more individuals, a balanced social constellation exists when we like someone whose relationships with others parallel our own. Thus, we want to like the friends of our friends and the enemies of our enemies (Aronson & Cope, 1968). If you've ever had a good friend who dated someone you detested, then you know just how awkward and unpleasant an *un*balanced relationship can be. The fact is, we don't expect our friends and enemies to get along (Chapdelaine et al., 1994).

Between two people, a state of balance exists when the relationship is characterized by **reciprocity**—a mutual exchange between what we give and what we receive. Liking is mutual, which is why we tend to like others who indicate that they like us. In one experiment, Rebecca Curtis and Kim Miller (1986) brought pairs of students into the laboratory, arranged for them to talk, and then "revealed" to one

matching hypothesis The proposition that people are attracted to others who are similar in physical attractiveness.

reciprocity A mutual exchange between what we give and receive—for example, liking those who like us.

When Julia Roberts and Lyle Lovett married, the popular press had a field day. Their pairing did not fit the expectations we tend to hold about the matching hypothesis.

member in each pair that he or she was liked by the partner or disliked. When the students were later reunited for conversation, those who thought that they were liked were, in turn, warmer, more agreeable, and more self-disclosing. Feeling liked is important. When groups of men and women were asked to reflect on how they fell in love or developed friendships with specific people, many spontaneously said they had been turned on initially by the realization that they were liked (Aron et al., 1989).

But wait. Does reciprocity mean, simply, that the more people like us, the more we will like them back? Elliot Aronson and Darwyn Linder (1965) conducted an interesting study in which female students met in pairs several times to discuss various topics. In each pair, one student was a research participant, and her partner was a confederate. After each meeting, the participant overheard a follow-up conversation between the experimenter and the confederate in which she was discussed and evaluated. Over time, the confederate's evaluation of the participant either was consistently positive or negative or underwent a change—either from negative to positive (gain) or from positive to negative (loss). Put yourself in the participant's shoes. All else being equal, in which condition would you like your partner most? In this study, participants liked the partner more when her evaluation changed from negative to positive than when it was positive all along. As long as the "conversion" is gradual and believable, people like others more when their affection takes time to earn than when it comes easily.

Pursuing Those Who Are Hard to Get The Aronson and Linder (1965) finding suggests that we like others who are socially selective. This seems to support an old popular notion that you can spark romantic interest by playing hard to get. For example, Ellen Fein and Sherri Schneider (1996) wrote a paperback book for women seductively titled *The Rules: Time-Tested Secrets for Capturing the Heart of Mr. Right.* What were the rules? Here's one: "Don't call him and rarely return his calls." Here's another: "Let him take the lead." In all cases, the theme was that men are charmed by women who are hard to get. It's an interesting hypothesis. Yet researchers have found that the **hard-to-get effect** is harder to get than they had originally anticipated (Walster et al., 1973). One problem is that we prefer people who are moderately selective compared with those who are nonselective (they have no taste, or no standards) or too selective (they are arrogant). Another is that we are turned *off* by those who reject us because they are committed to someone else or have no interest in us (Wright & Contrada, 1986).

But now suppose that someone you are interested in is hard to get for external reasons. What if a desired relationship is opposed or forbidden by parents, as in the story of Romeo and Juliet? What about a relationship threatened by catastrophe, as in the love story portrayed in the movie *Titanic*? What about distance, a lack of time, or renewed interest from a partner's old flame? As you may recall from Chapter 6, the theory of psychological reactance states that people are motivated to protect their freedom to choose and behave as they please. When a valued freedom is threatened, people reassert themselves, often by over-wanting the endangered behaviour—like the proverbial forbidden fruit (Brehm & Brehm, 1981).

hard-to-get effect The tendency to prefer people who are highly selective in their social choices over those who are more readily available.

Consistent with reactance theory, studies conducted in bars like this one have shown that men and women who are not in committed relationships see each other as more attractive as the night wears on.

Consider what happens when you think that your chance to get a date for the evening is slipping away. Is it true, to quote country-and-western musician Mickey Gilley, that "the girls all get prettier at closing time"? To find out, researchers entered some bars in Texas and asked patrons three times during the night to rate the physical attractiveness of other patrons of the same and opposite sex. As Gilley's lyrics suggested, people of the opposite sex were seen as more attractive as the night wore on (Pennebaker et al., 1979). The study is cute, but the correlation between time and attraction can be interpreted in other ways (perhaps attractiveness ratings rise with blood-alcohol levels!). More recently, however, Scott Madey and his colleagues (1996) also had patrons in a bar make attractiveness ratings throughout the night. They found that these ratings increased as the night wore on only among patrons who were not committed to a relationship. As reactance theory would predict, closing time posed a threat—which sparked desire—only to those on the lookout for a late-night date.

Another possible instance of passion fuelled by reactance can be seen in "the allure of secret relationships." In a fascinating experiment, Daniel Wegner and others (1994) paired up male and female students to play bridge. Within each foursome, one couple was instructed in writing to play footsie under the table—either secretly or in the open. Got the picture? After a few minutes, the game was stopped, and the players were asked to indicate privately how attracted they were to their own partner and to the opposite-sex member of the other team. The result: Students who played footsie in secret were more attracted to each other than those who played in the open or not at all. This finding is certainly consistent with reactance theory. But there may be more to it. As we'll see later, the thrill of engaging in a forbidden act, or the sheer excitement of having to keep a secret, may help fan the flames of attraction.

"Love ceases to be a pleasure when it ceases to be a secret."
—Aphra Behn

Finally, it's important to realize that there are situations in which reactance reduces interpersonal attraction. Think about it. Have you ever tried to play the matchmaker by insisting that two of your unattached single friends get together? Be forewarned: Setting people up can backfire. Determined to preserve the freedom to make their own romantic choices, your friends may become *less* attracted to each other than they would have been without your encouragement (Wright et al., 1992).

Mate Selection: The Evolution of Desire

Before moving onto the topic of close relationships, let's stop and ponder this question: When it comes to the search for a short-term or long-term mate, are men and women similarly motivated? If not, what are the differences? Later in this chapter, we'll see that most men appear more sex-driven than most women—desiring more frequent and more casual sex, more partners, and more variety, all of which leads researchers in the area to conclude that "men desire sex more than women" (Baumeister et al., 2001, p. 270).

In 1999, Ron Harris—a fashion photographer and horse breeder—opened Ron's Angels, a Web site on which he sells the ovarian eggs of beautiful models in Internet auctions. In answer to critics who say that this enterprise is distasteful, Harris says, "This is Darwin at his very best. It's the butterfly that's the prettiest that gets the guys."

The Evolutionary Perspective Why do these differences exist, and what do they mean? In *The Evolution of Desire*, David Buss (2003) argues that the answer can be derived from evolutionary psychology. According to this perspective, human beings all over the world exhibit mate-selection patterns that favour the conception, birth, and survival of their offspring—and women and men, by necessity, employ different strategies to achieve that common goal (Buss & Schmitt, 1993; Gangestad & Simpson, 2000; Trivers, 1972).

According to Buss, women must be highly selective because they are biologically limited in the number of children they can bear and raise in a lifetime. A woman must, therefore, protect those she has and so searches for a mate who possesses (or has the potential to possess) economic resources and is willing to commit those resources to support her offspring. The result is that women should be attracted to men who are older and financially secure or who have ambition, intelligence, stability, and other traits predictive of future success.

In contrast, men can father an unlimited number of children and ensure their reproductive success by inseminating many women. Men are restricted, however, by their ability to attract fertile partners and by their lack of certainty as to whether the babies born are actually their own. With these motives springing from their evolutionary past, men seek out women who are young and physically attractive (having smooth skin, full lips, lustrous hair, good muscle tone, and other youthful features)—attributes that signal health and reproductive fertility. To minimize their paternal uncertainty, men should also favour chastity, pursuing women they think will be sexually faithful rather than promiscuous.

To test this theory, Buss (1989) and a team of researchers surveyed 10 047 men and women in 37 cultures in North and South America, Asia, Africa, Eastern and Western Europe, and the Pacific. All respondents were asked to rank-order and rate the importance of various attributes in choosing a mate. The results were consistent with predictions. Both men and women gave equally high ratings to certain attributes, such as "having a pleasant disposition." But in the vast majority of countries, "good looks" and "no previous experience in sexual intercourse" were valued more by men, whereas "good financial prospect" and "ambitious and industrious" were more important to women. Analyses of personal ads appearing in magazines and newspapers have also revealed that in the dating marketplace the "deal" is that women offer beauty, while men offer wealth (Feingold, 1992a; Rajecki et al., 1991; Sprecher et al., 1994). In the words of one investigator, the search for a heterosexual mate seems to feature "men as success objects and women as sex objects" (Davis, 1990).

Some researchers have suggested that these gendered preferences are not mere luxuries, but necessities in the mating marketplace. In Buss's (1989) study, men were more likely to prefer good looks, and women were more likely to prefer good financial prospects, but both sexes saw other characteristics—such as funny, dependable, and kind—as more important. But what happens in real life, where mate seekers who can't have it all must prioritize their desires? Studying "the necessities and luxuries in mate preferences," Norman Li and others (2002) asked research participants to design their ideal marriage partner by purchasing different characteristics using "mate dollars." In some cases, they were granted a large budget to

FIGURE 9.5

Sex Differences in Mate Preference: Evolutionary Necessities?

In this study, participants built an ideal mate by purchasing characteristics. Given a large budget, men spent a somewhat higher percentage of money on physical attractiveness and women spent somewhat more on social status—relative to other characteristics. On a low budget, however, men spent even more on physical attractiveness and women spent even more on social status. *(Li et al., 2002.)*

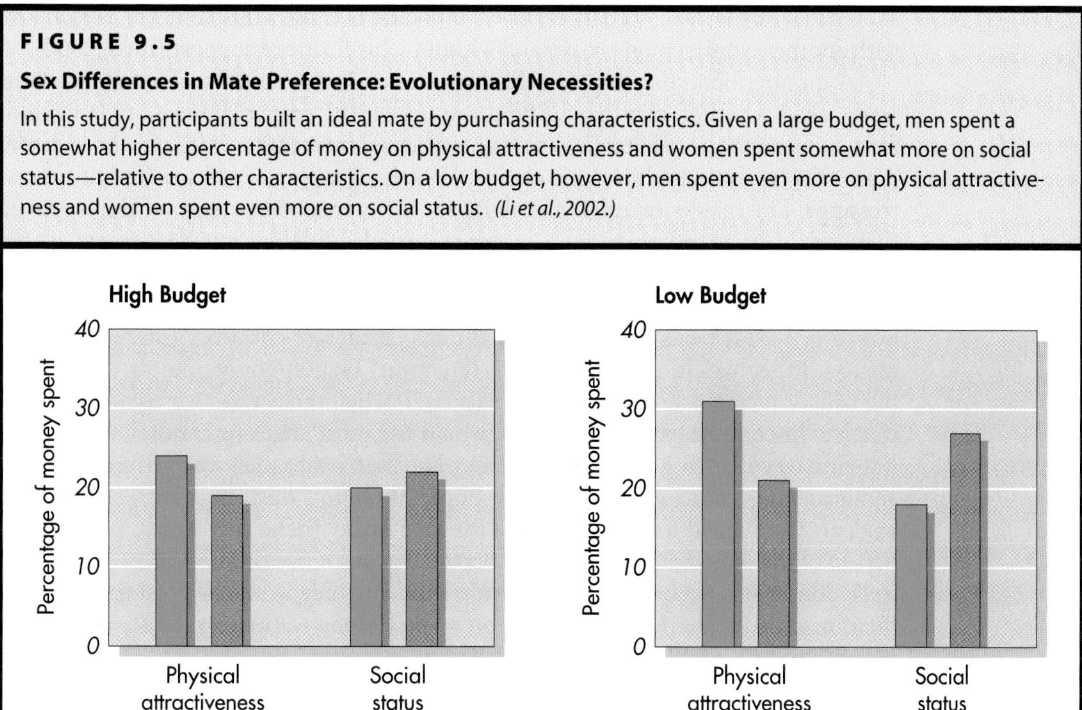

work with; in other cases, the budget was limited. In the large-budget condition, men spent somewhat more play money on physical attractiveness and women spent somewhat more on social status—but both were just as interested in a partner who was kind, lively, and creative. In the low-budget condition, however, men spent even more of their play money on physical attractiveness and women spent even more on social status. When mate seekers can't have it all and must therefore focus on what's most important, they prioritize their choices in the ways predicted by evolutionary theory (see Figure 9.5).

"Men seek to propagate widely, whereas women seek to propagate wisely."
—Robert Hinde

Also consistent with the evolutionary perspective is a universal tendency for men to seek younger women (who are most likely to be fertile) and for women to desire older men (who are most likely to have financial resources). Buss (1989) found this age-preference discrepancy in all the cultures he studied, with men on average wanting to marry women who were 2.7 years younger and women wanting men who were 3.4 years older. Based on their analysis of personal ads, Douglas Kenrick and Richard Keefe (1992) found that men in their twenties are equally interested in younger women and slightly older women still of fertile age. But men in their thirties seek out women who are five years younger, while men in their fifties prefer women 10 to 20 years younger. In contrast, girls and women of all ages are attracted to men who are older than they are. These patterns can also be seen in marriage statistics taken from different cultures and generations. There is one interesting exception: Teenage boys say they are most attracted to women who are slightly *older* than they are, women in their fertile twenties (Kenrick et al., 1996).

Also supportive of evolutionary theory is research on *jealousy*, "the dangerous passion"—a negative emotional state that arises from a perceived threat to one's relationship. Although jealousy is a common and normal human reaction, men and women may well be aroused by different triggering events. According to the theory, a man should be most upset by *sexual* infidelity because a wife's extramarital affair increases the risk that the children he supports are not his own. In contrast, a woman should feel threatened more by *emotional* infidelity because a husband who falls in love with another woman might leave and withdraw his financial support (Buss, 2000).

A number of studies support this hypothesis. In one, male and female students were asked whether they would be more upset if their romantic partner were to form a deep emotional attachment or have sexual intercourse with another person. Think for a moment about this choice. Which situation would *you* find more distressing? The results revealed a striking sex difference: 60 percent of the men said they would be more upset by a partner's sexual infidelity, but 83 percent of the women felt that emotional infidelity was worse (Buss et al., 1992).

In a second study, newly married husbands and wives were interviewed about how they would react if they suspected their partner of cheating. Interestingly, the men said they would use more "mate-retention" tactics (concealing or threatening the wife or taking action against the male rival) when their wives were young and attractive. In contrast, women said they would use more mate-retention tactics (being watchful or enhancing their appearance) when married to men who strived for status and made more money (Buss & Shackelford, 1997). In a third study, male and female students were asked to imagine their girlfriend or boyfriend flirting at a party with a person of the opposite sex—someone depicted as attractive or unattractive, and as socially dominant or submissive. The result: Men said they would be most jealous when their imagined male rival was dominant, while women were most jealous when their female rival was physically attractive (Dijkstra & Buunk, 1998).

Sociocultural Perspectives Although the differences between the sexes are intriguing, critics of the evolutionary approach are quick to argue that some of the results can be interpreted in terms that are "psychological" rather than "evolutionary." One common argument is that women trade youth and beauty for money not for reproductive purposes but, rather, because they often lack *direct* access to economic power. With this hypothesis in mind, Steven Gangestad (1993) examined women's access to wealth in each of the countries in Buss's cross-cultural study. He found that the more economic power women had, the more important male physical attractiveness was to them. This result suggests that it may be the generally low social and economic status of women relative to men that leads them to care less about the physical attributes of a potential mate.

Another argument concerns the finding that men are more fearful of a mate's sexual infidelity (which threatens paternal certainty), while women worry more about emotional infidelity (which threatens future support). The difference is consistent, but exactly what does it mean? There are two criticisms. First, in contrast to the explanation provided by evolutionary theory, some researchers have found that men become more upset over sexual infidelity not because of uncertain paternity but because they reasonably assume that a married woman who has a sexual affair is also likely to have intimate feelings for her extramarital partner. In other words, the man's concern, like the woman's, may be over the threat to the relationship—not fatherhood issues (DeSteno & Salovey, 1996; Harris & Christenfeld, 1996). Second, although men and women react differently when asked to imagine a partner's sexual or emotional infidelity, they are equally more upset by emotional infidelity when asked to recall actual experiences from a past relationship (Harris, 2002).

A third argument is that the differences typically found between the sexes are small compared to the similarities. This is an important point. In Buss's cross-cultural study, both men and women gave their highest ratings to such attributes as kindness, dependability, a good sense of humour, and a pleasant disposition (physical attractiveness and financial prospects did not top the lists). In fact, research shows that women desire physical attractiveness as much as men do when asked about what they want in a short-term casual sex partner (Regan & Berscheid, 1997).

Finally, the sex differences often observed are neither predictable nor universal. Human societies are remarkably flexible in terms of the ways people adapt to their environments—and there are revealing exceptions to the rules that are supposed to govern human play on the evolutionary field. For example, David Geary (2000) points out that while human fathers spend less time at child care than mothers do, they are unique among mammals—including baboons and chimpanzees, our evolutionary cousins—in the amount of care they give to their offspring. Geary speculates that human men care for their children in part because they enjoy more paternal certainty than do other male primates. Consider, too, the puzzling observation that most women of the Bari tribe in Venezuela are highly promiscuous. From an evolutionary standpoint, this behaviour does not seem adaptive since women who "sleep around" may scare off potential mates fearful of wasting their resources on children who are not their own. So why is female promiscuity the norm in this culture? In *Cultures of Multiple Fathers*, anthropologists Stephen Beckerman, Paul Valentine, and others note that the Bari—and some other aboriginal people in lowland South America—believe that a baby can have multiple fathers and that all men who have sex with a pregnant woman make a biological contribution to the unborn child (some groups assume that more than one father, or at least more than one insemination, are *required* to form a fetus). Thus, by taking many lovers a woman increases the number of men who provide for her child. It appears that this strategy works. A multifathered Bari child is 16 percent more likely than a single-fathered child to survive to the age of 15 (Beckerman & Valentine, 2002).

Summing Up The evolutionary perspective offers social psychologists a fascinating but controversial perspective on relationships. The approach continues to draw criticism that the results are weak, limited, or explainable by nonevolutionary means (Harris, 2003; Hazan & Diamond, 2000; Pedersen et al., 2002). However, it also continues to generate new and interesting ideas. At present, scientists in this area are studying a range of issues—such as the possible links between facial appearance and health and fertility (Fink & Penton-Voak, 2002); the flexibility or "plasticity" of sexual orientation in men and women (Baumeister, 2000); the potentially deadly link between sexual jealousy and violence (Buss, 2000); monogamy and extra-relationship affairs (Barash & Lipton, 2001); and mate poachers who seek sex partners from already committed relationships (Schmitt & Buss, 2001; Schmitt & Shackelford, 2003). Interested in the cognitive mechanisms that underlie mate selection behaviour, one clever researcher found that after university-age men are visually exposed to highly attractive young women, they begin to report more favourable attitudes toward wealth and more ambition—precisely the attributes said to be desired by women. This result suggests that people know what others consider attractive and then try to present themselves accordingly when primed to do so (Roney, 2003).

Close Relationships

Being attracted to people can be exhilarating or frustrating depending on how the initial encounters develop. How important is a good relationship to you? Researchers asked 300 students to weigh the importance of having a satisfying romantic relationship against the importance of other life goals (such as getting a good education, having a successful career, contributing to a better society) and found that 73 percent said they would sacrifice most other goals before giving up a good relationship (Hammersla & Frease-McMahan, 1990).

People have many significant relationships in their lives, but social psychologists have concentrated on adult friends, dating partners, lovers, and married couples (Berscheid & Regan, 2005; Brehm et al., 2001; Hendrick & Hendrick, 2000).

These **intimate relationships** often involve three basic components: (1) feelings of attachment, affection, and love; (2) the fulfillment of psychological needs; and (3) interdependence between partners, each of whom has a meaningful influence on the other.

Not all intimate relationships contain all these ingredients. A summer romance is emotionally intense; but in the fall, both partners resume their separate lives. An "empty shell" marriage revolves around coordinated daily activities; but emotional attachment is weak, and psychological needs go unmet. Clearly, relationships come in different shapes and sizes. Some are sexual; others are not. Some involve partners of the same sex; others, partners of the opposite sex. Some partners commit to a future together; others drop by for a brief stay. Feelings run the gamut from joyful to painful and from loving to hateful—with emotional intensity ranging all the way from mild to megawatt.

How do we advance from our first encounters to the intimate relationships that warm our lives? Do we proceed in stages, step by step, or by leaps and bounds? According to one perspective, relationships progress in order through a series of stages. For example, Bernard Murstein's (1986) *stimulus-value-role (SVR) theory* says there are three: (1) the stimulus stage, in which attraction is sparked by external attributes such as physical appearance; (2) the value stage, in which attachment is based on similarity of values and beliefs; and (3) the role stage, in which commitment is based on the performance of such roles as husband and wife. All three factors are important throughout a relationship, but each one is said to be first and foremost during only one stage.

In evaluating any stage theory, the critical issue is *sequence*. Does the value stage always precede the role stage, or might a couple work out roles before exploring whether their values are compatible? Most researchers do not believe that intimate relationships progress through a fixed sequence of stages. What then accounts for how they change? Every relationship has a developmental history with ups, downs, stalls, and accelerations. What pushes a relationship up, pulls it down, or keeps it steady? One common answer is *rewards*. Love, like attraction, depends on the experience of positive emotions in the presence of a partner. Step by step, as the rewards pile up, love develops. Or, as rewards diminish, love erodes. In reward theories of love, quantity counts. But some would disagree. Think about your own relationships. Are your feelings toward someone you love simply a more intense version of your feelings toward someone you like? Is the love of a close friend the same as the love of a romantic partner? If not, then you can appreciate that there are qualitative differences among relationships. Both views have something to offer. Progress on the road from attraction to love depends on the quantity of fuel in the tank *and* on the kind of engine providing the power. The next section examines the reward-based approach to building a relationship. Then we consider differences among the various types of relationships.

The Intimate Marketplace: Tracking the Gains and Losses

Earlier, we saw that people are initially attracted to others who provide them with direct or indirect rewards. But is "What's in it for me?" still important in a relationship that has blossomed and grown? Can an economic approach be used to predict the future of a close relationship?

Social Exchange Theory **Social exchange theory** is an economic model of human behaviour according to which people are motivated by a desire to maximize profit and minimize loss in their social relationships just as they are in business (Homans, 1961; Thibaut & Kelley, 1959). The basic premise of social exchange

intimate relationship A close relationship between two adults involving emotional attachment, fulfillment of psychological needs, or interdependence.

social exchange theory A perspective that views people as motivated to maximize benefits and minimize costs in their relationships with others.

theory is simple: Relationships that provide more rewards and fewer costs will be more satisfying and endure longer. Between intimates, the rewards include love, companionship, consolation in times of distress, and sexual gratification if the relationship is of this nature. The costs include the work it takes to maintain a relationship, conflict, compromise, and the sacrifice of opportunities elsewhere.

The development of an intimate relationship is very clearly associated with the overall level of rewards and costs. Research has shown that dating couples who experience greater increases in rewards as their relationship progresses are more likely to stay together than are those who experience small increases or declines (Berg & McQuinn, 1986). People do not worry about costs during the honeymoon phase of a relationship (Hays, 1985). After a few months, however, both rewards and costs contribute to levels of satisfaction—both in married couples (Margolin & Wampold, 1981) and in gay and lesbian couples living together (Kurdek, 1991a).

Rewards and costs do not arise in a psychological vacuum. People bring to their relationships certain expectations about the balance sheet to which they are entitled. John Thibaut and Harold Kelley (1959) coined the term *comparison level (CL)* to refer to this average expected outcome in relationships. A person with a high CL expects his or her relationships to be rewarding; someone with a low CL does not. Situations that meet or exceed a person's expectations are more satisfying than those that fall short. Even a bad relationship can look pretty good to someone who has a low CL.

According to Thibaut and Kelley, a second kind of expectation is also important. They coined the term *comparison level for alternatives (CLalt)* to refer to people's expectations about what they would receive in an alternative situation. If the rewards available elsewhere are believed to be high, a person will be less committed to staying in the present relationship (Drigotas & Rusbult, 1992). If people perceive few acceptable alternatives (a low CLalt), they will tend to remain—even in an unsatisfying relationship that fails to meet expectations (CL). Of course, just as these alternatives can influence our commitment, commitment can influence our perceptions of the alternatives. If you have ever been in love, you probably were not cold, calculating, and altogether objective in your perceptions of the alternatives. In close and intimate relationships, we act like lovers, not scientists, and harbour positive illusions. Research shows that people who are in love see other prospective partners as less appealing (Johnson & Rusbult, 1989; Simpson et al., 1990). They also tend to see their own partners and relationships through rose-coloured glasses (Collins & Feeney, 2000; Gagne & Lydon, 2001; Sanderson & Evans, 2001). Those who have positive illusions about their romantic partners tend to report more satisfaction, love, and trust in their relationships (Murray et al., 1996; Murray & Holmes, 1999). It seems that seeing one's partner through those rose-coloured glasses is conducive to happy, stable relationships.

A third element in the social exchange is investment. An *investment* is something a person puts into a relationship that he or she cannot recover if the relationship ends. If you don't like the way an intimate relationship is working out, you can pack your clothes, grab your laptop or CD player, and drive away. But what about the time you put into trying to make it last? What about all the romantic and career opportunities you sacrificed along the way? As you might expect, investments increase commitment. Because of those things we can't take with us, we're more likely to stay (Rusbult & Buunk, 1993).

Over the years, research has shown that the building blocks of the social exchange framework—as depicted in Figure 9.6, and as incorporated into Caryl Rusbult et al.'s (1998) Investment Model—can be used to determine the level of commitment that partners bring to a relationship (Le & Agnew, 2003). This is important because commitment levels predict how long relationships will last. In studies of dating and married couples, research shows that the best-adjusted ones are those in which each partner is committed and sees the other as mutually committed

FIGURE 9.6

Relational Building Blocks

The building blocks of social exchange are rewards, costs, comparison level, comparison level for alternatives, and investments. These factors are strongly associated with the satisfaction and commitment partners experience in their relationship.

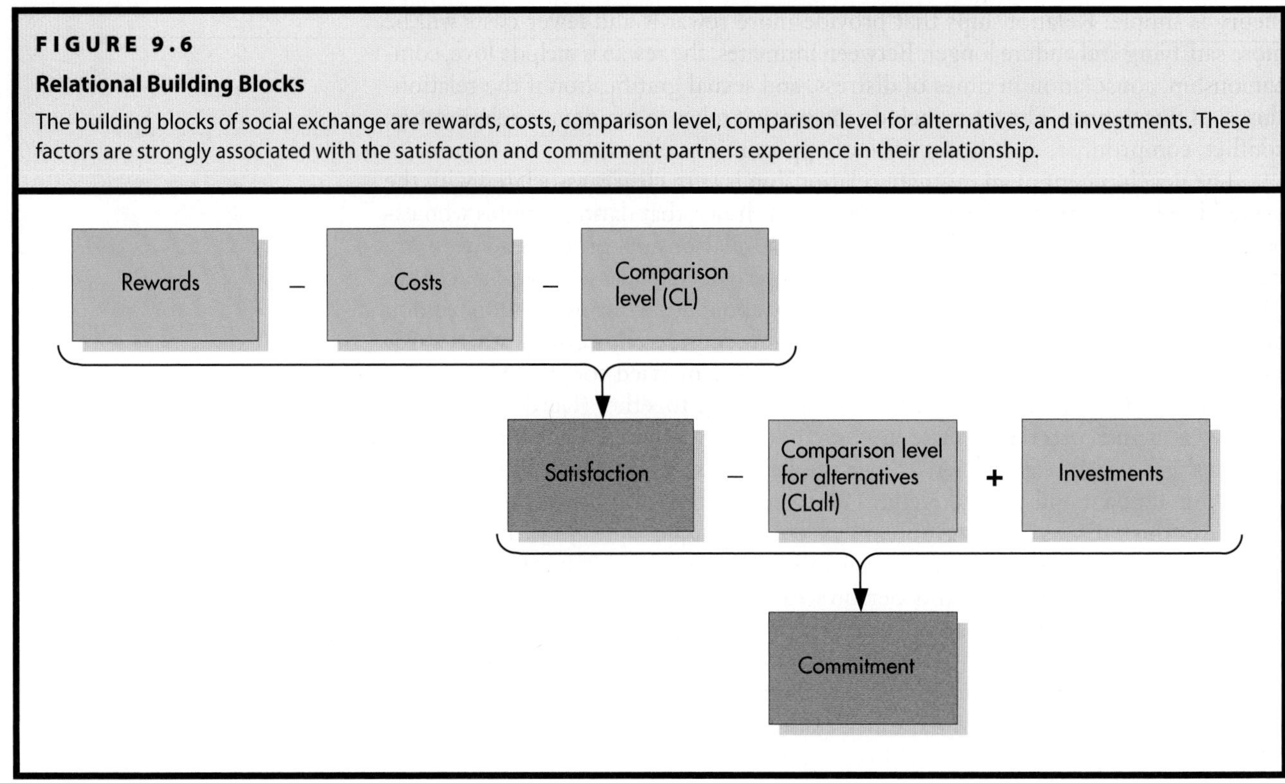

(Drigotas et al., 1999). Studies also show that people who are committed to their relationship often engage in pro-relationship behaviours—being flexible, generous, and self-sacrificing—which builds trust (Wieselquist et al., 1999). Particularly important for the durability of a relationship, people who are committed are more likely to forgive and forget when their partners betray a spoken or unspoken relationship norm by flirting, lying, forgetting an anniversary, revealing an embarrassing story in public, or having an affair (Finkel et al., 2002).

Equity Theory **Equity theory** is a specific version of how social exchange operates in interpersonal interactions (Adams, 1965; Messick & Cook, 1983; Walster et al., 1978). According to this theory, people are most content with a relationship when the ratio between what they get out of it (benefits) and what they put into it (contributions) is similar for both partners. Thus, the basic equity formula is:

$$\frac{\text{Your Benefits}}{\text{Your Contribution}} = \frac{\text{Your Partner's Benefit}}{\text{Your Partner's Contribution}}$$

Equity is different from equality. According to equity theory, the balance is what counts. So if one partner benefits more from a relationship but also makes a greater contribution, then the situation is equitable. In an *in*equitable relationship, the balance is disturbed: One partner (called the *overbenefited*) receives more benefits than he or she deserves on the basis of contributions made, while the other partner (aptly called the *underbenefited*) receives fewer benefits than deserved.

Both overbenefit and underbenefit are unstable and often unhappy states. Underbenefited partners feel angry and resentful because they are giving more than their partner for the benefits they receive. At the same time, overbenefited partners feel guilty because they are profiting unfairly. Both kinds of inequity are associated with negative emotions in dating couples (Walster et al., 1978), married couples

equity theory The theory that people are most satisfied with a relationship when the ratio between benefits and contributions is similar for both partners.

(Schafer & Keith, 1980), and the friendships of elderly widows (Rook, 1987). When it comes to satisfaction with a relationship, however, it is more unpleasant to feel underbenefited than overbenefited. People prefer to receive too much in life rather than too little—even if they feel bad about it (Grote & Clark, 2001; Hatfied et al., 1982; Sprecher, 2001).

It may strike you that although equity is important, determining whether or not a given relationship is equitable can be difficult. You have to tally up your own benefits, tally up your contributions, compute your partner's benefits and contributions, and compare the two. Rodney Cate and Sally Lloyd (1992) wondered whether people really go to all this trouble when much simpler calculations might suffice. In a series of studies, they found that the absolute level of rewarding outcomes was actually a better predictor of relationship satisfaction and endurance than was either an equality of rewards or equity. Simply put, the more good things people said they received from a relationship, the better they felt about it.

Types of Relationships

Social exchange models focus on quantity: The more (rewards, equity), the better (satisfaction, endurance). But is reward always necessary? And what about the qualitative differences in our relationships? Does more reward turn casual acquaintances into friends, and friends into lovers, or are these types of relationships different from each other in other ways?

Exchange and Communal Relationships According to Margaret Clark and her colleagues, people operate by a reward-based model when they are in **exchange relationships**, which are characterized by an immediate tit-for-tat repayment of benefits. In these situations, people want costs to be quickly offset by compensation, leaving the balance at zero. But not all relationships fit this mould. Clark maintains that in **communal relationships**, partners respond to each other's needs and well being over time, without regard for whether they have given or received a benefit (Clark, 1984; Clark & Mills, 1979).

Exchange relationships most often exist between strangers and casual acquaintances and in certain long-term arrangements such as business partnerships. In contrast, strong communal relationships are usually limited to close friends, romantic partners, and family members (Clark & Mills, 1993). Based on fieldwork in West Africa, Alan Fiske (1992) is convinced that this distinction applies to human interactions all over the world. But the cynics among us wonder: Are communal relationships truly free of social exchange considerations? Can people really give without any desire to receive, or do partners in a communal relationship follow a more subtle version of social exchange, assuming that the benefits will balance out in the long run? Clark and Judson Mills (1993) believe that true communal relationships do exist—that once a communal norm has been adopted in a relationship, regardless of how it started, the motivation to respond to the other's needs becomes automatic.

Secure and Insecure Attachment Styles Another interesting approach to understanding relationships is provided by Phillip Shaver, Cindy Hazan, and their colleagues, who have theorized that just as infants display different kinds of attachment toward their parents, so do adults exhibit specific **attachment styles** in their romantic relationships (Cassidy & Shaver, 1999).

For many years, child development psychologists had noticed that infants form intense, exclusive bonds with their primary caretakers. This first relationship is highly charged with emotion, and it emerges with regularity from one culture to the next. By observing the way babies react to both separations from and reunions with the primary caretaker, usually the mother, researchers also noticed that babies

exchange relationship A relationship in which the participants expect and desire strict reciprocity in their interactions.

communal relationship A relationship in which the participants expect and desire mutual responsiveness to each other's needs.

attachment style The way a person typically interacts with significant others.

have different attachment styles. Those with *secure* attachments cry in distress when the mother leaves and then beam with sheer delight when she returns. Those with insecure attachments show one of two patterns. Some, described as *anxious*, cling and cry when the mother leaves but then greet her with anger or apathy upon her return. Others are generally more detached and *avoidant*, not reacting much on either occasion (Ainsworth et al., 1978).

How important is this first attachment? Does a secure and trusting bond in the first year of life lay a foundation for close relationships later in life? John Bowlby (1988), a psychiatrist and influential theorist, argues that there is a link—that infants form "internal working models" of attachment figures, and that these models guide their relationships later in life. Research shows that infants classified as securely attached are later more positive in their outlook toward others (Cassidy et al., 1996). Looking back, adults with a secure attachment style described having positive family relationships, while avoidant and anxious adults recalled having problems with one or both parents (Feeney & Noller, 1990; Hazan & Shaver, 1987).

Whether or not adult attachment styles are rooted in the first year of life, the distinction among adults has proved to be a useful one. Read the descriptions of three attachment types in Table 9.1. Which fits you best? Hazan and Shaver (1987) presented this task initially in a "love quiz" that appeared in a newspaper and then in a study of university students. As shown in Table 9.1, the distribution of responses was similar in the two samples, and it proved similar again in a later US-wide sample of 8000 adults (Mickelson et al., 1997). In addition, the researchers found that

TABLE 9.1
Attachment Style *(Hazan & Shaver, 1987.)*

Question: Which of the following best describes your feelings?

Answers and Percentages	Newspaper Sample	University Sample
Secure I find it relatively easy to get close to others and am comfortable depending on them and having them depend on me. I don't often worry about being abandoned or about someone getting too close to me.	56%	56%
Avoidant I am somewhat uncomfortable being close to others; I find it difficult to trust them completely, difficult to allow myself to depend on them. I am nervous when anyone gets too close, and often, love partners want me to be more intimate than I feel comfortable being.	25%	23%
Anxious I find that others are reluctant to get as close as I would like. I often worry that my partner doesn't really love me or won't want to stay with me. I want to merge completely with another person, and this desire sometimes scares people away.	19%	21%

people who have a secure attachment style report having satisfying relationships that are happy, friendly, based on mutual trust, and enduring. Cognitively, they see people as good-hearted; and they believe in romantic love. In contrast, avoidant lovers fear intimacy and believe that romantic love is doomed to fade; and anxious lovers report a love life full of emotional highs and lows, obsessive preoccupation, a greater willingness than others to make long-term commitments, and extreme sexual attraction and jealousy.

To some extent, our attachment styles can be seen in our everyday behaviour. For example, Jeffrey Simpson and others (1996) videotaped dating couples as they tried to resolve various conflicts and then showed the tapes to outside observers. They found that men classified as having an insecure-avoidant attachment style were the least warm and supportive and that women with an insecure-anxious style were the most upset and negative in their behaviour. In another study, Campbell, Simpson, Boldry, and Kashy (2005) asked dating partners at the University of Western Ontario to keep a 14-day diary, and then videotaped the couples discussing a problem. They found that anxiously attached individuals were more likely to feel that there was greater conflict in the relationship and that the problems were escalating; independent raters noted that these individuals were more likely to be responsible for the escalation of conflict.

What about the future? Does the attachment style you endorse today foretell relational outcomes tomorrow? On this question, the evidence is mixed. People who are secure do tend to have more lasting relationships. But the prognosis for those classified as insecure is harder to predict, with the results less consistent. What's important to realize is that although styles of attachment are somewhat stable over time—perhaps as holdovers from infancy and childhood—they are not fixed, or completely set in stone. For instance, Lee Kirkpatrick and Cindy Hazan (1994) tracked down participants from an earlier study and found, four years later, that 30 percent had different attachment styles. In keeping with the central theme of social psychology—that people are profoundly shaped by the situations they are in—research suggests that people may continuously revise their attachment styles in response to their own relationship experiences (Baldwin & Fehr, 1995; Keelan et al., 1994; Scharfe & Bartholomew, 1994).

"I have studied love because it is my life's most difficult problem. Although I have made much progress, the 'impossible dream' of a truly fulfilling mutual love remains a goal I have yet to achieve."
—John Alan Lee

How Do I Love Thee? Counting the Ways

The poet Elizabeth Barrett Browning asked, "How do I love thee?" and then went on to "count the ways"—of which there are many. When students were asked to list all the kinds of love that came to mind, they produced 216 items—such as friendship, parental, brotherly, sisterly, romantic, sexual, spiritual, obsessive, possessive, and puppy love (Fehr & Russell, 1991).

Over the years, various schemes for classifying different types of love have been proposed (Sternberg & Barnes, 1998). On the basis of ancient writings, sociologist John Alan Lee (1988) identified three primary love styles—*eros* (erotic love), *ludus* (game-playing, uncommitted love), and *storge* (friendship love). As with primary colours, Lee theorized, these three styles can be blended together to form new secondary types of love, such as *mania* (demanding and possessive love), *pragma* (pragmatic love), and *agape* (other-oriented, altruistic love). On a scale designed to measure these "colours of love," men tend to score higher than women on *ludus*, while women score higher on *storge*, *mania*, and *pragma* (Hendrick & Hendrick, 1995).

Another popular taxonomy is derived from Robert Sternberg's (1986) **triangular theory of love**. According to Sternberg, there are eight basic subtypes of love (seven different forms of love and an eighth combination that results in non-love)—and all can be derived from the presence or absence of three components. The

triangular theory of love A theory proposing that love has three basic components—intimacy, passion, and commitment—which can be combined to produce eight subtypes.

FIGURE 9.7

Sternberg's Triangular Theory of Love

According to Sternberg, various combinations of passion, intimacy, and commitment give rise to seven different types of love (although not shown, the absence of all three components produces an eighth result, non-love). *(Sternberg, 1986.)*

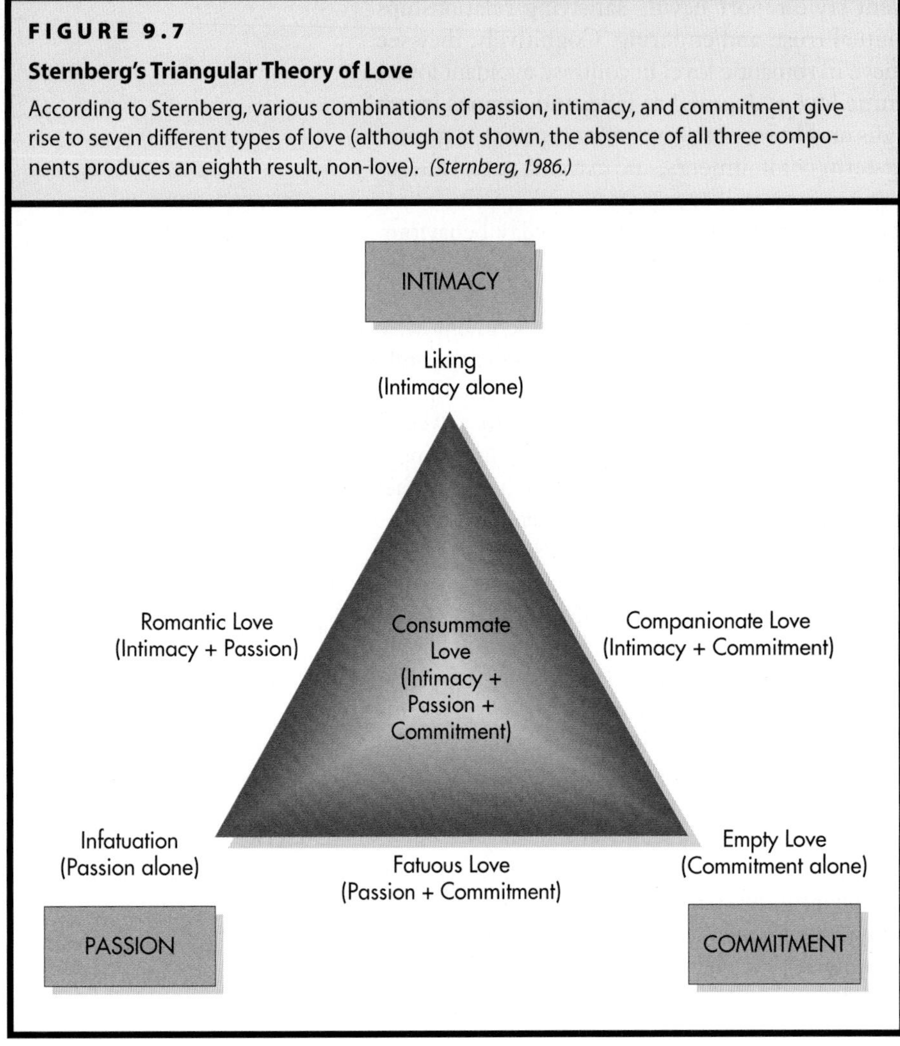

combination can thus be viewed as the vertices of a triangle (see Figure 9.7). These three components—and sample items used to measure each one—are described below:

Intimacy: The emotional component, which involves liking and feelings of closeness. ("I have a comfortable relationship with ___.")

Passion: The motivational component, which contains drives that trigger attraction, romance, and sexual desire. ("Just seeing ___ is exciting for me.")

Commitment: The cognitive component, which reflects the decision to make a long-term commitment to a loved partner. ("I will always feel a strong responsibility for ___.")

Research provides good support for this tri-component model of love (Sternberg, 1999). In one study, Arthur Aron and Lori Westbay (1996) asked people to rate 68 prototypical features of love and found that all the various features fell into three categories: passion *(gazing at the other, euphoria, butterflies in the stomach)*, intimacy *(feeling free to talk about anything, supportive, understanding)*, and commitment *(devotion, putting the other first, long-lasting)*. In a second study, Sternberg (1997) asked people to indicate what they see as important in different kinds of relationships and found that the results were consistent with the theory. For example, "ideal lover" scored high on all three components, "friend" scored high on intimacy and commitment but low on passion, and "sibling" scored high on commitment but low on intimacy and passion.

In light of infant attachments, colours, triangles, and other love classification schemes that have been proposed over the years, one wonders: How many types of love are there, really? It's hard to tell. But there are two basic types that are built into all models: *liking*, the type of feeling you would have for a platonic friend, and *loving*, the kind of feeling you would have for a romantic partner. According to Zick Rubin (1973), liking and loving are two distinct reactions to an intimate relationship. There is some question, however, about how sharp the difference is. Kenneth and Karen Dion (1976) questioned casual daters, exclusive daters, engaged couples, and married couples. Although casual daters reported more liking than loving, liking and loving did not differ among those in the more committed dating relationships. More pointed is the two-pronged distinction made by Elaine Hatfield (1988) and others between passionate love and companionate love. According to Hatfield, **passionate love** is an emotionally intense *and often erotic* state of absorption in another person, whereas **companionate love** is a secure, trusting, and stable partnership, similar to what Rubin called liking.

passionate love Romantic love characterized by high arousal, intense attraction, and fear of rejection.

companionate love A secure, trusting, stable partnership.

According to excitation transfer theory, bodily arousal triggered by one stimulus can be misattributed to another stimulus. This theory suggests that the energy that springs from dancing may intensify a person's feelings for their partner, fanning the flames of passion.

Passionate Love: The Thrill of It Passionate love is an intense emotional state of absorption in another person. From ecstatic highs to agonizing lows, it is the bittersweet stuff of romance paperbacks, popular music, poems, and soap operas. What is passionate love, and where does it come from? According to Ellen Berscheid and Elaine Walster (later Hatfield) (1974), the key to understanding passionate love is to recognize that it is an emotion—and can be analyzed like any other emotion. Drawing on Schachter's (1964) two-factor theory of emotion (see Chapter 3), they theorized that passionate love requires two key ingredients: (1) a heightened state of physiological *arousal* and (2) the *belief* that this arousal was triggered by the beloved person.

Sometimes, the arousal-love connection is obvious—as when a person feels a surge of sexual desire at the sight of a romantic partner. At other times, however, the symptoms of arousal—such as a pounding heart, sweaty palms, and weak knees—can be hard to interpret. In the company of an attractive person, these symptoms may be attributed or "misattributed" to passionate love. Dolf Zillmann (1984) calls the process **excitation transfer**. According to Zillmann, arousal triggered by one stimulus can be transferred or added to the arousal from a second stimulus. The combined arousal is then perceived as having been caused only by the second stimulus.

Donald Dutton and Arthur Aron (1974) first tested this provocative hypothesis in a field study that took place on two bridges above British Columbia's Capilano River. One was a narrow, wobbly suspension bridge (137 metres long and 1.5 metres wide, with a low handrail) that sways 70 metres above rocky rapids—a nightmare for anyone the least bit afraid of heights. The other bridge was wide, sturdy, and only 3 metres from the ground. Whenever an unaccompanied young man walked across one of these bridges, he was met by an attractive young woman who introduced herself as a research assistant, asked him to fill out a brief questionnaire, and gave her phone number in case he wanted more information about the project. As predicted, men who crossed the scary bridge were later more likely to call her than those who crossed the stable bridge. In an amusement park study of "love at first fright," Cindy Meston and Penny Frohlich (2003) similarly found that men and women who were not with a romantic partner rated a pictured person of the opposite sex as more attractive just after they rode on a roller coaster than before they began the ride. Perhaps terror can fan the hot flames of romance.

Or maybe not. Maybe it's just a relief to be with someone when we're in distress. To rule out the possibility that it's relief rather than arousal that fuels attraction, Gregory White and his colleagues (1981) had to create arousal without distress. How? A little exercise can do it. Male participants ran in place for either two minutes or 15 seconds and then saw a videotape of a woman they expected to meet. The woman had been made up to look physically attractive or unattractive. After watching the video, participants rated her appearance. The result: Those who exercised for two minutes as opposed to only 15 seconds saw the physically attractive woman as even more attractive and the unattractive woman as less attractive. This

excitation transfer The process whereby arousal caused by one stimulus is added to arousal from a second stimulus and the combined arousal is attributed to the second stimulus.

study, and others like it (Allen et al., 1989), showed that arousal—even without distress—intensifies emotional reactions, positive or negative.

The implication of this research—that our passions are at the mercy of bridges, roller coasters, exercise, and anything else that causes the heart to race—is intriguing. It is certainly consistent with the common observation that people are vulnerable to falling in love when their lives are turbulent. But does the effect occur, as theorized, because people *mis*attribute their arousal to a person they have just met? Yes and no. Based on their review of 33 experiments, Craig Foster and others (1998) confirmed that the arousal-attraction effect does exist. They also found, however, that the effect occurs even when people know the actual source of their arousal—in other words, even without misattribution. According to these investigators, just being aroused, even if we know why, facilitates whatever is the most natural response. If the person we meet is good-looking and of the right sex, we become more attracted. If the person is not good-looking or is of the wrong sex, we become less attracted. No thought is required. The response is automatic.

Whatever its moment-by-moment determinants, passionate love is a widespread, probably universal, human phenomenon. Looking at anthropological research on 166 cultures, William Jankowiak and Edward Fischer (1992) detected at least some indications of passionate love in 147 of them. In light of the highly sexual nature of passionate love, this should come as no surprise. In a book entitled *Lust: What We Know About Human Sexual Desire*, Pamela Regan and Ellen Berscheid (1999) present compelling evidence for the proposition that intense sexual desire and excitement are a vital part of the experience. In this regard, they are quick to note that "to love" is different from "being in love." To illustrate, Berscheid and Meyers (1996) asked men and women to make three lists: people they loved, people they were in love with, and people they were sexually attracted to. As it turned out, only 2 percent of those in the "love" category also appeared in the sex list. Yet among those in the "in love" category, the overlap with sex was 85 percent. And when Regan and her colleagues (1998) asked people to list the characteristics of romantic love, two-thirds cited sexual desire—more than the number who put happiness, loyalty, communication, sharing, or commitment on the list.

Although most people in the world agree that sexual desire is what injects the passion into passionate love, not everyone sees it as necessary for marriage. Think about this question: If a man or woman had all other qualities you desired, would you marry this person if you were *not* in love? When American students were surveyed in 1967, 35 percent of men and 76 percent of women said yes. Twenty years later, only 14 percent of men and 20 percent of women said they would marry someone with whom they were not in love (Simpson et al., 1986). The shift among women may reflect the pragmatic point that marrying for love is an economic luxury that few women of the past could afford.

In a wedding ceremony that took place in Bombay, Tushar Agarwal and his bride Richa are married. Fulfilling a tradition that seems strange to most North Americans, for whom being in love is essential, this Indian marriage was arranged.

The willingness to marry without love is also subject to cultural variation. Today, that number ranges from 4 percent in the United States, 5 percent in Australia, and 8 percent in

England up to 49 percent in India and 51 percent in Pakistan (Levine, 1993). Culture's influence on love is interesting. On the one hand, it could be argued that the rugged individualism found in western cultures would inhibit the tendency to become intimate and interdependent with others. On the other hand, this same individualistic orientation leads people to give priority in making marital decisions to their own feelings—rather than to family concerns, social obligations, religious constraints, income, and the like (Dion & Dion, 1996).

"True love never grows old."
—proverb

Even in North America, home of a strong and consistent romantic ideology, people have doubts about the staying power of passionate love. Does the fire within a relationship burn hot and bright over time, or is it just a passing fancy? Comparisons of couples at different stages of their relationships and longitudinal studies that measure changes in the same couples over time suggest that passionate love does diminish somewhat over time (Acker & Davis, 1992; Tucker & Aron, 1993).

Companionate Love: The Self-Disclosure in It In contrast to the intense, emotional, and erotic nature of passionate love, companionate love is a form of affection found between close friends as well as lovers. Companionate relationships rest more on a foundation of mutual trust, caring, respect, friendship, and long-term commitment—characteristics that John Harvey and Julie Omarzu (2000) see as necessary for "minding the close relationship."

Compared with the passionate form of love, companionate love is less intense but in some respects deeper and more enduring. Susan Sprecher and Pamela Regan (1998) administered passionate and companionate love scales to heterosexual couples who had been together for varying amounts of time and found that passionate love scores of both men and women initially rose over time but then peaked and declined somewhat during marriage. Companionate love scores, however, did not similarly decline. In fact, in couples that stay together, partners are likely to report that "I love you more today than yesterday" (Sprecher, 1999). Like the sturdy, steady tortoise in Aesop's fable, companionate love may seem outpaced by the flashier start of passionate love, but it can still cross the finish line well ahead.

Companionate love is characterized by high levels of **self-disclosure**, a willingness to open up and share intimate facts and feelings. In a way, self-disclosure is to companionate love what arousal is to passionate love. Think for a moment about your most embarrassing moment, your most cherished ambitions, or your sex life. Would you bare your soul on these private matters to a complete stranger? What about an acquaintance, date, friend, or lover? Whether or not to self-disclose—what, when, how much, and to whom—is a decision that each of us makes based on a consideration of what we stand to gain and lose in a relationship (Omarzu, 2000).

Still, it is the willingness to disclose intimate facts and feelings that lies at the heart of our closest and most intimate relationships (Derlega et al., 1993). Research shows that the more emotionally involved people are in a close relationship, the more they self-disclose to each other. Nancy Collins and Lynn Miller (1994) note three possible reasons for this correlation: (1) We disclose to people we like, (2) we like people who disclose to us, and (3) we like people to whom we have disclosed. Thus, among pairs of students brought together in a laboratory for brief getting-acquainted conversations, the more they self-disclosed, the better they felt about each other afterward (Vittengl & Holt, 2000).

Over the years, researchers have made three major observations about self-disclosure patterns in relationships. One is that partners reveal more to each other as their relationship grows over time. According to Irving Altman and Dalmas Taylor (1973), self-disclosure is a basic form of social exchange that unfolds as relationships develop. Their *social penetration theory* holds that relationships progress from superficial exchanges to more intimate ones. At first, people give relatively little of themselves to each other and receive little in return. If the initial encounters prove rewarding, however, the exchanges become both *broader* (covering more areas of

self-disclosure Revelations about the self that a person makes to others.

FIGURE 9.8

From a Sliver to a Wedge

According to the theory of social penetration, as a relationship becomes closer, partners increase both the breadth (covering a wider range of topics) and depth (revealing more intimate information) of their exchanges.

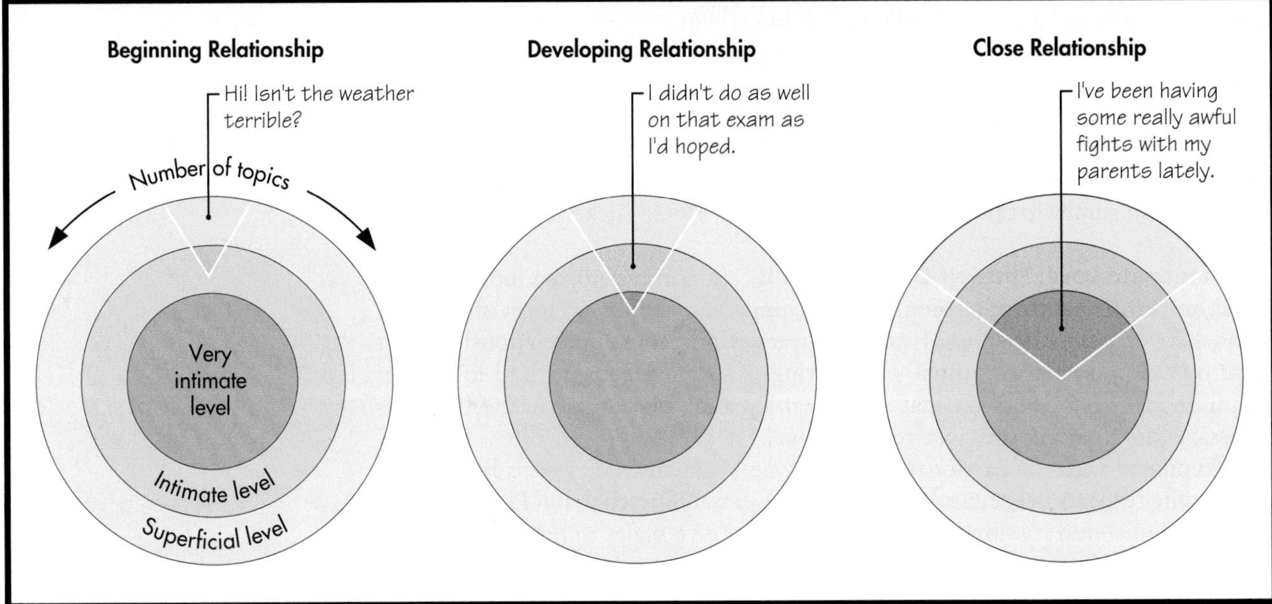

their lives) and *deeper* (involving more sensitive areas). As shown in Figure 9.8, social interaction grows from a narrow, shallow sliver to a wider, more penetrating wedge.

This increase in self-disclosure can be seen in the fact that the more intimate people are in a relationship, the less likely they are to lie to each other. In a naturalistic study of this point, Bella DePaulo and Deborah Kashy (1998) asked people to keep a one-week diary of all social encounters and record every instance in which they tried to mislead someone—regardless of how self-serving or well-meaning the intent (some lies are told to advance the liar's self-interest, and others are told for the other person's benefit). As it turned out, the rate of lying among participants decreased according to the closeness of their relationships. On average, they lied most to strangers, followed by casual acquaintances, then family members and friends. Also consistent with the presumed patterns of self-disclosure is that unmarried participants lied three times more often to their romantic partners than married participants did to their spouses. These results are presented in Figure 9.9.

A second observation is that patterns of self-disclosure change according to the state of a relationship. During a first encounter, and in the budding stages of a new relationship, people tend to reciprocate another's self-disclosure with their own—at a comparable level of intimacy. If a new acquaintance opens up, it is polite to match that self-disclosure by revealing more of ourselves. Once a relationship is well established, however, strict reciprocity occurs less frequently (Altman, 1973; Derlega et al., 1976). Among couples in distress, two different self-disclosure patterns have been observed. For some, both breadth and depth decrease as partners withdraw from each other and cease to communicate (Baxter, 1987). For others, the breadth of self-disclosure declines, but depth increases as the partners hurl cruel and angry statements at each other (Tolstedt & Stokes, 1984). In this case, the social *de*penetration process resembles neither the sliver of a superficial affiliation nor the wedge of a close relationship—but, rather, a long, thin dagger of discontent.

A third common observation is that individuals differ in the tendency to share private, intimate thoughts with others. For example, Kathryn Dindia and Mike Allen (1992) conducted a meta-analysis of 205 studies involving 23 702 white North Americans and found, on average, that women are more open than men—and that people in general are more self-disclosing to women than to men. This being the case, it comes as no surprise that women rate their same-sex friendships more highly than men rate theirs. At least in North America, male friends seem to bond more by taking part in common activities, while female friends engage more in a sharing of feelings (Duck & Wright, 1993). As Paul Wright (1982) put it, women tend to interact "face-to-face;" men go "side-by-side."

FIGURE 9.9

To Whom Do People Lie?

For one week, people recorded every instance in which they tried to mislead someone. As you can see, they lied most to strangers, followed by acquaintances, family members, and friends (left). Also shown is that people lied more often to their unmarried romantic partners than to their spouses (right). These results suggest that the closer two people are, the less likely they are to lie to each other. *(Data from DePaulo & Kashy, 1998.)*

Rate of lying: 0, 10, 20, 30, 40, 50, 60, 70

Strangers Acquaintances Friends Family | Romantic partners Spouses

Types of Relationships

Relationship Issues: The Male-Female "Connection"

Browse the shelves of any bookstore, and you'll see one paperback title after another on the general topic of gender. There are books for men and books for women, books that preach the masculine ideal and books that tell us how to be more feminine, books that portray men and women as similar and books that focus on differences, the so-called gender gap. Is it true, to borrow John Gray's (1997) provocative book title, that *Men Are from Mars, Women Are from Venus?* And if so, what are the implications when it comes to male-female relationships?

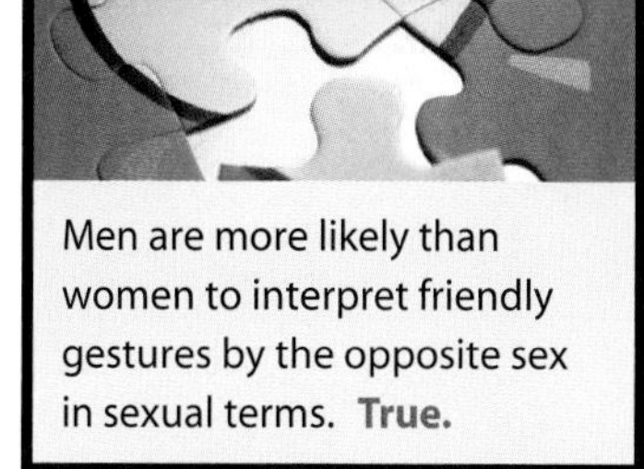

Men are more likely than women to interpret friendly gestures by the opposite sex in sexual terms. **True.**

Sexuality One hundred years ago, Sigmund Freud shocked the scientific community by proposing psychoanalytic theory, which placed great emphasis on sex as a driving force in human behaviour. At the time, Freud's closest associates rejected this focus on sexual motivation. But was he wrong? Sexual images and themes pop up, quite literally, in our dreams, in the jokes we tell, in the TV shows we watch, in the novels we read, in the music we hear, and in the sex scandals that swirl around public figures in the news. It's no wonder that advertisers use sex to sell everything from blue jeans to perfumes, soft drinks, and cars.

With sex the most private aspect of human relations, it is difficult to study systematically. During the 1940s, biologist Alfred Kinsey and colleagues (1948, 1953) conducted the first large-scale survey of sexual practices in the United States. Based on confidential interviews of more than 17 000 men and women, these researchers sought for the first time to describe what nobody would openly talk about: sexual activity. Many of his results were shocking, with reported sexual activity more frequent and more varied than anyone had expected. His books were instant best-sellers. Certain aspects of his methodology were flawed, however. For example,

TABLE 9.2

What Constitutes "Having Sex"?

In this study, male and female students were asked, "Would you say you *had sex* with someone if the most intimate behaviour you engaged in was . . . ?" As you can see, there was consensus for some behaviours but disagreement for others. *(Sanders & Reinisch, 1999.)*

Contact %	Who Said Yes
Deep kissing	2%
Oral contact with breasts	3%
Touching genitals	14%
Oral contact with genitals	40%
Anal intercourse	81%
Vaginal intercourse	99%

participants were mostly young, white, urban, and middle class—hardly a representative sample. He also asked leading questions to enable respondents to report on sexual activities—or make up stories (Jones, 1997). Kinsey died in 1954, but his Institute for Sex Research at Indiana University remains a major centre for the study of human sexuality (Bancroft, 1997).

Since Kinsey's groundbreaking study, many sex surveys have been conducted, and they form part of the research history chronicled in *Kiss and Tell: Surveying Sex in the Twentieth Century* (Ericksen & Steffen, 1999). The limits of self-reports—regardless of whether they are taken in face-to-face interviews, telephone surveys, or the Internet—is that we can never know for sure how accurate the results are. Part of the problem is that respondents may not be honest in their disclosures. But also problematic is that people differ in their interpretations of survey questions. Consider this deceptively simple question: What does it mean to say you had sex? In an article published in the *Journal of the American Medical Association*, Stephanie Sanders and June Reinisch (1999) asked university students from 29 states, "Would you say you *had sex* with someone if the most intimate behaviour you engaged in was . . . ?" The results showed that most students agreed that vaginal and anal intercourse constitute having sex—and that deep kissing, oral contact with breasts, and manual contact with genitals do not. Yet there was little consensus about oral-genital contact. This finding suggests that there is some ambiguity in this regard (see Table 9.2).

In recent years, researchers have used an array of methods to measure sexual attitudes and behaviour. Studies of everyday interactions reveal that men view the world in more "sexualized" terms. Antonia Abbey (1982) arranged for pairs of male and female students to talk for five minutes, while other students observed the sessions. When she later questioned the actors and observers, Abbey found that the males were more sexually attracted to the females than vice versa. The males also rated the female actors as being more seductive and more flirtatious than the women had rated themselves as being. Among men more than women, eye contact, a compliment, a friendly remark, a brush against the arm, and an innocent smile are often interpreted as sexual come-ons (Kowalski, 1993). These differing perceptions occur not only in the laboratory but also between strangers, acquaintances, and casual friends who meet at parties, at school, at work, and in other settings (Abbey, 1987; Saal et al., 1989).

Gender differences are particularly common in self-report surveys, where men report being more promiscuous, more likely to think about sex, more permissive, more likely to enjoy casual sex without emotional commitment, and more likely to fantasize about sex with multiple partners (Oliver & Hyde, 1993). When asked to select ten private wishes from a list, for example, most men and women similarly wanted love, health, peace on earth, unlimited ability, and wealth. But more men than women also wanted "to have sex with anyone I choose" (Ehrlichman & Eichenstein, 1992). In a large-scale study of 16 000 respondents from 52 countries all over the world, David Schmitt (2003) found that men desire more sex partners and more sexual variety than women do—regardless of their relationship status or sexual orientation. Based on all this research, Roy Baumeister and others (2001) concluded that "men desire sex more than women" (p. 270).

sexual orientation One's sexual preference for members of the same sex, opposite sex, or both sexes.

Sexual Orientation No discussion of human sexuality is complete without consideration of individual differences in **sexual orientation**—defined as one's sexual preference for members of the same sex (homosexuality), opposite sex (heterosexuality), or both sexes (bisexuality). How common is homosexuality, and where does it come from? Throughout history, and in all cultures, a vast majority of people have been heterosexual in their orientation. But how vast a majority is a subject of some debate. In a survey of Canadian men and women, 1.3 percent of men and 0.7 percent of women identified themselves as gay or lesbian; the combined prevalence was 1.0 percent. This number rose to 2 percent among those in the 18–35 age bracket, and dropped to 1.2 percent among those in the 45–59 age range (Statistics Canada, 2003). Together, large-scale surveys in the United States, Europe, Asia, and the Pacific suggest that the exclusively homosexual population in the world is 3 or 4 percent among men and about half that number among women (Diamond, 1993).

Although researchers can only estimate the population prevalence of homosexuality, many men and women are openly gay. It isn't always easy, of course. In 2002, Marc Hall became the centre of a media story when school officials refused to allow him to bring his boyfriend to the high school prom. He fought the ruling, and won.

Although an exclusive homosexual orientation is rare among humans and other animals, homosexual *behaviours* are more common. In *Biological Exuberance*, Bruce Bagemihl (1999) reports that sexual encounters among male-male and female-female pairs have been observed in more than 450 species—including giraffes, goats, birds, chimpanzees, and lizards. Among humans, the incidence of homosexual behaviour varies from one generation and culture to the next, depending on prevailing attitudes. In *Same Sex, Different Cultures*, Gilbert Herdt (1998) notes that in part of the world, stretching from Sumatra to Melanesia, it's common for adolescent males to engage in homosexual activities before being of age for marriage—even though homosexuality as a permanent trait is rare. It's important, then, to realize that sexual orientation cannot be viewed in black-or-white terms but along a continuum. In the centre of that continuum, 1 percent of people describe themselves as actively *bi*sexual.

To explain the roots of homosexuality, various theories have been proposed. The Greek philosopher Aristotle believed that it was inborn but strengthened by habit; psychoanalysts argue that it stems from family dynamics and a child's overattachment to a parent of the same or opposite sex; social learning theorists point to rewarding sexual experiences with same-sex peers in childhood. Yet there is little evidence to support these claims. In a particularly comprehensive study, Alan Bell and others (1981) interviewed 1 500 homosexual and heterosexual adults about their lives. There were no differences in past family backgrounds, absence of a male or female parent, relationship with parents, sex abuse, age of onset of puberty, or high school dating patterns. Except for the fact that homosexual adults described themselves as less conforming as children, the two groups could not be distinguished by past experiences. Both groups strongly felt that their sexual orientation was set long before it was "official."

Increasingly, there is scientific evidence of a biological disposition. In a highly publicized study, neurobiologist Simon LeVay (1991) autopsied the brains of 19 homosexual men who had died of AIDS, 16 heterosexual men (some of whom had died of AIDS), and six heterosexual women. LeVay examined a tiny nucleus in the hypothalamus known to be involved in regulating sexual behaviour and known to be larger in heterosexual men than in women. The specimens were numerically coded, so LeVay did not know whether the donor he was examining was male or female, straight or gay. The result: In the male homosexual brains he studied, the nucleus was half the size as in male heterosexual brains—and comparable to those found in female heterosexual brains. This research is fully described in LeVay's (1993) book *The Sexual Brain.*

It's important to recognize that this study revealed only a correlation between sexual orientation and the brain and cannot be used to draw conclusions about cause and effect. More convincing support for the biological roots of sexual orientation comes from twin studies suggesting that there is a genetic predisposition. Michael

Bailey and Richard Pillard (1991) surveyed 167 gay men and their twins and adopted brothers. Overall, 52 percent of the identical twins were gay, compared to only 22 percent of fraternal twins and 11 percent of adoptive brothers. Two years later, Bailey and others (1993) conducted a companion study of lesbians with similar results.

The origins of sexual orientation are complex for two reasons. First, it's not clear that sexual orientation for men and women are similarly rooted. In Australia, Bailey and others (2000) had hundreds of pairs of twins rate their own sexuality on a seven-point continuum that ranged from "exclusively heterosexual" to "exclusively homosexual." Overall, 92 percent of both men and women saw themselves as exclusively heterosexual. Among the others, however, more women said that they had bisexual tendencies and more men said they were exclusively homosexual. In another study, a longitudinal investigation of 18- to 25-year-old women, Lisa Diamond (2003) found that more than a quarter of those who had initially identified themselves as lesbian or bisexual changed their orientation over the next five years—far more than is ever reported among men. These findings, and others, compel the conclusion that women are sexually more flexible than men, having more *erotic plasticity*. Simply put, women are more likely to change sexual preferences over the course of a lifetime (Baumeister, 2000; Peplau, 2003).

A second complicating factor is that although there is evidence for a biological disposition, this does not mean that there's a "gay gene" (Hamer et al., 1999). Daryl Bem (1996, 2000) sees the development of sexual orientation as a *psycho*biological process. According to Bem, genes determine a person's temperament at birth, leading some infants and young children to be naturally more active, energetic, and aggressive than others. These differences in temperament draw some children toward male playmates and "masculine" activities and others toward female playmates and "feminine" activities. Bem refers to children who prefer same-sex playmates as gender-conformists and to those who prefer opposite-sex playmates as gender-nonconformists ("sissies" and "tomboys").

Activity preferences in childhood may be biologically rooted, but what happens next is the psychological part. According to Bem, gender-conforming children come to see members of the opposite sex as different, unfamiliar, and arousing, even "exotic." Gender-nonconforming children, in contrast, come to see same-sex peers as different, unfamiliar, arousing, and exotic. Later, at puberty, as children become physically and sexually mature, they find that they are attracted to members of the same or opposite sex—depending on which is the more exotic. Bem describes his proposed chain of events as the "exotic becomes erotic" theory of sexual orientation.

At present, there is only sketchy support for this theory. It is true that genetic makeup can influence temperament and predispose a child to favour certain kinds of activities over others (Kagan, 1994). It is also true that gay men are more likely to have been "sissies" and that lesbians are more likely to have been "tomboys" as children (Bell et al., 1981; Bailey & Zucker, 1995). It may even be true that people are genetically hardwired to become sissies and tomboys as children (Bailey et al., 2000). But do peer preferences in childhood alter adult sexual orientation, as Bem suggests, because exotic becomes erotic? Or, is there a "gay gene" that fosters gender nonconformity in childhood as well as homosexuality in adolescence and adulthood? And can a single theory explain homosexuality in both men and women, or are separate theories needed, as some have suggested (Peplau et al., 1998)? At present, more research is needed to answer these questions and tease apart the biological and psychological influences. Either way, one point looms large: People do not seem to wilfully choose their sexual orientation, nor can they easily change it.

The Marital Trajectory Because we are social beings, having close relationships is important to us all—for our happiness and emotional well-being and even for our physical health and longevity. Yet sadly, we live in a society where 40 to 50 percent of first marriages are likely to end in divorce. With at least one previously divorced

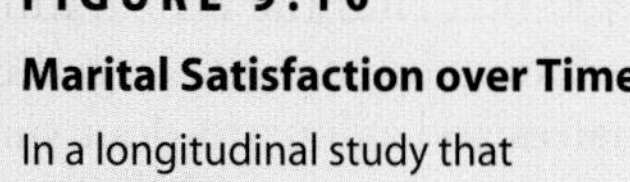

FIGURE 9.10

Marital Satisfaction over Time

In a longitudinal study that spanned ten years, married couples rated the quality of their marriages. On average, these ratings were high, but they declined among both husbands and wives. As you can see, there were two steep drops, occurring during the first and eighth years of marriage. *(Kurdek, 1999.)*

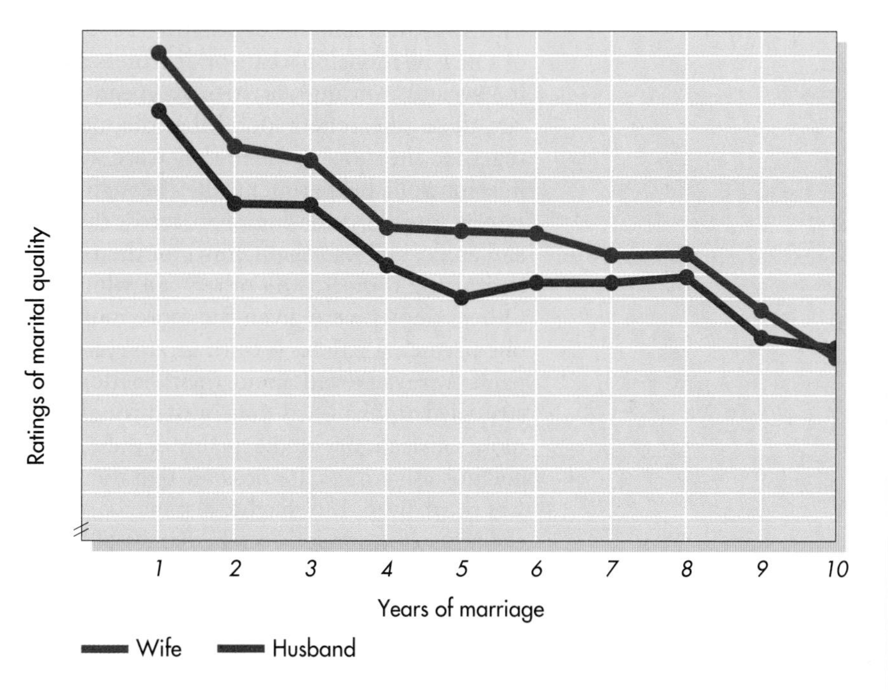

partner, the odds of divorce are even greater (Gottman, 1998). This discrepancy—between the endurance most people want and the disruption they may have to confront—is dramatic. Couples break up, separate, and divorce. How do marriages evolve over time, and why do some last while others dissolve?

Ellen Berscheid and Harry Reis (1998) say that for social psychologists who study intimate relationships, this is the most frequently asked and vexing question. Is there a typical developmental pattern? No and yes. No, it's clear that all marriages are different and cannot be squeezed into a single mould. But yes, certain patterns do emerge when survey results are combined from large numbers of married couples that are studied over long periods of time. Recently, Lawrence Kurdek (1999) reported on a longitudinal study of married couples in which he measured each spouse's satisfaction every year for ten years (out of 522 couples he started with, 93 completed the study). Look at Figure 9.10, and you'll see that there is an overall trajectory of decline in ratings of marital quality—and that the ratings given by husbands and wives were very similar. Look more closely and you'll also see that there are two particularly sharp periods of decline. The first occurs during the first year of marriage. Apparently, while newlyweds tend to idealize each other and to enjoy an initial state of marital bliss (Murray et al., 1996), this "honeymoon" is soon followed by a decline in satisfaction (Bradbury, 1998). After some stabilization, a second decline is then observed at about the eighth year of marriage—a finding that is consistent with the popular belief in a "seven-year itch" (Kovacs, 1983).

Are there specific factors that predict future outcomes? To address this question, Benjamin Karney and Thomas Bradbury (1995) reviewed 115 longitudinal studies of more than 45 000 married couples and found only that certain positively valued variables (education, employment, constructive behaviours, similarity in attitudes) are somewhat predictive of positive outcomes. They did find, however, that the steeper the initial decline in satisfaction, the more likely couples are to break up later. This decline is, in part, related to the stress of having and raising children—a stress that is common among newly married couples.

After the honeymoon period, there is an overall decline in levels of marital satisfaction. **True.**

Is there anything a couple can do to keep the honeymoon alive? Perhaps there is. Arthur Aron and his colleagues (2000) have theorized that after the exhilaration of a new relationship wears off, partners can combat boredom by engaging together in new and arousing activities. By means of questionnaires and a door-to-door survey, these researchers found that the more new experiences spouses said they had together, the more satisfied they were with their marriages. To test this hypothesis in a controlled experiment, they brought randomly selected couples into the laboratory, spread gymnasium mats across the floor, tied the partners together at a wrist and ankle, and had them crawl on their hands and knees, over a barrier, from one end of the room to the other—all while carrying a pillow between their bodies. Other couples were given the more mundane task of rolling a ball across the mat, one partner at a time. A third group received no assignment. Afterward, all participants were surveyed about their relationships. As predicted, the couples that had struggled and laughed their way through the novel and arousing activity reported more satisfaction with the quality of their relationships than did those in the mundane and no-task groups. It's possible that the benefit of shared participation in this study was short-lived. But maybe, just maybe, a steady and changing diet of exciting new experiences can help keep the flames of love burning.

Communication and Conflict Disagreements about sex, children, in-laws, and other matters can stir conflict in close relationships. Research shows that economic pressures, in particular, put an enormous amount of strain on marital relations (Conger et al., 1999). Whatever the cause, all couples experience some degree of friction. The issue is not whether it occurs but how we respond to it. One source of conflict is the difficulty some people have talking about their disagreements. When relationships break up, communication problems are indeed among the most common causes cited by heterosexual and homosexual couples alike (Kurdek, 1991b; Sprecher, 1994). But what constitutes "bad communication"? Comparisons between happy and distressed couples have revealed a number of communication patterns that often occur in troubled relationships (Fincham, 2003).

One common pattern is called *negative affect reciprocity*—a tit-for-tat exchange of expressions of negative feelings. Generally speaking, expressions of negative affect within a couple trigger more in-kind responses than do expressions of positive affect. But negative affect reciprocity, especially in nonverbal behaviour, is greater in couples that are unhappy, distressed, and locked into a duel. For couples in distress, smiles pass by unnoticed, but every glare, every disgusted look, provokes a sharp reflex-like response. The result, as observed in unhappy couples around the world, is an inability to break the vicious cycle and terminate unpleasant interactions (Gottman, 1998).

Men and women react differently to conflict. Women usually report more intense emotions and are more expressive (Grossman & Wood, 1993). She tells him to "warm up," while he urges her to "calm down." Thus, unhappy marriages also tend to be characterized by a *demand/withdraw interaction pattern*, in which the wife demands to discuss the relationship problems, only to become frustrated when her husband withdraws from such discussions (Christensen & Heavey, 1993). This configuration is not unique to married couples. When dating partners were asked about how they typically deal with problems, the same female-demand/male-withdraw pattern was found (Vogel et al., 1999). Married or not, then, it's clear that couples caught in this bind often find themselves echoing the title of Deborah Tannen's (1990) popular book on gender differences in communication, *You Just Don't Understand*. According to John Gottman (1994), there is nothing wrong with either approach to dealing with conflict. The problem, he says, lies in the discrepancy—that healthy relationships are most likely when both partners have similar styles of dealing with conflict.

Whatever one's style, there are two basic approaches to reducing the negative effects of conflict. The first is so obvious that it is often overlooked: Increase rewarding behaviour in other aspects of the relationship. According to Gottman and Levenson (1992), marital stability rests on a "fairly high balance of positive to negative behaviours" (p. 230). If there's conflict over one issue, partners can and should search for other ways to reward each other. As the balance of positives to negatives improves, so should overall satisfaction, which can reduce conflict (Huston & Vangelisti, 1991). The second approach is to try to understand the other's point of view. Being sensitive to what the partner thinks and how he or she feels enhances the quality of the relationship (Honeycutt et al., 1993; Long & Andrews, 1990). What motivates individuals in the heat of battle to make that effort to understand? For starters, it helps if they agree that there is, in fact, a communication problem.

The attributions that partners make for each other's behaviours are correlated with the quality of their relationship (Bradbury & Fincham, 1992; Harvey & Manusov, 2001). As you might expect, happy couples make *relationship-enhancing attributions:* They see the partner's undesirable behaviours as caused by factors that are situational ("a bad day"), temporary ("It'll pass"), and limited in scope ("That's just a sore spot"). Yet they see desirable behaviours as caused by factors that are inherent in the partner, permanent, and generalizable to other aspects of the relationship. In contrast, unhappy couples flip the attributional coin on its tail by making the opposite attributions, called *distress-maintaining attributions.* Thus, while happy couples minimize the bad and maximize the good, distressed couples don't give an inch. In light of these differing attributional patterns, it would seem, over time, that happy couples would get happier and miserable couples more miserable. Do they? Yes. By tracking married couples in multi-year longitudinal studies, researchers have found that husbands and wives who made distress-maintaining causal attributions early in their marriage reported less satisfaction at a later point in time (Fincham et al., 2000; Karney & Bradbury, 2000). The link between causal attributions and marital bliss or distress may be reciprocal, with each influencing the other.

Breaking Up When an intimate relationship ends, the effect can be traumatic (Kitson & Morgan, 1990). How do people cope? The answer is, it depends on the nature of the loss. One vital factor is the closeness of a relationship, or the extent to which the line between self and other becomes so blurred that mine and yours are one and the same. Indeed, Aron and others (1992) found that the longevity of a romantic relationship can be predicted by which diagram in Figure 9.11 people choose to describe their relationship. The more one incorporates a partner into the self, the more lasting the relationship is likely to be—but the more distress one anticipates if there is a break-up.

Another important factor in this regard is interdependence—the social glue that bonds us together. Research shows that the more interdependent couples are (as measured by the amount of time spent together, the variety of shared activities, and the degree of influence each partner has on the other), and the more invested they are in the relationship, the longer it is likely to last (Berscheid et al., 1989; Rusbult & Buunk, 1993)—and the more devastated they become when it ends (Fine & Sacher, 1997; Simpson, 1987). People also differ in the extent to which their associations with others are important to their identity. Among students who had recently experienced a romantic break-up, those for whom relationships play a more central role in identity were more upset (Smith & Cohen, 1993).

An ironic theme runs through much of the research on coping. We are, to put it mildly, darned if we do and darned if we don't. Those factors that contribute to the endurance of a relationship (closeness, interdependence, and the importance of the relationship to one's own identity) turn out to be the same factors that intensify

FIGURE 9.11

How Close Is Your Relationship?

The Inclusion of Other in the Self (IOS) Scale is a one-item, pictorial measure of relationship closeness. Choosing a picture with less overlap between the circles indicates less closeness; choosing one with more overlap indicates more closeness. *(Aron et al., 1992.)*

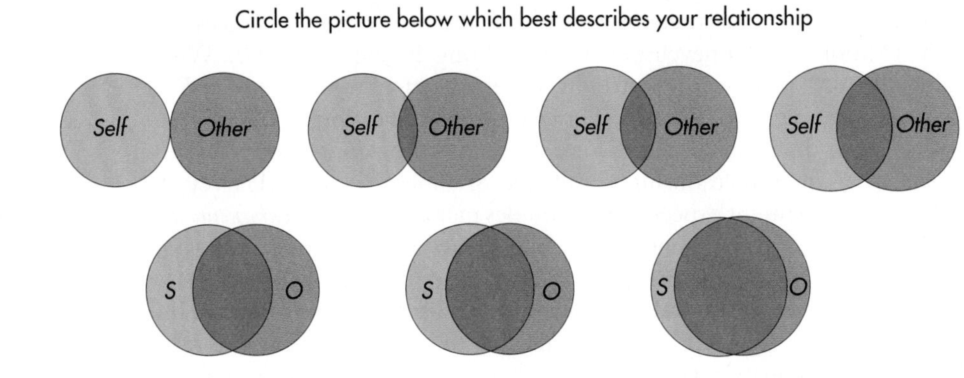

distress and make coping more difficult after a relationship ends. So, how do you balance making the psychological investment necessary for a lasting relationship against holding back enough for self-protection?

In Canada and other western countries, various demographic markers indicate how problematic traditional forms of commitment have become: a high divorce rate, more single-parent families, more couples living together, and more never-married individuals. Yet the desire for long-term intimate relationships has never wavered or disappeared. To the contrary, gays and lesbians seek legal recognition of same-sex marriages, the vast majority of divorced individuals remarry, and stepfamilies forge a new sense of what it means to be a "family." It seems that we are in the midst of a great and compelling search, as millions of men and women try to find ways to affiliate with, attract, get closer to, love, and commit themselves with permanence to others.

Review

Being with Others: A Fundamental Human Motive

- The need to belong is a basic human motive, a pervasive drive to form and maintain lasting relationships.

The Thrill of Affiliation

- This social motivation begins with the need for affiliation, a desire to establish social contact with others.
- People differ in the strength of their affiliative needs.
- Stressful situations in particular motivate us to affiliate with others who face a similar threat.

The Agony of Loneliness

- Shyness is a pervasive problem that sets people up to have unrewarding interactions with others.
- People who are painfully shy are at risk for loneliness, a feeling of isolation, and social deprivation.

The Initial Attraction

- According to one perspective, people are attracted to others with whom the relationship is rewarding; rewards can be direct or indirect.
- Evolutionary psychologists argue that human beings exhibit patterns of attraction and mate selection that favour the passing on of their own genes.

Familiarity: Being There

- Proximity sets the stage for social interaction, which is why friendships are most likely to form between people who live near each other.
- Supporting the mere exposure effect, studies show that the more often people see a stimulus, the more they come to like it.
- We do not have to be aware of our prior exposures for the increase in liking to occur.

Physical Attractiveness: Getting Drawn In

- In a wide range of social settings, people respond more favourably to men and women who are physically attractive.
- Some researchers believe that certain faces (averaged and symmetrical) are inherently attractive—across cultures and to infants as well as adults.
- Others argue that beauty is in the eye of the beholder and point to the influences of culture, time, and context.
- One reason for the bias toward beauty is that it's rewarding to be in the company of others who are attractive.
- A second reason is that people associate beauty with other positive qualities, a belief known as the what-is-beautiful-is-good stereotype.
- People seen as physically attractive are more popular, more sexually experienced, and more socially skilled; however, they are not happier or higher in self-esteem.
- One reason for the latter finding is that people who see themselves as attractive often discount the praise they get for nonsocial endeavours.
- Another problem with having beauty as a social asset is that people, notably women, feel pressured to keep up their appearance and are often dissatisfied with how they look.

First Encounters: Getting Acquainted

- People tend to associate with, befriend, and marry others who are similar in their demographic backgrounds, attitudes, and interests.
- People first avoid others who are dissimilar and then are drawn to those remaining who are most similar.
- Supporting the matching hypothesis, people tend to become romantically involved with others who are equivalent in physical attractiveness.
- Contrary to popular belief, complementarity in needs or personality does not spark attraction.
- Indicating the effects of reciprocity, we tend to like others who indicate that they like us.
- But indiscriminate likers can be taken for granted and not liked as much.
- Research on the hard-to-get-effect shows that people like others best who are moderately selective in their social choices.

Mate Selection: The Evolution of Desire

- Evolutionary psychologists say that women seek men with financial security or traits predictive of future success in order to ensure the survival of their offspring.
- In contrast, men seek women who are young and attractive (physical attributes that signal health and fertility)—and not promiscuous (an attribute that diminishes certainty of paternity).
- Cross-cultural studies tend to support these predicted sex differences, but critics note that many results are not that strong and can be viewed in terms that are more psychological than evolutionary.

Close Relationships

- Intimate relationships include at least one of three components: feelings of attachment, fulfillment of psychological needs, and interdependence.
- Stage theories propose that close relationships go through specific stages, but evidence for a fixed sequence is weak.
- Two other views emphasize either a gradual accumulation of rewards or a sharp distinction between types of relationships.

The Intimate Marketplace: Tracking the Gains and Losses

- According to social exchange theory, people seek to maximize gains and minimize costs in their relationships.
- Higher rewards, lower costs, and an outcome that meets or exceeds a partner's comparison level (CL) predict high levels of satisfaction.
- Lower expectations about alternatives (CLalt) and more investment in the relationship are associated with higher levels of commitment.
- Equity theory holds that satisfaction is greatest when the ratio between benefits and contributions is similar for both partners.
- Both overbenefit and underbenefit elicit negative emotions, but the underbenefited are usually less satisfied.

Types of Relationships

- In exchange relationships, people are oriented toward reward and immediate reciprocity; in communal relationships, partners are responsive to each other's needs.

- People with secure attachment styles have more satisfying romantic relationships than do those with insecure (anxious or avoidant) styles.

How Do I Love Thee? Counting the Ways

- According to the triangular theory of love, there are eight subtypes of love produced by the combinations of intimacy, passion, and commitment.
- Inherent in all classifications of love are two types: passionate and companionate.
- Passionate love is an intense, emotional, often erotic state of positive absorption in another person.
- In one theory, passionate love is sparked by physiological arousal and the belief that the arousal was caused by the loved person.
- Consistent with excitation transfer, arousal can increase or decrease attraction, depending on the initial attractiveness of the person whom one is with.
- Compared with passionate love, companionate love is less intense but in some respects deeper and more enduring.
- Companionate love rests on mutual trust, caring, friendship, commitment, and willingness to share intimate facts and feelings.
- Self-disclosure between partners often becomes broader and deeper over time, though self-disclosure varies with the state of the relationship.

Relationship Issues: The Male-Female "Connection"

- People vary in how they define what it means to "have sex."
- On average, men report being more sexually active than women and see opposite-sex interactions in more sexualized terms.
- An estimated 3 or 4 percent of men and 2 percent of women are exclusively homosexual in orientation.
- Both biological and environmental theories are used to explain the origins of homosexuality.
- When relationships break up, communication problems are among the most common causes.
- Unhappy couples engage often in negative affect reciprocity and exhibit a demand/withdraw interaction pattern.
- During conflict, women are more likely to be demanding; men are more likely to withdraw.
- Partners can reduce conflict by behaving in rewarding ways in other areas and by trying to understand each other's point of view.
- Happy couples make relationship-enhancing attributions, while unhappy couples make distress-maintaining attributions.
- On average, marital satisfaction starts high, declines during the first year, stabilizes, and then declines again at about the eighth year.
- Partners who are close and interdependent and for whom relationships are important to the self-concept (characteristics that normally promote stability) suffer more after breaking up.

Key Terms

attachment style *(317)*
communal relationship *(317)*
companionate love *(320)*
equity theory *(316)*
exchange relationship *(317)*
excitation transfer *(321)*
hard-to-get effect *(308)*
intimate relationship *(314)*
loneliness *(296)*
matching hypothesis *(307)*
mere exposure effect *(298)*
need for affiliation *(294)*
passionate love *(320)*
reciprocity *(307)*
self-disclosure *(323)*
sexual orientation *(326)*
social exchange theory *(314)*
triangular theory of love *(319)*
what-is-beautiful-is-good stereotype *(302)*

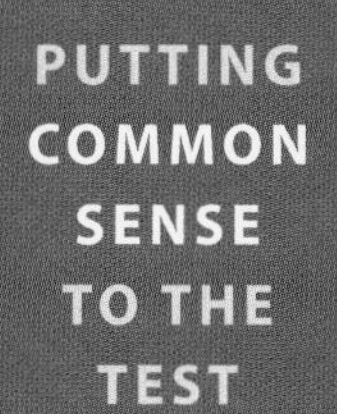

People seek out the company of others, even strangers, in times of stress.

True. *Research has shown that external threat causes stress and leads people to affiliate with others who are facing or have faced a similar threat.*

Infants do not discriminate between faces considered attractive and unattractive in their culture.

False. *Two-month-old infants spend more time gazing at attractive than unattractive faces, indicating that they do make the distinction.*

People who are physically attractive are happier and have higher self-esteem than those who are unattractive.

False. *Attractive people are at an advantage in their social lives, but they are not happier, better adjusted, or higher in self-esteem.*

When it comes to romantic relationships, opposites attract.

False. *Consistently, people are attracted to others who are similar—not opposite or complementary—on a whole range of dimensions.*

Men are more likely than women to interpret friendly gestures by the opposite sex in sexual terms.

True. *Experiments have shown that men are more likely than women to interpret friendly opposite-sex interactions as sexual come-ons.*

After the honeymoon period, there is an overall decline in levels of marital satisfaction.

True. *High marital satisfaction levels among newlyweds are often followed by a measurable decline during the first year and then, after a period of stabilization, by another decline at about the eighth year—a pattern found among parents and nonparents alike.*

10 Helping Others

OUTLINE

PREVIEW

THIS CHAPTER describes the social psychology of giving and receiving help. First, we examine the *evolutionary, motivational, situational, personal,* and *interpersonal* factors that predict whether a potential helper will provide assistance to a person in need. Then, we consider people's *reactions to receiving help*. In the concluding section, we discuss the *helping connection*, the role of social ties in promoting helpfulness to others.

It was their bravery that compelled them to risk their lives, but it was their compassion that ultimately saved them. Six firefighters from New York City's Ladder Company Six were among the numerous firefighters, police officers, and other rescue workers who courageously climbed up the stairs of the World Trade Center on September 11, 2001. The jets that had flown into each of the Twin Towers of the skyscraper were hemorrhaging fuel, causing an inferno of unprecedented proportion. A massive stream of people trying to flee raced down the narrow stairs, passing the firefighters who were going up. Awed by their courage and resolve, people yelled encouragement and blessings to the firefighters as they passed them. Under the burden of more than 100 pounds of equipment, the men of Company Six reached the 27th floor of the North Tower when they heard the horrifying sound of the South Tower collapsing. Their captain ordered them to turn back, realizing that if the other tower could collapse, so could theirs.

On their way down, around the 14th or 15th floor, they encountered a frail woman named Josephine Harris. She had walked down almost 60 flights already, and she was exhausted. The firefighters helped her walk, but she was slowing them down dangerously. Their captain, John Jonas, was growing more anxious: "I could hear the clock ticking in the back of my head. I'm thinking, 'C'mon, c'mon. We've got to keep moving.'" But none of the six men considered leaving her—or any of the rest of the group—behind, so they slowly walked down together. Josephine didn't think she could go on, but one of the firefighters asked her about her family and told her that her children and grandchildren wanted to see her again. She continued, but finally collapsed as they got near the 4th floor. On the 4th floor they tried to find a chair to carry her in. And then, the 110-story skyscraper collapsed.

Other rescue workers who had passed this slow-moving group on the stairs were killed on the floors below them. Virtually everyone who was still above them was killed. And yet somehow this group survived, trapped in an inexplicable pocket of safety amidst the unimaginable wreckage, along with two other firefighters, a Fire Department chief, and a Port Authority police officer. After a harrowing search for a way out, eventually they found a small ray of light—a literal ray of hope—and followed it to safety.

The firefighters later called Josephine Harris their guardian angel and thanked *her* for saving *their* lives. They realized that had they not encountered her, they would have gone down the stairs faster, and had she not kept walking despite exhaustion,

PUTTING COMMON SENSE TO THE TEST

T / F

____ **People are more likely to help someone in an emergency if the potential rewards seem high and the potential costs seem low.**

____ **In an emergency, a person who needs help has a much better chance of getting it if three other people are present than if only one other person is present.**

____ **People are much more likely to help someone when they're in a good mood.**

____ **People are much less likely to help someone when they're in a bad mood.**

____ **Attractive people have a better chance than unattractive people of getting help when they need it.**

____ **In any situation, people are more likely to help a friend succeed than a stranger.**

____ **Women seek help more often than men do.**

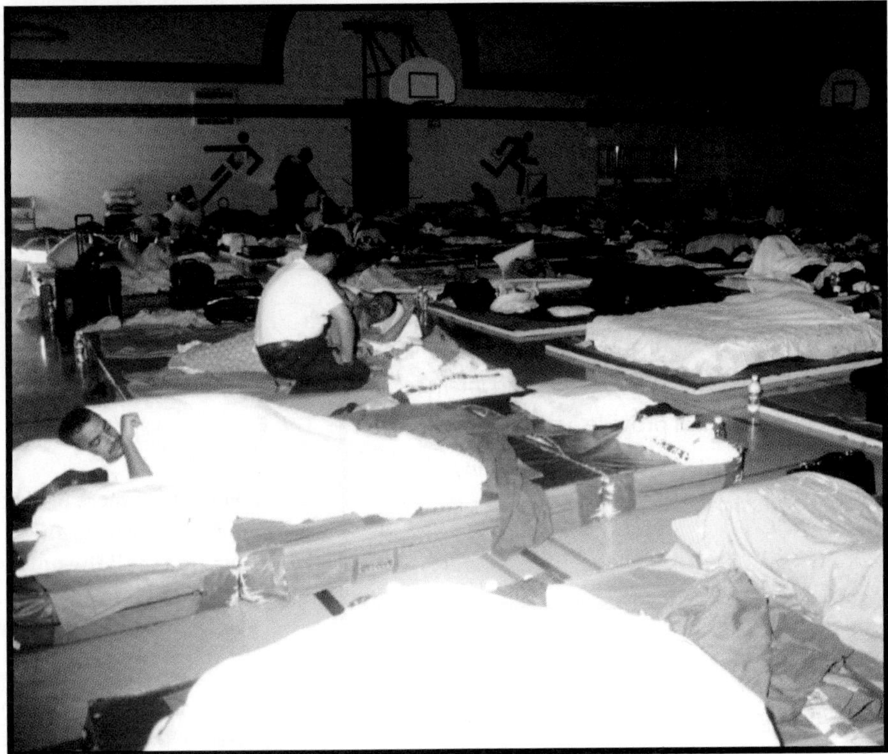

When all North American aircraft were grounded in the aftermath of the terrorist attacks in New York on September 11, 2001, Gander, Newfoundland, opened their schools, churches, and hearts to those that were stranded.

they would have been a few floors above—either way, they would have been killed. But Josephine Harris knew that she owed her life to these brave men, who risked seeing their own children again so that she could see hers.

There were many other heroes that day, including ordinary citizens whose acts of self-sacrifice to help others were not part of their job descriptions. Some of the help was dramatically heroic, like that of the passengers aboard hijacked United Airlines Flight 93. They decided to fight the terrorists on their flight and sacrifice their own lives in order to try to prevent the terrorists from killing many more people on the ground. And much of the help was behind the scenes, as in the cases of people volunteering endless hours doing the gruelling work of cleaning up the disaster area, helping the injured and the grieving, and donating money, clothes, and other resources. When American airspace was closed in response to the terrorist attacks, 240 flights were re-routed to Canada. Thirty-eight of those planes landed in Gander, Newfoundland, which has a population of approximately 10 000 people. According to passenger reports, the people of Gander could not have been more helpful. Consider this letter written to the Cleveland *Plain Dealer* thanking the people of Gander for their assistance:

> *Everyone was extraordinarily thoughtful of each other. One woman must have put her life on hold and was constantly checking on us. She even came to the airport when we finally left to make sure we all were fine. I never saw her without a smile. The lady who ran the cafeteria along with many neighbors made hot meals and brought in casseroles each day. Students helped us to use e-mail, and we were able to use the phone to call our family. No organization with financial backing was behind this—this was a call to neighbors and friends to come and help those of us in need. We will never be able to think of Gander, Newfoundland, without remembering all the goodness and kindness that was showered upon us by our neighbors and friends from Canada.* (Sweet, 2001, p. B6)

When people read stories such as these, it is natural for them to wonder what they would have done. What makes some people, at some times, act to help others? The wonderful acts of helping during the chaos of 9/11 are inspiring, to be sure. But there were also many stories that day of people who turned their backs on others, even on people who had just helped them.

Every day there are numerous unheralded acts of helping others and of failing to help others. A volunteer works tirelessly in an AIDS clinic, a university student tutors a child, a congregation raises money for a religious cause, an older sister lets her little brother win at checkers. And yet every day someone ignores the screams outside his or her window, drives past motorists stranded on the side of a road, or tries to avoid making eye contact with a homeless person on the street. Every few months we see a story like the man who was driving on an Edmonton highway in

June 2006 when he witnesses a collision between a truck and a car. The man stopped and pulled two injured people from the truck as their vehicle caught fire. The man, who asked not to be identified, stated "I was glad that I was there and able to help out" (*cbc.ca*, 2006). And every few months we also learn of a story like Breann Voth's, a 19-year-old who was attacked and killed while she was walking home at dawn in December 2002 near Vancouver. Police discovered that at least three neighbours had heard her screaming for more than ten minutes, and yet no one intervened or called the police (*Ottawa Citizen*, 2002).

There is no simple answer to the question of why some help and others don't or why some situations lead to quick assistance and others to shocking displays of inaction. The determinants of helping behaviour are complex and multifaceted. But social psychologists have learned a great deal about these determinants over the last three decades; and as you will see in the pages to come, some of their findings are quite surprising.

In this chapter, we examine several questions about helping: *Why* do people help? *When* do they help? *Who* is likely to help? *Whom* do they help? We then explore the other side of helping: how people react to the help they receive. The concluding section concentrates on a major, recurring theme—social connection—that underlies much of the theory and research on helping.

Evolutionary and Motivational Factors: Why Do People Help?

Although few individuals reach the heights of heroic helping, virtually everyone helps somebody sometime. People give their friends a ride on a bad car day; donate money, food, and clothing for disaster relief; babysit for a relative; work as a volunteer for charitable organizations; pick up the mail for a neighbour who's out of town. The list of **prosocial behaviours**—actions intended to benefit others—is endless. But *why* do people help? Several factors have an impact.

In a survey conducted by Statistics Canada in 2004 asking about charitable activities in the previous 12 months, 45 percent of the population over the age of 15 indicated they had volunteered their time with their contributions totalling almost 2 billion hours. In addition, 85 percent of the Canadian population made a charitable donation (Canada Survey of Giving, Volunteering and Participating, 2004).

prosocial behaviours Actions intended to benefit others.

Evolutionary Factors in Helping

We begin with evolution. Evolutionary psychologists and biologists use principles of evolution to understand human social behaviour. Can evolutionary principles help explain why people help? At first glance, some may think it unlikely. From an evolutionary perspective, what possible function can there be in helping others, especially at the risk of one's own life? Doesn't risking one's life for others fly in the face of evolutionary principles like "survival of the fittest"?

The "Selfish Gene" In fact, evolutionary perspectives emphasize not the survival of the fittest individuals but the survival of the individuals' genes (Dawkins, 1989; Hamilton, 1964). From the perspective of evolution, then, human social behaviour should be analyzed in terms of its contribution to reproductive success in ancestral environments: the conception, birth, and survival of offspring over the course of many generations. If a specific social behaviour enhances reproductive success, the genetic underpinnings of that behaviour are more likely to be passed on to subsequent generations. In this way, the behaviour can eventually become part of the common inheritance of the species.

Of course, in order to reproduce, the individual must survive long enough to do so. Being helped *by* others should increase the chances of survival. But what

Many animals groom each other, whether they are chimpanzees in Tanzania or schoolgirls in North America. According to evolutionary psychologists, such behaviour often reflects reciprocal altruism.

about being helpful to others? Since helping others can be costly in terms of time and effort, and is sometimes dangerous to the helper, being helpful would seem to decrease one's chances of survival. Shouldn't any genetically based propensities for helping have dropped out of the gene pool long ago?

No. There is an alternative to individual survival. You can also preserve your genes by promoting the survival of those who share your genetic make-up, even if you perish in the effort to help them. By means of this indirect route to genetic survival, the tendency to help genetic relatives, called **kinship selection**, could become an innate characteristic—that is, a characteristic that is not contingent on learning for its development, although it can be influenced by learning, culture, and other factors. Kinship selection is evident in the behaviour of many organisms. Just as humans often risk their lives to save close relatives, squirrels emit an alarm to nearby relatives to warn them of a predator—which helps their relatives but makes the squirrel who sounds the alarm more vulnerable to attack (Hauber & Sherman, 1998; Sherman, 1981). In what at first glance might seem to defy evolutionary principles, in some species, individuals delay breeding in order to stay close to home and assist their parents in raising younger siblings. Why would they delay reproducing their own genes to help raise genetically related, but not identical, kin? In the conditions in which this *cooperative breeding* typically occurs, this strategy actually is advantageous, helping these individuals perpetuate their own genes at a time and place in which they would be unable to rear their own offspring (Baglione et al., 2003; Gardner et al., 2003; Griffin & West, 2003).

Because kinship selection serves the function of genetic survival, preferential helping of genetic relatives should be strongest when the biological stakes are particularly high. This appears to be the case. Eugene Burnstein and others (1994) conducted a series of studies testing several predictions based on evolutionary theory. These researchers asked students in the United States and Japan to report how they would respond to a variety of situations in which someone needed help. Consistent with predictions based on kinship selection, participants indicated they were more likely to help a person who was closely related (for example, a sibling or parent) than a person who was more distantly related (for example, an uncle or grandmother)—especially in life-and-death situations as opposed to more everyday situations. In addition, intentions to help kin in life-threatening situations were influenced by reproductive-related factors; for example, participants reported they would help youthful relatives more than older adults, and healthy relatives more than those in poor health. In a more recent study involving more than 600 partici-

kinship selection Preferential helping of genetic relatives, so that genes held in common will survive.

pants from an ethnically diverse sample, Daniel Kruger (2003) also found strong support for the role of kinship in individuals' intentions to perform a risky rescue behaviour. The importance of kin selection can also be seen in the helping intentions indicated by children. Marie and John Tisak (1996) found that children in fourth, sixth, and eighth grades reported greater likelihood of helping a sibling in a threatening situation than helping a friend. Do these intentions to help translate to actual behaviours? According to Yossi Shavit and others (1994), they can. These researchers asked residents of metropolitan Haifa, Israel, to report from whom they received support during the missile attacks in the 1991 Gulf War. Although residents reported receiving comfort and advice from friends as well as kin, more immediate and direct aid was much more likely to come from kin.

"Scratch my back and I'll scratch yours."

—proverb

Reciprocal Altruism At best, however, kinship selection provides only a partial explanation for helping. Relatives are not always helpful to each other. And even though relatives may get preferential treatment, most people help out non-kin as well. What's the reproductive advantage of helping someone who isn't related to you? The most common answer is reciprocity. Through *reciprocal altruism*, helping someone else can be in your best interests because it increases the likelihood that you will be helped in return (Krebs, 1987; Trivers, 1985). If Chris helps Sandy and Sandy helps Chris, both Chris and Sandy increase their chances of survival and reproductive success. Over the course of evolution, therefore, individuals who engage in reciprocal altruism should survive and reproduce more than individuals who do not, thus enabling this kind of altruism to flourish.

Robert Trivers (1971) cites several examples of reciprocal altruism in animals. Many animals groom each other; for instance, monkeys groom other monkeys and cats groom other cats. Large fish (such as groupers) allow small fish (such as wrasses) to swim in their mouths without eating them; the small fish get food for themselves and at the same time remove parasites from the larger fish. And chimps who share with other chimps at one feeding are repaid by the other chimps at another feeding; those who are selfish are rebuffed, sometimes violently, at a later feeding (de Waal, 1996; de Waal et al., 2002). An additional illustration is provided by Robert Seyfarth and Dorothy Cheney (1984). In a creative field experiment, these researchers audiotaped female vervet monkeys calling out for help and then played the recorded vocalizations near other female monkeys. Half of these other monkeys heard a female who had recently groomed them; the other half heard a female who had not recently done so. Consistent with the idea of reciprocal altruism, they were significantly more likely to respond attentively to the request for help if the solicitor had just groomed them than if she had not. Interestingly, if the solicitor was genetically related to the monkeys who heard the tape, the monkeys' response was equally strong whether or not she had groomed them.

Franz de Waal (2003) observed a group of chimpanzees engaged in nearly 7000 interactions and recorded their grooming and food-sharing behaviours. He noted striking evidence of reciprocal altruism among these chimps. If Chimp A groomed Chimp B, for instance, B was much more likely to then share his or her food with A than if A had not groomed B first, or than B would with some other chimp. Moreover, Chimp A would be relatively unlikely to share his or her own food with Chimp B before B had reciprocated—after all, A had already groomed B, and now it was B's turn to help A! It's interesting that these chimps were able to negotiate this kind of reciprocity across acts—in grooming and food sharing. It was as if they were operating under a norm of "You scratch my back, I'll scratch yours—or maybe I'll give you some of my apples." In another study, de Waal and Michelle Berger (2000) observed same-sex pairs of capuchin monkeys working cooperatively in a test chamber to obtain a tray of food. The two monkeys were separated from each other by a mesh partition. One monkey by itself could not pull the tray, but the two monkeys could accomplish the task cooperatively. When successful, the monkey that wound

Among the Amish, cooperation within the group is an essential feature of their way of life. Some evolutionary theorists believe that helping other members of one's social group is an innate tendency among all human beings.

up with the food consistently shared it with its helper. When rewarded in this way, the monkeys became even more likely to help each other subsequently.

In some human environments, reciprocal altruism is essential for survival even today. Burnstein and his colleagues (1994) cite the !Kung people of Africa as an example. The !Kung have been pushed by other groups into barren lands where food and water are scarce. As a result, the !Kung share all resources within the band. An individual who gets food will share with the others and will expect the same in return. "The idea of eating alone is shocking to the !Kung. It makes them shriek with an uneasy laughter. Lions could do that, they say, not men" (Marshall, 1979, p. 357).

Reciprocal altruism is not restricted to basic needs such as food acquisition. The passengers of one of those flights diverted to Gander after the 9/11 attacks were so grateful for the kindness and assistance they received that they created a scholarship for Gander students; it is now worth more than $20 000. In addition, the swapping of music and videos online through services like Kazaa and Morpheus may be considered a form of reciprocal altruism, since an individual makes his or her own files available to others so that he or she can have access to theirs. (Of course, the record labels and movie studios have other terms for these activities, such as *criminal* and *unethical.*) Strong norms often develop in these peer-to-peer networks. An individual who downloads songs or videos from others' computers but doesn't make his or her own files available is likely to be chastised quickly and emphatically. Indeed, the development of norms and the punishment of individuals who deviate from the norm are key factors in maintaining reciprocal altruism, especially in groups of non-kin. Even though in some situations individuals risk personal costs in order to punish violators, they do so anyway to preserve a norm that tends to benefit everyone in the group (Fehr & Gaechter, 2002; Gintis et al., 2003).

The Cooperative Group Kinship selection and reciprocal altruism emphasize helping specific others based on genetic relatedness or the probability of being helped in return. But much helping goes beyond these limits. For example, injured or sick animals are often aided by others in their group, even if they are unrelated and there is little chance that the recipients will return the favour (de Waal, 1996). Can altruism operate at a broader level than specific genes or specific reciprocal relationships between individuals? Some evolutionary theorists believe that natural selection operates across the full biological hierarchy, from genes, to organisms, to groups, to species (Gould, 1992).

According to Elliott Sober and David Wilson (1998; Wilson & Sober, 1994), group selection may play a role in accounting for the evolution of human psychology: Human beings can sometimes increase their reproductive success by protecting their own self-interest in relation to other individuals *and* by protecting their group's interest in relation to other groups. Kinship selection is a form of group selection that occurs only in groups of genetic relatives. But the kind of group selection proposed by Wilson and Sober can also operate in groups of unrelated individuals, producing helping behaviour based on a social connection rather than a genetic relationship. Thus, cooperation and helpfulness among members of a social group (especially when the group faces an external threat) could be an innate, universal tendency. Franz de Waal (1996) reports remarkable instances of within-group helping among animals—for example, a Japanese monkey born without hands and feet who was fully accepted and helped by the other monkeys in its group and a mentally retarded rhesus monkey given special care by the other monkeys in its group. There is considerable evidence that human beings also cooperate with and help others to a much greater extent if they consider these others to be members of their ingroup (Cadenhead & Richman, 1996; Dovidio et al., 1997). Humans' strong need to belong to groups and to maintain strong social identities may stem in part from these evolutionary roots (Baumeister & Leary, 1995; Caporael, 1997).

Rewards of Helping: Helping Others to Help Oneself

People are more likely to help someone in an emergency if the potential rewards seem high and the potential costs seem low. **True.**

Whether or not it can be traced to evolutionary factors, one important reason why people help others is because it often is rewarding. We all like the idea of being the hero, lifted onto the shoulders of our peers for coming to the rescue of someone in distress. Helping helps the helper.

The empirical evidence on this point is clear: People are much more likely to help when the potential rewards of helping seem high relative to the potential costs (Dovidio, 1984; Fritzsche et al., 2000; Piliavin et al., 1975; Shotland & Stebbins, 1983). This effect does not appear to be limited to the very individualistic cultures of Canada, the United States, and Western Europe; evidence has also been found in Sudan and in Japan, for example (Hedge & Yousif, 1992; Imai, 1991). The research of Jane Piliavin, John Dovidio, and their colleagues suggests that potential helpers conduct a cost-benefit analysis not only when making deliberate decisions to behave prosocially, as when donating blood, but also in more impulsive, sudden decisions to intervene in an emergency (Dovidio et al., 1991; Piliavin et al., 1981). Indeed, the **arousal: cost-reward model** of helping stipulates that both emotional and cognitive factors determine whether bystanders to an emergency will intervene. Emotionally, bystanders experience the shock and alarm of personal distress; this unpleasant state of arousal motivates them to do something to reduce it. What they do, however, depends on the "bystander calculus," their computation of the costs and rewards associated with helping. When potential rewards (to self and victim) outweigh potential costs (to self and victim), bystanders will help. But raise those costs and lower those rewards, and victims stand a good chance of having to do without (Fritzsche et al., 2000).

Feeling Good Helping often simply *feels* good (Smith et al., 1989; Williamson & Clark, 1992). People whose high self-esteem has been threatened by failure become particularly helpful, presumably because they feel the need to reclaim their positive feelings about themselves and they realize that they can achieve this by helping others (Brown & Smart, 1991). Similarly, feeling guilty about something—for example, after hurting someone's feelings or damaging someone's property—often motivates people to behave prosocially and help others (Estrada-Hollenbeck & Heatherton, 1998; D. T. Regan et al., 1972; J. W. Regan, 1971).

A growing body of recent research has pointed to a strong relationship between giving help and feeling better, including on measures of mental *and* physical health (Dulin & Hill, 2003; Piliavin, 2003; Schwartz et al., 2003). Stephanie Brown and others (2003), for example, studied a sample of 846 elderly individuals for five years. The researchers found that the people in this sample who early on had reported helping others were only about half as likely to die during these five years as those

arousal: cost-reward model The proposition that people react to emergency situations by acting in the most cost-effective way to reduce the arousal of shock and alarm.

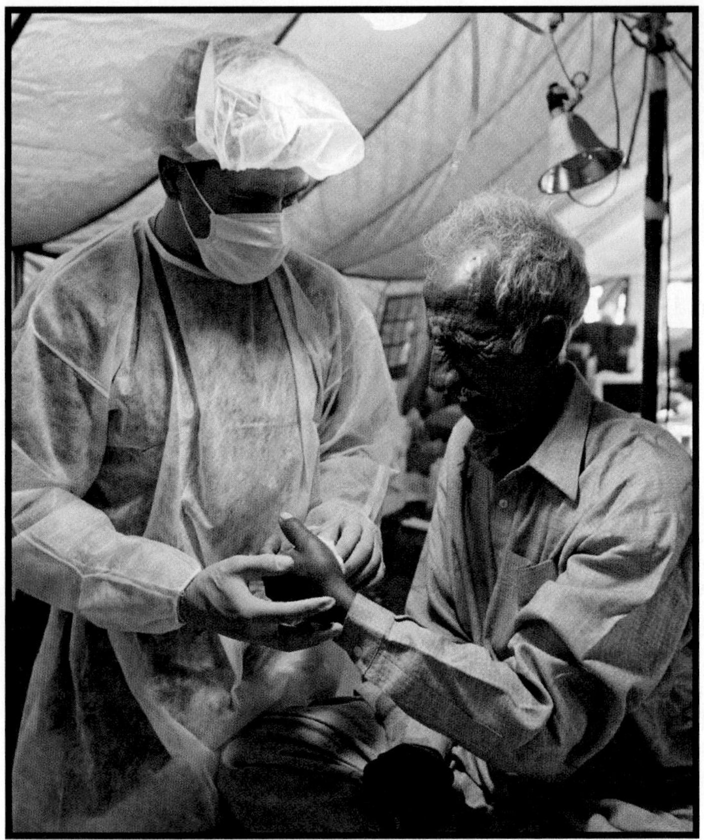

Volunteering one's time, energy, and skills to help others can make one feel good about oneself. Even if not financial, the rewards can be tremendous.

who did not. This helping could consist of a variety of behaviours, from helping with errands to giving emotional support. Of course, with a correlational finding such as this, we cannot know whether the helping behaviours *caused* the better health, but the researchers did analyze and effectively rule out a number of plausible other causes for this correlation. If helping does help the helper's health, how does it do so? The researchers draw on two established research findings to answer this: (1) Helping does tend to feel good, as we have just discussed, improving people's moods and lowering their stress; and (2) positive affect and lowered stress can have a positive effect on one's health.

In a provocative set of studies using brain-imaging techniques, James Rilling and others (2002) examined the brain activity of women playing a Prisoner's Dilemma game, which, as was discussed in Chapter 8, is a game in which individuals compete or cooperate with each other for individual and joint payoffs. The researchers found that when the women were engaged in mutual cooperation during the game, activation was observed in areas of the brain that are linked to processing rewards. Despite the fact that these individuals could earn more money by competing with their partner after their partner had cooperated, their brain activity suggested that cooperation was intrinsically rewarding, and this feeling could reinforce altruism and inhibit selfishness.

Even when helping doesn't feel good immediately, it can pay off in the long run. When parents reluctantly sacrifice relaxing with a good book or DVD at the end of a hard day in order to help their child finish some homework, they might not feel immediate joy from giving help; but in the long run, they will reap the benefits of their behaviour (Salovey et al., 1991). Evidence in support of this conclusion is provided by Carolyn Schwartz and Meir Sendor (1999), who, in a study of peer supporters of people with multiple sclerosis, found that the supporters showed significant improvement on several dimensions—including confidence, self-awareness, self-esteem, and relief from depression—three years after first being surveyed.

Children learn that helping others can be rewarding (Grusec, 1991). Younger children focus on the rewards they get from parents and others; but as they develop into adolescence, they begin to reward themselves for helping, taking pride in their actions. Their helpful behaviour can then be internally motivated, leading them to help even without the promise of immediate material or social rewards (Cialdini et al., 1981; Piliavin & Callero, 1991).

The process of helping others to feel good about oneself is often not conscious, but it can be. For example, participants in one study rated the relative importance of a number of considerations in deciding whether to help someone else. Two of the three considerations that the participants rated as most important concerned the rewards ("It would make me feel good about myself") and costs ("I might get hurt") of helping. The other consideration was "It's the right thing to do" (Smitherman, 1992). People's awareness that helping feels good is evident in the words offered by no less an authority than the venerable "Dear Abby," the world's most famous syndicated advice columnist. She recently offered this advice to her readers: "The surest way to forget your own troubles is to do something nice for those less fortunate. The adrenaline rush you'll get is more powerful than speed, and the 'high' is perfectly legal" ("Dear Abby," 2003).

Being, or Appearing to Be, Good In addition to the rewards of helping, the consideration that "It's the right thing to do" reflects, at least in part, a sense of moral obligation or duty. Being motivated to behave in ways consistent with moral principles may drive people to help each other, and affirming one's morality in this way can make one feel good about oneself. Conversely, inhibiting or disengaging oneself from such moral concerns may be the critical factor in enabling humans to act inhumanely toward one another, through violence, terrorism, discrimination, and other acts of destruction (Bandura, 1999; Staub, 1996). Another motive for helping has the appearance of morality but reflects a more selfish desire to reap the social rewards of helping. The reference here is to *moral hypocrisy*, whereby people try to convince themselves and others that they are driven to help others by moral principles when in actuality they are motivated to benefit themselves by *appearing* to be moral. For example, imagine that you and a friend meet a musician you both admire and she gives you a back-stage pass for her next concert. There's just the one pass, and it's in your hands. Do you keep it, or do you flip a coin for it? Furthermore, what if you know that if you flip the coin, you can increase the likelihood that you're going to win? If you are motivated by moral hypocrisy, you might make a big, noble show of your willingness to flip the coin—as long as you know that you're probably going to win. Truly moral motivation, on the other hand, would compel you to ask a disinterested third person to flip the coin under perfectly fair conditions, even though you might suffer a cost. Using experimental scenarios that mimicked dilemmas similar to this one, Daniel Batson, Diane Kobrynowicz, and others (1997) demonstrated the prevalence of moral hypocrisy in their research. They found that participants were likely to act morally when their action benefited themselves; but when it did not benefit them, and if the situation permitted them to behave in a self-interested way without appearing selfish, they were much less likely to take the moral action.

A particularly disturbing version of moral hypocrisy can be seen when individuals deliberately hurt or endanger others so that they can swoop in and apparently try to save the day. A case in point was Kristen Gilbert, a nurse and mother of two, who was sentenced to life in prison in 2001 for killing four patients at a Veterans Affairs hospital in Massachusetts. She killed the patients by injecting them with epinephrine, a stimulant that caused their hearts to beat out of control. Why did she do it? According to her lawyers, "Her aim was to cause a medical emergency so she could become a hero" (Bayles, 2001). Another kind of hypocrisy involves *overhelping*. Picture the following: A child who feels threatened by the attention given to a younger sibling proceeds to "help" the toddler right off his or her feet and onto the floor with a crash. "Oops," says the older child. "I was only trying to help." Adults can be subtler in their approach, but they may have a similar motivation: to appear to help another only to hurt him or her. According to Daniel Gilbert and David Silvera (1996), people sometimes offer help to another who doesn't really need it, or they offer more help than the recipient needs, in order to raise suspicions about the recipient's successful performance. Thus the adult version of the previous situation might play out like this: Ryan knows that Christina doesn't need any help on a project she's completing, but he makes a public display of assistance, hoping that she'll get less of the credit than she deserves. He hopes others will say, "Sure, Christina did a great job on the project, but I wonder if she could have done it without Ryan."

Costs of Helping, or of Not Helping Clearly, helping has its rewards; but it has its costs as well. The firefighters in Ladder Company Six who risked their lives to help Josephine Harris were among the lucky ones. Not everyone is so lucky; in January 2004, 23-year-old Rachel Davis came to the aid of a young man being beaten outside of a Vancouver nightclub. After leaning over the man—a stranger to her—she was shot and killed by one of his assailants.

Other helpers have done more sustained and deliberate helping, such as the people who helped guide runaway slaves in the nineteenth-century American South through the underground railroad to places such as Canada or Mexico where they could live as free citizens, or the people who helped hide Jews during the Holocaust. Sharon Shepela and others (1999) call this type of thoughtful helping in the face of potentially enormous costs *courageous resistance*. And although giving help is often associated with positive affect and health, when the help involves constant and exhausting demands, which is often the case when taking long-term care of a very ill person, the effects on the helper's physical and mental health can be quite negative (Schwartz et al., 2003).

To shift the balance between the costs and benefits of helping more toward the benefits, several provinces have created "Good Samaritan" laws that encourage people to provide or summon aid in an emergency—so long as they do not endanger themselves in the process. A component of such a law is that the would-be helper cannot be sued for coming to the aid of a victim should something not go according to plan. However, the province of Quebec actually *requires* an individual to come to the aid of someone in need, unless it means putting themselves at risk. Such laws are not uncommon in Europe. In fact, several photographers were initially accused by French authorities of breaking France's Good Samaritan laws following the automobile crash that killed Princess Diana, her companion, and their driver in Paris in 1997. Reportedly, these photographers arrived early at the crash scene and took pictures rather than attempting to help the victims.

Altruism or Egoism: The Great Debate

At the end of 1996, *People* magazine honoured Binti Jua as one of the 25 "most intriguing people" of the year; and *Newsweek* named her "hero of the year." On August 16, while caring for her own 17-month-old daughter, Binti came across a three-year-old boy who had fallen about 6 metres onto a cement floor and been knocked unconscious. She picked up the boy and gently held him, rocking him softly, and then turned him over to paramedics. The "intriguing" thing about Binti was that she is a gorilla.

When the boy climbed over a fence and fell into the primate exhibit at the Brookfield Zoo, near Chicago, witnesses feared the worst. One paramedic said, "I didn't know if she was going to treat him like a doll or a toy." With her own daughter clinging to her back the entire time, Binti "protected the toddler as if he were her own," keeping other gorillas at bay and eventually placing him gently at the entrance where zookeepers and paramedics could get to him. "I could not believe how gentle she was," observed a zoo director (O'Neill et al., 1996, p. 72).

It was, of course, a terrific story; and it soon sparked national debate; was Binti's act a heartwarming example of altruism, motivated by kindness and compassion, or was it that Binti had received training in infant care before the birth of her own baby and had simply acted as she had been trained to act—with no kindness or compassion involved?

The same debate exists about human behaviour. Are humans ever truly **altruistic**—motivated by the desire to increase another's welfare? Or are our helpful behaviours always **egoistic**—motivated by selfish concerns or simple conformity to socialized norms? Although most psychological theories assume an egoistic, self-interested bottom line, not everyone is content with this account of the motives of human behaviour. Consider, for example, the many students who participate in volunteer activities: tutoring refugees and disadvantaged youngsters, serving meals at food kitchens, signing up potential bone-marrow donors, working in community service agencies—the list goes on and on. Are they all just looking out for number one?

altruistic Motivated by the desire to increase another's welfare.

egoistic Motivated by the desire to increase one's own welfare.

Daniel Batson (2002) thinks not. He believes that the motivation behind some helpful actions is at least in part truly altruistic. Batson defines *altruistic* as we defined it previously: motivated by the desire to increase another's welfare. This definition is narrower than some, which characterize any helpful action in the absence of a clear external reward as altruistic. At the same time, it is broader than others, which restrict altruism to helpful actions requiring personal sacrifice by the helper. According to this perspective, it's the nature of the helper's motive that counts, not whether the helper receives benefits or suffers costs for helping.

Binti Jua, a gorilla in the Brookfield Zoo, near Chicago, gently rocks a three-year-old boy who had fallen 6 metres into the primate exhibit. The gorilla was acclaimed a hero for her role in saving the boy. Did Binti Jua act out of kindness and empathy? Or did she simply do what she was taught to do—care for an infant? This episode brings the altruism debate to life—even in the animal world.

The Empathy-Altruism Hypothesis Batson's model of altruism is based on his view of the consequences of empathy, which has long been viewed as a basic factor in promoting positive behaviour toward others. Although the definition of *empathy* has been much debated, most researchers regard empathy as a complex phenomenon with both cognitive and emotional components (Davis, 1994; Eisenberg et al., 1996). The major cognitive component of empathy is *perspective taking:* using the power of imagination to try to see the world through someone else's eyes. A key emotional component of empathy is *empathic concern*, which involves other-oriented feelings, such as sympathy, compassion, and tenderness. In contrast to empathic concern is *personal distress*, which involves self-oriented reactions to a person in need, such as feeling alarmed, troubled, or upset.

According to Batson, perspective taking is the first step toward altruism. If you perceive someone in need and imagine how *that person* feels, you are likely to experience other-oriented feelings of empathic concern, which in turn produce the altruistic motive to reduce the other person's distress. However, if you perceive someone in need and focus on your *own* feelings or on how *you* would feel in that person's situation, you are not adopting the perspective of the needy person; rather, you will experience self-oriented feelings of personal distress, which elicit the egoistic motive to reduce your distress (Batson et al., 1997; Stotland, 1969). The basic features of Batson's **empathy-altruism hypothesis** are outlined in Figure 10.1.

Now comes the hard part. How can we tell the difference between egoistic and altruistic motives? In both cases, people help someone else, but the helpers' reasons are different. Confronted with this puzzle, Batson came up with an elegant solution. It depends, he says, on how easy it is to escape from a helping situation. When a person's motive is egoistic, helping should decline if it's easy for the individual to escape from the situation. When a person's motive is altruistic, however, help will be given regardless of the ease of escape.

Batson and others have conducted numerous experiments in support of this hypothesis. Imagine that you are a participant in one of these studies (Batson et al., 1981). You are paired with a woman named Elaine, whom you are led to believe is another participant. Through what appears to be random assignment, you are placed in the observer condition, whereas Elaine is asked to try to complete an unpleasant task. Via a TV monitor you then observe Elaine being hooked up to a machine that, a short time later, seems to be delivering painful electric shocks to her as she works. After receiving a number of shocks, she appears quite uncomfortable. Asking for a glass of water, she tells the experimenter about a frightening childhood experience when she was thrown from a horse against an electric fence. For Elaine, the shocks she is now receiving are very unpleasant, but she says she wants to go on.

empathy-altruism hypothesis The proposition that empathic concern for a person in need produces an altruistic motive for helping.

FIGURE 10.1

The Empathy-Altruism Hypothesis

According to the empathy-altruism hypothesis, taking the perspective of a person in need creates feelings of empathic concern, which produce the altruistic motive to reduce the other person's distress. When people do *not* take the other's perspective, they experience feelings of personal distress, which produce the egoistic motive to reduce their own discomfort. *(Based on Batson, 1991.)*

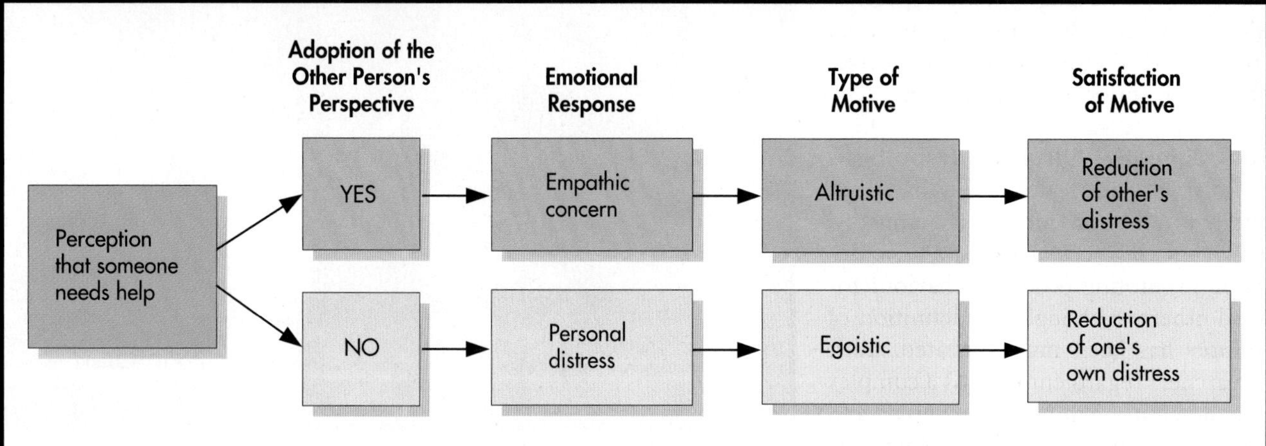

The experimenter hesitates; perhaps Elaine should stop at this point. And then the experimenter has a bright idea: Would *you* be willing to trade places with Elaine?

Actually, Elaine was a trained confederate and never got shocked. But the experimental procedures created a compelling dilemma for participants. Would they suffer for someone else? The answer rests on the combinations of *empathic concern* and *difficulty of escape* manipulated in the experiment.

- Because similarity increases empathic thoughts and feelings, half of the participants were told that Elaine's personal values and interests were very similar to their own. The other half were told they were quite different.
- To create an easy-escape condition, half the participants were informed that they could leave after witnessing two of the ten trials during which Elaine would receive random shocks. Those in the difficult-escape condition were required to witness all ten trials. The experimenter's invitation to trade places came at the end of two trials, letting easy-escape participants off the hook but keeping difficult-escape participants still dangling.

So, who agreed to trade places with Elaine? As you can see in Figure 10.2, the vast majority of high-empathic-concern participants helped out, regardless of the ease or difficulty of escape. For the low-empathic-concern participants, in contrast, the ease or difficulty of escape did make a difference: Most of them helped if they thought they would have to continue to watch Elaine suffer unless they took her place, but most did not come to Elaine's rescue if they believed they could leave right away. Just as the empathy-altruism hypothesis predicted, when the escape hatch was wide open, participants with little empathic concern took the easy way out. Those with high empathic concern stayed to help.

In subsequent research, Batson and his colleagues have manipulated empathic concern in other ways, such as by having the experimenter or the person in need of help appeal to the participants either to remain objective and "not get caught up" in what the person in need is experiencing (low empathy) or to try to imagine what the person in need is feeling (high empathy). In more than two dozen experiments, these researchers have demonstrated that empathy promotes altruistic motivation (Batson, 2002; Batson et al., 1997).

Egoistic Alternatives Can we conclude, then, that altruism really does exist? Batson and his colleagues believe so. Others are not so sure and offer egoistic alternatives.

One alternative is that empathy encourages helping not because of concern for the other but because of concern about the costs to the *self* of not helping. People may learn that they will feel guilty after experiencing empathy for others in need but failing to help them. Having learned to anticipate such guilt, these people may help others simply to avoid it. The work of Batson and his colleagues, however, suggests that guilt cannot account for the helpful inclinations associated with empathic concern (Batson, 1991; Batson & Weeks, 1996).

A second alternative is that empathy highlights the potential *rewards* for helping others. As we noted earlier in this chapter, helping makes people feel good. In their **negative state relief model**, Robert Cialdini and his colleagues (1987) propose that because of this positive effect of helping, people who are feeling bad may be inclined to help others in order to improve their mood. Thus, perhaps empathy promotes helping in the following way: Empathic concern for a person in need increases feelings of sadness, which in turn increase the need for mood enhancement, which in turn brings about helping behaviour. This egoistic account has generated a flurry of studies—some that support it and others that do not (Batson, 2002; Maner et al., 2002).

Another egoistic alternative involving empathy-specific rewards emphasizes positive well-being rather than negative relief. Kyle Smith and his colleagues (1989) maintain that empathic concern enhances the helper's sensitivity to the good feelings experienced by the person receiving help, causing the helper to experience *empathic joy*. Thus, we help those with whom we empathize because helping them makes us feel especially good. Here again, some evidence has supported the egoism side of the debate (Smith et al., 1989), other evidence, the empathy altruism side (Batson, 1998, 2002).

FIGURE 10.2

When Empathy Helps

These results supported the predictions made by the empathy-altruism hypothesis. When empathic concern was high, most people helped regardless of whether escape was easy or difficult. But among those with low levels of empathic concern, fewer people helped when escape was easy than when it was difficult. *(Based on Batson et al., 1981.)*

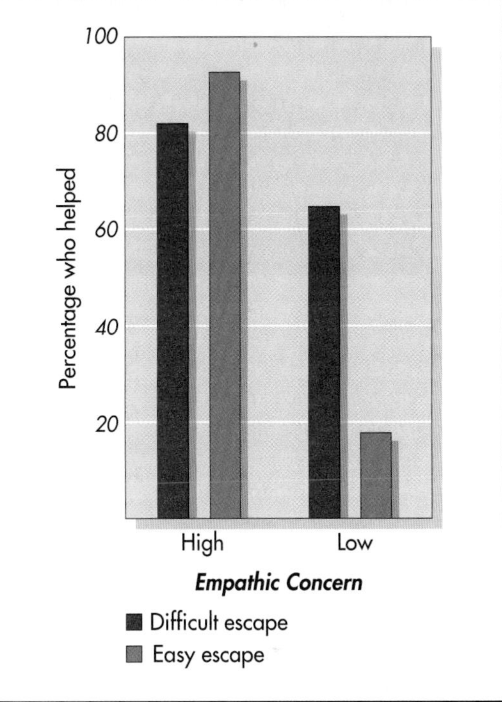

Altruism Versus Egoism: Limits and Convergence Despite the egoistic alternatives that have been proposed, the evidence for the empathy-altruism hypothesis is quite strong. Nevertheless, it has its limits. First of all, Batson has never claimed that *all* helping is altruistically motivated. No doubt, there are multiple motives for helping, and many helpful acts are best explained in terms of the processes we consider elsewhere in this chapter. And any single helpful action can be the result of a mixture of egoistic and altruistic motives. Mark Snyder (1993) suggests, for example, that the most effective way to increase helping is to encourage people to recognize and feel comfortable with the convergence of self-oriented and other-oriented concerns.

Another limit is created by the fact that motives do not guarantee behaviour. Empathy leads to altruistic motivations, but not necessarily to helpful behaviours. For example, someone with empathic concern for another might not help this person if he or she fears that the potential cost of offering the help is very high (Batson et al., 1983). When egoistic costs are greater than the altruistic motive can bear, the other-oriented impulse cannot prevail. Perhaps in order to avoid such internal conflicts, people who anticipate being asked for high-cost assistance often avoid empathy-inducing experiences (Shaw et al., 1994).

A possible third limitation cuts even closer to the fundamental nature of altruism. Distinguishing between egoistic and altruistic motives requires the assumption that there is a clear divide between the self and the other. But what if there isn't?

negative state relief model The proposition that people help others in order to counteract their own feelings of sadness.

The Canadian Cancer Society sponsors "Cops for Cancer"—fundraising events where police officers publicly shave their heads to raise money for the charity. According to the empathy-altruism hypothesis, taking the perspective of someone in need is the first step toward altruism.

What if, as Daniel Wegner (1980, p. 133) suggests, empathy reflects "a basic confusion between ourselves and others"? What if, as Arthur and Elaine Aron (2001) propose, those in close relationships incorporate the other into the self? When one and one equals "oneness" or "we-ness," helping this close other person may be seen as helping oneself, or at least helping an important part of oneself (Maner et al., 2002; Piliavin et al., 1981). Cialdini and his colleagues believe that in such situations, helping is caused by the recognition of the self in the other, not by empathic concern for the other; Batson and his colleagues counter that empathy triggers altruism regardless of feelings of oneness. But perhaps there is a different way to think about the debate on oneness: Perhaps the egoistic account and the altruistic account actually merge on this point. In relationships in which the self-other distinction is virtually eliminated and you feel someone else's needs as deeply as you feel your own, the distinction between an egoistic motive and an altruistic one may be eliminated as well.

Distinguishing Among the Motivations to Help: Why Does It Matter?

On the surface, the debate between altruistic and egoistic accounts of helping may seem to be irrelevant quibbling about semantics or philosophy. After all, if someone pulls you out of a burning car, you don't care if your rescuer did it to increase the chances that your similar genes will be passed down to future generations, to be lauded as a hero as the action news team approaches with its cameras, or simply because he or she was concerned for your safety. You just are thankful that the person helped, no matter what the motivation. So why does it matter whether we attribute the motivation of the helper to altruism or egoism?

Perhaps the most important reason to consider people's motivations is that they help us determine whether or not the helping will occur in the first place. Recall the previous example—but this time imagine that there is a witness to your accident. If this witness is motivated by egoistic concern, then he or she is likely to help only if they expect to benefit from doing so, as the recipients of some material or psychological reward. If they are motivated by altruism, they may try to help you despite the potential costs, particularly if they feel empathy for you. And, according to Batson's research, if they do not feel empathy for you, they might fail to help if there is an easy way for them to escape the situation and avoid experiencing personal distress.

Motivational factors also play important roles in more long-term helping behaviour, such as volunteerism. Research has found a number of important motivations underlying volunteering, including those associated with empathy, such as perspective taking and empathic concern, and more egoistic goals, such as career aspirations, relieving aversive emotions, and conforming to prosocial norms (Ferrari et al., 1999; Penner & Finkelstein, 1998; Snyder et al., 2000; Snyder & Clary, 2004; Unger & Thumuluri, 1997). Goals can be as simple as wanting to enhance one's resumé (Dickinson, 1999), or more lofty, as wanting to gain knowledge and understanding about AIDS and the communities most affected by it—which were found in independent studies to be positive predictors of volunteering for AIDS prevention or care services (Reeder et al., 2001; Simon et al., 2000).

Table 10.1 lists five categories of motives that Allen Omoto and Mark Snyder (1995) found compelled people to volunteer to help persons with AIDS. AIDS volunteers who had initially endorsed self-oriented motives, such as gaining understanding and developing personal skills, remained active volunteers longer than did those who had initially emphasized other-oriented motives, such as humanitarian values and community concern. Why were the more egoistic goals associated with longer service? As Mark Snyder notes, "The good, and perhaps romanticized, intentions related to humanitarian concern simply may not be strong enough to sustain volunteers faced with the tough realities and personal costs of working with [persons with AIDS]" (Snyder, 1993, p. 258). When helping demands more of us, self-interest may keep us going.

Self-interest as a motive for helping, therefore, is not necessarily a bad thing. Indeed, the fact that many people find helping others to be so personally rewarding is a positive aspect of human nature. One's feelings of empathic concern for others are usually limited to a few other people at a time and perhaps to relatively brief periods. Those people who derive a great deal of personal satisfaction from helping others, however, may be motivated much more frequently and consistently to engage in helping behaviours. Indeed, commitment to prosocial actions can become an important part of one's identity (Piliavin et al., 2002).

TABLE 10.1

Motivations to Volunteer to Help People with AIDS

Allen Omoto and Mark Snyder identified five categories of motivations underlying people's initial decisions to volunteer to help people with AIDS. Within each category, three examples of specific statements representative of the general motive are presented. *(Omoto & Snyder, 1995.)*

Values

Because of my humanitarian obligation to help others
Because I enjoy helping other people
Because I consider myself a loving and caring person

Understanding

To learn more about how to prevent AIDS
To learn how to help people with AIDS
To deal with my personal fears and anxiety about AIDS

Personal Development

To get to know people who are similar to myself
To meet new people and make new friends
To gain experience dealing with emotionally difficult topics

Community Concern

Because of my sense of obligation to the gay community
Because I consider myself an advocate for gay-related issues
Because of my concern and worry about the gay community

Esteem Enhancement

To feel better about myself
To escape other pressures and stress in my life
To feel less lonely

Situational Influences: When Do People Help?

Thus far, we have focused on *why* people help others. We now turn to the question of *when* people help. We begin by discussing a remarkably creative and provocative set of research findings that make a surprising point: If you need help in an emergency, you may be better off if there is only one witness to your plight than if there are several. We then focus on a wide range of other situational factors on helping, including where we live, whether we are experiencing time pressure, what kind of mood we're in, and whether we've been exposed to particular role models or social norms.

The Unhelpful Crowd

At about 3:20 on the morning of March 13, 1964, 28-year-old Kitty Genovese was returning home from her job as a bar manager. Suddenly, a man attacked her with a knife. She was stalked, stabbed, and sexually assaulted just 35 yards from her own

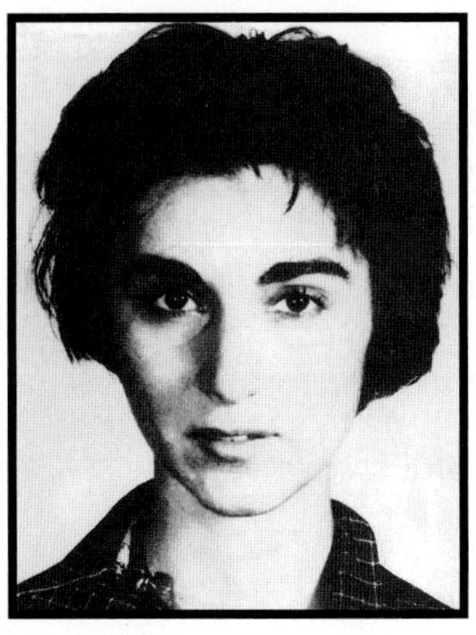

How could 38 witnesses stand by and do nothing while Kitty Genovese was being murdered? Research conducted in the aftermath of the tragedy suggests that if there had been only one witness rather than almost 40, she might have had a better chance of receiving help, and she might be alive today.

apartment building in the New York City borough of Queens. Lights went on and windows went up as she screamed, "Oh my God! He stabbed me! Please help me!" She broke free from her attacker twice, but only briefly. Thirty-eight of her neighbours witnessed her ordeal, but not one intervened. Finally, after nearly 45 minutes of terror, one man called the police; but by then, Genovese was dead.

The murder of Kitty Genovese shocked the nation. Were her neighbours to blame? It seemed unlikely that all 38 of them could have been moral monsters. Most of the media attention focused on the decline of morals and values in contemporary society and on the anonymity and apathy seen in large American cities such as New York. A few days after the incident, Bibb Latané and John Darley discussed over dinner the events and the explanations being offered for it. They were not convinced that these explanations were sufficient to account for why Kitty Genovese didn't get the help she needed; and they wondered if other, social psychological processes might have been at work. They speculated that because each witness to the attack could see that many other witnesses had turned on their lights and were looking out their windows, each witness might have assumed that others would, or should, take responsibility and call the police. To test their ideas, Latané and Darley (1970) set out to see if they could produce unresponsive bystanders under laboratory conditions. Let's take a look at one of their studies.

When a participant arrived, he or she was taken to one of a series of small rooms located along a corridor. Speaking over an intercom, the experimenter explained that he wanted participants to discuss personal problems often faced by students. Participants were told that, to protect confidentiality, the group discussion would take place over the intercom system, and the experimenter would not be listening. They were required to speak one at a time, taking turns. Some participants were assigned to talk with one other person; others joined larger groups of three or six people.

Although one participant did mention in passing that he suffered from a seizure disorder that was sometimes triggered by study pressures, the opening moments of the conversation were uneventful. But soon, an unexpected problem developed. When the time came for this person to speak again, he stuttered badly, had a hard time speaking clearly, and sounded as if he were in very serious trouble:

> *I could really-er-use some help so if somebody would-er-give me a little h-help-uh-erer-er-er c-could somebody-er-er-help-er-uh-uh-uh [choking sounds]. . . . I'm gonna die-er-er-I'm . . . gonna die-er-help-er-er-seizure-er [chokes, then quiet].*

Confronted with this situation, what would *you* do? Would you interrupt the experiment, dash out of your cubicle, and try to find the experimenter? Or would you sit there—concerned, but unsure how to react?

As it turns out, participants' responses to this emergency were strongly influenced by the size of their group. Actually, all participants were participating alone, but tape-recorded material led them to believe that others were present. All the participants who thought that only they knew about the emergency left the room quickly to try to get help. In the larger groups, however, participants were less likely and slower to intervene. Indeed, 38 percent of the participants in the six-person groups never left the room at all! This research led Latané and Darley to a chilling conclusion: The more bystanders, the *less* likely the victim will be helped. This is the **bystander effect**, whereby the presence of others inhibits helping.

Before the pioneering work of Latané and Darley, most people would have assumed just the opposite. Isn't there safety in numbers? Don't we feel more secure rushing in to help when others are around to lend their support? Latané and Darley overturned this common-sense assumption and provided a careful, step-by-step analysis of the decision-making process involved in emergency interventions. In the following sections, we examine each of five steps in this process: noticing something unusual, interpreting it as an emergency, taking responsibility for getting help, de-

bystander effect The effect whereby the presence of others inhibits helping.

ciding how to help, and providing assistance. We also consider the reasons why people sometimes fail to take one of these steps and, therefore, do not help. These steps, and the obstacles along the way, are summarized in Figure 10.3.

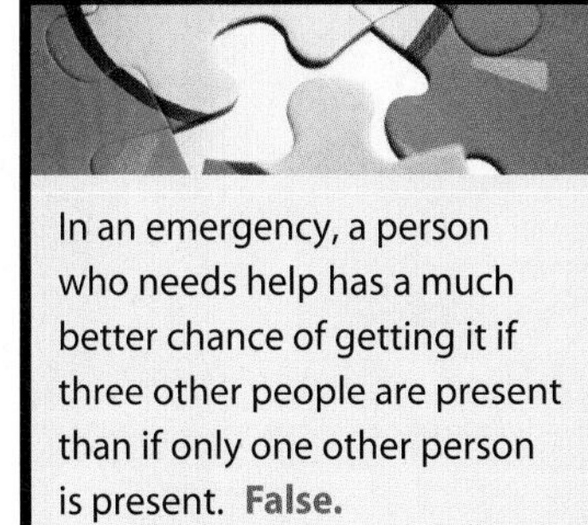

In an emergency, a person who needs help has a much better chance of getting it if three other people are present than if only one other person is present. **False.**

Noticing The first step toward being a helpful bystander is to notice that someone needs help or, at least, that something out of the ordinary is happening. Participants in the seizure study could not help but notice the emergency. In many situations, however, the problem isn't always perceived. The presence of others can be distracting and can divert attention away from indications of a victim's plight. In addition, people may fail to notice that someone needs help because they are caught up in their own self-concerns. People who live in big cities and noisy environments may become so used to seeing people lying on sidewalks or hearing screams that they begin to tune them out, becoming susceptible to what Stanley Milgram (1970) called *stimulus overload.*

FIGURE 10.3

The Five Steps to Helping in an Emergency

On the basis of their analysis of the decision-making process in emergency interventions, Latané and Darley (1970) outlined five steps that lead to providing assistance. But there are obstacles that can interfere; and if a step is missed, the victim won't be helped.

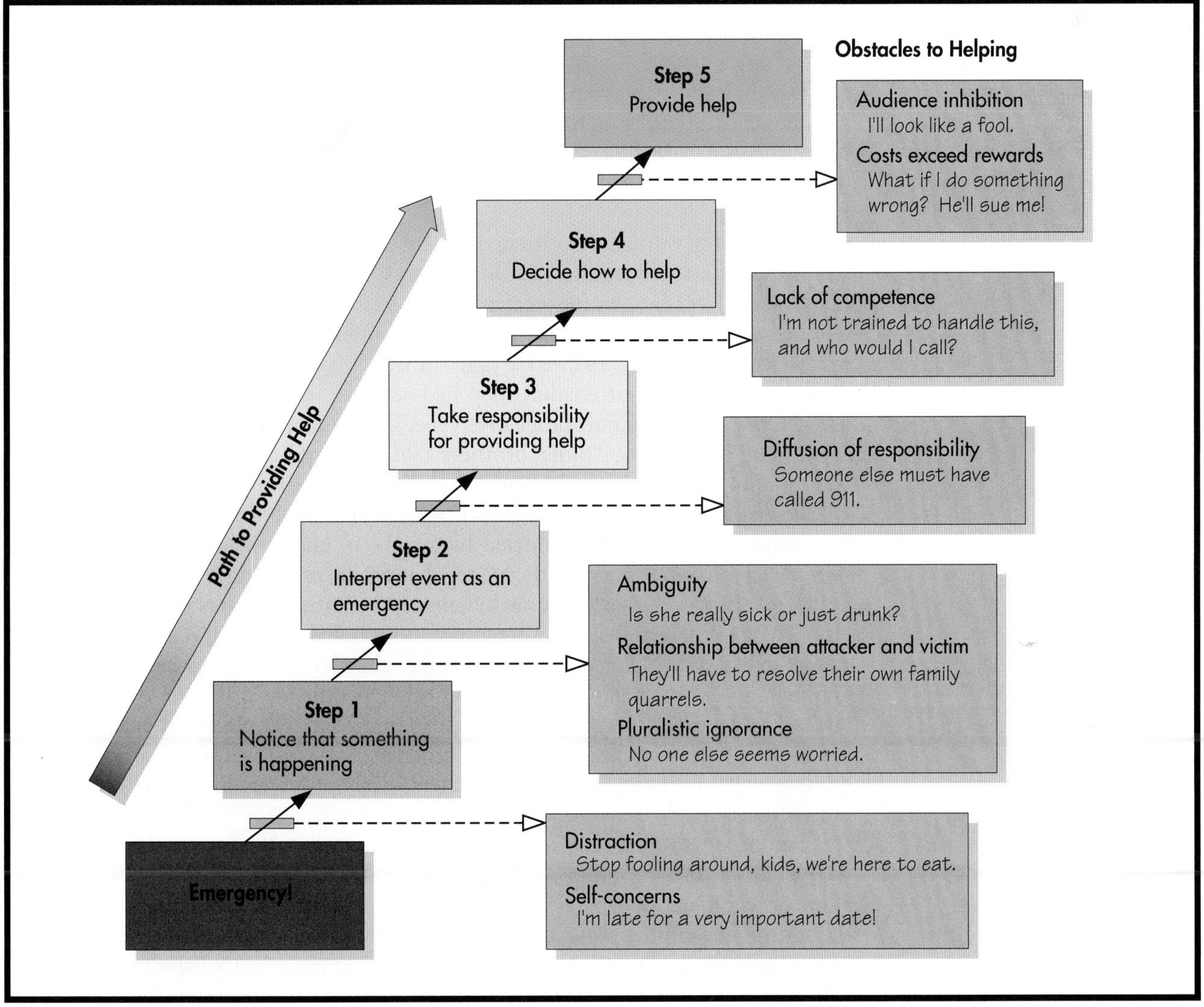

Path to Providing Help

Obstacles to Helping

Emergency!

Step 1
Notice that something is happening

Distraction
Stop fooling around, kids, we're here to eat.
Self-concerns
I'm late for a very important date!

Step 2
Interpret event as an emergency

Ambiguity
Is she really sick or just drunk?
Relationship between attacker and victim
They'll have to resolve their own family quarrels.
Pluralistic ignorance
No one else seems worried.

Step 3
Take responsibility for providing help

Diffusion of responsibility
Someone else must have called 911.

Step 4
Decide how to help

Lack of competence
I'm not trained to handle this, and who would I call?

Step 5
Provide help

Audience inhibition
I'll look like a fool.
Costs exceed rewards
What if I do something wrong? He'll sue me!

The first step toward providing help is to notice that someone needs assistance. These people become "invisible" to potential helpers who pass them each day as they make their way to school or work, distracted by their own concerns or by the overwhelming stimuli of a big, bustling city.

Interpreting Noticing the victim is a necessary first step toward helping, but it is not enough. People must interpret the meaning of what they notice. Cries of pain can be mistaken for shrieks of laughter; heart-attack victims can appear to be drunk. So observers wonder: Does that person really need help? In general, the more ambiguous the situation, the less likely it is that bystanders will intervene (Clark & Word, 1972).

Interpretations of the relationship between a victim and an attacker also affect whether help will be provided. Consider, for example, how people react when they see a woman attacked by a man. Research by Lance Shotland and Margaret Straw (1976) indicates that many observers of such an incident believe that the attacker and the victim have a close relationship as dates, lovers, or spouses—even when no information about the relationship is actually available. This inference can have very serious implications, since—as Shotland and Straw documented—intervening in domestic violence is perceived to be more dangerous to the helper and less desired by the victim than is intervening in an attack by a stranger. Given such beliefs, the response to a scene staged by Shotland and Straw was predictable: In the scene, a woman was supposedly being assaulted either by a stranger or by her husband. More than three times as many observers tried to stop the assault by the stranger.

It's not only women who are in danger if they are perceived as having a close relationship with their attacker: Children also suffer. The 1993 murder of two-year-old James Bulger by two ten-year-old boys was the British equivalent of the Kitty Genovese slaying. James was dragged, kicking and screaming, for two and a half miles from a shopping mall to a railroad track, where he was battered to death. Sixty-one people admitted that they had seen the boys. Most did nothing. One asked a few questions but didn't intervene. The reason? As one witness put it, he thought the boys were "older brothers taking a little one home." When people think "family," they think, "It's OK, it's safe." But sometimes it isn't.

Perhaps the most powerful information available during an emergency is the behaviour of other people. Startled by a sudden, unexpected, possibly dangerous event, each person looks quickly to see what others are doing. As everyone looks at everyone else for clues about how to behave, the entire group is paralyzed by indecision. When this happens, the person needing help is a victim of **pluralistic ignorance.** In this state of ignorance, each individual believes that his or her own thoughts and feelings are different from those of other people, even though everyone's behaviour is the same. Each bystander thinks that other people aren't acting because somehow they know there isn't an emergency. Actually, everyone is confused and hesitant; but, imputing wisdom to others, each observer concludes that help is not required.

pluralistic ignorance The state in which people mistakenly believe that their own thoughts and feelings are different from those of others, even though everyone's behaviour is the same.

Latané and Darley (1968) put this phenomenon to the test in an experiment in which participants completed a questionnaire in a room in which they were either alone or with two other participants. A few minutes after participants had started to fill out the questionnaire, smoke began to seep into the room through a vent. Was this an emergency? How do you think you would respond? Within four minutes, half of the participants who were working alone took some action, such as leaving the room to report the smoke to someone. Within six minutes—the maximum time allotted before the researchers terminated the experiment—three-quarters of these participants took action. Clearly, they interpreted the smoke as a potential emergency. But what about the participants working in groups of three? Common sense suggests that the chances that somebody will take action should be greater when more people are present. But only one of the 24 participants in this condition took action within four minutes, and only three did so before the end of the study—even though, at that point, the smoke was so thick they had to fan it away from their faces to see the questionnaire. If these participants had interpreted the smoke as a potential emergency, they would have acted, because their own lives would have been at stake. But instead, they quickly, coolly looked at the reactions of the others in the room, saw that nobody else seemed too concerned, and so became convinced that nothing could be wrong.

Pluralistic ignorance is not restricted to emergency situations (Miller & McFarland, 1987; Miller et al., 2000; Monin & Norton, 2003; Sabini et al., 1999; Suls & Green, 2003). Have you ever sat through a class feeling totally lost? You want to ask a question, but you're too embarrassed. No one else is saying anything, so you assume they all find the material a snap. Finally, you dare to ask a question. And suddenly, hands shoot up in the air all over the classroom. No one understood the material, yet everyone assumed that everyone else was breezing along. Pluralistic ignorance in the classroom interferes with learning. In an emergency situation, it can lead to disaster—unless someone breaks out of the pack and dares to help. Then others are likely to follow.

Taking Responsibility Noticing a victim and recognizing an emergency are crucial steps; but by themselves, they don't ensure that a bystander will come to the rescue. The issue of responsibility remains. When help is needed, who is responsible for providing it? If a person knows that others are around, it's all too easy to place the responsibility on *them*. People often fail to help because of the **diffusion of responsibility**—the belief that others will or should intervene. Presumably, each of those 38 people who watched and listened to Kitty Genovese's murder thought someone else would do something to stop the attack. But remember those helpful participants in the seizure study who thought that they alone heard the other person's cry for help? Diffusion of responsibility cannot occur if an individual believes that only he or she is aware of the victim's need.

An interesting set of experiments by Stephen Garcia and others (2002) found that the presence of others can promote diffusion of responsibility even when they are present only in one's mind! Garcia and his colleagues (including John Darley) had participants simply *imagine* being in a crowd or being alone, and soon after, these participants were given an opportunity to help someone. The results indicated that participants who had just thought of being with many other people were less likely to help than were the participants who had imagined themselves alone. In one study, for example, some students were asked to imagine themselves at dinner with ten friends; others were asked to imagine themselves at dinner with one friend; and others were asked a nonsocial question. Soon after, the students were asked if they would be willing to volunteer to help with an experiment in another room. Figure 10.4 depicts the average number of minutes the students in each condition volunteered to spend on this other experiment. As can be seen, those students who had imagined going out to dinner with a big group of friends tended to volunteer less of their time to help out with the subsequent experiment than did students who had imagined being out with only one friend, or who had not imagined being out with friends at all. In another experiment, these researchers found that having students think about being in a crowd made concepts like *unaccountable* and *exempt* more accessible in the students' minds, suggesting that merely thinking about the presence of others can promote diffusion of responsibility relatively automatically.

diffusion of responsibility
The belief that others will or should take the responsibility for providing assistance to a person in need.

FIGURE 10.4

The Implicit Bystander Effect

Students in this study imagined having dinner with either one person or with a large group of friends, or they were not asked to imagine a social situation (neutral control group). Later they were asked if they would be willing to volunteer some of their time to help in a different experiment. The students who had imagined a large group volunteered the least amount of time. This result was consistent with the idea that even imagining being in a crowd can prompt thoughts of a lack of responsibility and create a bystander effect. *(Garcia et al., 2002.)*

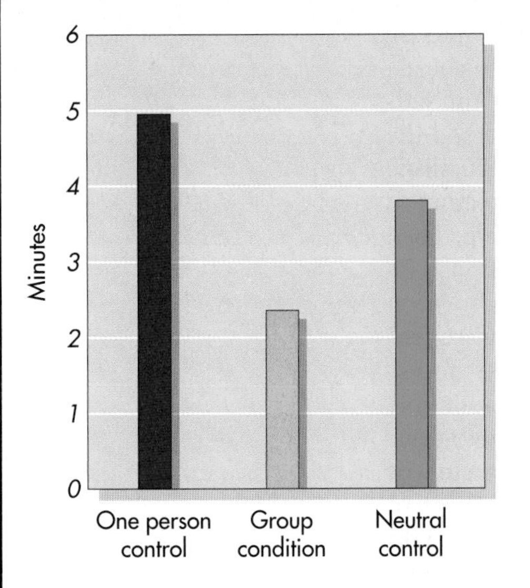

Diffusion of responsibility usually takes place under conditions of anonymity. Bystanders who do not know the victim personally are more likely to see others as responsible for providing help. Accordingly, if the psychological distance between a bystander and the victim is reduced, there will be less diffusion of responsibility and more help. Reducing the psychological distance among bystanders can also counteract the diffusion of responsibility. Established groups in which the members know each other are usually more helpful than groups of strangers (Rutkowski et al., 1983).

In addition, the diffusion of responsibility can be defeated by a person's role. A group leader, even if only recently assigned to that position, is more likely than other group members to act in an emergency (Baumeister et al., 1988). And some occupational roles increase the likelihood of intervention. Registered nurses, for example, do not diffuse responsibility when confronted by a possible physical injury (Cramer et al., 1988). Even when there's no direct relationship between one's occupation and the type of assistance that's needed, job requirements can still influence helping behaviour. In 1994, Jack Santos, a YMCA security guard, ran across two highways, passed a dozen passive observers, and put out the fire from the burning clothes of Jack Ordner, who had been thrown from his gasoline tanker when it overturned and burst into flames. Santos was neither a professional firefighter nor a medical specialist, but he was used to taking charge during an emergency.

Deciding How to Help Having assumed the responsibility to help, the person must now decide how to help. Bystanders are more likely to offer direct help when they feel competent to perform the actions required. For instance, individuals who have received Red Cross training in first-aid techniques are more likely to provide direct assistance to a bleeding victim than are those without training (Shotland & Heinold, 1985).

But people who do not possess the skills that would make them feel competent to intervene directly often do have an option available. They can decide to help indirectly by calling for assistance from others. In many situations, indirect helping is by far the wiser course of action. Physical injuries are best treated by medical personnel; dangerous situations such as domestic violence are best handled by police officers; and that friendly-looking individual standing by the side of a stalled car on a lonely road is best picked up by the highway patrol. Even people trained in CPR are now advised to call 911 before starting CPR on an adult victim. Calling others in to help is safe, simple, and effective. A prompt phone call can be a lifeline. Such a call might have saved Kitty Genovese's life.

Providing Help The final step in the intervention process is to take action. Here, too, the presence of others can have an impact. Latané and Darley point out that people sometimes feel too socially awkward and embarrassed to act helpfully in a public setting. When observers do not act in an emergency because they fear making a bad impression on other observers, they are under the influence of **audience inhibition**. Worrying about how others will view us does not, however, always reduce helping. When people think others will scorn them for failing to help, the presence of an audience *increases* their helpful actions (Schwartz & Gottlieb, 1980).

Social scorn or approval is but one cost-benefit factor that can influence helping in an emergency. As we discussed earlier, the likelihood that people will engage in short-term or long-term helping is affected by a variety of potential costs and rewards for the action.

audience inhibition Reluctance to help for fear of making a bad impression on observers.

The Legacy of the Bystander Effect Research As you can see in Figure 10.3, providing help in an emergency is a challenging process. At each step along the way, barriers and diversions can prevent a potential helper from becoming an actual one. Most of these obstacles are social in nature, demonstrating Latané and Darley's point that an individual is less likely to intervene in an emergency when others are present than when he or she is alone with the victim.

Although not physically in the same room, the virtual presence of others in an Internet chatroom is enough to create the right conditions for the bystander effect to occur.

The bystander effect apparently made it into the world of cyberspace, as news spread in February 2003 of the death of 21-year-old Brandon Vedas. Vedas overdosed on drugs and lay dying in front of a room crowded with people many of whom egged him on to take even more drugs. The modern-day twist was that this room was virtual—it was a chat room, and the bystanders watched Vedas, who used the name "Ripper" online, poison himself to death via the webcam in his Phoenix, Arizona, bedroom. "That's not much," said a teenager from rural Oklahoma whose alias was "Smoke2K." "Eat more. I wanna see if you survive or if you just black out." Another wrote in, "Ripper—you should try to pass out in front of the cam." Not everyone was so callous. Some wrote in warning Ripper to be careful; one wrote, "Don't OD on us, Ripper." One person did begin to call the police, but, astonishingly, others talked her out of it. Vedas posted his cell number with the instructions, "Call if I look dead." The last coherent words Vedas wrote were "I told u I was hardcore" (Kennedy, 2003, p. 5).

This incident was different from the Kitty Genovese one in several ways, including the fact that it was not clear if the onlookers could have done anything about this. Without knowing Ripper's real name or address, the police probably would not have been able to find him in time even had someone called promptly. But several processes central to Darley and Latané's research clearly were evident. Several witnesses suggested that "somebody" call poison control or the police but did not do so themselves. Some questioned whether Ripper was really dying or had just passed out. One person told another *not* to call the police because that could get Ripper arrested. Together, these Internet bystanders were struggling on the decision tree, spreading doubt and diffusion of responsibility. And newspapers throughout the world would soon be referring to Kitty Genovese once again, for a fourth decade.

Many of us who teach social psychology have stories of former students who witnessed an emergency and jumped in to help while consciously thinking of the lessons they'd learned about the bystander effect in their social psychology classes. Indeed, one of the authors of this book remembers being at a colloquium in a room filled with social psychologists when a loud crash suddenly emanated from an adjacent room. After a few seconds of delay, dozens of social psychologists burst out of their chairs, almost trampling each other as they rushed to see if there was an emergency. And the only ones of us who were not explicitly thinking "Darley & Latané" while doing so were the ones thinking "Latané & Darley."

Getting Help in a Crowd: What Should You Do? But what do all these stories and experiments teach you about what to do if you need help in the presence of many people? Is there anything you can do to enhance the chances that someone will come to your aid? Try to counteract the ambiguity of the situation by making it very

FIGURE 10.5

Cyberhelping

In a study that extends Latané and Darley's research on the bystander effect by bringing it into cyberspace, individuals participating in an online chat room saw a plea for help from another person in the chat room. Consistent with Latané and Darley's findings, individuals responded more slowly if they thought many other people were in the chat room than if they thought there were few others present. However, if an individual's name was specified in the request for help, then that person responded quickly regardless of how many other people were in the chat room. *(Source: Markey, 2000.)*

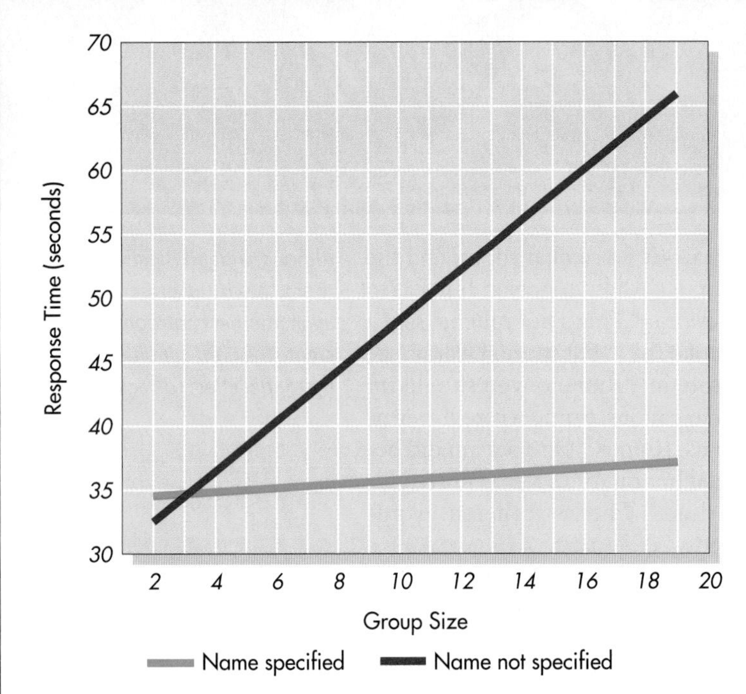

clear that you do need help, and try to reduce diffusion of responsibility by singling out particular individuals for help, such as with eye contact, pointing, or direct requests (Moriarty, 1975; Shotland & Stebbins, 1980). Consistent with this advice, and with Latané and Darley's research, are the results of a recent study by P. M. Markey (2000) involving people in Internet chat rooms: As the number of people present in each chat room group grew larger, individuals took increasingly more time to respond to someone's plea for help; however, this effect was eliminated when the person asking for help specified a particular individual's name (see Figure 10.5). In light of Brandon Vedas's overdose a few years later, this study of diffusion of responsibility in Internet chat rooms was chillingly prophetic.

Time Pressure

The presence of others can create obstacles at each step on the way toward helping in an emergency. Other factors, too, can affect multiple steps in this process. Our good intentions to help those in need can sometimes conflict with other motivations. One such source of conflict is time pressure. When we are in a hurry or have a lot on our minds, we may be so preoccupied that we fail to notice others who need help, we may become less likely to accept responsibility for helping someone, or we may decide that the costs of helping are too high because of the precious time that will be lost. When we have other demands on us that seem very important, getting involved in someone else's problems may seem like a luxury we can't afford (Batson et al., 1978). John Darley and Daniel Batson (1973) examined the role of time pressure in an experiment that produced what may be the most ironic finding in the history of social psychology.

Their study was based on the parable of the Good Samaritan, from the Bible. This parable tells the story of three different people—a priest, a Levite, and a Samaritan—each traveling on the road from Jerusalem to Jericho. Each encounters a man lying half-dead by the roadside. The priest and the Levite—both considered busy, important, and relatively holy people—pass by the man without stopping. The only one who helps is the Samaritan, a social and religious outcast of that time. A moral of the tale is that people with low status are sometimes more virtuous than those enjoying high status and prestige. Why? Perhaps in part because high-status individuals tend to be busy people, preoccupied with their own concerns and rushing around to various engagements. Such characteristics may prevent them from noticing or deciding to help a victim in need of assistance.

Darley and Batson brought this ancient story to life. They asked seminary students to think about what they wanted to say in an upcoming talk. Half of them were told that the talk was to be based on the parable of the Good Samaritan; the other half expected to discuss the jobs that seminary students like best. All participants were then instructed to walk over to a nearby building where the speech would be recorded. At this point, participants were told that they were running ahead of schedule, that they were right on time, or that they were already a few minutes behind schedule. On the way to the other building, all participants passed a research confederate slumped in a doorway, coughing and groaning. Which of these future ministers stopped to lend a helping hand?

Perhaps surprisingly, the topic of the upcoming speech had little effect on helping. The pressure of time, however, made a real difference. Of those who thought they were ahead of schedule, 63 percent offered help—compared with 45 percent of those who believed they were on time and only 10 percent of those who had been told they were late. In describing the events that took place in their study, Darley and Batson noted that "on several occasions a seminary student going to give his talk on the parable of the Good Samaritan literally stepped over the victim as he hurried on his way!" These seminary students unwittingly demonstrated the very point that the parable they would be discussing warns against.

Location and Culture

If the presence of others often inhibits helping, do individuals have a worse chance of being helped in an emergency in a big city than in a small town? In the midst of the hectic pace and large crowds of a big city, are pleas for help more likely to go unanswered?

Although place of residence does not seem to affect how much those in close relationships help each other (Franck, 1980; Korte, 1980), a large city does have a number of characteristics that might reduce help to strangers. For example, as we discussed earlier in the context of "noticing" an emergency, Stanley Milgram (1970) proposed that cities produce stimulus overload among their inhabitants. Bombarded by sights and sounds, city residents may wear a coat of unresponsive armour to protect themselves from being overwhelmed by stimulation (Korte et al., 1975). Claude Fischer (1976) noted that the residents of large urban areas are a heterogeneous group—composed of diverse nationalities, races, and ethnic backgrounds. Such diversity could diminish the sense of similarity with others, reduce empathic concern, and result in less helping. Also, people may feel more anonymous and less accountable for their actions in large cities than in smaller communities in which people are more likely to know their neighbours.

Whatever the exact causes, people are less likely to help in urban areas than in rural ones. This relationship has been found in several countries, including Canada, Israel, Great Britain, and the Sudan (Hedge & Yousif, 1992; Steblay, 1987). For example, Paul Amato (1983) studied 55 Australian communities, and he found that spontaneous, informal help to strangers was greater where the population was smaller. Interestingly, a recent *Reader's Digest* poll rated the world's most "polite" cities and ranked Toronto third in the world, behind New York and Zurich. Part of the survey involved a confederate dropping a folder of papers in a busy location to see if anyone helped to pick them up. One of the testers for *Reader's Digest*, noted that "Courtesy is the social lubricant that allows us—in these densely packed urban areas—to get along with each other," he said. "And without it, we'd be at each other's throats" (*Reader's Digest*, 2006). Around the world as well, some cities seem to have more helpful citizens than others. Robert Levine and others (2001) conducted field experiments in a major city in each of 23 large countries around the world. In each city, experimenters would position themselves near a passer-by and drop a pen, drop a pile of magazines (while limping with an apparently injured leg), or play the role of a blind person needing help crossing a street. Would pedestrians help? Table 10.2 reports how the cities ranked in their propensity to help, with pedestrians in Rio de Janeiro, Brazil, exhibiting the highest rates of helping and pedestrians in Kuala Lampur, Malaysia, the lowest rates. Levine and his colleagues examined a number of measures of each city to try to determine what factors

TABLE 10.2

Helping Around the World

Three types of spontaneous helping—helping someone who dropped a pen, who dropped a pile of magazines, or who needed help crossing the street—were examined in field experiments in a major city in each of 23 different countries around the world. The top six and bottom six cities are listed below, along with their respective ranks on a measure of economic prosperity, relative to the 22 cities for which there were available data. Cities with asterisks are considered to have *simpatia* cultural values, which are characterized by a concern with the social well being of others. *(Based on Levine et al., 2001.)*

Top Six Cities for Helping

City	Helping Rank	Economic Rank
*Rio de Janeiro, Brazil	1	16
*San Jose, Costa Rica	2	15
Lilongwe, Malawi	3	22
Calcutta, India	4	21
Vienna, Austria	5	4
*Madrid, Spain	6	9

Bottom Six Cities for Helping

City	Helping Rank	Economic Rank
Taipei, Taiwan	18	[data unavailable]
Sofia, Bulgaria	19	17
Amsterdam, Netherlands	20	6
Singapore, Singapore	21	2
New York, United States	22	1
Kuala Lampur, Malaysia	23	10

predicted these differences in helping, such as how hectic the pace of life seemed to be (as determined by pedestrians' walking speed) or how individualistic or collectivistic the culture was. Only two measures correlated with helping rates. One was a measure of economic well-being—cities from countries with the greatest levels of economic well-being tended to exhibit the least helping, although this relationship was not very strong.

The other variable that predicted helping concerned the notion of what is called *simpatia* in Spanish or *simpatico* in Portuguese. Some researchers report that this is an important element of Spanish and Latin American cultures and involves a concern with the social well-being of others (Markus & Lin, 1999; Sanchez-Burks et al., 2000). The five *simpatia* cultures in Levine et al.'s study did tend to show higher rates of helping than the non-*simpatia* cultures.

You may find it surprising that collectivism was not a predictor of helping, but the research on the relationship between individualism-collectivism and prosocial behaviour is quite mixed at this time. This inconsistency may stem in part from differences in the kinds of helping studied. Relative to individualists, collectivists may be more likely to help ingroup members, but they are less likely to help outgroup members (Conway et al., 2001; Schwartz, 1990). Lucian Conway and others (2001) studied differences in people's levels of individualism and collectivism within the United States. They found that collectivism was positively associated with the kind of direct, spontaneous, non-serious help assessed in the Levine et al. (2001) cross-cultural study described previously, such as picking up a dropped pen for a stranger. However, for helping that is less spontaneous and more deliberate, such as mailing a sealed and stamped letter that someone (unseen) had apparently dropped or making contributions to a particular charity, collectivism was associated with *less* helping. These correlations did not seem to be due to differences in economic variables. Conway et al. speculate that a possible explanation for these results is that collectivists are more responsive to the immediate needs of a person near them but less responsive in the more abstract situations, as in the found letter situation or making charitable contributions.

Moods and Helping

Helping someone can put people in a better mood, but can being in a good mood increase people's likelihood of helping someone? Are we less likely to help if we're in a bad mood? What's your prediction?

Good Moods and Doing Good Over the course of a year, pedestrians in the US were stopped and asked to participate in a survey of social opinions. When Michael Cunningham (1979) tabulated their responses according to the weather conditions, he discovered that people answered more questions on sunny days than on cloudy ones. Moving his investigation indoors, Cunningham found that sunshine is truly golden: The more the sun was shining, the more generous were the tips left by restaurant customers. Sunshine and helping seem to go together, but what's the connection? Probably it's the mood we're in, as a sunny day cheers us up and a cloudy day damps us down.

People are much more likely to help someone when they're in a good mood. **True.**

When the sun is not shining, many people head for the mall. One of the more powerful sensations you can count on experiencing while strolling through the mall comes when you pass a bakery or coffee shop, the pleasant aroma of freshly baked chocolate chip cookies or freshly brewed French roast stopping you in your tracks. Robert Baron (1997) believed that these pleasant scents put people in a good mood, and he wondered if this good mood would make them more likely to help someone in need. He tested this with passers-by in a large shopping mall. Each selected passer-by was approached by a member of the research team and asked for change for a dollar. This interaction took place in a location containing either strong, pleasant odours (such as near a bakery or a coffee-roasting cafe) or no discernible odour (such as near a clothing store). As can be seen in Figure 10.6, people approached in a pleasant-smelling location were much more likely to help than people approached in a neutral-smelling location. Baron also found that people were in a better mood when they were in the pleasant-smelling environments. This effect on their mood appears to have caused their greater tendency to help.

FIGURE 10.6

Scents and Sensibilities

People walking in a mall were approached by someone who asked them for change. This encounter took place in areas of the mall with either pleasant ambient odours or no clear odours. The stranger also gave the individuals a questionnaire that measured their moods on a five-point scale, ranging from 1 (very bad) to 5 (very good). As shown on the left, the people approached in a pleasant-smelling area were in a better mood than those approached in neutral-smelling locations. In addition (right), people were more likely to help the stranger by giving him change if they were in a pleasant-smelling area than if they were in a neutral-smelling area. *(Data from Baron, 1997.)*

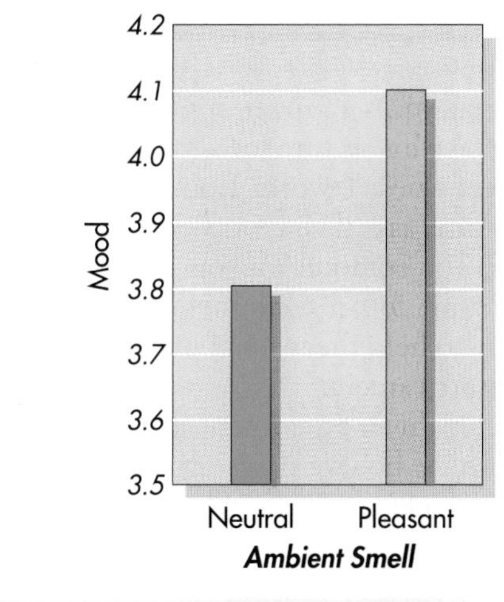

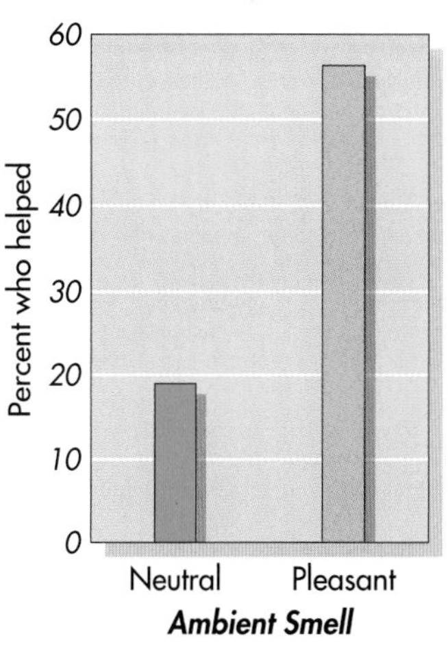

Of course, sunshine and sweet scents are not the only enhancers of mood and helping. In fact, helping is increased by all kinds of pleasant, mood-lifting experiences, such as being successful on a task, reading pleasant positive statements, being offered a cookie, imagining a Hawaiian vacation, and listening to a comedy routine (Aderman, 1972; Isen, 1970; Isen & Levin, 1972; Rosenhan et al., 1981; Wilson, 1981). On the job, being in a good mood seems to be the major determinant of a wide range of behaviours (such as helping coworkers, making constructive suggestions, and spreading good will) that improve workplace quality and increase organizational effectiveness (George & Brief, 1992). When we're happy, we're helpful—a state of affairs known as the **good mood effect.**

Why do good moods increase helping? There seem to be several factors at work. Table 10.3 summarizes some of the reasons why feeling good often leads to doing good, and it also describes some of the forks in this road that can lead away from helping. Whatever its exact cause, the good mood effect kicks in quite early in

good mood effect The effect whereby a good mood increases helping behaviour.

TABLE 10.3

Good Moods Lead to Helping: Reasons and Limitations

Research shows that people in positive moods are more likely to help someone in need than are people in neutral moods. There are several explanations for this effect, as well as some limiting conditions that can weaken or reverse the help-promoting effects of good moods.

Why Feeling Good Leads to Doing Good

- *Desire to maintain one's good mood.* When we are in a good mood, we are motivated to maintain that mood. Helping others makes us feel good, and so it can help maintain a positive mood.
- *Positive expectations about helping.* If we have more positive expectations about the rewards of helping, we are more likely to help.
- *Positive thoughts.* Positive moods trigger positive thoughts, and if we have positive thoughts about others, we should like them more, which makes us more likely to help them.
- *Positive thoughts and expectations about social activities.* Positive moods trigger positive thoughts and expectations about interacting with others and engaging in social activities. These positive thoughts and expectations can promote interacting with others in prosocial ways, including helping them.

When Feeling Good Might Not Lead to Doing Good

- *Costs of helping are high.* If the anticipated costs of helping in a particular situation seem high, helping would put our good mood at risk. In this case, if we can avoid getting involved and thus maintain our good mood (for example, if we can justify our failure to help), we are less likely to help.
- *Positive thoughts about other social activities that conflict with helping.* If our good mood makes us want to go out and party with our friends, our motivation to engage in this social activity may prevent us from taking the time to notice or take responsibility for helping someone in need.

life. It occurs among people of all ages, and even young children help more when they feel happy and cheerful (Moore et al., 1973).

Bad Moods and Doing Good Since a good mood increases helping, does a bad mood decrease it? Not necessarily. Under many circumstances, negative feelings can elicit positive behaviour toward others (Carlson & Miller, 1987). One such circumstance is when people feel guilt. We feel guilty when we believe that we have violated our own personal standards or fear that others may perceive such a violation. Have you ever felt guilty about getting too worked up during a trivial disagreement with a friend? Did you gratefully seize the next available opportunity to help that individual? In such cases, being helpful restores an existing relationship that we value (Estrada-Hollenbeck & Heatherton, 1998). But the impact of guilt on helping can be much more widespread.

Imagine yourself in the following situation. A stranger approaches you on the street and asks you to use his camera to take his picture for a school project. You get ready, aim, and . . . nothing. The camera doesn't work. Looking concerned, the stranger says the camera is rather delicate, asks if you touched any of the dials, and informs you that it will have to be fixed. You continue on your way down the street. As you pass a young woman, she drops a file folder containing some papers. Now, here's the question: Are you more likely to help the woman pick up her papers because you think you broke the other person's camera?

Probably. In an experiment that used this setup, 80 percent of participants who had been led to believe that they had broken the man's camera helped the woman pick up her papers; only 40 percent of participants who had had no broken-camera experience stopped to help (Cunningham et al., 1980). Thus, participants who unintentionally harmed one individual were more helpful to the next person. According to Roy Baumeister and others (1994), such spillover effects provide an especially vivid demonstration of the interpersonal nature of guilt and its function of enhancing, maintaining, and repairing relationships. Feeling guilty, they contend, motivates us to strengthen whatever social relations are at hand.

More generally, negative moods often promote helping. Why might this be? As noted earlier, people know that helping makes them feel good. Recall that in our discussion of the motivations that promote helping, we described the negative state relief model, which holds that people who are feeling bad are motivated to repair their mood and they realize that one way to do it is by helping others. This model seems reasonable, but the evidence is mixed—leading to a vigorous debate on the pros and cons of the negative state relief model (Cialdini & Fultz, 1990; Miller & Carlson, 1990).

An interesting aspect of the negative state relief model involves children. Although young children are more helpful when they are happy, they do not help more when they are sad. Robert Cialdini and his colleagues (1981) propose that helping is not as rewarding to young children as it is to older children and adults. As they develop, children become not only more empathic but also more aware of the potential benefits of helping, which may in turn make them more likely to try to help others to make themselves feel better (Shorr & McClelland, 1998).

TABLE 10.4

Bad Moods and Helping: When Does Feeling Bad Lead to Doing Good, and When Doesn't It?

Research shows that people in negative moods are often more likely to help someone in need than are people in neutral moods. However, there are several limitations to this effect. This table summarizes some of the factors that make it more or less likely for people to do good when they feel bad.

When Negative Moods Make Us More Likely to Help Others

- If we take responsibility for what caused our bad mood ("I feel guilty for what I did")
- If we focus on other people ("Wow, those people have suffered so much")
- If we are made to think about our personal values that promote helping ("I really shouldn't act like such a jerk next time; I have to be nicer")

When Negative Moods Make Us Less Likely to Help Others

- If we blame others for our bad mood ("I feel so angry at that jerk who put me in this situation")
- If we become very self-focused ("I am so depressed")
- If we are made to think about our personal values that do not promote helping ("I have to wise up and start thinking about my own needs more")

In sum, the relationship between good moods and helping is a strong and consistent one. The relationship between negative moods and helping is more complex. Although feeling bad often leads to helping behaviour, there are several limits to this effect (see Table 10.4). One important variable is whether people accept responsibility for their bad feelings (Rogers et al., 1982). Negative moods are less likely to promote helping if we blame others for them (such as when we're angry at another person) than if we take personal responsibility (such as when we regret a poor decision we just made). In addition, negative moods are less likely to increase helping if they cause us to become very self-focused (such as when we experience intense grief or depression or when we dwell on our own problems and concerns) than if they direct our focus outward (such as when we feel sad after watching a public service advertisement about child abuse) (Bagozzi & Moore, 1994; Tangney et al., 1996; Wood et al., 1990).

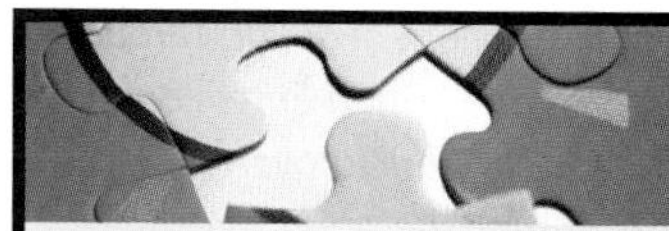

People are much less likely to help someone when they're in a bad mood. **False.**

Role Models and Social Norms: A Helpful Standard

We mentioned earlier that children become more aware as they get older of the potential benefits of helping. How, in general, do children learn about helping? One important way is through role models. Seeing important people in their lives behave prosocially, or antisocially, encourages children to follow suit. Role models can be real people in children's lives or characters they see on television (Moriarty & McCabe, 1977; Rushton, 1981a; Sprafkin et al., 1975). Indeed, although politicians, educators, researchers, and parents pay a great deal of attention to the negative effects of TV on children (discussed in Chapter 11 on Aggression), TV can also have positive effects on children through the modeling of prosocial behaviour. After reviewing an extensive research literature, Susan Hearold (1986) concluded that the effect of prosocial TV on prosocial behaviour was about twice as large as the effect of TV violence on aggressive behaviour. She argued that rather than advocating primarily to "eliminate the negative" by removing shows with sex and violence, the

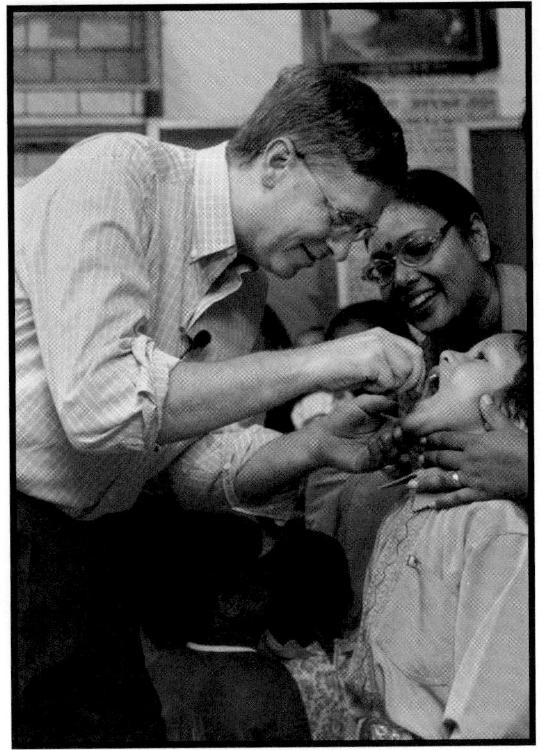

Microsoft chairman Bill Gates has donated billions of dollars through the Bill and Melinda Gates Foundation to help reduce poverty and disease around the world. Here he administers an oral polio vaccine to Nikunj Kumar, 5, of New Delhi, India.

public should focus more on "accentuating the positive" by encouraging the creation of more shows with prosocial themes and positive role models (p. 116).

Helpful models are important not only for children but for all of us. Observing helpful models increases helping in a variety of situations (Bryan & Test, 1967; Macaulay, 1970; Sarason et al., 1991).

Why do models of other people helping inspire us to help? Three reasons stand out. First, they provide an example of behaviour for us to imitate directly. Second, when they are rewarded for their helpful behaviour, models teach us that helping is valued and rewarding, which strengthens our own inclination to be helpful. Third, the behaviour of models makes us think about and become more aware of the standards of conduct in our society.

General rules of conduct established by society are called **social norms**. These norms embody standards of socially approved and disapproved behaviour. Two sets of social norms bear directly on when people are likely to help. The first consists of norms based on fairness. As we mentioned in Chapter 7, the *norm of reciprocity* establishes quid-pro-quo transactions as a socially approved standard: People who give to you should be paid back (Schopler, 1970). Accordingly, people usually help those who have helped them, especially when the initial assistance was given voluntarily (Gross & Latané, 1974; Whatley et al., 1999). Equity is the basis of another norm calling for fairness in our treatment of others. The *norm of equity* prescribes that when people are in a situation in which they feel overbenefited (receiving more benefits than earned), they should help those who are underbenefited (receiving fewer benefits than earned). Such help restores an equitable balance (Walster et al., 1978).

Other help-relevant social norms go beyond an immediate sense of fairness to a larger sense of what is right. The **norm of social responsibility** dictates that people should help those who need assistance. This norm creates a sense of duty and obligation, to which people respond by giving more help to those in greater need of it (Berkowitz, 1972; Bornstein, 1994). When people are more motivated by concerns about *justice* or *fairness*, however, their intentions to help someone will be driven more by their belief that this person *deserves* their assistance than by their belief that he or she simply needs it (Lerner, 1998).

Concerns with reciprocity, equity, social responsibility, and justice can have powerful effects. Yet sometimes they fail to produce the helpful behaviour they prescribe. Why? One problem with social norms is their generality. They are so general, so abstract, that it is not clear when they apply. When you encounter two people fighting, should you follow the norm prescribing "Help those in need" or the one instructing you to "Mind your own business"? (Darley & Latané, 1970).

Another norm that can promote social behaviour might surprise you. Rebecca Ratner and Dale Miller (2001) propose that in individualistic cultures there is a strong **norm of self-interest**, indicating that people's attitudes and behaviours are highly influenced by their self-interest, and that this norm can play a somewhat ironic role in promoting prosocial behaviours. People in individualistic cultures are more likely to help others when they themselves can gain something as well. This is not terribly surprising, of course. But what may be surprising is that this norm is so strong that when people work for a social cause intended to help others but that is not consistent with their own apparent self-interest, it can elicit surprise and even anger. Participants in one study by Ratner and Miller predicted that they would be evaluated more negatively if they took action for a cause that was against or irrelevant to their self-interest, and participants in another study did indeed react more negatively to an individual's prosocial actions when it did not appear consistent with

social norm A general rule of conduct reflecting standards of social approval and disapproval.

norm of social responsibility A moral standard emphasizing that people should help those who need assistance.

norm of self-interest The sense in individualistic cultures that people's attitudes and behaviours are, and should be, highly influenced by their self-interest.

his or her self-interest. According to John Holmes and his colleagues (2002), this norm can cause individuals to sometimes hide their altruistic intent under "a cloak of self-interest." For example, students in one of their studies donated more money to a charity when offered a product in exchange—even though the product held little appeal for them. The researchers called this an *exchange fiction*—the donors didn't care about the product they got in exchange for their donation, but they did care about not appearing to violate the norm of self-interest.

Such a concern with violating a norm of self-interest most likely would seem quite odd in less individualistic cultures. Indeed, social norms can vary dramatically across cultures. As we discussed earlier, inhibiting or disengaging from one's concerns with morality can be a critical step away from prosocial behaviour and toward destructive and violent transgressions. Albert Bandura (1999) documents a variety of factors that facilitate this moral disengagement. For example, the use of euphemistic labelling, such as "surgical strikes" instead of bombing missions or "casualties" instead of "deaths" in war, may reduce people's moral concerns with such actions. Similarly, through stereotypes and prejudice, people may exclude certain other groups from their moral concerns and end up rationalizing inhumane actions against them (Staub, 1996). What can be done to increase the likelihood that people will help rather than hurt outgroups? Whereas ignoring the humanity of others makes it easier to hurt them, emphasizing the humanity of one or more members of the group, such as through empathy or friendship, may have the opposite effect. Indeed, a recent wave of research suggests that individuals who are induced to feel empathy or a strong sense of connection with a particular outgroup member or to simply take the perspective of an outgroup member, become more likely to help members of the outgroup (Batson et al., 2002; Esses & Dovidio, 2002; Galinsky & Ku, 2004; Galinsky & Moskowitz, 2000; Pettigrew & Tropp, 2000; Stephan & Finlay, 1999; Wright et al., 1997).

Personal Influences: Who Is Likely to Help?

As we have just seen, social psychological research addressing the question "When do people help?" has been quite productive. What about the question "Who is likely to help?" When we think about extreme acts of helping, or of failing to help, or when we think about long-term, well-planned acts of helping such as volunteering at a clinic or shelter or serving as a Big Brother or Big Sister, we tend to wonder not about the situational influences but about the nature of the people involved. In this section, we consider some of the individual differences between people that address the question "Who is likely to help?" Researchers interested in this question have tried to identify an *altruistic personality* that distinguishes people who help from those who don't. Some of their research has focused on whether certain people tend to be more helpful across situations than others and whether and to what extent these differences might be genetically based. Other research has sought to identify what general personality characteristics and traits constitute the altruistic personality. In this section, we review both of these lines of research.

Are Some People More Helpful than Others?

What led to 12-year-old Craig Kielburger creating the "Free the Children" organization? One day Craig read a Toronto newspaper that detailed the plight of another boy his age a world away in Pakistan; Iqbal worked in a carpet factory

"The purpose of human life is to serve and to show compassion and the will to help others."

—Albert Schweitzer

12 hours a day, six days a week. He and his friends began to discuss the case of Iqbal, and others like him, and his crusade for children's rights began. Free the Children, now a worldwide organization, has been nominated for a Nobel Peace Prize three times. Although situational factors clearly can overwhelm individual differences in influencing helping behaviours in many contexts (Latané & Darley, 1970), researchers have demonstrated some evidence of individual differences in helping tendencies that endure across at least some situations. People who are more helpful than others in one situation are likely to be more helpful in other situations as well (Hampson, 1984; Rushton, 1981b). In addition, a longitudinal study by Nancy Eisenberg and others (1999) suggests that this individual difference may be relatively stable over time. Specifically, they found that the degree to which preschool children exhibited spontaneous helping behaviour predicted how helpful they would be in later childhood and early adulthood.

According to J. Philippe Rushton and his colleagues (1984), this individual difference in helpfulness is in part genetically based. Studies of twins offer some support for Rushton's argument. Genetically identical (monozygotic) twins are more similar to each other in their helpful behavioural tendencies and their helping-related emotions and reactions, such as empathy, than are fraternal (dizygotic) twins, who share only a portion of their genetic make-up (Davis et al., 1994; Rushton et al., 1986; Zahn-Wexler et al., 1992). These findings suggest that there may be a heritable component to helpfulness.

What Is the Altruistic Personality?

Even if we identify some people who help others a lot and other people who don't, we have not addressed the question of what distinguishes people who help from those who don't—other than their helpfulness, of course. What are the various components of the altruistic personality? Can we predict who is likely to be altruistic by looking at people's overall personalities?

Two qualities that the research thus far suggests are most essential for an altruistic personality are empathy and advanced moral reasoning (e.g., Hoffman, 2000). We have already discussed empathy in this chapter, such as in the context of Batson's empathy-altruism hypothesis. Empathic individuals witnessing someone suffering are likely to suffer along with that person and to feel sympathy and compassion for him or her. Being able to take the perspective of others and experience empathy are associated positively with helping and other prosocial behaviours in children and adults (Batson, 1998; Davis et al., 1999; Eisenberg, 2000; Litvack et al., 1997; Unger & Thumuluri, 1997).

The second characteristic associated with helping is moral reasoning. Children and adults who exhibit internalized and advanced levels of moral reasoning behave more altruistically than others. Such moral reasoning involves adhering to moral standards independent of external social controls, and taking into account the needs of others when

Every year, Edwin "Honest Ed" Mirvish and his family, owners of a large discount department store in Toronto, hand out hundreds of free turkeys and Christmas cakes to needy families.

making decisions about courses of action. In contrast, people whose reasoning is focused on their own needs or on the concrete personal consequences that their actions are likely to have tend not to engage in many helping behaviours (Carlo et al., 1996; Krebs & Rosenwald, 1994; Midlarsky et al., 1999; Schonert-Reichl, 1999).

The combination of empathy and advanced moral reasoning may be an especially strong predictor of helping tendencies. Paul Miller and his colleagues (1996) propose that "cold" cognitive moral principles may not be enough to trigger self-sacrificing prosocial action; when these principles are activated together with the experience of "hot" empathic or sympathetic emotional responses to another's suffering, however, helping is much more likely. In one study, preschool children (four- to five-year-olds) watched a film in which a boy and girl were hurt in a fall. The children's empathic responses were measured through their facial reactions while they watched the film as well as through verbal and nonverbal self-reports of their feelings. The children's prosocial moral reasoning was assessed by their responses to a series of moral reasoning dilemmas in which the needs of the self are in conflict with those of another.

FIGURE 10.7

Children's Empathy and Moral Reasoning

Children learned about a boy and a girl who were hurt in an accident and were then given an opportunity to help the boy and girl by collecting crayons for them. The more they worked on helping the boy and girl, the less time they had to play with toys themselves. Children high in *both* empathy *and* other-oriented moral reasoning were the most helpful toward the boy and girl. Neither high empathy alone nor other-oriented moral reasoning alone was associated with a significant amount of helping. *(Based on data from Miller et al., 1996.)*

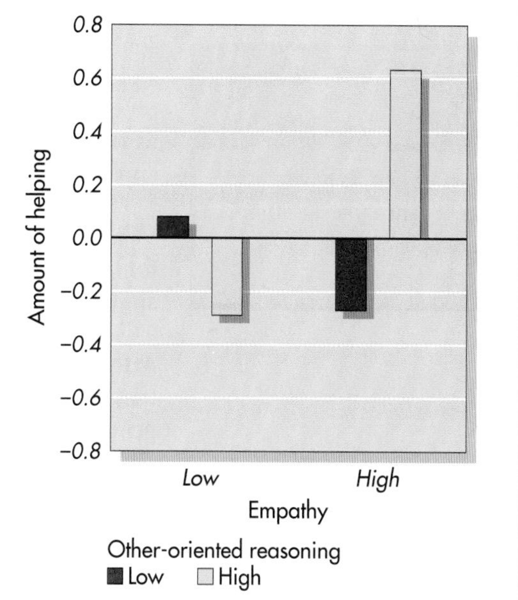

"True kindness presupposes the faculty of imagining as one's own the suffering and joy of others."

—André Gide

To measure the children's helping behaviour, the experimenter told them that the boy and the girl from the film were in the hospital recovering from their fall, feeling fine but bored because there was nothing for them to do. The experimenter gave the children the option of either playing with very attractive toys or helping the boy and girl in the hospital by putting loose crayons into crayon boxes to send to them. Figure 10.7 illustrates the results. The children who were high in *both* moral reasoning and empathic emotions were especially likely to help the injured children by forgoing their own playing time to provide the hospitalized child with crayons.

Interpersonal Influences: Whom Do People Help?

However influential they might be, personal factors alone do not a helper make. The characteristics of the person in need are important as well. Are some people more likely than others to receive help? Are some helpers particularly responsive to certain kinds of individuals who need assistance? Here, we explore some of the interpersonal aspects of helping.

Perceived Characteristics of the Person in Need

Although many characteristics of a person in need might affect whether that individual is helped, researchers have paid special attention to two: the personal attractiveness of the person in need and whether or not the person seems responsible for being in the position of needing assistance.

Attractiveness In Chapter 9, we described the social advantages enjoyed by physically attractive individuals. The bias for beauty also affects helping, as Peter Benson and his colleagues (1976) observed in a large metropolitan airport. Darting into a phone booth to make a call, each of 604 travelers discovered some materials supposedly left behind accidentally by the previous caller (but actually planted by the experimenters): a completed graduate school application form, a photograph of the applicant, and a stamped, addressed envelope. In some packets, the photo depicted a physically attractive individual; in others, the person was relatively unattractive. What was a busy traveler to do? When the researchers checked their mail, they found that people were more likely to send in the materials of the good-looking applicants than those of the less attractive applicants.

Attractive people have a better chance than unattractive people of getting help when they need it. **True.**

Attributions of Responsibility At some time or another, most students have had the experience of being asked to lend their class notes to a classmate. Has this ever happened to you? If so, you can compare your reactions with those of the students in a study conducted by Richard Barnes and his colleagues (1979). In this research, students received a call from an experimental confederate posing as another student, who asked to borrow their class notes to prepare for an upcoming exam. The reason for this request varied. To some students, the caller said, "I just don't seem to have the ability to take good notes. I really try to take good notes, but sometimes I just can't do it." Other students were told that "I just don't seem to have the motivation to take good notes. I really can take good notes, but sometimes I just don't try." You probably won't be surprised to learn that the caller received much more help from those who were informed he had tried yet failed than from those who were told he hadn't tried at all.

Bluntly stating that you didn't even try to help yourself may seem like an obvious way to ensure that others won't help you out. But even when the circumstances are more complex and the causes more subtle, people's beliefs about the needy individual's responsibility influence helping. For example, participants in an experiment by Pamela Dooley (1995) read scenarios about someone who had just been diagnosed with AIDS. If the participants read that the person had contracted the disease through a blood transfusion rather than through sexual activity or drug use, they considered the situation less controllable, and they felt more pity for the person. In addition, those who felt pity indicated a greater desire to engage in helping behaviours. Similarly, Mary DePalma and others (1999) found that students given an opportunity to help a medical patient were significantly more likely to do so if the individual was portrayed as not responsible for the onset of his or her disease. This effect was particularly strong among individuals who believed in a just world, in which people tend to get what they deserve.

The Fit Between Giver and Receiver

Some potential helpers are particularly responsive to some kinds of potential recipients. In this section, we look at a variety of ways in which helping depends on the fit between a giver and a receiver.

Similarity: Helping Those Just Like Us We are more likely to help others who are similar to us. All kinds of similarity—from dress to attitudes to nationality—increase our willingness to help, and signs of dissimilarity decrease it (Dovidio, 1984).

The influence of similarity could even be a form of kinship selection. If similarity in appearance reflects the degree of genetic overlap (or, at least, if people think it does), then evolutionary psychologists and biologists would expect people to help similar-looking relatives more than dissimilar ones (Segal, 1993). We might also help similar, though biologically unrelated, individuals because we over-generalize the assumption that what looks alike must genetically be alike (Krebs, 1987).

The effects of similarity on helping suggest that members of the same race should help each other more than members of different races. However, research on black-white helping indicates that the effects of racial similarity are highly inconsistent (Crosby et al., 1980). What accounts for these inconsistencies? First, although helping can be a compassionate response to another, it can also be seen as a sign of superiority over the person who needs help (Rosen et al., 1986). Thus, cross-racial helping isn't always a sign of egalitarian attitudes. Second, public displays of racial prejudice risk social disapproval, and prejudiced individuals may bend over backward, in public at least, to avoid revealing their attitudes. As discussed in Chapter 5, however, modern racism relies on more subtle forms of discrimination. For example, if people are provided with an excuse not to help, racial discrimination in helping is more likely (Frey & Gaertner, 1986).

Intergroup biases in helping can be reduced significantly, however, if the members of the different groups can perceive themselves as members of a common group. Through fostering perceptions of shared identities, encouraging meaningful contact that defies group boundaries, and highlighting similarities on other dimensions unrelated to group distinctions, an ingroup and an outgroup can begin to see each other as more similar than different, thereby promoting helping and other positive behaviours (Gaertner & Dovidio, 2000).

Closeness: A Little Help for Our Friends As we would expect, people are usually more helpful toward those they know and care about than toward strangers or superficial acquaintances (Bell et al., 1995; Clark & Mills, 1993). People in a *communal* relationship, such as close friends or romantic partners, feel mutual responsibility for each other's needs. People in an *exchange* relationship, such as acquaintances or business associates, give help with the expectation of receiving comparable benefits in return—"If I help you move your furniture, you'd better give me a ride to the airport." When people are, or desire to be, in a communal relationship with each other, they attend more to each other's needs, are more likely to help, and are less likely to be concerned with keeping track of rewards and costs. People in a communal relationship also feel better about having helped the other, and they feel worse if they were unable to help (Williamson et al., 1996).

So, common sense seems correct here: People help their friends more than strangers or acquaintances. But there may be an exception to this general rule: What if a person's ego is threatened? According to the *self-evaluation maintenance model* (Erber & Tesser, 1994), we can respond in two very different ways to superior performance by a significant other. If the achievement occurs in an area not relevant to our own ego, we can indulge in the delight of BIRGing—basking in reflected glory, as described in Chapter 3. If the area is relevant to our own ego, however, we may experience envy and resentment.

To apply this perspective to helping behaviour, suppose you have just finished working on a task and are told that you performed "a little below average." Then two other people take their turns at the same task; one of them is a stranger, and the other a close friend. You are asked to give some clues to each individual. The available clues differ in their level of difficulty. Some are easy and will boost the person's performance; others are so difficult that they will interfere with a good performance. Will you give your friend easier, more helpful clues than you give to the stranger?

As the self-evaluation maintenance model would predict, it depends on the task. When participants found themselves in the situation we've just described, those who believed that the task was a trivial game helped their friend more than they helped the stranger (Tesser & Smith, 1980). But when the task was important and relevant to their own self-esteem, participants were slightly less helpful to their friend than to the stranger (see Figure 10.8). In a conflict between our own egos and the welfare of a friend, the need to protect our self-esteem can sometimes overcome our helpful inclinations. The self-evaluation maintenance model applies even to very close relationships, such as married couples (Beach et al., 1996; Lockwood et al., 2004). Note, however, that superior performance by a close other on an important

In any situation, people are more likely to help a friend succeed than a stranger.
False.

FIGURE 10.8

Not Giving Much Help to Our Friends

People usually help their friends more than they help strangers, but not always. In this study, people who thought they had performed poorly on a task gave clues on the same task to a friend and to a stranger. When the task was not important for participants' self-esteem, they gave more helpful clues to the friend than to the stranger. When the task was highly ego-relevant, they gave slightly less helpful clues to the friend than to the stranger. *(Data from Tesser & Smith, 1980.)*

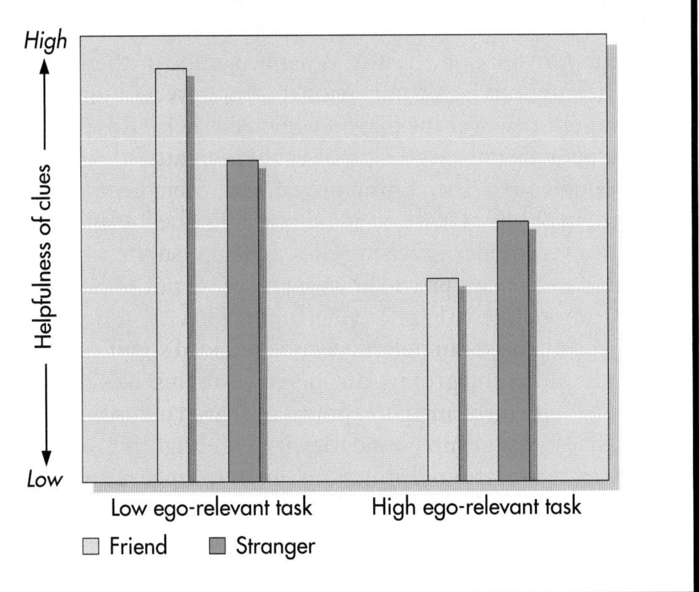

task is not always threatening. Indeed, Hart Blanton and others (2000) found that when an ingroup member's superior performance challenged negative stereotypes about that group's abilities, other members of his or her group felt better rather than worse about themselves.

Gender and Helping

Here's a quick, one-question quiz: Who helps more, men or women? Before you answer, consider the following situations:

A. Two strangers pass on the street. Suddenly, one of them needs help that might be dangerous to give. Other people are watching. The person in need is female.

B. Two individuals have a close relationship. Every so often, one of them needs assistance that takes time and energy to provide but is not physically dangerous. No one else is around to notice whether help is given. The person who needs help is either male or female.

Men are less likely to seek help than women, possibly because it is more threatening to their self-esteem.

Is your answer the same for both situations? It shouldn't be. Situation A is a classic male-helper scenario. Here, the helper is a "knight in shining armour"—physically brave and chivalrous, rescuing a lady in distress. Because social psychologists have tended to focus on these kinds of emergency situations, their research has found that, on the average, men are more helpful than women and women receive more help than do men (Eagly & Crowley, 1986).

Situation B is the classic female-helper scenario. Every day, millions of women—mothers, sisters, wives, and female friends—provide support for their friends and loved ones, and they are more likely to provide this kind of help than are men (George et al., 1998; McGuire, 1994). Though it lacks the high drama of an emergency intervention, this type of helping, called "social support," plays a crucial role in the quality of our lives.

Gender is related not only to differences in helping behaviour but also to differences in the willingness to *seek* help. Remember the time you and a member of the opposite sex got lost while driving in unfamiliar territory? Who wanted to stop early on and ask for directions? Who kept insisting that help wasn't necessary? In this case, the male stereotype is true: For relatively minor problems, at least, men ask for help less frequently than do women (McMullen & Gross, 1983). Less socially acceptable for men, help-seeking is more threatening to their self-esteem (Wills & DePaulo, 1991).

Women seek help more often than men. **True.**

As we will see in the following section, reactions to receiving help are more complex than one might think.

Reactions to Receiving Help

Thus far, we've described factors that influence whether helping will occur. Now, we turn to what happens after it takes place. The last time someone helped you, how did you feel? Grateful, relieved, comforted—anything else? Embarrassed, obligated, inferior? Receiving help is often a positive experience, but sometimes it has drawbacks for the recipient. There are costs in providing help, and there can be costs in receiving it.

Jeffrey Fisher and Arie Nadler have extensively examined people's reactions to receiving help (Fisher et al., 1982; Nadler & Fisher, 1986). According to their **threat-to-self-esteem model**, receiving help is experienced as *self-supportive* when the recipient feels appreciated and cared for, but as *self-threatening* when the recipient feels inferior and overly dependent. If recipients feel supported by the help they receive, they respond positively: feeling good, accepting the help, and being grateful to the donor. If, however, recipients feel threatened, they have a negative emotional reaction and evaluate both the help and the helper unfavourably.

There are three conditions under which receiving help is most likely to be perceived as threatening. First, individuals with high self-esteem tend to react more negatively to receiving help than do those with low self-esteem. Presumably, people who regard themselves as highly competent are especially sensitive to the implication that they are unable to take care of themselves. Second, being helped by a similar other highlights the contrast between the recipient's need for assistance and the competence of the provider. This one difference between people alike in other ways may imply that the recipient is inferior. The third condition under which receiving help can be threatening involves the type of relationship the recipient has with the provider and the area in which help has been received. As would be expected from the self-evaluation maintenance model, receiving help from a significant other on an ego-relevant task can be threatening to an individual's self-esteem.

Usually, however, help from those who are close to us will be seen as supportive. High self-esteem does not appear to prompt negative reactions to assistance by a sibling (Searcy & Eisenberg, 1992). And the negative effects of similarity probably do not apply to close relationships, in which similarity is expected and desired (Wills, 1992). Even ego-relevant help may elicit positive, rather than negative, reactions from partners in an interdependent relationship (Clark, 1983; Cook & Pelfrey, 1985). In such relationships, feelings of inferiority are less likely to arise, as each person sometimes helps, sometimes receives help. Mutuality makes receiving help less threatening. So does a very young age. Because dependency is more acceptable for children than for adolescents and adults, children less often react negatively to being helped (Shell & Eisenberg, 1992).

threat-to-self-esteem model The theory that reactions to receiving assistance depend on whether help is perceived as supportive or threatening.

People who are stigmatized by being the targets of negative stereotypes and feeling devalued in the larger society often face a difficult attributional dilemma when they receive help from members of nonstigmatized groups: Is the helping sincere and unassuming, is it well intentioned but patronizing, or is it controlling and designed to keep the recipient dependent? These are questions that members of nonstigmatized groups aren't as likely to consider when they receive help from another. Members of stigmatized groups may feel worse about themselves after receiving help from an outgroup member, particularly if the help was unsolicited (Blaine et al., 1995; Schneider et al., 1996).

The Helping Connection

Although whether or not people help others can be quite variable, there is a consistent theme that appears repeatedly in this chapter: a sense of connection.

The importance of a sense of connection is vividly demonstrated by a cross-cultural comparison. First, consider one of the great social tragedies of our time: homelessness. In Canada, one of the richest countries on earth, thousands of men, women, and children are without a home. Many sleep on the street, carry their belongings in grocery carts, and rummage through piles of garbage to find food.

Now, compare Canada's homelessness with an anthropologist's account of life among the Moose (pronounced "MOH-say") in West Africa:

> *Moose welcome anyone who wishes to join the community and move into the village. New arrivals have only to say where they wish to build their homes, and the user of the land in question gives it up for the newcomer's residence. . . . Each of the two years that I lived there, the well ran dry and villagers had to walk miles to get water for themselves and their stock from other villages, carrying it home on their heads. Each of these other villages shared their water until their wells were nearly dry, without expecting any reciprocation for the water. Even in these circumstances, any stranger who comes into the village may ask for a drink, and any visitor is offered water. (Fiske, 1991, pp. 190–191)*

Among some of the poorest people on earth, no one goes without shelter or remains thirsty as long as anyone has water to drink.

How can we account for the extraordinary difference between Canadian homelessness and Moose hospitality? Homelessness is, of course, a complex phenomenon affected by many specific economic and political factors. But it may also be a symptom of a profound loss of social connection in North American society (Wuthnow, 1991). Among the Moose, no such loss has occurred. Their sense of being intimately connected to others binds them to those who live in their village and to strangers who arrive in their midst.

The relationship between helping and interpersonal connection runs like a bright red thread through much of the research on helping. For example:

- Evolutionary perspectives emphasize the genetic connection of reciprocal, kinship, and within-group helping.
- Two kinds of connections lie at the heart of the empathy-altruism hypothesis: the cognitive connection of perspective taking and the emotional connection of empathic concern.
- In an emergency, bystanders who know the victim or know each other are more likely to intervene.

- People who respond empathically to another's suffering and consider the plight of others in their own moral reasoning are more likely to help than are others.
- Perceived similarity increases helping.
- In a close relationship, it's easier to give and more comfortable to receive.

Taken as a whole, these theories and research findings suggest that helping requires the recognition of individual human beings with whom we can have a meaningful connection. Which brings us back to Ladder Company Six, and the many others who risked, and even lost, their lives that day. Most of the people didn't know the others they were helping. But unexpectedly, horribly, fate had thrown them together, and suddenly their lives deeply mattered to each other. They felt responsible for each other. Many of those who helped in the face of grave danger may never have read the words that English poet John Donne wrote almost 400 years ago. But they would have understood them:

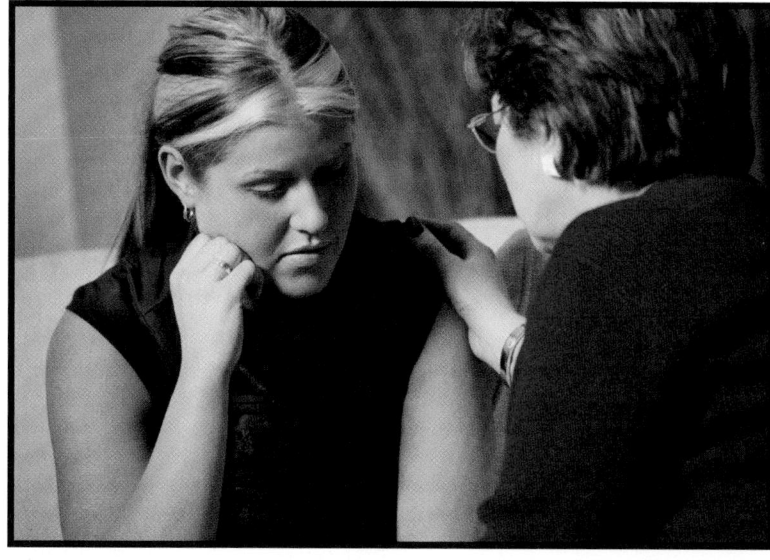

Before we can help others, we must feel a sense of connection. This may sometimes be lost in our busy North American society, but if we can empathize with the suffering of another person, we are much more likely to help them in their time of need.

> *No man is an island, entire of itself. Every man is a piece of the continent, a part of the main. If a clod be washed away by the sea, Europe is the less, as well as if a promontory were, as well as if a manor of thy friends or of thine own were. Any man's death diminishes me, because I am involved in mankind. And therefore never send to know for whom the bell tolls; it tolls for thee.*

Review

Evolutionary and Motivational Factors: Why Do People Help?

Evolutionary Factors in Helping

- Evolutionary perspectives emphasize three ways in which helping could become an innate, universal behavioural tendency: kinship selection, in which individuals protect their own genes by helping close relatives; reciprocal altruism, in which those who give also receive; and group selection, in which members of a social group help each other survive.

Rewards of Helping: Helping Others to Help Oneself

- People are much more likely to help when the potential rewards of helping seem high relative to the potential costs.
- Helping others often makes the helper feel good, it can relieve negative feelings such as guilt, and it is associated with better health.
- People sometimes help in order to appear to be moral, or to take credit away from someone else, rather than because of more sincere motivations.
- Emphasizing the costs of helping, or the costs of not helping, can affect people's decisions about whether to offer help.

Altruism or Egoism: The Great Debate

- According to the empathy-altruism hypothesis, taking the perspective of a person perceived to be in need creates the other-oriented emotion of empathic concern, which in turn produces the altruistic motive to reduce the other's distress.
- The self-oriented emotion of personal distress produces the egoistic motive to reduce one's own distress.
- When people are altruistically motivated, they will help even when escaping from the helping situation is easy.
- Alternatives to the empathy-altruism hypothesis include empathy-specific punishments for not helping and empathy-specific rewards for helping, such as negative state relief and empathic joy.
- In relationships in which the self-other distinction is eliminated and one person feels the other's needs as deeply as his or her own, the difference between altruistic and egoistic motivations may disappear.

Distinguishing Among the Motivations to Help: Why Does It Matter?

- People's motivations influence whether or not they are likely to help someone in a particular situation.
- People who help someone for egoistic reasons will feel good or bad about their actions to the extent that they are rewarded for the actions, whereas people who help someone for altruistic reasons will feel good or bad as a function of the other person's fate.
- Longer-term acts of helping, such as volunteerism, reflect both altruistic and egoistic motivations. Self-interested goals in this context can be a good thing in that they promote a commitment to helping behaviour to the extent that such goals are met.

Situational Influences: When Do People Help?

The Unhelpful Crowd

- Research on the bystander effect, in which the presence of others inhibits helping in an emergency, indicates why the five steps necessary for helping—noticing, interpreting, taking responsibility, deciding how to help, and providing help—may not be taken.
- The distractions of others and our own self-concerns may impair our ability to notice that someone needs help.
- Under ambiguous circumstances, some interpretations—such as the belief that an attacker and a victim have a close relationship or the mistaken inferences drawn from pluralistic ignorance—reduce bystander intervention.
- People may fail to take responsibility because they assume that others will—a phenomenon called diffusion of responsibility.
- Bystanders are less likely to offer direct aid when they do not feel competent to do so. They can, however, call for assistance from others.
- Even if people want to help, they may not do so if they fear that behaving in a helpful fashion will make them look foolish.

Time Pressure

- When people are in a hurry, they are less likely to notice or choose to help others in need.

Location and Culture

- Residents of densely populated areas are less likely to provide spontaneous, informal help to strangers than are residents of smaller or less densely populated communities.
- Cross-cultural research has found variation in the helping rates of people in cities around the world. According to one study, people in cities with relatively low levels of economic well-being were somewhat more likely to help strangers, and people from *simpatia* cultures were more likely to help strangers than people from non-*simpatia* cultures.
- Research concerning the relationship between individualism-collectivism and helping has yielded rather mixed results. According to one analysis, collectivists may be more responsive than individualists to the immediate needs of a particular person but less helpful in more abstract situations.

Moods and Helping

- A good mood increases helpfulness.
- People in a good mood may help in order to maintain their positive mood or because they have more positive thoughts and expectations about helpful behaviour, the person in need, or social activities in general.
- A bad mood can often increase helpfulness, such as when people feel guilty about something.
- People in a bad mood may be motivated to help others in order to improve their mood.
- A bad mood is less likely to increase helpfulness if the bad mood is attributed to the fault of others, or if it causes the person to become very self-focused.

Role Models and Social Norms: A Helpful Standard

- Observing a helpful model increases helping.
- Social norms that promote helping are based on a sense of fairness or on standards about what is right.
- The norm of self-interest is strong in individualistic cultures and can promote prosocial actions when they are in a person's self-interest. When people are motivated toward such actions even when the actions would not be in their self-interest, they may hide their altruistic motives under the guise of an apparent self-interest.
- Cultural differences exist in how people interpret and apply social norms.
- De-emphasizing the humanity of outgroup members can facilitate destructive actions against them, whereas recognizing their humanity can facilitate positive attitudes and behaviours toward them.

Personal Influences: Who Is Likely to Help?

Are Some People More Helpful than Others?

- There is some evidence of relatively stable individual differences in helping tendencies.

What Is the Altruistic Personality?

- Some personality traits are associated with helpful behavioural tendencies, but no one set of traits appears to define the altruistic personality.
- Two qualities that do predict helping behaviours are empathy and advanced moral reasoning.

Interpersonal Influences: Whom Do People Help?

Perceived Characteristics of the Person in Need

- Attractive individuals are more likely to receive help than are those who are less attractive.

- People are more willing to help when they attribute a person's need for assistance to uncontrollable causes rather than to events under the person's control.

The Fit Between Giver and Receiver

- In general, perceived similarity to a person in need increases willingness to help. But research on racial similarity has yielded inconsistent results.
- People usually help significant others more than strangers, except when helping threatens their own egos.

Gender and Helping

- Men help female strangers in potentially dangerous situations more than women do; women help friends and relations in everyday situations more than men do.
- Compared to women, men are more hesitant to seek help, especially for relatively minor problems.

Reactions to Receiving Help

- The threat-to-self-esteem model distinguishes between help perceived as supportive, which produces positive reactions, and help perceived as threatening, which creates negative reactions.
- Help is most likely to be perceived as threatening by a recipient with high self-esteem who receives help from a similar provider or from a significant other on an ego-relevant task.
- In close, interdependent relationships, receiving help is usually a positive experience.
- Members of stigmatized groups sometimes feel threatened and depressed after receiving unsolicited help from members of nonstigmatized groups.

The Helping Connection

- Theory and research seem to indicate that helping requires the recognition of meaningful connections among individuals.

Key Terms

altruistic *(346)*
arousal: cost-reward model *(343)*
audience inhibition *(356)*
bystander effect *(352)*
diffusion of responsibility *(355)*
egoistic *(346)*
empathy-altruism hypothesis *(347)*
good mood effect *(361)*
kinship selection *(340)*
negative state relief model *(349)*
norm of self-interest *(364)*
norm of social responsibility *(364)*
pluralistic ignorance *(354)*
prosocial behaviours *(339)*
social norm *(364)*
threat-to-self-esteem model *(371)*

PUTTING COMMON SENSE TO THE TEST

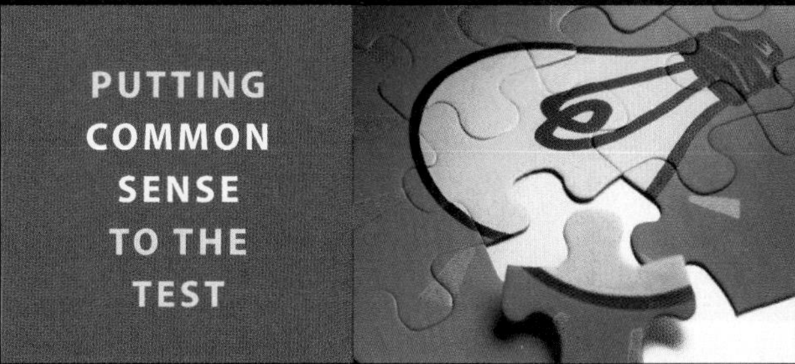

People are more likely to help someone in an emergency if the potential rewards seem high and the potential costs seem low.

True. *For both emergency situations and more long-term, well-planned helping, people's helping behaviours are determined in part by a cost-benefit analysis.*

In an emergency, a person who needs help has a much better chance of getting it if three other people are present than if only one other person is present.

False. *In several ways, the presence of others inhibits helping.*

People are much more likely to help someone when they're in a good mood.

True. *Compared to neutral moods, good moods tend to elicit more helping and other prosocial behaviours.*

People are much less likely to help someone when they're in a bad mood.

False. *Compared to neutral moods, negative moods often elicit more helping and prosocial behaviours. This effect depends on a number of factors, including whether people take responsibility for their bad mood or blame it on others; but in many circumstances, feeling bad leads to doing good.*

Attractive people have a better chance than unattractive people of getting help when they need it.

True. *People are more likely to help those who are attractive. This attractiveness can be based on physical appearance or friendliness.*

In any situation, people are more likely to help a friend succeed than a stranger.

False. *Although we tend to help those closest to us more than we help others, this tendency is often eliminated or even reversed if the task is very important to our own self-esteem and if our friend's success is threatening to our ego.*

Women seek help more often than men.

True. *At least for relatively minor problems, men ask for help less frequently than women do.*

11 Aggression

OUTLINE

PREVIEW

IN THIS CHAPTER, we examine a disturbing aspect of human behaviour: aggression. First, we ask, *"What is aggression?"* and consider its definition. After describing *cultural and gender differences,* we examine various theories concerning the *origins of aggression.* We then explore a variety of *situational factors* that influence when people are likely to behave aggressively. Next, we focus on two critically important issues in our society: the *effects of media violence and pornography* on aggression and the *intimate violence* that can occur in close relationships. We conclude by discussing ways of *reducing violence.*

PUTTING COMMON SENSE TO THE TEST

T / F

____ **In virtually every culture, males are more violent than females.**

____ **For virtually any category of aggression, males are more aggressive than females.**

____ **Children who are spanked or otherwise physically disciplined (but not abused) for behaving aggressively tend to become less aggressive.**

____ **Blowing off steam by engaging in safe but aggressive activities (such as sports) makes people less likely to aggress later.**

____ **Exposure to TV violence in childhood is related to aggression later in life.**

____ **Men are much more likely than women to aggress against their spouses or partners.**

____ **Adults who as children were abused by their parents are less likely to inflict abuse on their own children than are other adults.**

On December 26, 2005, 15-year-old Jane Creba was doing some Boxing Day shopping with her sister in downtown Toronto. When she crossed the street to visit a sporting goods store, she found herself in the middle of a gun battle—she was shot in the chest, and died a short time later. While police followed leads, the reality was that between 10 and 15 youths were likely involved in the gunplay. How then, to try to find the killer? And how to explain why an innocent bystander shopping in the middle of the afternoon on a busy street ends up a victim of youth violence in Canada? As mentioned in Chapter 2, incidents such as the school shooting in Taber, Alberta, following on the heels of the shootings at Columbine High School in Littleton, Colorado, provide us with dramatic illustrations of the reality of aggression and violence in society.

Profound questions are raised by this tragedy and the other school shootings before and since. Was Creba's death due to lax rules at the border allowing illegal guns to enter Canada? Were the youths involved in the crime from "broken" homes or "bad" neighbourhoods? Did they spend their days watching violent videogames, just looking for the chance to act them out for real? What triggered the Columbine massacre? Was it the fact that the two adolescent gunmen, members of the so-called "trench-coat" mafia, were social outcasts in school? Was it the fact that they idolized Hitler, spent hours playing vicious videogames, and had ready access to an arsenal of weapons? These are some of the issues that social psychologists grapple with in their research, which, in turn, is the focus of this chapter.

Would you consider the following statistics to be good news or bad news? Based on statistics collected by the World Health Organization, 1.6 million people worldwide died prematurely and violently in 2000. While rates of youth homicides decreased in Canada and Western Europe, the United States saw a dramatic increase. There were just over 27 000 sexual assaults reported in Canada in 2000, and 622 murders in 2004. Do these numbers seem high or low to you? As a basis of comparison, the United States reported 16 000 murders and 95 000 forcible rapes in 2002, both of these statistics representing a dramatic decrease from the previous few years. Keep in mind, of course, that the US has a much larger population than Canada. Despite this, Canada has for many years enjoyed a positive comparison in

In the early afternoon of September 13, 2006, a young man entered Montreal's Dawson College and, without saying a word, opened fire. Within a few minutes, he had killed one student and seriously injured 20 others before taking his own life.

terms of crime statistics—rates of crimes in major Canadian cities are much lower than those found in similarly sized American cities. In the past couple of years, however, cities such as Toronto have seen a large increase in gun violence attributed to youth gangs. Behind these statistics (see Table 11.1) are tragic stories. Think of someone you care deeply about—a parent, a brother or sister, a special teacher or coach, your best friend. Imagine that this person was taken away from you forever because of violence. Now imagine how many other people would suffer, too, because of the loss of this person.

And it is not only murder and other violent crimes that take their toll. For instance, look at schools in many countries around the world, and you're likely to see numerous acts of aggressive bullying (Olweus, 2003). According to one extensive program of research, more than one in five 12-year-olds are repeatedly either bullies, victims, or both (Juvonen et al., 2003). Wendy Craig and others (2000) set up hidden video cameras and microphones to get an unfiltered peek into aggression in schoolyards in Canada, and they saw bullying in midsized schools at a rate of 4.5 episodes per hour. Another researcher estimates that 75 percent of adolescents in the United States have been bullied at school (Peterson, 1999). And 27 percent of respondents in a study involving a middle school in Hunan Province, China, reported bullying others (Zheng, 2000). These seemingly ordinary rites of childhood can lead to extraordinary suffering. Sonia Sharp (1995) found that approximately one-third of the secondary school students she studied in England reported incidents of being bullied that left them with feelings of panic or nervousness in school, recurring memories of the incidents, and impaired concentration in school. Chronic peer abuse appears to be a risk factor in suicidal behaviour, depression, and poor mental health among adolescents (Carney, 2000; Rigby, 2000; West & Salmon, 2000). The injurious psychological effects of bullying are felt especially intensely by children with low self-esteem (Sharp, 1996; Sharp et al., 2000). It is worth noting that in most of the instances of school shootings during the past several years, the shooters had reportedly felt bullied or picked on by peers.

There are few safe havens from aggression. Take a drive, and you might be another victim of "road rage," as aggressive drivers cut each other off and exchange heated words, gestures, and even gunshots. Go to work and you may experience or observe "desk rage," as work-related stress drives people to tears, hostility, and violence. Read a university newspaper and learn about the violent hazing endured by fraternity pledges. Watch sports on TV and see clips of the latest fight between a player and another player, coach, or fan—or perhaps between a coach and an umpire at a Little League game.

TABLE 11.1

The Violent Crime Clock

The World Health Organization (2002) reported the following worldwide statistics:

■ One MURDER	every 60 seconds
■ One DEATH DUE TO ARMED CONFLICT	every 100 seconds
■ One AGGRAVATED ASSAULT	every 35 seconds
■ One SUICIDE	every 40 seconds

As the twenty-first century began, the world hoped for a more peaceful century than the previous one, with its world wars, genocide, and so-called ethnic cleansing. But with new wars, terrorism, and the constant fear of weapons of mass destruction, biological and chemical warfare, and suicide bombings, it is clear that the human animal is as aggressive as ever.

What can account for this aggression? This chapter examines the origins and immediate triggers of aggression, as well as factors that reduce aggression. It focuses primarily on aggression by individuals; aggression by groups, such as rampaging mobs and warring nations, was discussed in Chapter 8.

"The most persistent sound which reverberates through men's history is the beating of war drums."

—Arthur Koestler

What Is Aggression?

The word is a familiar one, part of our everyday vocabulary, but the concept of "aggression" can be surprisingly hard to pin down. Consider, for example, the following actions. Which ones do you think are aggressive?

- Accidentally injuring someone
- Working tenaciously to try to sell a product to a customer
- Biting someone on the neck
- Swinging a stick at someone but missing
- Hurling insults at someone
- Deliberately failing to prevent harm
- Murdering for money
- Hiring someone to break a competitor's kneecaps
- Hitting others while in a rage.

Researchers, too, have engaged in classification exercises like this in order to determine the meaning of aggression. Not everyone agrees on every point; by 1983, there were more than 250 different definitions of aggression in the psychological literature (Harré & Lamb, 1983). Most definitions used today share a number of common features, however. Putting them together, we can define **aggression** as behaviour that is intended to harm another individual.

This definition rules out the first example in our list. Accidentally injuring someone is not an aggressive act, because there is no intent to harm. People commonly refer to the second example as aggressive behaviour ("She is a very aggressive salesperson"), but social psychologists classify this behaviour as *assertive* rather than aggressive because there is no intent to injure. Actions that produce harm as an unintended by-product are not aggressive; a physician who administers a painful treatment does not act aggressively. In contrast, actions that do not cause harm but were intended to do so are aggressive. Swinging a stick to injure someone is an aggressive act, even if there is no contact.

Of course, any definition that relies on an individual's intentions has a serious drawback. We can't see another person's intentions, so how do we know what they are? And whose view do we accept if people disagree about someone's intentions? When defined in terms of intent, aggression lies ultimately in the eye of the beholder. The consequences of a harmful act may be obvious to everyone, but its characterization as aggressive is a matter of subjective judgment.

Aggressive behaviours come in many forms. Words as well as deeds can be aggressive. Quarrelling couples who intend their spiteful remarks to hurt are behaving aggressively. Even failure to act can be aggressive. If you know that someone is about to do something that will lead to her being humiliated but you don't warn her because you want to see this happen to her, your inaction could be considered aggression.

To distinguish them from less harmful behaviours, extreme acts of aggression are called *violence*. Some other terms in the language of aggression refer to emotions and attitudes. *Anger* consists of strong feelings of displeasure in response to a perceived

aggression Behaviour intended to harm another individual.

During their heavyweight boxing championship fight in June 1997, former champion Mike Tyson viciously bites champion Evander Holyfield's ear. After chewing off pieces of both of Holyfield's ears, Tyson was disqualified, and a near-riot ensued in the ring. Was Tyson's attack an instance of instrumental aggression, in which he bit Holyfield's ears in order to stop a fight he felt he could not win, or emotional aggression, in which he lost his composure and snapped due to the frustration and pain he was experiencing?

injury; the exact nature of these feelings (for example, outrage, hate, or irritation) depends on the specific situation. *Hostility* is a negative, antagonistic attitude toward another person or group. Anger and hostility are often closely connected to aggression, but not always. People can be angry at others and regard them with great hostility without ever trying to harm them. And aggression can occur without a trace of anger or hostility, as when a contract killer murders a perfect stranger in order to "make a killing" financially.

The aggression of a hired gun is an example of **instrumental aggression**, in which harm is inflicted as a means to a desired end. Aggression aimed at harming someone for personal gain, attention, or even self-defence fits this definition. If the aggressor believes that there is an easier way to obtain the goal, aggression would not occur.

In **emotional aggression**, the means and the end coincide. Harm is inflicted for its own sake. Emotional aggression is often impulsive, carried out in the heat of the moment. The jealous lover strikes out in rage; fans of rival soccer teams go at each other with fists and clubs. Emotional aggression, however, can also be calm, cool, and calculating. Revenge, so the saying goes, is a dish best served cold.

Of course, sometimes it is hard to distinguish between instrumental and emotional aggression. Why did Mike Tyson viciously bite Evander Holyfield's ear during their 1997 championship boxing match? Was it a deliberate attempt to escape the embarrassment of being beaten by his opponent for the second time, or did he simply lose control and lash out against him in frustration? Perhaps no one, not even Tyson himself, can answer this question—in part because it is difficult to know where to draw the line. Indeed, some scholars believe that all aggression is fundamentally instrumental, serving some need, and still others suggest that instrumental and emotional aggression are not distinct categories but endpoints on a continuum (Anderson, 2004a; Anderson & Huesmann, 2003; Tedeschi & Bond, 2001).

Cultural and Gender Differences

Just as not all types of aggression are alike, not all groups of people are alike in their attitudes and propensities toward aggression. Before we discuss the sources of aggression and what can be done about it, we need to consider how aggression is similar and how it differs across cultures and gender.

instrumental aggression Inflicting harm in order to obtain something of value.

emotional aggression Inflicting harm for its own sake.

Cultural Variation

Cultures vary dramatically in how, and how much, their members aggress against each other. We can see this variation across societies and across specific groups, or subcultures, within a society.

Comparisons Across Societies The United States continues to be an exceptionally violent country. Its murder rate is one of the highest among industrialized nations, far worse than those in Canada, Australia, New Zealand, and much of Western Europe. However, several countries in Eastern Europe, Africa, Asia, and the Americas have worse rates than the United States. Figure 11.1 illustrates some of the variation in homicide rates around the world.

FIGURE 11.1

Violence Around the World

These figures indicate the number of murders in one year per 100 000 people in each of several countries, according to United Nations statistics published in 2002. As can be seen, the frequency of murders varies widely around the world.

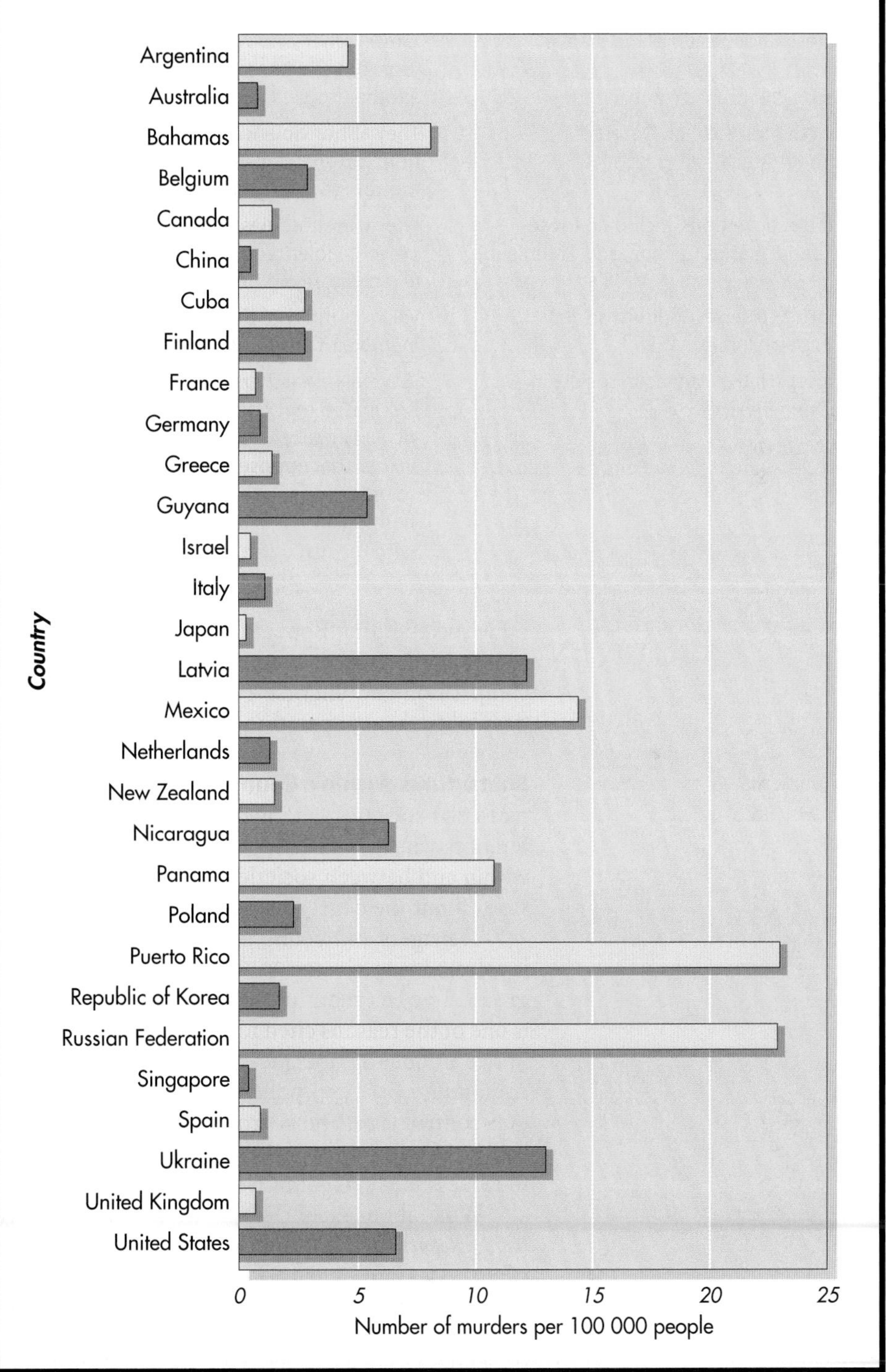

The forms violence typically takes, and people's attitudes toward various kinds of aggression, also differ internationally. Relative to most of the world, the United States has a tremendous amount of gun-related violence, and this violence tends to involve individuals rather than groups of people. Groups attacking other groups in political, ethnic, tribal, or other institutionalized conflict are seen throughout the world but are particularly associated with the Middle East, Africa, Eastern Europe, and parts of South America. And violent mobs of European football (what North Americans call "soccer") fans are not uncommon in England and other parts of Europe—behaviour rarely seen at North American sports events.

Cultures also differ in aggression involving children. For example, in Japan, it has been relatively common for Japanese adult businessmen to grope schoolgirls on public transportation—a practice that would be considered aggressive and unacceptable in many other cultures (Mcginty, 2000; Moshavi, 2001). Another example concerns female genital mutilation—any of several procedures in which, according to some estimates, approximately 6 000 girls a day have their genitals cut in many countries of Africa and Asia, as well as in

TABLE 11.2

Nonviolent Societies

In addition to those discussed in the text, this table lists a few of the other societies that Bruce Bonta (1997) identified as nonviolent.

Society	Comments
Balinese (Indonesian island of Bali)	A researcher who was there for four years never witnessed one boy beating another boy.
G/wi (Central Kalahari Desert of southern Africa)	They abhor violence and take pleasure from fortunate events only if they are in the company of group members.
Inuit (Arctic regions, including those in Siberia, Alaska, Canada, and Greenland)	They use strategies to control anger and prevent violence; they have a strong fear of aggression.
Ladakhis (Tibetan Buddhist society in northern India)	Villagers indicate that they have no memory of any fighting in the village.
Zapotec (Native American society in southern Mexico)	"Several researchers have been fascinated that one community is particularly peaceful, with very strong values that oppose violence, in contrast to other communities nearby where fighting and machismo are comparable with the rest of Mexico" (p. 320).

New Zealand. The cultures that practice this consider it an important, sacred ritual; but the cultures that condemn it consider it an inhumane act of violence and have vigorously called for a worldwide ban (Gross, 2000; Swain, 1997).

Although violence seems to be just about everywhere, a handful of societies stand out as nonviolent exceptions. Bruce Bonta (1997) describes 25 societies around the world that are almost completely without violence. For example, the Chewong, who live in the mountains of the Malay Peninsula, do not even have words in their language for quarrelling, fighting, aggression, or warfare. The Amish, the Hutterites, and the Mennonites are all societies that reside in Canada and the relatively violent United States but remain remarkably nonviolent. Table 11.2 lists some of the other societies that Bonta identified as nonviolent. What makes all of these societies so peaceful? According to Bonta, all but two of these 25 societies strongly oppose competition and endorse cooperation in all aspects of their lives. This raises the possibility that cooperation and lack of competition may promote nonviolence.

Subcultures Within a Country There are important variations in aggression within particular societies as a function of age, class, race, and region. Identifying these differences can be critically important in understanding why crime rates vary both within and between societies, and why overall crime rates do not tell the complete story about the degree of violence that different groups of people are experiencing.

Teenagers and young adults, aged 14 through 24, have a much greater rate of involvement in violent crime—as both offenders and victims—than any other age group. The fact that the North American population has been aging in recent years is one of the reasons cited for the drop in violent crime rates. (Other factors that are noted frequently include longer jail sentences for criminals, more visible and community-oriented policing, a decline in the market for crack cocaine, tougher gun-control laws, and a strong economy.) As the post-World War II baby boomers began entering their forties and fifties in the mid-1990s, this large group became much less likely to commit acts of aggression and violence.

What about race? The National Parole Board of Canada's *Performance Monitoring Report* for 2004 indicated that aboriginal offenders represented 16.2 percent of the federal offender population (compared to their overall representation in the population of 3.3 percent), and Blacks 6.1 percent (who comprise 2.2 percent of the Canadian population). Among incidents involving one victim and one offender in the United States in 1999, 94 percent of black murder victims were killed by black offenders, and 85 percent of white murder victims were slain by white offenders. Nevertheless, black Americans live in a much more violent America than do Whites. FBI analyses in 1999 projected that 1 in 40 black males, and 1 in 199 black females, are likely to be murdered in their lifetime, compared to 1 in 280 white males and 1 in 794 white females.

Regional differences are also striking. In the United States, the murder rate is consistently highest in the South, followed by the West. Some scholars have attributed the greater violence in the South and West to a "culture of honour" that is prevalent among white males in these regions. The culture of honour encourages violent responses to perceived threats against one's status as an honourable, powerful man (Cohen et al., 1998; Vandello & Cohen, 2005). We will focus more on the culture of honour later in the chapter.

Gender Differences

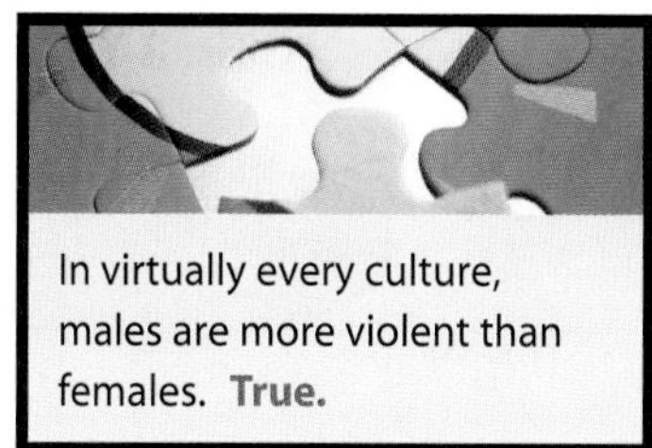

In virtually every culture, males are more violent than females. **True.**

Despite all the variation across cultures, one thing is universal: Men are more violent than women. This has been found in virtually all cultures studied around the world. According to Canadian statistics, women represent only 4 percent of the offender population in Canada. World Health Organization data indicate that, compared to women, men are almost four times more likely to be murdered in the United States, two times more likely in Finland, four times more likely in the Russian Federation, and nine times more likely in Mexico (Bulatao & VandenBos, 1996). Despite the significant variation in total violence from one country to another, the gender difference remains remarkably stable over time and place: Men commit the very large majority of homicides, and men comprise the very large majority of murder victims (Buss, 2004; Daly & Wilson, 1989). And in the spate of school shootings discussed at the beginning of this chapter, all of the perpetrators were boys.

What about aggression in general, as opposed to violence? In a recent series of meta-analyses involving hundreds of samples from more than 20 countries, John Archer (2005) found that males are consistently more physically aggressive than females. Females were as likely to feel anger as males, but they were much less likely to act on their anger in aggressive ways. Even among children between three and six years old, boys show higher rates of physical aggression than girls (Loeber & Hay, 1997). Young boys play more aggressive games (mock fighting, cops and robbers) than girls, who tend to prefer more nurturant play (Jukes & Goldstein, 1993; Singer, 1994). Two-year-olds show different preferences for books: Boys like stories of violence and horror, and girls like more romantic tales (Collins-Standley et al., 1996). Indeed, even infants differ, with infant boys showing more anger and poorer regulation of their emotional states than infant girls (Weinberg & Tronick, 1997).

Men are more physically aggressive than women in most societies, but women, too, commit acts of physical violence. Here, a young woman is being brutally initiated into a gang by other female gang members.

So, does all this mean that the stereotype of males as more aggressive than females is correct? Not necessarily. As Deborah Richardson and Georgina Hammock (2005) concluded, the answer to this question "will almost always be 'it depends.'" Most of the research has focused on the aggression typical of males: physical aggression. But think back to our definition of aggression: It concerns intent

FIGURE 11.2

Gender and Indirect Versus Direct Aggression in Four Countries

In this study involving 8- and 15-year-old children from a variety of ethnic groups in Finland, Israel, Poland, and Italy, same-sex peers estimated how much physical, verbal, and indirect aggression boys and girls engaged in. Across all of these cultural groups, the results suggested that girls are much more likely to use indirect aggression than boys and that boys are much more likely to use physical aggression than girls. *(Based on Oesterman et al., 1998.)*

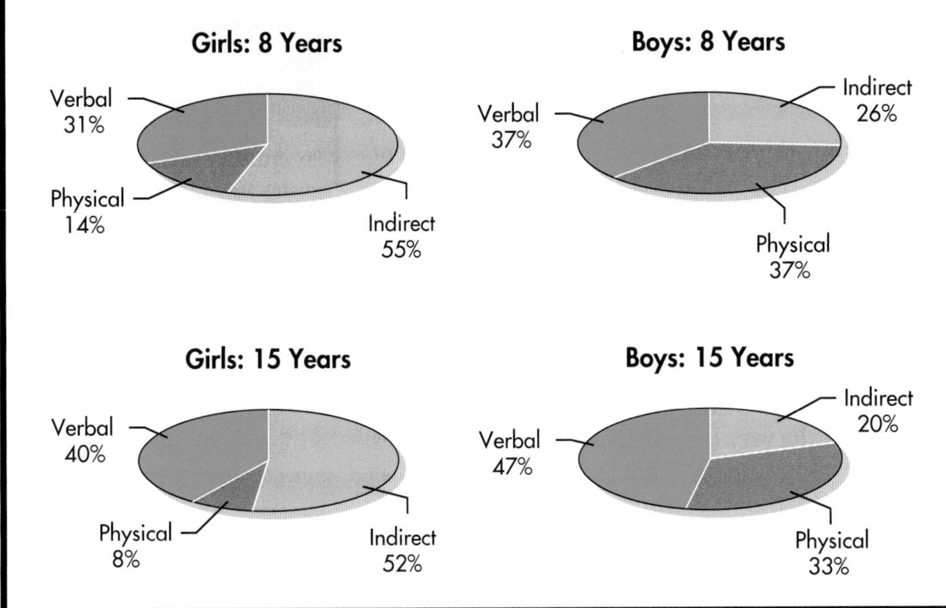

to harm. There are many ways to harm someone other than through physical means. Recent research has recognized this, and the results challenge the notion that males are more aggressive than females. The findings emerging can be summarized by a remark noted by Britt Galen and Marion Underwood (1997) in their research on aggression among adolescent girls and boys: "Boys may use their fists to fight, but at least it's over with quickly; girls use their tongues, and it goes on forever" (p. 589).

This research reveals that although boys tend to be more *overtly* aggressive than girls, girls often are more *indirectly*, or *relationally*, aggressive than boys. Indirect forms of aggression include acts such as telling lies to get someone in trouble or shutting them out of desired activities. Relational aggression is one kind of indirect aggression, particularly targeting a person's relationships and social status, such as by threatening to end a friendship, engaging in gossip and backbiting, and trying to get others to dislike the target. Why are girls more likely to use relational aggression than boys? Nikki Crick and others (Crick & Rose, 2000; Crick et al., 1999; Morales et al., 2005) believe it is because females typically care more about relationships and intimacy than males do and so may see injuring someone socially as particularly effective.

In studies conducted in several countries, including Finland, Argentina, Italy, Australia, Indonesia, and the United States, females were found to engage in indirect aggression more often than males (Archer, 2005; Björkqvist et al., 1992; Crick et al., 1997; French et al., 2002; Galen & Underwood, 1997; Huesmann et al., 2003; Owens et al., 2000). For example, while observing samples from Finland, Israel, Poland, and Italy, Karin Oesterman and others (1998) recorded the frequency with which individual boys and girls of various ages engaged in different forms of aggression, as estimated by their peers. Across all of these samples, girls were consistently more likely to use indirect aggression than physical aggression—and vice versa (see Figure 11.2). Indeed, girls as young as preschool age tend to be more relationally aggressive than their male peers. The gender difference is clear through the school years, particularly from about age 11. The difference begins to decline as the girls and boys become young adults, primarily because boys show a marked decrease in physical aggression from the age of 15 to 18 and a corresponding increase in their use of verbal and indirect aggression. Recent research also suggests that adult women use relational aggression more often than adult men, who, in turn, aggress verbally more often than they aggress relationally (Archer, 2005; Crick & Rose, 2000; Geen, 1998; Huesmann et al., 2003).

Even the well-established gender difference in overt aggression appears to be an oversimplification. In a meta-analysis of 64 experiments, Ann Bettencourt and Norman Miller (1996) found that men consistently were more aggressive than women under neutral conditions but that this difference diminished significantly under conditions in which there was some clear provocation for the aggression, such as if the participants had been frustrated, insulted, or threatened. In many everyday life situations, however, males are quicker to aggress than females because they are more likely to interpret ambiguous situations as provoking.

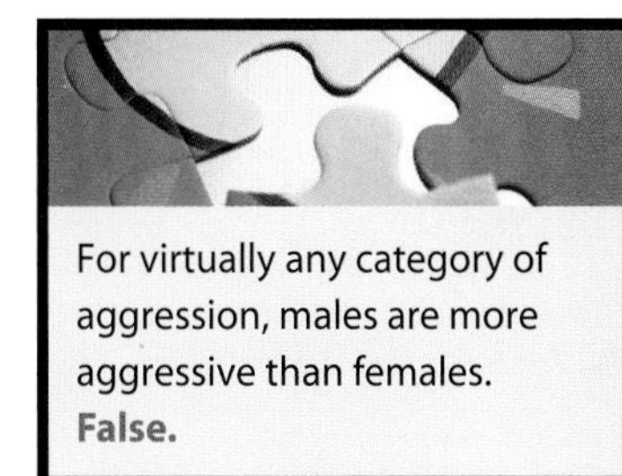

For virtually any category of aggression, males are more aggressive than females. **False.**

Origins of Aggression

Regardless of these various cultural and gender differences, aggression has been a prevalent part of human interaction throughout human history and around the world. It is not surprising that many have speculated about the origins of aggression. Where does it come from? Are we *born* aggressive, or are we *taught* to be aggressive? Many have argued for one side or the other of the "nature-nurture" debate—the "nature" side holding that aggression is an innate characteristic of human beings and the "nurture" side holding that aggression is learned through experience. In this section, we look at the theory and research most relevant to tracing the origins of human aggression. In reviewing each perspective, we examine how well it can account for the overall prevalence of aggression, as well as for the cultural and gender differences that we have discussed.

Is Aggression Innate?

Innate characteristics are not contingent on learning for their development, although they can be influenced by learning, culture, and other factors. Here, we examine three approaches to the issue of whether aggression is innate: instinct theories; evolutionary psychology accounts; and biological factors, including genes, hormones, and neurotransmitters.

Instinct Theories On November 11, 1918, a human catastrophe finally ended. Covered in mud, lungs blasted by gas, millions of soldiers had died to gain bits and pieces of contested territory. For an Austrian physician named Sigmund Freud, the slaughter on the battlefields of Europe during World War I marked a turning point. Rejecting his prewar version of psychoanalysis, Freud (1920) proposed a grim new concept: the *death instinct*—a profound, unconscious desire to escape the tensions of living by becoming still, inanimate, dead. This impulse toward self-destruction does not, according to Freud, exist unchallenged. There is also a life instinct, which motivates human beings to preserve and reproduce themselves. Paradoxically, Freud considered aggression toward others to be a momentary victory for the life instinct. In aggression, the force of the death instinct is deflected outward at others rather than aimed inward toward the original target, the self.

Like Freud, Konrad Lorenz (1966) regarded aggression as an innate, instinctual motivation. Unlike Freud, who believed that the life and death instincts are antagonistic, Lorenz saw the will to live and the will to aggress as entirely compatible. Based on his observations of animals in their natural habitat, Lorenz argued that aggression secures an advantage in the struggle to survive. The individual who successfully aggresses against others gains access to valuable resources such as food, territory, and desirable mates. Because only those who survive are able to reproduce, natural selection would produce an aggressive instinct in humans as well as in other animals.

Despite the widespread attention that these theories received at the time they were formulated, they no longer have much influence on scientific research. The primary reason for their fall from favour is their reliance on circular reasoning. Why do people aggress? Because they have an aggressive instinct. How do we know that aggression is instinctive? Because people aggress. Case closed. But shut off from the exploration of testable alternatives, circular reasoning is a logical and scientific dead end. In addition, instinct theories cannot account adequately for the cultural and gender differences in aggression—except through more circular reasoning.

Evolutionary Psychology There are clear similarities between Lorenz's instinct theory and evolutionary psychology, which uses principles of evolution to understand human social behaviour. For example, John Tooby and Leda Cosmides (1988) share Lorenz's belief that human warfare originated in attempts to obtain valuable resources. These investigators, however, maintain that the earliest battles between men were fought over women rather than over food or land. To be well fed and have a safe territory can prolong life and indirectly enhance reproductive success—but having a mate is essential.

In contrast to Lorenz, evolutionary accounts emphasize genetic survival rather than survival of the individual. Because at least some of a person's genes can be transmitted through the reproductive success of genetic relatives, evolution should have favoured the inhibition of aggression against those who are genetically related to us. For example, according to Martin Daly and Margo Wilson (1988, 1994, 1996, 2000), birth parents are much less likely to abuse or murder their own offspring than stepparents are to harm stepchildren. In two samples studied, preschool children living with a stepparent or foster parent were 70 to 100 times more likely to be fatally abused than were children living with both biological parents.

What can account for the gender differences in aggression? From a strictly evolutionary perspective, for males to best ensure the survival of their genes, they should mate with attractive, healthy females and invest their time and resources only in offspring who are genetically related to them. Males are competitive with each other because females select high-status males for mating, and aggression is a means by which males traditionally have been able to achieve and maintain status. In addition, because human men, unlike women, cannot be sure that they are the true genetic parents of their children, men are predisposed to sexual jealousy. Behaviours triggered by sexual jealousy, including aggression and the threat of aggression, may be designed to enhance the male's confidence in his paternity of offspring. Consistent with evolutionary reasoning, crime statistics indicate that male-to-male violence is most likely to occur when one is perceived as challenging the other's status or social power, such as by attempting to humiliate him or to challenge his sexual relationships. Male-to-female violence is predominantly triggered by sexual jealousy (Buss, 2004; Buss & Duntley, 2005; Shackelford et al., 2003; Wilson & Daly, 1996).

Of course, as noted earlier, women also aggress. From an evolutionary perspective, reproductive success is dependent on the survival of one's offspring, and because women are much more limited than men in terms of the number of children they can have, evolution presumably favoured those women who were committed to protecting their children. Indeed, much research on aggression by females has focused on maternal aggression, whereby females aggress to defend their offspring against threats by others. For example, females in a variety of species have been observed to attack male strangers who come too close to their offspring (Ferreira et al., 2000; Gammie et al., 2000). In a similar vein, Anne Campbell (1999) proposes that females tend to place a higher value on protecting their own lives—again, so as to protect their offspring. This hypothesis may explain not only why human males engage more often in risky, potentially self-destructive behaviours, but also why human females, when they do aggress, are more likely to use less obvious, and thus less dangerous, means—such as indirect or relational aggression rather than overt, physical aggression.

Evolutionary accounts have been challenged for a variety of reasons, including the historical and cultural diversity of human aggression (Ruback & Weiner, 1995). Within any society, the amount of aggression varies across time; and between societies, as illustrated in Figure 11.1, there are large differences in rates of violence. If aggression is innate and universal, how could people differ so much in when and where they display it? Faced with such variation, even some researchers who believe that aggression is an evolved characteristic have concluded that its occurrence is primarily determined by social factors (Lore & Schultz, 1993).

Responding to these challenges, evolutionary psychologists argue that the presence of cultural and historical variation is not inconsistent with evolution-based theories. Rather, evolutionary and social factors should be seen as compatible and complementary. Evolved psychological mechanisms develop in response to specific environmental contexts. David Buss (1995) points out, for example, that few doubt that our ability to develop calluses on our skin is an evolved physical reaction to environmental influences. Just because some people have lots of calluses and others don't does not invalidate the argument that evolutionary factors played a role in causing humans to evolve mechanisms that produce calluses to protect their skin. Similarly, the argument goes, one should not deny the role of evolution in human aggression just because some cultures are more violent than others. In addition, cultural differences themselves may be products of evolution, traced to different environmental pressures that required dissimilar adaptive responses (Buss & Malamuth, 1996).

Behaviour Genetics Evolutionary psychology involves tying together evolution, genetic transmission, and behaviour. Behaviour genetics settles for the complexities of connecting the latter two. Early in life, aggressiveness becomes a relatively stable personality characteristic—relative to other children, those who are high in aggressiveness when they are about eight years old are more likely to be aggressive later in life (Huesmann, 2005; Huesmann & Guerra, 1997; Olweus, 1979). Can this aggressive personality type be due to genes?

To trace a line of genetic transmission (heritability), scientists examine differences between individuals or groups. Two types of studies are typically employed in research on humans. In twin studies, monozygotic twins (who are identical in their genetic make-up) are compared with dizygotic twins (who share only part of their genes). On any heritable trait, monozygotic twins will be more similar than dizygotic twins. Adoptee studies are also used in behaviour genetics research. On any inherited trait, adopted children will resemble their biological parents more than they resemble their adoptive parents. Although twin and adoptee studies have produced some evidence supporting the heritability of human aggressive behaviour, the results overall have been somewhat mixed (Hines & Saudino, 2002; Miles & Carey, 1997). More research, and particularly more research that uses diverse methods, needs to be done before a clearer picture of the heritability of aggression can be drawn.

The Role of Testosterone In addition to the question of heritability, researchers have long been interested in determining what specific biological factors influence aggression (Renfrew, 1997). Because of the persistent sex differences in physical aggression found among humans and other animals, many researchers have wondered if testosterone plays a role. Although men and women both have this "male sex hormone," men usually have higher levels than do women. If testosterone affects aggressive behaviour, then it could serve as the connection between biological sex and human aggression. Research conducted on a variety of animals has found a strong correlation between testosterone levels and aggression. The relationship is far weaker among humans, however. Even so, a number of studies have documented an association between testosterone and aggression. Using diverse samples of people, such as young boys, prison inmates, university students, and elderly men with dementias such as Alzheimer's disease, these studies tend to show a strong positive correlation between testosterone levels and physical aggression or violence (Book et al., 2001; Chance et al., 2000; Dabbs & Dabbs, 2005; Dabbs et al., 1995; Orengo et al., 1997). One study found that fraternities whose members tended to have higher testosterone levels were more rambunctious and exhibited more crude behaviour than other fraternities; fraternities with lower testosterone levels tended to be more academically successful and socially responsible, and their members smiled more (Dabbs et al., 1996). The relationship between testosterone and aggression is not limited to males. Studies have also shown a positive relationship between testosterone and aggression and related behaviours (such as competitiveness) in women (Cashdan, 2003; Dabbs & Dabbs, 2005; von der Pahlen et al., 2002).

Intriguing as they are, such correlational findings cannot prove that testosterone causes aggression. There are alternative explanations. For example, aggression itself can cause temporary increases in testosterone—if the aggression is successful. Even a game, such as tennis, chess, or a laboratory task, can temporarily increase the testosterone levels of winners and decrease the levels of losers (Gladue et al., 1989; Mazur et al., 1992). Stress may also be involved: Higher levels of stress are associated with higher levels of testosterone (Thompson et al., 1990). Testosterone levels are better predictors of antisocial behaviour for individuals low in socioeconomic status than for those with greater income and education (Dabbs & Morris, 1990; Dabbs et al., 1990). Perhaps people who are poor and badly educated are more vulnerable to the kinds of stressors that simultaneously elevate both testosterone and aggression.

For ethical reasons, researchers do not manipulate people's levels of testosterone to measure its effects on aggression and other behaviours. But Stephanie Van Goozen and others (1995; Cohen-Ketteinis & Van Goozen, 1997) have studied individuals who were voluntarily manipulating their sex hormones—transsexuals undergoing sex reassignment treatments. The researchers administered tests of aggression to 35 female-to-male transsexuals and 15 male-to-female transsexuals shortly before and three months after the start of cross-sex hormone treatment in a Dutch hospital. With their increase in male hormones, the female-to-male transsexuals exhibited increased aggression-proneness. In contrast, the deprivation of these hormones in the male-to-female group was associated with a decrease in aggression-proneness. It is important to note, however, that these changes in aggressiveness may have been caused not by the hormone treatment per se but, rather, by indirect factors such as the transsexuals' expectations or other people's reactions to them.

The Role of Serotonin Testosterone is not the only biological factor linked to human aggression. There has been an explosion of interest recently in the role of the neurotransmitter serotonin. Neurotransmitters such as serotonin act as chemical messengers in the nervous system, transmitting information. Serotonin appears to work like a braking mechanism to restrain impulsive acts of aggression. Low levels of serotonin in the nervous systems of humans and many animals are associated with high levels of aggression. Drugs that boost serotonin's activity can dampen aggressiveness, along with a range of other impulsive and socially deviant behaviours (Cleare & Bond, 2000; Fishbein, 2000; Holmes et al., 2003; Oquendo & Mann, 2000; Soloff et al., 2000). Such drugs have even been used to treat "road rage"—people's impulsive acts of aggression and violence while driving.

Is the lack of serotonin, then, an innate cause of aggression? Like testosterone, serotonin appears to be both a cause and a consequence of behaviours relevant to social status and dominance. In their work with vervet monkeys, for example, Gary Brammer and his colleagues (1994) found that individuals' social status influenced their levels of serotonin at least as much as their serotonin levels influenced their social status. Here again, biological and social factors interact with each other.

The interaction of biological and social factors is also evident in recent work by Craig Ferris (2005). His research with hamsters suggests that serotonin interacts with the hormone vasopressin in regulating aggression, and that both the serotonin and vasopressin systems are affected by daily stress, such as stress associated with the threat of attack. For these hamsters, stress during adolescence can have long-term effects later in life on aggression-related behaviour and on the interaction of serotonin and vasopressin systems.

Is Aggression Learned?

Regardless of the precise contribution of genetic and biological factors, the importance of experience is clear: Aggressive behaviour is strongly affected by learning (Bandura, 1973). Rewards obtained by aggression today increase its use tomorrow. Such rewards come in two flavours: *positive reinforcement*, when aggression produces desired outcomes, and *negative reinforcement*, when aggression prevents or stops undesirable outcomes. The child who gets a toy by hitting the toy's owner is likely to hit again. So, too, the child who can stop other children from teasing by shoving them away has learned the fateful lesson that aggression pays. Children who see aggression producing more good outcomes, and fewer bad ones, are more aggressive than other children (Boldizar et al., 1989).

Rewards are one part of the learning equation, but what about punishment? Punishment is often promoted as a way to reduce aggressive behaviour. Can people learn not to act aggressively through punishment? Jennifer Hall and others (1998) found among a sample of children from relatively poor economic backgrounds that those children who most expected to be punished for bad behaviour scored lower on self-reported aggression. Punishment is most likely to decrease aggression when it (1) immediately follows the aggressive behaviour, (2) is strong enough to deter the aggressor, and (3) is consistently applied and perceived as fair and legitimate by the aggressor. However, such stringent conditions are seldom met, and when they are not met, punishment can backfire. When courts are overburdened and prisons are overcrowded, the relationship between crime and punishment can seem more like a lottery than a rational system in which the punishment fits the crime. In short, the *certainty* of punishment is more important than its *severity* (Berkowitz, 1998).

There are some other problems with punishment as well. Punishment perceived as unfair or arbitrary can provoke retaliation, creating an escalating cycle of aggression. Perhaps most troubling is that punishment, especially when delivered in an angry or hostile manner, offers a model to imitate. Murray Straus and his colleagues (Straus, 2000; Straus & Stewart, 1999) have been outspoken critics of the use of *corporal punishment*—physical force (such as spanking, hitting, and pinching) intended to cause a child pain, but not injury, for the purpose of controlling or correcting the child's behaviour. It is difficult to find data on the rates of spanking in Canada; most of the data is derived from American studies that indicate that the majority of children in the United States experience spanking and other forms of corporal punishment. Numerous studies, however, report a *positive* relationship between corporal punishment and the likelihood of aggression: more corporal punishment is associated with more aggression. Elizabeth Gershoff (2002) investigated this issue with a meta-analysis of 88 studies conducted over six decades and involving more than 36 000 participants. Her analysis revealed strong evidence for a positive correlation between corporal punishment and several antisocial behaviours, such as aggression as a child, aggression as an adult, and adult criminal behaviour.

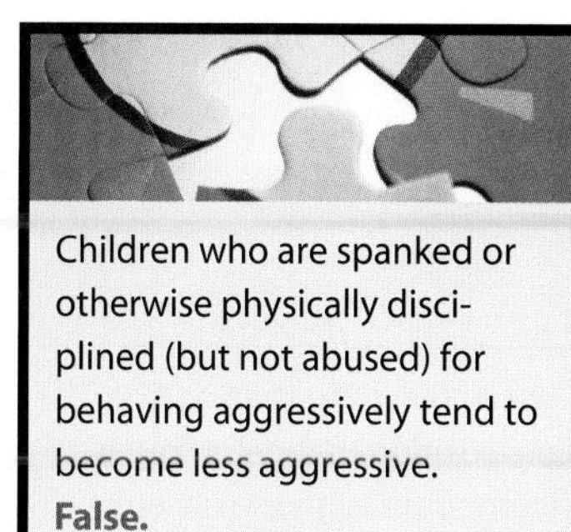

Children who are spanked or otherwise physically disciplined (but not abused) for behaving aggressively tend to become less aggressive.
False.

Correlational findings do not prove causality, however, and experiments using random assignment cannot be conducted to investigate the effects of spanking

FIGURE 11.3

Spanking by Parents and Subsequent Antisocial Behaviour by Children

In this study, researchers recorded the number of times in a week that children were spanked by parents and then measured the change after two years in the children's antisocial behaviour. As you can see, the more the children were spanked, the more antisocial their behaviour was two years later. *(Straus et al., 1997.)*

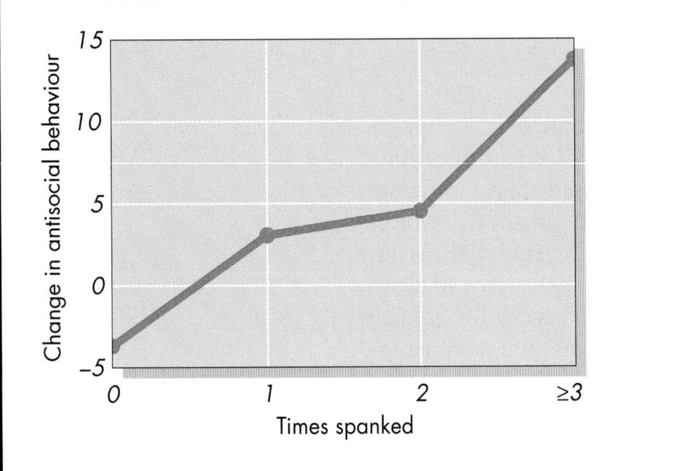

children. It is very possible that the aggressiveness of the children leads to more spanking, rather than the other way around. Some studies that have looked at this relationship longitudinally—measuring the use of corporal punishment and aggression at one time and measuring aggression at some later point—suggest that corporal punishment may indeed increase subsequent aggression. One study reported that boys who received harsh punishment when they were 8 years old were more aggressive than other males 22 years later on several measures of aggression, such as number of arrests, tendency to hit their spouses, and self-reported serious aggression (Eron et al., 1991). Another study (Straus et al., 1997) found that the more times a child was spanked during one week (as reported by the child's mother), the more likely the child was to display antisocial behaviour, including aggression, two years later—even with the effects of the child's earlier antisocial behaviour, gender, and ethnic background and the family's socioeconomic status controlled for. In fact, the researchers found that children who were spanked even once during that first week showed an increase in antisocial behaviour two years later (Figure 11.3).

The relationship between parental corporal punishment and children's subsequent aggression is influenced by a number of factors, including the overall family environment, the emotions displayed by the parents during the punishment, and cultural and ethnic differences (Benjet & Kazdin, 2003; Pinderhughes et al., 2000). For example, corporal punishment is less likely to increase aggressiveness when it is administered in the context of an overall warm and supportive parent-child relationship (Baumrind, 1997; Deater-Deckard et al., 1998).

Social Learning Theory One of the authors of this book remembers many a late, cold afternoon during his middle school and high school years playing informal but competitive games of football and hockey with friends. Both games were played without protective equipment and were quite rough, but the way he and his friends played them, football was the more physically brutal of the two. Yet despite the fact that virtually every play culminated in a pile of boys jumping on the flattened body of an opponent, it was very rare that an actual fight would break out. When this same group of friends played hockey, on the other hand, virtually every single game they played featured at least one fight. Why? Although he was years away from his first social psychology class, this future social psychologist was quite sure that he and his friends were basing their behaviour on role models. Rarely had they seen professional football players stop and fight on the field. But rarely had they seen a professional hockey game in which that *didn't* happen.

The power of models to modify behaviour is a crucial tenet of Albert Bandura's (1977) **social learning theory**. Social learning theory emphasizes that we learn from the example of others as well as from direct experience with rewards and punishments. Models influence the prosocial, helpful behaviour described in Chapter 10. They also affect antisocial, aggressive behaviour. In a classic study, Bandura and his associates (1961) observed the behaviour of mildly frustrated children. Those who had previously watched an adult throw around, punch, and kick an inflatable doll were more aggressive when they later played with the doll than were those who

social learning theory The proposition that behaviour is learned through the observation of others as well as through the direct experience of rewards and punishments.

had watched a quiet, subdued adult. These children followed the adult model's lead not only in degree of aggression but also in the kinds of aggression they exhibited. Subsequent research has amply demonstrated that a wide range of aggressive models can elicit a wide range of aggressive imitations. Furthermore, these models do not have to be present; people on TV—and even cartoon characters—can serve as powerful models of aggression (Bandura, 1983; Baron & Richardson, 1994; Berkowitz, 1993).

Iraqi boys in Baghdad play with toy guns in January 2004, imitating the adult behaviour they have observed in their war-torn country.

Models who obtain desired goals through the use of aggression and are not punished for their behaviour are the most likely to increase aggression among observers. But even those who are punished can have an effect. Postwar increases in homicide rates have been documented not only in rewarded, victorious countries that watched their soldiers prevail, but also in punished, defeated nations that saw their soldiers overwhelmed (Archer & Gartner, 1984).

People learn more than specific aggressive behaviours from aggressive models. They also develop more positive attitudes and beliefs about aggression in general, and they construct aggressive "scripts" that serve as guides for how to behave and solve social problems. These scripts can be activated automatically in various situations, leading to quick, often unthinking aggressive responses that follow the scripts we have been taught (Guerra et al., 2003; Huesmann, 1998).

Fortunately, changing the model can change the consequences: Nonaggressive models decrease aggressive behaviour. Observing a nonaggressive response to a provoking situation teaches a peaceful alternative and strengthens existing restraints against aggression. In addition, observing someone who is calm and reasonable may help an angry person settle down rather than strike out. Aggression can spread like wildfire. But nonviolence and prosocial behaviour, too, can be contagious (Donnerstein & Donnerstein, 1976; Gibbons & Ebbeck, 1997).

Bandura's social learning theory has been one of the most important social psychological approaches to the study of human aggression since his classic early experiments in the early 1960s. Its simplicity should not obscure the fact that it can help explain a great amount of human behaviour. Daniel Batson and Adam Powell (2003) recently wrote that social learning theory "has probably come closer to [the goal of accounting for the most facts with the fewest principles] than has any other theory in the history of social psychology" (p. 466).

Socialization and Gender Differences: "Boys Will Be Boys" To account for gender differences in aggression, learning approaches emphasize that males and females are taught different lessons about aggression—they are rewarded and punished differently for aggression and are presented with different models. Whether or not gender differences in aggressive behaviour originated from innate biological factors, today they are maintained and perpetuated through lessons that are passed on from one generation to the next about the acceptability of various kinds and degrees of aggression.

Most researchers agree that social roles have a strong influence on gender differences in physical aggression. As described in Chapter 5, males and females are socialized to fill different roles in society. Overt aggression tends to be more socially acceptable in stereotypically male roles than in female roles. Indeed, as Philip Rodkin and others (2000) report, highly aggressive boys are often among the most popular and socially connected children in elementary school. Boys who use their fists to deal with conflict are much more likely to be rewarded with increased social status than are girls, who might suffer scorn and ridicule for fighting. On the other hand, a girl who successfully uses relational aggression, such as through social manipulation, can reap social benefits more easily than a boy (Crick & Rose, 2000).

These different social norms may underlie an interesting gender difference observed in longitudinal research. Although in general individuals who are more aggressive than their peers as children tend to be relatively aggressive as adults, this *continuity of aggression* is less true of females than males (Huesmann, 2005). Although males' and females' levels of aggression at age 8 correlate with their aggression at age 19, the correlations remain high for males but get weaker for females at ages 30 and 48. Huesmann notes also that the weaker relationship between childhood and adult aggressiveness among women is more due to females who were aggressive as children becoming relatively less aggressive as adults than to females becoming more aggressive. Males tend to show the opposite pattern. The reason may be that a girl's aggressiveness is less likely to be rewarded and reinforced by her environment than is a boy's, and so she is less likely to remain relatively aggressive.

US Marine paratroopers earn a pair of gold pins upon completion of ten training jumps. In February 1997, it was revealed, as captured on videotape, that this achievement is sometimes marked by "blood pinning"—a brutal hazing in which veteran Marines punch, pound, and grind the pins into the chests of the new initiates, who scream and writhe in pain. As military leaders try to crack down on this violent "rite of passage," others defend it as an important part of the "macho," honour-bound culture of the Marines.

Socialization and Cultural Differences: Cultures of Honour Socialization of aggression also varies from culture to culture. In support of this statement is a study by Giovanna Tomada and Barry Schneider (1997) who report that adolescent boys in traditional villages in Italy are encouraged to aggress as an indication of their sexual prowess and preparation for their dominant role in the household. These authors believe that this is why schoolyard bullying among elementary schoolboys is significantly higher in Central and Southern Italy than it is in Norway, England, Spain, or Japan. Similarly, some researchers believe that *machismo*—which in its most stereotyped characterization prescribes that challenges, abuse, and even differences of opinion "must be met with fists or other weapons" (Ingoldsby, 1991, p. 57)—contributes to the fact that rates of violence are higher among Latin American men than European American men (Harris, 1995).

Machismo may represent one form of what anthropologists call a *culture of honour*, which emphasizes honour and social status, particularly for males, and the role of aggression in protecting that honour. Even minor conflicts or disputes are often seen as challenges to social status and reputation and can therefore trigger aggressive responses. Several such subcultures exist in the United States. In an extensive series of studies, Dov

Cohen and Richard Nisbett have focused on the culture of honour among white men in the American South. Nisbett and Cohen (1996) report that rates of violence are consistently higher in the South than in all other regions. They have collected data from surveys, field experiments, and laboratory experiments suggesting that the culture of honour persists today, and that this culture promotes violent behaviour. Southerners are more likely than northerners to agree that "a man has the right to kill" in order to defend his family and house; and they are more accepting of using violence to protect one's honour than are people from other parts of the country. (Note, however, that southerners are *not* more likely than other Americans to accept violence unrelated to the protection of honour.)

In one series of experiments (Cohen et al., 1996), researchers investigated how white male students who had grown up either in the North or in the South responded to insults. The experiments, conducted on a large midwestern campus, involved an encounter that took place as the participant and a confederate were passing each other in a narrow hallway. The confederate did not give way to the participant, bumped into him, and hurled an insult. Compared with northerners, southerners were more likely to think that their masculine reputations had been threatened; exhibited greater physiological signs of being upset; appeared more physiologically primed for aggression (their testosterone levels rose); and engaged in more aggressive and dominant subsequent behaviour (gave firmer handshakes) and were more unwilling to yield to a subsequent confederate as they walked toward each other in a very narrow hallway (see Figure 11.4).

Institutions support norms about the acceptability of honour-based violence. Cohen and Nisbett (1997) sent letters to employers all over the United States from a fictitious job applicant who admitted having been convicted of a felony. To half

FIGURE 11.4

Insult, Aggression, and the Southern Culture of Honour

White male participants from either North or South regions of the United States either were bumped and insulted by a male confederate, or they passed the confederate without incident (control condition). As you can see, the incident had a greater effect on southern participants. Specifically, they thought that they would be seen as less masculine (left); their testosterone levels increased more (centre); and they were slower to yield to a confederate who later approached them in a narrow corridor (right). *(Cohen et al., 1996.)*

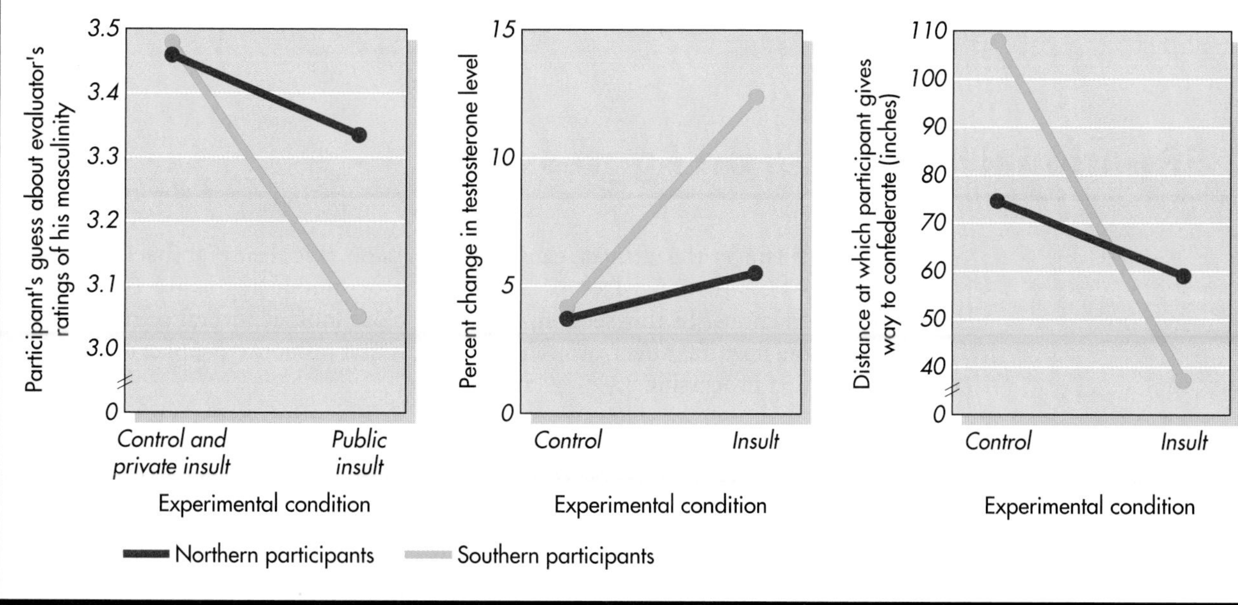

the employers, the applicant reported that he had impulsively killed a man who had been having an affair with his fiancée and then taunted him about it in a crowded bar. To the other half, the applicant reported that he had stolen a car because he needed the money to pay off debts. Employers from the South and the West (which has a culture of honour similar to the South's) were more likely than their northern counterparts to respond in an understanding and cooperative way to the letter from the convicted killer—but not from the auto thief.

In Chapter 2 we discussed more recent work on cultures of honour and aggression by Joseph Vandello and Dov Cohen (2003, 2005). Brazil, rather than the US South, was the culture of honour examined in this research. Vandello and Cohen found that a wife's infidelity harmed a man's reputation more in the eyes of Brazilian students than in the eyes of students from the northern United States. These researchers propose that because the reputations of men from cultures of honour are so important to them and are perceived to be more vulnerable, men from these cultures may be more likely than men from other cultures to react to their wives' and girlfriends' honour-threatening behaviours with violence, both as a way to prevent infidelity and to restore their own honour.

Nature Versus Nurture: A False Debate?

The origins of aggression are a source not only of scientific disagreement but also of political controversy. Heated debates about funding research and treatment programs frequently occur among politicians who disagree strongly on whether aggression is, to any significant extent, attributable to genetic inheritance or stable biological characteristics present at birth. However important it may be, this contentious issue should not obscure the considerable agreement that exists on other points. The effects of learning are not disputed; aggression is, at least to some extent, "made" by experience. Nor is there any doubt that in aggression, as in all human behaviour, biology and environment interact. Evolutionary accounts emphasize genetic predispositions as well as adaptations to immediate environmental contexts. Biological factors affect, and are affected by, social interactions. Social and cultural norms may have their roots in evolutionary and biological phenomena, but they exert direct influences on individuals today largely independent of their contemporary adaptive or biological significance. The debate between nature and nurture may rage on politically, but scientifically it is clear that the origins of human aggression represent a profound interaction of innate predispositions and environmental and social factors.

Situational Influences on Aggression

Whatever the ultimate causes of aggression, it is clear that specific, immediate situational factors can promote or inhibit aggressive thoughts and actions. In this section, we take a close look at several of these factors: frustration, negative affect, arousal, and factors that influence people's thoughts and information processing.

Frustration: Aggression as a Drive

In 1939, the year that World War II began, John Dollard and his colleagues published *Frustration and Aggression*, one of the most influential books on aggression ever written. This book sets forth two major propositions, which taken together are called the **frustration-aggression hypothesis**: (1) Frustration produced by interrupting a person's progress toward an expected goal will always elicit the motive to aggress and (2) All aggression is caused by frustration.

Aggressive behaviour on the road—what has been labelled "road rage"—is now a major problem in Canada as well as in many parts of the world. A poll conducted by the Canadian Automobile Association (CAA, 2000) found that 47 percent of their respondents had been a victim of road rage. A large majority of these acts of aggression stem from frustration—such as frustration about being stuck in traffic or cut off by another driver.

Dollard and his colleagues claimed that the motive to aggress is a psychological drive that resembles physiological drives like hunger. According to this theory, just as food deprivation elicits a hunger drive, so frustration elicits an aggressive drive. Just as the hunger drive prompts the search for food, so the aggressive drive prompts the attempt to inflict injury. But what if we're unable to aggress against the source of our frustration? After all, we can't hit the boss; nor can we strike out against abstractions such as health problems or financial setbacks. Dollard and his colleagues believed that in such instances the aggressive drive can seep out in the form of **displacement**. Here, the inclination to aggress is deflected from the real target only to land on a substitute. After a bad day at work or at school, do you sometimes come home and yell at the first available target—be it man, woman, or beast? If so, what is the effect on you? Does yelling at an innocent bystander reduce your inclination to take revenge on the person who gave you a hard time?

The efficacy of such substitute actions was warmly endorsed by Dollard and his colleagues in their notion of **catharsis**. Just as hunger can be satisfied by hamburgers as well as by caviar, so any aggressive act should reduce the motive to engage in any other aggressive behaviour. Since the Dollard group defined aggression quite broadly—to include making hostile jokes, telling violent stories, cursing, and observing the aggression of others, real or fictional—they held out the hope that engaging in some relatively harmless pursuit could drain away energy from more violent tendencies.

The Frustration-Aggression Hypothesis: Does the Evidence Support It? Obviously, there is a connection between frustration and aggression. Break into a line of shoppers at the supermarket or interrupt a student cramming for an exam, and you can see it for yourself. On a more extreme level, it was clear that Dylan Klebold and Eric Harris in the Columbine killing, had been feeling extremely frustrated—as a result of their exclusion from popular cliques. Indeed, in 13 of the 15 school shootings between 1995 and 2001 that Mark Leary and others (2003) examined, the shooters had apparently been frustrated by social rejection.

Soon after the frustration-aggression theory was proposed, however, critics pointed out that the Dollard group had overstated their case. Early on, Neal Miller (1941), one of the originators of the hypothesis, acknowledged that frustration does not always produce aggressive inclinations. The other absolute, that all aggression is caused by frustration, was soon overturned as well. In the following pages, we will consider many other causes of aggression.

The concept of displacement was also subjected to close scrutiny. In 1940, Carl Hovland and Robert Sears proposed that aggression by Whites against Blacks reflected the displacement of aggressive tendencies actually caused by economic frustration. Reviewing information on 14 southern states from 1882 to 1930, these

frustration-aggression hypothesis The idea that (1) frustration always elicits the motive to aggress and (2) all aggression is caused by frustration.

displacement Aggressing against a substitute target because aggressive acts against the source of the frustration are inhibited by fear or lack of access.

catharsis A reduction of the motive to aggress that is said to result from any imagined, observed, or actual act of aggression.

investigators found a strong negative correlation between economic indicators and the number of lynchings of black men. When the southern economy declined, more lynchings occurred. However, subsequent analyses, using more sophisticated statistical techniques to examine both the original data and the relationship between economic conditions and recent hate crimes, have failed to find a reliable association (Green et al., 1998).

Ervin Staub (1996, 2004) has proposed that genocide and mass killing, such as during the Holocaust, the "ethnic cleansing" in the former Yugoslavia, and recent acts of terrorism, may typically have their roots in societal frustrations arising from economic and social difficulties. These frustrations give rise to *scapegoating*—or blaming a particular minority group or groups for the problems the overall society is facing. In contrast, when the economy and social conditions are improving, aggression may decrease.

However, these correlational findings do not prove the validity of the concept of displacement. Indeed, acceptance of displacement's role in channelling aggressive behaviour quickly diminished within the field after scholars pointed to theoretical weaknesses and inconclusive empirical evidence (Marcus-Newhall et al., 2000; Zillmann, 1979). Yet recent work by Norman Miller and others (2003) may revive interest in it. In one pair of experiments, for example, a relatively trivial frustration caused by one person triggered displaced aggression by participants who had earlier been provoked by a different person (Pedersen et al., 2000). And a meta-analysis of 49 published articles has found reliable evidence for displaced aggression in response to provocation (Marcus-Newhall et al., 2000).

The concept of catharsis also received a great deal of attention, perhaps because it seemed to offer a way to control aggression. Dollard and his colleagues described catharsis as a two-step sequence. First, aggression reduces the level of physiological arousal. Second, because arousal is reduced, people are less angry and less likely to aggress further. It sounds logical, and many people believe it. For example, Gordon Russell and his colleagues (1995) reported that more than two-thirds of Canadian respondents in their research agreed with statements reflecting a belief in the effectiveness of catharsis (such as the statement that participating in aggressive sports is a good way to get rid of aggressive urges). Catharsis has also been used by school administrators and others to justify violent sports (Bennett, 1991).

But, put to the test, catharsis has not lived up to its advertisement. Most researchers have concluded that the catharsis idea is a myth. It is more counterproductive than effective in reducing subsequent aggression (Bushman, 2002; Geen & Quanty, 1977). Here's why:

- Imagined aggression or the observation of aggressive models is more likely to increase arousal and aggression than to reduce them. Indeed, this is a central point of social learning theory.
- Actual aggression can lower arousal levels. However, if aggressive intent remains, "cold-blooded" aggression can still occur. Furthermore, if aggression-produced reduction of arousal feels good to the aggressor, this reward makes it more likely that aggression will occur again—another important point from social learning theory.
- Blowing off steam by hitting a punching bag or screaming may feel good to people who intuitively believe in catharsis. Yet their feelings of hostility and anger may persist—and possibly even increase.
- Even relatively low levels of aggression can chip away at restraints against more violent behaviour.

Aggressive behaviour may sometimes reduce the likelihood of further immediate aggression—but so can just letting the frustration simply dissipate over time. For that matter, a response incompatible with aggression, such as distracting oneself with laughter, can be more effective. In the long run, however, successful aggression sets the stage for more aggression later. In sum, relying on catharsis is dangerous medicine—more likely to inflame aggression than to put it out.

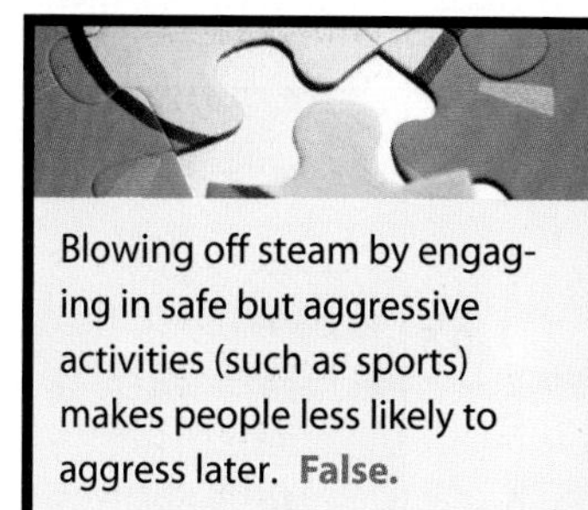

Blowing off steam by engaging in safe but aggressive activities (such as sports) makes people less likely to aggress later. **False.**

Frustration-Aggression Theory Revised After bearing so much criticism, the frustration-aggression hypothesis seemed torn and tattered. But Leonard Berkowitz's (1989) reformulation put the hypothesis in a new perspective. According to Berkowitz, frustration is but one of many unpleasant experiences that can lead to aggression by creating negative, uncomfortable feelings. It is these negative feelings, not the frustration itself that can trigger aggression. And as we'll see, negative feelings play a major role in influencing aggression.

Negative Affect

The key concept of negative affect opens all sorts of aggressive doors. In addition to frustrating experiences, a wide variety of noxious stimuli can create negative feelings and increase aggression: noise, crowding, physical pain, threatened self-esteem, bad odours, and having your home team lose a professional football playoff game (Baumeister et al., 2000; Berkowitz, 1998; Fisher et al., 1984; Geen & McCown, 1984; Panee & Ballard, 2002; Verona et al., 2002). Reactions to a very common unpleasant condition, hot weather, are especially intriguing. Many people assume that temperature and tempers rise together, while others think it's just a myth. Who is right?

Heat and Aggression: Losing Your Cool Craig Anderson and others have conducted extensive research on the question of whether heat leads to aggression; and data across time, cultures, and methodologies strongly support the notion that people lose their cool in hot temperatures and behave more aggressively (Anderson et al., 2000; Bushman et al., 2005). More violent crimes occur in the summer than in the winter, during hot years than in cooler years, and in hot cities than in cooler cities at any given time of year. The numbers of political uprisings, riots, homicides, assaults, rapes, and reports of violence all peak in the summer months (see Figure 11.5).

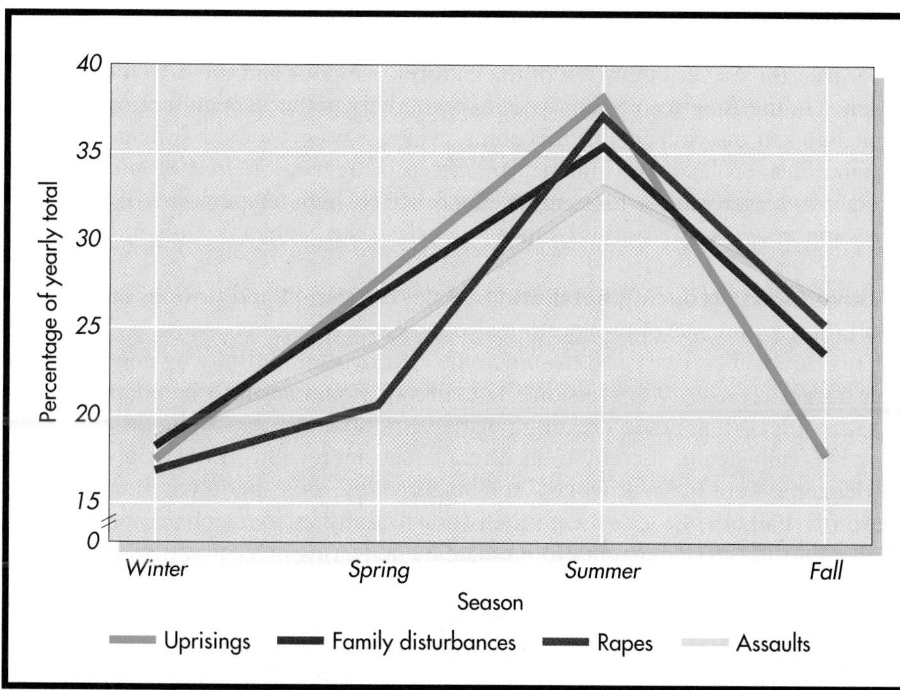

FIGURE 11.5

The Link Between Heat and Violence

Worldwide weather records and crime statistics reveal that more violent crimes are committed during the summer than in the other seasons. *(Anderson, 1989.)*

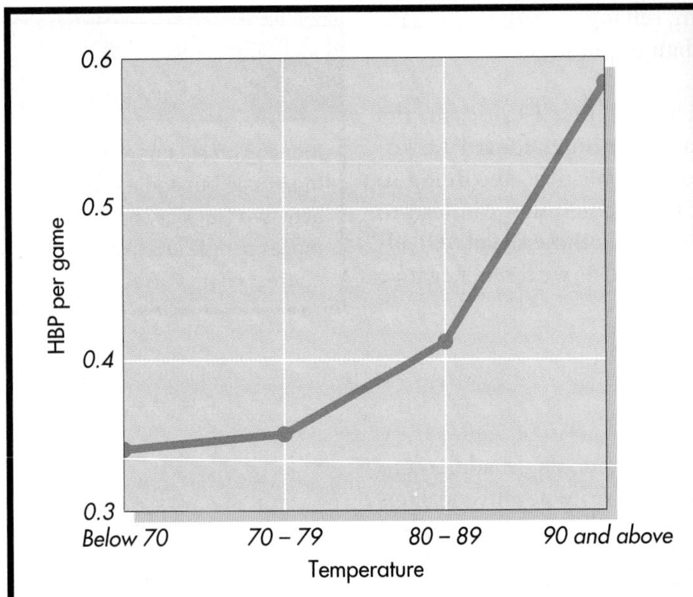

FIGURE 11.6

Temper and Temperature in Baseball

This figure shows the average number of players hit by pitches (HBPs) per game during the 1986 through 1988 Major League Baseball seasons. As the temperature increased, so did the likelihood that pitchers would hit batters (with balls often thrown around 90 miles per hour and often thrown at a batter's head). Players' general wildness or fatigue, as measured by walks, wild pitches, passed balls, and errors, did not increase with temperature, suggesting that the heat-HBP correlation may be due to hotter temperatures—and hotter tempers. *(Reifman et al., 1991.)*

Indirect acts of aggression also increase in excessive heat. As temperatures rise to uncomfortable levels, laboratory participants become more likely to interpret ambiguous events in hostile terms (Rule et al., 1987), and drivers in cars without air-conditioning become more likely to honk their horns at motorists whose cars are stalled in front of them (Kenrick & MacFarlane, 1986). Alan Reifman and others (1991) found that as the temperature rises, Major League Baseball pitchers are more likely to hit batters with a pitch; the pitchers aren't wilder in general (such as in their number of walks or wild pitches)—just more likely to hit batters (see Figure 11.6).

Interestingly, uncomfortably cold temperatures may also increase aggressiveness, although people typically are better able to find relief from the cold than from the heat. In laboratory settings in which such escape is not available, aversively cold conditions do increase aggression (Anderson et al., 2000).

Given the earlier discussion of the culture of honour and the high incidence of violence in the American South, you may wonder whether it is culture or heat that contributes to the violence. At this point, evidence points to both influences as important. Each probably has independent effects on aggression. In addition, they may interact with each other—for example, the relatively high temperatures of the region may support aggressive norms (Anderson et al., 2000; Nisbett & Cohen, 1996).

Positive Affect: Reducing Retaliation Like frustration and noxious stimuli, the unpleasant experience of provocation also increases aggression. Most aggressive incidents can be directly linked to some type of provocation. But why does provocation trigger retaliatory aggression? The answer would seem to be a familiar one: negative affect. If so, then creating positive emotional reactions should cancel out negative feelings and thereby reduce retaliatory aggression. It does. In one study, participants were first provoked and angered by an experimental confederate (Baron & Ball, 1974). They were then shown funny cartoons or neutral pictures. Presented with an opportunity to retaliate by delivering electric shocks as part of a supposed learning experiment, those who had seen the cartoons delivered fewer shocks. Feeling good appears to be incompatible with anger and aggression. Feeling concerned about others has similar effects. An empathic response to another person reduces aggression against that individual (Miller & Eisenberg, 1988).

		Intensity of Physiological Arousal	
		Low	High
Type of Emotion	Negative	Aggression increases	Aggression greatly increases
	Neutral	No effect	Aggression increases
	Positive	Aggression decreases	Aggression increases or Aggression decreases

FIGURE 11.7

The Arousal-Affect Model

According to this model, aggression is influenced by both the intensity of physiological arousal and the type of emotion produced by a stimulus.

Arousal: "Wired" for Action

Research on affect clearly indicates that the type of emotion (positive or negative) influences aggression. The intensity of arousal is important as well. In Chapter 9, we described the process of *excitation transfer*, in which the arousal created by one stimulus can intensify an individual's emotional response to another stimulus (Meston & Frohlich, 2003; Zillmann, 1996, 2003). For example, men who engaged in vigorous exercise were later more attracted to an attractive female than were those who had barely moved (White et al., 1981). Physical exercise is a highly arousing but emotionally neutral experience. Can it increase aggression as well as attraction? The research of Dolf Zillmann (1983) suggests that it can. The scope of excitation transfer is not limited to physical exercise. Noise, violent motion pictures, arousing music—all have been shown to increase aggression. Heat has an interesting effect on arousal: Although people believe that heat lowers arousal, it actually increases it. This misperception makes heat a prime candidate for excitation transfer, as people are likely to misattribute arousal caused by heat to something else, such as anger, which can then lead to aggression (Anderson et al., 1996). Later in this chapter, we describe the effects of another arousing stimulus—pornography—on the inclination to aggress.

Thus far, we have treated the type of emotion and the intensity of physiological arousal as separate territories. But they can be unified. Focusing primarily on retaliatory aggression, the **arousal-affect model** (Sapolsky, 1984; Zillmann & Bryant, 1984) provides a systematic integration that summarizes a number of the findings we've discussed. As you can see in Figure 11.7, experiences that create negative emotions increase aggression; add high arousal, and the combination could be lethal. Experiences that are emotionally neutral have little impact on aggression, *unless* they are highly arousing. Experiences that create positive emotions and low arousal decrease aggression. Now comes the hard part: experiences that produce positive emotions and high arousal. Will aggression decrease because a positive emotional experience is incompatible with unpleasant angry feelings? Or will aggression increase because there's a lot of arousal available for transfer? It's a tough call and could go either way—depending on the individual, the situation, and the thoughts that come to mind. What is more clear, however, is that reducing arousal can reduce aggression. Using physiological models, Paul Tyson (1998) has proposed that relaxation techniques may be particularly effective in reducing aggressive responses to anger and arousal. Indeed, Christopher Lopata (2003) found that progressive muscle relaxation reduced the aggressiveness of elementary schoolchildren who had been classified as having emotional disabilities.

arousal-affect model The proposal that aggression is influenced by both the intensity of arousal and the type of emotion produced by a stimulus.

Thought: Automatic and Deliberate

Step by step, we have been making our way toward a comprehensive theory of social and situational influences on aggression, particularly emotional aggression. We've examined several kinds of unpleasant experiences (frustration, noxious stimuli, and provocation) that create negative affect. We've considered how changes in negative affect (decreasing it by positive emotions, intensifying it by high arousal) produce corresponding changes in aggression. The next step is to add cognition. People don't just feel; they also think. What is the role of thought in aggressive behaviour?

According to Leonard Berkowitz's **cognitive neoassociation analysis**, thought has a starring role. This theory proposes that feelings and thoughts interact. Negative affect automatically stimulates various thoughts, memories, and other reactions that are relevant to two basic tendencies: fight and flight. These automatic thoughts and reactions give rise to basic emotional experiences of anger and fear. How individuals ultimately respond to these automatic thoughts and emotions is influenced by subsequent higher-order cognitive processing. People interpret the situation they are in ("Was that an insult or a joke?"), think about how they feel ("How angry am I?"), make causal attributions for what led them to feel this way ("I'm angry because of that remark"), and weigh the consequences of acting on their feelings ("What would be the risk of retaliation?"). These thoughts produce more clearly differentiated feelings of anger or fear, as well as intentions to act (Berkowitz, 1993).

Let's take a closer look at two major influences on cognition: situational cues, which trigger automatic thoughts, and cognitive mediators, which influence more deliberate, higher-order thinking.

Automatic Cognition: Situational Cues The deadliest aggression in the United States comes from the barrel of a gun. The statistics are staggering. No other stable, industrialized country in the world comes even close to the United States in terms of the prevalence of guns used in violent crime. In fact, the large majority of murders in that country are committed with guns. According to one report, every day over 100 000 children carry guns to school, and gun-related violence kills an American child every three hours (Geen & Donnerstein, 1998). In contrast, Canada, which has strict gun laws, saw a total of 842 gun-related deaths across the country in 2001.

Faced with the gruesome American statistics, the National Rifle Association (NRA) responds that guns should not be blamed. People, the NRA says, pull the trigger. Guns are the instrument, not the cause. But are guns entirely neutral? Or does the presence of a weapon act as a situational cue that automatically triggers aggressive thoughts and feelings, thereby increasing the likelihood of aggression? In a classic study designed to address these questions, male participants who had been provoked by an experimental confederate delivered more shocks to him when a revolver and rifle were present (allegedly for use in a different study) than when badminton racquets and shuttlecocks were scattered about (Berkowitz & LePage, 1967). This tendency for the presence of guns to increase aggression is called the **weapons effect**. As Berkowitz put it: "The finger pulls the trigger, but the trigger may also be pulling the finger" (1968, p. 22).

More recent studies by Craig Anderson and others (1998) have provided data in support of the weapons effect. In these studies, participants exposed to pictures of guns automatically activated aggression-related thoughts. They were more likely to have words like *assault*, *butcher*, *punch*, and *torture* accessible in their minds than were participants exposed to neutral pictures.

In general, any object or external characteristic that is associated with (1) successful aggression or (2) the negative affect of pain or unpleasantness can serve as an aggression-enhancing situational cue (Berkowitz, 1993, 1998). Such cues can have

cognitive neoassociation analysis The view that unpleasant experiences create negative affect, which in turn stimulates associations connected with anger and fear. Emotional and behavioural outcomes then depend, at least in part, on higher-order cognitive processing.

weapons effect The tendency of weapons to increase the likelihood of aggression by their mere presence.

very strong effects, increasing people's hostility and likelihood of aggressing. In addition, stimuli that would not serve as aggression-enhancing cues for some people can be aggression-enhancing cues for others. People who tend to be aggressive associate significantly more cues with aggression and hostility than do people who are not as chronically aggressive; thus, they are particularly prone to automatically activating aggression-related thoughts (Bushman, 1996, 1998).

Higher-Order Cognition: Cognitive Control Situational cues affect a network of automatic associations. More complex information about one's situation, however, influences the deliberate, thoughtful consideration that we call higher-order cognitive processing. For example, an angry person might refrain from acting aggressively if the potential costs of fighting seem too high. In this case, the person might choose to flee rather than fight. In addition, people whose cognitive beliefs about the acceptability of aggression imply that aggression is inappropriate in a particular situation, or whose moral values and principles mandate nonviolent behaviour, may realize that better alternatives to aggression exist (Bandura et al., 1996; Huesmann & Guerra, 1997). The behaviour of other people in the immediate situation can also influence an individual's considerations. If one or more others in a group are reacting aggressively to the situation, aggression can be contagious (Levy & Nail, 1993).

People's thoughts about the intentions of other people can determine whether they are likely to respond aggressively. For example, what if a person who has injured you claims that the action was unintentional? You have to think it over and decide whether you're convinced. If you are, the person may get a pass, and you are less likely to be angry or aggressive in response. **Mitigating information** indicating that an individual should not be held responsible for aggressive acts should also diminish perceived intent to harm—particularly if the other person is aware of the mitigating information before being provoked. Sometimes, however, mitigating information is "too little, too late" (Dill & Anderson, 1995, Zillmann, 1996).

Perhaps because it reduces the perception of intent, apologizing for having hurt someone reduces the victim's tendency to retaliate (Ohbuchi et al., 1989). Indeed, one strategy suggested to curb "road rage" is to encourage drivers to offer nonverbal apologies to other drivers whom they may have angered. A company in Scotland marketed a road rage–reducing electronic device that mounted inside a car's rear window and flashed friendly messages such as "Thanks" and "Sorry" to other motorists (Johnson, 2000).

Some people react to apologies with understanding. Others—especially those who exhibit a **hostile attribution bias**—tend to perceive hostile intent in others. For example, socially maladjusted children who are chronically aggressive and have been rejected by their peers see hostile intent where others don't (Crick & Dodge, 1994). Such perceptions then increase their aggression, and their peers respond by rejecting them further, locking these children into an ever-escalating vicious cycle. Chronically aggressive adults, too, tend to expect and perceive hostility in others' motives and behaviours (Dill et al., 1997). Individuals also differ in terms of how they manage and express their anger. Some people tend to react to anger in constructive ways, such as by initiating communication designed to resolve conflict. Others react more destructively, lashing out at those around them (Eisenberg et al., 1992; Tangney et al., 1996).

Alcohol Some conditions make it more difficult to engage in the higher-order processing that can inhibit aggressive impulses. High arousal, for example, impairs the cognitive control of aggression (Zillmann et al., 1975). So does alcohol. Alcohol is implicated in the majority of violent crimes, suicides, and automobile fatalities. The evidence is quite clear about this point: Alcohol consumption often increases aggressive behaviour (Bushman & Cooper, 1990; Leonard et al., 2003). Even

mitigating information Information about a person's situation indicating that he or she should not be held fully responsible for aggressive actions.

hostile attribution bias The tendency to perceive hostile intent in others.

FIGURE 11.8

A Model of Situational Influences on Emotional Aggression

Unpleasant experiences and situational cues can trigger negative affect, high arousal, and aggression-related thoughts. Due to individual differences, some people are more likely than others to experience these feelings and thoughts. Higher-order thinking then shapes these feelings and thoughts into more well-defined emotions and behavioural intentions. Depending on the outcome of this thinking (which can occur beneath the individual's conscious awareness and can be affected by factors such as alcohol or stress), the individual may choose to aggress. *(Based on Anderson et al., 1996.)*

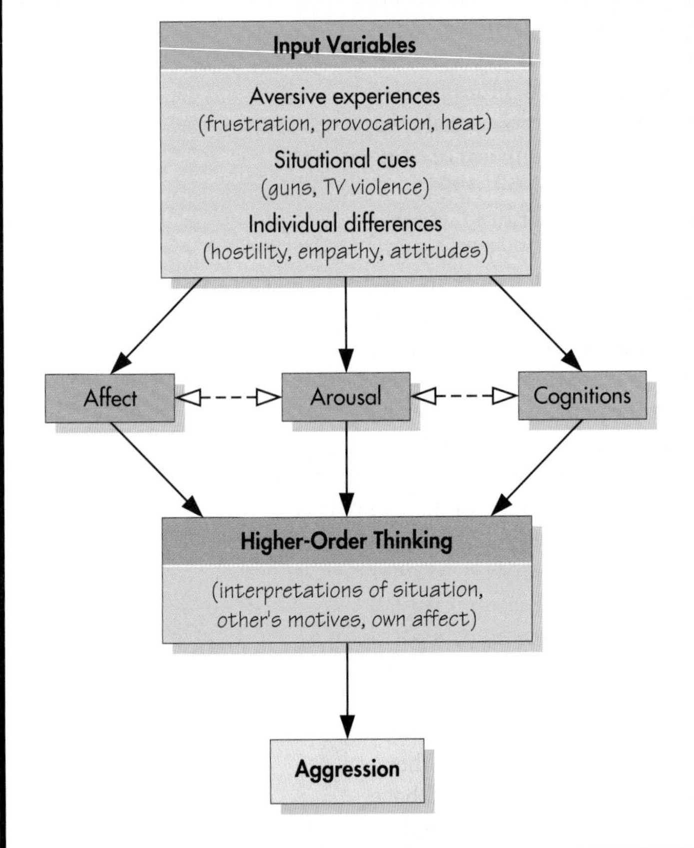

among individuals who are usually not aggressive, those who drink more, aggress more (Bailey & Taylor, 1991; Pihl et al., 1997). However, Hoaken and Pihl (2000) found that when highly provoked, both sober and intoxicated women behaved in a similar fashion to intoxicated men; thus alcohol is not always a determining factor.

But *how* does alcohol increase aggression? A meta-analysis of 49 studies indicates that alcohol reduces anxiety, which in turn lowers people's inhibitions against aggressing (Ito et al., 1996). In addition, drinking disrupts the way we process information (Leonard, 1989). For example, Claude Steele and Robert Josephs (1990) propose that intoxication causes *alcohol myopia.* That is, it narrows people's focus of attention. Intoxicated people respond to initial, salient information about the situation but often miss later, more subtle indicators. Alcohol myopia is related to potentially destructive behaviour other than aggression, such as intentions to engage in risky sexual behaviour (MacDonald et al., 2000). In combination with the reduced inhibitions that alcohol can produce, this behaviour can be lethal.

Situational Influences: Putting It All Together

We have seen that negative affect, arousal, and aggression-related thoughts can lead to aggression. And a number of factors influence whether one is likely to experience negative affect, arousal, and aggressive thoughts, such as aversive experiences (frustration, crowding, heat, provocation), situational cues (guns, violent movies), and individual and cultural differences (chronic hostility, cultures of honour). Figure 11.8 diagrams how these various factors interact to lead to emotional aggression.

Media Effects: Scenes of Violence

Having looked at origins and specific factors that contribute to aggression, we now focus on a special topic that has been a major concern of politicians, families, and social scientists alike for many years: violence in television, film, and other media. We explore two types of mass media presentations—nonsexual violence and pornography—in which the display of aggression may elicit more of it.

Violence in TV, Movies, Music Lyrics, and Video Games

According to a recent review of television and violence, there are more television sets in the North America than there are toilets (Bushman & Huesmann, 2001). And according to many observers, it is the toilet where much of the TV content belongs.

Can playing violent video games cause children and young adults to become more aggressive and violent? A growing body of research suggests that it can.

Violence depicted in the media has been a target of attack and counterattack for decades. But the amount, intensity, and graphic nature of the violence have continued to escalate. One Canadian study examined almost 700 shows on six different networks during one week in March over four years. They recorded over 10 000 acts of physical and psychological violence and noted that violent acts had increased 50 percent between 1995 and 1998. Private networks in particular were three times more likely to show violent shows than were public networks. Interestingly, it is estimated that 80 percent of the violent programming in Canada originates in the US (Paquette & de Guise, 2006).

The most violent TV shows ironically enough are targeted to children directly—namely, cartoons and other children's programming (*National Television Violence Study*, 1998). At the same time, children and adolescents are heavily exposed to violent depictions in movies, video games, and virtual reality games. Particularly popular among young males is "professional" wrestling, which in recent years has become increasingly violent and graphic. Young men and women are also heavy consumers of music that includes violent imagery in its lyrics and accompanying videos.

There is no question, then, that children, as well as adults, are exposed to a tremendous amount of violence through the media. People in industrialized societies spend more of their leisure time with electronic media than with any other activity, and it is clear that violent imagery is rampant. But does exposure to such imagery have any effect on real-world aggression and violence? If consumers didn't enjoy violence in their steady diet of TV, film, music, and video games, these media would not be featuring it. So can it really be harmful? We explore this question in the sections that follow.

Linking Media Violence to Real-World Violence Does life imitate art? Sometimes it seems that way. Brad Bushman, whose work is cited in several places in this chapter, first became interested in research on media violence when a store owner he knew was the victim of a heinous crime: Two armed men came into the store and forced the owner and customers into the basement, forced them to drink Drano (a highly corrosive, toxic fluid used to clean plumbing pipes), and put duct tape over their mouths. The day prior to the attack, these men had allegedly watched (three times) the Clint Eastwood movie *Magnum Force*, which features a scene depicting this very act of brutality (Leland, 1995). In Ottawa in 1994, a 21-year-old man died after lying in the middle of a highway; he reportedly got the idea from the movie *The Program* where this particular act was glorified as a way to earn respect and show team spirit. In January 2006, two Toronto teenagers were in court facing charges that their street-racing led to the death of a cab driver. A copy of the video game "Need for Speed"—a game about drag racing and evading police—was found in one of the cars. Yet no one can ever prove that a specific fictional depiction was the primary cause of a specific act of violence. There are always other possibilities.

If you ask people whether exposure to media violence causes real aggression, most would probably say that they doubt that it does, or that there has never been clear evidence one way or another on this question. When this issue is discussed on the news or in the media in general, the reports tend to conclude that the relevant scientific evidence is weak and mixed, at best. Defenders of the entertainment industry consistently argue that there is no evidence that viewing media violence causes real-world aggression.

But what does the social psychological research *really* say on this matter? Here, we do not need to qualify the answer with "It depends." Although media violence is neither a necessary nor a sufficient cause of real-world aggression and violence (that is, exposure to media violence does not necessarily cause one to aggress, nor is it ever the only cause of an act of aggression or violence), the evidence is impressive and clear: Media violence contributes to real aggression and violence. In one review, Brad Bushman and Rowell Huesmann (2001) asked and answered this question emphatically: "Does TV violence have any effect on aggressive and violent behaviour of children? The answer is yes! The scientific evidence . . . is overwhelming on this point. The relation between TV violence and aggression is about as strong as the relation between smoking and cancer" (p. 223). Figure 11.9 illustrates the relative magnitude of the correlation between TV violence and aggression.

What is the evidence behind these numbers and conclusions? Studying the effects of media violence on real-world aggression is particularly challenging because

FIGURE 11.9

How Strong Is the Relationship Between Media Violence and Real-World Aggression?

The correlation between exposure to violence in the media and aggressive behaviour is compared here to the correlations of several other well-established relationships. This comparison illustrates the relative magnitude of the link between media violence and aggressive behaviour. *(Bushman & Huesmann, 2001.)*

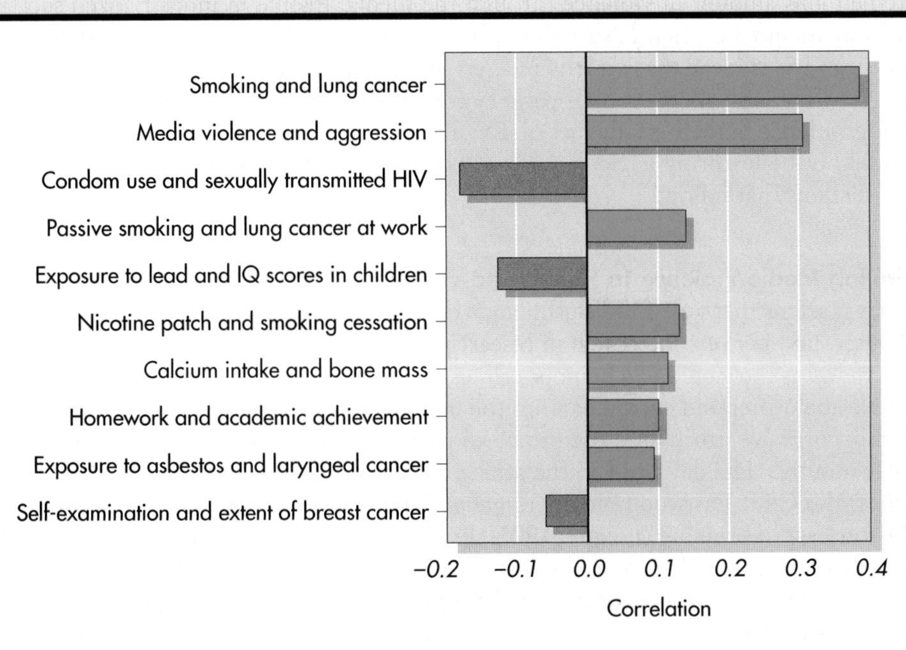

while correlational studies cannot determine causality, experiments are limited due to practical and ethical constraints. For instance, ethical considerations would not allow researchers to conduct experiments to study the kinds of real-world aggression that we want to understand. Therefore, the measures of aggression that are used in experiments may seem far removed from real-world murder and mayhem, such as participants' ratings of someone harshly or how much electric shock they decide to administer to another person. The best way to investigate the issue of media violence, therefore, is to use multiple methods, each of which has different sets of strengths and weaknesses. This is exactly what researchers in this area have done. What has been particularly impressive about this research is that the results have been strikingly consistent across methods.

Researchers have employed laboratory experiments, field experiments, cross-sectional surveys (which look, at one point in time, at the relation between individuals' exposure to violent media and their aggressive behaviour), and longitudinal studies (which examine individuals' exposure to violent media early in life and then examine their real-world aggression years later). Laboratory experiments offer the best control of variables and insight into causality, whereas the surveys and longitudinal studies are the most naturalistic and assess the most serious kinds of aggression and violence. In one extensive review, researchers examined the relationship between exposure to media violence and real aggression in 46 longitudinal studies, 86 cross-sectional surveys, 28 field experiments, and 124 laboratory experiments—totalling more than 50 000 participants. As can be seen in Figure 11.10, the magnitude of the positive relationship between exposure to media violence and real aggressive behaviour was consistent across all four types of studies, with the laboratory experiments tending to show the strongest effects and the other three types of studies showing only slightly weaker relationships (Anderson & Bushman, 2002a; Anderson et al., 2004).

Of course, the media do not operate in a vacuum. People are influenced by their families, peers, social values, and opportunities for education and employment. Nor are all individuals the same; differences in personality can heat up or tone down the impact of exposure to aggressive displays. Media effects tend to be especially strong among people who are high in trait aggressiveness, irritability, or hostility as well as among those who lack empathy (Anderson & Bushman, 2002b; Bushman & Huesmann, 2001; Fein & Eustis, 2001; Zillmann & Weaver, 1997).

The effects of media violence can be immediate as well as long-term. We consider both types of effects in the following section.

Immediate Effects Research under controlled conditions in the laboratory has amply documented that aggressive models, live or on film, increase aggressive behaviour among children and adults (Bushman & Huesmann, 2001; Smith & Donnerstein, 1998). When exposure to violent images is manipulated in an experiment, the causal effect is clear. With control, however, comes artificiality—causing some to doubt whether what is found in the lab will also occur in the real world (e.g., Freedman, 1988). Others, however, defend laboratory experiments

FIGURE 11.10

Media Violence Effects Across Types of Studies

This figure depicts the correlation between exposure to media violence and real aggression in laboratory experiments, field experiments, cross-sectional surveys, and longitudinal studies. Despite the very different methods used in these types of studies, the effect sizes are quite consistent—pointing to a positive association between media violence and real aggression. *(Anderson & Bushman, 2002a.)*

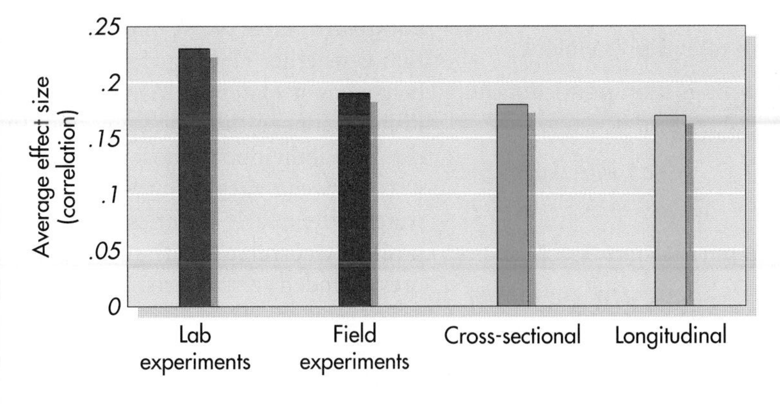

Rap star 50 Cent has achieved a great deal of popularity and acclaim over the past several years, while at the same time sparking controversy because of the violent nature of many of his songs. In December 2005, he was granted a temporary resident visa so that he could perform in Canada, after a Canadian MP tried to keep him out of Canada based on his criminal record and violent lyrics.

as valid and meaningful (Anderson et al., 1999). Field experiments in a real-world setting such as a school offer one way to address this issue. When Wendy Wood and her colleagues (1991) examined both laboratory and field experiments conducted with children and adolescents, they found that exposure to aggressive films increased aggressive behaviour in the laboratory, the classroom, the lunchroom, the playground, and the athletic field. Although the laboratory experiments produced somewhat stronger results than those conducted in natural environments, the aggression-inducing effects of filmed models occurred in both types of settings.

Researchers have also looked at effects of violent imagery in the music industry. Many music videos and song lyrics depict violence and sexual aggression or promote negative, hostile attitudes toward women (and, to a lesser extent, toward men). Rap and heavy metal music have received particular attention in this regard. James Johnson and his colleagues (1995) found that young black men expressed greater acceptance of violence in general and violence toward women in particular—and a higher probability that they would engage in violence—if they had recently been exposed to violent rap music videos than if they had not. Several other studies have illustrated similar effects of gangsta rap and rock music videos (Hansen, 1995). Craig Anderson and others (2003) found across a series of experiments using different types of songs that students who heard songs with violent lyrics felt more hostile and had more aggressive thoughts than did students who heard nonviolent songs.

Today's video games are not only more popular than ever before but also are more graphically violent. Here, too, the statistics are staggering. North American youth spend countless hours playing these games, many of which involve a "first-person shooter" format whereby players view the action through a character's eyes, rehearsing extremely violent behaviours over and over. Research has yielded evidence that suggests both a strong correlation and a causal relationship between playing these games and behaving aggressively. A recent meta-analysis of video game studies, consisting of both experimental and correlational methods, reports that exposure to violent video games is significantly linked to increases in aggressive behaviour, aggressive cognitions, aggressive affect, and physiological arousal, and to decreases in helping behaviour (Anderson, 2004b). Because of the sexual and sexist overtones of many video games, they may also promote sexist attitudes and behaviours (Dietz, 1998). Steven Fein and Emily Eustis (2001) found that among male students with higher-than-average levels of hostility, the attitudes they expressed were more sexist following their participation in a video game that featured sexist behaviour.

"I see television's violent content as therapeutic for the population."

—Jib Fowles, author of *The Case for Television Violence*

"The pervasiveness of false beliefs about catharsis makes them potentially harmful."

—Social psychologists Brad Bushman and Roy Baumeister

Long-Term Effects A question that has received a tremendous amount of attention is whether viewing violence at an early age is associated with more aggressive behaviour at a later age. Most of the relevant research aimed at answering this question has concentrated on television. In one ambitious longitudinal study, for example, 329 individuals whose TV viewing habits had first been assessed when they were between ages 6 and 9 were studied approximately 15 years later, when they were in their early twenties. Their exposure to TV violence at ages six to nine was positively correlated with measures of their aggression as adults (these adult measures included self-reports, reports of them given by others, and archival data such as criminal records). The relationship was especially strong among individuals who had identified strongly with aggressive same-sex TV characters as children or who had perceived the TV violence as realistic. The connection between childhood TV viewing and adult aggression was evident for both males and females. The relationship also held true for measures of indirect aggression among women (Huesmann et al., 2003).

In an extensive cross-cultural study, Rowell Huesmann and Leonard Eron (1986) collaborated with researchers around the world to examine the relationship between TV violence and aggression among children in five different countries: Australia, Finland, Israel, Poland, and the United States. They found evidence of a connection between early viewing of TV violence and later aggression for children in Finland, Poland, the United States, and urban areas in Israel. No such connection was established for Australian children or for those living on kibbutzim in Israel. The researchers believe that the correlation found among the children living on kibbutzim was weak because in this setting children watch very little violent TV. When they do, it is likely followed by a discussion of the implications of the violence—which may offer a lesson for all of us (Donnerstein, 2005).

These findings raise another question as well: How can childhood exposure to violent images have long-term effects on adult aggression? One way is by influencing our values and attitudes toward aggression, making it seem more legitimate and even necessary for social interaction and resolution of social conflicts. Through the processes of social learning, children may learn that aggression and violence are common, normal ways of dealing with threats or problems and may even be rewarding. Frequent exposure to such imagery fuels the aggression scripts that children and adolescents develop, which they subsequently use to guide their behaviour (Anderson & Huesmann, 2003).

Attitudes can also be affected through the process of **habituation**. A novel stimulus gets our attention and, if it's sufficiently interesting or exciting, elicits physiological arousal. But when we get used to something, our reactions diminish. Familiarity with violence reduces physiological arousal to new incidents of violence (Geen, 1981; Thomas, 1982). Desensitized to violence, we may become more accepting of it. For example, in one study, fourth- and fifth-grade girls and boys watched either a condensed version of the movie *The Karate Kid*, which depicts several brutal fights, or nonviolent scenes of Olympic competition. The students then saw two children on a TV monitor (the children supposedly were in an adjacent room) become violent toward each other. The students who had watched *The Karate Kid* were slower to seek out help, tolerating the violence more than the other children did (Molitor & Hirsch, 1994).

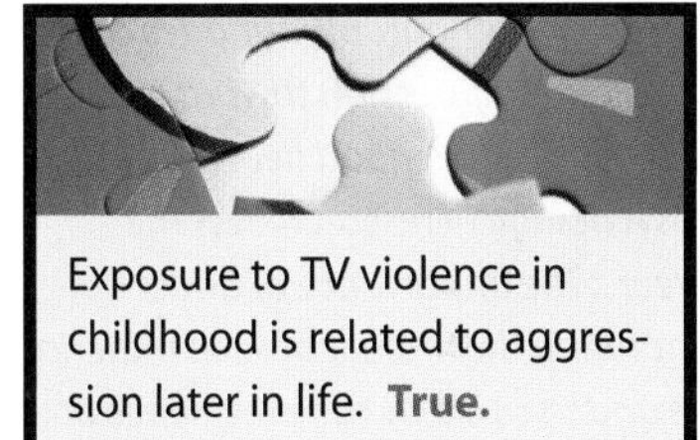

Exposure to TV violence in childhood is related to aggression later in life. **True.**

Another way that depictions of violence could change values and attitudes is through what George Gerbner and his colleagues (1986) call **cultivation**. Cultivation refers to the capacity of the mass media to construct a social reality that people perceive as true, even if it isn't. The media tend to depict the world as much more violent than it actually is. This can make people become more fearful, more distrustful, more likely to arm themselves, and more likely to behave aggressively in what they perceive as a threatening situation (Nabi & Sullivan, 2001).

Pornography

Just as citizens, scientists, and politicians have been concerned about the consequences of mass media presentations of violence, they have also been troubled by mass media displays of sexual material. Such displays are highly visible and widely available. Books, magazines, videos, and Internet sites cater to a wide range of sexual interests. Heavy metal, electronica, and rap groups often rely on obscenities to get their fans' attention. Dial-a-porn lines rake in millions of dollars. Opposition to pornography is equally prominent. Parents, religious leaders, consumer groups, and feminist activists lobby legislators and go to court to obtain greater restraints on the availability of sexually explicit materials.

In a recent meta-analysis of 46 published studies, Elizabeth Oddone-Paolucci

habituation Adaptation to something familiar, so that both physiological and psychological responses are reduced.

cultivation The process by which the mass media (particularly television) construct a version of social reality for the public.

The question of whether exposure to erotic or pornographic images can influence aggression toward women has triggered a good deal of social psychological research over the years. The importance of understanding the impact of such material is underscored by the prevalence of such images in our society, such as this billboard in Windsor, Ontario. It was part of a series of ads that featured women in suggestive poses holding air hoses, hammers, and tape measures.

and others (2000) found that men were significantly more likely to report sexually aggressive behaviours and attitudes if they also reported exposure to pornography. Of course, this correlational evidence does not prove that pornography caused these behaviours and attitudes; indeed, such evidence must be supported by experimental research, which we review later. But it is important to recognize the challenges of conducting research on such a controversial and sensitive issue. Even defining the variables is rarely straightforward. Attempts to ban specific works, such as James Joyce's novel *Ulysses* and Robert Mapplethorpe's photos, indicate that the definitions of such terms as *obscenity*, *erotica*, and *pornography* are often a matter of personal opinion. One person's smut is another person's masterpiece. Because of the subjectivity in such definitions, the term **pornography** is used here to refer to explicit sexual material, regardless of its moral or aesthetic qualities. It is crucial, however, to distinguish between nonviolent and violent pornography in discussing the relationship between pornographic displays and aggression.

Nonviolent Pornography Earlier in this chapter, we described the arousal-affect model, which proposes that both the type of emotion and the intensity of arousal produced by a stimulus influence aggression. The results of research on nonviolent pornography confirm the importance of these factors (Donnerstein et al., 1987). For many people, viewing attractive nudes elicits a pleasant emotional response and low levels of sexual arousal. Such materials usually reduce retaliatory aggression against a same-sex confederate. However, most people are more disturbed by crude displays of sexual activities. Their emotional response is negative, and their arousal is heightened by alarm, sexual feelings, or both. These kinds of pornographic materials usually increase aggression toward a same-sex confederate.

But what about aggression toward the opposite sex? Since the vast majority of pornography is designed to appeal to heterosexual males, investigators have been especially interested in whether pornographic materials have a specific effect on men's aggression against women. It does, but only when restraints that ordinarily inhibit male-to-female aggression are reduced such as when there are repeated opportunities to aggress (Donnerstein & Hallam, 1978).

In general, though, according to Michael Seto and colleagues (2001), there is little support for a direct causal link between pornography use and sexual aggression. These researchers do note, however, that men who are already predisposed to sexually offend are the most likely to be affected by pornography exposure. This latter point is also consistent with a conclusion reached by Neil Malamuth and others (2000). They propose that relatively aggressive men may interpret and react to the same images differently than less aggressive men, making them more likely to be affected by them in negative ways.

pornography Explicit sexual material.

Violent Pornography Adding violence to pornography greatly increases the possibility of harmful effects. Violent pornography is a triple threat: It brings together high arousal; negative emotional reactions such as shock, alarm, and disgust; and aggressive thoughts. According to a meta-analysis of 217 studies on the relationship between TV violence and aggression, violent pornography had a stronger effect than any other type of program (Paik & Comstock, 1994). And there is substantial evidence that this effect is gender-specific. Male-to-male aggression is no greater after exposure to violent pornography than after exposure to highly arousing but nonviolent pornography. Male-to-female aggression, however, is markedly increased (Donnerstein & Malamuth, 1997; Linz et al., 1987; Malamuth & Donnerstein, 1982).

Like most experiences that intensify arousal (such as physical exercise), nonviolent pornography increases aggression only among individuals who have been provoked. But, like guns and alcohol, some violent pornography can increase aggression even in the absence of provocation. The prime ingredient in such materials is the portrayal of women as willing participants who "enjoy" their own victimization. In one study (Donnerstein & Berkowitz, 1981), violent pornography that emphasized the victim's suffering increased aggression only among men who had been provoked. But films that depicted female sexual arousal in response to acts of sexual violence increased aggression among both provoked and unprovoked male participants (see Figure 11.11).

Not everyone is affected by violent pornography in the same way. Neil Malamuth has developed what he calls the "rapist's profile." Men fit the profile if they have relatively high levels of sexual arousal in response to violent pornography and also express attitudes and opinions indicating acceptance of violence toward women (see Table 11.3). These individuals report more sexually coercive behaviour in the past and more sexually aggressive intentions for the future. Among male students given an opportunity to retaliate against a female confederate who had angered them, those who fit the rapist's profile were more aggressive (Malamuth, 1983, 1986). In another study illustrating the volatile mix of negative attitudes and violent pornography, Dano Demaré and his colleagues (1993) found that male students'

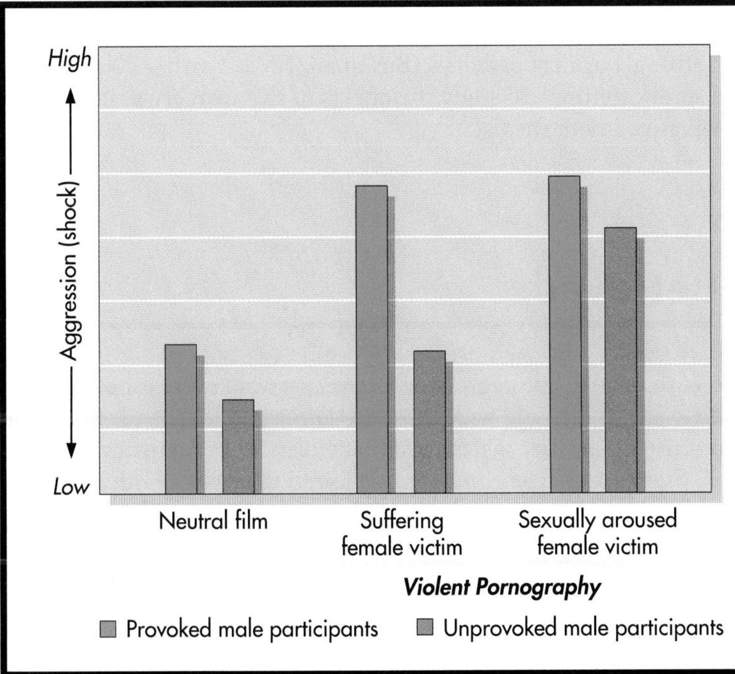

FIGURE 11.11

When Provocation Isn't Necessary

Arousing stimuli usually increase aggression only when someone is angry because of a previous provocation. Accordingly, violent pornography depicting a suffering female victim significantly increased aggression only among provoked male participants in this study. As you can see, however, violent pornographic films depicting a sexually aroused female victim increased aggression even among unprovoked men. *(Data from Donnerstein & Berkowitz, 1981; figure adapted from Donnerstein et al., 1987.)*

TABLE 11.3

Attitudes About Sex and Aggression

Widely used in research on pornography, these two scales assess attitudes about violence toward women and beliefs about the nature of rape. A few items from each scale are shown here. *(Based on Burt, 1980.)*

Acceptance of Interpersonal Violence (Toward Women): AIV Scale

1. Being roughed up is sexually stimulating to many women.
2. Many times a woman will pretend she doesn't want to have intercourse because she doesn't want to seem loose, but she's really hoping the man will force her.
3. A man is never justified in hitting his wife.

Scoring: Persons scoring high in acceptance of violence toward women agree with items 1 and 2 but disagree with item 3.

Rape Myth Acceptance: RMA Scale

1. If a woman engages in necking or petting and she lets things get out of hand, it is her own fault if her partner forces sex on her.
2. Any female can get raped.
3. Many women have an unconscious wish to be raped, and may then unconsciously set up a situation in which they are likely to be attacked.
4. In the majority of rapes, the victim is promiscuous or has a bad reputation.

Scoring: Persons scoring high in acceptance of rape myths agree with items 1, 3, and 4 but disagree with item 2.

negative attitudes toward women and their frequent consumption of violent pornography each predicted the students' self-reported sexually aggressive intentions; the best prediction, however, was obtained when both pornography *and* attitudes were included in the equation.

The potential dangers of mixing violence and sexual arousal are not limited to the pornography industry. Many popular movies, video games, and music videos also mix the two frequently and strategically. This has been true in the movie industry since the time of silent movies, in which the hero saves the damsel in distress, who is perhaps tied to the train tracks; and it continues a century later as action movies try to top each other with increasingly arousing, graphic scenes of fighting and sex. Meanwhile, professional wrestling organizations have become notorious for their accelerating use of violence and sexual imagery targeted to young males. Numerous Internet sites—including many that are free and can be viewed easily by minors—focus specifically on images of sexual violence against women, and they use the many depictions of women's pain as a selling point (Gossett & Byrne, 2002). Defenders claim that viewing such material is harmless at worst—and at best offers a cathartic release for viewers, thereby reducing real-world violence. Opponents cite evidence pointing strongly against catharsis (Bushman, 2002; Fowles, 2000). Social psychologists will surely continue to study the effects of this imagery as it becomes more and more pervasive in our media.

Intimate Violence: Trust Betrayed

All violence is shocking, but aggression between intimates is especially disturbing. We want to feel safe with those we know and love; and yet far too often, that sense of security is destroyed by violence. In Statistics Canada's *1999 General Social Survey on Victimization*, it was found that while both Canadian men and women encounter similar rates of violence in their relationships, the severity of the violence is much greater for women. For example, women are six times more likely to report being sexually assaulted by their partner, and more than twice as likely to report being beaten. The victims of intimate violence are children as well as adults, and the assault that takes place is often sexual as well as physical. In this section, we examine three major types of intimate violence: sexual aggression among students, physical aggression between partners, and child abuse.

Sexual Aggression Among University Students

Acquaintance rape (often called "date rape") is a serious problem among university students. In Canada, more than 20 percent of women on university campuses said they had had unwanted sexual intercourse because they were overwhelmed by their male partner. When all types of unwanted sexual interactions are included, a majority of women and about a third of men say they have experienced coercive sexual contact (Cate & Lloyd, 1992; De Keseredy et al., 1993); Struckman-Johnson & Struckman-Johnson, 1994).

A number of factors are associated with sexual aggression among university students. Two of the most important are gender and alcohol. First, both men and women report that men are more likely to engage in coercive behaviour—psychological as well as physical—in order to obtain sex (Poppen & Segal, 1988). Second, alcohol consumption is involved in a majority of sexually aggressive incidents between university students (Cate & Lloyd, 1992). Not only does actual consumption increase aggressive behaviour, but the mere *belief* that one has consumed alcohol (even if one hasn't) heightens sexual arousal and sexual interest (Baron & Richardson, 1994). The cognitive effects of intoxication, in which salient cues are noticed but subtle ones are missed, may disrupt interpersonal communication; and the anxiety-reducing effects of intoxication may weaken inhibitions against aggressive behaviour. These conclusions are consistent with the results of an experiment by Brian Marx and others (1999) in which male students listened to an audiotape of a simulated date rape. As illustrated in Figure 11.12, those participants who had consumed alcohol took significantly longer to determine that the man should refrain from attempting further sexual contact with the woman. A recent particularly disturbing development has been the growing use of so-called date-rape drugs, such as Rohypnol (sometimes called "Roofies") or Gamma Hydroxy Butyrate (GHB, sometimes called "Liquid Ecstasy"), to render a person, often a date, helpless. Numerous stories around the world have documented its use in acquaintance rape, such as by secretly putting the drug in a target's drink at a club or party.

A third important factor concerns attitudes toward rape and toward women. As we indicated earlier, men who fit Malamuth's concept of the rapist's profile—relatively high sexual arousal in response to violent pornography and attitudes indicating acceptance of violence toward women—report using more sexually coercive behaviour. Both men and women who express greater acceptance of rape myths (again, see Table 11.4) also report greater use of coercive and aggressive tactics of sexual influence. Men's rape myth attitudes are also associated with hostility toward women, which itself promotes the use of these aggressive tactics (Malamuth, 1996). Men who are self-centred rather than sensitive to others' needs and who have very impersonal, noncommittal, game-playing orientations in sexual relations are also more likely to engage in sexually aggressive behaviour (Dean & Malamuth, 1997; Malamuth, 1996). In light of these findings, it is encouraging that rape-awareness workshops appear to reduce acceptance of rape myths and increase sympathy for female rape victims (Hong, 2000; Proto-Campise et al., 1998). Education has a crucial role to play in reducing sexual aggression.

FIGURE 11.12

Alcohol and Perception of Sexual Aggression

Male students listened to an audiotape of what was designed to sound like a date rape. Before listening to the tape, some of the men consumed alcohol and others did not. The experimenter recorded how long it took each participant to determine that the man on the tape should stop attempting further sexual contact with the woman. Students who consumed alcohol took significantly longer to determine that the man should refrain from attempting further sexual contact. *(Marx et al. 1999.)*

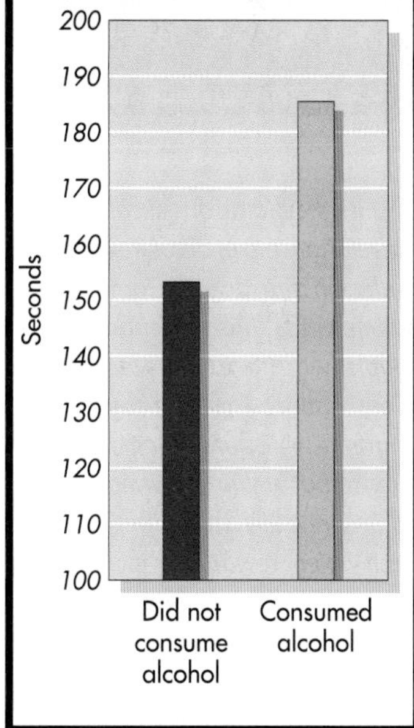

Physical Aggression Between Partners

In 2000, there were 67 Canadians who were killed by their either their current or former spouse, according to a Statistics Canada report. This was an overall decrease of 65 percent based on 1974 statistics. Partner abuse is not limited to Canada; it is a worldwide phenomenon. Neither is it a new development; it has occurred throughout history. Indeed, evolutionary psychologists point to a number of factors that predict such behaviour from an evolutionary perspective, including males' concerns about

Men are much more likely than women to aggress against their spouses or partners. **False.**

Despite their fame and wealth, the relationship of actor Pamela Anderson and rock star Tommy Lee has elements shared by many couples who have been scarred by spousal abuse. The early days of their marriage were passionate and intense, but within a few years Pamela revealed that Tommy had been violent toward her, including in front of their two young children. In 1998 Tommy was sentenced to six months in prison for felony spousal abuse. Pamela said that she feared for the children's safety and divorced Tommy. Several years later, Pamela briefly accepted Tommy back into her life as they appeared together (above) in October 2003, at the premiere of her movie, Scary Movie 3.

paternity (in particular, uncertainty over whether they are the biological fathers of their children). These concerns are known to fuel intense sexual jealousy and distrust, both of which have been implicated in a large percentage of spousal homicides and acts of physical aggression (Buss & Duntley, 2005; Shackelford, 2001; Shackelford & Goetz, 2005). Only in recent years, however, has a concerted effort been made to document the extent of this often very private form of violence—for example, through national surveys.

One of the most surprising results of national surveys in 1975 and 1985 was the high level of wife-to-husband violence, which in terms of severe violence (such as kicking, hitting, beating, threatening with a weapon, and using a weapon) was consistently higher than the level of husband-to-wife abuse. Prospective research on aggression during the first years of marriage also found higher rates of wife-to-husband abuse (O'Leary et al., 1989). These statistics were initially met with doubt, but they have since received support from the results of research by Murray Straus and his colleagues (Straus, 1999; Straus & Ramirez, 2005) and from a series of meta-analyses conducted by John Archer (2000, 2005), involving more than 80 published articles, books, and other sources of data concerning aggression between heterosexual partners in Canada, the United States, the United Kingdom, and three other countries.

These statistics tell only part of the story. Although women may aggress against men in intimate relationships as much or somewhat more than vice versa, the consequences of aggression between partners tend to be much more damaging to women, who are more often killed, seriously injured, or sexually assaulted during domestic disputes than are men (Archer, 2000, 2005; Straus & Ramirez, 2005). As Barbara Morse (1995) put it, "Women were more often the victims of severe partner assault and injury not because men strike more often, but because men strike harder" (p. 251).

Like most aggressive actions, violence between partners is caused by multiple factors. Among the factors associated with increased partner aggression are personal characteristics (such as age, attitudes toward violence, drug and alcohol abuse, and personality), socioeconomic status (which includes income and education), interpersonal conflict, stress, social isolation, and the experience of growing up in a violent family (Herzberger, 1996, 2005; Tjaden & Thoennes, 2000).

Child Abuse

Children who grow up in a violent family not only witness aggression; they often bear the brunt of it. Tragically, child abuse is not a rare occurrence. While it is difficult to get accurate estimates of child abuse, due to the hidden nature of the crime, a 1998 study estimated that more than 135 000 Canadian children had been abused. In 2001, there were 89 murders of children across Canada; 32 were killed by their biological mother or father. David Finkelhor and Jennifer Dziuba-Leatherman (1994) conclude that the available evidence "strongly suggests that children are more victimized than adults are" (p. 173).

Children are abused by strangers as well as by family members, but severe abuse, particularly of young children, is more often inflicted by parents and caretakers. Boys suffer more physical abuse than do girls, and mothers are more likely than fathers to physically abuse their children (Straus et al., 1980). In contrast, girls suffer more sexual abuse than do boys, and fathers are more likely than mothers to sexually abuse their children (Russell, 1984).

Like partner aggression, child abuse is multiply determined. Among the factors associated with increased child abuse are personal characteristics of the abusing parent (such as personality and substance abuse) and of the child (younger children are more often abused by family members); the family's socioeconomic status; stressful experiences; social isolation; marital conflict; and the abusing parent's having been abused as a child (Belsky, 1993; Davies & Cummings, 1994; Herzberger, 1996, 2005).

The Cycle of Family Violence At this point, you should begin to see a pattern emerging: the connection between violence in childhood and violence as an adult. This connection is called the **cycle of family violence**. Children who witness parental violence or who are themselves abused are more likely as adults to inflict abuse on intimate partners or their children, or, perhaps, to be victims of intimate violence (Brems & Namyniuk, 2002; Heyman & Slep, 2002; Malinosky-Rummell & Hansen, 1993; Simons et al., 1993; Tjaden & Thoennes, 2000). In turn, their children are more likely to interact violently with each other and to aggress against their parents (Patterson, 1984; Peek et al., 1985). This intergenerational transmission of domestic violence is by no means inevitable, however. Most people who witness or experience abuse in their families of origin are not abusive or abused in their families of procreation. The cycle of family violence refers to a greater tendency, not an absolute certainty.

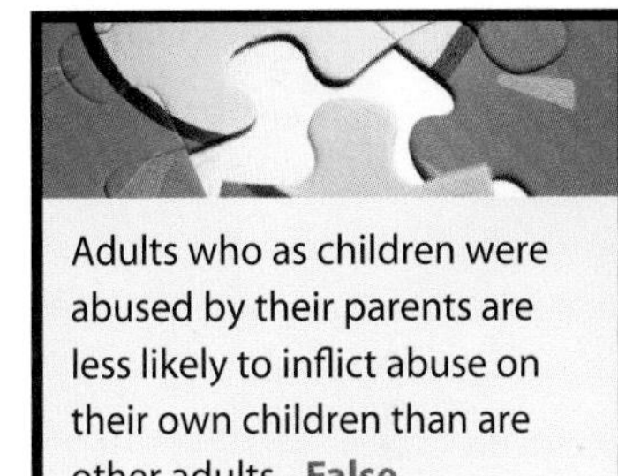

Adults who as children were abused by their parents are less likely to inflict abuse on their own children than are other adults. **False.**

Reducing Violence

Multiple Causes, Multiple Cures

A variety of factors can contribute to aggression—and, as we have seen, the impact of any one factor often involves other factors simultaneously. Hot temperatures, for instance, influence arousal and aggressive thoughts as well as affect. The effects of watching violence in the media may depend on the chronic level of hostility that a viewer has. Thus we cannot hope for a single, simple cure. The most effective strategies for reducing aggression recognize this complexity and work on multiple levels (Goldstein, 1999). Indeed, one of the most successful treatment programs for violent juvenile delinquents is called *multisystemic therapy*. This approach addresses individuals' problems at several different levels, including the needs of the adolescents and the many contexts in which they are embedded, such as family, peer group, school, and neighbourhood (Borduin et al., 2003; Huey et al., 2000).

Situational and Sociocultural Factors What about steps to reduce aggression more generally? Given that negative affect and thinking contribute to aggression, reducing stressors such as frustration, discomfort, and provocation should reduce aggression. Toward this end, an improved economy, healthier living conditions, and social support are extremely important. The prevalence of weapons has also been

cycle of family violence
The transmission of domestic violence across generations.

associated with aggressive thoughts and emotions. Reducing the number of guns may reduce not only access to the weapons but also the incidence of such thoughts and emotions. At the same time, teaching and modeling nonviolent responses to frustrations and social problems—and encouraging thoughtful responses incompatible with anger, such as humour and relaxation—are among the most effective things we can do for our society's children, and for each other.

Having observed the relative nonviolence of cultures that emphasize cooperation over competitiveness, social psychologists have concluded that cooperation and shared goals across groups are effective methods for reducing intergroup hostilities and aggression. In addition, because communities beset by broken windows and petty crime reveal a loss of control and support—thus possibly signalling to those who live there that aggression and antisocial behaviour are left unpunished—police departments in numerous cities have begun to crack down on relatively minor acts of vandalism and aggression in the hope that doing so will prevent more serious acts of violence (Taylor, 2000). Finally, changing the cost-reward payoffs associated with aggression can have profound effects on the aggressive tendencies exhibited within a culture. Socialization practices that reward prosocial rather than antisocial behaviour therefore have the potential to greatly reduce the tendency among boys, in particular, to engage in bullying, fighting, and other aggressive behaviours. Conversely, when violence is legitimized, we are all at risk.

Media Effects The media, of course, play an important role in legitimizing—even glorifying—violence. What, then, can we do about it? Government censorship is one answer; but it is not a very popular one, for a number of reasons. Another alternative is to use public pressure to increase media self-censorship. Of course, the most powerful kind of public pressure would be a commercial boycott. If violence did not sell, the media would not produce it. Unfortunately, however, violence continues to be a moneymaker.

At this point, education may well be the most effective approach. For example, treatment programs have been developed to curb children's undesirable reactions to TV (Eron, 1986; Singer & Singer, 1983). These programs recommend that parents select shows that provide compelling, vivid prosocial models for their children. An extensive review by Susan Hearold (1986) is encouraging in this regard. As discussed in Chapter 10, her analysis indicated that prosocial TV programs produce stronger effects on behaviour than do antisocial TV programs. Parents have also been advised to watch television with their children and to teach them how TV differs from real life, how imitating TV characters can produce undesirable outcomes, and how children might be harmed by watching TV (Huesmann et al., 1983). This kind of ongoing parental tutorial takes significant time and effort. But given the extent of media depictions of violence in our society, strengthening children's critical viewing skills is a wise investment.

The question of what to do about the potentially harmful effects of pornography leads to the same options described for depictions of nonsexual violence. Should pornography be banned? Should consumers be educated? Banning pornography raises a number of philosophical, political, and practical concerns. In addition, banning explicit sexual material would not prevent dehumanizing portrayals of women as sex objects or titillating but fully clothed scenes of rape and sexual assault.

According to Daniel Linz and his colleagues (1992), the real villains are violence, sexual or not, and the demeaning and degrading messages about women contained in pornographic depictions, violent or not. These researchers encourage educational efforts to increase viewers' critical skills in evaluating media depictions of violence and sex. A model for such efforts can be found in the debriefing provided to research participants exposed to violent pornography in experiments

(Donnerstein et al., 1987). This debriefing emphasizes that rape myths are inaccurate and that violent pornography is unrealistic. Among individuals presented with this information, there are long-term reductions in acceptance of rape myths.

Intimate Violence Sex-education programs that emphasize the desirability of being respectful and considerate toward one's sexual partner, in addition to rape-awareness programs that debunk various rape myths and increase sensitivity can be important tools in the effort to reduce sexual aggression. Many university campuses experience persistent problems with alcohol abuse, which can be a key factor in many rapes and other forms of sexual aggression. Preventing and treating alcohol abuse, therefore, can make for healthier, safer campuses.

Family violence, too, is a matter of grave societal concern; and, since it is caused by multiple factors, it must be addressed by a variety of approaches. Laws and programs that protect victims of abuse and reduce the likelihood of continued violence by abusers are vitally important. But family violence takes place in a larger context. According to Jay Belsky (1993), poverty is "undoubtedly the major risk for child abuse and neglect" (p. 428). Thus, protecting families from violence also requires providing family members with educational and employment opportunities. Furthermore, because abuse of alcohol and other drugs so often leads to family violence, better education about the effects of such substances, as well as support for individuals who need help dealing with them, would be a worthy investment not only for these individuals but also for the people around them.

Ultimately, effective communication is the key to reducing intimate violence. Jealousy and distrust contribute to much of the violence that occurs between intimate partners. Insensitivities to others' needs and fears, as well as acceptance of myths about rape, play important roles in sexual aggression. And children who grow up in abusive homes may learn aggressive scripts that teach them that the best way to respond to social problems is through aggression. Better communication can help address all of these problems.

Conclusions

We conclude where we began, by discussing the recent wave of gun violence in Canada. A review of this chapter will reveal social psychological research in each section that is relevant to various aspects of the lives of the children involved in these shootings. Some of the perpetrators grew up in a "culture of honour" that may have glorified violence in response to perceived threats to their status and manhood. Many experienced great frustrations in their lives, felt isolated and lonely, had easy access to weapons and hate-filled propaganda, and were "consumers" of brutal violence in TV shows, movies, and video games. Some were exposed to abuse within their families.

> **"Since war begins in the minds of men, it is in the minds of men that the defenses of peace must be constructed."**
>
> —Constitution of UNESCO

There exists no single profile of the kind of student who is most likely to lash out violently. Rather, the best way to predict those most likely to aggress is to listen to what the students themselves have to say, as many of them reveal, in one way or another, their aggressive thoughts and hostile attitudes. This conclusion parallels the crucial point we have already stated: Communication and social support are critically important factors in reducing violence.

Table 11.4 lists some of the possible steps suggested by the research we've reviewed. Personally, you may not agree that all of these actions are desirable—and you may prefer others that are not mentioned. What's important is to realize that each of us can do something to reduce aggression. There are many paths to take toward this common goal. And because aggression is caused by multiple factors, it is only through multiple paths that we can reach this goal.

TABLE 11.4

Some Steps to Reduce Aggression and Violence

Although there may be reasons to endorse or reject these ideas, social psychological research on aggression suggests that each has the potential to reduce aggression.

- Enlarge opportunities to achieve the goals valued by society (such as social approval, status, financial success) through nonviolent means.
- Reward nonaggressive behaviour.
- Provide attractive models of peaceful behaviour.
- Reduce all forms of aggression in our society, including physical punishment of children, capital punishment of criminals, and war.
- Reduce frustration by improving the quality of life in housing, health care, employment, and child care.
- Provide fans and air-conditioned shelters when it's hot.
- Reduce access to and display of weapons.
- Apologize when you've angered someone, and regard apologies as a sign of strength—not weakness. Encourage others to do likewise.
- Stop and think when you feel your temper rising. Control it instead of letting it control you.
- Discourage excessive drinking of alcohol and support efforts to provide treatment for alcohol abuse.
- Develop good communication skills in families and relationships, thereby helping to avoid misperceptions, jealousy, and distrust.
- Pay attention and respond to warning signs of trouble in adolescents, including social isolation, talk of violence, and consumption of violence-filled literature and other media.

Review

What Is Aggression?

- Aggression is behaviour intended to harm another individual.
- Anger is an emotional response to perceived injury; hostility is an antagonistic attitude.
- Instrumental aggression is a means to obtain a desired outcome.
- In emotional aggression, harm is inflicted for its own sake.

Cultural and Gender Differences

Cultural Variation

- The rates of violence and the forms violence takes vary dramatically from one society to another.
- Within a society, different subcultures exhibit different norms concerning aggression.
- Teenagers and young adults, and people in the Southern US (compared to northern states) are the groups most prone to violence.

Gender Differences

- Men are more violent than women in virtually every culture and time period that has been studied.
- Males tend to be more overtly, physically aggressive than females.
- Females are often more indirectly, or relationally, aggressive than males.
- When clearly provoked, women are often as overtly aggressive as men.

Origins of Aggression

Is Aggression Innate?

- Both Freud and Lorenz regarded aggression as an innate instinct, but the circular reasoning of such instinct theories is unscientific.
- Evolutionary psychology views aggression as a universal, innate characteristic that has evolved from natural and sexual selection pressures.
- Evolutionary accounts propose that gender differences in aggression can be traced to competition for status (and the most desirable mates) and sexual jealousy.
- Some research suggests that individual differences in aggression are produced by genetic inheritance, but the overall evidence is somewhat mixed.
- The sex hormone testosterone and the neurotransmitter serotonin appear to play roles in human aggression.
- Biological factors interact with social factors in producing or regulating aggression.

Is Aggression Learned?

- Aggression is increased by rewards.
- Aggression is decreased by punishment only under specific conditions that are often not met in the real world.
- Physical punishment of children is associated with increases in their subsequent aggressive behaviour.
- Social learning theory emphasizes the influence of models on the behaviour of observers.
- Models who obtain desired goals through the use of aggression and are not punished for their behaviour are the most likely to be imitated. But even punished models may encourage aggression by observers.
- Aggressive models teach not only specific behaviours but also more general attitudes and ideas about aggression.
- Peaceful models can decrease aggressive responses by observers.
- Gender and cultural differences in human aggression may be due in part to differences in socialization practices—lessons taught, reinforcements and punishments given, models offered, and roles and norms emphasized.
- A culture of honour promotes status-protecting aggression among white males in the American South and West, as well as among men in other parts of the world, such as in Brazil.

Nature Versus Nurture: A False Debate?

- Human aggression clearly is affected by learning and experience.
- In aggression, as in all human behaviour, biological and environmental influences interact.

Situational Influences on Aggression

Frustration: Aggression as a Drive

- The frustration-aggression hypothesis proposes that frustration produces the motive to aggress and that aggression is caused by frustration.
- But, in fact, frustration produces many motives, and aggression is caused by many factors.
- According to the frustration-aggression hypothesis, displacement occurs if aggression against the source of frustration is inhibited.
- The frustration-aggression hypothesis holds that engaging in any aggressive action reduces the motive to engage in further aggression, a process called catharsis.
- In the long run, however, aggression now is likely to increase aggression later.
- Frustration is only one of a number of unpleasant experiences that produce negative affect and increase aggression.
- Some studies support the idea of displacement of aggression; however, most research does not support the idea of catharsis as an effective means to reduce aggression.

Negative Affect

- A wide variety of noxious stimuli can create negative feelings and increase aggression.
- Hot temperatures are associated with increased aggression and violence.
- Being attacked or insulted by someone is another experience that produces negative affect, and retaliation to provocation is a major source of aggressive behaviour.
- Positive emotional responses are incompatible with negative affect and reduce retaliatory aggression.

Arousal: "Wired" for Action

- Highly arousing stimuli, neutral as well as negative, increase retaliatory aggression.
- The arousal-affect model proposes that both the type of emotion and the intensity of arousal influence aggression, which is greatest in response to experiences that combine negative affect and high arousal.

Thought: Automatic and Deliberate

- Berkowitz's cognitive-neoassociation analysis of aggression proposes that unpleasant experiences create negative affect, which in turn stimulates automatic associations connected with anger and fear. Behavioural and emotional outcomes then depend, at least in part, on higher-order cognitive processing.
- Situational cues associated with aggression, such as the presence of a gun, can automatically activate aggression-related thoughts and increase aggressive behaviour.

- More deliberate thoughts that affect aggression include the perception of intent, which is reduced by mitigating information indicating that a person was not fully responsible for harmful acts.
- Individual differences, such as in chronic aggressiveness, influence how individuals interpret the aggression-related motives of others and how they react to mitigating information.
- High arousal impairs the cognitive control of aggression, as does alcohol.

Situational Influences: Putting It All Together

- Aggression is influenced by separate and interactive influences of affect, arousal, and cognitions.

Media Effects: Scenes of Violence

Violence in TV, Movies, Music Lyrics, and Video Games

- There is a tremendous amount of violence depicted in the media, and much of it is targeted to children and adolescents.
- A large number of studies, using a variety of different methods, have by now shown a significant positive relationship between exposure to media violence and real-world aggressive cognitions and behaviours.
- In laboratory and field experiments, exposure to aggressive models increases aggressive behaviour among adults and children.
- Exposure to TV violence in childhood is related to aggression later in life.
- Observing violence in the media can encourage imitation and the development of aggressive scripts, which can guide subsequent behaviour.
- Since we habituate to familiar stimuli, repeated observations of violence reduce physiological arousal to new incidents but may make aggression more acceptable.
- Through cultivation of a social reality, the mass media can intensify fear of aggression and encourage aggressive behaviour.

Pornography

- Nonviolent pornography that is only mildly arousing reduces retaliatory aggression against someone of the same sex.
- When normative restraints against male-to-female aggression are reduced, nonviolent but arousing pornography increases male-to-female aggression more than male-to-male aggression.
- In general, the evidence pointing to a causal link between viewing nonviolent pornography and aggressive behaviour is weak, but the effect is stronger among individuals who are already predisposed to sexual aggression.
- Violent pornography increases male-to-female aggression more than male-to-male aggression.
- When a female is portrayed as enjoying violent sex, even unprovoked men become more aggressive and more accepting of violence against women.
- The combination of interest in violent pornography and negative attitudes toward women is a strong predictor of self-reported sexual aggression in the past and sexually aggressive intentions for the future.

Intimate Violence: Trust Betrayed

Sexual Aggression Among University Students

- Men are more likely than women to engage in sexually coercive behaviour.
- Alcohol consumption is involved in a majority of sexually aggressive incidents.
- Attitudes toward rape and toward women are associated with coercive sexual behaviour.

Physical Aggression Between Partners

- Sexual jealousy and distrust fuel a great deal of violence between intimate partners.
- National surveys reveal that women engage in more aggressive behaviour against a partner than do men; but women are more likely to be killed, seriously injured, or sexually abused by a partner.

Child Abuse

- A shockingly high number of children are victimized—often by parents and caretakers.
- Children who witness parental violence or are themselves abused are more likely as adults to abuse their partners and their own children. But most people escape from this cycle of family violence.

Reducing Violence

Multiple Causes, Multiple Cures

- Recognizing that aggression has multiple levels of causes, multisystemic therapy has been effective in reducing aggressive behaviours among violent adolescents.
- Situational and sociocultural factors that can help reduce violence include avoidance of negative affect, aggressive thinking, the presence of weapons, competitiveness, minor acts of aggression and vandalism, and social rewards for aggressive behaviour. Also useful is the modeling of nonviolent responses to social problems.
- Educational efforts emphasizing the unrealistic nature of

violent pornography have proved effective in reducing acceptance of rape myths.

- Sex-education and rape-awareness programs can be effective in helping prevent sexual aggression.
- Because of the role of alcohol in rape and other forms of sexual aggression, it is all the more important for university campuses to develop more effective prevention and treatments of alcohol abuse.
- Protecting the victims of family violence and preventing its recurrence require a wide range of interventions.

Conclusions

- Communication and social support are critically important factors in reducing violence.

Key Terms

aggression *(379)*
arousal-affect model *(399)*
catharsis *(395)*
cognitive neoassociation analysis *(400)*
cultivation *(407)*
cycle of family violence *(413)*
displacement *(395)*
emotional aggression *(380)*
frustration-aggression hypothesis *(395)*
habituation *(407)*
hostile attribution bias *(401)*
instrumental aggression *(380)*
mitigating information *(401)*
pornography *(408)*
social learning theory *(390)*
weapons effect *(400)*

In virtually every culture, males are more violent than females.

True. *In almost every culture and time period that have been studied, men commit the large majority of violent crimes.*

For virtually any category of aggression, males are more aggressive than females.

False. *Girls are often more indirectly, or relationally, aggressive than boys; and women often exhibit levels of aggression similar to men's when they have been provoked or when they feel relatively anonymous and deindividuated.*

Children who are spanked or otherwise physically disciplined (but not abused) for behaving aggressively tend to become less aggressive.

False. *Evidence indicates that the use of even a little physical punishment to discipline children is associated with increases in subsequent aggressive and antisocial behaviour by the children, even years later, although this relationship may depend on a variety of other factors.*

Blowing off steam by engaging in safe but aggressive activities (such as sports) makes people less likely to aggress later.

False. *Although people may be less likely to aggress immediately after such activities, initial aggression makes future aggression more, not less, likely.*

Exposure to TV violence in childhood is related to aggression later in life.

True. *Laboratory experiments, field experiments, and correlational research all suggest a link between exposure to violence on TV and subsequent aggressive behaviour.*

Men are much more likely than women to aggress against their spouses or partners.

False. *Some evidence suggests that women engage in more acts of serious aggression against their partners than men do; but men are much more likely to injure, sexually abuse, or kill their partners.*

Adults who as children were abused by their parents are less likely to inflict abuse on their own children than are other adults.

False. *Although most people who have experienced such abuse do break the cycle of family violence, on average they are more likely to abuse their own children than are people who have never experienced parental abuse.*

12 Law

OUTLINE

PREVIEW

THIS CHAPTER examines applications of social psychology to the law. First, we consider three stages in the life of a jury trial: *jury selection,* an often controversial process; *the courtroom drama* in which confessions, eyewitness identifications, and other types of evidence are presented; and *jury deliberation,* where the jury reaches a group decision. Next, we consider *post-trial factors* such as sentencing and prison, the possible result of a guilty verdict. Finally, we discuss *perceptions of justice* both inside and outside the courtroom.

PUTTING COMMON SENSE TO THE TEST

T / F

___ **Contrary to popular opinion, women are harsher as criminal trial jurors than men are.**

___ **Without being beaten or threatened, innocent people sometimes confess to crimes they did not commit.**

___ **A person can fool a lie-detector test by suppressing arousal when questions about the crime are asked.**

___ **Eyewitnesses find it relatively difficult to recognize members of a race other than their own.**

___ **The more confident an eyewitness is about an identification, the more accurate it is likely to be.**

___ **One can usually predict a jury's final verdict by knowing where the individual jurors stand the first time they vote.**

It seems there is always a high-profile trial in the news that spotlights a crime of sex, violence, money, passion, or celebrity, and captures our interest. The twenty-first century is still young, and yet we have already witnessed the very public legal woes of media mogul Conrad Black facing charges of money laundering and racketeering; the bizarre child molestation case in California against pop star Michael Jackson; the US government securities fraud and obstruction case against Martha Stewart, the well-known TV homemaker and former CEO of Martha Stewart Living; and the trial for Robert Pickton, the British Columbia pig farmer accused of murdering at least 26 women who disappeared from downtown Vancouver between 1995 and 2002, is well underway. Overseas, ex-president Saddam Hussein, defeated in war and captured, was tried in Baghdad for crimes committed against the people of Iraq and executed.

Regardless of how you feel about these cases, they illustrate the profound importance of social psychology at work in the legal system. There are many questions raised, at least in the Canadian cases: What kinds of people do lawyers think make good jurors, and why? Can partisans set aside their biases in decision-making? How reliable are confessions, eyewitnesses, and other types of evidence presented in court? Are decision makers contaminated by pretrial publicity and other information not in evidence? How do judges and juries reach their decisions after days, weeks, or months of presentations, often followed by exhausting deliberation? In this chapter, we take social psychology into the courtroom to answer these questions. But first, let's place the trial process in a broader context.

In the North American criminal justice system, trials are just the tip of an iceberg. Once a crime takes place, it must be detected and reported if it is to receive further attention. Through investigation, the police must then find a suspect and decide whether to make an arrest. If they do, the suspect is jailed or bail is set, and then the courts decide if there is sufficient evidence for a formal accusation. If there is, the Crown counsel and defence lawyers begin a lengthy process known as "discovery," during which they gather evidence. At this point, many defendants plead guilty as part of a deal negotiated by the lawyers. In cases that do go to trial, the ordeal does not then end with a verdict. After conviction, the judge imposes a sentence, and the defendant decides whether to appeal to a higher court. For those in prison, decisions concerning their release are made by parole boards.

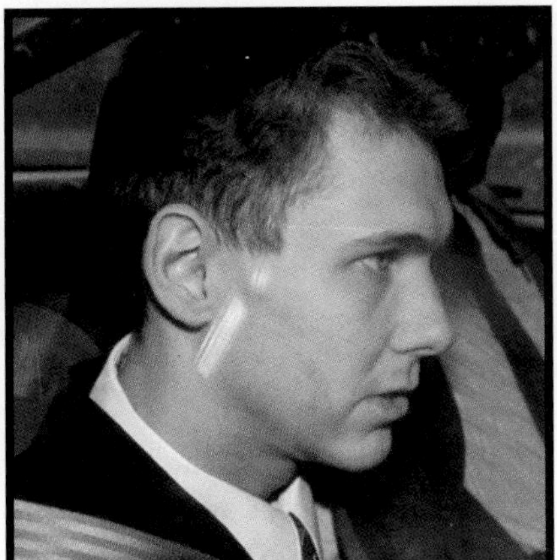

North Americans are fascinated by trials, particularly when they involve celebrities, sensational details, and horrific crimes. In recent years, high-profile trials involved Martha Stewart, the famous TV homemaker who was found guilty of lying in a securities fraud investigation (left); Paul Bernardo (middle), responsible for the murders of two young school girls; and Kobe Bryant, the NBA basketball star who was accused of rape in a Colorado hotel (right).

The criminal justice apparatus is complex, and the actors behind the scenes are numerous. Yet through it all, the trial—a relatively infrequent event—is the heart and soul of the system. The threat of trial motivates parties to gather evidence and, later, to negotiate a deal. And when it's over, the trial by judge or jury forms the basis for sentencing and appeals decisions. Social psychologists have a lot to say about trials and other aspects of the legal system as well (Costa, 2004; Memo et al., 2003; Wrightsman et al., 2002). At present, for example, researchers are looking at the extent to which law enforcement professionals can tell when someone is lying (Vrij, 2000), at how juries make decisions in civil cases involving large sums of money (Greene & Bornstein, 2003; Sustain et al., 2002), at how jurors view alibi evidence provided by a defendant (Burke et al., 2006), at how children's and adults' ability to identify a suspect is affected by the culprit changing his appearance (Pozzulo & Balfour, 2006), and at how the legal system can make juries more competent through procedural innovations (Diamond et al., 2003; Horowitz et al., 2001). In the coming pages, we divide this event into three basic stages: jury selection, the presentation of evidence, and the jury's deliberations.

Jury Selection

If you're ever accused of a crime in Canada, or involved in a lawsuit, the *Canadian Charter of Rights and Freedoms* guarantees you many rights including being presumed innocent until proven guilty; being tried within a reasonable time; and the right to a jury trial if the maximum punishment for the offense is imprisonment for five years or more. Such rights are considered essential to doing justice within a democracy. Yet it often seems that whenever a controversial verdict is reached in a high-profile case, people, right or wrong, blame the 12 individuals who constituted the jury. That's why it is important to know how juries are elected.

Voir Dire

Jury selection is a three-stage process. First, the Sheriff's office is in charge of contacting the eligible jurors, based on voter registration lists and other sources to compile a master list of eligible citizens who live in the community. Second, so that a representative sample can be obtained, a certain number of people from the list are randomly drawn and summoned for duty. Before people who appear in court are placed on a jury, the court ensures that they don't know any of the people involved in the trial, including victims, the accused, and even the police officers overseeing the case. This screening process is formally known as the **voir dire,** but its use is very limited in Canada, compared to what you might find in the United States. For example, if you have ever read a John Grisham novel, you will have read about lawyers investigating prospective jurors, learning everything they can about them before they ever come to the trial. While this makes for thrilling reading, the process is typically far less dramatic. For example, if you are called for jury duty in Canada, it is likely that all that will be known about you is your name, address, and occupation. In most cases, based on this very limited information, the lawyers can either accept the juror (and they become part of the jury in this case) or they can "challenge" (reject) them. Each side (Crown and Defense) is given a limited number of what are called **peremptory challenges**; they don't need a reason to reject a juror, but can excuse them nonetheless. What guides the decision to accept some jurors and reject others? These questions make the process of voir dire particularly interesting to social psychologists (Hans & Vidmar, 1986; Kassin & Wrightsman, 1988).

There are also unlimited challenges for "cause"; if one side feels that jurors may be biased for a particular reason, such as the ethnicity or sexual orientation of the defendant, they may ask the judge to grant them the opportunity to challenge (ask further questions of) the jurors on these issues. In order for such challenges to be granted, the need for it must be proven first; if a juror does then appear to be biased, they are excused. In fact, if it can be demonstrated that an entire community is biased, perhaps because of pretrial publicity, then the trial might be postponed or moved to another location.

Trial Lawyers as Intuitive Psychologists

Trial lawyers have been known to have some unusual ideas about who—or what—makes for a good juror. Under pressure to make choices quickly and without much information, lawyers may rely on implicit personality theories and stereotypes. As described in Chapter 4, an implicit personality theory is a set of assumptions that people make about how certain attributes are related to each other and to behaviour. When people believe that all members of a group share the same attributes, these implicit theories are called stereotypes.

Contrary to popular opinion, women are harsher as criminal trial jurors than men are. **False.**

As far as trial practice is concerned, many how-to books claim that the astute lawyer can predict a juror's verdict by his or her gender, race, occupation, ethnic heritage, and other simple demographics (Fulero & Penrod, 1990). It has been suggested, for example, that athletes lack sympathy for fragile and injured victims, that engineers are unemotional, that men with beards resist authority, and that cabinetmakers are so meticulous in their work that they are never completely satisfied with the evidence. Other lawyers have theorized that women are more skeptical as jurors than men—particularly in response to attractive female witnesses. Still others offer selection advice based on faces, body language, and clothing. Perhaps the most interesting rule of thumb is also the simplest: "If you don't like a juror's face, chances are he doesn't like yours either!" (Wishman, 1986, pp. 72–73).

If assumptions based on surface appearances were correct, it would be easy to predict how jurors would vote. But the folk wisdom of trial lawyers is not supported by research, as demographic factors such as gender, age, race, income, education, marital status, and occupation do not consistently predict juror verdicts (Hastie et al., 1983). Research has also shown that jurors who have an authoritarian personality—which leads them to identify with figures of authority, while being punitive and intolerant of others who are nonconventional—are also generally prone to convict (Narby et al., 1993).

voir dire The pretrial examination of prospective jurors by the judge or opposing lawyers to uncover signs of bias.

peremptory challenge A means by which lawyers can exclude a limited number of prospective jurors without the judge's approval.

On Saturday, December 9, 2006, more than 600 people were summoned as potential jurors in the trial of Robert "Willy" Pickton, accused of a series of grisly murders in the Vancouver area. Though the field for selection was large, the selection process lasted just two days.

Clearly, there are individual differences among jurors. But just as clearly, simple and general cookbook recipes—such as "women are tougher than men in rape cases"—can prove hopelessly misleading. Research on race effects illustrates the point. In one study, Norbert Kerr and others (1995) tested the most intuitive hypothesis of all, that jurors favour defendants who are similar to themselves. They presented mixed-race groups with a strong or weak case involving a black or white defendant. They found that when the evidence was weak, the participants were more lenient in their verdicts toward the defendant of the same race. Yet when the evidence was strong, they were harsher against that similar defendant—as if distancing themselves from his wrongdoing. In a second study, Samuel Sommers and Phoebe Ellsworth (2001) tested the popular notion that race would matter particularly for crimes that involved race and racism. Yet they found the opposite pattern. When race was a prominent issue at trial, white jurors did not want to appear prejudiced and did not discriminate. When race was not an overt issue, however, white jurors did not bend over backward to avoid prejudice, treating the defendant more favourably when he was white than when he was black. Mitchell, Haw, Pfeifer and Meissner (2005) studied this issue from a slightly different perspective; rather than focusing on a particular minority group (i.e. black or white), they instead defined racial bias as negative treatment of a member of an outgroup. When framed in this way, bias is no longer viewed as specifically a minority issue, but instead acknowledges that such treatment can occur to any member of an outgroup. Their results, based on a meta-analytic review of research in this area, found a small but reliable effect of racial bias as part of the juror decision-making process.

Clearly, the intuitive approach to jury selection is flawed. Thus, while some experienced trial attorneys take pride in their jury-selection skills, researchers have found that lawyers cannot effectively predict how jurors will vote (Kerr et al., 1991; Olczak et al., 1991; Zeisel & Diamond, 1978). Apparently, whether a juror characteristic predicts verdicts depends on the specifics of each and every case.

The Courtroom Drama

Once a jury is selected, the trial officially begins, and much of the evidence previously gathered comes to life. The evidence produced in the courtroom can range far and wide, from confessions to autopsy results, medical tests, bloodstains, hair samples, handwriting samples, diaries, fingerprints, photographs, and business documents. The trial itself is a well-orchestrated event. Lawyers for both sides make opening statements. Witnesses then answer questions under oath. Lawyers make closing arguments. The judge instructs the jury. Yet there are many problems in this all-too-human enterprise: The evidence may not be accurate or reliable, jurors may be biased by extraneous factors, and judges' instructions may fall on deaf ears. In this section, we identify some of the problems and possible solutions.

Confession Evidence

Every now and then, an extraordinary event comes along that shakes the way you think. The Central Park jogger case was one of these events. In 1989, five boys, 14 to 16 years old, were found guilty of a monstrous assault and rape of a female jogger in New York's Central Park after they confessed, four of them on videotape, in vivid detail. Thirteen years later, a serial rapist named Matias Reyes stepped forward from prison to say that he alone, not the boys, had committed the crime. As part of an investigation of Reyes's claim, the district attorney DNA-tested the semen from the crime scene and found that it was a match: Reyes was the rapist. The five boys, now men, were innocent. Their confessions were false and the convictions were vacated (Kassin, 2002; Saulny, 2002). As these events unfolded, questions mounted: Why would five boys, or anyone else for that matter, confess to a crime they did not commit? Sometimes, a false confession is voluntarily given by a suspect who perhaps is looking for some attention or notoriety. In 1967, already in prison on a robbery charge, Romeo Phillion confessed to the murder of Ottawa firefighter Leopold Roy. He immediately recanted that confession, claiming it was only meant as a "bad joke"; however that confession, joke or not, ultimately led to him spending the next 32 years in prison. More recently, police in the United States believed they had finally solved one of the most mysterious and notorious crimes of the last century when John Mark Karr confessed to the 1996 beating death of six-year-old JonBenet Ramsey. Once the forensic evidence was examined, however, it became clear he was not the killer. Besides the attention or notoriety aspect, why would anyone confess to a crime they did not commit?

Police Interrogations: Social Influence Under Pressure In general, what social influences are brought to bear on suspects interrogated by police? Many years ago, police detectives would use bright lights, brute force, the rubber hose, and physical intimidation to get confessions. Today, however, the *Charter of Rights and Freedoms* requires the police to inform suspects of their rights to silence and to legal counsel—and the "third degree" tactics they use are more psychological in nature. In *Criminal Interrogation and Confessions*, the most popular how-to manual written for the police, and used extensively throughout North America, Fred Inbau and others (2001) advise interrogators to put suspects into a small, bare, soundproof room—a physical environment designed to arouse feelings of social isolation, helplessness, and discomfort. Next, they present a vivid nine-step procedure designed to get suspects to confess (see Table 12.1). These steps are part of what is commonly referred to as the "Reid Technique."

TABLE 12.1

The Nine Steps of Interrogation *(Inbau et al., 2001.)*

1. Confront the suspect with assertions of his or her guilt.
2. Develop "themes" that appear to justify or excuse the crime.
3. Interrupt all statements of innocence and denial.
4. Overcome all of the suspect's objections to the charges.
5. Keep the increasingly passive suspect from tuning out.
6. Show sympathy and understanding, and urge the suspect to tell all.
7. Offer the suspect a face-saving explanation for his or her guilty action.
8. Get the suspect to recount the details of the crime.
9. Convert that statement into a full written confession.

In general, there are two approaches contained within this method of interrogation. One approach is to pressure the suspect into submission by expressing certainty of his or her guilt and even, at times, claiming to have damaging evidence such as fingerprints or an eyewitness. In this way, the accused is led to believe that it is futile to mount a defence. A second approach is to befriend the suspect, offer sympathy and friendly advice, and "minimize" the offence by offering face-saving excuses or blaming the victim. Lulled into a false sense of security, and led to expect leniency, the suspect caves in. These police tactics may sound as if they come from a television script, but in real life they are frequently used (Gudjonsson, 2003; Kassin,

Prisoners' rights advocates Joyce Milgaard and Ruban (Hurricane) Carter (left) outside court in Winnipeg, Manitoba, in 2003, where they were working to exonerate Jim Driskell, who they believe was wrongly convicted in 1991 for the first-degree murder of his friend Perry Harder. In 2006 a federal justice minister quashed his original conviction and ordered a new trial, but the Manitoba government has decided not to pursue this course of action.

1997; Kassin & Wrightsman, 1985; Lassiter, 2004). In an observational study of 182 live and videotaped interrogations, for example, Richard Leo (1996) found that detectives used an average of five to six tactics per suspect. Interestingly, there is nothing under Canadian law that guarantees a suspect that their solicitor will be present while they are being interrogated, *unless they specifically request it*, in which case the police must immediately comply.

The Risk of False Confessions It could be argued that the use of trickery and deception does not pose a serious problem because innocent people never confess to crimes they did not commit. This assumption, however, is not always correct. As hard as it is to believe, there are a number of chilling cases on record. In fact, among prisoners convicted and later proved innocent by DNA evidence, 20 to 25 percent had given false confessions (**www.innocenceproject.org/**).

Sometimes innocent suspects confess as an act of *compliance*, merely to escape a bad situation. Douglas Firemoon and Joel Labadie were both charged (along with another youth) in the murder of 14-year-old Regina native Darrelle Exner, after admitting they had started to walk her home the night she was killed. All three suspects were subjected to the Reid technique; after hours and hours of interrogation, they each provided details of how they committed the crime—the problem was, they were innocent. In the Central Park jogger case, the boys were in custody and interrogated by several detectives for 14 to 30 hours before giving their videotaped confessions (most interrogations last an hour or two). Very long periods of time bring fatigue, despair, and a deprivation of sleep and other need states. The jogger detectives and suspects disagree about what transpired during these unrecorded hours, so it is impossible to know for sure. The defendants claimed that they were threatened, that promises were made in exchange for cooperation, and that the crime details that appeared in their confessions were suggested to them. Put simply, they said they cooperated, thinking they would go home.

There are other instances in which interrogation causes innocent suspects to believe that they might be guilty of the crime, illustrating an even stronger form of social influence known as *internalization*. This process was evident in the story of Paul Ingram, a police officer charged with rape and a host of satanic ritual cult crimes. For a period of six months, Ingram was hypnotized, informed of graphic crime details, told by a police psychologist that sex offenders typically repress their offences, and urged by the minister of his church to confess. Eventually he "recalled" crime scenes to specification, pleaded guilty, and was sentenced to prison. In fact, there was no physical evidence that the alleged events had even occurred, and an expert who reviewed the case concluded that Ingram had been "brainwashed." At one point, this expert accused Ingram of a phoney crime. Ingram denied the charge at first, but eventually he confessed—and embellished the story in the process (Ofshe & Watters, 1994).

Is it really possible to convince people that they are guilty of an act they did not commit? Based on an analysis of actual cases, Saul Kassin and Katherine Kiechel (1996) theorized that two factors can increase this risk: (1) a suspect who lacks a clear memory of the event in question and (2) the presentation of false evidence. To test this hypothesis, they recruited pairs of students to work on a fast- or slow-paced computer task. At one point, the computer crashed, and students were accused of having caused the damage by pressing a key they had been specifically instructed to avoid. All students were truly innocent and denied the charge. In half the sessions, however, the second student (who was really a confederate) said that she had seen the student hit the forbidden key. Demonstrating the process of compliance, many students confronted by this false witness agreed to sign a confession handwritten by the experimenter. Next, demonstrating the process of internalization, some students later "admitted" their guilt to a stranger (also a confederate) after the experiment was supposedly over and the two were alone. In short, innocent people who are vulnerable to suggestion can be induced to confess and to internalize guilt by the presentation of false evidence—an interrogation tactic commonly used by the police (see Table 12.2). In this situation, false confessions have also been observed in the Netherlands, even when participants thought they would have to pay for the damage (Horselenberg et al., 2003)—and are particularly pronounced among young adolescents (Redlich & Goodman, 2003).

TABLE 12.2

Factors That Promote False Confessions

As participants worked on a fast- or slow-paced task, the computer crashed, and they were accused of causing the damage. A confederate then said that she had or had not seen the participants hit the forbidden key. As shown, many participants signed a confession (compliance), and some even "admitted" their guilt in private to another confederate (internalization). Despite their innocence, many participants in the fast-false witness condition confessed on both measures. *(Kassin & Kiechel, 1996.)*

	Control		False Witness	
	Slow	Fast	Slow	Fast
Compliance	35%	65%	89%	100%
Internalization	0%	12%	44%	65%

Confessions and the Jury: An Attributional Dilemma How does the legal system treat confessions brought out by various methods of interrogation? The procedure is straightforward. Whenever a suspect confesses but then withdraws the statement and goes to trial, the judge must determine whether the statement was voluntary or coerced. If the confession was clearly coerced—as when a suspect is isolated for a long period of time, deprived of food or sleep, threatened, or abused—it is excluded. If not, it is admitted into evidence for the jury to evaluate. Juries are thus confronted with a classic attributional dilemma: A suspect's statement may indicate guilt (personal attribution), or it may simply be a way to avoid the aversive consequences of silence (situational attribution). According to attribution theory, jurors should reject all confessions made in response to external pressure. But wait. Remember the fundamental attribution error? In Chapter 4, we saw that people tend to overattribute behaviour to persons and overlook the influence of situational forces. Is it similarly possible that jurors view suspects who confess as guilty even if they were highly pressured to confess during interrogation?

To examine this question, Kassin and Holly Sukel (1997) had mock jurors read one of three versions of a murder trial. In a control version that did not contain a confession, only 19 percent voted guilty. In a low-pressure version in which the defendant was said to have confessed immediately upon questioning, the conviction rate rose considerably, to 62 percent. But there was a third, high-pressure condition in which participants were told that the defendant had confessed out of fear and with his hands cuffed painfully behind his back. How did participants in this situation react? Reasonably, they judged the confession to be coerced, and they said it did not influence their

"Before we begin, may I ask which of you is the good cop, and which is the bad?"

verdicts. Yet the conviction rate in this situation significantly increased, this time to 50 percent. Apparently, people are powerfully influenced by evidence of a confession—even, sometimes, when they concede that this confession was coerced.

The jury's reaction to confession evidence may also depend on how that evidence is presented. Today, many police departments videotape confessions for presentation in court. But how are these events staged for the camera? As described in Chapter 4, research has shown that observers who watch two people engage in a conversation overemphasize the impact on that interaction of the person who is visually salient. Similarly, in a series of experiments, Daniel Lassiter and his colleagues (2001) taped mock confessions from three different camera angles so that either the suspect or the interrogator or both were visible. All participants heard the same exchanges of words, but those who watched the suspects saw the situations as less coercive than did those who focused on the interrogators. The practical implications are striking. When the camera directs all eyes at the accused, jurors are likely to underestimate the amount of pressure exerted by the "hidden" interrogator.

Without being beaten or threatened, innocent people sometimes confess to crimes they did not commit. **True.**

The Lie-Detector Test

Often, people confess after being told that they have failed the **polygraph**, or lie-detector test. A polygraph is an electronic instrument that simultaneously records multiple channels of physiological arousal. The signals are picked up by sensors attached to different parts of the body. For example, rubber tubes are strapped around a suspect's torso to measure breathing; blood pressure cuffs are wrapped around the upper arm to measure pulse rate; and electrodes are placed on the fingertips to record sweat-gland activity, or perspiration. These signals are then boosted by amplifiers and converted into a visual display.

The polygraph is used to detect deception on the assumption that when people lie, they become anxious in ways that can be measured. Here's how the test is conducted. After convincing a suspect that the polygraph works and establishing his or her baseline level of arousal, the examiner asks a series of yes-no questions and compares how the suspect reacts to emotionally arousing *crime-relevant questions* ("Did you steal the money?") and *control questions* that are arousing but not relevant to the crime ("Did you take anything that did not belong to you when you were young?"). In theory, suspects who are innocent—whose denials are truthful—should be more aroused by the control questions, while guilty suspects—whose denials are false—should be more aroused by the crime-relevant questions.

Does the lie-detector test really work? Many people think it is foolproof, but scientific opinion is split (Iacono & Lykken, 1997). Some researchers report accuracy rates of up to 80 to 90 percent (Honts, 1996; Raskin, 1986). Others say that such claims are exaggerated and misleading (Lykken, 1998). One well-documented problem is that truthful persons too often fail the test. A second problem is that the test can be faked. Studies show that you can beat the polygraph by tensing your muscles, squeezing your toes, or using other countermeasures while answering the *control* questions. By artificially inflating the responses to "innocent" questions, one can mask the stress that is aroused by lying on the crime-relevant questions (Honts et al., 1994).

What, then, are we to conclude? Careful reviews of the research suggest that there is no simple answer (Furedy & Heslegrave, 1991; Hont et al., 2002; Saxe et al., 1985). Under certain conditions—for example, when the suspect is naive and the examiner is competent— it is possible for the polygraph to detect truth and deception at fairly high levels of accuracy. Still, the problems are hard to overcome, which is why the Supreme Court of Canada ruled, in 1987, that polygraph test results are not admissible in courts of law. As an alternative, researchers are now trying to develop tests that distinguish between truth and deception through the measurement of involuntary electrical activity in the brain (Bashore & Rapp, 1993),

polygraph A mechanical instrument that records physiological arousal from multiple channels; it is often used as a lie-detector test.

pupil dilation when the person being tested is asked to lie, which requires more cognitive effort than telling the truth (Dionisio et al., 2001), and involuntary muscle movements in the face that betray grimaces and other expressions too subtle to detect with the naked eye (Bartlett et al., 1999). Research suggests it may even be possible to judge truth and deception by measuring how long it takes people to react to crime-relevant information, with guilty suspects taking longer to react than innocent ones (Seymour et al., 2000). Watkins and Turtle (2003) discuss the differences between research results on people's deception-detection abilities and what law enforcement training manuals often claim. Gaze aversion, for example, is often claimed to be a potential indicator of deception, yet research typically shows that there is often no difference in eye contact between deceivers and truth-tellers. And when there is a difference, it tends to be in the other direction.

A person can fool a lie-detector test by suppressing arousal when questions about the crime are asked. **False.**

Eyewitness Testimony

"I'll never forget that face!" When these words are uttered, police officers, judges, and juries all take notice. Often, however, eyewitnesses make mistakes. Consider the story of Thomas Sophonow, charged with murdering Barbara Stoppel while visiting his sister in Winnipeg, Manitoba, in 1981. Several eyewitnesses picked Sophonow out of a lineup. It seemed that the police had their killer. Sophonow spent four years in prison for this crime, although he maintained his innocence throughout. While he was eventually freed four years later, it took another 15 years before he was officially found innocent. We will discuss the factors that helped to wrongfully convict him, below.

According to Rod Lindsay of Queen's University in Kingston, Ontario, as few as 40 and as many as 300 people are wrongfully convicted each year in Canada, primarily on the basis of mistaken eyewitness identification. US figures suggest that 77 000 people a year are charged with crimes solely on the basis of eyewitness evidence (Goldstein et al., 1989). Many of these eyewitness accounts are accurate, but many are not. Studies of wrongful convictions—cases in which an individual is convicted, but later exonerated by DNA evidence—have demonstrated that the number one reason people are wrongfully convicted is mistaken eyewitness identification (CBC News: Disclosure, 2003; Connors et al., 1996; Scheck et al., 2000). In 1999, the US Department of Justice took a bold step in response to this problem, assembling a group of police, prosecutors, defence attorneys, and research psychologists (including two from Canada) to devise a set of "how-to" guidelines. Led by Gary Wells, this technical working group went on to publish *Eyewitness Evidence: A Guide for Law Enforcement* (US Department of Justice, 1999; Wells et al., 2000). Turtle, Lindsay, and Wells (2003) provide detailed explanations for the recommendations outlined in this guide.

Thomas Sophonow, despite an alibi and no physical evidence linking him to the crime, was wrongfully convicted for the murder of a 16-year-old waitress and spent four years in jail.

As eyewitnesses, people can be called upon to remember just about anything—perhaps a face, an accident, or a conversation. Over the years, hundreds of tightly controlled studies have been conducted. Based on this research, three conclusions can be drawn: (1) Eyewitnesses are imperfect, (2) certain personal and situational factors systematically influence their performance, and (3) judges, juries, and lawyers are not well informed about these factors (Cutler & Penrod, 1995; Sporer et al., 1996; Thompson et al., 1998; Wells & Olson, 2003).

People tend to think that human memory is like a videotape camera: If you turn on the power and focus the lens, all events will be recorded for subsequent playback. Unfortunately, it's not that simple. Over the years, researchers have found it useful to view memory as a three-stage process involving the *acquisition*, *storage*, and *retrieval* of information. The first of these stages, acquisition, refers to a witness's perceptions at the time of the event in question. Second, the witness stores that information in memory to avoid forgetting. Third, the witness retrieves the information from storage when needed. This model suggests that errors can occur at three different points.

Acquisition Some kinds of persons and events are more difficult to perceive than others. Common sense tells us that brief exposure time, poor lighting, distance, physical disguise, and distraction can all limit a witness's perceptions. Research has uncovered other, less obvious factors as well.

Consider the effects of a witness's emotional state. Often people are asked to recall a bloody shooting, or a car wreck, or an assault—emotional events that trigger high levels of stress. Arousal has a complex effect on memory. Realizing the importance of what they are seeing, highly aroused witnesses zoom in on the central features of an event—perhaps the culprit, the victim, or a weapon. As a direct result of this narrowed field of attention, however, arousal impairs a witness's memory for other less central details (Brown, 2003; Christianson, 1992). Alcohol, a drug often involved in crime, also causes problems. When participants in one study witnessed a live staged crime, those who had earlier consumed fruit juice were more accurate in their recollections than were those who had been served an alcoholic beverage (Yuille & Tollestrup, 1990). Under the influence of alcohol, people can recognize the perpetrator in a lineup—but they too often make false identifications when the actual perpetrator is absent (Dysart et al., 2002).

The **weapon-focus effect** is also an important factor. Across a wide range of settings, research shows that when a criminal pulls out a gun, a razor blade, or a knife, witnesses are less able to identify that culprit than if no weapon is present (Pickel, 1999; Steblay, 1992). There are two reasons for this effect. First, people are agitated by the sight of a menacing stimulus—as when participants in one study were approached by an experimenter holding a syringe or threatening to administer an injection (Maass & Kohnken, 1989). Second, even in a harmless situation, a witness's eyes lock in on a weapon like magnets—drawing attention away from the face. To demonstrate, Elizabeth Loftus and others (1987) showed people slides of a customer who walked up to a bank teller and pulled out either a pistol or a chequebook. By tracking eye movements, these researchers found that people spent more time looking at the gun than at the chequebook. The net result was an impairment in their ability to identify the criminal in a lineup.

There is still another important consideration. By varying the racial make-up of participants and target persons in laboratory and real-life interactions, researchers discovered that people find it relatively difficult to recognize members of a race other than their own—an effect known as the **cross-race identification bias** (Malpass & Kravitz, 1969). The finding that "they all look alike" (referring to members of other groups) is found reliably and in many different racial and ethnic groups. Indeed, Christian Meissner and John Brigham (2001) statistically combined the results of 39 studies involving a total of 5000 mock witnesses. As it turns out, these witnesses were consistently less accurate and more prone to making false identifications when they tried to recognize target persons from racial and ethnic groups other than their own.

weapon-focus effect The tendency for the presence of a weapon to draw attention and impair a witness's ability to identify the culprit.

cross-race identification bias The tendency for people to have difficulty identifying members of a race other than their own.

Storage Typically, there is a delay between when a crime occurs, and when a witness is called to court to testify about that event. It could take a few months, or it could even take a few years. Can remembrances of the remote past be trusted?

As you might expect, memory for faces and events tends to decline with the passage of time. Longer intervals between an event and its retrieval are generally associated with increased forgetting (Shapiro & Penrod, 1986). But not all recollec-

FIGURE 12.1

Biasing Eyewitness Reports with Loaded Questions

Participants viewed a film of a traffic accident and then answered this question: "About how fast were these cars going when they (hit, smashed, or contacted) each other?" As shown, the wording of the question influenced speed estimates (top). One week later, it also caused participants to reconstruct their memory of other aspects of the accident (bottom). *(Loftus & Palmer, 1974.)*

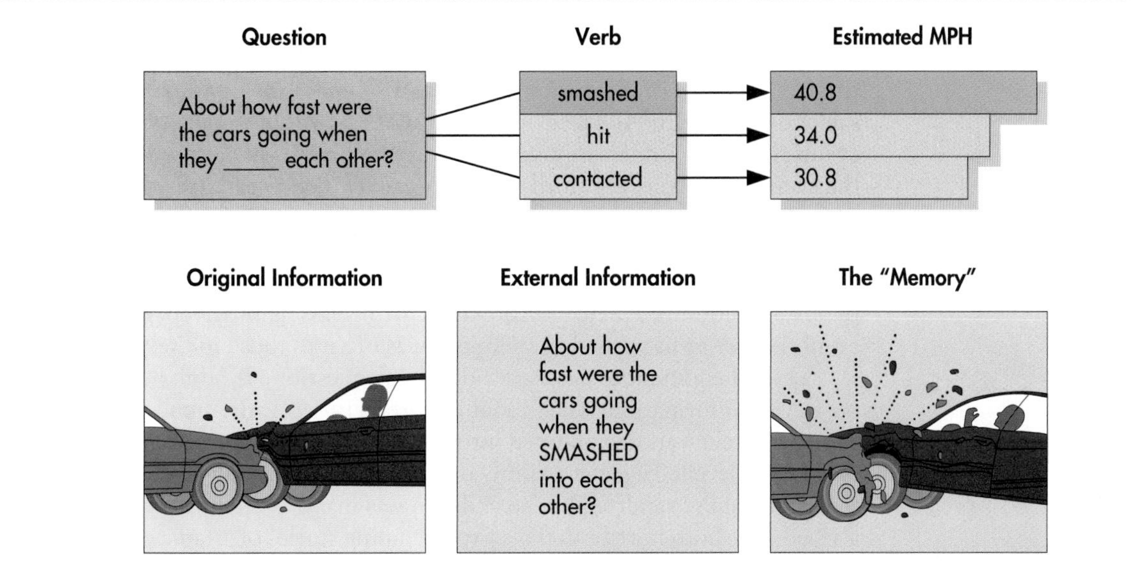

tions fade, and time alone does not cause memory slippage. Consider the plight of bystanders who witness firsthand such incidents as terrorist bombings, shootings, plane crashes, or fatal car accidents. Afterward, they may talk about what they saw, read about it, hear what other bystanders have to say, and answer questions from investigators and reporters. By the time witnesses to these events are officially questioned, they are likely to have been exposed to so much post-event information that one wonders if their original memory is still "pure."

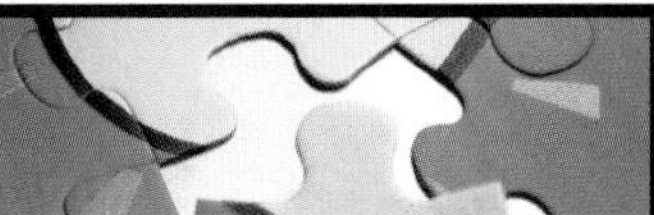

Eyewitnesses find it relatively difficult to recognize members of a race other than their own. **True.**

According to Elizabeth Loftus (1996), it probably is not. Many years ago, based on her studies of eyewitness testimony, Loftus proposed a theory of reconstructive memory. After people observe an event, she said, later information about that event—whether it's true or not—becomes integrated into the fabric of their memory. A classic experiment by Loftus and John Palmer (1974) illustrates the point. Participants viewed a film of a traffic accident and then answered questions, including: "About how fast were the cars going when they hit each other?" Other participants answered the same question, except that the verb *hit* was replaced by *smashed*, *collided*, *bumped*, or *contacted*. All participants saw the same accident, yet the wording of the question affected their reports. Figure 12.1 shows that participants given the "smashed" question estimated the highest average speed and those responding to the "contacted" question estimated the lowest. But there's more. One week later, participants were called back for more probing. Had the wording of the questions caused them to reconstruct their memories of the accident? Yes. When asked whether they had seen broken glass at the accident (none was actually present), 32 percent of the "smashed" participants said they had. As Loftus had predicted, what these participants remembered of the accident was based on two sources: the event itself and post-event information.

This **misinformation effect** has aroused much controversy. It's clear that eyewitnesses can be compromised when they get post-event information—as when

misinformation effect
The tendency for false post-event information to become integrated into people's memory of an event.

they are told, for example, what other witnesses had reported (Shaw et al., 1997). But does post-event information actually alter a witness's real memory, so that it can never be retrieved again? Or do participants merely follow the experimenter's suggestion, leaving their true memory intact for retrieval under other conditions? Either way, whether memory is truly altered or not, eyewitness *reports* are hopelessly biased by post-event information. This effect can be hard to erase (Johnson & Seifert, 1998). It can also be dramatic. In one laboratory study, people were led through a process of imagination to create false memories of having performed some bizarre behaviours two weeks earlier—like balancing a spoon on the nose, sitting on dice, and rubbing lotion on a chair (Thomas & Loftus, 2002). Steve Lindsay and others (2004) asked undergraduates to recall details of three childhood events, based on information provided by the parents of the students. Only two of the events were true; the third event, created by the researchers, was about the student playing a prank on their teacher. As a memory cue, half of the participants were also provided with their school class photos for the years during which the events were to have taken place. They found that rates of false memories soared in the class photo condition. Participants provided with class photos reported details of an event that never happened to them twice as often as those in the no-photo group.

This phenomenon raises an additional question. If adults can be misled by post-event information, what about children? In 1991, the small town of Martensville, Saskatchewan was plunged into the media spotlight after allegations of sexual abuse were levelled against a family operating an unlicensed daycare centre. The extent of the abuse reported by the children was massive, and the particular events described were both horrific and bizarre, including stories of satanic rituals and torture.

Were the children's stories accurate? On the one hand, there were striking consistencies in the testimonies of the child witnesses. On the other hand, the therapists and investigators who conducted the interviews often prompted the children with suggestive leading questions, urged them to describe acts they had initially denied, offered bribes for disclosures, and pressured those who claimed ignorance. Except for this testimony, there was no physical evidence of abuse and no other witnesses—even though the acts were supposed to have occurred during school hours. Can suggestive interview procedures cause young children to confuse appearance and reality? In recent years, thousands of sex abuse charges have been filed against babysitters, preschool teachers, and family members. In some of these cases, the suspects were falsely accused of performing ritual abuse as part of satanic cults (Bottoms & Davis, 1997). In light of these events, judges struggle to decide: Are preschoolers competent to take the witness stand, or are they too suggestible, too prone to confuse reality and fantasy? To provide guidance to the courts, researchers have studied children's eyewitness memory (Bruck & Ceci, 1999).

This research has evolved through several stages. At first, simple laboratory experiments showed that preschoolers were more likely than older children and adults to incorporate misleading "trick" questions into their memories for simple stories (Ceci et al., 1987). Other studies showed that interviewers could get young children to change their memories, or at least their answers, simply by repeating a question over and over—a situation that implies that the answer given is not good enough (Poole & White, 1991). But are young children similarly suggestible about stressful real-life experiences?

In one study, Michelle Leichtman and Stephen Ceci (1995) told nursery school children about a clumsy man named Sam Stone who always broke things. A month later, a man visited the school, spent time in the classroom, and left. The next day, the children were shown a ripped book and a soiled teddy bear and asked what happened. Reasonably, no one said that they saw Stone cause the damage. But then, over the next ten weeks, they were asked suggestive questions ("I wonder if Sam Stone was wearing long pants or short pants when he ripped the book?"). The result: When a new interviewer asked the children in the class to tell what happened, 72 percent of the three- and four-year-olds blamed Stone for the damage, and

45 percent said they saw him do it. One child "recalled" that Stone took a paintbrush and painted melted chocolate on the bear. Others "saw" him spill coffee, throw toys in the air, rip the book in anger, and soak the book in warm water until it fell apart. It's important to realize that false memories in children are not necessarily a by-product of bad questioning procedures. Even when interviews are fair and neutral, false reports can stem from young children's exposure to misinformation from outside sources—such as television (Principe et al., 2000), parents (Poole & Lindsay, 2001), and classmates (Principe & Ceci, 2002).

To summarize, research shows that repetition, misinformation, and leading questions can bias a child's memory report—and that preschoolers are particularly vulnerable in this regard. The effects can be dramatic. In dozens of studies, these procedures have led children to falsely report that they were touched, hit, kissed, and hugged; that a thief came into their classroom; that something "yukky" was put into their mouth; and even that a doctor had cut a bone from their nose to stop it from bleeding. Somehow, the courts must distinguish between true and false claims—and do so on a case-by-case basis. To assist in this endeavour, researchers have proposed that interviewing guidelines be set so that future child witnesses are questioned in an objective, nonbiasing manner (Poole & Lamb, 1998).

"Do you swear to tell your version of the truth as you perceive it, clouded perhaps by the passage of time and preconceived notions?"

Retrieval For eyewitnesses, testifying is only the last in a series of efforts to retrieve what they saw from memory. Before witnesses reach the courtroom, they are questioned by police and lawyers, view a lineup or mug shots, and even assist in the construction of a facial composite or an artist's sketch of the perpetrator. Yet each of these experiences increases the risk of error and distortion.

Nothing an eyewitness does has greater impact than an identification from a lineup. When the police make an arrest, they often call on witnesses to view a photographic lineup that includes the suspect and five to seven other individuals. This procedure may take place within days of a crime or months later. Either way, the lineup often results in tragic cases of mistaken identity. Through the application of eyewitness research findings, as we'll see, this risk can be reduced (Wells et al., 1998).

Basically, four factors affect identification performance. The first is the lineup *construction*. Many years ago, comedian Richard Pryor performed in a skit on the TV show *Saturday Night Live* in which he stood in a lineup next to a nun, a refrigerator, and a duck. Lo and behold, the eyewitness—having described a male criminal—picked Pryor. It obviously doesn't take a social psychologist to see the problem with this particular situation. To be fair, a lineup should contain four to eight innocent persons, or "foils," who match the witness's general description of the culprit or resemble the suspect in general appearance. Anything that makes a suspect distinctive, compared with the others, increases his or her chance of being selected (Buckhout, 1974). This is what happened to Thomas Sophonow; his picture stood out like a sore thumb. The culprit had been described as being quite tall, but Sophonow was the tallest person shown to the witnesses. His photo was the only one taken outdoors (wearing a cowboy hat), whereas the rest were taken indoors. Further, he was the only person from the photo lineup to then be asked to appear in a live lineup; it is no wonder that some of the witnesses found him to be "familiar" (Loftus, 2003)!

Second, lineup *instructions* to the witness are important. In a study by Roy Malpass and Patricia Devine (1981), students saw a staged act of vandalism, after which they attended a lineup. Half of the students received "biased" instructions: They were led to believe that the culprit was in the lineup. The others were told that he might or might not be present. Lineups were then presented either with or without the culprit. When the students received biased instructions, they felt compelled to identify *someone*—and

TABLE 12.3

Effects of Lineup and Instructions on False Identifications

After witnessing a crime, participants were told either that the culprit was in the lineup (biased instruction) or that he might or might not be present (unbiased instruction). Participants then viewed a lineup in which the real culprit was present or absent. Notice the percentage of participants in each group who identified an innocent person. Those who received the biased instruction were more likely to make a false identification, picking an innocent person rather than no one at all—especially when the real culprit was not in the lineup. *(Malpass & Devine, 1981.)*

	Percentage of False Identifications	
	Unbiased Instructions	Biased Instructions
Culprit present	0	25
Culprit absent	33	78

often picked an innocent person (see Table 12.3). Additional studies have consistently confirmed this basic result (Steblay, 1997).

Third, the *format* of a lineup also influences whether a witness feels compelled to make a selection. When witnesses are presented with a spread of photographs, they tend to make relative, multiple-choice-like judgments by picking the target who looks most like the criminal—a strategy that increases the risk of making a false identification. The solution: When the same photos are shown sequentially, one at a time, witnesses tend to make absolute judgments by comparing each target person with their memory of the criminal. This situation diminishes the risk of a forced and often false identification (Lindsay & Bellinger, 1999; Lindsay et al., 1991; Lindsay & Wells, 1985). Indeed, in a procedure known as a *showup*—in which the police bring the suspect in alone, without foils—witnesses become cautious and make judgments that are more absolute than relative (Steblay et al., 2003).

The fourth factor is perhaps the most subtle, as it pertains to *familiarity-induced biases*. Research shows that people often remember a face but forget the circumstances in which they saw that face. In one study, for example, participants witnessed a staged crime and then looked through mug shots. A few days later, they were asked to view a lineup. The result was startling: Participants were just as likely to identify an innocent person whose photograph was in the mug shots as they were to pick the actual criminal (Brown et al., 1977)! This familiarity effect has been observed in many different studies (Brigham & Cairns, 1988; Gorenstein & Ellsworth, 1980). In fact, people are also likely to misidentify as the criminal an innocent bystander who happened to be at the crime scene (Ross et al., 1994).

Courtroom Testimony Eyewitnesses can be inaccurate, but that's only part of the problem. The other part is that their testimony in court is persuasive and not easy to evaluate. To examine how juries view eyewitness testimony, Gary Wells, Rod Lindsay, and others conducted a series of experiments in which they staged the theft of a calculator in front of unsuspecting research participants, who were later cross-examined after trying to pick the culprit from a photo spread. Other participants, who served as mock jurors, observed the questioning and judged the witnesses. The results were sobering: Jurors overestimated how accurate the eyewitnesses were and could not distinguish between witnesses whose identifications were correct and those whose identifications were incorrect (Lindsay et al., 1981; Wells et al., 1979).

There appear to be two problems. First, the subject of human memory is not something people know about through common sense. Brian Cutler and others (1988) found that mock jurors were not sensitive enough to the effects of lineup instructions, weapon focus, and other aspects of an eyewitnessing situation. Others found that mock jurors did not account for the cross-race bias in evaluating the testimony of an eyewitness (Abshire & Bernstein, 2003). Yet a witness's behaviour may provide clues to his or her accuracy. One possible way to distinguish between accurate and inaccurate identifications is by asking witnesses to describe the decision-making process. David Dunning and Lisa Beth Stern (1994) staged a crime and found that witnesses who made a correct identification from photographs described the judgment as quick, effortless, and automatic ("His face just popped out at me"). Those who were inaccurate described a more careful and deliberate process-of-elimination strategy ("I compared the photos with each other to narrow the choices"). The witness who recognizes the culprit's face is most likely to do so instantly, without very much thought (Sporer, 1993). In fact, Dunning and Perretta (2002) discovered that there is a 10- to 12-second rule. In a series of studies, they found that witnesses making identifications in faster than 10 to 12 seconds were nearly 90 percent accurate, while those who took longer were only 50 percent accurate.

The second problem is that participants in this study—and in others as well—based their judgments largely on how *confident* the witness was, a factor that only modestly predicts accuracy. This statement may seem surprising, but studies have shown that the witness who declares "I am absolutely certain" is often not more likely to be right than the one who appears unsure (Bothwell et al., 1987; Penrod & Cutler, 1995; Sporer et al., 1995; Wells & Murray, 1984). Why are eyewitness confidence and accuracy not highly related? The reason is that confidence levels can be raised and lowered by factors that do not have an impact on identification accuracy.

To demonstrate, Elizabeth Lüüs and Wells (1994) staged a theft in front of pairs of participants and then had each separately identify the culprit from a photographic lineup. After the participants made their identifications, the experimenters led them to believe that their partner, a cowitness, either had picked the same person, a similar-looking different person, or a dissimilar-looking different person, or had said that the thief was not in the lineup. Participants were then questioned by a police officer who asked, "On a scale from one to ten, how confident are you in your identification?" The result: Participants became more confident when told that a cowitness picked the same person or a dissimilar alternative and less confident when told that the cowitness selected a similar alternative or none at all. Other research confirms how important post-identification feedback can be. In fact, John Shaw (1996) found that witnesses who are repeatedly questioned about their observations become increasingly confident over time but not more accurate.

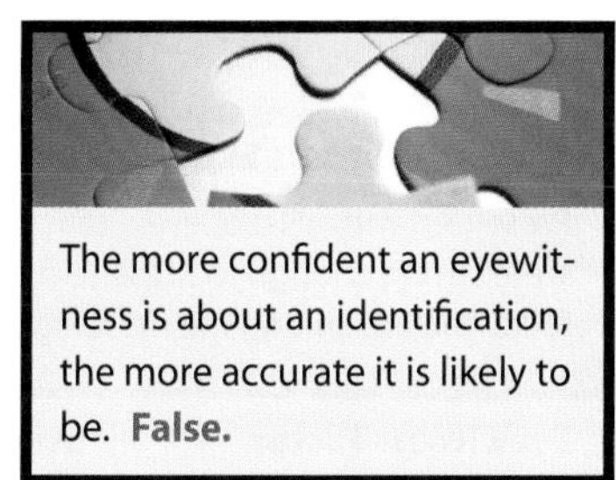

The more confident an eyewitness is about an identification, the more accurate it is likely to be. **False.**

Gary Wells and Amy Bradfield (1998) then found that eyewitnesses who were given positive feedback about their false identifications also went on to reconstruct other aspects of their eyewitnessing experience. In a series of studies, they showed participants a security camera videotape of a man who shoots a guard followed by a set of photographs that did not contain the actual gunman (in other words, all identifications made were false). The experimenter then said to some witnesses, but not to others,

FIGURE 12.2

Biasing Effects of Post-Identification Feedback

Participants saw a gunman on videotape and then tried to make an identification from a set of photographs in which he was absent. Afterward, the experimenter gave some witnesses but not others confirming feedback about their selection. As shown, those given the confirming feedback later recalled that they had paid more *attention* to the event, had a better *view* of it, could make out *details* of the culprit's face, and found it *easier* to make the identification. They were also more willing to testify in court. *(Wells & Bradfield, 1998.)*

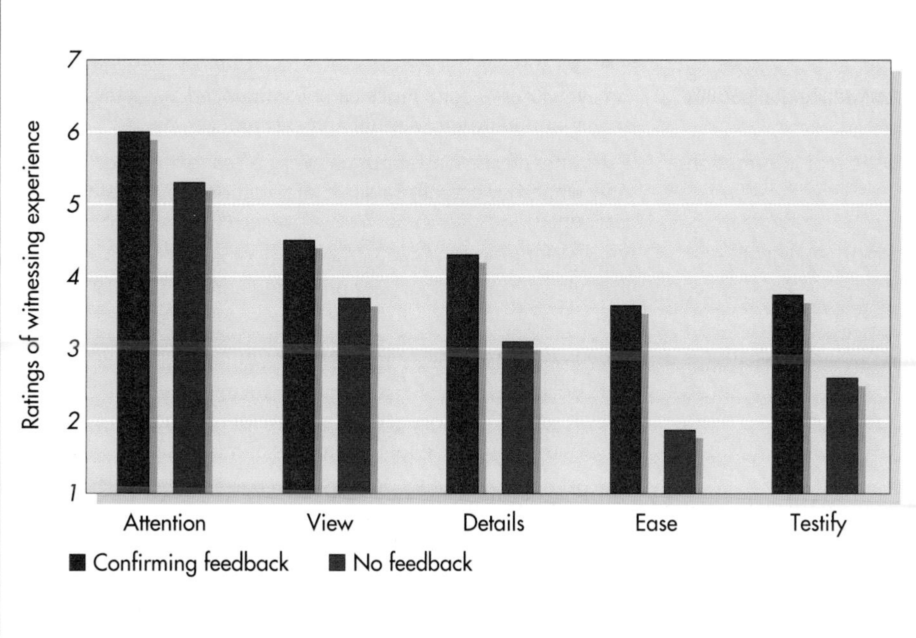

"Oh good. You identified the actual murder suspect." When witnesses were later asked about the whole experience, those given the confirming feedback recalled that they had paid more attention to the event, had a better view of the culprit, and found it easier to make the identification (see Figure 12.2). Apparently, an eyewitness's confidence about the entire experience can be raised or lowered by social feedback—and this makes confidence even less predictive of accuracy (Bradfield et al., 2002).

The Eyewitness Expert Having described the problems with information obtained from eyewitnesses, social psychologists are in a position to put their knowledge to use by educating juries so they can better evaluate the evidence. But can this goal be achieved? Like medical doctors who testify about a patient's physical condition, economists who testify on monopolies and other antitrust matters, and architectural engineers who testify on the structural integrity of buildings, psychologists are often called by one party or the other to tell the jury about relevant aspects of human perception, memory, and behaviour (Leippe, 1995). What, specifically, do these experts say to the jury? What findings do they present in court? Recently, researchers surveyed 64 eyewitness experts, many of whose studies are described in this chapter. The principles listed in Table 12.4 were seen by the vast majority as highly reliable and worthy of expert testimony (Kassin et al., 2001).

Does the jury need to be informed? In some cases, yes. Researchers have found that there's a great deal about eyewitnesses that the average person does not know as a matter of common sense (Devenport et al., 1997). In fact, judges and lawyers themselves are not aware of many of the factors that influence eyewitness performance. To demonstrate, Veronica Stinson and others (1996, 1997) presented large groups of Florida judges and defence lawyers with hypothetical cases that included a lineup identification that varied in important ways. In general, the judges and lawyers were able to reasonably distinguish between lineups and instructions that were fair as opposed to suggestive. But they did not understand that witnesses are more likely to pick someone from photographs—even someone innocent—when the pictures are shown all at once (which leads people to make relative judgments) than when they are shown sequentially, one at a time (which leads people to make absolute judgments). Getting it backward, the judges and lawyers criticized the sequential format for not allowing witnesses to compare photographs—which is precisely what should not be done.

TABLE 12.4

What Eyewitness Experts Say in Court

Presented with a list of eyewitness factors, 64 experts were asked what research findings were strong enough to present in court. In order of how much support they elicited, the following are among the most highly regarded topics of expert testimony. *(Kassin et al., 2001.)*

Eyewitness Factor	Statement
Wording of questions	An eyewitness's testimony about an event can be affected by how the questions put to the witness are worded.
Lineup instructions	Police instructions can affect an eyewitness's willingness to make an identification.
Mug shot-induced bias	Exposure to mug shots of a suspect increases the likelihood that the witness will later choose that suspect in a lineup.
Confidence malleability	An eyewitness's confidence can be influenced by factors that are unrelated to identification accuracy.
Post-event information	Eyewitness testimony about an event often reflects not only what they actually saw but information they obtained later on.
Child suggestibility	Young children are more vulnerable than adults to interviewer suggestion, peer pressures, and other social influences.
Alcoholic intoxication	Alcoholic intoxication impairs an eyewitness's later ability to recall persons and events.
Cross-race bias	Eyewitnesses are more accurate when identifying members of their own race than members of other races.
Weapon focus	The presence of a weapon impairs an eyewitness's ability to accurately identify the perpetrator's face.
Accuracy-confidence	An eyewitness's confidence is not a good predictor of his or her identification accuracy.

Psychologists disagree over whether advice from experts can help the jury—and whether they should testify. People in general put too much faith in eyewitnesses, so it can't hurt to make juries more critical, informed consumers of this type of evidence.

Nonevidentiary Influences

A trial is a well-orchestrated event that follows strict rules of evidence and procedure. The goal is to ensure that juries base their verdicts solely on the evidence and testimony presented in court—not on rumours, newspaper stories, a defendant's attire, and other information. The question is: To what extent is this goal achieved, and to what extent are jury verdicts tainted by nonevidentiary influences?

"It is a capital mistake to theorize before you have all the evidence. It biases the judgment."
—Sir Arthur Conan Doyle

Pretrial Publicity Many cases find their way into newspapers and other mass media long before they appear in court, particularly when they involve celebrities or high profile crimes. In each instance, the legal system struggles with this dilemma: Does exposure to pretrial news stories corrupt prospective jurors? Public opinion surveys consistently show that the more people know about a case, the more likely they are to presume the defendant guilty, even when they claim to be impartial (Kovera, 2002; Moran & Cutler, 1991). There is nothing particularly mysterious about this result. The information in news reports usually comes from the police or Crown counsel's office, so it often reveals facts unfavourable to the defence. The real question is whether these reports have an impact on juries that go on to receive hard evidence in court and deliberate to a verdict.

To examine the effects of pretrial publicity, Geoffrey Kramer and his colleagues (1990) played a videotaped re-enactment of an armed robbery trial to hundreds of people participating in 108 mock juries. Before watching the tape, participants were exposed to news clippings about the case. Some read material that was neutral. Others read information that was incriminating—revealing, for example, that the defendant had a prior record or implicating him in a hit-and-run accident in which a small child was killed. Even though participants were instructed to base their decisions solely on the evidence, pretrial publicity had a marked effect. Among those exposed to neutral material, 33 percent voted guilty after deliberating in a jury. Among those exposed to the prejudicial material, that figure increased to 48 percent. What's worse, judges and defence lawyers could not identify in a simulated voir dire which jurors were biased by the publicity. As shown in Figure 12.3, 48 percent of those who were questioned and not challenged—jurors who said they were unaffected—went on to vote guilty (Kerr et al., 1991). The impact of pretrial publicity is even more powerful when the news is seen on television rather than in print (Ogloff & Vidmar, 1994). In Canada, it is not uncommon for a judge to issue a publication ban on evidence surrounding a case as a way to increase the chances of a defendant getting a fair trial, or to otherwise protect those involved in the case. For example, when Paul Bernardo and Karla Homolka were charged with the murders of two young schoolgirls, a ban was issued prohibiting the Canadian media from reporting on any of the evidence until after the trial. Despite this ban, however, the Internet was full of gruesome details of their crimes (many of the details were false, but that didn't stop the flow of information). In addition, some of the US media did not honour the ban, allowing those that lived close to the US border access to the lurid details presented in court. In this case at least, the publication ban did little to limit the amount of information available to potential jurors (Freedman & Burke, 1996).

Pretrial publicity is potentially dangerous in two respects. First, it often divulges information that is not later allowed into the trial record. Freedman and Burke (1996) suggested that pretrial publicity is more likely to have an effect in such circumstances, as any potentially damaging information never officially becomes evidence and so can never be refuted in court. Second is the matter of timing. Because many news

FIGURE 12.3

Contaminating Effects of Pretrial Publicity

In this study, participants were exposed to prejudicial or neutral news reports about a defendant, watched a videotaped trial, and voted before and after participating in a mock jury deliberation. As shown, pretrial publicity increased the conviction rate slightly before deliberations (left). After deliberations, however, it more clearly increased the conviction rate—even among participants perceived as impartial by judges and lawyers (right). *(Kerr et al., 1991.)*

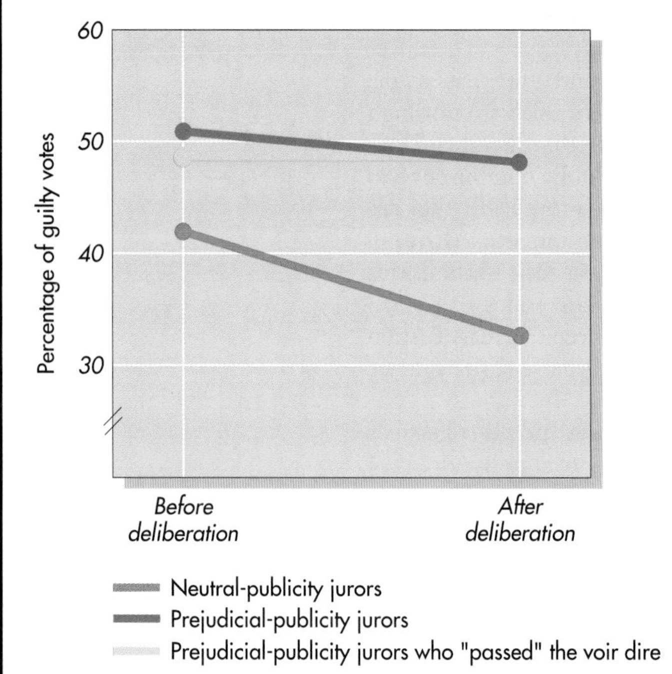

stories precede the actual trial, jurors learn certain facts even before they enter the courtroom. If jurors receive prejudicial news information about a defendant *before* trial, the concern is that this information will distort the way they interpret the facts of the case. Given that the results of many studies indicate that the biasing effects persist despite the practices of jury selection, the presentation of hard evidence, cautionary words from the judge, and jury deliberations, justice may demand that highly publicized cases be postponed or moved to other, less informed communities (Steblay et al., 1999; Studebaker & Penrod, 1997) as was done in the Bernardo trial.

Inadmissible Testimony Just as jurors are biased by news stories, so they occasionally receive extralegal information within the trial itself. Imagine that you are a juror in a case, and right after hearing some really powerful piece of evidence, one of the lawyers jumps up and says "I object. Move to strike." The learned judge leans over and tells the jury to disregard the information that was just presented. Could you do it? Can people really strike information from their minds the way court reporters can strike it from the record? Can people resist the forbidden fruit of inadmissible testimony? Although common sense suggests they cannot, the research is mixed. In one study, a group of mock jurors read about a murder case based on evidence so weak that not a single juror voted guilty. A second group read the same case, except that the prosecution introduced an illegally obtained tape recording of a phone call made by the defendant: "I finally got the money to pay you off. . . . When you read the papers tomorrow, you'll know what I mean." The defence argued that the illegal tape should not be admissible, but the judge disagreed. At this point, the conviction rate increased to 26 percent. In a third group, as in the second, the tape was brought in and the defence objected. Yet this time, the judge sustained the objection and told jurors to disregard the tape. The result: 35 percent voted for conviction (Sue et al., 1973). Other studies as well have revealed that "limiting instructions" do not deter jurors (Greene & Dodge, 1995; Pickel, 1995).

Why do people not follow a judge's order to disregard inadmissible evidence? There are a number of possible explanations (Lieberman & Arndt, 2000). Imagine yourself in the jury box, and three reasons will become apparent. First, the added instruction draws attention to the information in controversy. It's like being told *not* to think about white bears. As we saw in Chapter 3, trying to suppress a specific thought increases its tendency to intrude upon our consciousness (Wegner, 1994). A second reason is that a judge's instruction to disregard, much like censorship, restricts a juror's decision-making freedom. Accordingly, it can backfire by arousing reactance. Thus, when a judge emphasizes the ruling by *forbidding* jurors from considering the information ("You have no choice but to disregard it"), they become even *more* likely to use it (Wolf & Montgomery, 1977). The third reason is the easiest to understand: Jurors want to reach the right decision. If they stumble onto relevant information, they want to use it—whether it satisfies the law's technical rules or not. In other words, jurors find it hard to ignore information that seems relevant to a case (Wissler & Saks, 1985).

To test this third hypothesis, Kassin and Samuel Sommers (1997) had mock jurors read a transcript of a double-murder trial that was based on weak evidence, leading only 24 percent to vote guilty. Three other groups read the same case except that the state's evidence included a wiretapped phone conversation in which the defendant confessed to a friend. In all cases, the defence lawyer objected to the disclosure. When the judge ruled to admit the tape into evidence, the conviction rate increased considerably, to 79 percent. But when the judge excluded the tape and instructed jurors to disregard it, their reaction depended on the reason for the tape's being excluded. When told to disregard the tape because it was barely audible and could not be trusted, participants mentally erased the information, as they should, and delivered the same 24 percent conviction rate as in the no-tape control group. But when told to disregard the item because it had been illegally obtained, 55 percent voted guilty. Despite the judge's warning, these latter participants were unwilling to ignore testimony they saw as highly relevant merely because of a legal "technicality." Fortunately, additional studies indicate that jurors in this situation comply with a judge's instruction to disregard when the technicality involves a *serious* violation of the defendant's rights (Fleming et al., 1999)—and that the process of deliberation increases compliance, which minimizes the bias (London & Nunez, 2000).

The Judge's Instructions

One of the most important rituals in any trial is the judge's instruction to the jury. It is through these instructions that juries are educated about relevant legal concepts, informed of the verdict options, admonished to disregard extralegal factors, and advised on how to conduct their deliberations. To make verdicts adhere to the law, juries are supposed to comply with these instructions. The task seems simple enough, but there are problems.

To begin with, the jury's intellectual competence has been called into question. For years, the courts have doubted whether jurors understood their instructions. One skeptical judge put it bluntly when he said that "these words may as well be spoken in a foreign language" (Frank, 1949, p. 181). To some extent, he was right. When actual instructions are tested with mock jurors, the results reveal high levels of misunderstanding—a serious problem in light of the fact that jurors seem to have many preconceptions about crimes and the requirements of the law. Rose and Ogloff (2001) compared the ability of undergraduate students, volunteers from jury panels, and first year law students from British Columbia to understand the judge's instructions in a drug conspiracy case. They found that comprehension levels were highest among the law-school students (approximately 70 percent), while students did about as well as jurors (in the 60- to 70-percent range). They described these overall levels of comprehension as "abysmally low" (p. 429). There is, however, reason for hope. Research has shown that when conventional instructions (which are poorly structured, esoteric, and filled with complex legal terms) are rewritten in plain English, comprehension rates increase markedly (Elwork et al., 1982; English & Sales, 1997).

Comprehension is a necessary first step, but presentation factors are also important. Consider the following study (Kassin & Wrightsman, 1979). Participants watched an auto-theft trial that included, for the defence, an all-important instruction stating that the defendant is presumed innocent and that the prosecutor must prove guilt beyond a reasonable doubt. The statement itself was easy to understand. The key, however, was its *timing*. Among mock jurors who never received the instruction, 63 percent voted guilty. When the instruction followed the evidence, as is the custom in most courts, the conviction rate remained high at 59 percent. Only when the instruction preceded the evidence did the rate drop, to 37 percent. Why did the post-evidence instructions have so little impact? The researchers asked half of the participants for their opinions at various points during the trial and found that these mid-trial opinions were predictive of final verdicts. In other words, it was simply too late for a presumption-of-innocence instruction because many participants had already made up their minds. Indeed, Lynne ForsterLee and others (1993) found that pre-evidence instructions generally increased the decision-making competence of mock jurors in a complex civil case.

A lack of comprehension and poor timing are two reasons that a judge's instruction may have little impact. But there's a third reason: Sometimes juries disagree with the law, thus raising the controversial issue of **jury nullification**. You may not realize it, but juries, because they deliberate in private, can choose to disregard, or "nullify," the judge's instructions. The pages of history are filled with poignant examples. Consider the case of someone tried for euthanasia, or "mercy killing." By law, it is murder. But to the defendant, it might be a noble act on behalf of a loved one. For example, when Saskatchewan farmer Robert Latimer was charged with the murder of his 12-year-old severely disabled daughter Tracy in 1993, he did not deny that he had done it. Instead, he explained to authorities that he did it to save her any more suffering. Faced with this kind of conflict—an explosive moral issue on which public opinion is sharply divided—juries often evaluate the issue in human terms, use their own notions of common-sense justice, and vote despite the law for acquittal (Finkel, 1995; Horowitz & Willging, 1991; Niedermeier et al., 1999). Latimer was convicted of second-degree murder, and under Canadian law, there is a mandatory minimum sentence of 25 years, with no chance of parole for 10 years. However, the jury recommended that he be eligible for parole after only one year. While such a recommendation broke new legal ground, it was short-lived; the Saskatchewan court of appeal overturned this decision, re-instating the mandatory minimum penalty.

Jury Deliberation

Anyone who has seen *Twelve Angry Men* can appreciate how colourful and passionate a jury's deliberation can be. This film classic opens with a jury eager to convict a young man of murder—no ifs, ands, or buts. The group selects a foreperson and takes a show-of-hands vote. The result is an 11-to-1 majority, with actor Henry Fonda the lone dissenter. After many tense moments, Fonda manages to convert his peers, and the jury votes unanimously for acquittal.

It is often said that the unique power of the jury stems from the fact that individuals come together privately as one *group*. Is this assumption justified? *Twelve Angry Men* is a work of fiction, but does it realistically portray what transpires in the jury room? And in what ways does the legal system influence the group dynamics? By interviewing jurors after trials, and by recruiting people to participate on mock juries and then recording their deliberations, researchers have learned a great deal about the ways in which juries make their decisions.

Leadership in the Jury Room

In theory, all jurors are created equal. In practice, however, it is common for dominance hierarchies to develop. As in other decision-making groups, a handful of individuals lead the discussion, while others join in at a lower rate or watch from the sidelines, speaking only to cast their votes (Hastie et al., 1983). It's almost as if there is a jury within the jury. The question is, what kinds of people emerge as leaders?

jury nullification The jury's power to disregard, or "nullify," the law when it conflicts with personal conceptions of justice.

It is often assumed that the foreperson is the leader. The foreperson, after all, calls for votes, acts as a liaison between the judge and jury, and announces the verdict in court. It seems like a position of importance, yet the selection process is very quick and casual. It's interesting that foreperson selection outcomes do follow a predictable pattern (Stasser et al., 1982). People of higher occupational status or with prior experience on a jury are frequently chosen. Sex differences are also common. Norbert Kerr and others (1982) examined the records of 179 trials held in San Diego and found that 50 percent of the jurors were female but 90 percent of the forepersons were male. Other patterns, too, are evident. The first person who speaks is often chosen as foreperson (Strodtbeck et al., 1957). And when jurors deliberate around a rectangular table, those who sit at the heads of the table are more likely to be chosen than are those seated in the middle (Bray et al., 1978; Strodtbeck & Hook, 1961). Adding to the complete picture is the fact that men are more likely than women to speak first and to take the prominent seats (Nemeth et al., 1976).

In the classic movie, Twelve Angry Men, *Henry Fonda plays a lone juror who single-handedly converts his 11 guilty-voting peers to vote for acquittal. Sometimes life imitates art; in this case, it does not. Research shows that majorities on the first jury vote usually prevail in the final verdict.*

If you find such inequalities bothersome, fear not: Forepersons may act as nominal leaders, but they do *not* exert more than their fair share of influence over the group. In fact, although they spend more time than other jurors talking about procedural matters, they spend less time expressing opinions on the verdict (Hastie et al., 1983). Thus, it may be most accurate to think of the foreperson not as the jury's leader but as its moderator. In *Twelve Angry Men*, actor Martin Balsam—not Henry Fonda—was the foreperson. He was also among the least influential members of the jury.

The Dynamics of Deliberation

If the walls of the jury room could talk, they would tell us that the decision-making process typically passes through three stages (Hastie et al., 1983; Stasser et al., 1982). Like other problem-solving groups, juries begin in a relaxed *orientation* period during which they set an agenda, talk in open-ended terms, raise questions, and explore the facts. Then, once differences of opinion are revealed—usually after the first vote is taken—factions develop, and the group shifts abruptly into a period of *open conflict*. With the battle lines sharply drawn, discussion takes on a more focused, argumentative tone. Together, jurors scrutinize the evidence, construct stories to account for that evidence, and discuss the judge's instructions (Pennington & Hastie, 1992). If all jurors agree, they return a verdict. If not, the majority tries to achieve a consensus by converting the holdouts through information and social pressure. If unanimity is achieved, the group enters a period of *reconciliation*, during which it smoothes over the conflicts and affirms its satisfaction with the outcome. If

FIGURE 12.4

Jury Deliberations: The Process

Juries move through various tasks en route to a verdict. They begin by setting and reviewing the case. If all jurors agree, they return a verdict. If not, they continue to discuss the case until they reach a consensus. If the holdouts refuse to vote with the majority, the jury declares itself hung.

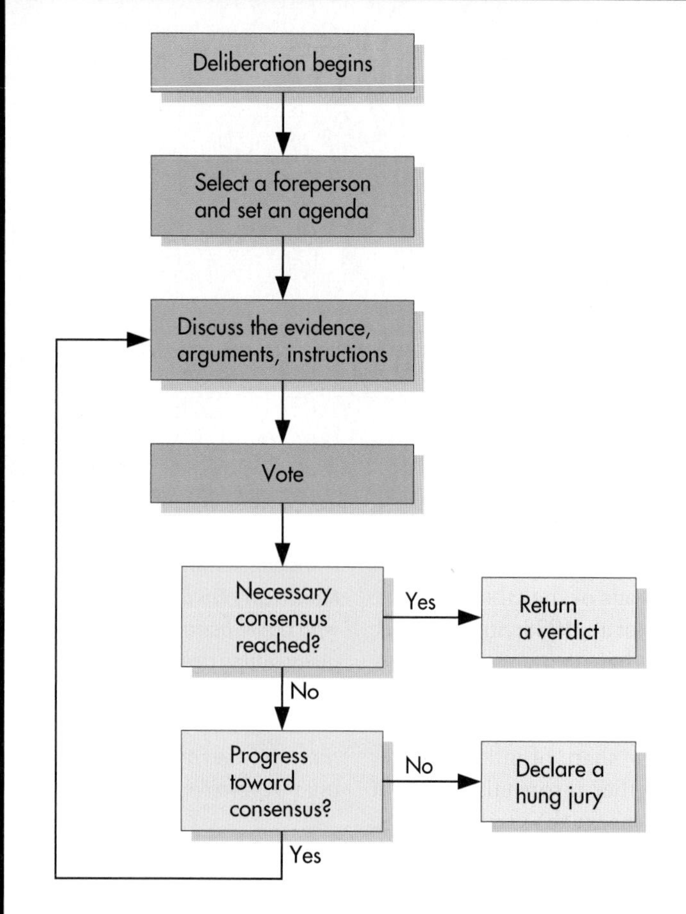

the holdouts continue to disagree, the jury declares itself hung. This process is diagrammed in Figure 12.4.

When it comes to decision-making *outcomes*, deliberations follow a predictable course first discovered by Harry Kalven and Hans Zeisel (1966). By interviewing the members of 225 juries, they were able to reconstruct how these juries split on their very first vote. Out of 215 juries that opened with an initial majority, 209 reached a final verdict consistent with that first vote. This finding—later bolstered by the results of mock jury studies (Kerr, 1981; Stasser & Davis, 1981; see Table 12.5)—led Kalven and Zeisel to conclude that "the deliberation process might well be likened to what the developer does for an exposed film; it brings out the picture, but the outcome is predetermined" (1966, p. 489). Henry Fonda's *Twelve Angry Men* heroics notwithstanding, one can usually predict the final verdict by knowing where the individual jurors stand the first time they vote. Indeed, juries are not generally more or less subject to bias than the individuals who comprise the groups (Kerr et al., 1999).

There is one reliable exception to this majority-wins rule. It is that in criminal trials, deliberation tends to produce a **leniency bias** favouring the defendant. All other factors being equal, individual jurors are more likely to vote guilty on their own than in a group; they are also more prone to convict before deliberations than after (MacCoun & Kerr, 1988). Look again at Table 12.5, and you'll see that juries that are equally divided in their initial vote are ultimately likely to return not-guilty verdicts. Perhaps it is easier to raise a "reasonable doubt" in other people's minds than to erase all doubt. In this regard, it is interesting to note that in their classic study entitled *The American Jury* (1966), Kalven and Zeisel surveyed 555 judges who reported how they would have voted in some 3 500 jury trials. Judges agreed with their juries 78 percent of the time. When they disagreed, it was usually because the jury acquitted a defendant thought to be guilty by the judge. Perhaps these disagreements are due, in part, to the fact that juries decide as groups; and judges, as individuals.

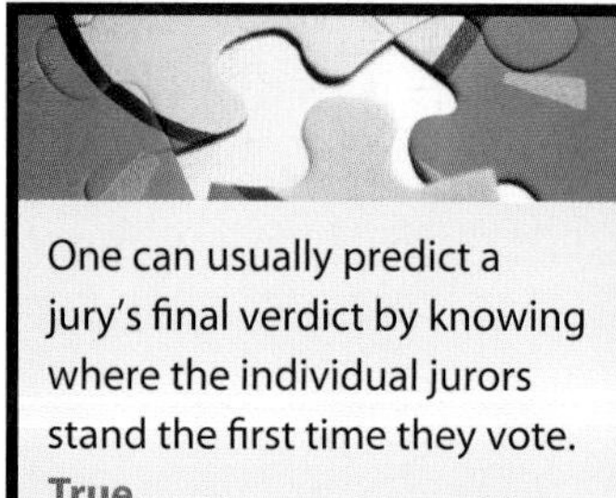

One can usually predict a jury's final verdict by knowing where the individual jurors stand the first time they vote. **True.**

Knowing that the majority tends to prevail doesn't tell us how juries manage to resolve disagreements en route to a verdict. From the conformity studies discussed in Chapter 7, we know that there are two possibilities. Sometimes, people conform because, through a process of *informational influence,* they are genuinely persuaded by what others say. At other times, people yield to the pressures of *normative influence* by changing their overt behaviour in the majority's direction even though they disagree in private. When it comes to the decision-making of juries, justice demands that they reach a consensus through a vigorous exchange of views and information, not by heavy-handed social pressure. But is that how it works? Research shows that juries achieve unanimity not by one process or the other but by a combination of both (Kaplan & Schersching, 1981). Research also shows that certain factors can upset the delicate balance between informational and normative influ-

leniency bias The tendency for jury deliberation to produce a tilt toward acquittal.

ence. Social pressure is increased, for example, in juries that vote by a public roll call or show of hands (Davis et al., 1989) and in deadlocked juries that are called into the courtroom and urged by the judge to resolve their differences (Smith & Kassin, 1993).

Of course, how members of a jury proceed in any given case can only be inferred from the results of studies using mock-jurors, archival research, or post-trial interviews with jurors in the US, as jurors in Canada are strictly forbidden from discussing anything about the trial or their deliberations.

TABLE 12.5

The Road to Agreement: From Individual Votes to a Group Verdict

Research has shown how verdicts are reached by mock juries that begin with different combinations of initial votes. You can see that the results support the majority-wins rule. But also note the evidence for a leniency bias: When the initial vote is split, juries gravitate toward acquittal. *(Kerr, 1981, as cited in Stasser et al., 1982.)*

	Final Jury Verdicts (percent)		
Initial Votes (Guilty–Not Guilty)	Conviction	Acquittal	Hung
6–0	100	0	0
5–1	78	7	16
4–2	44	26	30
3–3	9	51	40
2–4	4	79	17
1–5	0	93	7
0–6	0	100	0

Jury Size

How many people does it take to form a jury? In keeping with the British tradition, 12 has long been the magic number and is still the norm in Canada. The American courts are today permitted to cut trial costs by using six-person juries in cases that do not involve the death penalty.

What is the impact of a six-person jury? The US Supreme Court approached this question as a social psychologist would. It sought to determine whether the change would affect the decision-making process. Unfortunately, the Court misinterpreted the available research so badly that Michael Saks concluded it "would not win a passing grade in a high school psychology class" (1974, p. 18). Consider whether a reduction in size affects the ability of those in the voting minority to resist normative pressures. The Court did not think it would. Citing Asch's (1956) conformity studies, the Court argued that an individual juror's resistance depends on the *proportional* size of the majority. But is that true? Is the lone dissenter caught in a 5-to-1 bind as well insulated from the group norm as the minority in a 10-to-2 split? The Court argued that these 83-to-17 percent divisions are psychologically identical. But wait. Asch's research showed exactly the opposite—that the mere presence of a single ally enables dissenters to keep their independence better than anything else. Research has shown that the size of a jury has other effects too. Michael Saks and Molli Marti (1997) conducted a meta-analysis of studies involving 15000 mock jurors who deliberated in over 2000 6-person or 12-person juries. Overall, they found that the smaller juries were less likely to represent minority segments of the population. They were also more likely to reach a unanimous verdict and to do so despite deliberating for shorter periods of time. Even in civil trials—in which juries have to make complex decisions on how much money to award the plaintiff—six-person groups spend less time discussing the case (Davis et al., 1997).

Post-Trial: To Prison and Beyond

The Sentencing Process

For defendants convicted of crimes, the jury's verdict is followed by a sentence. Sentencing decisions—usually made by judges, not juries—are often controversial. One reason for the controversy is that many people see judges as being too lenient

(Stalans & Diamond, 1990). Another reason is that people disagree on the goals served by imprisonment. For many judges, the goal of a prison sentence is a practical one: to incapacitate offenders and deter them from committing future crimes. For many citizens, however, there is a more powerful motive at work: to exact retribution, or revenge, against the offender for his or her misdeeds. Research shows that people are driven by this "just desserts" motive, recommending sentences of increasing harshness for crimes of increasing severity—regardless of whether the offender is seen as likely to strike again (Darley et al., 2000; Carlsmith et al., 2002).

Judges also disagree about sentencing-related issues. Thus, a common public complaint is that there is too much **sentencing disparity**—that punishments are inconsistent from one judge to the next. To document the problem, Anthony Partridge and William Eldridge (1974) compiled identical sets of files from 20 actual cases, sent them to 50 federal judges, and found major disparities in the sentences they said they would impose. In one case, for example, judges had read about a man who was convicted of extortion and tax evasion. One judge recommended a three-year prison sentence, while another recommended 20 years in prison and a fine of $65 000. It's hard to believe these two judges read the same case. But other studies have uncovered similar differences.

The Prison Experience

It is no secret that many prisons are overcrowded and that the situation has worsened as a result of recently toughened sentencing guidelines. It is also no secret that prison life can be cruel, violent, and degrading. The setting is highly oppressive and regimented, many prison guards are abusive, and many inmates fall into a state of despair (Paulus, 1988). Indeed, many are psychologically disturbed and in need of treatment they do not receive (Kupers, 1999). Thus, it is natural for social psychologists to wonder: Is there something in the situation that leads guards and prisoners to behave as they do? Would the rest of us react in the same way?

For ethical reasons, one obviously cannot place research participants inside a real prison. So, many years ago, a team of researchers from Stanford University did the next best thing. They constructed their own prison in the basement of the psychology department building (Haney et al., 1973; Haney & Zimbardo, 1998; Zimbardo et al., 1973). Complete with iron-barred cells, a solitary-confinement closet, and a recreation area for guards, the facility housed 21 participants—all healthy and stable men between the ages of 17 and 30 who had answered a newspaper ad promising $15 a day for a two-week study of prison life. By the flip of a coin, half the participants were designated as guards; the other half became prisoners. Neither group was told specifically how to fulfill its role.

On the first day, each of the participant prisoners was unexpectedly "arrested" at his home, booked, fingerprinted, and driven to the simulated prison by officers of the local police department. These prisoners were then stripped, searched, and dressed in loose-fitting smocks with an identification number, a nylon stocking to cover their hair, rubber sandals, and a chain bolted to ankle shackles. The guards were dressed in khaki uniforms and supplied with nightsticks, handcuffs, reflector sunglasses, keys, and whistles. The rules specified that prisoners were to be called by number, routinely lined up to be counted, fed three bland meals, and permitted three supervised toilet visits per day. The stage was set. It remained to be seen just how seriously the participants would take their roles and react to one another in this novel setting.

The events of the next few days were startling. Filled with a sense of power and authority, a few guards became progressively more abusive. They harassed the inmates, forced them into crowded cells, woke them during the night, and subjected them to hard labour and solitary confinement. These guards were particularly cruel when they thought they were alone with a prisoner. The prisoners themselves were

sentencing disparity
Inconsistency of sentences for the same offence from one judge to another.

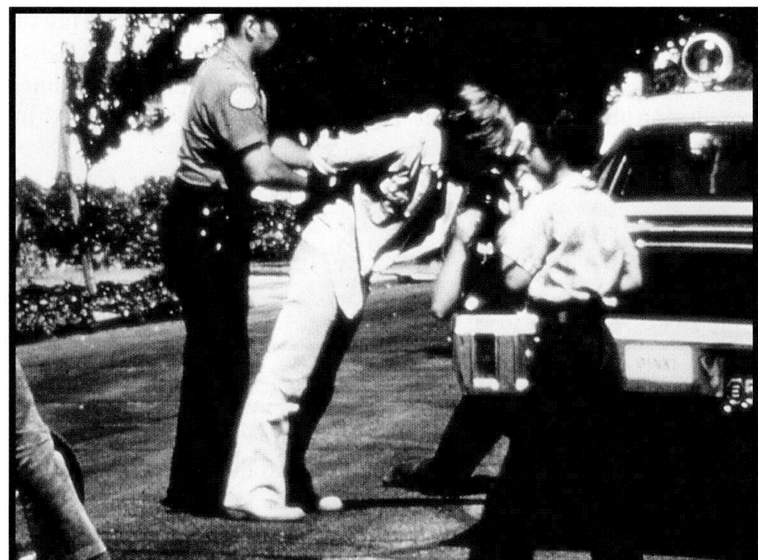

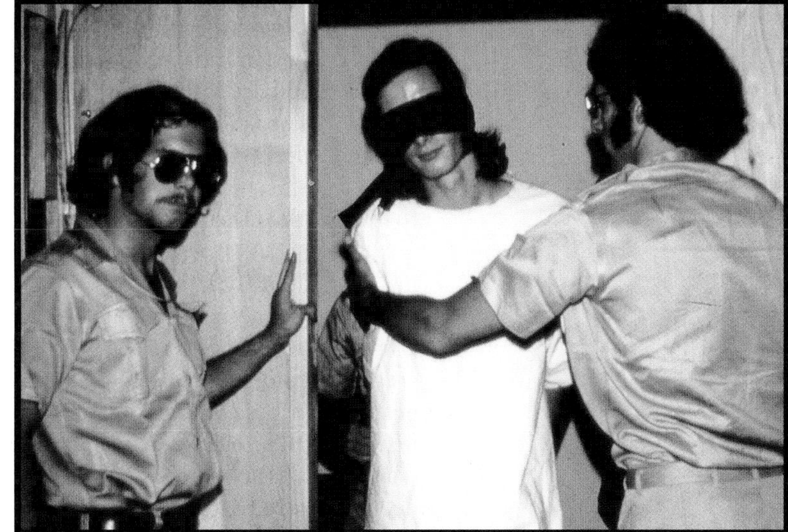

In this simulation study of prison behaviour, participants were arbitrarily assigned to be prisoners or guards. Local police officers arrested the prisoners, who were brought to a jail constructed at Stanford University. After several days, the guards took on cruel, authoritarian roles that demoralized the prisoners to such an extent that the experiment was terminated.

rebellious at first, but their efforts were met with retaliation. Soon they all became passive and demoralized. After 36 hours, the experimenters had to release their first prisoner, who was suffering from acute depression. On subsequent days, other prisoners had to be released. By the sixth day, those who remained were so shaken by the experience that the study was terminated. It is reassuring, if not remarkable, that after a series of debriefing sessions, participants seemed to show no signs of lasting distress.

This study has been criticized on both methodological and ethical grounds (Banuazizi & Movahedi, 1975; Savin, 1973). Still, in some ways, the results are impressive. Within a brief period of time, under relatively mild conditions, and with a group of men not prone to violence, the Stanford study re-created some of the prisoner and guard behaviours actually found behind prison walls. But would the same results occur today, in the twenty-first century? To find out, social psychologists Alex Haslam and Steve Reicher worked in the spring of 2002 with the British Broadcasting Corporation to create a *Survivor*-like reality TV special called *The Experiment*, modeled after Zimbardo's study. Shown in four episodes entitled Conflict, Order, Rebellion, and Tyranny, they brought together 15 men, all carefully screened, forewarned that they would be exposed to hardships, and randomly assigned to prisoner and guard roles. Determined to set limits, monitor events

"It only makes a man worse to go to prison and be corrupted."

—E.M. Forster

closely, and adhere to ethical guidelines for research with human subjects, Haslam and Reicher did not fully re-create the conditions of the original study, and they did not observe the same brutality from the guards. In their view, the findings challenge the conclusion that normal people could so easily be dehumanized by institutional roles.

Justice: A Matter of Procedure?

People tend to measure the success of a legal system by its ability to produce fair and accurate results. But is that all there is to justice? Let's step back for a moment from the specifics and ask if it is possible to define justice in a way that is unrelated to outcomes.

In a book entitled *Procedural Justice* (1975), John Thibaut and Laurens Walker proposed that our satisfaction with the way disputes are resolved—legal or otherwise—depends not only on outcomes but also on the procedures used to achieve those outcomes. Two aspects of procedure are important in this regard: One is *decision control*—whether a procedure affords the involved parties the power to accept, reject, or otherwise influence the final decision. The other is *process control*—whether it offers the parties an opportunity to present their case to a third-party decision maker. In the courtroom, of course, the disputants are limited in their decision control. Thus, their satisfaction must depend on whether they feel that they had a chance to express their views.

There are two ways to look at the effects of process control on perceptions of justice. Originally, it was thought that people want an opportunity to express their opinions only because having a voice in the process improves the odds of achieving a favourable ruling. In this view, process control is satisfying only because it increases decision control (Thibaut & Walker, 1978). Recent research, however, suggests that people value the chance to present their side of a story to an impartial decision maker even when they do not prevail in the ultimate outcome. In other words, process control is more than just an instrumental means to an end. When people believe that they had a voice in the proceedings, were treated with respect, and were judged by an impartial decision maker, process control can be an end in itself (Lind et al., 1990).

This aspect of the legal system is very important. It means, for example, that regardless of whether people agree or disagree with how a case turns out, they can find solace in the fact that both sides had their "day in court"—at least when the decision maker is seen as impartial. Yet certain members of the legal community are openly critical of that so-called day in court. As law professor Alan Dershowitz once put it, "Nobody really wants justice. Winning is the only thing to most participants in the criminal justice system, just as it is to professional athletes" (1982, p. xvi). Dershowitz's skepticism is centred on something that many of us take for granted: the **adversarial model** of justice. In the adversarial system—as practised in North America, Great Britain, and a handful of other countries—the prosecution and defence oppose each other, each presenting one side of the story in an effort to win a favourable verdict. In contrast, most other countries use an **inquisitorial model**, in which a neutral investigator gathers the evidence from both sides and presents the findings in court. With two such different methods of doing justice, social psychologists could not resist the temptation to make comparisons. Which system, they ask, do people prefer?

adversarial model A dispute-resolution system in which the prosecution and defence present opposing sides of the story.

inquisitorial model A dispute-resolution system in which a neutral investigator gathers evidence from both sides and presents the findings in court.

To find out, Laurens Walker and others (1974) constructed a business simulation in which two companies competed for a cash prize. Assigned to the role of president of a company, participants learned that someone on their staff was accused of spying on the competition. To resolve the dispute, a "trial" was held. In some cases, the trial followed an adversarial procedure in which the two sides were presented by law students who were chosen by participants and whose payment was contingent on winning. Other cases followed an inquisitorial model in which a single law student—appointed by the experimenter and paid regardless of the outcome—presented both sides. Regardless of whether they had won or lost the verdict, participants who took part in an adversarial trial were more satisfied than those involved in an inquisitorial trial. Even impartial observers preferred the adversarial proceedings.

It seems that any method that offers participants a voice in the proceedings—including methods that are nonadversarial—is seen as fair and just (Folger & Greenberg, 1985; Sheppard, 1985). Process control is desirable even among Chinese people, whose culture emphasizes social harmony and the resolution of disputes in ways that minimize conflict (Leung, 1987). Procedural concerns about voice and an impartial decision maker are important not only among North Americans and Western Europeans but among the peoples of the once-communist countries of Bulgaria, Hungary, Poland, and Russia (Cohn et al., 2000). In matters of justice, people all over the world are motivated not only by the desire for personal gain but also by their need to be recognized, respected, and treated fairly by others (Tyler & Lind, 2001).

Closing Statement

This chapter focuses on the trial process, the events that precede it, and the events that follow from it. Yet we've only scratched the surface. In recent years, more and more judges, lawyers, and policy makers have come to recognize that social psychology can make important contributions to the legal system. Thus, with increasing frequency, social psychologists are called on for expert advice in and out of court and are cited in the opinions written by judges. Clearly, the gathering, presentation, and evaluation of evidence are imperfect human enterprises and subject to bias. Through an understanding of social psychology, however, we can now identify some of the problems—and perhaps even the solutions.

Review

- Embedded in a large criminal justice system, relatively few cases come to trial.
- Yet the trial is the heart and soul of the system.

Jury Selection

Voir Dire

- Once called for service, prospective jurors are questioned by the judge or lawyers in a process known as voir dire.
- Those who exhibit a clear bias are excluded. Lawyers may also strike a limited number through the use of peremptory challenges.

Trial Lawyers as Intuitive Psychologists

- Pressured to make juror selections quickly, lawyers rely on implicit personality theories and stereotypes.
- But general demographic factors do not reliably predict how jurors will vote.

The Courtroom Drama

- Once the jury is selected, evidence previously gathered is presented in court.

Confession Evidence

- The police employ various methods of interrogation.
- One method is to befriend the suspect and "minimize" the offence; a second is to scare the suspect into believing that it is futile to deny the charges.
- Under pressure, people sometimes confess to crimes they did not commit.
- Although juries are supposed to reject coerced confessions, their verdicts are still influenced by such evidence.

The Lie-Detector Test

- By recording physiological arousal, the polygraph can be used as a lie-detector.
- Polygraphers report high rates of accuracy; but truthful persons are too often judged guilty, and the test can be fooled.

Eyewitness Testimony

- Eyewitness memory is a three-stage process involving acquisition, storage, and retrieval.
- During acquisition, witnesses who are highly aroused zoom in on the central features of an event but lose memory for peripheral details.
- The presence of a weapon hinders a witness's ability to identify the perpetrator.
- Witnesses have trouble recognizing members of a race other than their own.
- During storage, misleading post-event information biases eyewitness memory.
- Young children are particularly suggestible in this regard.
- Lineups are biased when a suspect is distinctive, when the police imply that the criminal is in the lineup, when witnesses make relative judgments, and when the suspect is familiar for other reasons.
- In court, jurors overestimate eyewitnesses' accuracy and cannot distinguish between accurate and inaccurate witnesses.
- People are too readily persuaded by a witness's confidence—a factor that does not reliably predict identification accuracy.
- Psychologists are sometimes called to testify as experts on eyewitness evidence.

Nonevidentiary Influences

- The more pretrial knowledge people have about a case, the more likely they are to presume the defendant guilty.
- Research shows that pretrial publicity can bias jury verdicts.
- Once inadmissible testimony leaks out in court, the jury is contaminated by it.
- A judge's cautionary instruction may worsen the situation by drawing attention to the forbidden testimony, arousing reactance, or leading jurors to see the information as relevant.

The Judge's Instructions

- The judge's instructions often have little impact, in part because they are often incomprehensible.
- The instructions are usually delivered after the evidence—after many jurors have formed an opinion.
- Jurors may not follow instructions that conflict with their own conceptions of justice, a phenomenon known as jury nullification.

Jury Deliberation

Leadership in the Jury Room

- Dominance hierarchies develop in the jury room.
- Certain people are more likely than others to be elected foreperson, but the foreperson tends to play the role of moderator rather than group leader.

The Dynamics of Deliberation

- Jury deliberations pass through three stages: orientation, open conflict, and reconciliation.
- The period of open conflict is filled with informational and normative pressures.
- When it comes to outcomes, the initial majority typically wins, although deliberation tends to produce a leniency bias.

Jury Size

- While the US Supreme Court has ruled that the use of 6-person juries is acceptable, the norm in Canada is still 12 people.
- But these smaller groups do not deliberate for as long as 12-person juries and contain less minority representation.

Post-Trial: To Prison and Beyond

The Sentencing Process

- Many people believe that judges are too lenient and that punishments for the same offence are often inconsistent from one case to another.
- Part of the problem is that people have different views of the goals of sentencing and punishment.

The Prison Experience

- Stanford researchers built a simulated prison and recruited male adults to act as guards and prisoners.
- Some guards were abusive, prisoners became passive, and the study had to be terminated.

Justice: A Matter of Procedure?

- Satisfaction with justice depends not only on winning and losing but also on the procedures used to achieve the outcome.
- People of all cultures prefer models of justice that offer participants a voice in the proceedings and the opportunity to be judged by an impartial decision maker.

Closing Statement

- Increasingly, social psychologists have become involved in studying the legal system—identifying the problems and seeking solutions.

Key Terms

adversarial model *(446)*
cross-race identification bias *(430)*
inquisitorial model *(446)*
jury nullification *(440)*
leniency bias *(442)*
misinformation effect *(431)*
peremptory challenge *(423)*
polygraph *(428)*
sentencing disparity *(444)*
voir dire *(422)*
weapon-focus effect *(430)*

Contrary to popular opinion, women are harsher as criminal trial jurors than men are.

False. *Demographic factors such as gender do not consistently predict juror verdicts; men may be harsher in some cases, women in others.*

Without being beaten or threatened, innocent people sometimes confess to crimes they did not commit.

True. *Innocent suspects sometimes confess—either to escape an unpleasant situation or because they are led to believe they committed a crime they cannot recall.*

A person can fool a lie-detector test by suppressing arousal when questions about the crime are asked.

False. *It is possible to beat a lie-detector test—but by elevating arousal when "innocent" questions are asked, not by trying to suppress arousal in response to "guilty" questions.*

Eyewitnesses find it relatively difficult to recognize members of a race other than their own.

True. *Researchers have observed this cross-race identification bias in both laboratory and field settings.*

The more confident an eyewitness is about an identification, the more accurate it is likely to be.

False. *Studies have shown that eyewitness confidence does not reliably predict accuracy, in part because confidence is influenced by post-identification factors.*

One can usually predict a jury's final verdict by knowing where the individual jurors stand the first time they vote.

True. *As a result of both informational and normative group influences, the preference of the initial voting majority usually prevails.*

GLOSSARY

actor-observer effect The tendency to attribute our own behaviour to situational causes and the behaviour of others to personal factors.

adversarial model A dispute-resolution system in which the Crown and defence present opposing sides of the story.

affective forecasting The process of predicting how one would feel in response to future emotional events.

aggression Behaviour intended to harm another individual.

altruistic Motivated by the desire to improve another's welfare.

ambivalent sexism A form of sexism characterized by attitudes about women that reflect both negative, resentful beliefs and feelings and affectionate, chivalrous, but potentially patronizing beliefs and feelings.

applied research Research designed to enlarge the understanding of naturally occurring events and to find solutions to practical problems.

arousal-affect model The proposition that aggression is influenced by both the intensity of arousal and the type of emotion produced by a stimulus.

arousal: cost-reward model The proposition that people react to emergency situations by acting in the most cost-effective way to reduce the arousal of shock and alarm.

attachment style The way a person typically interacts with significant others.

attitude A positive, negative, or mixed reaction to a person, object, or idea.

attitude scale A multiple-item questionnaire designed to measure a person's attitude toward some object.

attribution theory A group of theories that describe how people explain the causes of behaviour.

audience inhibition Reluctance to help for fear of making a bad impression on observers.

availability heuristic The tendency to estimate the likelihood that an event will occur by how easily instances of it come to mind.

base-rate fallacy The finding that people are relatively insensitive to consensus information presented in the form of numerical base rates.

basic research Research designed to increase the understanding of human behaviour, often by testing hypotheses based on a theory.

bask in reflected glory (BIRG) To increase self-esteem by associating with others who are successful.

behavioural genetics A subfield of psychology that examines the role of genetic factors in behaviour.

belief in a just world The belief that individuals get what they deserve in life, an orientation that leads people to disparage victims.

belief perseverance The tendency to maintain beliefs even after they have been discredited.

bogus pipeline A phoney lie-detector device that is sometimes used to get respondents to give truthful answers to sensitive questions.

brainstorming A technique that attempts to increase the production of creative ideas by encouraging group members to speak freely without criticizing their own or others' contributions.

bystander effect The effect whereby the presence of others inhibits helping.

catharsis A reduction of the motive to aggress that is said to result from any imagined, observed, or actual act of aggression.

central route to persuasion The process by which a person thinks carefully about a communication and is influenced by the strength of its arguments.

central traits Traits that exert a powerful influence on overall impressions.

cognitive dissonance theory The theory that holding inconsistent cognitions arouses psychological tension that people become motivated to reduce.

cognitive neoassociation analysis The view that unpleasant experiences create negative affect, which in turn stimulates associations connected with anger and fear. Emotional and behavioural outcomes then depend, at least in part, on higher-order cognitive processing.

collective People engaged in common activities but having minimal direct interaction.

collective effort model The theory that individuals will exert effort on a collective task to the degree that they think their individual efforts will be important, relevant, and meaningful for achieving outcomes that they value.

collectivism A cultural orientation in which interdependence, cooperation, and social harmony take priority over personal goals.

communal relationship A relationship in which the participants expect and desire mutual responsiveness to each other's needs.

companionate love A secure, trusting, stable partnership.

compliance Changes in behaviour that are elicited by direct requests.

confederate Accomplice of an experimenter who, in dealing with the real participants in an experiment, acts as if he or she is also a participant.

confirmation bias The tendency to seek, interpret, and create information that verifies existing beliefs.

conformity The tendency to change our perceptions, opinions, or behaviour in ways that are consistent with group norms.

construct validity The extent to which the measures used in a study measure the variables they were designed to measure and the manipulations in an experiment manipulate the variables they were designed to manipulate.
contact hypothesis The theory that direct contact between hostile groups will reduce prejudice under certain conditions.
contrast effect The tendency to perceive stimuli that differ from expectations as being even more different than they really are.
correlational research Research designed to measure the association between variables that are not manipulated by the researcher.
correlation coefficient A statistical measure of the strength and direction of the association between two variables.
counterfactual thinking The tendency to imagine alternative events or outcomes that might have occurred but did not.
covariation principle A principle of attribution theory holding that people attribute behaviour to factors that are present when a behaviour occurs and absent when it does not.
cross-cultural research Research designed to compare and contrast people of different cultures.
cross-race identification bias The tendency for people to have difficulty identifying members of a race other than their own.
cultivation The process by which the mass media (particularly television) construct a version of social reality for the public.
cycle of family violence The transmission of domestic violence across generations.

debriefing A disclosure, made to participants after research procedures are completed, in which the researcher explains the purpose of the research, attempts to resolve any negative feelings, and emphasizes the scientific contribution made by the participants' involvement.
deception In the context of research, a method that provides false information to participants.
deindividuation The loss of a person's sense of individuality and the reduction of normal constraints against deviant behaviour.
dependent variable In an experiment, a factor that experimenters measure to see if it is affected by the independent variable.
diffusion of responsibility The belief that others will or should take the responsibility for providing assistance to a person in need.
discrimination Any behaviour directed against persons because of their membership in a particular group.
displacement Aggressing against a substitute target because aggressive acts against the source of the frustration are inhibited by fear or lack of access.
distraction-conflict theory A theory holding that the presence of others will produce social facilitation effects only when those others distract from the task and create attentional conflict.
door-in-the-face technique A two-step compliance technique in which an influencer prefaces the real request with one that is so large that it is rejected.
downward social comparison The defensive tendency to compare ourselves with others who are worse off than we are.

egoistic Motivated by the desire to increase one's own welfare.
elaboration The process of thinking about and scrutinizing the arguments contained in a persuasive communication.
emotional aggression Inflicting harm for its own sake.
empathy-altruism hypothesis The proposition that empathic concern for a person in need produces an altruistic motive for helping.
entity theorists People who tend to see social groups as relatively fixed, static entities and the borders between groups as relatively clear and rigid.
equity theory The theory that people are most satisfied with a relationship when the ratio between benefits and contributions is similar for both partners.
escalation effect The condition in which commitments to a failing course of action are increased to justify investments already made.
evaluation apprehension theory A theory holding that the presence of others will produce social facilitation effects only when those others are seen as potential evaluators.
evolutionary psychology A subfield of psychology that uses the principles of evolution to understand human social behaviour.
exchange relationship A relationship in which the participants expect and desire strict reciprocity in their interactions.
excitation transfer The process whereby arousal caused by one stimulus is added to arousal from a second stimulus and the combined arousal is attributed to the second stimulus.
experiment A form of research that can demonstrate causal relationships because the experimenter has control over the events that occur and participants are randomly assigned to conditions.
experimental realism The degree to which experimental procedures are involving to participants and lead them to behave naturally and spontaneously.
experimenter expectancy effects The effects produced when an experimenter's expectations about the results of an experiment affect his or her behaviour toward a participant and thereby influence the participant's responses.
external validity The degree to which there can be reasonable confidence that the results of a study would be obtained for other people and in other situations.

facial electromyograph (EMG) An electronic instrument that records facial muscle activity associated with emotions and attitudes.
facial feedback hypothesis The hypothesis that changes in facial expression can lead to corresponding changes in emotion.
false-consensus effect The tendency for people to overestimate the extent to which others share their opinions, attributes, and behaviours.
foot-in-the-door technique A two-step compliance technique in which an influencer sets the stage for the real request by first getting a person to comply with a much smaller request.
frustration-aggression hypothesis The idea that frustration always elicits the motive to aggress and all aggression is caused by frustration.
fundamental attribution error The tendency to focus on the role of personal causes and underestimate the impact of situations on other people's behaviour.

good mood effect The effect whereby a good mood increases helping behaviour.

graduated and reciprocated initiatives in tension-reduction (GRIT) A strategy for unilateral, persistent efforts to establish trust and cooperation between opposing parties.

group Two or more persons perceived as related because of their interactions, membership in the same social category, or common fate.

group polarization The exaggeration through group discussion of initial tendencies in the thinking of group members.

groupthink A group decision-making style characterized by an excessive tendency among group members to seek concurrence.

habituation Adaptation to something familiar, so that both physiological and psychological responses are reduced.

hard-to-get effect The tendency to prefer people who are highly selective in their social choices over those who are more readily available.

hostile attribution bias The tendency to perceive hostile intent in others.

hypothesis A testable prediction about the conditions under which an event will occur.

idiosyncrasy credits Interpersonal "credits" that a person earns by following group norms.

illusory correlation An overestimate of the association between variables that are only slightly or not at all correlated.

implicit association test (IAT) A covert measure of unconscious attitudes, it is derived from the speed at which people respond to pairings of concepts—such as *black* or *white* with *good* or *bad.*

implicit attitude An attitude—such as prejudice—that one is not aware of having.

implicit egotism A nonconscious form of self-enhancement.

implicit personality theory A network of assumptions people make about the relationships among traits and behaviours.

impression formation The process of integrating information about a person to form a coherent impression.

incremental theorists People who tend to see social groups as relatively dynamic and changeable, with less consistency within groups and more malleability between groups.

independent variable In an experiment, a factor that experimenters manipulate to see if it affects the dependent variable.

individualism A cultural orientation in which independence, autonomy, and self-reliance take priority over group allegiances.

informational influence Influence that produces conformity when a person believes others are correct in their judgments.

information integration theory The theory that impressions are based on perceiver dispositions and a weighted average of a target person's traits.

informed consent An individual's deliberate, voluntary decision to participate in research, based on the researcher's description of what will be required during such participation.

ingroup favouritism The tendency to discriminate in favour of ingroups over outgroups.

ingroups Groups with which an individual feels a sense of membership, belonging, and identity.

inoculation hypothesis The idea that exposure to weak versions of a persuasive argument increases later resistance to that argument.

inquisitorial model A dispute-resolution system in which a neutral investigator gathers evidence from both sides and presents the findings in court.

instrumental aggression Inflicting harm in order to obtain something of value.

insufficient deterrence A condition in which people refrain from engaging in a desirable activity, even when only mild punishment is threatened.

insufficient justification A condition in which people freely perform an attitude-discrepant behaviour without receiving a large reward.

integrative agreement A negotiated resolution to a conflict in which all parties obtain outcomes that are superior to what they would have obtained from an equal division of the contested resources.

interaction A statistical term indicating the change in the effect of each independent variable as a function of other independent variables.

interactionist perspective An emphasis on how both an individual's personality and environmental characteristics influence behaviour.

internal validity The degree to which there can be reasonable certainty that the independent variables in an experiment caused the effects obtained on the dependent variables.

interrater reliability The degree to which different observers agree on their observations.

intimate relationship A close relationship between two adults involving emotional attachment, fulfillment of psychological needs, or interdependence.

jigsaw classroom A cooperative learning method used to reduce racial prejudice through interaction in group efforts.

jury nullification The jury's power to disregard, or "nullify," the law when it conflicts with personal conceptions of justice.

kinship selection Preferential helping of genetic relatives, so that genes held in common will survive.

learned helplessness A phenomenon in which experience with an uncontrollable event creates passive behaviour toward a subsequent threat to well-being.

leniency bias The tendency for jury deliberation to produce a tilt toward acquittal.

loneliness A feeling of deprivation about existing social relations.

low-balling A two-step compliance technique in which the influencer secures agreement with a request but then increases the size of that request by revealing hidden costs.

main effect A statistical term indicating the overall effect that an independent variable has on the dependent variable, ignoring all other independent variables.

matching hypothesis The proposition that people are attracted to others who are similar in physical attractiveness.

mere exposure effect The phenomenon whereby the more often people are exposed to a stimulus, the more positively they evaluate that stimulus.

mere presence theory The proposition that the mere presence of others is sufficient to produce social facilitation effects.

meta-analysis A set of statistical procedures used to review a body of evidence by combining the results of individual studies to measure the overall reliability and strength of particular effects.

minority influence The process by which dissenters produce change within a group.

misinformation effect The tendency for false post-event misinformation to become integrated into people's memory of an event.

mitigating information Information about a person's situation indicating that he or she should not be held fully responsible for aggressive actions.

modern racism A form of prejudice that surfaces in subtle ways when it is safe, socially acceptable, and easy to rationalize.

multicultural research Research designed to examine racial and ethnic groups within cultures.

mundane realism The degree to which the experimental situation resembles places and events in the real world.

need for affiliation The desire to establish and maintain many rewarding interpersonal relationships.

need for closure The desire to reduce cognitive uncertainty, which heightens the importance of first impressions.

need for cognition (NC) A personality variable that distinguishes people on the basis of how much they enjoy effortful cognitive activities.

negative state relief model The proposition that people help others in order to counteract their own feelings of sadness.

nonverbal behaviour Behaviour that reveals a person's feelings without words—through facial expressions, body language, and vocal cues.

normative influence Influence that produces conformity when a person fears the negative social consequences of appearing deviant.

norm of self-interest The sense in individualistic cultures that people's attitudes and behaviours are, and should be, highly influenced by their self-interest.

norm of social responsibility A moral standard emphasizing that people should help those who need assistance.

obedience Behaviour change produced by the commands of authority.

operational definition The specific procedures for manipulating or measuring a conceptual variable.

outgroup homogeneity effect The tendency to assume that there is greater similarity among members of outgroups than among members of ingroups.

outgroups Groups with which an individual does not feel a sense of membership, belonging, or identity.

overjustification effect The tendency for intrinsic motivation to diminish for activities that have become associated with reward or other extrinsic factors.

passionate love Romantic love characterized by high arousal, intense attraction, and fear of rejection.

peremptory challenge A means by which lawyers can exclude a limited number of prospective jurors without the judge's approval.

peripheral route to persuasion The process by which a person does not think carefully about a communication and is influenced instead by superficial cues.

personal attribution Attribution to internal characteristics of an actor, such as ability, personality, mood, or effort.

persuasion The process by which attitudes are changed.

pluralistic ignorance The state in which people mistakenly believe that their own thoughts and feelings are different from those of others, even when everyone's behaviour is the same.

polygraph A mechanical instrument that records physiological arousal from multiple channels; it is often used as a lie-detector test.

pornography Explicit sexual material.

prejudice Negative feelings toward persons based on their membership in certain groups.

primacy effect The tendency for information presented early in a sequence to have more impact on impressions than information presented later.

priming The tendency for recently used or perceived words or ideas to come to mind easily and influence the interpretation of new information.

Prisoner's Dilemma A type of dilemma in which one party must make either cooperative or competitive moves in relation to another party; typically designed in such a way that competitive moves are more beneficial to either side, but if both sides make competitive moves, they are both worse off than if they both cooperated.

private conformity The change of beliefs that occurs when a person privately accepts the position taken by others.

private self-consciousness A personality characteristic of individuals who are introspective, often attending to their own inner states.

process loss The reduction in group performance due to obstacles created by group processes, such as problems of coordination and motivation.

prosocial behaviours Actions intended to benefit others.

psychological reactance The theory that people react against threats to their freedom by asserting themselves and perceiving the threatened freedom as more attractive.

public conformity A superficial change in overt behaviour, without a corresponding change of opinion, produced by real or imagined group pressure.

public self-consciousness A personality characteristic of individuals who focus on themselves as social objects, as seen by others.

racism Prejudice and discrimination based on a person's racial background.

random assignment A method of assigning participants to the various conditions of an experiment so that each participant in the experiment has an equal chance of being in any of the conditions.

random sampling A method of selecting participants for a study so that everyone in a population has an equal chance of being in the study.

realistic conflict theory The theory that hostility between groups is caused by direct competition for limited resources.

reciprocity A mutual exchange between what we give and receive—for example, liking those who like us.

relative deprivation Feelings of discontent aroused by the belief that one fares poorly compared with others.

resource dilemmas Social dilemmas concerning how two or more people share a limited resource.

self-awareness theory The theory that self-focused attention leads people to notice self-discrepancies, thereby motivating either an escape from self-awareness or a change in behaviour.

self-concept The sum total of an individual's beliefs about his or her own personal attributes.

self-disclosure Revelations about the self that a person makes to others.

self-efficacy A person's belief that he or she is capable of the specific behaviour required to produce a desired outcome in a given situation.

self-esteem An affective component of the self, consisting of a person's positive and negative self-evaluations.

self-fulfilling prophecy The process by which one's expectations about a person eventually lead that person to behave in ways that confirm those expectations.

self-handicapping Behaviours designed to sabotage one's own performance in order to provide a subsequent excuse for failure.

self-monitoring The tendency to change behaviour in response to the self-presentation concerns of the situation.

self-perception theory The theory that when internal cues are difficult to interpret, people gain self-insight by observing their own behaviour.

self-presentation Strategies people use to shape what others think of them.

self-schema A belief people hold about themselves that guides the processing of self-relevant information.

sentencing disparity Inconsistency of sentences for the same offence from one judge to another.

sexism Prejudice and discrimination based on a person's gender.

sexual orientation A person's preference for members of the same sex (homosexuality), opposite sex (heterosexuality), or both sexes (bisexuality).

situational attribution Attribution to factors external to an actor, such as the task, other people, or luck.

sleeper effect A delayed increase in the persuasive impact of a noncredible source.

social categorization The classification of persons into groups on the basis of common attributes.

social cognition The study of how people perceive, remember, and interpret information about themselves and others.

social comparison theory The theory that people evaluate their own abilities and opinions by comparing themselves to others.

social dilemma A situation in which a self-interested choice by everyone creates the worst outcome for everyone.

social dominance orientation A desire to see one's ingroups as dominant over other groups and a willingness to adopt cultural values that facilitate oppression over other groups.

social exchange theory A perspective that views people as motivated to maximize benefits and minimize costs in their relationships with others.

social facilitation A process whereby the presence of others enhances performance on easy tasks but impairs performance on difficult tasks.

social identity theory The theory that people favour ingroups over outgroups in order to enhance their self-esteem.

social impact theory The theory that social influence depends on the strength, immediacy, and number of source persons relative to target persons.

social learning theory The theory that behaviour is learned through the observation of others as well as through the direct experience of rewards and punishments.

social loafing A group-produced reduction in individual output on easy tasks where contributions are pooled.

social neuroscience The study of the relationship between neural and social processes.

social norm A general rule of conduct reflecting standards of social approval and disapproval.

social perception A general term for the processes by which people come to understand one another.

social psychology The scientific study of how individuals think, feel, and behave in regard to other people and how individuals' thoughts, feelings, and behaviours are affected by other people.

social role theory The theory that small gender differences are magnified in perception by the contrasting social roles occupied by men and women.

stereotype A belief that associates a group of people with certain traits.

subject variable A variable that characterizes pre-existing differences among the participants in a study.

subliminal presentation A method of presenting stimuli so faintly or rapidly that people do not have any conscious awareness of having been exposed to them.

superordinate goal A shared goal that can be achieved only through cooperation among individuals or groups.

that's-not-all technique A two-step compliance technique in which the influencer begins with an inflated request, then decreases its apparent size by offering a discount or bonus.

theory An organized set of principles used to explain observed phenomena.

theory of planned behaviour The theory that attitudes toward a specific behaviour combine with subjective norms and perceived control to influence a person's actions.

threat-to-self-esteem model The theory that reactions to receiving assistance depend on whether help is perceived as supportive or threatening.

transactive memory A shared system for remembering information that enables multiple people to remember information together more efficiently than they could alone.

triangular theory of love A theory proposing that love has three basic components—intimacy, passion, and commitment—which can be combined to produce eight subtypes.

two-factor theory of emotion The theory that the experience of emotion is based on two factors: physiological arousal and a cognitive interpretation of that arousal.

voir dire The pretrial examination of prospective jurors by the judge or opposing lawyers to uncover signs of bias.

weapon-focus effect The tendency for the presence of a weapon to draw attention and impair a witness's ability to identify the culprit.

weapons effect The tendency of weapons to increase the likelihood of aggression by their mere presence.

what-is-beautiful-is-good stereotype The belief that physically attractive individuals also possess desirable personality characteristics.

References

Abbey, A. (1982). Sex differences in attributions for friendly behavior: Do males misperceive females' friendliness? *Journal of Personality and Social Psychology, 42*, 830–838.

Abbey, A. (1987). Misperceptions of friendly behavior as sexual interest: A survey of naturally occurring incidents. *Psychology of Women Quarterly, 11*, 173–194.

ABCNews.com (September 12, 2000). Democrats smell a rat.

Abelson, R. P. (1981). Psychological status of the script concept. *American Psychologist, 36*, 715–729.

Abelson, R. P., Aronson, E., McGuire, W. J., Newcomb, T. M., Rosenberg, M. J., & Tannenbaum, P. H. (1968). *Theories of cognitive consistency: A sourcebook.* Chicago: Rand McNally.

Aberson, C. L., Healy, M., & Romero, V. (2000). Ingroup bias and self-esteem: A meta-analysis. *Personality and Social Psychology Review, 4*, 157–173.

Aberson, C. L., & Howanski, L. M. (2002). Effects of self-esteem, status, and identification on two forms of ingroup bias. *Current Research in Social Psychology, 7*, 225–243.

Abshire, J., & Bernstein, B. H. (2003). Juror sensitivity to the cross-race effect. *Law and Human Behavior, 27*, 471–480.

Acker, M., & Davis, M. H. (1992). Intimacy, passion, and commitment in adult romantic relationships: A test of the triangular theory of love. *Journal of Social and Personal Relationships, 9*, 21–50.

Adair, J. G. (2005). The origins and development of social psychology in Canada. *International Journal of Psychology, 40*, 277–288.

Adams, J. S. (1965). Equity in social exchange. *Advances in Experimental Social Psychology, 2*, 267–299.

Aderman, D. (1972). Elation, depression, and helping behavior. *Journal of Personality and Social Psychology, 24*, 91–101.

Adorno, T., Frenkel-Brunswik, E., Levinson, D., & Sanford, R. N. (1950). *The authoritarian personality.* New York: Harper.

Aharpour, S., & Brown, R. (2002). Functions of group identification: An exploratory analysis. *Revue Internationale de Psychologie Sociale, 15*, 157–186.

Ahlfinger, N. R., & Esser, J. K. (2001). Testing the groupthink model: Effects of promotional leadership and conformity predisposition. *Social Behavior and Personality, 29*, 31–41.

Aiello, J. R., & Douthitt, E. A. (2001). Social facilitation from Triplett to electronic performance monitoring. *Group Dynamics, 5*, 163–180.

Ainsworth, M., Blehar, M. C., Waters, E., & Wall, S. (1978). *Patterns of attachment: A psychological study of the strange situation.* Hillsdale, NJ: Erlbaum.

Ajzen, I. (1991). The theory of planned behavior. *Organizational Behavior and Human Decision Processes, 50*, 179–211.

Ajzen, I. (2001). Nature and operation of attitudes. *Annual Review of Psychology, 52*, 27–58.

Ajzen, I., & Fishbein, M. (1977). Attitude-behavior relations: A theoretical analysis and review of empirical research. *Psychological Bulletin, 84*, 888–918.

Akimoto, S. A., & Sanbinmatsu, D. M. (1999). Differences in self-effacing behavior between European and Japanese Americans: Effect on competence evaluations. *Journal of Cross-Cultural Psychology, 30*, 159–177.

Albarracin, D., Johnson, B. T., Fishbein, M., & Muellerleile, P. A. (2001). Theories of reasoned action and planned behavior as models of condom use: A meta-analysis. *Psychological Bulletin, 127*, 142–161.

Alderson, A. (2001, November 11). Mother blames herself for the White Mischief copycat murder of her son. *Sunday Telegraph (London)*, p. 6.

Alexander, G. M. (2003). An evolutionary perspective of sex-typed toy preferences: Pink, blue, and the brain. *Archives of Sexual Behavior, 32*, 7–14.

Alexander, G. M., & Hines, M. (2002). Sex differences in response to children's toys in nonhuman primates *(Cercopithecus aethiops sabaeus). Evolution and Human Behavior, 23*, 467–479.

Alexander, M. G., & Fisher, T. D. (2003). Truth and consequences: Using the bogus pipeline to examine sex differences in self-reported sexuality. *Journal of Sex Research, 40*, 27–35.

Alicke, M. D., & Largo, E. (1995). The role of the self in the false consensus effect. *Journal of Experimental Social Psychology, 31*, 28–47.

Allen, B. (1995). Gender stereotypes are not accurate: A replication of Martin (1987) using diagnostic vs. self-report and behavioral criteria. *Sex Roles, 32*, 583–600.

Allen, J. B., Kenrick, D. T., Linder, D. E., & McCall, M. A. (1989). Arousal and attribution: A response-facilitation alternative to misattribution and negative-reinforcement models. *Journal of Personality and Social Psychology, 57*, 261–270.

Allen, V. L. (1965). Situational factors in conformity. In L. Berkowitz (Ed.), *Advances in Experimental Social Psychology, 2*, 133–175.

Allen, V. L., & Levine, J. M. (1969). Consensus and conformity. *Journal of Experimental Social Psychology, 5*, 389–399.

Allen, V. L., & Levine, J. M. (1971). Social support and conformity: The role of independent assessment of reality. *Journal of Experimental Social Psychology, 7*, 48–58.

Alley, T. R. (1988). *Social and applied aspects of perceiving faces.* Hillsdale, NJ: Erlbaum.

Allport, F. H. (1924). *Social psychology.* Boston: Houghton Mifflin.

Allport, F. H., et al. (1953). The effects of segregation and the consequences of desegregation: A social science statement. *Minneapolis Law Review, 37*, 429–440.

Allport, G. W. (1954). *The nature of prejudice.* Reading, MA: Addison-Wesley.

Allport, G. W. (1985). The historical background of social psychology. In G. Lindzey & E. Aronson (Eds.), *Handbook of social psychology* (3rd ed., Vol. I, pp. 1–46). New York: Random House.

Allport, G. W., & Postman, L. J. (1947). *The psychology of rumor.* New York: Holt.

Altemeyer, R. (2004) Highly dominating, highly authoritarian personalities. *Journal of Social Psychology, 144,* 421–447.

Altman, I. (1973). Reciprocity of interpersonal exchange. *Journal for Theory of Social Behavior, 3,* 249–261.

Altman, I., & Taylor, D. A. (1973). *Social penetration: The development of interpersonal relationships.* New York: Holt, Rinehart and Winston.

Alvidrez, A., & Weinstein, R. S. (1999). Early teacher perceptions and later student academic achievement. *Journal of Educational Psychology, 91,* 731–746.

Amabile, T. M. (1996). *Creativity in context.* New York: Westview.

Amabile, T. M., Hill, K. G., Hennessey, B. A., & Tighe, E. M. (1994). The work preference inventory: Assessing intrinsic and extrinsic motivation orientations. *Journal of Personality and Social Psychology, 66,* 950–967.

Amato, P. R. (1983). Helping behavior in urban and rural environments: Field studies based on a taxonomic organization of helping episodes. *Journal of Personality and Social Psychology, 45,* 571–586.

Ambady, N., & Rosenthal, R. (1993). Half a minute: Predicting teacher evaluations from thin slices of nonverbal behavior and physical attractiveness. *Journal of Personality and Social Psychology, 64,* 431–441.

Andersen, S. M., & Chen, S. (2002). The relational self: An interpersonal social-cognitive theory. *Psychological Review, 109,* 619–645.

Anderson, C. A. (2004a). Aggression. In E. Borgatta (Ed.), *The encyclopedia of sociology* (rev. ed.). New York: Macmillan.

Anderson, C. A. (2004b). An update on the effects of playing violent video games. *Journal of Adolescence, 27,* 113–122.

Anderson, C. A., Anderson, K. B., & Deuser, W. E. (1996). Examining an affective framework: Weapon and temperature effects on aggressive thoughts, affect, and attitudes. *Personality and Social Psychology Bulletin, 22,* 366–376.

Anderson, C. A., Anderson, K. B., Dorr, N., DeNeve, K. M., & Flanagan, M. (2000). Temperature and aggression. In M. P. Zanna (Ed.), *Advances in experimental social psychology* (Vol. 32, pp. 63–133). San Diego, CA: Academic Press.

Anderson, C. A., Benjamin, A. J. Jr., & Bartholow, B. D. (1998). Does the gun pull the trigger? Automatic priming effects of weapon pictures and weapon names. *Psychological Science, 9,* 308–314.

Anderson, C. A., Berkowitz, L., Donnerstein, E., Huesmann, L. R., Johnson, J., Linz, D., Malamuth, N., & Wartella, E. (2001). The influence of media violence on youth. *Psychological Science in the Public Interest, 4,* 81–110.

Anderson, C. A., & Bushman, B. J. (2002a). The effects of media violence on society. *Science, 295,* 2377–2379.

Anderson, C. A., & Bushman, B. J. (2002b). The general aggression model: An integrated social-cognitive model of human aggression. *Annual Review of Psychology, 53,* 27–51.

Anderson, C. A., Carnagey, N. L., & Eubanks, J. (2003). Exposure to violent media: The effects of songs with violent lyrics on aggressive thoughts and feelings. *Journal of Personality and Social Psychology, 84,* 960–971.

Anderson, C. A., Carnagey, N. L., Flanagan, M., Benjamin, A. J., Eubanks, J., & Valentine, J. C. (2004). Violent video games: Specific effects of violent content on aggressive thoughts and behavior. In M. Zanna (Ed.), *Advances in experimental social psychology.* San Diego, CA: Academic Press.

Anderson, C. A., & Huesmann, L. R. (2003). Human aggression: A social-cognitive view. In M. A. Hogg & J. Cooper (Eds.), *Handbook of social psychology* (pp. 296–323). London: Sage.

Anderson, C. A., Lepper, M. R., & Ross, L. (1980). Perseverance of social theories: The role of explanation in the persistence of discredited information. *Journal of Personality and Social Psychology, 39,* 1037–1049.

Anderson, C. A., Lindsay, J. J., & Bushman, B. J. (1999). Research in the psychological laboratory: Truth or triviality? *Current Directions in Psychological Science, 8,* 3–9.

Anderson, C. A., Miller, R. S., Riger, A. L., Dill, J. C., & Sedikides, C. (1994). Behavioral and characterological attributional styles as predictors of depression and loneliness: Review, refinement, and test. *Journal of Personality and Social Psychology, 66,* 549–558.

Anderson, C. A., & Sechler, E. S. (1986). Effects of explanation and counterexplanation on the development and use of social theories. *Journal of Personality and Social Psychology, 50,* 24–34.

Anderson, D. E., DePaulo, B. M., Ansfield, M. E., Tickle, J. J., & Green, E. (1999). Beliefs about cues to deception: Mindless stereotypes or untapped wisdom? *Journal of Nonverbal Behavior, 23,* 67–89.

Anderson, J. L., Crawford, C. B., Nadeau, J., & Lindberg, T. (1992). Was the Duchess of Windsor right? A cross-cultural review of the socioecology of ideals of female body shape. *Ethology and Sociobiology, 13,* 197–227.

Anderson, N. H. (1965). Averaging versus adding as a stimulus combination rule in impression formation. *Journal of Experimental Social Psychology, 70,* 394–400.

Anderson, N. H. (1968). Likableness ratings of 555 personality-trait words. *Journal of Personality and Social Psychology, 9,* 272–279.

Anderson, N. H. (1981). *Foundations of information integration theory.* New York: Academic Press.

Anderson, N. H., & Hubert, S. (1963). Effects of concomitant verbal recall on order effects in personality impression formation. *Journal of Verbal Learning and Verbal Behavior, 2,* 379–391.

Archer, D., & Gartner, R. (1984). *Violence and crime in crossnational perspective.* New Haven, CT: Yale University Press.

Archer, J. (2000). Sex differences in aggression between heterosexual partners: A meta-analytic review. *Psychological Bulletin, 126,* 651–680.

Archer, J. (2005). Are women or men the more aggressive sex? In S. Fein, G. R. Goethals, & M. J. Sandstrom (Eds.), *Gender and aggression: Interdisciplinary perspectives.* Mahwah, NJ: Erlbaum.

Archibald, F. S., Bartholomew, K., & Marx, R. (1995). Loneliness in early adolescence: A test of the cognitive discrepancy model of loneliness. *Personality and Social Psychology Bulletin, 21,* 296–301.

Ardts, J., Jansen, P., & van der Velde, M. (2001). The breaking in of new employees: Effectiveness of socialization tactics and personnel instruments. *Journal of Management Development, 20,* 159–167.

Arendt, H. (1963). *Eichmann in Jerusalem: A report on the banality of evil.* New York: Viking.

Argote, L., Devadas, R., & Melone, N. (1990). The base-rate fallacy: Contrasting processes and outcomes of group and individual judgment. *Organizational Behavior and Human Decision Processes, 46,* 296–310.

Argote, L., Insko, C. A., Yovetich, N., & Romero, A. A. (1995). Group learning curves: The effects of turnover and task complexity on group performance. *Journal of Applied Social Psychology, 25,* 512–529.

Arkin, R. M. (1981). Self-presentation styles. In J. T. Tedeschi (Ed.), *Impression management theory and social psychological research* (pp. 311–333). New York: Academic Press.

Armour, S. (1998, February 17). Office ethics: Teams make it hard to tattle. *USA Today,* p. 6B.

Armstrong, S. J., Allinson, C. W., & Hayes, J. (2002). Formal mentoring systems: An examination of the effects of mentor/protege cognitive styles on the mentoring process. *Journal of Management Studies, 39,* 1111–1137.

Arndt, J., Greenberg, J., Schimel, J., Pyszczynski, T., & Solomon, S. (2002). To belong or not to belong, that is the question: Terror management and identification with gender and ethnicity. *Journal of Personality and Social Psychology, 83,* 26–43.

Aron, A., & Aron, E. N. (2001). The self-expansion model: Motivation and including other in the self. In W. Ickes & S. Duck (Eds.), *The social psychology of personal relationships.* Chichester, England: Wiley.

Aron, A., Aron, E. N., & Smollan, D. (1992). Inclusion of Other in the Self Scale and the structure of interpersonal closeness. *Journal of Personality and Social Psychology, 63,* 596–612.

Aron, A., Aron, E. N., Tudor, M., & Nelson, G. (1991). Close relationships as including other in the self. *Journal of Personality and Social Psychology, 60,* 241–253.

Aron, A., Dutton, D. G., Aron, E. N., & Iverson, A. (1989). Experiences of falling in love. *Journal of Social and Personal Relationships, 6,* 243–257.

Aron, A., Norman, C. C., Aron, E. N., McKenna, C., & Heyman, R. E. (2000). Couples' shared participation in novel and arousing activities and experienced relationship quality. *Journal of Personality and Social Psychology, 78,* 273–284.

Aron, A., & Westbay, L. (1996). Dimensions of the prototype of love. *Journal of Personality and Social Psychology, 70,* 535–551.

Aronoff, J., Barclay, A. M., & Stevenson, L. A. (1988). The recognition of threatening facial stimuli. *Journal of Personality and Social Psychology, 54,* 647–655.

Aronoff, J., Woike, B. A., & Hyman, L. M. (1992). Which are the stimuli in facial displays of anger and happiness? *Journal of Personality and Social Psychology, 62,* 1050–1066.

Aronson, E. (1992). Stateways can change folkways. In R. M. Baird & S. E. Rosenbaum (Eds.), *Bigotry, prejudice, and hatred: Definitions, causes, and solutions* (pp. 185–201). Buffalo, NY: Prometheus.

Aronson, E. (1999). Dissonance, hypocrisy, and the self-concept. In E. Harmon-Jones & J. Mills (Eds.), *Cognitive dissonance: Progress on a pivotal theory in social psychology* (pp. 103–126). Washington, DC: American Psychological Association.

Aronson, E., Blaney, N., Stephan, C., Sikes, J., & Snapp, M. (1978). *The jigsaw classroom.* Beverly Hills, CA: Sage.

Aronson, E., & Carlsmith, J. M. (1963). Effect of severity of threat on the devaluation of forbidden behavior. *Journal of Abnormal and Social Psychology, 66,* 584–588.

Aronson, E., & Carlsmith, J. M. (1968). Experimentation in social psychology. In G. Lindzey & E. Aronson (Eds.), *Handbook of social psychology* (Vol. 2, 2nd ed., pp. 1–79). Reading, MA: Addison-Wesley.

Aronson, E., & Cope, V. (1968). My enemy's enemy is my friend. *Journal of Personality and Social Psychology, 8,* 8–12.

Aronson, E., & Linder, D. (1965). Gain and loss of esteem as determinants of interpersonal attractiveness. *Journal of Experimental Social Psychology, 1,* 156–172.

Aronson, E., & Mills, J. (1959). The effect of severity of initiation on liking for a group. *Journal of Abnormal and Social Psychology, 59,* 177–181.

Aronson, J., Lustina, M. J., Good, C., Keough, K., Steele, C. M., & Brown, J. (1999). When white men can't do math: Necessary and sufficient factors in stereotype threat. *Journal of Experimental Social Psychology, 35,* 29–46.

Arrow, H., & Burns, K. L. (2004). Self-organizing culture: How norms emerge in small groups. In M. Schaller & C. S. Crandall (Eds.), *The psychological foundations of culture* (pp. 171–199). Mahwah, NJ: Erlbaum.

Arunachalam, V., Wall, J. A., Jr., & Chan, C. (1998). Hong Kong versus U.S. negotiations: Effects of culture, alternatives, outcome scales, and mediation. *Journal of Applied Social Psychology, 28,* 1219–1244.

Asch, S. E. (1946). Forming impressions of personality. *Journal of Abnormal and Social Psychology, 41,* 258–290.

Asch, S. E. (1951). Effects of group pressure upon the modification and distortion of judgments. In H. Guetzkow (Ed.), *Groups, leadership, and men.* Pittsburgh, PA: Carnegie Press.

Asch, S. E. (1955, November). Opinions and social pressure. *Scientific American,* pp. 31–35.

Asch, S. E. (1956). Studies of independence and conformity: A minority of one against a unanimous majority. *Psychological Monographs, 70,* 416.

Asch, S. E., & Zukier, H. (1984). Thinking about persons. *Journal of Personality and Social Psychology, 46,* 1230–1240.

Askenasy, H. (1978). *Are we all Nazis?* Secaucus, NJ: Lyle Stuart.

Aspinwall, L. G., & Taylor, S. E. (1993). The effects of social comparison direction, threat, and self-esteem on affect, self-evaluation, and expected success. *Journal of Personality and Social Psychology, 64,* 708–722.

Aspinwall, L. G., & Taylor, S. E. (1997). A stitch in time: Self-regulation and proactive coping. *Psychological Bulletin, 121,* 417–436.

Associated Press. (1988, October 10). Skirting the issue? *The National Law Journal,* p. 43.

Au, W. T., & Komorita, S. S. (2002). Effects of initial choices in the prisoner's dilemma. *Journal of Behavioral Decision Making, 15,* 343–359.

Austin, J. R. (2003). Transactive memory in organizational groups: The effects of content, consensus, specialization, and accuracy on group performance. *Journal of Applied Psychology, 88,* 866–878.

Axelrod, R. (1984). *The evolution of cooperation.* New York: Basic Books.

Axsom, D., & Cooper, J. (1985). Cognitive dissonance and psychotherapy: The role of effort justification in inducing weight loss. *Journal of Experimental Social Psychology, 21,* 149–160.

Axtell, R. E. (1993). *Do's and taboos around the world* (3rd ed.). New York: John Wiley.

Bagemihl, B. (1999). *Biological exuberance: Animal homosexuality and natural diversity.* New York: St. Martin's Press.

Baglione, V., Canestrari, D., Marcos, J. M., & Ekman, J. (2003). Kin selection in cooperative alliances of carrion crows. *Science, 300,* 1947–1949.

Bagozzi, R. P., & Moore, D. J. (1994). Public service advertisements: Emotions and empathy guide prosocial behavior. *Journal of Marketing, 58,* 56–70.

Bahrick, H. P., Hall, L. K., & Berger, S. A. (1996). Accuracy and distortion in memory for high school grades. *Psychological Science,* 7, 265–271.

Bailenson, J. N., Blascovich, J., Beall, A. C., & Loomis, J. M. (2003). Interpersonal distance in immersive virtual environments. *Personality and Social Psychology Bulletin, 29,* 819–833.

Bailey, D. S., & Taylor, S. P. (1991). Effects of alcohol and aggressive disposition on human physical aggression. *Journal of Research in Personality, 25,* 334–342.

Bailey, J. M., Dunne, M. P., & Martin, N. G. (2000). Genetic and environmental influences on sexual orientation and its correlates in an Australian twin sample. *Journal of Personality and Social Psychology 78,* 524–536.

Bailey, J. M., & Pillard, R. C. (1991). A genetic study of male sexual orientation. *Archives of General Psychiatry, 48,* 1089–1096.

Bailey, J. M., Pillard, R. C., Neale, M. C., & Agyei, Y. (1993). Heritable factors influence sexual orientation in women. *Archives of General Psychiatry, 50,* 217–223.

Bailey, J. M., & Zucker, K. J. (1995). Childhood sex-typed behavior and sexual orientation: A conceptual analysis and quantitative review. *Development Psychology, 31,* 43–55.

Baldwin, M. (1994). Primed relational schemas as a source of self-evaluative reactions. *Journal of Social and Clinical Psychology, 3,* 380–403.

Baldwin, M., & Fehr, B. (1995). On the instability of attachment style ratings. *Personal Relationships, 2,* 247–261.

Baldwin, M. W., & Sinclair, L. (1996). Self-esteem and "if . . . then" contingencies of interpersonal acceptance. *Journal of Personality and Social Psychology, 71,* 1130–1141.

Bales, R. F. (1958). Task roles and social roles in problem-solving groups. In E. E. Maccoby, T. M. Newcomb, & E. L. Hartley (Eds.), *Readings in social psychology* (3rd ed., pp. 437–447). New York: Holt.

Banaji, M. R., & Hardin, C. D. (1996). Automatic gender stereotyping. *Psychological Science,* 7, 136–141.

Banaji, M. R., Hardin, C., & Rothman, A. J. (1993). Implicit stereotyping in person judgment. *Journal of Personality and Social Psychology, 65,* 272–281.

Banaji, M. R., & Steele, C. M. (1989). Alcohol and self-evaluation: Is a social cognition approach beneficial? *Social Cognition,* 7, 137–151.

Bancroft, J. (Ed.) (1997). *Researching sexual behavior: Methodological issues.* Bloomington: Indiana University Press.

Bandura, A. (1973). *Aggression: A social learning analysis.* Englewood Cliffs, NJ: Prentice-Hall.

Bandura, A. (1977). *Social learning theory.* Englewood Cliffs, NJ: Prentice-Hall.

Bandura, A. (1983). Psychological mechanisms of aggression. In R. G. Green & E. I. Donnerstein (Eds.), *Aggression: Theoretical and empirical reviews: Vol. l. Theoretical and methodological issues* (pp. 1–40). New York: Academic Press.

Bandura, A. (1997). *Self-efficacy: The exercise of control.* New York: W. H. Freeman.

Bandura, A. (1999). A sociocognitive analysis of substance abuse: An agentic perspective. *Psychological Science, 10,* 214–218.

Bandura, A. (1999). Moral disengagement in the perpetration of inhumanities. *Personality and Social Psychology Review, 3,* 193–209.

Bandura, A. (2002). Selective moral disengagement in the exercise of moral agency. *Journal of Moral Education, 31,* 101–119.

Bandura, A. (2004). The role of selective moral disengagement in terrorism and counterterrorism. In F. M. Moghaddam & A. J. Marsella (Eds.), *Understanding terrorism: Psychosocial roots, consequences, and interventions* (pp. 121–150). Washington, DC: American Psychological Association.

Bandura, A., Barbaranelli, C., Caprara, G. V., & Pastorelli, C. (1996). Mechanisms of moral disengagement in the exercise of moral agency. *Journal of Personality and Social Psychology, 71,* 364–374.

Bandura, A., Ross, R., & Ross, S. (1961). Transmission of aggression through imitation of aggressive models. *Journal of Abnormal and Social Psychology, 63,* 575–582.

Banuazizi, A., & Movahedi, S. (1975). Interpersonal dynamics in a simulated prison: A methodological analysis. *American Psychologist, 30,* 152–160.

Barash, D. P., & Lipton, J. E. (2001). *The myth of monogamy.* New York: Freeman.

Bargh, J. A. (1997). The automaticity of everyday life. In R. S. Wyer (Ed.), *The automaticity of everyday life: Advances in social cognition* (Vol. 10, pp. 1–61). Mahwah, NJ: Erlbaum.

Bargh, J. A., Chaiken, S., Govender, R., & Pratto, F. (1992). The generality of the automatic attitude activation effect. *Journal of Personality and Social Psychology, 62,* 893–912.

Bargh, J. A., Chaiken, S., Raymond, P., & Hymes, C. (1996). The automatic evaluation effect: Unconditional automatic attitude activation with a pronunciation task. *Journal of Experimental Social Psychology, 31,* 104–128.

Bargh, J. A., & Chartrand, T. L. (1999). The unbearable automaticity of being. *American Psychologist, 54,* 462–479.

Bargh, J. A., & Chartrand, T. L. (2000). The mind in the middle: A practical guide for priming and automaticity research. In H. T. Reis and C. M. Judd (Eds.), *Handbook of research methods in social and personality psychology* (pp. 253–285). New York: Cambridge University Press.

Bargh, J. A., Chen, M., & Burrows, L. (1996). Automaticity of social behavior: Direct effects of trait construct and stereotype activation on action. *Journal of Personality and Social Psychology, 71,* 230–244.

Bargh, J. A., Fitzsimons, G. M., & McKenna, K. Y. A. (2003). The self, online. In S. J. Spencer, S. Fein, M. P. Zanna, & J. P. Olson (Eds.), *Motivated social perception: The Ontario symposium,* (Vol. 9, pp. 195–213). Mahwah, NJ: Erlbaum.

Bargh, J. A., Lombardi, W. J., & Higgins, E. T. (1988). Automaticity of chronically accessible constructs in person × situation effects on person perception: It's just a matter of time. *Journal of Personality and Social Psychology, 55,* 599–605.

Bargh, J.A., & McKenna, K. Y. A. (2004). The internet and social life. *Annual Review of Psychology, 55,* 20.1–20.18.

Bargh, J. A., & Pietromonaco, P. (1982). Automatic information processing and social perception: The influence of trait information presented outside of conscious awareness on impression formation. *Journal of Personality and Social Psychology, 43,* 437–449.

Barnes, R. D., Ickes, W., & Kidd, R. F. (1979). Effects of the perceived intentionality and stability of another's dependency on helping behavior. *Personality and Social Psychology Bulletin, 5,* 367–372.

Baron, J., & Miller, J. G. (2000). Limiting the scope of moral obligations to help: A cross-cultural investigation. *Journal of Cross Cultural Psychology, 31,* 703–725.

Baron, R., Logan, H., Lilly, J., Inman, M., & Brennan, M. (1994). Negative emotion and message processing. *Journal of Experimental Social Psychology, 30,* 181–201.

Baron, R. A. (1997). The sweet smell of . . . helping: Effects of pleasant ambient fragrance on prosocial behavior in shopping malls. *Personality and Social Psychology Bulletin, 23,* 498–503.

Baron, R. A., & Ball, R. L. (1974). The aggression-inhibiting influence of nonhostile behavior. *Journal of Experimental Social Psychology, 10,* 23–33.

Baron, R. A., & Richardson, D. R. (1994). *Human aggression* (2nd ed.). New York: Plenum.

Baron, R. S. (1986). Distraction-conflict theory: Progress and problems. In L. Berkowitz (Ed.), *Advances in experimental social psychology* (Vol. 19, pp. 1–40). Orlando, FL: Academic Press.

Baron, R. S., Hoppe, S. I., Kao, C. F., Brunsman, B., Linneweh, B., & Rogers, D. (1996). Social corroboration and opinion extremity. *Journal of Experimental Social Psychology, 32,* 537–560.

Baron, R. S., Vandello, J. A., & Brunsman, B. (1996). The forgotten variable in conformity research: Impact of task importance on social influence. *Journal of Personality and Social Psychology, 71,* 915–927.

Bar-Tal, D. (1996). Development of social categories and stereotypes in early childhood: The case of "the Arab" concept formation, stereotype and attitudes by Jewish children in Israel. *International Journal of Intercultural Relations, 20,* 341–370.

Bartlett, M. S., Hagar, J. C., Ekman, P., & Sejnowski, T. J. (1999). Measuring facial expressions by computer image analysis. *Psychophysiology, 36,* 253–263.

Bartsch, R. A., Burnett, T., Diller, T. R., & Rankin-Williams, E. E. (2000). Gender representation in television commercials: Updating an update. *Sex Roles, 43,* 735–743.

Bartsch, R. A., Judd, C. M., Louw, D. A., Park, B., & Ryan, C. S. (1997). Cross-national outgroup homogeneity: United States and South African stereotypes. *South African Journal of Psychology, 27,* 166–170.

Basden, B. H., Basden, D. R., Bryner, S., & Thomas, R. L. III. (1997). A comparison of group and individual remembering: Does collaboration disrupt retrieval strategies? *Journal of Experimental Psychology: Learning, Memory, and Cognition, 23,* 1176–1191.

Bashore, T. R., & Rapp, P. E. (1993). Are there alternatives to traditional polygraph procedures? *Psychological Bulletin, 113,* 3–22.

Bassili, J. N. (2003). The minority slowness effect: Subtle inhibitions in the expression of views not shared by others. *Journal of Personality and Social Psychology, 84,* 261–276.

Bassili, J. N., & Provencal, A. (1988). Perceiving minorities: A factor-analytic approach. *Personality and Social Psychology Bulletin, 14,* 5–15.

Batson, C. D. (1991). *The altruism question.* Hillsdale, NJ: Erlbaum.

Batson, C. D. (1998). Altruism and prosocial behavior. In D. T. Gilbert, S. T. Fiske, & G. Lindzey (Eds.), *The handbook of social psychology* (4th ed., Vol. 2, pp. 282–316). New York: McGraw-Hill.

Batson, C. D. (2002). Addressing the altruism question experimentally. In S. G. Post & L. G. Underwood (Eds.), *Altruism and altruistic love: Science, philosophy, and religion in dialogue* (pp. 89–105). London: Oxford University Press.

Batson, C. D., Chang, J., Orr, R., & Rowland, J. (2001). Empathy, attitudes, and action: Can feeling for a member of a stigmatized group motivate one to help the group? *Personality and Social Psychology Bulletin, 28,* 1656–1666.

Batson, C. D., Cochran, P. J., Biederman, M. F., Blosser, J. L., Ryan, M. J., & Vogt, B. (1978). Failure to help when in a hurry: Callousness or conflict? *Personality and Social Psychology Bulletin, 4,* 97–101.

Batson, C. D., Duncan, B. D., Ackerman, P., Buckley, T., & Birch, K. (1981). Is empathic emotion a source of altruistic motivation? *Journal of Personality and Social Psychology, 40,* 290–302.

Batson, C. D., Early, S., & Salvarani, G. (1997). Perspective taking: Imagining how another feels versus imagining how you would feel. *Personality and Social Psychology Bulletin, 23,* 751–758.

Batson, C. D., Kobrynowicz, D., Dinnerstein, J. L., & Kampf, H. C. (1997). In a very different voice: Unmasking moral hypocrisy. *Journal of Personality and Social Psychology, 72,* 1335–1348.

Batson, C. D., O'Quin, K., Fultz, J., Vanderplas, M., & Isen, A. M. (1983). Influence of self-reported distress and empathy on egoistic versus altruistic motivation to help. *Journal of Personality and Social Psychology, 45,* 706–718.

Batson, C. D., Polycarpou, M. P., Harmon-Jones, E., Imhoff, H. J., Mitchener, E. C., Bednar, L. L., Klein, T. R., & Highberger, L. (1997). Empathy and attitudes: Can feeling for a member of a stigmatized group improve feelings toward the group? *Journal of Personality and Social Psychology, 72,* 105–118.

Batson, C. D., & Powell, A. A. (2003). Altruism and prosocial behavior. In T. Millon & M. J. Lerner (Eds.), *Handbook of psychology: Personality and social psychology* (Vol. 5, pp. 463–484). New York: Wiley.

Batson, C. D., Sager, K., Garst, E., Kang, M., Rubchinsky, K., & Dawson, K. (1997). Is empathy-induced helping due to self-other merging? *Journal of Personality and Social Psychology, 73,* 495–509.

Batson, C. D., Thompson, E. R., & Chen, H. (2002). Moral hypocrisy: Addressing some alternatives. *Journal of Personality and Social Psychology, 83,* 330–339.

Batson, C. D., & Weeks, J. L. (1996). Mood effects of unsuccessful helping: Another test of the empathy-altruism hypothesis. *Personality and Social Psychology Bulletin, 22,* 148–157.

Baugh, S. G., & Graen, G. B. (1997). Effects of team gender and racial composition on perceptions of team performance in cross-functional teams. *Group and Organization Management, 22,* 366–383.

Baumeister, R. F. (1982). A self-presentational view of social phenomena. *Psychological Bulletin, 91,* 3–26.

Baumeister, R. F. (1984). Choking under pressure: Self-consciousness and paradoxical effects of incentives on skillful performance. *Journal of Personality and Social Psychology, 46,* 610–620.

Baumeister, R. F. (1991). *Escaping the self.* New York: Basic Books.

Baumeister, R. F. (Ed.) (1999). *The self in social psychology.* Philadelphia: Taylor & Francis.

Baumeister, R. F. (2000). Gender differences in erotic plasticity: The female sex drive as socially flexible and responsive. *Psychological Bulletin, 126,* 347–374.

Baumeister, R. F., Bushman, B. J., & Campbell, W. K. (2000). Self-esteem, narcissism, and aggression: Does violence result from low self-esteem or from threatened egotism? *Current Directions in Psychological Science, 9*, 26–29.

Baumeister, R. F., Catanese, K. R., & Vohs, K. D. (2001). Is there a gender difference in the strength of sex drive? Theoretical views, conceptual distinctions, and a review of relevant evidence. *Personality and Social Psychology Review, 5*, 242–273.

Baumeister, R. F., Chesner, S. P., Sanders, P. S., & Tice, D. M. (1988). Who's in charge here? Group leaders do lend help in emergencies. *Personality and Social Psychology Bulletin, 14*, 17–22.

Baumeister, R. F., & Leary, M. R. (1995). The need to belong: Desire for interpersonal attachments as a fundamental human motivation. *Psychological Bulletin, 117*, 497–529.

Baumeister, R. F., & Scher, S. J. (1988). Self-defeating behavior patterns among normal individuals: Review and analysis of common self-destructive tendencies. *Psychological Bulletin, 104*, 3–22.

Baumeister, R., Stillwell, A. M., & Hetherington, T. F. (1994). Guilt: An interpersonal approach. *Psychological Bulletin, 115*, 243–267.

Baumeister, R. F., & Tice, D. M. (1984). Role of self-presentation and choice in cognitive dissonance under forced compliance: Necessary or sufficient causes? *Journal of Personality and Social Psychology, 46*, 5–13.

Baumeister, R. F., & Twenge, J. M. (2003). The social self. In T. Millon & M. J. Lerner (Eds.), *Handbook of psychology: Personality and social psychology* (Vol. 5, pp. 327–352). New York: Wiley.

Baumeister, R. F., & Vohs, K. D. (Eds.) (2004). *Handbook of self-regulation.* New York: Guilford.

Baumrind, D. (1997). Necessary distinctions. *Psychological Inquiry, 8*, 176–229.

Baxter, L. A. (1987). Self-disclosure and disengagement. In V. J. Derleg & J. H. Berg (Eds.), *Self-disclosure: Theory, research, and therapy* (pp. 155–174). New York: Plenum.

Bayles, F. (2001, March 27). Nurse gets life in prison for killing 4 veterans. Experts explore motives of medical murderers. *USA Today*, p. 6A.

Bazerman, M. H., Curhan, J. R., Moore, D. A., Valley, K. L. (2000). Negotiation. *Annual Review of Psychology, 51*, 279–314.

Bazerman, M. H., & Neale, M. A. (1992). *Negotiating rationally.* New York: Free Press.

Beach, S. R. H., Tesser, A., Mendolia, M., Anderson, P., et al. (1996). Self-evaluation maintenance in marriage: Toward a performance ecology of the marital relationship. *Journal of Family Psychology, 10*, 379–396.

Beaman, A. L., Klentz, B., Diener, E., & Svanum, S. (1979). Objective self-awareness and transgression in children: A field study. *Journal of Personality and Social Psychology, 37*, 1835–1846.

Beckerman, S., & Valentine, P. (Eds.) (2002). *Cultures of multiple fathers: The theory and practice of partible paternity in lowland South America.* Gainesville: University Press of Florida.

Beidel, D. C., & Turner, S. M. (1998). *Shy children, phobic adults: Nature and treatment of social phobia.* Washington, DC: American Psychological Association.

Beilock, S. L., & Carr, T. H. (2001). On the fragility of skilled performance: What governs choking under pressure? *Journal of Experimental Psychology: General, 130*, 701–725.

Bell, A. P., Weinberg, M. S., & Hammersmith, S. K. (1981). *Sexual preference: Its development in men and women.* Bloomington: Indiana University Press.

Bell, J., Grekul, J., Lamba, N., Minas, C., & Harrell, W. A. (1995). The impact of cost on student helping behavior. *Journal of Social Psychology, 135*, 49–56.

Belmore, S. M. (1987). Determinants of attention during impression formation. *Journal of Experimental Psychology: Learning, Memory, and Cognition, 13*, 480–489.

Belsky, J. (1993). Etiology of child maltreatment: A developmental-ecological analysis. *Psychological Bulletin, 114*, 413–434.

Bem, D. J. (1965). An experimental analysis of self-persuasion. *Journal of Experimental Social Psychology, 1*, 199–218.

Bem, D. J. (1967). Self-perception: An alternative interpretation of cognitive dissonance phenomena. *Psychological Review, 74*, 183–200.

Bem, D. J. (1972). Self-perception theory. In L. Berkowitz (Ed.), *Advances in experimental social psychology* (Vol. 6, pp. 1–62). New York: Academic Press.

Bem, D. J. (1996). Exotic becomes erotic: A developmental theory of sexual orientation. *Psychological Review, 103*, 320–335.

Bem, D. J. (2000). Exotic becomes erotic: Interpreting the biological correlates of sexual orientation. *Archives of Sexual Behavior, 29*, 531–548.

Bem, S. L. (1981). Gender schema theory: A cognitive account of sex typing. *Psychological Review, 88*, 354–364.

Benjet, C., & Kazdin, A. E. (2003). Spanking children: The controversies, findings and new directions. *Clinical Psychology Review, 23*, 197–224.

Bennett, J. C. (1991). The irrationality of the catharsis theory of aggression as justification for educators' support of interscholastic football. *Perceptual and Motor Skills, 72*, 415–418.

Benson, P. L., Karabenick, S. A., & Lerner, R. M. (1976). Pretty pleases: The effects of physical attractiveness, race, and sex on receiving help. *Journal of Experimental Social Psychology, 12*, 409–415.

Ben-Zeev, T., Fein, S., & Inzlicht, M. (2005). Arousal and stereotype threat. *Journal of Experimental Social Psychology, 41*, 174–181.

Bercovitch, J., & Houston, A. (2000). Why do they do it like this? An analysis of the factors influencing mediation behavior in international conflicts. *Journal of Conflict Resolution, 44*, 170–202.

Berg, J. H., & McQuinn, R. D. (1986). Attraction and exchange in continuing and noncontinuing dating relationships. *Journal of Personality and Social Psychology, 50*, 942–952.

Berglas, S., & Jones, E. E. (1978). Drug choice as a self-handicapping strategy in response to noncontingent success. *Journal of Personality and Social Psychology, 36*, 405–417.

Berkowitz, L. (1965). Some aspects of observed aggression. *Journal of Personality and Social Psychology, 2*, 359–369.

Berkowitz, L. (1968). Impulse, aggression, and the gun. *Psychology Today, 2*(4), pp. 18–22.

Berkowitz, L. (1972). Social norms, feelings, and other factors affecting helping and altruism. In L. Berkowitz (Ed.), *Advances in experimental social psychology.* (Vol. 6, pp. 63–108). New York: Academic Press.

Berkowitz, L. (1989). Frustration-aggression hypothesis: Examination and reformulation. *Psychological Bulletin, 106*, 59–73.

Berkowitz, L. (1993). *Aggression: Its causes, consequences, and control.* New York: McGraw-Hill.

Berkowitz, L. (1998). Affective aggression: The role of stress, pain, and negative affect. In R. G. Geen & E. Donnerstein

(Eds.), *Human aggression: Theories, research, and implications for social policy* (pp. 49–72). San Diego: Academic Press.
Berkowitz, L., & Donnerstein, E. (1982). External validity is more than skin deep: Some answers to criticisms of laboratory experiments. *American Psychologist, 37,* 245–257.
Berkowitz, L., & LePage, A. (1967). Weapons as aggression-eliciting stimuli. *Journal of Personality and Social Psychology, 7,* 202–207.
Berndsen, M., Spears, R., Pligt, J., & McGarty, C. (2002). Illusory correlation and stereotype formation: Making sense of group differences and cognitive biases. In C. McGarty, V. Y. Yzerbyt, & R. Spears (Eds.), *Stereotypes as explanations: The formation of meaningful beliefs about social groups* (pp. 90–110). Cambridge, UK: Cambridge University Press.
Bernhardt, P. C., Dabbs, J. M., Fielden, J. A., & Lutter, C. D. (1998). Testosterone changes during vicarious experiences of winning and losing among fans at sporting events. *Physiology and Behavior, 65,* 59–62.
Berntson, G. G., & Cacioppo, J. T. (2004). Heart rate variability: Stress and psychiatric conditions. In M. Malik & A. J. Camm (Eds.), *Dynamic Electrocardiography* (pp. 56–63). New York: Futura.
Berry, D. S., & Finch Wero, J. L. (1993). Accuracy in face perception: A view from ecological psychology. *Journal of Personality, 61,* 497–520.
Berry, D. S., & Zebrowitz-McArthur, L. (1986). Perceiving character in faces: The impact of age-related craniofacial changes in social perception. *Psychological Bulletin, 100,* 3–18.
Berry, J. W. (1979). A cultural ecology of social behavior. *Advances in Experimental Social Psychology, 12,* 177–206.
Berry, J. W., Poortinga, Y. H., Segall, M. H., & Dasen, P. R. (1992). *Cross-cultural psychology: Research and application.* Cambridge, UK: Cambridge University Press.
Berscheid, E. (1966). Opinion change and communicator-communicatee similarity and dissimilarity. *Journal of Personality and Social Psychology, 4,* 670–680.
Berscheid, E., Dion, K., Walster, E., & Walster, G. W. (1971). Physical attractiveness and dating choice: A test of the matching hypothesis. *Journal of Experimental Social Psychology, 7,* 173–189.
Berscheid, E., & Meyers, S. A. (1996). A social categorical approach to a question about love. *Personal Relationships, 3,* 19–43.
Berscheid, E., & Regan, P. C. (2005). *The psychology of interpersonal relationships.* Upper Saddle River, NJ: Prentice Hall.
Berscheid, E., & Reis, H. T. (1998). Attraction and close relationships. In D. Gilbert, S. Fiske, & G. Lindzey (Eds.), *Handbook of social psychology* (4th ed.). New York: McGraw-Hill.
Berscheid, E., Snyder, M., & Omoto, A. M. (1989). The relationship closeness inventory: Assessing the closeness of interpersonal relationships. *Journal of Personality and Social Psychology, 57,* 792–807.
Berscheid, E., & Walster, E. (1974). A little bit about love. In T. Huston (Ed.), *Foundations of interpersonal attraction* (pp. 355–381). New York: Academic Press.
Berscheid, E., Walster, E., & Campbell, R. (1972). *Grow old along with me.* Unpublished manuscript, Department of Psychology, University of Minnesota.
Bersoff, D. N. (Ed.) (2003). *Ethical conflicts in psychology* (3rd ed.). Washington, DC: American Psychological Association.
Bersoff, D. N., & Ogden, D. W. (1987). In the Supreme Court of the United States: *Lockhart v. McCree. American Psychologist, 42,* 59–68.
Bettencourt, B. A., & Dorr, N. (1998). Cooperative interaction and intergroup bias: Effects of numerical representation and cross-cut role assignment. *Personality and Social Psychology Bulletin, 24,* 1276–1293.
Bettencourt, B. A., & Miller, N. (1996). Gender differences in aggression as a function of provocation: A meta-analysis. *Psychological Bulletin, 119,* 422–447.
Bettencourt, B. A., & Sheldon, K. (2001). Social roles as mechanism for psychological need satisfaction within social groups. *Journal of Personality and Social Psychology, 81,* 1131–1143.
Bickman, L. (1974). The social power of a uniform. *Journal of Applied Social Psychology, 4,* 47–61.
Björkqvist, K., Österman, K., & Kaukiainen, A. (1992). The development of direct and indirect aggressive strategies in males and females. In K. Björkqvist & P. Niemelä (Eds.), *Of mice and women: Aspects of female aggression* (pp. 51–64). San Diego: Academic Press.
Blaine, B., Crocker, J., & Major, B. (1995). The unintended negative consequences of sympathy for the stigmatized. *Journal of Applied Social Psychology, 25,* 889–905.
Blair, I. V. (2001). Implicit stereotypes and prejudice. In G. B. Moskowitz (Ed.), *Cognitive social psychology: On the future of social cognition* (pp. 359–374). Mahwah, NJ: Erlbaum.
Blair, I. V. (2002). The malleability of automatic stereotypes and prejudice. *Personality and Social Psychology Review, 6,* 242–261.
Blair, I. V., Judd, C. M., Sadler, M. S., & Jenkins, C. (2002). The role of Afrocentric features in person perception: Judging by features and categories. *Journal of Personality and Social Psychology, 83,* 5–25.
Blair, I. V., Ma, J. E., & Lenton, A. P. (2001). Imagining stereotypes away: The moderation of implicit stereotypes through mental imagery. *Journal of Personality and Social Psychology, 81,* 828–841.
Blair, I. V., Park, B., & Bachelor, J. (2003). Understanding intergroup anxiety: Are some people more anxious than others? *Group Processes and Intergroup Relations, 6,* 151–169.
Blanton, H., Crocker, J., & Miller, Dale T. (2000). The effects of in-group versus out-group social comparison on self-esteem in the context of a negative stereotype. *Journal of Experimental Social Psychology, 36,* 519–530.
Blascovich, J., Mendes, W. B., Hunter, S. B., & Salomon, K. (1999). Social "facilitation" as challenge and threat. *Journal of Personality and Social Psychology, 77,* 68–77.
Blascovich, J., Spencer, S. J., Quinn, D., & Steele, C. (2001). African Americans and high blood pressure: The role of stereotype threat. *Psychological Science, 12,* 225–229.
Blass, T. (1991). Understanding behavior in the Milgram obedience experiment: The role of personality, situations, and their interactions. *Journal of Personality and Social Psychology, 60,* 398–413.
Blass, T. (1992). The social psychology of Stanley Milgram. *Advances in Experimental Social Psychology, 25,* 227–329.
Blass, T. (1999). The Milgram paradigm after 35 years: Some things we now know about obedience to authority. *Journal of Applied Social Psychology, 25,* 955–978.
Blass, T. (Ed.) (2000). *Obedience to authority: Current perspectives on the Milgram paradigm.* Mahwah, NJ: Erlbaum.
Blass, T. (2004). *The man who shocked the world.* New York: Basic Books.

Bless, H., Schwarz, N., & Wieland, R. (1996). Mood and the impact of category membership and individuating information. *European Journal of Social Psychology, 26,* 935–959.

Bochner, S. (1994). Cross-cultural differences in the self-concept: A test of Hofstede's individualism/collectivism distinction. *Journal of Cross Cultural Psychology, 25,* 273–283.

Bochner, S., & Insko, C. A. (1966). Communicator discrepancy, source credibility, and opinion change. *Journal of Personality and Social Psychology, 4,* 614–621.

Bodenhausen, G. V. (1990). Stereotypes as judgmental heuristics: Evidence of circadian variations in discrimination. *Psychological Science, 1,* 319–322.

Bodenhausen, G. V., & Macrae, C. N. (1998). Stereotype activation and inhibition. In R. S. Wyer, Jr. (Ed.), *Stereotype activation and inhibition: Advances in Social Cognition* (Vol. 11, pp. 1–52). Mahwah, NJ: Erlbaum.

Bodenhausen, G. V., Macrae, C. N., & Hugenberg, K. (2003). Social cognition. In T. Millon & M. J. Lerner (Eds.), *Handbook of psychology: Personality and social psychology* (Vol. 5., pp. 257–282). New York: Wiley.

Bogart, L. M., & Helgeson, V. S. (2000). Social comparisons among women with breast cancer: A longitudinal investigation. *Journal of Applied Social Psychology, 30,* 547–575.

Boldero, J., & Francis, J. (2000). The relation between self-discrepancies and emotion: The moderating roles of self-guide importance, location relevance, and social self-domain centrality. *Journal of Personality and Social Psychology, 78,* 38–52.

Boldizar, J. P., Perry, D. G., & Perry, L. (1989). Outcome values and aggression. *Child Development, 60,* 571–579.

Bond, C. F., Jr., & Titus, L. T. (1983). Social facilitation: A meta-analysis of 241 studies. *Psychological Bulletin, 94,* 265–292.

Bond, R., & Smith, P. B. (1996). Culture and conformity: A meta-analysis of studies using Asch's (1952b, 1956) line judgment task. *Psychological Bulletin, 119,* 111–137.

Boninger, D. S., Brock, T. C., Cook, T. D., Gruder, C. L., & Romer, D. (1990). Discovery of reliable attitude change persistence resulting from a transmitter tuning set. *Psychological Science, 1,* 268–271.

Boninger, D. S., Krosnick, J. A., & Berent, M. K. (1995). Origins of attitude importance: Self-interest, social identification, and value relevance. *Journal of Personality and Social Psychology, 68,* 61–80.

Bonner, B. L., Baumann, M. R., & Dalal, R. S. (2002). The effects of member expertise on group decision-making and performance. *Organizational Behavior and Human Decision Processes, 88,* 719–736.

Bonnie, K. E., & de Waal, F. B. M. (2004). Primate social reciprocity and the origin of gratitude. In R. A. Emmons & M. E. McCullough (Eds.), *The psychology of gratitude.* Oxford: Oxford University Press.

Bonta, B. D. (1997). Cooperation and competition in peaceful societies. *Psychological Bulletin, 121,* 299–320.

Book, A. S., Starzyk, K. B., & Quinsey, V. L. (2001). The relationship between testosterone and aggression: A meta-analysis. *Aggression and Violent Behavior, 6,* 579–599.

Borduin, C. M., Schaeffer, C. M., & Ronis, S. T. (2003). Multisystemic treatment of serious antisocial behavior in adolescents. In C. A. Essau (Ed.), *Conduct and oppositional defiant disorders: Epidemiology, risk factors, and treatment* (pp. 299–318). Mahwah, NJ: Erlbaum.

Borgida, E., & Campbell, B. (1982). Belief relevance and attitude-behavior consistency: The moderating role of personal experience. *Journal of Personality and Social Psychology, 42,* 239–247.

Bornstein, R. F. (1989). Exposure and affect: Overview and meta-analysis of research, 1968–1987. *Psychological Bulletin, 106,* 265–289.

Bornstein, R. F. (1994). Dependency as a social cue: A meta-analytic review of research on the dependency-helping relationship. *Journal of Research in Personality, 28,* 182–213.

Bornstein, R. F., & D'Agostino, P. R. (1992). Stimulus recognition and the mere exposure effect. *Journal of Personality and Social Psychology, 63,* 545–552.

Bosacki, S., Innerd, W., & Towson, S. (1997). Field independence–dependence and self-esteem in preadolescents: does gender make a difference? *Journal of Youth and Adolescence, 26,* 1573–6601.

Bothwell, R. K., Deffenbacher, K. A., & Brigham, J. C. (1987). Correlation of eyewitness accuracy and confidence: Optimality hypothesis revisited. *Journal of Applied Psychology, 72,* 691–695.

Bottoms, B. L., & Davis, S. L. (1997). The creation of satanic ritual abuse. *Journal of Social and Clinical Psychology, 16,* 112–132.

Bowlby, J. (1988). *A secure base.* New York: Basic Books.

Bowling, D., & Hoffman, D. (2000). Bringing peace into the room: The personal qualities of the mediator and their impact on the mediation. *Negotiation Journal, 16,* 5–28.

Boysen, S. T., & Himes, G. T. (1999). Current issues and emerging theories in animal cognition. *Annual Review of Psychology 50,* 683–705.

Bradbury, T. N. (Ed.) (1998). *The developmental course of marital dysfunction.* New York: Cambridge University Press.

Bradbury, T. N., & Fincham, F. D. (1992). Attributions and behavior in marital interaction. *Journal of Personality and Social Psychology, 63,* 613–628.

Bradfield, A. L., Wells, G. L., & Olson, E. A. (2002). The damaging effect of confirming feedback on the relation between eyewitness certainty and identification accuracy. *Journal of Applied Psychology, 87,* 112–120.

Brammer, G. L., Raleigh, M. J., & McGuire, M. T. (1994). Neurotransmitters and social status. In L. Ellis (Ed.), *Social stratification and socioeconomic inequality, Vol. 2: Reproductive and interpersonal aspects of dominance and status* (pp. 75–91). Westport, CT: Praeger/Greenwood.

Branscombe, N. R., Wann, D. L., Noel, J. G., & Coleman, J. (1993). In-group or out-group extremity: Importance of the threatened social identity. *Personality and Social Psychology Bulletin, 19,* 381–388.

Brauer, M., Judd, C. M., & Gliner, M. D. (1995). The effects of repeated expressions on attitude polarization during group discussions. *Journal of Personality and Social Psychology, 68,* 1014–1029.

Bray, R. M., Johnson, D., & Chilstrom, J. T., Jr. (1982). Social influence by group members with minority opinions: A comparison of Hollander & Moscovici. *Journal of Personality and Social Psychology, 43,* 78–88.

Bray, R. M., Struckman-Johnson, C., Osborne, M., McFarlane, J., & Scott, J. (1978). The effects of defendant status on decisions of student and community juries. *Social Psychology, 41,* 256–260.

Brean, H. (1958, March 31). What hidden sell is all about. *Life,* pp. 104–114.

Brehm, J. W. (1956). Post-decision changes in desirability of alternatives. *Journal of Abnormal and Social Psychology, 52,* 384–389.

Brehm, S. S., & Brehm, J. W. (1981). *Psychological reactance: A theory of freedom and control.* New York: Academic Press.

Brehm, S. S., Miller R., Perlman, D., & Campbell, S. M. (2001). *Intimate relationships* (3rd ed.). New York: McGraw-Hill.

Bremner, J. G. (2002). The nature of imitation by infants. *Infant Behavior & Development, 25,* 65–67.

Brems, C., & Namyniuk, L. (2002). The relationship of childhood abuse history and substance use in an Alaska sample. *Substance Use and Misuse, 37,* 473–494.

Bressan, P., & Martello, M. F. D. (2002). *Talis Pater, Talis Filius:* Perceived resemblance and the belief in genetic relatedness. *Psychological Science, 13,* 213–218.

Brett, J. M., Shapiro, D. L., & Lytle, A. L. (1998). Breaking the bonds of reciprocity in negotiations. *Academy of Management Journal, 41,* 410–424.

Brewer, M. B. (1988). A dual process model of impression formation. In T. K. Srull, & R. S. Wyer, Jr. (Eds.), *A dual process model of impression formation. Advances in social cognition* (Vol. 1, pp. 1–36). Hillsdale, NJ: Erlbaum.

Brewer, M. B. (2000). Reducing prejudice through cross-categorization: Effects of multiple social identities. In S. Oskamp (Ed.), *Reducing prejudice and discrimination* (pp. 165–183). Mahwah, NJ: Erlbaum.

Brewer, M. B. (2003). Optimal distinctiveness, social identity, and the self. In M. R. Leary & J. P. Tangney (Eds.), *Handbook of self and identity* (pp. 480–491). New York: Guilford.

Brewer, M. B., & Brown, R. J. (1998). Intergroup relations. In D. T. Gilbert, S. T. Fiske, & G. Lindzey (Eds.), *The handbook of social psychology* (4th ed., Vol. 2, pp. 554–594). New York: McGraw-Hill.

Brewer, M. B., Hong, Y., & Li, Q. (2004). Dynamic entitivity: Perceiving groups as actors. In C. Judd, V. Yzerbyt, & O. Corneille (Eds.), *The psychology of group perception: Contributions to the study of homogeneity, entitivity, and essentialism* (pp. 25–38). Philadelphia, PA: Psychology Press.

Brewer, M. B., & Pickett, C. L. (1999). Distinctiveness motives as a source of the social self. In T. R. Tyler & R. M. Kramer (Eds.), *The psychology of the social self: Applied social research* (pp. 71–87). Mahwah, NJ: Erlbaum.

Brewin, C. R., & Beaton, A. (2002). Thought suppression, intelligence, and working memory capacity. *Behavior Research and Therapy, 40,* 923–930.

Brigham, J. C., & Cairns, D. L. (1988). The effect of mugshot inspections on eyewitness identification accuracy. *Journal of Applied Social Psychology, 18,* 1394–1410.

Brinthaupt, R. M., Moreland, R. L., & Levine, J. M. (1991). Sources of optimism among prospective group members. *Personality and Social Psychology Bulletin, 17,* 36–43.

Brockner, J. (1983). Low self-esteem and behavioral plasticity: Some implications. In L. Wheeler & P. Shaver (Eds.), *Review of personality and social psychology* (Vol. 4, pp. 237–271). Beverly Hills, CA: Sage.

Brodkey, H. (1993, July 5). The central face. *The New Yorker,* p. 31.

Bronfenbrenner, U. (1961). The mirror-image in Soviet-American relations. *Journal of Social Issues, 17,* 45–56.

Brooks, P. (2000). *Troubling confessions.* Chicago: University of Chicago Press.

Brooks, X. (2002, December 20). Natural born copycats: Eight murders have been blamed on Oliver Stone's evil 1995 film. *The Guardian (London),* p. 10.

Brown, E., Deffenbacher, K., & Sturgill, W. (1977). Memory for faces and the circumstances of encounter. *Journal of Applied Psychology, 62,* 311–318.

Brown, J. D. (1998). *The self.* New York: McGraw-Hill.

Brown, J. D., & Dutton, K. A. (1995). The thrill of victory, the complexity of defeat: Self-esteem and people's emotional reactions to success and failure. *Journal of Personality and Social Psychology, 68,* 712–722.

Brown, J. D., & Smart, S. A. (1991). The self and social conduct: Linking self-representations to prosocial behavior. *Journal of Personality and Social Psychology, 60,* 368–375.

Brown, J. M. (2003). Eyewitness memory for arousing events: Putting things into context. *Applied Cognitive Psychology, 17,* 93–106.

Brown, R. (1986). *Social psychology* (2nd ed.). New York: Free Press.

Brown, R., & Kulik, J. (1977). Flashbulb memories. *Cognition, 5,* 73–99.

Brown, S. L., Nesse, R. M., Vinokur, A. D., & Smith, D. M. (2003). Providing social support may be more beneficial than receiving it: Results from a prospective study of mortality. *Psychological Science, 14,* 320–327.

Brown, S. M. (1999). Good Samaritan laws: Protection and limits. *RN, 62,* 65–67.

Bruch, M. A., Gorsky, J. M., Collins, T. M., & Berger, P. A. (1989). Shyness and sociability examined: A multicomponent analysis. *Journal of Personality and Social Psychology, 57,* 904–915.

Bruck, M., & Ceci, S. J. (1999). The suggestibility of children's memory. *Annual Review of Psychology, 50,* 419–439.

Bruner, J. S., & Potter, M. C. (1964). Interference in visual recognition. *Science, 144,* 424–425.

Bruner, J. S., & Tagiuri, R. (1954). Person perception. In G. Lindzey (Ed.), *Handbook of social psychology* (Vol. 2, pp. 634–654). Reading, MA: Addison-Wesley.

Bryan, J. H., & Test, M. A. (1967). Models and helping: Naturalistic studies in aiding behavior. *Journal of Personality and Social Psychology, 6,* 400–407.

Buckhout, R. (1974, December). Eyewitness testimony. *Scientific American,* pp. 23–31.

Buehler, R., & Griffin, D. (1994). Change-of-meaning effects in conformity and dissent: Observing construal processes over time. *Journal of Personality and Social Psychology, 67,* 984–996.

Bulatao, E. Q., & VandenBos, G. R. (1996). Workplace violence: Its scope and the issues. In G. R. VandenBos & E. Q. Bulatao (Eds.), *Violence on the job: Identifying risks and developing solutions* (pp. 1–23). Washington, DC: American Psychological Association.

Burke, T. M., Turtle, J. W., & Olson, E. (2006). A psychological approach to the study of alibis. In M. Toglia, J. D. Read, D. Ross, & R. C. L. Lindsay (Eds.), *The Handbook of Eyewitness Psychology.* Mahwah, NJ: Erlbaum.

Burger, J. M. (1986). Increasing compliance by improving the deal: The that's-not-all technique. *Journal of Personality and Social Psychology, 51,* 277–283.

Burger, J. M. (1999). The foot-in-the-door compliance procedure: A multiple-process analysis and review. *Personality and Social Psychology Review, 3,* 303–325.

Burger, J. M., & Cornelius, T. (2003). Raising the price of agreement: Public commitment and the low-ball compliance procedure. *Journal of Applied Social Psychology, 33,* 923–934.

Burger, J. M., Horita, M., Kinoshita, L., Roberts, K., & Vera, C. (1997). Effects of time on the norm of reciprocity. *Basic and Applied Social Psychology, 19*, 91–100.

Burger, J. M., & Petty, R. E. (1981). The low-ball compliance technique: Task or person commitment? *Journal of Personality and Social Psychology, 40*, 492–500.

Burman, B., & Margolin, G. (1992). An analysis of the association between marital relationships and health problems: An interactional perspective. *Psychological Bulletin, 112*, 39–63.

Burnstein, E., Crandall, C., & Kitayama, S. (1994). Some neo-Darwinian decision rules for altruism: Weighing cues for inclusive fitness as a function of the biological importance of the decision. *Journal of Personality and Social Psychology, 67*, 773–789.

Burnstein, E., & Schul, Y. (1982). The informational basis of social judgments: The operations in forming an impression of another person. *Journal of Experimental Social Psychology, 18*, 217–234.

Burt, M. C. (1980). Cultural myths and supports for rape. *Journal of Personality and Social Psychology, 38*, 217–230.

Bushman, B. J. (1988). The effects of apparel on compliance: A field experiment with a female authority figure. *Personality and Social Psychology Bulletin, 14*, 459–467.

Bushman, B. J. (1996). Individual differences in the extent and development of aggressive cognitive-associative networks. *Personality and Social Psychology Bulletin, 22*, 811–819.

Bushman, B. J. (1998). Priming effects of violent media on the accessibility of aggressive constructs in memory. *Personality and Social Psychology Bulletin, 24*, 537–545.

Bushman, B. J. (2002). Does venting anger feed or extinguish the flame? Catharsis, rumination, distraction, anger, and aggressive responding. *Personality and Social Psychology Bulletin, 28*, 724–731.

Bushman, B. J., & Baumeister, R. F. (1998). Threatened egotism, narcissism, self-esteem, and direct and displaced aggression: Does self-love or self-hate lead to violence? *Journal of Personality and Social Psychology, 75*, 219–229.

Bushman, B. J., & Cooper, H. M. (1990). Effects of alcohol on human aggression: An integrative research review. *Psychological Bulletin, 107*, 341–354.

Bushman, B. J., & Huesmann, L. R. (2001). Effects of televised violence on aggression. In D. G. Singer & J. L. Singer (Eds.), *Handbook of children and the media* (pp. 223–254). Thousand Oaks, CA: Sage.

Bushman, B. J., Wang, M. C., & Anderson, C. A. (2005). Is the curve relating temperature to aggression linear or curvilinear? A response to Bell (2005) and to Cohn and Rotton (2005). *Journal of Personality and Social Psychology, 89*, 74–77.

Buss, A. H. (1980). *Self-consciousness and social anxiety.* San Francisco: Freeman.

Buss, D. M. (1989). Sex differences in human mate preferences: Evolutionary hypotheses tested in 37 cultures. *Behavioral and Brain Sciences, 12*, 1–14.

Buss, D. M. (1995). Evolutionary psychology: A new paradigm for psychological science. *Psychological Inquiry, 6*, 1–30.

Buss, D. M. (2000). *The dangerous passion: Why jealousy is as necessary as love and sex.* New York: Free Press.

Buss, D. M. (2003). *The evolution of desire: Strategies of human mating* (rev. ed.). New York: Basic Books.

Buss, D. M. (2004). *Evolutionary psychology: The new science of the mind* (2nd ed.). Boston: Allyn & Bacon.

Buss, D. M., & Duntley, J. D. (2005). The evolution of gender differences in aggression. In S. Fein, G. R. Goethals, & M. J. Sandstrom (Eds.), *Gender and aggression: Interdisciplinary perspectives.* Mahwah, NJ: Erlbaum.

Buss, D. M., Larsen, R. J., Westen, D., & Semmelroth, J. (1992). Sex differences in jealousy: Evolution, physiology, and psychology. *Psychological Science, 3*, 251–255.

Buss, D. M., & Malamuth, N. M. (Eds.) (1996). *Sex, power, conflict: Evolutionary and feminist perspectives.* New York: Oxford University.

Buss, D. M., & Schmitt, D. P. (1993). Sexual strategies theory: An evolutionary perspective on human mating. *Psychological Review, 100*, 204–232.

Buss, D. M., & Shackelford, T. K. (1997). From vigilance to violence: Mate retention tactics in married couples. *Journal of Personality and Social Psychology, 72*, 346–361.

Byrne, D. (1971). *The attraction paradigm.* New York: Academic Press.

Byrne, D. (1997). An overview (and underview) of research and theory within the attraction paradigm. *Journal of Social and Personal Relationships, 14*, 417–431.

Byrne, D., & Clore, G. L. (1970). A reinforcement model of evaluative processes. *Personality: An International Journal, 1*, 103–128.

Byrne, D., Clore, G. L., & Smeaton, G. (1986). The attraction hypothesis: Do similar attitudes affect anything? *Journal of Personality and Social Psychology, 51*, 1167–1170.

Byrne, R. M. J., & McEleney, A. (2000). Counterfactual thinking about actions and failures to act. *Journal of Experimental Psychology: Learning Memory, and Cognition, 26*, 1318–1331.

CBC News: Disclosure (November 26, 2003). Unreliable Evidence.

Cacioppo, J. T., Crites, S. L., Berntson, G. G., & Coles, M. G. H. (1993). If attitudes affect how stimuli are processed, should they not affect the event-related brain potential? *Psychological Science, 4*, 108–112.

Cacioppo, J. T., Gardner, W. L., & Bernston, G. G. (1997). Beyond bipolar conceptualizations and measures: The case of attitudes and evaluative space. *Personality and Social Psychology Review, 1*, 3–25.

Cacioppo, J. T., Hawkley, L. C., & Bernston, G. G. (2003). The anatomy of loneliness. *Current Directions in Psychological Science, 12*, 71–74.

Cacioppo, J. T., & Petty, R. E. (1981). Electromyograms as measures of extent and affectivity of information processing. *American Psychologist, 36*, 441–456.

Cacioppo, J. T., & Petty, R. E. (1982). The need for cognition. *Journal of Personality and Social Psychology, 42*, 116–131.

Cacioppo, J. T., Petty, R. E., Feinstein, J. A., & Jarvis, W. B. G. (1996). Dispositional differences in cognitive motivation: The life and times of individuals varying in need for cognition. *Psychological Bulletin, 119*, 197–253.

Cacioppo, J. T., Petty, R. E., Losch, M. E., & Kim, H. S. (1986). Electromyographic activity over facial muscle regions can differentiate the valence and intensity of affective reactions. *Journal of Personality and Social Psychology, 50*, 260–268.

Cacioppo, J. T., Petty, R. E., & Morris, K. (1983). Effects of need for cognition on message evaluation, recall, and persuasion. *Journal of Personality and Social Psychology, 45*, 805–818.

Cacioppo, J. T., Priester, J. R., & Bernston, G. G. (1993). Rudimentary determinants of attitudes. II. Arm flexion and extension have differential effects on attitudes. *Journal of Personality and Social Psychology, 65*, 5–17.

Cadenhead, A. C., & Richman, C. L. (1996). The effects of interpersonal trust and group status on prosocial and aggressive behaviors. *Social Behavior and Personality, 24*, 169–184.

Callaway, M. R., Marriott, R. G., & Esser, J. K. (1985). Effects of dominance on group decision making: Toward a stress-reduction explanation of groupthink. *Journal of Personality and Social Psychology, 49*, 949–952.

Cameron, J., & Pierce, W. D. (1994). Reinforcement, reward, and intrinsic motivation: A meta-analysis. *Review of Educational Research, 64*, 363–423.

Campbell, A. (1999). Staying alive: Evolution, culture, and women's intrasexual aggression. *Behavioral and Brain Sciences, 22*, 203–252.

Campbell, L., Simpson, J. A., Boldry, J., & Kashy, D. A. (2005). Perceptions of conflict and support in romantic relationships: The role of attachment anxiety. *Journal of Personality and Social Psychology, 88*, 510–531

Canadian Automobile Association. *Membership Survey, April 2000.*

Canadian Community Health Survey (CCHS): Mental Health and Well-Being, 2002.

Canadian Psychological Association. (2000). *Canadian Code of Ethics for Psychologists* (3rd ed.). Ottawa.

Caporael, L. R. (1997). The evolution of truly social cognition: The core configurations model. *Personality and Social Psychology Review, 1*, 276–298.

Capozza, D., & Brown, R. (2000). *Social identity processes: Trends in theory and research.* London: Sage.

Capozza, D., Voci, A., & Licciardello, O. (2000). Individualism, collectivism, and social identity theory. In D. Capozza & R. Brown (Eds)., *Social identity processes: Trends in theory and research.* London: Sage.

Carless, S. A., & De-Paola, C. (2000). The measurement of cohesion in work teams. *Small Group Research, 31*, 71–88.

Carlo, G., Koller, S. H., Eisenberg, N., Da Silva, M. S., & Frohlich, C. B. (1996). A cross-national study on the relations among prosocial moral reasoning, gender role orientations, and prosocial behaviors. *Developmental Psychology, 32*, 231–240.

Carlsmith, K. M., Darley, J. M., & Robinson, P. H. (2002). Why do we punish?: Deterrence and just desserts as motives for punishment. *Journal of Personality and Social Psychology, 83*, 284–299.

Carlson, M., & Miller, N. (1987). Explanation of the relation between negative mood and helping. *Psychological Bulletin, 102*, 91–108.

Carnegie, D. (1936). *How to win friends and influence people.* New York: Pocket Books. (Reprinted in 1972)

Carnevale, P. J. (2002). Mediating from strength. In J. Bercovitch (Ed.), *Studies in international mediation: Essays in honor of Jeffrey Z. Rubin* (pp. 25–40). London: Palgrave-MacMillan.

Carnevale, P. J., & Leung, K. (2001). Cultural dimensions of negotiation. In M. Hogg & S. Tindale (Eds.), *Blackwell handbook of social psychology, Vol. 3: Group processes* (pp. 482–496). Oxford, UK: Blackwell.

Carney, J. V. (2000). Bullied to death: Perceptions of peer abuse and suicidal behaviour during adolescence. *School Psychology International, 21*, 213–223.

Carr, S. C., & MacLachlan, M. (1998). Psychology in developing countries: Reassessing its impact. *Psychology and Development Societies, 10*, 1–20.

Carron, A. V., Colman, M. M., Wheeler, J., & Stevens, D. (2002). Cohesion and performance in sport: A meta analysis. *Journal of Sport and Exercise Psychology, 24*, 168–188.

Carter, S. L. (1991). *Reflections of an affirmative action baby.* New York: Basic Books.

Cartwright, D. (1971). Risk taking by individuals and groups: An assessment of research employing choice dilemmas. *Journal of Personality and Social Psychology, 20*, 245–261.

Cartwright, D. (1979). Contemporary social psychology in historical perspective. *Social Psychology Quarterly, 42*, 82–93.

Cartwright, D., & Zander, A. (1960). Group cohesiveness: Introduction. In D. Cartwright & A. Zander (Eds.), *Group dynamics: Research and theory* (2nd ed., pp. 69–94). Evanston, IL: Row, Peterson.

Carver, C. S., & Scheier, M. F. (1981). *Attention and self-regulation: A control-theory approach to human behavior.* New York: Springer-Verlag.

Carver, C. S., & Scheier, M. F. (1990). Origins and functions of positive and negative affect: A control-process view. *Psychological Review, 97*, 19–35.

Carver, C. S., & Scheier, M. F. (1998). *On the self-regulation of behavior.* New York: Cambridge University Press.

Cashdan, E. (2003). Hormones and competitive aggression in women. *Aggressive Behavior, 29*, 107–115.

Caspi, A. (2000). The child is the father of man: Personality continuities from childhood to adulthood. *Journal of Personality and Social Psychology, 78*, 158–172.

Cassidy, J., Kirsh, S. J., Scolton, K. L., & Parke, R. D. (1996). Attachment and representations of peer relationships. *Developmental Psychology, 32*, 892–904.

Cassidy, J., & Shaver, P. R. (Eds.) (1999). *Handbook of attachment: Theory, research, and clinical applications.* New York: Guilford Press.

Castano, E., Sacchi, S., & Gries, P. H. (2003). The perception of the other in international relations: Evidence for the polarizing effect of entitativity. *Political Psychology, 24*, 449–468.

Castano, E., Yzerbyt, V. Y., Bourguignon, D., & Seron, E. (2002). Who may enter? The impact of in-group identification on in-group/out-group categorization. *Journal of Experimental Social Psychology, 38*, 315–322.

Castano, E., Yzerbyt, V. Y., Paladino, M. P., & Sacchi, S. (2002). I belong, therefore, I exist: Ingroup identification, ingroup entitativity, and ingroup bias. *Personality and Social Psychology Bulletin, 28*, 135–143.

Castelli, L., Arcuri, L., & Zogmaister, C. (2003). Perceiving ingroup members who use stereotypes: Implicit conformity and similarity. *European Journal of Social Psychology, 33*, 163–175.

Cate, R. M., & Lloyd, S. A. (1988). Courtship. In S. Duck (Ed.), *Handbook of personal relationships: Theory, research, and interventions* (pp. 409–427). New York: Wiley.

Cate, R. M., & Lloyd, S. A. (1992). *Courtship.* Newbury Park, CA: Sage.

Ceci, S. J., Peters, D., & Plotkin, J. (1985). Human subjects review, personal values, and the regulation of social science research. *American Psychologist, 40*, 994–1002.

Ceci, S. J., Ross, D. F., & Toglia, M. P. (1987). Suggestibility of children's memory: Psycholegal implications. *Journal of Experimental Psychology, 116*, 38–49.

Centers for Disease Control Vietnam Experience Study. (1988). Health status of Vietnam veterans: I. Psychosocial characteristics. *Journal of the American Medical Association, 259*, 2701–2707.

Chaiken, S. (1979). Communicator physical attractiveness and persuasion. *Journal of Personality and Social Psychology, 37,* 1387–1397.

Chaiken, S. (1980). Heuristic versus systematic information processing and the use of source versus message cues in persuasion. *Journal of Personality and Social Psychology, 39,* 752–766.

Chaiken, S. (1987). The heuristic model of persuasion. In M. P. Zanna, J. M. Olson, & C. P. Herman (Eds.), *Social influence: The Ontario symposium* (Vol. 5, pp. 3–39). Hillsdale, NJ: Erlbaum.

Chaiken, S., & Baldwin, M. W. (1981). Affective-cognitive consistency and the effect of salient behavioral information on the self-perception of attitudes. *Journal of Personality and Social Psychology, 41,* 1–12.

Chaiken, S., & Maheswaran, D. (1994). Heuristic processing can bias systematic processing: Effects of source credibility, argument ambiguity, and task importance on attitude judgment. *Journal of Personality and Social Psychology, 66,* 460–473.

Chaiken, S., & Trope, Y. (Eds.) (1999). *Dual-process theories in social psychology.* NY: Guilford.

Chance, S. E., Brown, R. T., Dabbs, J. M., Jr., & Casey, R. (2000). Testosterone, intelligence and behavior disorders in young boys. *Personality and Individual Differences, 28,* 437–445.

Chandrashekaran, M., Walker, B. A., Ward, J. C., & Reingen, P. H. (1996). Modeling individual preference evolution and choice in a dynamic group setting. *Journal of Marketing Research, 33,* 211–223.

Chapdelaine, A., Kenny, D. A., & LaFontana, K. M. (1994). Matchmaker, matchmaker, can you make me a match? Predicting liking between two unacquainted persons. *Journal of Personality and Social Psychology, 67,* 83–91.

Chaplin, W. F., Phillips, J. B., Brown, J. D., Clanton, N. R., & Stein, J. L. (2000). *Journal of Personality and Social Psychology, 79,* 110–117.

Chapman, L. J. (1967). Illusory correlation in observational report. *Journal of Verbal Learning and Verbal Behavior, 6,* 151–155.

Chartrand, T. L., & Bargh, J. A. (1999). The chameleon effect: The perception-behavior link and social interaction. *Journal of Personality and Social Psychology, 76,* 893–910.

Chastain, G., & Landrum, R. E. (Eds.) (1999). *Protecting human subjects: Departmental subject pools and institutional review boards.* Washington, DC: American Psychological Association.

Chatman, C. M., & von Hippel, W. (2001). Attributional mediation of in-group bias. *Journal of Experimental Social Psychology, 37,* 267–272.

Cheah, C. S. L., & Nelson, L. J. (2004). The role of acculturation in the emerging adulthood of Aboriginal college students. *International Journal of Behavioral Development, 28,* 495–507.

Cheek, J. M., & Melchior, L. A. (1990). Shyness, self-esteem, and self-consciousness. In H. Leitenberg (Ed.), *Handbook of social and evaluation anxiety.* New York: Plenum.

Chen, F. F., & Kenrick, D. T. (2002). Repulsion or attraction: Group membership and assumed attitude similarity. *Journal of Personality and Social Psychology, 83,* 111–125.

Chen, M., & Bargh, J. A. (1997). Nonconscious behavioral confirmation processes: The self-fulfilling consequences of automatic stereotype activation. *Journal of Experimental Social Psychology, 33,* 541–560.

Chen, S., & Chaiken, S. (1999). The heuristic-systematic model in its broader context. In S. Chaiken & Y. Trope (Eds.), *Dual-process theories in social psychology* (pp. 73–96). New York: Guilford.

Chen, Y-R., Brockner, J., & Chen, X-P. (2002). Individual-collective primacy and ingroup favoritism: Enhancement and protection effects. *Journal of Experimental Social Psychology, 38,* 482–491.

Cheng, P. W., & Novick, L. R. (1990). A probabilistic contrast model of causal induction. *Journal of Personality and Social Psychology, 58,* 545–567.

Cheryan, S., & Bodenhausen, G. V. (2000). When positive stereotypes threaten intellectual performance: The psychological hazards of "model minority" status. *Psychological Science, 11,* 399–402.

Chidambaram, L., & Bostrom, R. P. (1997). Group development (I): A review and synthesis of development models. *Group Decision and Negotiation, 6,* 159–187.

Chiu, C., Morris, M. W., Hong, Y., & Menon, T. (2000). Motivated cultural cognition: The impact of implicit cultural theories on dispositional attribution varies as a function of need for closure. *Journal of Personality and Social Psychology, 78,* 247–259.

Choi, I., Nisbett, R. E., & Norenzayan, A. (1999). Causal attribution across cultures: Variation and universality. *Psychological Bulletin, 125,* 47–63.

Choi, J. N., & Kim, M. U. (1999). The organizational application of groupthink and its limitations in organizations. *Journal of Applied Psychology, 84,* 297–306.

Christensen, A., & Heavey, C. L. (1993). Gender differences in marital conflict: The demand/withdraw interaction pattern. In S. Oskamp & M. Costanzo (Eds.), *Gender issues in contemporary society* (pp. 113–141). Newbury Park, CA: Sage.

Christensen, L. (1988). Deception in psychological research: When is its use justified? *Personality and Social Psychology Bulletin, 14,* 664–675.

Christianson, S. (1992). Emotional stress and eyewitness memory: A critical review. *Psychological Bulletin, 112,* 284–309.

Chun, W. Y., & Lee, H. K. (1999). Effects of the difference in the amount of group preferential information on illusory correlation. *Personality and Social Psychology Bulletin, 25,* 1463–1475.

Cialdini, R. B. (2001). *Influence: Science and practice* (4th ed.). Needham Heights, MA: Allyn & Bacon.

Cialdini, R. B., & Ascani, K. (1976). Test of a concession procedure for inducing verbal, behavioral, and further compliance with a request to give blood. *Journal of Applied Psychology, 61,* 295–300.

Cialdini, R. B., Baumann, D. J., & Kenrick, D. T. (1981). Insights from sadness: A three-step model of the development of altruism as hedonism. *Developmental Review, 1,* 207–223.

Cialdini, R. B., Borden, R. J., Thorne, A., Walker, M. R., Freeman, S., & Sloan, L. R. (1976). Basking in reflected glory: Three (football) field studies. *Journal of Personality and Social Psychology, 34,* 366–375.

Cialdini, R. B., Cacioppo, J. T., Bassett, R., & Miller, J. A. (1978). Low-ball procedure for producing compliance: Commitment then cost. *Journal of Personality and Social Psychology, 36,* 463–476.

Cialdini, R. B., & De Nicholas, M. E. (1989). Self-presentation by association. *Journal of Personality and Social Psychology, 57,* 626–631.

Cialdini, R. B., & Fultz, J. (1990). Interpreting the negative mood-helping literature via "mega" analysis: A contrary view. *Psychological Bulletin, 107,* 210–214.

Cialdini, R. B., & Goldstein, N. J. (2004). Social influence: Compliance and conformity. *Annual Review of Psychology, 55,* 591–621.

Cialdini, R. B., Kallgren, C. A., & Reno, R. R. (1991). A focus theory of normative conduct: A theoretical refinement and reevaluation of the role of norms in human behavior. *Advances in Experimental Social Psychology, 24,* 201–234.

Cialdini, R. B., Reno, R. R., & Kallgren, C. A. (1990). A focus theory of normative conduct: Recycling the concept of norms to reduce littering in public places. *Journal of Personality and Social Psychology, 58,* 1015–1026.

Cialdini, R. B., Schaller, M., Houlihan, D., Arps, K., Fultz, J., & Beaman, A. L. (1987). Empathy-based helping: Is it selflessly or selfishly motivated? *Journal of Personality and Social Psychology, 52,* 749–758.

Cialdini, R. B., Trost, M. R., & Newsom, J. T. (1995). Preference for consistency: The development of a valid measure and the discovery of surprising behavioral implications. *Journal of Personality and Social Psychology, 69,* 318–328.

Cialdini, R. B., Vincent, J. E., Lewis, S. K., Catalan, J., Wheeler, D., & Darby, B. L. (1975). Reciprocal concessions procedure for inducing compliance: The door-in-the-face technique. *Journal of Personality and Social Psychology, 31,* 206–215.

Clark, M. S. (1983). Reactions to aid in communal and exchange relationships. In J. D. Fisher, A. Nadler, & B. DePaulo (Eds.), *New directions in helping: Vol. 1. Recipient reactions to aid* (pp. 281–304). New York: Academic Press.

Clark, M. S. (1984). Record keeping in two types of relationships. *Journal of Personality and Social Psychology, 47,* 549–557.

Clark, M. S., & Mills, J. (1979). Interpersonal attraction in exchange and communal relationships. *Journal of Personality and Social Psychology, 37,* 12–24.

Clark, M. S., & Mills, J. (1993). The difference between communal and exchange relationships: What it is and is not. *Personality and Social Psychology Bulletin, 19,* 684–691.

Clark, R. D., III. (2001). Effects of majority defection and multiple minority sources on minority influence. *Group Dynamics, 5,* 57–62.

Clark, R. D., III, & Maass, A. (1990). The effects of majority size on minority influence: *European Journal of Psychology, 20,* 99–117.

Clark, R. D., III, & Word, L. E. (1972). Why don't bystanders help? Because of ambiguity? *Journal of Personality and Social Psychology, 24,* 392–400.

Cleare, A. J., & Bond, A. J. (2000). Experimental evidence that the aggressive effect of tryptophan depletion is mediated via the 5-HT-sub-1A receptor. *Psychopharmacology, 147,* 439–441.

Clifford, M. M., & Walster, E. H. (1973). The effect of physical attractiveness on teacher expectations. *Sociology of Education, 46,* 248–258.

Cohen, D., & Nisbett, R. E. (1997). Field experiments examining the culture of honor: The role of institutions in perpetuating norms about violence. *Personality and Social Psychology Bulletin, 23,* 1188–1199.

Cohen, D., Nisbett, R. E., Bowdle, B. F., & Schwarz, N. (1996). Insult, aggression, and the southern culture of honor: An "experimental ethnography." *Journal of Personality and Social Psychology, 70,* 945–960.

Cohen, D., Vandello, J., & Rantilla, A. K. (1998). The sacred and the social: Cultures of honor and violence. In P. Gilbert & B. Andrews (Eds.), *Shame: Interpersonal behavior, psychopathology, and culture* (pp. 261–282). Cambridge: Oxford University Press.

Cohen, G. L., Steele, C. M., & Ross, L. D. (1999). The mentor's dilemma: Providing critical feedback across the racial divide. *Personality and Social Psychology Bulletin, 25,* 1302–1318.

Cohen-Ketteinis, P. T., & Van Goozen, S. H. M. (1997). Sex reassignment of adolescent transsexuals: A follow-up study. *Journal of the American Academy of Child and Adolescent Psychiatry, 36,* 263–271.

Cohn, E. G., & Rotton, J. (1997). Assault as a function of time and temperature: A moderator-variable time-series analysis. *Journal of Personality and Social Psychology, 72,* 1322–1334.

Cohn, E. S., White, S. O., & Sanders, J. (2000). Distributive and procedural justice in seven nations. *Law and Human Behavior, 24,* 553–580.

Cokley, K. O. (2002). Ethnicity, gender and academic self-concept: A preliminary examination of academic disidentification and implications for psychologists. *Cultural Diversity and Ethnic Minority Psychology, 8,* 378–388.

Collins, N. L., & Feeney, B. C. (2000). A safe haven: An attachment theory perspective on support seeking and caregiving in intimate relationships. *Journal of Personality and Social Psychology, 78,* 1053–1073.

Collins, N. L., & Miller, L. C. (1994). Self-disclosure and liking: a meta-analytic review. *Psychological Bulletin, 116,* 457–475.

Collins-Standley, T., Gan, S., Yu, H., & Zilmann, D. (1996). Choice of romantic, violent, and scary fairy-tale books by preschool girls and boys. *Child Study Journal, 26,* 279–302.

Coltraine, S., & Messineo, M. (2000). The perpetuation of subtle prejudice: Race and gender imagery in 1990s television advertising. *Sex Roles, 42,* 363–389.

Conner, M., Norman, P., & Bell, R. (2002). The theory of planned behavior and healthy eating. *Health Psychology, 21,* 194–201.

Connolly, D. A., Price, H. L., & Read, J D. (2006) Predicting expert social science testimony in criminal prosecutions of historic child sexual abuse *Legal and Criminological Psychology, 11,* 55–74

Connors, E., Lundregan, T., Miller, N., & McEwen, T. (1996). *Convicted by juries, exonerated by science: Case studies in the use of DNA evidence to establish innocence after trial.* Washington, DC: U.S. Department of Justice.

Conway, L. G., Ryder, A. G., Tweed, R. G., & Sokol, B. W. (2001). Intranational cultural variation: Exploring further implications of collectivism within the United States. *Journal of Cross-Cultural Psychology, 32,* 681–697.

Conway, M. A. (1995). *Flashbulb memories.* Mahwah, NJ: Erlbaum.

Conway, M. A., & Pleydell-Pearce, C. W. (2000). The construction of autobiographical memories in the self-memory system. *Psychological Review, 107,* 261–288.

Cook, S. W. (1985). Experimenting on social issues: The case of school desegregation. *American Psychologist, 40,* 452–460.

Cook, S. W., & Pelfrey, M. (1985). Reactions to being helped in cooperating interracial groups: A context effect. *Journal of Personality and Social Psychology, 49,* 1231–1245.

Cook, T. D., & Campbell, D. T. (1979). *Quasi-experimentation:*

Design and analysis issues for field settings. Chicago: Rand McNally.

Cooley, C. H. (1902). *Human nature and the social order.* New York: Schocken Books. (Reprinted in 1964)

Cooper, J., & Fazio, R. H. (1984). A new look at dissonance theory. In L. Berkowitz (Ed.), *Advances in experimental social psychology* (Vol. 17, pp. 229–267). New York: Academic Press.

Cooper, J., & Neuhaus, I. M. (2000). The "hired gun" effect: Assessing the effect of pay, frequency of testifying, and credentials on the perception of expert testimony. *Law and Human Behavior, 24,* 149–171.

Cooper, J., Zanna, M. P., & Goethals, G. R. (1974). Mistreatment of an esteemed other as a consequence affecting dissonance reduction. *Journal of Experimental Social Psychology, 10,* 224–233.

Cooper, M. L., Frone, M. R., Russell, M., & Mudar, P. (1995). Drinking to regulate positive and negative emotions: A motivational model of alcohol use. *Journal of Personality and Social Psychology, 69,* 990–1005.

Coopersmith, S. (1967). *The antecedents of self-esteem.* San Francisco: Freeman.

Copeland, J. T. (1994). Prophecies of power: Motivational implications of social power for behavioral confirmation. *Journal of Personality and Social Psychology, 67,* 264–277.

Corneille, O., Yzerbyt, V. Y., Rogier, A., & Buidin, G. (2001). Threat and the group attribution error: When threat elicits judgments of extremity and homogeneity. *Personality and Social Psychology Bulletin, 27,* 437–446.

Correll, J., Spencer, S. J. & Zanna, M. P. (2004). An affirmed self and an open mind: Self-affirmation and sensitivity to argument strength. *Journal of Experimental Social Psychology, 40,* 350–356.

Cose, E. (1997). *Color-blind: Seeing beyond race in a race-obsessed world.* New York: HarperCollins.

Cosmides, L., & Tooby, J. (2004). *What is evolutionary psychology: Explaining the new science of the mind.* New Haven, CT: Yale University Press.

Costanzo, M. (1997). *Just revenge: Costs and consequences of the death penalty.* New York: St. Martin's Press.

Costanzo, M. (2004). *Psychology applied to law.* Belmont, CA: Wadsworth/Thomson.

Cota, A. A., Evans, C. R., Dion, K. L., Kilik, L., & Longman, R. S. (1995). The structure of group cohesion. *Personality and Social Psychology Bulletin, 21,* 572–580.

Cottrell, N. B., Wack, D. L., Sekerak, G. J., & Rittle, R. H. (1968). Social facilitation of dominant responses by the presence of an audience and the mere presence of others. *Journal of Personality and Social Psychology, 9,* 245–250.

Covington, M. V. (2000). Intrinsic versus extrinsic motivation in schools: A reconciliation. *Current Directions in Psychological Science, 9,* 22–25.

Cowan, C. L., Thompson, W. C., & Ellsworth, P. C. (1984). The effects of death qualification on jurors' predisposition to convict and on the quality of deliberation. *Law and Human Behavior, 8,* 53–80.

Cox, M., & Tanford, S. (1989). An alternative method of capital jury selection. *Law and Human Behavior, 13,* 167–183.

Cox, T. H., Lobel, S. A., & McLeod, P. L. (1991). Effects of ethnic group cultural differences on cooperative and competitive behavior on a group task. *Academy of Management Journal, 34,* 827–847.

Coyne, J. C. (1994). Self-reported distress: Analog or ersatz depression? *Psychological Bulletin, 116,* 29–45.

Craig, W. M., Pepler, D., & Atlas, R. (2000). Observations of bullying in the playground and in the classroom. *School Psychology International, 21,* 22–36.

Cramer, R. E., McMaster, M. R., Bartell, P. A., & Dragna, M. (1988). Subject competence and the minimization of the bystander effect. *Journal of Applied Social Psychology, 18,* 1133–1148.

Crandall, C. S., & Eshleman, A. (2003). A justification-suppression of the expression and experience of prejudice. *Psychological Bulletin, 129,* 414–446.

Crandall, C. S., Eshleman, A., & O'Brien, L. (2002). Social norms and the expression and suppression of prejudice: The struggle for internalization. *Journal of Personality and Social Psychology, 82,* 359–378.

Crano, W. D. (2000). Milestones in the psychological analysis of social influence. *Group Dynamics: Theory, Research, and Practice, 4,* 68–80.

Crawford, M. T., Sherman, S. J., & Hamilton, D. L. (2002). Perceived entitativity, stereotype formation, and the interchangeability of group. *Journal of Personality and Social Psychology, 83,* 1076–1094.

Crick, N. R., Casas, J. F., & Mosher, M. (1997). Relational and overt aggression in preschool. *Developmental Psychology, 33,* 579–588.

Crick, N. R., & Dodge, K. A. (1994). A review and reformulation of social information-processing mechanisms in children's social adjustment. *Psychological Bulletin, 115,* 74–101.

Crick, N. R., & Rose, A. J. (2000). Toward a gender-balanced approach to the study of social-emotional development: A look at relational aggression. In R. G. Geen & E. Donnerstein (Eds.), *Human aggression: Theories, research, and implications for social policy* (pp. 153–168). San Diego: Academic Press.

Crick, N. R., Werner, N. E., Casas, J. F., O'Brien, K. M., Nelson, D. A., Grotpeter, J. K., & Markon, K. (1999). Childhood aggression and gender: A new look at an old problem. In D. Bernstein (Ed.), *Nebraska symposium on motivation* (vol. 45, pp. 75–141). Lincoln: University of Nebraska Press.

Crocker, J., & Quinn, D. M. (2000). Social stigma and the self: Meanings, situations, and self-esteem. In T. F. Heatherton & R. E. Kleck (Eds.), *The social psychology of stigma* (pp. 153–183). New York: Guilford.

Crocker, J., Voelkl, K., Testa, M., & Major, B. (1991). Social stigma: The affective consequences of attributional ambiguity. *Journal of Personality and Social Psychology, 60,* 218–228.

Croizet, J. C., & Claire, T. (1998). Extending the concept of stereotype and threat to social class: The intellectual underperformance of students from low socioeconomic backgrounds. *Personality and Social Psychology Bulletin, 24,* 588–594.

Croizet, J. C., Després, G., Gauzins, M. E., Huguet, P., Leyens, J.-P., & Meot, A. (2004). Stereotype threat undermines intellectual performance by triggering a disruptive mental load. *Personality and Social Psychology Bulletin, 30,* 721–731.

Cronbach, L. J. (1955). Processes affecting scores on "understanding of others" and "assumed similarity." *Psychological Bulletin, 52,* 177–193.

Crosby, F., Bromley, S., & Saxe, L. (1980). Recent unobtrusive studies of black and white discrimination and prejudice: A literature review. *Psychological Bulletin, 87,* 546–563.

Crozier, W. R. (Ed.) (2001). *Shyness: Development, consolidation, and change*. London: Routledge.

Crozier, W. R., & Alden, L. E. (Eds.) (2001). *International handbook of social anxiety: Concepts, research, and interventions relating to the self and shyness*. West Sussex, England: Wiley.

Crutchfield, R. S. (1955). Conformity and character. *American Psychologist, 10*, 195–198.

Csikszentmihalyi, M., & Figurski, T. J. (1982). Self-awareness and aversive experience in everyday life. *Journal of Personality, 50*, 15–28.

Cuddy, A. J. C., Norton, M. I., & Fiske, S. T. (2005). This old stereotype: The pervasiveness and persistence of the elderly stereotype. *Journal of Social Issues, 61*, 267.

Cunningham, M. R. (1979). Weather, mood, and helping behavior: Quasi experiments with the sunshine Samaritan. *Journal of Personality and Social Psychology, 37*, 1947–1956.

Cunningham, M. R., Roberts, A. R., Wu, C., Barbee, A. P., & Druen, P. B. (1995). "Their ideas of beauty are, on the whole, the same as ours": Consistency and variability in the cross-cultural perception of female physical attractiveness. *Journal of Personality and Social Psychology, 68*, 261–279.

Cunningham, M. R., Steinberg, J., & Grev, R. (1980). Wanting to and having to help: Separate motivations for positive mood and guilt-induced helping. *Journal of Personality and Social Psychology, 38*, 181–192.

Cunningham, W. A., Johnson, M. K., Gatenby, J. C., Gore, J. C., & Banaji, M. R. (2003). Neural components of social evaluation. *Journal of Personality and Social Psychology, 85*, 639–649.

Cunningham, W. A., Johnson, M. K., Raye, C. L., Gatenby, J., Gore, J. C., Banaji, M. (2004). Separable neural components in the processing of black and white faces. *Psychological Science, 15*, 806–813.

Curtis, R. C., & Miller, K. (1986). Believing another likes or dislikes you: Behaviors making the beliefs come true. *Journal of Personality and Social Psychology, 51*, 284–290.

Cutler, B. L., & Penrod, S. D. (1995). *Mistaken identification: The eyewitness, psychology, and the law*. New York: Cambridge University Press.

Cutler, B. L., Penrod, S. D., & Stuve, T. E. (1988). Juror decision making in eyewitness identification cases. Law and *Human Behavior, 12*, 41–55.

Dabbs, J. M., Jr., Carr, T. S., Frady, R. L., & Riad, J. K. (1995). Testosterone, crime, and misbehavior among 692 male prison inmates. *Personality and Individual Differences, 18*, 627–633.

Dabbs, J. M., & Dabbs, M. G. (2005). Why men and women fight: The role of testosterone in mate relations. In S. Fein, G. R. Goethals, & M. J. Sandstrom (Eds.), *Gender and aggression: Interdisciplinary perspectives*. Mahwah, NJ: Erlbaum.

Dabbs, J. M., Jr., Hargrove, M. F., & Heusel, C. (1996). Testosterone differences among college fraternities: Well-behaved vs. rambunctious. *Personality and Individual Differences, 20*, 157–161.

Dabbs, J. M., Jr., Hopper, C. H., & Jurkovic, G. J. (1990). Testosterone and personality among college students and military veterans. *Personality and Individual Differences, 11*, 1263–1269.

Dabbs, J. M., Jr., & Morris, R. (1990). Testosterone, social class, and antisocial behavior in a sample of 4,462 men. *Psychological Science, 1*, 209–211.

Daly, M., & Wilson, M. (1988). *Homicide*. New York: Aldine de Gruyter.

Daly, M., & Wilson, M. (1989). Homicide and cultural evolution. *Ethology and Sociobiology, 10*, 99–110.

Daly, M., & Wilson, M. (1994). Some differential attributes of lethal assaults on small children by stepfathers versus genetic fathers. *Ethology and Sociobiology, 15*, 207–217.

Daly, M., & Wilson, M. (1996). Violence against stepchildren. *Current Directions in Psychological Science, 5*, 77–81.

Daly, M., & Wilson, M. (2000). Not quite right. *American Psychologist, 55*, 679–680.

Danheiser, P. R., & Graziano, W. G. (1982). Self-monitoring and cooperation as a self-presentational strategy. *Journal of Personality and Social Psychology, 42*, 497–505.

Darby, B. L. (1975). Reciprocal concessions procedure for inducing compliance: The door-in-the-face technique. *Journal of Personality and Social Psychology, 31*, 206–215.

Darley, J. M., & Batson, C. D. (1973). From Jerusalem to Jericho: A study of situational and dispositional variables in helping behavior. *Journal of Personality and Social Psychology, 27*, 100–108.

Darley, J. M., Carlsmith, K. M., & Robinson, P. H. (2000). Incapacitation and just desserts as motives for punishment. *Law and Human Behavior, 24*, 659–684.

Darley, J. M., & Fazio, R. (1980). Expectancy confirmation processes arising in the social interaction sequence. *American Psychologist, 35*, 867–881.

Darley, J. M., & Gross, P. H. (1983). A hypothesis-confirming bias in labeling effects. *Journal of Personality and Social Psychology, 44*, 20–33.

Darley, J. M., & Latané, B. (1970). Norms and normative behavior: Field studies of social interdependence. In J. Macauley & L. Berkowitz (Eds.), *Altruism and helping behavior* (pp. 83–101). New York: Academic Press.

Darwin, C. (1872). *The expression of the emotions in man and animals*. London: John Murray.

Das, E. H. H. J., de Wit, J. B. F., & Stroebe, W. (2003). Fear appeals motivate acceptance of action recommendations: Evidence for a positive bias in the processing of persuasive messages. *Personality and Social Psychology Bulletin, 29*, 650–664.

Davidson, A. R., & Jaccard, J. J. (1979). Variables that moderate the attitude-behavior relation: Results of a longitudinal survey. *Journal of Personality and Social Psychology, 37*, 1364–1376.

Davies, P. G., Spencer, S. J., Quinn, D. M., & Gerhardstein, R. (2002). Consuming images: How television commercials that elicit stereotype threat can restrain women academically and professionally. *Personality and Social Psychology Bulletin, 28*, 1615–1628.

Davies, P. T., & Cummings, E. M. (1994). Marital conflict and child adjustment: An emotional security hypothesis. *Psychological Bulletin, 116*, 387–411.

Davis, B. P., & Knowles, E. S. (1999). A Disrupt-Then-Reframe technique of social influence. *Journal of Personality and Social Psychology, 76*, 192–199.

Davis, J. H., Au, W. T., Hulbert, L., Chen, X., & Zarnoth, P. (1997). Effects of group size and procedural influence on consensual judgments of quantity: The example of damage awards and mock civil juries. *Journal of Personality and Social Psychology, 73*, 703–718.

Davis, J. H., Kameda, T., Parks, C., Stasson, M., & Zimmerman, S. (1989). Some social mechanics of group decision-making: The distribution of opinion, polling sequence, and implications for consensus. *Journal of Personality and Social Psychology, 57*, 1000–1012.

Davis, J. L., & Rusbult, C. E. (2001). Attitude alignment in close relationships. *Journal of Personality and Social Psychology, 81*, 65–84.

Davis, M. H. (1994). *Empathy: A social psychological approach.* Madison, WI: Browon & Benchmark.

Davis, M. H., Luce, C., & Kraus, S. J. (1994). The heritability of characteristics associated with dispositional empathy. *Journal of Personality, 62*, 369–391.

Davis, M. H., Mitchell, K. V., Hall, J. A., Lothert, J., Snapp, T., & Meyer, M. (1999). Empathy, expectations, and situational preferences: Personality influences on the decision to participate in volunteer helping behaviors. *Journal of Personality, 67*, 469–503.

Davis, S. (1990). Men as success objects and women as sex objects: A study of personal advertisements. *Sex Roles, 23*, 43–50.

Dawes, R. M. (1980). Social dilemmas. *Annual Review of Psychology, 31*, 169–193.

Dawkins, R. (1989). *The selfish gene* (2nd ed.). Oxford: Oxford University Press.

De Cremer, D., & Leonardelli, G. J. (2003). Cooperation in social dilemmas and the need to belong: The moderating effect of group size. *Group Dynamics, 7*, 168–174.

De Cremer, D., & van Lange, P. A. M. (2001). Why prosocials exhibit greater cooperation than proselfs: The roles of social responsibility and reciprocity. *European Journal of Personality, 15*, S5–S18.

De Dreu, C., & De Vries, N. (Eds.) (2001). *Group Consensus and Minority Influence: Implications for innovation.* London: Blackwell.

De Dreu, C. K. W., & Carnevale, P. J. (2003). Motivational bases of information processing and strategy in negotiation and social conflict. In M. P. Zanna (Ed.), *Advances in experimental social psychology* (Vol. 35). New York: Academic Press.

De Raad, B. (2000). *The big five personality factors: Theory and applications.* Germany: Hogrefe & Huber.

De Veer, M. W., Gallup, G. G., Theall, L. A., van den Bos, R., & Povinelli, D. J. (2003). An 8-year longitudinal study of mirror self-recognition in chimpanzees *(Pan troglodytes). Neuropsychologia, 41*, 229–234.

de Waal, F. B. M. (1996). *Good natured: The origins of right and wrong in humans and other animals.* Cambridge, MA: Harvard University Press.

de Waal, F. B. M. (2003). The chimpanzee's service economy: Evidence for cognition-based reciprocal exchange. In E. Ostrom & J. Walker (Eds.), *Trust and reciprocity: Interdisciplinary lessons from experimental research* (pp. 128–143). New York: Russell Sage.

de Waal, F. B., & Berger, M. L. (2000). Payment for labor in monkeys. *Nature, 404*, 563.

Dean, K. E., & Malamuth, N. M. (1997). Characteristics of men who aggress sexually and of men who imagine aggressing: Risk and moderating variables. *Journal of Personality and Social Psychology, 72*, 449–455.

Dear Abby (2003, December 17). *The Berkshire Eagle*, p. C7.

Deater-Deckard, K., Dodge, K. A., Bates, J. E., & Pettit, G. S. (1998). Multiple-risk factors in the development of externalizing behavior problems: Group and individual differences. *Development and Psychopathology, 10*, 469–493.

Deaux, K., & Emswiller, T. (1974). Explanations for successful performance on sex-linked tasks: What is skill for the male is luck for the female. *Journal of Personality and Social Psychology, 29*, 80–85.

Deaux, K., & Lewis, L. L. (1984). The structure of gender stereotypes: Interrelationships among components and gender label. *Journal of Personality and Social Psychology, 46*, 991–1004.

Deaux, K., & Major, B. (1987). Putting gender into context: An interactive model of gender-related behavior. *Psychological Review, 94*, 369–389.

DeBono, K. G., Leavitt, A., & Backus, J. (2003). Product packaging and product evaluation: An individual difference approach. *Journal of Applied Social Psychology, 33*, 513–521.

Deci, E. L., & Ryan, R. M. (1985). *Intrinsic motivation and self-determination in human behavior.* New York: Plenum.

DeCramer, D. (2001). Relations of self-esteem concerns, group identification, and self-stereotyping to in-group favoritism. *Journal of Social Psychology, 141*, 389–400.

DeKeseredy, W. S., Schwartz, M. D., & Tait, K. (1993) Sexual assault and stranger aggression on a Canadian university campus. *Sex Roles, 28*, 263–277

Demaré, D., Lips, H. M., & Briere, J. (1993). Sexually violent pornography, anti-women attitudes, and sexual aggression: A structural equation model. *Journal of Research in Personality, 27*, 285–300.

Dennis, A. R., & Williams, M. L. (2003). Electronic brainstorming: Theory, research, and future directions. In P. B. Paulus & B. A. Nijstad (Eds.), *Group creativity: Innovation through collaboration* (pp. 160–178). New York: Oxford University Press.

DePalma, M. T., Madey, S. F., Tillman, T. C., & Wheeler, J. (1999). Perceived patient responsibility and belief in a just world affect helping. *Basic and Applied Social Psychology, 21*, 131–137.

DePaulo, B. M. (1994). Spotting lies: Can humans do better? *Current Directions in Psychological Science, 3*, 83–86.

DePaulo, B. M., Charlton, K., Cooper, H., Lindsay, J. J., & Muhlenbruck, L. (1997). The accuracy-confidence correlation in the detection of deception. *Personality and Social Psychology Review, 1*, 346–357.

DePaulo, B. M., & Kashy, D. A. (1998). Everyday lies in close and casual relationships. *Journal of Personality and Social Psychology, 74*, 63–79.

DePaulo, B. M., Lassiter, G. D., & Stone, J. I. (1982). Attentional determinants of success at detecting deception and truth. *Personality and Social Psychology Bulletin, 8*, 273–279.

DePaulo, B. M., Lindsay, J. J., Malone, B. E., Muhlenbruck, L., Charlton, K., & Cooper, H. (2003). Cues to deception. *Psychological Bulletin, 129*, 74–112.

Deppe, R. K., & Harackiewicz, J. M. (1996). Self-handicapping and intrinsic motivation: Buffering intrinsic motivation from the threat of failure. *Journal of Personality and Social Psychology, 70*, 868–876.

Depret, E., & Fiske, S. T. (1999). Perceiving the powerful: Intriguing individuals versus threatening groups. *Journal of Experimental Social Psychology, 35*, 461–480.

Derlega, V. J., Metts, S., Petronio, S., & Margulis, S. T. (1993). *Self-disclosure.* Newbury Park, CA: Sage.

Derlega, V. J., Wilson, M., & Chaikin, A. L. (1976). Friendship and disclosure reciprocity. *Journal of Personality and Social Psychology, 34*, 578–587.

Dershowitz, A. M. (1982). *The best defense.* New York: Vintage Books.
DeSteno, D. A., & Salovey, P. (1996). Evolutionary origins of sex differences in jealousy? Questioning the "fitness" model. *Psychological Science, 7,* 367–372.
Deutsch, F. M. (1989). The false consensus effect: Is the self-justification hypothesis justified? *Basic and Applied Social Psychology, 10,* 83–99.
Deutsch, M., & Gerard, H. B. (1955). A study of normative and informational social influences upon individual judgment. *Journal of Abnormal and Social Psychology, 51,* 629–636.
Deutsch, M., & Krauss, R. M. (1960). The effect of threat upon interpersonal bargaining. *Journal of Abnormal and Social Psychology, 61,* 181–189.
Devenport, J. L., Penrod, S. D., & Cutler, B. L. (1997). Eyewitness identification evidence: Evaluating commonsense evaluations. *Psychology, Public Policy, and Law, 3,* 338–361.
Devine, D. J., Clayton, L. D., Dunford, B. B., Seying, R., & Pryce, J. (2001). Jury decision making: 45 years of empirical research on deliberating groups. *Psychology, Public Policy, and Law, 7,* 622–727.
Devine, P. G. (1989). Stereotypes and prejudice: Their automatic and controlled components. *Journal of Personality and Social Psychology, 56,* 5–18.
Devine, P. G., Brodish, A. B., & Vance, S. L. (2004). Self-regulatory processes in interracial interactions: The role of internal and external motivation to respond without prejudice. In J. P. Forgas, K. D. Williams, & W. von Hippel (Eds.), *Social motivation: Conscious and unconscious processes.* New York: Psychology Press.
Diamond, L. M. (2003). Was it a phase? Young women's relinquishment of lesbian/bisexual identities over a 5-year period. *Journal of Personality and Social Psychology, 84,* 352–364.
Diamond, M. (1993). Homosexuality and bisexuality in different populations. *Archives of Sexual Behavior, 22,* 291–310.
Diamond, S., Vidmar, N., Rose, M. R., Ellis, L., & Murphy, E. (2003). Juror discussions during civil trials: Studying an Arizona innovation. *University of Arizona Law Review, 45,* 1.
Dickinson, M. J. (1999). Do gooders or do betters? An analysis of the motivation of student tutors. *Educational Research, 41,* 221–227.
Diekman, A. B., Eagly, A. H., & Kulesa, P. (2002). Accuracy and bias in stereotypes about the social and political attitudes of women and men. *Journal of Experimental Social Psychology, 38,* 268–282.
Diekmann, K. A., Tenbrunsel, A. E., & Galinsky, A. D. (2003). From self-prediction to self-defeat: Behavioral forecasting, self-fulfilling prophecies, and the effect of competitive expectations. *Journal of Personality and Social Psychology, 85,* 672–683.
Diener, E. (1979). Deindividuation, self-awareness, and disinhibition. *Journal of Personality and Social Psychology, 37,* 1160–1171.
Diener, E. (1980). Deindividuation: The absence of self-awareness and self-regulation in group members. In P. B. Paulus (Ed.), *Psychology of group influence* (pp. 209–242). Hillsdale, NJ: Erlbaum.
Diener, E., Fraser, S. C., Beaman, A. L., & Kelem, R. T. (1976). Effects of deindividuation variables on stealing among Halloween trick-or-treaters. *Journal of Personality and Social Psychology, 33,* 178–183.
Diener, E., Wolsic, B., & Fujita, F. (1995). Physical attractiveness and subjective well-being. *Journal of Personality and Social Psychology, 69,* 120–129.
Dietz, T. L. (1998). An examination of violence and gender role portrayals in video games: Implications for gender socialization and aggressive behavior. *Sex Roles, 38,* 425–442.
Dietz-Uhler, B. (1996). The escalation of commitment in political decision-making groups: A social identity approach. *European Journal of Social Psychology, 26,* 611–629.
Dijksterhuis, A., & Aarts, H. (2003). Of wildebeests and humans: The preferential detection of negative stimuli. *Psychological Science, 14,* 14–18.
Dijksterhuis, A., & van Knippenberg, A. (1996). The knife that cuts both ways: Facilitated and inhibited access to traits as a result of stereotype activation. *Journal of Experimental and Social Psychology, 32,* 271–288.
Dijkstra, P., & Buunk, B. P. (1998). Jealousy as a function of rival characteristics: An evolutionary perspective. *Personality and Social Psychology Bulletin, 24,* 1158–1166.
Dill, J. C., & Anderson, C. A. (1995). Effects of frustration justification on hostile aggression. *Aggressive Behavior, 21,* 359–369.
Dill, K. E., Anderson, C. A., Anderson, K. B., & Deuser, W. E. (1997). Effects of aggressive personality on social expectations and social perceptions. *Journal of Research in Personality, 31,* 272–292.
Dimberg, U., & Ohman, A. (1996). Behold the wrath: Psychophysiological responses to facial stimuli. *Motivation and Emotion, 20,* 149–181.
Dimberg, U., Thunberg, M., & Elmehed, K. (2000). Unconscious facial reactions to emotional facial expressions. *Psychological Science, 11,* 86–89.
Dindia, K., & Allen, M. (1992). Sex differences in self-disclosure: A meta-analysis. *Psychological Bulletin, 112,* 106–124.
Dion, K. K., Berscheid, E., & Walster, E. (1972). What is beautiful is good. *Journal of Personality and Social Psychology, 24,* 285–290.
Dion, K. K., & Dion, K. L. (1996). Cultural perspectives on romantic love. *Personal Relationships, 3,* 5–17.
Dion, K. L. (1979). Intergroup conflict and intragroup cohesiveness. In W. G. Austin & S. Worchel (Eds.), *The social psychology of intergroup relations* (pp. 211–224). Pacific Grove, CA: Brooks/Cole.
Dion, K. L. (2000). Group cohesion: From "field of forces" to multidimensional construct. *Group Dynamics, 4,* 7–26.
Dion, K. L., & Cota, A. A. (1991). The Ms. stereotype: Its domain and the role of explicitness in title preference. *Psychology of Women Quarterly, 15,* 403–410.
Dion, K. L., & Dion, K. K. (1976). Love, liking and trust in heterosexual relationships. *Personality and Social Psychology Bulletin, 2,* 187–190.
Dionisio, D. P., Granholm, E., Hillix, W. A., & Perrine, W. F. (2001). Differentiation of deception using pupillary responses as an index of cognitive processing. *Psychophysiology, 38,* 205–211.
Dodd, D. K. (1985). Robbers in the classroom: A deindividuation exercise. *Teaching in Psychology, 12,* 89–91.
Dolinski, D. (2000). On inferring one's beliefs from one's attempt and consequences for subsequent compliance. *Journal of Personality and Social Psychology, 78,* 260–272.
Dollard, J., Doob, L. W., Miller, N. E., Mowrer, O. H., & Sears, R. R. (1939). *Frustration and aggression.* New Haven, CT: Yale University Press.

Donne, J. (1975). Meditation, 17. In A. Raspa (Ed.), *Devotions upon emergent occasions* (p. 87). Montreal: McGill-Queen's University Press. (Original work published 1624)

Donnerstein, E. (2005). Media violence: Theory, effects, and context. In S. Fein, G. R. Goethals, & M. J. Sandstrom (Eds.), *Gender and aggression: Interdisciplinary perspectives.* Mahwah, NJ: Erlbaum.

Donnerstein, E., & Berkowitz, L. (1981). Victim reactions in aggressive erotic films as a factor in violence against women. *Journal of Personality and Social Psychology, 41,* 710–724.

Donnerstein, E., & Donnerstein, M. (1976). Research in the control of interracial aggression. In R. G. Geen and E. C. O'Neal (Eds.), *Perspectives on aggression* (pp. 133–168). New York: Academic Press.

Donnerstein, E., & Hallam, J. (1978). Facilitating effects of erotica on aggression against women. *Journal of Personality and Social Psychology, 36,* 1270–1277.

Donnerstein, E., Linz, D., & Penrod, S. (1987). *The question of pornography.* New York: Free Press.

Donnerstein, E., & Malamuth, N. (1997). Pornography: Its consequences on the observer. In L. B. Schlesinger & E. Revitch (Eds.), *Sexual dynamics of anti-social behavior* (2nd ed., pp. 30–49). Springfield, IL: Charles C Thomas.

Dooley, P. A. (1995). Perceptions of the onset controllability of AIDS and helping judgments: An attributional analysis. *Journal of Applied Social Psychology, 25,* 858–869.

Doosje, B., & Branscombe, N. (2003). Attributions for the negative historical actions of a group. *European Journal of Social Psychology, 33,* 235–248.

Dornbusch, S. M., Hastorf, A. H., Richardson, S. A., Muzzy, R. E., & Vreeland, R. S. (1965). The perceiver and the perceived: Their relative influence on categories of interpersonal perception. *Journal of Personality and Social Psychology, 1,* 434–440.

Douglas, K. M., & McGarty, C. (2002). Internet identifiability and beyond: A model of the effects of identifiability on communicative behavior. *Group Dynamics, 6,* 17–26.

Dovidio, J. F. (1984). Helping behavior and altruism: An empirical and conceptual overview. In L. Berkowitz (Ed.), *Advances in experimental social psychology* (Vol. 17, pp. 361–427). New York: Academic Press.

Dovidio, J. F., Brigham, J. C., Johnson, B. T., & Gaertner, S. L. (1996). Stereotyping, prejudice, and discrimination: Another look. In C. N. Macrae, C. Stangor, & M. Hewstone (Eds.), *Stereotypes and stereotyping* (pp. 276–319). New York: Guilford.

Dovidio, J. F., & Gaertner, S. L. (1998). On the nature of contemporary prejudice: The causes, consequences, and challenges of aversive racism. In J. L. Eberhardt, & S. T. Fiske (Eds.), *Confronting racism: The problem and the response* (pp. 3–32). Thousand Oaks, CA: Sage.

Dovidio, J. F., & Gaertner, S. L. (1999). Reducing prejudice: Combating intergroup biases. *Current Directions in Psychological Science, 8,* 101–105.

Dovidio, J. F., & Gaertner, S. L. (2000). Aversive racism and selection decisions: 1989 and 1999. *Psychological Science, 11,* 319–323.

Dovidio, J. F., Gaertner, S. E., Kawakami, K., & Hodson, G. (2002). Why can't we just get along? Interpersonal biases and interracial distrust. *Cultural Diversity and Ethnic Minority Psychology, 8,* 88–102.

Dovidio, J. F., Gaertner, S. L., Validzic, A., Matoka, K., Johnson, B., & Frazier, S. (1997). Extending the benefits of recategorization: Evaluations, self-disclosure, and helping. *Journal of Experimental Social Psychology, 33,* 401–420.

Dovidio, J. F., Kawakami, K., & Gaertner, S. L. (2002). Implicit and explicit prejudice and interracial interaction. *Journal of Personality and Social Psychology, 82,* 62–68.

Dovidio, J. F., Kawakami, K., Johnson, C., Johnson, B., & Howard, A. (1997). On the nature of prejudice: Automatic and controlled processes. *Journal of Experimental Social Psychology, 33,* 510–540.

Dovidio, J. F., Piliavin, J. A., Gaertner, S. L., Schroeder, D. A., & Clark, R. D., II. (1991). The arousal: cost-reward model and the process of intervention: A review of the evidence. In M. S. Clark (Ed.), *Review of personality and social psychology 12: Prosocial behavior* (pp. 86–118). Newbury Park, CA: Sage.

Dovidio, J. F., Smith, J. K., Donnella, A. G., & Gaertner, S. L. (1997). Racial attitudes and the death penalty. *Journal of Applied Social Psychology, 27,* 1468–1487.

Downs, A. C., & Lyons, P. M. (1991). Natural observations of the links between attractiveness and initial legal judgments. *Personality and Social Psychology Bulletin, 17,* 541–547.

Drigotas, S. M., & Rusbult, C. E. (1992). Shall I stay or should I go? A dependence model of breakups. *Journal of Personality and Social Psychology, 62,* 62–87.

Drigotas, S. M., Rusbult, C. E., & Verette, J. (1999). Level of commitment, mutuality of commitment, and couple well-being. *Personal Relationships, 6,* 389–409.

Duck, S., & Wright, P. H. (1993). Reexamining gender differences in same-gender friendships: A close look at two kinds of data. *Sex Roles, 28,* 709–727.

Duckitt, J., & Mphuthing, T. (1998). Group identification and intergroup attitudes: A longitudinal analysis in South Africa. *Journal of Personality and Social Psychology, 74,* 80–85.

Duckworth, K. L., Bargh, J. A., Garcia, M., & Chaiken, S. (2002). The automatic evaluation of novel stimuli. *Psychological Science, 13,* 513–519.

Duclos, S. E., Laird, J. D., Schneider, E., Sexter, M., Stern, L., & Van Lighten, O. (1989). Emotion-specific effects of facial expressions and postures on emotional experience. *Journal of Personality and Social Psychology, 57,* 100–108.

Duff, K. J., & Newman, L. S. (1997). Individual differences in the spontaneous construal of behavior: Idiocentrism and the automatization of the trait inference process. *Social Cognition, 15,* 217–241.

Duffy, M. K., & Shaw, J. D. (2000). The Salieri Syndrome: Consequences of envy in groups. *Small Group Research, 31,* 3–23.

Dulin, P. L., & Hill, R. D. (2003). Relationships between altruistic activity and positive and negative affect among low-income older adult service providers. *Aging and Mental Health, 7,* 294–299.

Dunning, D. (1999). A newer look: Motivated social cognition and the schematic representation of social concepts. *Psychological Inquiry, 10,* 1–11.

Dunning, D. (2002). The zealous self-affirmer: How and why the self lurks so pervasively behind social judgment. In S. J. Spencer, S. Fein, M. Zanna, & J. M. Olson (Eds.), *Motivated social perception: The Ontario symposium* (Vol. 9). Mahwah, NJ: Erlbaum.

Dunning, D., Griffin, D. W., Milojkovic, J. D., & Ross, L. (1990). The overconfidence effect in social prediction. *Journal of Personality and Social Psychology, 58,* 568–581.

Dunning, D., & Hayes, A. F. (1996). Evidence for egocentric

comparison in social judgment. *Journal of Personality and Social Psychology, 71,* 213–229.

Dunning, D., Johnson, K., Ehrlinger, J., & Kruger, J. (2003). Why people fail to recognize their own incompetence. *Current Directions in Psychological Science, 12,* 83–87.

Dunning, D., & Perretta, S. (2002). Automaticity and eyewitness accuracy: A 10- to 12-second rule for distinguishing accurate from inaccurate positive identifications. *Journal of Applied Psychology, 87,* 951–962.

Dunning, D., & Sherman, D. A. (1997). Stereotypes and tacit inference. *Journal of Personality and Social Psychology, 73,* 459–471.

Dunning, D., & Stern, L. B. (1994). Distinguishing accurate from inaccurate eyewitness identifications via inquiries about decision processes. *Journal of Personality and Social Psychology, 67,* 818–835.

Dunton, B. C., & Fazio, R. H. (1997). An individual difference measure of motivation to control prejudiced reactions. *Personality and Social Psychology Bulletin, 23,* 316–326.

Dutton, D. G., & Aron, A. P. (1974). Some evidence for heightened sexual attraction under conditions of high anxiety. *Journal of Personality and Social Psychology, 30,* 510–517.

Duval, S., & Wicklund, R. A. (1972). *A theory of objective self-awareness.* New York: Academic Press.

Duval, S., Duval, V. H., & Mulilis, J. P. (1992). Effects of self-focus, discrepancy between self and standard, and outcome expectancy favorability on the tendency to match self to standard or to withdraw. *Journal of Personality and Social Psychology, 62,* 340–348.

Dysart, J. E., Lindsay, R. C. L., MacDonald, T. K., & Wicke, C. (2002). The intoxicated witness: Effects of alcohol on identification accuracy from showups. *Journal of Applied Psychology, 87,* 170–175.

Eagly, A. H. (1987). *Sex differences in social behavior: A social-role interpretation.* Hillsdale, NJ: Erlbaum.

Eagly, A. H. (2004). Few women at the top: How role incongruity produces prejudice and the glass ceiling. In D. van Knippenberg & M. A. Hogg (Eds.), *Identity, leadership, and power.* London: Sage.

Eagly, A. H. (2004). Prejudice: Toward a more inclusive understanding. In A. Eagly, R. M. Baron, & V. L. Hamilton (Eds.), *The social psychology of group identity and social conflict: Theory, application, and practice.* Washington, DC: APA Books.

Eagly, A. H., Ashmore, R. D., Makhijani, M. G., & Longo, L. C. (1991). What is beautiful is good, but . . . : A meta-analytic review of research on the physical attractiveness stereotype. *Psychology Bulletin, 110,* 107–128.

Eagly, A. H., & Carli, L. L. (1981). Sex of researchers and sex-typed communications as determinants of sex differences in influenceability: A meta-analysis of social influence studies. *Psychological Bulletin, 90,* 1–20.

Eagly, A. H., & Chaiken, S. (1998). Attitude structure and function. In D. Gilbert, S. Fiske, & G. Lindzey (Eds.), *Handbook of social psychology* (4th ed.) (pp. 269–322). New York: McGraw-Hill.

Eagly, A. H., Chen, S., Chaiken, S., & Shaw-Barnes, K. (1999). The impact of attitudes on memory: An affair to remember. *Psychological Bulletin, 125,* 64–89.

Eagly, A. H., & Chravala, C. (1986). Sex differences in conformity: Status and gender-role interpretations. *Psychology of Women Quarterly, 10,* 203–220.

Eagly, A. H., & Crowley, M. (1986). Gender and helping behavior: A meta-analytic review of the social psychological literature. *Psychological Bulletin, 100,* 283–308.

Eagly, A. H, Mladinic, A., & Otto, S. (1994). Are women evaluated more favorably than men? An analysis of attitudes, beliefs, and emotions. *Psychology of Women Quarterly, 15,* 203–216.

Eagly, A. H., & Steffen, V. J. (1986). Gender and aggressive behavior: A meta-analytic review of the social psychology literature. *Psychological Bulletin, 100,* 309–330.

Eagly, A. H., Wood, W., & Chaiken, S. (1978). Causal inferences about communicators and their effect on opinion change. *Journal of Personality and Social Psychology, 36,* 424–435.

Eagly, A. H., Wood, W., & Fishbaugh, L. (1981). Sex differences in conformity: Surveillance by the group as a determinant of male nonconformity. *Journal of Personality and Social Psychology, 40,* 384–394.

Eagly, A. H., Wood, W., & Johannesen-Schmidt, M. C. (2004). Social role theory of sex differences and similarities: Implications for the partner preferences of women and men. In A. H. Eagly, A. Beall, & R. J. Sternberg (Eds.), *The psychology of gender* (2nd ed.). New York: Guilford.

Eaton, J. (2001). Management communication: The threat of groupthink. *Corporate Communications, 6,* 183–192.

Eberhardt, J. L., Dasgupta, N., & Banaszynski, T. L. (2002). Believing is seeing: The effects of racial labels and implicit beliefs on face perception. *Personality and Social Psychology Bulletin, 29,* 360–370.

Eberhardt, J. L., & Goff, P. A. (2004). Seeing race. In C. S. Crandall & M. Schaller (Eds.), *The social psychology of prejudice: Historical perspectives.* Seattle, WA: Lewinian.

Eberhardt, J. L., Goff, P. A., Purdie, V. J., & Davies, P. G. (2004). *Seeing black: Race, crime, and visual processing. Journal of Personality and Social Psychology, 87,* 876–963.

Eckes, T. (2002). Paternalistic and envious gender stereotypes: Testing predictions from the stereotype content model. *Sex Roles, 47,* 99–114.

Eden, D. (1990). Pygmalion without interpersonal contrast effects: Whole groups gain from raising manager expectations. *Journal of Applied Psychology, 75,* 394–398.

Edwards, K. (1990). The interplay of affect and cognition in attitude formation and change. *Journal of Personality and Social Psychology, 59,* 202–216.

Edwards, K., & Smith, E. E. (1996). A disconfirmation bias in the evaluation of arguments. *Journal of Personality and Social Psychology, 71,* 5–24.

Egan, J. (2003, November 23). Love in the time of no time. *New York Times Magazine,* Section 6, p. 66.

Ehrlichman, H., & Eichenstein, R. (1992). Private wishes: Gender similarities and differences. *Sex Roles, 26,* 399–422.

Eisenberg, N. (2000). Emotion, regulation, and moral development. *Annual Review of Psychology, 51,* 665–697.

Eisenberg, N., Fabes, R. A., Carlo, G., & Karbon, M. (1992). Emotional responsivity to others: Behavioral correlates and socialization antecedents. In N. Eisenberg & R. A. Fabes (Eds.), *Emotion and its regulation in early development* (pp. 57–73). San Francisco: Jossey-Bass.

Eisenberg, N., Fabes, R. A., Murphy, B., Karbon, M., Smith, M., & Maszk, P. (1996). The relations of children's dispositional empathy-related responding to their emotionality regulation, and social functioning. *Developmental Psychology, 32,* 195–209.

Eisenberg, N., Guthrie, I. K., Murphy, B. C., Shepard, S. A., Cumberland, A., & Carlo, G. (1999). Consistency and development of prosocial dispositions: A longitudinal study. *Child Development, 70,* 1360–1372.

Eisenberger, N. I., Lieberman, M. I., & Williams, K. D. (2003). Does rejection hurt? An fMRI study of social exclusion. *Science, 302,* 290–292.

Eisenberger, R., & Cameron, J. (1996). Detrimental effects of reward: Reality or myth? *American Psychologist, 51,* 1153–1166.

Eisenberger, R., Cotterell, N., & Marvel, J. (1987). Reciprocation ideology. *Journal of Personality and Social Psychology, 53,* 743–750.

Ekman, P., & Davidson, R. J. (1993). Voluntary smiling changes regional brain activity. *Psychological Science, 22,* 342–345.

Ekman, P., & Friesen, W. V. (1974). Detecting deception from the body or face. *Journal of Personality and Social Psychology, 29,* 288–298.

Ekman, P., Friesen, W. V., O'Sullivan, M., Chan, A., Diacoyanni-Tarlatzis, I., Heider, K., Krause, R., LeCompte, W. A., Pitcairn, T., Ricci-Bitti, P., Scherer, K., Tomita, M., & Tzavaras, A. (1987). Universals and cultural differences in the judgments of facial expressions of emotion. *Journal of Personality and Social Psychology, 53,* 712–717.

Ekman, P., & O'Sullivan, M. (1991). Who can catch a liar? *American Psychologist, 46,* 913–920.

Elfenbein, H. A., & Ambady, N. (2002). On the universality and cultural specificity of emotion recognition: A meta-analysis. *Psychological Bulletin, 128,* 203–235.

Elkin, R. A., & Leippe, M. R. (1986). Physiological arousal, dissonance, and attitude change: Evidence for a dissonance-arousal link and a "don't remind me" effect. *Journal of Personality and Social Psychology, 51,* 55–65.

Ellemers, N., & Bos, A. E. R. (1998). Social identity, relative deprivation, and coping with the threat of position loss: A field study among native shopkeepers in Amsterdam. *Journal of Applied Social Psychology, 28,* 1987–2006.

Elliot, A. J., & Devine, P. G. (1994). On the motivational nature of cognitive dissonance: Dissonance as psychological discomfort. *Journal of Personality and Social Psychology, 67,* 382–394.

Elliott, M. A., Armitage, C. J., & Baughan, C. J. (2003). Drivers' compliance with speed limits: An application of the theory of planned behavior. *Journal of Applied Psychology, 88,* 964–972.

Elliott, R. (1991). Social science data and the APA: The Lockhart brief as a case in point. *Law and Human Behavior, 15,* 59–76.

Elloy, D. F., & Smith, C. R. (2003). Patterns of stress, work-family conflict, role conflict, role ambiguity and overload among dual-career and single-career couples: An Australian study. *Cross-Cultural Management, 10,* 55–66.

Ellsworth, P. C. (1991). To tell what we know or wait for Godot? *Law and Human Behavior, 15,* 77–90.

Elms, A., & Milgram, S. (1966). Personality characteristics associated with obedience and defiance toward authoritative command. *Journal of Experimental Research in Personality, 1,* 282–289.

Elwork, A., Sales, B. D., & Alfini, J. J. (1982). *Making jury instructions understandable.* Charlottesville, VA: Miche.

English, P. W., & Sales, B. D. (1997). A ceiling or consistency effect for the comprehension of jury instructions. *Psychology, Public Policy, and Law, 3,* 381–401.

Enzle, M. E., & Anderson, S. C. (1993). Surveillant intentions and intrinsic motivation. *Journal of Personality and Social Psychology, 64,* 257–266.

Epley, N., & Huff, C. (1998). Suspicion, affective response, and educational benefit as a result of deception in psychology research. *Personality and Social Psychology Bulletin, 24,* 759–768.

Erber, R., & Tesser, A. (1994). Self-evaluation maintenance: A social psychological approach to interpersonal relationships. In R. Erber & R. Gilmour (Eds.), *Theoretical frameworks for personal relationships* (pp. 211–233). Hillsdale, NJ: Erlbaum.

Ericksen, J. A., & Steffen, S. A. (1999). *Kiss and tell: Surveying sex in the twentieth century.* Cambridge, MA: Harvard University Press.

Eron, L. D. (1986). Interventions to mitigate the psychological effects of media violence on aggressive behavior. In L. R. Huesmann & N. M. Malamuth (Eds.), *Journal of Social Issues: Media Violence and Antisocial Behavior, 42*(3), 155–169.

Eron, L. D., Huesmann, L. R., & Zelli, A. (1991). The role of parental variables in the learning of aggression. In. D. J. Pepler & K. H. Rubin (Eds.), *The development and treatment of childhood aggression* (pp. 169–188). Hillsdale, NJ: Erlbaum.

Esser, J. K. (1998). Alive and well after 25 years: A review of groupthink research. *Organizational Behavior and Human Decision Processes, 73,* 116–141.

Esses, V. M., & Dovidio, J. F. (2002). The role of emotions in determining willingness to engage in intergroup contact. *Personality and Social Psychology Bulletin, 28,* 1202–1214.

Estrada-Hollenbeck, M., & Heatherton, T. F. (1998). Avoiding and alleviating guilt through prosocial behavior. In J. Bybee (Ed.), *Guilt and children* (pp. 215–231). San Diego: Academic Press.

Etcoff, N. (1999). *Survival of the prettiest: The science of beauty.* New York: Doubleday.

Fairburn, C. G., & Brownell, K. D. (Eds.) (2002). *Eating disorders and obesity: A comprehensive handbook.* New York: Guilford Press.

Fazio, R. H. (1987). Self-perception theory: A current perspective. In M. P. Zanna, J. M. Olson, & C. P. Herman (Eds.), *Social influence: The Ontario symposium* (Vol. 5, pp. 129–150). Hillsdale, NJ: Erlbaum.

Fazio, R. H. (1990). Multiple processes by which attitudes guide behavior: The MODE model as an integrative framework. In M. P. Zanna (Ed.), *Advances in experimental social psychology* (Vol. 23, pp. 75–109). New York: Academic Press.

Fazio, R. H., Effrein, E. A., & Falender, V. J. (1981). Self-perceptions following social interactions. *Journal of Personality and Social Psychology, 41,* 232–242.

Fazio, R. H., Jackson, J. R., Dunton, B. C., & Williams, C. J. (1995). Variability in automatic activation as an unobtrusive measure of racial attitudes. A bona fide pipeline? *Journal of Personality and Social Psychology, 69,* 1013–1027.

Fazio, R. H., Ledbetter, J. E., & Towles-Schwen, T. (2000). On the costs of accessible attitudes: Detecting that the attitude object has changed. *Journal of Personality and Social Psychology, 78,* 197–210.

Fazio, R. H., & Olson, M. A. (2003). Implicit measures in social cognition research: Their meaning and use. *Annual Review of Psychology, 54,* 297–327.

Fazio, R. H., & Towles-Schwen, T. (1999). The MODE model

of attitude-behavior processes. In S. Chaiken & Y. Trope (Eds.), *Dual-process theories in social psychology* (pp. 97–116). New York: Guilford.

Fazio, R. H., & Zanna, M. P. (1981). Direct experience and attitude-behavior consistency. In L. Berkowitz (Ed.), *Advances in experimental social psychology* (Vol. 14, pp. 162–202). New York: Academic Press.

Fazio, R. H., Zanna, M. P., & Cooper, J. (1977). Dissonance and self perception: An integrative view of each theory's proper domain of application. *Journal of Experimental Social Psychology, 13*, 464–479.

Feeney, J. A., & Noller, P. (1990). Attachment style as a predictor of adult romantic relationships. *Journal of Personality and Social Psychology, 58*, 281–291.

Fehr, B., & Russell, J. A. (1991). The concept of love viewed from a prototype perspective. *Journal of Personality and Social Psychology, 60*, 425–438.

Fehr, E., & Gaechter, S. (2002). Altruistic punishment in humans. *Nature, 415*, 137–140.

Fein, E., & Schneider, S. (1996). *The rules: Time-tested secrets for capturing the heart of Mr. Right.* New York: Warner Books.

Fein, S., & Eustis, E. F. (2001). *Effects of violent and sexist content in video games on men's sexist attitudes and judgments.* Paper presented at the second annual meeting of the Society of Personality and Social Psychology, San Antonio, TX.

Fein, S., Goethals, G. R., & Kassin, S. M. (2002). *Group influence on political judgments: The case of presidential debates.* Unpublished manuscript, Williams College.

Fein, S., Goethals, G. R., & Sandstrom, M. J. (Eds.) (2005). *Gender and aggression: Interdisciplinary perspectives.* Mahwah, NJ: Erlbaum.

Fein, S., Hoshino-Browne, E., Davies, P. G., & Spencer, S. J. (2003). Self-image maintenance goals and sociocultural norms in motivated social perception. In S. J. Spencer, S. Fein, M. P. Zanna, & J. M. Olson (Eds.), *Motivated social perception: The Ontario symposium* (Vol. 9, pp. 21–44). Mahwah, NJ: Erlbaum.

Fein, S., Morgan, S. J., Norton, M. I., & Sommers, S. R. (1997). Hype and suspicion: The effects of pretrial publicity, race, and suspicion on jurors' verdicts. *Journal of Social Issues, 53*, 487–502.

Fein, S., & Spencer, S. J. (1997). Prejudice as self-image maintenance: Affirming the self through derogating others. *Journal of Personality and Social Psychology, 73*, 31–44.

Fein, S., von Hippel, W., & Spencer, S. J. (1999). To stereotype or not to stereotype: Motivation and stereotype activation, application, and inhibition. *Psychological Inquiry, 10*, 49–54.

Feingold, A. (1988). Matching for attractiveness in romantic partners and same-sex friends: A meta-analysis and theoretical critique. *Psychological Bulletin, 104*, 226–235.

Feingold, A. (1992a). Gender differences in mate selection preferences: A test of the parental investment model. *Psychological Bulletin, 112*, 125–139.

Feingold, A. (1992b). Good-looking people are not what we think. *Psychological Bulletin, 111*, 304–341.

Fejfar, M. C., & Hoyle, R. H. (2000). Effect of private self-awareness on negative affect and self-referent attribution: A quantitative review. *Personality and Social Psychology Review, 4*, 132–142.

Felson, R. B. (1989). Parents and the reflected appraisal process: A longitudinal analysis. *Journal of Personality and Social Psychology, 56*, 965–971.

Fenigstein, A., & Abrams, D. (1993). Self-attention and the egocentric assumption of shared perspectives. *Journal of Experimental Social Psychology, 29*, 287–303.

Fenigstein, A., Scheier, M. F., & Buss, A. H. (1975). Public and private self-consciousness: Assessment and theory. *Journal of Consulting and Clinical Psychology, 43*, 522–527.

Ferguson, G. A. (1992) Psychology in Canada: 1939–1945. *Canadian Psychology. 33*, 697–705

Ferrari, J. R. (1998). Procrastination. In H. S. Friedman (Ed.), *Encyclopedia of Mental Health* (pp. 5.1–5.7). San Diego: Academic Press.

Ferrari, J. R., Loftus, M. M., & Pesek, J. (1999). Young and older caregivers at homeless animal and human shelters: Selfish and selfless motives in helping others. *Journal of Social Distress and the Homeless, 8*, 37–49.

Ferreira, A., Picazo, O., Uriarte, N., Pereira, M., & Fernandez-Guasti, A. (2000). Inhibitory effect of buspirone and diazepam, but not of 8-OH-DPAT, on maternal behavior and aggression. *Pharmacology, Biochemistry and Behavior, 66*, 389–396.

Ferris, C. F. (2005). Adolescent stress, aggression, and neural plasticity. In S. Fein, G. R. Goethals, & M. J. Sandstrom (Eds.), *Gender and aggression: Interdisciplinary perspectives.* Mahwah, NJ: Erlbaum.

Fershtman, M. (1997). Cohesive group detection in a social network by the segregation matrix index. *Social Networks, 19*, 193–208.

Festinger, L. (1950). Informal social communication. *Psychological Review, 57*, 271–282.

Festinger, L. (1954). A theory of social comparison processes. *Human Relations, 7*, 117–140.

Festinger, L. (1957). *A theory of cognitive dissonance.* Stanford, CA: Stanford University Press.

Festinger, L., & Carlsmith, J. M. (1959). Cognitive consequences of forced compliance. *Journal of Abnormal and Social Psychology, 58*, 203–210.

Festinger, L., Pepitone, A., & Newcomb, T. (1952). Some consequences of de-individuation in a group. *Journal of Abnormal and Social Psychology, 47*, 382–389.

Festinger, L., Schachter, S., & Back, K. W. (1950). *Social pressures in informal groups: A study of human factors in housing.* New York: Harper.

Fincham, F. D. (2003). Marital conflict, correlates, structure, and context. *Current Directions in Psychological Science, 12*, 23–27.

Fincham, F. D., Harold, G. T., & Gano-Phillips, S. (2000). The longitudinal association between attributions and marital satisfaction: Direction of effects and role of efficacy expectations. *Journal of Family Psychology, 14*, 267–285.

Fine, M. A., & Sacher, J. A. (1997). Predictors of distress following relationship termination among dating couples. *Journal of Social and Clinical Psychology, 16*, 381–388.

Fink, B., & Penton-Voak, I. (2002). Evolutionary psychology of facial attractiveness. *Current Directions in Psychological Science, 11*, 154–158.

Fink, J. S., & Kensicki, L. J. (2002). An imperceptible difference: Visual and textual constructions of femininity in *Sports Illustrated* and *Sports Illustrated for Women. Mass Communication and Society, 5*, 317–339.

Finkel, E. J., Rusbult, C. E., Kumashiro, M., & Hannon, P. A. (2002). Dealing with betrayal in close relationships: Does commitment promote forgiveness? *Journal of Personality and Social Psychology, 82*, 956–974.

Finkel, N. J. (1995). *Commonsense justice: Jurors' notions of the law.* Cambridge, MA: Harvard University Press.

Finkelhor, D., & Dziuba-Leatherman, J. (1994). Victimization of children. *American Psychologist, 49,* 173–183.

Fischer, C. S. (1976). *The urban experience.* New York: Harcourt Brace Jovanovich.

Fishbein, D. H. (Ed.) (2000). *The science, treatment, and prevention of antisocial behaviors: Application to the criminal justice system.* Kingston, NJ: Civic Research Institute.

Fishbein, M. (1980). A theory of reasoned action: Some applications and implications. In H. E. Howe & M. M. Page (Eds.), *Nebraska symposium on motivation* (Vol. 27, pp. 65–116). Lincoln: University of Nebraska Press.

Fishbein, M., & Ajzen, I. (1972). Attitudes and opinions. In P. H. Mussen & M. R. Rosenzweig (Eds.), *Annual Review of Psychology, 23,* 487–544.

Fishbein, M., & Ajzen, I. (1975). *Beliefs, attitudes, intention, and behavior: An introduction to theory and research.* Reading, MA: Addison-Wesley.

Fisher, J. D., Bell, P. A., & Baum, A. (1984). *Environmental psychology* (2nd ed.). New York: Holt, Rinehart and Winston.

Fisher, J. D., Nadler, A., & Whitcher-Alagna, S. (1982). Recipient reactions to aid. *Psychological Bulletin, 91,* 27–54.

Fiske, A. P. (1991). The cultural relativity of selfish individualism: Anthropological evidence that humans are inherently sociable. In M. S. Clark (Ed.), *Review of personality and social psychology: Vol. 12. Prosocial behavior* (pp. 176–214). Newbury Park, CA: Sage.

Fiske, A. P. (1992). The four elementary forms of sociality: Framework for a unified theory of social relations. *Psychological Review, 99,* 689–723.

Fiske, S. T. (2000). Interdependence reduces prejudice and stereotyping. In S. Oskamp (Ed.), *Reducing prejudice and discrimination* (pp. 115–135). Mahwah, NJ: Erlbaum.

Fiske, S. T., Bersoff, D. N., Borgida, E., Deaux, K., & Heilman, M. E. (1991). Social science research on trial: Use of sex stereotyping research in Price Waterhouse v. Hopkins. *American Psychologist, 46,* 1049–1060.

Fiske, S. T., Bersoff, D. N., Borgida, E., Deaux, K., & Heilman, M. E. (1997). What constitutes a scientific review? A majority reply to Barrett and Morris. In M. R. Walsh (Ed.), *Women, men, and gender: Ongoing debates.* New Haven, CT: Yale University Press.

Fiske, S. T., Cuddy, A. J. C., Glick, P., & Xu, J. (2002). A model of (often mixed) stereotype content: Competence and warmth respectively follow from perceived status and competition. *Journal of Personality and Social Psychology, 82,* 878–902.

Fiske, S. T., Lin, M., & Neuberg, S. L. (1999). The continuum model: Ten years later. In S. Chaiken & Y. Trope (Eds.), *Dual-process theories in social psychology* (pp. 231–254). New York: Guilford.

Fiske, S. T., & Neuberg, S. L. (1990). A continuum model of impression formation: From category-based to individuating processes: Influence of information and motivation on attention and interpretation. In M. P. Zanna (Ed.), *Advances in experimental social psychology* (Vol. 23, pp. 1–74). San Diego, CA: Academic Press.

Fitzgerald, J. M. (1988). Vivid memories and the reminiscence phenomenon: The role of self-narrative. *Human Development, 31,* 261–273.

Fitzgerald, R., & Ellsworth, P. C. (1984). Due process vs. crime control: Death qualification and jury attitudes. *Law and Human Behavior, 8,* 31–52.

Fivush, R., Haden, C. A., & Dimmick, J. W. (Eds.) (2003). *Autobiographical memory and the construction of a narrative self: Developmental and cultural perspectives.* Mahwah, NJ: Erlbaum.

Flack, W. F., Jr., Laird, J. D., & Cavallaro, L. A. (1999). Separate and combined effects of facial expressions and bodily postures on emotional feelings. *European Journal of Social Psychology, 29,* 203–217.

Fleming, M. A., Wegener, D. T., & Petty, R. E. (1999). Procedural and legal motivations to correct for perceived judicial biases. *Journal of Experimental Social Psychology, 35,* 186–203.

Fletcher, G. J. O., Danilovics, P., Fernandez, G., Peterson, D., & Reeder, G. D. (1986). Attributional complexity: An individual differences measure. *Journal of Personality and Social Psychology, 51,* 875–884.

Flory, J. D., Raikkonen, K., Matthews, K. A., & Owens, J. F. (2000). Self-focused attention and mood during everyday social interactions. *Personality and Social Psychology Bulletin, 26,* 875–883.

Folger, R., & Greenberg, J. (1985). Procedural justice: An interpretive analysis of personnel systems. In K. Rowland & G. Ferris (Eds.), *Research in personnel and human resource management* (Vol. 3, pp. 141–183). Greenwich, CT: JAI Press.

Folkes, V. S. (1982). Forming relationships and the matching hypothesis. *Personality and Social Psychology Bulletin, 8,* 631–636.

Follett, M. P. (1942). Constructive conflict. In H. C. Metcalf & L. Urwick (Eds.), *Dynamic administration: The collected papers of Mary Parker Follett* (pp. 30–49). New York: Harper.

Ford, T. E., Ferguson, M. A., Brooks, J. L., & Hagadone, K. M. (2004). Coping sense of humor reduces effects of stereotype threat on women's math performance. *Personality and Social Psychology Bulletin, 30,* 643–653.

Ford, T. E., & Tonander, G. R. (1998). The role of differentiation between groups and social identity in stereotype formation. *Social Psychology Quarterly, 61,* 372–384.

Forgas, J. P. (1992). Mood and the perception of atypical people: Affect and prototypicality in person memory and impressions. *Journal of Personality and Social Psychology, 62,* 863–875.

Forgas, J. P. (Ed.) (2000). *Feeling and thinking: Affective influences on social cognition.* New York: Cambridge University Press.

Forgas, J. P., & Bower, G. H. (1987). Mood effects on person perception judgments. *Journal of Personality and Social Psychology, 53,* 53–60.

Forgas, J. P., Williams, K. D., & von Hippel, W. (2004). *Social motivation: Conscious and unconscious processes.* London: Cambridge University Press.

ForsterLee, L., Horowitz, I. A., & Bourgeois, M. J. (1993). Juror competence in civil trials: Effects of preinstruction and evidence technicality. *Journal of Applied Psychology, 78,* 14–21.

Forsyth, D. R. (1999). *Group dynamics* (3rd ed.). Belmont, CA: Wadsworth.

Forsythe, S. M. (1990). Effects of applicant's clothing on interviewer's decision to hire. *Journal of Applied Social Psychology, 20,* 1579–1595.

Foster, C. A., Witcher, B. S., Campbell, W. K., & Green, J. D. (1998). Arousal and attraction: Evidence for automatic and controlled processes. *Journal of Personality and Social Psychology, 74,* 86–101.

Fosterling, F. (1992). The Kelley model as an analysis of variance analogy: How far can it be taken? *Journal of Experimental Social Psychology, 28,* 475–490.

Fowles, J. (2000). *The case for television violence: Academic duplicity and cultural conflict.* Thousand Oaks, CA: Sage.

Frable, D. E. S. (1989). Sex typing and gender ideology: Two facets of the individual's gender psychology that go together. *Journal of Personality and Social Psychology, 56,* 95–108.

Franck, K. A. (1980). Friends and strangers: The social experience of living in urban and non-urban settings. *Journal of Social Issues, 36*(3), 52–71.

Frank, J. (1949). *Courts on trial.* Princeton, NJ: Princeton University Press.

Frank, M. G., & Ekman, P. (1997). The ability to detect deceit generalizes across different types of high-stake lies. *Journal of Personality and Social Psychology,* 72, 1429–1439.

Frank, M. G., Ekman, P., & Friesen, W. V. (1993). Behavioral markers and recognizability of the smile of enjoyment. *Journal of Personality and Social Psychology, 64,* 83–93.

Fredrickson, B. L., Roberts, T. A., Noll, S. M., Quinn, D. M., & Twenge, J. M. (1998). The swimsuit becomes you: Sex differences in self-objectification, restrained eating, and math performance. *Journal of Personality and Social Psychology, 75,* 269–284.

Freedman, J. L. (1988). Television violence and aggression: What the evidence shows. *Applied Social Psychology Annual, 8,* 144–162.

Freedman, J. L., & Burke, T.M. (1996). The effect of pretrial publicity: The Bernardo case. *Canadian Journal of Criminology, 38, 253–270.*

Freedman, J. L., & Fraser, S. C. (1966). Compliance without pressure: The foot-in-the-door technique. *Journal of Personality and Social Psychology, 4,* 195–202.

Freedman, J. L., & Sears, D. O. (1965). Warning, distraction, and resistance to influence. *Journal of Personality and Social Psychology, 1,* 262–266.

French, D. C., Jansen, E. A., & Pidada, S. (2002). United States and Indonesian children's and adolescents' reports of relational aggression by disliked peers. *Child Development,* 73, 1143–1150.

Freud, S. (1905). Fragments of an analysis of a case of hysteria. *Collected papers* (Vol. 3). New York: Basic Books. (Reprinted in 1959)

Freud, S. (1920). *Beyond the pleasure principle: A study of the death instinct in human aggression* (J. Strachey, Trans.). New York: Bantam Books. (Reprinted in 1959)

Frey, D. L., & Gaertner, S. L. (1986). Helping and the avoidance of inappropriate interracial behavior: A strategy that perpetuates a nonprejudiced self-image. *Journal of Personality and Social Psychology, 50,* 1083–1090.

Frey, D., & Schulz-Hardt, S. (2001). Confirmation bias in group information seeking and its implications for decision making in administration, business and politics. In F. Butera & G. Mugny (Eds.), *Social influence in social reality: Promoting individual and social change* (pp. 53–73). Ashland, OH: Hogrefe & Huber.

Friedrich, J., Fethersonhaugh, D., Casey, S., & Gallagher, D. (1996). Argument integration and attitude change: Suppression effects in the integration of one-sided arguments that vary in persuasiveness. *Personality and Social Psychology Bulletin, 22,* 179–191.

Friend, R., Rafferty, Y., & Bramel, D. (1990). A puzzling misinterpretation of the Asch "conformity" study. *European Journal of Social Psychology, 20,* 29–44.

Fritzsche, B. A., Finkelstein, M. A., & Penner, L. A. (2000). To help or not to help: Capturing individuals' decision policies. *Social Behavior and Personality, 28,* 561–578.

Froehle, T. C., Mullen, C., Pappas, V., Tracy, M., & Chait, J. (1999). Using group decision support systems to brainstorm and evaluate prospective consultation interventions. *Consulting Psychology Journal: Practice and Research, 5,* 181–190.

Fuente-Fernandez, R., Ruth, T. R., Sossi, V., Schulzer, M., Calne, D. B., & Stoessl, A. J. (2001). Expectation and dopamine release: Mechanism of the placebo effect in Parkinson's disease. *Science, 293,* 1164–1166.

Fulero, S., & Penrod, S. D. (1990). Attorney jury selection folklore: What do they think and how can psychology help? *Forensic Reports, 3,* 223–259.

Furedy, J. J. and Heslegrave, R. J. (1991). The Forensic Use of the Polygraph: A Psychophysiological Analysis of Current Trends and Future Prospects In P. K. Ackles, J. R. Jennings, & M. G. H. Coles (Eds), *Advances in Psychophysiology,* (Vol.4), London: Jessica Kingsley Publishers.

Furnham, A. (2003). Belief in a just world: Research progress over the past decade. *Personality and Individual Differences, 34,* 795–817.

Furnham, A., Pallangyo, A. E., & Gunter, B. (2001). Genderrole stereotyping in Zimbabwean television advertisements. *South African Journal of Psychology, 31,* 21–29.

Gabbert, F., Memon, A., & Allan, K. (2003). Memory conformity: Can eyewitnesses influence each other's memories for an event? *Applied Cognitive Psychology, 17,* 533–543.

Gaertner, S. L., & Dovidio, J. F. (2000). *Reducing intergroup bias: The common ingroup identity model.* Philadelphia, PA: Psychology Press.

Gagne, F. M., & Lyndon, J. E. (2001). Mindset and relationship illusions: The moderating effects of domain specificity and relationship commitment. *Personality and Social Psychology Bulletin, 27,* 1144–1155.

Gagnon, A., & Bourhis, R. Y. (1996). Discrimination in the minimal group paradigm: Social identity or self-interest? *Personality and Social Psychology Bulletin, 22,* 1289–1301.

Galanter, M. (1999). *Cults: Faith, healing, and coercion* (2nd ed.). New York: Oxford University Press.

Galen, B. R., & Underwood, M. K. (1997). *Developmental Psychology, 33,* 589–600.

Galinsky, A. D., & Kray, L. J. (2004). From thinking about what might have been to sharing what we know: The role of counterfactual mind-sets in information sharing in groups. *Journal of Experimental Social Psychology, 40,* 606–618.

Galinsky, A. D., & Ku, G. (2004). The effects of perspective-taking on prejudice: The moderating role of self-evaluation. *Personality and Social Psychology Bulletin, 30,* 594–604.

Galinsky, A. D., Martorana, P. V., & Ku, G. (2003). To control or not to control stereotypes: Separating the implicit and explicit processes of perspective-taking and suppression. In J. P. Forgas, K. D. Williams, & W. von Hippel (Eds.), *Social judgments: Implicit and explicit processes* (pp. 343–363). New York: Cambridge University Press.

Galinsky, A. D., & Moskowitz, G. B. (2000). Perspective-taking: Decreasing stereotype expression, stereotype accessibility, and in-group favoritism. *Journal of Personality and Social Psychology, 78,* 708–724.

Galinsky, A. D., Stone, J., & Cooper, J. (2000). The reinstatement of dissonance and psychological discomfort following failed affirmations. *European Journal of Social Psychology, 30,* 123–147.

Gallup, G. G., Jr. (1977). Self-recognition in primates: A comparative approach to the bidirectional properties of consciousness. *American Psychologist, 32,* 329–337.

Gallup Poll Editors (2002). *Gallup poll of the Islamic world: Subscriber report.* Princeton, NJ: Gallup Press.

Game, F., Carchon, I., & Vital-Durand, F. (2003). The effect of stimulus attractiveness on visual tracking in 2- to 6-month-old infants. *Infant Behavior & Development, 26,* 135–150.

Gammie, S. C., Olaghere-da-Silva, U. B., & Nelson, R. J. (2000). 3-Bromo-7-nitroindazole, a neuronal nitric oxide synthase inhibitor, impairs maternal aggression and citrulline immunoreactivity in prairie voles. *Brain Research, 870,* 80–86.

Gamson, W. A., Fireman, B., & Rytina, S. (1982). *Encounters with unjust authority.* Homewood, IL: Dorsey.

Gan, S., Zillmann, D., & Mitrook, M. (1997). Stereotyping effect of Black women's sexual rap on White audiences. *Basic and Applied Social Psychology, 19,* 381–399.

Gangestad, S. W. (1993). Sexual selection and physical attractiveness: Implications for mating dynamics. *Human Nature, 4,* 205–235.

Gangestad, S. W., & Simpson, J. A. (2000). The evolution of human mating: Trade-offs and strategic pluralism. *Behavioral and Brain Sciences, 23,* 573–587.

Gangestad, S. W., & Snyder, M. (1991). Taxonomic analysis redux: Some statistical considerations for testing a latent class model. *Journal of Personality and Social Psychology, 61,* 141–146.

Gangestad, S. W., & Snyder, M. (2000). Self-monitoring: Appraisal and reappraisal. *Psychological Bulletin, 126,* 530–555.

Gannon, T. A. (2006). Increasing Honest Responding on Cognitive Distortions in Child Molesters: The Bogus Pipeline Procedure. *Journal of Interpersonal Violence, 21,* 358–375

Garcia, S. M., Weaver, K., Moskowitz, G. B., & Darley, J. M. (2002). Crowded minds: The implicit bystander effect. *Journal of Personality and Social Psychology, 83,* 843–853.

Gardner, J. L., Magrath, R. D., & Kokko, H. (2003). Stepping stones of life: Natal dispersal in the group-living but noncooperative speckled warbler. *Animal Behaviour, 66,* 521–530.

Gardner, W. L., Gabriel, S., & Hochschild, L. (2002). When you and I are "we," you are not threatening: The role of self-expansion in social comparison. *Journal of Personality and Social Psychology, 82,* 239–251.

Geary, D. C. (2000). Evolution and proximate expression of human paternal investment. *Psychological Bulletin, 126,* 55–77.

Green, R. G. (1981). Behavioral and physiological reactions to observed violence: Effects of prior exposure to aggressive stimuli. *Journal of Personality and Social Psychology, 40,* 868–875.

Geen, R. G. (1991). Social motivation. *Annual Review of Psychology, 42,* 377–399.

Geen, R. G. (1998). Aggression and antisocial behavior. In D. T. Gilbert, S. T. Fiske, & G. Lindzey (Eds.), *The handbook of social psychology* (4th ed., Vol. 2, pp. 317–356). New York: McGraw-Hill.

Geen, R. G., & Donnerstein, E. (Eds.) (1998). *Human aggression: Theories, research, and implications for social policy.* San Diego, CA: Academic Press.

Geen, R. G., & McCown, E. J. (1984). Effects of noise and attack on aggression and physiological arousal. *Motivation and Emotion, 8,* 231–241.

Geen, R. G., & Quanty, M. B. (1977). The catharsis of aggression: An evaluation of a hypothesis. In L. Berkowitz (Ed.), *Advances in experimental social psychology* (Vol. 10, pp. 1–37). New York: Academic Press.

Geis, F. L., Brown, V., Jennings (Walstedt), J., & Porter, N. (1984). TV commercials as achievement scripts for women. *Sex Roles, 10,* 513–525.

Geiselman, R. E., Haight, N. A., & Kimata, L. G. (1984). Context effects in the perceived physical attractiveness of faces. *Journal of Experimental Social Psychology, 20,* 409–424.

Gelfand, M., & Brett, J. (Eds.) (2003). *Culture and negotiation: Integrative approaches to theory and research.* Palo Alto, CA: Stanford University Press.

Gelfand, M. J., & Christakopoulou, S. (1999). Culture and negotiator cognition: Judgment accuracy and negotiation processes in individualistic and collectivistic cultures. *Organizational Behavior and Human Decision Processes, 71,* 248–269.

George, D. M., Carroll, P., Kersnick, R., & Calderon, K. (1998). Gender-related patterns of helping among friends. *Psychology of Women Quarterly, 22,* 685–704.

George, J. M., & Brief, A. P. (1992). Feeling good–doing good: A conceptual analysis of the mood at work–organizational spontaneity relationship. *Psychological Bulletin, 112,* 310–329.

Gerard, H. B., Whilhelmy, R. A., & Connolley, R. S. (1968). Conformity and group size. *Journal of Personality and Social Psychology, 8,* 79–82.

Gerbner, G., Gross, L., Morgan, M., & Signorielli, N. (1986). Living with television: The dynamics of the cultivation process. In J. Bryant & D. Zillmann (Eds.), *Perspectives on media effects* (pp. 17–40). Hillsdale, NJ: Erlbaum.

Gergen, K. J. (1973). Social psychology as history. *Journal of Personality and Social Psychology, 26,* 309–320.

Gergen, K. J. (1994). Exploring the postmodern: Perils or potentials? *American Psychologist, 49,* 412–416.

Gershoff, E. T. (2002). Corporal punishment by parents and associated child behaviors and experiences: A meta-analytic and theoretical review. *Psychological Bulletin, 128,* 539–579.

Gersick, C. J. G. (1988). Time and transition in work teams: Toward a new model of group development. *Academy of Management Journal, 21,* 9–41.

Gersick, C. J. G. (1994). Pacing strategic change: The case of a new venture. *Academy of Management Journal, 37,* 9–45.

Gibbons, F. X. (1978). Sexual standards and reactions to pornography: Enhancing behavioral consistency through self-focused attention. *Journal of Personality and Social Psychology, 36,* 976–987.

Gibbons, F. X. (1990). Self-attention and behavior: A review and theoretical update. In M. P. Zanna (Ed.), *Advances in experimental social psychology* (Vol. 23, pp. 249–303). New York: Academic Press.

Gibbons, F. X., Lane, D. J., Gerrard, M., Reis-Bergan, M., Lautrup, C., Pexa, N., & Blanton, H. (2002). Comparison level preferences after performance: Is downward comparison theory still useful? *Journal of Personality and Social Psychology, 83,* 865–880.

Gibbons, F. X., & McCoy, S. B. (1991). Self-esteem, similarity, and reactions to active versus passive downward comparison. *Journal of Personality and Social Psychology, 60,* 414–424.

Gibbons, S. L., & Ebbeck, V. (1997). The effect of different teaching strategies on the moral development of physical education students. *Journal of Teaching in Physical Education, 17,* 85–98.

Gibson, B., & Sachau, D. (2000). Sandbagging as a self-presentational strategy: Claiming to be less than you are. *Personality and Social Psychology Bulletin, 26,* 56–70.

Giesler, R. B., & Swann, W. B., Jr. (1999). Striving for confirmation: The role of self-verification in depression. In T. Joiner & J. C. Coyne (Eds.), *The interactional nature of depression: Advances in interpersonal approaches* (pp. 189–217). Washington, DC: American Psychological Association.

Giesler, R. B., Josephs, R. A., & Swann, W. B., Jr. (1996). Self-verification in clinical depression: The desire for negative evaluation. *Journal of Abnormal Psychology, 105,* 358–368.

Gigerenzer, G., Todd, P. M., & the ABC Research Group (1999). *Simple heuristics that make us smart.* New York: Oxford University Press.

Gigone, D., & Hastie, R. (1993). The common knowledge effect: Information sharing and group judgment. *Journal of Personality and Social Psychology, 65,* 959–974.

Gigone, D., & Hastie, R. (1997). The impact of information on small group choice. *Journal of Personality and Social Psychology, 72,* 132–140.

Gilbert, D. T., Giesler, R. B., & Morris, K. A. (1995). When comparisons arise. *Journal of Personality and Social Psychology, 69,* 227–236.

Gilbert, D. T., & Hixon, J. G. (1991). The trouble of thinking: Activation and application of stereotypic beliefs. *Journal of Personality and Social Psychology, 60,* 509–517.

Gilbert, D. T., & Jones, E. E. (1986). Perceiver-induced constraint: Interpretations of self-generated reality. *Journal of Personality and Social Psychology, 50,* 269–280.

Gilbert, D. T., & Krull, D. S. (1988). Seeing less and knowing more: The benefits of perceptual ignorance. *Journal of Personality and Social Psychology, 54,* 193–202.

Gilbert, D. T., & Malone, P. S. (1995). The correspondence bias. *Psychological Bulletin, 117,* 21–38.

Gilbert, D. T., McNulty, S. E., Giuliano, T. A., & Benson, J. E. (1992). Blurry words and fuzzy deeds: The attribution of obscure behavior. *Journal of Personality and Social Psychology, 62,* 18–25.

Gilbert, D. T., Pelham, B. W., & Krull, D. S. (1988). On cognitive busyness: When person perceivers meet persons perceived. *Journal of Personality and Social Psychology, 54,* 733–740.

Gilbert, D. T., & Silvera, D. H. (1996). Overhelping. *Journal of Personality and Social Psychology, 70,* 678–690.

Gilbert, S. J. (1981). Another look at the Milgram obedience studies: The role of the gradated series of shocks. *Personality and Social Psychology Bulletin, 7,* 690–695.

Gillig, P. M., & Greenwald, A. G. (1974). Is it time to lay the sleeper effect to rest? *Journal of Personality and Social Psychology, 29,* 132–139.

Gilovich, T. (1991). *How we know what isn't so: The fallibility of human reason in everyday life.* New York: Free Press.

Gilovich, T., Grifin, D., & Kahneman, D. (Eds.) (2002). *Heuristics and biases: The psychology of intuitive judgment.* New York: Cambridge University Press.

Gilovich, T., Medvec, V. H., & Savitsky, K. (2000). The spotlight effect in social judgment: An egocentric bias in estimates of the salience of one's own actions and appearance. *Journal of Personality and Social Psychology, 78,* 211–222.

Giner-Sorolla, R., & Chaiken, S. (1997). Selective use of heuristic and systematic processing under defensive motivation. *Personality and Social Psychology Bulletin, 23,* 84–97.

Gintis, H., Bowles, S., Boyd, R., & Fehr, E. (2003). Explaining altruistic behavior in humans. *Evolution and Human Behavior, 24,* 153–172.

Gladue, B. A., Boechler, M., & McCaul, K. D. (1989). Hormonal response to competition in human males. *Aggressive Behavior, 15,* 409–422.

Glanz, J., & Schwartz, J. (September 26, 2003). Dogged engineer's effort to assess shuttle damage. *New York Times,* p. A1.

Gleick, E. (1997). The marker we've been waiting for. *Time* (April 7, 1997), pp. 31–36.

Glick, P., & Fiske, S. T. (2001a). Ambivalent sexism. In M. P. Zanna (Ed.), *Advances in experimental social psychology* (Vol. 33, pp. 115–188). San Diego, CA: Academic Press.

Glick, P., & Fiske, S. T. (2001b). Ambivalent stereotypes as legitimizing ideologies: Differentiating paternalistic and resentful prejudice. In J. T. Jost & B. Major (Eds.), *The psychology of legitimacy: Emerging perspectives on ideology, justice, and intergroup relations* (pp. 278–306). New York: Cambridge University Press.

Glick, P., Fiske, S. T., et al. (2000). Beyond prejudice as simple antipathy: Hostile and benevolent sexism across cultures. *Journal of Personality and Social Psychology, 79,* 763–775.

Godfrey, D. K., Jones, E. E., & Lord, C. G. (1986). Self-promotion is not ingratiating. *Journal of Personality and Social Psychology, 50,* 106–115.

Goethals, G. R., Cooper, J., & Naficy, A. (1979). Role of foreseen, foreseeable, and unforeseeable behavioral consequences in the arousal of cognitive dissonance. *Journal of Personality and Social Psychology, 37,* 1179–1185.

Goethals, G. R., & Darley, J. (1977). Social comparison theory: An attributional approach. In J. M. Suls & R. L. Miller (Eds.), *Social comparison processes: Theoretical and empirical perspectives* (pp. 259–278). Washington, DC: Hemisphere.

Goethals, G. R., & Reckman, R. (1973). The perception of consistency in attitudes. *Journal of Experimental Social Psychology, 9,* 491–501.

Goffman, E. (1955). On face-work: An analysis of ritual elements in social interaction. *Psychiatry, 18,* 213–231.

Goffman, E. (1959). *The presentation of self in everyday life.* Garden City: Doubleday.

Goldberg, L. R. (1978). Differential attribution of trait-descriptive terms to oneself as compared to well-liked, neutral, and disliked others: A psychometric analysis. *Journal of Personality and Social Psychology, 36,* 1012–1028.

Goldberg, P. (1968). Are women prejudiced against women? *Transaction, 5,* 28–30.

Goldhagen, D. J. (1996). *Hitler's willing executioners: Ordinary Germans and the Holocaust.* New York: Knopf.

Goldstein, A. G., Chance, J. E., & Schneller, G. R. (1989). Frequency of eyewitness identification in criminal cases: A survey of prosecutors. *Bulletin of the Psychonomic Society, 27,* 71–74.

Goldstein, A. P. (1999). Aggression reduction strategies: Effective and ineffective. *Social Psychology Quarterly, 14,* 40–58.

Goldstein, D. G., & Gigerenzer, G. (2002). Models of ecological rationality: The recognition heuristic. *Psychological Review, 109,* 75–90.

Gollwitzer, P. M., & Schaal, B. (2001). How goals and plans affect action. In J. M. Collis & S. Messick (Eds.), *Intelligence and personality: Bridging the gap in theory and measurement* (pp. 139–161). Mahwah, NJ: Erlbaum.

Golombok, S., & Hines, M. (2002). Sex differences in social behavior. In P. K. Smith & C. H. Hart (Eds.), *Blackwell handbook of childhood social development* (pp. 117–136). Malden, MA: Blackwell.

Gonzales, P. M., Blanton, H., & Williams, K. J. (2002). The effects of stereotype threat and double-minority status on the test performance of Latino women. *Personality and Social Psychology Bulletin, 28,* 659–670.

Goode, E. (2000, June 17). To Yankee second baseman, throwing is no idle thought. *New York Times,* p. A1.

Goodwin, S. A., Fiske, S. T., Rosen, L. D., & Rosenthal, A. M. (2002). The eye of the beholder: Romantic goals and impression biases. *Journal of Experimental Social Psychology, 38,* 232–241.

Goodwin, S. A., Gubin, A., Fiske, S. T., & Yzerbyt, V. (2000). Power can bias impression formation: Stereotyping subordinates by default and by design. *Group Processes and Intergroup Relations, 3,* 227–256.

Gopnik, A., Meltzoff, A. N., & Kuhl, P. K. (1999). *The scientist in the crib: Minds, brains, and how children learn.* New York: Morrow.

Gorenstein, G. W., & Ellsworth, P. C. (1980). Effect of choosing an incorrect photograph on a later identification by an eyewitness. *Journal of Applied Psychology, 65,* 616–622.

Gorman, C. (1994, September 19). Let's not be too hasty. *Time,* p. 71.

Gosselin, P., Kirouac, G., & Dore, F. Y. (1995). Components and recognition of facial expression in the communication of emotion by actors. *Journal of Personality and Social Psychology, 68,* 83–96.

Gossett, J. L., & Byrne, S. (2002). "CLICK HERE": A content analysis of Internet rape sites. *Gender and Society, 16,* 689–709.

Gottman, J. M. (1994). *What predicts divorce?* Hillsdale, NJ: Erlbaum.

Gottman, J. M. (1998). Psychology and the study of marital processes. *Annual Review of Psychology, 49,* 169–197.

Gottman, J. M., & Levenson, R. W. (1992). Marital processes predictive of later dissolution: Behavior, physiology, and health. *Journal of Personality and Social Psychology, 63,* 221–233.

Gould, S. J. (1992, November 19). The confusion over evolution. *New York Review of Books,* pp. 47–54.

Gouldner, A. W. (1960). The norm of reciprocity: A preliminary statement. *American Sociological Review, 25,* 161–178.

Graham, K., & Wells, S. (2001). The two worlds of aggression for men and women. *Sex Roles, 45,* 595–622.

Graham, S. (1992). "Most of the subjects were white and middle class": Trends in published research on African Americans in selected APA journals, 1970–1989. *American Psychologist, 47,* 629–639.

Grammer, K., & Thornhill, R. (1994). Human facial attractiveness and sexual selection: The role of averageness and symmetry. *Journal of Comparative Psychology, 108,* 233–242.

Grant, M. J., Button, C. M., Hannah, T. E., & Ross, A. S. (2002). Uncovering the multidimensional nature of stereotype inferences: A within-participants study of gender, age, and physical attractiveness. *Current Research in Social Psychology, 8,* 19–39.

Gray, J. (1997). *Men are from Mars, women are from Venus.* New York: HarperCollins.

Gray-Little, B., & Hafdahl, A. R. (2000). Factors influencing racial comparisons of self-esteem: A quantitative review. *Psychological Bulletin, 126,* 26–54.

Green, D. P., Glaser, J., & Rich, A. (1998). From lynching to gay bashing: The elusive connection between economic conditions and hate crime. *Journal of Personality and Social Psychology, 75,* 82–92.

Greenberg, J., & Pyszczynski, T. (1985). The effects of an overheard ethnic slur on evaluations of the target: How to spread a social disease. *Journal of Experimental Social Psychology, 21,* 61–72.

Greenberg, J., Pyszczynski, T., Solomon, S., Rosenblatt, A., et al. (1990). Evidence for terror management theory II: The effects of mortality salience on reactions to those who threaten or bolster the cultural worldview. *Journal of Personality and Social Psychology, 58,* 308–318.

Greenberg, J., Solomon, S., & Pyszczynski, T. (1997). Terror management theory of self-esteem and cultural worldviews: Empirical assessments and conceptual refinements. *Advances in Experimental Social Psychology, 29,* 61–139.

Greenberg, M. S., & Westcott, D. R. (1983). Indebtedness as a mediator of reactions to aid. In J. D. Fisher, A. Nadler, & B. M. DePaulo (Eds.), *New directions in helping: Vol. 1. Recipient reactions to aid* (pp. 85–112). New York: Academic Press.

Greene, E., & Bornstein, B. (2003). *Determining damages: The psychology of jury awards.* Washington, DC: American Psychological Association.

Greene, E., & Dodge, M. (1995). The influence of prior record evidence on juror decision-making. *Law and Human Behavior, 19,* 67–78.

Greenhause, S. (2001, September 1). Report shows Americans have more "Labor Days." *New York Times,* p. A6.

Greenwald, A. G. (1968). Cognitive learning, cognitive responses to persuasion, and attitude change. In A. Greenwald, T. Brock, & T. Ostrom (Eds.), *Psychological foundations of attitudes* (pp. 147–170). New York: Academic Press.

Greenwald, A. G. (1980). The totalitarian ego: Fabrication and revision of personal history. *American Psychologist, 35,* 603–618.

Greenwald, A. G. (1992). New look 3: Unconscious cognition reclaimed. *American Psychologist, 47,* 766–779.

Greenwald, A. G., & Farnham, S. D. (2000). Using the Implicit Association Test to measure self-esteem and self-concept. *Journal of Personality and Social Psychology, 79,* 1022–1038.

Greenwald, A. G., McGhee, D. E., & Schwartz, J. L. K. (1998). Measuring individual differences in implicit cognition: The implicit association test. *Journal of Personality and Social Psychology, 74,* 1464–1480.

Greenwald, A. G., Nosek, B. A., & Banaji, M. R. (2003). Understanding and using the Implicit Association Test: I. An improved scoring algorithm. *Journal of Personality and Social Psychology, 85,* 197–216.

Greenwald, A. G., Oakes, M. A., & Hoffman, H. G. (2003). Targets of discrimination: Effects of race on responses to weapons holders. *Journal of Experimental Social Psychology, 39,* 399–405.

Greenwald, A. G., Pratkanis, A. R., Leippe, M. R., & Baumgardner, M. H. (1986). Under what conditions does theory obstruct research progress? *Psychological Review, 93,* 216–229.

Greenwald, A. G., Spangenberg, E. R., Pratkanis, A. R., &

Eskenazi, J. (1991). Double-blind tests of subliminal self-help audiotapes. *Psychological Science, 2,* 119–122.

Griffin, A. S., & West, S. A. (2003). Kin discrimination and the benefit of helping in cooperatively breeding vertebrates. *Science, 302,* 634–636.

Griffiths, R. A., Beumont, P. J. V., Giannakopoulos, E., Russell, J., Schotte, D., Thornton, C., Touyz, S. W., & Varano, P. (1999). Measuring self-esteem in dieting disordered patients: The validity of the Rosenberg and Coopersmith contrasted. *International Journal of Eating Disorders, 25,* 227–231.

Gross, A. E., & Crofton, C. (1977). What is good is beautiful. *Sociometry, 40,* 85–90.

Gross, A. E., & Latané, J. G. (1974). Receiving help, reciprocation, and interpersonal attraction. *Journal of Applied Social Psychology, 4,* 210–223.

Gross, J. (2000, May 31). Public lives: Uniting the world against violence to women. *New York Times,* p. B2.

Grossman, M., & Wood, W. (1993). Sex differences in intensity of emotional experience: A social role interpretation. *Journal of Personality and Social Psychology, 65,* 1010–1020.

Grote, N. K., & Clark, M. S. (2001). Perceiving unfairness in the family: Cause or consequence of marital distress? *Journal of Personality and Social Psychology, 80,* 281–293.

Gruder, C. L., Cook, T. D., Hennigan, K. M., Flay, B. R., Alessis, C., & Halamaj, J. (1978). Empirical tests of the absolute sleeper effect predicted from the discounting cue hypothesis. *Journal of Personality and Social Psychology, 36,* 1061–1074.

Grusec, J. E. (1991). The socialization of altruism. In M. S. Clark (Ed.), *Prosocial behavior. Review of personality and social psychology* (Vol. 12, pp. 9–33). Newbury Park, CA: Sage.

Gudjonsson, G. H. (2003). *The psychology of interrogations and confessions.* London: Wiley.

Gudykunst, W., & Bond, M. H. (1997). Intergroup relations across cultures. In J. W. Berry, M. H. Segall, & C. Kagitçibasi (Eds.), *Handbook of cross-cultural psychology: Social behavior and applications* (2nd ed., Vol. 3, pp. 119–161). Needham Heights, MA: Allyn & Bacon.

Guerin, B. (2003). Social behaviors as determined by different arrangements of social consequences: Diffusion of responsibility effects with competition. *Journal of Social Psychology, 143,* 313–329.

Guerra, N. G., Huesmann, L. R., & Spindler, A. (2003). Community violence exposure, social cognition, and aggression among urban elementary school children. *Child Development, 74,* 1561–1576.

Guimond, S. (2000). Group socialization and prejudice: The social transmission of intergroup attitudes and beliefs. *European Journal of Social Psychology,* 30, 335–354.

Gully, S. M., Devine, D. J., & Whitney, D. J. (1995). A meta-analysis of cohesion and performance: Effects of level of analysis and task interdependence. *Small Group Research, 26,* 497–520.

Gump, B. B., & Kulik, J. A. (1997). Stress, affiliation, and emotional contagion. *Journal of Personality and Social Psychology, 72,* 305–319.

Haberstroh, S., Oyserman, D., Schwarz, N., Kuehnen, U., & Ji, L. J. (2002). Is the interdependent self more sensitive to question context than the independent self? Self-construal and the observation of conversational norms. *Journal of Experimental Social Psychology, 38,* 323–329.

Hafer, C. L. (2000). Do innocent victims threaten the belief in a just world? Evidence from a modified Stroop task. *Journal of Personality and Social Psychology, 79,* 165–173.

Hafer, C. L., Begue, L., Choma, B. L.& Dempsey, J. L. (2005). Belief in a just world and commitment to long-term deserved outcomes. *Social Justice Research, 18,* 429–444.

Hagerty, M. R. (2000). Social comparisons of income in one's community: Evidence from national surveys of income and happiness. *Journal of Personality and Social Psychology, 78,* 761–771.

Hakmiller, K. L. (1966). Threat as a determinant of downward comparison. *Journal of Experimental Social Psychology* (Suppl. 1), 32–39.

Halberstadt, J., & Rhodes, G. (2000). The attractiveness of nonface averages: Implications for an evolutionary explanation of the attractiveness of average faces. *Psychological Science, 11,* 285–289.

Halberstadt, J., & Rhodes, G. (2003). It's not just average faces that are attractive: Computer-manipulated averageness makes birds, fish, and automobiles attractive. *Psychonomic Bulletin and Review, 10,* 149–156.

Halberstam, D. (1972). *The best and the brightest.* New York: Random House.

Hall, J. A., Herzberger, S. D., & Skowronski, K. J. (1998). Outcome expectancies and outcome values as predictors of children's aggression. *Aggressive Behavior, 24,* 439–454.

Hamer, D. H., Rice, G., Risch, N., & Ebers, G. (1999). Genetics and male sexual orientation. *Science, 285,* 803.

Hamermesh, D. S., & Biddle, J. E. (1994). Beauty and the labor market. *American Economic Review, 84,* 1174–1195.

Hamilton, D. L., & Gifford, R. K. (1976). Illusory correlation in interpersonal perception: A cognitive basis of stereotypic judgments. *Journal of Experimental Social Psychology, 12,* 392–407.

Hamilton, D. L., & Rose, T. L. (1980). Illusory correlation and the maintenance of stereotypic beliefs. *Journal of Personality and Social Psychology, 39,* 832–845.

Hamilton, W. D. (1964). The genetical evolution of social behavior: I and II. *Journal of Theoretical Biology,* 7, 1–52.

Hammersla, J. F., & Frease-McMahan, L. (1990). University students' priorities: Life goals vs. relationships. *Sex Roles, 23,* 1–14.

Hampson, R. B. (1984). Adolescent prosocial behavior: Peer-group and situational factors associated with helping. *Journal of Personality and Social Psychology, 46,* 153–162.

Han, G., & Park, B. (1995). Children's choice in conflict: Application of the theory of individualism-collectivism. *Journal of Cross-Cultural Psychology, 26,* 298–313.

Han, S., & Shavitt, S. (1994). Persuasion and culture: Advertising appeals in individualistic and collectivistic societies. *Journal of Experimental Social Psychology, 30,* 326–350.

Haney, C. (1984). On the selection of capital juries: The biasing effects of the death-qualification process. *Law and Human Behavior, 8,* 121–132.

Haney, C., Banks, C., & Zimbardo, P. (1973). Interpersonal dynamics in a simulated prison. *International Journal of Criminology and Penology, 1,* 69–97.

Haney, C., Hurtado, A., & Vega, L. (1994). "Modern" death qualification: New data on its biasing effects. *Law and Human Behavior, 18,* 619–633.

Haney, C., & Zimbardo, P. G. (1998). The past and future of U.S. prison policy: Twenty-five years after the Stanford Prison Experiment. *American Psychologist, 53,* 709–727.

Hannaford, P. L., Hans, V. P., & Munsterman, G. T. (2000). Permitting jury discussions during trial: Impact on the Arizona reform. *Law and Human Behavior, 24,* 359–380.

Hans, V. P. (2000). *Business on trial: The civil jury and corporate responsibility.* New Haven, CT: Yale University Press.

Hans, V. P., & Vidmar, N. (1986). *Judging the jury.* New York: Plenum.

Hansen, C. H. (1995). Predicting cognitive and behavioral effects of gangsta rap. *Basic and Applied Social Psychology, 16,* 43–52.

Harackiewicz, J. M., & Elliot, A. J. (1993). Achievement goals and intrinsic motivation. *Journal of Personality and Social Psychology, 65,* 904–915.

Hardin, G. (1968). The tragedy of the commons. *Science, 162,* 1243–1248.

Haritos-Fatouros, M. (2002). *Psychological origins of institutionalized torture.* London: Routledge.

Harkins, S. G., & Lowe, M. D. (2000). The effects of self-set goals on task performance. *Journal of Applied Social Psychology, 30,* 1–40.

Harkins, S. G., & Petty, R. E. (1981). Effects of source magnification of cognitive effort on attitudes: An information processing view. *Journal of Personality and Social Psychology, 40,* 401–413.

Harkins, S. G., & Petty, R. E. (1987). Information utility and the multiple source effect. *Journal of Personality and Social Psychology, 52,* 260–268.

Harkins, S. G., & Szymanski, K. (1987). Social loafing and social facilitation: New wine in old bottles. In C. Hendrick (Ed.), *Review of personality and social psychology: Group processes and intergroup relations* (Vol. 9, pp. 167–188). Beverly Hills, CA: Sage.

Harmon-Jones, E., Brehm, J. W., Greenberg, J., Simon, L., & Nelson, D. E. (1996). Evidence that the production of aversive consequences is not necessary to create cognitive dissonance. *Journal of Personality and Social Psychology, 70,* 5–16.

Harmon-Jones, E., & Mills, J. (Eds.) (1999). *Cognitive dissonance: Progress on a pivotal theory in social psychology.* Washington, DC: American Psychological Association.

Harré, R., & Lamb, R. (1983). *The encyclopedic dictionary of psychology.* Oxford, England: Basil Blackwell.

Harris, C. R. (2002). Sexual and romantic jealousy in heterosexual and homosexual adults. *Psychological Science, 13,* 7–12.

Harris, C. R. (2003). A review of sex differences in sexual jealousy, including self-report data, psychophysiological responses, interpersonal violence, and morbid jealousy. *Personality and Social Psychology Review, 7,* 102–128.

Harris, C. R., & Christenfeld, N. (1996). Gender, jealousy, and reason. *Psychological Science, 7,* 364–366.

Harris, M. B. (1995). Ethnicity, gender, and evaluations of aggression. *Aggressive Behavior, 21,* 343–357.

Harris, M. J., & Perkins, R. (1995). Effects of distraction on interpersonal expectancy effects: A social interaction test of the cognitive busyness hypothesis. *Social Cognition, 13,* 163–182.

Harris, M. J., & Rosenthal, R. (1985). Mediation of interpersonal expectancy effects. *Psychological Bulletin, 97,* 363–386.

Harrison, A. A., & Connors, M. M. (1984). Groups in exotic environments. In L. Berkowitz (Ed.), *Advances in experimental social psychology* (Vol. 8, pp. 49–87). Orlando, FL: Academic Press.

Hart, A. J. (1995). Naturally occurring expectation effects. *Journal of Personality and Social Psychology, 68,* 109–115.

Hart, A. J., Whalen, P. J., Shin, L. M., McInerney, S. C., Fischer, H., & Rauch, S. L. (2000). Differential response in the human amygdala to racial outgroup vs ingroup face stimuli. *NeuroReport, 11,* 2351–2355.

Harvey, J. H., & Manusov, V. L. (Eds.) (2001). *Attribution, communication behavior, and close relationships.* New York: Cambridge University Press.

Harvey, J. H., & Omarzu, J. (2000). *Minding the close relationship: A theory of relationship enhancement.* New York: Cambridge University Press.

Hass, R. G. (1981). Effects of source characteristics on the cognitive processing of persuasive messages and attitude change. In R. Petty, T. Ostrom, & T. Brock (Eds.), *Cognitive responses in persuasion* (pp. 141–172). Hillsdale, NJ: Erlbaum.

Hass, R. G. (1984). Perspective taking and self-awareness: Drawing an E on your forehead. *Journal of Personality and Social Psychology, 46,* 788–798.

Hass, R. G., & Eisenstadt, D. (1990). The effects of self-focused attention on perspective-taking and anxiety. *Anxiety Research, 2,* 165–176.

Hass, R. G., & Grady, K. (1975). Temporal delay, type of forewarning, and resistance to influence. *Journal of Experimental Social Psychology, 11,* 459–469.

Hass, R. G., Katz, I., Rizzo, N., Bailey, J., & Moore, L. (1992). When racial ambivalence evokes negative affect, using a disguised measure of mood. *Personality and Social Psychology Bulletin, 18,* 786–797.

Hassin, R., & Trope, Y. (2000). Facing faces: Studies on the cognitive aspects of physiognomy. *Journal of Personality and Social Psychology, 78,* 837–852.

Hastie, R. (1984). Causes and effects of causal attribution. *Journal of Personality and Social Psychology, 46,* 44–56.

Hastie, R., Penrod, S. D., & Pennington, N. (1983). *Inside the jury.* Cambridge, MA: Harvard University Press.

Hatfield, E. (1988). Passionate and companionate love. In R. J. Sternberg & M. L. Barnes (Ed.), *The psychology of love* (pp. 191–217). New Haven, CT: Yale University Press.

Hatfield, E., Greenberger, E., Traupmann, J., & Lambert, P. (1982). Equity and sexual satisfaction in recently married couples. *Journal of Sex Research, 18,* 18–32.

Hatfield, E., & Rapson, R. L. (1993). *Love, sex, and intimacy: Their psychology, biology, and history.* New York: HarperCollins.

Hatfield, E., & Sprecher, S. (1986). *Mirror, mirror. . . . The importance of looks in everyday life.* Albany, NY: State University of New York Press.

Hauber, M. E., & Sherman, P. W. (1998). Nepotism and marmot alarm calling. *Animal Behaviour, 56,* 1049–1052.

Haupt, A. L., & Leary, M. R. (1997). The appeal of worthless groups: Moderating effects of trait self-esteem. *Group Dynamics, 1,* 124–132.

Haverkamp, B. E. (1993). Confirmatory bias in hypothesis testing for client-identified and counselor self-generated hypotheses. *Journal of Counseling Psychology, 40,* 303–315.

Hawkins, D. L., Pepler, D. J., & Craig, W. M. (2001). Naturalistic observations of peer interventions in bullying. *Social Development, 10,* 512–527.

Hays, R. B. (1985). A longitudinal study of friendship development. *Journal of Personality and Social Psychology, 48,* 909–924.

Hazan, C., & Diamond, L. M. (2000). The place of attachment in human mating. *Review of General Psychology, 4,* 186–204.

Hazan, C., & Shaver, P. (1987). Romantic love conceptualized as an attachment process. *Journal of Personality and Social Psychology, 52,* 511–524.

Hearold, S. (1986). A synthesis of 1043 effects of television on social behavior. In G. Comstock (Ed.), *Public communication and behavior* (Vol. 1, pp. 65–133). Orlando, FL: Academic Press.

Heatherton, T. F., & Polivy, J. (1991). Development and validation of a scale for measuring state self-esteem. *Journal of Personality and Social Psychology, 60,* 895–910.

Heatherton, T. F., & Vohs, K. D. (2000). Interpersonal evaluations following threats to self: Role of self-esteem. *Journal of Personality and Social Psychology, 78,* 725–736.

Heatherton, T. F., & Wyland, C. L. (2003). Assessing self-esteem. In S. J. Lopez & C. R. Snyder (Eds.), *Positive psychological assessment: A handbook of models and measures* (pp. 219–233). Washington, DC: American Psychological Association.

Hechanova, R., Beehr, T. A., & Christiansen, N. D. (2003). Antecedents and consequences of employees' adjustment to overseas assignment: A meta-analytic review. *Applied Psychology: An International Review, 52,* 213–236.

Hedge, A., & Yousif, Y. H. (1992). Effects of urban size, urgency, and cost on helpfulness: A cross-cultural comparison between the United Kingdom and the Sudan. *Journal of Cross Cultural Psychology, 23,* 107–115.

Heider, F. (1958). *The psychology of interpersonal relations.* New York: Wiley.

Heilman, M. E., Rivero, J. C., & Brett, J. F. (1991). Skirting the competence issue: Effects of sex-based preferential selection on task choices of women and men. *Journal of Applied Psychology, 76,* 99–105.

Heine, S. J. (2005). Constructing good selves in Japan and North America. In R. Sorrentino, D. Cohen, J. M. Olson, & M. P. Zanna (Eds.), *Culture and social behavior: The Ontario symposium,* (Vol. 10). Mahwah, NJ: Erlbaum.

Heine, S. J., & Lehman, D. R. (1997). The cultural construction of self-enhancement: An examination of group-serving biases. *Journal of Personality and Social Psychology, 72,* 1268–1283.

Heine, S. J., & Lehman, D. R. (1997) Culture, dissonance, and self-affirmation. *Personality and Social Psychology Bulletin, 23,* 389–400.

Heine, S. J., Lehman, D. R., Markus, H. R., & Kitayama, S. (1999). Is there a universal need for positive self-regard? *Psychological Review, 106,* 756–794.

Heine, S. J., Takata, T., & Lehman, D. R. (2000). Beyond self-presentation: Evidence for self-criticism among Japanese. *Personality and Social Psychology Bulletin, 26,* 71–78.

Heller, J. F., Pallak, M. S., & Picek, J. M. (1973). The interactive effects of intent and threat on boomerang attitude change. *Journal of Personality and Social Psychology, 26,* 273–279.

Helweg-Larsen, M., & Shepperd, J. A. (2001). Do moderators of the optimistic bias affect personal or target risk estimates? A review of the literature. *Personality and Social Psychology Review, 5,* 74–95.

Henchy, T., & Glass, D. C. (1968). Evaluation apprehension and the social facilitation of dominant and subordinate responses. *Journal of Personality and Social Psychology, 10,* 446–454.

Henderlong, J., & Lepper, M. R. (2002). The effects of praise on children's intrinsic motivation: A review and synthesis. *Psychological Bulletin, 128,* 774–795.

Henderson, L., & Zimbardo, P. (1998). Shyness. In H. S. Friedman (Ed.), *Encyclopedia of Mental Health.* San Diego: Academic Press.

Henderson-King, D., Henderson-King, E., & Hoffman, L. (2001). Media images and women's self-evaluations: Social context and importance of attractiveness as moderators. *Personality and Social Psychology Bulletin, 27,* 1407–1416.

Henderson-King, E., & Henderson-King, D. (1997). Media effects on women's body esteem: Social and individual differences factors. *Journal of Applied Social Psychology, 27,* 399–417.

Hendrick, C., & Hendrick, S. S. (Eds.) (2000). *Close relationships: A sourcebook.* Thousand Oaks, CA: Sage.

Hendrick, S. S., & Hendrick, C. (1993). Lovers as friends. *Journal of Social and Personal Relationships, 10,* 459–466.

Hendrick, S. S., & Hendrick, C. (1995). Gender differences and similarities in sex and love. *Personal Relationships, 2,* 55–65.

Henley, N. M. (1977). *Body politics: Power, sex, and nonverbal communication.* Englewood Cliffs, NJ: Prentice-Hall.

Henry, R. A., Strickland, O. J., Yorges, S. L., & Ladd, D. (1996). Helping groups determine their most accurate member: The role of outcome feedback. *Journal of Applied Social Psychology, 26,* 1153–1170.

Herdt, G. (1998). *Same sex, different cultures: Exploring gay and lesbian lives.* Boulder, CO: Westview Press.

Herman, C. P., Zanna, M. P., & Higgins, E. T. (1986). *Physical appearance, stigma, and social behavior: The Ontario symposium* (Vol. 3). Hillsdale, NJ: Erlbaum.

Herzberger, S. D. (1996). *Violence within the family: Social psychological perspectives.* Madison, WI: Brown & Benchmark.

Herzberger, S. D. (2005). Snips, snails, sugar, and spice: Decisions about family violence through the lens of gender. In S. Fein, G. R. Goethals, & M. J. Sandstrom (Eds.), *Gender and aggression: Interdisciplinary perspectives.* Mahwah, NJ: Erlbaum.

Hewitt, P. L., Flett, G. L., Sherry, S. B., Habke, M., Parkin, M., Lam, R., McMurtry, B., Ediger, E., Fairlie, P., & Stein, M. B. (2003). The interpersonal expression of perfection: Perfectionistic self-presentation and psychological distress. *Journal of Personality and Social Psychology, 84,* 1303–1325.

Hewstone, M., & Lord, C. G. (1998). Changing intergroup cognitions and intergroup behavior: The role of typicality. In C. Sedikides, J. Schopler, & C. A. Insko (Eds.), *Intergroup cognition and intergroup behavior* (pp. 367–392). Mahwah, NJ: Erlbaum.

Heyman, R. E., & Slep, A. M. S. (2002). Do child abuse and interparental violence lead to adulthood family violence? *Journal of Marriage and Family, 64,* 864–870.

Higgins, E. T. (1989). Self-discrepancy theory: What patterns of self-beliefs cause people to suffer? In L. Berkowitz (Ed.), *Advances in experimental social psychology* (Vol. 22, pp. 93–136). New York: Academic Press.

Higgins, E. T. (1999). Self-discrepancy: A theory relating self and affect. In R. F. Baumeister (Ed.), *The self in social psychology* (pp. 150–181). Philadelphia, PA: Psychology Press/ Taylor & Francis.

Higgins, E. T., King, G. A., & Mavin, G. H. (1982). Individual construct accessibility and subjective impressions and recall. *Journal of Personality and Social Psychology, 43,* 35–47.

Higgins, E. T., Rholes, C. R., & Jones, C. R. (1977). Category accessibility and impression formation. *Journal of Experimental Social Psychology, 13,* 141–154.

Higgins, E. T., & Rholes, W. S. (1978). "Saying is believing": Effects of message modification on memory and liking for the person described. *Journal of Experimental Social Psychology, 14*, 363–378.

Higgins, R. L., & Harris, R. N. (1988). Strategic "alcohol" use: Drinking to self-handicap. *Journal of Social and Clinical Psychology, 6*, 191–202.

Hill, C. A. (1987). Affiliation motivation: People who need people . . . but in different ways. *Journal of Personality and Social Psychology, 52*, 1008–1018.

Hilton, J. L., & Darley, J. M. (1985). Constructing other persons: A limit on the effect. *Journal of Experimental Social Psychology, 21*, 1–18.

Hilton, J. L., & Darley, J. M. (1991). The effects of interaction goals on person perception. *Advances in Experimental Social Psychology, 24*, 235–267.

Hilton, J. L., & Fein, S. (1989). The role of typical diagnosticity in stereotype-based judgments. *Journal of Personality and Social Psychology, 57*, 201–211.

Hilton, J. L., Fein, S., & Miller, D. T. (1993). Suspicion and dispositional inference. *Personality and Social Psychology Bulletin, 19*, 501–512.

Hines, D. A., & Saudino, K. J. (2002). Intergenerational transmission of intimate partner violence: A behavioral genetic perspective. *Trauma Violence and Abuse, 3*, 210–225.

Hing, L. S. S., Li, W., & Zanna, M. P. (2002). Inducing hypocrisy to reduce prejudicial responses among aversive racists. *Journal of Experimental Social Psychology, 38*, 71–78.

Hinkle, S., Taylor, L. A., Fox-Cardamone, L., & Ely, P. G. (1998). Social identity and aspects of social creativity: Shifting to new dimensions of intergroup comparison. In S. Worchel & J. F. Morales (Eds.), *Social identity: International perspectives* (pp. 166–179). London: Sage.

Hinsz, V. B. (1995). Group and individual decision making for task performance goals: Processes in the establishment of goals in groups. *Journal of Applied Social Psychology, 25*, 353–370.

Hinsz, V. B., Tindale, R. S., & Vollrath, D. A. (1997). The emerging conceptualization of groups as information processors. *Psychological Bulletin, 121*, 43–64.

Hirt, E. R., Deppe, R. K., & Gordon, L. J. (1991). Self-reported versus behavioral self-handicapping: Empirical evidence for a theoretical distinction. *Journal of Personality and Social Psychology, 61*, 981–991.

Hirt, E. R., McCrea, S. M., & Boris, H. I. (2003). "I know you self-handicapped last exam": Gender differences in reactions to self-handicapping. *Journal of Personality and Social Psychology, 84*, 177–193.

Hirt, E. R., Zillman, D., Erickson, G. A., & Kennedy, C. (1992). Costs and benefits of allegiance: Changes in fans' self-ascribed competencies after team victory versus defeat. *Journal of Personality and Social Psychology, 63*, 724–738.

Hitler, A. (1933). *Mein Kampf* (E. T. S. Dugdale, Trans.). Cambridge, MA: Riverside.

Hixon, J. G., & Swann, W. B., Jr. (1993). When does introspection bear fruit? Self-reflection, self-insight, and interpersonal choices. *Journal of Personality and Social Psychology, 64*, 35–43.

Hoaken, P. N. S. & Pihl, R. O. (2000). The effects of alcohol intoxication on aggressive responses in men and women. *Alcohol and Alcoholism, 35*, 471–477.

Hoffman, M. L. (2000). *Empathy and moral development: Implications for caring and justice.* New York: Cambridge University Press.

Hofling, C. K., Brotzman, E., Dalrymple, S., Graves, N., & Pierce, C. (1966). An experimental study of nurse-physician relations. *Journal of Nervous and Mental Disease, 143*, 171–180.

Hofstede, Geert. (2001) *Culture's consequences, comparing values, behaviors, institutions, and organizations across nations*, 2nd ed. Newbury Park, CA: Sage.

Hogg, M. A., & Ridgeway, C. L. (2003). Social identity: Sociological and social psychological perspectives. *Social Psychology Quarterly, 66*, 97–100.

Hogg, M. A., Turner, J. C., & Davidson, B. (1990). Polarized norms and social frames of reference: A test of the self-categorization theory of group polarization. *Basic and Applied Social Psychology, 11*, 77–100.

Hollander, E. P. (1958). Conformity, status, and idiosyncrasy credit. *Psychological Review, 65*, 117–127.

Hollingshead, A. B., & Fraidin, S. (2003). Gender stereotypes and assumptions about expertise in transactive memory. *Journal of Experimental Social Psychology, 39*, 355–363.

Holmes, A., Murphy, D. L., & Crawley, J. N. (2003). Abnormal behavioral phenotypes of serotonin transporter knockout mice: Parallels with human anxiety and depression. *Biological Psychiatry, 54*, 953–959.

Holmes, J. G., Miller, D. T., & Lerner, M. J. (2002). Committing altruism under the cloak of self-interest: The exchange fiction. *Journal of Experimental Social Psychology, 38*, 144–151.

Homans, G. C. (1961). *Social behavior*. New York: Harcourt, Brace & World.

Honeycutt, J. M., Woods, B. L., & Fontenot, K. (1993). The endorsement of communication conflict rules as a function of engagement, marriage and marital ideology. *Journal of Social and Personal Relationships, 10*, 285–304.

Hong, L. (2000). Toward a transformed approach to prevention: Breaking the link between masculinity and violence. *Journal of American College Health, 48*, 269–279.

Hong, Y., Chan, G., Chiu, C., Wong, R. Y. M., Hansen, I. G., Lee, S., Tong, Y., & Fu, H. (2004). How are social identities linked to self-conception and intergroup orientation? The moderating effect of implicit theories. *Journal of Personality and Social Psychology, 85*, 1147–1160.

Hong, Y., Morris, M. W., Chiu, C., & Benet-Martinez, V. (2000). Multicultural minds: A dynamic constructivist approach to culture and cognition. *American Psychologist, 55*, 709–720.

Hong, Y., Wong, R. Y. M., & Liu, J. H. (2001). The history of war strengthens ethnic identification. *Journal of Psychology in Chinese Societies, 2*, 77–105.

Honts, C. R. (1996). Criterion development and validity of the CQT in field application. *Journal of General Psychology, 123*, 309–324.

Honts, C. R., Raskin, D. C., & Kircher, J. C. (1994). Mental and physical countermeasures reduce the accuracy of polygraph tests. *Journal of Applied Psychology, 79*, 252–259.

Honts, C. R., Raskin, D. C., & Kircher, J. C. (2002). The scientific status of research on polygraph techniques: The case for polygraph tests (pp. 446–483). In D. L. Faigman, D. Kaye, M. J. Saks, & J. Sanders (Eds.), *Modern scientific evidence: The law and science of expert testimony.* St. Paul, MN: West.

Hoorens, V., & Nuttin, J. M. (1993). Overvaluation of own attributes: Mere ownership or subjective frequency? *Social Cognition, 11,* 177–200.

Horowitz, I. A., & ForsterLee, L. (2001). The effects of note-taking and trial transcript access on mock jury decisions in a complex civil trial. *Law and Human Behavior, 25,* 373–391.

Horowitz, I. A., & Willging, T. E. (1991). Changing views of jury power: The nullification debate, 1787–1988. *Law and Human Behavior, 15,* 165–182.

Horselenberg, R., Merckelbach, H., & Josephs, S. (2003). Individual differences and false confessions: A conceptual replication of Kassin and Kiechel (1996). *Psychology, Crime & Law, 9,* 1–8.

Hosoda, M., Stone-Romero, E. F., & Coats, G. (2003). The effects of physical attractiveness on job-related outcomes: A meta-analysis of experimental studies. *Personnel Psychology, 56,* 431–462.

Houldsworth, C., & Mathews, B. P. (2000). Group composition, performance and educational attainment. *Education and Training, 42,* 40–53.

Houts, A. C., Cook, T. D., & Shadish, W. R., Jr. (1986). The person-situation debate: A critical multiplist perspective. *Journal of Personality, 54,* 52–105.

Houts, R. M., Robins, E., & Huston, T. L. (1996). Compatibility and the development of premarital relationships. *Journal of Marriage and the Family, 58,* 7–20.

Hovland, C. I., & Sears, R. R. (1940). Minor studies in aggression: VI. Correlation of lynchings with economic indices. *Journal of Psychology, 9,* 301–310.

Hovland, C. I., & Weiss, W. (1951). The influence of source credibility on communication effectiveness. *Public Opinion Quarterly, 15,* 635–650.

Hovland, C. I., Janis, I. L., & Kelley, H. H. (1953). *Communication and persuasion: Psychological studies of opinion change.* New Haven, CT: Yale University Press.

Hovland, C. I., Lumsdaine, A. A., & Sheffield, F. D. (1949). *Experiments on mass communication.* Princeton, NJ: Princeton University Press.

Howard, D. J. (1990a). The influence of verbal responses to common greetings on compliance behavior: The foot-in-the-mouth effect. *Journal of Applied Social Psychology, 20,* 1185–1196.

Howard, D. J. (1990b). Rhetorical question effects on message processing and persuasion: The role of information availability and the elicitation of judgment. *Journal of Experimental Social Psychology, 26,* 217–239.

Hrobjartsson, A., & Gotzsche, P. C. (2001). Is the placebo powerless?: An analysis of clinical trials comparing placebo with no treatment. *New England Journal of Medicine, 344,* 1594–1602.

Huang, W. W., Wei, K. K., Watson, R. T., & Tan, B. C. Y. (2003). Supporting virtual team-building with a GSS: An empirical investigation. *Decision Support Systems, 34,* 359–367.

Huesmann, L. R. (1988). An information processing model for the development of aggression. *Aggressive Behavior, 14,* 13–24.

Huesmann, L. R. (1998). The role of social information processing and cognitive schema in the acquisition and maintenance of habitual aggressive behavior. In R. G. Geen & E. Donnerstein (Eds.), *Human aggression: Theories, research, and implications for social policy* (pp. 73–109). San Diego: Academic Press.

Huesmann, L. R. (2005). Gender differences in the continuity of aggression from childhood to adulthood: Evidence from some recent longitudinal studies. In S. Fein, G. R. Goethals, & M. J. Sandstrom (Eds.), *Gender and aggression: Interdisciplinary perspectives.* Mahwah, NJ: Erlbaum.

Huesmann, L. R., & Eron, L. D. (Eds.) (1986). *Television and the aggressive child: A cross-national comparison.* Hillsdale, NJ: Erlbaum.

Huesmann, L. R., Eron, L. D., Klein, R., Brice, P., & Fischer, P. (1983). Mitigating the imitation of aggressive behaviors by changing children's attitudes about media violence. *Journal of Personality and Social Psychology, 44,* 899–910.

Huesmann, L. R., & Guerra, N. G. (1997). Children's normative beliefs about aggression and aggressive behavior. *Journal of Personality and Social Psychology, 72,* 408–419.

Huesmann, L. R., Moise-Titus, J., Podolski, C. P., & Eron, L. D. (2003). Longitudinal relations between children's exposure to TV violence and their aggressive and violent behavior in young adulthood: 1977–1992. *Developmental Psychology, 39,* 201–229.

Huey, S. J. Jr., Henggeler, S. W., Brondino, M. J., & Pickrel, S. G. (2000). Mechanisms of change in multisystemic therapy: Reducing delinquent behavior through therapist adherence and improved family and peer functioning. *Journal of Consulting and Clinical Psychology, 68,* 451–467.

Hugenberg, K., & Bodenhausen, G. V. (2003). Facing prejudice: Implicit prejudice and the perception of facial threat. *Psychological Science, 14,* 640–643.

Hugenberg, K., & Bodenhausen, G. V. (2004). Ambiguity in social categorization: The role of prejudice and facial affect in race categorization. *Psychological Science, 15,* 342–345.

Huguet, P., Galvaing, M. P., Monteil, J. M., & Dumas, F. (1999). Social presence effects in the Stroop task: Further evidence for an attentional view of social facilitation. *Journal of Personality and Social Psychology,* 77, 1011–1025.

Hull, J. G., & Young, R. D. (1983). Self-consciousness, self-esteem, and success-failure as determinants of alcohol consumption in male social drinkers. *Journal of Personality and Social Psychology, 44,* 1097–1109.

Hull, J. G., Young, R. D., & Jouriles, E. (1986). Applications of the self-awareness model of alcohol consumption: Predicting patterns of use and abuse. *Journal of Personality and Social Psychology, 51,* 790–796.

Huston, T. L., & Vangelisti, A. L. (1991). Socioemotional behavior and satisfaction in marital relationships: A longitudinal study. *Journal of Personality and Social Psychology, 61,* 721–733.

Iacono, W. G., & Lykken, D. T. (1997). The validity of the lie-detector test: Two surveys of scientific opinion. *Journal of Applied Psychology, 82,* 426–433.

Ickes, W., Bissonnette, V., Garcia, S., & Stinson, L. L. (1990). Implementing and using the Dyadic Interaction Paradigm. In C. Hendrick & M. S. Clark (Eds.), *Review of personality and social psychology: Vol. 11. Research methods in personality and social psychology* (pp. 16–44). Newbury Park, CA: Sage.

Imai, Y. (1991). Effects of influence strategies, perceived social power and cost on compliance with requests. *Japanese Psychological Research, 33,* 134–144.

Inbau, F. E., Reid, J. E., Buckley, J. P., & Jayne, B. C. (2001). *Criminal interrogation and confessions* (4th ed.). Gaithersburg, MD: Aspen.

Ingham, A. G., Levinger, G., Graves, J., & Peckham, V. (1974). The Ringelmann effect: Studies of group size and group performance. *Journal of Experimental Social Psychology, 10,* 371–384.

Ingoldsby, B. B. (1991). The Latin American family: Familism vs. machismo. *Journal of Comparative Family Studies, 23,* 47–62.

Ingram, R. E. (1990). Self-focused attention in clinical disorders: Review and a conceptual model. *Psychological Bulletin, 107,* 156–176.

Insko, C. A., Drenan, S., Solomon, M. R., Smith, R., & Wade, T. J. (1983). Conformity as a function of the consistency of positive self-evaluation with being liked and being right. *Journal of Experimental Social Psychology, 19,* 341–358.

Insko, C. A., Sedlak, A. J., & Lipsitz, A. (1982). A two-valued logic or two-valued balance resolution of the challenge of agreement and attraction effects in p-o-x triads, and a theoretical perspective on conformity and hedonism. *European Journal of Social Psychology, 12,* 143–167.

Isen, A. M. (1970). Success, failure, attention, and reaction to others: The warm glow of success. *Journal of Personality and Social Psychology, 15,* 294–301.

Isen, A. M. (1984). Toward understanding the role of affect in cognition. In R. S. Wyer & T. K. Srull (Eds.), *Handbook of social cognition* (Vol. 3, pp. 179–236). Hillsdale, NJ: Erlbaum.

Isen, A. M., & Levin, P. A. (1972). Effect of feeling good on helping: Cookies and kindness. *Journal of Personality and Social Psychology, 21,* 384–388.

Ishii, K., Reyes, J., & Kitayama, S. (2003). Spontaneous attention to word content versus emotional tone: Differences among three cultures. *Psychological Science, 14,* 39–46.

Ito, T. A., Larsen, J. T., Smith, N. K., & Cacioppo, J. T. (1998). Negative information weighs more heavily on the brain: The negativity bias in evaluative categorizations. *Journal of Personality and Social Psychology, 75,* 887–900.

Ito, T. A., Miller, N., & Pollock, V. E. (1996). Alcohol and aggression: A meta-analysis on the moderating effects of inhibitory cues, triggering events, and self-focused attention. *Psychological Bulletin, 120,* 60–82.

Jacks, J. Z., & Cameron, K. A. (2003). Strategies for resisting persuasion. *Basic and Applied Social Psychology, 25,* 145–161.

Jackson, J. M. (1986). In defense of social impact theory: Comment on Mullin. *Journal of Personality and Social Psychology, 50,* 511–513.

Jackson, J. M., & Williams, K. D. (1985). Social loafing on difficult tasks: Working collectively can improve performance. *Journal of Personality and Social Psychology, 49,* 937–942.

Jackson, L. M., Esses, V. M., & Burris, C. T. (2001). Contemporary sexism and discrimination: The importance of respect for men and women. *Personality and Social Psychology Bulletin, 27,* 48–61.

Jackson, S. E., May, K. E., & Whiteney, K. (1995). Understanding the dynamics of diversity in decision making teams. In R. A. Guzzo & E. Salas (Eds.), *Team effectiveness and decision making in organizations* (pp. 204–261). San Francisco: Jossey-Bass.

Jackson, S. E., & Schuler, R. S. (1985). A meta-analysis and conceptual critique of research on role ambiguity and role conflict in work settings. *Organizational Behavior, 36,* 16–78.

Jackson, T., Fritch, A., Nagasaka, T., & Gunderson, J. (2002). Towards explaining the association between shyness and loneliness: A path analysis with American college students. *Social Behavior and Personality, 30,* 263–270.

James, W. (1890). *Principles of psychology* (Vols. 1–2). New York: Holt.

Janis, I. L. (1968). Attitude change via role playing. In R. Abelson, E. Aronson, W. McGuire, T. Newcomb, M. Rosenberg, & P. Tennenbaum (Eds.), *Theories of cognitive consistency: A sourcebook* (pp. 810–818). Chicago: Rand McNally.

Janis, I. L. (1982). *Groupthink* (2nd ed.). Boston: Houghton Mifflin.

Janis, I. L., & Feshbach, S. (1953). Effects of fear arousing communications. *Journal of Abnormal and Social Psychology, 48,* 78–92.

Janis, I. L., Kaye, D., & Kirschner, P. (1965). Facilitating effects of "eating while reading" on responsiveness to persuasive communications. *Journal of Personality and Social Psychology, 1,* 181–186.

Janis, I. L., & King, B. T. (1954). The influence of role playing on opinion change. *Journal of Abnormal and Social Psychology, 49,* 211–218.

Jankowiak, W. R., & Fischer, E. F. (1992). A cross-cultural perspective on romantic love. *Ethnology, 31,* 149–155.

Jansari, A., & Parkin, A. J. (1996). Things that go bump in your life: Explaining the reminiscence bump in autobiographical memory. *Psychology and Aging, 11,* 85–91.

Jarvis, W. B. G., & Petty, R. E. (1996). The need to evaluate. *Journal of Personality and Social Psychology, 70,* 172–194.

Jennings (Walstedt), J., Geis, F. L., & Brown, V. (1980). Influence of television commercials on women's self-confidence and independent judgment. *Journal of Personality and Social Psychology, 38,* 203–210.

Jepson, C., & Chaiken, S. (1990). Chronic issue-specific fear inhibits systematic processing of persuasive communications. *Journal of Social Behavior and Personality, 5,* 61–84.

Johannesen-Schmidt, M. C., & Eagly, A. H. (2002). Diminishing returns: The effects of income on the content stereotypes of wage earners. *Personality and Social Psychology Bulletin, 28,* 1538–1545.

Johansson, G., von Hofsten, C., & Jansson, G. (1980). Event perception. *Annual Review of Psychology, 31,* 27–53.

Johnson, A. (2000, April 27). Road-rage remedy? Flashing rear window message says "sorry." *Milwaukee Journal Sentinel,* p. 1A.

Johnson, B. T., & Eagly, A. H. (1989). Effects of involvement on persuasion: A meta-analysis. *Psychological Bulletin, 106,* 290–314.

Johnson, D. J., & Rusbult, C. E. (1989). Resisting temptation: Devaluation of alternative partners as a means of maintaining commitment in close relationships. *Journal of Personality and Social Psychology, 57,* 967–980.

Johnson, H. M., & Seifert, C. M. (1998). Updating accounts following a correction of misinformation. *Journal of Experimental Psychology: Learning, Memory, and Cognition, 24,* 1483–1494.

Johnson, J. D., Jackson, L. A., & Gatto, L. (1995). Violent attitudes and deferred academic aspirations: Deleterious effects of exposure to rap music. *Basic and Applied Social Psychology, 16,* 27–41.

Johnson, R. D., & Downing, L. L. (1979). Deindividuation and valance of cues: Effects on prosocial and antisocial behavior. *Journal of Personality and Social Psychology, 37,* 1532–1538.

Johnson, R. W., Kelly, R. J., & LeBlane, B. A. (1995). Motivational basis of dissonance: Aversive consequences or inconsistency. *Personality and Social Psychology Bulletin, 21,* 850–855.

Johnson, T., Kulesa, P., Cho, Y., & Shavitt, S. (2005). The relation between culture and response styles: Evidence from 19 countries. *Journal of Cross-Cultural Psychology, 36,* 264–277

Johnston, K. E., & Jacobs, J. E. (2003). Children's illusory correlations: The role of attentional bias in group impression formation. *Journal of Cognition and Development, 4,* 129–160.

Johnston, K. L., & White, K. M. (2003). Binge-drinking: A test of the role of group norms in the theory of planned behaviour. *Psychology and Health, 18,* 63–77.

Johnston, L. C., & Macrae, C. N. (1994). Changing social stereotypes: The case of the information seeker. *European Journal of Social Psychology, 24,* 581–592.

Joireman, J. A., Kuhlman, D. M., van Lange, P. A. M., Doi, T., & Shelley, G. P. (2003). Perceived rationality, morality, and power of social choice as a function of interdependence structure and social value orientation. *European Journal of Social Psychology, 33,* 413–437.

Jones, E. E. (1964). *Ingratiation: A social psychological analysis.* New York: Appleton-Century-Crofts.

Jones, E. E. (1990). *Interpersonal perception.* New York: Freeman.

Jones, E. E. & Davis, K. E. (1965). From acts to dispositions: The attribution process in person perception. *Advances in Experimental Psychology, 2,* 219–266.

Jones, E. E., Davis, K. E., & Gergen, K. (1961). Role playing variations and their informational value for person perception. *Journal of Abnormal and Social Psychology, 63,* 302–310.

Jones, E. E., & Harris, V. A. (1967). The attribution of attitudes. *Journal of Experimental Social Psychology, 3,* 1–24.

Jones, E. E., & Nisbett, R. E. (1972). The actor and the observer: Divergent perceptions of causality. In E. E. Jones, D. E. Kanouse, H. H. Kelley, R. E. Nisbett, S. Valins, & B. Weiner (Eds.), *Attribution: Perceiving the causes of behavior* (pp. 79–94). Morristown, NJ: General Learning Press.

Jones, E. E., & Pittman, T. S. (1982). Toward a general theory of strategic self presentation. In J. Suls (Ed.), *Psychological perspectives on the self.* Hillsdale, NJ: Erlbaum.

Jones, E. E., Rhodewalt, F., Berglas, S., & Skelton, J. A. (1981). Effects of strategic self-presentation on subsequent self-esteem. *Journal of Personality and Social Psychology, 41,* 407–421.

Jones, E. E., Rock, L., Shaver, K. G., Goethals, G. R., & Ward, L. M. (1968). Pattern of performance and ability attribution: An unexpected primary effect. *Journal of Personality and Social Psychology, 10,* 317–340.

Jones, E. E., & Sigall, H. (1971). The bogus pipeline: A new paradigm for measuring affect and attitude. *Psychological Bulletin, 76,* 349–364.

Jones, J. H. (1997). *Alfred C. Kinsey: A Public/Private Life.* New York: Norton.

Jones, T. F., et al. (2000). Mass psychogenic illness attributed to toxic exposure at a high school. *New England Journal of Medicine, 342,* 96–100.

Jordan, C. H., Spencer, S. J., & Zanna, M. P. (2005). Types of high self-esteem and prejudice: How implicit self-esteem relates to racial discrimination among high explicit self-esteem individuals. *Personality and Social Psychology Bulletin, 31,* 693–702.

Jorgensen, S., Fichten, C. S., Havel, A., Lamb, D., James, C., & Barile, M. (2005). Academic performance of college students with and without disabilities: An archival study. *Canadian Journal of Counselling, 39,* 101–117

Josephs, R. A., Bosson, J. K., & Jacobs, C. G. (2003). Self-esteem maintenance processes: When low self-esteem may be resistant to change. *Personality and Social Psychology Bulletin, 29,* 920–933.

Jost, J. T., Banaji, M. R., & Nosek, B. A. (2004). A decade of system justification theory: Accumulated evidence of conscious and unconscious bolstering of the status quo. *Political Psychology, 25,* 881–919.

Jukes, J. A., & Goldstein, J. H. (1993). Preference for aggressive toys. *International Play Journal, 1,* 81–91.

Jussim, L., Eccles, J., & Madon, S. (1998). Social perception, social stereotypes, and teacher expectations: The quest for the powerful self-fulfilling prophecy. In M. P. Zanna (Ed.), *Advances in experimental social psychology* (Vol. 28, pp. 281–388). San Diego, CA: Academic Press.

Juvonen, J., Graham, S., & Schuster, M. A. (2003). Bullying among young adolescents: The strong, the weak, and the troubled. *Pediatrics, 112,* 1231–1237.

Kafer, R., Hodkin, B., Furrow, D. & Landry, T. (1993). What do the Montreal murders mean? Attitudinal and demographic predictors of attribution. *Canadian Journal of Behavioural Science, 25,* 541–558.

Kagan, J. (1994). *Galen's prophecy: Temperament in human nature.* New York: Basic Books.

Kahle, L. R., & Homer, P. M. (1985). Physical attractiveness of the celebrity endorser: A social adaptation perspective. *Journal of Consumer Research, 11,* 954–961.

Kahneman, D., & Miller, D. T. (1986). Norm theory: Comparing reality to its alternatives. *Psychological Review, 93,* 136–153.

Kahneman, D., Slovic, P., & Tversky, A. (Eds.) (1982). *Judgment under uncertainty: Heuristics and biases.* New York: Cambridge University Press.

Kahneman, D., & Tversky, A. (1979). Prospect theory: An analysis of decisions under risk. *Econometrika, 47,* 263–291.

Kahneman, D., & Tversky, A. (1982). The simulation heuristic. In D. Kahneman, P. Slovic, & A. Tversky, (Eds.), *Judgment under uncertainty: Heuristics and biases* (pp. 201–208). New York: Cambridge University Press.

Kalick, S. M., & Hamilton, T. E., III. (1986). The matching hypothesis revisited. *Journal of Personality and Social Psychology, 51,* 673–682.

Kalin, R., & Berry, J. W. (1995). Ethnic and civic self-identity in Canada: analyses of 1974 and 1991 national surveys. *Canadian Ethnic Studies, 27,* 1–15.

Kallgren, C. A., Rena, R. R., & Cialdini, R. B. (2000). A focus theory of normative conduct: When norms do and do not affect behavior. *Personality and Social Psychology Bulletin, 26,* 1002–1012.

Kallgren, C. A., & Wood, W. (1986). Access to attitude-relevant information in memory as a determinant of attitude-behavior consistency. *Journal of Experimental Social Psychology, 22,* 328–338.

Kalven, H., & Zeisel, H. (1966). *The American jury.* Boston: Little, Brown.

Kampe, K. K. W., Frith, C. D., Dolan, R. J., & Frith, U.

(2001). Reward value of attractiveness and gaze. *Nature, 413,* 589–590.

Kang, M. E. (1997). The portrayal of women's images in magazine advertisements: Goffman's gender analysis revisited. *Sex Roles, 37,* 979–996.

Kaplan, M. F., & Schersching, C. (1981). Juror deliberation: An information integration analysis. In B. Sales (Ed.), *The trial process* (pp. 235–262). New York: Plenum.

Karau, S. J., & Williams, K. D. (1993). Social loafing: A meta-analytic review and theoretical integration. *Journal of Personality and Social Psychology, 65,* 681–706.

Karau, S. J., & Williams, K. D. (2001). Understanding individual motivation in groups: The collective effort model. In M. E. Turner (Ed.), *Groups at work: Theory and research. Applied social research* (pp. 113–141). Mahwah, NJ: Erlbaum.

Karlsson, N., Asgeir, J., Grankvist, G., & Gaerling, T. (2002). Impact of decision goal on escalation. *Acta Psychologica, 111,* 309–322.

Karney, B. R., & Bradbury, T. N. (1995). The longitudinal course of marital quality and stability: A review of theory, method, and research. *Psychological Bulletin, 118,* 3–34.

Karney, B. R., & Bradbury, T. N. (1997). Neuroticism, marital interaction, and the trajectory of marital satisfaction. *Journal of Personality and Social Psychology, 72,* 1075–1092.

Karney, B. R., & Bradbury, T. N. (2000). Attributions in marriage: State or trait? A growth curve analysis. *Journal of Personality and Social Psychology, 78,* 295–309.

Karniol, R. (2003). Egocentrism versus protocentrism: The status of self in social prediction. *Psychological Review, 110,* 564–580.

Karpinski, A. T., & von Hippel, W. (1996). The role of the linguistic intergroup bias in expectancy maintenance. *Social Cognition, 14,* 141–163.

Kashima, Y., & Kerekes, A. R. Z. (1994). A distributed memory model of averaging phenomena in person impression formation. *Journal of Experimental Social Psychology, 30,* 407–455.

Kassin, S. M. (1997). The psychology of confession evidence. *American Psychologist, 52,* 221–233.

Kassin, S. M. (2002, November 1). False confessions and the jogger case. *New York Times,* p. A31.

Kassin, S. M., Goldstein, C. J., & Savitsky, K. (2003). Behavioral confirmation in the interrogation room: On the dangers of presuming guilt. *Law and Human Behavior, 27,* 187–203.

Kassin, S. M., & Kiechel, K. L. (1996). The social psychology of false confessions: Compliance, internalization, and confabulation. *Psychological Science, 7,* 125–128.

Kassin, S. M., & Sommers, S. R. (1997). Inadmissible testimony, instructions to disregard, and the jury: Substantive versus procedural considerations. *Personality and Social Psychology Bulletin, 23,* 1046–1054.

Kassin, S. M., & Sukel, H. (1997). Coerced confessions and the jury: An experimental test of the "harmless error" rule. *Law and Human Behavior, 21,* 27–46.

Kassin, S. M., Tubb, V. A., Hosch, H. M., & Memon, A. (2001). On the "general acceptance" of eyewitness testimony research: A new survey of the experts. *American Psychologist, 56,* 405–416.

Kassin, S. M., & Wrightsman, L. S. (1979). On the requirements of proof: The timing of judicial instruction and mock juror verdicts. *Journal of Personality and Social Psychology, 37,* 1877–1887.

Kassin, S. M., & Wrightsman, L. S. (1983). The construction and validation of a Juror Bias Scale. *Journal of Research in Personality, 17,* 423–442.

Kassin, S. M., & Wrightsman, L. S. (1985). Confession evidence. In S. Kassin & L. Wrightsman (Eds.), *The psychology of evidence and trial procedure.* Beverly Hills: Sage Books.

Kassin, S. M., & Wrightsman, L. S. (1988). *The American jury on trial: Psychological perspectives.* Washington, DC: Hemisphere.

Katz, D., & Braly, K. W. (1933). Racial stereotypes of 100 college students. *Journal of Abnormal and Social Psychology, 28,* 280–290.

Kaufman, D. Q., Stasson, M. F., & Hart, J. W. (1999). Are the tabloids always wrong or is that just what we think? Need for cognition and perceptions of articles in print media. *Journal of Applied Social Psychology, 29,* 1984–1997.

Kawakami, K., Dion, K. L., & Dovidio, J. F. (1998). Racial prejudice and stereotype activation. *Personality and Social Psychology Bulletin, 24,* 407–416.

Kawakami, K., & Dovidio, J. F. (2001). The reliability of implicit stereotyping. *Personality and Social Psychology Bulletin, 27,* 212–225.

Kawakami, K., Dovidio, J. F., Moll, J., Hermsen, S., & Russin, A. (2000). Just say no (to stereotyping): Effects of training in the negation of stereotypic association on stereotype activation. *Journal of Personality and Social Psychology, 78,* 871–888.

Keelan, J. P. R., Dion, K. L., & Dion, K. K. (1994). Attachment style and heterosexual relationships among young adults: A short-term panel study. *Journal of Social and Personal Relationships, 11,* 201–214.

Keillor, J. M., Barrett, A. M., Crucian, G. P., Kortenkamp, S., & Heilman, K. M. (2003). Emotional experience and perception in the absence of facial feedback. *Journal of the International Neurological Society, 8,* 130–135.

Keller, P. A. (1999). Converting the unconverted: The effect of inclination and opportunity to discount health-related fear appeals. *Journal of Applied Psychology, 84,* 403–415.

Kelley, H. H. (1950). The warm-cold variable in first impressions of persons. *Journal of Personality, 18,* 431–439.

Kelley, H. H. (1967). Attribution in social psychology. *Nebraska symposium on motivation, 15,* 192–238.

Kelley, H. H., & Stahelski, A. J. (1970). Social interaction basis of cooperators' and competitors' beliefs about others. *Journal of Personality and Social Psychology, 16,* 66–91.

Kelman, H. C. (1961). Processes of opinion change. *Public Opinion Quarterly, 25,* 57–78.

Kelman, H. C. (1967). Human use of human subjects: The problem of deception in social psychology experiments. *Psychological Bulletin, 67,* 1–11.

Kelman, H. C., & Hamilton, V. L. (1989). *Crimes of obedience: Toward a social psychology of authority and responsibility.* New Haven, CT: Yale University Press.

Kelman, H. C., & Hovland, C. I. (1953). "Reinstatement" of the communicator in delayed measurement of opinion change. *Journal of Abnormal and Social Psychology, 48,* 327–335.

Kennedy, H. (2003). He takes fatal OD as internet pals watch: Chatroom vultures egged him to pop more Rx pills. *New York Daily News,* February 2, p. 5.

Kenny, D. A. (1994). *Interpersonal perception: A social relations analysis.* New York: Guilford.

Kenny, D. A., & Acitelli, L. K. (2001). Accuracy and bias of perceptions of the partner in close relationships. *Journal of Personality and Social Psychology.*

Kenny, D. A., Albright, L., Malloy, T. E., & Kashy, D. A. (1994). Consensus in interpersonal perception: Acquaintance and the Big Five. *Psychological Bulletin, 116,* 245–258.

Kenny, D. A., & DePaulo, B. M. (1993). Do people know how others view them? An empirical and theoretical account. *Psychological Bulletin, 114,* 145–161.

Kenny, D. A., Horner, C., Kashy, D. A., & Chu, L. (1992). Consensus at zero acquaintance: Replication, behavioral cues, and stability. *Journal of Personality and Social Psychology, 62,* 88–97.

Kenrick, D. T., Gabrielidis, C., Keefe, R. C., & Cornelius, J. S. (1996). Adolescents' age preferences for dating partners: Support for an evolutionary model of life-history strategies. *Child Development, 67,* 1499–1511.

Kenrick, D. T., Gutierres, S. E., & Goldberg, L. L. (1989). Influence of popular erotica on judgments of strangers and mates. *Journal of Experimental Social Psychology, 25,* 159–167.

Kenrick, D. T., & Keefe, R. C. (1992). Age preferences in mates reflect sex differences in human reproductive strategies. *Behavioral and Brain Sciences, 15,* 75–133.

Kenrick, D. T., & MacFarlane, S. W. (1986). Ambient temperature and horn honking: A field study of the heat/aggression relationship. *Environment and Behavior, 18,* 179–191.

Kenrick, D. T., Montello, D. R., Gutierres, S. E., & Trost, M. R. (1993). Effects of physical attractiveness on affect and perceptual judgments: When social comparison overrides social reinforcement. *Personality and Social Psychology Bulletin, 19,* 195–199.

Kernis, M. H., & Waschull, S. B. (1995). The interactive roles of stability and level of self-esteem: Research and theory. *Advances in Experimental Social Psychology, 27,* 93–141.

Kerr, N. L. (1981). Social transition schemes: Charting the group's road to agreement. *Journal of Personality and Social Psychology, 41,* 684–702.

Kerr, N. L. (1983). Motivation losses in small groups: A social dilemma analysis. *Journal of Personality and Social Psychology, 45,* 819–828.

Kerr, N. L. (1992). Issue importance and group decision making. In S. Worchel, W. Wood, & J. A. Simpson (Eds.), *Group process and productivity* (pp. 68–88). Newbury Park, CA: Sage.

Kerr, N. L., Harmon, D. L., & Graves, J. K. (1982). Independence of multiple verdicts by jurors and juries. *Journal of Applied Social Psychology, 12,* 12–29.

Kerr, N. L., Hymes, R. W., Anderson, A. B., & Weathers, J. E. (1995). Defendant-juror similarity in mock juror judgments. *Law and Human Behavior, 19,* 545–567.

Kerr, N. L., Kramer, G. P., Carroll, J. S., & Alfini, J. J. (1991). On the effectiveness of voir dire in criminal cases with prejudicial pretrial publicity: An empirical study. *American University Law Review, 40,* 665–701.

Kerr, N. L., Niedermeier, K. E., & Kaplan, M. F. (1999). Bias in jurors vs. bias in juries: New evidence from the SDS perspective. *Organizational Behavior and Human Decision Processes, 80,* 70–86.

Kessler, R. C., Sonnega, A., Bromet, E., Hughes, M., & Nelson, C. B. (1995). Posttraumatic stress disorder in the National Comorbidity Survey. *Archives of General Psychiatry, 52,* 1048–1060.

Key, W. B. (1973). *Subliminal seduction.* Englewood Cliffs, NJ: Signet.

Key, W. B. (1989). *The age of manipulation.* New York: Holt.

Keysar, B., & Henly, A. S. (2002). Speakers' overestimation of their effectiveness. *Psychological Science, 13,* 207–212.

Kiecolt-Glaser, J. K., Marucha, P. T., Atkinson, C., & Glaser, R. (2001). Hypnosis as a modulator of cellular immune dysregulation during acute stress. *Journal of Consulting and Clinical Psychology, 69,* 674–682.

Kierein, N. M., & Gold, M. A. (2000). Pygmalion in work organizations: A meta-analysis. *Journal of Organizational Behavior, 21,* 913–928.

Kiesler, C. A. (1971). *The psychology of commitment.* New York: Academic Press.

Kiesler, C. A., & Kiesler, S. B. (1969). *Conformity.* Reading, MA: Addison-Wesley.

Kilham, W., & Mann, L. (1974). Level of destructive obedience as a function of transmitter and executant roles in the Milgram obedience paradigm. *Journal of Personality and Social Psychology, 29,* 696–702.

Kilianski, S. E., & Rudman, L. A. (1998). Wanting it both ways: Do women approve of benevolent sexism? *Sex Roles, 39,* 333–352.

Kim, H., & Markus, H. R. (1999). Deviance or uniqueness, harmony or conformity? A cultural analysis. *Journal of Personality and Social Psychology,* 77, 785–800.

Kim, H. S., & Markus, H. R. (2002). Freedom of speech and freedom of silence: An analysis of talking as a cultural practice. In R. A. Shweder, M. Minow, & H. R. Markus (Eds.), *Engaging cultural differences: The multicultural challenge in liberal democracies* (pp. 432–452). New York: Russell Sage.

Kimmel, P. R. (1994). Cultural perspectives on international negotiations. *Journal of Social Issues, 50,* 179–196.

Kimmel, P. R. (2000). Culture and conflict. In M. Deutsch & P. T. Coleman (Eds.), *The handbook of conflict resolution: Theory and practice* (pp. 453–474). San Francisco, CA: Jossey-Bass.

Kinsey, A. C., Pomeroy, W. B., & Martin, C. E. (1948). *Sexual behavior in the human male.* Philadelphia: Saunders.

Kinsey, A. C., Pomeroy, W. B., Martin, C. E., & Gebhard, P. H. (1953). *Sexual behavior in the human female.* Philadelphia: Saunders.

Kinzer, S. (1999, September 13). A sudden friendship blossoms between Greece and Turkey. *New York Times* (http:www.nytimes.com/library/world/europe/091399greece-turkey.html).

Kirkpatrick, L. A., & Hazan, C. (1994). Attachment styles and close relationships: A four-year prospective study. *Personal Relationships, 1,* 123–142.

Kitayama, S., Duffy, S., Kawamura, T., & Larsen, J. T. (2003). Perceiving an object and its context in different cultures: A cultural look at New Look. *Psychological Science, 14,* 201–206.

Kitayama, S., Markus, H. R., Matsumoto, H., & Norasakkunkit, V. (1997). Individual and collective processes in the construction of the self: Self-enhancement in the United States and self-criticism in Japan. *Journal of Personality and Social Psychology, 72,* 1245–1267.

Kitson, G. C., & Morgan, L. A. (1990). The multiple consequences of divorce: A decade review. *Journal of Marriage and the Family, 52,* 913–924.

Klein, J. G. (1991). Negativity effects in impression formation: A test in the political arena. *Personality and Social Psychology Bulletin, 17,* 412–418.

Klein, O., Licata, L., Azzi, A. E., & Durala, I. (2003). "How European am I?" Prejudice expression and the presentation of social identity. *Self and Identity, 2,* 251–264.

Klein, W. M. (1997). Objective standards are not enough: Affective, self-evaluative, and behavioral responses to social comparison information. *Journal of Personality and Social Psychology, 72*, 763–774.

Klein, W. M. P., Monin, M. M., Steers-Wentzell, K. L., & Buckingham, J. T. (2006). Effects of standards on self-enhancing interpretations of ambiguous social comparison information. *Basic and Applied Social Psychology, 28*, 65–79.

Kleinke, C. L. (1986). Gaze and eye contact: A research review. *Psychological Bulletin, 100*, 78–100.

Knowles, E. S. (1983). Social physics and the effects of others: Tests of the effects of audience size and distance on social judgments and behavior. *Journal of Personality and Social Psychology, 45*, 1263–1279.

Knox, R. E., & Inskter, J. A. (1968). Postdecision dissonance at post time. *Journal of Personality and Social Psychology, 8*, 319–323.

Knox, R. E., & Safford, R. K. (1976). Group caution at the race track. *Journal of Experimental Social Psychology, 12*, 317–324.

Kohn, A. (1993). *Punished by rewards.* Boston: Houghton Mifflin.

Kolditz, T. A., & Arkin, R. M. (1982). An impression management interpretation of the self-handicapping strategy. *Journal of Personality and Social Psychology, 43*, 492–502.

Komorita, S. S., Chan, D. K-S., & Parks, C. (1993). The effects of reward structure and reciprocity in social dilemmas. *Journal of Experimental Social Psychology, 29*, 252–267.

Konecni, V. J., & Ebbesen, E. B. (1982). *The criminal justice system: A social-psychological analysis.* San Francisco: Freeman.

Korte, C. (1980). Urban-nonurban differences in social behavior and social psychological models of urban impact. *Journal of Social Issues, 36* (3), 29–51.

Korte, C., Ypma, I., & Toppen, A. (1975). Helpfulness in Dutch society as a function of urbanization and environmental input level. *Journal of Personality and Social Psychology, 32*, 996–1003.

Kosonen, P., & Winne, P. (1995). Effects of teaching statistical laws of reasoning about everyday problems. *Journal of Educational Psychology, 87*, 33–46.

Kovacs, L. (1983). A conceptualization of marital development. *Family Therapy, 3*, 183–210.

Kovera, M. B. (2002). The effects of general pretrial publicity on juror decisions: An examination of moderators and mediating mechanisms. *Law and Human Behavior, 26*, 43–72.

Kowalski, R. M. (1993). Inferring sexual interest from behavioral cues: Effects of gender and sexually relevant attitudes. *Sex Roles, 29*, 13–36.

Kowalski, R. M. (1996). Complaints and complaining: Functions, antecedents, and consequences. *Psychological Bulletin, 119*, 179–196.

Kraines, D., & Kraines, V. (1995). Evolution of learning among Pavlov strategies in a competitive environment with noise. *Journal of Conflict Resolution, 39*, 439–466.

Kramer, G. P., Kerr, N. L., & Carroll, J. S. (1990). Pretrial publicity, judicial remedies, and jury bias. *Law and Human Behavior, 14*, 409–438.

Kramer, R. M. (1998). Revisiting the Bay of Pigs and Vietnam decisions 25 years later: How well has the groupthink hypothesis stood the test of time? *Organizational Behavior and Human Decision Processes, 73*, 236–271.

Kramer, R. M., & Brewer, M. B. (1984). Effects of group identity on resource use in a simulated commons dilemma. *Journal of Personality and Social Psychology, 46*, 1044–1057.

Kramer, T. J, Fleming, G. P., & Mannis, S. M. (2001). Improving face-to-face brainstorming through modeling and facilitation. *Small Group Research, 32*, 529–553.

Kraus, S. J. (1995). Attitudes and the prediction of behavior: A meta-analysis of the empirical literature. *Personality and Social Psychology Bulletin, 21*, 58–75.

Krauss, R. M., Chen, Y., & Chawla, P. (1996). Nonverbal behavior and nonverbal communication: What do conversational hand gestures tell us? *Advances in Experimental Social Psychology, 28*, 389–450.

Kravitz, D. A., & Martin, B. (1986). Ringelmann rediscovered: The original article. *Journal of Personality and Social Psychology, 50*, 936–941.

Kray, L. J., & Galinsky, A. D. (2003). The debiasing effect of counterfactual mind-sets on group decisions: Increasing the search for disconfirmatory information in group decisions. *Organizational Behavior and Human Decision Processes, 91*, 69–81.

Kray, L. J., Galinsky, A. D., & Thompson, L. (2002). Reversing the gender gap in negotiations: An exploration of stereotype regeneration. *Organizational Behavior and Human Decision Processes, 87*, 386–409.

Kray, L. J., Rebb, J., Galinsky, A. D., & Thompson, L. (2004). Stereotype reactance at the bargaining table: The effect of stereotype activation and power on claiming and creating value. *Personality and Social Psychology Bulletin, 30*, 399–411.

Krebs, D. (1987). The challenge of altruism in biology and psychology. In C. Crawford, M. Smith, & D. Krebs (Eds.), *Sociobiology and psychology: Ideas, issues, and applications* (pp. 81–118). Hillsdale, NJ: Erlbaum.

Krebs, D., & Rosenwald, A. (1994). Moral reasoning and moral behavior in conventional adults. In B. Puka (Ed.), *Fundamental research in moral development* (pp. 111–121). New York: Garland.

Kressel, N. J., & Kressel, D. F. (2002). *Stack and sway: The new science of jury consulting.* Boulder, CO: Westview Press.

Kroon, M. B. R., 't Hart, P., & van Kreveld, D. (1991). Managing group decision making processes: Individual versus collective accountability and groupthink. *International Journal of Conflict Management, 2*, 91–115.

Kruger, D. J. (2003). Evolution and altruism: Combining psychological mediators with naturally selected tendencies. *Evolution and Human Behavior, 24*, 118–125.

Krueger, J. (1998). On the perception of social consensus. *Advances in Experimental Social Psychology, 30*, 163–240.

Krueger, J., & Clement, R. W. (1994). The truly false consensus effect: An ineradicable and egocentric bias in social perception. *Journal of Personality and Social Psychology, 67*, 596–610.

Krueger, J., Rothbart, M., & Sriram, N. (1989). Category learning and change: Differences in sensitivity to information that enhances or reduces intercategory distinctions. *Journal of Personality and Social Psychology, 56*, 866–875.

Krueger, J. I., Hasman, J. F., Acevedo, M., & Villano, P. (2003). Perceptions of trait typicality in gender stereotypes: Examining the role of attribution and categorization processes. *Personality and Social Psychology Bulletin, 29*, 108–116.

Krueger, R. F., Hicks, B. M., & McGue, M. (2001). Altruism and antisocial behavior: Independent tendencies, unique personality correlates, distinct etiologies. *Psychological Science, 12*, 397–402.

Kruger, J., & Dunning, D. (1999). Unskilled and unaware of it: How difficulties in recognizing one's own incompetence lead to inflated self-assessments. *Journal of Personality and Social Psychology, 77,* 1121–1134.

Kruglanski, A. W. (2001). That "vision thing": The state of theory in social and personality psychology at the edge of the new millennium. *Journal of Personality and Social Psychology, 80,* 871–875.

Kruglanski, A. W., & Freund, T. (1983). The freezing and unfreezing of lay-inferences: Effects of impressional primacy, ethnic stereotyping, and numerical anchoring. *Journal of Experimental Social Psychology, 19,* 448–468.

Kruglanski, A. W., & Mayseless, O. (1988). Contextual effects in hypothesis testing: The role of competing alternatives and epistemic motivations. *Social Cognition, 6,* 1–20.

Kruglanski, A. W., Shah, J. Y., Fishbach, A., Friedman, R., Chun, W. Y., & Sleeth-Keppler, D. (2002). A theory of goal systems. In M. Zanna (Ed.), *Advances in experimental social psychology* (Vol. 34, pp. 331–378). San Diego, CA: Academic Press.

Kruglanski, A. W., & Webster, D. M. (1996). Motivated closing of the mind: "Seizing" and "freezing." *Psychological Review, 103,* 263–283.

Kugihara, N. (1999). Gender and social loafing in Japan. *Journal of Social Psychology, 139,* 516–526.

Kulik, J. A., & Mahler, H. I. M. (1989). Stress and affiliation in a hospital setting: Preoperative roommate preferences. *Personality and Social Psychology Bulletin, 15,* 183–193.

Kulik, J. A., Mahler, H. I. M., & Earnest, A. (1994). Social comparison and affiliation under threat: Going beyond the affiliate-choice paradigm. *Journal of Personality and Social Psychology, 66,* 301–309.

Kulik, J. A., Mahler, H. I. M., & Moore, P. J. (1996). Social comparison and affiliation under threat: Effects of recovery from major surgery. *Journal of Personality and Social Psychology, 71,* 967–979.

Kunda, Z. (1987). Motivated inference: Self-serving generation and evaluation of causal theories. *Journal of Personality and Social Psychology, 53,* 636–647.

Kunda, Z. (1990). The case of motivated reasoning. *Psychological Bulletin, 108,* 480–498.

Kunda, Z., Adams, B., Davies, P. G., Hoshino-Browne, E., & Jordan, C. (2003). The impact of comprehension goals on the ebb and flow of stereotype activation during interaction. In Spencer, S. J., Fein, S., Zanna, M. P., & Olson, J. M. (Eds.), *Motivated social perception: The Ontario symposium* (Vol. 9, pp. 1–20). Mahwah, NJ: Erlbaum.

Kunda, Z., Davies, P. G., Adams, B. D., & Spencer, S. J. (2002). The dynamic time course of stereotype activation: Activation, dissipation, and resurrection. *Journal of Personality and Social Psychology, 82,* 283–299.

Kunda, Z., & Oleson, K. C. (1995) Maintaining stereotypes in the face of discrimination: Constructing grounds for subtyping deviants. *Journal of Personality and Social Psychology, 68,* 565–579.

Kunda, Z., & Sinclair, L. (1999). Motivated reasoning with stereotypes: Activation, application, and inhibition. *Psychological Inquiry, 10,* 12–22.

Kunda, Z., Sinclair, L., & Griffin, D. (1997). Equal ratings but separate meanings: Stereotypes and the construal of traits. *Journal of Personality and Social Psychology, 72,* 720–734.

Kunda, Z., & Spencer, S. J. (2003). When do stereotypes come to mind and when do they color judgment? A goal-based theoretical framework for stereotype activation and application. *Psychological Bulletin, 129,* 522–544.

Kuntz-Wilson, W., & Zajonc, R. B. (1980). Affective discrimination of stimuli that cannot be recognized. *Science, 207,* 557–558.

Kupers, T. A. (1999). *Prison madness: The mental health crisis behind bars and what we must do about it.* New York: Jossey-Bass.

Kurdek, L. A. (1991a). Correlates of relationship satisfaction in cohabiting gay and lesbian couples: Interpretation of contextual, investment, and problem-solving models. *Journal of Personality and Social Psychology, 61,* 910–922.

Kurdek, L. A. (1991b). The dissolution of gay and lesbian couples. *Journal of Social and Personal Relationships, 8,* 265–278.

Kurdek, L. A. (1999). The nature and predictors of the trajectory of change in marital quality for husbands and wives over the first 10 years of marriage. *Developmental Psychology, 35,* 1283–1296.

Kurdek, L. A. (2000). Attractions and constraints as determinants of relationship commitment: Longitudinal evidence from gay, lesbian, and heterosexual couples. *Personal Relationships, 7,* 245–262.

Kurzban, R., & Leary, M. R. (2001). Evolutionary origins of stigmatization: The functions of social exclusion. *Psychological Bulletin, 127,* 187–208.

LaFrance, M., Hecht, M. A., & Paluck, E. L. (2003). The contingent smile: A meta-analysis of sex differences in smiling. *Psychological Bulletin, 129,* 305–334.

Laird, J. D. (1974). Self-attribution of emotion: The effects of expressive behavior on the quality of emotional experience. *Journal of Personality and Social Psychology, 29,* 475–486.

Lakin, J. L., & Chartrand, T. L. (2003). Using nonconscious behavioral mimicry to create affiliation and rapport. *Psychological Science, 14,* 334–339.

Lalonde, R. N. (2002). Testing the social identity-intergroup differentiation hypothesis: "We're not American eh!" *British Journal of Social Psychology, 41,* 611–630.

Lam, K. C. H., Buehler, R., McFarland, C., Ross, M., & Cheung, I. (2005). Culture and affective forecasting. *Personality and Social Psychology Bulletin, 31,* 1296–1309.

Lam, S. S. K., & Schaubroeck, J. (2000). Improving group decisions by better pooling information: A comparative advantage of group decision support systems. *Journal of Applied Psychology, 85,* 565–573.

Lambert, A. J., Payne, B. K., Jacoby, L. L., Shaffer, L. M., Chasteen, A. L., & Khan, S. R. (2003). Stereotypes as dominant responses: On the "social facilitation" of prejudice in anticipated public contexts. *Journal of Personality and Social Psychology, 84,* 277–295.

Lamm, H., & Myers, D. G. (1978). Group-induced polarization of attitudes and behavior. In L. Berkowitz (Ed.), *Advances in experimental social psychology* (Vol. 11, pp. 145–195). New York: Academic Press.

Landau, T. (1989). *About faces: The evolution of the human face.* New York: Anchor Books.

Langer, E. J. (1975). The illusion of control. *Journal of Personality and Social Psychology, 32,* 311–328.

Langer, E. J. (1989). *Mindfulness.* Reading, MA: Addison-Wesley.

Langer, E. J., Blank, A., & Chanowitz, B. (1978). The mindlessness of ostensibly thoughtful action. *Journal of Personality and Social Psychology, 36,* 635–642.

Langfred, C. W. (1998). Is group cohesiveness a double-edged sword? An investigation of the effects of cohesiveness on performance. *Small Group Research, 29,* 124–143.

Langlois, J. H., Kalakanis, L., Rubenstein, A. J., Larson, A., Hallam, M., & Smoot, M. (2000). Maxims or myths of beauty? A meta-analytic and theoretical review. *Psychological Bulletin, 126,* 390–423.

Langlois, J. H., Ritter, J. M., Roggman, L. A., & Vaughn, L. S. (1991). Facial diversity and infant preferences for attractive faces. *Developmental Psychology, 27,* 79–84.

Langlois, J. H., & Roggman, L. A. (1990). Attractive faces are only average. *Psychological Science, 1,* 115–121.

Langlois, J. H., Roggman, L. A., & Musselman, L. (1994). What is average and what is not average about attractive faces? *Psychological Science, 5,* 214–220.

Langton, S. R. H., Watt, R. J., & Bruce, V. (2000). Do the eyes have it? Cues to the direction of social attention. *Trends in Cognitive Sciences, 4,* 50–59.

Lanzetta, J. T. (1955). Group behavior under stress. *Human Relations, 8,* 29–52.

Lanzetta, J. T., & Englis, B. G. (1989). Expectations of cooperation and competition and their effects on observers' vicarious emotional responses. *Journal of Personality and Social Psychology, 56,* 543–554.

LaPiere, R. T. (1934). Attitudes vs. action. *Social Forces, 13,* 230–237.

Larsen, K. S. (1990). The Asch conformity experiment: Replication and transhistorical comparisons. *Journal of Social Behavior and Personality, 5,* 163–168.

Larson, J. R., Jr., Foster-Fishman, P. G., & Franz, T. M. (1998). Leadership style and the discussion of shared and unshared information in decision-making groups. *Personality and Social Psychology Bulletin, 24,* 482–495.

Lassiter, G. D. (1988). Behavior perception, affect, and memory. *Social Cognition, 6,* 150–176.

Lassiter, G. D. (Ed.) (2004). *Interrogations, confessions, and entrapment.* New York: Kluwer Academic.

Lassiter, G. D., Geers, A. L., Munhall, P. J., Handley, I. M., & Beers, M. J. (2001). Videotaped confessions: Is guilt in the eye of the camera? *Advances in Experimental Social Psychology, 33,* 189–254.

Lassiter, G. D., Stone, J. I., & Rogers, S. L. (1988). Memorial consequences of variation in behavior perception. *Journal of Experimental Social Psychology, 24,* 222–239.

Latané, B. (1981). The psychology of social impact. *American Psychologist, 36,* 343–356.

Latané, B., & Darley, J. M. (1968). Group inhibition of bystander intervention. *Journal of Personality and Social Psychology, 10,* 215–221.

Latané, B., & Darley, J. M. (1970). *The unresponsive bystander: Why doesn't he help?* New York: Appleton-Century-Crofts.

Latané, B., & L'Herrou, T. (1996). Spatial clustering in the conformity game: Dynamic social impact in electronic groups. *Journal of Personality and Social Psychology, 70,* 1218–1230.

Latané, B., Liu, J. H., Nowak, A., Bonevento, M., & Zheng, L. (1995). Distance matters: Physical space and social impact. *Personality and Social Psychology Bulletin, 21,* 795–805.

Latané, B., & Werner, C. (1978). Regulation of social contact in laboratory rats: Time, not distance. *Journal of Personality and Social Psychology, 36,* 1128–1137.

Latané, B., Williams, K., & Harkins, S. (1979). Many hands make light the work: The causes and consequences of social loafing. *Journal of Personality and Social Psychology, 37,* 822–832.

Latané, B., & Wolf, S. (1981). The social impact of majorities and minorities. *Psychological Review, 88,* 438–453.

Lau, R. R. (1985). Two explanations for negativity effects in political behavior. *American Journal of Political Science, 29,* 119–138.

Laughlin, P. R., & Bonner, B. L. (1999). Collective induction: Effects of multiple hypotheses and multiple evidence in two problem domains. *Journal of Personality and Social Psychology, 77,* 1163–1172.

Laughlin, P. R., Bonner, B. L., & Miner, A. G. (2002). Groups perform better than the best individuals on Letters-to-Numbers problems. *Organizational Behavior and Human Decision Processes, 88,* 605–620.

Laughlin, P. R., & Ellis, A. L. (1986). Demonstrability and social combination processes on mathematical intellective tasks. *Journal of Experimental Social Psychology, 22,* 177–189.

Lawson, E. (2001). Informational and relational meanings of deception: Implications for deception methods in research. *Ethics and Behavior, 11,* 115–130.

Le, B., & Agnew, C. R. (2003). Commitment and its theorized determinants: A meta-analysis of the investment model. *Personal Relationships, 10,* 37–57.

Le Bon, G. (1895). *Psychologie des foules.* Paris: Félix Alcan.

Leana, C. R. (1985). A partial test of Janis' groupthink model: Effects of group cohesiveness and leader behavior on defective decision making. *Journal of Management, 11,* 5–17.

Leary, M. R. (Ed.) (2001). *Interpersonal rejection.* New York: Oxford University Press.

Leary, M. R., & Baumeister, R. F. (2000). The nature and function of self-esteem: Sociometer theory. *Advances in Experimental Social Psychology.*

Leary, M. R., Haupt, A. L., Strausser, K. S., & Chokel, J. T. (1998). Calibrating the sociometer: The relationship between interpersonal appraisals and state self-esteem. *Journal of Personality and Social Psychology, 74,* 1290–1299.

Leary, M. R., & Kowalski, R. M. (1990). Impression management: A literature review and two-component model. *Psychological Bulletin, 107,* 34–47.

Leary, M. R., & Kowalski, R. M. (1995). *Social anxiety.* New York: Guilford Press.

Leary, M. R., Kowalski, R. M., Smith, L., & Phillips, S. (2003). Teasing, rejection, and violence: Case studies of the school shootings. *Aggressive Behavior, 29,* 202–214.

Leary, M. R., & Tangney, J. P. (Eds.) (2003). *Handbook of self and identity.* New York: Guilford.

Leary, M. R., Tchividjian, L. R., & Kraxberger, B. E. (1994). Self-presentation can be hazardous to your health: Impression management and health risk. *Health Psychology, 13,* 461–470.

Lee, J. A. (1977). A typology of styles of loving. *Personality and Social Psychology Bulletin, 3,* 173–182.

Lee, J. A. (1988). Love-styles. In R. J. Sternberg & M. L. Barnes (Ed.), *The psychology of love* (pp. 38–67). New Haven, CT: Yale University Press.

Lee, Y. T., & Ottati, V. (1995). Perceived in-group homogeneity as a function of group membership salience and stereotype threat. *Personality and Social Psychology Bulletin, 21,* 610–619.

Lehman, D. R., Lempert, R. O., & Nisbett, R. E. (1988). The effects of graduate training on reasoning: Formal discipline and thinking about everyday-life events. *American Psychologist, 43*, 431–442.

Leichtman, M. D., & Ceci, S. J. (1995). The effects of stereotypes and suggestions on preschoolers' reports. *Developmental Psychology, 31*, 568–578.

Leigh, B. C., & Stacy, A. W. (1993). Alcohol outcome expectancies: Scale construction and predictive utility in higher-order confirmatory models. *Psychological Assessment, 5*, 216–229.

Leinbach, M. D., & Fagot, B. I. (1993). Categorical habituation to male and female faces: Gender schematic processing in infancy. *Infant Behavior and Development, 16*, 317–332.

Leippe, M. R. (1995). The case for expert testimony about eyewitness memory. *Psychology, Public Policy, and Law, 1*, 909–959.

Leippe, M. R., & Eisenstadt, D. (1994). Generalization of dissonance reduction: Decreasing prejudice through induced compliance. *Journal of Personality and Social Psychology, 67*, 395–413.

Leland, J. (1995, December 11). "Copycat" crimes in New York's subways reignite the debate: Do TV and movies cause actual mayhem? *Newsweek*, p. 46.

Leo, R. A. (1996). Inside the interrogation room. *The Journal of Criminal Law and Criminology, 86*, 266–303.

Leonard, K. E. (1989). The impact of explicit aggressive and implicit nonaggressive cues on aggression in intoxicated and sober roles. *Personality and Social Psychology Bulletin, 15*, 390–400.

Leonard, K. E., Collins, R. L., & Quigley, B. M. (2003). Alcohol consumption and the occurrence and severity of aggression: An event-based analysis of male-to-male barroom violence. *Aggressive Behavior, 29*, 346–365.

Lepore, L., & Brown, R. (1997). Category and stereotype activation: Is prejudice inevitable? *Journal of Personality and Social Psychology, 72*, 275–287.

Lepore, L., & Brown, R. (2002). The role of awareness: Divergent automatic stereotype activation and implicit judgment correction. *Social Cognition, 20*, 321–351.

Lepper, M. R., Greene, D., & Nisbett, R. E. (1973). Undermining children's intrinsic interest with extrinsic reward: A test of the "overjustification" hypothesis. *Journal of Personality and Social Psychology, 28*, 129–137.

Lerner, M. J. (1980). *The belief in a just world: A fundamental delusion.* New York: Plenum.

Lerner, M. J. (1998). The two forms of belief in a just world: Some thoughts on why and how people care about justice. In L. Montada, & M. J. Lerner (Eds.), *Responses to victimization and belief in a just world: Critical issues in social justice* (pp. 247–269). NY: Plenum.

Lerner, M. J., & Simmons, C. H. (1966). Observers' reaction to the "innocent victim": Compassion or rejection? *Journal of Personality and Social Psychology, 4*, 203–210.

Leung, K. (1987). Some determinants of reactions to procedural models for conflict resolution: A cross-national study. *Journal of Personality and Social Psychology, 53*, 898–908.

LeVay, S. (1991). A difference in hypothalamic structure between heterosexual and homosexual men. *Science, 253*, 1034–1037.

LeVay, S. (1993). *The sexual brain.* Cambridge, MA: MIT Press.

Leventhal, H. (1970). Findings and theory in the study of fear communications. In L. Berkowitz (Ed.), *Advances in experimental social psychology* (Vol. 5, pp. 119–186). New York: Academic Press.

Leventhal, H., Watts, J. C., & Pagano, F. (1967). Effects of fear and instructions on how to cope with danger. *Journal of Personality and Social Psychology, 6*, 313–321.

Levesque, M. J. (1997). Meta-accuracy among acquainted individuals: A social relations analysis of interpersonal perception and metaperception. *Journal of Personality and Social Psychology, 72*, 66–74.

Levin, S. (2004). Perceived group differences and the effects of gender, ethnicity, and religion on social dominance orientation. *Political Psychology, 25*, 31–48.

Levin, S., Henry, P. J., Pratto, F., & Sidanius, J. (2003). Social dominance and social identity in Lebanon: Implications for support of violence against the West. *Group Processes and Intergroup Relations, 6*, 353–368.

Levine, J. M. (1989). Reaction to opinion deviance in small groups. In P. B. Paulus (Ed.), *Psychology of group influence* (2nd ed., pp. 187–231). Hillsdale, NJ: Erlbaum.

Levine, J. M., & Moreland, R. L. (1990). Progress in small group research. *Annual Review of Psychology, 41*, 585–634.

Levine, J. M., & Moreland, R. L. (1998). Small groups. In D. T. Gilbert, S. T. Fiske, & G. Lindzey (Eds.), *The handbook of social psychology* (4th ed., Vol. 2, pp. 415–469). New York: McGraw-Hill.

Levine, J. M., Moreland, R. L., & Hausmann, L. R. M. (2004). Managing group composition: Inclusive and exclusive role transitions. In D. Abrams, J. M. Marques, & M.A. Hogg (Eds.), *The social psychology of inclusion and exclusion.* Philadelphia: Psychology Press.

Levine, J. M., Moreland, R. L., & Ryan, C. S. (1998). Group socialization and intergroup relations. In C. Sedikides, J. Schopler, & C. A. Insko (Eds.), *Intergroup Cognition and Intergroup Behavior.* Mahwah, NJ: Erlbaum, pp. 283–308.

Levine, R. A., & Campbell, D. T. (1972). *Ethnocentrism: Theories of conflict, ethnic attitudes, and group behavior.* New York: Wiley.

Levine, R. B. (1993). Is love a luxury? *American Demographics, 15* (2), 27–28.

Levine, R. V., Martinez, T. S., Brase, G., & Sorenson, K. (1994). Helping in 36 U.S. cities. *Journal of Personality and Social Psychology, 67* (1), 69–82.

Levine, R. V., Norenzayan, A., & Philbrick, K. (2001). Crosscultural differences in helping strangers. *Journal of Cross-Cultural Psychology, 32*, 543–560.

Levy, D. A., & Nail, P. R. (1993). Contagion: A theoretical and empirical review and reconceptualization. *Genetic, Social, and General Psychology Monographs, 119*, 233–284.

Levy, G. D., & Haaf, R. A. (1994). Detection of gender-related categories by 10-month-old infants. *Infant Behavior and Development, 17*, 457–459.

Levy, S. R., Plaks, J. E., Hong, Y., Chiu, C., & Dweck, C. S. (2001). Static versus dynamic theories and the perception of groups: Different routes to different destinations. *Personality and Social Psychology Review, 5*, 156–168.

Levy, S. R., Stroessner, S. J., & Dweck, C. S. (1998). Stereotype formation and endorsement: The role of implicit theories. *Journal of Personality and Social Psychology, 74*, 1421–1436.

Lewicki, R. J., Saunders, D. M., & Minton, J. W. (1999). *Negotiation: Reading, exercises, and cases* (3rd ed.), Boston: Irwin/McGraw-Hill.

Lewin, K. (1935). *A dynamic theory of personality.* New York: McGraw-Hill.

Lewin, K. (1947). Group decision and social change. In T. M. Newcomb & E. L. Hartley (Eds.), *Readings in social psychology* (pp. 330–344). New York: Holt.

Lewin, K. (1951). Problems of research in social psychology. In D. Cartwright (Ed.), *Field theory in social science* (pp. 155–169). New York: Harper & Row.

Lewis, B. P., & Linder, D. E. (1997). Thinking about choking? Attentional processes and paradoxical performance. *Personality and Social Psychology Bulletin, 23*, 937–944.

Lewis, K. (2003). Measuring transactive memory systems in the field: Scale development and validation. *Journal of Applied Psychology, 88*, 587–604.

Lewis, M., & Brooks-Gunn, J. (1979). *Social cognition and the acquisition of self.* New York: Plenum.

Leyens, J.-Ph., Cortes, B. P., Demoulin, S., Dovidio, J., Fiske, S. T., Gaunt, R., Paladino, M. P., Rodriquez-Perez, A., Rodriquez-Torres, R., & Vaes, V. (2003). Emotional prejudice, essentialism, and nationalism. *European Journal of Experimental Social Psychology, 23*, 703–717.

Li, N. P., Bailey, J. M., Kenrick, D. T., & Linsenmeier, J. A. W. (2002). The necessities and luxuries of mate preferences: Testing the tradeoffs. *Journal of Personality and Social Psychology, 82*, 947–955.

Lickel, B., Hamilton, D. L., Wieczorkowska, G., Lewis, A., Sherman, S. J., & Uhles, A. N. (2000). Varieties of groups and the perception of group entitativity. *Journal of Personality and Social Psychology, 78*, 223–246.

Lieberman, J. D. (1999). Terror management, illusory correlation, and perception of minority groups. *Basic and Applied Social Psychology, 21*, 13–23.

Lieberman, J. D., & Arndt, J. (2000). Understanding the limits of limiting instructions. *Psychology, Public Policy, and Law, 6*, 677–711.

Lieberman, M. D., Gaunt, R., Gilbert, D. T., & Trope, Y. (2004). Reflection and reflexion: A social cognitive neuroscience approach to attributional inference. In M. P. Zanna (Ed.), *Advances in experimental social psychology* (Vol. 34, pp. 199–249). San Diego, CA: Academic Press.

Lieberman, M. D., Ochsner, K. N., Gilbert, D. T., & Schacter, D. L. (2001). Do amnesics exhibit cognitive dissonance reduction? The role of explicit memory and attention in attitude change. *Psychological Science, 12*, 135–140.

Lifton, R. J. (1986). *The Nazi doctors: Medical killing and the psychology of genocide.* New York: Basic Books.

Likert, R. (1932). A technique for the measurement of attitudes. *Archives of Psychology, 140*, 1–55.

Liljenquist, K. A., Galinsky, A. D., & Kray, L. J. (2004). The differential impact of individual and group level activation of counterfactual mind-sets on information sharing, group processes, and judgment accuracy. In E. M. Wong & L. J. Kray (Chairs), *Counterfactual thinking in organizations: A multi-level analysis.* Symposium presented at the annual conference of the Academy of Management, New Orleans.

Lind, E. A., Kanfer, R., & Farley, P. C. (1990). Voice, control, and procedural justice: Instrumental and noninstrumental concerns in fairness judgments. *Journal of Personality and Social Psychology, 59*, 952–959.

Linder, D. E., Cooper, J., & Jones, E. E. (1967). Decision freedom as a determinant of the role of incentive magnitude in attitude change. *Journal of Personality and Social Psychology, 6*, 245–254.

Lindsay, D. S., Hagen, L., Read, J. D., Wade, K. A., & Garry, M. (2004). True photographs and false memories. *Psychological Science, 15*, 149–154.

Lindsay, R. C. L., & Bellinger, K. (1999). Alternatives to the sequential lineup: The importance of controlling the pictures. *Journal of Applied Psychology, 84*, 315–321.

Lindsay, R. C. L., Lea, J. A., & Fulford, J. A. (1991). Sequential lineup presentation: Technique matters. *Journal of Applied Psychology, 76*, 741–745.

Lindsay, R. C. L., & Wells, G. L. (1985). Improving eyewitness identifications from lineups: Simultaneous versus sequential lineup presentations. *Journal of Applied Psychology, 70*, 556–564.

Lindsay, R. C. L., Wells, G. L., & Rumpel, C. M. (1981). Can people detect eyewitness-identification accuracy within and across situations? *Journal of Applied Psychology, 66*, 79–89.

Lindskold, S., & Han, G. (1988). GRIT as a foundation for integrative bargaining. *Personality and Social Psychology Bulletin, 14*, 335–345.

Linville, P. (1998). The heterogeneity of homogeneity. In J. Cooper & J. Darley (Eds.), *Attribution processes, person perception, and social interaction: The legacy of Ned Jones.* Washington, DC: American Psychological Association.

Linville, P. W., & Jones, E. E. (1980). Polarized appraisals of out-group members. *Journal of Personality and Social Psychology, 38*, 689–703.

Linville, P. W., Fischer, G. W., & Fischoff, B. (1992). Perceived risk and decision making involving AIDS. In J. B. Pryor & G. D. Reeder (Eds.), *The social psychology of HIV infection.* Hillsdale, NJ: Erlbaum.

Linville, P. W., Fischer, G. W., & Salovey, P. (1989). Perceived distributions of the characteristics of in-group and out-group members: Empirical evidence and a computer simulation. *Journal of Personality and Social Psychology, 57*, 165–188.

Linz, D., Donnerstein, E., & Penrod, S. (1987). The findings and recommendations of the Attorney General's Commission on Pornography: Do the psychological "facts" fit the political fury? *American Psychologist, 42*, 946–953.

Linz, D., Wilson, B. J., & Donnerstein, E. (1992). Sexual violence in the mass media: Legal solutions, warnings, and mitigation through education. *Journal of Social Issues, 48*, 145–171.

Lipponen, J., Helkama, K., & Juslin, M. (2003). Subgroup identification, superordinate identification and intergroup bias between the subgroups. *Group Processes and Intergroup Relations, 6*, 239–250.

Liquori, S. A., Kreh, M. L., Holzapfel, L. L., & Fein, S. (2001). *Ad it up: Effects of sexy images of women in advertising on women's math performance in same-sex and mixed-sex groups.* Paper presented at the second annual meeting of the Society of Personality and Social Psychology, San Antonio, TX.

Litvack, M. W., McDougall, D., & Romney, D. M. (1997). The structure of empathy during middle childhood and its relationship to prosocial behavior. *Genetic, Social and General Psychology Monographs, 123*, 303–324.

Lockhart v. McCree, 54 U.S.L.W. 4449 (1986).

Locksley, A., Borgida, E., Brekke, N., & Hepburn, C. (1980). Sex stereotypes and social judgment. *Journal of Personality and Social Psychology, 39*, 821–831.

Lockwood, P., Dolderman, D., Sadler, P., & Gerchak, L. (2004). Feeling better about doing worse: Social comparisons within romantic relationships. *Journal of Personality and Social Psychology, 87*, 80–95.

Lockwood, P. & Kunda, Z. (2000). Outstanding role models: Do they inspire or demoralize us? In A. Tesser, J. Suls, & R. Felson (Eds.), *Psychological perspectives on self and identity*, pp. 147–171. Washington, D. C. APA Press.

Loeber, R., & Hay, D. (1997). Key issues in the development of aggression and violence from childhood to early adulthood. *Annual Review of Psychology, 48*, 371–410.

Loewenstein, G. F., Weber, E. U., Hsee, C. K., & Welch, N. (2001). Risk as feelings. *Psychological Bulletin, 127*, 267–286.

Loftus, E. F. (1996). *Eyewitness testimony* (reprint ed.). Cambridge, MA: Harvard University Press.

Loftus, E. F. (2003). Memory in Canadian courts of law. *Canadian Psychology, 44*, 207–212.

Loftus, E. F., Loftus, G. R., & Messo, J. (1987). Some facts about "weapon focus." *Law and Human Behavior, 11*, 55–62.

Loftus, E. F., & Palmer, J. C. (1974). Reconstruction of automobile destruction: An example of the interaction between language and memory. *Journal of Verbal Learning and Verbal Behavior, 13*, 585–589.

London, K., & Nunez, N. (2000). The effect of jury deliberations on jurors' propensity to disregard inadmissible evidence. *Journal of Applied Psychology, 85*, 932–939.

Long, E. C. J., & Andrews, D. W. (1990). Perspective taking as a predictor of marital adjustment. *Journal of Personality and Social Psychology, 59*, 126–131.

Lopata, C. (2003). Progressive muscle relaxation and aggression among elementary students with emotional or behavioral disorders. *Behavioral Disorders, 28*, 162–172.

Lore, R. K., & Schultz, L. A. (1993). Control of human aggression: A comparative perspective. *American Psychologist, 48*, 16–25.

Lorenz, K. (1966). *On aggression.* New York: Harcourt, Brace & World.

Lorenzi-Cioldi, F., Deaux, K., & Dafflon, A. C. (1998). Group homogeneity as a function of relative social status. *Swiss Journal of Psychology, 57*, 255–273.

Lortie-Lussier, M. (1987). Minority influence and idiosyncrasy credit: A new comparison of the Moscovici and Hollander theories of innovation. *European Journal of Social Psychology, 17*, 431–446.

Losch, M. E., & Cacioppo, J. T. (1990). Cognitive dissonance may enhance sympathetic tonus, but attitudes are changed to reduce negative affect rather than arousal. *Journal of Experimental Social Psychology, 26*, 289–304.

Lott, A. J., & Lott, B. E. (1974). The role of reward in the formation of positive interpersonal attitudes. In T. L. Huston (Ed.), *Foundations of interpersonal attraction* (pp. 171–189). New York: Academic Press.

Lott, B. (1985). The devaluation of women's competence. *Journal of Social Issues, 41*, 43–60.

Lubow, R. E., & Fein, O. (1996). Pupillary size in response to a visual guilty knowledge test: A new technique for the detection of deception. *Journal of Experimental Psychology: Applied, 2*, 164–177.

Lüüs, C. A. E., & Wells, G. L. (1991). Eyewitness identification and the selection of distractors for lineups. *Law and Human Behavior, 15*, 43–58.

Lüüs, C. A. E., & Wells, G. L. (1994). The malleability of eyewitness confidence: Co-witness and perseverance effects. *Journal of Applied Psychology, 79*, 714–723.

Lykken, D. T. (1998). *A tremor in the blood: Uses and abuses of the lie detector* (2nd ed.). Cambridge, MA: Perseus.

Lykken, D. T., & Tellegen, A. (1993). Is human mating adventitious or the result of lawful choice? A twin study of mate selection. *Journal of Personality and Social Psychology, 65*, 56–68.

Lyons, A., & Kashima, Y. (2001). The representation of culture: Communication processes tend to maintain cultural stereotypes. *Social Cognition, 19*, 372–394.

Maass, A., & Clark, R. D., III. (1984). Hidden impact of minorities: Fifteen years of minority influence research. *Psychological Bulletin, 95*, 428–450.

Maass, A., & Kohnken, G. (1989). Eyewitness identification: Simulating the "weapon effect." *Law and Human Behavior, 13*, 397–408.

Maass, A., Volpato, C., & Mucchi-Faina, A. (1996). Social influence and the verifiability of the issue under discussion: Attitudinal versus objective items. *British Journal of Social Psychology, 35*, 15–26.

Macaulay, J. R. (1970). A shill for charity. In J. Macaulay & L. Berkowitz (Eds.), *Altruism and helping behavior* (pp. 43–59). New York: Academic Press.

MacCoun, R. J., & Kerr, N. L. (1988). Asymmetric influence in mock jury deliberation: Jurors' bias for leniency. *Journal of Personality and Social Psychology, 54*, 21–33.

MacDonald, G. & Leary M. R. (2005). Why does social exclusion hurt? The relationship between social and physical pain. *Psychological Bulletin, 131*, 202–223.

MacDonald, T. K., Fong, G. T., Zanna, M. P., & Martineau, A. M. (2000). Alcohol myopia and condom use: Can alcohol intoxication be associated with more prudent behavior? *Journal of Personality and Social Psychology, 78*, 605–619.

MacDonald, T. K., Zanna, M. P. (1998). Cross-dimension ambivalence toward social groups: Can ambivalence affect intentions to hire feminists? *Personality and Social Psychology Bulletin, 24*, 427–441.

Macionis, J. J. (2003). *Sociology* (9th ed.). Upper Saddle River, NJ: Prentice Hall.

Mackie, D. M., Asuncion, A. G., & Rosselli, F. (1992). Impact of positive affect on persuasion processes. *Review of Personality and Social Psychology, 14*, 247–270.

Mackie, D. M., & Cooper, J. (1984). Attitude polarization: Effects of group membership. *Journal of Personality and Social Psychology, 46*, 575–585.

Mackie, D. M., & Worth, L. T. (1989). Processing deficits and the mediation of positive affect in persuasion. *Journal of Personality and Social Psychology, 57*, 27–40.

MacLeod, C., & Campbell, L. (1992). Memory accessibility and probability judgments: An experimental evaluation of the availability heuristic. *Journal of Personality and Social Psychology, 63*, 890–902.

Macrae, C. N., Bodenhausen, G. V., & Milne, A. B. (1995). The dissection of selection in person perception: Inhibitory processes in social stereotyping. *Journal of Personality and Social Psychology, 69*, 397–407.

Macrae, C. N., Bodenhausen, G. V., & Milne, A. B. (1998). Saying no to unwanted thoughts: Self-focus and the regulation of mental life. *Journal of Personality and Social Psychology, 74*, 578–589.

Macrae, C. N., Bodenhausen, G. V., Milne, A. B., & Jetten, J. (1994). Out of mind but back in sight: Stereotypes on the rebound. *Journal of Personality and Social Psychology, 67*, 808–817.

Madden, T. J., Ellen, P. S., & Ajzen, I. (1992). A comparison of the theory of planned behavior and the theory of reasoned action. *Personality and Social Psychology Bulletin, 18*, 3–9.

Maddux, J. E., & Rogers, R. W. (1980). Effects of source

expertness, physical attractiveness, and supporting arguments on persuasion: A case of brains over beauty. *Journal of Personality and Social Psychology, 39,* 235–244.

Madey, S. F., Simo, M., Dillworth, D., Kemper, D., Toczynski, A., & Perella, A. (1996). They do get more attractive at closing time, but only when you are not in a relationship. *Basic and Applied Social Psychology, 18,* 387–393.

Madon, S., Guyll, M., Spoth, R., Cross, S. E., & Hilbert, S. J. (2003). The self-fulfilling influence of mother expectations on children's underage drinking. *Journal of Personality and Social Psychology, 84,* 1188–1205.

Madon, S., Jussim, L., Keiper, S., Eccles, J., Smith, A., & Palumbo, P. (1998). The accuracy and power of sex, social class, and ethnic stereotypes: A naturalistic study in person perception. *Personality and Social Psychology Bulletin, 24,* 1304–1318.

Maio, G., & Olson, J. M. (Eds.) (2000). *Why we evaluate: Functions of attitudes.* Mahwah, NJ: Erlbaum.

Major, B., Carrington, P. I., & Carnevale, P. J. D. (1984). Physical attractiveness and self-esteem: Attributions for praise from an other-sex evaluator. *Personality and Social Psychology Bulletin, 10,* 43–50.

Major, B., & Crocker, J. (1993). Social stigma: The affective consequences of attributional ambiguity. In D. M. Mackie & D. L. Hamilton (Eds.), *Affect, cognition, and stereotyping: Interactive processes in intergroup perception* (pp. 345–370). New York: Academic Press.

Major, B., McCoy, S. K., Kaiser, C. R., & Quinton, W. J. (2004). Prejudice and self-esteem: A transactional model. *European Review of Social Psychology, 14,* 77–104.

Major, B., McFarlin, D. B., & Gagnon, D. (1984). Overworked and underpaid: On the nature of gender differences in personal entitlement. *Journal of Personality and Social Psychology, 47,* 1399–1412.

Major, B., Quinton, W. J., & McCoy, S. K. (2002). Antecedents and consequences of attributions to discrimination: Theoretical and empirical advances. In M. Zanna (Ed.), *Advances in experimental social psychology* (Vol. 34, pp. 251–330). San Diego, CA: Academic Press.

Major, B., Quinton, W. J., & Schmader, T. (2003). Attributions to discrimination and self-esteem: Impact of group identification and situational ambiguity. *Journal of Experimental Social Psychology, 39,* 220–231.

Malamuth, N. M. (1983). Factors associated with rape as predictors of laboratory aggression against women. *Journal of Personality and Social Psychology, 45,* 432–442.

Malamuth, N. M. (1986). Predictors of naturalistic sexual aggression. *Journal of Personality and Social Psychology, 50,* 953–962.

Malamuth, N. M. (1996). The confluence model of sexual aggression: Feminist and evolutionary perspectives. In D. M. Buss & N. M. Malamuth (Eds.), *Sex, power, conflict: Evolutionary and feminist perspectives* (pp. 269–295). New York: Oxford University Press.

Malamuth, N. M., Addison, T., & Koss, M. (2000). Pornography and sexual aggression: Are there reliable effects and can we understand them? *Annual Review of Sex Research, 11,* 26–91.

Malamuth, N. M., & Billings, V. (1986). The function and effects of pornography: Sexual communications versus the feminist model in light of research findings. In J. Bryant & D. Zillmann (Eds.), *Perspectives on media effects* (pp. 83–108). Hillsdale, NJ: Erlbaum.

Malamuth, N. M., & Donnerstein, E. I. (1982). The effects of aggressive-pornographic mass media stimuli. In L. Berkowitz (Ed.), *Advances in experimental social psychology* (Vol. 15, pp. 103–136). New York: Academic Press.

Malinoski, P. T., & Lynn, S. J. (1999). The plasticity of early memory reports: Social pressure, hypnotizability, compliance, and interrogative suggestibility. *International Journal of Clinical and Experimental Hypnosis, 47,* 320–345.

Malinosky-Rummell, R., & Hansen, D. J. (1993). Long-term consequences of childhood physical abuse. *Psychological Bulletin, 114,* 68–79.

Malle, B. F., & Knobe, J. (1997). Which behaviors do people explain? A basic actor-observer asymmetry. *Journal of Personality and Social Psychology, 72,* 288–304.

Malle, B. F., Knobe, J., O'Laughlin, M. J., Pearce, G. E., & Nelson, S. E. (2000). Conceptual structure and social functions of behavior explanations: Beyond person-situation attributions. *Journal of Personality and Social Psychology, 79,* 309–326.

Malloy, T. E., & Albright, L. (1990). Interpersonal perception in a social context. *Journal of Personality and Social Psychology, 58,* 419–428.

Malpass, R. S., & Devine, P. G. (1981). Eyewitness identification: Lineup instructions and the absence of the offender. *Journal of Applied Psychology, 66,* 482–489.

Malpass, R. S., & Kravitz, J. (1969). Recognition for faces of own and other race. *Journal of Personality and Social Psychology, 13,* 330–334.

Manasian, D. (2003). Digital dilemmas: A survey of the Internet society. *Economist, 25,* 1–26.

Maner, J. K., Luce, C. L., Neuberg, S. L., Cialdini, R. B., Brown, S., & Sagarin, B. J. (2002). The effects of perspective taking on motivations for helping: Still no evidence for altruism. *Personality and Social Psychology Bulletin, 28,* 1601–1610.

Mann, L. (1981). The baiting crowd in episodes of threatened suicide. *Journal of Personality and Social Psychology, 41,* 703–709.

Marcus-Newhall, A., Pedersen, W. C., Carlson, M., & Miller, N. (2000). Displaced aggression is alive and well: A meta-analytic review. *Journal of Personality and Social Psychology, 78,* 670–689.

Margolin, G., & Wampold, B. E. (1981). A sequential analysis of conflict and accord in distressed and nondistressed marital partners. *Journal of Consulting and Clinical Psychology, 49,* 554–567.

Markey, P. M. (2000). Bystander intervention in computer-mediated communication. *Computers in Human Behavior, 16,* 183–188.

Markman, K. D., & Weary, G. (1996). The influence of chronic control concerns on counterfactual thought. *Social Cognition, 14,* 292–316.

Marks, J. (1995). *Human biodiversity: Genes, race, and history.* New York: Aldine de Gruyter.

Markus, H. (1977). Self-schemata and processing information about the self. *Journal of Personality and Social Psychology, 35,* 63–78.

Markus, H., Hamill, R., & Sentis, K. P. (1987). Thinking fat: Self-schemas for body weight and the processing of weight-relevant information. *Journal of Applied Social Psychology, 17,* 50–71.

Markus, H. R., & Kitayama, S. (1991). Culture and the self: Implications for cognition, emotion, and motivation. *Psychological Review, 98,* 224–253.

Markus, H. R., & Lin, L. R. (1999). Conflictways: Cultural diversity in the meanings and practices of conflict. In D. A. Prentice & D. T. Miller (Eds.), *Cultural divides: Understanding and overcoming group conflict* (pp. 302–333). New York: Russell Sage.

Marques, J. M., Yzerbyt, V. Y., & Rijsman, J. B. (1988). Context effects on intergroup discrimination: In-group bias as a function of experimenter's provenance. *British Journal of Social Psychology, 27*, 301–318.

Marshall, L. (1979). Sharing, talking, and giving: Relief of social tensions among !Kung Bushmen. In R. B. Lee & I. DeVore (Eds.), *Kalahari hunter-gatherers: Studies of the !Kung San and their neighbors* (pp. 349–372). Cambridge, England: Cambridge University Press.

Martin, C. L., Eisenbud, L., & Rose, H. (1995). Children's gender-based reasoning about toys. *Child Development, 66*, 1453–1471.

Martin, C. L., Wood, C. H., & Little, J. K. (1990). The development of gender stereotype components. *Child Development, 61*, 1891–1904.

Marx, B. P., Gross, A. M., & Adams, H. E. (1999). The effect of alcohol on the responses of sexually coercive and noncoercive men to an experimental rape analogue. *Sexual Abuse: Journal of Research and Treatment, 11*, 131–145.

Maslach, C. (1979). Negative emotional biasing of unexplained arousal. *Journal of Personality and Social Psychology, 37*, 953–969.

Masuda, T., & Nisbett, R. E. (2001). Attending holistically vs. analytically: Comparing the context sensitivity of Japanese and Americans. *Journal of Personality and Social Psychology, 81*, 922–934.

Mathur, M., & Chattopadhyay, A. (1991). The impact of moods generated by TV programs on responses to advertising. *Psychology and Marketing, 8*, 59–77.

Mayberg, H. S., Silva, J. A., Brannan, S. K., Tekell, J. L., Mahurin, R. K., McGinnis, S., & Jerabek, P. A. (2002). The functional neuroanatomy of the placebo effect. *American Journal of Psychiatry, 159*, 728–737.

Maznevski, M. L. (1994). Understanding our differences: Performance in decision-making groups with diverse members. *Human Relations, 47*, 531–552.

Mazur, A., Booth, A., & Dabbs, J. M. (1992). Testosterone and chess competition. *Social Psychology Quarterly, 55*, 70–77.

McAdams, D. P. (1989). *Intimacy: The need to be close.* New York: Doubleday.

McArthur, L. A. (1972). The how and what of why: Some determinants and consequences of causal attribution. *Journal of Personality and Social Psychology, 22*, 171–193.

McAuliffe, B. J., Jetten, J., Hornsey, M. J., & Hogg, M. A. (2003). Individualist and collectivist norms: When it's ok to go your own way. *European Journal of Social Psychology, 33*, 57–70.

McCabe, M. P., Ricciardelli, L. A., & Finemore, J. (2002). The role of puberty, media and popularity with peers on strategies to increase weight, decrease weight and increase muscle tone among adolescent boys and girls. *Journal of Psychosomatic Research, 52*, 145–154.

McConahay, J. B. (1986). Modern racism, ambivalence, and the modern racism scale. In J. F. Dovidio & S. L. Gaertner (Eds.), *Prejudice, discrimination, and racism: Theory and research* (pp. 91–125). Orlando, FL: Academic Press.

McConnell, A. R. (2001). Implicit theories: Consequences for social judgments of individuals. *Journal of Experimental Social Psychology, 37*, 215–227.

McCrae, R. R., & Costa, P. T., Jr. (1997). Personality trait structure as a human universal. *American Psychologist, 52*, 509–516.

McDougall, W. (1908). *An introduction to social psychology.* London: Methuen.

McElwee, R. O., Dunning, D., Tan, P. L., & Hollmann, S. (2001). Evaluating others: The role of who we are versus what we think traits mean. *Basic and Applied Social Psychology, 23*, 123–136.

McFarland, C., & Buehler, R. (1995). Collective self-esteem as a moderator of the frog-pond effect in reactions to performance feedback. *Journal of Personality and Social Psychology, 68*, 1055–1070.

McFarland, L. A., Lev-Arey, D. M., & Ziegert, J. C. (2003). An examination of stereotype threat in a motivational context. *Human Performance, 16*, 181–205.

McGarty, C., Turner, J. C., Hogg, M. A., David, B., et al. (1992). Group polarization as conformity to the prototypical group member. *British Journal of Social Psychology, 31*, 1–19.

McGillicuddy, N. B., Pruitt, D. G., & Syna, H. (1984). Perceptions of fairness and strength of negotiation. *Personality and Social Psychology Bulletin, 10*, 402–409.

McGinty, S. (2000, August 31). Japan's darkest secrets: The dark side of the orient. *The Scotsman*, p. 2.

McGrew, J. F., Bilotta, J. G., & Deeney, J. M. (1999). Software team formation and decay: Extending the standard model for small groups. *Small Group Research, 30*, 209–234.

McGuire, A. M. (1994). Helping behaviors in the natural environment: Dimensions and correlates of helping. *Personality and Social Psychology Bulletin, 20*, 45–56.

McGuire, W. J. (1964). Inducing resistance to persuasion. In L. Berkowitz (Ed.), *Advances in experimental social psychology* (Vol. 1, pp. 192–229). New York: Academic Press.

McGuire, W. J. (1967). Some impending reorientations in social psychology: Some thoughts provoked by Kenneth Ring. *Journal of Experimental Social Psychology, 3*, 124–139.

McGuire, W. J. (1968). Personality and susceptibility to social influence. In E. F. Borgatta & W.W. Lambert (Eds.), *Handbook of personality theory and research* (pp. 1130–1187). Chicago: Rand McNally.

McGuire, W. J. (1969). The nature of attitudes and attitude change. In G. Lindzey & E. Aronson (Eds.), *Handbook of social psychology* (2nd ed., Vol. 3, pp. 136–314). Reading, MA: Addison-Wesley.

McGuire, W. J., & McGuire, C. V. (1988). Content and process in the experience of self. In L. Berkowitz (Ed.), *Advances in experimental social psychology* (Vol. 20, pp. 97–144). New York: Academic Press.

McIntyre, R. B., Paulson, R. M., & Lord, C. G. (2003). Alleviating women's mathematics stereotype threat through salience of group achievements. *Journal of Experimental Social Psychology, 39*, 83–90.

McKenna, K. Y. A., & Bargh, J. A. (1998). Coming out in the age of the Internet: "Demarginalization" through virtual group participation. *Journal of Personality and Social Psychology, 75*, 681–694.

McKenna, K. Y. A., & Bargh, J. A. (2000). Plan 9 from cyberspace: The implications of the Internet for personality and social psychology. *Personality and Social Psychology Review, 4*, 57–75.

McKenna, K. Y. A., & Bargh, J. A. (2002). The self, on-line: Motivated social perception on the Internet. In S. J. Spencer, S. Fein, M. Zanna, & J. M. Olson (Eds.), *Motivated social perception: The Ontario symposium* (Vol. 9). Mahwah, NJ: Erlbaum.

McLeod, P. L., Lobel, S. A., & Cox, Jr., T. H. (1996). Ethnic diversity and creativity in small groups. *Small Group Research, 27*, 248–264.

McMullen, P. A., & Gross, A. E. (1983). Sex differences, sex roles, and health-related help-seeking. In B. M. DePaulo, A. Nadler, & J. D. Fisher (Eds.), *New directions in helping: Vol. 2. Help-Seeking* (pp. 233–263). New York: Academic Press.

McNatt, D. B. (2000). Ancient Pygmalion joins contemporary management: A meta-analysis of the result. *Journal of Applied Psychology, 85*, 314–322.

McPherson, M., Smith-Lovin, L., & Cook, J. M. (2001). Birds of a feather: Homophily in social networks. *Annual Review of Sociology, 27*, 415–444.

Mead, G. H. (1934). *Mind, self, and society*. Chicago: University of Chicago Press.

Mealey, L., Bridgstock, R., & Townsend, G. C. (1999). Symmetry and perceived facial attractiveness: A monozygotic co-twin comparison. *Journal of Personality and Social Psychology, 76*, 151–158.

Medvec, V. H., Madey, S. F., & Gilovich, T. (1995). When less is more: Counterfactual thinking and satisfaction among olympic medalists. *Journal of Personality and Social Psychology, 69*, 603–610.

Medvec, V. H., & Savitsky, K. (1997). When doing better means feeling worse: The effects of categorical cutoff points on counterfactual thinking and satisfaction. *Journal of Personality and Social Psychology, 72*, 1284–1296.

Medved, M. (1996, September 21). *Daily Telegraph*, p. 5.

Meeres, S. L., & Grant, P. R. (1999). Enhancing collective and personal self-esteem through differentiation: Further exploration of Hinkle & Brown's taxonomy. *British Journal of Social Psychology, 38*, 21–34.

Meeus, W. H. J., & Raaijmakers, Q. A. W. (1995). Obedience in modern society: The Utrecht studies. *Journal of Social Issues, 51*, 155–175.

Mehl, M. R., & Pennebaker, J. W. (2003). The sounds of social life: A psychometric analysis of students' daily social environments and natural conversations. *Journal of Personality and Social Psychology, 84*, 857–870.

Meissner, C. A., & Brigham, J. C. (2001). 30 years of investigating the own-race bias in memory for faces: A meta-analytic review. *Psychology, Public Policy, and Law, 7*, 3–35.

Memon, A., Vrij, A., & Bull, R. (2003). *Psychology and law: Truthfulness, accuracy and credibility* (2nd ed.). London: Wiley.

Mendes, W. B., Blascovich, J., Lickel, B., & Hunter, S. (2002). Challenge and threat during social interaction with white and black men. *Personality and Social Psychology Bulletin, 28*, 939–952.

Merikle, P., & Skanes, H. E. (1992). Subliminal self-help audiotapes: A search for placebo effects. *Journal of Applied Psychology, 77*, 772–776.

Merton, R. (1948). The self-fulfilling prophecy. *Antioch Review, 8*, 193–210.

Messick, D. M., & Cook, K. S. (Eds.) (1983). *Equity theory: Psychological and sociological perspectives*. New York: Praeger.

Messick, D. M., Wilke, H., Brewer, M. B., Kramer, R. M., Zemke, P. E., & Lui, L. (1983). Individual adaptation and structural change as solutions to social dilemmas. *Journal of Personality and Social Psychology, 44*, 294–309.

Meston, C. M., & Frohlich, P. F. (2003). Love at first sight: Partner salience moderates roller-coaster-induced excitation transfer. *Archives of Sexual Behavior, 32*, 537–544.

Mickelson, K. D., Kessler, R. C., & Shaver, P. R. (1997). Adult attachment in a nationally representative sample. *Journal of Personality and Social Psychology, 73*, 1092–1106.

Midlarsky, E., Kahana, E., Corley, R., Nemeroff, R., & Schonbar, R. A. (1999). Altruistic moral judgment among older adults. *International Journal of Aging and Human Development, 49*, 27–41.

Miles, D. R., & Carey, G. (1997). Genetic and environmental architecture on human aggression. *Journal of Personality and Social Psychology, 72*, 207–217.

Miles, J. A., & Greenberg, J. (1993). Using punishment threats to attenuate social loafing effects among swimmers. *Organizational Behavior and Human Decision Processes, 56*, 246–265.

Milgram, S. (1963). Behavioral study of obedience. *Journal of Abnormal and Social Psychology, 67*, 371–378.

Milgram, S. (1970). The experience of living in cities. *Science, 167*, 1461–1468.

Milgram, S. (1974). *Obedience to authority: An experimental view*. New York: Harper & Row.

Milgram, S., Bickman, L., & Berkowitz, L. (1969). Note on the drawing power of crowds of different size. *Journal of Personality and Social Psychology, 13*, 79–82.

Milgram, S., & Sabini, J. (1978). On maintaining urban norms: A field experiment in the subway. In A. Baum, J. E. Singer, & S. Valins (Eds.), *Advances in environmental psychology* (Vol. 1). Hillsdale, NJ: Erlbaum.

Milgram, S., & Toch, H. (1969). Collective behavior: Crowds and social movements. In G. Lindzey & E. Aronson (Eds.), *The handbook of social psychology* (2nd ed., Vol. 4, pp. 507–610). Reading, MA: Addison-Wesley.

Milkie, M. (1999). Social comparisons, reflected appraisals, and mass media: The impact of pervasive beauty images on black and white girls' self concepts. *Social Psychology Quarterly, 62*, 190–210.

Millar, M. (2002). Effects of guilt induction and guilt reduction on door in the face. *Communication Research, 29*, 666–680.

Millar, M. G., & Millar, K. U. (1990). Attitude change as a function of attitude type and argument type. *Journal of Personality and Social Psychology, 59*, 217–228.

Miller, A. G. (1986). *The obedience experiments: A case study of controversy in social science*. New York: Praeger.

Miller, A. G., Gordon, A. K., & Buddie, A. M. (1999). Accounting for evil and cruelty: Is to explain to condone? *Personality and Social Psychology Review, 3*, 254–268.

Miller, A. G., Jones, E. E., & Hinkle, S. (1981). A robust attribution error in the personality domain. *Journal of Experimental Social Psychology, 17*, 587–600.

Miller, C. T. (1984). Self-schemas, gender, and social comparison: A clarification of the related attributes hypothesis. *Journal of Personality and Social Psychology, 46*, 1222–1229.

Miller, C. T., & Myers, A. M. (1998). Compensating for prejudice: How heavyweight people (and others) control outcomes despite prejudice. In J. K. Swim & C. Stangor (Eds.), *Prejudice: The target's perspective* (pp. 191–218). San Diego: Academic Press.

Miller, D. T., & McFarland, C. (1987). Pluralistic ignorance: When similarity is interpreted as dissimilarity. *Journal of Personality and Social Psychology, 53*, 298–305.

Miller, D. T., Monin, B., & Prentice, D. A. (2000). Pluralistic ignorance and inconsistency between private attitudes and public behaviors. In D. J. Terry, M. A. Hogg, & K. M. White (Eds.), *Attitudes, behavior, and social context: The role of norms and group membership* (pp. 95–113). Mahwah, NJ: Erlbaum.

Miller, E. M. (2000). Homosexuality, birth order, and evolution: Toward an equilibrium reproductive economics of homosexuality. *Archives of Sexual Behavior, 29,* 1–34.

Miller, J. G. (1984). Culture and the development of everyday social explanation. *Journal of Personality and Social Psychology, 46,* 961–978.

Miller, M. L., & Thayer, J. F. (1989). On the existence of discrete classes in personality: Is self-monitoring the correct joint to carve? *Journal of Personality and Social Psychology, 57,* 143–155.

Miller, N., & Campbell, D. T. (1959). Recency and primacy in persuasion as a function of the timing of speeches and measurements. *Journal of Abnormal and Social Psychology, 59,* 1–9.

Miller, N., & Carlson, M. (1990). Valid theory-testing meta-analyses further question the negative state relief model of helping. *Psychological Bulletin, 107,* 215–225.

Miller, N. E. (1941). The frustration-aggression hypothesis. *Psychological Review, 48,* 337–342.

Miller, N., Pedersen, W. C., Earleywine, M., & Pollock, V. E. (2003). A theoretical model of triggered displaced aggression. *Personality and Social Psychology Review, 7,* 75–97.

Miller, P. A., & Eisenberg, N. (1988). The relation of empathy to aggressive and externalizing/antisocial behavior. *Psychological Bulletin, 103,* 324–344.

Miller, P. A., Eisenberg, N., Fabes, R. A., & Shell, R. (1996). Relations of moral reasoning and vicarious emotion to young children's prosocial behavior toward peers and adults. *Developmental Psychology, 32,* 210–219.

Miller, T. Q., Smith, T. W., Turner, C. W., Guijarro, M. L., & Hallet, A. J. (1996). A meta-analytic review of research on hostility and physical health. *Psychological Bulletin, 119,* 322–348.

Miller-Loessi, K., & Parker, J. N. (2003). Cross-cultural social psychology. In J. Delamater (Ed.), *Handbooks of sociology and social research* (pp. 529–553). New York: Kluwer.

Miranda, S. M. (1994). Avoidance of groupthink: Meeting management using group support systems. *Small Group Research, 25,* 105–136.

Mita, T. H., Dermer, M., & Knight, J. (1977). Reversed facial images and the mere exposure hypothesis. *Journal of Personality and Social Psychology, 35,* 597–601.

Mitchell, T. L., Haw, R. M., Pfeifer, J. E., & Meissner, C. A. (2005). Racial bias in juror decision-making: A meta-analytic review of defendant treatment. *Law & Human Behavior, 29,* 621–637.

Miyamoto, Y., & Kitayama, S. (2002). Cultural variation in correspondence bias: The critical role of attitude diagnosticity of socially constrained behavior. *Journal of Personality and Social Psychology, 83,* 1239–1248.

Moghaddam, F. M., Taylor, D. M., & Wright, S. C. (1993). *Social psychology in cross-cultural perspective,* New York: W. H. Freeman.

Molitor, F., & Hirsch, K. W. (1994). Children's toleration of real-life aggression after exposure to media violence: A replication of the Drabman and Thomas studies. *Child Study Journal, 24,* 191–207.

Mondschein, E. R., Adolph, K. E., & Tamis-LeMonda, C. S. (2000). Gender bias in mothers' expectations about infant crawling. *Journal of Experimental Child Psychology, 77,* 304–316.

Monin, B., & Miller, D. T. (2001). Moral credentials and the expression of prejudice. *Journal of Personality and Social Psychology, 81,* 33–43.

Monin, B., & Norton, M. I. (2003). Perceptions of a fluid consensus: Uniqueness bias, false consensus, false polarization, and pluralistic ignorance in a water conservation crisis. *Personality and Social Psychology Bulletin, 29,* 559–567.

Montada, L. & M. J. Lerner (Eds.), *Responses to victimizations and belief in a just world: Critical issues in social justice* (pp. 247–269). NY: Plenum.

Monteith, M. J., Ashburn-Nardo, L., Voils, C. I., & Czopp, A. M. (2002). Putting the brakes on prejudice: On the development and operation of cues for control. *Journal of Personality and Social Psychology, 83,* 1029–1050.

Monteith. M. J., Sherman, J. W., & Devine, P. G. (1998). Suppression as a stereotype control strategy. *Personality and Social Psychology Review, 2,* 63–82.

Monteith, M. J., & Voils, C. I. (2001). Exerting control over prejudiced responses. In G. B. Moskowitz (Ed.), *Cognitive social psychology: On the future of social cognition* (pp. 375–388). Mahwah, NJ: Erlbaum.

Montepare, J. M., & McArthur, L. Z. (1988). Impressions of people created by age-related qualities of their gaits. *Journal of Personality and Social Psychology, 55,* 547–556.

Moore, B. S., Underwood, B., & Rosenhan, D. L. (1973). Affect and altruism. *Developmental Psychology, 8,* 99–104.

Moore, T. E. (1982). Subliminal advertising: What you see is what you get. *Journal of Marketing, 46,* 38–47.

Mor, N., & Winquist, J. (2002). Self-focused attention and negative affect: A meta-analysis. *Psychological Bulletin, 128,* 638–662.

Morales, J. R., Cullerton-Sen, C., & Crick, N. R. (2005). Relational aggression and victimization in dyadic peer relationships: Once I ran to you, now I run from you. In S. Fein, G. R. Goethals, & M. J. Sandstrom (Eds.), *Gender and aggression: Interdisciplinary perspectives.* Mahwah, NJ: Erlbaum.

Moran, G., & Comfort, C. (1986). Neither "tentative" nor "fragmentary": Verdict preference of impaneled felony jurors as a function of attitude toward capital punishment. *Journal of Applied Psychology, 71,* 146–155.

Moran, G., & Cutler, B. L. (1991). The prejudicial impact of pretrial publicity. *Journal of Applied Social Psychology, 21,* 345–367.

Moray, N. (1959). Attention in dichotic listening: Affective cues and the influence of instructions. *Quarterly Journal of Experimental Psychology, 11,* 56–60.

Moreland, R. L., & Beach, S. R. (1992). Exposure effects in the classroom: The development of affinity among students. *Journal of Experimental Social Psychology, 28,* 255–276.

Moreland, R. L., Hogg, M. A., & Hains, S. C. (1994). Back to the future: Social psychological research on groups. *Journal of Experimental Social Psychology 30,* 527–555.

Moreland, R. L., & Levine, J. M. (2002). Socialization and trust in work groups. *Group Processes and Intergroup Relations, 5,* 185–201.

Moreland, R. L., & McMinn, J. G. (2004). Entitativity and social integration: Managing beliefs about the reality of groups. In V. Y. Yzerbyt, C. Judd, & O. Corneille (Eds.), *The psychology of group perception: Contributions to the study of homogeneity, entitivity, and essentialism.* Philadelphia: Psychology Press.

Moriarty, D., & McCabe, A. E. (1977). Studies of television and youth sport. In *Ontario Royal Commission on Violence in the Communications Industry report* (Vol. 5). Toronto: Queen's Printer for Ontario.

Moriarty, T. (1975). Crime, commitment, and the responsive bystander: Two field experiments. *Journal of Personality and Social Psychology, 31*, 370–376.

Morris, M. W., & Peng, K. (1994). Culture and cause: American and Chinese attributions for social and physical events. *Journal of Personality and Social Psychology, 67*, 949–971.

Morrongiello, B. A., & Dawber, T. (2000). Mothers' responses to sons and daughters engaging in injury-risk behaviors on a playground: Implications for sex differences in injury rates. *Journal of Experimental Child Psychology, 76*, 89–103.

Morrongiello, B. A., Midgett, C., & Stanton, K. L. (2000). Gender biases in children's appraisals of injury risk and other children's risk-taking behaviors. *Journal of Experimental Child Psychology, 77*, 317–336.

Morse, B. J. (1995). Beyond the Conflict Tactics Scale: Assessing gender differences in partner violence. *Violence and Victims, 10*, 251–272.

Moscovici, S. (1980). Toward a theory of conversion behavior. In L. Berkowitz (Ed.), *Advances in Experimental Social Psychology, 6*, 149–202.

Moscovici, S., Lage, E., & Naffrechoux, M. (1969). Influence of a consistent minority on the responses of a majority in a color perception task. *Sociometry, 32*, 365–380.

Moscovici, S., Mugny, G., & Van Avermaet, E. (Eds.) (1985). *Perspectives on minority influence.* New York: Cambridge University Press.

Moscovici, S., & Personnaz, B. (1991). Studies in social influence VI: Is Lenin orange or red? Imagery and social influence. *European Journal of Social Psychology, 21*, 101–118.

Moscovici, S., & Zavalloni, M. (1969). The group as a polarizer of attitudes. *Journal of Personality and Social Psychology, 12*, 125–135.

Moshavi, S. (2001, July 4). In Japan, a grope-free ride: Female commuters finally get a break from men's feelings. *Boston Globe*, p. A8.

Moskalenko, S., & Heine, S. J. (2003). Watching your troubles away: Television viewing as a stimulus for subjective self-awareness. *Personality and Social Psychology Bulletin, 29*, 76–85.

Moskowitz, G. B. (1996). The mediational effects of attributions and information processing in minority social influence. *British Journal of Social Psychology, 35*, 47–66.

Moskowitz, G. B. (2001). Preconscious control and compensatory cognition. In G. B. Moskowitz (Ed.), *Cognitive social psychology: The Princeton symposium on the legacy and future of social cognition* (pp. 333–358). NJ: Lawrence Erlbaum Associates, Inc.

Moskowitz, G. B., Li, P., & Kirk, E. R. (2004). The implicit volition model: On the preconscious regulation of temporarily adopted goals. In M. P. Zanna (Ed.), *Advances in experimental social psychology.* San Diego, CA: Academic Press.

Mouton, J., Blake, R., & Olmstead, J. (1956). The relationship between frequency of yielding and the disclosure of personal identity. *Journal of Personality, 24*, 339–347.

Mueller, J. H. (1982). Self-awareness and access to material rated as self-descriptive and nondescriptive. *Bulletin of the Psychonomic Society, 19*, 323–326.

Mugny, G. (1982). *The power of minorities.* London: Academic Press.

Mugny, G., & Perez, J. A. (1991). *Social psychology of minority influence.* Cambridge: Cambridge University Press.

Mullen, B. (1983). Operationalizing the effect of the group on the individual: A self-attention perspective. *Journal of Experimental Social Psychology, 19*, 295–322.

Mullen, B. (1985). Strength and immediacy of sources: A meta-analytic evaluation of the forgotten elements of social impact theory. *Journal of Personality and Social Psychology, 48*, 1458–1466.

Mullen, B. (1986). Atrocity as a function of lynch mob composition: A self-attention perspective. *Personality and Social Psychology Bulletin, 12*, 187–197.

Mullen, B., Anthony, T., Salas, E., & Driskell, J. E. (1994). Group cohesiveness and quality of decision making: An integration of tests of the groupthink hypothesis. *Small Group Research, 25*, 189–204.

Mullen, B., & Copper, C. (1994). The relation between group cohesiveness and performance: An integration. *Psychological Bulletin, 115*, 210–227.

Mullen, B., Dovidio, J. F., Johnson, C., & Copper, C. (1992). In-group and out-group differences in social projection. *Journal of Experimental Social Psychology, 28*, 422–440.

Mullen, B., Johnson, C., & Salas, E. (1991). Productivity loss in brainstorming groups: A meta-analytic integration. *Basic and Applied Social Psychology, 12*, 3–23.

Muraven, M., & Baumeister, R. F. (1998). Self-control as a limited resource: Regulatory depletion patterns. *Journal of Personality and Social Psychology, 74*, 774–789.

Muraven, M., & Baumeister, R. F. (2000). Self-regulation and depletion of limited resources: Does self-control resemble a muscle? *Psychological Bulletin, 126*, 247–259.

Murray, C. B., Kaiser, R., & Taylor, S. (1997). The O. J. Simpson verdict: Predictors of beliefs about innocence or guilt. *Journal of Social Issues, 53*, 455–475.

Murray, S. L., Griffin, D. W., Rose, P., & Bellavia, G. M. (2003). Calibrating the sociometer: The relational contingencies of self-esteem. *Journal of Personality and Social Psychology, 85*, 63–84.

Murray, S. L., & Holmes, J. G. (1999). The (mental) ties that bind: Cognitive structures that predict relationship resilience. *Journal of Personality and Social Psychology, 77*, 1228–1244.

Murray, S. L., Holmes, J. G., & Griffin, D. W. (1996). The benefits of positive illusions: Idealization and the construction of satisfaction in close relationships. *Journal of Personality and Social Psychology, 70*, 79–98.

Murstein, B. I. (1972). Physical attractiveness and marital choice. *Journal of Personality and Social Psychology, 22*, 8–12.

Murstein, B. I. (1986). *Paths to marriage.* Beverly Hills, CA: Sage.

Murstein, B. I. (1987). A clarification and extension of the SVR theory of dyadic pairing. *Journal of Marriage and the Family, 49*, 929–933.

Mussweiler, T., & Ruter, K. (2003). What friends are for! The use of routine standards in social comparison. *Journal of Personality and Social Psychology, 85*, 467–481.

Mussweiler, T., & Strack, F. (2000). The "relative self": Informational and judgmental consequences of comparative self-evaluation. *Journal of Personality and Social Psychology, 79*, 23–38.

Myers, D. G., & Bishop, G. D. (1970). Discussion effects on racial attitudes. *Science, 169*, 778–779.

Myers, D. G., & Lamm, H. (1976). The group polarization phenomenon. *Psychological Bulletin, 83*, 602–627.

Nabi, R. L., & Sullivan, J. L. (2001). Does television viewing relate to engagement in protective action against crime? A cultivation analysis from a theory of reasoned action perspective. *Communication Research, 28,* 802–825.

Nacoste, R. W. (1994). If empowerment is the goal . . . : Affirmative action and social interaction. *Basic and Applied Social Psychology, 15,* 87–112.

Nadler, A., & Fisher, J. D. (1986). The role of threat to self-esteem and perceived control in recipient reactions to help: Theory development and empirical validation. In L. Berkowitz (Ed.), *Advances in experimental social psychology* (Vol. 19, pp. 81–122). New York: Academic Press.

Nando Times, (1997, September 5). Good Samaritan Laws, pp. 1–2.

Narby, D. J., Cutler, B. L., & Moran, G. (1993). A meta-analysis of the association between authoritarianism and jurors' perceptions of defendant culpability. *Journal of Applied Psychology, 78,* 34–42.

National Law Journal (1990). Rock group not liable for deaths (September 10), p. 33.

National Parole Board of Canada (2004). *Performance Monitoring Report for 2004.*

National Television Violence Study, Vol. 2 (1998). Thousand Oaks, CA: Sage.

Neighbors, C., Dillard, A. J., Lewis, M. A., Bergstrom, R. L., & Neil, T. A. (2006). Normative misperceptions and temporal precedence of perceived norms and drinking. *Journal of Studies on Alcohol, 67,* 290–299.

Nemeth, C. (1986). Differential contributions of majority and minority influence. *Psychological Review, 93,* 23–32.

Nemeth, C., & Brilmayer, A. G. (1987). Negotiation versus influence. *European Journal of Social Psychology, 17,* 45–56.

Nemeth, C., Endicott, J., & Wachtler, J. (1976). From the '50s to the '70s: Women in jury deliberations. *Sociometry, 39,* 38–56.

Nemeth, C., & Kwan, J. (1987). Minority influence, divergent thinking, and detection of correct solutions. *Journal of Applied Social Psychology, 17,* 788–799.

Nemeth, C., Mayseless, O., Sherman, J., & Brown, Y. (1990). Exposure to dissent and recall of information. *Journal of Personality and Social Psychology, 58,* 429–437.

Nemeth, C. J., & Nemeth-Brown, B. (2003). Better than individuals? The potential benefits of dissent and diversity for group creativity. In P. B. Paulus & B. A. Nijstad (Eds.), *Group creativity: Innovation through collaboration* (pp. 63–84). New York: Oxford University.

Neuberg, S. L. (1989). The goal of forming accurate impressions during social interactions: Attenuating the impact of negative expectancies. *Journal of Personality and Social Psychology, 56,* 374–386.

Neumann, R., & Strack, F. (2000). "Mood contagion": The automatic transfer of mood between persons. *Journal of Personality and Social Psychology, 79,* 211–223.

Newby-Clark, I. R., & Ross, M. (2003). Conceiving the past and future. *Personality and Social Psychology Bulletin, 29,* 807–818.

Newcomb, T. M. (1961). *The acquaintance process.* New York: Holt, Rinehart and Winston.

Newman, C. (2000, January). The enigma of beauty. *National Geographic,* pp. 94–121.

Newman, L. S. (1993). How individualists interpret behavior: Idiocentrism and spontaneous trait inference. *Social Cognition, 11,* 243–269.

Newman, L. S., & Uleman, J. S. (1989). Spontaneous trait inference. In J. S. Uleman & J. A. Bargh (Eds.), *Unintended thought* (pp. 155–188). New York: Guilford.

Newtson, D. (1974). Dispositional inference from effects of actions: Effects chosen and effects foregone. *Journal of Experimental Social Psychology, 10,* 487–496.

Newtson, D., Hairfield, J., Bloomingdale, J., & Cutino, S. (1987). The structure of action and interaction. *Social Cognition, 5,* 191–237.

Nezlek, J. B. (2003). Using multilevel random coefficient modeling to analyze social interaction diary data. *Journal of Social and Personal Relationships, 20,* 437–469.

Nezlek, J. B., & Leary, M. R. (2002). Individual differences in self-presentational motives in daily social interaction. *Personality and Social Psychology Bulletin, 28,* 211–223.

Niedermeier, K. E., Horowitz, I. A., & Kerr, N. L. (1999). Informing jurors of their nullification power: A route to a just verdict or judicial chaos? *Law and Human Behavior, 23,* 331–351.

Nier, J. A., Gaertner, S. L., Dovidio, J. F., Banker, B. S., Ward, C. M., & Rust, M. C. (2001). Changing interracial evaluations and behavior: The effects of a common group identity. *Group Processes and Intergroup Relations, 4,* 299–316.

Nieva, V. F., & Gutek, B. A. (1981). *Women and work: A psychological perspective.* New York: Praeger.

Nijstad, B. A., Diehl, M., & Stroebe, W. (2003). Cognitive stimulation and interference in idea-generating groups. In P. B. Paulus & B. A. Nijstad (Eds.), *Group creativity: Innovation through collaboration* (pp. 137–159). New York: Oxford University Press.

Nisbett, R. E. (2003). *The geography of thought: How Asians and Westerners think differently . . . and why.* New York: Free Press.

Nisbett, R. E., & Cohen, D. (1996). *Culture of honor: The psychology of violence in the South.* Boulder, CO: Westview.

Nisbett, R. E., Fong, G. T., Lehman, D. R., & Cheng, P.W. (1987). Teaching reasoning. *Science, 238,* 625–631.

Nisbett, R. E., & Ross, L. (1980). *Human inference: Strategies and shortcomings of social judgment.* Englewood Cliffs, NJ: Prentice-Hall.

Nisbett, R. E., & Wilson, T. D. (1977). Telling more than we can know: Verbal reports on mental processes. *Psychological Review, 84,* 231–259.

Noel, J. G., Wann, D. L., & Branscombe, N. R. (1995). Peripheral ingroup membership status and public negativity toward outgroups. *Journal of Personality and Social Psychology, 68,* 127–137.

Norenzayan, A., & Nisbett, R.E. (2000). Culture and causal cognition. *Current Directions in Psychological Science, 9,* 132–135.

North, A. C., Hargreaves, D. J., & McKendrick, J. (1999). The influence of in-store music on wine selections. *Journal of Applied Psychology, 84,* 271–276.

North, A. C., Linley, A., & Hargreaves, D. J. (2000). Social loafing in a co-operative classroom task. *Educational Psychology, 20,* 389–392.

Norton, K. I., Olds, T. S., Olive, S., & Dank, S. (1996). Ken and Barbie at life size. *Sex Roles, 34,* 287–294.

Norton, M. I., Monin, B., Cooper, J., & Hogg, M. A. (2003). Vicarious dissonance: Attitude change from the inconsistency of others. *Journal of Personality and Social Psychology, 85,* 47–62.

Nosek, B. (2003). Personal communication.

Nosek, B. A., & Banaji, M. R. (2001). The Go/No-go Association Task. *Social Cognition, 19,* 625–666.

Nosek, B. A., Banaji, M. R., & Greenwald, A. G. (2002). Harvesting implicit attitudes and stereotype data from the Implicit Association Test website. *Group Dynamics, 6,* 101–115.

Nowak, M., & Sigmund, K. (1993). A strategy of win-stay, lose-shift that outperforms tit-for-tat in the Prisoner's Dilemma game. *Nature, 364,* 56–58.

O'Brien, L. T., & Crandall, C. S. (2003). Stereotype threat and arousal: Effects on women's math performance. *Personality and Social Psychology Bulletin, 29,* 782–789.

Ochsner, K. N., & Lieberman, M. D. (2001). The emergence of social cognitive neruroscience. *American Psychologist, 56,* 717–734.

O'Connor, S. C., & Rosenblood, L. K. (1996). Affiliation motivation in everyday experience: A theoretical comparison. *Journal of Personality and Social Psychology, 70,* 513–522.

O'Keefe, D. J., & Figge, M. (1997). A guilt-based explanation of the door-in-the-face influence strategy. *Human Communication Research, 42,* 64–81.

O'Leary, K. D., Barling, J., Arias, I., Rosenbaum, A., Malone, J., & Tyree, A. (1989). Prevalence and stability of physical aggression between spouses: A longitudinal analysis. *Journal of Consulting and Clinical Psychology, 57,* 263–268.

O'Leary, K. D., & Smith, D. A. (1991). Marital interaction. *Annual Review of Psychology, 42,* 191–212.

O'Leary-Kelly, A. M., Martocchio, J. J., & Frink, D. D. (1994). A review of the influence of group goals on group performance. *Academy of Management Journal, 37,* 1285–1301.

Oliver, M. G., & Hyde, J. S. (1993). Gender differences in sexuality: A meta-analysis. *Psychological Bulletin, 114,* 29–51.

Olweus, D. (2003). Social problems in school. In A. Slater & G. Bremmer (Eds.), *An introduction to developmental psychology* (pp. 434–454). Malden, MA: Blackwell.

O'Neill, A. M., Green, M., & Cuadros, P. (1996, September 2). *People,* p. 72.

Oddone-Paolucci, E., Genuis, M., & Violato, C. (2000). A meta-analysis of the published research on the effects of pornography. In C. Violato & E. Oddone-Paolucci (Eds.), *The changing family and child development* (pp. 48–59). Aldershot, England: Ashgate.

Oesterman, K., Bjorkqvist, K., Lagerspetz, K. M. J., Kaukiainen, A., Landau, S. F., Fraczek, A., & Caprara, G. V. (1998). Cross-cultural evidence of female indirect aggression. *Aggressive Behavior, 24,* 1–8.

Ofshe, R., & Watters, E. (1994). *Making monsters: False memories, psychotherapy, and sexual hysteria.* New York: Charles Scribner's Sons.

Ogilvy, D. (1985). *Ogilvy on advertising.* New York: Vintage Books.

Ogloff, J. R. P., & Vidmar, N. (1994). The impact of pretrial publicity on jurors: A study to compare the relative effects of television and print media in a child sex abuse case. *Law and Human Behavior, 18,* 507–525.

Ohbuchi, K., Kameda, M., & Agarie, N. (1989). Apology as aggression control: Its role in mediating appraisal of and response to harm. *Journal of Personality and Social Psychology, 56,* 219–227.

Olczak, P. V., Kaplan, M. F., & Penrod, S. (1991). Attorneys' lay psychology and its effectiveness in selecting jurors: Three empirical studies. *Journal of Social Behavior and Personality, 6,* 431–452.

Olson, J. M., Vernon, P. A., Harris, J. A., & Jang, K. L. (2001). The heritability of attitudes: A study of twins. *Journal of Personality and Social Psychology,* in press.

Olson, M. (1965). *The logic of collective action.* Cambridge, MA: Harvard University Press.

Olweus, D. (1979). Stability of aggression patterns in males: A review. *Psychological Bulletin, 86,* 852–875.

Omarzu, J. (2000). A disclosure decision model: Determining how and when individuals will self-disclose. *Personality and Social Psychology Review, 4,* 174–185.

Omoto, A. M., & Snyder, M. (1995). Sustained helping without obligation: Motivation, longevity of service, and perceived attitude change among AIDS volunteers. *Journal of Personality and Social Psychology, 68,* 671–686.

Operario, D., & Fiske, S. T. (2001). Effects of trait dominance on powerholders' judgments of subordinates. *Social Cognition, 19,* 161–180.

Opotow, S. (2001). Reconciliation in times of impunity: Challenges for social justice. *Social Justice Research, 14,* 149–170.

Oquendo, M. A., & Mann, J. J. (2000). The biology of impulsivity and suicidality. *Psychiatric Clinics of North America, 23,* 11–25.

Orbell, J., Dawes, R., & Schwartz-Shea, P. (1994). Trust, social categories, and individuals: The case of gender. *Motivation and Emotion, 18,* 109–128.

Ore, T. E. (2000). *The social construction of difference and inequality: Race, gender, and sexuality.* Mountain View, CA: Mayfield.

Orengo, C. A., Kunik, M. E., Ghusn, H., & Yudofsky, S. C. (1997). Correlation of testosterone with aggression in demented elderly men. *Journal of Nervous and Mental Disease, 185,* 349–351.

Orenstein, P. (1994). *Schoolgirls: Young women, self-esteem, and the confidence gap.* New York: Anchor Books.

Orne, M. T. (1962). On the social psychology of the psychological experiment: With particular reference to demand characteristics and their implications. *American Psychologist, 17,* 776–783.

Ortmann, A., & Hertwig, R. (1997). Is deception acceptable? *American Psychologist, 52,* 746–747.

Orwell, G. (1942). Looking back on the Spanish War. In S. Orwell & I. Angus (Eds.), *The collected essays, journalism and letters of George Orwell: Vol. 2. My country right or left, 1940–1943* (pp. 249–267). New York: Harcourt, Brace & World. (Reprinted in 1968)

Osbaldiston, R., & Sheldon, K. M. (2002). Social dilemmas and sustainability: Promoting peoples' motivation to "cooperate with the future." In P. Schmuck & W. P. Schultz (Eds.), *Psychology of sustainable development* (pp. 37–57). Dordrecht, Netherlands: Kluwer Academic.

Osborn, A. F. (1953). *Applied imagination.* New York: Scribner.

Osgood, C. E. (1962). *An alternative to war or surrender.* Urbana: University of Illinois Press.

Ostrom, T. M., & Sedikides, C. (1992). Out-group homogeneity effects in natural and minimal groups. *Psychological Bulletin, 112,* 536–552.

Oswald, D. L., & Harvey, R. D. (2000–2001). Hostile environments, stereotype threat, and math performance among undergraduate women. *Current Psychology: Developmental, Learning, Personality, Social, 19,* 338–356.

Otto, A. L., Penrod, S. D., & Dexter, H. R. (1994). The biasing impact of pretrial publicity on juror judgments. *Law and Human Behavior, 18,* 453–469.

Owens, L., Shute, R., & Slee, P. (2000). "Guess what I just heard!": Indirect aggression among teenage girls in Australia. *Aggressive Behavior, 26,* 67–83.

Oyserman, D., Coon, H. M., & Kemmelmeier, M. (2002). Rethinking individualism and collectivism: Evaluation of theoretical assumptions and meta-analyses. *Psychological Bulletin, 128,* 3–72.

Oyserman, D., & Lauffer, A. (2002). Examining the implications of cultural frames on social movements and group actions. In L. S. Newman & R. Erber (Ed.), *Understanding genocide: The social psychology of the Holocaust* (pp. 162–187). London: Oxford University Press.

Packard, V. (1957). *The hidden persuaders.* New York: Pocket Books.

Páez, D., Martinez-Taboada, C., Arrospide, J. J., Insua, P., & Ayestaran, S. (1998). Constructing social identity: The role of status, collective values, collective self-esteem, perception and social behaviour. In S. Worchel, J. F. Morales, D. Páez, & J. C. Deschemps (Eds.), *Social identity: International perspectives* (pp. 211–229). London: Sage.

Paik, H., & Comstock, G. (1994). The effects of television violence on antisocial behavior: A meta-analysis. *Communication Research, 21,* 516–546.

Pallak, S. R. (1983). Salience of a communicator's physical attractiveness and persuasion: A heuristic versus systematic processing interpretation. *Social Cognition, 2,* 158–170.

Panee, C. D., & Ballard, M. E. (2002). High versus low aggressive priming during video-game training: Effects on violent action during game play, hostility, heart rate, and blood pressure. *Journal of Applied Social Psychology, 32,* 2458–2474.

Paquette, G., & de Guise, J. (2002). *La violence à la télévision canadienne, 1993–1998: Analyse des émissions de fiction diffusées par les six réseaux generalists.* Centre for Media Studies, Laval University.

Park, B. (1986). A method for studying the development of impressions of real people. *Journal of Personality and Social Psychology, 51,* 907–917.

Parkinson, S. (1994). Scientific or ethical quality? *Psychological Science, 5,* 137–138.

Parks, C. D. (1994). The predictive ability of social values in resource dilemmas and public goods games. *Personality and Social Psychology Bulletin, 20,* 431–438.

Parks, C. D., Sanna, L. J., & Posey, D. C. (2003). Retrospection in social dilemmas: How thinking about the past affects future cooperation. *Journal of Personality and Social Psychology, 84,* 988–996.

Partridge, A., & Eldridge, W. B. (1974). *The second circuit sentencing study: A report to the judges of the second circuit.* Washington, DC: Federal Judicial Center.

Patterson, G. R. (1984). Siblings: Fellow travelers in coercive family processes. In R. J. Blanchard & D. C. Blanchard (Eds.), *Advances in the study of aggression* (Vol. 1, pp. 173–215). New York: Academic Press.

Patterson, M. L. (1983). *Nonverbal behavior: A functional perspective.* New York: Springer-Verlag.

Paulhus, D. L. (1998). Interpersonal and intrapsychic adaptiveness of trait self-enhancement: A mixed blessing? *Journal of Personality and Social Psychology, 74,* 1197–1208.

Paulhus, D., Graf, P., & Van Selst, M. (1989). Attentional load increases the positivity of self-presentation. *Social Cognition, 7,* 389–400.

Paulus, P. B. (2000). Groups, teams, and creativity: The creative potential of idea-generating groups. *Applied Psychology: An International Review, 49,* 237–262.

Paulus, P. B., & Brown, V. R. (2003). Enhancing ideational creativity in groups: Lessons from research on brainstorming. In P. B. Paulus & B. A. Nijstad (Eds.), *Group creativity: Innovation through collaboration* (pp. 110–136). New York: Oxford University Press.

Paulus, P. B., Dzindolet, M. T., Poletes, G., & Camacho, L. M. (1993). Perception of performance in group brainstorming: The illusion of group productivity. *Personality and Social Psychology Bulletin, 19,* 78–89.

Paulus, P. B., Larey, T. S., Putman, V. L., & Leggett, K. L. (1996). Social influence processes in computer brainstorming. *Basic and Applied Social Psychology, 18,* 3–14.

Paulus, P. B., & Paulus, L. E. (1997). Implications of research on group brainstorming for gifted education. *Roeper Review, 19,* 225–229.

Pavitt, C. (1994). Another view of group polarizing: The "reasons for" one-sided oral argumentation. *Communication Research, 21,* 625–642.

Pawlowski, B., Dunbar, R. I. M., & Lipowicz, A. (2000). Evolutionary fitness: Tall men have more reproductive success. *Nature, 403,* 156.

Pedersen, W. C., Gonzales, C., & Miller, N. (2000). The moderating effect of trivial triggering provocation on displaced aggression. *Journal of Personality and Social Psychology, 78,* 913–927.

Pedersen, W. C., Miller, L. C., Putch-Bhagavatula, A. D., & Yang, Y. (2002). Evolved sex differences in the number of partners desired? The long and the short of it. *Psychological Science, 13,* 157–161.

Peek, C. W., Fischer, J. L., & Kidwell, J. S. (1985). Teenage violence toward parents: A neglected dimension of family violence. *Journal of Marriage and the Family, 47,* 1051–1058.

Pelham, B. W. (1995). Self-investment and self-esteem: Evidence for a Jamesian model of self-worth. *Journal of Personality and Social Psychology, 69,* 1141–1150.

Pelham, B.W., Mirenberg, M.C., & Jones, J.T. (2002). Why Susie sells seashells by the seashore: Implicit egotism and major life decisions. *Journal of Personality and Social Psychology, 82,* 469–487.

Pelham, B. W., & Swann, W. B., Jr. (1989). From self-conceptions to self-worth: The sources and structure of self-esteem. *Journal of Personality and Social Psychology, 57,* 672–680.

Pendry, L. F., & Macrae, C. N. (1994). Stereotypes and mental life: The case of the motivated but thwarted tactician. *Journal of Experimental Social Psychology, 30,* 303–325.

Pendry, L. F., & Macrae, C. N. (1996). What the disinterested perceiver overlooks: Goal-directed social categorization. *Personality and Social Psychology Bulletin, 22,* 249–256.

Peng, K., & Knowles, E. D. (2003). Culture, education, and the attribution of physical causality. *Personality and Social Psychology Bulletin, 29,* 1272–1284.

Pennebaker, J. W. (1997). Writing about emotional experiences as a therapeutic process. *Psychological Science, 8,* 162–166.

Pennebaker, J. W., Colder, M., & Sharp, L. K. (1990). Accelerating the coping process. *Journal of Personality and Social Psychology, 58,* 528–537.

Pennebaker, J. W., Dyer, M. A., Caulkins, R. J., Litowitz, D. L., Ackreman, P. L., Anderson, D. B., & McGraw, K. M. (1979). Don't the girls get prettier at closing time: A country and western application to psychology. *Personality and Social Psychology Bulletin, 5*, 122–125.

Penner, L. A., & Finkelstein, M. A. (1998). Dispositional and structural determinants of volunteerism. *Journal of Personality and Social Psychology, 74*, 525–537.

Penner, L. A., Fritzsche, B. A., Craiger, J. P., & Freifeld, T. S. (1995). Measuring the prosocial personality. In J. Butcher & C. Spielberger (Eds.), *Advances in personality assessment* (Vol. 10, pp. 147–163). Hillsdale, NJ: Erlbaum.

Pennington, N., & Hastie, R. (1992). Explaining the evidence: Tests of the story model for juror decision making. *Journal of Personality and Social Psychology, 62*, 189–206.

Penrod, S. D., & Cutler, B. (1995). Witness confidence and witness accuracy: Assessing their forensic relation. *Psychology, Public Policy, and Law, 1*, 817–845.

People (1996, December 30). She gave a helping hand to a distant—very distant—relation. p. 66.

Peplau, L. A. (2003). Human sexuality: How do men and women differ? *Current Directions in Psychological Science, 12*, 37–40.

Peplau, L. A., Garnets, L. D., Spalding, L. R., Conley, T. D., & Veniegas, R. C. (1998). A critique of Bem's "Exotic becomes erotic" theory of sexual orientation. *Psychogical Review, 105*, 387–394.

Peplau, L. A., & Perlman, D. (Eds.) (1982). *Loneliness: A sourcebook of current theory, research, and therapy.* New York: Wiley.

Pepler, D. J., & Craig, W. M. (1995). A peek behind the fence: Naturalistic observations of aggressive children with remote audiovisual recording. *Developmental Psychology, 31*, 548–553.

Perdue, C. W., Dovidio, J. F., Gurtman, M. B., & Tyler, R. B. (1990). Us and them: Social categorization and the process of intergroup bias. *Journal of Personality and Social Psychology, 59*, 475–486.

Petersen, L. E., & Blank, H. (2003). Ingroup bias in the minimal group paradigm shown by three-person groups with high or low state self-esteem. *European Journal of Social Psychology, 33*, 149–162.

Peterson, K. S. (1999, September 8). Bullies, victims grow into roles that can last a lifetime. *USA Today*, p. 7D.

Peterson, R. S., Owens, P. D., Tetlock, P. E., Fan, E. T., & Martorana, P. (1998). Group dynamics in top management teams: Groupthink, vigilance, and alternative models of organizational failure and success. *Organizational Behavior and Human Decision Processes, 73*, 272–305.

Pettigrew, T. F. (1958). Personality and sociocultural factors in intergroup attitudes: A cross-national comparison. *Journal of Conflict Resolution, 2*, 29–42.

Pettigrew, T. F. (1998a). Intergroup contact theory. *Annual Review of Psychology, 49*, 65–85.

Pettigrew, T. F. (1998b). Reactions toward the new minorities of Western Europe. *Annual Review of Sociology, 24*, 77–103.

Pettigrew, T. F., & Martin, J. (1987). Shaping the organizational context for black American inclusion. *Journal of Social Issues, 43*, 41–78.

Pettigrew, T. F., & Meertens, R. W. (1995). Subtle and blatant prejudice in western Europe. *European Journal of Social Psychology, 25*, 57–75.

Pettigrew, T. F., & Tropp, L. R. (2000). Does intergroup contact reduce prejudice: Recent meta-analytic findings. In S. Oskamp (Ed.), *Reducing prejudice and discrimination: The Claremont symposium on applied social psychology* (pp. 93–114). Mahwah, NJ: Erlbaum.

Petty, R. E., & Cacioppo, J. T. (1983). The role of bodily responses in attitude measurement and change. In J. Cacioppo & R. Petty (Eds.), *Social psychophysiology: A sourcebook* (pp. 51–101). New York: Guilford.

Petty, R. E., & Cacioppo, J. T. (1984). The effects of involvement on response to argument quantity and quality: Central and peripheral routes to persuasion. *Journal of Personality and Social Psychology, 46*, 69–81.

Petty, R. E., & Cacioppo, J. T. (1986). *Communication and persuasion: Central and peripheral routes to attitude change.* New York: Springer-Verlag.

Petty, R. E., Cacioppo, J. T., & Goldman, R. (1981). Personal involvement as a determinant of argument-based persuasion. *Journal of Personality and Social Psychology, 41*, 847–855.

Petty, R. E., & Chaiken, S. (Eds.) (2004). *Key readings in attitudes and persuasion.* London: Taylor & Francis.

Petty, R. E., & Krosnick, J. A. (Eds.) (1995). *Attitude strength: Antecedents and consequences.* Mahwah, NJ: Erlbaum.

Petty, R. E., Schumann, D. W., Richman, S. A., & Strathman, A. J. (1993). Positive mood and persuasion: Different roles for affect under high-and low-elaboration conditions. *Journal of Personality and Social Psychology, 64*, 5–20.

Petty, R. E., & Wegener, D. T. (1999). The Elaboration Likelihood Model: Current status and controversies. In S. Chaiken & Y. Trope (Eds.), *Dual-process theories in social psychology* (pp. 41–72). New York: Guilford.

Petty, R. E., Wegener, D. T., & Fabrigar, L. R. (1997). Attitudes and attitude change. *Annual Review of Psychology, 48*, 609–647.

Petty, R. E., Wegener, D. T., & White, P. (1998). Flexible correction processes in persuasion. *Social Cognition, 16*, 93–113.

Pezdek, K., Blandon-Gitlin, I., & Moore, C. (2003). Children's face recognition memory: More evidence for the cross-race effect. *Journal of Applied Psychology, 88*, 760–763.

Pfau, M., Kenski, H. C., Nitz, M., & Sorenson, J. (1990). Efficacy of inoculation strategies in promoting resistance to political attack messages: Application to direct mail. *Communication Monographs, 57*, 25–43.

Phelps, E. A., O'Connor, K. J., Cunningham, W. A., Funayama, E. S., Gatenby, J. C., Gore, J. C., & Banaji, M. R. (2000). Performance on indirect measures of race evaluation predicts amygdala activation. *Journal of Cognitive Neuroscience, 12*, 729–738

Pickel, K. L. (1995). Inducing jurors to disregard inadmissible evidence: A legal explanation does not help. *Law and Human Behavior, 19*, 407–424.

Pickel, K. L. (1999). The influence of context on the "weapon focus" effect. *Law and Human Behavior, 23*, 299–311.

Pickett, C. L., & Brewer, M. B. (2001). Assimilation and differentiation needs as motivational determinants of perceived in-group and out-group homogeneity. *Journal of Experimental Social Psychology, 37*, 341–348.

Pihl, R. O., Lau, M. L., & Assaad, J. M. (1997). Aggressive disposition, alcohol, and aggression. *Aggressive Behavior, 23*, 11–18.

Piliavin, I. M., Piliavin, J. A., & Rodin, J. (1975). Costs, diffusion, and the stigmatized victim. *Journal of Personality and Social Psychology, 32*, 429–438.

Piliavin, J. A. (2003). Doing well by doing good: Benefits for the benefactor. In C. L. M. Keyes & J. Haidt (Eds.), *Flourishing: Positive psychology and the life well-lived* (pp. 227–247). Washington, DC: American Psychological Association.

Piliavin, J. A., & Callero, P. L. (1991). *Giving blood: The development of an altruistic identity.* Baltimore: Johns Hopkins.

Piliavin, J. A., Dovidio, J. F., Gaertner, S. L., & Clark, R. D., III. (1981). *Emergency intervention.* New York: Academic Press.

Piliavin, J. A., Grube, J. A., & Callero, P. L. (2002). Role as a resource for action in public service. *Journal of Social Issues, 58,* 469–485.

Pinderhughes, E. E., Dodge, K. A., Bates, J. E.. Pettit, G. S., & Zelli, A. (2000). Discipline responses: Influences of parents' socioeconomic status, ethnicity, beliefs about parenting, stress, and cognitive-emotional processes. *Journal of Family Psychology, 14,* 380–400.

Pittman, T. S. (1975). Attribution of arousal as a mediator of dissonance reduction. *Journal of Experimental Social Psychology, 11,* 53–63.

Pittman, T. S., & Heller, J. F. (1987). Social motivation. *Annual Review of Psychology, 38,* 461–489.

Plaks, J. E., & Higgins, E. T. (2000). Pragmatic use of stereotyping in teamwork: Social loafing and compensation as a function of inferred partner-situation fit. *Journal of Personality and Social Psychology, 79,* 962–974.

Plant, E. A., & Devine, P. G. (1998). Internal and external motivation to respond without prejudice. *Journal of Personality and Social Psychology, 75,* 811–832.

Plant, E. A., & Devine, P. G. (2003). The antecedents and implications of interracial anxiety. *Personality and Social Psychology Bulletin, 29,* 790–801.

Plant, E. A., Devine, P. G., & Brazy, P. C. (2003). The bogus pipeline and motivations to respond without prejudice: Revisiting the fading and faking of racial prejudice. *Group Processes and Intergroup Relations, 6,* 187–200.

Polivy, J., Garner, D. M., & Garfinkel, P. E. (1986). Causes and consequences of the current preference for thin female physiques. In C. P. Herman, M. P. Zanna, & E. T. Higgins (Eds.), *The Ontario symposium: Vol. 3. Physical appearance, stigma, and social behavior* (pp. 89–112). Hillsdale, NJ: Erlbaum.

Pontari, B. A., & Schlenker, B. R. (2000). The influence of cognitive load on self-presentation: Can cognitive busyness help as well as harm social performance? *Journal of Personality and Social Psychology, 78,* 1092–1108.

Poole, D. A., & Lamb, M. E. (1998). *Investigative interviews of children: A guide for helping professionals.* Washington, DC: American Psychological Association.

Poole, D. A., & White, L. T. (1991). Effects of question repetition on the eyewitness testimony of children and adults. *Developmental Psychology, 27,* 975–986.

Poole, D., & Lindsay, D. S. (2001). Children's eyewitness reports after exposure to misinformation from parents. *Journal of Experimental Psychology: Applied, 7,* 27–50.

Pope, H. G., Jr., Phillips, K. A., & Olivardia, R. (2000). *The Adonis complex: The secret crisis of male body obsession.* New York: Free Press.

Poppen, P. J., & Segal, N. J. (1988). The influence of sex and sex role orientation on sexual coercion. *Sex Roles, 19,* 689–701.

Posavac, H. D., Posavac, S. S., & Posavac, E. J. (1998). Exposure to media images of female attractiveness and concern with body weight among young women. *Sex Roles, 38,* 187–201.

Postmes, T., & Lea, M. (2000). Social processes and group decision making: Anonymity in group decision support systems. *Ergonomics, 43,* 1252–1274.

Postmes, T., & Spears, R. (2002). Behavior online: Does anonymous computer communication reduce gender inequality? *Personality and Social Psychology Bulletin, 28,* 1073–1083.

Postmes, T., Spears, R., & Cihangir, S. (2001). Quality of decision making and group norms. *Journal of Personality and Social Psychology, 80,* 918–930.

Povinelli, D. J., Gallup, G. G. Jr., Eddy, T. J., Bierschwale, D. T., Engstrom, M. C., Perilloux, H. K., & Toxopeus, I. B. (1997). Chimpanzees recognize themselves in mirrors. *Animal Behaviour, 53,* 1083–1088.

Powell, M. C., & Fazio, R. M. (1984). Attitude accessibility as a function of repeated attitudinal expression. *Personality and Social Psychology Bulletin, 10,* 139–148.

Powlishta, K. K. (1995). Intergroup processes in childhood: Social categorization and sex role development. *Developmental Psychology, 31,* 781–788.

Pozzulo, J.D., & Balfour, J. (2006). The impact of change in appearance on children's eyewitness identification accuracy: Comparing simultaneous and elimination lineup procedures. *Legal and Criminological Psychology, 11,* 25–34.

Prapavessis, H., & Carron, A. V. (1997). Sacrifice, cohesion, and conformity to norms in sport teams. *Group Dynamics, 1,* 231–240.

Pratkanis, A. R. (1992). The cargo-cult science of subliminal persuasion. *Skeptical Inquirer, 16,* 260–272.

Pratkanis, A., & Aronson, E. (1992). *Age of propaganda: The everyday use and abuse of persuasion.* San Francisco: Freeman.

Pratkanis, A. R., Greenwald, A. G., Leippe, M. R., & Baumgardner, M. H. (1988). In search of reliable persuasion effects: III. The sleeper effect is dead. Long live the sleeper effect. *Journal of Personality and Social Psychology, 54,* 203–218.

Pratkanis, A. R., & Turner, M. E. (1994). Nine principles of successful affirmative action: Mr. Branch Rickey, Mr. Jackie Robinson, and the integration of baseball. *Nine: A Journal of Baseball History and Social Policy Perspectives, 3,* 36–65.

Pratto, F. (2002). Integrating experimental and social constructivist social psychology: Some of us are already doing it. *Personality and Social Psychology Review, 6,* 194–198.

Pratto, F., & John, O. P. (1991). Automatic vigilance: The attention-grabbing power of negative social information. *Journal of Personality and Social Psychology, 61,* 380–391.

Pratto, F., Liu, J. H., Levin, S., Sidanius, J., Shih, M., Bachrach, H., & Hegarty, P. (2000). Social dominance orientation and the legitimization of inequality across cultures. *Journal of Cross Cultural Psychology, 31,* 369–409.

Prentice, D. A., & Carranza, E. (2002). What women should be, shouldn't be, are allowed to be, and don't have to be: The contents of prescriptive gender stereotypes. *Psychology of Women Quarterly, 26,* 269–281.

Prentice, D. A., & Miller, D. T. (1996). Pluralistic ignorance and the perpetuation of social norms by unwitting actors. *Advances in Experimental Social Psychology, 28,* 161–209.

Prentice-Dunn, S., & Rogers, R. W. (1982). Effects of public and private self-awareness on deindividuation and aggression. *Journal of Personality and Social Psychology, 43,* 503–513.

Prentice-Dunn, S., & Rogers, R. W. (1983). Deindividuation in aggression. In R. G. Geen & E. I. Donnerstein (Eds.), *Aggression: Theoretical and empirical reviews: Vol. 2. Issues in research* (pp. 155–171). New York: Academic Press.

Priester, J. R., Cacioppo, J. T., & Petty, R. E. (1996). The influence of motor processes on attitudes toward novel versus familiar semantic stimuli. *Personality and Social Psychology Bulletin, 22*, 442–447.

Priester, J. R., & Petty, R. E. (1995). Source attributions and persuasion: Perceived honesty as a determinant of message scrutiny. *Personality and Social Psychology Bulletin, 21*, 637–654.

Principe, G. F., & Ceci, S. J. (2002). "I saw it with my own ears": The effects of peer conversations on preschoolers' reports of nonexperienced events. *Journal of Experimental Child Psychology, 83*, 1–25.

Principe, G. F., Ornstein, P. A., Baker-Ward, L., & Gordon, B. N. (2000). The effects of intervening experiences on children's memory for a physical examination. *Applied Cognitive Psychology 14*, 59–80.

Pronin, E., Steele, C. M., & Ross, L. (2004). Identity bifurcation in response to stereotype threat: Women and mathematics. *Journal of Experimental Social Psychology, 40*, 152–168.

Propp, K. M. (1995). An experimental examination of biological sex as a status cue in decision-making groups and its influence on information use. *Small Group Research, 26*, 451–474.

Proto-Campise, L., Belknap, J., & Wooldredge, J. (1998). High school students' adherence to rape myths and the effectiveness of high school rape-awareness programs. *Violence Against Women, 4*, 308–328.

Pruitt, D. G. (1998). Social conflict. In D. T. Gilbert, S. T. Fiske, & G. Lindzey (Eds.), *The handbook of social psychology* (4th ed., Vol. 2, pp. 410–503). New York: McGraw-Hill.

Pryor, J. B., & Merluzzi, T. V. (1985). The role of expertise in processing social interaction scripts. *Journal of Experimental Social Psychology, 21*, 362–379.

Pyszczynski, T., & Greenberg, J. (1987). Self-regulatory preservation and the depressive self-focusing style: A self-awareness theory of reactive depression. *Psychological Bulletin, 201*, 122–138.

Pyszczynski, T. A., Solomon, S., & Greenberg, J. (2003). *In the wake of 9/11: The psychology of terror.* Washington, DC: American Psychological Association.

Qualter, T. H. (1962). *Propaganda and psychological warfare.* New York: Random House.

Quattrone, G. A. (1986). On the perception of a group's variability. In S. Worchel & W. G. Austin (Eds.), *Psychology of intergroup relations* (2nd ed., pp. 25–48). Chicago: Nelson Hall.

Quinn, D. M., Kahng, S. K., & Crocker, J. (2004). Discreditable: Stigma effects of revealing a mental illness history on test performance. *Personality and Social Psychology Bulletin, 30*, 803–815.

Rajecki, D. W., Bledsoe, S. B., & Rasmussen, J. L. (1991). Successful personal ads: Gender differences and similarities in offers, stipulations, and outcomes. *Basic and Applied Social Psychology, 12*, 457–469.

Raskin, D. C. (1986). The polygraph in 1986: Scientific, professional, and legal issues surrounding application and acceptance of polygraph evidence. *Utah Law Review*, 29–74.

Ratner, R. K., & Miller, D. T. (2001). The norm of self-interest and its effects on social action. *Journal of Personality and Social Psychology, 81*, 5–16.

Read, S. J. (1987). Constructing causal scenarios: A knowledge structure approach to causal reasoning. *Journal of Personality and Social Psychology, 52*, 288–302.

Read, S. J., & Urada, D. I. (2003). A neural network simulation of the outgroup homogeneity effect. *Personality and Social Psychology Review*, 7, 146–159.

Reader's Digest. *How polite are we?* July, 2006

Redlich, A. D., & Goodman, G. S. (2003). Taking responsibility for an act not committed: The influence of age and suggestibility. *Law and Human Behavior, 27*, 141–156.

Reeder, G. D. (1993). Trait-behavior relations and dispositional inference. *Personality and Social Psychology Bulletin, 19*, 586–593.

Reeder, G. D., & Brewer, M. B. (1979). A schematic model of dispositional attribution in interpersonal perception. *Psychological Review, 86*, 61–79.

Reeder, G. D., Davison, D. M., Gipson, K. L., & Hesson-McInnis, M. S. (2001). Identifying the motivations of African American volunteers working to prevent HIV/AIDS. *AIDS Education and Prevention, 13*, 343–354.

Regan, D. T. (1971). Effects of a favor and liking on compliance. *Journal of Experimental Social Psychology*, 7, 627–639.

Regan, D. T., & Kilduff, M. (1988). Optimism about elections: Dissonance reduction at the ballot box. *Political Psychology, 9*, 101–107.

Regan, D. T., Williams, M., & Sparling, S. (1972). Voluntary expiation of guilt: A field experiment. *Journal of Personality and Social Psychology, 24*, 42–45.

Regan, J. W. (1971). Guilt, perceived injustice, and altruistic behavior. *Journal of Personality and Social Psychology, 18*, 124–132.

Regan, P. C., & Berscheid, E. (1997). Gender differences in characteristics desired in a potential sexual and marriage partner. *Journal of Psychology and Human Sexuality, 9*, 25–37.

Regan, P. C., & Berscheid, E. (1999). *Lust: What we know about human sexual desire.* Thousand Oaks, CA: Sage.

Regan, P. C., & Gutierrez, D. M. (2005). Effects of participants' sex and targets' perceived need on supermarket helping behavior. *Perceptual and Motor Skills, 101*, 617–620.

Regan, P. C., Kocan, E. R., & Whitlock, T. (1998). Ain't love grand! A prototype analysis of the concept of romantic love. *Journal of Social and Personal Relationships, 15*, 411–420.

Reicher, S. D. (2001). The St. Pauls' riot: An explanation of the limits of crowd action in terms of a social identity model. In M. A. Hogg & D. Abrams (Eds.), *Intergroup relations: Essential readings. Key readings in social psychology* (pp. 302–315). Philadelphia: Psychology Press.

Reifman, A. S., Larrick, R. P., & Fein, S. (1991). Temper and temperature on the diamond: The heat-aggression relationship in major-league baseball. *Personality and Social Psychology Bulletin, 17*, 580–585.

Reifman, A., Klein, J. G., & Murphy, S. T. (1989). Self-monitoring and age. *Psychology and Aging, 4*, 245–246.

Reisenzein, R. (1983). The Schachter theory of emotion: Two decades later. *Psychological Bulletin, 94*, 239–264.

Remley, A. (1988, October). The great parental value shift: From obedience to independence. *Psychology Today*, 56–59.

Renfrew, J. W. (1997). *Aggression and its causes: A biopsychosocial approach.* New York: Oxford University Press.

Responsible citizenship. (2002, December 31). *Ottawa Citizen*, p. A14.

Rhee, E., Uleman, J. S., Lee, H. K., & Roman, R. J. (1995). Spontaneous self-descriptions and ethnic identities in individualistic and collectivistic cultures. *Journal of Personality and Social Psychology, 69*, 142–152.

Rhoden, W. C. (1996, December 24). A two-hour psychological test turns into Giants' lightning rod. *New York Times*, pp. B1, B10.

Rhodes, G., Sumich, A., & Byatt, G. (1999). Are average facial configurations attractive only because of their symmetry? *Psychological Science, 10*, 52–58.

Rhodes, G., & Zebrowitz, L. A. (Eds.) (2002). *Facial attractiveness: Evolutionary, cognitive, and social perspectives.* Norwood, NJ: Ablex.

Rhodes, G., Zebrowitz, L. A., Clark, A., Kalick, S. M., Hightower, A., & McKay, R. (2001). Do facial averageness and symmetry signal health? *Evolution and Human Behavior, 22*, 31–46.

Rhodes, N., & Wood, W. (1992). Self-esteem and intelligence affect influenceability: The mediating role of message reception. *Psychological Bulletin, 111*, 156–171.

Rhodewalt, F. (1990). Self-handicappers: Individual differences in the preference for anticipatory, self-protective acts. In R. L. Higgins, C. R. Synder, & S. Berglas (Eds.), *Self-handicapping: The paradox that isn't* (pp. 69–106). New York: Plenum.

Rhodewalt, F., & Agustsdottir, S. (1986). Effects of self-presentation on the phenomenal self. *Journal of Personality and Social Psychology, 50*, 47–55.

Rhodewalt, F., Sandonmatsu, D. M., Tschanz, B., Feick, D. L., & Waller, A. (1995). Self-handicapping and interpersonal trade-offs: The effects of claimed self-handicaps on observers' performance evaluations and feedback. *Personality and Social Psychology Bulletin, 21*, 1042–1050.

Ricciardelli, L. A., McCabe, M. P., & Banfield, S. (2000). Sociocultural influences on body image and body change methods. *Journal of Adolescent Health, 26*, 3–4.

Richardson, D. S., & Hammock, G. (2005). Social context of human aggression: Are we paying too much attention to gender? In S. Fein, G. R. Goethals, & M. J. Sandstrom (Eds.), *Gender and aggression: Interdisciplinary perspectives.* Mahwah, NJ: Erlbaum.

Richeson, J. A., Baird, A. A., Gordon, H. L., Heatherton, T. F., Wyland, C. L., Trawalter, S., & Shelton, J. N. (2003). An fMRI investigation of the impact of interracial contact on executive function. *Nature Neuroscience, 6*, 1323–1328.

Richeson, J. A., & Shelton, J. N. (2003). When prejudice does not pay: Effects of interracial contact on executive function. *Psychological Science, 14*, 287–290.

Rigby, K. (2000). Effects of peer victimization in schools and perceived social support on adolescent well-being. *Journal of Adolescence, 23*, 57–68.

Rilling, J. K., Gutman, D. A., Zeh, T. R., Pagnoni, G., Berns, G. S., & Kilts, C. D. (2002). A neural basis for social cooperation. *Neuron, 35*, 395–405.

Rind, B., & Strohmetz, D. B. (2001). Effect on restaurant tipping of a helpful message written on the back of customers' checks. *Journal of Applied Social Psychology, 31*, 1379–1384.

Ringelmann, M. (1913). Recherches sur les moteurs animés: Travail de l'homme. *Annales de l'Institut National Agronomique, 2e série, tom XII*, 1–40.

Ritter, D., & Eslea, M. (2005). Hot sauce, toy guns, and graffiti: A critical account of current laboratory aggression paradigms. *Aggressive Behavior, 31*, 407–419.

Robins, R. W., Hendin, H. M., & Trzesniewski, K. H. (2001). Measuring global self-esteem: Construct validation of a single-item measure and the Rosenberg self-esteem scale. *Personality and Social Psychology Bulletin, 27*, 151–161.

Robinson, I., Ziss, K., Ganza, B., Katz, S, & Robinson, E. (1991). Twenty years of the sexual revolution, 1965–1985: An update. *Journal of Marriage and the Family, 53*, 216–220.

Robinson, J. P., Shaver, P. R., & Wrightsman, L. S. (Eds.) (1991). *Measures of personality and social psychological attitudes.* New York: Academic Press.

Robinson, J. P., Shaver, P. R., & Wrightsman, L. S. (Eds.) (1998). *Measures of political attitudes.* New York: Academic Press.

Roccas, S. (2003). Identification and status revisited: The moderating role of self-enhancement and self-transcendence values. *Personality and Social Psychology Bulletin, 29*, 726–736.

Rodkin, P. C., Farmer, T. W., Pearl, R., & van Acker, R. (2000). Heterogeneity of popular boys: Antisocial and prosocial configurations. *Developmental Psychology, 36*, 14–24.

Roediger, H. L., Meade, M. L., & Bergman, E. T. (2001). Social contagion of memory. *Psychonomic Bulletin and Review, 8*, 365–371.

Roesch, S. C., & Amirkhan, J. H. (1997). Boundary conditions for self-serving attributions: Another look at the sports pages. *Journal of Applied Social Psychology, 27*, 245–261.

Roese, N. J. (1997). Counterfactual thinking. *Psychological Bulletin, 121*, 133–148.

Roese, N. J., & Jamieson, D. W. (1993). Twenty years of bogus pipeline research: A critical review and meta-analysis. *Psychological Bulletin, 114*, 363–375.

Roese, N. J., & Olson, J. M. (Eds.) (1995). *What might have been: The social psychology of counterfactual thinking.* Hillsdale, NJ: Erlbaum.

Rofé, Y. (1984). Stress and affiliation: A utility theory. *Psychological Review, 91*, 235–250.

Rogers, M., Miller, N., Mayer, F. S., & Duval, S. (1982). Personal responsibility and salience of the request for help: Determinants of the relation between negative affect and helping behavior. *Journal of Personality and Social Psychology, 43*, 956–970.

Rogers, R. W. (1983). Cognitive and psychological processes in fear appeals and attitude change: A revised theory of protection motivation. In J. Cacioppo & R. Petty (Eds.), *Social psychophysiology: A sourcebook* (pp. 153–176). New York: Guilford.

Rogers, R. W., & Mewborn, R. C. (1976). Fear appeals and attitude change: Effects of a threat's noxiousness, probability of occurrence, and the efficacy of coping responses. *Journal of Personality and Social Psychology, 34*, 54–61.

Rohrer, J. H., Baron, S. H., Hoffman, E. L., & Swander, D. V. (1954). The stability of autokinetic judgments. *Journal of Abnormal and Social Psychology, 49*, 595–597.

Roney, J. R. (2003). Effects of visual exposure to the opposite sex: Cognitive aspects of mate attraction in human males. *Personality and Social Psychology Bulletin, 29*, 393–404.

Rook, K. S. (1987). Reciprocity of social exchange and social satisfaction among older women. *Journal of Personality and Social Psychology, 52*, 145–154.

Rook, K. S., & Peplau, L. A. (1982). Perspectives on helping the lonely. In L. A. Peplau & D. Perlman (Eds.), *Loneliness: A sourcebook of current theory, research and therapy* (pp. 351–378). New York: Wiley.

Rose, V. G., & Ogloff, J. R. P. (2001). Evaluating the comprehensibility of jury instructions: A method and an example. *Law and Human Behavior, 25*, 409–431.

Rosen, S., Tomarelli, M. M., Kidda, M. L., Jr., & Medvin, N. (1986). Effects of motive for helping, recipient's inability to reciprocate, and sex on devaluation of the recipient's competence. *Journal of Personality and Social Psychology, 50,* 729–736.

Rosenbaum, M. E. (1986). The repulsion hypothesis: On the nondevelopment of relationships. *Journal of Personality and Social Psychology, 51,* 1156–1166.

Rosenberg, M. (1965). *Society and the adolescent self-image.* Princeton, NJ: Princeton University Press.

Rosenhan, D. L., Salovey, P., & Hargis, K. (1981). The joys of helping: Focus of attention mediates the impact of positive affect on altruism. *Journal of Personality and Social Psychology, 40,* 899–905.

Rosenthal, R. (1976). *Experimenter effects in behavioral research.* New York: Irvington.

Rosenthal, R. (1985). From unconscious experimenter bias to teacher expectancy effects. In J. B. Dusek, V. C. Hall, & W. J. Meyer (Eds.), *Teacher expectancies* (pp. 37–65). Hillsdale, NJ: Erlbaum.

Rosenthal, R. (2002). Covert communication in classrooms, clinics, courtrooms, and cubicles. *American Psychologist, 57,* 839–849.

Rosenthal, R., & Jacobson, L. (1968). *Pygmalion in the classroom: Teacher expectation and pupils' intellectual development.* New York: Holt, Rinehart and Winston.

Rosnow, R. L., & Rosenthal, R. (1993). *Beginning behavioral research: A conceptual primer.* New York: Macmillan.

Ross, D. F., Ceci, S. J., Dunning, D., & Toglia, M. P. (1994). Unconscious transference and mistaken identity: When a witness misidentifies a familiar but innocent person. *Journal of Applied Psychology, 79,* 918–930.

Ross, E. A. (1908). *Social psychology: An outline and source book.* New York: Macmillan.

Ross, J., & Staw, B. M. (1986). Expo 86: An escalation prototype. *Administrative Science Quarterly, 31,* 274–297.

Ross, L. (1977). The intuitive psychologist and his shortcomings: Distortions in the attribution process. In L. Berkowitz (Ed.), *Advances in experimental social psychology* (Vol. 10, pp. 174–221). New York: Academic Press.

Ross, L., Amabile, T. M., & Steinmetz, J. L. (1977). Social roles, social control, and biases in social-perception processes. *Journal of Personality and Social Psychology, 35,* 485–494.

Ross, L., Bierbrauer, G., & Hoffman, S. (1976). The role of attribution processes in conformity and dissent. *American Psychologist, 31,* 148–157.

Ross, L., Greene, D., & House, P. (1977). The false consensus phenomenon: An attributional bias in self-perception and social-perception processes. *Journal of Experimental Social Psychology, 13,* 279–301.

Ross, M. (1989). The relation of implicit theories to the construction of personal histories. *Psychological Review, 96,* 341–357.

Ross, M., & Sicoly, F. (1979). Egocentric biases in availability and attribution. *Journal of Personality and Social Psychology, 37,* 322–336.

Ross, M., Xun, W. Q., & Wilson, A. E. (2002). Language and the bicultural self. *Personality and Social Psychology Bulletin, 28,* 1040–1050.

Rowatt, W. C., Cunningham, M. R., & Druen, P. B. (1999). Lying to get a date: The effect of facial physical attractiveness on the willingness to deceive prospective dating partners. *Journal of Social and Personal Relationships, 16,* 209–223.

Rowe, D. C., Almeida, D. M., & Jacobson, K. C. (1999). School context and genetic influences on aggression in adolescence. *Psychological Science, 10,* 277–280.

Rozin, P., & Fallon, A. E. (1987). A perspective on disgust. *Psychological Review, 94,* 23–41.

Rozin, P., Haidt, J., & McCauley, C. R. (2000). Disgust. In M. Lewis & J. Haviland-Jones (Eds.), *Handbook of emotions* (2nd ed., pp. 637–653). New York: Guilford.

Rozin, P., & Royzman, E. B. (2001). Negativity bias, negativity dominance, and contagion. *Personality and Social Psychology Review, 5,* 296–320.

Ruback, R. B., & Weiner, N. A. (Eds.) (1995). *Interpersonal violent behaviors: Social and cultural aspects.* New York: Springer Publishing.

Rubin, D. C. (Ed.) (1996). *Remembering our past: Studies in autobiographical memory.* New York: Cambridge University Press.

Rubin, J. Z., Provenzano, F. J., & Luria, Z. (1974). The eye of the beholder: Parents' views on sex of newborns. *American Journal of Orthopsychiatry, 44,* 512–519.

Rubin, J. Z., Pruitt, D. G., & Kim, S. H. (1994). *Social conflict: Escalation, stalemate, and settlement.* New York: McGraw-Hill.

Rubin, M., & Hewstone, M. (1998). Social identity theory's self-esteem hypothesis: A review and some suggestions for clarification. *Personality and Social Psychology Review, 2,* 40–62.

Rubin, Z. (1973). *Liking and loving.* New York: Holt, Rinehart and Winston.

Rudman, L. A., & Borgida, E. (1995). The afterglow of construct accessibility: The behavioral consequences of priming men to view women as sexual objects. *Journal of Experimental Social Psychology, 31,* 493–517.

Rudman, L. A., & Glick, P. (2001). Prescriptive gender stereotypes and backlash toward agentic women. *Journal of Social Issues, 57,* 743–762.

Rule, B. G., Taylor, B. R., & Dobbs, A. R. (1987). Priming effects of heat on aggressive thoughts. *Social Cognition, 5,* 131–143.

Rusbult, C. E., & Buunk, B. P. (1993). Commitment processes in close relationships: An interdependence analysis. *Journal of Social and Personal Relationships, 10,* 175–204.

Rusbult, C. E., Martz, J. M., & Agnew, C. R. (1998). The investment model scale: Measuring commitment level, satisfaction level, quality of alternatives, and investment size. *Personal Relationships, 5,* 357–391.

Rusbult, C. E., & van Lange, P. A. M. (2003). Interdependence, interaction and relationships. *Annual Review of Psychology, 54,* 351–375.

Ruscher, J. B. (1998). Prejudice and stereotyping in everyday communication. In M. P. Zanna (Ed.), *Advances in experimental social psychology* (Vol. 30, pp. 241–307). San Diego: Academic Press.

Ruscher, J. B., Fiske, S. T., & Schnake, S. B. (2000). The motivated tactician's juggling act: Compatible vs. incompatible impression goals. *British Journal of Social Psychology, 39,* 241–256.

Rushton, J. P. (1981a). Television as a socializer. In J. P. Rushton & R. M. Sorrentino (Eds.), *Altruism and helping behavior: Social, personality, and developmental perspectives* (pp. 91–108). Hillsdale, NJ: Erlbaum.

Rushton, J. P. (1981b). The altruistic personality. In J. P. Rushton & R. M. Sorrentino (Eds.), *Altruism and helping behavior: Social, personality, and developmental perspectives* (pp. 251–266). Hillsdale, NJ: Erlbaum.

Rushton, J. P., Fulker, D. W., Neale, M. C., Nias, D. K. B., & Eysenck, H. J. (1986). Altruism and aggression: The heritability of individual differences. *Journal of Personality and Social Psychology, 50,* 1192–1198.

Rushton, J. P., Russell, R. J. H., & Wells, P. A. (1984). Genetic similarity theory: Beyond kin selection. *Behavior Genetics, 14,* 179–193.

Russell, D., Peplau, L. A., & Cutrona, C. E. (1980). The revised UCLA Loneliness Scale: Concurrent and discriminant validity evidence. *Journal of Personality and Social Psychology, 39,* 472–480.

Russell, D. E. H. (1984). *Sexual exploitation.* Beverly Hills, CA: Sage.

Russell, G. W., Arms, R. L., & Bibby, R. W. (1995). Canadians' belief in catharsis. *Social Behavior and Personality, 23,* 223–228.

Russell, J. A. (1994). Is there universal recognition of emotion from facial expression? A review of cross-cultural studies. *Psychological Bulletin, 115,* 102–141.

Rutkowski, G. K., Gruder, C. L., & Romer, D. (1983). Group cohesiveness, social norms, and bystander intervention. *Journal of Personality and Social Psychology, 44,* 545–552.

Ryan, C. S., & Bogart, L. M. (1997). Development of new group members' ingroup and outgroup stereotypes: Changes in perceived group variability and ethnocentrism. *Journal of Personality and Social Psychology, 73,* 719–732.

Saal, F. E., Johnson, C. B., & Weber, N. (1989). Friendly or sexy? It may depend on whom you ask. *Psychology of Women Quarterly, 13,* 263–276.

Sabini, J., Cosmas, K., Siepmann, M., & Stein, J. (1999). Underestimates and truly false consensus effects in estimates of embarrassment and other emotions. *Basic and Applied Social Psychology, 21,* 223–241.

Sacks, O. (1985). *The man who mistook his wife for a hat.* New York: Summit.

Saenz, D. S. (1994). Token status and problem-solving deficits: Detrimental effects of distinctiveness and performance monitoring. *Social Cognition, 12,* 61–74.

Sagar, H. A., & Schofield, J. W. (1980). Racial and behavioral cues in black and white children's perceptions of ambiguously aggressive acts. *Journal of Personality and Social Psychology, 39,* 590–598.

Saks, M. J. (1974). Ignorance of science is no excuse. *Trial, 10,* 18–20.

Saks, M. J., & Marti, M. W. (1997). A meta-analysis of the effects of jury size. *Law and Human Behavior, 21,* 451–468.

Salovey, P., Mayer, J. D., & Rosenhan, D. L. (1991). Mood and helping: Mood as a motivator of helping and helping as a regulator of mood. In M. S. Clark (Ed.), *Prosocial behavior* (Vol. 12, pp. 215–237). Newbury Park, CA: Sage.

Salovey, P., & Rodin, J. (1984). Some antecedents and consequences of social-comparison jealousy. *Journal of Personality and Social Psychology, 47,* 780–792.

Salzer, M. S. (2000). Toward a narrative conceptualization of stereotypes: Contextualizing perceptions of public housing residents. *Journal of Community and Applied Social Psychology, 10,* 123–137.

Sanchez-Burks, J., Nisbett, R. E., & Ybarra, O. (2000). Relational schemas, cultural styles, and prejudice against outgroups. *Journal of Personality and Social Psychology, 79,* 174–189.

Sanders, G. S. (1981). Driven by distraction: An integrative review of social facilitation theory and research. *Journal of Experimental Social Psychology, 17,* 227–251.

Sanders, G. S., & Baron, R. S. (1977). Is social comparison irrelevant for producing choice shifts? *Journal of Experimental Social Psychology, 13,* 303–314.

Sanders, S. A., & Reinisch, J. M. (1999). Would you say you "had sex" if . . . ? *Journal of the American Medical Association, 281,* 275–277.

Sanderson, C. A., & Evans, S. M. (2001). Seeing one's partner through intimacy-colored glasses: An examination of the processes underlying the intimacy goals-relationship satisfaction link. *Personality and Social Psychology Bulletin, 27,* 463–473.

Sanderson, D. W. (1993). *Smileys.* Sebastopol, CA: O'Reilly.

Sani, F., & Todman, J. (2002). Should we stay or should we go? A social psychological model of schisms in groups. *Personality and Social Psychology Bulletin, 28,* 1647–1655.

Sanna, L. J. (1992). Self-efficacy theory: Implications for social facilitation and social loafing. *Journal of Personality and Social Psychology, 62,* 774–786.

Sanna, L. J., Parks, C. D., & Chang, E. C. (2003). Mixed-motive conflict in social dilemmas: Mood as input to competitive and cooperative goals. *Group Dynamics, 7,* 26–40.

Sanna, L. J., Turley-Ames, K. J., & Meier, S. (1999). Mood, self-esteem, and simulated alternatives: Thought-provoking affective influences on counterfactual direction. *Journal of Personality and Social Psychology, 76,* 543–558.

Sanoff, A. P., & Leight, K. (1994). Altruism is in style. *U.S. News and World Report (America's Best Colleges: 1994 College Guide),* pp. 25–28.

Sansone, C., & Harackiewicz, J. M. (Eds.) (2000). *Intrinsic and extrinsic motivation: The search for optimal motivation and performance.* New York: Academic Press.

Santos, M. D., Leve, C., & Pratkanis, A. R. (1994). Hey buddy, can you spare seventeen cents? Mindful persuasion and the pique technique. *Journal of Applied Social Psychology, 24,* 755–764.

Sapolsky, B. S. (1984). Arousal, affect, and the aggression-moderating effect of erotica. In N. M. Malamuth & E. I. Donnerstein (Eds.), *Pornography and sexual aggression* (pp. 85–113). New York: Academic Press.

Sarason, I. G., Sarason, B. R., Pierce, G. R., Shearin, E. N., & Sayers, M. H. (1991). A social learning approach to increasing blood donations. *Journal of Applied Social Psychology, 21,* 896–918.

Sarnoff, I., & Zimbardo, P. (1961). Anxiety, fear, and social affiliation. *Journal of Abnormal and Social Psychology, 62,* 356–363.

Sassenberg, K. (2002). Common bond and common identity groups on the Internet: Attachment and normative behavior in on-topic and off-topic chats. *Group Dynamics, 6,* 27–37.

Saulnier, K., & Perlman, D. (1981). The actor-observer bias is alive and well in prison: A sequel to Wells. *Personality and Social Psychology Bulletin, 7,* 559–564.

Saulny, S. (2002). Why confess to what you didn't do? *The New York Times,* December 8, Section 4.

Savin, H. B. (1973). Professors and psychological researchers: Conflicting values in conflicting roles. *Cognition, 2,* 147–149.

Savitsky, K., Epley, N., & Gilovich, T. (2001). Do others judge us as harshly as we think? Overestimating the impact of our failures, shortcomings, and mishaps. *Journal of Personality and Social Psychology, 81,* 44–56.

Savitsky, K., Gilovich, T., Berger, G., & Medvec, V. H. (2003).

Is our absence as conspicuous as we think? Overestimating the salience and impact of one's absence from a group. *Journal of Experimental Social Psychology, 39,* 386–392.

Saxe, L., Dougherty, D., & Cross, T. (1985). The validity of polygraph testing: Scientific analysis and public controversy. *American Psychologist, 38,* 355–366.

Schachter, S. (1951). Deviation, rejection, and communication. *Journal of Abnormal and Social Psychology, 46,* 190–207.

Schachter, S. (1959). *The psychology of affiliation: Experimental studies of the sources of gregariousness.* Stanford, CA: Stanford University Press.

Schachter, S. (1964). The interaction of cognitive and physiological determinants of emotional state. In L. Berkowitz (Ed.), *Advances in experimental social psychology* (Vol. 1, pp. 49–80). New York: Academic Press.

Schachter, S., Ouellette, R., Whittle, B., & Gerin, W. (1987). Effects of trends and of profit or loss on the tendency to sell stock. *Basic and Applied Social Psychology, 8,* 259–271.

Schachter, S., & Singer, J. (1962). Cognitive, social, and physiological determinants of the emotional state. *Psychological Review, 69,* 379–399.

Schachter, S., & Singer, J. (1979). Comments on the Maslach and Marshall-Zimbardo experiments. *Journal of Personality and Social Psychology, 37,* 989–995.

Schafer, R. B., & Keith, P. M. (1980). Equity and depression among married couples. *Social Psychology Quarterly, 43,* 430–435.

Schaller, M. (1991). Social categorization and the formation of social stereotypes: Further evidence for biased information processing in the perception of group-behavior correlations. *European Journal of Social Psychology, 21,* 25–35.

Schaller, M., Conway, L. G., & Tanchuk, T. L. (2002). Selective pressures on the once and future contents of ethnic stereotypes: Effects of the communicability of traits. *Journal of Personality and Social Psychology, 82,* 861–877.

Schaller, M., & Conway, L. G., III (1999). Influence of impression-management goals on the emerging contents of group stereotypes: Support for a social-evolutionary process. *Personality and Social Psychology Bulletin, 25,* 819–833.

Schaller, M., & Conway, L. G., III (2001). From cognition to culture: The origins of stereotypes that really matter. In G. Moscowitz (Ed.), *Cognitive social psychology: On the tenure and future of social cognition* (pp. 163–176). Mahwah, NJ: Erlbaum.

Scharfe, E., & Bartholomew, K. (1994). Reliability and stability of adult attachment patterns. *Personal Relationships, 1,* 23–43.

Scheck, B., Neufeld, P., & Dwyer, J. (2000). *Actual innocence: Five days to execution and other dispatches from the wrongly convicted.* New York: Doubleday.

Scheier, M. F., & Carver, C. S. (1983). Two sides of the self: One for you and one for me. In J. Suls and A. G. Greenwald (Eds.), *Psychological perspectives on the self* (Vol. 2, pp. 123–157). Hillsdale, NJ: Erlbaum.

Scheier, M. F., Carver, C. S., & Gibbons, F. X. (1979). Self-directed attention, awareness of bodily states, and suggestibility. *Journal of Personality and Social Psychology, 37,* 1576–1588.

Scher, S. J., & Cooper, J. (1989). Motivational basis of dissonance: The singular role of behavioral consequences. *Journal of Personality and Social Psychology, 56,* 899–906.

Schimel, J., Arndt, J., Pyszczynski, T., & Greenberg, J. (2001). Being accepted for who we are: Evidence that social validation of the intrinsic self reduces general defensiveness. *Journal of Personality and Social Psychology, 80,* 35–52.

Schittekatte, M., & van Hiel, A. (1996). Effects of partially shared information and awareness of unshared information on information sampling. *Small Group Research, 27,* 431–448.

Schlenker, B. R. (1982). Translating actions into attitudes: An identity-analytic approach to the explanation of social conduct. In L. Berkowitz (Ed.), *Advances in experimental social psychology* (Vol. 15, pp. 193–247). New York: Academic Press.

Schlenker, B. R. (2003). Self-presentation. In M. R. Leary & J. P. Tangney (Eds.), *Handbook of self and identity* (pp. 492–518). New York: Guilford.

Schlenker, B. R., & Trudeau, J. V. (1990). The impact of self-presentations on private self-beliefs: Effects of prior self-beliefs and misattribution. *Journal of Personality and Social Psychology, 58,* 22–32.

Schlenker, B. R., Weigold, M. F., & Hallam, J. R. (1990). Self-serving attributions in social context: Effects of self-esteem and social pressure. *Journal of Personality and Social Psychology, 58,* 855–863.

Schmader, T. (2002). Gender identification moderates stereotype threat effects on women's math performance. *Journal of Experimental Social Psychology, 38,* 194–201.

Schmader, T., & Johns, M. (2003). Converging evidence that stereotype threat reduces working memory capacity. *Journal of Personality and Social Psychology, 85,* 440–452.

Schmitt, D. P. (2003). Universal sex differences in the desire for sexual variety: Tests from 52 nations, 6 continents, and 13 islands. *Journal of Personality and Social Psychology, 85,* 85–104.

Schmitt, D. P., & Buss, D. M. (2001). Human mate poaching: Tactics and temptations for infiltrating existing mateships. *Journal of Personality and Social Psychology, 80,* 894–917.

Schmitt, D. P., & Shackelford, T. K. (2003). Nifty ways to leave your lover: The tactics people use to entice and disguise the process of human mate poaching. *Personality and Social Psychology Bulletin, 29,* 1018–1035.

Schmitt, M. T., Branscombe, N. R., & Kappen, D. M. (2003). Attitudes toward group-based inequality: Social dominance or social identity? *British Journal of Social Psychology, 42,* 161–186.

Schmitt, M. T., Branscrombe, N. R., Kobrynowicz, D., & Owen, S. (2002). Perceiving discrimination against one's gender group has different implications for well-being in women and men. *Personality and Social Psychology Bulletin, 28,* 197–210.

Schmitt, M. T., & Maes, J. (2002). Stereotypic ingroup bias as self-defense against relative deprivation: Evidence from a longitudinal study of the German unification process. *European Journal of Social Psychology, 32,* 309–326.

Schmitt, M. T., Spears, R., & Branscombe, N. R. (2003). Constructing a minority group identity out of shared rejection: The case of international students. *European Journal of Social Psychology, 33,* 1–12.

Schnake, S. B., & Ruscher, J. B. (1998). Modern racism as a predictor of the linguistic intergroup bias. *Journal of Language and Social Psychology, 17,* 484–491.

Schneider, D. J. (1973). Implicit personality theory: A review. *Psychological Bulletin, 79,* 294–309.

Schneider, D. M., & Watkins, M. J. (1996). Response conformity in recognition testing. *Psychonomic Bulletin & Review, 3,* 481–485.

Schneider, M. E., Major, B., Luhtanen, R., & Crocker, J. (1996). Social stigma and the potential costs of assumptive help. *Personality and Social Psychology Bulletin, 22,* 201–209.

Schneiderman, N., Antoni, M. H., Saab, P. G., & Ironson, G.

(2001). Health psychology: Psychosocial and biobehavioral aspects of chronic disease management. *Annual Review of Psychology, 52*, 555–580.

Schofield, P. E., Pattison, P. E., Hill, D. J., & Borland, R. (2001). The influence of group identification on the adoption of peer group smoking norms. *Psychology and Health, 16*, 1–16.

Schofield, P. E., Pattison, P. E., Hill, D. J., & Borland, R. (2003). Youth culture and smoking: Integrating social group processes and individual cognitive processes in a model of health-related behaviours. *Journal of Health Psychology, 8*, 291–306.

Schonert-Reichl, K. A. (1999). Relations of peer acceptance, friendship adjustment, and social behavior to moral reasoning during early adolescence. *Journal of Early Adolescence, 19*, 249–279.

Schopler, J. (1970). An attribution analysis of some determinants of reciprocating a benefit. In J. R. Macaulay & L. Berkowitz (Eds.), *Altruism and helping behavior* (pp. 231–238). New York: Academic Press.

Schultheiss, O. C., & Brunstein, J. C. (2000). Choice of difficult tasks as a strategy of compensating for identity-relevant failure. *Journal of Research in Personality, 34*, 269–277.

Schultz, B., Ketrow, S. M., & Urban, D. M. (1995). Improving decision quality in the small group: The role of the reminder. *Small Group Research, 26*, 521–541.

Schwartz, C., Meisenhelder, J. B., Ma, Y., & Reed, G. (2003). Altruistic social interest behaviors are associated with better mental health. *Psychosomatic Medicine, 65*, 778–785.

Schwartz, C. E., & Sendor, M. (1999). Helping others helps oneself: Response shift effects in peer support. *Social Science and Medicine, 48*, 1563–1575.

Schwartz, S. H. (1990). Individualism-collectivism: Critique and proposed refinements. *Journal of Cross-Cultural Psychology, 21*, 139–157.

Schwartz, S. H., & Gottlieb, A. (1980). Bystander anonymity and reaction to emergencies. *Journal of Personality and Social Psychology, 39*, 418–430.

Schwarz, N. (1990). Feelings as information: Information and motivational functions as affective states. In E. T. Higgins et al. (Eds.), *Handbook of motivation and cognition: Foundations of social behavior* (Vol. 2, pp. 527–561). New York: Guilford.

Schwarz, N. (1999). Self-reports: How the questions shape the answers. *American Psychologist, 54*, 93–105.

Schwarz, N. (2003). Self-reports in consumer research: The challenge of comparing cohorts and cultures. *Journal of Consumer Research, 29*, 588–594.

Schwarz, N., Bless, H., & Bohner, G. (1991). Mood and persuasion: Affective states influence the processing of persuasive communications. In M. P. Zanna (Ed.), *Advances in experimental social psychology* (Vol. 24, pp. 161–199). New York: Academic Press.

Schwarz, N., Hippler, H. J., Deutsch, B., & Strack, F. (1985). Response scales: Effects of category range on reported behavior and comparative judgments. *Public Opinion Quarterly, 49*, 388–395.

Schwarz, N., Strack, F., Hilton, D., & Naderer, G. (1991). Base rates, representativeness, and the logic of conversation: The contextual relevance of "irrelevant" information. *Social Cognition, 9*, 67–84.

Schwarzwald, J., Raz, M., & Zvibel, M. (1979). The applicability of the door-in-the-face technique when established behavioral customs exist. *Journal of Applied Social Psychology, 9*, 576–586.

Scott, L., & O'Hara, M. W. (1993). Self-discrepancies in clinically anxious and depressed university students. *Journal of Abnormal Psychology, 102*, 282–287.

Scott, W. D., Ingram, R. E., & Shadel, W. G. (2003). Hostile and sad moods in dysphoria: Evidence for cognitive specificity in attributions. *Journal of Social and Clinical Psychology, 22*, 233–252.

Searcy, E., & Eisenberg, N. (1992). Defensiveness in response to aid from a sibling. *Journal of Personality and Social Psychology, 62*, 422–433.

Sears, D. O. (1986). College sophomores in the laboratory: Influences of a narrow data base on social psychology's view of human nature. *Journal of Personality and Social Psychology, 51*, 515–530.

Sears, D. O., & Kinder, D. R. (1985). Whites' opposition to busing: On conceptualizing and operationalizing group conflict. *Journal of Personality and Social Psychology, 48*, 1141–1147.

Sedikides, C. (1993). Assessment, enhancement, and verification determinants of the self-evaluation process. *Journal of Personality and Social Psychology, 65*, 317–338.

Sedikides, C., & Anderson, C. A. (1994). Causal perceptions of intertrait relations: The glue that holds person types together. *Personality and Social Psychology Bulletin, 20*, 294–302.

Sedikides, C., & Brewer, M. B. (Eds.) (2001). *Individual self, relational self, collective self.* Philadelphia: Psychology Press.

Sedikides, C., Gaertner, L., & Toguchi, Y. (2003). Pancultural self-enhancement. *Journal of Personality and Social Psychology, 84*, 60–79.

Sedikides, C., & Jackson, J. M. (1990). Social impact theory: A field test of source strength, source immediacy and number of targets. *Basic and Applied Social Psychology, 11*, 273–281.

Sedikides, C., & Skowronski, J. J. (1997). The symbolic self in evolutionary context. *Personality and Social Psychology Review, 1*, 80–102.

Seers, A., & Woodruff, S. (1997). Temporal pacing in task forces: Group development or deadline pressure? *Journal of Management, 23*, 169–187.

Segal, N. L. (1993). Twin, sibling, and adoption methods: Tests of evolutionary hypotheses. *American Psychologist, 48*, 943–956.

Seijts, G. H., & Latham, G. P. (2000). The effects of goal setting and group size on performance in a social dilemma. *Canadian Journal of Behavioural Science, 32*, 104–116.

Sekaquaptewa, D., Espinoza, P., Thompson, M., Vargas, P., & von Hippel, W. (2003). Stereotypic explanatory bias: Implicit stereotyping as a predictor of discrimination. *Journal of Experimental Social Psychology, 39*, 75–82.

Sekaquaptewa, D., & Thompson, M. (2003). Solo status, stereotype threat, and performance expectancies: Their effects on women's performance. *Journal of Experimental Social Psychology, 39*, 68–74.

Seligman, M. E. P. (1975). *On depression, development, and death.* San Francisco: Freeman.

Sellers, R. M., & Shelton, J. N. (2003). The role of racial identity in perceived racial discrimination. *Journal of Personality and Social Psychology, 84*, 1079–1092.

Selvan, M. S., Ross, M. W., Kapadia, A. S., Mathai, R., & Hira, S. (2001). Study of perceived norms, beliefs and intended sexual behaviour among higher secondary school students in India. *AIDS Care, 13*, 779–788.

Selye, H. (1936). A syndrome produced by diverse nocuous agents. *Nature, 138*, 32.

Serbin, L. A., Poulin-Dubois, D., & Eichstedt, J. A. (2002). Infants' response to gender-inconsistent events. *Infancy, 3,* 531–542.

Seto, M. C., Marc, A., & Barbaree, H. E. (2001). The role of pornography in the etiology of sexual aggression. *Aggression and Violent Behavior, 6,* 35–53.

Seyfarth, R. M., & Cheney, D. L. (1984). Grooming, alliances and reciprocal altruism in vervet monkeys. *Nature, 308,* 541–543.

Seymour, T. L., Seifert, C. M., Shafto, M. G., & Mosmann, A. L. (2000). Using response-time measures to assess "guilty knowledge." *Journal of Applied Psychology, 85,* 30–47.

Shackelford, T. K. (2001). Cohabitation, marriage, and murder: Woman-killing by male romantic partners. *Aggressive Behavior, 27,* 284–291.

Shackelford, T. K., Buss, D. M., & Weekes-Shackelford, V. A. (2003). Wife killings committed in the context of a lovers triangle. *Basic and Applied Social Psychology, 25,* 137–143.

Shackelford, T. K., & Goetz, A. T. (2005). When we hurt the ones we love: Predicting violence against women from men's mate retention tactics. In S. M. Platek & T. K. Shackelford (Eds.), *Human paternal uncertainty and anti-cuckoldry tactics: How males deal with female infidelity.* Cambridge: Cambridge University Press.

Shackelford, T. K., & Larsen, R. J. (1999). Facial attractiveness and physical health. *Evolution and Human Behavior, 20,* 71–76.

Shaffer, D. R., Smith, J. E., & Tomarelli, M. (1982). Self-monitoring as a determinant of self-disclosure reciprocity during the acquaintance process. *Journal of Personality and Social Psychology, 43,* 163–175.

Shakun, M. F. (1999). An ESD computer culture for intercultural problem solving and negotiation. *Group Decision and Negotiation, 8,* 237–249.

Shanab, M. E., & Yahya, K. A. (1977). A behavioral study of obedience in children. *Journal of Personality and Social Psychology, 35,* 530–536.

Shanab, M. E., & Yahya, K. A. (1978). A cross cultural study of obedience. *Bulletin of the Psychonomic Society, 11,* 267–269.

Shapiro, P. N., & Penrod, S. (1986). Meta-analysis of facial identification studies. *Psychological Bulletin, 100,* 139–156.

Sharp, S. (1995). How much does bullying hurt? The effects of bullying on the personal well-being and educational progress of secondary aged students. *Educational and Child Psychology, 12* (2), 81–88.

Sharp, S. (1996). Self-esteem, response style and victimization: Possible ways of preventing victimization through parenting and school based training programmes. *School Psychology International, 17,* 347–357.

Sharp, S., Thompson, D., & Arora, T. (2000). How long before it hurts? An investigation into long-term bullying. *School Psychology International, 21,* 37–46.

Shaver, K. G. (1970). Defensive attribution: Effects of severity and relevance on the responsibility assigned for an accident. *Journal of Personality and Social Psychology, 14,* 101–113.

Shaver, P., & Rubenstein, E. (1980). Childhood attachment experience and adult loneliness. In L. Wheeler (Ed.), *Review of personality and social psychology* (Vol. 1, pp. 42–73). Beverly Hills, CA: Sage.

Shavit, Y., Fischer, C. S., & Koresh, Y. (1994). Kin and nonkin under collective threat: Israeli networks during the Gulf War. *Social Forces, 72,* 1197–1215.

Shavitt, S., Sanbonmatsu, D. M., Smittipatana, S., & Posavac, S. S. (1999). Broadening the conditions for illusory correlation formation: Implications for judging minority groups. *Basic and Applied Social Psychology, 21,* 263–279.

Shavitt, S., Swan, S., Lowery, T. M., & Wanke, M. (1994). The interaction of endorser attractiveness and involvement in persuasion depends on the goal that guides message processing. *Journal of Consumer Psychology, 3,* 137–162.

Shaw, J. S., III (1996). Increases in eyewitness confidence resulting from postevent questioning. *Journal of Experimental Psychology: Applied, 2,* 126–146.

Shaw, J. S., III., Garven, S., & Wood, J. M. (1997). Co-witness information can have immediate effects on eyewitness memory reports. *Law and Human Behavior, 21,* 503–523.

Shaw, L. L., Batson, C. D., & Todd, R. M. (1994). Empathy avoidance: Forestalling feeling for another in order to escape the motivational consequences. *Journal of Personality and Social Psychology, 67,* 879–887.

Shell, R. M., & Eisenberg, N. (1992). A developmental model of recipients' reactions to aid. *Psychological Bulletin, 111,* 413–433.

Shelton, J. N. (2003). Interpersonal concerns in social encounters between majority and minority group members. *Group Processes and Intergroup Relations, 6,* 171–185.

Shepela, S. T., Cook, J., Horlitz, E., Leal, R., Luciano, S., Lutfy, E., Miller, C., Mitchell, G., & Worden, E. (1999). Courageous resistance: A special case of altruism. *Theory and Psychology, 9,* 787–805.

Sheppard, B. H. (1985). Justice is no simple matter: Case for elaborating our model of procedural fairness. *Journal of Personality and Social Psychology, 49,* 953–962.

Shepperd, J. A. (1993a). Productivity loss in performance groups: A motivation analysis. *Psychological Bulletin, 113,* 67–81.

Shepperd, J. A., & Taylor, K. M. (1999). Social loafing and expectancy-value theory. *Personality and Social Psychology Bulletin, 25,* 1147–1158.

Sherif, M. (1936). *The psychology of social norms.* New York: Harper.

Sherif, M. (1966). *In common predicament: Social psychology of intergroup conflict and cooperation.* Boston: Houghton Mifflin.

Sherif, M., Harvey, L. J., White, B. J., Hood, W. R., & Sherif, C.W. (1961). *The Robbers Cave experiment: Intergroup conflict and cooperation.* Middletown, CT: Wesleyan University Press. (Reprinted in 1988)

Sherman, J. W., Conrey, F. R., & Groom, C. J. (2004). Encoding flexibility revisited: Evidence for enhanced encoding of stereotype-inconsistent information under cognitive load. *Social Cognition, 22,* 214–232.

Sherman, P. W. (1981). Kinship, demography, and Belding's ground squirrel nepotism. *Behavioral Ecology and Sociobiology, 8,* 251–259.

Shih, M., Pittinsky, T. L., & Ambady, N. (1999). Stereotype susceptibility: Identity salience and shifts in quantitative performance. *Psychological Science, 10,* 80–83.

Shorr, D. N., & McClelland, S. E. (1998). Children's recognition of pride and guilt as consequences of helping and not helping. *Child Study Journal, 28,* 123–136.

Shotland, R. L., & Heinold, W. D. (1985). Bystander response to arterial bleeding: Helping skills, the decision-making process, and differentiating the helping response. *Journal of Personality and Social Psychology, 49,* 347–356.

Shotland, R. L., & Stebbins, C. A. (1980). Bystander response to rape: Can a victim attract help? *Journal of Applied Social Psychology, 10,* 510–527.

Shotland, R. L., & Stebbins, C. A. (1983). Emergency and cost as determinants of helping behavior and the slow accumulation of social psychological knowledge. *Social Psychology Quarterly, 46*, 36–46.

Shotland, R. L., & Straw, M. K. (1976). Bystander response to an assault: When a man attacks a woman. *Journal of Personality and Social Psychology, 34*, 990–999.

Shrauger, J. S., & Schoeneman, T. (1979). Symbolic interactionist view of the self-concept: Through the looking-glass darkly. *Psychological Bulletin, 86*, 549–573.

Sidanius, J., Levin, S., Federico, C. M., & Pratto, F. (2001). Legitimizing ideologies: The social dominance approach. J. T. Jost & B. Major (Eds.), *The psychology of legitimacy: Emerging perspectives on ideology, justice, and intergroup relations* (pp. 307–331). New York: Cambridge University Press.

Sidanius, J., Levin, S., Liu, J., & Pratto, F. (2000). Social dominance orientation, anti-egalitarianism and the political psychology of gender: An extension and cross-cultural replication. *European Journal of Social Psychology, 30*, 41–67.

Sidanius, J., Pratto, F., van Laar, C., & Levin, S. (2004). Social dominance theory: Its agenda and method. *Political Psychology, 25*, 845–880.

Signorielli, N., McLeod, D., & Healy, E. (1994). Gender stereotypes in MTV commercials: The beat goes on. *Journal of Broadcasting and Electronic Media, 38*, 91–101.

Silke, A. (2003). Deindividuation, anonymity, and violence: Findings from Northern Ireland. *Journal of Social Psychology, 143*, 493–499.

Silverstein, B., Perdue, L., Peterson, B., & Kelly, E. (1986). The role of the mass media in promoting a thin standard of bodily attractiveness for women. *Sex Roles, 14*, 519–532.

Simmons, R. G. (1978). Blacks and high self-esteem: A puzzle. *Social Psychology, 41*, 54–57.

Simon, B., Stuermer, S., & Steffens, K. (2000). Helping individuals or group members? The role of individual and collective identification in AIDS volunteerism. *Personality and Social Psychology Bulletin, 26*, 497–506.

Simon, H. A. (1956). Rational choice and the structure of the environment. *Psychological Review, 63*, 129–138.

Simons, R. L., Johnson, C., Beaman, J., & Conger, R. D. (1993). Explaining women's double jeopardy: Factors that mediate the association between harsh treatment as a child and violence by a husband. *Journal of Marriage and the Family, 55*, 713–723.

Simpson, J. A. (1987). The dissolution of romantic relationships: Factors involved in relationship stability and emotional distress. *Journal of Personality and Social Psychology, 53*, 683–692.

Simpson, J. A., Campbell, B., & Berscheid, E. (1986). The association between romantic love and marriage: Kephart (1967) twice revisited. *Personality and Social Psychology Bulletin, 12*, 363–372.

Simpson, J. A., & Gangestad, S. W. (1992). Sociosexuality and romantic partner choice. *Journal of Personality, 60*, 31–51.

Simpson, J. A., Gangestad, S. W., & Lerma, M. (1990). Perception of physical attractiveness: Mechanisms involved in the maintenance of romantic relationships. *Journal of Personality and Social Psychology, 59*, 1192–1201.

Simpson, J. A., & Kenrick, D. T. (Eds.) (1997). *Evolutionary social psychology*. Mahwah, NJ: Erlbaum.

Simpson, J. A., Rholes, W. S., & Phillips, D. (1996). Conflicts in close relationships: An attachment perspective. *Journal of Personality and Social Psychology, 71*, 899–914.

Sinclair, L., & Kunda, Z. (1999). Reactions to a black professional: Motivated inhibition and activation of conflicting stereotypes. *Journal of Personality and Social Psychology, 77*, 885–904.

Sinclair, L., & Kunda, Z. (2000). Motivated stereotyping of women: She's fine if she praised me but incompetent if she criticized me. *Personality and Social Psychology Bulletin, 26*, 1329–1342.

Sinclair, R. C., Hoffman, C., Mark, M. M., Martin, L. M., & Pickering, T. L. (1994). Construct accessibility and the misattribution of arousal: Schachter and Singer revisited. *Psychological Science, 5*, 15–19.

Sinclair, R. C., Mark, M. M., Moore, S. E., Lavis, C. A., & Soldat, A. S. (2000). An electoral butterfly effect. *Nature, 408*, 665–666.

Singelis, T. M. (1994). The measurement of independent and interdependent self-construals. *Personality and Social Psychology Bulletin, 20*, 580–591.

Singer, J. L. (1994). Imaginative play and adaptive development. In J. H. Goldstein (Ed.), *Toys, play, and child development* (pp. 6–26). New York: Cambridge University Press.

Singer, J. L., & Singer, D. G. (1983). Psychologists look at television: Cognitive, developmental, personality, and social policy implications. *American Psychologist, 38*, 826–834.

Singh, D. (1995). Female judgment of male attractiveness and desirability for relationships: Role of waist-to-hip ratio and financial status. *Journal of Personality and Social Psychology, 69*, 1089–1101.

Singh-Manoux, A., Richards, M., & Marmot, M. (2003). Leisure activities and cognitive function in middle age: Evidence from the Whitehall II study. *Journal of Epidemiology and Community Health, 57*, 907–913.

Sistrunk, F., & McDavid, J. W. (1971). Sex variable in conforming behavior. *Journal of Personality and Social Psychology, 17*, 200–207.

Skitka, L. J. (1999). Ideological and attributional boundaries on public compassion: Reactions to individuals and communities affected by a natural disaster. *Personality and Social Psychology Bulletin, 25*, 793–808.

Skov, R. B., & Sherman, S. J. (1986). Information-gathering processes: Diagnosticity, hypothesis confirmatory strategies, and perceived hypothesis confirmation. *Journal of Experimental Social Psychology, 22*, 93–121.

Skowronski, J. J., & Carlston, D. E. (1989). Negativity and extremity biases in impression formation: A review of explanations. *Psychology Bulletin, 105*, 131–142.

Slamecka, N. J., & Graff, P. (1978). The generation effect: Delineation of a phenomenon. *Journal of Experimental Psychology: Human Learning and Memory, 4*, 592–604.

Slone, A. E., Brigham, J. C., & Meissner, C. A. (2000). Social and cognitive factors affecting the own-race bias in Whites. *Basic and Applied Social Psychology, 22*, 71–84.

Slovic, P. (2000). *The perception of risk*. London: Earthscan.

Slovic, P., Fischhoff, B., & Lichtenstein, S. (1982). Facts versus fears: Understanding perceived risk. In D. Kahneman, P. Slovic, & A. Tversky (Eds.), *Judgment under uncertainty: Heuristics and biases* (pp. 463–489). New York: Cambridge University Press.

Smeaton, G., Byrne, D., & Murnen, S. K. (1989). The repulsion hypothesis revisited: Similarity irrelevance or dissimilarity bias? *Journal of Personality and Social Psychology, 56*, 54–59.

Smeesters, D., Warlop, L., van Avermaet, E., Corneille, O., & Yzerbyt, V. (2003). Do not prime hawks with doves: The interplay of construct activation and consistency of social value orientation on cooperative behavior. *Journal of Personality and Social Psychology, 84*, 972–987.

Smith, A., Jussim, L., & Eccles, J. (1999). Do self-fulfilling prophecies accumulate, dissipate, or remain stable over time? *Journal of Personality and Social Psychology*, 77, 548–565.

Smith, B. N., Kerr, N. A., Markus, M. J., & Stasson, M. F. (2001). Individual differences in social loafing: Need for cognition as a motivator in collective performance. *Group Dynamics, 5*, 150–158.

Smith, E. R., Jackson, J. W., & Sparks, C. W. (2003). Effects of inequality and reasons for inequality on group identification and cooperation in social dilemmas. *Group Processes and Intergroup Relations, 6*, 201–220.

Smith, H. J., Spears, R., & Hamstra, I. J. (1999). Social identity and the context of relative deprivation. In N. Ellemers, R. Spears, & I. J. Hamstra (Eds.), *Social identity: Context, commitment, content* (pp. 205–229). Oxford, England: Blackwell.

Smith, H. J., & Tyler, T. R. (1997). Choosing the right pond: The impact of group membership on self-esteem and group-oriented behavior. *Journal of Experimental Social Psychology, 33*, 146–170.

Smith, H. S., & Cohen, L. H. (1993). Self-complexity and reactions to a relationship breakup. *Journal of Social and Clinical Psychology, 12*, 367–384.

Smith, K. D., Keating, J. P., & Stotland, E. (1989). Altruism reconsidered: The effect of denying feedback on a victim's status to empathic witnesses. *Journal of Personality and Social Psychology, 57*, 641–650.

Smith, N. K., Cacioppo, J. T., Larsen, J. T., & Chartrand, T. L. (2003). May I have your attention, please: Electrocortical responses to positive and negative stimuli. *Neuropsychologia, 41*, 171–183.

Smith, P. B., & Bond, M. H. (1993). *Social psychology across cultures: Analysis and perspective.* New York: Harvester/Wheatsheaf.

Smith, P. K., Morita, Y., Junger-Tas, J., Olweus, D., Catalano, R. F., & Slee, P. (Eds.) (1998). *The nature of school bullying: A cross-national perspective.* New York: Routledge.

Smith, S. L., & Donnerstein, E. (1998). Harmful effects of exposure to media violence: Learning of aggression, emotional desensitization, and fear. In R. G. Geen & E. Donnerstein (Eds.), *Human aggression: Theories, research, and implications for social policy* (pp. 167–202). San Diego, CA: Academic Press.

Smith, S. M., McIntosh, W. D., & Bazzani, D. G. (1999). Are the beautiful good in Hollywood? An investigation of the beauty-and-goodness stereotype on film. *Basic and Applied Social Psychology, 21*, 69–80.

Smith, S. S., & Richardson, D. (1983). Amelioration of deception and harm in psychological research: The important role of debriefing. *Journal of Personality and Social Psychology, 44*, 1075–1082.

Smith, T.W., Snyder, C. R., & Perkins, S. C. (1983). The self-serving function of hypochondriacal complaints: Physical symptoms as self-handicapping strategies. *Journal of Personality and Social Psychology, 44*, 787–797.

Smith, V. L., & Kassin, S. M. (1993). Effects of the dynamite charge on the deliberations of deadlocked mock juries. *Law and Human Behavior, 17*, 625–643.

Smitherman, H. O. (1992). Helping: The importance of cost/reward considerations on likelihood to help. *Psychological Reports, 71*, 305–306.

Smyth, J., & Lepore, S. J. (2002). *The writing cure: How expressive writing promotes health and emotional well-being.* Washington, DC: American Psychological Association.

Snyder, C. R., & Higgins, R. L. (1988). Excuses: Their effective role in the negotiation of reality. *Psychological Bulletin, 104*, 23–35.

Snyder, C. R., Higgins, R. L., & Stucky, R. J. (1983). *Excuses: Masquerades in search of grace.* New York: Wiley.

Snyder, C. R., Lassegard, M. A., & Ford, C. E. (1986). Distancing after group success and failure: Basking in reflected glory and cutting off reflected failure. *Journal of Personality and Social Psychology, 51*, 382–388.

Snyder, M. (1974). The self-monitoring of expressive behavior. *Journal of Personality and Social Psychology, 30*, 526–537.

Snyder, M. (1987). *Public appearances private/realities: The psychology of self-monitoring.* New York: Freeman.

Snyder, M. (1993). Basic research and practical problems: The promise of a "functional" personality and social psychology. *Personality and Social Psychology Bulletin, 19*, 251–264.

Snyder, M., & Clary, E. G. (2004). Volunteerism and the generative society. In E. de St. Aubin & D. P. McAdams (Eds.), *The generative society: Caring for future generations* (pp. 221–237). Washington, DC: American Psychological Association.

Snyder, M., Clary, E. G., & Stukas, A. A. (2000). The functional approach to volunteerism. In G. R. Maio & J. M. Olson (Eds.), *Why we evaluate: Functions of attitudes* (pp. 365–393). Mahwah, NJ: Erlbaum.

Snyder, M., & DeBono, K. (1985). Appeals to image and claims about quality: Understanding the psychology of advertising. *Journal of Personality and Social Psychology, 49*, 586–597.

Snyder, M., & Gangestad, S. (1986). On the nature of self-monitoring: Matters of assessment, matters of validity. *Journal of Personality and Social Psychology, 51*, 125–139.

Snyder, M., & Monson, T. C. (1975). Persons, situations, and the control of social behavior. *Journal of Personality and Social Psychology, 32*, 637–644.

Snyder, M., & Stukas, A. A. (1999). Interpersonal processes: The interplay of cognitive, motivational, and behavioral activities in social interaction. *Annual Review of Psychology, 50*, 273–303.

Snyder, M., & Swann, W. B., Jr. (1978). Behavioral confirmation in social interaction: From social perception to social reality. *Journal of Personality and Social Psychology, 36*, 1202–1212.

Snyder, M., Tanke, E. D., & Berscheid, E. (1977). Social perception and interpersonal behavior: On the self-fulfilling nature of social stereotypes. *Journal of Personality and Social Psychology, 35*, 656–666.

Sober, E., & Wilson, D. S. (1998). *Unto others: The evolution and psychology of unselfish behavior.* Cambridge, MA: Harvard University Press.

Soloff, P. H., Meltzer, C. C., Greer, P. J., Constantine, D., & Kelly, T. M. (2000). A fenfluramine-activated FDG-PET study of borderline personality disorder. *Biological Psychiatry, 47*, 540–547.

Sommer, K. L., & Baumeister, R. F. (2002). Self-evaluation, persistence, and performance following implicit rejection: The role of trait self-esteem. *Personality and Social Psychology Bulletin, 28*, 926–938.

Sommers, S. R., & Ellsworth, P. C. (2001). White juror bias: An investigation of racial prejudice against Black defendants in the American courtroom. *Psychology, Public Policy, and Law, 7*, 201–229.

Son Hing, L. S., Li, W., & Zanna, M. P. (2002). Inducing hypocrisy to reduce prejudicial responses among aversive racists. *Journal of Experimental Social Psychology, 38*, 71–78.

Spears, R. (2002). Four degrees of stereotype formation: Differentiation by any means necessary. In C. McGarty, V. Y. Yzerbyt, & R. Spears (Eds.), *Stereotypes as explanations: The formation of meaningful beliefs about social groups* (pp. 127–156). Cambridge, UK: Cambridge University Press.

Spears, R., Postmes, T., Lea, M., & Watt, S. E. (2001). A SIDE view of social influence. In J. P. Forgas & K. D. Williams (Eds.), *Social influence: Direct and indirect processes. The Sydney symposium of social psychology* (pp. 331–350). Philadelphia: Psychology Press.

Special report: A crime as American as a Colt .45. (1995, August 15). *Newsweek*, 22–23, 45.

Spencer, S. J., Fein, S., Wolfe, C. T., Fong, C., & Dunn, M. A. (1998). Automatic activation of stereotypes: The role of self-image threat. *Personality and Social Psychology Bulletin, 24*, 1139–1152.

Spencer, S. J., Fein, S., Zanna, M., & Olson, J.M. (Eds.) (2003). *Motivated social perception: The Ontario symposium* (Vol. 9). Mahwah, NJ: Erlbaum.

Spencer, S. J., Steele, C. M., & Quinn, D. M. (1999). Stereotype threat and women's math performance. *Journal of Experimental Social Psychology, 35*, 4–28.

Spivey, C. B., & Prentice-Dunn, S. (1990). Assessing the directionality of deindividuated behavior: Effects of deindividuation, modeling, and private self-consciousness on aggressive and prosocial responses. *Basic and Applied Social Psychology, 11*, 387–403.

Sporer, S. L. (1993). Eyewitness identification accuracy, confidence, and decision times in simultaneous and sequential lineups. *Journal of Applied Psychology, 78*, 22–33.

Sporer, S. L., Malpass, R. S., & Koehnken, G. (Eds.) (1996). *Psychological issues in eyewitness identification.* Mahwah, NJ: Erlbaum.

Sporer, S. L., Penrod, S. D., Read, J. D., & Cutler, B. L. (1995). Choosing, confidence, and accuracy: A meta-analysis of the confidence-accuracy relation in eyewitness identification studies. *Psychological Bulletin, 118*, 315–327.

Sprafkin, J. N., Liebert, R. M., & Poulos, R. W. (1975). Effects of a prosocial televised example on children's helping. *Journal of Experimental Child Psychology, 20*, 119–126.

Sprecher, S. (1994). Two sides to the breakup of dating relationships. *Personal Relationships, 1*, 199–222.

Sprecher, S. (1999). "I love you more today than yesterday": Romantic partners' perceptions of changes in love and related affect over time. *Journal of Personality and Social Psychology, 76*, 46–53.

Sprecher, S. (2001). Equity and social exchange in dating couples: Associations with satisfaction, commitment, and stability. *Journal of Marriage and the Family, 63*, 599–613.

Sprecher, S., & Regan, P. C. (1998). Passionate and companionate love in courting and young married couples. *Sociological Inquiry, 68*, 163–185.

Sprecher, S., Sullivan, Q., & Hatfield, E. (1994). Mate selection preferences: Gender differences examined in a national sample. *Journal of Personality and Social Psychology, 66*, 1074–1080.

Sproull, L., Subramani, M., Kiesler, S., Walker, J. H., & Waters, K. (1996). When the interface is a face. *Human Computer Interaction, 11*, 97–124.

Sraus, M. A. (1999). The controversy over domestic violence by women: A methological, theoretical, and sociology of science analysis. In X. B. Arriaga & S. Oskamp (Eds.), *Violence in intimate relationships* (pp. 17–44). Thousand Oaks, CA: Sage.

Stalans, L. J., & Diamond, S. S. (1990). Formation and change in lay evaluations of criminal sentencing: Misperception and discontent. *Law and Human Behavior, 14*, 199–214.

Stangor, C., & Lange, J. E. (1994). Mental representations of social groups: Advances in understanding stereotypes and stereotyping. In M. P. Zanna (Ed.), *Advances in experimental social psychology* (Vol. 26, pp. 357–416). San Diego, CA: Academic Press.

Stangor, C., Lynch, L., Changming, D., & Glass, B. (1992). Categorization of individuals on the basis of multiple social features. *Journal of Personality and Social Psychology, 62*, 207–218.

Stapel, D. A., & Koomen, W. (2000). How far do we go beyond the information given? The impact of knowledge activation on interpretation and inference. *Journal of Personality and Social Psychology, 78*, 19–37.

Stasser, G. (1992). Pooling of unshared information during group discussions. In S. Worchel, W. Wood, & J. A. Simpson (Eds.), *Group process and productivity* (pp. 48–67). Newbury Park, CA: Sage.

Stasser, G., & Birchmeier, Z. (2003). Group creativity and collective choice. In P. B. Paulus & B. A. Nijstad (Eds.), *Group creativity: Innovation through collaboration* (pp. 85–109). New York: Oxford University.

Stasser, G., & Davis, J. H. (1981). Group decision making and social influence: A social interaction sequence model. *Psychological Review, 88*, 523–551.

Stasser, G., Kerr, N. L., & Bray, R. M. (1982). The social psychology of jury deliberations: Structure, process, and product. In N. Kerr & R. Bray (Eds.), *The psychology of the courtroom* (pp. 221–256). New York: Academic Press.

Stasser, G., Stewart, D. D., & Wittenbaum, G. M. (1995). Expert roles and information exchange during discussion: The importance of knowing who knows what. *Journal of Experimental Social Psychology, 31*, 244–265.

Stasson, M. F., & Bradshaw, S. D. (1995). Explanations of individual-group performance differences: What sort of "bonus" can be gained through group interaction? *Small Group Research, 26*, 296–308.

Statistics Canada (1999). *General Social Survey on Victimization.*

Statistics Canada (2004). *Canada Survey of Giving, Volunteering and Participating.*

Staub, E. (1996). Cultural-societal roots of violence: The examples of genocidal violence and of contemporary youth violence in the United States. *American Psychologist, 51*, 117–132.

Staub, E. (2004). Understanding and responding to group violence: Genocide, mass killing, and terrorism. In F. M. Moghaddam, & A. J. Marsella (Eds.), *Understanding terrorism: Psychosocial roots, consequences, and interventions* (pp. 151–168). Washington, DC: American Psychological Association.

Staw, B. M. (1997). The escalation of commitment: An update and appraisal. In Z. Shapira (Ed.), *Organizational decision making. Cambridge series on judgement and decision making* (pp. 191–215). New York: Cambridge University Press.

Steblay, N., Besirevic, J., Fulero, S., & Jiminez-Lorente, B. (1999). The effects of pretrial publicity on juror verdicts: A meta-analytic review. *Law and Human Behavior, 23*, 219–235.

Steblay, N., Dysart, J., Fulero, S., & Lindsay, R. C. L. (2003). Eyewitness accuracy rates in police showup and lineup presentations: A meta-analytic comparison. *Law and Human Behavior, 27*, 523–540.

Steblay, N. M. (1987). Helping behavior in rural and urban environments: A meta-analysis. *Psychological Bulletin, 102*, 346–356.

Steblay, N. M. (1992). A meta-analytic review of the weapon-focus effect. *Law and Human Behavior, 16*, 413–424.

Steblay, N. M. (1997). Social influence in eyewitness recall: A meta-analytic review of lineup instruction effects. *Law and Human Behavior, 21*, 283–297.

Steele, C. M. (1988). The psychology of self-affirmation: Sustaining the integrity of the self. In L. Berkowitz (Ed.), *Advances in experimental social psychology* (Vol. 21, pp. 261–302). New York: Academic Press.

Steele, C. M. (1997). A threat in the air: How stereotypes shape intellectual identity and performance. *American Psychologist, 52*, 613–629.

Steele, C. M. (1999). Thin ice: "Stereotype threat" and black college students. *Atlantic Monthly, 284*, 44–47, 50–54.

Steele, C. M., & Aronson, J. (1995). Stereotype vulnerability and the intellectual test performance of African Americans. *Journal of Personality and Social Psychology, 69*, 797–811.

Steele, C. M., & Josephs, R. A. (1990). Alcohol myopia: Its prized and dangerous effects. *American Psychologist, 45*, 921–933.

Steele, C. M., Spencer, S. J., & Aronson, J. (2003). Contending with group image: The psychology of stereotype and social identity threat. In M. P. Zanna (Ed.), *Advances in experimental social psychology* (Vol. 34, pp. 379–440). San Diego, CA: Academic Press.

Steele, C. M., Spencer, S. J., & Lynch, M. (1993). Self-image resilience and dissonance: The role of affirmational resources. *Journal of Personality and Social Psychology, 64*, 885–896.

Stein, M. B., Walker, J. R., & Forde, D. R. (1996). Public-speaking fears in a community sample. *Archives of General Psychiatry, 53*, 169–174.

Steiner, I. D. (1972). *Group process and productivity.* New York: Academic Press.

Stempfle, J., Huebner, O., & Badke-Schaub, P. (2001). A functional theory of task role distribution in work groups. *Group Processes and Intergroup Relations, 4*, 138–159.

Stephan, W. G. (1986). The effects of school desegregation: An evaluation 30 years after Brown. In M. J. Saks & L. Saxe (Eds.), *Advances in applied social psychology* (Vol. 3, pp. 181–206). Hillsdale, NJ: Erlbaum.

Stephan, W. G., & Finlay, K. (1999). The role of empathy in improving intergroup relations. *Journal of Social Issues, 55*, 729–743.

Stephan, W. G., Ybarra, O., & Bachman, G. (1999). Prejudice toward immigrants. *Journal of Applied Social Psychology, 29*, 2221–2237.

Stepper, S., & Strack, F. (1993). Proprioceptive determinants of emotional and nonemotional feelings. *Journal of Personality and Social Psychology, 64*, 211–220.

Sternberg, R. J. (1986). A triangular theory of love. *Psychological Review, 93*, 119–135.

Sternberg, R. J. (1997). *Successful intelligence: How practical and creative intelligence determine success in life.* New York: Plume.

Sternberg, R. J. (1999). *Cupid's arrow: The course of love through time.* New York: Cambridge University Press.

Sternberg, R. J., & Barnes, M. L. (Eds.) (1998). *The psychology of love.* New Haven, CT: Yale University Press.

Stets, J. E., & Straus, M. A. (1989). The marriage license as a hitting license: A comparison of assaults in dating, cohabiting, and married couples. *Journal of Family Violence, 41*, 33–52.

Stinson, V., Devenport, J. L., Cutler, B. L., & Kravitz, D. A. (1996). How effective is the presence-of-counsel safeguard? Attorney perceptions of suggestiveness, fairness, and correctability of biased lineup procedures. *Journal of Applied Psychology, 81*, 64–75.

Stinson, V., Devenport, J. L., Cutler, B. L., & Kravitz, D. A. (1997). How effective is the motion-to-suppress safeguard? Judges perceptions of the suggestiveness and fairness of biased lineup procedures. *Journal of Applied Psychology, 82*, 26–43.

Stogdill, R. (1972). Group productivity, drive, and cohesiveness. *Organizational Behavior and Human Performance, 8*, 26–43.

Stoltzfus, N. (1996). *Resistance of the heart: Intermarriage and the Rosenstrasse protest in Nazi Germany.* New York: Norton.

Stone, B., Jones, C., & Betz, B. (1996). Response of cooperators and competitors in a simulated arms race. *Psychological Reports, 79*, 1101–1102.

Stone, J. (2002). Battling doubt by avoiding practice: The effects of stereotype threat on self-handicapping in white athletes. *Personality and Social Psychology Bulletin, 28*, 1667–1678.

Stone, J. (2003). Self-consistency for low self-esteem in dissonance processes: The role of self-standards. *Personality and Social Psychology Bulletin, 29*, 846–858.

Stone, J., Lynch, C. I., Sjomeling, M., & Darley, J. M. (1999). Stereotype threat effects on black and white athletic performance. *Journal of Personality and Social Psychology, 77*, 1213–1227.

Stone J., Perry, Z. W., & Darley, J. M. (1997). "White men can't jump": Evidence for the perceptual confirmation of racial stereotypes following a basketball game. *Basic and Applied Social Psychology, 19*, 291–306.

Stone, J., Wiegand, A. W., Cooper, J., & Aronson, E. (1997). When exemplification fails: Hypocrisy and the motive for self-integrity. *Journal of Personality and Social Psychology, 72*, 54–65.

Stone, W. F., Lederer, G., & Christie, R. (Eds.) (1993). *Strength and weakness: The authoritarian personality today.* New York: Springer-Verlag.

Stoner, J. A. F. (1961). *A comparison of individual and group decisions involving risk.* Unpublished manuscript, Massachusetts Institute of Technology, Cambridge, MA.

Stotland, E. (1969). Exploratory investigations of empathy. In L. Berkowitz (Ed.), *Advances in experimental social psychology* (Vol. 4, pp. 271–313). New York: Academic Press.

Strahan, E. J., Spencer, S. J., & Zanna, M. P. (2002). Subliminal priming and persuasion: Striking while the iron is hot. *Journal of Experimental Social Psychology, 38*, 556–568.

Strauman, T. J. (1992). Self-guides, autobiographical memory, and anxiety and dysphoria: Toward a cognitive model of vulnerability to emotional distress. *Journal of Abnormal Psychology, 101*, 87–95.

Strauman, T. J., Lemieux, A. M., & Coe, C. L. (1993). Self-discrepancy and natural killer cell activity: Immunological consequences of negative self-evaluation. *Journal of Personality and Social Psychology, 64*, 1042–1052.

Straus, M. A. (1999). The controversy over domestic violence by women: A methodical, theoretical, and sociology of science analysis. In X. B. Arriaga & S. Oskamp (Eds.), *Violence in intimate relationships* (pp. 17–44). Thousand Oaks, CA: Sage.

Straus, M. A. (2000). *Beating the devil out of them: Corporal punishment in American families and its effects on children* (2nd ed.). New Brunswick, NJ: Transaction Publishers.

Straus, M. A., Gelles, R. J., & Steinmetz, S. K. (1980). *Behind closed doors.* Garden City, NY: Anchor Books.

Straus, M. A., & Mouradian, V. E. (1998). Impulsive corporal punishment by mothers and antisocial behavior and impulsiveness of children. *Behavioral Sciences and the Law, 16*, 353–374.

Straus, M. A., & Ramirez, I. L. (2005). Gender symmetry in prevalence, severity, and chronicity of physical aggression against dating partners by University students in Mexico and the USA. In S. Fein, G. R. Goethals, & M. J. Sandstrom (Eds.), *Gender and aggression: Interdisciplinary perspectives.* Mahwah, NJ: Erlbaum.

Straus, M. A., & Stewart, J. H. (1999). Corporal punishment by American parents: National data on prevalence, chronicity, severity, and duration, in relation to child and family characteristics. *Clinical Child and Family Psychology Review, 2, 55–70.*

Straus, M. A., Sugarman, D. B., & Giles-Sims, J. (1997). Spanking by parents and subsequent antisocial behavior of children. *Archives of Pediatrics and Adolescent Medicine, 151*, 761–767.

Striegel-Moore, R., & Smolak, L. (Eds.) (2001). *Eating disorders: Innovative directions in research and practice.* Washington, DC: American Psychological Association.

Strier, F. (1999). Wither trial consulting: Issues and projections. *Law and Human Behavior, 23*, 93–115.

Strodtbeck, F. L., & Hook, L. (1961). The social dimensions of a twelve-man jury table. *Sociometry, 24*, 397–415.

Strodtbeck, F. L., James, R., & Hawkins, C. (1957). Social status in jury deliberations. *American Sociological Review, 22*, 713–719.

Stroebe, W., & Diehl, M. (1994). Why groups are less effective than their members: On productivity losses in idea generating groups. In W. Stroebe & M. Hewstone (Eds.), *European Review of Social Psychology* (Vol. 5, pp. 272–303). Chichester, England: Wiley.

Stroessner, S. J., & Plaks, J. E. (2001). Illusory correlation and stereotype formation: Tracing the arc of research over a quarter century. In G. B. Moskowitz (Ed.), *Cognitive social psychology: The Princeton symposium on the legacy and future of social cognition* (pp. 247–259). Mahwah, NJ: Erlbaum.

Strohmetz, D. B., Rind, B., Fisher, R., & Lynn, M. (2002). Sweetening the till: The use of candy to increase restaurant tipping. *Journal of Applied Social Psychology, 32*, 300–309.

Struckman-Johnson, C., & Struckman-Johnson, D. (1994). Men pressured and forced into sexual experience. *Archives of Sexual Behavior, 23*, 93–114.

Studebaker, C. A., & Penrod, S. D. (1997). Pretrial publicity: The media, the law, and common sense. *Psychology, Public Policy, and Law, 3*, 428–460.

Sue, S., Smith, R. E., & Caldwell, C. (1973). Effects of inadmissible evidence on the decisions of simulated jurors: A moral dilemma. *Journal of Applied Social Psychology, 3*, 345–353.

Suls, J., & Green, P. (2003). Pluralistic ignorance and college student perceptions of gender-specific alcohol norms. *Health Psychology, 22*, 479–486.

Suls, J., Wan, C. K., & Sanders, G. S. (1988). False consensus and false uniqueness in estimating the prevalence of health-protective behaviors. *Journal of Applied Social Psychology, 18*, 66–79.

Suls, J. M., & Wheeler, L. (Eds.) (2000). *Handbook of social comparison: Theory and research.* New York: Plenum.

Sunstein, C. R., Hastie, R., Payne, J. W., Schkade, D. A., & Viscusi, W. K. (2002). *Punitive damages: How juries decide.* Chicago: University of Chicago Press.

Swain, P. (1997, October 25). Culture battle over a cruel mutilation. *The Dominion* (Wellington), p. 25.

Swann, W. B., Jr. (1984). Quest for accuracy in person perception: A matter of pragmatics. *Psychological Review, 91*, 457–477.

Swann, W. B., Jr. (1987). Identity negotiation: Where two roads meet. *Journal of Personality and Social Psychology, 53*, 1038–1051.

Swann, W. B., Jr. (1997). The trouble with change: Self-verification and allegiance to the self. *Psychological Science, 8*, 177–180.

Swann, W. B., Jr. (1999). *Resilient identities: Self, relationships, and the construction of social reality.* New York: Basic Books.

Swann, W. B., Jr., & Ely, R. J. (1984). A battle of wills: Self-verification versus behavioral confirmation. *Journal of Personality and Social Psychology, 46*, 1287–1302.

Swann, W. B., Jr., & Hill, C. A. (1982). When our identities are mistaken: Reaffirming self-conceptions through social interaction. *Journal of Personality and Social Psychology, 43*, 59–66.

Swann, W. B., Jr., Hixon, J. G., & De La Ronde, C. (1992). Embracing the bitter "truth": Negative self-concepts and marital commitment. *Psychological Science, 3*, 118–121.

Swann, W. B., Jr., Kwan, V. S. Y., Polzer, J. T., & Milton, L. P. (2003). Fostering group identification and creativity in diverse groups: The role of individuation and self-verification. *Personality and Social Psychology Bulletin, 29*, 1396–1406.

Swann, W. B., Jr., Stein-Seroussi, A., & Giesler, B. J. (1992). Why people self-verify. *Journal of Personality and Social Psychology, 62*, 392–401.

Sweet, P. R. (October 1, 2001). "Surely, Canada Is Our Best Friend, Closest Ally." *The Cleveland Plain Dealer.* p. B6.

Swim, J. K., & Sanna, L. J. (1996). He's skilled, she's lucky: A meta-analysis of observers' attributions for women's and men's successes and failures. *Personality and Social Psychology Bulletin, 22*, 507–519.

Swim, J. K., Aikin, K. J., Hall, W. S., & Hunter, B. A. (1995). Sexism and racism: Old-fashioned and modern prejudices. *Journal of Personality and Social Psychology, 68*, 199–214.

Swim, J. K., Borgida, E., Maruyama, G., & Myers, D. G. (1989). Joan McKay versus John McKay: Do gender stereotypes bias evaluations? *Psychological Bulletin, 105*, 409–429.

't Hart, P. (1998). Preventing groupthink revisited: Evaluating and reforming groups in government. *Organizational Behavior and Human Decision Processes, 73*, 306–326.

't Hart, P., Stern, E., & Sundelius, B. (1995). *Beyond groupthink.* Stockholm: Stockholm Center for Organizational Research.

Tajfel, H. (1982). Social psychology of intergroup relations. *Annual Review of Psychology, 33,* 1–39.

Tajfel, H., Billig, M. G., Bundy, R. P., & Flament, C. (1971). Social categorization and intergroup behavior. *European Journal of Social Psychology, 1,* 149–178.

Tan, H. T., & Yates, J. F. (2002). Financial budgets and escalation effects. *Organizational Behavior and Human Decision Processes, 87,* 300–322.

Tanford, S., & Penrod, S. (1984). Social influence model: A formal integration of research on majority and minority influence processes. *Psychological Bulletin, 95,* 189–225.

Tang, S., & Hall, V. C. (1995). The overjustification effect: A meta-analysis. *Applied Cognitive Psychology, 9,* 365–404.

Tangney, J. P., Wagner, P. E., Hill-Barlow, D., Marschall, D. E., & Gramzow, R. (1996). Relation of shame and guilt to constructive versus destructive responses to anger across the lifespan. *Journal of Personality and Social Psychology, 70,* 797–809.

Tannen, D. (1990). *You just don't understand: Women and men in conversation.* New York: Morrow.

Tarde, G. (1890). *Les lois de l'imitation. Étude sociologique.* Paris: Félix Alcan.

Tassinary, L. G., & Cacioppo, J. T. (1992). Unobservable facial actions and emotion. *Psychological Science, 3,* 28–33.

Tate, D. C., Reppucci, N. D., & Mulvey, E. P. (1995). Violent juvenile delinquents: Treatment effectiveness and implications for future action. *American Psychologist, 50,* 777–781.

Taubman-Ben-Ari, O., Findler, L., & Mikulincer, M. (2002). The effects of mortality salience on relationship strivings and beliefs: The moderating role of attachment style. *British Journal of Social Psychology, 41,* 419–441.

Taylor, D. M., & Moghaddam, F. M. (1994). *Theories of intergroup relations* (2nd ed.). Westport, CT: Praeger.

Taylor, R. B. (2000). *Breaking away from broken windows: Baltimore neighborhoods and the nationwide fight against crime, grime, fear, and decline.* Boulder, CO: Westview Press.

Taylor, S. E. (1989). *Positive illusions: Creative self-deceptions and the healthy mind.* New York: Basic Books.

Taylor, S. E. (1991). Asymmetrical effects of positive and negative events: The mobilization-minimization hypothesis. *Psychological Bulletin, 110,* 67–85.

Taylor, S. E., & Brown, J. D. (1988). Illusion and well-being: A social psychological perspective on mental health. *Psychological Bulletin, 103,* 193–210.

Taylor, S. E., & Fiske, S. T. (1975). Point of view and perceptions of causality. *Journal of Personality and Social Psychology, 32,* 439–445.

Taylor, S. E., Kemeny, M. E., Reed, G. M., Bower, J. E., & Gruenewald, T. L. (2000). Psychological resources, positive illusions, and health. *American Psychologist, 55,* 99–109.

Taylor, S. E., Klein, L. C., Lewis, B. P., Gruenewald, T. L., Guring, R. A. R., & Updegraff, J. A. (2000). Biobehavioral responses to stress in females: Tend-and-befriend, not fight-or-flight. *Psychological Review, 107,* 411–429.

Taylor, S. E., Lerner, J. S., Sherman, D. K., Sage, R. M., & McDowell, N. K. (2003). Portrait of the self-enhancer: Well adjusted and well liked or maladjusted and friendless? *Journal of Personality and Social Psychology, 84,* 165–176.

Taylor, S. E., & Lobel, M. (1989). Social comparison activity under threat: Downward evaluation and upward contacts. *Psychological Review, 96,* 569–575.

Taylor, S. P., & Hulsizer, M. R. (1998). Psychoactive drugs and human aggression. In R. G. Geen & E. Donnerstein (Eds.), *Human aggression: Theories, research, and implications for social policy* (pp. 139–165). San Diego: Academic Press.

Tedeschi, J. T. (Ed.) (1981). *Impression management theory and social psychological research.* New York: Academic Press.

Tedeschi, J. T., & Bond, M. H. (2001). Aversive behavior and aggression in cultural perspective. In R. M. Kowalski (Ed.), *Behaving badly: Aversive behaviors in interpersonal relationships* (pp. 257–293). Washington, DC: American Psychological Association.

Tedeschi, J. T., & Quigley, B. M. (2000). A further comment on the construct validity of laboratory aggression paradigms: A response to Giancola and Chermack. *Aggression and Violent Behavior, 5,* 127–136.

Tedeschi, J. T., Schlenker, B. R., & Bonoma, T. V. (1971). Cognitive dissonance: Private ratiocination or public spectacle? *American Psychologist, 26,* 685–695.

Tenenbaum, H. R., & Leaper, C. (2002). Are parents' gender schemas related to their children's gender-related cognitions? A meta-analysis. *Developmental Psychology, 38,* 615–630.

Terkel, S. (1992). *Race: How blacks and whites think and feel about the American obsession.* New York: New Press.

Tesser, A. (1978). Self-generated attitude change. In L. Berkowitz (Ed.), *Advances in experimental social psychology* (Vol. 11, pp. 288–338). New York: Academic Press.

Tesser, A. (1988). Toward a self-evaluation maintenance model of social behavior. In L. Berkowitz (Ed.), *Advances in experimental social psychology* (Vol. 21, pp. 181–227). New York: Academic Press.

Tesser, A. (1993). The importance of heritability in psychological research: The case of attitudes. *Psychological Review, 100,* 129–142.

Tesser, A., & Collins, J. E. (1988). Emotion in social reflection and comparison situations: Intuitive, systematic, and exploratory approaches. *Journal of Personality and Social Psychology, 55,* 695–709.

Tesser, A., Pilkington, C. J., & McIntosh, W. D. (1989). Self-evaluation maintenance and the mediational role of emotion: The perception of friends and strangers. *Journal of Personality and Social Psychology, 57,* 442–456.

Tesser, A., & Smith, J. (1980). Some effects of task relevance and friendship on helping: You don't always help the one you like. *Journal of Experimental Social Psychology, 16,* 582–590.

Tesser, A., Stapel, D. A., & Wood, J. V. (Eds.) (2002). *Self and motivation: Emerging psychological perspectives.* Washington, DC: American Psychological Association.

Tetlock, P. E. (1998). Social psychology and world politics. In D. T. Gilbert, S. T. Fiske, & G. Lindzey (Eds.), *The handbook of social psychology* (4th ed., Vol. 2, pp. 868–912). New York: McGraw-Hill.

Thibaut, J. W., & Kelley, H. H. (1959). *The social psychology of groups.* New York: Wiley.

Thibaut, J., & Walker, L. (1975). *Procedural justice: A psychological analysis.* Hillsdale, NJ: Erlbaum.

Thibaut, J., & Walker, L. (1978). A theory of procedure. *California Law Review, 66,* 541–566.

Thomas, A. K., & Loftus, E. F. (2002). Creating bizarre false memories through imagination. *Memory and Cognition, 30,* 423–431.

Thomas, M. H. (1982). Physiological arousal, exposure to a relatively lengthy aggressive film, and aggressive behavior. *Journal of Research in Personality, 16,* 72–81.

Thomas, S. L., Skitka, L. J., Christen, S., & Jurgena, M. (2002).

Social facilitation and impression formation. *Basic and Applied Social Psychology, 24*, 67–70.

Thompson, C. P., Herrmann, D. J., Read, J. D., Bruce, D., Payne, D. G., & Toglia, M. P. (Eds.) (1998). *Autobiographical memory: Theoretical and applied perspectives.* Mahwah, NJ: Erlbaum.

Thompson, C. P., Herrmann, D. J., Read, J. D., Bruce, D., Payne, D. G., & Toglia, M. P. (Eds.) (1998). *Eyewitness memory: Theoretical and applied perspectives.* Mahwah, NJ: Erlbaum.

Thompson, J. K., & Heinberg, L. J. (1999). The media's influence on body image disturbance and eating disorders: We've reviled them, now can we rehabilitate them? *Journal of Social Issues, 55*, 339–353.

Thompson, L. (1990). Negotiation behavior and outcomes: Empirical evidence and theoretical issues. *Psychological Bulletin, 108*, 515–532.

Thompson, L. (1991). Information exchange in negotiation. *Journal of Experimental Social Psychology, 27*, 161–179.

Thompson, L. (1995). "They saw a negotiation": Partisanship and involvement. *Journal of Personality and Social Psychology, 68*, 839–853.

Thompson, L., Gentner, D., & Loewenstein, J. (2000). Avoiding missed opportunities in managerial life: Analogical training more powerful than individual case training. *Organizational Behavior and Human Decision Processes, 82*, 60–75.

Thompson, L., & Hrebec, D. (1996). Lose-lose agreements in interdependent decision making. *Psychological Bulletin, 120*, 396–409.

Thompson, S. C. (1999). Illusions of control: How we overestimate our personal influence. *Current Directions in Psychological Science, 8*, 187–190.

Thompson, W. M., Dabbs, J. M., Jr., & Frady, R. L. (1990). Changes in saliva testosterone levels during a 90-day shock incarceration program. *Criminal Justice and Behavior, 17*, 246–252.

Thornhill, R., & Gangestad, S. W. (1993). Human facial beauty: Averageness, symmetry, and parasite resistance. *Human Nature, 4*, 237–269.

Thornton, B. (1992). Repression and its mediating influence on the defensive attribution of responsibility. *Journal of Research in Personality, 26*, 44–57.

Thornton, B., & Moore, S. (1993). Physical attractiveness contrast effect: Implications for self-esteem and evaluation of the social self. *Personality and Social Psychology Bulletin, 19*, 474–480.

Thurstone, L. L. (1928). Attitudes can be measured. *American Journal of Sociology, 33*, 529–544.

Tice, D. M. (1991). Esteem protection or enhancement? Self-handicapping motives and attributions differ by trait self-esteem. *Journal of Personality and Social Psychology, 60*, 711–725.

Tice, D. M., & Wallace, H. M. (2003). The reflected self: Creating yourself as (you think) others see you. In M. R. Leary & J. P. Tangney (Eds.), *Handbook of self and identity* (pp. 91–105). New York: Guilford.

Tilker, H. A. (1970). Socially responsible behavior as a function of observer responsibility and victim feedback. *Journal of Personality and Social Psychology, 14*, 95–100.

Tisak, M. S., & Tisak, J. (1996). My sibling's but not my friend's keeper: Reasoning about responses to aggressive acts. *Journal of Early Adolescence, 16*, 324–339.

Tjaden, P., & Thoennes, N. 2000. *Extent, nature, and consequences of intimate partner violence.* Washington, DC: U.S. Department of Justice.

Todorov, A., & Uleman, J. S. (2002). Spontaneous trait inferences are bound to actors' faces: Evidence from a false recognition paradigm. *Journal of Personality and Social Psychology, 83*, 1051–1065.

Tolstedt, B. E., & Stokes, J. P. (1984). Self-disclosure, intimacy, and the depenetration process. *Journal of Personality and Social Psychology, 46*, 84–90.

Tomada, G., & Schneider, B. H. (1997). Relational aggression, gender, and peer acceptance: Invariance across culture, stability over time, and concordance among informants. *Developmental Psychology, 33*, 601–609.

Toobin, J. (1996, September 9). The Marcia Clark verdict. *New Yorker,* pp. 58–71.

Tooby, J., & Cosmides, L. (1988). *The evolution of war and its cognitive foundations.* Institute for Evolutionary Studies, Technical Report No. 88-1.

Top, T. J. (1991). Sex bias in the evaluation of performance in the scientific, artistic, and literary professions: A review. *Sex Roles, 24*, 73–106.

Tormala, Z. L., & Petty, R. E. (2002). What doesn't kill me makes me stronger: The effects of resisting persuasion on attitude certainty. *Journal of Personality and Social Psychology, 83*, 1298–1313.

Tougas, F., Brown, R., Beaton, A. M., & Joly, S. (1995). Neosexism: Plus ça change, plus c'est pareil. *Personality and Social Psychology Bulletin, 21*, 842–849.

Tourangeau, R., Rips, L. J., & Rasinksi, K. (2000). *The psychology of survey response.* New York: Cambridge University Press.

Tourangeau, R., Smith, T. W., & Rasinski, K. A. (1997). Motivation to report sensitive behaviors on surveys: Evidence from a bogus pipeline experiment. *Journal of Applied Social Psychology, 27*, 209–222.

Trafimow, D., Triandis, H. C., & Goto, S. G. (1991). Some tests of the distinction between the private and collective self. *Journal of Personality and Social Psychology, 60*, 649–655.

Triandis, H. C. (1994). *Culture and social behavior.* New York: McGraw-Hill.

Triandis, H. C. (1995). *Individualism and collectivism.* Boulder, CO: Westview.

Triandis, H., Chen, X. P., & Chan, D. K. (1998). Scenarios for the measurement of collectivism and individualism. *Journal of Cross-Cultural Psychology, 29*, 275–289.

Triplett, N. (1897–1898). The dynamogenic factors in pacemaking and competition. *American Journal of Psychology, 9*, 507–533.

Tripp, C., Jensen, T. D., & Carlson, L. (1994). The effects of multiple product endorsements by celebrities on consumers' attitudes and intentions. *Journal of Consumer Research, 20*, 535–547.

Trivers, R. L. (1971). The evolution of reciprocal altruism. *Quarterly Review of Biology, 46*, 35–57.

Trivers, R. L. (1972). Parental investment and sexual selection. In B. Campbell (Ed.), *Sexual selection and the descent of man* (pp. 136–179). Chicago: Aldine-Atherton.

Trivers, R. L. (1985). *Social evolution.* Menlo Park, CA: Benjamin/Cummings.

Troll, L. E., & Skaff, M. M. (1997). Perceived continuity of self in very old age. *Psychology and Aging, 12*, 162–169.

Trope, Y. (1986). Identification and inferential processes in dispositional attribution. *Psychological Review, 93*, 239–257.

Trope, Y., & Alfieri, T. (1997). Effortfulness and flexibility of dispositional judgment processes. *Journal of Personality and Social Psychology, 73*, 662–674.

Trope, Y., Bassock, M., & Alon, E. (1984). The questions lay interviewers ask. *Journal of Personality, 52,* 90–106.

Trope, Y., & Thompson, E. P. (1997). Looking for truth in all the wrong places? Asymmetric search of individuating information about stereotyped group members. *Journal of Personality and Social Psychology, 73,* 229–241.

Tropp, L. R., & Wright, S. C. (2003). Evaluations and perceptions of self, ingroup, and outgroup: Comparisons between Mexican-American and European-American children. *Self and Identity, 2,* 203–221.

Trzesniewski, K. H., Donnellan, M. B., & Robins, R. W. (2003). Stability of self-esteem across the life span. *Journal of Personality and Social Psychology, 84,* 205–220.

Tubre, T. C., & Collins, J. M. (2000). Jackson and Schuler (1985) revisited: A meta-analysis of the relationships between role ambiguity, role conflict, and job performance. *Journal of Management, 26,* 155–169.

Tucker, P., & Aron, A. (1993). Passionate love and marital satisfaction at key transition points in the family life cycle. *Journal of Social and Clinical Psychology, 12,* 135–147.

Tuckman, B. W. (1965). Developmental sequence in small groups. *Psychological Bulletin, 63,* 384–399.

Tuckman, B. W., & Jensen, M. A. (1977). Stages of small-group development revisited. *Group and Organization Studies, 2,* 419–427.

Turner, J. C. (1987). *Rediscovering the social group: A self-categorization theory.* Oxford, England: Basil Blackwell.

Turner, J. C. (1991). *Social influence.* Pacific Grove, CA: Brooks/Cole.

Turner, J. C., & Oakes, P. J. (1989). Self-categorization theory and social influence. In P. B. Paulus (Ed.), *Psychology of group influence* (2nd ed., pp. 233–275). Hillsdale, NJ: Erlbaum.

Turner, M. E., & Pratkanis, A. R. (1994). Affirmative action as help: A review of recipient reactions to preferential selection and affirmative action. *Basic and Applied Social Psychology, 15,* 43–70.

Turner-Bowker, D. M. (1996). Gender stereotyped descriptors in children's picture books: Does "curious Jane" exist in the literature? *Sex Roles, 35,* 461–488.

Turtle, J., Lindsay, R. C. L., & Wells, G. L. (2003). Best practice recommendations for eyewitness evidence procedures: New ideas for the oldest way to solve a case. *Canadian Journal of Police and Security Services, 1,* 5–18.

Tversky, A., & Kahneman, D. (1973). Availability: A heuristic for judging frequency and probability. *Cognitive Psychology, 5,* 207–232.

Twenge, J., & Crocker, J. (2002). Race and Self-Esteem. *Psychological Bulletin, 128,* 371–408.

Tyler, T. R., & Lind, E. A. (2001). Procedural justice. In J. Sanders and V. L. Hamilton (Eds.), *Justice in socio-legal contexts.* New York: Plenum.

Tyler, T., Lind, E. A., Ohbuchi, K., Sugawara, I., & Huo, Y. J. (1998). Conflict with outsiders: Disputing within and across cultural boundaries. *Personality and Social Psychology Bulletin, 24,* 137–146.

Tyson, P. D. (1998). Physiological arousal, reactive aggression, and the induction of an incompatible relaxation response. *Aggression and Violent Behavior, 2,* 143–158.

U.S. Bureau of the Census (1994). *Statistical Abstract of the United States: 1994.* Washington, DC: The Reference Press.

U.S. Department of Health, Education, and Welfare. (1974, May 30). *Protection of human subjects.* Federal Register, 39(105): 18914–20 (45CFR, part 46).

U.S. Department of Justice (1999). *Eyewitness evidence: A guide for law enforcement.* Washington, DC: U.S. Department of Justice.

Uleman, J. S., Rhee, E., Bardoliwalla, N., Semin, G., & Toyama, M. (2000). The relational self: Closeness to ingroups depends on who they are, culture, and the type of closeness. *Asian Journal of Social Psychology, 3,* 1–17.

Underwood, J., & Pezdek, K. (1998). Memory suggestibility as an example of the sleeper effect. *Psychonomic Bulletin and Review, 5,* 449–453.

Unger, L. S., & Thumuluri, L. K. (1997). Trait empathy and continuous helping: The case of voluntarism. *Journal of Social Behavior and Personality, 12,* 785–800.

USA Today (1999, February 3).

Vaes, J., Paladino, M. P., Castelli, L., Leyens, J.-P., & Giovanazzi, A. (2003). On the behavioral consequences of infrahumanization: The implicit role of uniquely human emotions in intergroup relations. *Journal of Personality and Social Psychology, 85,* 1016–1034.

Vallacher, R. R., Read, S. J., & Nowak, A. (2002). The dynamical perspective in personality and social psychology. *Personality and Social Psychology Review, 6,* 264–273.

Van Dyne, L., & Saavedra, R. (1996). A naturalistic minority influence experiment: Effects on divergent thinking, conflict, and originality in work-groups. *British Journal of Social Psychology, 35,* 151–167.

Van Goozen, S. H. M., Cohen-Kettenis, P. T., Gooren, L. J. G., & Frijda, N. H., et al. (1995). Gender differences in behaviour: Activating effects of cross-sex hormones. *Psychoneuroendocrinology, 20,* 343–363.

Van Lange, P. A. M., Van Vugt, M., Meertens, R. M., & Ruiter, R. A. C. (1998). A social dilemma analysis of commuting preferences: The roles of social value orientation and trust. *Journal of Applied Social Psychology, 28,* 796–820.

Vandello, J. A., & Cohen, D. (2003). Male honor and female fidelity: Implicit cultural scripts that perpetuate domestic violence. *Journal of Personality and Social Psychology, 84,* 997–1010.

Vandello, J. A., & Cohen, D. (2005). Tenuous manhood and domestic violence against women. In S. Fein, G. R. Goethals, & M. J. Sandstrom (Eds.), *Gender and aggression: Interdisciplinary approaches.* Mahwah, NJ: Erlbaum.

VanderStoep, S. W., & Shaughnessy, J. J. (1997). Taking a course in research methods improves reasoning about real-life events. *Teaching of Psychology, 24,* 122–124.

VanderZee, K. I., Buunk, B. P., DeRuiter, J. H., Tempelaar, R., VanSonderen, E., & Sanderman, R. (1996). Social comparison and the subjective well-being of cancer patients. *Basic and Applied Social Psychology, 18,* 453–468.

Vaughn, L. A., & Weary, G. (2002). Roles of the availability of explanations, feelings of ease, and dysphoria in judgments about the future. *Journal of Social and Clinical Psychology, 21,* 686–704.

Verkuyten, M. (2005). The puzzle of high self-esteem among ethnic minorities: Comparing explicit and implicit self-esteem. *Self and Identity, 4,* 171–192.

Verona, E., Patrick, C. J., & Lang, A. R. (2002). A direct assessment of the role of state and trait negative emotion in aggressive behavior. *Journal of Abnormal Psychology, 111,* 249–258.

Vescio, T. K., Hewstone, M., Crisp, R. J., & Rubin, M. (1999). Perceiving and responding to multiply categorizable individuals: Cognitive processes and affective intergroup bias. In D. Abrams & M. Hogg (Eds.), *Social identity and social cognition* (pp. 111–140). Oxford: Blackwell.

Vinokur, A., & Burnstein, E. (1974). Effects of partially shared persuasive arguments on group-induced shifts: A group-problem-solving approach. *Journal of Personality and Social Psychology, 29*, 305–315.

Visintainer, M., Volpicelli, J., & Seligman, M. (1982). Tumor rejection in rats after inescapable or escapable shock. *Science, 216*, 437–439.

Vittengl, J. R., & Holt, C. S. (2000). Getting acquainted: The relationship of self-disclosure and social attraction to positive affect. *Journal of Social and Personal Relationships, 17*, 53–66.

Vogel, D. L., Wester, S. R., & Heesacker, M. (1999). Dating relationships and the demand/withdraw pattern of communication. *Sex Roles, 41*, 297–306.

Vohs, K. D., & Heatherton, T. F. (2000). Self-regulatory failure: A resource-depletion approach. *Psychological Science, 11*, 249–252.

Vohs, K. D., & Heatherton, T. F. (2001). Self-esteem and threats to the self: Implications for self-construals and interpersonal perceptions. *Journal of Personality and Social Psychology, 81*, 1103–1118.

von der Pahlen, B., Lindman, R., Sarkola, T., Maekisalo, H., & Eriksson, C. J. P. (2002). An exploratory study on self-evaluated aggression and androgens in women. *Aggressive Behavior, 28*, 273–280.

von Hippel, W., Sekaquaptewa, D., & Vargas, P. (1995). On the role of encoding processes in stereotype maintenance. In M. P. Zanna (Ed.), *Advances in experimental social psychology* (Vol. 27, pp. 177–254). San Diego, CA: Academic Press.

von Hippel, W., Silver, L. A., & Lynch, M. E. (2000). Stereotyping against your will: The role of inhibitory ability in stereotyping and prejudice among the elderly. *Personality and Social Psychology Bulletin, 26*, 523–532.

Von Lang, J., & Sibyll, C. (Eds.) (1983). *Eichmann interrogated* (R. Manheim, Trans.). New York: Farrar, Straus & Giroux.

Vonk, R. (1998). The slime effect: Suspicion and dislike of likeable behavior toward superiors. *Journal of Personality and Social Psychology, 74*, 849–864.

Vonk, R., & van Knippenberg, A. (1995). Processing attitude statements from in-group and out-group members: Effects of within-group and within-person inconsistencies on reading times. *Journal of Personality and Social Psychology, 68*, 215–227.

Voracek, M., & Fisher, M. L. (2002). Shapely centrefolds? Temporal change in body measures: Trend analysis. *British Medical Journal, 325*, 1447–1448.

Vorauer, J. D. (2003). Dominant group members in intergroup interaction: Safety or vulnerability in numbers? *Personality and Social Psychology Bulletin, 29*, 498–511.

Vorauer, J. D., Cameron, J. J., Holmes, J. G., & Pearce, D. G. (2003). Invisible overtures: Fears of rejection and the signal amplification bias. *Journal of Personality and Social Psychology, 84*, 793–812.

Vorauer, J. D., & Claude, S. D. (1998). Perceived versus actual transparency of goals in negotiation. *Personality and Social Psychology Bulletin, 24*, 371–385.

Vrij, A. (1997). Wearing black clothes: The impact of offenders' and suspects' clothing on impression formation. *Applied Cognitive Psychology, 11*, 47–53.

Vrij, A. (2000). *Detecting lies and deceit: The psychology of lying and the implications for professional practice.* Chichester, New York: John Wiley.

Waid, L. D., & Frazier, L. D. (2003). Cultural differences in possible selves during later life. *Journal of Aging Studies, 17*, 251–268.

Walker, I., & Smith, H. J. (2002). *Relative deprivation: Specification, development, and integration.* Cambridge, UK: Cambridge University Press.

Walker, L., LaTour, S., Lind, E. A., & Thibaut, J. (1974). Reactions of participants and observers to modes of adjudication. *Journal of Applied Social Psychology, 4*, 295–310.

Wallace, P. (1999). *The psychology of the Internet.* New York: Cambridge University Press.

Walster, E. (1966). Assignment of responsibility for important events. *Journal of Personality and Social Psychology, 3*, 73–79.

Walster, E., Aronson, V., Abrahams, D., & Rottman, L. (1966). The importance of physical attractiveness in dating behavior. *Journal of Personality and Social Psychology, 4*, 508–516.

Walster, E., & Festinger, L. (1962). The effectiveness of "overheard" persuasive communications. *Journal of Abnormal and Social Psychology, 65*, 395–402.

Walster, E., Walster, G. W., & Berscheid, E. (1978). *Equity: Theory and research.* Boston: Allyn & Bacon.

Walster, E., Walster, G. W., Piliavin, J., & Schmidt, L. (1973). "Playing hard-to-get": Understanding an elusive phenomenon. *Journal of Personality and Social Psychology, 26*, 113–121.

Walster, E., Walster, G. W., & Traupmann, J. (1978). Equity and premarital sex. *Journal of Personality, 36*, 82–92.

Walther, E. (2002). Guilty by mere association: Evaluative conditioning and the spreading attitude effect. *Journal of Personality and Social Psychology, 82*, 919–934.

Walton, G., & Cohen, G. (2004). Stereotype lift. *Journal of Experimental Social Psychology, 39*, 456–467.

Wang, C. L., Bristol, T., Mowen, J. C., & Chakraborty, G. (2000). Alternative modes of self-construal: Dimensions of connectedness-separateness and advertising appeals to the cultural and gender-specific self. *Journal of Consumer Psychology, 9*, 107–115.

Wang, H., Liu, Y., & Zhang, K. (2003). The effects of group decision support system (GDSS) and group discussion on group decision making. *Acta Psychologica Sinica, 35*, 190–194.

Warren, B. L. (1966). A multiple variable approach to the assortive mating phenomenon. *Eugenics Quarterly, 13*, 285–298.

Watkins, K., & Turtle, J. (2003). Investigative interviewing and the detection of deception: Who is deceiving whom? *Canadian Journal of Police and Security Services, 1*, 115–123.

Watson, D. (1982). The actor and the observer: How are their perceptions of causality divergent? *Psychological Bulletin, 92*, 682–700.

Weary, G., & Edwards, J. A. (1994). Individual differences in causal uncertainty. *Journal of Personality and Social Psychology, 67*, 308–318.

Weber, R., & Crocker, J. C. (1983). Cognitive processes in the revision of stereotypic beliefs. *Journal of Personality and Social Psychology, 45*, 961–967.

Webster, D. M., Richter, L., & Kruglanski, A. W. (1996). On leaping to conclusions when feeling tired: Mental fatigue effects on impressional primacy. *Journal of Experimental Social Psychology, 32*, 181–195.

Wegener, D. T., & Petty, R. E. (1994). Mood management across affective states: The hedonic contingency hypothesis. *Journal of Personality and Social Psychology, 66*, 1034–1048.

Wegener, D. T., Petty, R. E., & Smith, S. M. (1995). Positive mood can increase or decrease message scrutiny: The hedonic contingency view of mood and message processing. *Journal of Personality and Social Psychology, 69*, 5–15.

Wegge, J. (2000). Participation in group goal setting: Some novel findings and a comprehensive model as a new ending to an old story. *Applied Psychology: An International Review, 49*, 498–516.

Wegner, D. M. (1980). The self in prosocial action. In D. M. Wegner & R. R. Vallacher (Eds.), *The self in social psychology* (pp. 131–157). New York: Oxford University Press.

Wegner, D. M. (1994). Ironic processes of mental control. *Psychological Review, 101*, 34–52.

Wegner, D. M. (1997). When the antidote is the poison: Ironic mental control processes. *Psychological Science, 8*, 148–153.

Wegner, D. M. (2003). The mind's best trick: How we experience conscious will. *Trends in Cognitive Science, 7*, 65–69.

Wegner, D. M., Ansfield, M., & Pilloff, D. (1998). The putt and the pendulum: Ironic effects of the mental control of action. *Psychological Science, 9*, 196–199.

Wegner, D. M., Erber, R., & Raymond, P. (1991). Transactive memory in close relationships. *Journal of Personality and Social Psychology, 61*, 923–929.

Wegner, D. M., Lane, J. D., & Dimitri, S. (1994). The allure of secret relationships. *Journal of Personality and Social Psychology, 66*, 287–300.

Weinberg, K. M., & Tronick, E. Z. (1997). Maternal depression and infant maladjustment: A failure of mutual regulation. In J. Noshpitz (Ed.), *The handbook of child and adolescent psychiatry*. New York: Wiley.

Weiner, B. (1985). "Spontaneous" causal thinking. *Psychological Bulletin, 97*, 74–84.

Weinstein, N. D. (1980). Unrealistic optimism about future life events. *Journal of Personality and Social Psychology, 39*, 806–820.

Weiss, D. E. (1991). *The great divide*. New York: Simon & Schuster.

Weldon, M. S., & Bellinger, K. D. (1997). Collective memory: Collaborative and individual processes in remembering. *Journal of Experimental Psychology: Learning, Memory, and Cognition, 23*, 1160–1175.

Weldon, M. S., Blair, C., & Huebsch, D. (2000). Group remembering: Does social loafing underlie collaborative inhibition? *Journal of Experimental Psychology: Learning, Memory, and Cognition, 26*, 1568–1577.

Wells, G. L., & Bradfield, A. L. (1998). "Good, you identified the suspect": Feedback to eyewitnesses distorts their reports of the witnessing experience. *Journal of Applied Psychology, 83*, 360–376.

Wells, G. L., & Bradfield, A. L. (1999). Distortions in eyewitnesses' recollections: Can the post-identification feedback effect be moderated? *Psychological Science, 10*, 138–144.

Wells, G. L., Lindsay, R. C. L., & Ferguson, T. J. (1979). Accuracy, confidence, and juror perceptions in eyewitness identification. *Journal of Applied Psychology, 64*, 440–448.

Wells, G. L., Malpass, R. S., Lindsay, R. C. L., Fisher, R. P., Turtle, J. W., & Fulero, S. M. (2000). From the lab to the police station: A successful application of eyewitness research. *American Psychologist, 55*, 581–598.

Wells, G. L., & Murray, D. M. (1984). Eyewitness confidence. In G. Wells & E. Loftus (Eds.), *Eyewitness testimony: Psychological perspectives* (pp. 155–170). New York: Cambridge University Press.

Wells, G. L., & Olson, E. A. (2003). Eyewitness testimony. *Annual Review of Psychology, 54*, 277–295.

Wells, G. L., Olson, E. A., & Charman, S. D. (2003). Distorted retrospective eyewitness reports as functions of feedback and delay. *Journal of Experimental Psychology: Applied, 9*, 42–52.

Wells, G. L., & Petty, R. E. (1980). The effects of overt head-movements on persuasion: Compatibility and incompatibility of responses. *Basic and Applied Social Psychology, 1*, 219–230.

Wells, G. L., Small, M., Penrod, S., Malpass, R. S., Fulero, S. M., & Brimacombe, C. A. E. (1998). Eyewitness identification procedures: Recommendations for lineups and photospreads, *Law and Human Behavior, 22*, 603–648.

Wenzlaff, R. M., & Wegner, D. M. (2000). Thought suppression. *Annual Review of Psychology, 51*, 59–91.

West, A., & Salmon, G. (2000). Bullying and depression: A case report. *International Journal of Psychiatry in Clinical Practice, 4*, 73–75.

Whatley, M. A., Webster, J. M., Smith, R. H., & Rhodes, A. (1999). The effect of a favor on public and private compliance: How internalized is the norm of reciprocity? *Basic and Applied Social Psychology, 21*, 251–259.

Wheeler, L., & Kim, Y. (1997). What is beautiful is culturally good: The physical attractiveness stereotype has different content in collectivist cultures. *Personality and Social Psychology Bulletin, 23*, 795–800.

Wheeler, L., Koestner, R., & Driver, R. E. (1982). Related attributes in the choice of comparison others. *Journal of Experimental Social Psychology, 18*, 489–500.

Whitbeck, L. B., & Hoyt, D. R. (1994). Social prestige and assortive mating: A comparison of students from 1956 and 1988. *Journal of Social and Personal Relationships, 11*, 137–145.

White, G. L., Fishbein, S., & Rutstein, J. (1981). Passionate love: The misattribution of arousal. *Journal of Personality and Social Psychology, 41*, 56–62.

Whyte, G. (1993). Escalating commitment in individual and group decision making: A prospect theory approach. *Organizational Behavior and Human Decision Processes, 54*, 430–455.

Whyte, G. (1998). Recasting Janis's groupthink model: The key role of collective efficacy in decision fiascoes. *Organizational Behavior and Human Decision Processes, 73*, 185–209.

Wicker, A. W. (1969). Attitudes versus actions: The relationship between verbal and overt behavioral responses to attitude objects. *Journal of Social Issues, 25(4)*, 41–78.

Wicker, B., Keysers, C., Plailly, J., Royet, J. P., Gallese, V., & Rizzolatti, G. (2003). Both of us disgusted in *my* insula: The common neural basis of seeing and feeling disgust. *Neuron, 40*, 655–664.

Wicklund, R. A. (1975). Objective self-awareness. In L. Berkowitz (Ed.), *Advances in experimental social psychology* (Vol. 8, pp. 233–275). New York: Academic Press.

Wicklund, R. A., & Frey, D. (1980). Self-awareness theory: When the self makes a difference. In D. M. Wegner & R. R. Vallacher (Eds.), *The self in social psychology* (pp. 31–54). New York: Oxford University Press.

Widmeyer, W. N., & Loy, J. W. (1988). When you're hot, you're hot! Warm-cold effects in first impressions of persons and teaching effectiveness. *Journal of Educational Psychology, 80*, 118–121.

Wieselquist, J., Rusbult, C. E., Foster, C. A., & Agnew, C. R. (1999). Commitment, pro-relationship behavior, and trust in close relationships. *Journal of Personality and Social Psychology, 77,* 942–966.

Wigboldus, D. H. J., Sherman, J. W., Franzese, H. L., & van Knippenberg, A. (2004). Capacity and comprehension: Spontaneous stereotyping under cognitive load. *Social Cognition,* in press.

Wiggins, J. S. (Ed.) (1996). *The five-factor model of personality: Theoretical perspectives.* New York: Guilford.

Wilder, D. A. (1977). Perception of groups, size of opposition, and social influence. *Journal of Experimental Social Psychology, 13,* 253–268.

Wilder, D. A., Simon, A. F., & Myles, F. (1996). Enhancing the impact of counterstereotypic information: Dispositional attributions for deviance. *Journal of Personality and Social Psychology, 71,* 276–287.

Wildschut, T., Pinter, B., Vevea, J. L., Insko, C. A., & Schopler, J. (2003). Beyond the group mind: A quantitative review of the interindividual intergroup discontinuity effect. *Psychological Bulletin, 129,* 698–722.

Wilkenfeld, J., Young, K., Asal, V., & Quinn, D. (2003). Mediating international crises: Cross-national and experimental perspectives. *Journal of Conflict Resolution, 47,* 279–301.

Williams, J. E., & Best, D. L. (1982). *Measuring sex stereotypes: A thirty nation study.* Beverly Hills, CA: Sage.

Williams, K. D. (2001). *Ostracism: The power of silence.* New York: Guilford.

Williams, K. D. (2003). Ostracism: The power of silence. *Journal of Social and Personal Relationships, 20,* 141–142.

Williams, K. D., Cheung, C., & Choi, W. (2000). Cyberostracism: Effects of being ignored over the internet. *Journal of Personality and Social Psychology, 79,* 748–762.

Williams, K. D., Govan, C. L., Croker, V., Tynan, D., Cruickshank, M., & Lam, A. (2002). Investigations into differences between social-and cyberostracism. *Group Dynamics: Theory, Research, and Practice, 6,* 65–77.

Williams, R. (1993). *Anger kills.* New York: Times Books.

Williamson, G. M., & Clark, M. S. (1992). Impact of desired relationship type on affective reactions to choosing and being required to help. *Personality and Social Psychology Bulletin, 18,* 10–18.

Williamson, G. M., Clark, M. S., Pegalis, L. J., & Behan, A. (1996). Affective consequences of refusing to help in communal and exchange relationships. *Personality and Social Psychology Bulletin, 22,* 34–47.

Wills, T. A. (1981). Downward comparison principles in social psychology. *Psychological Bulletin, 90,* 245–271.

Wills, T. A. (1992). The helping process in the context of personal relationships. In S. Spacapan & S. Oskamp (Eds.), *Helping and being helped: Naturalistic studies* (pp. 17–48). Newbury Park, CA: Sage.

Wills, T. A., & DePaulo, B. M. (1991). Interpersonal analysis of the help-seeking process. In C. R. Snyder & D. R. Forsyth (Eds.), *Handbook of social and clinical psychology: The health perspective* (pp. 350–375). New York: Pergamon Press.

Wilson, A. E., & Ross, M. (2000). The frequency of temporal and social comparisons in people's personal appraisals. *Journal of Personality and Social Psychology, 78,* 928–942.

Wilson, A. E., & Ross, M. (2003). The identity function of autobiographical memory: Time is on our side. *Invited paper in Memory: Special Issue Exploring the Functions of Autobiographical Memory, 11,* 137–149.

Wilson, D. S., & Sober, E. (1994). Reintroducing group selection to the human behavioral sciences. *Behavioral and Brain Sciences, 17,* 585–654.

Wilson, D. W. (1981). Is helping a laughing matter? *Psychology, 18,* 6–9.

Wilson, M. I., & Daly, M. (1996). Male sexual proprietariness and violence against wives. *Current Directions in Psychological Science, 5,* 2–7.

Wilson, T. D. (2002). *Strangers to ourselves: Discovering the adaptive unconscious.* Cambridge, MA: Belknap Press.

Wilson, T. D., & Gilbert, D. T. (2003). Affective forecasting. *Advances in Experimental Social Psychology, 35,* 345–411.

Wilson, T. D., Lindsey, S., & Schooler, T. Y. (2000). A model of dual attitudes. *Psychological Review, 107,* 101–126.

Wilson, T. D., Wheatley, T., Meyers, J. M., Gilbert, D. T., & Axsom, D. (2000). Focalism: A source of durability bias in affective forecasting. *Journal of Personality and Social Psychology, 78,* 821–836.

Winch, R. F., Ktsanes, I., & Ktsanes, V. (1954). The theory of complementary needs in mate selection: An analytic and descriptive study. *American Sociological Review, 19,* 241–249.

Wishman, S. (1986). *Anatomy of a jury: The system on trial.* New York: Times Books.

Wissler, R. L., & Saks, M. J. (1985). On the inefficacy of limiting instructions: When jurors use prior conviction evidence to decide on guilt. *Law and Human Behavior, 9,* 37–48.

Witte, K. (1992). Putting the fear back into fear appeals: The extended parallel process model. *Communication Monographs, 59,* 329–349.

Wittenbrink, B., Judd. C. M., & Park, B. (1997). Evidence for racial prejudice at the implicit level and its relationship with questionnaire measures. *Journal of Personality and Social Psychology, 72,* 262–274.

Wolf, S., & Montgomery, D. A. (1977). Effects of inadmissible evidence and level of judicial admonishment to disregard on the judgments of mock jurors. *Journal of Applied Social Psychology, 7,* 205–219.

Wolfe, C., & Crocker, J. (2003). What does the self want? Contingencies of self-worth and goals. In S. J. Spencer, S. Fein, M. P. Zanna, & J. M. Olson (Eds.), *Motivated social perception: The Ontario symposium* (Vol. 9., pp. 147–170). Mahwah, NJ: Erlbaum.

Wood, J. V. (1989). Theory and research concerning social comparisons of personal attributes. *Psychological Bulletin, 106,* 231–248.

Wood, J. V., Saltzberg, J. A., & Goldsamt, L. A. (1990). Does affect induce self-focused attention? *Journal of Personality and Social Psychology, 58,* 899–908.

Wood, N., & Cowan, N. (1995). The cocktail party phenomenon revisited: How frequent are attention shifts to one's name in an irrelevant auditory channel? *Journal of Experimental Psychology: Learning, Memory, and Cognition, 21,* 255–260.

Wood, W. (2000). Attitude change: Persuasion and social influence. *Annual Review of Psychology, 51,* 539–570.

Wood, W., Kallgren, C. A., & Preisler, R. M. (1985). Access to attitude-relevant information in memory as a determinant of persuasion: The role of message attributes. *Journal of Experimental Social Psychology, 21,* 73–85.

Wood, W., Lundgren, S., Ouellette, J. A., Busceme, S., & Blackstone, T. (1994). Minority influence: A meta-analytic review of social influence processes. *Psychological Bulletin, 115,* 323–345.

Wood, W., Pool, G. J., Leck, K., & Purvis, D. (1996). Self-definition, defensive processing, and influence: The normative impact of majority and minority groups. *Journal of Personality and Social Psychology, 71,* 1181–1193.

Wood, W., & Quinn, J. M. (2003). Forewarned and forearmed? Two meta-analysis syntheses of forewarnings of influence appeals. *Psychological Bulletin, 129,* 119–138.

Wood, W., Wong, F. Y., & Chachere, J. G. (1991). Effects of media violence on viewers' aggression in unconstrained social interaction. *Psychological Bulletin, 109,* 371–383.

Word, C. O., Zanna, M. P., & Cooper, J. (1974). The nonverbal mediation of self-fulfilling prophecies in interracial interaction. *Journal of Experimental Social Psychology, 10,* 109–120.

World Health Organization. *World Report on Violence and Health,* October 3, 2002.

Worth, L. T., & Mackie, D. M. (1987). Cognitive mediation of positive affect in persuasion. *Social Cognition, 5,* 76–94.

Wright, D. B., Boyd, C. E., & Tredoux, C. G. (2003). Inter-racial contact and the own-race bias for face recognition in South Africa and England. *Applied Cognitive Psychology, 17,* 365–373.

Wright, P. H. (1982). Men's friendships, women's friendships and the alleged inferiority of the latter. *Sex Roles, 8,* 1–20.

Wright, R. A., & Contrada, R. J. (1986). Dating selectivity and interpersonal attraction: Toward a better understanding of the "elusive phenomenon." *Journal of Social and Personal Relationships, 3,* 131–148.

Wright, R. A., Wadley, V. G., Danner, M., & Phillips, P. N. (1992). Persuasion, reactance, and judgments of interpersonal appeal. *European Journal of Social Psychology, 22,* 85–91.

Wright, S. C., Aron, A., McLaughlin-Volpe, T., & Ropp, S. A. (1997). The extended contact effect: Knowledge of cross-group friendships and prejudice. *Journal of Personality and Social Psychology, 73,* 73–90.

Wrightsman, L. S., & Kassin, S. M. (1993). *Confessions in the courtroom.* Newbury Park, CA: Sage.

Wrightsman, L. S., Nietzel, M. T., Fortune, W. H., & Greene, E. (2002). *Psychology in the legal system* (5th ed.). Pacific Grove, CA: Brooks/Cole.

Wuthnow, R. (1991). *Acts of compassion.* Princeton, NJ: Princeton University Press.

Wyer, N. A. (2004). Not all stereotypic biases are created equal: Evidence for a stereotype *dis*confirmation bias. *Personality and Social Psychology Bulletin, 30,* 706–720.

Wyer, N. A., Sadler, M. S., & Judd, C. M. (2002). Contrast effects in stereotype formation and change: The role of comparative context. *Journal of Experimental Social Psychology, 38,* 443–458.

Wyer, N. A., Sherman, J. W., & Stroessner, S. J. (2000). The roles of motivation and ability in controlling the consequences of stereotype suppression. *Personality and Social Psychology Bulletin, 26,* 13–25.

Young, R. K., Kennedy, A. H., Newhouse, A., Browne, P., & Thiessen, D. (1993). The effects of names on perceptions of intelligence, popularity, and competence. *Journal of Applied Social Psychology, 23,* 1770–1788.

Yu, D. W., & Shepard, G. H. (1998). Is beauty in the eye of the beholder? *Nature, 296,* 321–322.

Yuille, J. C., & Tollestrup, P. A. (1990). Some effects of alcohol on eyewitness memory. *Journal of Applied Psychology, 75,* 268–273.

Yzerbyt, V. Y., Dardenne, B., & Leyens, J.-Ph. (1998). Social judgeability concerns in impression formation. In V. Y. Yzerbyt, G. Lories, & B. Dardenne (Eds.), *Metacognition: Cognitive and social dimensions* (pp. 126–156). London: Sage.

Yzerbyt, V. Y., & Rocher, S. (2002). Subjective essentialism and the emergence of stereotypes. In C. McGarty, V. Y. Yzerbyt, & R. Spears (Eds.), *Stereotypes as explanations: The formation of meaningful beliefs about social groups* (pp. 38–66). Cambridge, UK: Cambridge University Press.

Zahn-Wexler, C., Robinson, J. L., & Emde, R. N. (1992). The development of empathy in twins. *Developmental Psychology, 28,* 1038–1047.

Zajonc, R. B. (1965). Social facilitation. *Science, 149,* 269–274.

Zajonc, R. B. (1968). Attitudinal effects of mere exposure. *Journal of Personality and Social Psychology Monograph Supplement, 9(2),* 1–27.

Zajonc, R. B. (1980). Compresence. In P. B. Paulus (Ed.), *Psychology of group influence* (pp. 35–60). Hillsdale, NJ: Erlbaum.

Zajonc, R. B. (1993). Brain temperature and subjective emotional experience. In M. Lewis & J. M. Haviland (Eds.), *Handbook of emotions* (pp. 209–220). New York: Guilford.

Zajonc, R. B. (2001). Mere exposure: A gateway to the subliminal. *Current Directions in Psychological Science, 10,* 224–228.

Zajonc, R. B., Heingartner, A., & Herman, E. M. (1969). Social enhancement and impairment of performance in the cock-roach. *Journal of Personality and Social Psychology, 13,* 82–92.

Zanna, M. P., & Cooper, J. (1974). Dissonance and the pill: An attribution approach to studying the arousal properties of dissonance. *Journal of Personality and Social Psychology, 29,* 703–709.

Zárate, M. A., & Sanders, J. D. (1999). Face categorization, graded priming, and the mediating influences of similarity. *Social Cognition, 17,* 367–389.

Zebrowitz, L.A. (1997). *Reading faces: Window to the soul?* Boulder, CO: Westview Press.

Zebrowitz, L. A., Fellous, J. M., Mignault, A., & Andreoletti, C. (2003). Trait impressions as overgeneralized responses to adaptively significant facial qualities: Evidence from connectionist modeling. *Personality and Social Psychology Review,* 7, 194–215.

Zebrowitz, L. A., & McDonald, S. M. (1991). The impact of litigants' babyfacedness and attractiveness on adjudications in small claims courts. *Law and Human Behavior, 15,* 603–624.

Zebrowitz, L. A., Tenenbaum, D. R., & Goldstein, L. H. (1991). The impact of job applicants' facial maturity, gender, and academic achievement on hiring recommendations. *Journal of Applied Social Psychology, 21,* 525–548.

Zeelenberg, M., van der Pligt, J., & Manstead, A. S. R. (1998). Undoing regret on Dutch television: Apologizing for interpersonal regrets involving actions or inactions. *Personality and Social Psychology Bulletin, 24,* 1113–1119.

Zeisel, H., & Diamond, S. (1978). The effect of peremptory challenges on jury and verdict: An experiment in a federal district court. *Stanford Law Review, 30,* 491–531.

Zheng, X. (2000). A research on middle school students' bullying. *Psychological Science China, 23,* 73–76.

Zillmann, D. (1979). *Hostility and aggression.* Hillsdale, NJ: Erlbaum.

Zillmann, D. (1983). Arousal and aggression. In R. G. Geen & E. I. Donnerstein (Eds.), *Aggression: Theoretical and empirical reviews: Vol. l. Theoretical and methodological issues* (pp. 75–101). New York: Academic Press.
Zillmann, D. (1984). *Connections between sex and aggression.* Hillsdale, NJ: Erlbaum.
Zillmann, D. (1996). Sequential dependencies in emotional experience and behavior. In R. D. Kavanaugh, B. Zimmerberg, & S. Fein (Eds.), *Emotion: Interdisciplinary perspectives* (pp. 243–272). Mahwah, NJ: Erlbaum.
Zillmann, D. (2003). Theory of affective dynamics: Emotions and moods. In J. Bryant, D. Roskos-Ewoldsen, & J. Cantor (Eds.), *Communication and emotion: Essays in honor of Dolf Zillmann* (pp. 533–567). Mahwah, NJ: Erlbaum.
Zillmann, D., & Bryant, J. (1984). Effects of massive exposure to pornography. In N. M. Malamuth & E. I. Donnerstein (Eds.), *Pornography and sexual aggression* (pp. 115–138). New York: Academic Press.
Zillmann, D., Bryant, J., Cantor, J. R., & Day, K. D. (1975). Irrelevance of mitigating circumstances in retaliatory behavior at high levels of excitation. *Journal of Research in Personality, 9,* 282–293.
Zillmann, D., & Weaver, J. B., III. (1997). Psychoticism in the effect of prolonged exposure to gratuitous media violence on the acceptance of violence as a preferred means of conflict resolution. *Personality and Individual Differences, 22,* 613–627.
Zimbardo, P. G. (1969). The human choice: Individuation, reason, and order versus deindividuation, impulse, and chaos. *Nebraska symposium on motivation, 17,* 237–307.
Zimbardo, P. G., Banks, W. C., Haney, C., & Jaffe, D. (1973, April 8). The mind is a formidable jailer: A Pirandellian prison. *New York Times Magazine,* pp. 38–60.
Zimbardo, P. G., LaBerge, S., & Butler, L. D. (1993). Psychophysiological consequences of unexplained arousal: A posthypnotic suggestion paradigm. *Journal of Abnormal Psychology, 102,* 466–473.
Zuckerman, M., DePaulo, B. M., & Rosenthal, R. (1981). Verbal and nonverbal communication of deception. In L. Berkowitz (Ed.), *Advances in experimental social psychology* (Vol. 14, pp. 1–59). New York: Academic Press.
Zuckerman, M., Knee, C. R., Hodgins, H. S., & Miyake, K. (1995). Hypothesis confirmation: The joint effect of positive test strategy and acquiescence response set. *Journal of Personality and Social Psychology, 68,* 52–60.
Zuwerink, J. R., & Devine, P. G. (1996). Attitude importance and resistance to persuasion: It's not just the thought that counts. *Journal of Personality and Social Psychology, 70,* 931–944.

Credits

Photo Credits

Chapter 1: **p. 2** *(Opener)* Bob Mahoney/The Image Works. **p. 3:** CP/Toronto star/Rick Madonik. **p. 4:** CP/Belleville Intelligencer/Jeremy Ashley. **p. 5:** Stewart Cohen/Stone/Getty Images. **p. 6:** CP/Montreal Gazette/Dave Sidaway. **p. 11:** Skjold Photography/The Image Works. **p. 13:** AP/Wide World Photos. **p. 14:** Jim West/The Image Works. **p. 17:** Lorne Resnick/Stone/Getty Images. **p. 21:** Dan McCoy/Rainbow. **p. 18:** Marty Heitner/The Image Works.

Chapter 2: **p. 24** *(Opener)* Barry Rosenthal/Image Bank/Getty Images. **p. 26:** Chung Sung-Jun **p. 27:** CP/ Jeff McIntosh. **p. 30:** Kate Connell/Stone Getty Images. **p. 31:** Kayte M. Deioma/PhotoEdit. **p. 32:** © The New Yorker Collection 2003 Dean Vietor from cartoonbank.com. All right reserved. **p. 33:** Jeff Greenberg/The Image Works, Inc. **p. 34:** Image13/Photonica/Getty Images. **p. 35:** © The New Yorker Collection 2003 Matthew Diffee from cartoonbank.com. All rights reserved. **p. 36:** Richard B. Levine. **p. 37:** UPI/Corbis-Bettmann. **p. 38:** Anthony Edgeworth/Corbis Stock Market. **p. 42:** Ariel Skelley/Corbis. **p. 46:** Jane Alexander Atwood/L'Agence VU. **p. 49:** The Far Side ® by Gary Larson © 1993 FarWorks, Inc. All rights reserved. Used with permission.

Chapter 3: **p. 52** *(Opener)* Claire Artman/zefa/Corbis. **p. 55:** Ursula Markus/Photo Researchers. **p. 57:** © The New Yorker Collection 1998 Robert Mankoff from cartoonbank.com. All rights reserved. **p. 56:** © The New Yorker Collection 1991 Ed Frascino from cartoonbank.com. All rights reserved. **p. 58:** Howard Pyle/zefa/Corbis. **p. 63:** HS Photos provided by Yearbook Archives/ClassMates.com. **p. 63:** HS Photos provided by Yearbook Archives/ClassMates.com. **p. 64 (left):** J.P. Laffont/Corbis Sygma. **p. 64 (right):** CP/Moose Jaw Times/Mark Taylor. **p. 67:** © The New Yorker Collection 1996 Mike Twohy from cartoonbank.com. All rights reserved. **p. 75 (bottom):** Shaun Best/Reuters/Corbis. **p. 75 (top):** Bartlomiej Zborowisk/epa/Corbis. **p. 77:** Lara Solt/Dallas Morning News/Corbis. **p. 79:** AFP/Getty Images. **p. 84:** © The New Yorker Collection 1992 Mischa Richter from cartoonbank.com. All rights reserved.

Chapter 4: **p. 90** *(Opener)* Timli/Getty Images. **p. 91:** CP/Chuck Stoody. **p. 93 (top):** Caterina Bernardi/Corbis. **p. 93 (bottom):** Corbis/Bettmann. **p. 94:** Timothy Archibald. **p. 95:** Copyright by Paul Ekman 1975. American Psychological Association. **p. 97:** Al Bello/Allsport/Getty Images. **p. 99:** © The New Yorker Collection 1997 Robert Mankoff from cartoonbank.com. All Rights Reserved. **p. 107:** The Everett Collection. **p. 108:** James T. Spencer/Photo Researchers. **p. 110:** AP/Wide World Photos. **p. 112:** CP/Ryan Remiorz. **p. 115 (left):** Bill Ross/Corbis Images. **p. 115 (right):** Francoise de Mulder/Corbis Images.

Chapter 5: **p. 128** *(Opener)* Francis Dean/The Image Works. **p. 130:** CP/London Free Press/Sue Reeve. **p. 133:** Reuters/Corbis. **p. 135:** Mark Ludak/The Image Works, Inc. **p. 137:** CP/Ryan Remiorz. **p. 141:** CP/Tim Hanson. **p. 146:** CP/John Hasyn. **p. 149:** Patrik Giardino/Corbis. **p. 152 (top):** James Leynse/Corbis SABA. **p. 152 (bottom):** Michael Newman/ PhotoEdit, Inc. **p. 154 (left):** David Reed/Corbis. **p. 154 (right):** Jack Dabaghian/Reuters Picture Archive. **p. 159:** CP/Aaron Harris. **p. 162:** Courtesy of Jennifer Richeson. **p. 168:** Rocky Widner/NBAE/Getty Images. **p. 169 (left):** AP/Wide World Photos. **p. 169 (right):** AP/Wide World Photos.

Chapter 6: **p. 176** *(Opener)* Image Source/RF/Corbis. **p. 179:** Donald Weber/Stringer/Getty Images. **p. 180:** Don MacKinnon/Getty Images. **p. 186:** T.K. Wanstal/The Image Works, Inc. **p. 187:** Jim Young/Reuters/Corbis. **p. 190:** Reprinted with permission of Pepsi Cola. **p. 191:** Allen Einstein/Getty Images. **p. 196:** CP/Ryan Remiorz. **p. 198:** Courtesy of American Association of Advertising Agencies. **p. 201:** Reprinted with permission from Apple Computer Corp. All rights reserved. **p. 204:** Larry Hirshowitz/Corbis. **p. 205:** From the Wall Street Journal. Permission, Cartoon Features Syndicate. All rights reserved. **p. 208:** Getty Images.

Chapter 7: **p. 216** *(Opener)* Kevin Miller/Stone/Getty Images. **p. 218:** Oliver Coret/In Visu/Corbis. **p. 219:** Pete Stone/Corbis. **p. 221:** William Vandivert. **p. 222:** David Turnley/Corbis. **p. 226 (left):** David Frazier/Photo Researchers, Inc. **p. 226 (right):** Ashley Cooper/Corbis. **p. 228:** John Moore/The Image Works. **p. 231:** © 2004 Robert Mankoff from cartoonbank.com. All Rights Reserved. **p. 234:** Tim Boyle/Getty Images. **p. 236:** © The New Yorker Collection 1999 Michael Crawford from cartoonbank.com. All Rights Reserved. **p. 238** *(Opener)* Syndicated Features Limited/The Image Works, Inc. **p. 239 (left):** From the film *Obedience* by Stanley Milgram copyright 1965 and distributed by The Penn State University Audio Visual Services. **p. 239 (right):** From the film *Obedience* by Stanley Milgram copyright 1965 and distributed by The Penn State University Audio Visual Services. **p. 244:** Saul Porto/Reuters/Corbis. **p. 246:** Jennie Woodcock/Reflections Library/Corbis. **p. 247:** Omar Sobhani/Reuters/Corbis.

Chapter 8: **p. 250** *(Opener)* CP/COC/Jonathan Hayword. **p. 252:** Anthony Redpath/Corbis. **p. 255:** David Alan Harvey/Magnum Photos. **p. 258:** © The New Yorker Collection 1995 Sam Gross from cartoonbank.com. All rights reserved. **p. 260:** Tom Sobolk/Black Star Picture Collection Inc./The Web Stock House. **p. 262:** Reuters/Corbis. **p. 264:** CP/London Free Press/Dave Chidley. **p. 267:** Walter Hodges/Corbis. **p. 268:** Corbis/Sygma. **p. 272:** © The New Yorker Collection 1997 Richard Cline from cartoonbank.com. All rights reserved. **p. 273:** The Image Bank/Getty Images. **p. 278:** CP/Toronto Star/Steve

Russell. **p. 279:** AP/Wide World Photos. **p. 284:** Ami Vitale/Getty Images. **p. 285:** Jason Reed/Reuters/Corbis. **p. 288:** Reuters/Corbis-Bettmann.

Chapter 9: **p. 292** *(Opener)* Ariel Skelley/Corbis. **p. 295:** JLP/Sylvia Torres/Corbis. **p. 297:** AP/Wide World Photos. **p. 300 (far left):** Luis Villota/Corbis Stock Market. **p. 300 (middle left):** Art Wolfe Photography. **p. 300 (middle right):** John Callahan/Photo Resource Hawaii, Inc. **p. 300 (far right):** The Kobal Collection. **p. 301:** Courtesy of Dr. Judith Langlois; University of Texas, Austin. **p. 303:** Christie's Image/Corbis. **p. 308:** Trapper Frank/Corbis. **p. 309:** © The New Yorker Collection 1998 Jack Ziegler from cartoonbank.com. All Rights Reserved. **p. 310:** AP/Wide World photos. **p. 321:** Lawrence Manning/Corbis. **p. 322:** DPA/The Image Works, Inc. **p. 327:** CP/Aaron Harris.

Chapter 10: **p. 336** *(Opener)* Kevin Dodge/Corbis. **p. 338:** CP/Scott Cook. **p. 340 (left):** Keenan Ward/ Corbis Stock Market. **p. 340 (right):** Ellen Senisi/The Image Works, Inc. **p. 342:** Jeff Irwin/Photo Researchers. **p. 344:** CP/Ryan Remiorz. **p. 347:** © 1996 Robert Allison/Contact Press Images. **p. 350:** CP/Peterborough Examiner/Clifford Skarstedt. **p. 352:** NY Times Pictures. **p. 354:** CP/Victoria Times Colonist/Debra Brash. **p. 357:** Ellen B. Sensi/The Image Works. **p. 364:** Jeff Christensen/Getty Images. **p. 366:** CP/CP Toronto Star/Ken Faught. **p. 370:** Flynn Larson/Phototonica/Getty Images. **p. 373:** RF/Don Hammond/Design Pics/Corbis.

Chapter 11: **p. 376** *(Opener)* Roger Lemoyne/Getty Images. **p. 378:** CP/Paul Chiasson. **p. 380:** Photo by Clint Karlsen/Courtesy Las Vegas Review-Journal. **p. 383:** Roger Yager/Stone/Getty Images. **p. 391:** Mario Tama/Getty Images. **p. 392:** NBC News Archives. **p. 395:** RF/Ford Smith/Corbis. **p. 403:** Jonathan Nourak/PhotoEdit, Inc. **p. 406:** AP Photo/Jim Cooper. **p. 408:** CP/The Windsor Star/Dan Janisse. **p. 412:** Frank Trapper/Corbis.

Chapter 12: **p. 420** *(Opener)* First Light/RF. **p. 422 (left):** Ciniglio Lorenzo/Corbis. **p. 422 (middle):** Toronto Star/Corbis/Sygma. **p. 422 (right):** AP/Wide World Photos. **p. 424:** CP/Chuck Stoody. **p. 426:** CP/Ruth Bonneville. **p. 427:** © The New Yorker Collection 2000 Michael Maslin from cartoonbank.com. All Rights Reserved. **p. 429:** CP/Aaron Harris. **p. 433:** © 1989 Sidney Harris. **p. 441:** The Everett Collection. **p. 445 (top left):** P.G. Zimbardo, Inc. Stanford, CA. **p. 445 (top right):** P.G. Zimbardo, Inc. Stanford, CA. **p. 445 (bottom):** P.G. Zimbardo, Inc. Stanford, CA.

Text Credits

Chapter 3 **p. 60** ***Figure 3.1*:** From M.R. Lepper, D. Greene, and K.E. Nisbett (1973) "Undermining Children's Intrinsic Interest with Extrinsic Reward: A Test of the 'Overjustification' Hypothesis," *Journal of Personality and Social Psychology*, 28, 129–137. Copyright © 1973 by the American Psychological Association. Reprinted with permission. **p. 63** ***Figure 3.2*:** From Bahrick et al., *Psychological Science*, 1996, Vol. 7, pp. 266–271. Copyright © 1996 Blackwell Publishing. Reprinted with permission. **p. 65** ***Figure 3.3*:** From H.R. Markus and S. Kitayama (1991) "Culture and the Self: Implications for Cognition, Emotion, and Motivation," *Psychological Review*, 98, 226. Copyright © 1991 by the American Psychological Association. Reprinted with permission. **p. 66** ***Figure 3.4*:** From H. Kim and H.R. Marcus (1999) "Deviance or Uniqueness, Harmony or Conformity? A Cultural Analysis," *Journal of Personality and Social Psychology*, 77, 785–800. Copyright © 1999 by the American Psychological Association. Reprinted with permission. **p. 71** ***Figure 3.5*:** From J.M. Twenge and J. Crocker (2002) "Race and Self-Esteem: Meta-Analysis Comparing Whites, Blacks, Hispanics, Asians, and American Indians," *Psychological Bulletin*, 128, 371–408. Copyright © 2002 by the American Psychological Association. Reprinted with permission. **p. 72** ***Table 3.1*:** From A. Fenigstein, M.F. Scheier, and A.H. Buss (1975) "Public and Private Self-Consciousness: Assessment and Theory," *Journal of Consulting and Clinical Psychology*, 43, 522–527. Copyright © 1975 by the American Psychological Association. Reprinted with permission. **p. 86** ***Table 3.2*:** From M. Snyder and S. Gangestad (1986) "On the Nature of Self-Monitoring: Matters of Assessment, Matters of Validity," *Journal of Personality and Social Psychology*, 51, 125–139. Copyright © 1986 by the American Psychological Association. Reprinted with permission.

Chapter 4 **p. 96** ***Figure 4.1*:** From H.A. Elfenbein and N. Ambady (2002) "On the Universality and Cultural Specificity of Emotion Recognition: A Meta-Analysis," *Psychological Bulletin*, 128, 203–235. Copyright © 2002 by the American Psychological Association. Adapted with permission. **p. 97** ***Figure 4.2*:** Reprinted with permission from "Smileys" © 1996, O'Reilly Media, Inc. All rights reserved. Orders and Information: 800–998–9938, www.oreilly.com. **p. 101** ***Figure 4.3*:** Reprinted from *Journal of Experimental Social Psychology*, Vol. 3, "The Attribution of Attitudes," by E.G. Jones and K.E. Harris, pp. 1–24. Copyright © 1967, with permission from Elsevier. **p. 106** ***Figure 4.5*:** From L. Ross, T.M. Amabile, and J.L. Steinmetz (1977) "Social Roles, Social Control, and Biases in Social Perception Processes," *Journal of Personality and Social Psychology*, 35, 485–494. Copyright © by the American Psychological Association. Adapted with permission. **p. 108** ***Figure 4.7*:** From J.G. Miller (1984) "Culture and the Development of Everyday Social Explanation," *Journal of Personality and Social Psychology*, 46, 961–978. Copyright © 1984 by the American Psychological Association. Adapted with permission. **p. 109** ***Figure 4.8*:** From Y. Hong, M.W. Morris, C. Chiu and V. Benet-Martinez (2000) "Multicultural Minds: A Dynamic Constructivist Approach to Culture and Cognition," *American Psychologist*, 55, 709–720. Copyright © 2000 by the American Psychological Association. Reprinted with permission. **p. 114** ***Figure 4.9*:** From J.A. Bargh, M. Chen and L. Burrows (1996) "Automaticity of Social Behavior: Direct Effects of Trait Construct and Stereotype Activation on Action," *Journal of Personality and Social Psychology*, 71, 230–244. Copyright © 1996 by the American Psychological Association. Reprinted with permission.

Chapter 5 **p. 142** ***Figure 5.4*:** From L. Sinclair and Z. Kunda "Reactions to a Black Professional: Motivated Inhibition and Activation of Conflicting Stereotypes," *Journal of Personality and Social Psychology*, 77, 885–904. Copyright © by the American Psychological Association. Reprinted with permission. **p. 165** ***Figure 5.10*:** From

B. Major, S.K. McCoy, C.R. Kaiser and W.J. Quinton, "Prejudice and Self-Esteem: A Transactional Model," *European Review of Social Psychology*, 2003, Vol. 14, 77–104. Reprinted by permission of European Association of Experimental Social Psychology, http:www.tandf.co.uk/journals. **p. 166 *Figure 5.11*:** From Claude Steele (1995) *Journal of Personality and Social Psychology*, 69, 797–811. Copyright © 1995 by the American Psychological Association. Reprinted with permission. **p. 167 *Figure 5.13*:** From B.L. Fredrickson, T.A. Roberts, S.M. Noll, D.A. Quinn and J.M. Twenge (1998) "That Swimsuit Becomes You: Sex Differences in Self-Objectification, Restrained Eating, and Math Performance," *Journal of Personality and Social Psychology*. Copyright © 1998 by the American Psychological Association. Reprinted with permission.

Chapter 6 **p. 181 *Figure 6.2*:** From J.T. Cacioppo and R.E. Petty (1981) "Electromyograms as Measures of Extent and Affectivity of Information Processing," *American Psychologist*, 36, 441–456. Copyright © 1981 by the American Psychological Association. Reprinted with permission. **p. 182 *Figure 6.3*:** From *Essentials of Psychology* by Saul Kassin, Copyright © 2004. Reprinted by permission of Pearson Education, Inc., Upper Saddle River, NJ. **p. 184 *Figure 6.4*:** Reprinted from *Organizational Behavior and Human Decision Processes*, Vol. 50, Professor Ajzen, pp. 179–211. Copyright © 1991, with permission from Elsevier. **p. 193 *Figure 6.7*:** Reprinted by permission from Richard E. Petty. **p. 200 *Table 6.3*:** From J.T. Cacioppo and R.E. Petty (1982) "The Need for Cognition," *Journal of Personality and Social Psychology*, 42, 116–131. Copyright © 1982 by the American Psychological Association. Reprinted with permission. **p. 201 *Figure 6.10*:** From J.M. Snyder and K.G. DeBono (1985) "Appeals to Image and Claims About Quality: Understanding the Psychology of Advertising," *Journal of Personality and Social Psychology*, 49, 586–597. Copyright © 1985 by the American Psychological Association. Adapted with permission. **p. 206 *Figure 6.11*:** From "Cognitive Consequences of Forced Compliance," by L. Festinger and J.M. Carlsmith (1959), *Journal of Abnormal and Social Psychology*, 58, 203.210. Reprinted with permission.

Chapter 7 **p. 219 *Figure 7.2*:** From *Psychology*, 3rd Edition by Saul Kassin. Copyright © 1997. Reprinted by permission of Prentice-Hall, Inc., Upper Saddle River, NJ. **p. 224 *Figure 7.5*:** From Robert Baron et al., (1996) *Journal of Personality and Social Psychology*, 71, 915–927. Copyright © 1996 by the American Psychological Association. Adapted with permission. **p. 240 *Table 7.3*:** From Stanley Milgram, *Obedience to Authority*, 1974. Reprinted with permission. **p. 241 *Table 7.4*:** Based on Stanley Milgram, *Obedience to Authority*, 1974. Reprinted with permission. **p. 242 *Figure 7.6*:** Based on Stanley Milgram, *Obedience to Authority*, 1974. Reprinted with permission. **p. 246 *Figure 7.7*:** From B. Latane (1981) "The Psychology of Social Impact," *American Psychologist*, 36, 344. Copyright © 1981 by the American Psychological Association. Reprinted with permission.

Chapter 8 **p. 257 *Figure 8.2*:** Reprinted from *Journal of Experimental Social Psychology*, "Arousal and Stereotype Threat," by T. Ben-Zeev, S. Fein and M. Inzlicht. Copyright © 2004, with permission from Elsevier. **p. 263 *Figure 8.5*:** From R.D. Johnson and L.L. Downing (1979) "Deindividuation and Valance of Cues: Effects on Prosocial and Antisocial Behavior," *Journal of Personality and Social Psychology*, 37, 1532–1538. Copyright © 1979 by the American Psychological Association. Adapted with permission. **p. 277 *Figure 8.7*:** From T. Postmes, R. Spears, and S. Cihagir (2001) "Quality of Decision Making and Group Norms," *Journal of Personality and Social Psychology*, 80, 918–930. Copyright © 2001 by the American Psychological Association. Reprinted with permission.

Chapter 9 **p. 302 *Figure 9.1*:** From D.T. Kenrick, D.R. Montello, S.E. Gutierres, and M.R. Trost, "Effects of Physical Attractiveness on Affect and Perceptual Judgments: When Social Comparison Overrides Social Reinforcement," *Personality and Social Psychology Bulletin*, Vol. 19, pp. 195–196. By permission of author. **p. 304 *Figure 9.3*:** From *Academy of Management Journal* by B. Major and E. Konar. Copyright © 1984 by Academy of Management. Reproduced with permission of Academy of Management via Copyright Clearance Center. **p. 318 *Table 9.1*:** From C. Hazan and P. Shaver (1987) "Romantic Love Conceptualized as an Attachment Process," *Journal of Personality and Social Psychology*, 52, 511–524. Copyright © 1997 by the American Psychological Association. Reprinted with permission. **p. 320 *Figure 9.7*:** From R. Sternberg and M.L. Barnes (eds.) *The Psychology of Love*, Yale University Press, 1986. Reprinted with permission of Yale University Press. **p. 325 *Figure 9.9*:** From B.M. DePaulo and D.A. Kashy (1998) "Everyday Lies in Close and Casual Relationships," *Journal of Personality and Social Psychology*, 74, 63–79. Copyright © 1998 by the American Psychological Association. Adapted with permission. **p. 326 *Table 9.2*:** From S.A. Sanders and J.M. Reinisch "Would You Say You 'Had Sex' If . . . ," *Journal of the American Medical Association*, 281, pp. 275–277. Copyright © 1999 American Medical Association. All rights reserved. **p. 329 *Figure 9.10*:** From L.A. Kurdek (1999) "The Nature and Predictors of the Trajectory of Change in Marital Quality for Husbands and Wives Over the First 10 Years of Marriage," *Developmental Psychology*, 35, 1283–1296. Copyright © 1999 by the American Psychological Association. Reprinted with permission. **p. 332 *Figure 9.11*:** From A. Aron, E. Aron, and D. Smollan (1992) "Inclusion of the Other in the Self Scale and the Structure of Interpersonal Closeness," *Journal of Personality and Social Psychology*, 63, 596–612. Copyright © 1992 by the American Psychological Association. Reprinted with permission.

Chapter 10 **p. 348 *Figure 10.1*:** From C.D. Batson, *The Altruism Question*, 1991. Reprinted with permission of Lawrence Erlbaum Associates, Inc. **p. 348 *Figure 10.2*:** From C.D. Batson, B.D. Duncan, P. Ackerman, T. Buckley, and K. Birch (1981) "Is Empathetic Emotion a Source of Altruistic Motivation?" *Journal of Personality and Social Psychology*, 40, 290–302. Copyright © 1981 by the American Psychological Association. Adapted with permission. **p. 349 *Table 10.2*:** Helping in the U.S., from "Helpfulness Index: How U.S. Cities Rank," *The Boston Globe*, July 7, 1994. Copyright © 1994 The Boston Globe. Reprinted courtesy of The Boston Globe. **p. 351 *Table 10.1*:** From A.M. Omoto and M. Snyder (1995) "Sustained Helping Without Obligation: Motivation, Longevity of Service, and Perceived Attitude Change Among AIDS Volunteers," *Journal of Personality and Social Psychology*, 68, 671–686. Copyright ©

1995 by the American Psychological Association. Reprinted with permission. **p. 356** ***Figure 10.4***: From S.M. Garcia, K. Weaver, G.B. Moskowitz, and J.M. Darley (2002) "Crowded Minds: The Implicit Bystander Effect," *Journal of Personality and Social Psychology*, 83, 843–853. Copyright © 2002 by the American Psychological Association. Reprinted with permission. **p. 358** ***Figure 10.5***: Reprinted from *Computers in Human Behavior* Vol. 16, P.M. Markey, pp. 183–188. Copyright © 2000, with permission from Elsevier. **p. 360** ***Table 10.3***: Based on R.V. Levine, A. Norenzayan and K. Philbrock, "Cross-Cultural Differences in Helping Strangers," *Journal of Cross-Cultural Psychology*, Vol. 32, pp. 543–560. Copyright © 2001 by Sage Publications, Inc. Reprinted by permission of Sage Publications, Inc. **p. 361** ***Figure 10.6***: From R.A. Baron, "The Sweet Smell of . . . Helping: Effects of Pleasant Ambient Fragrance on Prosocial Behavior in Shopping Malls," *Personality and Social Psychology Bulletin*, Vol. 23, pp. 498–503. Copyright © 1997 by Sage Publications, Inc. Reprinted by permission of Sage Publications, Inc.

Chapter 11 **p. 382** ***Table 11.2***: From Bruce Bonta (1997) "Cooperation and Competition in Non-Violent Societies" *Psychological Bulletin*, 121, 299–320. Copyright © 1997 by the American Psychological Association. Reprinted with permission. **p. 384** ***Figure 11.2***: From K. Oesterman, et al., "Cross-Cultural Evidence of Female Indirect Aggression," *Aggressive Behavior*, Vol. 24. Copyright © 1998 by Wiley-Liss, Inc. Reprinted by permission of Wiley-Liss, Inc., a subsidiary of John Wiley & Sons, Inc. **p. 390** ***Figure 11.3***: From M.A. Straus, D.B. Sugarman, J. Giles-Sims, "Spanking by Parents and Subsequent Antisocial Behavior by Children," *Archives of Pediatrics and Adolescent Medicine*, 151, pp. 761–767. Copyright © 1997 American Medical Association. All rights reserved. **p. 393** ***Figure 11.4***: From D. Cohen, R.E. Nisbett, B.F. Bowdle, and N. Schwart (1996) "Insult, Aggression, and the Southern Culture of Honor: An 'Experimental Ethnography'" *Journal of Personality and Social Psychology*, 70, 945–960. Copyright © 1996 by the American Psychological Association. Reprinted with permission. **p. 397** ***Figure 11.5***: From C.A. Anderson (1989) "Temperature and Aggression: Ubiquitous Effects of Heat on Occurrence of Human Violence," *Psychological Bulletin*, 106, 74–96. Copyright © 1989 by the American Psychological Association. Reprinted with permission. **p. 398** ***Figure 11.6***: From A.S. Reifman, R.P. Larrick, and S. Fein, "Temper and Temperature on the Diamond: The Heat-Aggression Relationship in Major-League Baseball," *Personality and Social Psychology Bulletin*, Vol. 17, pp. 580–585. Copyright © 1991 by Sage Publications, Inc. Reprinted by permission of Sage Publications, Inc. **p. 402** ***Figure 11.8***: From C.A. Anderson, K.B. Anderson, and W.E. Deuser, "Examining an Affective Framework: Weapon and Temperature Effects on Aggressive Thoughts, Affect, and Attitudes," *Personality and Social Psychology Bulletin*, Vol. 22, pp. 366–376. Copyright © 1996 by Sage Publications, Inc. Reprinted by permission of Sage Publications, Inc. **p. 404** ***Figure 11.9***: From Dorothy G. Singer and Jerome L. singer (eds.), *Handbook of Children and the Media*. Copyright © 2001 by Sage Publications, Inc. Reprinted by permission of Sage Publications, Inc. **p. 405** ***Figure 11.10***: Reprinted with permission from C.A. Anderson and B.J. Bushman, "The Effects of Media Violence on Society," *Science*, Vol. 295, 2377–2379. Copyright © 2002 AAAS. **p. 409** ***Figure 11.11***: Adapted with the permission of The Free Press, a Division of Simon & Schuster Adult Publishing Group, from *The Question of Pornography: Research Findings and Policy Implications* by Edward Donnerstein, Daniel Linz, Steven Penrod. Copyright © 1987 by The Free Press. All rights reserved. **p. 410** ***Table 11.4***: From M.C. Burt (1980) "Cultural Myths and Supports for Rape," *Journal of Personality and Social Psychology*, 28, 217–230. Copyright © 1980 by the American Psychological Association. Reprinted with permission.

Chapter 12 **p. 427** ***Table 12.3***: From S.M. Kassin and K.L. Kiechel, "The Social Psychology of False Confessions: Compliance, Internalization, and Confabulation," *Psychological Science*, 1996. Reprinted with permission of Blackwell Publishing Ltd. **p. 431** ***Figure 12.1***: (Top Portion) Adapted from E.F. Loftus and J.C. Palmer, "Reconstruction of Automobile Destruction: An Example of the Interaction Between Language and Memory," *Journal of Verbal Learning and Verbal Behavior*, Vol. 13, 1974, pp. 585–589. (Bottom Portion) From G.R. Loftus and E.F. Loftus, *Human Memory: The Processing of Information*. Copyright © 1976 by Lawrence Erlbaum Associates, Inc. Reprinted with permission. **p. 434** ***Table 12.4***: From R. Malpass and P. Devine (1981) "Eyewitness Identification: Lineup Instructions and the Absence of the Offender," *Journal of Applied Psychology*, 66, 482–489. Copyright © 1981 by the American Psychological Association. Reprinted with permission. **p. 436** ***Table 12.5***: From S.M. Kassin, V.A. Tubb, H.M. Hosch, and A. Memon (2001) "On The 'General Acceptance' of Eyewitness Testimony Research: A New Survey of the Experts," *American Psychologist*. Copyright © 2001 by the American Psychological Association. Reprinted with permission. **p. 438** ***Figure 12.4***: From N.I. Kerr, G.P. Kramer, J.S. Carroll and J.J. Alfinin, (1982), "On the Effectiveness of Voir Dire in Criminal Cases with Prejudicial Pretrial Publicity: An Empirical Study," *American University Law Review*, 40, pp. 665–701. Reprinted with permission.

Name Index

Page numbers followed by *c* indicate captions; page numbers followed by *f* indicate figures; page numbers followed by *t* indicate tables.

Subject Index

Page numbers followed by *c* indicate captions; page numbers followed by *f* indicate figures; page numbers followed by *t* indicate tables.